For the new couple

_____

On your special day

_____

*Wishing you much love, joy, and
happiness, from*

_____

Better Homes and Gardens®

New CookBook

Bridal Edition

WILEY

John Wiley & Sons, Inc.

To the Newlyweds

It started with three little words —"I love you."

Now that the vows have been exchanged, the tuxes returned, and the two of you have crossed the threshold of an exciting life together, three new little words come into play. "What's for dinner?"

Whether cooking for each other, in tandem, or preparing meals for friends and family, the Bridal Edition of Better Homes and Gardens® New Cook Book will help you answer that question with a cornucopia of wonderful recipes and scores of helpful tips and techniques that make cooking at home easy and fun.

This special edition is packed with advice that will help you cook your way through your first year of marriage and beyond. You'll find the basics, such as handy tips on organizing your first kitchen, stretching your grocery budget, and doubling the efficiency of your kitchen time. And there's a cache of recipes especially selected for newlyweds that will get you off to a terrific start for anything from fast weeknight meals to your first holiday feast.

Whether you're seasoned cooks or beginners, this book will keep your family happy and well fed for years. May the kitchen be the heart of your home.

Credits for Bridal Section:
Editor: Carlos Acevedo **Writer:** Wini Moranville **Contributing Writer:** Deborah Wagman
Design Director: Ken Carlson, Waterbury Publications, Inc. **Recipe Developer:** Lois White **Contributing Copy
Editor:** Susan Kling **Contributing Proofreader:** Gretchen Kauffman **Photographers:** Jason Donnelly, Marty
Baldwin **Contributing Food Stylists:** Susan Draudt, Janet Pittman **Contributing Prop Stylist:** Sue Mitchell

CHICKEN AND VEGGIE WRAPS, PAGE A-21

CHEESE MANICOTTI WITH ROASTED
PEPPER SAUCE, PAGE A-31

TOASTED RAVIOLI NIBBLERS, PAGE A-41

CITRUS GRANITAS, PAGE A-56

Contents

WOODEN SPOONS

FINE-MESH SIEVES

GLASS BOWLS

ALUMINUM FOIL

CHEF'S KNIFE

FOOD PROCESSOR

My First Kitchen

Six Go-To Tools

The more you cook, the more you'll appreciate gadgets that make your kitchen time more productive and enjoyable. However, when you're just starting out, it's nice to know that you can get a lot of cooking done with just a handful of essentials. Before you roll up your sleeves, stock up on these six multifunctional gadgets—and get to know what these "power tools" can do for you. (To further supplement your kitchen toolbox, refer to the list of equipment on page 8.)

Chef's Knife

The sharp edge of this all-purpose, wedge-shape knife can handle most of your slicing, dicing, chopping, and mincing and can also be used to cut up large pieces of meat. However, the blade's flat side can also come in handy for other chores, such as crushing olives to remove their pits and smashing garlic cloves.

Food Processor

This countertop appliance makes quick work of slicing, chopping, and pureeing anything from vegetables and herbs to nuts and seeds. It's also a real boon for bakers. Once you've used it to knead dough and cut fat into dry ingredients for pastries and crumble toppings, you'll have a hard time going back to doing those tasks by hand.

Glass Bowls

When you see bowls, mixing and tossing ingredients comes to mind, but you can also use them to rise dough or as makeshift punch bowls. Covered with plastic wrap, they work for storing ingredients in the refrigerator. Turned upside down, they can be used to cover and protect a cake or pie on the kitchen counter.

Fine-Mesh Sieves

You'll often reach for these to drain cooked pasta and vegetables. They are also useful for sifting flour or powdered sugar (simply put the food in the strainer and tap it over a bowl). And if you have to fish an ingredient out of a pot of cooking liquids, you'll be glad you have this tool on hand.

Wooden Spoons

This most basic of kitchen tools is absolutely essential. You'll reach for one often to stir liquids, batters, and doughs, so keep several on hand in a convenient spot while cooking. You can also use wooden spoons to lift and turn meats and vegetables when sauteing and for lifting foods from pan to plate. Use the handle end to crimp piecrusts or muddle ingredients, such as fresh mint leaves, for your favorite cocktail.

Aluminum Foil

While its obvious function is to cover or wrap foods, aluminum foil will serve you in many other ways. When you need to bake a casserole but don't have a lid for the dish, cover it with aluminum foil instead. Cover roasted, grilled, and sauteed meats with aluminum foil and allow them to stand to distribute the meat juices for succulent results. For easy cleanup, line pans with aluminum foil when making bar cookies. Also keep it on hand for foil-packet cooking on the grill or in the oven.

Six Go-To Ingredients

Once you start cooking, you'll be surprised at how a handful of ingredients in your refrigerator and on the shelf can add up to a thoroughly enjoyable meal. The trick is to keep a stock of versatile staples on hand to help. Here are six items you'll find yourself pulling off the shelf again and again.

Garlic

Many a good dish starts with a clove of garlic. Whisk it into a vinaigrette for a quick salad to savor before the greens in your crisper wilt. Saute it in olive oil for an improvisational stir-fry, tossing in whatever veggies you have on hand. Rub cut cloves across slices of toasted French bread, drizzle with olive oil, and sprinkle with herbs for a quick bruschetta to serve with a soup supper.

Eggs

Even at the end of "one of those days," you can probably rustle up enough energy to cook eggs. Whether poached, fried, hard-cooked, or scrambled, it doesn't take much to turn them into meals. Saute potatoes, toast some bread, and you're set. Eggs are also indispensible for baking, so make sure you always have some fresh ones ready to crack.

Potatoes

Whether you serve them baked, boiled, roasted, mashed, or fried or go gourmet with gnocchi or au gratin, potatoes are among the all-time most gratifying ways to add heartiness to a meal. You can also make them into a meal with the Baked Potato Soup, page 587, served with a platter of cured meats and cheeses.

Chicken Broth

Broth, canned or reconstituted from bouillon cubes or a chicken-base product, makes a flavorful base for soups. Also use it to deglaze a pan to make a sauce (see Chicken with Pan Sauce, page 478) or as a poaching liquid. And whenever something you're cooking seems a little dry or could use a flavor boost, chicken broth can come to the rescue.

Shaped Pasta

Check out the many forms of shaped pasta available (such as those on pages 420–421) and stock up! Use them to anchor quick pasta tosses made with fresh produce and cheeses you have on hand or in baked pasta dishes such as Macaroni and Cheese, page 236, and Baked Ziti with Three Cheeses, page 440. Toss cooked, cooled pasta with leftover meats and vegetables and your favorite dressing for a filling main-dish salad. For a quick side dish, toss cooked pasta with a little butter and sprinkle with herbs.

Cheese

Semifirm and hard cheeses have long shelf lives in the refrigerator and come in handy for grating on top of salads, soups, vegetables, and pasta; adding to omelets and scrambled eggs; and tucking into sandwiches. Have a couple varieties available, along with some good-quality crackers, a bottle of wine, and a jar of olives, to serve guests for impromptu entertaining.

SHAPED PASTA

CHEESE

GARLIC

CHICKEN BROTH

EGGS

My Green Kitchen

As we start to see the impact our choices have on the planet, it's clear that taking even the tiniest steps in an environmentally sustainable direction can have a big impact. If you two are thinking of "greening" your home, the kitchen is a smart place to start. It's filled with great, easy-to-accomplish opportunities for saving power, reducing waste, and keeping our planet clean and healthy.

Fresh and Local

Do your best to eat fruits and vegetables in season rather that serving fresh raspberries in December when they must be air-freighted from warmer climates. Use a recipe with frozen or preserved raspberries or fresh produce from local farms and orchards, which tastes better, costs less, and reduces the production of greenhouse gasses.

Clean Green

Save money and protect the environment by using natural kitchen-cleaning products. A spray bottle filled with equal parts of water and distilled vinegar may be used as an all-purpose cleaner on everything from windows and countertops to sinks and fixtures.

Power Trip

Making minor, easy-to-accomplish adjustments that increase energy efficiency will make a big impact—on the environment as well as your gas and electric bills.

* *If your oven has a convection option, use it whenever you can. Because it continually circulates air, convection cooking uses about 20 percent less energy than conventional baking or roasting.*

* *Choose the right pan. Using a 6-inch pan on an 8-inch burner can waste up to 40 percent of the burner's heat. Match the pan to burner size.*

* *If you have a dishwasher, let it do the dishes—machines use less water than washing by hand. To save even more energy, turn off the dishwasher's drying cycle and run the machine only when it is full.*

* *Save with slow cooking. Slow cookers use about 250 watts of electricity, while ovens may use as much as 4,000 watts. The appliance is good for your grocery budget as well—low, slow heat coddles inexpensive cuts of meat, making them savory and succulent.*

* *Cook once and eat twice. Make efficient use of your oven and stovetop by cooking dishes that make more than one meal. (See pages A-22 to A-27 for a week's worth of creative cook once, eat twice recipes.)*

Reduce, Reuse, Recycle

Put these three verbs into everyday action to help conserve natural resources, landfill space, and energy. Even something as simple as taking your own shopping bags to the grocery store can have a big impact.

Left: For storing food, use glass! Plastic uses petroleum, a nonrenewable resource. Right: Recycle food scraps, such as coffee grounds, banana peels, and eggshells, to become rich compost for houseplants.

Left: Small appliances are energy-efficient, so use hotpots, microwaves, and toasters when you can. Right: Most dishes do not need rinsing before washing in the dishwasher, which saves gallons of water per load.

Drink Clean! A water-filtering pitcher or faucet-mounted system filters contaminants such as lead and chloroform. When compared to buying bottled water, these devices also help you save money while cutting down on plastic containers.

Everyday Cooking

A Table for Two

The first years of married life often coincide with those early, hard-charging years in a career. The load will be lighter when you know that at the end of each workday, the best is yet to come. Take the time to talk, laugh, cook, and dine together into the evening and you'll nourish each other in so many ways. The recipes, tips, and techniques in this section will get you started on a lifetime of meaningful everyday meals.

Shopping for Two

When it's just the two of you at home, consider these shopping strategies.

Fruits and Vegetables: It may cost more per pound, but fresh, ready-to-eat produce at the supermarket salad bar may save money in the long run. Buy just what you need for tonight's meal rather than ending up with a drawer full of extras wilting in your fridge's crisper.

Meat, Poultry, and Fish: Most supermarkets let you buy these items in any amount you wish. If you do buy prepackaged meat, divide it into perfect-for-two portions when you get home and freeze any meat you won't use within the next two days.

Breads: Most yeast breads are packaged for a family; fortunately they freeze well. Freeze rolls, sandwich buns, and slices of bread in airtight containers or freezer bags until you need them. Most will thaw quickly at room temperature.

Frozen Foods: Loose-pack vegetables are the way to go; you can cook just what you need and return the rest to the freezer.

Canned Foods: If you don't use an entire can of tomatoes, broth, or spaghetti sauce, refrigerate the remainder in an airtight container up to 3 days or freeze up to 3 months.

Cooking for Two

Many recipes yield four to six servings—too much for just the two of you. Fortunately, leftovers from most recipes freeze well; at the end of a long day, you'll appreciate having a home-cooked meal ready and waiting to quickly reheat in the microwave. See page 32 for guidelines on how to freeze foods.

However, for those times when you don't really feel like cooking for a crowd, most recipes can be halved. Just divide each ingredient by two (for a refresher on weights and measures, see page 16) and follow these tips:

* For recipes where exact measures are less crucial, such as salads and soups, round measurements down to the nearest ¼ or ⅓ cup; for example, if a soup recipe calls for ¾ cup sliced carrot, use ⅓ cup.

* When halving recipes, you'll likely need to use a smaller saucepan than the original recipe calls for; otherwise, the food can cook too quickly and burn. However, the pan must be large enough to hold the food without overflowing.

* One egg is equivalent to about 4 tablespoons. When halving a recipe that calls for one egg, crack the egg into a bowl, stir it with a fork, and measure out 2 tablespoons.

* Halving recipes for baked goods, such as cakes and breads, is tricky. Instead, bake the whole recipe and freeze the leftovers.

A Little Help, Please!

Ideally, you're both wizards in the kitchen; but if that's not the case, don't let that keep you from sharing in the fun. Cook side by side (see Couples Cooking, pages A-28 to A-31) so the more experienced of you can show the other how it's done.

Choose a handful of easy recipes and keep the ingredients for these dishes on hand. Good options include Make-It-Mine Chili, page 574, Baked Cavatelli, page 440, and Chicken Burritos, page 484.

When you get home from the supermarket, divide large packages of meat into portions and freeze some in sealable bags. Label with the date they were frozen. Raw hamburger can be frozen up to 3 to 4 months.

Three Cooking Stategies

Think of roasting, sauteing, and tossing pasta as your culinary ABCs—once you get the hang of these three ways to cook, they'll open up volumes of wonderful meals to enjoy together. These three no-fail recipes will help you tap into key concepts for each approach.

ROAST

Roasting might seem a little daunting, but fear not. The technique is easy to learn and gives food a deliciously browned exterior while developing a moist, succulent interior.

Spice-Rubbed Chicken with Roasted Onions

PREP: 20 MINUTES **ROAST:** 2 HOURS
STAND: 15 MINUTES **OVEN:** 350°F
MAKES: 6 TO 8 SERVINGS

- 4 cups thickly sliced or quartered red, white, and/or yellow onions and/or boiling or cipollini onions, peeled
- ¼ teaspoon salt
- 1 5- to 6-pound whole roasting chicken
- 1 teaspoon sugar
- 1 teaspoon garlic powder
- 1 teaspoon ground cumin
- 1 teaspoon paprika
- 1 teaspoon ground coriander
- ½ teaspoon salt
- ¼ teaspoon ground cinnamon
- ¼ teaspoon black pepper
- ⅛ teaspoon ground nutmeg
- 2 tablespoons olive oil

1 Preheat oven to 350°F. Place half of the onions in a large shallow roasting pan. Sprinkle with the ¼ teaspoon salt; set aside.

2 Rinse chicken body cavity; pat dry with paper towels. Skewer neck skin to back; tie legs to tail. Twist wing tips under back. In a small bowl combine sugar, garlic powder, cumin, paprika, coriander, the ½ teaspoon salt, the cinnamon, pepper, and nutmeg. Brush chicken with oil. Sprinkle with spice mixture; rub in with fingers.

3 Place chicken, breast side up, on onions in roasting pan. If desired, insert a meat thermometer into center of an inside thigh muscle. (Thermometer should not touch bone.) Loosely cover with foil. Roast for 1 hour. Remove foil.

4 Add the remaining onions to roasting pan. Roast, uncovered, for 30 minutes; cut string between legs. Roast, uncovered, for 30 to 45 minutes more or until legs move easily in their sockets and chicken is no longer pink (180°F).

5 Remove from oven. Cover; let stand for 15 minutes before carving. Serve chicken with roasted onions. Slice or chop the remaining chicken; place in a storage container. Cover and refrigerate for up to 3 days or freeze for up to 1 month for another use.

PER 6 OUNCES CHICKEN + ¾ CUP ONIONS: 618 cal., 42 g total fat (11 g sat. fat, 0 g trans fat), 191 mg chol., 438 mg sodium, 9 g carbo., 1 g fiber, 49 g pro.
EXCHANGES: 1 Vegetable, 7 Medium-Fat Meat, 2 Fat

Foolproof Roasting

Always make sure your oven is preheated to the required temperature before you pop the meat into the oven. This helps promote that appealing golden-brown exterior that is the hallmark of a beautiful roast.

SPICE-RUBBED CHICKEN WITH ROASTED ONIONS

Spice-Rubbed Chicken with Roasted Onions, Step-by-Step

1. Use your fingers to rub the spice rub into the chicken—brushing the bird with oil first helps the spices adhere.
2. Using kitchen string, available at kitchenware shops, tie the legs together. 3. Before carving, let the roasted
chicken stand 15 minutes. This will allow juices to redistribute for a tastier bird and also makes it easier to slice.

SESAME HAM AND NOODLE SALAD

Steak with Sauteed Onions, Step-by-Step

1. Near the end of cooking time, check the doneness of the steak by inserting an instant-read thermometer into the side. A digital instant-read thermometer should be inserted at least 1 inch into the steak.   2. It only takes a touch of cream to add richness to the onions.   3. Top the steaks with purchased onion marmalade, available from gourmet markets.

1

2

3

STEAK WITH SAUTEED ONIONS

SAUTE

Sauteing is cooking food in a skillet over direct heat in a small amount of oil or other fat. Sauteed dinners are easy, fast, and very tasty.

Steak with Sauteed Onions

START TO FINISH: 25 MINUTES
MAKES: 2 SERVINGS

- 2 4-ounce beef tenderloin steaks, cut 1 inch thick
- ¼ teaspoon salt
- ¼ teaspoon black pepper
- 1 tablespoon butter
- 1 small onion, cut into 6 wedges
- 1 teaspoon bottled minced garlic (2 cloves)
- 1 teaspoon dried basil, crushed
- ½ teaspoon dried oregano, crushed
- 1 tablespoon whipping cream
- 2 tablespoons onion marmalade or orange marmalade
   Snipped fresh parsley (optional)

1 Trim fat from steaks. Sprinkle steaks with salt and pepper; set aside. In a skillet melt butter over medium heat. Add onion and garlic. Cook for 6 to 8 minutes or until onion is tender, stirring frequently. Remove onion mixture from skillet; set aside.

2 Add steaks to hot skillet. Cook over medium heat for 10 to 13 minutes for medium rare (145°F) to medium (160°F), turning once. If steaks brown too quickly, reduce heat to medium-low. Sprinkle with basil and oregano for the last 2 minutes of cooking.

3 Remove steaks from skillet; cover and keep warm. Return onion mixture to skillet; heat through. Remove from heat. Stir in cream.

4 To serve, divide steaks between two dinner plates. Top with marmalade and onion mixture. If desired, sprinkle with parsley.

PER STEAK + 1 TABLESPOON SAUCE: 300 cal., 15 g total fat (7 g sat. fat, 0 g trans fat), 79 mg chol., 209 mg sodium, 17 g carbo., 1 g fiber, 25 g pro.
EXCHANGES: 1 Other Carbo., 3 Lean Meat, 2 Fat

PASTA TOSS

Mixing cooked pasta with simple ingredients is a method used the world over to create flavorful dishes quickly with whatever's on hand.

Sesame Ham and Noodle Salad

START TO FINISH: 15 MINUTES
MAKES: 2 SERVINGS

- ½ of a 3-ounce package chicken-flavor ramen noodles
- 6 ounces cooked ham, cut into strips
- 1½ cups shredded napa cabbage or green cabbage
- ½ cup broccoli florets
- ½ cup packaged fresh julienned carrots
- ¼ cup sliced green onions (2)
- ¼ cup bottled Asian-style salad dressing with sesame and ginger
   Honey-roasted peanuts, chopped (optional)
   Lime wedges

1 In a medium saucepan cook ramen noodles (omit seasoning packet) according to package directions for 2 minutes; drain. Transfer noodles to a large bowl. Add ham, cabbage, broccoli, carrots, and green onions. Add dressing; toss to coat. If desired, sprinkle with chopped peanuts. Serve with lime wedges.

PER SERVING: 325 cal., 16 g total fat (4 g sat. fat, 0 g trans fat), 41 mg chol., 1,415 mg sodium, 28 g carbo., 3 g fiber, 18 g pro.
EXCHANGES: 2 Vegetable, 1 Starch, 2 Lean Meat, 3 Fat

Fast, Faster, Fastest

When you find yourselves hungry at the end of a long workday, it's time for some dinnertime magic. These half-dozen mealtime miracles will soon have the two of you reconnecting over a delectable dish.

FAST

Chipotle Pork and White Bean Chili

START TO FINISH: 30 MINUTES
MAKES: 2 SERVINGS

    8 ounces pork tenderloin, cut into ½-inch
        cubes (about 1½ cups)*
    ½ cup chopped onion (1 medium)
    1 tablespoon vegetable oil
    1 15-ounce can cannellini (white kidney)
        beans, rinsed and drained
    1 14.5-ounce can diced tomatoes,
        undrained
    ½ cup beer or chicken broth
    1 teaspoon dried Italian seasoning, crushed
    ¾ teaspoon finely chopped canned chipotle
        chile pepper in adobo sauce**
        Dairy sour cream
        Fresh cilantro sprigs (optional)

1 In a large saucepan cook pork and onion in hot oil over medium-high heat until pork is browned and onion is tender.

2 Stir in beans, undrained tomatoes, beer, Italian seasoning, and chile pepper. Bring to boiling; reduce heat. Simmer, covered, for 20 minutes. To serve, top with sour cream. If desired, garnish with cilantro.

*Tip: Or use leftover Grilled Pork Tenderloin (page A-52), cut into ½-inch pieces, and omit Italian seasoning. Add the grilled pork with the beans in Step 2.

**Tip: If you prefer, use a few dashes bottled chipotle hot pepper sauce.

PER 2½ CUPS: 412 cal., 14 g total fat (3 g sat. fat, 0 g trans fat), 78 mg chol., 1,055 mg sodium, 43 g carbo., 11 g fiber, 37 g pro.
EXCHANGES: 2 Vegetable, 2 Starch, 4 Lean Meat, 1 Fat

FAST

Chicken-Stuffed Zucchini

PREP: 20 MINUTES **BAKE:** 10 MINUTES
OVEN: 400°F **MAKES:** 4 SERVINGS

    4 medium zucchini (about 8 ounces each)
    1½ cups chopped cooked chicken or turkey
    1 cup chopped steamed vegetables (such as
        sweet pepper, eggplant, and/or zucchini)
    ½ cup chopped tomato (1 medium)
    6 tablespoons finely shredded Parmesan
        cheese
    1 teaspoon Mediterranean seasoning or
        other herb seasoning blend

1 In a Dutch oven or large saucepan cook whole zucchini in a large amount of boiling, lightly salted water for 5 minutes; drain and cool slightly.

2 Preheat oven to 400°F. Cut a lengthwise slice from the top of each zucchini. Using a spoon, carefully scoop out pulp, leaving shells about ¼ inch thick.

3 For filling, in a medium bowl stir together cooked chicken, steamed vegetables, tomato, 4 tablespoons of the Parmesan cheese, and the Mediterranean seasoning. Spoon filling into zucchini shells. Place stuffed shells in a shallow baking pan. Sprinkle with the remaining 2 tablespoons Parmesan cheese.

4 Bake for 10 to 15 minutes or until heated through.

PER STUFFED ZUCCHINI: 184 cal., 6 g total fat (2 g sat. fat, 0 g trans fat), 52 mg chol., 270 mg sodium, 10 g carbo., 3 g fiber, 21 g pro.
EXCHANGES: 2 Vegetable, 2½ Lean Meat, ½ Fat

CHIPOTLE PORK AND WHITE BEAN CHILI

Extra Pork? *Pork tenderloins are often sold in packages of two. Another night, when you have a little more time, roast the extra tenderloin according to the directions on pages 414–415.*

CHICKEN-STUFFED ZUCCHINI

FASTER

Quick Meatball Minestrone

START TO FINISH: 25 MINUTES
MAKES: 6 TO 8 SERVINGS

- 1 12- to 16-ounce package frozen cooked Italian-style meatballs
- 3 14.5-ounce cans lower-sodium beef broth
- 1 15- to 16-ounce can Great Northern beans or cannellini (white kidney) beans, rinsed* and drained
- 1 14.5-ounce can diced tomatoes with basil, garlic, and oregano, undrained
- 1 10-ounce package frozen mixed vegetables
- 1 cup packaged dried small pasta (such as macaroni, small shells, mini penne, or rotini)
- 1 teaspoon sugar
   Finely shredded Parmesan cheese (optional)
   Italian bread (optional)

1 In a 4-quart Dutch oven stir together meatballs, broth, beans, undrained tomatoes, and mixed vegetables. Bring to boiling. Stir in pasta. Return to boiling; reduce heat. Simmer, uncovered, about 10 minutes or until pasta is tender and meatballs are heated through. Stir in sugar. If desired, sprinkle each serving with Parmesan cheese. If desired, serve with sliced Italian bread.
2 Place remaining soup in a storage container. Cover and refrigerate for up to 3 days or freeze for up to 1 month.

*Tip: To rinse canned beans, just empty the can's contents into a colander. Run water over beans to rinse well.

PER 1⅔ CUPS: 345 cal., 13 g total fat (6 g sat. fat, 0 g trans fat), 37 mg chol., 1,264 mg sodium, 40 g carbo., 8 g fiber, 20 g pro.
EXCHANGES: 2 Vegetable, 2 Starch, 2 Medium-Fat Meat

FASTER

Salmon and Asparagus Linguine

START TO FINISH: 25 MINUTES
MAKES: 2 SERVINGS

- 1 8-ounce fresh salmon fillet, skin removed
- 1 teaspoon olive oil
- 4 ounces linguine
- 1 cup chopped asparagus tips and stems
- ½ cup purchased Alfredo sauce
- 5 cherry tomatoes, halved
- 2 tablespoons freshly grated Parmesan cheese
   Freshly ground black pepper

1 Rinse salmon; pat dry with paper towels. Brush salmon with olive oil. Season with *salt* and *pepper*. In a large nonstick skillet add the salmon fillet and saute over medium heat until browned and cooked through, about 3 minutes per side for medium. Flake salmon with a fork and set aside.

2 In a large saucepan cook pasta according to package directions, adding asparagus during the last 5 minutes of cooking time. Drain; return mixture to pan. Add Alfredo sauce, stirring to coat. Gently toss in salmon and tomatoes; heat through. Sprinkle each serving with Parmesan cheese. Season to taste with pepper.

PER 1½ CUPS: 565 cal., 23 g total fat (9 g sat. fat, 0 g trans fat), 102 mg chol., 669 mg sodium, 51 g carbo., 4 g fiber, 38 g pro.
EXCHANGES: 1 Vegetable, 3 Starch, 4 Medium-Fat Meat

Tailored to Your Tastes (and Time)

As a substitute for salmon, use leftover chicken, pork, or beef in the above recipe. Or skip the meat and add extra asparagus.

10 to Try–Hearty Dinner Salad

Start with Chef's Salad, page 502, and your favorite salad dressing.

1. LAMB: Add 6 ounces sliced cooked lamb and ½ cup crumbled feta cheese. **2. CRAB LOUIS:** Omit meat and cheese. Add 6 ounces lump crabmeat and 2 slices cooked bacon. **3. ASIAN TOFU:** Omit meat and cheese. Add ½ cup each cubed firm tofu, shredded carrots, and snow peas. **4. ANTIPASTO:** Add ½ cup each mozzarella, salami, and roasted red sweet peppers.
5. FRUIT-FILLED: Add ½ cup each diced apple, grapes, strawberries, diced watermelon, and dried cranberries. **6. COWBOY:** Combine 1 cup shredded cooked chicken, and ¼ cup barbecue sauce. Add ½ cup canned drained black beans, and ½ cup cooked whole kernel corn. **7. TUNA AND WHITE BEAN:** Combine two 5-ounce cans tuna, drained, ½ cup canned drained white beans. **8. HAWAIIAN SHRIMP:** Omit meat. Add 8 ounces cooked, peeled, and deveined shrimp. Top with ½ cup each diced mango and pineapple. **9. BLACK 'N' BLUE:** Omit meat, cheese, and eggs. Add 1 cup sliced cooked beef steak and ½ cup crumbled blue cheese.
10. VEGGIN' OUT: Omit meat. Add ½ cup each sliced cucumber, zucchini, and radishes. Top with ¼ cup sunflower kernels.

CHICKEN AND VEGGIE WRAPS

Dinner in 15? It's no problem when the meat's precooked like the refrigerated grilled chicken breast strips and the andouille smoked sausage links in these recipes.

CAJUN RICE WITH SAUSAGE

FASTEST

Chicken and Veggie Wraps

START TO FINISH: 15 MINUTES
MAKES: 4 WRAPS

- ½ cup mayonnaise or salad dressing
- 3 to 4 tablespoons refrigerated dried tomato pesto
- 8 to 12 6-inch corn tortillas or 7- to 8-inch flour tortillas
- 2 6-ounce packages refrigerated grilled chicken breast strips
- 2 small yellow summer squash or zucchini (8 ounces total), cut into thin bite-size strips
- 1 medium green or red sweet pepper, cut into strips
  Fresh cilantro sprigs (optional)

1 In a small bowl stir together mayonnaise and pesto; set aside. Place tortillas on a microwave-safe plate; cover with paper towels. Microwave on 100% power (high) for 30 to 45 seconds or until tortillas are warm.

2 Divide warm tortillas, chicken, and vegetable strips among four shallow bowls. If desired, top with cilantro. Spoon pesto mixture over all.

PER WRAP: 467 cal., 28 g total fat (5 g sat. fat, 0 g trans fat), 66 mg chol., 657 mg sodium, 33 g carbo., 5 g fiber, 24 g pro. EXCHANGES: 1 Vegetable, 2 Starch, 3 Lean Meat, 3½ Fat

Wrap It Up

If wraps or tortillas are brittle or dry, layer them between damp paper towels and heat for 30 seconds in the microwave.

FASTEST

Cajun Rice with Sausage

START TO FINISH: 15 MINUTES
MAKES: 2 SERVINGS

- 1 slice bacon
- 3 ounces andouille smoked sausage links, chopped (½ cup)
- ¼ cup chopped onion
- ¼ cup chopped celery
- 1 clove garlic, minced
- 1 8.8-ounce package cooked long grain white rice
- ⅔ cup frozen sliced okra, thawed
- ½ teaspoon Cajun seasoning

1 In a medium skillet cook bacon over medium heat until crisp. Transfer to a paper towel-lined plate to drain. Crumble and set aside.

2 Add sausage, onion, celery, and garlic to same skillet. Cook and stir for 3 to 4 minutes or until vegetables are tender and sausage begins to brown. Stir in cooked rice, thawed okra, Cajun seasoning, and crumbled bacon; heat through.

PER 1¼ CUPS: 307 cal., 7 g total fat (1 g sat. fat, 0 g trans fat), 39 mg chol., 486 mg sodium, 46 g carbo., 2 g fiber, 14 g pro. EXCHANGES: 2 Starch, 1 Medium-Fat Meat

---

WEEKNIGHT DESSERTS

END WITH SOMETHING SWEET:

■ When you have extra time, bake and freeze some brownies or bar cookies. Bring them out, two by two, to thaw while you're cooking and eating dinner.

■ Toss strawberries with sugar; let them stand one hour. Drizzle with balsamic vinegar and top with sweetened mascarpone cheese.

■ Toss in-season fruits with sugar and a splash of liqueur or fruit juice. Top with sweetened whipped cream and a sprinkling of toasted nuts.

Cook Once, Eat Twice

The way to kitchen finesse isn't through hard work. It's through smart work by preparing food for tonight and tomorrow at the same time. Start with the double-duty recipes here: Each pair makes a bonus batch, which becomes a jump-start to another night's meal when you add a few flourishes.

TONIGHT

Roasted Chicken with Honey-Ginger Carrots

START TO FINISH: 25 MINUTES
MAKES: 2 SERVINGS + RESERVES

- 1 2- to 2¼-pound purchased roasted chicken
- 2 cups water
- ¼ teaspoon salt
- 8 ounces medium carrots, halved lengthwise and cut into 2-inch pieces, or 1½ cups packaged peeled fresh baby carrots
- 1 tablespoon butter or margarine
- ¼ teaspoon ground ginger
- 1 tablespoon honey
   Snipped fresh thyme

1 Cut up chicken, reserving thighs to use in Step 3; cover and keep warm. Slice chicken breast meat; place sliced chicken in a storage container. Cover and refrigerate for up to 3 days to use in Chicken-Avocado Clubs. Slice or chop the remaining chicken; place in a storage container. Cover and refrigerate up to 3 days or freeze up to 1 month for another use.

2 For carrots, in a saucepan combine the water and salt. Bring to boiling. Add carrots. Return to boiling; reduce heat. Simmer, covered, for 8 to 10 minutes or until crisp-tender. Drain carrots.

3 In the same saucepan melt butter over medium heat. Add ginger; cook 30 seconds, stirring constantly. Carefully add carrots and honey. Toss gently for 2 to 3 minutes or until carrots are thoroughly coated with glaze and heated through. Serve carrots with the reserved chicken thighs and drumsticks. Sprinkle with thyme.

PER 2 PIECES CHICKEN + ¾ CUP CARROTS: 329 cal., 19 g total fat (7 g sat. fat, 0 g trans fat), 128 mg chol., 704 mg sodium, 20 g carbo., 3 g fiber, 21 g pro. EXCHANGES: 1 Vegetable, ½ Other Carbo., 3 Lean Meat, 3 Fat

TOMORROW

Chicken-Avocado Clubs

START TO FINISH: 25 MINUTES
MAKES: 2 SERVINGS

- 2 tablespoons mayonnaise or light mayonnaise
- 1 teaspoon purchased basil pesto
- 1 to 2 slices bacon or turkey bacon, halved crosswise
- 4 slices whole grain bread, lightly toasted
- 2 lettuce leaves
- 2 slices Swiss cheese (1½ ounces total)
   Reserved thinly sliced chicken breast from Roasted Chicken with Honey-Ginger Carrots
- ½ of a ripe avocado, halved, seeded, peeled, and sliced
- 1 medium orange, peeled and sliced

1 In a small bowl stir together mayonnaise and pesto; set aside. Cook bacon according to package directions; drain well on paper towels. Cut bacon into large pieces.

2 Spread pesto mixture on one side of each bread slice; top two of the bread slices with lettuce, cheese, and chicken. Add avocado and orange slices. Top with bacon and add remaining bread slices, spread sides down. To serve, cut each sandwich in half.

PER SANDWICH: 619 cal., 32 g total fat (9 g sat. fat, 0 g trans fat), 86 mg chol., 1,131 mg sodium, 44 g carbo., 12 g fiber, 39 g pro. EXCHANGES: ½ Fruit, 2½ Starch, 4 Lean Meat, 5 Fat

Cook Now, Eat Later

You don't have to cook the second recipe right away the following night. Meat and poultry leftovers will keep in the refrigerator for three days. Just be sure to chill them promptly.

TONIGHT | **TOMORROW**

Roasted Chicken with Honey-Ginger Carrots, Step-by-Step

1. Carve the leg-thigh portions off the chicken for tonight's recipe. Slice the breast and store it in the refrigerator for Chicken-Avocado Clubs to enjoy another night.   2. Melt the butter in the saucepan, but do not allow it to brown. 3. A touch of honey adds sweetness and coats the carrots with a glistening glaze.

TONIGHT | **TOMORROW**

Braised Beef Ragout with Noodles, Step-by-Step

1. When browning meat, make sure your pan is large enough to accommodate the meat easily but not so large that the fat drippings will burn. 2. As the cooking liquids simmer, they will reduce and thicken, making a rich sauce for the meat. 3. Separate the meat into shreds by pulling it in opposite directions using two forks.

Cook Once, Eat Twice (continued)

TONIGHT

Braised Beef Ragout with Noodles

PREP: 45 MINUTES   **COOK:** 2 HOURS
MAKES: 2 SERVINGS + RESERVES (BEEF)

- 1   1½-pound boneless beef chuck pot roast
- ½   teaspoon salt
- ¼   teaspoon freshly ground black pepper
- 2   tablespoons olive oil
- ½   cup chopped onion (1 medium)
- ½   cup chopped carrot (1 medium)
- 2   cloves garlic, minced
- ¾   cup dry red wine or beef broth
- 1   14.5-ounce can diced tomatoes, undrained
- 1   tablespoon tomato paste
- 1   teaspoon dried oregano, crushed
- 2   tablespoons whipping cream

1   Trim fat from meat. Sprinkle meat with salt and pepper. In a 4-quart Dutch oven cook meat in hot oil about 10 minutes or until brown on all sides, turning to brown evenly. Transfer meat to a platter; reserve drippings in Dutch oven.

2   Add onion, carrot, and garlic to drippings in Dutch oven. Cook and stir about 5 minutes or until light brown. Add the wine and simmer, uncovered, for 1 minute. Stir in undrained tomatoes, tomato paste, and oregano. Return meat to Dutch oven. Bring to boiling; reduce heat. Simmer, covered, about 2 hours or until meat is tender.

3   Remove meat from Dutch oven; keep warm. For sauce, skim fat from cooking liquid. Return cooking liquid to the Dutch oven. To reduce cooking liquid, simmer, uncovered, until mixture measures about 2 cups. Stir in cream.

4   Meanwhile, using two forks, pull meat apart into shreds; place half of the shredded meat in a storage container. Cover and refrigerate for up to 3 days to use in Shredded Beef Taco Salad with Corn Salsa. Add the remaining meat to sauce mixture in Dutch oven; heat through. Serve over *hot cooked noodles*.

PER 2 OUNCES MEAT + 1 CUP SAUCE: 786 cal.,
42 g total fat (14 g sat. fat, 0 g trans fat), 140 mg chol.,
885 mg sodium, 52 g carbo., 7 g fiber, 35 g pro.
EXCHANGES: 2 Vegetable, 2½ Starch, 3½ Lean Meat, 7 Fat

TOMORROW

Shredded Beef Taco Salad with Corn Salsa

PREP: 20 MINUTES   **COOK:** 10 MINUTES
MAKES: 2 SERVINGS

- ½   cup fresh or frozen whole kernel corn
- 2   large roma tomatoes, seeded and chopped
- 1   teaspoon ground cumin
- 1   teaspoon chili powder
- ½   teaspoon garlic powder
- ⅓   cup water
-     Reserved shredded cooked beef from Braised Beef Ragout with Noodles
- 2   teaspoons snipped fresh cilantro
-     Few dashes bottled hot pepper sauce
- 2   cups torn romaine lettuce
-     Corn chips or tortilla chips
-     Refrigerated avocado dip (guacamole)

1   Thaw corn, if frozen. In a medium saucepan combine one of the tomatoes, the cumin, chili powder, and garlic powder. Stir in the water. Add beef. Bring to boiling; reduce heat. Simmer, covered, for 10 minutes.

2   Meanwhile, for corn salsa, combine the remaining tomato, the corn, cilantro, and hot pepper sauce. Set aside.

3   To serve, pile romaine on serving plates. Top with beef mixture and corn salsa. Serve with chips and avocado dip.

PER SERVING: 560 cal., 33 g total fat (9 g sat. fat, 0 g trans fat),
84 mg chol., 621 mg sodium, 37 g carbo., 8 g fiber, 31 g pro.
EXCHANGES: 2 Vegetable, 2 Starch, 3 Lean Meat, 5 Fat

Love Those Leftovers
Some dishes, such as soups and stews, become better after a day or two in the fridge. The extra time allows the flavors to meld and become richer and bolder as they stand.

TONIGHT

Veggie-Lover's Shepherd's Pies

PREP: 35 MINUTES **COOK:** 20 MINUTES
BAKE: 15 MINUTES **OVEN:** 400°F
MAKES: 2 SERVINGS + RESERVES

- 1 pound potatoes (2 or 3 medium), peeled and halved
- ¼ cup whipping cream
- 1 tablespoon butter, melted
- 1 clove garlic, minced
- ¼ teaspoon salt
- ¼ teaspoon black pepper
- 1¼ cups chicken broth
- ¼ cup brown lentils, rinsed and drained
- 1 teaspoon snipped fresh thyme or ¼ teaspoon dried thyme, crushed
- 1 medium tomato, peeled, seeded, and chopped
- 1 tablespoon tomato paste
- ½ cup coarsely chopped parsnip
- ½ cup coarsely chopped carrot (1 medium)
- 2 tablespoons shredded Parmesan cheese
- 2 tablespoons chopped bottled roasted red sweet peppers
  Shredded Parmesan cheese (optional)

1 For garlic mashed potatoes, in a saucepan cook potatoes, covered, in a large amount of boiling lightly salted water for 20 to 25 minutes or until tender; drain. In a medium bowl mash potatoes with a potato masher (or press potatoes through a potato ricer into a medium bowl). Stir in cream, butter, garlic, salt, and black pepper. Set aside 1 cup of the mashed potatoes. Place another 1-cup portion of the mashed potatoes in a storage container. Cover and refrigerate for up to 3 days to use in Smashed Potato, Ham, and Leek Soup.

2 Meanwhile, in a medium saucepan combine broth, lentils, and, if using, dried thyme. Bring mixture to boiling; reduce heat. Simmer, covered, for 10 minutes. Add tomato, tomato paste, parsnip, carrot, and, if using, fresh thyme. Return to boiling. Simmer, covered, for 15 to 20 minutes more or until lentils are tender. Transfer mixture to two 10- to 12-ounce ramekins.

3 Preheat oven to 400°F. In a medium bowl combine the reserved 1 cup garlic mashed potatoes, the 2 tablespoons Parmesan cheese, and the chopped roasted sweet peppers. Spoon mounds of the mashed potato mixture onto vegetable mixture in ramekins. Place ramekins on a baking sheet. If desired, sprinkle additional Parmesan cheese onto potato mounds. Bake about 15 minutes or until heated through and golden brown on top.

PER PIE: 339 cal., 11 g total fat (6 g sat. fat, 0 g trans fat), 34 mg chol., 957 mg sodium, 49 g carbo., 13 g fiber, 13 g pro. EXCHANGES: 1 Vegetable, 3 Starch, 1½ Fat

TOMORROW

Smashed Potato, Ham, and Leek Soup

START TO FINISH: 20 MINUTES
MAKES: 2 SERVINGS

- 1 tablespoon butter or margarine
- ½ cup thinly sliced leek
- 1 cup reduced-sodium chicken broth
  Reserved garlic mashed potatoes from Veggie-Lover's Shepherd's Pies
- 1 cup coarsely chopped cooked ham
- 2 tablespoons whipping cream, half-and-half, or light cream
  Fresh dill sprigs or fresh chives (optional)

1 In a medium saucepan melt butter over medium heat. Add leek; cook for 5 minutes, stirring occasionally. Add broth, potatoes, and ham. Bring mixture just to boiling. Stir in whipping cream. If desired, garnish with dill sprigs or chives.

PER 1⅓ CUPS: 400 cal., 26 g total fat (14 g sat. fat, 0 g trans fat), 102 mg chol., 1,395 mg sodium, 27 g carbo., 3 g fiber, 16 g pro. EXCHANGES: 2 Starch, 1½ Lean Meat, 4 Fat

TONIGHT | **TOMORROW**

Veggie-Lover's Shepherd's Pies, Step-by-Step

1. Gently stir the veggie mixture occasionally while it simmers, checking to make sure the heat isn't too high. 2. Use two large spoons to top the pies with the potato mixture—one to scoop the potatoes, the other to push them over the veggies.
3. Place the baking dishes on a shallow baking pan to catch any filling that bubbles over.

Couples Cooking

Long gone are the days when meal making fell on just one pair of shoulders. Couples today have discovered that cooking together can be a way to have fun, unwind, and turn a commonplace task into a treasured part of the day.

Split Work and Share Fun

There are many ways to heat up the kitchen! Choose what works best for the two of you, whether you each prepare a different dish, one preps while the other takes over the stove, or you just tag-team the whole magnificent meal while having a great conversation in the process.

To turn any dinner into a date night, consider these tips.

Tandem Tastes: Plan menus together, combining each of your favorite flavors into a meal that both of you love. For fun, take inspiration from cable cooking shows, stir in a few favorites that your moms used to make, or try to duplicate a dish from your favorite restaurant.

Keep It Simple: While you're getting comfortable in your kitchen and developing your skills, choose simple, frustration-free recipes.

Mix In Some Music: Cooking and music go together like fish and water. Put some favorite tunes in the rotation, pour a little wine or your favorite microbrews, and make it a mini party.

Share Cleanup: Make sure that nobody gets left with the least enjoyable part of the gig. Clean as you go to minimize after-dinner tasks. And remember—if other activities beckon, just put away the perishables, shut the door, and forget the mess. Soaked overnight, those final pots and pans will wash easily while your morning coffee brews.

Apricot-Glazed Pork Chops

START TO FINISH: 25 MINUTES
MAKES: 4 SERVINGS

- 4 ½-inch bone-in pork chops
  Salt and black pepper
- 2 teaspoons olive oil
- 1 large onion, cut into thin wedges
- ½ cup apricot preserves
- ¼ cup water
- 1 tablespoon Dijon-style mustard or spicy mustard
- ½ teaspoon ground nutmeg
  Fresh sage leaves (optional)

1 Sprinkle pork chops with salt and pepper. In a very large skillet heat oil over medium-high heat. Add chops and onion wedges to skillet. Cook for 3 minutes; turn chops and onion. Cook for 3 minutes more.

2 Meanwhile, in a small microwave-safe bowl combine preserves, the water, mustard, and nutmeg. Microwave on 100% power (high) for 1 to 2 minutes or until preserves melt. Pour over chops in skillet. Reduce heat to medium. Cook, covered, about 10 minutes or until chops are cooked through and juices run clear. If desired, garnish with sage.

PER CHOP: 503 cal., 32 g total fat (11 g sat. fat, 0 g trans fat), 89 mg chol., 314 mg sodium, 31 g carbo., 1 g fiber, 20 g pro.
EXCHANGES: 2 Other Carbo., 3 Lean Meat, 4 Fat

The More the Merrier

If you plan to cook together, keep some extra knives, cutting boards, measuring spoons, and cups on hand. You have more enjoyable things to talk about than trying to figure out who misplaced that need-it-now utensil!

Cooking in Tandem. *Have the more confident cook take care of sauteing the chops while the other cook preps the glaze and chooses the tunes.*

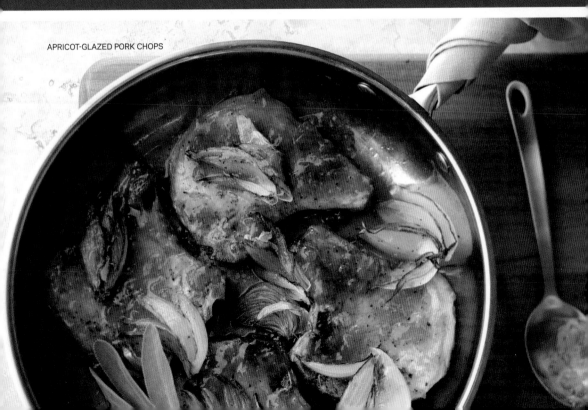

APRICOT-GLAZED PORK CHOPS

Mini Chicken-Artichoke Potpies

PREP: 25 MINUTES **BAKE:** 20 MINUTES
OVEN: 425°F **MAKES:** 2 SERVINGS

- ½ of a 17.3-ounce package (1 sheet) frozen puff pastry
- 1 tablespoon butter or margarine
- 1 tablespoon all-purpose flour
- ¾ cup milk
- 1 cup chopped cooked chicken
- ½ cup coarsely chopped canned artichokes
- ¼ cup frozen peas
- ¼ cup grated Parmesan cheese
- 1 teaspoon snipped fresh Italian parsley

1 Thaw the sheet of puff pastry according to package directions.

2 Preheat oven to 425°F. In a medium saucepan melt butter over medium-high heat. Stir in flour. Add milk all at once. Cook and stir until thickened and bubbly. Stir in chicken, artichokes, peas, Parmesan cheese, and parsley; heat through. Keep warm while preparing pastry.

3 For pastry, unfold puff pastry sheet. On a lightly floured surface roll pastry sheet into an 11-inch square. Cut into four equal squares; set aside two of the squares for another use.* Transfer the hot chicken mixture to two 8- to 10-ounce individual casseroles. Place one of the remaining pastry squares on top of each casserole (pastry squares will hang over edges of dishes). Cut slits in pastry for steam to escape. Place casseroles in a 15×10×1-inch baking pan.

Cheese Manicotti with Roasted Red Pepper Sauce, Step-by-Step

1. This recipe neatly divides the work into two steps. One cook can boil and stuff the manicotti. 2. The other can make the sauce, shred the cheeses, and mix up cocktails to enjoy while the pasta bakes.

4 Bake for 20 to 25 minutes or until crust is puffed and golden brown.

PER POTPIE: 580 cal., 35 g total fat (8 g sat. fat, 0 g trans fat), 94 mg chol., 610 mg sodium, 34 g carbo., 2 g fiber, 32 g pro. EXCHANGES: 1 Vegetable, 2 Starch, 3 Medium-Fat Meat, 6 Fat

Tip: For a sweet treat, preheat oven to 425°F. Sprinkle remaining two puff pastry squares with sugar mixed with ground cinnamon; sprinkle with miniature semisweet chocolate pieces. Fold each square diagonally in half to make a triangle; seal with the tines of a fork. Prick tops with fork; brush with milk. Bake about 15 minutes or until golden brown.

Cheese Manicotti with Roasted Pepper Sauce

PREP: 30 MINUTES **BAKE:** 30 MINUTES
STAND: 10 MINUTES **OVEN:** 350°F
MAKES: 4 SERVINGS

- 8 packaged dried manicotti shells
  Nonstick cooking spray
- 1 cup chopped fresh mushrooms
- ¾ cup shredded carrots
- 3 to 4 cloves garlic, minced
- 1 cup light ricotta cheese or low-fat cream-style cottage cheese
- ¾ cup shredded reduced-fat mozzarella cheese (3 ounces)
- 2 eggs, lightly beaten
- ¼ cup grated Parmesan cheese
- 2 teaspoons dried Italian seasoning, crushed
- 1 14.5-ounce can no-salt-added diced tomatoes with basil, garlic, and oregano, undrained
- 1 cup roasted red sweet peppers, drained and chopped

1 Preheat oven to 350°F. Cook manicotti shells according to package directions; drain. Rinse with cold water; drain again.

2 Meanwhile, for filling, coat a large nonstick skillet with cooking spray. Heat skillet over medium heat. Add mushrooms, carrots, and garlic to hot skillet; cook for 3 to 5 minutes or just until vegetables are tender, stirring occasionally. Remove from heat; cool slightly. Stir in ricotta cheese, ½ cup of the mozzarella cheese, the eggs, Parmesan cheese, and Italian seasoning. Using a small spoon, carefully spoon filling into cooked manicotti shells.

3 For sauce, place undrained tomatoes in a blender. Cover and blend until smooth. Stir in roasted peppers. Spread about ⅓ cup of the sauce in the bottom of each of four ungreased 12- to 16-ounce individual baking dishes or one 2-quart rectangular baking dish. Arrange filled manicotti shells in baking dishes, overlapping shells slightly if necessary. Pour the remaining sauce over shells.

4 Bake, covered, for 25 minutes for individual baking dishes, 35 minutes for large baking dish, or until heated through. Sprinkle with the remaining ¼ cup mozzarella cheese. Bake, uncovered, for 5 minutes more. Let stand for 10 minutes before serving.

PER 2 MANICOTTI: 377 cal., 13 g total fat (7 g sat. fat, 0 g trans fat), 140 mg chol., 370 mg sodium, 43 g carbo., 9 g fiber, 22 g pro. EXCHANGES: 2 Vegetable, 2 Starch, 2 Medium-Fat Meat

Your House Vinaigrette

A green salad goes well with so many dishes. Make yours a go-to specialty by coming up with your own formula for a vinaigrette. Start with the recipe on page 502 and tinker with the varieties of herbs and vinegars until you develop your own house style.

Celebrations

It's Your Turn to Host

Whether you host friends for drinks, nibbles, and laughs, or entertain in-laws for your first holiday meal as a couple, plan well so you can move out of the kitchen and into your groove the minute guests walk through your door.

Choosing the Food

Novice hosts knock themselves out for guests; experts do no such thing. After all, you set the tone for your party—the more fun you have, the better it will be for everyone. Here's how to stay in your comfort zone whenever you host.

Go with What You Know Choose a menu mostly based on recipes you've made and enjoyed. If you want to energize the menu with a few new items, give them a test run or make sure you have plenty other dishes to offer in case the trial recipe doesn't turn out as you'd hoped.

Make Some/Buy Some Purchased items from your favorite deli, bakery, or caterer can round out the homemade offerings.

Get a Head Start Eyeball recipes to find steps that can be done in advance, from cutting veggies to prebaking a quiche crust. Notice that the appetizer recipes on the following pages offer clear make-ahead angles.

Just Say "Yes" Friends who ask to bring something probably aren't simply being polite. Good cooks enjoy sharing a favorite recipe without having to host a whole party. So say "yes, please" to the offer.

Added Advice Check out our party-planning strategies, including how much food to make and how many beverages to buy, on page 39.

Setting the Mood

What do you remember most about the best parties you've been to? Chances are, it wasn't just the food but also the laughter, conversation, and camaraderie you enjoyed with friends. There's an art to orchestrating a good time that's easily mastered when you keep your guests in mind:

* When you invite guests, let them know what to expect, whether it's an appetizer-and-drinks party or an entire meal. That will help them plan their evening.

* Try your best to accommodate dietary needs. You don't have to plan an entire meatless menu around a vegetarian, but you should offer a hearty nonmeat option along with some vegetables that everyone can enjoy.

* Get the good times rolling. Offer guests refreshments the moment they arrive. A thoughtful quaff and some nibbles will put guests at ease.

* Time it right. If you're serving dinner, limit cocktail hour to just that. You don't want your guests to get too hungry before dinner is served.

* Minimize mishaps. So the steak is a bit over-cooked and the piecrust is overbrowned. If you don't let it spoil your evening, your guests won't either.

* Never press those who pass. Guests who decline something you serve—from drinks to dessert—may have personal reasons for doing so. Respect their wishes graciously.

* Move it along. After dinner is over, invite every-one to regroup in another room. Your guests will appreciate the change in scenery and the chance to swap conversation partners.

Keep an entertaining journal. Make shopping and to-do lists and draw up a timeline for your party. Keep the information on hand for future gatherings.

It's a good idea to buy more food than you think you need and to hold some of the items back. When you need to, you can replenish the table with fresh food.

Wine Guide for Newlyweds

You may have received some nifty wineglasses for your wedding gifts. Now, raise a glass to something you'll both be glad to know. Enjoying wine is easy. All you need to know to enjoy a casual glass, together or with friends, is right here.

Aging Wines

Don't bother. Most wineries release bottles only when they're ready to drink. Exceptions include high-end and collectible wines. If those intrigue you, get to know a local wine merchant who can offer advice on cellaring.

Storing Wines

Wine keeps best when the bottles are stored in a dark, cool place free of vibrations. A temperature-controlled wine storage unit would be ideal, but a box in a closet away from heat and light will work just fine.

A Good Chill

Reds can use about 30 minutes in the refrigerator before serving; whites should be fully chilled but taken out of the refrigerator 20 minutes before serving—a too-cool temperature keeps the wine's flavors and aromas from showing off at their most expressive best.

Pairing Wine and Food

To keep it simple, remember that, in general, as the food gets heavier, wine should too. For example, bright Sauvignon Blanc goes well with summer salads; bold reds mesh with meaty stews. There are exceptions—elegant Rieslings go well with robust sausages and cured meats.

When in doubt, reach for Riesling, Pinot Noir, and Pinot Grigio—wines that will never let you down with food.

Trust Your Intuition

What wine comes to mind as you prepare a dish? Chances are it'll be a fine match with the food. And you'll get better at this with every cork you pull.

What to Do with Leftover Wine

There's no need to polish off a whole bottle in one sitting—most wines stay fresh for at least a day or two. Recork the bottle with its original cork and store it in the refrigerator, whether white or red. Let reds warm up a little at room temperature before re-serving.

Sparkling wines will generally stay fizzy for one day after opening—or at least long enough to enjoy the bubbles at brunch. You won't be able to recork the bottle with the same cork (it will have expanded upon opening); use another stopper.

If you have unopened bottles of chilled wine after a party, it's generally fine to re-store them at room temperature; only the most fragile of wines will be the worse for wear.

Finding Affordable Favorites

To find wines you love, learn a little bit about the grapes. Page 88 offers an overview of eight popular varietals. The next step is to find everyday-priced wines—bottles that cost under $12 but drink like they cost $20 or more. Here are the regions that produce bargains:

* *Australia:* If plush, fruity reds are your passion, look for well-priced bottles from here.
* *Chile:* Snag great values in reds (Carmenere, Merlot, Cabernet, and Syrah) and keep an eye out for Sauvingon Blanc and Chardonnay.
* *Italy:* Look for lesser-known (and undervalued) dry, crisp whites, such as Vermentino and Orvieto, as well as Asti, a generously fruity sparkling wine.
* *Spain:* The sparkling wines (cava) are inexpensive enough to serve a crowd yet dashing enough to impress everyone.
* *Washington State:* Balanced, finesse-filled Rieslings rival those of Germany and France—at a fraction of the price.

STEMMED RED WINE GLASS

STEMMED WHITE WINE GLASS

STEMMED CHAMPAGNE FLUTE

STEMLESS RED WINE GLASS

STEMLESS WHITE WINE GLASS

STEMLESS CHAMPAGNE FLUTE

Uncorking and Recorking a Bottle, Step-by-Step

1. Use the small knife attached to a waiter's corkscrew to cut off the top of the foil covering. Once the metal spiral has made it through the cork's center, place the lever on the lip of the bottle and squeeze the lever against the bottle while using the handle to pull the cork up. 3. Recork unused wine with purchased bottle stoppers; store in the refrigerator.

1

2

3

POMEGRANATE FIZZES

Your signature drink. *Choose one specialty cocktail to serve at your party and you won't need to play bartender all night. Round out the offerings with sodas, beer, and wine.*

HONEYDEW-BASIL NOJITOS

GOLDEN SPARKLERS

Mocktails to Cocktails

A stylish cocktail makes for a dashing way to kick off an evening, but you should always be ready to serve something festive to nondrinkers (club soda with lime just doesn't cut it!). Each of these recipes works two ways—with alcohol or without.

Pomegranate Fizzes

PREP: 15 MINUTES **CHILL:** 2 HOURS
MAKES: ABOUT 20 SERVINGS

- ¼ cup fresh mint leaves
- 4 cups pomegranate juice or cranberry juice
- ¼ cup sugar
- 2 1-liter bottles carbonated water
- ½ cup vodka (optional)
  Fresh mint sprigs (optional)

1 Place mint leaves in a pitcher. Using a wooden spoon, crush mint leaves. Add pomegranate juice and sugar; stir until sugar dissolves. Cover and chill for at least 2 hours to blend flavors. Using a slotted spoon, remove and discard mint leaves.

2 For each serving, in a small glass combine ¼ cup of the juice mixture, a splash of vodka (if desired), and ¼ cup of the carbonated water; add *ice cubes*. If desired, garnish with mint sprigs. Serve immediately.

PER 4 OUNCES: 37 cal., 0 g total fat, 0 mg chol., 6 mg sodium, 9 g carbo., 0 g fiber, 0 g pro.
EXCHANGES: ½ Fruit

Golden Sparklers

START TO FINISH: 15 MINUTES
MAKES: ABOUT 10 SERVINGS

- 1½ cups orange juice, chilled
- 1½ cups apricot nectar, chilled
- ¼ cup whiskey (optional)
- 1 375-milliliter bottle sparkling water, chilled
  Thinly sliced orange or lime (optional)

1 Place 1 cup *ice cubes* in a large pitcher. Pour orange juice, apricot nectar, and, if desired, whiskey over the ice cubes. Slowly add sparkling water, stirring gently. Fill 10 glasses with *ice*. Pour mixture into ice-filled glasses. If desired, garnish with orange or lime slices. Serve immediately.

PER 4 OUNCES: 38 cal., 0 g total fat, 0 mg chol., 2 mg sodium, 9 g carbo., 0 g fiber, 0 g pro.
EXCHANGES: ½ Other Carbo.

Honeydew-Basil Nojitos

START TO FINISH: 25 MINUTES
MAKES: 8 SERVINGS

- ½ cup large fresh basil leaves, torn
- ½ cup lime juice
- 2 teaspoons granulated sugar
- 2 3-pound honeydew melons, peeled, seeded, and cubed
  Lime wedges (optional)
  Superfine granulated sugar (optional)
  Carbonated water (optional)
- ¼ cup white rum (optional)
  Honeydew melon spears or balls (optional)

1 In a large pitcher combine basil leaves, lime juice, and granulated sugar. Using a muddler or the back of a wooden spoon, mash ingredients together well, making sure most of the sugar is dissolved. Set aside.

2 Place about one-fourth of the melon cubes in a food processor or blender. Cover and process or blend until smooth. Press puree through a fine-mesh sieve; discard solids. Repeat with the remaining melon cubes, one-fourth at a time (you should have 4 cups total juice). Add melon juice to the pitcher.

3 If desired, rub a lime wedge around rims of eight glasses and dip rims in superfine sugar. Fill glasses with *ice*. Pour juice mixture into ice-filled glasses. If desired, add a splash of carbonated water, rum, and/or melon spears or balls to each glass. Serve immediately.

PER 10 OUNCES: 65 cal., 0 g total fat, 0 mg chol., 29 mg sodium, 17 g carbo., 1 g fiber, 1 g pro.
EXCHANGES: 1 Fruit

Easy Appetizers

If you're new to hosting, an appetizer party is the best place to begin. They're easy-to-master, sure-fire hits as long as you fill the room with the most interesting people you know and fill the buffet table with a variety of intriguing nibbles, such as the up-to-date bites on pages A-38 to A-43.

Thai Chicken Wings with Peanut Sauce

PREP: 25 MINUTES **BAKE:** 20 MINUTES
COOK: 5 MINUTES **OVEN:** 400°F
MAKES: 20 DRUMMETTES

- 2¼ pounds chicken wing drummettes (about 20)
- ½ cup bottled salsa
- 2 tablespoons creamy peanut butter
- 1 tablespoon lime juice
- 2 teaspoons soy sauce
- 2 teaspoons grated fresh ginger
- ¼ cup sugar
- ¼ cup creamy peanut butter
- 3 tablespoons soy sauce
- 3 tablespoons water
- 2 cloves garlic, minced

1 Preheat oven to 400°F. Place drummettes in a large bowl. Combine salsa, the 2 tablespoons peanut butter, the lime juice, the 2 teaspoons soy sauce, and ginger. Pour over drummettes, tossing to coat.

2 Arrange drummettes in a single layer in a roasting pan lined with foil. Bake for 20 minutes or until tender and no longer pink.

3 Meanwhile, for the peanut sauce, in a small saucepan stir together sugar, the ¼ cup peanut butter, the 3 tablespoons soy sauce, the water, and garlic. Cook over medium-low heat until sugar dissolves and mixture is smooth. Serve with drummettes (mixture will thicken as it stands).

Slow Cooker Method: Place drummettes in a 3½- or 4-quart slow cooker. Add salsa mixture, tossing to coat. Cover and cook on low-heat setting for 5 to 6 hours or on high-heat setting for 2½ to 3 hours. Drain drummettes; discard liquid. Return drummettes to slow cooker. Gently stir in peanut sauce. To serve, keep drummettes warm in a covered cooker on low-heat setting for up to 2 hours.

Make-Ahead Tip: If using the slow cooker method, combine drummettes and salsa mixture in the slow cooker insert. Cover and chill up to 24 hours. Replace insert in the slow cooker; cook as directed.

PER 2 DRUMMETTES: 191 cal., 13 g total fat (3 g sat. fat, 0 g trans fat), 58 mg chol., 432 mg sodium, 7 g carbo., 1 g fiber, 12 g pro.
EXCHANGES: ½ Starch, 1½ High-Fat Meat

Avocado Pesto-Stuffed Tomatoes

PREP: 40 MINUTES **STAND:** 30 MINUTES
MAKES: 30 APPETIZERS

- 30 cherry tomatoes (about 1¼ pints)
- ½ of a medium avocado, seeded, peeled, and cut up
- 2 ounces cream cheese, softened
- 2 tablespoons basil pesto
- 1 teaspoon lemon juice
  Snipped fresh basil (optional)
  Fresh basil leaves (optional)

1 Cut a thin slice from the top of each tomato. (If desired, cut a thin slice from the bottom of each tomato so it stands upright.) Using a very small spoon or a small melon baller, carefully hollow out tomatoes. Line a baking sheet with paper towels. Invert tomatoes onto the towels. Let stand for 30 minutes to drain.

2 Meanwhile, for filling, in a food processor combine avocado, cream cheese, pesto, and lemon juice. Cover and process just until combined.

3 Place tomatoes, open sides up, on a serving platter. Spoon filling into the tomato cups. If desired, cover loosely with plastic wrap and chill for up to 4 hours. If desired, sprinkle with snipped basil before serving and serve on basil leaves.

PER APPETIZER: 18 cal., 1 g total fat (1 g sat. fat, 0 g trans fat), 2 mg chol., 16 mg sodium, 1 g carbo., 0 g fiber, 0 g pro.
EXCHANGES: Free

10 to Try–Hummus

Start with Hummus, page 45.
1. ROASTED PEPPER: Add ½ cup bottled roasted sweet peppers and 1 teaspoon snipped fresh oregano to the food processor. **2. CILANTRO AND CURRY:** Stir ¼ cup snipped fresh cilantro and 1 tablespoon curry powder into pureed mixture. **3. PEAS AND CHEESE:** Add 1 cup peas to the food processor. Top with 2 tablespoons feta cheese. **4. TOFU-LICIOUS:** Add 4 ounces (about ½ cup) soft silken tofu to the food processor. **5. TOMATO:** Add ¼ cup chopped oil-packed dried tomatoes to food processor. **6. SMOKIN'-HOT:** Omit the ¼ teaspoon paprika. Add 2 teaspoons smoked paprika, 1 teaspoon ground cumin, and ¼ teaspoon cayenne pepper to the food processor. **7. GUACAMOLE:** Add 1 cup chopped avocado and ½ cup snipped fresh cilantro to the food processor. **8. CAPERS AND RED ONION:** Stir ¼ cup each chopped capers and red onion into the pureed mixture. **9. GO GREEN:** Add 1 cup cooked sweet soybeans (edamame), ½ teaspoons prepared wasabi paste, and 1½ teaspoons soy sauce to the food processor. **10. MUSTARD-TARRAGON:** Stir 1 tablespoon snipped fresh tarragon and 2 teaspoons mustard into the pureed mixture.

TOASTED RAVIOLI NIBBLERS

Don't Knock Yourself Out. It's easy to get overly ambitious when planning appetizer parties. The best strategy is to make one or two little bites and accompany the spread with purchased nibbles.

BBQ PHYLLO BITES

MINI MARGHERITA PIZZAS

BBQ Phyllo Bites

PREP: 15 MINUTES **BAKE:** 20 MINUTES
OVEN: 375°F **MAKES:** 15 PHYLLO BITES

- 1 1.9-ounce package baked miniature phyllo dough shells
- 2 ounces smoked cheddar cheese, cut into 15 cubes
- ¾ cup refrigerated cooked shredded pork or chicken in original barbecue sauce
   Dairy sour cream
   Snipped fresh cilantro

1   Preheat oven to 375°F. Place phyllo dough shells in a 15×10×1-inch baking pan. Place a cheese cube into each phyllo shell.

2   Divide shredded pork evenly among shells. Bake about 20 minutes or until heated through. Top with sour cream and cilantro.

Make-Ahead Tip: Prepare as directed in Step 1. Cover and chill up to 8 hours. Continue as directed in Step 2.

PER PHYLLO BITE: 60 cal., 3 g total fat (1 g sat. fat, 0 g trans fat), 9 mg chol., 124 mg sodium, 4 g carbo., 0 g fiber, 3 g pro. EXCHANGES: ½ Medium-Fat Meat, ½ Fat

Toasted Ravioli Nibblers

START TO FINISH: 30 MINUTES
MAKES: 25 APPETIZERS

- 1 16-ounce package purchased frozen breaded cheese-filled ravioli (about 25)
- 25 fresh mozzarella bocconcini balls and/or fresh mozzarella or provolone cheese cubes
- 25 small fresh basil leaves
- 25 cherry tomatoes
   Flavored dipping oil or purchased marinara sauce

1   Bake ravioli according to package directions.

2   Thread a baked ravioli, a cherry tomato, a basil leaf, and a cheese ball or cube on each of twenty-five 6-inch skewers. Serve immediately with your choice of flavored dipping oil or sauce.

Make-Ahead Tip: Thread a cheese ball or cube, a basil leaf, and a cherry tomato (not the ravioli) onto twenty-five 6-inch skewers. Cover and chill for up to 2 hours before serving. Just before serving bake frozen ravioli according to package directions. Add to skewers. Serve immediately.

PER APPETIZER: 127 cal., 9 g total fat (3 g sat. fat, 0 g trans fat), 15 mg chol., 171 mg sodium, 7 g carbo., 0 g fiber, 5 g pro. EXCHANGES: ½ Starch, ½ Medium-Fat Meat, 1 Fat

Mini Margherita Pizzas

PREP: 25 MINUTES **BAKE:** 8 MINUTES
OVEN: 450°F **MAKES:** 18 TO 20 MINI PIZZAS

- 1 14-ounce package (12-inch) Italian bread shell (such as Boboli brand)
- ½ cup purchased roasted sweet pepper bruschetta topper, Kalamata olive bruschetta topper, or desired pizza sauce
- 6 ounces fresh mozzarella cheese, sliced
- 2 roma tomatoes, thinly sliced
   Freshly ground black pepper
   Small fresh basil leaves

1   Preheat oven to 450°F. Line a baking sheet with foil; set aside. For pizza crusts, use a 2-inch round cookie cutter to cut Italian bread shell into 18 to 20 circles (or cut into 20 pieces). Arrange circles on prepared baking sheet.

2   Spread bruschetta topper over pizza crusts. Top with sliced mozzarella cheese and tomatoes. (If necessary, cut cheese and tomatoes to fit.)

3   Bake for 8 to 10 minutes or until cheese melts and pizza crusts are crisp. To serve, sprinkle with black pepper and top with small basil leaves.

Make-Ahead Tip: Cut bread shell into circles or pieces. Place in a storage container; cover and let stand at room temperature for 24 hours before serving.

PER MINI PIZZA: 83 cal., 4 g total fat (1 g sat. fat, 0 g trans fat), 8 mg chol., 159 mg sodium, 9 g carbo., 0 g fiber, 4 g pro. EXCHANGES: ½ Starch, 1 Fat

Shrimp-and-Bacon-Stuffed Baby Potatoes

PREP: 35 MINUTES **BAKE:** 42 MINUTES
OVEN: 425°F **MAKES:** 28 APPETIZERS

- 14 tiny new potatoes (about 1¼ pounds)
- 2 tablespoons Dijon-style mustard
- 1 tablespoon olive oil
- 1 teaspoon Old Bay seasoning (seafood seasoning)*
- 1 7- to 8-ounce package frozen peeled cooked shrimp, thawed, drained, and chopped
- ½ of an 8-ounce package cream cheese, softened
- 1 cup shredded Gouda cheese (4 ounces)
- 5 slices bacon, crisp-cooked, drained, and crumbled
- 1 teaspoon Old Bay seasoning (seafood seasoning)*
- ¼ cup snipped fresh chives (optional)

1 Preheat oven to 425°F. Cut potatoes in half lengthwise. Using a small melon baller or a very small spoon, scoop out potato pulp, leaving ¼-inch shells. Cut a thin slice from the bottom of each potato half so it stands upright. Place potatoes, cut sides up, in a 15⊠10⊠1-inch baking pan.

2 In a small bowl combine mustard, oil, and 1 teaspoon Old Bay seasoning. Brush insides of potato shells with mustard mixture. Bake about 30 minutes or until potatoes are tender.

3 Meanwhile, for filling, in a small bowl combine shrimp, cream cheese, Gouda cheese, bacon, and 1 teaspoon Old Bay seasoning. Spoon filling into potato shells, mounding slightly.

4 Bake for 12 to 15 minutes more or until filling is heated through and cheese is melted. Serve warm or at room temperature. If desired, garnish with chives.

*Tip: If seasoning is coarse, crush before using in recipe.

PER APPETIZER: 63 cal., 4 g total fat (2 g sat. fat, 0 g trans fat), 24 mg chol., 169 mg sodium, 3 g carbo., 0 g fiber, 4 g pro. EXCHANGES: ½ Lean Meat, 1 Fat

Polenta with Olives and Basil

PREP: 20 MINUTES **BAKE:** 15 MINUTES
OVEN: 350°F **MAKES:** 12 APPETIZERS

- 1 16-ounce tube refrigerated cooked polenta
- 1 tablespoon olive oil
- ½ cup finely shredded Parmesan cheese
- ½ cup chopped, pitted Kalamata olives*
- 1 tablespoon snipped fresh basil or Italian parsley*

1 Preheat oven to 350°F. Trim ends of polenta; discard trimmings. Cut polenta into twelve ½-inch slices. Brush both sides of each polenta slice with oil. Place polenta slices on a baking sheet.

2 Bake for 10 minutes. Sprinkle slices with Parmesan cheese. Bake about 5 minutes more or until cheese melts.

3 To serve, top polenta slices with olives and sprinkle with snipped basil.

Make-Ahead Tip: Prepare as directed in Step 1. Cover baking sheet and chill for up to 4 hours. Continue as directed in Step 3.

PER APPETIZER: 66 cal., 3 g total fat (1 g sat. fat, 0 g trans fat), 2 mg chol., 266 mg sodium, 8 g carbo., 1 g fiber, 2 g pro. EXCHANGES: ½ Starch, ½ Fat

*Other Topping Ideas: Instead of olives, use ¾ cup marinated artichoke hearts, drained and chopped; ¾ cup pepperoni slices, slivered; ½ cup flaked smoked salmon; or ½ cup salsa and ⅓ cup canned refried beans. Instead of basil, use 1½ teaspoons snipped fresh rosemary or 2 teaspoons snipped fresh oregano.

Boosting the Bounty

To offer more choice at your party (without more cooking), pick up cheeses, cured meats, olives, and artisanal breads from the grocery store. Buy prepared deviled eggs and dress them up as shown on page 42.

10 to Try— Soda Fix-Ups

1. ICED COLA COFFEE: Combine 4 cups each chilled coffee and *cream soda*. Serve over ice with a splash of half-and-half. **2. ROOT BEER FRAPPE:** Puree 6 cups ice and 1 cup sweetened condensed milk in a blender. Add 4 cups *root beer*. **3. LEMON FREEZE:** Puree 1 pint each lemon sorbet and vanilla ice cream with ½ cup vodka. Add 4 cups *lemon-lime soda*.
4. BERRY SANGRIA: Combine 1 cup raspberries, 1 bottle dry red wine, 4 cups *cherry cola*, and ice.
5. POMEGRANATE: Combine 3 cups pomegranate juice and 3 cups chilled *orange soda*. Serve over ice.
6. CUCUMBER-MINT: Puree 2 peeled cucumbers, ½ cup cold water, and ¼ cup mint leaves. Strain and add 4 cups chilled *ginger ale*.
7. CHOCO-CHERRY: Place 2 scoops chocolate ice cream into a glass and fill with *cherry cola*.
8. PEACH SANGRIA: Combine sliced peaches, 1 bottle white wine, 4 cups *lemon-lime soda*, and ice.
9. CREAMSICLE: Place 1 to 2 scoops orange sherbet or sorbet into a glass and top with *cream soda*. **10. STRAWBERRY LIMEADE:** Combine 4 cups *strawberry soda* and 1 cup lime juice.

Our First Holiday Dinner

So this is your very first time making a holiday dinner—and you're not quite sure how to pull it off. Fear no more. Although inviting friends and family to your new home for a dinner may seem daunting you can do it. It's all a matter of using tried-and-true recipes, creating a plan, and following your plan step-by-step.

First Things First

A few reminders. The best thing about holiday meals is that your table will be filled with family and friends—an easy audience already so fond of you that they won't even notice if anything is less than perfect.

Craft the meal as a couple. You'll halve the work and share in the applause. Remember too that you do not have to fly solo on a meal of this magnitude. Does your mom make the world's best pecan pie? Does your mother-in-law bake dinner rolls to die for? If so, ask them to donate their time and talent to the festivities. They'll be flattered you asked.

Make a Game Plan

With pencil and paper in hand, along with these pages and trusted recipes, plan your menu. For sure success, make the menu included here—tailor-made to be easy and delicious.

Customize the menu with your specialties or traditional family favorites. Go for it, as long as the dishes you choose have pretty, contrasting colors and varied textures—from smooth and creamy to crisp and crunchy.

Countdown to Success

One trick to hosting the holiday meal is figuring out what to do in what order, then following the plan. Here are some of the tasks you can do in advance:

TWO WEEKS AHEAD

* Buy all foods with long shelf lives, including spices, nuts, canned and frozen goods, and beverages.

1 TO 2 DAYS AHEAD

* Purchase your turkey breast; thaw in the refrigerator according to size. Allow at least 1 day of thawing for every 4 pounds of turkey.
* Prepare turkey rub; store in airtight container.
* Choose linens, serving vessels, and tableware; ensure they're in ready-to-use shape.
* Purchase all perishable items.

1 DAY AHEAD

* Prepare mushroom gravy and bread stuffing; cover and refrigerate.
* Cook the Green Beans with Lemon and Walnuts and the Glazed Carrots with Pistachios through Step 1 of each recipe; cover and refrigerate. (The next day, reheat green beans in the microwave to continue with recipe; continue as directed for the carrots.)
* Toast the pistachios for the Glazed Carrots with Pistachios; cover and store at room temperature up to 24 hours.

A sieve is handy for removing green beans from boiling water. To make them ahead, prepare through Step 1, then place in a storage bowl, cover tightly, and chill up to 24 hours. Reheat in the microwave.

Left: Purchase the turkey a week before Thanksgiving to give it time to thaw in the refrigerator. Right: Prep the carrots up to 24 hours in advance, then saute to warm them just before serving.

Left: The stuffing can be assembled 24 hours before baking; refrigerate, covered, until ready to reheat. Right: Toast pistachios; cool, then cover and store at room temperature to sprinkle over carrots.

Make-Ahead Carrots. *Prepare the Glazed Carrots with Pistachios as directed through Step 2. Place carrots and nuts in seperate airtight containers and chill up to 24 hours. When ready, continue as directed in Step 3.*

Glazed Carrots with Pistachios

PREP: 20 MINUTES **COOK:** 10 MINUTES
BAKE: 8 MINUTES **OVEN:** 350°F
MAKES: 8 SERVINGS

- 2 pounds small carrots with tops
- 2 cups water
- ¼ teaspoon salt
- ⅓ cup pistachio nuts
- ⅓ cup butter
- ¼ cup packed brown sugar
- 1 teaspoon snipped fresh thyme

1 Preheat oven to 350°F. Trim carrots, leaving about 1 inch of the tops. In an extra-large skillet combine the water and salt. Bring to boiling. Add carrots. Return to boiling; reduce heat. Simmer, covered, for 10 to 12 minutes or just until carrots are tender. Drain carrots in a large colander; cool.

2 Meanwhile, to toast pistachio nuts, spread on a baking sheet; bake for 8 to 10 minutes or until nuts are lightly toasted, stirring once. Cool.

3 In an extra-large skillet melt butter over medium heat. Add brown sugar and thyme, stirring until combined. Add carrots and cook, uncovered, over medium-low heat about 10 minutes or just until carrots are glazed, stirring occasionally. Transfer carrots to a serving platter or bowl. Sprinkle with toasted nuts.

PER SERVING: 163 cal., 10 g total fat (5 g sat. fat, 0 g trans fat), 20 mg chol., 196 mg sodium, 17 g carbo., 3 g fiber, 2 g pro.
EXCHANGES: 1 Vegetable, 1 Other Carbo., 2 Fat

Green Beans with Lemon and Walnuts

START TO FINISH: 25 MINUTES
MAKES: 8 SERVINGS

- 1½ pounds fresh green beans, trimmed and sliced lengthwise, or frozen French-cut green beans
- 2 tablespoons butter
- ½ cup chopped walnuts
- 2 teaspoons grated fresh ginger
- ½ teaspoon finely shredded lemon peel
- 2 teaspoons lemon juice

1 In a large saucepan cook beans, covered, in boiling salted water for 5 to 10 minutes or until crisp-tender; drain.

2 Meanwhile, in a small saucepan melt butter over medium heat. Add walnuts and ginger; cook for 2 to 3 minutes or until nuts are toasted. Remove from heat; stir in lemon peel and lemon juice. Stir nut mixture into cooked beans.

PER ¾ CUP: 97 cal., 8 g total fat (2 g sat. fat, 0 g trans fat), 8 mg chol., 25 mg sodium, 7 g carbo., 3 g fiber, 3 g pro.
EXCHANGES: 1 Vegetable, 1½ Fat

Your First Holiday Dessert

If making a from-scratch dessert just isn't in the picture, pumpkin pie from the grocery store, bakery, or holiday dessert maker can also be served with pride. Serve it on your prettiest plates and top with a flourish, such as whipped cream, a sprinkling of nutmeg, jewel-toned pomegranate seeds, toasted hazelnuts, and/or shavings of white chocolate.

Artisanal Bread Stuffing

PREP: 50 MINUTES **BAKE:** 70 MINUTES
OVEN: 325°F **MAKES:** 10 SERVINGS

- 12 cups ½- to ¾-inch cubes artisanal bread (such as rosemary, dried tomato, or cheese bread) (about a 1¼-pound loaf)
- ½ cup pine nuts
  Nonstick cooking spray
- 6 tablespoons butter
- 4½ cups coarsely chopped, cored fennel bulb
- 1½ cups chopped onion (3 medium)
- 1½ cups sliced Kalamata olives
- 3 tablespoons snipped fresh thyme or 1 tablespoon dried thyme, crushed
- ¾ teaspoon coarsely ground black pepper
- 2¼ cups chicken broth or chicken stock

1 Preheat oven to 325°F. Place bread cubes and pine nuts in a large roasting pan. Toast in the oven for 15 to 20 minutes or until bread cubes are crisp and pine nuts are light brown, tossing once. Set aside to cool.

2 Meanwhile, lightly coat a 3-quart casserole with cooking spray; set aside. In a large skillet melt butter over medium-high heat. Add fennel and onion; cook about 10 minutes or until vegetables are tender, stirring occasionally. Stir in olives, thyme, and pepper. Transfer mixture to an extra-large bowl. Add bread cubes and pine nuts, tossing to combine. Add chicken broth, stirring until moistened. Spoon bread mixture into prepared casserole.

3 Cover with foil. Bake for 45 minutes. Remove the foil. Bake about 25 minutes more or until the stuffing is heated through. Serve warm.

Make-Ahead Tip: Toast the bread cubes and pine nuts and store in an airtight container at room temperature up to 1 day ahead. Chop the fennel and onion; place in separate airtight containers and chill up to 6 hours before preparing the stuffing.

Make-Ahead Directions: Prepare as directed through Step 2. Cover casserole tightly with plastic wrap; chill for up to 24 hours. To serve, preheat oven to 325°F. Remove plastic wrap. If desired, drizzle stuffing with an additional ¼ cup chicken broth to moisten. Cover with foil. Bake for 55 to 60 minutes. Remove the foil. Bake about 25 minutes more or until heated through.

PER 1½ CUPS: 322 cal., 19 g total fat (7 g sat. fat, 0 g trans fat), 30 mg chol., 836 mg sodium, 29 g carbo., 4 g fiber, 7 g pro. EXCHANGES: ½ Vegetable, 2 Starch, 3½ Fat

Herbed Turkey Breast

PREP: 25 MINUTES **ROAST:** 1 HOUR 20 MINUTES
STAND: 10 MINUTES **OVEN:** 400°F/350°F
MAKES: 10 SERVINGS

- 2 3- to 3½-lb. fresh or frozen bone-in turkey breast halves
  Nonstick cooking spray
- ¼ cup butter, room temperature (½ stick)
- 2 tablespoons snipped fresh sage
- 2 tablespoons snipped fresh parsley
- 2 teaspoons snipped fresh thyme
- 2 teaspoons salt
- 1½ teaspoons black pepper

1 Thaw turkey, if frozen. Preheat oven to 400°F. Coat a large roasting pan and rack with cooking spray. Set aside. In small bowl combine butter, sage, parsley, thyme, salt, and pepper. Set aside.

2 Place turkey breast halves on cutting board. Slip fingers between skin and meat to loosen skin, leaving skin partially attached at edges. Lift skin and spread all but 1 tablespoon herb mixture evenly under skin over breast meat. Rub remaining herb mixture on outside of turkey. Insert oven-going meat thermometer into thickest part of breast, without touching bone. Place turkey breast halves, bone sides down, on roasting rack in prepared pan.

3 Roast, uncovered, on lower rack of oven for 20 minutes. Reduce oven temperature to 350°F. Roast 1 to 1½ hours longer or until thermometer registers 170°F, juices run clear, and turkey is no longer pink, occasionally spooning pan juices over turkey. If necessary, place foil over turkey breast the last 30 minutes of roasting to prevent burning. Let stand, covered with foil, for 10 minutes before slicing. Place sliced turkey on platter.

PER 7 OUNCES: 311 cal., 6 g total fat (2 g sat. fat, 0 g trans fat), 167 mg chol., 440 mg sodium, 4 g carbo., 0 g fiber, 57 g pro.
EXCHANGES: 8 Lean Meat

Turkey—Today and Tomorrow

Cooking the holiday meal offers the benefit of tasty leftovers! Sliced turkey will keep up to 3 days in the refrigerator and up to 4 months in the freezer. Enjoy it well into the new year in casseroles, salads, and sandwiches.

Herbed Turkey Breast, Step-by-Step

1. Slide the herb butter mixture between the skin and the breast meat, covering the meat as evenly as you can.
2. Place the oven-going meat thermometer at least 2 to 2½ inches into the thickest part of the meat, but do not touch the bone. 3. Use a deep spoon or ladle to pour pan juices over turkey occasionally while cooking. Wash the utensil well with warm soapy water after each use.

Pumpkin-Pear Cake, Step-by-Step

1. Place a serving platter or a baking pan over the top of the baking pan. (For the prettiest presentation, use a large serving platter with raised sides; if that's not available, use a 15×10×1-inch baking pan.) 2. Flip the cake pan over; tap bottom of the cake pan, if needed, to release the cake onto the platter.

1

2

PUMPKIN-PEAR CAKE

Easy Mushroom Gravy

START TO FINISH: 20 MINUTES
MAKES: 4 CUPS

- 6 cups sliced wild mushrooms, such as cremini or shiitake, or button mushrooms
- 2 tablespoons olive oil or vegetable oil
- 2 12-ounce jars turkey gravy
- 1 cup dairy sour cream or light dairy sour cream
- 1 teaspoon dried sage or thyme, crushed

1 In a large skillet cook mushrooms in hot oil until tender. In a medium bowl whisk together gravy, sour cream, and sage; add to mushrooms in skillet. Cook and stir until heated through. Serve over roasted meat, poultry, or potatoes.

PER ¼ CUP: 65 cal., 5 g total fat (2 g sat. fat, 0 g trans fat), 6 mg chol., 287 mg sodium, 4 g carbo., 0 g fiber, 2 g pro.
EXCHANGES: 1 Fat

Garlic and Herb Mashed Potatoes

START TO FINISH: 10 MINUTES
MAKES: 8 SERVINGS

- 2 24-ounce packages refrigerated mashed potatoes or 6 cups prepared instant mashed potatoes
- 2 5.2-ounce containers semisoft cheese with garlic and herbs (such as Boursin brand)
- ⅓ cup snipped fresh parsley
  Canned french-fried onions (optional)

1 Heat refrigerated potatoes according to package directions. Transfer warm potatoes to a serving bowl.

2 Stir in cheese and parsley. If desired, sprinkle with french-fried onions.

PER ¾ CUP: 280 cal., 18 g total fat (11 g sat. fat, g trans fat), 1 mg chol., 475 mg sodium, 24 g carbo., 1 g fiber, 6 g pro.
EXCHANGES: 1½ Starch, 3½ Fat

Pumpkin-Pear Cake

PREP: 25 MINUTES **BAKE:** 35 MINUTES
COOL: 35 MINUTES **OVEN:** 350°F.
MAKES: 16 SERVINGS

- 1 cup packed brown sugar
- ⅓ cup butter, melted
- 1½ teaspoons cornstarch
- 2 15-ounce cans pear halves in light syrup
- ½ cup coarsely chopped pecans
- 1 2-layer-size spice cake mix
- 1 cup canned pumpkin

1 Preheat oven to 350°F. In a small bowl combine brown sugar, butter, and cornstarch. Drain pears, reserving 3 tablespoons of the syrup. Stir reserved syrup into brown sugar mixture. Pour mixture into a 13×9×2-inch baking pan. If desired, cut pear halves into fans by making three or four lengthwise cuts ¼ inch from the stem end of each pear half to the bottom of the pear half. Arrange whole or fanned pear halves on top of syrup in pan, cored sides down. Sprinkle pecans evenly into pan.

2 Prepare cake mix according to package directions, except decrease oil to 2 tablespoons and add pumpkin. Slowly pour cake batter into pan, spreading evenly.

3 Bake for 35 to 40 minutes or until a wooden toothpick inserted near center comes out clean. Cool in pan on a wire rack for 5 minutes. Run a thin metal spatula around edges of cake. Carefully invert cake into a 15×10×1-inch baking pan or onto a very large serving platter with slightly raised sides. Cool about 30 minutes before serving. Serve warm. Place any leftover cake in a storage container. Cover and refrigerate up to 3 days or freeze for up to 1 month.

PER SLICE: 333 cal., 15 g total fat (4 g sat. fat, 0 g trans fat), 51 mg chol., 254 mg sodium, 50 g carbo., 2 g fiber, 3 g pro.
EXCHANGES: 1 Fruit, 1 Starch, 1½ Other Carbo., 2 Fat

Cooking Up Romance

How fast time goes by. Be thankful that each year brings two days, Valentine's Day and your anniversary, to slow down and take note of your love for each other. Make the most of these days with two enchanting menus, one that she cooks for him, another that he cooks for her.

SHE COOKS FOR HIM

It's long been said that the way to a man's heart is through his stomach, and you may find the old adage rings true, especially when you charm him with helpings of up-to-date fare such as this hearty, grilled menu.

Grilled Pork Tenderloin

PREP: 10 MINUTES **GRILL:** 30 MINUTES
STAND: 45 MINUTES **MAKES:** 2 SERVINGS +
2 LEFTOVER SERVINGS

 1   1-pound pork tenderloin
 2   teaspoons olive oil
1½ teaspoons garlic salt
1½ teaspoons dried oregano, crushed
1½ teaspoons ground cumin
1½ teaspoons ground coriander
1½ teaspoons dried thyme, crushed
      Fresh thyme sprigs (optional)

1   Trim fat from pork tenderloin. Rub tenderloin with oil. In a small bowl combine garlic salt, oregano, cumin, coriander, and thyme. Sprinkle oregano mixture evenly over tenderloin; rub in with your fingers. Let stand at room temperature for 30 minutes (or cover and chill for up to 2 hours).

2   For a charcoal grill, arrange hot coals around a drip pan. Test for medium-hot heat above the pan. Place tenderloin on a greased grill rack over pan. Cover and grill for 30 to 35 minutes or until an instant-read thermometer inserted in center of tenderloin registers 155°F. (For a gas grill, pre-heat grill. Reduce heat to medium-high. Adjust for indirect cooking. Place tenderloin on greased rack over burner that is turned off. Grill as directed.)

3   Remove tenderloin from grill. Cover with foil; let stand for 15 minutes.

4   Cut tenderloin in half crosswise. Place one half in an airtight storage container. Cover and chill for up to 3 days to use in another recipe. Cut the remaining tenderloin half into ½-inch slices. If desired, garnish with fresh thyme sprigs.

PER 3 OUNCES: 163 cal., 7 g total fat (2 g sat. fat, 0 g trans fat), 74 mg chol., 421 mg sodium, 1 g carbo., 1 g fiber, 24 g pro. EXCHANGES: 3½ Medium-Fat Meat

Veggie Kabobs

PREP: 15 MINUTES **COOK:** 10 MINUTES
GRILL: 8 MINUTES **MAKES:** 2 SERVINGS

 4   tiny new potatoes
 1   ear of corn, cut crosswise into
      1-inch pieces
 2   green onions, cut into 2-inch pieces
 2   tablespoons olive oil
 2   tablespoons snipped fresh basil,
      rosemary, and/or Italian parsley
 1   tablespoon butter, melted

1   In a medium saucepan cook potatoes, covered, in lightly salted boiling water for 10 to 12 minutes or just until tender. Drain. Set aside; cool slightly.

2   On two 8- to 10-inch skewers alternately thread potatoes, corn, and green onions, leaving a ¼-inch space between pieces. In a small bowl combine olive oil and herb; brush about half of the oil mixture on the vegetables. Set aside the remaining oil mixture.

3   For a charcoal grill, place kabobs on the rack of a grill with a cover directly over medium coals. Cover and grill for 8 to 12 minutes or until vegetables are tender, turning kabobs once half-way through grilling. (For a gas grill, preheat grill. Reduce heat to medium. Place kabobs on grill rack over heat. Grill as directed.)

4   Transfer kabobs to serving plates. Stir melted butter into the reserved oil mixture; drizzle over kabobs.

PER KABOB: 326 cal., 20 g total fat (6 g sat. fat, 0 g trans fat), 15 mg chol., 60 mg sodium, 35 g carbo., 4 g fiber, 5 g pro. EXCHANGES: 2 Starch, 4 Fat

Cheesy Potato Balls

PREP: 20 MINUTES **COOK:** 3 MINUTES
STAND: 15 MINUTES **MAKES:** 2 SERVINGS

- 1 cup cooked mashed potatoes, chilled
- ⅓ cup shredded Gruyère cheese
- 2 tablespoons finely chopped green onion (1)
- ½ teaspoon salt
- 1 egg
- ⅔ cup panko (Japanese-style bread crumbs) or soft bread crumbs
- 1 tablespoon snipped fresh parsley
  Vegetable oil

1 Let potatoes stand at room temperature for 15 minutes. Stir cheese, green onion, and salt into potatoes. Divide potato mixture into four portions; roll each portion into a ball.

2 In a small bowl beat egg with a whisk. In another shallow bowl combine bread crumbs and parsley. Dip each potato ball into beaten egg, then into crumb mixture. Dip ball in egg and crumb mixture again to double coat.

3 Heat 2 inches of oil in a skillet and fry potato balls in oil for 3 to 4 minutes or until golden brown, turning occasionally. Using a slotted spoon, transfer to a plate lined with paper towels.

Oven Directions: Preheat oven to 400°F. Prepare as directed through Step 2. Lightly coat the coated potato balls with nonstick cooking spray. Place potato balls on a foil-lined baking sheet. Bake for 20 to 25 minutes or until golden brown and heated through.

PER 2 BALLS: 410 cal., 25 g total fat (7 g sat. fat, 0 g trans fat), 132 mg chol., 1,066 mg sodium, 33 g carbo., 2 g fiber, 15 g pro.
EXCHANGES: 2 Starch, 1 Medium-Fat Meat, 4 Fat

Good Timing. *The tenderloin needs to rest 15 minutes before carving, which leaves you time to sizzle up the kabobs, fry the potato balls, and pour two glasses of wine.*

HE COOKS FOR HER

When cooking for a woman, it's all in the flourishes. Make the food look and taste as captivating to her as she is to you. Opt for colorful, nutritious dishes that pretty up the plate and offer unique textures and tastes—such as the three delightful dishes here.

Grilled Herbed Salmon with Garlicky Orange Mayo

PREP: 15 MINUTES **GRILL:** 8 MINUTES
MAKES: 2 SERVINGS

- 1 12-ounce fresh or frozen salmon fillet with skin
- 1 tablespoon olive oil
- 1 tablespoon snipped fresh basil, rosemary, and/or Italian parsley
    Sea salt
    Coarsely ground black pepper
- 1 recipe Garlicky Orange Mayo

1 Thaw salmon, if frozen. Rinse salmon; pat dry with paper towels. Brush salmon with olive oil. Sprinkle with herbs, salt, and pepper.

2 For a charcoal grill, place salmon, skin side down, on the greased rack of a grill with a cover directly over medium coals. Cover and grill for 8 to 12 minutes or until fish begins to flake when tested with a fork. Do not turn fish. (For a gas grill, preheat grill. Reduce heat to medium. Place salmon on a greased grill rack over heat. Grill as directed.)

3 Serve salmon with Garlicky-Orange Mayo.

Garlicky Orange Mayo: In a bowl combine ¼ cup mayonnaise; 1 clove garlic, minced; ½ teaspoon finely shredded orange peel; and 1 tablespoon orange juice. Chill mayo until ready to serve.

PER 6 OUNCES SALMON + 2 TABLESPOONS SAUCE: 506 cal., 39 g total fat (6 g sat. fat, 0 g trans fat), 104 mg chol., 230 mg sodium, 2 g carbo., 0 g fiber, 34 g pro.
EXCHANGES: 5 Medium-Fat Meat, 3 Fat

Spinach and Almond Rice Pilaf

START TO FINISH: 30 MINUTES
MAKES: 2 SERVINGS

- ¾ cup water
- ¼ cup apple juice
- ½ cup uncooked long grain or basmati rice
- ¼ teaspoon salt
- 1 tablespoon butter
- 2 tablespoons sliced green onion (1)
- 1 tablespoon chopped red sweet pepper or shredded carrot
- 1 clove garlic, minced
- 1 cup slivered fresh spinach leaves
- ¼ teaspoon finely shredded lemon peel
- 1 tablespoon slivered almonds, toasted
    Salt and black pepper

1 In a medium saucepan combine the water and apple juice; stir in rice and salt. Bring to boiling; reduce heat. Simmer, covered, for 20 minutes or until rice is tender and liquid is absorbed.

2 Meanwhile, in a medium skillet melt butter over medium heat. Add onion, sweet pepper, and garlic; cook until tender. Stir in cooked rice, spinach, and lemon peel. Cook until heated through and spinach is slightly wilted. Stir in almonds. Season to taste with salt and pepper.

PER 1¼ CUP: 263 cal., 8 g total fat (4 g sat. fat, 0 g trans fat), 15 mg chol., 496 mg sodium, 43 g carbo., 2 g fiber, 5 g pro.
EXCHANGES: 1 Vegetable, 2½ Starch, 1 Fat

An Unforgettable Finale

For dessert, consider the romantic recipe on the next page. Short on time? Pick up your spouse's favorite cookies (French macaroons, for example) and serve with ice cream.

Maple Nectarine Relish

PREP: 15 MINUTES **GRILL:** 8 MINUTES
MAKES: 2 SERVINGS

 2 tablespoons pure maple syrup
 1 tablespoon balsamic vinegar
 2 nectarines, halved and pitted
 1 red sweet pepper, quartered
 1 ½-inch-thick slice red onion

1 In a small saucepan combine maple syrup and balsamic vinegar; cook and stir until heated through. Brush nectarine halves, pepper quarters, and onion slice with about half of the maple syrup mixture; set remaining mixture aside.

2 For a charcoal grill, grill pepper quarters and onion directly over medium coals for 8 to 10 minutes or just until tender and light brown, turning once. Add nectarine halves to the grill, cut sides down, for the last 5 to 6 minutes of grilling or until softened and just warmed through. Remove from grill; cool slightly. (For a gas grill, preheat grill. Reduce heat to medium. Place peppers and onion, and later nectarine halves, on grill rack over heat. Cover and grill as directed.)

3 Add pepper quarters, onion, and nectarines to food processor. Cover and pulse just until coarsely chopped. Spoon nectarine mixture into a small serving bowl; add the remaining maple syrup mixture and toss to mix. Serve with grilled salmon.

PER ½ CUP: 143 cal., 1 g total fat (0 g sat. fat, 0 g trans fat), 0 mg chol., 6 mg sodium, 34 g carbo., 4 g fiber, 2 g pro.
EXCHANGES: 1 Vegetable, 1 Fruit, 1 Other Carbo.

Salmon—or Something Else? *This preparation would go well with other firm, meaty fish varieties, such as swordfish, Arctic char, or tuna. You may need to adjust cooking time.*

Date Night Desserts

Make your treasured evenings even sweeter with an after-dinner indulgence. Cozy up around a fondue pot while you savor the world's most seductive flavor: chocolate. Or go for a tingly, citrus-sparked granita that will send shivers down your spines.

Citrus Granitas

PREP: 15 MINUTES **COOL:** 30 MINUTES
FREEZE: 6 HOURS **STAND:** 5 MINUTES
MAKES: 2 SERVINGS

- ¾ cup orange juice
- 2 tablespoons sugar
- 2 tablespoons lemon juice or lime juice
- ½ of a medium orange, peeled, sectioned, and finely chopped
- ½ of a small lemon or lime, peeled, sectioned, and finely chopped
-    Lemon, lime, and/or orange wedges (optional)
-    Fresh mint sprigs (optional)

1   For syrup, in a small saucepan combine orange juice and sugar. Cook and stir over medium heat until sugar dissolves. Remove from heat. Stir in lemon juice; set syrup aside to cool for 30 minutes.

2   Stir finely chopped orange and lemon into syrup mixture. Pour orange mixture into an 8×8×2-inch baking pan. Freeze for 2 hours, stirring and scraping frozen mixture from sides of pan every 20 minutes. Cover and freeze, without stirring, about 4 hours or until firm.

3   To serve, let granita stand at room temperature for 5 to 10 minutes. Using the tines of a fork, scrape across the surface of the granita. Spoon granita into chilled dessert dishes. If desired, garnish with lemon wedges and/or mint sprigs.

PER ½ CUP: 115 cal., 0 g total fat, 0 mg chol., 2 mg sodium, 30 g carbo., 2 g fiber, 1 g pro.
EXCHANGES: 1 Fruit, 1 Other Carbo.

S'mores Fondue

START TO FINISH: 20 MINUTES **MAKES:** 3½ CUPS

- ⅓ cup unsweetened cocoa powder
- ¼ cup sugar
- 2 tablespoons cornstarch
- ¼ teaspoon ground cinnamon
- 2½ cups low-fat milk
- ⅔ cup marshmallow creme
-    Low-fat milk
-    Graham cracker sticks and/or assorted fruit dippers (such as strawberries, banana chunks, and/or apple wedges)

1   In a medium saucepan combine cocoa powder, sugar, cornstarch, and cinnamon. Gradually whisk in the 2½ cups milk. Cook and stir over medium heat until thickened and bubbly; reduce heat. Cook and stir for 2 minutes more. Remove from heat. Whisk in marshmallow creme until well mixed.

2   Transfer chocolate mixture to a 1- or 1½-quart slow cooker or a fondue pot. Keep warm for up to 2 hours on low heat. Stir occasionally, adding additional milk to thin as needed. Serve warm with graham cracker sticks and/or fruit dippers.

PER ¼ CUP FONDUE: 61 cal., 1 g total fat (1 g sat. fat, 0 g trans fat), 4 mg chol., 19 mg sodium, 12 g carbo., 1 g fiber, 2 g pro.
EXCHANGES: ½ Starch, ½ Other Carbo.

More to Love
Save leftover fondue to warm in the microwave and serve over ice cream another night. Store, covered, in the refrigerator.

ORANGE GRANITAS

Fondue delights. *Get creative with the dippers. Try angel food cake, pound cake, short-bread cookies, pineapple, cherries—anything that tastes good with a dab of chocolate.*

S'MORES FONDUE

BAKED BEEF RAVIOLI

Potluck Tip. When toting dishes to a potluck, take not only a crowd-pleasing dish but also the proper serving utensils. The host may not have enough serving spoons for a crowd.

SAUCY BOW TIE PASTA CASSEROLE

Potluck Parties, Italian Style

From bowl-game parties to end-year holidays that stretch from Thanksgiving to New Year's, many of the most enjoyable gatherings are bring-a-dish affairs. Next time you're invited to such a celebration, tote something Italian. Your dish will likely be one of the first devoured.

Baked Beef Ravioli

PREP: 20 MINUTES **BAKE:** 20 MINUTES
OVEN: 375°F **MAKES:** 8 TO 10 SERVINGS

- 2 9-ounce packages refrigerated cheese-filled ravioli
- 1½ pounds ground beef
- 1 cup chopped onion (1 large)
- 6 cloves garlic, minced
- 1 14.5-ounce can diced tomatoes, undrained
- 1 10.75-ounce can condensed tomato soup
- 1 teaspoon dried basil, crushed
- 1 teaspoon dried oregano, crushed
- 1½ cups shredded mozzarella cheese (6 ounces)
- ½ cup finely shredded Parmesan cheese (2 ounces)

1 Preheat oven to 375°F. Cook ravioli according to package directions; drain. Return to hot pan; cover and keep warm.

2 Meanwhile, in a large skillet cook ground beef, onion, and garlic over medium heat until meat is brown and onion is tender, using a wooden spoon to break up meat as it cooks. Drain off fat. Stir undrained tomatoes, soup, basil, and oregano into meat mixture in skillet. Gently stir in cooked ravioli.

3 Spoon mixture into an ungreased 3-quart baking dish. Sprinkle with mozzarella cheese and Parmesan cheese. Bake about 20 minutes or until heated through.

PER 1 CUP: 503 cal., 24 g total fat (12 g sat. fat, 1 g trans fat), 130 mg chol., 932 mg sodium, 34 g carbo., 1 g fiber, 37 g pro. EXCHANGES: 1 Vegetable, 2 Starch, 4 Medium-Fat Meat

Food Safety on the Go

Follow the safetly guidelines on page 31 to ensure your dish arrives at it's best.

Saucy Bow Tie Pasta Casserole

PREP: 35 MINUTES **BAKE:** 35 MINUTES
STAND: 5 MINUTES **OVEN:** 350°F/400°F
MAKES: 8 SERVINGS

- 3 cups dried bow tie, penne, or ziti pasta (8 ounces)
- 2 medium red onions, cut into thin wedges, or 5 medium leeks, sliced (about 2 cups)
- 2 cloves garlic, minced
- 1 tablespoon butter or margarine
- 1 24- to 26-ounce jar tomato pasta sauce
- 1 8-ounce can tomato sauce
- 1 10-ounce package frozen chopped spinach, thawed and well drained
- 1½ cups cubed lean cooked ham
- 2 medium tomatoes, seeded and chopped
- ⅓ cup grated Parmesan cheese (3 ounces)
- 2 cups mozzarella or Muenster cheese (8 ounces)
  Grated Parmesan cheese (optional)
  Italian parsley sprigs (optional)

1 Preheat oven to 350°F. In a large pot cook pasta according to the package directions. Drain; rinse pasta with cold water. Drain again.

2 In the same pan cook onions and garlic, covered, in hot butter for 8 to 10 minutes or until onion is tender, stirring occasionally. Stir in the cooked pasta, pasta sauce, tomato sauce, spinach, ham, tomatoes, and ⅓ cup Parmesan cheese. Spoon mixture into a 3-quart rectangular baking dish. Cover dish with foil.

3 Bake for 30 minutes or until heated through. Increase oven temperature to 400°F. Top with mozzarella cheese and, if desired, additional Parmesan cheese. Bake, uncovered, about 5 minutes more or until cheese is melted. Let stand for 5 minutes. If desired, garnish with parsley.

PER 1¼ CUP: 296 cal., 12 g total fat (6 g sat. fat, 0 g trans fat), 35 mg chol., 1,141 mg sodium, 31 g carbo., 5 g fiber, 20 g pro. EXCHANGES: 1 Vegetable, 1½ Starch, 2 Lean Meat, 1½ Fat

Apple-Sausage Rigatoni

START TO FINISH: 25 MINUTES
MAKES: 8 SERVINGS

- 12 ounces packaged dried rigatoni (about 2 cups)
- 1 pound cooked smoked sausage, halved lengthwise and cut into 1-inch pieces
- 3 pounds red MacIntosh or Braeburn apples, cored and cut into ½-inch slices
- 1 cup whipping cream
- 1 cup crumbled Gorgonzola cheese (4 ounces)
  Fresh herbs (optional)

1 In a 5- to 6-quart Dutch oven cook pasta according to package directions. Drain; set aside.

2 In the same Dutch oven cook sausage until light brown. Add apples; cook about 5 minutes or until apples are lightly golden, stirring occasionally. Stir in the cooked pasta, whipping cream, and cheese. Heat through. If desired, garnish with fresh herbs.

PER 1⅔ CUPS: 568 cal., 31 g total fat (17 g sat. fat, 0 g trans fat), 92 mg chol., 847 mg sodium, 55 g carbo., 5 g fiber, 18 g pro. EXCHANGES: 1 Fruit, 2½ Starch, 2 High-Fat Meat, 3 Fat

Butternut Squash Lasagna

PREP: 50 MINUTES **BAKE:** 50 MINUTES
STAND: 10 MINUTES **OVEN:** 425°F/375°F
MAKES: 8 TO 10 SERVINGS

- 3 pounds butternut squash, peeled, seeded, and cut into ¼- to ½-inch slices
- 3 tablespoons olive oil
- ½ teaspoon salt
- ¼ cup butter or margarine
- 6 cloves garlic, minced
- ¼ cup all-purpose flour
- ½ teaspoon salt
- 4 cups milk
- 1 tablespoon snipped fresh rosemary
- 9 no-boil lasagna noodles
- 1⅓ cups finely shredded Parmesan cheese
- 1 cup whipping cream

1 Preheat oven to 425°F. Lightly grease a 15×10×1-inch baking pan. Place squash in the prepared baking pan. Add oil and ½ teaspoon salt; toss gently to coat. Spread in an even layer. Roast, uncovered, for 25 to 30 minutes or until squash is tender, stirring once. Reduce oven temperature to 375°F.

2 Meanwhile, for sauce, in a large saucepan melt butter over medium heat. Add garlic; cook and stir for 1 minute. Stir in flour and ½ teaspoon salt. Gradually stir in milk. Cook and stir until thickened and bubbly. Stir in squash and rosemary.

3 Lightly grease a 3-quart rectangular baking dish. To assemble lasagna, spread about 1 cup of the sauce over the bottom of the prepared baking dish. Layer three of the uncooked noodles in dish. Spread with one-third of the remaining sauce. Sprinkle with ⅓ cup of the Parmesan cheese. Repeat layering noodles, sauce, and Parmesan cheese two more times. Pour whipping cream evenly over layers in dish. Sprinkle with the remaining ⅓ cup Parmesan cheese.

4 Cover dish with foil. Bake for 40 minutes. Remove the foil. Bake about 10 minutes more or until edges are bubbly and top is light brown. Let stand for 10 minutes before serving.

Make-Ahead Directions: Prepare as directed through Step 3. Cover unbaked lasagna with foil; chill for 2 to 24 hours. To serve, preheat oven to 375°F. Bake, covered, for 45 minutes. Remove the foil. Bake for 10 to 15 minutes more or until edges are bubbly and top is lightly browned. Let stand for 10 minutes before serving.

PER SERVING: 512 cal., 29 g total fat (15 g sat. fat, 0 g trans fat), 76 mg chol., 627 mg sodium, 50 g carbo., 3 g fiber, 16 g pro. EXCHANGES: 3 Starch, 1½ Medium-Fat Meat, 3½ Fat

Butternut Squash Lasagna, Step-by-Step

1. When making white sauce, stir the flour and salt into the butter and garlic; cook, stirring occasionally. Do not allow the flour to brown. Gradually add the milk, whisking constantly as you pour. 2. As you layer ingredients, spread the sauce and cheese layers as evenly as possible. Pour whipping cream over the entire dish.

Bridal Edition Index

New CookBook

15th edition

WILEY

John Wiley & Sons, Inc.

BEST BASIC CHALLAH, PAGE 110

BALSAMIC-GLAZED FLANK STEAK WITH FALL FRUIT SALSA, PAGE 392

MAKE-IT-MINE CHEESECAKE, PAGE 301

SALMON AND PASTA TOSS, PAGE 323

CONTENTS

TRIED & TRUE, FRESH & NEW

MY KITCHEN MEMORIES—GOING BACK TO WHEN I HAD TO STAND ON MY TIPTOES TO PEER OVER THE COUNTER—ARE SO WARM AND WONDERFUL THAT THEY'VE SHAPED THE WAY I FEEL ABOUT MY KITCHEN TODAY.

It's still my favorite place. I love cooking there, chatting with my daughter there, and how visiting friends and family gravitate to the spot where I enjoy their company most. Often I find myself standing at a counter performing tasks that have nothing to do with cooking because in the kitchen—the heart of my home—everything feels right with the world.

I feel the same way about the Better Homes and Gardens Test Kitchen, the heart of our editorial home. It was central to our efforts to update our treasured Red Plaid cookbook and transform it into the book you hold in your hands today.

The entire Red Plaid team—home economists, food editors, and stylists—gathered together there like a family to perfect each of the recipes that made their way into this cookbook. Huddled around a stove or seated at a table, our diverse team—some from large rural families, others single and urban, some old enough to have decades' worth of Red Plaid memories, others young enough to own Red Plaids without one stained or tattered page—sampled dishes together.

Our collective ideas make this book relevant to the way you cook today. We retained tried-and-true classics—each as delicious as you remember—while infusing the book with creations that utilize the new ingredients and multiethnic flavors we're fond of now. We gave special attention to creating recipes that allow you to add your own personal touches. The Make It Mine recipes—found in every chapter—offer inspiring variations that fit every family's tastes.

Our 10 to Try sections provide fresh ideas for bringing excitement to classic recipes. Take a peek at the scrumptious veggie toppers on page 605 and the super swift chicken pan sauces on page 479.

We didn't forget practicality. Busy cooks will love the Cook Once, Eat Twice sections. Intended to make cooking efficient, these duos—like my favorites, Pasta Margherita and Chicken and Spinach Pasta Salad (page 431)—make incredible meals one night with leftovers that can be transformed into different dishes the next night.

And because we know that often we all need a leg up on dinner, we packed the "Convenience Cooking" chapter with simple recipes based on the excellent time-saving purchased ingredients available today.

Finally—because we know that an essential part of our heritage is to ensure your success in the kitchen—we have included more how-to photos and detailed step-by-step directions than ever. We're confident that every recipe created in our kitchen will work wonderfully in yours.

Thank you for inviting us into the heart of your home. We look forward to spending many happy hours with you there.

Jan Miller

Editor

COOKING BASICS

KNIVES

THIS CHAPTER OPENS WITH THE TOPIC OF KNIVES FOR A REASON—THEY'RE A MAJOR PLAYER IN KITCHEN SUCCESS.

You can make do without a lot of kitchen gadgets and appliances, but a good set of knives is almost invaluable. Although high-quality cutlery can be expensive, if you invest in the best set you can afford, then hand-wash and dry them, and keep them professionally sharpened, your knives will last for years. Choose knives that feel balanced and comfortable in your hand. Good, practical knives have high-carbon, stainless-steel blades.

NECESSITIES

1 SERRATED BREAD KNIFE Use a sawing motion with a serrated blade to cut through crusty breads or tender cakes.

2 CHEF'S KNIFE Slice, dice, chop, and mince with this all-purpose wedge-shape blade.

3 UTILITY KNIFE The thin, ultrasharp blade is perfect for delicate tasks, such as cutting fish, soft fruits, and cheeses.

4 SCISSORS Keep a pair solely for the kitchen. Use for everything from opening packages to cutting chicken and snipping fresh herbs—you'll wonder how you ever lived without them.

5 PARING KNIFE This small knife is ideal for coring, peeling, and cutting. Keep a few on hand so you'll always have a clean one to reach for as you cook.

USEFUL EXTRAS

6 CARVING KNIFE Slicing meats is simple with this long, thin-bladed knife.

7 TOMATO KNIFE Ever try to slice a tomato and have the pulp squeeze out all over the counter? That won't happen with this knife—its scalloped edge cleanly slices through the soft skin of tomatoes and other fruits and vegetables.

8 SANTOKU KNIFE Hollowed-out impressions in the Japanese-style blade minimize sticking, making it versatile in your kitchen.

CUTTING BOARD PROS AND CONS

A PLASTIC These are affordable and easy to clean, though sharp knives can scuff them up.

B WOOD Wood lasts longer and doesn't dull sharp knives as quickly as plastic. Check instructions before running through the dishwasher.

C BAMBOO Bamboo boards absorb less moisture and show fewer cut marks than wood or plastic ones, but they're also pricier.

KITCHEN TOOLBOX

THESE GO-TO TOOLS MAKE IT EASIER FOR YOU TO COOK MORE GOOD THINGS MORE OFTEN.

NECESSITIES

1 LARGE LIQUID MEASURES With the 8-cup measure, you can measure large amounts of liquids when making soups or measure multiple liquids together. Also use them to hold ingredients while you prepare other foods.

2, 3 SMALL LIQUID MEASURES The 1-cup and 2-cup measures are a must for any kitchen.

4 GRADUATED MEASURING CUPS Use these only for dry ingredients, such as flour and sugar, and soft solids, such as shortening. They're also known as dry measuring cups.

5 KITCHEN TONGS Toss a salad, serve spaghetti, flip cutlets in a frying pan, or snag pickles out of the jar with this handy tool.

6 CAN OPENER A no-brainer—just remember that after opening a can, handle the lid with caution; it can be as sharp as a knife.

7 MEASURING SPOONS Use these spoons for both dry and liquid ingredients.

8 HEAT-RESISTANT TONGS An alternative to No. 5, these offer two advantages: They stay cooler than all-metal tongs and are friendlier to nonstick cookware.

9 VEGETABLE PEELER Its obvious function is to remove the skin from vegetables, but it can also be used to make long shavings of cheese or strips of citrus peel for cooking and garnishing.

10 SILICONE SCRAPERS These work to mix, stir, and fold ingredients, and to scrape up every bit of whatever is in your bowl, jar, or pan. They're heat-resistant too.

11 TURNER/SPATULA Flip and serve anything you have grilled, broiled, baked, or pan-fried.

12 EGG SEPARATOR Separating the yolk from the white by tossing the yolk from shell to shell can spread harmful bacteria. This handy gadget cradles the yolk over a cup that catches the white.

13 WOODEN SPOONS Stirring thick batter and dough is an easy task for these sturdy spoons. Because they're made of wood, they stay cool and don't scratch nonstick cookware.

14 BOX GRATER The sides with the larger slits or holes are for shredding foods; the sides with the smaller slits or holes are for grating foods.

15 COLANDER Use to drain boiled foods or pasta and to hold foods while rinsing.

16 WIRE WHISK This tool is a must for beating eggs and other ingredients. Also use it for smoothing out lumpy sauces.

USEFUL EXTRAS

17 MEAT MALLET The smooth side flattens meat; the spiked side both flattens and tenderizes.

18 MORTAR AND PESTLE Crush herbs and spices to boost their fresh flavors in your cooking.

19, 20 POTATO MASHERS Use one of these low-tech tools to achieve fluffy mashed potatoes. They're also good for mashing bananas for baking.

21 FINE-MESH SIEVE When straining foods that have fine particles, use this instead of a colander. You can also use it for sifting.

22 CHEESE SLICER Most have an adjustable wire to cut thin to thick slices.

23 CITRUS JUICER Choose one with a sieve to easily strain pulp and seeds.

24, 25 HANDHELD GRATERS These are especially handy when you want to grate or shred a food directly over a pan, plate, or bowl.

26 KITCHEN TIMER Keep track of the minutes with this classic wind-up timer. To get timings down to the second, go with a digital model.

27 PASTRY BLENDER Pie and biscuit bakers use this time-honored gadget to cut butter or shortening into flour for masterfully flaky results.

28 PASTRY BRUSH Use this to grease a baking pan and brush barbecue sauce on meat (as directed in recipes), butter on sheets of phyllo dough, and glazes on baked goods.

29 SLOTTED SPOON This spoon is useful for removing solids from liquids, such as vegetables from a broth. Use it for stirring too.

30 ROLLING PIN This helps you roll out everything from piecrusts and puff pastry to pizza and cookie dough. Although rolling pins can be made of a variety of materials, the Test Kitchen pros prefer those made of wood.

31 PIZZA CUTTER Whether you like slices or squares, this lets you cut pizza your way.

GET TWO—OR A FEW BUY MULTIPLES OF YOUR MOST OFTEN-USED GADGETS, INCLUDING MEASURING CUPS AND SPOONS. THAT WAY YOU'LL ALWAYS HAVE CLEAN ONES TO REACH FOR WHILE COOKING.

THERMOMETERS

TO ACHIEVE SAFETY AND SUCCESS WHEN COOKING RELY ON AN ACCURATE THERMOMETER.

Clockwise from top:

ELECTRONIC CORD THERMOMETER: Use for larger cuts of meat. Insert the stainless-steel probe into meat before roasting; its cord leads to a digital display that remains outside of the oven.

DIAL OVEN-SAFE MEAT THERMOMETER: Use for larger cuts of meat, such as roasts. Insert it into meat before roasting; leave it in the entire time.

INSTANT-READ THERMOMETER: This digital or dial thermometer gives an internal reading within seconds. Do not leave thermometer in food while cooking, unless your model is designed for this.

CANDY THERMOMETER: Marked with candy-making stages, these can measure extra-high temperatures. Most have a clip that attaches to the pan. For more information see page 183.

TWO MORE TO LOOK FOR

APPLIANCE THERMOMETERS HELP YOU COOK AND STORE FOODS SAFELY.

OVEN THERMOMETER: This lets you make sure your oven temperature is accurate.

REFRIGERATER-FREEZER THERMOMETERS: Use these to ensure your appliance is chilling correctly (0ºF or below for freezers and no higher than 40ºF for refrigerators).

MISSING A TOOL? TRY THESE EASY KITCHEN SWAPS

1. Tool: Juicer. **Swap:** Fork. **How It's Done:** Insert the fork into cut fruit. While gently squeezing the fruit, lift and lower fork to extract juice. **2. Tool:** Pastry Brush. **Swap:** Paper towel or small plastic bag. **How It's Done:** If using the paper towel, fold in edges to thicken spreading surface of the towel. Dip towel into shortening and spread it evenly on the pan. If using a plastic bag, insert your hand into the bag and dip your covered fingers into the shortening; spread it evenly on the pan. **3. Tool:** Egg separator. **Swap:** Your fingers. **How It's Done:** After cracking the egg into a separate bowl, gently lift the yolk with your fingers and allow the white to slide from the yolk. **4. Tool:** Mortar and pestle. **Swap:** Your hands. **How It's Done:** Place the larger dried herbs and spices in palm of one hand. Crush the herbs gently between your thumb and fingers of the opposite hand.

SMALL APPLIANCES

WITH A PUSH OF A BUTTON OR A FLIP OF A SWITCH, FOOD PREP CAN BE FASTER, EASIER, BETTER.

NECESSITIES

1 HAND MIXER This is a must-have for everything from making whipped cream to beating egg whites. Choose one that has at least five speeds and enough power to mix a reasonably stiff dough.

2 SLOW COOKER This ultimate unwatched pot helps you enjoy a home-cooked meal even on your busiest days. For essential information on how to use one, see pages 549–550.

3 BLENDER For quick smoothies, protein shakes, and pureed soups, a blender can't be beat. It also can be used for some tasks normally done in a food processor.

4 STAND MIXER If you bake often, you might want to invest in a stand mixer, which can handle large amounts of thick dough or batter. This big guy also allows you freedom to move about the kitchen while the ingredients are being mixed.

USEFUL EXTRAS

FOOD PROCESSOR This chopping, mincing, and pureeing machine shaves valuable minutes off recipe prep times. Look for an 8- to 10-cup bowl for most kitchen tasks; go larger if you plan to make yeast bread dough with it.

IMMERSION BLENDER Pureeing hot soups with a blender can be a little bit tricky (see page 567 to learn how to do this). An easier way is with this handy gadget. It lets you puree right in the pan, which is not only safer but saves on cleanup duty.

PANINI PRESS You're just minutes to an easy, hot, pressed, grilled sandwich when you have one of these popular appliances in your kitchen lineup. It can also be used as an indoor grill.

COOKWARE

IF YOU BUY GOOD-QUALITY PANS, THESE WORKHORSES WILL SERVE YOU WELL FOR YEARS TO COME.

NECESSITIES

1 LARGE NONSTICK SKILLET WITH SLOPED SIDES The sides allow for easier tossing and flipping of foods you're preparing. The nonstick coating allows you to cook with less fat.

2 POT Cook pasta and make big batches of broth, soup, stew, and chili in this vessel. Look for one with a volume of 6 to 8 quarts.

3 MEDIUM SAUCEPAN Saucepans have tall straight sides with tight-fitting lids. A midsize saucepan (2 quarts) works well for tasks such as making sauces and cooking rice.

4 LARGE SAUCEPAN A large saucepan holds 3 to 4 quarts and is perfect for small-batch soups and stews.

5 SMALL SAUCEPAN Use the smallest saucepan (1 to 1½ quarts) for small-volume tasks, such as melting chocolate or butter.

6 LARGE STRAIGHT-SIDED SKILLET (WITH LID) Sometimes called a saute pan, this straight-sided skillet is often interchangeable with a slope-sided skillet. However, with its lid, this one works better for braising meats, such as bone-in chicken, on the stovetop. Either can handle most pan-frying jobs.

7 DUTCH OVEN With this stovetop-to-oven pot, you can brown foods, then bake them in the same vessel. The one shown is made of porcelain enamel-coated cast iron. A 4- to 6-quart size with a lid will handle many jobs.

METAL MATTERS

HERE ARE THE KINDS OF PANS USED TO TEST RECIPES FOR THIS BOOK.

Pans are made in a variety of metals. Heavy stainless-steel pans, enameled cast-iron pans, hard-anondized aluminum, and Tri-Ply pans are all good choices for the home cook. Note that some recipes, such as those for puddings and custards, call specifically for a heavy saucepan. In this case, any of these types of pan may be used.

USEFUL EXTRAS

1 OMELET PAN The nonstick surface and sloped sides make folding the eggs and sliding omelets from pan to plate a cinch.

2 WOK Whether it has a flat or rounded bottom, the wok's deep, sloped sides help keep the bite-size pieces of food in the pan while stir-frying.

3 GRILL PAN Get the appealing grill marks and low-fat results of grilling without having to stand outside. The grooves in the heavy stovetop pan allow fat to drain off the food.

4 GRIDDLE PAN Make Saturday morning breakfast—bacon, eggs, and pancakes—on this flat, low-rim pan.

BAKEWARE

WITH JUST A FEW ESSENTIALS, YOU CAN COOK ALL KINDS OF PIES, TARTS, CAKES, COOKIES, BREADS, AND CASSEROLES.

PAN OR DISH—WHAT'S WHAT

In this book, a baking pan refers to a metal container, and a baking dish means an oven-safe glass or ceramic vessel.

BAKING PANS (METAL) Aluminum—nonstick or not—is a great choice for baking pans. It's lightweight and conducts heat well for even baking and browning. Also use aluminum or other metal baking pans when broiling; high temperatures might cause glass or ceramic to shatter.

BAKING DISHES (GLASS OR CERAMIC) Use when called for and when baking egg dishes or acidic foods, such as tomatoes and lemons. Metal pans can cause these foods to discolor.

NECESSITIES (See page 15.)

1 LOAF PAN You will need at least one if you're a fan of zucchini or banana bread or meat loaf. The most common size is 8×4×2 inches, though the larger 9×5×3-inch pan comes in handy too.

2 ROUND CASSEROLE DISH Sized in 1½, 2, or 3 quarts, these usually come with a lid. If you don't have a lid, use foil to cover the dish.

3 PIE PLATE The pie recipes in this book call for 9-inch pie plates; they can be made of glass, ceramic, stoneware, aluminum, or tin.

4 RECTANGULAR AND SQUARE PANS AND DISHES Stock up on rectangular (9×13×2-inch) and square (8×8×2-inch or 9×9×2-inch) baking pans, as well as rectangular (3-quart) and square (2-quart) baking dishes for lasagna, casseroles, brownies, cakes, bars, and more.

5 ROUND CAKE PANS Though two will do for baking standard birthday cakes, fancier recipes often call for three pans. Choose pans with an 8- or 9-inch diameter that are 1½ inches deep.

6 JELLY-ROLL PAN You might never make a jelly roll, but you still need this 15×10×1-inch pan for other tasks, such as bar cookies and brownies.

7 COOKIE SHEET This low- or no-sided pan allows heat to circulate around the cookies.

8 MUFFIN PAN Though many recipes yield more than 12 cupcakes, that's how many cups you'll find in a standard muffin pan. Bake in batches or buy two pans. Mini muffin pans also come in handy for baking small tassie-style cookies.

USEFUL EXTRAS (See below.)

1 TUBE PAN Also called an angel food cake pan, this has a hollow center tube that ensures even baking; most have a removable bottom.

2 RAMEKINS Use these for cooking custards and other individual desserts. They're also great for holding prepped and measured ingredients to have them ready to go in a quick-moving recipe.

3 TART PANS WITH REMOVABLE BOTTOMS These help you bake beautiful tarts with fancifully fluted sides and move them easily from pan to serving plate. They come in a variety of sizes.

4 SPRINGFORM PAN This pan has a latch that springs open, making it easy to remove its sides from a baked dessert. When a recipe calls for this pan, don't even think of substituting another—you'll be hard-pressed to get your dessert out of the pan.

5 FLUTED TUBE PAN These pans add depth and texture to pound cakes and coffee cakes.

6 SOUFFLÉ DISH Steep, straight sides help soufflés rise to the occasion. You'll also find this dish surprisingly versatile for making other desserts and for serving side dishes.

MEASURING

KNOWING HOW TO MEASURE INGREDIENTS PROPERLY IS KEY TO RECIPE SUCCESS.

When it comes to measuring, what you use is most important: Use liquid measuring cups for liquid ingredients and graduated measuring cups for dry ingredients. Information on these and other measuring tools can be found on page 8.

MEASURING DRY INGREDIENTS

Before measuring a dry ingredient, such as flour, stir it in its original container. Using a large spoon, fill the measuring cup without shaking or packing (see top). With the back edge of a knife blade or with the flat edge of a spatula, level off the excess into a bowl you're not using for the recipe (see center) or back into the container. Pack brown sugar into a dry measuring cup. Use your fingers to press it firmly into the cup (see bottom).

MEASURING LIQUID INGREDIENTS

Pour the liquid into a liquid measuring cup set on a level surface. To confirm the measurement, bend down so your eye is level with the markings on the sides of the cup. When measuring 1 tablespoon or less, fill the appropriate-size measuring spoon to the rim without letting liquid spill over.

EXTRA KNOW-HOW

BUTTER AND BLOCK-STYLE CREAM CHEESE: These ingredients have tablespoon markings on the wrapper. If your butter or cream cheese does not come in a marked wrapper, measure as you would shortening.

SHORTENING: Spoon shortening into a graduated measuring cup. Pack it firmly into the cup and level off the top.

STICKY LIQUIDS: For syrups, molasses, and other liquids that cling to the sides of the measuring cup, be sure to use a spatula to scrape every last bit from the cup.

WEIGHTS AND MEASURES

Tablespoon Math

3 teaspoons = 1 tablespoon	
4 tablespoons = ¼ cup	
5 tablespoons + 1 teaspoon = ⅓ cup	
8 tablespoons = ½ cup	
10 tablespoons + 2 teaspoons = ⅔ cup	
12 tablespoons = ¾ cup	
16 tablespoons = 1 cup	

Measure	Equivalent Measure	Equivalent Ounces
1 tablespoon		½ fluid ounce
1 cup	½ pint	8 fluid ounces
2 cups	1 pint	16 fluid ounces
2 pints (4 cups)	1 quart	32 fluid ounces
4 quarts (16 cups)	1 gallon	128 fluid ounces

EGGS

SIMPLE AND WHOLESOME, EGGS PLAY A KEY ROLE IN MANY RECIPES. FOLLOW THE GUIDELINES BELOW TO MAKE THE MOST OF THIS IMPORTANT INGREDIENT.

Before adding eggs in a recipe, crack them into a separate bowl to ensure no eggshells get into your finished food. To crack an egg, tap it firmly on a flat countertop or on the rim of a bowl. If a shell piece gets in the raw egg, use a spoon to fish it out. When separating yolk and white, use an egg separator (see right and No. 12, page 9) .

HOW TO PASTEURIZE EGG WHITES

For food safety, when preparing recipes that use raw or undercooked egg whites, use purchased pasteurized egg whites or pasteurize egg whites as follows. Note that unless otherwise specified, you do not need to pasteurize egg whites for recipes in this book.

■ In a small saucepan stir together 2 egg whites, 2 tablespoons granulated sugar, 1 teaspoon water, and ⅛ teaspoon cream of tartar just until combined but not foamy. Heat and stir over low heat until mixture registers 160°F on an instant-read thermometer. You might see a few small bits of cooked white in the mixture.

■ Remove from heat and place saucepan in a large bowl half-filled with ice water (see above). Stir for 2 minutes to cool mixture quickly.

BEATING EGGS AND EGG WHITES, STEP-BY-STEP

1. For a lightly beaten egg, use a fork to beat a whole egg. It's ready when it's pale yellow with no streaks of white or yolk. **2.** For beaten egg yolks, beat on high speed about 5 minutes or until they're thick and have a lemon color. **3.** For soft peaks, beat the egg whites with a mixer on medium speed until peaks form with tips that curl when the beaters are lifted. **4.** For stiff peaks, beat on high speed until egg whites form peaks with tips that stand straight when the beaters are lifted. Take care not to overbeat egg whites—they can get lumpy and won't blend well with other ingredients.

COOKING METHODS

THESE COOKING TERMS APPEAR
OFTEN IN OUR RECIPES. HERE'S
WHAT THEY MEAN.

1 SAUTE From the French word *sautér* ("to
jump"), saute means to cook and stir foods in a
small amount of fat or oil over fairly high heat in
an open shallow pan. It's best to cut food into
uniform-size pieces to ensure even cooking.

2 STIR-FRY This is a method of quickly cooking
small, uniform pieces of food in a little hot oil in a
wok or large skillet over medium-high heat. Stir
foods constantly to prevent burning. This technique is usually used to cook vegetables and to
prepare many Asian-style dishes.

3 STEAM Food is placed in a steamer basket,
set over boiling water, and covered. In this relatively fast cooking method, steam from boiling water
cooks the food, usually vegetables, while helping
to retain color and nutrients.

4 BROIL With this method, food is cooked below
direct, dry heat. To broil, position the broiler pan
and its rack so that the surface of the food (not
the rack) is the specified distance from the heat
source. Before heating the broiler, use a ruler to
measure the distance in a cold oven.

5 PAN-FRY This refers to cooking food, often
lightly coated or breaded, in a skillet with a small
amount of hot fat or oil. The surface of the food
should brown and, if coated, become crisp. Thin
cuts of fish or chicken work well for pan-frying.

6 ROAST With this method, food is cooked with
dry heat, uncovered, in an oven. Roasting works
best with tender meats that have internal or surface fat to keep them moist. Large items, such as
turkey or beef roasts, are often placed on a rack in
a roasting pan to allow the melted fat to drip away.

BROIL, ROAST, OR BRAISE?
TO LEARN WHICH COOKING
METHODS BEST SUIT EACH
CUT OF MEAT, CHECK OUT THE
PHOTOS ON PAGES 380-381,
396-397, AND 408.

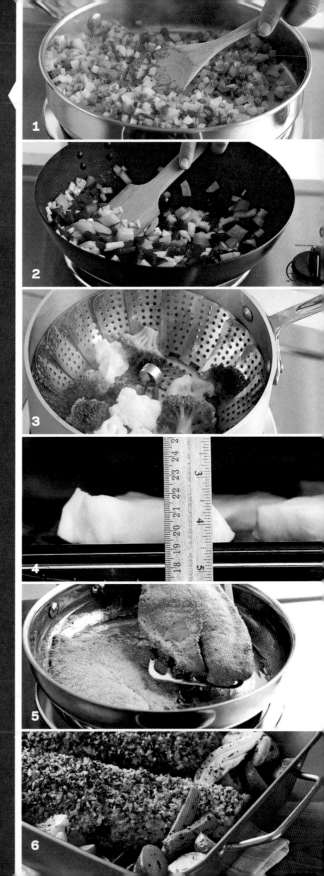

TECHNIQUES & TIPS

WITH JUST A FEW BASIC SKILLS
AND TRICKS, YOU CAN COOK
MANY GOOD THINGS TO EAT. FOR
MORE KNOW-HOW, CHECK THE
GLOSSARY, PAGES 633–634.

CUTTING IN BUTTER

Piecrusts, biscuits, and
other flaky baked goods
call for cutting cold butter
or shortening into the dry
ingredients. To do this,
start by slicing the butter
into ½- to 1-inch chunks; add them to the dry mixture. Using a pastry blender, gently press and cut
the butter into smaller and smaller pieces until the
mixture looks like coarse crumbs.

WITHOUT A PASTRY
BLENDER? A pastry
blender is the best method
for combining flour with
shortening or butter. If you
don't have one, use two
butter knives. Cross the
tips of the knives in the middle of the flour and butter or shortening mixture. Pull the knives toward the
edges of the bowl in a cutting motion; repeat until
the butter or shortening is cut into the flour.

ROLLING DOUGH

Form the dough for
piecrusts and cutout cookies into a small, flattened
circle. Coat your counter
surface and rolling pin with
flour and start rolling the
dough from the middle toward the outside edge of
the circle. Continue by bringing the pin back to the
center area of the dough and rolling outward until
dough is rolled to the thickness specified.

MAKING SOUR MILK

For baking recipes that
call for buttermilk, you can
generally use sour milk as
a substitute. To make
1 cup sour milk, place
1 tablespoon lemon juice
or vinegar in a glass measuring cup. Add enough
milk to make 1 cup total liquid; stir. Let the mixture
stand for 5 minutes before using it in a recipe.

FOLDING

This method calls for mixing light ingredients with
heavy ingredients without
decreasing their volume.
Use a spatula to cut down
vertically through the mix-
ture. Move spatula across bottom of bowl; bring it
back up other side, carrying some of the mixture
from the bottom over the surface. Repeat, rotating bowl, until ingredients are combined.

WHIPPING CREAM, STEP-BY-STEP

1. In a chilled mixing bowl
combine 1 cup whipping cream,
2 tablespoons sugar, and
½ teaspoon vanilla. Beat with
an electric mixer on medium
speed until soft peaks form
(tips curl). Serve whipped cream
at this stage if you wish to
softly drape it over a dessert.
2. Or you can continue beating
until stiff peaks form (tips stand
straight). Do not overbeat or it
will turn to butter.

NUTS

TOASTING NUTS AND COCONUT: To toast whole nuts or large pieces, spread them in a shallow pan. Bake them in a 350°F oven for 5 to 10 minutes, shaking the pan once or twice. (Toast coconut the same way, but watch closely to avoid burning it.) Toast finely chopped or ground nuts or sesame seeds in a dry skillet over medium heat. Stir often so they don't burn.

CHOPPING NUTS: Many types of nuts can be purchased already chopped—look for them in the baking aisle of the supermarket. If you buy nuts whole, you can chop them the size your recipe specifies.

■ Coarsely chopped nuts are large, irregular pieces that are more than ¼ inch in size.

■ Chopped nuts are medium, irregular pieces about ¼ inch in size.

■ Finely chopped nuts are small, irregular pieces that are about ⅛ inch in size.

MAKING GROUND NUTS: Use a blender or food processer to grind nuts, adding 1 tablespoon of the sugar or flour from recipe for each cup of nuts to help absorb some of the oil. Use a quick start-and-stop motion to help prevent overprocessing the nuts, which can turn them into nut butter.

CUBES AND CRUMBS

CRACKER CRUMBS: For 1 cup of crumbs, you'll need about 28 saltine crackers, 14 graham crackers, or 24 rich round crackers. To make the crumbs, place the crackers in a food processor fitted with the blade attachment. Process using on/off pulses until crumbs are of desired consistency.

SOFT (FRESH) BREAD CRUMBS: Cut bread into cubes and process as you would cracker crumbs. Use one slice of fresh bread for every ¾ cup crumbs.

FINE DRY BREAD CRUMBS: First, make dry bread cubes (see below). Process the cubes as you would cracker crumbs. One slice of bread yields ¼ cup fine dry crumbs.

WHEN TO USE SOFT OR DRY CRUMBS: Dry bread crumbs and cracker crumbs are usually used for breading foods that are to be fried. Soft bread crumbs tend to be used for crispy toppings on casseroles and filler in ground meat dishes, such as meat loaf and meatballs.

DRY BREAD CUBES: Often called for in stuffing and casserole recipes, dry bread cubes can be made from just about any type of bread. To make, stack a few slices and cut the bread into ½-inch strips using a serrated knife. Cut the strips crosswise into ½-inch cubes. Preheat the oven to 300°F. Arrange cubes in a single layer on a baking pan. Bake for 10 to 15 minutes or until golden, stirring once or twice. Let cool.

CRUMBS ON CALL IF YOUR BREAD HAS TURNED THE CORNER FROM FRESH TO DRY, FREEZE IT. THAT WAY, YOU'LL HAVE SOME BREAD TO THAW AND MAKE INTO DRY CRUMBS OR CUBES AS NEEDED.

CUTTING

JULIENNE: Cut food into matchlike sticks by slicing the food into 2x¼-inch pieces. Stack slices and cut them lengthwise into ⅛- to ¼-inch-wide strips.

DICE: Use a chef's knife to cut foods into uniform pieces that are about ⅛ to ¼ inch on all sides.

CUBE: Use a chef's knife to cut foods into uniform pieces that are about ½ inch on all sides.

CHOP: Use a chef's knife or food processor to cut foods into irregular pieces that are fine (⅛ inch or smaller), medium (¼ inch), or coarse (more than ¼ inch).

WEDGE: Put your food, flat side down, on the cutting board and cut the pieces at an angle.

SIMPLE CITRUS

CITRUS ZEST: To remove zest, draw the fruit across a fruit zester or grater; avoid the bitter white membrane (the pith).

PEELING CITRUS: You can use a vegetable peeler, as shown, to cut the outer layer of skin from the fruit. If you don't have a peeler, use a paring knife.

SECTIONING CITRUS: Using a paring knife, cut off a thin slice from both ends of an orange (or grapefruit). Place a flat end of the orange (see right) on a cutting board and cut away the peel and the white part of the rind, working from top to bottom. Tip the orange to its side and cut into center between one section and membrane (see right). Cut along the other side of the section next to the membrane to free the section.

MICROWAVE TIPS

YES, YOUR MICROWAVE DOES MORE THAN BOIL WATER AND REHEAT LEFTOVERS. HERE ARE WAYS TO USE IT TO GET YOUR INGREDIENTS RECIPE-READY IN SECONDS.

MELTING CHOCOLATE OR CANDY COATING: In a small microwave-safe bowl microwave 1 cup semi-sweet or milk chocolate pieces or 1 ounce chopped unsweetened or semi-sweet chocolate, uncovered, on 70% power for 1 minute; stir. Microwave at the same power for 1½ to 3 minutes more, stirring every 15 seconds until the chocolate is melted and smooth.

SOFTENING BUTTER: If you forget to set your butter out to soften, put it in a microwave-safe dish; microwave on 30% power (defrost) for 15 seconds. Check and repeat, if necessary. If you accidentally melt the butter, start over with another stick—do not use melted butter when softened butter is called for in a recipe.

MELTING BUTTER: Slice your butter into ½-inch-thick pieces and arrange evenly in a microwave-safe dish. Cover the dish with a paper towel. Microwave at 70% power for 30 seconds, checking and stirring every 5 to 10 seconds. Do this until evenly melted; avoid burning the butter.

SOFTENING CREAM CHEESE: Microwave in an uncovered microwave-safe bowl on 100% power. Allow 10 to 20 seconds for 3 to 8 ounces. Let stand before using.

SOFTENING TORTILLAS: Before microwaving, place tortillas between paper towels. Microwave on 100% power for 20 to 40 seconds.

THE PANTRY

CONSIDER YOUR PANTRY MORE OF A STRATEGY THAN A PARTICULAR PLACE IN YOUR KITCHEN. A WELL-STOCKED ONE WILL MAKE YOUR COOKING LIFE A LOT EASIER.

Though it's a grandmotherly word—conjuring up a quaint storage room with shelf upon shelf of home-canned goods—a pantry is actually anywhere you store food, from the cupboard to the refrigerator and the freezer. When you keep a well-stocked pantry, those time-eating trips to the supermarket become less frequent. Even if you do need to go to the store for fresh meat or produce, the time you spend there will be minimized if you don't have to chase down staples on every trip.

These lists show basic ingredients that are often used in recipes in this book. They're also ingredients that keep relatively well compared to more perishable items. Buy what you think you will eat fairly often and buy in small quantities so foods stay fresh. Tailor your pantry according to foods you love; fill it with recipe ingredients that you use again and again and you'll be surprised how much easier it is to motivate yourself to cook a meal rather than ordering pizza (again!).

SKIP THE DRIVE-THROUGH
KEEP INGREDIENTS ON HAND FOR AT LEAST ONE QUICK MEAL—SUCH AS A PASTA TOSS OR A STIR-FRY—AND YOU'LL BE LESS TEMPTED TO DINE OUT BY DEFAULT.

ITEMS FOR A WELL-STOCKED PANTRY

FOR THE CUPBOARD

Baking powder and soda

Canned beans (kidney, black, cannellini)

Canned tuna

Cornstarch

Couscous

Dried fruits

Egg noodles, dried

Flour (all-purpose)

Garlic

Honey

Hot pepper sauce

Milk (evaporated, sweetened condensed)

Nonstick cooking spray

Nuts (almonds, pecans, walnuts)

Oil (vegetable, olive)

Onions

Pasta, dried

Pasta sauce

Peanut butter

Pizza sauce

Rice

Salsa

Salt, pepper, herbs, and spices (the ones you use most often)

Sugar (granulated, brown)

Tomatoes, canned

Vinegar (cider, red and white wine, balsamic)

FOR THE REFRIGERATOR

Barbecue sauce

Bottled salad dressing

Butter or margarine

Carrots

Celery

Cheese (cheddar, Parmesan, Swiss)

Cream cheese

Eggs

Jams and jellies

Ketchup

Lemons

Mayonnaise

Meats with long shelf lives (such as smoked sausage, corned beef)

Milk

Mustard

Orange juice

Pesto

Precut vegetables

Salad greens

Soy sauce

Syrup, maple

Tortillas

FOR THE FREEZER

Chicken breasts

Ground beef

Vegetables, frozen

REFRIGERATOR/FREEZER STORAGE

Purchase products by "sell by" or expiration dates and follow these guidelines for storing them.

Product:	To store:	Refrigerate (40°F) up to:	Freeze (0°F) up to:
DAIRY			
Butter	Refrigerate in original packaging. Overwrap with moisture- and vaporproof wrap to freeze.	1 month	6 months
Buttermilk	Refrigerate in original packaging. To freeze, transfer to freezer containers; allow for headspace.	7 days	Up to 3 months Use for baking and cooking only.
Cheese, cottage and ricotta	Refrigerate in original packaging.	Use by date on container or within 5 days of purchase.	Not recommended.
Cheese, hard and semifirm	Wrap in plastic wrap. Overwrap in freezer wrap to freeze.	4 to 6 weeks If cheese molds, cut ½ inch below the mold and discard molded portion.	1 month Use only for cooking.
Sour Cream and Yogurt	Refrigerate in original packaging.	7 days	Not recommended.
EGGS			
Hard-cooked, in shells	Refrigerate.	7 days	Not recommended.
Whites	Refrigerate in tightly covered containers; transfer to freezer containers to freeze.	4 days	6 months
Whole, in shells	Store whole eggs in carton placed in coldest part of refrigerator. Do not wash; do not store in refrigerator door.	5 weeks after packing date.	Do not freeze eggs in shells.
COOKED MEATS			
Ham; Hot dogs; Lunch meats; Sausage, smoked links and patties	Refrigerate in original wrapping. Overwrap in freezer wrap to freeze.	7 days	1 month
UNCOOKED MEAT, POULTRY, AND FISH			
Meat (roasts, steaks, chops), Poultry (whole and pieces)	Refrigerate in original wrapping. Overwrap in freezer wrap to freeze.	3 days	3 to 6 months
Meat and Poultry (ground)	Refrigerate in original wrapping. Overwrap in freezer wrap to freeze.	1 to 2 days	3 months
Fish and Shellfish	Store in moisture- and vaporproof wrap in coldest part of refrigerator. Overwrap in freezer wrap to freeze.	1 to 2 days	3 months

CHILE PEPPERS

THESE BEAUTIES MAKE RECIPES POP WITH FLAVOR AND COLOR.

When buying peppers, whether sweet or hot, pick peppers that are glossy, have bright color, and are a good shape for the variety. Avoid those that are shriveled or bruised or have soft spots.

Most chile peppers can be stored in the refrigerator, unwashed and wrapped in paper towels in a plastic bag, for up to 10 days. Serrano peppers are an exception—keep these in a vegetable crisper; do not store in plastic. To clean peppers before using, rinse thoroughly and scrub with a clean produce brush; prepare as needed. The seeds and membrane are the hottest part; remove or use them depending on how much you like the heat.

Poblano

Banana wax peppers

Jalapeño

Serrano

CAUTION—HOT STUFF!
THE OILS THAT GIVE CHILES THEIR BURN CAN ALSO DO THE SAME TO YOU.
Fresh chile peppers contain volatile oils that can burn your skin and eyes, so avoid direct contact with them as much as possible. When working with fresh chile peppers, wear disposable plastic or rubber gloves. If your bare hands do touch the chiles, wash your hands and nails thoroughly with soap and hot water. If you get chile oil in your eyes, flush them with cool water.

OLIVES & CAPERS

FLAVOR-PACKED OLIVES ARE A MUST FOR COOKING AND FOR PARTY HORS D'OEUVRES.

These days many supermarkets and specialty food shops have olive bars brimming with all kinds of these colorful, flavor-packed orbs. When cooking, you generally need to pit olives before adding them to a recipe. To do so, gently crush the long side of the unpitted olive with your thumb or the broad side of a chef's knife. The pit will then present itself—just pop it out.

Found next to olives in the supermarket, capers are the buds of a spiny shrub. They have an assertive flavor often described as a marriage of citrus and olive plus a tang from their packaging brine.

Queen

Niçoise

Kalamata

Capers

Pimiento-stuffed green

California ripe olives

FLAVORINGS

THE MORE YOU COOK, THE MORE YOU'LL LOVE GETTING TO KNOW THE VARIETY OF SPICE BLENDS, SPICES, AND HERBS AVAILABLE.

Spices are the seeds, bark, fruit, or flowers of a plant. For photographs of the spices common in a well-stocked pantry, see page 26; for herbs, see page 29.

SPICE BLENDS

Consider stocking up on the following spice and herb blends; they let you add time-honored combinations to your recipes with one easy measure.

CAJUN SEASONING Though this mix differs from brand to brand, most blends are peppery hot and include onion, garlic, salt, and the classic Cajun pepper trio of white, black, and red. Sprinkle it into crumb coatings or directly onto fish, poultry, or meat before cooking.

FINES HERBES (feenz ERB) This combo of chervil, parsley, chives, and tarragon adds unmistakable French finesse to egg dishes as well as gravies, sauces, and creamy soups.

FIVE-SPICE POWDER Brands vary, but this mix usually includes cinnamon, anise, fennel, Szechwan or black pepper, and cloves.

GARAM MASALA "Garam" means warm or hot; "masala" means spice blend. While garam masala is not fiery hot, the Indian blend does add a warm spiciness to a dish. Though versions vary, the mix can include cumin, coriander, fennel, cardamom, cinnamon, cloves, dried chiles, and black pepper, among other spices. Look for it at Indian markets, spice shops, or import food shops.

HERBES DE PROVENCE Common in the South of France, this mélange of dried herbs usually includes basil, fennel, lavender, marjoram, rosemary, sage, savory, and thyme. These flavors complement pork, chicken, and lamb.

ITALIAN SEASONING Herbs often found in this blend include basil, oregano, thyme, and rosemary; sometimes garlic and red pepper are added. Enjoy this in tomato-based pasta or pizza sauces and as a rub for roast chicken.

JAMAICAN JERK SEASONING Add spice to fish, meat marinades, and just about anything you cook on a grill with this lively mix that can include salt, sugar, allspice, thyme, cloves, ginger, cinnamon, onion, and chile peppers.

LEMON-PEPPER SEASONING Give fish and poultry a fresh, delicate lemon flavor with this mixture made of salt with black pepper and dried grated lemon peel.

MEXICAN SEASONING This spicy blend often includes cumin, chile peppers, salt, onion, sweet peppers, garlic, and oregano. It's always a great add-in for Mexican specialties, from huevos rancheros to salsa.

STORING DRIED HERBS AND SPICES

It's best to buy dried herbs and spices in small amounts because they lose flavor over time. Most whole spices and herbs keep 1 to 2 years (whole cloves, nutmeg, and cinnamon sticks will last slightly longer). Ground herbs and spices maintain good quality and aroma for 6 months. Keep them as fresh as possible by storing all dried herbs and spices in airtight containers in a dry place away from sunlight and heat. Refrigerate red spices, such as paprika, to preserve color and flavor.

BOUQUET GARNI
HERE'S HOW TO BUNDLE YOUR HERBS—AND WHY IT'S WORTHWHILE.

WHAT? A bouquet garni (boo-KAY gar-NEE) is a French term for a group of herbs that is tied together or bundled in cheesecloth. Traditionally,  the herbs used were thyme, parsley, and bay leaf, but you can create one from just about any herb, fresh or dried.

HOW? Bundle the herbs in several thicknesses of 100-percent-cotton cheesecloth. Tie the cheesecloth closed with kitchen string to form a bag.

WHY? After extended cooking, fresh herbs can lose their color, and dried herbs can muddy up the look of a dish. A bouquet garni allows the herbs to flavor a recipe and makes it easy to remove the herbs before the dish is served. Whether or not you use a bouquet garni, bay leaves should always be removed from a dish before serving.

Here are popular spices and top forms to use them. Note that some cooks prefer buying spices in their whole form, then crushing or grinding them for the most intense flavor. **1. CINNAMON STICKS:** Use to infuse hot drinks with cinnamon flavor. **2. GROUND CINNAMON:** Meats, breads, desserts. **3. CARDAMOM PODS/4.GROUND CARDAMOM:** Curried dishes, baked goods. **5. CAYENNE PEPPER:** Stews, barbecue rubs and sauces, egg and cheese dishes. **6. CHILI POWDER/ 7. CHIPOTLE POWDER:** Stews, marinades, meats. **8. GROUND CLOVES/9. WHOLE CLOVES:** Meats, desserts, spiced beverages. **10. CUMIN SEED/11. GROUND CUMIN:** Meats, poultry, soups, stews. **12. CURRY POWDER:** Meats, sauces, stews. **13. FENNEL SEED:** Meat, sausage, poultry, breads. **14. GROUND GINGER:** Marinades, baked goods. **15. CRYSTALLIZED GINGER:** Add as a finishing touch to desserts. **16. WHOLE NUTMEG/17. GROUND NUTMEG:** Baked goods, white sauces, custard. **18. GROUND MUSTARD:** Salad dressings, egg and cheese dishes. **19. MUSTARD SEEDS:** Pickling, relishes. **20. PAPRIKA:** Meat, fish, chicken, egg dishes. **21. FRESH GINGER:** Stir-fries, soups, sauces, beverages.

Finely ground pepper

Coarsely ground pepper

Peppercorns

PEPPER

The photo above shows whole peppercorns, as well as two forms this must-have ingredient is often called for in recipes (clockwise from bottom):

PEPPERCORNS: Because pepper can lose flavor after it's ground, many cooks prefer to purchase whole peppercorns and grind them as needed. To do this, you need a pepper mill; most come with settings that allow coarse to finely ground pepper.

COARSELY GROUND BLACK PEPPER: Larger flakes lend a distinct peppery appeal to a recipe.

FINELY GROUND BLACK PEPPER: Smaller flakes are called for when the peppery notes are meant to blend more seamlessly with the other flavors.

GARLIC

Although you can purchase minced garlic by the jar, you will get the best flavor if you use a fresh bulb.

■ Pick firm and plump bulbs; the skin should be papery and dry.

■ Store it in a cool, dry, dark place, such as a garlic keeper on the counter or a brown paper bag in the pantry. Store no longer than 4 months.

■ Leave bulbs whole so that individual cloves won't dry too quickly.

■ For minced garlic, remove the cloves from the head. Peel away the papery skin and finely mince with a sharp knife or use a garlic press.

GARLIC MATH:

1 bulb of garlic = between 10 and 20 cloves
1 clove of garlic = ½ teaspoon minced or
⅛ teaspoon garlic powder

HERB AND SPICE SWAPS

If you find yourself lacking a particular herb or spice called for in a recipe, there's usually another choice that can be successfully substituted. Here are some easy swaps to use in popular styles of ethnic cooking.

Don't have	Swap with
MEXICAN	
Cilantro	Though it won't replace the flavor, Italian parsley will add freshness to your dish.
Chili powder	Combine oregano, cumin, and either red pepper flakes or hot sauce.
Cumin	Coriander
ITALIAN	
Basil	Oregano
Fennel	Anise seeds
Garlic	Garlic powder
Oregano	Marjoram or thyme
GREEK	
Bay leaf	Thyme
Marjoram	Oregano or sage
Rosemary	Savory or thyme
Dill	Tarragon
INDIAN	
Curry powder	Use a blend of turmeric, ginger, black pepper, coriander, cumin, and chili powder.
Cardamom	Equal parts cloves and cinnamon
Cinnamon	Mace, allspice, or a smaller amount of nutmeg

VANILLA BEANS

Vanilla extract is convenient and commonly called for in recipes for baked goods and ice cream. Sometimes, though, a recipe starts with vanilla beans. These long, thin pods should not be eaten; rather, the tiny, dark seeds inside are used to bring intense vanilla flavor and a confetti-like sprinkle to a dish. To remove seeds, cut the pod lengthwise with a paring knife; scrape out the tiny seeds.

HERBS

IT'S AMAZING HOW A SIMPLE DOSE OF SOMETHING GREEN CAN ADD SO MUCH FRESH FLAVOR TO YOUR COOKING.

USING DRIED HERBS

Before using a dried herb in any recipe, crush with a mortar and pestle to release its aromatic oils and bring out the flavor. If you don't have one, place the dried herb in the palm of your hand and press and rub it with your thumb. Another method is to rub the herbs between your thumb and two fingers (see photo 4, page 10).

USING DRIED HERBS FOR FRESH

Some recipes specify using fresh herbs. However, sometimes fresh herbs aren't available, or it just isn't practical to buy a bunch when only a teaspoon is needed. In such cases, dried herbs can usually be substituted. To do so, use one-third the amount of dried herb for the fresh herb called for in the recipe. (For example, substitute 1 teaspoon of a dried herb for 1 table-spoon of a fresh herb.) When substituting a ground herb for dried leaf herb, use about half of the amount of the dried leaf herb called for in the recipe.

Add the dried herb to a recipe at the beginning of the cooking time; this allows its flavors to seep into the dish.

USING FRESH HERBS

1 STRIPPING To remove leaves from the herb's stem, hold onto stem with one hand and strip the leaves into a bowl, using the thumb and forefinger of the other hand.

2 SNIPPING To cut large leaves, place them in a measuring cup or bowl and snip them with kitchen shears. Use quick, short strokes. For herbs with tough stems, such as rosemary, strip leaves from the stem first.

3 CHIFFONADE The term literally means "made of rags," but in herb-speak, it refers to herbs cut into strips or shreds. To do this, roll up larger leaves and cut across the roll.

4 STORING To store fresh herbs, cut ½ inch from the bottom of stems; stand them in a jar with water. Loosely cover leaves with a plastic bag. Store the herbs in the refrigerator (except basil, which should be stored at room temperature).

1

2

3

4

Here are some of the most commonly used culinary herbs, along with foods they complement particularly well.
1. SAGE: Poultry, sausage, pork, stuffing, and vegetables. **2. TARRAGON:** Poultry, fish, grilled meats, and vinaigrettes. **3. THYME:** Chicken, beef, vegetables, and sauces. **4. ROSEMARY:** Lamb, pork, fish, and breads. **5. FLAT-LEAF (ITALIAN) PARSLEY:** Brings a mild, fresh herb taste to almost any dish. **6. BASIL:** Sauces, salads, tomato dishes, and pesto. **7. MARJORAM:** Lamb, veal, and vegetables. **8. MINT:** Salads, marinades, dressings; also use as an edible garnish for desserts. **9. DILL:** Fish, seafood, vegetables, and pickles. **10. CHIVES:** Eggs, salad dressings, potatoes, and seafood. **11. CURLY-LEAF PARSLEY:** Interchangeable with flat-leaf parsley. **12. OREGANO:** Pizza, pasta, bean soups, sauces, and pasta salads. **13. CILANTRO:** Asian, Indian, and Mexican cuisines.

FOOD SAFETY

THE PLEASURE OF COOKING FOR FRIENDS AND FAMILY COMES WITH THE RESPONSIBILITY OF MAKING SURE EVERYTHING YOU SERVE IS SAFE TO EAT.

TEMPERATURE TIPS

You cannot see, taste, or smell most bacteria that cause foodborne illnesses, so it's wise to prevent the bacteria from growing in the first place. A key step in doing this is to keep hot foods hot and cold foods cold. Store cold foods at 40°F or below and serve hot foods immediately or keep them at 140°F or above. It's between these temperatures that illness-causing bacteria thrive and multiply; therefore, keep foods out of this danger zone.

SEPARATE, DON'T CROSS-CONTAMINATE

Cross-contamination occurs when ready-to-eat foods pick up bacteria from other foods, unclean hands, cutting boards, knives, or other utensils. To avoid cross-contamination, keep raw meat, poultry, eggs, fish, shellfish, and the juices away from other foods. Here are guidelines.

■ Keep raw meat, poultry, fish, and shellfish separate from other foods in your grocery cart and shopping bags.

■ Once home, store raw meat, poultry, fish, and shellfish in sealed containers or plastic bags so the juices don't drip onto other foods. Place whole roasts and poultry on a tray or pan that's large enough to catch any juices that might leak.

■ If possible, purchase two different cutting boards. Use one only for raw meats, poultry, fish, and shellfish. Use the other for ready-to-eat foods, such as breads and vegetables.

■ Don't wash raw beef, pork, lamb, poultry, or veal before cooking. Rinsing these foods poses a risk of cross-contamination with other foods and utensils in the kitchen. Bacteria that might be present are destroyed with proper cooking.

■ Place cooked foods on a clean plate. Never reuse the unwashed dish that held the raw meat, poultry, fish, or shellfish.

■ Keep your hands and all surfaces and utensils that come into contact with food clean.

WHEN IN DOUBT, THROW IT OUT

If food hasn't been properly handled, even cooking it correctly won't make it safe. If you aren't sure that food has been prepared, served, or stored safely, throw it out. Never taste food to see if it's safe—contaminated food can taste, smell, and look good enough to eat. But eating even a small amount can make you sick.

THAW SAFELY

Thawing foods properly is another piece of the food-safety puzzle. Here are key concepts.

■ Thaw foods in the refrigerator, never at room temperature (a few exceptions include breads and sweets that specifically call for thawing at room temperature). Make sure that thawing foods don't drip onto other foods.

■ Some foods can be successfully thawed in a microwave. Follow the manufacturer's instructions and cook the food immediately after thawing.

■ You can also thaw by placing food in a leak-proof plastic bag and immersing it in cold tap

SAFE FOOD TEMPERATURES

Always use a food thermometer to ensure that food has reached a high enough temperature to destroy harmful bacteria. Here are recommended internal temperatures for meats and other foods.

Food	Final Doneness Temperature
Beef, lamb, and veal steaks, chops, and roasts	
medium rare	145°F
medium	160°F
Hamburger, meat loaf, ground pork, veal, and lamb	160°F
Pork chops, ribs, and roasts	160°F
Egg dishes	160°F
Ground turkey and chicken	165°F
Stuffing and casseroles	165°F
Leftovers	165°F
Chicken and turkey breasts	170°F
Chicken and turkey, whole bird, legs, thighs, and wings	180°F
Duck and goose	180°F

water in the sink, changing the water every half hour to keep it cold. When changing the water, flip the bag if it's not fully submerged. Cook food immediately after thawing.

THE TWO-HOUR TIME LIMIT

To make sure that leftovers stay bacteria-free, refrigerate them immediately after the meal is finished. Discard any food that has been left out more than 2 hours (1 hour if the temperature is higher than 80°F).

QUESTIONS? CALL THE REGULATORS

To get the latest information on ever-changing food safety regulations and precautions call:

■ the USDA Meat and Poultry Hotline at 800/535-4555

■ the U.S. FDA Center for Food Safety and Applied Nutrition Outreach Center at 888/723-3366

■ your health care provider

You can also get information at the government's website, *foodsafety.gov.*

FOOD SAFETY—IN SHORT

KEEP HANDS, SURFACES, AND UTENSILS CLEAN; DON'T CROSS-CONTAMINATE; COOK TO PROPER TEMPERATURES; AND REFRIGERATE PROMPTLY.

SAFE SERVING AND TOTING

These tips will help you keep food out of the "danger zone" when transporting and serving them.

■ When toting hot foods to a picnic or party, use heavy-duty foil (see below), layers of newspaper (see right), or a heavy towel (see below right) to wrap the container well. Place the wrapped container in an insulated container to keep the food at or above 140°F.

■ When serving hot foods buffet-style, use chafing dishes, slow cookers, and warming trays to keep food above 140°F.

■ Buy cold, perishable foods last when shopping. Go straight home and refrigerate them immediately; follow packaging labels for safe handling.

■ When serving cold foods on a buffet, place the foods on a tray over ice. Discard after 2 hours (1 hour if temperature is over 80°F).

■ When toting cold perishable foods, keep them at 40°F or lower by packing them in a well-insulated cooler with plenty of ice. A full cooler will maintain its cold temperature longer than a partially filled one.

FREEZING FOODS

GOOD FOODS SUCCESSFULLY STORED IN THE FREEZER ARE CULINARY GIFTS TO OPEN AND ENJOY WHEN YOU NEED THEM MOST.

COLD ENOUGH

Check the temperature of your freezer to ensure that it maintains the proper temperature for food storage. Freezers should maintain a temp of 0°F.

COOL IT, STORE IT, FREEZE IT

To keep bacteria from growing, foods that are to be frozen must be cooled quickly first. To freeze soups and stews, see page 567. To freeze other foods, divide them into small portions in shallow containers. Arrange containers in a single layer in freezer to allow cold air to circulate around packages until frozen. Stack after completely frozen. These vessels are best for freezer-bound foods:

FREEZER-SAFE CONTAINERS: Look for a phrase or an icon on the label or container bottom indicating they are designed for freezer use.

BAKING DISHES: Use freezer-to-oven or freezer-to-microwave dishes and cover them with plastic freezer wrap or heavy-duty foil.*

GLASS JARS WITH TIGHT-FITTING LIDS: All major brands of canning jars are acceptable for use in the refrigerator and freezer. Leave headspace in the jar for the food to expand if you plan to freeze liquids or semi-liquids.

SELF-SEALING STORAGE BAGS AND PLASTIC WRAP: Buy products made for freezer use.

HEAVY-DUTY FOIL: Regular foil won't make the cut when it comes to storing foods in the freezer.

*NOTE: Foods that contain acidic ingredients, such as tomatoes, should not be wrapped and stored in foil. To freeze dishes with acidic ingredients, wrap the food in plastic wrap first; cover with foil. Remove plastic before heating.

LABEL IT

Take a moment to label foods before storing them. Use a wax crayon or waterproof marking pen to note the name of the food item or recipe, the quantity, the date it was frozen, and any special information about its use.

THAW AND REHEAT

Reheat food to a safe internal temperature before serving. To do so, follow these guidelines.

- Bring sauces, soups, and gravies to a rolling boil in a covered saucepan. Stir occasionally.
- Heat leftovers to 165°F.
- See page 30 for helpful thawing tips.

FOODS NOT TO FREEZE

These foods lose flavor, texture, and overall quality when frozen.

- Battered and fried foods
- Cooked egg whites and yolks, as well as icings made with egg whites
- Cottage and ricotta cheeses
- Custard and cream pies or desserts with cream fillings
- Soups and stews made with potatoes, which can darken and become mushy
- Stews thickened with cornstarch or flour
- Sour cream, mayonnaise, and salad dressings
- Stuffed chops or chicken breasts
- Whole eggs in the shell, raw or cooked

MAKE-AND-FREEZE RECIPES

THESE RECIPES ARE PARTICULARLY WELL SUITED TO FREEZING.

- Cheesy Italian Meatball Casserole, page 231
- Simple Stromboli, page 246
- Spice-Rubbed Beef Tenderloin, page 341
- Spiced-and-Sassy Beef Ribs, page 362
- Pulled Pork Shoulder, page 363
- Ham Balls in Barbecue Sauce, page 406
- Baked Ziti with Three Cheeses, page 440
- Turkey Meat Loaf, page 484
- Citrus-Marinated Turkey Breast, page 489
- Sloppy Joes, page 522
- French Dip Sandwiches, page 523
- Barley-Beef Soup, page 569
- Lamb Cassoulet, page 572
- Make-It-Mine Chili, page 574
- Ham and Bean Soup, page 575
- Lentil and Sausage Soup, page 577

RECIPE NUTRITION GUIDE

EACH RECIPE COMES WITH INFORMATION TO HELP YOU DECIDE IF IT FITS YOUR NUTRITION NEEDS.

NUTRITION INFORMATION GUIDE

The nutrition analysis for a single serving is listed at the end of each recipe. Here's an example.

PER 3 SHRIMP: 473 cal., 15 g total fat (3 g sat. fat, 0 g trans fat), 65 mg chol., 1,533 mg sodium, 60 g carbo., 5 g fiber, 18 g pro. **EXCHANGES:** 1½ Vegetable, 3½ Starch, 1 Lean Meat, 2 Fat

Read what each of the entries refers to and use the guidelines to help you make smart food choices at every meal.

cal. Total calories per serving. The estimated calorie requirements per day range by age and gender. For example, the requirement for moderately active women between the ages of 31 and 50 is 2,000 calories; for moderately active men in that age group, the number is 2,400 to 2,600.

total fat The amount of all fat per serving, which includes saturated, polyunsaturated, monounsaturated, and trans fats. For a healthy diet, strive to keep fat intake between 20 percent to 35 percent of daily calories.

sat. fat Saturated fat per serving. Limit saturated fat to 10 percent of daily calories.

trans fat Trans fat per serving. Limit trans fat to 1 percent of your total daily calories.

chol. Cholesterol per serving. Limit this to 300 milligrams per day.

sodium Sodium per serving. Based on the Dietary Guidelines for Americans, keep sodium under 2,300 milligrams per day.

carbo. Carbohydrates per serving. Strive to consume carbohydrates from unrefined sources such as whole grains. If you consume foods and beverages high in added sugars, you tend to consume more calories, which may lead to weight gain.

fiber Total fiber per serving. This amount includes soluble and insoluble fiber. Strive to get 25 grams of fiber per day if you're on a 2,000-calorie diet (30 grams if you're on a 2,500-calorie diet).

pro. Protein per serving. Look for lean meats and poultry, and vary your protein sources with fish, beans, peas, nuts, and seeds.

HOW RECIPE ANALYSES IS CALCULATED

To determine nutritional values in each recipe, the Better Homes and Gardens® Test Kitchen uses nutrition-analysis software. When looking at the analyses, keep these factors in mind.

■ When an ingredient is listed as optional, such as a garnish, it is not included in the analysis.

■ When ingredient choices appear, the first choice is used to calculate the analysis.

■ When there is a range in the number of servings (4 to 6 servings), the first (smaller) number is used.

■ For marinade, it is assumed most of the marinade is discarded.

■ When milk is a recipe ingredient, the analysis is calculated using 2 percent (reduced-fat) milk.

■ Diabetic exchanges, listed with the nutrition facts for each recipe, are based on the exchange list developed by the American Dietetic Association and the American Diabetes Association.

LOOK FOR THESE SYMBOLS

If you are searching for a specific type of recipe, use these symbols above the recipe title to find what you are looking for.

BEST EVER Favorite takes on the classics.

FAST These recipes will take 30 minutes or less.

WHOLE GRAIN Look for this symbol to include a good source of whole grain in your meal.

LOW FAT To qualify for this designation, appetizers must have 2 grams of fat or less per serving. Main-dish recipes must have 12 grams of fat or less. Salads must have 5 grams of fat or less. Breads and vegetable side dishes must have 3 grams of fat or less. Cookies must have 2 grams of fat or less per cookie.

HEALTHY These recipes adhere to specific guidelines. **Fat:** Less than or equal to 35 percent of total calories or less than 1 gram per serving. **Sat. fat:** Less than 10 percent of calories or less than 1 gram per serving. (To figure either fat, multiply the grams of the fat in the serving by 9; divide that number by the total calories in the serving.) **Trans fat:** 0 grams. **Cholesterol:** Less than or equal to 60 milligrams. **Sodium:** Less than or equal to 480 milligrams.

EATING HEALTHY

EATING WELL MEANS EATING
FOODS YOU ENJOY AS WELL AS
FOODS THAT ARE GOOD FOR YOU.
HERE ARE WAYS TO DO BOTH.

KNOW YOUR FATS

Fats are an essential part of your diet and should make up 20 to 35 percent of your dietary calories. Fats help with nutrient absorption. But when consumed in excess, they can contribute to weight gain, heart disease, and cancer.

However, not all fats are created equal. Some can contribute to heart disease, but others—when consumed in appropriate amounts—can have beneficial effects. Here's the breakdown.

GOOD FATS

MONOUNSATURATED FAT: This fat is typically found in foods high in vitamin E, which is an antioxidant that helps keep your cells healthy. Monounsaturated fat can help decrease total cholesterol when substituted for saturated fat. Good sources include olive oil, canola oil, sunflower oil, avocado, and peanut butter.

POLYUNSATURATED FAT: This fat can help decrease total cholesterol. Omega-3 fatty acids are included in this group. In addition to helping maintain healthy heart function, omega-3s are necessary for healthy cell development and brain function. Good sources are soybean oil, salmon and other fatty fish, walnuts, and ground flaxseed.

BAD FATS

SATURATED FAT: Too much saturated fat in your diet will raise cholesterol levels which may increase your risk of heart disease and stroke. Common sources of saturated fat are butter and other dairy products made from whole or reduced-fat milk, beef, pork, palm oil, and coconut oil.

TRANS FAT: This fat can increase your risk of heart disease by lowering HDL (good cholesterol) levels while increasing LDL (bad cholesterol) levels. Most trans fats are artificially made and can be found in fried foods, processed goods, and food items with partially hydrogenated oils in the ingredients list.

MARGARINE VS. BUTTER

When it comes to a healthy choice, margarine usually beats butter. Margarine is made from vegetable oil, so it doesn't contain cholesterol. It's also higher in polyunsaturated and monounsaturated fats (the good fats). Butter is made mostly from animal fat, so it contains cholesterol and high levels of saturated fat.

However, most margarine is processed using hydrogenation, which results in unhealthy trans fat. Therefore, when looking for a healthy choice, select a margarine with the lowest trans fat content possible and less than 2 grams total of saturated plus trans fats. Because trans-fat-free margarine might not last as long as one that was made with artificial trans fat, be sure to check the package for expiration date and proper storage.

One caveat: While spreading toast with margarine products with better-than-butter fat profiles is an easy swap, butter is recommended for baking, as it brings the best flavor and texture to the results. Enjoy in moderation.

IS FRESH BETTER?

FROZEN AND CANNED FRUITS AND VEGGIES RETAIN THEIR NUTRIENTS OFTEN TIMES AS WELL AS FRESH PRODUCE.

Canned and frozen vegetable and fruit options make the goal of eating the recommended 4½ cups of fruits and vegetables per day much more attainable. Many of the health benefits are still available in canned and frozen options and they are often less expensive. Before purchasing, consider these tips.

■ Rinse and drain canned fruits and vegetables before using.

■ Buy no-salt-added canned vegetables.

■ Opt for canned fruits in light syrup or canned in the fruit's natural juices.

■ Pick frozen vegetables that have no salt or sodium added.

■ Choose frozen vegetable packs that do not have sauces, butter, or flavorings added. Buy frozen fruit that has no sugar added.

THE IMPORTANCE OF WHOLE GRAINS

Health experts advise that at least half of the grains you eat should be whole grains. Fortunately, many tasty ingredients fall into the whole grain camp. These include barley, brown rice, bulgur, oats, quinoa, wheat germ, wheat berries, and millet. These and other whole grains contain disease-fighting phytochemicals and anti-oxidants. Eating whole grains regularly can help lower your risk of obesity and lower cholesterol levels, which in turn lowers your risk for type 2 diabetes and heart disease. Whole grains can also help you feel more full and satisfied after a meal, making it easier to give junk food a pass. Unsure how to bring whole grains to your table? Look for the **WHOLE GRAIN** symbol for the great recipes in this book that are rife with whole grains.

LIGHTEN UP YOUR FAVORITES

CALL ON THESE SIMPLE SWAPS TO SHAVE FAT AND CALORIES.

■ Opt for the reduced-fat or low-fat versions of products you commonly use, such as milk, sour cream, peanut butter, and salad dressing. Compare labels before purchasing new, lower-fat products to ensure you're saving calories and fat grams.

■ Swap lean ground turkey for ground beef to cut the fat from hamburgers and tacos. Meatless crumbles are a good vegetarian option and have four times less fat and 0 mg cholesterol.

POWER FOODS

Healthy eating isn't just about the foods you avoid; it's about the foods you love too. Use the following tasty, satisfying foods to help build a diet that protects your heart and total body health.

QUINOA: The nutrients in this gluten-free, bead-like whole grain help repair damaged body tissue. Quinoa (KEEN-wah) is also considered a power-house food because it's a complete protein and is high in magnesium, which helps relax muscles and lower blood pressure.

BERRIES: Blackberries, blueberries, and raspberries are packed with antioxidants, potassium, and fiber. Studies have shown that berries also significantly reduce blood pressure, increase HDL (good cholesterol), and reduce platelet activity, which helps blood flow better. Berries are also sweet, simple, easy-to-enjoy foods.

DARK LEAFY GREENS: Spinach is a power-packed leafy green that's widely available, cost-efficient, and loaded with important vitamins and minerals, such as calcium and iron.

BEANS: Black and kidney beans stand out among the healthy legume choices; they are cholesterol-free, as well as a good source of protein and fiber. They also can lower cholesterol and blood pressure, and help you lose weight. Mash some for a sandwich spread, use some to add satisfying heft to a simple salad, or serve as an easy side dish.

WALNUTS AND ALMONDS: Walnuts contain protein, antioxidants, and omega-3 fatty acids, which help reduce the risk of heart disease. Almonds are an easy snack and provide a healthy amount of monounsaturated fat. Use them in small amounts and in combination with healthful foods. For example, sprinkle nuts on a salad with fat-free dressing.

PLAN YOUR PLATE TO WORK MORE NUTRIENTS AND FIBER INTO YOUR DIET, FILL THREE-FOURTHS OF YOUR PLATE WITH A VARIETY OF WHOLE GRAINS AND COLORFUL FRUITS AND VEGGIES.

TABLE SETTING 101

PLACING FLATWARE PROPERLY ON THE TABLE SHOWS GUESTS YOU CARE ABOUT THEIR EASE AND ENJOYMENT.

1 CASUAL MEALS This simple setting is perfect for everyday lunches and dinners. Having soup? Simply place the bowl on the plate. This setting can also be used for casual entertaining for close friends or family.

2 INFORMAL DINNERS OR LUNCHEONS This setting adds a wineglass and bread and/ or salad plate. Use it for a special brunch, ladies' luncheon, or a celebratory dinner at home.

3 FORMAL MEALS This setting is for holiday meals and formal entertaining. Before serving dessert, first clear all unnecessary plates, utensils, and glasses.

Glass

Dinner fork

Dinner plate

Teaspoon

Napkin

Knife

1

Bread & salad plate

Water goblet

Wineglass

Salad fork

Dinner fork

Dinner plate

Knife

Teaspoon

Napkin

2

3

Water goblet

Bread & salad plate

Dessert spoon

Dessert fork

Red wineglass

Butter knife

White wineglass

Salad fork

Dinner plate

Napkin

Dinner fork

Knife

Teaspoon

Soup spoon

APPETIZERS & SNACKS

SHRIMP SPRING ROLLS WITH
CHIMICHURRI SAUCE, PAGE 62

APPETIZERS & SNACKS

CASUAL APPETIZER PARTIES RANK AMONG THE EASIEST AND MOST ENJOYABLE OF GATHERINGS. HERE'S HOW TO PULL ONE OFF.

MENU PLANNER

■ Choose a combination of crowd-pleasing recipes you feel confident serving alongside a newbie or two to create a little buzz come party time.

■ Anchor your appetizer buffet with one or two hearty bites, such as cocktail meatballs, fondue, and/or chicken drumettes.

■ Don't knock yourself out—complement the recipes you choose to cook with foods that require little or no prep, such as a cheese tray or a platter of cured meats.

■ Relax. Keep in mind that many party foods taste better when served closer to room temperature than piping hot or ice cold. That means you don't have to rush foods from oven (or fridge) to the table. However, perishable foods should not stand at room temperature longer than 2 hours.

BEVERAGE PLANNER

■ Rather than offering a full bar, consider serving one stylish cocktail or punch plus beer, wine, and plenty of nonalcoholic beverages. That way, you won't need to mix drinks all night.

■ Plan on serving one 750-milliliter bottle of wine for every two guests. Chill more white wines than you think you'll need. Generally, inexpensive and moderately priced wines that have been chilled can be returned to room-temperature storage without damage.

■ Allow 12 ounces of beer per guest for every half hour to an hour of party time.

■ Purchase about 1 pound of ice per guest. Store it in coolers during the party.

A SATISFYING SOIREE This chart gives you an idea of how much food to make or purchase. In general, plan on about 12 appetizer servings per person for cocktail parties. Purchase more food than you think you'll need—keep no-prep fixes such as cured meats and cheeses in the fridge to bring out if necessary.

Food	Per Guest	For 12	For 24	For 48
Chicken Wings	2	2 pounds	4 pounds	8 pounds
Cocktail Meatballs	2	1 pound	2 pounds	4 pounds
Crackers	4	8 ounces	1 pound	2 pounds
Dips/Spreads	2 tablespoons	1½ cups	3 cups	6 cups
Fondue/Chili con Queso	¼ cup	3 cups	6 cups	12 cups
Nuts	1 ounce	¾ pound	1½ pounds	3 pounds
Shrimp (large)	4	1 pound	2 pounds	4 pounds
Stuffed Mushrooms	2	1 pound	2 pounds	4 pounds
Veggie Dippers	2 pieces	24 pieces	48 pieces	96 pieces

CRAB DIP, PAGE 44

DISH IT OUT—AGAIN AND AGAIN BE SURE TO HAVE ALMOST TWICE AS MANY GLASSES AND APPETIZER PLATES ON HAND AS THERE ARE GUESTS.

BRUSCHETTA

PREP: 30 MINUTES **BROIL:** 2 MINUTES PER BATCH
MAKES: 36 APPETIZERS

- 3 tablespoons olive oil
- 1 tablespoon snipped fresh chives
- 1 tablespoon snipped fresh basil
- 1 tablespoon lemon juice
- 1 clove garlic, minced
- 2 cups chopped, seeded roma tomatoes
- ½ cup finely chopped red onion
- 1 8-ounce loaf baguette-style French bread
  Snipped fresh basil (optional)

1 Preheat broiler. In a bowl combine 1 tablespoon of the olive oil, the chives, 1 tablespoon basil, lemon juice, and garlic. Stir in tomatoes and onion. Season with *salt* and *pepper*; set aside.

2 Cut the bread into 36 slices; arrange on two large baking sheets. Brush one side of each slice with some of the remaining 2 tablespoons oil. Broil bread, one pan at a time, 3 to 4 inches from heat for 2 to 3 minutes or until toasted, turning once.

3 Using a slotted spoon, spoon tomato mixture onto oiled side of each toast. If desired, top with additional fresh basil. Serve within 30 minutes.

SEAFOOD BRUSCHETTA: Prepare as directed, except decrease tomatoes to 1 cup. Add 6 ounces lump crabmeat and 1 tablespoon snipped fresh dill to the tomato mixture.

WHITE BEAN BRUSCHETTA: Prepare as directed, except substitute snipped fresh thyme for the chives and snipped fresh oregano for the basil; decrease tomatoes to 1 cup. Add one 15-ounce can cannellini beans, rinsed and drained, to the tomato mixture. Drizzle assembled toasts with an additional 2 tablespoons olive oil. Top with additional snipped fresh thyme.

PER APPETIZER PLAIN, SEAFOOD, OR WHITE BEAN VARIATIONS: 31 cal., 1 g total fat (0 g sat. fat, 0 g trans fat), 0 mg chol., 50 mg sodium, 4 g carbo., 0 g fiber, 1 g pro. EXCHANGES: ½ Starch

ANTIPASTI PLATTER

START TO FINISH: 30 MINUTES
MAKES: 12 SERVINGS

- 1 pound assorted sliced deli meats (such as salami, spicy capocollo, prosciutto, and/or mortadella)
- 8 ounces assorted cheeses, cubed (such as Parmesan, Asiago, fresh mozzarella, provolone, and/or blue cheese)
- 1½ cups Marinated Olives (below), purchased marinated olives, and/or marinated artichoke hearts
- 1 12-ounce jar roasted red and/or yellow sweet peppers, drained and cut into ½-inch-wide strips
- 1 cup cherry and/or grape tomatoes, halved or quartered, if desired
  Snipped fresh basil (optional)
- ½ cup olive oil
- ¼ teaspoon coarse kosher salt
- ¼ teaspoon freshly ground black pepper
- 1 8-ounce loaf Italian bread, sliced

1 Arrange meats, cheese, olives, roasted peppers, and tomatoes on a large platter. If desired, sprinkle with fresh basil. Place oil in a shallow dish. Sprinkle with salt and black pepper. Drizzle some of the oil mixture over the meats, cheese, and vegetables. Serve remaining oil mixture beside platter for dipping or drizzling. Serve with bread.

PER SERVING: 363 cal., 27 g total fat (8 g sat. fat, 0 g trans fat), 46 mg chol., 1,100 mg sodium, 14 g carbo., 1 g fiber, 17 g pro. EXCHANGES: 1 Starch, 2 High-Fat Meat, 2 Fat

MARINATED OLIVES

PREP: 10 MINUTES **CHILL:** 2 DAYS **STAND:** 1 HOUR
MAKES: 8 TO 10 SERVINGS

- 2 cups black and/or green olives, pitted, rinsed, and drained
- ½ cup extra virgin olive oil
- 2 3×½-inch strips of lemon peel
- ½ cup lemon juice
- 4 to 6 cloves garlic, sliced
- 2 teaspoons snipped fresh oregano or 1 teaspoon dried oregano, crushed
- 1 bay leaf
- ½ teaspoon crushed red pepper

1 In a 1-quart jar with a screw-top lid combine olives, olive oil, lemon peel, lemon juice, garlic, oregano, bay leaf, and red pepper. Cover and shake to coat olives with marinade. Refrigerate for 2 days, shaking jar occasionally.

2 Before serving, let stand at room temperature for 1 to 2 hours. Remove olives from marinade. Store in the refrigerator for up to 2 weeks.

PER ¼ CUP: 70 cal., 7 g total fat (1 g sat. fat, 0 g trans fat), 0 mg chol., 293 mg sodium, 3 g carbo., 1 g fiber, 0 g pro. EXCHANGES: 1½ Fat

BRUSCHETTA

BEAUTIFUL BITES SHORT ON TIME? THAT'S JUST FINE. MANY PARTY FOODS, SUCH AS THE ANTIPASTI PLATTER, ARE MORE ABOUT QUICK, ARTFUL ARRANGING THAN COMPLICATED, ALL-DAY COOKING.

ANTIPASTI PLATTER

10 TO TRY— DEVILED EGGS

Start with Deviled Eggs, page 43.

1. SALMON: Top with smoked salmon, sour cream, and chives.

2. MEXICAN: Substitute Mexican-style sour cream dip for mayo. Top with avocado and cilantro.

3. GREEK: Add 2 teaspoons snipped oregano to filling. Top with olives, feta, and snipped oregano.

4. TUNA: Substitute lemon juice for vinegar; add ¼ cup flaked tuna and 1 tablespoon pickle relish to filling. **5. GERMAN:** Use brown mustard; add 2 cooked tiny potatoes, chopped, and 1 tablespoon chopped red onion to filling.

6. BLUE CHEESE: Add ¼ cup chopped apple, 1 tablespoon blue cheese, and 1 tablespoon chopped walnuts to filling. **7. BACON:** Add 2 slices cooked bacon, crumbled, and 1 tablespoon snipped basil to filling. Top with tomato and basil.

8. SHRIMP: Substitute lemon juice for vinegar and add ¼ cup chopped cooked shrimp to filling. Top with cucumber and snipped thyme. **9. CONFETTI:** Substitute ranch dressing for mayo. Top with sweet pepper. **10. ASPARAGUS:** Substitute lemon juice for vinegar and add ¼ cup chopped cooked asparagus and 1 tablespoon diced ham to filling.

DEVILED EGGS

PREP: 25 MINUTES **MAKES:** 12 SERVINGS

   6 Hard-Cooked Eggs (page 134)
   ¼ cup mayonnaise
   1 teaspoon yellow mustard
   1 teaspoon vinegar
      Paprika or parsley sprigs (optional)

1 Halve hard-cooked eggs lengthwise and remove yolks. Set whites aside. Place yolks in a small bowl; mash with a fork. Add mayonnaise, mustard, and vinegar; mix well. If desired, season with *salt* and *black pepper*. Stuff egg white halves with yolk mixture. Cover and chill until serving time (up to 24 hours). If desired, garnish with paprika and/or parsley.

PER DEVILED EGG: 72 cal., 6 g total fat (1 g sat. fat, 0 g trans fat), 109 mg chol., 62 mg sodium, 0 g carbo., 0 g fiber, 3 g pro. EXCHANGES: ½ Medium-Fat Meat, 1 Fat

WRAP-AND-ROLL BASIL PINWHEELS

PREP: 20 MINUTES **CHILL:** 2 TO 4 HOURS
MAKES: 18 TO 20 PINWHEELS

   3 7- or 8-inch flour tortillas
   1 5.2-ounce container semisoft cheese with
      garlic and herbs
  12 large fresh basil leaves
   ½ of a 7-ounce jar roasted red sweet
      peppers, cut into ¼-inch-wide strips
      (⅓ cup)
   4 ounces thinly sliced cooked ham, roast
      beef, or turkey
      Fresh basil leaves (optional)

1 Spread each tortilla evenly with one-third of the cheese (if cheese seems crumbly, stir it until smooth). Add a layer of large basil leaves to cover cheese. Arrange roasted red pepper strips over basil leaves. Top with meat slices. Tightly roll up each tortilla into a spiral, tucking in meat as you roll. Wrap each roll in plastic wrap. Chill rolls in the refrigerator for 2 to 4 hours.

2 To serve, remove plastic wrap from rolls. Trim ends of rolls; cut rolls into 1-inch slices. If desired, skewer each slice on a pick or short decorative skewer. Arrange slices on a platter. If desired, garnish platter with additional fresh basil leaves.

PER PINWHEEL: 68 cal., 5 g total fat (3 g sat. fat, 0 g trans fat), 4 mg chol., 172 mg sodium, 5 g carbo., 0 g fiber, 2 g pro. EXCHANGES: 1 Fat

TAPENADE

START TO FINISH: 25 MINUTES
MAKES: 1 CUP

   ½ cup pimiento-stuffed green olives
   ½ cup pitted Kalamata olives
   1 tablespoon olive oil
   2 teaspoons balsamic vinegar
   1 teaspoon Dijon-style mustard
   2 cloves garlic, minced
   ½ cup finely chopped, seeded tomato
   2 tablespoons thinly sliced green onion (1)
   1 teaspoon snipped fresh rosemary (optional)
      Toasted baguette slices

1 In a blender or food processor combine green olives, Kalamata olives, olive oil, vinegar, mustard, and garlic. Cover and blend or process until nearly smooth, scraping down sides of container as necessary. Stir in tomato, green onion, and, if desired, rosemary. Serve with bread slices.

PER 1 TABLESPOON (WITH BREAD): 43 cal., 2 g total fat (0 g sat. fat, 0 g trans fat), 0 mg chol., 139 mg sodium, 6 g carbo., 1 g fiber, 1 g pro. EXCHANGES: ½ Starch

CREAMY DIP FOR FRUIT

PREP: 15 MINUTES **CHILL:** 60 MINUTES
MAKES: 2 CUPS

   1 8-ounce package cream cheese, softened
   1 8-ounce carton dairy sour cream*
   ¼ cup packed brown sugar
   1 teaspoon vanilla
   2 to 3 tablespoons milk
      Assorted fruit, such as cherries, sliced
      apple, pear, banana, and/or strawberries

1 In a small mixing bowl beat the cream cheese with an electric mixer on low speed until smooth. Gradually add the sour cream, beating until combined. Add the brown sugar and vanilla; beat just until combined. Stir in enough milk to make dipping consistency. Cover; chill at least 60 minutes before serving. Serve with assorted fruit.

*NOTE: For a lighter version of the dip, use one 6-ounce carton plain yogurt instead of dairy sour cream.

SPICE DIP: Prepare as directed, except add ½ teaspoon ground cinnamon or pumpkin pie spice.

PER ¼ CUP PLAIN OR SPICE VARIATION: 181 cal., 15 g total fat (9 g sat. fat, 0 g trans fat), 46 mg chol., 117 mg sodium, 9 g carbo., 0 g fiber, 2 g pro. EXCHANGES: ½ Other Carbo., 3 Fat

DILL DIP

PREP: 10 MINUTES **CHILL:** 1 TO 24 HOURS
MAKES: ABOUT 2 CUPS

- 1 8-ounce package cream cheese, softened
- 1 8-ounce carton dairy sour cream
- 2 tablespoons finely chopped green onion (1)
- 2 tablespoons snipped fresh dill or 2 teaspoons dried dillweed
- ½ teaspoon seasoned salt or salt
  Milk (optional)
  Assorted vegetable dippers, crackers, or potato chips

1 In a medium mixing bowl beat cream cheese, sour cream, green onion, dill, and seasoned salt with an electric mixer on low speed until fluffy. Cover and chill for 1 to 24 hours. If dip thickens after chilling, stir in 1 to 2 tablespoons milk. Serve with vegetable dippers, crackers, or chips.

CREAMY BLUE CHEESE DIP: Prepare as directed, except omit dill and seasoned salt or salt. Stir ½ cup crumbled blue cheese (2 ounces) and ⅓ cup finely chopped toasted walnuts into the beaten cream cheese mixture.

SPINACH-DILL DIP: Prepare as directed, except stir half of a 10-ounce package frozen chopped spinach, thawed and well-drained, into the beaten cream cheese mixture.

PER 1 TABLESPOON DIP PLAIN, BLUE CHEESE, OR SPINACH VARIATIONS: 38 cal., 4 g total fat (2 g sat. fat, 0 g trans fat), 11 mg chol., 52 mg sodium, 1 g carbo., 0 g fiber, 1 g pro.
EXCHANGES: 1 Fat

CRAB DIP (photo, page 39)

PREP: 20 MINUTES **CHILL:** 2 TO 24 HOURS
MAKES: ABOUT 1⅓ CUPS

- 1 cup cooked crabmeat or one 6-ounce can crabmeat, drained, flaked, and cartilage removed
- ½ cup mayonnaise
- ½ cup dairy sour cream
- 2 tablespoons finely chopped red onion or green onion
- 1 tablespoon snipped fresh dill or 1 teaspoon dried dillweed
- 1 teaspoon finely shredded lemon peel
- 1 teaspoon lemon juice or lime juice
  Several dashes bottled hot pepper sauce
  Dash cayenne pepper (optional)

  Salt and black pepper
  Finely chopped red or green onion (optional)
  Assorted crackers and/or vegetable dippers

1 In a small bowl stir together crab, mayonnaise, sour cream, the 2 tablespoons onion, dill, lemon peel, lemon juice, hot pepper sauce, and, if desired, cayenne pepper. Season to taste with salt and black pepper.

2 Transfer dip to a serving dish. Cover and chill for 2 to 24 hours. If desired, garnish with finely chopped red or green onion. Serve with crackers and/or vegetable dippers.

PER 2 TABLESPOONS: 117 cal., 11 g total fat (3 g sat. fat, 0 g trans fat), 26 mg chol., 145 mg sodium, 1 g carbo., 0 g fiber, 4 g pro.
EXCHANGES: ½ Very Lean Meat, 2 Fat

CRAB TARTLETS: Prepare dip as directed through Step 1. Spoon dip into 30 miniature phyllo dough shells (two 2.1-ounce packages). For a hot appetizer, place the filled phyllo dough shells on a large baking sheet. Bake in a 350°F oven for 5 to 8 minutes or until heated through. If desired, garnish with finely shredded lemon peel and fresh dill sprigs.

PER TARTLET: 62 cal., 5 g total fat (1 g sat. fat, 0 g trans fat), 9 mg chol., 58 mg sodium, 3 g carbo., 0 g fiber, 2 g pro.
EXCHANGES: 1 Fat

FAST

SMOKED SALMON DIP

PREP: 15 MINUTES **STAND:** 15 MINUTES
MAKES: 1½ TO 1¾ CUPS

- 4 ounces smoked salmon, skin and bones removed, or lox-style salmon
- ⅓ cup finely chopped red onion
- 1 to 1½ tablespoons prepared horseradish
- 1 8-ounce carton dairy sour cream or whipped cream cheese, or one 6-ounce carton plain Greek yogurt
  Salt and black pepper
  Snipped fresh chives
  Assorted vegetable dippers

1 In a medium bowl finely flake salmon (or chop lox-style salmon); stir in the onion, horseradish, and sour cream. Season with salt and pepper. Let stand for at least 15 minutes or chill for up to 24 hours.

2 Stir before serving. Top with chives and serve with vegetable dippers.

PER 2 TABLESPOONS: 50 cal., 4 g total fat (2 g sat. fat, 0 g trans fat), 12 mg chol., 117 mg sodium, 1 g carbo., 0 g fiber, 2 g pro. EXCHANGES: 1 Fat

SMOKED SALMON SPREAD: Prepare as directed on page 44, except substitute one 8-ounce package softened cream cheese or reduced-fat cream cheese (Neufchâtel) for the sour cream. Use as a spread on crackers or baguette slices. Makes 1¾ cups.

PER 2 TABLESPOONS: 67 cal., 6 g total fat (3 g sat. fat, 0 g trans fat), 20 mg chol., 140 mg sodium, 1 g carbo., 0 g fiber, 2 g pro. EXCHANGES: 1½ Fat

FAST

HUMMUS

START TO FINISH: 15 MINUTES
MAKES: ABOUT 1¾ CUPS

- 1 15-ounce can garbanzo beans (chickpeas), rinsed and drained
- 1 clove garlic, minced
- ¼ cup tahini (sesame seed paste)
- ¼ cup lemon juice
- ¼ cup olive oil
- ½ teaspoon salt
- ¼ teaspoon paprika

  Stir-ins such as ¼ cup sliced green onions; ¼ cup crumbled feta cheese; ⅓ cup chopped ripe olives or Kalamata olives; ⅓ cup chopped roasted red sweet peppers; 2 to 3 chopped chipotle peppers; 1 tablespoon snipped fresh dill; and/or ¼ cup purchased basil pesto (optional)
- 1 tablespoon snipped fresh parsley
- 2 to 3 teaspoons olive oil (optional)
- 2 tablespoons pine nuts, toasted (see tip, page 20) (optional)

  Toasted pita wedges and/or assorted vegetable dippers

1 In a blender or food processor combine garbanzo beans, garlic, tahini, lemon juice, ¼ cup oil, salt, and paprika. Cover and blend or process until smooth, scraping sides as necessary.

2 If desired, add one or more stir-ins. Spoon hummus onto a serving platter. Top with parsley. If desired, drizzle with oil and sprinkle with pine nuts. Serve with pita wedges and/or vegetable dippers.

PER 2 TABLESPOONS: 97 cal., 6 g total fat (1 g sat. fat, 0 g trans fat), 0 mg chol., 176 mg sodium, 8 g carbo., 2 g fiber, 2 g pro. EXCHANGES: ½ Starch, 1 Fat

LAYERED GREEK DIP

BEST EVER

LAYERED GREEK DIP

PREP: 20 MINUTES **CHILL:** 2 TO 24 HOURS
MAKES: ABOUT 2½ CUPS

- 1 8-ounce package cream cheese, softened
- 1 tablespoon lemon juice
- 1 teaspoon dried Italian seasoning
- 3 cloves garlic, minced
- 1½ cups Hummus (left) or purchased hummus
- 1 cup chopped cucumber
- 1 cup chopped tomato
- ½ cup chopped pitted Kalamata olives
- ½ cup crumbled feta cheese
- ⅓ cup sliced green onions (3)

  Pita chips and/or multigrain tortilla chips

1 In a medium bowl beat cream cheese, lemon juice, Italian seasoning, and garlic with an electric mixer on medium speed until smooth.

2 Spread cream cheese mixture into a deep 9-inch pie plate or shallow serving dish. Evenly spread hummus on cream cheese layer. Top with cucumber, tomato, olives, feta cheese, and green onions. Cover and chill for 2 to 24 hours. Serve with pita chips and/or multigrain tortilla chips.

PER 2½ TABLESPOONS: 113 cal., 8 g total fat (4 g sat. fat, 0 g trans fat), 20 mg chol., 201 mg sodium, 7 g carbo., 1 g fiber, 3 g pro. EXCHANGES: ½ Starch, ½ Medium-Fat Meat, 1 Fat

GUACAMOLE

PREP: 15 MINUTES **CHILL:** UP TO 8 HOURS
MAKES: ABOUT 1¼ CUPS

- 2 ripe avocados,* halved, seeded, peeled, (see photos 1 and 2, below), and coarsely mashed**
- 2 tablespoons dairy sour cream
- 2 tablespoons snipped fresh cilantro
- 1 tablespoon lime juice
- ¼ teaspoon salt
- Several drops bottled hot pepper sauce (optional)
- Sliced green onions
- Chopped tomatoes
- Tortilla chips

1 In a medium bowl combine avocados, sour cream, cilantro, lime juice, salt, and, if desired, bottled hot pepper sauce.** Cover surface with plastic wrap; chill until ready to use (up to 8 hours).

2 Before serving, sprinkle with onions and tomatoes. Serve with tortilla chips.

***NOTE:** Ripe avocados feel soft under gentle palm pressure. (Don't press them with your finger or they'll bruise.) To speed ripening, place avocados in a closed paper bag at room temperature.

****TIP:** Do not mash avocados. Place avocado meat, sour cream, cilantro, lime juice, salt, and bottled hot pepper sauce, if using, in a sturdy resealable plastic bag. Seal bag. Knead bag with your hands to combine ingredients (see photo 3, below). Place in refrigerator until ready to use (up to 8 hours). To serve, arrange chips on a serving platter. Snip a hole in one corner of the bag. Squeeze avocado mixture onto chips. Sprinkle with green onions and tomatoes.

TOASTED-CUMIN GUACAMOLE: In a small dry skillet heat 2 teaspoons cumin seeds over medium-high heat for 1 to 2 minutes or until lightly toasted, shaking skillet occasionally. Remove seeds from skillet; cool. Coarsely crush the cumin seeds; stir into guacamole mixture.

PER 1 TABLESPOON GUACAMOLE OR TOASTED-CUMIN VARIATION: 25 cal., 2 g total fat (0 g sat. fat, 0 g trans fat), 1 mg chol., 17 mg sodium, 1 g carbo., 1 g fiber, 0 g pro. EXCHANGES: ½ Fat

PREPARING GUACAMOLE, STEP-BY-STEP

1. Cut the avocado lengthwise around the seed. Twist the two halves to separate. Place the avocado half on a clean dish towel and carefully strike the pit with a knife. Use the knife to twist and pull out the pit of the avocado. **2.** Using a spoon, scrape the avocado meat into a large resealable bag. **3.** Seal bag and use your hands to mash the ingredients together.

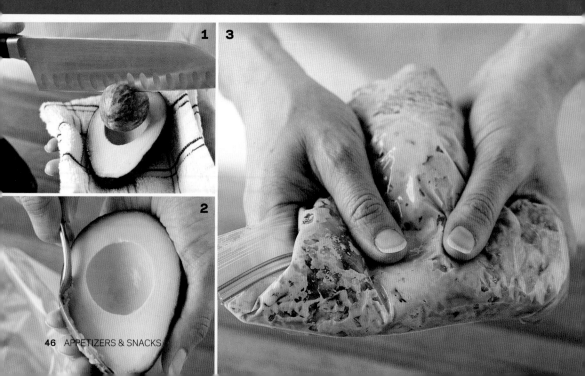

FRESH TOMATO SALSA

START TO FINISH: 30 MINUTES **MAKES:** 3 CUPS

    6 roma tomatoes, coarsely chopped
    1 small red onion, coarsely chopped
    1 large fresh poblano chile pepper, seeded
       and coarsely chopped*
    1 to 2 large fresh jalapeño chile peppers,
       seeded and coarsely chopped*
    2 tablespoons lime juice
    1 tablespoon canola oil or cooking oil
    1 teaspoon cumin seeds, toasted and
       ground,** or ½ teaspoon ground cumin
    1 teaspoon coriander seeds, toasted
       and ground,** or ½ teaspoon ground
       coriander
    ½ teaspoon kosher salt or salt
    ¼ teaspoon black pepper

1 In a food processor combine all ingredients. Cover; process with on/off turns until finely chopped. Cover and chill up to 3 days.

***NOTE:** Because chile peppers contain volatile oils that can burn your skin and eyes, avoid direct contact with them as much as possible. When working with chile peppers, wear plastic or rubber gloves. If your bare hands do touch the peppers, wash your hands and nails well with soap and warm water.

****NOTE:** To toast seeds: In a small dry skillet heat the cumin and coriander seeds over medium heat for 1 to 2 minutes or until lightly toasted, shaking skillet occasionally. Remove seeds from heat; allow to cool before grinding with a spice grinder or a mortar and pestle.

PER ¼ CUP: 28 cal., 1 g total fat (0 g sat. fat, 0 g trans fat), 0 mg chol., 84 mg sodium, 4 g carbo., 1 g fiber, 1 g pro. EXCHANGES: ½ Vegetable

MEXICAN SEVEN-LAYER DIP

PREP: 20 MINUTES **CHILL:** 4 TO 24 HOURS
MAKES: 16 SERVINGS

    1 16-ounce can refried beans
    ½ cup bottled salsa
    ½ of a 14-ounce package refrigerated
       guacamole
    1 8-ounce carton dairy sour cream
    1 cup shredded cheddar cheese (4 ounces)
    ¼ cup sliced green onions (2)
    ¼ cup sliced pitted ripe olives
    1 cup chopped, seeded tomato (1 large)
    8 cups tortilla chips or crackers

1 In a medium bowl combine refried beans and salsa; spread onto a 12-inch platter or a in 2-quart rectangular baking dish. Carefully layer guacamole and sour cream over bean mixture. Top with cheese, green onions, and olives. Cover and chill for 4 to 24 hours.

2 Before serving, sprinkle with chopped tomato. Serve with tortilla chips.

PER ¼ CUP DIP AND ½ CUP CHIPS: 179 cal., 11 g total fat (4 g sat. fat, 0 g trans fat), 15 mg chol., 340 mg sodium, 16 g carbo., 3 g fiber, 5 g pro. EXCHANGES: 1 Starch, 2 Fat

BEST EVER

SMOKY CHEESE BALL

PREP: 30 MINUTES **CHILL:** 4 TO 24 HOURS
STAND: 45 MINUTES **MAKES:** 3½ CUPS

    2 8-ounce packages cream cheese
    2 cups finely shredded smoked cheddar,
       Swiss, or Gouda cheese (8 ounces)
    ½ cup butter or margarine
    2 tablespoons milk
    2 teaspoons steak sauce
    1 cup finely chopped toasted nuts (see tip,
       page 20)
       Assorted crackers

1 In a medium bowl let cream cheese, shredded cheese, and butter stand at room temperature for 30 minutes. Add milk and steak sauce; beat until fluffy. Cover and chill for 4 to 24 hours.

2 Shape mixture into a ball; roll in nuts. Let stand for 15 minutes. Serve with crackers.

MAKE-AHEAD DIRECTIONS: Prepare as directed, except do not roll in nuts. Wrap cheese ball in moisture- and vapor-proof plastic wrap. Freeze for up to 1 month. To serve, thaw cheese ball in refrigerator overnight. Roll in nuts. Let stand for 30 minutes at room temperature before serving.

PER 1 TABLESPOON: 73 cal., 7 g total fat (4 g sat. fat, 0 g trans fat), 18 mg chol., 66 mg sodium, 1 g carbo., 0 g fiber, 2 g pro. EXCHANGES: 1½ Fat

LOCAL FLAVORS

ANY SEMIFIRM CHEESE YOU LOVE CAN BE USED IN A CHEESE BALL. TRY SWITCHING A REGIONALLY PRODUCED FAVORITE FOR THE CHEDDAR.

PIMIENTO CHEESE

PREP: 10 MINUTES **CHILL:** 4 TO 24 HOURS
MAKES: 2⅓ CUPS

- 3 cups shredded cheddar cheese
  (12 ounces)
- ⅔ cup mayonnaise
- 1 4-ounce jar sliced pimiento, drained and
  chopped
- 1 teaspoon Worcestershire sauce
- 1 teaspoon yellow mustard
- ¼ teaspoon garlic powder
  Assorted crackers

1 In a large bowl stir together cheese, mayonnaise, pimiento, Worcestershire, mustard, and garlic powder, mashing mixture with the back of a spoon as you mix (mixture will be chunky). Transfer to a serving bowl. Cover with plastic wrap and chill for 4 to 24 hours. Serve as a spread with crackers.

JALAPEÑO CHEESE: Prepare as directed, except omit the pimiento and mustard. Substitute 12 ounces Colby and Monterey Jack cheese or 6 ounces Colby and Monterey Jack cheese and 6 ounces Monterey Jack cheese with jalapeño peppers for the cheddar cheese. Stir one 4-ounce can diced jalapeño peppers, drained, into the cheese mixture.

PER 2 TABLESPOONS PLAIN OR JALAPEÑO VARIATION:
137 cal., 13 g total fat (5 g sat. fat, 0 g trans fat), 23 mg chol.,
169 mg sodium, 1 g carbo., 0 g fiber, 5 g pro.
EXCHANGES: ½ High-Fat Meat, 1 Fat

BEEF AND PICKLE CHEESE: Prepare as directed, except omit the pimiento, Worcestershire, and mustard. Substitute Monterey Jack cheese for the cheddar cheese. Add one 3-ounce package cream cheese, softened; ½ cup chopped dill pickle; and ½ cup chopped dried beef or boiled ham (about 2½ ounces) to cheese mixture. If desired, serve with melba toasts or rye crackers. Makes 3 cups.

PER 2 TABLESPOONS: 114 cal., 10 g total fat (4 g sat. fat,
0 g trans fat), 21 mg chol., 231 mg sodium, 0 g carbo., 0 g fiber,
5 g pro.
EXCHANGES: ½ High-Fat Meat, 1½ Fat

CHEESY ARTICHOKE AND SPINACH DIP

PREP: 25 MINUTES **BAKE:** 30 MINUTES
OVEN: 350°F **MAKES:** 5½ CUPS

- ½ cup chopped onion
- ½ cup chopped red sweet pepper
- 2 cloves garlic, minced
- 1 tablespoon olive oil
- 2 8-ounce packages reduced-fat cream
  cheese (Neufchâtel), softened
- 1½ cups finely shredded Parmesan or
  Romano cheese
- ¼ cup milk
- ¼ cup mayonnaise
- ¼ cup light dairy sour cream
- 4 cups chopped fresh spinach leaves
- 1 14-ounce can artichoke hearts, drained
  and chopped
  Bagel chips, corn tortilla chips, or toasted
  baguette-style French bread slices

1 Preheat oven to 350°F. In a large skillet cook onion, sweet pepper, and garlic in hot oil over medium heat until tender, stirring often; set aside to let cool.

2 In a large bowl stir together cream cheese, Parmesan cheese, milk, mayonnaise, and sour cream. Add onion mixture, spinach, and chopped artichoke hearts; stir gently to combine. Spread mixture into a deep 9-inch pie plate or a 1½-quart baking dish.

3 Bake about 30 minutes or until bubbly. Serve with bagel chips, corn tortilla chips, or toasted bread slices.

MAKE-AHEAD DIRECTIONS: Prepare dip as directed through Step 2. Cover and chill up to 24 hours. Uncover and bake about 40 minutes or until heated through.

PER ¼ CUP: 113 cal., 9 g total fat (4 g sat. fat, 0 g trans fat),
21 mg chol., 243 mg sodium, 3 g carbo., 1 g fiber, 5 g pro.
EXCHANGES: ½ High-Fat Meat, 1 Fat

CHEESY SAUSAGE AND SPINACH DIP:
Prepare as directed, except omit olive oil and cook 8 ounces bulk sweet or hot Italian sausage with the onion, sweet pepper, and garlic in the large skillet until brown, stirring often. Drain off fat. Omit artichokes and add ⅓ cup mild banana pepper rings, drained and chopped, to the cream cheese mixture. Bake as directed.

PER ¼ CUP: 118 cal., 9 g total fat (4 g sat. fat, 0 g trans fat),
24 mg chol., 242 mg sodium, 2 g carbo., 0 g fiber, 6 g pro.
EXCHANGES: 1 High-Fat Meat, ½ Fat

SAVE SOME FOR YOU
EXTRA TAPENADE AND DIPS
TASTE GREAT IN OMELETS THE
NEXT MORNING AS YOU GO OVER
THE POST-PARTY PLAY-BY-PLAY.

PRALINE-TOPPED BRIE

PREP: 10 MINUTES **BAKE:** 15 MINUTES
OVEN: 350°F **MAKES:** 10 TO 12 SERVINGS

- 1 13- to 15-ounce round Brie or
Camembert cheese
- ½ cup fig or apricot preserves
- 2 tablespoons packed brown sugar
- ⅓ cup coarsely chopped pecans or almonds,
toasted (see tip, page 20)
   Baguette-style French bread slices,
toasted, and/or assorted plain crackers

1 Preheat oven to 350°F. Place the round of cheese in a shallow ovenproof serving dish or pie plate. In a small bowl stir together fig preserves and brown sugar. Spread on top of cheese. Sprinkle with toasted pecans.

2 Bake for 15 to 20 minutes or until cheese is slightly softened and topping is bubbly. Serve with baguette slices and/or crackers.

PER SERVING (WITH BREAD): 296 cal., 13 g total fat (7 g sat. fat, 0 g trans fat), 37 mg chol., 446 mg sodium, 32 g carbo., 1 g fiber, 12 g pro.
EXCHANGES: 2 Starch, 1 High-Fat Meat, ½ Fat

BRIE EN CROÛTE

PREP: 30 MINUTES **BAKE:** 20 MINUTES
STAND: 10 MINUTES **OVEN:** 400°F
MAKES: 2 ROUNDS (12 SERVINGS)

- ½ of a 17.3-ounce package frozen puff
pastry sheets, thawed (1 sheet)
- 2 tablespoons jalapeño pepper jelly, apple
jelly, or apricot jelly
- 2 4½-ounce rounds Brie or Camembert
cheese

- 2 tablespoons chopped nuts, toasted (see
tip, page 20)
- 1 egg, lightly beaten
- 1 tablespoon water
   Apple and/or pear slices (optional)

1 Preheat oven to 400°F. Grease a baking sheet; set aside. Unfold pastry on a lightly floured surface; roll into a 16×10-inch rectangle. Cut into two 8-inch circles (see photo 1, below); reserve trimmings.

2 Spread jelly over top of each cheese round. Sprinkle with nuts; lightly press nuts into jelly.

3 Combine egg and water; set aside. Place pastry circles over cheese rounds. Invert rounds and pastry. Brush edges of circles with a little of the egg mixture. Bring edges of pastry up and over cheese rounds, pleating and pinching edges to cover and seal. Trim excess pastry (see photo 2, below). Place rounds, smooth sides up, on prepared baking sheet. Brush egg mixture over tops and sides. Cut small slits for steam to escape. Using hors d'oeuvre cutters, cut shapes from reserved pastry. Brush shapes with egg mixture; place on top of rounds.

4 Bake for 20 to 25 minutes or until pastry is deep golden brown. Let stand for 10 to 20 minutes before serving. If desired, serve with apple and/or pear slices.

PER SERVING: 207 cal., 15 g total fat (6 g sat. fat, 0 g trans fat), 39 mg chol., 192 mg sodium, 12 g carbo., 0 g fiber, 7 g pro.
EXCHANGES: 1 Starch, ½ High-Fat Meat, 2 Fat

PREPARING BRIE EN CROÛTE, STEP-BY-STEP

1. Using an 8-inch round cake pan as a guide, cut two circles from the pastry. **2.** Carefully bring the puff pastry up and over each cheese round, pleating the edges as necessary to fit over the top of the cheese round. Use kitchen shears to trim excess pastry from the pleats to create an even thickness.

CHEESE 101

SOFT AND RINDLESS

Terrific in salads and quick-cooking dishes, these cheeses have a high moisture content, soft texture, and flavors that range from mild to tangy. Store, tightly covered, in their original containers and original liquid (if applicable) for up to 5 days.

SOFT-RIPENED/BLUE

Both styles are welcome additions to cheese platters to be enjoyed either as an appetizer or a cheese course after the main dish. Soft-ripened cheeses have a smooth interior and thin, bloomy rind. Blue cheeses contain blue veins created by the addition of mold during the cheesemaking process. Store soft-ripened cheeses wrapped in waxed paper, which allows them to breathe. Wrap blue cheeses in foil or waxed paper, then in plastic wrap.

SEMISOFT/SEMIFIRM

Semisoft cheeses have a high moisture content; their pliable texture makes them easy to slice and tuck into cold sandwiches. Semifirm cheeses have less moisture. They're often used in cooking because they melt well. Choose longer-aged semifirm cheeses for bolder and more complex flavors. To store semisoft and semifirm cheeses, wrap in waxed paper and place in an airtight container.

HARD

Great for grating, hard cheeses have been aged to remove moisture and allow the salt in the cheese to crystallize. This is what gives these cheeses their sharp flavor and slightly granular texture. Because they do not need to breathe, store hard cheeses wrapped tightly in plastic wrap in an airtight container.

FETA

CHÈVRE

FRESH MOZZARELLA

GORGONZOLA

MAYTAG BLUE

BRIE

SWISS

MUENSTER

CHEDDAR

PARMIGIANO-REGGIANO

ASIAGO

MANCHEGO

BEST EVER

SWISS FONDUE

START TO FINISH: 65 MINUTES **OVEN:** 350°F
MAKES: 4 CUPS

- 20 ounces Gruyère, Emmentaler, or Swiss cheese, shredded (5 cups)
- 1 clove garlic, halved
- 3 tablespoons all-purpose flour
- 3 to 4 ounces French bread, herb bread, or rye bread, cut into 1-inch cubes, and/or 4 cups vegetables (such as broccoli florets, cauliflower florets, cherry tomatoes, and/or tiny new potatoes)
- 1½ cups dry white wine
- ¼ cup milk
- 1 tablespoon cognac or brandy (optional)
- 1 teaspoon Dijon-style mustard
- ⅛ teaspoon ground nutmeg

1 Let shredded cheeses stand at room temperature for 30 minutes. Meanwhile, rub inside of a fondue pot with garlic; discard garlic. Set pan aside. Toss cheeses with flour; set aside.

2 Preheat oven to 350°F. Place bread cubes on a baking sheet. Bake for 5 to 7 minutes or until crisp and toasted; set aside. To precook vegetables, in a large saucepan bring a small amount of water to boiling; add broccoli or cauliflower florets. Simmer, covered, about 3 minutes or until crisp-tender. Drain and rinse with cold water; set aside. To cook potatoes, simmer, covered, 10 to 12 minutes or until tender.

3 In a large saucepan heat wine over medium heat until small bubbles rise to the surface. Just before wine boils, reduce heat to medium-low and stir in the cheese mixture, a little at a time, whisking constantly and making sure cheese is melted before adding more. Gradually stir in milk. Cook and stir until bubbles begin to form.

4 Stir in cognac (if desired), mustard, and nutmeg. Transfer cheese mixture to a fondue pot. Keep mixture bubbling gently over a fondue burner. (Mixture thickens if it cools; if mixture becomes too thick, reheat and stir in a little more milk.) Serve with toasted bread cubes and/or vegetables.

PER ¼ CUP (WITH BREAD): 188 cal., 12 g total fat (7 g sat. fat, 0 g trans fat), 39 mg chol., 164 mg sodium, 5 g carbo., 0 g fiber, 11 g pro.
EXCHANGES: 1½ High-Fat Meat

FAST

CHILI CON QUESO

PREP: 10 MINUTES **COOK:** 10 MINUTES
MAKES: 2⅔ CUPS

- ½ cup finely chopped onion (1 medium)
- 1 tablespoon butter
- 1⅓ cups chopped, seeded tomatoes (about 2 medium)
- 1 4-ounce can diced green chiles
- ½ teaspoon ground cumin
- 2 ounces Monterey Jack cheese with jalapeño peppers, shredded (½ cup)
- 1 teaspoon cornstarch
- 1 8-ounce package cream cheese, cubed
  Tortilla chips or corn chips

1 In a medium saucepan cook onion in butter until tender. Stir in tomatoes, chile peppers, and cumin. Heat to boiling; reduce heat. Simmer, uncovered, for 10 minutes, stirring occasionally.

2 Toss shredded cheese with cornstarch. Gradually add cheese mixture to saucepan, stirring until cheese is melted. Gradually add the cream cheese, stirring until cheese is melted and smooth. Heat through. Serve with chips.

SLOW COOKER DIRECTIONS: Prepare as directed. Transfer mixture to a 1½- or 2-quart slow cooker. Keep warm on low-heat setting, if available, up to 2 hours, stirring occasionally.

PER 2 TABLESPOONS: 58 cal., 5 g total fat (3 g sat. fat, 0 g trans fat), 16 mg chol., 79 mg sodium, 5 g carbo., 0 g fiber, 2 g pro.
EXCHANGES: 1 Fat

PARTY CHEESE

HERE'S HOW TO DESIGN A FASCINATING CHEESE TRAY FOR APPETIZER PARTIES.

■ Serve three to five different cheeses and purchase 3 to 4 ounces total per guest.

■ Vary the textures and flavors, serving at least one soft cheese, one soft-ripened or blue cheese, and a firm cheese.

■ Vary the cheeses by milk source, choosing at least one each of goat's, cow's, and sheep's milk.

■ Because most cheeses taste best at room temperature, arrange the tray and set it out for 30 minutes before serving.

■ Serve with crackers and/or breads and easy accompaniments such as olives and nuts or dried or fresh fruits.

SPINACH PHYLLO TRIANGLES

PREP: 50 MINUTES BAKE: 15 MINUTES
OVEN: 375°F MAKES: 36 TRIANGLES

- 1 10-ounce package frozen chopped spinach
- ½ cup finely chopped onion
- 1 clove garlic, minced
- 1½ cups finely crumbled feta cheese (6 ounces)
- ½ teaspoon dried oregano, crushed
- 24 sheets frozen phyllo dough (9×14-inch rectangles), thawed
- ½ cup butter, melted

1 Preheat oven to 375°F. For filling, cook the spinach, onion, and garlic according to spinach package directions. Drain well in a colander. Press mixture with the back of a spoon to remove excess moisture. Combine spinach mixture with feta cheese and oregano.

2 Place one sheet of phyllo dough on a cutting board or other flat surface. Lightly brush with some of the melted butter. Place another sheet of phyllo on top; brush with butter. (Keep remaining phyllo covered with plastic wrap until needed.)

3 Cut the two layered sheets lengthwise into three equal strips, each 14 inches long. Spoon 1 well-rounded teaspoon of filling about 1 inch from an end of each dough strip. To fold into a triangle, bring a corner over filling so the short edge lines up with the side edge. Continue folding the triangular shape along the strip until the end is reached. Repeat with remaining phyllo, butter, and filling.

4 Place triangles on a baking sheet; brush with butter. Bake about 15 minutes or until golden. Serve warm.

MAKE-AHEAD DIRECTIONS: Prepare as directed through Step 3. Place the unbaked triangles in a covered freezer container; freeze for up to 2 months. Brush with additional melted butter and bake as directed. Do not thaw the triangles before baking.

PER 2 TRIANGLES: 162 cal., 9 g total fat (5 g sat. fat, 0 g trans fat), 25 mg chol., 321 mg sodium, 15 g carbo., 1 g fiber, 4 g pro. EXCHANGES: 1 Starch, 1½ Fat

BALSAMIC SHALLOT AND GOAT CHEESE TART

PREP: 30 MINUTES BAKE: 18 MINUTES
STAND: 5 MINUTES OVEN: 400°F
MAKES: 9 SQUARES

- 3 tablespoons butter
- 8 small shallots, quartered lengthwise
- 3 tablespoons honey
- 3 tablespoons balsamic vinegar
- ½ teaspoon salt
- ½ teaspoon black pepper
- ½ of a 17.3-ounce package frozen puff pastry sheets, thawed (1 sheet)
- 1 egg yolk
- 2 teaspoons water
- 4 ounces goat cheese (chèvre), crumbled into small chunks
- 2 teaspoons snipped fresh Italian parsley

1 Preheat oven to 400°F. In a medium ovenproof skillet melt butter over medium heat. Stir in shallots and honey. Cook about 10 minutes or until shallots start to brown, stirring occasionally. Stir in balsamic vinegar, salt, and pepper.

2 Transfer skillet to oven. Bake for 15 to 20 minutes or until shallots are tender and liquid is syrupy. Remove from oven; set aside.

3 Meanwhile, on a large baking sheet unfold puff pastry. Trim a ½-inch-wide strip from each side of the pastry. In a small bowl combine egg yolk and water. Lightly brush edges of the pastry sheet with egg yolk mixture. Place the pastry strips on the edges of the pastry sheet to form a ridge, trimming any excess pastry (see photos 1 and 2, page 53). Lightly brush ridge with egg yolk mixture. Using a fork, generously prick bottom of pastry.

4 Bake for 15 to 20 minutes or until pastry is puffed and golden brown. Spread shallot mixture over bottom of pastry (see photo 3, page 53). (Pastry will sink when topped with the shallot mixture.) Top with cheese. Bake for 3 to 5 minutes more or until cheese is softened.

5 Transfer to a wire rack. Sprinkle with parsley. Let stand for 5 minutes. Cut into 9 squares.

PER SQUARE: 277 cal., 19 g total fat (8 g sat. fat, 0 g trans fat), 43 mg chol., 294 mg sodium, 23 g carbo., 0 g fiber, 6 g pro. EXCHANGES: 1½ Starch, 3½ Fat

BALSAMIC SHALLOT AND GOAT CHEESE TART

PREPARING THE TART, STEP-BY-STEP

1. Brush the edges of the pastry with the egg yolk mixture. Place the pastry strips over the pastry edge, creating a ridge. **2.** Using kitchen shears, trim the excess pastry at the corners. **3.** Spoon the shallot mixture into the prebaked pastry (the base will have puffed during cooking and will sink as you fill it). Spread mixture evenly to reach edges.

NACHOS

PREP: 15 MINUTES **BAKE:** 20 MINUTES
OVEN: 350°F **MAKES:** 8 SERVINGS

- 5 cups bite-size tortilla chips (6 ounces)
- 1 pound ground beef
- 1 15-ounce can black beans or pinto beans, rinsed and drained
- 1 cup bottled chunky salsa
- 1½ cups shredded cheddar, Colby and Monterey Jack, or Mexican cheese blend (6 ounces)

  Optional toppings (such as thinly sliced green onion, snipped fresh cilantro, seeded and chopped fresh jalapeño pepper (see tip, page 24), dairy sour cream, and/or bottled chunky salsa)

1 Preheat oven to 350°F. Spread half of the tortilla chips on an 11- or 12-inch ovenproof platter or pizza pan; set aside.

2 In a large skillet cook ground beef over medium heat until brown. Drain off fat.

3 Add the beans and the 1 cup salsa to the beef. Spoon half of the mixture over chips. Sprinkle with half the cheese. Bake about 10 minutes or until cheese melts. Remove from oven. Top with remaining chips, beef mixture, and cheese. Bake about 10 minutes more or until cheese melts.

4 If desired, top with green onion, cilantro, jalapeño pepper, sour cream, and/or additional salsa.

PER SERVING: 368 cal., 21 g total fat (8 g sat. fat, 1 g trans fat), 61 mg chol., 638 mg sodium, 26 g carbo., 5 g fiber, 23 g pro. EXCHANGES: 2 Starch, 2½ Lean Meat, 2 Fat

MEATLESS NACHOS: Prepare as directed, except omit beef and skip Step 2. Add another 15-ounce can black beans or pinto beans, rinsed and drained, to the bean mixture.

PER SERVING: 291 cal., 12 g total fat (5 g sat. fat, 0 g trans fat), 22 mg chol., 771 mg sodium, 35 g carbo., 8 g fiber, 16 g pro. EXCHANGES: 2 Starch, 1½ Lean Meat, 1 Fat

CHICKEN NACHOS: Prepare as directed, except substitute 1 pound skinless, boneless chicken breasts, cut into bite-size pieces, for the ground beef. Cook until chicken pieces are no longer pink.

PER SERVING: 309 cal., 13 g total fat (5 g sat. fat, 0 g trans fat), 55 mg chol., 637 mg sodium, 26 g carbo., 5 g fiber, 25 g pro. EXCHANGES: 2 Starch, 2½ Lean Meat, ½ Fat

CHEESE AND CHILE QUESADILLAS

PREP: 15 MINUTES **COOK:** 4 MINUTES PER BATCH
OVEN: 300°F **MAKES:** 9 SERVINGS

- 6 7- or 8-inch flour tortillas
  Vegetable oil or nonstick cooking spray
- 1½ cups shredded cheddar, Colby and Monterey Jack, or Monterey Jack cheese (6 ounces)
- 3 tablespoons canned diced green chiles, drained
- 1 tablespoon snipped fresh cilantro
  Salsa (optional)
  Dairy sour cream (optional)

1 Lightly brush one side of each tortilla with oil or lightly coat with cooking spray. Place 3 of the tortillas, oiled or sprayed sides down, on a cutting board or waxed paper. Sprinkle ½ cup of the cheese over each tortilla. Top with chiles and cilantro. Top with remaining tortillas, oiled sides up, pressing gently.

2 Heat a 10-inch nonstick skillet or grill pan over medium heat for 1 minute. Cook quesadillas, one at a time, over medium heat for 4 to 6 minutes or until light brown, turning once. Remove quesadillas from skillet; place on a baking sheet. Keep warm in a 300°F oven. Repeat with remaining quesadillas. To serve, cut each quesadilla into six wedges. If desired, serve with salsa and sour cream.

PER 2 WEDGES: 188 cal., 10 g total fat (4 g sat. fat, 0 g trans fat), 20 mg chol., 297 mg sodium, 17 g carbo., 0 g fiber, 7 g pro. EXCHANGES: 1 Starch, ½ High-Fat Meat, 1 Fat

FAJITA-STYLE QUESADILLAS: Prepare as directed, except in a large skillet heat 1 tablespoon vegetable oil over medium heat. Add 8 ounces beef flank steak or boneless beef sirloin steak, sliced across the grain into thin bite-size strips. Cook and stir for 2 minutes. Add 1 medium red and/or green sweet pepper, cut into bite-size strips, and 1 small onion, cut into thin wedges. Cook and stir for 4 to 5 minutes more or until vegetables are crisp-tender. Spoon on top of cheese in Step 1.

PER 2 WEDGES: 246 cal., 13 g total fat (5 g sat. fat, 0 g trans fat), 30 mg chol., 313 mg sodium, 19 g carbo., 1 g fiber, 13 g pro. EXCHANGES: 1 Starch, 1½ Medium-Fat Meat, 1 Fat

CHICKEN QUESADILLAS: Prepare as directed, except top cheese with 1 cup shredded cooked chicken.

PER 2 WEDGES: 217 cal., 11 g total fat (5 g sat. fat, 0 g trans fat), 34 mg chol., 311 mg sodium, 17 g carbo., 0 g fiber, 12 g pro. EXCHANGES: 1 Starch, 1 Medium-Fat Meat, 1 Fat

GINGERY APRICOT-GLAZED PORK RIBS

PREP: 35 MINUTES **MARINATE:** 6 TO 24 HOURS
BAKE: 75 MINUTES **OVEN:** 350°F
MAKES: 14 TO 16 SERVINGS

- 4 pounds pork loin back ribs, halved across the bones*
- 1 cup finely chopped onion
- ⅔ cup dry sherry
- ½ cup rice vinegar
- ½ cup soy sauce
- ¼ cup finely chopped fresh ginger
- 2 tablespoons finely chopped garlic (about 12 cloves)
- 1 teaspoon black pepper
- ⅔ cup apricot preserves
- 3 tablespoons spicy brown mustard
- 1 tablespoon toasted sesame oil
- ¼ teaspoon cayenne pepper
- 1 tablespoon toasted sesame seeds

1 Trim fat from ribs. Cut ribs into single-rib portions (see photo 1, below). Place rib pieces in a large resealable plastic bag set in a shallow dish.

For marinade, in a medium bowl combine onion, sherry, vinegar, soy sauce, ginger, garlic, and black pepper. Pour over ribs; seal bag and turn to coat ribs (see photo 2, below). Marinate in the refrigerator for 6 to 24 hours, turning bag occasionally.

2 Preheat oven to 350°F. Drain rib pieces, reserving ¼ cup of the marinade. Arrange rib pieces, meaty sides up, in a shallow roasting pan. Roast, uncovered, about 1 hour or until tender.

3 Meanwhile, in a small saucepan combine apricot preserves, mustard, oil, and cayenne pepper. Add the reserved marinade. Bring to boiling; reduce heat. Simmer, uncovered, for 3 minutes.

4 Brush ribs generously with sauce. Bake, uncovered, for 15 minutes, brushing once or twice with sauce during baking. Sprinkle with sesame seeds before serving. If desired, heat remaining sauce; serve with ribs.

*NOTE: Ask your butcher to cut ribs in half across the bones.

PER 2 RIBS: 292 cal., 20 g total fat (7 g sat. fat, 0 g trans fat), 65 mg chol., 262 mg sodium, 12 g carbo., 0 g fiber, 13 g pro. EXCHANGES: 1 Other Carbo., 2 Medium-Fat Meat, 2 Fat

PREPARING THE RIBS, STEP-BY-STEP

1. Place the ribs, bone sides up, onto a cutting board. Using a sharp knife, slice between each bone. **2.** Place the ribs in a sturdy resealable bag set in a shallow dish. Pour marinade over the ribs. Seal bag and turn to thoroughly coat each rib. **3.** If you like, heat the remaining sauce and serve it alongside the ribs for dipping.

BUFFALO WINGS

PREP: 20 MINUTES **MARINATE:** 30 MINUTES
BROIL: 20 MINUTES **MAKES:** 12 SERVINGS

- 12 chicken wings (about 2 pounds)
- 2 tablespoons butter or margarine, melted
- 3 tablespoons bottled hot pepper sauce
- 2 teaspoons paprika
- ¼ teaspoon salt
- ¼ teaspoon cayenne pepper
- 1 recipe Blue Cheese Dip
  Celery sticks (optional)

1 Cut off and discard tips of chicken wings. Cut wings at joints to form 24 pieces. Place chicken wing pieces in a resealable plastic bag set in a shallow dish.

2 For marinade, in a small bowl stir together melted butter, hot pepper sauce, paprika, salt, and cayenne pepper. Pour over chicken wings; seal bag. Marinate at room temperature for 30 minutes. Drain; discard marinade.

3 Preheat broiler. Place the chicken wing pieces on the unheated rack of a broiler pan. Broil 4 to 5 inches from the heat about 10 minutes or until light brown. Turn chicken wings. Broil for 10 to 15 minutes more or until chicken is tender and no longer pink. Serve with Blue Cheese Dip and, if desired, celery sticks.

BLUE CHEESE DIP: In a blender or food processor combine ½ cup dairy sour cream, ½ cup mayonnaise, ½ cup crumbled blue cheese, 1 tablespoon white wine vinegar or white vinegar, and 1 clove garlic, minced. Cover and blend or process until smooth. Cover and chill for up to 1 week. If desired, top with additional crumbled blue cheese before serving.

PER 2 PIECES WITH BLUE CHEESE DIP: 285 cal.,
24 g total fat (7 g sat. fat, 0 g trans fat), 75 mg chol.,
265 mg sodium, 1 g carbo., 0 g fiber, 15 g pro.
EXCHANGES: 2 Lean Meat, 3½ Fat

CRANBERRY-BARBECUE MEATBALLS

PREP: 15 MINUTES **COOK:** 4 HOURS ON LOW;
2 HOURS ON HIGH **MAKES:** 64 MEATBALLS

- 2 16-ounce packages frozen cooked plain meatballs, thawed (32 meatballs each)
- 1 16-ounce can jellied cranberry sauce
- 1 cup barbecue sauce

1 Place meatballs in a 3½- or 4-quart slow cooker. In a medium bowl combine cranberry sauce and barbecue sauce. Pour over meatballs in cooker; stir to coat.

2 Cover and cook on low-heat setting for 4 to 5 hours or on high-heat setting for 2 to 2½ hours. Serve meatballs with toothpicks. If desired, keep warm on low-heat setting for up to 2 hours.

CRANBERRY-CHIPOTLE MEATBALLS: Prepare as directed, except add 1 to 2 tablespoons finely chopped chipotle chile peppers in adobo sauce to the cranberry-barbecue sauce mixture.

PER MEATBALL PLAIN OR CHIPOTLE VARIATION: 60 cal.,
4 g total fat (2 g sat. fat, 0 g trans fat), 5 mg chol., 156 mg sodium,
5 g carbo., 0 g fiber, 2 g pro.
EXCHANGES: 1 Fat

APRICOT SWEET-AND-SOUR MEATBALLS:
Prepare as directed, except substitute one 12-ounce bottle chili sauce and one 18-ounce jar apricot preserves for the cranberry sauce and barbecue sauce. Add 1 tablespoon cider vinegar and ¼ teaspoon ground ginger.

PER MEATBALL: 71 cal., 4 g total fat (2 g sat. fat, 0 g trans fat),
5 mg chol., 185 mg sodium, 5 g carbo., 1 g fiber, 2 g pro.
EXCHANGES: ½ Other Carbo., 1 Fat

ZESTY SHRIMP COCKTAIL

PREP: 25 MINUTES **CHILL:** 2 HOURS
MAKES: 8 TO 10 SERVINGS

- 1½ pounds fresh or frozen large shrimp in shells
- ¼ cup ketchup
- 2 tablespoons orange juice
- 1 tablespoon vegetable oil
- 2 teaspoons prepared horseradish
- ⅛ teaspoon salt
- ⅛ teaspoon cayenne pepper

1 Thaw shrimp, if frozen. Peel and devein shrimp. Cook shrimp in lightly salted boiling water for 1 to 3 minutes or until shrimp turn opaque, stirring occasionally. Rinse in a colander under cold running water; drain again. Chill for 2 hours or overnight.

2 For sauce, in a small bowl whisk together ketchup, orange juice, vegetable oil, horseradish, salt, and cayenne pepper. Cover and chill until serving time. Serve shrimp with sauce.

PER SERVING: 115 cal., 3 g total fat (1 g sat. fat, 0 g trans fat),
129 mg chol., 250 mg sodium, 3 g carbo., 0 g fiber, 17 g pro.
EXCHANGES: 2½ Lean Meat

LEMON-GINGER-MARINATED SHRIMP BOWL

PREP: 25 MINUTES **COOK:** 1 MINUTE
CHILL: OVERNIGHT **MAKES:** ABOUT 20 SERVINGS

  5 pounds fresh large shrimp in shells, peeled and deveined
  ½ cup olive oil
  ½ cup white or red wine vinegar
  1½ teaspoons finely shredded lemon peel
  ¼ cup lemon juice
  2 tablespoons tomato paste
  1 tablespoon honey
  3 cloves garlic, minced
  2 teaspoons grated fresh ginger
  ½ teaspoon salt
  ¼ teaspoon cayenne pepper
    Lemon wedges (optional)

1 In a large pot bring 5 quarts water and 1 teaspoon *salt* to boiling. Add the shrimp. Bring to boiling; reduce heat. Simmer, uncovered, for 1 to 3 minutes or until shrimp turn opaque, stirring occasionally. Drain shrimp. Rinse in a colander under cold running water; drain again.

2 To arrange shrimp, use a glass bowl that is 7 to 8 inches in diameter and about 4 inches deep. Arrange the shrimp, tails toward the center, in a circle to make one flat layer. Only the round backs of shrimp should be visible from the outside of the bowl (see photo 1, below). Repeat layers until bowl is filled, pressing down every couple of layers with the bottom of a plate that will fit into the bowl. When bowl is full, press down with plate once again.

3 For marinade, in a screw-top jar combine the olive oil, wine vinegar, lemon peel, lemon juice, tomato paste, honey, garlic, ginger, salt, and cayenne pepper. Cover and shake well. Pour marinade over shrimp in bowl. Cover and chill overnight, occasionally placing a flat plate larger than the bowl tightly over the bowl and inverting it to redistribute marinade.

4 Before serving, hold the plate off-center and invert bowl slightly to drain off marinade. Repeat inverting and draining until all marinade is drained. Discard marinade.

5 Place serving platter with ½-inch sides over bowl, because shrimp will continue to water out a bit; carefully invert bowl to unmold (see photo 2, below). If desired, arrange lemon wedges around shrimp on serving platter.

SPICY MARINATED SHRIMP BOWL: Prepare as directed, except omit honey and ginger. Add 1 teaspoon black pepper and ½ teaspoon white pepper to marinade mixture. If desired, garnish with lime wedges.

SMALLER VERSION: Halve the amount of shrimp and marinade called for and arrange in a glass bowl that is 5 to 6 inches in diameter and about 3 inches deep. Makes about 10 appetizer servings.

PER SERVING PLAIN OR SPICY VARIATION: 133 cal., 3 g total fat (1 g sat. fat, 0 g trans fat), 172 mg chol., 186 mg sodium, 1 g carbo., 0 g fiber, 23 g pro.
EXCHANGES: 3 Lean Meat

PREPARING THE MARINATED SHRIMP BOWL, STEP-BY-STEP

1. Arrange cooked shrimp in the bowl, being sure to point the tails toward the center of the bowl to leave the curved backs exposed. **2.** After draining off marinade, place a round serving platter over the shrimp bowl and carefully invert the bowl onto the platter. (Use a serving platter with ½-inch sides because some marinade might pool around the shrimp.) Slowly remove the bowl.

PROSCIUTTO-WRAPPED SCALLOPS WITH ROASTED RED PEPPER AÏOLI

PREP: 35 MINUTES **STAND:** 30 MINUTES
BROIL: 6 MINUTES PER BATCH
MAKES: 20 APPETIZERS

- 10 fresh or frozen sea scallops
- 10 very thin slices prosciutto (6 to 7 ounces), halved lengthwise (see photo 2, below), or 10 slices center-cut bacon, halved crosswise
- 20 medium-size fresh basil leaves
  Freshly ground black pepper
- 1 recipe Roasted Red Pepper Aïoli
  Snipped fresh basil (optional)

1 Thaw scallops, if frozen. Soak twenty 6-inch wooden skewers in enough water to cover for at least 30 minutes; drain before using.

2 Meanwhile, preheat broiler. Rinse scallops; pat dry with paper towels. Cut scallops in half (see photo 1, below).

3 Lay prosciutto strips on a large cutting board. Top each strip with a medium-size basil leaf; add a scallop half. Starting from a short end, roll up each prosciutto strip around scallop (see photo 3, page 59). Thread each appetizer onto a skewer (see photo 4, page 59). Sprinkle with pepper.

4 Place the skewers on the lightly greased unheated rack of a broiler pan. Broil 4 to 5 inches from the heat for 6 to 8 minutes or until scallops are opaque and prosciutto is crisp, turning once.

5 Serve skewers with Roasted Red Pepper Aïoli for dipping. If desired, garnish aïoli with snipped fresh basil.

ROASTED RED PEPPER AÏOLI: In a blender or food processor combine ½ cup bottled roasted red sweet peppers, drained, and 2 cloves garlic, cut up. Cover and blend or process until nearly smooth. Add ⅓ cup mayonnaise. Cover and blend or process until smooth. With the blender or processor running, gradually add 2 tablespoons olive oil through the opening in lid or the feed tube, blending or processing until smooth. Transfer aïoli to a small bowl. Season with ⅛ teaspoon salt and a dash black pepper. Cover and chill until ready to serve.

PER APPETIZER: 92 cal., 7 g total fat (1 g sat. fat, 0 g trans fat), 11 mg chol., 231 mg sodium, 1 g carbo., 0 g fiber, 7 g pro.
EXCHANGES: 1 High-Fat Meat

BEST EVER

POTATO SKINS

PREP: 20 MINUTES **BAKE:** 50 MINUTES
OVEN: 425°F **MAKES:** 24 WEDGES

- 6 large baking potatoes (such as russet)
- 1 tablespoon vegetable oil
- 1 to 1½ teaspoons chili powder
  Several drops bottled hot pepper sauce
  Salt
- 8 slices crisp-cooked bacon, crumbled
- ⅔ cup finely chopped tomato (1 medium)
- 2 tablespoons finely chopped green onion (1)
- 1 cup shredded cheddar cheese (4 ounces)
- ½ cup dairy sour cream

1 Preheat oven to 425°F. Scrub potatoes and prick with a fork. Bake for 40 to 45 minutes or until tender; let cool.

PREPARING THE SCALLOPS, STEP-BY-STEP

1. Halve each scallop through the center. **2.** Cut each slice of prosciutto in half lengthwise. **3.** Lay a basil leaf over top of one prosciutto strip. Place a scallop half onto the basil and, starting from a short end, roll the prosciutto strip and basil around the scallop. **4.** Thread each wrapped scallop onto a 6-inch wooden skewer. **5.** Serve the scallops alongside Roasted Red Pepper Aïoli.

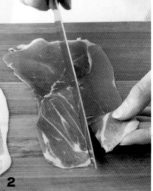

2 Cut each potato lengthwise into four wedges. Carefully scoop out the inside of each potato wedge, leaving a ¼-inch shell. Cover and chill the leftover white portion of the potato for another use.

3 Line a large baking sheet with foil; set aside. In a bowl combine the oil, chili powder, and hot pepper sauce. Using a pastry brush, brush the insides of the potato wedges with the oil mixture. Sprinkle with salt. Place the potato wedges in a single layer on prepared baking sheet. Sprinkle wedges with bacon, tomato, and green onion; top with cheese.

4 Bake about 10 minutes more or until cheese melts and potatoes are heated through. Serve with sour cream.

MAKE-AHEAD DIRECTIONS: Prepare as directed through Step 3. Cover; chill potato wedges for up to 24 hours. Uncover and bake as directed.

PER 2 WEDGES: 64 cal., 4 g total fat (2 g sat. fat, 0 g trans fat), 10 mg chol., 146 mg sodium, 4 g carbo., 1 g fiber, 3 g pro. EXCHANGES: 1 Fat

STUFFED MUSHROOMS

PREP: 20 MINUTES **BAKE:** 17 MINUTES
OVEN: 425°F **MAKES:** 24 MUSHROOMS

24 large fresh mushrooms, about 2 inches in diameter
½ cup seasoned fine dry bread crumbs
⅓ cup grated Parmesan cheese
⅓ cup dairy sour cream
2 cloves garlic, minced

2 tablespoons snipped fresh Italian parsley
¼ teaspoon black pepper
Nonstick cooking spray

1 Preheat oven to 425°F. Clean mushrooms. Remove stems from mushrooms; discard stems. Place mushroom caps, stem sides up, in a 15x10x1-inch baking pan; set aside.

2 In a small bowl stir together bread crumbs, Parmesan cheese, sour cream, garlic, parsley, and pepper. Spoon mixture into mushroom caps. Lightly coat mushrooms with nonstick cooking spray. Bake, uncovered, for 17 to 20 minutes or until light brown and heated through.

PER MUSHROOM: 25 cal., 1 g total fat (1 g sat. fat, 0 g trans fat), 2 mg chol., 64 mg sodium, 2 g carbo., 0 g fiber, 1 g pro. EXCHANGES: ½ Fat

BACON-CHEDDAR-STUFFED MUSHROOMS: Prepare as directed, except stir 4 slices bacon, crisp-cooked and crumbled, and ½ cup shredded cheddar cheese (2 ounces) into the filling.

PER MUSHROOM: 42 cal., 3 g total fat (1 g sat. fat, 0 g trans fat), 6 mg chol., 110 mg sodium, 2 g carbo., 0 g fiber, 3 g pro. EXCHANGES: ½ High-Fat Meat

BLUE CHEESE-AND-WALNUT-STUFFED MUSHROOMS: Prepare as directed, except stir ½ cup crumbled blue cheese and ¼ cup chopped toasted walnuts into the filling.

PER MUSHROOM: 43 cal., 3 g total fat (1 g sat. fat, 0 g trans fat), 5 mg chol., 103 mg sodium, 3 g carbo., 0 g fiber, 2 g pro. EXCHANGES: 1 Fat

ONION RINGS

PREP: 15 MINUTES **COOK:** 2 MINUTES PER BATCH
MAKES: 6 SERVINGS

- ¾ cup all-purpose flour
- ⅔ cup milk
- 1 egg
- 1 tablespoon vegetable oil
- ¼ teaspoon salt
  Vegetable oil for deep-fat frying
- 4 medium mild yellow or white onions, sliced ¼ inch thick and separated into rings (1¼ pounds)
  Salt
- 1 recipe Chipotle Ketchup or Curried Aïoli

1 For batter, in a medium bowl combine flour, milk, egg, the 1 tablespoon oil, and the ¼ teaspoon salt. Using a whisk or rotary beater, beat just until smooth.

2 In a deep-fat fryer or large deep skillet heat 1 inch oil to 365°F. Using a fork, dip onion rings into batter; drain off excess batter.* Fry onion rings, a few at a time, in a single layer in hot oil for 2 to 3 minutes or until golden, stirring once or twice with a fork to separate rings. Remove rings from oil; drain on paper towels. Sprinkle with additional salt.

***NOTE:** You might need to stir the last few onion slices into batter to coat them well.

CHIPOTLE KETCHUP: In a small bowl stir together 1 cup ketchup and 2 teaspoons finely chopped chipotle chile peppers in adobo sauce.

PER SERVING WITH CHIPOTLE KETCHUP: 657 cal., 58 g total fat (5 g sat. fat, 0 g trans fat), 37 mg chol., 771 mg sodium, 31 g carbo., 2 g fiber, 5 g pro.
EXCHANGES: 1 Vegetable, 1 Starch, 1 Other Carbo., 11½ Fat

CURRIED AÏOLI: In a medium bowl stir together ½ cup mayonnaise; 2 cloves garlic, minced; 1 teaspoon lemon juice; and ½ teaspoon curry powder. Slowly drizzle ⅓ cup olive oil in a thin stream into the mayonnaise mixture, whisking constantly.

PER SERVING WITH CURRIED AÏOLI: 859 cal., 85 g total fat (9 g sat. fat, 0 g trans fat), 44 mg chol., 418 mg sodium, 22 g carbo., 2 g fiber, 5 g pro.
EXCHANGES: 1 Starch, 1 Vegetable, 17 Fat

SAVORY NUTS

PREP: 10 MINUTES **BAKE:** 12 MINUTES
OVEN: 350°F **MAKES:** 2 CUPS

- 2 cups whole almonds, pecan halves, and/or cashews
- 2 tablespoons Worcestershire-style marinade for chicken
- 1 tablespoon olive oil
- 2 teaspoons snipped fresh thyme or ½ teaspoon dried thyme, crushed
- 1 teaspoon snipped fresh rosemary or ¼ teaspoon dried rosemary, crushed
- ¼ teaspoon salt
- ⅛ teaspoon cayenne pepper

1 Preheat oven to 350°F. Line a 13×9×2-inch baking pan with foil; lightly grease. Spread nuts in an even layer in pan. In a small bowl combine marinade, oil, thyme, rosemary, salt, and cayenne pepper. Drizzle over nuts; toss gently to coat.

2 Bake for 12 to 15 minutes or until nuts are toasted and appear dry, stirring occasionally. Spread nuts on a large sheet of foil; cool completely. Store in an airtight container at room temperature for up to 3 weeks.

PER ¼ CUP: 242 cal., 19 g total fat (1 g sat. fat, 0 g trans fat), 0 mg chol., 132 mg sodium, 8 g carbo., 4 g fiber, 8 g pro.
EXCHANGES: ½ Other Carbo., 1 High-Fat Meat, 2 Fat

WARM EDAMAME

START TO FINISH: 15 MINUTES
MAKES: 4 TO 6 SERVINGS

- 8 ounces fresh precooked or frozen edamame (sweet soybeans) in shells (2 cups)
- 1 teaspoon sesame seeds
- ½ teaspoon kosher salt
- ½ teaspoon coarsely ground black pepper
- ½ teaspoon toasted sesame oil
  Soy sauce (optional)

1 Place edamame in a steamer basket set in a large saucepan. Add water to just below basket. Bring to boiling; reduce heat. Cover; steam for 3 to 5 minutes or until tender. Transfer to a large bowl.

2 Add sesame seeds, salt, pepper, and sesame oil. Toss to coat. To serve, peel beans; discard shells. If desired, serve with soy sauce.

PER SERVING: 79 cal., 4 g total fat (0 g sat. fat, 0 g trans fat), 0 mg chol., 245 mg sodium, 6 g carbo., 3 g fiber, 6 g pro.
EXCHANGES: ½ Starch, ½ Lean Meat, ½ Fat

MAKE-IT-MINE PARTY MIX

PARTYGOERS HAVE EAGERLY MUNCHED ON NUT-AND-CEREAL MIXES FOR DECADES. NOW UPDATE THE CLASSIC WITH A FEW CONTEMPORARY FLOURISHES ALONG WITH THE BASIC INGREDIENTS YOU LIKE BEST.

BASIC INGREDIENTS

PREP: 20 MINUTES
BAKE: 45 MINUTES **OVEN:** 250°F
MAKES: 16 TO 18 CUPS

- 5 cups Crunchy Treat
- 4 cups round toasted oat cereal
- 3 cups Whole Nuts
- 8 cups Cereal
- 1 cup butter
- ¼ cup Worcestershire sauce
  Seasonings
  Several drops bottled hot pepper sauce (optional)

CRUNCHY TREAT

(PICK ONE)

Pretzel sticks
Small pretzel twists
Sesame sticks
Cheese crackers
Wasabi peas
Bagel crisps
Thin wheat crackers
Fish-shape crackers
Corn chips
Oyster crackers

WHOLE NUTS (PICK ONE)

Mixed nuts
Almonds
Cashews
Pecan halves
Soy nuts
Peanuts

CEREAL

(PICK TWO OR MORE OF THE FOLLOWING TO EQUAL 8 CUPS)

Sweetened oat square cereal
Puffed corn cereal
Bite-size corn square cereal
Bite-size rice square cereal
Bite-size wheat square cereal
Crispy corn and rice cereal

SEASONINGS (PICK ONE)

Italian: ½ cup grated Parmesan cheese plus 1 teaspoon garlic powder, and substitute bottled Italian vinaigrette for Worcestershire sauce

Ranch: One 1-ounce package ranch salad dressing mix

Cajun: 1 tablespoon Cajun seasoning plus 1 teaspoon garlic powder

Barbecue: 1 teaspoon garlic powder plus 1 teaspoon onion powder; substitute ½ cup barbecue sauce for Worcestershire sauce

Taco: One 1-ounce package taco seasoning mix plus 1 teaspoon ground cumin

BASIC INSTRUCTIONS

1 Preheat oven to 250°F. In a roasting pan* combine desired Crunchy Treat, round cereal, Nuts, and Cereal. Set aside.

2 In a small saucepan heat and stir butter, Worcestershire sauce, Seasonings, and bottled hot pepper sauce (if desired) until butter melts. Drizzle butter mixture over cereal mixture; stir gently to coat.

3 Bake for 45 minutes, stirring every 15 minutes. Spread on a large piece of foil to cool. Store in an airtight container at room temperature for up to 2 weeks or in the freezer for up to 3 months.

*__NOTE:__ If you don't have a roasting pan big enough to fit the party mix, purchase a large disposable roasting pan.

SHRIMP SPRING ROLLS WITH CHIMICHURRI SAUCE (photo, page 37)

PREP: 30 MINUTES **STAND:** 15 MINUTES
MAKES: 10 SPRING ROLLS

- 1 recipe Chimichurri Sauce
- 4 ounces cooked shrimp, peeled, deveined, and chopped
- 1 cup shredded romaine lettuce
- ¾ cup packaged coarsely shredded carrots
- ½ cup fresh cilantro leaves
- ½ cup fresh mint leaves
- 2 green onions, cut into thin bite-size strips
- 1 ounce dried rice vermicelli noodles
- 10 8-inch rice papers
- 10 sprigs fresh Italian parsley
  Soy sauce (optional)
  Crushed red pepper (optional)

1 Prepare Chimichurri Sauce. In a medium bowl combine the sauce, shrimp, lettuce, carrots, cilantro, mint, and green onions. Let stand for 15 to 30 minutes to allow shrimp and vegetables to soften slightly and absorb flavors from the sauce, stirring occasionally.

2 Meanwhile, in a medium saucepan cook the vermicelli in lightly salted boiling water for 3 minutes or just until tender; drain. Rinse under cold water; drain well. Use kitchen shears to snip the noodles into small pieces; set aside.

3 To assemble, pour warm water into a pie plate. Carefully dip a rice paper into the water; transfer to a clean round dinner plate. Let stand for several seconds to soften. Place a parsley sprig in the center of the paper. Spoon about ⅓ cup of the shrimp mixture just below the center. Arrange some of the vermicelli noodles across mixture. Tightly roll up rice paper from the bottom, tucking in sides as you roll.

4 Repeat with the remaining rice papers, parsley sprigs, shrimp mixture, and noodles. If desired, serve spring rolls with soy sauce sprinkled with crushed red pepper for dipping.

CHIMICHURRI SAUCE: In a blender or food processor combine 1½ cups lightly packed fresh Italian parsley; ¼ cup olive oil; ¼ cup rice vinegar; 4 to 6 cloves garlic, minced; ¼ teaspoon salt; ¼ teaspoon black pepper; and ¼ teaspoon crushed red pepper. Cover and blend or process with several on/off pulses until chopped but not pureed.

VEGETARIAN SPRING ROLLS: Prepare as directed, except omit shrimp and substitute ¾ cup diced firm tofu (fresh bean curd).

PER SPRING ROLL SHRIMP OR VEGETARIAN VARIATION: 128 cal., 6 g total fat (1 g sat. fat, 0 g trans fat), 22 mg chol., 312 mg sodium, 15 g carbo., 2 g fiber, 4 g pro. EXCHANGES: 1 Starch, 1 Fat

EGG ROLLS

PREP: 30 MINUTES **COOK:** 2 MINUTES PER BATCH
OVEN: 300°F **MAKES:** 8 EGG ROLLS

- 8 egg roll wrappers
- 1 recipe Filling
  Vegetable oil for deep-fat frying
- 1 cup Sweet-and-Sour Sauce (see page 542), bottled sweet-and-sour sauce, and/or ½ cup prepared Chinese-style hot mustard

1 Preheat oven to 300°F. To assemble, place an egg roll wrapper on a flat surface with a corner pointing toward you. Spoon ¼ cup Filling across and just below center of egg roll wrapper. Fold bottom corner over filling, tucking it under on the other side. Fold side corners over filling, forming an envelope shape. Roll egg roll toward remaining corner. Moisten top corner with water; press firmly to seal.

2 In a heavy saucepan or deep-fat fryer heat 1½ inches vegetable oil to 365°F. Fry egg rolls, a few at a time, for 2 to 3 minutes or until golden brown. Drain on paper towels. Keep warm in the oven while frying remaining egg rolls. Serve warm egg rolls with Sweet-and-Sour Sauce.

FILLING: In a large skillet cook 8 ounces ground pork until pork is brown, or cook 8 ounces cubed, drained firm tofu in 1 tablespoon hot vegetable oil until tofu is brown. Drain fat from pork, if using. Add 4 cups packaged shredded cabbage with carrot (coleslaw mix) or 3 cups packaged shredded broccoli (broccoli slaw mix); 2 tablespoons soy sauce; 2 teaspoons grated fresh ginger; 1 clove garlic, minced; and ¼ teaspoon salt. Cook and stir for 2 minutes.

PER EGG ROLL: 372 cal., 20 g total fat (3 g sat. fat, 0 g trans fat), 23 mg chol., 841 mg sodium, 38 g carbo., 2 g fiber, 10 g pro. EXCHANGES: 1 Vegetable, 1 Starch, 1 Other Carbo., 1 Lean Meat, 4 Fat

FAST FIND
LOOK FOR EGG ROLL WRAPPERS IN THE PRODUCE SECTION OF YOUR SUPERMARKET.

BEANS, RICE & GRAINS

LEMON-ASPARAGUS RISOTTO, PAGE 77

BEANS, RICE & GRAINS

LEARN HOW THESE HEARTY INGREDIENTS CAN BRING TEXTURE, FLAVOR, AND WHOLESOMENESS TO YOUR DIET.

BEAN TALK

High in fiber and phytonutrients and low in fat and saturated fat, beans and other legumes are inexpensive, easy-to-enjoy superfoods. Beans are also a good source of important vitamins and minerals.

STORING BEANS: Placed in an airtight container in a cool, dry, dark place, beans can be stored up to 1 year. However, the older they are, the longer they need to cook. For this reason, do not combine new packages of beans with older packages.

A RICE PRIMER

Here's a sampling of the rice varieties you can cook to go with almost anything you serve.

ARBORIO RICE: As it cooks, this short grain white rice releases starch, creating a creamy texture. It's often used for making risotto.

AROMATIC RICE: Great for adding fascinating fragrance to meals, these varieties include basmati, della, jasmine, Texmati, and wild pecan. Aromas range from flowers and nuts to popped corn.

BROWN RICE: Pleasantly chewy and nutlike in flavor, this rice retains the bran around the rice kernel. The longer cooking time pays off in wholesome goodness.

CONVERTED RICE: Also referred to as parboiled rice, this rice has been steamed, pressure-cooked, and dried before packaging. The process helps the nutrients stay within the grain and reduces surface starch, which keeps the rice from sticking together and helps retain a firm texture while cooking.

INSTANT AND QUICK-COOKING RICE: These are partially or fully cooked and dried before packaging, giving them a very short cooking time.

WHITE RICE: White rice has had the bran and germ removed and is available in short, medium, and long grain varieties. The shorter the grain, the more likely the rice will stick together when cooked.

WILD RICE: Actually a marsh grass, not a grain, wild rice has a nutty flavor.

WHOLE GRAIN GOODNESS

Grains that have not been refined are known as whole grains. Because they have not had the germ and bran removed, whole grains retain more of their nutrients than refined grains. They are especially good sources of fiber, which research suggests can reduce the risk of heart disease and help to maintain a healthy weight. To integrate whole grains into your diet, reach for brown rice as well as these and other whole grains.

BARLEY: Pleasantly chewy and mild in flavor, barley is one of the oldest grains and one of the richest sources of both soluble and insoluble fiber.

BULGUR: These are wheat kernels that have been boiled, dried, and cracked. With a tender, chewy texture and earthy flavor, bulgur is very high in fiber and rich in iron, phosphorus, zinc, manganese, selenium, and magnesium.

FARRO: Nutty and chewy, this Italian staple is high in protein, fiber, magnesium, and vitamins A, B, C, and E. It requires a long cooking time and can be found in flour form and used in baked goods.

MILLET: This tiny grain can be cooked and eaten like rice or used in baked goods. It's a good source of manganese, magnesium, and phosphorus.

QUINOA: Containing more protein than any other grain, quinoa is slightly chewy with a light, delicate flavor and texture.

SPELT: A distant cousin of wheat, spelt has a richer flavor, more of many nutrients, and higher protein content than wheat.

WHEAT BERRIES: These are whole, unprocessed kernels of wheat that are slightly sweet with a nutty flavor and pleasantly chewy texture.

BEANS, RICE & GRAINS

GOOD VALUE, GOOD NUTRITION, LONG SHELF LIFE—NO WONDER THESE
INGREDIENTS ENDURE AS CORNERSTONES TO MANY SATISFYING MEALS.

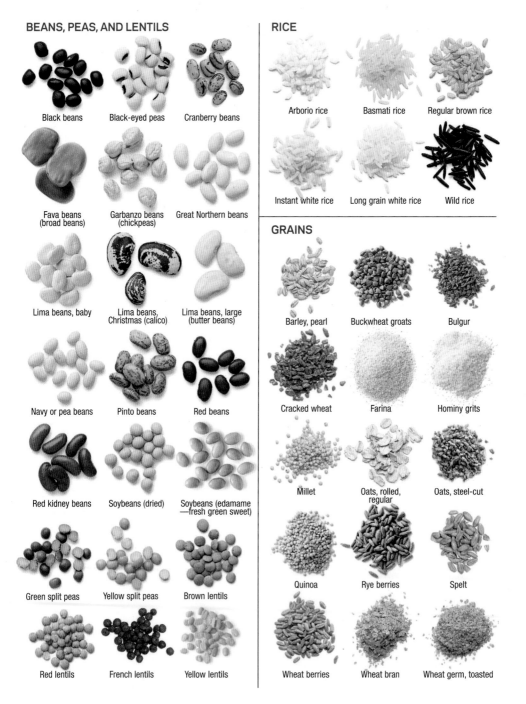

BEANS, PEAS, AND LENTILS

Black beans

Black-eyed peas

Cranberry beans

Fava beans
(broad beans)

Garbanzo beans
(chickpeas)

Great Northern beans

Lima beans, baby

Lima beans,
Christmas (calico)

Lima beans, large
(butter beans)

Navy or pea beans

Pinto beans

Red beans

Red kidney beans

Soybeans (dried)

Soybeans (edamame
—fresh green sweet)

Green split peas

Yellow split peas

Brown lentils

Red lentils

French lentils

Yellow lentils

RICE

Arborio rice

Basmati rice

Regular brown rice

Instant white rice

Long grain white rice

Wild rice

GRAINS

Barley, pearl

Buckwheat groats

Bulgur

Cracked wheat

Farina

Hominy grits

Millet

Oats, rolled,
regular

Oats, steel-cut

Quinoa

Rye berries

Spelt

Wheat berries

Wheat bran

Wheat germ, toasted

CUBAN RED BEANS AND RICE

START TO FINISH: 35 MINUTES
MAKES: 4 MAIN-DISH SERVINGS

- 1 large sweet onion, cut into thin wedges
- 1 cup chopped green or red sweet pepper (1 large)
- 4 cloves garlic, minced
- 1 tablespoon canola oil
- ½ cup snipped fresh cilantro
- ½ teaspoon dried oregano, crushed
- ½ teaspoon ground cumin
- ¼ teaspoon black pepper
- 2 15- to 16-ounce cans pinto beans and/or red kidney beans, rinsed and drained
- 1 cup vegetable broth*
- ¼ cup lime juice
- 1 8.8-ounce package cooked brown rice or 2 cups cooked brown rice
  Lime wedges and/or small hot chile peppers (optional)

1 In a large saucepan cook onion, sweet pepper, and garlic in hot oil over medium heat for 5 to 7 minutes or until tender, stirring occasionally. Add ¼ cup of the cilantro, the oregano, cumin, and black pepper. Cook and stir for 1 minute.

2 Add beans and broth. Bring to boiling; reduce heat. Simmer, uncovered, for 15 to 20 minutes or until liquid is thickened to desired consistency. Stir in lime juice. Prepare rice according to package directions. Serve beans over rice and sprinkle with remaining cilantro. If desired, serve with lime wedges and/or hot peppers.

*NOTE: Organic vegetable broth or vegetable stock is a good choice for lower sodium content.

PER 1 CUP + ½ CUP RICE: 369 cal., 6 g total fat (1 g sat. fat, 0 g trans fat), 0 mg chol., 933 mg sodium, 67 g carbo., 13 g fiber, 17 g pro.
EXCHANGES: ½ Vegetable, 4½ Starch, ½ Lean Meat

REFRIED BEANS

PREP: 20 MINUTES **STAND:** 60 MINUTES
COOK: 2½ HOURS + 8 MINUTES
MAKES: 4 SIDE-DISH SERVINGS

- ½ pound dried pinto beans (about 1¼ cups)
- 8 cups water
- ½ teaspoon salt
- 2 tablespoons bacon drippings or olive oil
- 2 cloves garlic, minced

1 Rinse beans. In a large saucepan or Dutch oven combine beans and 4 cups of the water.

CUBAN RED BEANS AND RICE

Bring to boiling; reduce heat. Simmer, covered, for 2 minutes. Remove from heat. Cover and let stand for 60 minutes. (Or place beans in water in pan. Cover and let soak in a cool place overnight.) Drain and rinse beans.

2 In the same saucepan or Dutch oven combine beans, remaining 4 cups fresh water, and the salt. Bring to boiling; reduce heat. Simmer, covered, for 2½ to 3 hours or until beans are very tender. Drain beans, reserving liquid.

3 In a large heavy skillet heat bacon drippings. Stir in garlic. Add beans; mash thoroughly with a potato masher. Stir in enough of the cooking liquid (about ¼ cup) to make a pastelike mixture. Cook, uncovered, over low heat for 8 to 10 minutes or until thick, stirring often. Season to taste with additional salt and *black pepper*.

PER ½ CUP: 257 cal., 7 g total fat (3 g sat. fat, 0 g trans fat), 6 mg chol., 321 mg sodium, 36 g carbo., 9 g fiber, 12 g pro.
EXCHANGES: 2½ Starch, ½ Lean Meat, 1 Fat

READY WHEN YOU ARE
GET A HEAD START ON RECIPES THAT BEGIN WITH DRIED BEANS BY SOAKING AND COOKING THE BEANS IN ADVANCE. COVER AND STORE IN THE REFRIGERATOR UP TO 3 DAYS.

WHITE BEANS AND WILTED SPINACH

START TO FINISH: 20 MINUTES
MAKES: 4 SIDE-DISH SERVINGS

- 1 medium onion, halved and thinly sliced
- 6 cloves garlic, minced (1 tablespoon)
- 1 tablespoon olive oil
- 1 15-ounce can cannellini (white kidney) or navy beans, rinsed and drained
- 1 14.5-ounce can diced tomatoes
- 1 tablespoon chopped fresh thyme
- 4 cups torn fresh spinach
- 2 slices turkey bacon, cooked, drained, and crumbled
- 4 teaspoons bottled balsamic or red wine vinaigrette
- Salt and freshly ground black pepper

1 In a large skillet cook onion and garlic in hot olive oil for 3 minutes or until tender. Stir in beans.

2 Drain tomatoes, reserving ⅓ cup liquid. Stir tomatoes, reserved tomato liquid (discard remaining liquid), and fresh thyme into onion mixture. Cook and stir over medium heat about 2 minutes or until heated through. Stir in 3 cups of the spinach and stir about 30 seconds or just until wilted. Stir in remaining spinach and bacon. Spoon mixture into four individual bowls. Drizzle each serving with 1 teaspoon vinaigrette. Season to taste with salt and pepper.

PER ⅔ CUP: 162 cal., 6 g total fat (1 g sat. fat, 0 g trans fat), 8 mg chol., 660 mg sodium, 25 g carbo., 8 g fiber, 9 g pro. EXCHANGES: 1 Vegetable, 1½ Starch, 1 Fat

SUCCOTASH

START TO FINISH: 25 MINUTES
MAKES: 6 SIDE-DISH SERVINGS

- 2 cups frozen lima beans
- 2 tablespoons butter
- 2 cups fresh corn kernels or frozen whole kernel corn
- ¼ teaspoon salt
- ⅛ teaspoon black pepper
- ¼ cup whipping cream
- ¼ cup diced cooked ham or crumbled, crisp-cooked bacon

1 Cook lima beans according to package directions; drain and set aside.

2 Heat butter in a large skillet over medium heat. Add corn, salt, and pepper. Cook and stir for

2 minutes. Add drained beans. Cook and stir for 1 minute more.

3 Add cream and ham. Bring to boiling; reduce heat. Simmer, uncovered, about 2 minutes or until cream thickens slightly.

PER ½ CUP: 182 cal., 9 g total fat (5 g sat. fat, 0 g trans fat), 27 mg chol., 207 mg sodium, 22 g carbo., 4 g fiber, 6 g pro. EXCHANGES: 1 Vegetable, 1 Starch, 1½ Fat

FALAFELS

START TO FINISH: 25 MINUTES
MAKES: 4 MAIN-DISH SERVINGS

- 1 15-ounce can garbanzo beans (chickpeas), rinsed and drained
- ¼ cup purchased julienned or coarsely shredded carrot
- 2 tablespoons all-purpose flour
- 2 tablespoons snipped fresh parsley
- 1 tablespoon olive oil
- 3 cloves garlic, halved
- 1 teaspoon ground coriander
- ½ teaspoon salt
- ½ teaspoon ground cumin
- ⅛ teaspoon black pepper
- 2 tablespoons olive oil
- ½ cup mayonnaise
- 1 clove garlic, minced
- ¼ teaspoon cayenne pepper
- 4 pita bread rounds
- 1 cup fresh spinach leaves, coarsely shredded

1 In a food processor combine beans, carrot, flour, parsley, 1 tablespoon olive oil, halved garlic, coriander, salt, cumin, and black pepper. Cover and process until finely chopped and mixture holds together (should have some visible pieces of garbanzo beans and carrots).

2 Shape mixture into four 3-inch patties. In a large skillet heat 2 tablespoons oil over medium-high heat. Add patties. Cook for 2 to 3 minutes per side or until browned and heated through.

3 Meanwhile, in a small bowl stir together mayonnaise, minced garlic, and cayenne pepper. Spread mixture over pita rounds. Top with spinach and patties.

PER PATTY: 607 cal., 34 g total fat (6 g sat. fat, 0 g trans fat), 10 mg chol., 1,093 mg sodium, 63 g carbo., 7 g fiber, 12 g pro. EXCHANGES: 4 Starch, 6 Fat

BLACK BEAN-CHIPOTLE BURGERS

PREP: 35 MINUTES **CHILL:** 60 MINUTES
COOK: 10 MINUTES **MAKES:** 4 BURGERS

- 1 15-ounce can black beans, rinsed and drained
- ½ cup frozen whole kernel corn, thawed
- 1 cup corn chips, finely crushed (about ½ cup crushed)
- ½ cup cooked brown rice
- ¼ cup finely chopped red onion
- ¼ cup bottled chunky salsa
- ½ to 1 teaspoon finely chopped canned chipotle peppers in adobo sauce
- ½ teaspoon ground cumin
- 1 clove garlic, minced
- 1 tablespoon olive oil
  Finely shredded green cabbage
- 4 tostada shells, heated according to package directions
  Bottled chunky salsa, dairy sour cream, fresh cilantro leaves, crumbled queso fresco, and/or avocado slices

1 In a medium bowl mash half the beans with a potato masher or pastry blender until well mashed (see photo 1, below). Add remaining beans, corn, corn chips, rice, onion, the ¼ cup salsa, chipotle peppers, cumin, and garlic.

2 Shape mixture into four 3½-inch patties, about ¾ inch thick (see photo 2, below). Place patties on a tray; cover and chill at least 60 minutes before cooking.

3 Brush both sides of patties with olive oil. Cook in a very large skillet over medium heat for 10 minutes or until heated through, turning once*.

4 Place some shredded cabbage on each tostada shell. Place the burgers on the cabbage and top with additional salsa, sour cream, cilantro, cheese, and/or avocado slices (see photo 3, below).

*BROILER DIRECTIONS: Preheat broiler. Place patties on the unheated rack of a broiler pan. Broil 4 inches from the heat about 10 minutes or until heated through, turning once.

PER BURGER: 362 cal., 17 g total fat (3 g sat. fat, 1 g trans fat), 6 mg chol., 600 mg sodium, 46 g carbo., 9 g fiber, 14 g pro.
EXCHANGES: ½ Vegetable, 3 Starch, ½ Lean Meat, 3 Fat

PREPARING BLACK BEAN-CHIPOTLE BURGERS, STEP-BY-STEP

1. Using a potato masher, mash half of the beans until well mashed. (This will help the burger mixture hold together.)
2. Use a measuring cup to uniformly shape the bean mixture into 3½-inch patties. **3.** Arrange shredded cabbage on each tostada shell. Place each patty on the cabbage and top with salsa, sour cream, cilantro, cheese, and/or avocado.

TERRIFIC TOFU BEFORE COOKING TOFU SLICES IN OIL, BLOT THEM WITH PAPER TOWELS TO REMOVE EXCESS MOISTURE. THIS PREVENTS SPATTERING WHILE ALLOWING THE TOFU TO BROWN EVENLY.

TOFU AND MUSHROOMS OVER GREENS

PASTA WITH SPINACH AND EDAMAME

START TO FINISH: 20 MINUTES
MAKES: 4 MAIN-DISH SERVINGS

- 1 9-ounce package refrigerated fettuccine
- 2 cups frozen sweet soybeans (edamame)
- ½ cup walnuts, broken
- ⅔ cup bottled Italian salad dressing with cheese
- ¼ teaspoon black pepper
- 4 cups fresh baby spinach

1 In a large pot cook pasta and soybeans according to pasta package directions; drain. Return pasta and soybeans to pan.

2 Meanwhile, in a medium skillet toast walnuts over medium heat for 3 to 4 minutes. Remove from heat; set aside.

3 Stir salad dressing and pepper into hot pasta mixture in pan. Add spinach and nuts; cook and toss over medium heat for 1 minute more.

PER 1¾ CUPS: 534 cal., 33 g total fat (5 g sat. fat, 0 g trans fat), 50 mg chol., 525 mg sodium, 43 g carbo., 7 g fiber, 20 g pro. EXCHANGES: 1 Vegetable, 2½ Starch, 1½ Lean Meat, 6 Fat

GINGERY VEGETABLE-TOFU STIR-FRY

START TO FINISH: 45 MINUTES
MAKES: 4 MAIN-DISH SERVINGS

- ¼ cup dry sherry or chicken broth
- 3 tablespoons soy sauce
- 1 tablespoon cornstarch
- ½ teaspoon sugar
- 1 tablespoon olive oil
- 2 teaspoons grated fresh ginger
- 1 pound fresh asparagus, cut into 1-inch pieces (2½ cups), or one 10-ounce package frozen cut asparagus, thawed and drained
- 1 small yellow summer squash, halved lengthwise and sliced (1¼ cups)
- ¼ cup sliced green onions (2)
- 1 10.5-ounce package extra-firm tofu (fresh bean curd), cut into ½-inch cubes
- ½ cup chopped almonds, toasted (see tip, page 20)
- 2 cups hot cooked brown rice

1 For sauce, in a small bowl stir together ¾ cup *water*, dry sherry, soy sauce, cornstarch, and sugar; set aside.

2 Pour olive oil into a wok or large skillet. (Add oil as necessary during cooking.) Preheat wok over medium-high heat. Stir-fry ginger in hot oil for

15 seconds. Add fresh asparagus (if using) and squash; stir-fry for 3 minutes. Add thawed asparagus (if using) and green onions; stir-fry 1½ minutes more or until asparagus is crisp-tender; remove.

3 Add tofu to hot wok. Stir-fry for 2 to 3 minutes or until light brown. Remove from wok. Stir sauce and add to hot wok. Cook and stir until thickened and bubbly. Return cooked vegetables and tofu to wok; stir to coat with sauce. Cover and cook about 1 minute more or until heated through. Stir in almonds. Serve over rice.

PER 1½ CUPS: 336 cal., 14 g total fat (2 g sat. fat, 0 g trans fat), 0 mg chol., 2 mg sodium, 34 g carbo., 6 g fiber, 16 g pro. EXCHANGES: 1½ Vegetable, 2 Starch, 1 Lean Meat, 2 Fat

TOFU AND MUSHROOMS OVER GREENS

START TO FINISH: 30 MINUTES
MAKES: 4 MAIN-DISH SERVINGS

- 8 ounces fresh button and/or cremini mushrooms, quartered
- 3 cloves garlic, minced
- 2 tablespoons olive oil
- 1 tablespoon butter
- 1 tablespoon snipped fresh thyme or 1 teaspoon dried thyme, crushed
- 12 ounces tofu (fresh bean curd), drained and cut into ½-inch-thick slices
- ¼ cup balsamic vinegar
- 6 cups torn mixed greens
- ¼ cup crumbled herbed feta cheese
  Toasted baguette-style French bread slices

1 In a large skillet cook mushrooms and garlic in hot olive oil and butter over medium heat until mushrooms are tender and liquid evaporates. Stir in thyme, ¼ teaspoon *salt,* and ⅛ teaspoon *black pepper.* Remove from skillet; keep warm.

2 Lightly season tofu slices with additional salt and black pepper. In the same skillet cook tofu slices, half at a time if necessary, over medium-high heat for 3 to 4 minutes or until light brown and heated through, turning once. Remove from skillet. Add balsamic vinegar to skillet; bring to boiling. Boil gently for 1 minute. Remove from heat.

3 To serve, arrange greens on serving plates. Top each with tofu slices. Drizzle with balsamic vinegar. Top tofu with mushrooms and cheese. Serve with bread slices.

PER SERVING: 271 cal., 13 g total fat (4 g sat. fat, 0 g trans fat), 9 mg chol., 415 mg sodium, 28 g carbo., 3 g fiber, 11 g pro. EXCHANGES: 1½ Vegetable, 1½ Starch, ½ Lean Meat, 2 Fat

BAKED BEANS WITH BACON

PREP: 30 MINUTES **STAND:** 60 MINUTES
COOK: 60 MINUTES **BAKE:** 90 MINUTES
OVEN: 300°F **MAKES:** 10 TO 12 SIDE-DISH SERVINGS

- 1 pound dried navy beans or Great Northern beans (2⅓ cups)
- 16 cups water
- 4 ounces bacon or pancetta, chopped
- 1 cup chopped onion (1 large)
- ¼ cup packed brown sugar
- ⅓ cup molasses or pure maple syrup
- ¼ cup Worcestershire sauce
- 1½ teaspoons dry mustard
- ½ teaspoon salt
- ¼ teaspoon black pepper
- 4 ounces bacon or pancetta, chopped, crisp-cooked, drained, and crumbled (optional)

1 Rinse beans. In a 4- to 5-quart oven-going Dutch oven combine beans and 8 cups of the water. Bring to boiling; reduce heat. Simmer, uncovered, for 2 minutes. Remove from heat. Cover and let stand for 1 hour. (Or place beans in water in Dutch oven. Cover and let soak in a cool place overnight.) Drain and rinse beans.

2 Return beans to Dutch oven. Stir in the remaining 8 cups fresh water. Bring to boiling; reduce heat. Cover and simmer for 60 to 90 minutes or until beans are tender, stirring occasionally. Drain beans, reserving liquid.

3 Preheat oven to 300°F. In the same Dutch oven cook the 4 ounces bacon and onion over medium heat until bacon is slightly crisp and onion is tender, stirring occasionally. Add brown sugar; cook and stir until sugar is dissolved. Stir in molasses, Worcestershire sauce, dry mustard, salt, and pepper. Stir in drained beans and 1¼ cups of the reserved bean liquid.

4 Bake, covered, for 60 minutes. Uncover and bake for 30 to 45 minutes or until desired consistency, stirring occasionally. Beans will thicken slightly as they cool. If necessary, stir in additional reserved bean liquid. If desired, sprinkle with additional cooked bacon.

PER ½ CUP: 267 cal., 6 g total fat (2 g sat. fat, 0 g trans fat), 8 mg chol., 282 mg sodium, 43 g carbo., 11 g fiber, 12 g pro. EXCHANGES: 2 Starch, 1 Other Carbo., 1 Medium-Fat Meat

CLASSIC BAKED BEANS

PREP: 20 MINUTES **BAKE:** 45 MINUTES
OVEN: 350°F **MAKES:** 8 SIDE-DISH SERVINGS

- 6 slices bacon
- ½ cup chopped onion
- 1 15- to 16-ounce can butter beans, rinsed and drained
- 1 15- to 16-ounce can pork and beans in tomato sauce
- 1 15- to 16-ounce can kidney or pinto beans, rinsed and drained
- ½ cup packed brown sugar
- ⅓ cup ketchup
- 2 tablespoons Worcestershire sauce

1 Preheat oven to 350°F. In a very large skillet cook bacon over medium heat until crisp. Drain on paper towels, reserving 2 tablespoons drippings in skillet. Crumble bacon and set aside. Add onion to reserved drippings; cook and stir over medium heat about 4 minutes or until tender.

2 In a 2-quart casserole combine butter beans, pork and beans in tomato sauce, kidney beans, brown sugar, ketchup, and Worcestershire sauce. Stir in bacon and onion mixture.

3 Bake, covered, about 45 minutes or until bubbly around edges.

PER 1 CUP: 259 cal., 6 g total fat (2 g sat. fat, 0 g trans fat), 14 mg chol., 809 mg sodium, 43 g carbo., 7 g fiber, 12 g pro. EXCHANGES: 3 Starch, ½ Lean Meat, ½ Fat

---

DRY VS. CANNED BEANS
YES, YOU CAN USE CANNED BEANS FOR DRY—HERE'S HOW TO DO THE MATH.

■ One pound (2¼ to 2½ cups) of dry, uncooked beans yields about 6 to 7 cups cooked beans. One 15-ounce can of beans equals about 1¾ cups drained beans. Therefore, use 3½ to four 15-ounce cans for each pound of dried beans called for.

■ Be sure to drain and rinse the canned beans under cold running water to eliminate the salty liquid.

10 TO TRY—
BAKED BEANS

Start with Classic Baked Beans, page 72. **1. APPLE:** Stir 1 tart apple, cut up, into bean mixture before baking. Sprinkle with ½ cup shredded smoked cheddar cheese (2 ounces) after baking. **2. BARBECUE:** Substitute bottled barbecue sauce for the ketchup. **3. HAWAIIAN:** Stir one 8-ounce can pineapple tidbits, undrained, into bean mixture before baking. Bake, uncovered, the last 10 minutes. **4. KIELBASA AND MUSTARD:** Stir ½ cup chopped cooked kielbasa and 1 tablespoon Dijon-style mustard into the beans before baking. **5. APRICOT:** Substitute apricot preserves for the brown sugar and stir ½ cup coarsely chopped dried apricots into bean mixture before baking. **6. CHEDDAR:** Sprinkle beans with ½ cup shredded cheddar cheese (2 ounces) after baking. **7. BEEFY:** Stir 8 ounces ground beef, cooked and drained, into bean mixture before baking. **8. MAPLE-PECAN:** Substitute maple syrup for the brown sugar. Sprinkle ½ cup chopped toasted pecans over bean mixture before serving. **9. SALSA:** Substitute black beans for the kidney beans and substitute salsa for the ketchup. Top with 1 cup coarsely crushed tortilla or corn chips before serving. **10. MOLASSES:** Substitute molasses for the brown sugar.

FRIED RICE

START TO FINISH: 30 MINUTES
MAKES: 6 SIDE-DISH SERVINGS

2 eggs

1 teaspoon soy sauce

1 teaspoon toasted sesame oil

1 clove garlic, minced

1 tablespoon vegetable oil

½ cup thinly bias-sliced celery (1 stalk)

¾ cup sliced fresh mushrooms

2 cups chilled cooked white rice

½ cup julienned carrots

½ cup frozen peas

2 tablespoons soy sauce

¼ cup sliced green onions (2)

1 In a small bowl beat eggs and 1 teaspoon soy sauce; set aside. Pour 1 teaspoon sesame oil into a wok or large skillet. Preheat over medium heat. Add garlic; cook 30 seconds. Add egg mixture; stir gently until set. Remove egg and slice (see photo 1, below). Remove wok from heat.

2 Pour 1 tablespoon vegetable oil into the wok. Heat over medium-high heat. Stir-fry celery in hot oil for 1 minute. Add mushrooms; stir-fry 1 to 2 minutes or until vegetables are crisp-tender.

3 Add rice, carrots, and peas. Pour 2 table-spoons soy sauce over all (see photo 2, below). Cook and stir for 4 to 6 minutes or until heated through. Add egg mixture and green onions; cook and stir about 1 minute or until heated through.

PER ½ CUP: 140 cal., 5 g total fat (1 g sat. fat, 0 g trans fat), 71 mg chol., 409 mg sodium, 18 g carbo., 2 g fiber, 6 g pro.
EXCHANGES: 1 Starch, ½ Lean Meat, 1 Fat

SPANISH RICE

PREP: 25 MINUTES **COOK:** 20 MINUTES
STAND: 5 MINUTES **MAKES:** 6 SIDE-DISH SERVINGS

4 ounces bacon, chopped (about 4 slices)

1 cup coarsely chopped onion (1 large)

¾ cup chopped green sweet pepper (1 medium)

1 clove garlic, minced

1 14.5-ounce can diced tomatoes, undrained

½ teaspoon black pepper

¼ teaspoon cayenne pepper

1 cup uncooked jasmine or long grain rice

2 teaspoons olive oil

¼ cup chopped green olives (optional)

1 cup shredded cheddar cheese (4 ounces)

1 In a large skillet cook bacon until crisp. Remove from skillet; drain on paper towels. Remove all but 1 tablespoon bacon drippings from skillet. Add onion, sweet pepper, and garlic. Cook and stir over medium heat until tender, 7 to 10 minutes. Add undrained tomatoes, black pepper, and cayenne pepper. Bring to boiling; reduce heat. Simmer, covered, for 20 minutes.

2 Meanwhile, in a medium saucepan stir together rice, oil, and ½ teaspoon *salt*. Add 2 cups *water*. Bring to boiling. Reduce heat to low and simmer, covered, about 15 minutes or until rice is tender.

3 Add the cooked rice, cooked bacon, and olives (if desired) to skillet. Top with cheese. Cover; let stand 5 minutes or until cheese melts.

PER ⅔ CUP: 273 cal., 12 g total fat (6 g sat. fat, 0 g trans fat), 28 mg chol., 577 mg sodium, 32 g carbo., 2 g fiber, 9 g pro.
EXCHANGES: ½ Vegetable, 2 Starch, 2 Fat

PREPARING FRIED RICE, STEP-BY-STEP

1. Use your hands to roll the cooked egg into a log. Use a sharp knife to slice the egg into strips.
2. Pour the soy sauce over the rice and vegetables in the skillet. Cook and stir just until the mixture is heated through and most of the soy sauce has been absorbed.

MAKE-IT-MINE RICE PILAF

TAKE A LOOK IN YOUR FRIDGE AND
CUPBOARD. CHANCES ARE YOU HAVE
THE INGREDIENTS YOU NEED TO CREATE
A RICE PILAF TO COMPLEMENT WHATEVER
YOU ARE SERVING FOR DINNER.

BASIC INGREDIENTS

PREP: 15 MINUTES
COOK: 15 TO 45 MINUTES
MAKES: 4 TO 6 SIDE-DISH SERVINGS

Rice or Grain
2 cloves garlic, minced
2 tablespoons butter
1 14-ounce can reduced-
    sodium chicken broth
¼ cup Dried Fruit (optional)
¼ cup Chopped Vegetable
¼ cup Liquid
1 to 2 teaspoons Fresh
    Herb or ¼ teaspoon
    Dried Herb
½ cup Stir-In

RICE OR GRAIN (PICK ONE)

¾ cup long grain rice or
    basmati rice
    ** (Cook 15 to 20 minutes.)
½ cup wild rice plus ⅓ cup
    regular barley
    ** (Cook 45 to 50 minutes.)

DRIED FRUIT (PICK ONE)

Cherries
Cranberries
Raisins
Snipped apricots

CHOPPED VEGETABLE
(PICK ONE)

Carrots
Celery
Mushrooms
Sweet peppers
Zucchini

LIQUID (PICK ONE)

Apple juice
Dry white wine
Water

FRESH OR DRIED HERB
(PICK ONE)

Basil
Oregano
Thyme

STIR-IN (PICK ONE)

Almonds
Crumbled crisp-cooked bacon
Pecans
Sliced green onions
Toasted chopped walnuts
Toasted pine nuts

BASIC INSTRUCTIONS

1 In a medium saucepan cook
and stir the uncooked desired
Rice or Grain and garlic in hot
butter for 3 minutes.* Carefully
stir in chicken broth, Dried Fruit
(if desired), Chopped Vegetable,
Liquid, and Dried Herb (if using).
Bring mixture to boiling; reduce
heat. Simmer, covered, for specified time** or until rice is tender
and liquid is absorbed. Add Stir-
In and Fresh Herb (if using).

*TIP: Toasting the rice or grain
adds a rich, earthy flavor to
the pilaf. Cook and stir it with
the garlic and hot butter until it
releases a nutty aroma.

COOK ONCE, EAT TWICE

TONIGHT'S GRATIFYING BOWL OF RISOTTO BECOMES ANOTHER NIGHT'S HEARTY CRUMB-COATED CAKES WITH A SPRIGHTLY SAUCE TO REALLY FRESHEN THINGS UP.

TONIGHT

VEGETABLE RISOTTO

PREP: 30 MINUTES **COOK:** 30 MINUTES
MAKES: 4 MAIN-DISH OR 8 SIDE-DISH SERVINGS

- 7 cups chicken broth
- 2 cups arborio rice or long grain rice
- 1 teaspoon paprika
- 2½ cups peeled and cubed butternut squash
- 2 small turnips, peeled and chopped
- 1½ cups chopped red sweet peppers (2)
- 1 cup coarsely chopped carrots (2 medium)
- 2 cups fresh cremini mushrooms, quartered
- 1¼ cups chopped zucchini (1 medium)
- ½ cup sliced green onions (4)
- 2 tablespoons olive oil
- Fresh thyme leaves

1 In a saucepan bring broth to boiling; reduce heat. Cover; keep warm. In a 4-quart pot combine rice, 1 cup *water*, and paprika; bring to boiling. Reduce heat; simmer and stir until most liquid is absorbed. Add squash, turnips, peppers, carrots, and 1 cup of the broth; bring to boiling. Reduce heat; simmer and stir until most liquid is absorbed. Add 5 cups of the broth, 1 cup at a time, stirring until liquid is absorbed (about 20 minutes).

2 Add mushrooms, zucchini, green onions, and remaining 1 cup broth. Cook and stir about 10 minutes or until liquid absorbs, vegetables are tender, and rice is tender yet slightly firm in center.

3 Remove from heat; stir in olive oil. Top with thyme. Serve half of the risotto. Reserve remaining half for Veggie Risotto Cakes in an airtight container in the refrigerator for up to 3 days.

PER 1½ CUPS: 495 cal., 7 g total fat (1 g sat. fat, 0 g trans fat), 0 mg chol., 1,711 mg sodium, 100 g carbo., 7 g fiber, 11 g pro. EXCHANGES: 3 Vegetable, 5½ Starch, ½ Fat

TOMORROW

VEGGIE RISOTTO CAKES

PREP: 30 MINUTES **COOK:** 16 MINUTES
OVEN: 300°F **MAKES:** 6 TO 7 MAIN-DISH SERVINGS

- ½ recipe Vegetable Risotto
- ½ cup grated Parmesan cheese
- 2 tablespoons snipped fresh Italian parsley
- 1 cup all-purpose flour
- 2 eggs, lightly beaten
- 1 cup fine dry bread crumbs
- 6 tablespoons olive oil
- 1 recipe Horseradish Sour Cream

1 Preheat oven to 300°F. In a large bowl stir together the Vegetable Risotto, Parmesan cheese, and parsley. Form mixture into 12 to fourteen ¾-inch-thick patties.

2 Place flour, eggs, and bread crumbs in three separate shallow dishes. Coat one patty with flour, tapping off excess. Coat in the eggs, letting excess drip off, then dip in the bread crumbs to coat. Repeat with remaining patties.

3 In a large skillet heat 3 tablespoons of the olive oil over medium heat. Add six to seven risotto patties in a single layer. Fry about 4 minutes or until golden on one side. Turn; fry about 4 minutes more or until second side is golden. Drain on paper towels. Repeat with remaining patties and oil. Keep risotto cakes warm in oven. Serve with Horseradish Sour Cream. Top with additional snipped parsley.

HORSERADISH SOUR CREAM: Stir together one 8-ounce carton dairy sour cream, 2 tablespoons prepared horseradish, and 2 teaspoons Dijon-style mustard.

PER 2 CAKES: 562 cal., 28 g total fat (8 g sat. fat, 0 g trans fat), 96 mg chol., 915 mg sodium, 64 g carbo., 4 g fiber, 14 g pro. EXCHANGES: 1 Vegetable, 4 Starch, 4½ Fat

RISOTTO

PREP: 10 MINUTES **COOK:** 15 MINUTES
MAKES: 4 SIDE-DISH SERVINGS

- ½ cup chopped onion (1 medium)
- 1 clove garlic, minced
- 2 tablespoons olive oil
- 2 tablespoons butter
- 1 cup arborio rice
- 2 14-ounce cans reduced-sodium chicken broth
- ½ cup finely shredded Parmesan or Asiago cheese
- ⅛ teaspoon black pepper

1 In a large saucepan cook onion and garlic in hot olive oil and 1 tablespoon of the butter until onion is tender; add rice. Cook and stir over medium heat for 2 to 3 minutes or until rice begins to brown.

2 Meanwhile, in another saucepan bring broth to boiling; reduce heat and simmer. Slowly add 1 cup of the broth to the rice mixture, stirring constantly. Continue to cook and stir over medium heat until liquid is absorbed. Add another ½ cup of the broth to the rice mixture, stirring constantly. Continue to cook and stir until the liquid is absorbed. Add remaining broth, ½ cup at a time, stirring constantly until the broth has been absorbed. (This should take 15 to 20 minutes.)

3 Stir in the remaining butter, Parmesan cheese, and pepper.

LEMON-ASPARAGUS RISOTTO: *(Photo, page 63.)* Prepare as directed, except add 1 cup chopped asparagus and 1 teaspoon finely shredded lemon peel to the risotto after half of the chicken broth has been stirred into the risotto.

PER ¾ CUP PLAIN OR LEMON-ASPARAGUS VARIATION: 289 cal., 15 g total fat (6 g sat. fat, 0 g trans fat), 22 mg chol., 683 mg sodium, 30 g carbo., 1 g fiber, 9 g pro. EXCHANGES: 2 Starch, ½ High-Fat Meat, 2 Fat

SPINACH-PEA RISOTTO: Prepare as directed, except stir 2 cups chopped fresh spinach, ½ cup frozen peas, and 2 teaspoons snipped fresh tarragon or ½ teaspoon dried tarragon, crushed, into the risotto with the butter, Parmesan cheese, and pepper. Cover and let stand 5 minutes.

PER ¾ CUP: 307 cal., 15 g total fat (6 g sat. fat, 0 g trans fat), 22 mg chol., 715 mg sodium, 33 g carbo., 2 g fiber, 10 g pro. EXCHANGES: 2 Starch, ½ Vegetable, ½ High-Fat Meat, 2 Fat

MUSHROOM RISOTTO: Prepare as directed, except cook 8 ounces sliced fresh assorted mushrooms (such as button, cremini, and/or stemmed shiitake) with the onion and garlic until tender and all liquid absorbs. If desired, substitute ½ cup dry white wine for ½ cup of the chicken broth. Stir in 1 tablespoon snipped fresh basil with the butter, Parmesan, and pepper.

PER ¾ CUP: 302 cal., 15 g total fat (6 g sat. fat, 0 g trans fat), 22 mg chol., 686 mg sodium, 32 g carbo., 1 g fiber, 11 g pro. EXCHANGES: 2 Starch, ½ Vegetable, ½ High-Fat Meat, 2 Fat

BAKED CHEESE GRITS

PREP: 15 MINUTES **BAKE:** 25 MINUTES
STAND: 5 MINUTES **OVEN:** 325°F
MAKES: 4 OR 5 SIDE-DISH SERVINGS

- 2 cups chicken broth
- ½ cup quick-cooking grits
- 1 egg, lightly beaten
- 1 cup shredded cheddar cheese (4 ounces)
- 2 tablespoons sliced green onion (1)
- 1 tablespoon butter
- ½ cup chopped fresh tomato (optional)
- 1 tablespoon snipped fresh cilantro (optional)

1 Preheat oven to 325°F. In a medium saucepan bring broth to boiling. Slowly add grits, stirring constantly. Gradually stir about ½ cup of the hot mixture into the egg. Return egg mixture to saucepan and stir to combine. Remove saucepan from heat. Stir cheese, green onion, and butter into grits until cheese and butter melt.

2 Pour grits mixture into an ungreased 1-quart casserole dish. Bake, uncovered, for 25 to 30 minutes or until a knife inserted near the center comes out clean. Let stand 5 minutes before serving. If desired, top with tomato and cilantro.

PER ⅔ CUP: 238 cal., 14 g total fat (8 g sat. fat, 0 g trans fat), 91 mg chol., 694 mg sodium, 17 g carbo., 0 g fiber, 11 g pro. EXCHANGES: 1 Starch, 1 High-Fat Meat, 1 Fat

THE NITTY-GRITTY ON GRITS
BE SURE TO PURCHASE QUICK-COOKING OR INSTANT GRITS TO USE IN THE ABOVE RECIPE. THE COARSER-GROUND VARIETY CAN TAKE MORE THAN TWICE AS LONG TO COOK.

POLENTA

PREP: 15 MINUTES **COOK:** 25 MINUTES
MAKES: 6 SIDE-DISH SERVINGS

1 cup coarse-ground yellow cornmeal*
1 cup cold water**
1 teaspoon salt

1 In a medium saucepan bring 2½ cups *water* to boiling. Meanwhile, in a medium bowl stir together cornmeal, the 1 cup cold water, and salt.

2 Slowly add cornmeal mixture to boiling water, stirring constantly. Cook and stir until mixture returns to boiling. Reduce heat to medium-low. Cook for 25 to 30 minutes or until mixture is very thick and tender, stirring frequently and adjusting heat as needed to maintain a slow boil. Spoon soft polenta into bowls.

*NOTE: TO USE REGULAR CORNMEAL: Increase water in saucepan to 2¾ cups; cook and stir just 10 to 15 minutes after mixture boils in Step 2.

**NOTE: For added flavor, use chicken broth in place of the water and omit the salt.

OPTIONAL STIR-INS:

■ Decrease salt to ½ teaspoon and stir in ½ cup shredded Parmesan, Romano, or fontina cheese (2 ounces) after cooking.

■ Stir in 2 tablespoons snipped fresh basil or Italian parsley or 1 teaspoon snipped fresh oregano or thyme after cooking.

■ Decrease salt to ½ teaspoon and stir in 2 tablespoons butter after cooking.

FIRM POLENTA: Prepare as directed, except pour the hot soft polenta into a 9-inch pie plate, spreading into an even layer. Let stand, uncovered, for 30 minutes. Cover and chill at least 1 hour or until firm. Preheat oven to 350°F. Bake polenta, uncovered, about 25 minutes or until heated through. Let stand on a wire rack for 5 minutes. Cut into six wedges to serve.

PER ½ CUP SOFT OR WEDGE FIRM POLENTA: 85 cal., 0 g total fat, 0 mg chol., 390 mg sodium, 18 g carbo., 1 g fiber, 2 g pro.
EXCHANGES: 1 Starch

FRIED POLENTA: Prepare as directed, except pour the hot soft polenta into a 7½×3½×2-inch or 8×4×2-inch loaf pan; cool. Cover and chill for at least 4 hours or overnight. Run a thin metal spatula around the edges of the pan. Remove polenta loaf from the pan and cut crosswise into 12 slices. In a large skillet or on a griddle heat 1 tablespoon butter over medium-high heat.

Reduce heat to medium. Cook half of the polenta slices for 16 to 20 minutes or until brown and crisp, turning once halfway through cooking. Repeat with remaining polenta slices, adding 1 tablespoon butter to skillet before adding polenta slices. If desired, serve with additional butter and honey or maple-flavored syrup.

PER 2 SLICES: 119 cal., 4 g total fat (2 g sat. fat, 0 g trans fat), 10 mg chol., 418 mg sodium, 18 g carbo., 1 g fiber, 2 g pro.
EXCHANGES: 1 Starch, 1 Fat

ROASTED VEGETABLES WITH POLENTA

PREP: 20 MINUTES **ROAST:** 15 MINUTES
OVEN: 425°F **MAKES:** 6 SIDE-DISH SERVINGS

6 cups vegetables, such as trimmed asparagus, thick slices red or green sweet peppers, sliced zucchini, quartered mushrooms, and/or red onion slices
¼ cup olive oil
¼ teaspoon salt
1 recipe Polenta (left) or one 16-ounce tube refrigerated cooked polenta
Shredded Parmesan cheese

1 Preheat oven to 425°F. In a shallow roasting pan combine vegetables, oil, and salt; toss to coat vegetables. Roast, uncovered, for 15 to 20 minutes or until vegetables are just tender; stirring once.

2 Meanwhile, prepare Polenta. Or slice refrigerated polenta and heat in skillet according to package directions.

3 To serve, spoon or arrange polenta into a shallow bowl. Spoon roasted vegetables on top of polenta. Sprinkle with Parmesan cheese.

PER ⅔ CUP VEGETABLES + ½ CUP POLENTA: 222 cal., 11 g total fat (2 g sat. fat, 0 g trans fat), 4 mg chol., 560 mg sodium, 25 g carbo., 4 g fiber, 6 g pro.
EXCHANGES: 1 Vegetable, 1½ Starch, 2 Fat

STIRRING SECRETS
AS YOU ADD THE CORNMEAL AND WATER MIXTURE TO THE BOILING WATER, WHISK IT CONSTANTLY. ONCE COMBINED, STIR WITH A WOODEN SPOON UNTIL IT REACHES A BOIL.

BABY SPINACH, COUSCOUS, AND BULGUR PLATTER

PREP: 30 MINUTES **CHILL:** 2 TO 24 HOURS
MAKES: 4 OR 5 MAIN-DISH SERVINGS

  2 cups vegetable broth or water
  ½ cup bulgur
  ½ teaspoon ground cumin
  ⅛ teaspoon black pepper
  ½ cup couscous
  1 15-ounce can garbanzo beans
      (chickpeas), rinsed and drained
  1 recipe Yogurt-Mint Salad Dressing
  5 cups prewashed packaged baby spinach
      or torn spinach
  1 cup coarsely chopped apple
  ½ of a small red onion, thinly sliced and
      separated into rings

1 In a medium saucepan combine broth, bulgur, cumin, ¼ teaspoon *salt*, and black pepper. Bring to boiling; reduce heat. Simmer, covered, about 10 minutes or until the bulgur is nearly tender. Remove from heat. Stir in couscous. Cover; let stand 5 minutes. Using a fork, fluff grain mixture. Transfer to a large bowl; cool slightly. Stir in beans. Cover; chill 2 to 24 hours or until completely chilled. Meanwhile, prepare Yogurt-Mint Salad Dressing.

2 To serve, arrange spinach on a serving platter or in bowls. Spoon grain mixture over spinach. Top with apple and onion. Drizzle dressing over salad.

YOGURT-MINT SALAD DRESSING: In a small bowl stir together ⅔ cup plain yogurt; ⅓ cup bottled red wine vinaigrette salad dressing; 2 tablespoons snipped fresh mint, cilantro, or Italian parsley; and ¼ teaspoon crushed red pepper. Serve immediately or cover and store in refrigerator for up to 1 week. Stir just before serving.

PER 1 CUP SPINACH + 1 CUP GRAIN MIXTURE: 354 cal., 9 g total fat (1 g sat. fat, 0 g trans fat), 2 mg chol., 1,318 mg sodium, 58 g carbo., 10 g fiber, 13 g pro.
EXCHANGES: 1 Vegetable, 3½ Starch, 1 Fat

KEEP IT PRETTY ONCE CUT, APPLES OXIDIZE AND TURN BROWN QUICKLY. TO SLOW THIS PROCESS, TOSS THE CHOPPED APPLES WITH LEMON JUICE BEFORE ADDING TO THE SALAD.

BABY SPINACH, COUSCOUS, AND BULGUR PLATTER

TABBOULEH

PREP: 25 MINUTES **CHILL:** 4 TO 24 HOURS
MAKES: 5 SIDE-DISH SERVINGS

- ¾ cup bulgur
- ¾ cup chopped cucumber
- ½ cup snipped fresh parsley
- ¼ cup thinly sliced green onions (2)
- 1 tablespoon snipped fresh mint
- 2 tablespoons water
- 3 tablespoons vegetable oil
- 3 tablespoons lemon juice
- ¼ teaspoon salt
- ¾ cup chopped tomato
- 4 Lettuce leaves
  Lemon slices (optional)

1 Place bulgur in a colander; rinse with cold water. In a large bowl combine bulgur, cucumber, parsley, green onions, and mint.

2 For dressing, in a screw-top jar combine water, oil, lemon juice, and salt. Cover and shake well. Drizzle dressing over bulgur mixture; toss to coat. Cover and chill for 4 to 24 hours. Stir tomato into bulgur mixture just before serving. Serve in a lettuce-lined bowl and, if desired, garnish with lemon slices.

PER 1 CUP: 161 cal., 9 g total fat (1 g sat. fat, 0 g trans fat), 0 mg chol., 128 mg sodium, 20 g carbo., 5 g fiber, 3 g pro. EXCHANGES: ½ Vegetable, 1 Starch, 1½ Fat

TABBOULEH WRAP OR PITA: To fill an 8-inch flour tortilla for a wrap, place several lettuce leaves in the center of the tortilla. Using a slotted spoon, top lettuce with ½ cup of the tabbouleh mixture. Fold bottom of tortilla halfway over the tabbouleh. Fold over sides and secure with a toothpick, forming a pocket. Or line pita bread halves with lettuce leaves. Place ½ cup of the tabbouleh mixture into the pocket of each bread half.

PER ½ CUP + WRAP: 240 cal., 8 g total fat (1 g sat. fat, 0 g trans fat), 0 mg chol., 323 mg sodium, 37 g carbo., 3 g fiber, 7.0 g pro. EXCHANGES: 2 Starch, ½ Vegetable, 1½ Fat

BEANS WITH PESTO BULGUR

PREP: 20 MINUTES **STAND:** 60 MINUTES
COOK: 75 MINUTES **MAKES:** 4 SIDE-DISH SERVINGS

- ¾ cup dried cranberry beans, dry Christmas (calico) lima beans, or dry pinto beans
- 1⅓ cups vegetable broth or chicken broth
- ⅔ cup bulgur
- ¾ cup chopped red sweet pepper (1 medium)
- ¼ cup thinly sliced green onions (2)
- ⅓ cup refrigerated basil pesto
  Lemon wedges

1 Rinse dry beans. In a large saucepan combine beans and 5 cups *water*. Bring to boiling; reduce heat. Simmer for 2 minutes. Remove from heat. Cover and let stand for 60 minutes. (Or place beans in water in a large saucepan. Cover and let soak in a cool place for 6 to 8 hours or overnight.)

2 Drain and rinse beans. Return beans to pan. Add 5 cups fresh *water*. Bring to boiling; reduce heat. Simmer, covered, for 75 to 90 minutes for cranberry or pinto beans, 45 to 60 minutes for Christmas limas, or until tender; drain.

3 Meanwhile, in a medium saucepan bring broth to boiling; add bulgur. Return to boiling; reduce heat. Simmer, covered, about 15 minutes or until most of the liquid is absorbed. Remove from heat. Stir in cooked beans, sweet pepper, green onions, and pesto. Season with *black pepper*. Serve warm or cover and refrigerate up to 3 days and serve chilled. Serve with lemon wedges.

SHORTCUT OPTION: Substitute one 15-ounce can pinto beans, drained, for the dried beans. Prepare as directed, except omit Steps 1 and 2.

PER ¾ CUP: 317 cal., 10 g total fat (2 g sat. fat, 0 g trans fat), 7 mg chol., 502 mg sodium, 46 g carbo., 15 g fiber, 14 g pro. EXCHANGES: 3 Starch, ½ Lean Meat, 1½ Fat

SQUASH, CORN, AND BARLEY SUCCOTASH

PREP: 20 MINUTES **COOK:** 40 MINUTES
MAKES: 12 SIDE-DISH SERVINGS

- 4 cups water
- ½ cup regular barley
- 1 teaspoon salt
- 1 tablespoon olive oil
- 1 cup finely chopped onion
- 1 2-pound butternut squash, peeled and cut into ½-inch cubes (about 4 cups)
- 1 cup reduced-sodium chicken broth
- ¼ teaspoon black pepper
- ⅛ teaspoon dried thyme, crushed
- 1 16-ounce package (about 3 cups) frozen whole kernel corn
- ¼ cup snipped fresh parsley

1 In a medium saucepan bring water to boiling. Add barley and ½ teaspoon of the salt. Return to boiling; reduce heat. Cover and simmer about 40 minutes or until barley is tender, stirring occasionally. Drain and set aside.

2 Meanwhile, in a very large skillet heat oil over medium-high heat. Add onion; cook and stir about 5 minutes or until tender. Stir in the remaining ½ teaspoon salt, squash, broth, pepper, and thyme. Bring to boiling; reduce heat. Cover and simmer 10 to 15 minutes or until squash is just tender. Stir in corn; cover and cook 5 minutes more. Stir in barley and parsley; heat through.

PER ⅔ CUP: 106 cal., 2 g total fat (0 g sat. fat, 0 g trans fat), 0 mg chol., 250 mg sodium, 22 g carbo., 4 g fiber, 3 g pro.
EXCHANGES: 1 Vegetable, 1 Starch

BEST EVER • WHOLE GRAIN

GREEK QUINOA AND AVOCADOS

PREP: 20 MINUTES **COOK:** 15 MINUTES
MAKES: 4 SIDE-DISH SERVINGS

- ½ cup uncooked quinoa, rinsed and drained
- 1 cup water
- 2 roma tomatoes, seeded and finely chopped
- ½ cup shredded fresh spinach
- ⅓ cup finely chopped red onion
- 2 tablespoons lemon juice
- 2 tablespoons olive oil
- ½ teaspoon salt
  Spinach leaves
- 2 ripe avocados, halved, seeded, peeled, and sliced*
- ⅓ cup crumbled feta cheese

1 In a small saucepan combine quinoa and water. Bring to boiling; reduce heat. Simmer, covered, about 15 minutes or until liquid is absorbed. Place quinoa in a medium bowl.

2 Add tomatoes, shredded spinach, and onion to quinoa; stir to combine. In a small bowl whisk together lemon juice, olive oil, and salt. Add to quinoa mixture; toss to coat.

3 Place spinach leaves on four salad plates. Arrange avocado slices on top of spinach leaves. Divide quinoa mixture evenly over avocado slices. Sprinkle each serving with some of the feta.

*NOTE: Brush avocado slices with additional lemon juice to prevent browning.

PER 1⅓ CUPS: 300 cal., 21 g total fat (4 g sat. fat, 0 g trans fat), 11 mg chol., 456 mg sodium, 24 g carbo., 7 g fiber, 7 g pro.
EXCHANGES: 1 Starch, 1½ Vegetable, 4 Fat

RINSED AND READY BE SURE TO RINSE QUINOA THOROUGHLY BEFORE COOKING TO REMOVE THE SAPONIN, A BITTER SUBSTANCE THAT COATS THE SEEDS.

SQUASH, CORN, AND BARLEY SUCCOTASH

GREEK QUINOA AND AVOCADOS

PEPPERS STUFFED
WITH QUINOA AND SPINACH

2 In a large skillet heat oil over medium-high heat. Add onion and garlic. Cook and stir 2 minutes. Add mushrooms. Cook and stir 4 to 5 minutes more or until mushrooms and onion are tender. Stir in ¼ teaspoon each salt and black pepper, undrained tomatoes, and spinach. Stir in quinoa mixture and ½ cup of the cheese. Remove from heat.

3 Cut peppers in half lengthwise. Remove and discard seeds and membranes from the peppers. Sprinkle insides of peppers lightly with additional salt and pepper. Fill pepper halves with quinoa mixture. Place peppers, filled sides up, in a 3-quart rectangular baking dish. Pour reserved cooking liquid into dish around peppers.

4 Bake, covered, 35 minutes. Uncover; top each with remaining cheese. Bake, uncovered, about 10 more minutes or until peppers are crisp-tender and cheese is brown.

PER 2 STUFFED PEPPER HALVES: 415 cal., 22 g total fat (10 g sat. fat, 0 g trans fat), 45 mg chol., 1,206 mg sodium, 39 g carbo., 9 g fiber, 19 g pro.
EXCHANGES: 3 Vegetable, 1½ Starch, 1 High-Fat Meat, 2½ Fat

WHOLE GRAIN

PEPPERS STUFFED WITH QUINOA AND SPINACH

PREP: 25 MINUTES **COOK:** 18 MINUTES
BAKE: 45 MINUTES **OVEN:** 400°F
MAKES: 4 MAIN-DISH SERVINGS OR
8 SIDE-DISH SERVINGS

- 1 14-ounce can vegetable broth
- ¼ cup quick-cooking barley
- ¼ cup uncooked quinoa, rinsed and drained
- 2 tablespoons olive oil
- ½ cup chopped onion (1 medium)
- 2 cloves garlic, minced
- 2 cups sliced fresh mushrooms
- ¼ teaspoon each salt and black pepper
- 1 14.5-ounce can diced tomatoes
- ½ of a 10-ounce package frozen chopped spinach, thawed and well drained
- 1½ cups Monterey Jack cheese with jalapeño peppers or Monterey Jack cheese, shredded (6 ounces)
- 4 large red sweet peppers
   Salt and black pepper

1 Preheat oven to 400°F. In a medium saucepan bring broth to boiling. Add barley and quinoa. Return to boiling; reduce heat. Cook, covered, about 12 minutes or until tender. Drain, reserving cooking liquid; set aside.

WHOLE GRAIN

SUMMER SPELT MEDLEY

PREP: 20 MINUTES **COOK:** 60 MINUTES
CHILL: 1 TO 24 HOURS **MAKES:** 8 SIDE-DISH SERVINGS

- 1½ cups uncooked spelt
   Water
- 1 cup chopped red sweet pepper
- 1 cup chopped, seeded cucumber
- ½ cup shredded carrot
- ¼ cup sliced green onions (2)
- ⅔ cup mayonnaise
- 2 tablespoons lemon juice
- ½ teaspoon salt
- ⅛ teaspoon cayenne pepper

1 In a medium saucepan combine spelt and enough water to cover by 2 inches. Bring to boiling; reduce heat. Simmer, covered, about 60 minutes or until tender. Drain well; place spelt in a large bowl.

2 Add sweet pepper, cucumber, carrots, and green onions to spelt; stir to combine. In a small bowl whisk together mayonnaise, lemon juice, salt, and cayenne pepper. Add to spelt mixture and toss to coat. Cover and refrigerate for 1 to 24 hours.

PER ¾ CUP: 276 cal., 16 g total fat (3 g sat. fat, 0 g trans fat), 7 mg chol., 255 mg sodium, 28 g carbo., 4 g fiber, 5 g pro.
EXCHANGES: 2 Starch, 3 Fat

COOKING GRAINS

Pour the measured amount of water into a medium saucepan. Bring the water to a full boil, unless the chart specifies otherwise. If desired, add ¼ teaspoon salt to the water. Slowly add the grain and return to boiling; reduce heat. Simmer, covered, for the time specified or until most of the water is absorbed and the grain is tender.

Grain	Amount of Grain	Amount of Water	Cooking Directions	Yield
Barley, quick-cooking pearl	1¼ cups	2 cups	Simmer, covered, for 10 to 12 minutes. Drain, if necessary.	3 cups
Barley, regular pearl	¾ cup	3 cups	Simmer, covered, about 45 minutes. Drain, if necessary.	3 cups
Buckwheat groats or kasha	⅔ cup	1½ cups	Add to cold water. Bring to boiling. Simmer, covered, for 6 to 8 minutes.	2¼ cups
Bulgur	1 cup	2 cups	Add to cold water. Bring to boiling. Simmer, covered, about 15 minutes.	3 cups
Farina, quick-cooking	¾ cup	3½ cups	Simmer, uncovered, for 2 to 3 minutes, stirring constantly.	3½ cups
Hominy grits, quick-cooking	¾ cup	3 cups	Simmer, covered, about 5 minutes, stirring occasionally.	3 cups
Millet	¾ cup	2 cups	Simmer, covered, for 15 to 20 minutes. Let stand, covered, for 5 minutes.	3 cups
Oats, rolled, quick-cooking	1½ cups	3 cups	Simmer, uncovered, for 1 minute. Let stand, covered, for 3 minutes.	3 cups
Oats, rolled, regular	1⅔ cups	3 cups	Simmer, uncovered, for 5 to 7 minutes. Let stand, covered, for 3 minutes.	3 cups
Oats, steel-cut	1⅓ cups	4 cups	Cook in large saucepan. Add ½ teaspoon salt. Simmer, covered, 25 to 30 minutes.	4 cups
Quinoa	¾ cup	1½ cups	Rinse well. Simmer, covered, about 15 minutes. Drain, if necessary.	1¾ cups
Rice, long grain white	1 cup	2 cups	Simmer, covered, about 15 minutes. Let stand, covered, for 5 minutes.	3 cups
Rice, regular brown	1 cup	2 cups	Simmer, covered, about 45 minutes. Let stand, covered, for 5 minutes.	3 cups
Rice, wild	1 cup	2 cups	Rinse well. Simmer, covered, about 40 minutes or until most of the water is absorbed. Drain, if necessary.	3 cups
Rye berries	¾ cup	2½ cups	Simmer, covered, about 60 minutes; drain. (Or soak berries in 2½ cups water in the refrigerator for 6 to 24 hours. Do not drain. Bring to boiling; reduce heat. Simmer, covered, for 30 minutes.)	2 cups
Spelt	1 cup	3 cups	Simmer, covered, for 50 to 60 minutes.	2½ cups
Wheat, cracked	⅔ cup	1½ cups	Add to cold water. Bring to boiling. Simmer, covered, for 12 to 15 minutes. Let stand, covered, for 5 minutes.	1¾ cups
Wheat berries	¾ cup	2½ cups	Simmer, covered, for 45 to 60 minutes; drain. (Or soak and cook as for rye berries.)	2 cups

COOKING DRY BEANS, LENTILS, AND SPLIT PEAS

Rinse beans, lentils, or split peas. (See special cooking instructions below for black-eyed peas, fava beans, lentils, and split peas.) In a large Dutch oven combine 1 pound beans and 8 cups cold water. Bring to boiling; reduce heat. Simmer for 2 minutes. Remove from heat. Cover and let stand for 60 minutes. (Or omit cooking step and soak beans in cold water overnight in a covered Dutch oven.) Drain and rinse. In the same Dutch oven combine beans and 8 cups fresh water. Bring to boiling; reduce heat. Simmer, covered, for time listed below or until beans are tender, stirring occasionally. Cooking time depends on the dryness of the beans.

Variety	Amount	Appearance	Cooking Time	Yield
Black beans	1 pound	Small, black, oval	60 to 90 minutes	6 cups
Black-eyed peas	1 pound	Small, cream color, oval (one side has a black oval with a cream-color dot in the center)	Do not presoak. Simmer, covered, for 45 minutes to 60 minutes.	7 cups
Cranberry beans	1 pound	Small, tan color with specks and streaks of burgundy, oval	75 to 90 minutes	7 cups
Fava or broad beans	1 pound	Large, brown, flat oval	Follow these soaking directions instead of those above: Bring beans to boiling; simmer, covered, 15 to 30 minutes to soften skins. Let stand 60 minutes. Drain and peel. To cook, combine peeled beans and 8 cups fresh water. Bring to boiling; simmer, covered, 45 to 50 minutes or until tender.	6 cups
Garbanzo beans (chickpeas)	1 pound	Medium, yellow or golden, round and irregular	90 minutes to 2 hours	6¼ cups
Great Northern beans	1 pound	Small to medium, white, kidney shape	60 to 90 minutes	7 cups
Kidney beans, red	1 pound	Medium to large, brownish red, kidney shape	60 to 90 minutes	6⅔ cups
Lentils (brown, French, red, or yellow)	1 pound	Tiny, disk shape	Do not presoak. Use 5 cups water. Simmer brown, French, and yellow, covered, 25 to 30 minutes; simmer red, covered, 5 to 10 minutes.	7 cups
Lima beans, baby	1 pound	Small, off-white, wide oval	45 minutes to 60 minutes	6½ cups
Lima beans, Christmas (calico)	1 pound	Medium, burgundy and cream color, wide oval	45 minutes to 60 minutes	6½ cups
Lima beans, large (butter beans)	1 pound	Medium, off-white, wide oval	60 to 75 minutes	6½ cups
Navy or pea beans	1 pound	Small, off-white, oval	60 to 90 minutes	6¼ cups
Pinto beans	1 pound	Small, tan color with brown specks, oval	75 to 90 minutes	6½ cups
Red beans	1 pound	Small, dark red, oval	60 to 90 minutes	6½ cups
Soybeans	1 pound	Small, cream color, oval	3 to 3½ hours	7 cups
Split peas	1 pound	Tiny, green or yellow, disk shape	Do not presoak. Use 5 cups water. Simmer, covered, about 45 minutes.	5½ cups

BEVERAGES

SUMMER FRUIT
DAIQUIRIS, PAGE 98

BEVERAGES

HERE'S HOW TO MAKE EVERYTHING YOU DRINK—FROM YOUR MORNING CUP OF JOE TO YOUR FAVORITE NIGHTCAP—MORE DASHING.

JAVA JIVE

Most coffee lovers are quite particular about their brew. Key into these concepts to make it *your* way:

■ The longer the beans are roasted, the darker they get. Choose light beans for lighter flavor, darker beans for stronger flavor.

■ Ground coffee loses its freshness quickly, so it's best to purchase beans whole and grind them fresh each time you make coffee.

■ Whole beans stay fresh about a week, so buy only what you'll need for the week. Store beans at room temperature in an airtight container.

■ Follow manufacturer's guidelines for your coffee maker for fine or coarse grind. Coffee too coarsely ground can result in weak flavor; if it's too finely ground, it can taste bitter and clog the filter.

COFFEE-MAKING EQUIPMENT

Automatic drip coffeemakers are convenient and make reliably good coffee, but coffee lovers often prefer to use a manual drip kind or a French press. These let you control the temperature of the water used to brew the coffee. A few hints:

■ For each 6-ounce cup, use ¾ cup fresh, cold water and 1 to 2 tablespoons ground coffee, depending on how strong you like your brew.

■ For manual drip makers, bring water to a full boil. Take the kettle off the heat and pause for a moment before pouring the water into the coffee. Water just under boiling (195°F to 205°F) releases coffee's compounds at their flavorful best.

■ To use a French press, measure coffee into the carafe. Heat water as for a manual drip maker. Pour water over coffee; place lid on carafe. Wait for 4 minutes; slowly press plunger to bottom of carafe, trapping the grounds, before serving.

TEA FOR YOU

Tea is available in bags or in loose-leaf form. Loose-leaf tea requires an infuser (such as a tea ball or spoon) or a strainer; bags do not.

HOT TEA: Use 1 bag or about 1 teaspoon loose-leaf tea per cup. Bring fresh, cool water to a full boil. If using loose-leaf tea, place it into an infuser. Warm a teapot by filling it with boiling water; let it stand a minute until pot is warmed. Empty the pot. Place infuser or tea bag(s) into the pot. If not using an infuser or bag(s), place tea directly into pot. Add more boiling water; cover pot and let steep for 3 to 5 minutes. Remove bag(s) or infuser, or pour loose tea through a strainer into teacup(s) to serve.

TRADITIONAL ICED TEA: Using 4 cups of water and 4 to 8 teaspoons loose tea or 4 to 8 tea bags, prepare tea as above. Steep as directed; remove bags and let tea cool for 2 hours at room temperature. Serve over ice; refrigerate leftovers.

REFRIGERATOR-BREWED TEA: Place 6 to 8 tea bags in 1½ quarts cold water; cover. Let "brew" in the refrigerator about 24 hours. Remove tea bags and serve tea over ice. In a hurry? Use instant tea or "cold brew" tea bags according to package directions.

A French press produces a richly textured coffee rife with natural oils. Some sediment will remain in the coffee—fans of the French press feel this adds character to the brew.

ANATOMY OF A COCKTAIL

In spite of their sophistication, cocktails require just a few basic concepts to make. Most cocktails consist of three basic parts plus finishing touches.

THE BASE: Spirits, such as bourbon, vodka, tequila, and gin.

MODIFIERS: Ingredients that enhance the drink without overpowering it, such as sodas, sparkling wines, and mild or sweet fruit juices.

ACCENTS: Stronger-flavor ingredients often used in small amounts. These include lemon and lime juice, liqueurs, bitters, and grenadine.

FINISHING TOUCHES: Cocktails usually get olives, cherries, or citrus curls or wedges added.

TOOLS OF THE TRADE

Though master mixologists take pride in owning all kinds of bar gadgets, you can make many classic drinks with the following simple tools.

■ A cocktail shaker to quickly chill the drink's ingredients without watering them down.

■ A strainer, fit over the mouth of the shaker, to catch the ice and solids when pouring into a glass.

■ A jigger to measure liquids. A standard jigger measures 1½ ounces; some jiggers have two ends, with a 1-ounce cup on one end and a 1½-ounce cup on the other. If you don't have a jigger, use a tablespoon measure (3 tablespoons equals 1½ ounces).

■ A juicer to squeeze fresh citrus juice and strain seeds. Note that using freshly squeezed citrus juices—rather than bottled juice—will greatly enhance your cocktails.

■ A bar spoon or long-handled spoon for stirring drinks directly in the glass.

■ Glassware. The three most essential bar glasses are the martini glass, the Collins (or highball) glass, and the rocks (or old-fashioned) glass.

EIGHT POPULAR WINES

Here are the general characteristics of eight easy-to-find wines, along with food pairing suggestions.

REDS

CABERNET SAUVIGNON: Bold and full, with cassis, black cherry, and sometimes cedarlike flavors. Pair with grilled and broiled steaks and lamb.

MERLOT: A soft and fruity wine; often less mouth-drying (tannic) than Cabernet Sauvignon. Try with beef, pork, burgers, red-sauced pasta, and pizza.

PINOT NOIR: A silky, elegant wine with bright, red-fruit flavors and sometimes earthy, smoky notes. Enjoy with salmon, poultry, and meat dishes, especially those featuring mushrooms.

SHIRAZ/SYRAH: Full-bodied, with vivid plum and black-fruit flavors and often smoky, spicy notes. Pair with lamb, pizza, burgers, and barbecue.

WHITES

CHARDONNAY: Exhibits pear, apple, and/or tropical fruit notes. Some styles are rich and buttery, sometimes with strong oak nuances. Enjoy with creamy pasta, seafood, and roast chicken.

PINOT GRIGIO: Light bodied, with mild peach and citrus notes. Try with light fish and chicken dishes.

RIESLING: Bright and fruity; ranges from sweet to dry and often has floral, peach, and citrus tones. Pair with pork, ham, chicken, and spicy foods.

SAUVIGNON BLANC: Bright and citrusy, often with grassy or herblike aromas. Enjoy with chicken and fish, flavored with tomatoes, herbs, and/or feta cheese.

MIX MASTER CREATE YOUR OWN HOUSE COCKTAIL WITH THIS BASIC FORMULA: 2 PARTS SPIRIT, 1 PART SWEETENER (LIQUEUR OR SUGAR), AND 1 PART JUICE, SUCH AS LEMON, LIME, OR ORANGE.

ICED GREEN TEA

PREP: 25 MINUTES **COOL:** SEVERAL HOURS
MAKES: 12 SERVINGS

    12 cups water
    ¼ to ½ cup sugar
     3 inches fresh ginger, peeled and thinly
        sliced
    12 green tea bags
        Ice cubes

1 In a large saucepan combine water, sugar, and ginger. Bring to boiling; reduce heat. Simmer, covered, for 5 minutes. Remove from heat. Add tea bags; cover and let stand for 3 minutes. Remove and discard tea bags. Strain ginger from tea; discard ginger. Transfer tea to a 2-gallon pitcher or punch bowl. Cover; cool for several hours. If desired, chill. Serve tea in tall glasses over ice.

PER 8 OUNCES: 18 cal., 0 g total fat, 0 mg chol., 8 mg sodium, 5 g carbo., 0 g fiber, 0 g pro.
EXCHANGES: Free

POMEGRANATE ICED GREEN TEA: Stir one 15.2-ounce bottle (1¾ cups) pomegranate juice into the tea mixture after straining ginger from tea. Continue as above. Makes 14 servings.

PER 8 OUNCES: 32 cal., 0 g total fat, 0 mg chol., 10 mg sodium, 8 carbo., 0 g fiber, 0 g pro.
EXCHANGES: ½ Other Carbo.

CHAI

START TO FINISH: 15 MINUTES
MAKES: 2 SERVINGS

     1 cup water
     2 black tea bags, such as orange pekoe,
        English breakfast, Lapsang Souchong,
        or Darjeeling
     1 3-inch piece stick cinnamon
     1 cup milk
     2 tablespoons raw sugar, granulated sugar,
        or honey
     1 teaspoon vanilla
    ¼ teaspoon ground ginger
    ⅛ teaspoon ground cardamom

1 In a small saucepan combine water, tea bags, and cinnamon stick. Bring to boiling. Remove from heat. Cover and let stand for 5 minutes. Remove and discard tea bags and cinnamon stick.

MOCHA COFFEE COOLER

2 Whisk the milk, sugar, vanilla, ginger, and cardamom into the tea. Heat and stir over medium heat just until heated through (do not boil).

PER 8 OUNCES: 122 cal., 2 g total fat (2 g sat. fat, 0 g trans fat), 10 mg chol., 55 mg sodium, 20 g carbo., 1 g fiber, 4 g pro.
EXCHANGES: ½ Milk, 1 Other Carbo., ½ Fat

MOCHA COFFEE COOLER

START TO FINISH: 5 MINUTES **MAKES:** 4 SERVINGS

     1 cup strong coffee, chilled
     1 cup half-and-half, light cream, or milk
     3 tablespoons chocolate-flavored syrup
     2 tablespoons sugar
     1 cup ice cubes
        Chocolate-flavored syrup (optional)

1 In a blender combine coffee, half-and-half, chocolate syrup, and sugar. Cover and blend until combined. Add ice cubes; cover and blend until nearly smooth. If desired, drizzle additional chocolate syrup around insides of glasses. Pour coffee mixture into glasses.

PER 7 OUNCES: 142 cal., 7 g total fat (4 g sat. fat, 0 g trans fat), 22 mg chol., 36 mg sodium, 18 g carbo., 0 g fiber, 2 g pro.
EXCHANGES: 1 Other Carbo., 1½ Fat

HOT ORANGE MOCHA

START TO FINISH: 20 MINUTES
MAKES: 6 SERVINGS

- 1 orange
- 5 cups hot strong coffee
- ½ cup unsweetened cocoa powder
- ½ cup packed brown sugar
- ¼ teaspoon ground cinnamon
- ½ cup whipping cream, half-and-half, or light cream
- 1 recipe Whipped Honey-Orange Topping
  Orange peel curls (optional)

1 Using a vegetable peeler, remove the peel from the orange in strips, being careful not to remove the white pith. In a large saucepan combine the peel and hot coffee. Let stand over medium-low heat for 5 minutes. Remove and discard orange peel.

2 Meanwhile, in a small bowl whisk together cocoa powder, brown sugar, and cinnamon. Whisk cocoa mixture into hot coffee until well combined. Stir in cream. If desired, use an immersion blender to froth the coffee mixture. Ladle coffee mixture into six coffee mugs. Top each serving with a spoonful of Whipped Honey-Orange Topping. If desired, garnish with orange peel curls.

WHIPPED HONEY-ORANGE TOPPING: In a mixing bowl combine ½ cup whipping cream, 1 tablespoon honey, and, if desired, 1 tablespoon (½ ounce) orange liqueur or orange juice. Beat with an electric mixer on low speed or beat with a whisk until soft peaks form (tips curl).

ICY ORANGE MOCHA: Prepare as directed, except cover and chill coffee mixture for up to 3 days. Serve in tall glasses over ice.

PER 7 OUNCES HOT OR ICY VARIATION: 246 cal., 16 g total fat (10 g sat. fat, 0 g trans fat), 55 mg chol., 26 mg sodium, 28 g carbo., 3 g fiber, 3 g pro.
EXCHANGES: 2 Other Carbo., 3 Fat

VANILLA CAFÉ LATTE

START TO FINISH: 5 MINUTES **MAKES:** 1 SERVING

- ¼ cup hot espresso or hot strong coffee
- 2 teaspoons vanilla-flavored syrup (syrup used to flavor beverages) or 1 teaspoon sugar and ¼ teaspoon vanilla
- 2 to 3 tablespoons steamed milk
- 2 tablespoons frothed milk*
  Ground cinnamon or grated chocolate

1 Pull the espresso or pour the coffee into a 6-ounce cup. Stir in vanilla syrup. Add steamed milk and top with frothed milk. Sprinkle with cinnamon.

***NOTE:** To make frothed milk, use the steam wand on your espresso machine to steam and froth the milk. Or place hot, but not boiling, milk in a blender. Cover and blend until froth forms on top of the milk. Or place the hot milk in a deep bowl and use an immersion blender to blend the milk until froth forms on top.

PER 4 OUNCES: 55 cal., 1 g total fat (1 g sat. fat, 0 g trans fat), 5 mg chol., 26 mg sodium, 9 g carbo., 0 g fiber, 2 g pro.
EXCHANGES: ½ Other Carbo.

HOT COFFEE LATTE EGGNOG

START TO FINISH: 30 MINUTES
MAKES: 8 SERVINGS

- 3 eggs, lightly beaten
- 2 cups whole milk
- 1 cup whipping cream
- ½ cup (4 ounces) coffee liqueur
- 2 tablespoons honey
- 1 tablespoon instant espresso coffee powder or 4 teaspoons instant coffee crystals
  Whipped cream (optional)
  Ground cinnamon
- 8 long cinnamon sticks (optional)

1 In a large heavy saucepan stir together the eggs, milk, whipping cream, coffee liqueur, honey, and espresso powder (see photo 1, page 91). Cook and stir over medium heat for 20 to 25 minutes or until milk mixture just coats a metal spoon (see photo 2, page 91); do not let boil. (Milk mixture should register 170°F on an instant-read thermometer.)

2 Pour hot eggnog into coffee cups or mugs. If desired, top each serving with whipped cream (see photo 3, page 91). Sprinkle with cinnamon and, if desired, serve with cinnamon sticks.

PER 4 OUNCES: 238 cal., 15 g total fat (9 g sat. fat, 0 g trans fat), 127 mg chol., 64 mg sodium, 14 g carbo., 0 g fiber, 5 g pro.
EXCHANGES: 1 Other Carbo., ½ Very Lean Meat, 3½ Fat

ALCOHOL-FREE COFFEE LATTE EGGNOG:
Prepare as directed, except omit the coffee liqueur and increase the milk to 2½ cups.

PER 4 OUNCES: 194 cal., 15 g total fat (9 g sat. fat, 0 g trans fat), 128 mg chol., 69 mg sodium, 9 carbo., 0 g fiber, 6 g pro.
EXCHANGES: ½ Other Carbo., ½ Lean Meat, 3 Fat

PREPARING HOT COFFEE LATTE EGGNOG, STEP-BY-STEP

1. Use a whisk to thoroughly combine the eggs, milk, cream, liqueur, honey, and espresso powder. Cook over heat that is just high enough to cook but not enough to boil. **2.** Dip a metal spoon into the mixture and swipe your finger across the back; your finger will leave a mark when the mixture is done. **3.** Drop a spoonful of whipped cream into each cup.

EGGNOG

PREP: 15 MINUTES **CHILL:** 4 TO 24 HOURS
MAKES: 7 SERVINGS

- 4 egg yolks, beaten
- 2 cups milk
- ⅓ cup sugar
- 1 cup whipping cream
- 2 tablespoons (1 ounce) light rum
- 2 tablespoons (1 ounce) bourbon
- 1 teaspoon vanilla
  Ground nutmeg

1 In a large saucepan stir together yolks, milk, and sugar. Cook and stir over medium heat until milk mixture just coats a metal spoon (see photo 2, page 91); do not let boil. Place pan in a sink or bowl of ice water; stir for 2 minutes. Stir in cream, rum, bourbon, and vanilla. Cover; chill for 4 to 24 hours. Serve in glasses. Sprinkle with nutmeg.

PER 4 OUNCES: 241 cal., 17 g total fat (10 g sat. fat, 0 g trans fat), 172 mg chol., 46 mg sodium, 14 g carbo., 0 g fiber, 5 g pro.
EXCHANGES: 1 Other Carbo., ½ Lean Meat, 3½ Fat

LOWER-FAT EGGNOG: Prepare as directed, except omit whipping cream and use 3 cups milk.

PER 4 OUNCES: 141 cal., 5 g total fat (2 g sat. fat, 0 g trans fat), 128 mg chol., 48 mg sodium, 15 g carbo., 0 g fiber, 5 g pro.
EXCHANGES: 1 Other Carbo., ½ Lean Meat, 1½ Fat

ALCOHOL-FREE EGGNOG: Prepare as directed, except omit the rum and bourbon and increase the milk to 2⅓ cups.

PER 4 OUNCES: 229 cal., 15 g total fat (10 g sat. fat, 0 trans fat), 173 mg chol., 51 mg sodium, 15 g carbo., 0 g fiber, 5 g pro.
EXCHANGES: 1 Other Carbo., ½ Lean Meat, 3 Fat

FAST

HOT CHOCOLATE MIX

START TO FINISH: 15 MINUTES
MAKES: 16 CUPS MIX (ENOUGH FOR 32 SERVINGS)

- 1 25.6-ounce package nonfat dry milk powder
- 1 16-ounce jar powdered nondairy creamer
- 1 8-ounce container unsweetened cocoa powder, sifted
- 2 cups powdered sugar
  Tiny marshmallows (optional)

1 In an extra-large bowl combine dry milk powder, nondairy creamer, cocoa powder, and sugar. Store in a tightly covered container for up to 3 months.

2 For one serving, place ½ cup of the mix in a mug or cup and add ½ cup boiling water. If desired, top with marshmallows.

PER 6 OUNCES: 197 cal., 5 g total fat (4 g sat. fat, 0 g trans fat), 4 mg chol., 126 mg sodium, 30 g carbo., 2 g fiber, 9 g pro.
EXCHANGES: 1 Milk, 1 Other Carbo., 1 Fat

MALTED HOT CHOCOLATE MIX: Prepare as directed, except add one 13-ounce jar malted milk powder to the dry mix. Makes about 18 cups mix (enough for 36 servings).

PER 6 OUNCES: 219 cal., 5 g total fat (4 g sat. fat, 0 trans fat), 6 mg chol., 154 mg sodium, 34 g carbo., 2 g fiber, 10 g pro.
EXCHANGES: 1 Milk, 1½ Other Carbo., 1 Fat

FAST

HOT CHOCOLATE

START TO FINISH: 15 MINUTES
MAKES: 6 SERVINGS

- 2 ounces semisweet chocolate, chopped, or ⅓ cup semisweet chocolate pieces
- ⅓ cup sugar
- 4 cups milk
- 1 tablespoon instant coffee crystals (optional)
  Whipped cream or tiny marshmallows (optional)

1 In a medium saucepan combine chocolate, sugar, and ½ cup of the milk. Cook and stir over medium heat until mixture just comes to boiling. Stir in remaining milk and, if desired, coffee crystals; heat through but do not boil. Remove from heat.

2 If desired, beat mixture with an immersion blender or rotary beater until frothy. Serve in mugs. If desired, top with whipped cream or tiny marshmallows.

SPICED HOT CHOCOLATE: Prepare as directed, except without coffee crystals; whisk ½ teaspoon ground cinnamon and ¼ teaspoon ground nutmeg into chocolate mixture with remaining milk.

PER 6 OUNCES PLAIN OR SPICED VARIATION: 170 cal., 6 g total fat (4 g sat. fat, 0 g trans fat), 13 mg chol., 68 mg sodium, 25 g carbo., 1 g fiber, 6 g pro.
EXCHANGES: ½ Milk, 1 Other Carbo., 1 Fat

LOW-FAT HOT CHOCOLATE: Prepare as directed, except substitute ¼ cup unsweetened cocoa powder for the chocolate and use fat-free milk.

PER 6 OUNCES: 106 cal., 1 g total fat (0 g sat. fat, 0 g trans fat), 3 mg chol., 69 mg sodium, 21 g carbo., 1 g fiber, 6 g pro.
EXCHANGES: ½ Milk, 1 Other Carbo.

HAZELNUT HOT CHOCOLATE: Prepare as directed on page 92, except substitute ⅓ cup chocolate-hazelnut spread for the chocolate. Whisk the hazelnut mixture together before bringing to boiling.

PER 6 OUNCES: 196 cal., 7 g total fat (2 g sat. fat, 0 g trans fat), 13 mg chol., 80 mg sodium, 27 g carbo., 0 g fiber, 6 g pro.
EXCHANGES: ½ Milk, 1½ Other Carbo., 1½ Fat

BEST EVER • FAST

WHITE HOT CHOCOLATE

START TO FINISH: 20 MINUTES
MAKES: 4 SERVINGS

- 3 ounces white baking chocolate with cocoa butter, chopped
- 2 cups milk, half-and-half, or light cream
- ⅓ cup hot strong coffee
- ½ teaspoon vanilla
  Vanilla ice cream (optional)
  Grated nutmeg or chocolate-flavored sprinkles (optional)

1 In a medium saucepan combine white chocolate and ⅓ cup of the milk. Cook and stir over low heat until chocolate melts. Add remaining milk. Stir until heated through. Add coffee and vanilla. Serve in mugs. If desired, top with ice cream and sprinkle with nutmeg.

PER 5½ OUNCES: 184 cal., 9 g total fat (6 g sat. fat, 0 g trans fat), 14 mg chol., 73 mg sodium, 18 g carbo., 0 g fiber, 6 g pro.
EXCHANGES: ½ Milk, ½ Other Carbo., 1½ Fat

BRANDIED WHITE HOT CHOCOLATE: Prepare as directed, except add 2 or 3 tablespoons (1 to 1½ ounces) brandy to the saucepan when adding coffee and vanilla.

PER 5½ OUNCES: 202 cal., 9 g total fat (6 g sat. fat, 0 g trans fat), 14 mg chol., 73 mg sodium, 18 g carbo., 0 g fiber, 6 g pro.
EXCHANGES: ½ Milk, ½ Other Carbo., 2½ Fat

FAST • LOW FAT • HEALTHY

HOT SPICED CIDER

PREP: 10 MINUTES **COOK:** 10 MINUTES
MAKES: 8 SERVINGS

- 8 cups apple cider or apple juice
- ¼ cup packed brown sugar
- 6 inches stick cinnamon
- 1 teaspoon whole allspice
- 1 teaspoon whole cloves
- 2 3×¾-inch strips orange peel
- 8 thin orange wedges (optional)

1 In a large saucepan combine cider and brown sugar. For spice bag, place cinnamon, allspice, cloves, and orange peel in the center of a double-thick, 6-inch square of 100-percent-cotton cheesecloth (see photo 1, below). Tie closed with clean kitchen string (see photo 2, below). Add bag to the saucepan. Bring to boiling; reduce heat. Simmer, covered, for 10 minutes. Remove and discard spice bag. Serve cider in mugs. If desired, garnish with orange wedges.

PER 8 OUNCES: 143 cal., 0 g total fat, 0 mg chol., 13 mg sodium, 35 g carbo., 1 g fiber, 0 g pro.
EXCHANGES: 2 Other Carbo.

PREPARING A SPICE BAG, STEP-BY-STEP

1. Layer two 6-inch squares of cheesecloth on a work surface. Pile the stick cinnamon, allspice, cloves, and orange peel in the middle of the cheesecloth. **2.** Gather the edges of the cheesecloth up around the spices to make a bundle. Tie the bundle closed with cotton kitchen string.

MAKE-IT-MINE PUNCH

ONE BEAUTIFUL PUNCH LETS YOU SERVE A CROWD WITHOUT SPENDING PRECIOUS PARTY TIME TAKING DRINK ORDERS. CUSTOMIZE YOUR OWN FESTIVE SIPPER AND SERVE IN GLASSES WITH FRUIT-FILLED ICE SHARDS OR IN A BOWL WITH AN ICE RING.

BASIC INGREDIENTS

PREP: 15 MINUTES
CHILL: 4 HOURS
MAKES: 16 TO 18 SERVINGS
(ABOUT 8 OUNCES EACH)

- 4 cups water
- 1 12-ounce can Frozen Juice Concentrate, thawed
- 1 cup sugar
- 2½ cups Juice Blend, chilled
- 1 2-liter bottle Carbonated Beverage, chilled
  Ice Shards, Ice Ring, or ice cubes
- 1 cup Stir-In (optional)

FROZEN JUICE CONCENTRATE (PICK ONE)

Cranberry juice
Lemonade
Limeade
Orange juice
Pineapple juice

JUICE BLEND (PICK ONE)

Cranberry-apple juice
Pineapple-orange-banana juice blend
Pink grapefruit juice
Pomegranate juice
Raspberry juice blend
Strawberry juice blend

CARBONATED BEVERAGE (PICK ONE)

Cream soda
Ginger ale
Lemon-lime carbonated beverage
Orange carbonated beverage
Strawberry carbonated beverage

STIR-IN (PICK ONE)

Citrus fruit slices
Kiwifruit slices
Rum, vodka, gin, bourbon, or tequila
Sherbet or sorbet
Sliced fresh strawberries

BASIC INSTRUCTIONS

1 In a large pitcher or bowl combine the water and desired Frozen Juice Concentrate. Add sugar; stir until dissolved. Cover and chill for at least 4 hours.

2 To serve, pour juice mixture into a very large punch bowl. Stir in Juice Blend. Slowly stir in Carbonated Beverage. Add Ice Ring and, if desired, Stir-In.

ICE SHARDS: In a 15×10×1-inch pan place 2 to 3 cups whole or sliced fruit, fresh mint leaves, and citrus peel curls. Add enough club soda or other beverage to surround fruit but not cover it. Freeze several hours or until firm. Add more club soda to cover (see top photo, below). Freeze until firm. To unmold, dip pan bottom in warm water to loosen ice. Invert over a cutting board. Using a mallet, break ice into small shards (see bottom photo, below). Place in glasses with punch.

ICE RING: Prepare as for ice shards, except place fruit in a fluted tube pan and freezing in layers as above. Unmold as above. Float frozen ring in punch in a punch bowl.

LEMONADE

START TO FINISH: 20 MINUTES
MAKES: 4 SERVINGS

   3 cups cold water
   1 cup lemon juice (5 to 6 lemons)
   ¾ cup sugar
   Ice cubes
   Lemon slices

1 In a 1½-quart pitcher stir together the water, lemon juice, and sugar until sugar dissolves. If desired, chill in the refrigerator. Serve in glasses over ice. Garnish with lemon slices.

GREEN TEA LEMONADE: Bring 1 cup of the water to boiling; add 2 green tea bags. Let steep for 5 minutes. Remove tea bags; let tea cool. Continue as above with remaining 2 cups water and remaining ingredients.

RASPBERRY LEMONADE: Prepare as directed, except place 1 cup fresh raspberries in a blender or food processor; cover and blend or process until mixture is pureed. Press mixture through a fine-mesh sieve; discard seeds. Add strained puree to pitcher. If desired, add additional sugar. Garnish with fresh raspberries.

PER 8 OUNCES PLAIN, GREEN TEA, OR RASPBERRY VARIATIONS: 163 cal., 0 g total fat, 0 mg chol., 6 mg sodium, 44 g carbo., 1 g fiber, 0 g pro.
EXCHANGES: 3 Other Carbo.

SWEET CHERRY SANGRIA

PREP: 20 MINUTES **CHILL:** 4 TO 24 HOURS
MAKES: 8 TO 10 SERVINGS

   1 750-milliliter bottle red wine, such as Beaujolais or Zinfandel
   4 cups freshly squeezed orange juice (about 12 oranges)
   1½ cups fresh dark sweet cherries, pitted and halved
   ¾ cup (6 ounces) cherry-flavored syrup (syrup used to flavor beverages)
   ½ cup (4 ounces) orange liqueur

1 In a large pitcher or glass jar stir together wine, orange juice, cherries, cherry syrup, and orange liqueur. Cover and refrigerate for at least 4 hours or up to 24 hours to blend flavors. Serve in glasses over ice.

PER 8 OUNCES: 274 cal., 0 g total fat, 0 mg chol., 13 mg sodium, 45 g carbo., 1 g fiber, 1 g pro.
EXCHANGES: 3 Other Carbo., 2 Fat

MIXED-BERRY
LIMONCELLO SANGRIA

BEST EVER

MIXED-BERRY LIMONCELLO SANGRIA

PREP: 15 MINUTES **CHILL:** 4 TO 24 HOURS
MAKES: 10 SERVINGS

   1 cup fresh raspberries
   1 cup halved fresh strawberries
   ½ cup fresh blackberries
   1 medium lemon, thinly sliced
   ½ of a 12-ounce can (¾ cup) frozen pink lemonade concentrate, thawed
   ½ cup (4 ounces) limoncello (lemon-flavored liqueur)
   2 750-milliliter bottles Prosecco or sparkling wine, chilled

1 In a large pitcher or glass jar combine raspberries, strawberries, blackberries, and lemon slices. Stir in lemonade concentrate and limoncello. Cover and refrigerate for at least 4 hours or up to 24 hours to blend flavors.

2 Just before serving, add Prosecco. Serve in glasses over ice.

PER 8 OUNCES: 181 cal., 0 g total fat, 0 mg chol., 9 mg sodium, 18 g carbo., 2 g fiber, 1 g pro.
EXCHANGES: 1 Other Carbo., 2½ Fat

10 TO TRY—SMOOTHIES

Start with Basic Smoothie, page 97. **1. PEANUT BUTTER-BANANA:** Substitute vanilla yogurt for plain, milk for orange juice, and add half of a ripe banana and 2 tablespoons creamy peanut butter. **2. TROPICAL:** Substitute piña colada-flavored yogurt for plain and add 2 peeled kiwifruits. **3. PEACH:** Add 1 cup frozen peach slices; omit ice. **4. MANGO:** Add ½ cup chopped fresh or frozen mango. **5. BANANA-CHOCOLATE:** Substitute vanilla yogurt for plain, milk for orange juice, and chocolate-flavored syrup for honey; add half of a ripe banana. **6. POMEGRANATE:** Substitute pomegranate juice for orange juice. **7. ORANGE DREAM:** Substitute orange yogurt for plain and add ½ cup mandarin orange sections. **8. MOCHA:** Substitute coffee-flavored yogurt for plain, milk for orange juice, and chocolate-flavored syrup for honey. **9. BANANA-BLUEBERRY:** Substitute blueberry yogurt for plain; add half a ripe banana and ½ cup fresh or frozen blueberries. **10. BERRY:** Add ½ cup halved fresh strawberries or raspberries.

BASIC SMOOTHIE

START TO FINISH: 10 MINUTES
MAKES: 2 SERVINGS

- 1 6-ounce carton plain yogurt
- ½ cup orange juice or orange juice blend
- 2 tablespoons honey or sugar
- ¼ teaspoon vanilla
- 1 cup small ice cubes or crushed ice

1 In a blender combine yogurt, orange juice, honey, vanilla, and ice cubes. Cover and blend until nearly smooth.

PER 8 OUNCES: 147 cal., 1 g total fat (1 g sat. fat, 0 g trans fat), 5 mg chol., 61 mg sodium, 30 g carbo., 0 g fiber, 5 g pro.
EXCHANGES: ½ Milk, 1½ Other Carbo.

MILK SHAKES

START TO FINISH: 5 MINUTES **MAKES:** 2 SERVINGS

- 1 pint vanilla ice cream
- ½ to ¾ cup milk
- 2 tablespoons malted milk powder (optional)

1 In a blender combine ice cream, milk, and, if using, malted milk powder. Cover and blend until smooth.

PER 8 OUNCES: 329 cal., 17 g total fat (11 g sat. fat, 0 g trans fat), 68 mg chol., 140 mg sodium, 37 g carbo., 3 g fiber, 10 g pro.
EXCHANGES: 1 Milk, 1½ Other Carbo., 3 Fat

PEANUT BUTTER-BANANA SHAKES: Prepare as directed, except increase milk to 1 cup and add 1 medium ripe banana, sliced, and 3 tablespoons creamy peanut butter with the milk. If desired, substitute chocolate ice cream for the vanilla ice cream. To make a malt, use chocolate malted milk powder rather than plain. Makes 3 servings.

PER 8 OUNCES: 368 cal., 20 g total fat (9 g sat. fat, 0 g trans fat), 0 g trans fat, 49 mg chol., 184 mg sodium, 39 g carbo., 3 g fiber, 10 g pro.
EXCHANGES: ½ Fruit, 1 Milk, 1½ Other Carbo., 4 Fat

FRUITY MILK SHAKES: Prepare as directed, except add 2 cups sliced fresh or frozen fruit, such as peeled peaches, strawberries, mango, and/or whole blueberries. Omit the malted milk powder. Makes 3 servings.

PER 8 OUNCES: 259 cal., 12 g total fat (7 g sat. fat, 0 g trans fat), 0 g trans fat, 45 mg chol., 93 mg sodium, 34 g carbo., 2 g fiber, 6 g pro.
EXCHANGES: ½ Fruit, ½ Milk, 1½ Other Carbo., 2 Fat

FROZEN GRASSHOPPERS

START TO FINISH: 5 MINUTES **MAKES:** 8 SERVINGS

- ½ cup (4 ounces) green crème de menthe
- ½ cup (4 ounces) white crème de cacao
- 1 pint (2 cups) vanilla ice cream
- 2 cups ice cubes
  Whipped cream (optional)
  Chopped layered chocolate-mint candies (optional)
  Fresh mint (optional)

1 In a blender combine crème de menthe, crème de cacao, ice cream, and about half of the ice. Cover and blend until smooth. Add the remaining ice; cover and blend until smooth.

2 Serve in small cocktail glasses. If desired, top with whipped cream, chopped candies, and a sprig of fresh mint.

PER 4 OUNCES: 177 cal., 4 g total fat (2 g sat. fat, 0 g trans fat), 16 mg chol., 30 mg sodium, 22 g carbo., 0 g fiber, 6 g pro.
EXCHANGES: ½ Milk, 1 Other Carbo., 1½ Fat

BRANDY-KISSED SNOWFLAKES

START TO FINISH: 10 MINUTES
MAKES: 8 SERVINGS

- ⅓ cup (about 3 ounces) brandy
- ¼ cup (2 ounces) white crème de cacao
- ¾ cup vanilla ice cream
- ½ cup ice cubes
  Whipped cream
  Ground cinnamon

1 In a blender combine brandy, crème de cacao, ice cream, and ice cubes. Cover and blend until mixture is smooth.

2 Spoon into eight 1½- to 2-ounce shot glasses. Top each with whipped cream and sprinkle lightly with cinnamon. Serve immediately or nest glasses in crushed ice.

PER 1½ OUNCES: 64 cal., 2 g total fat (1 g sat. fat, 0 g trans fat), 9 mg chol., 12 mg sodium, 4 g carbo., 0 g fiber, 1 g pro.
EXCHANGES: 1½ Fat

SUMMER FRUIT DAIQUIRIS *(photo, page 85)*

START TO FINISH: 15 MINUTES
MAKES: 6 TO 8 SERVINGS

- 3 cups fresh or frozen peeled peach slices, thawed; fresh or frozen unsweetened strawberries, thawed; fresh or frozen cubed mango, thawed; or cubed, seeded watermelon
- ½ of a 12-ounce can (¾ cup) frozen limeade or lemonade concentrate, thawed
- ¼ cup (2 ounces) light rum or orange juice
- 2 tablespoons powdered sugar
- 2 to 3 cups ice cubes

1 In a blender combine 3 cups fruit, limeade concentrate, rum, and powdered sugar. Cover and blend until smooth. With blender running, gradually add ice cubes through opening in lid until mixture is desired thickness. Serve in glasses. If desired, garnish with assorted *fruit* chunks threaded on wooden skewers.

PER 4 TO 5 OUNCES: 131 cal., 0 g total fat, 0 mg chol., 0 mg sodium, 28 g carbo., 1 g fiber, 1 g pro.
EXCHANGES: ½ Fruit, 1½ Other Carbo., ½ Fat

QUICK BLENDED MARGARITAS

START TO FINISH: 10 MINUTES
MAKES: 8 SERVINGS

- 1 or 2 limes
  Coarse salt
- 1 12-ounce can frozen limeade concentrate
- ⅔ cup (about 5 ounces) tequila
- ½ cup (4 ounces) orange liqueur
- 4 cups ice cubes

1 Cut a thick lime slice; cut slice in half. Rub halves around rims of eight glasses. Dip rims into a dish of coarse salt to coat; set aside. Slice remaining lime into 8 thin slices; set aside.

2 In a blender combine limeade concentrate, tequila, and orange liqueur. Cover and blend until combined. With blender running, add ice cubes, one at a time, through opening in lid, blending until mixture becomes slushy. Pour into prepared glasses. Garnish with the thin lime slices.

MAKE-AHEAD DIRECTIONS: Prepare Step 2 as directed. Pour into a 1½-quart freezer container. Cover; freeze overnight. To serve, prepare glasses as directed in Step 1. Use a large spoon to scrape the frozen surface and pile frozen mix into salt-rimmed glasses.

PER 6 OUNCES: 190 cal., 0 g total fat, 0 mg chol., 1,163 mg sodium, 32 g carbo., 0 g fiber, 0 g pro.
EXCHANGES: 2 Other Carbo., 1½ Fat

STRAWBERRY MARGARITAS: Prepare as directed, except substitute coarse sugar for the salt on the glasses and omit the lime garnish. Blend half of the mixture at a time, adding 1 cup frozen unsweetened whole strawberries and 2 cups of the ice cubes to each half.

PER 6 OUNCES: 209 cal., 0 g total fat, 0 mg chol., 1 mg sodium, 37 g carbo., 0 g fiber, 0 g pro.
EXCHANGES: 2 Other Carbo., 1½ Fat

PIÑA COLADA

START TO FINISH: 10 MINUTES
MAKES: 4 SERVINGS

- ½ cup (4 ounces) cream of coconut
- 1 8-ounce can crushed pineapple (juice pack), undrained
- ⅓ cup (about 3 ounces) dark or light rum
- 1 tablespoon lemon or lime juice
- 4 cups ice cubes

1 In a blender combine cream of coconut, pineapple, rum, and lemon juice. Cover and blend until smooth. With blender running, gradually add ice cubes through opening in lid until smooth.

PER 8 OUNCES: 210 cal., 6 g total fat (6 g sat. fat, 0 g trans fat), 0 mg chol., 14 mg sodium, 29 g carbo., 1 g fiber, 1 g pro.
EXCHANGES: 2 Other Carbo., 2 Fat

PINEAPPLE MIMOSAS

PREP: 10 MINUTES **CHILL:** 2 TO 24 HOURS
MAKES: 6 SERVINGS

- 1 12-ounce can frozen pineapple-orange-banana juice concentrate, thawed
- 1 cup cold water
- 1 750-milliliter bottle pink sparkling wine, sparkling wine, and/or sparkling apple juice, chilled
  Ice cubes
  Fresh pineapple spears (optional)

1 In a large pitcher combine juice concentrate and water. Cover; chill for 2 to 24 hours. Before serving, carefully add sparkling wine. Add ice to pitcher or each glass before serving. If desired, garnish each glass with a fresh pineapple spear.

PER 8 OUNCES: 147 cal., 0 g total fat, 0 mg chol., 5 mg sodium, 18 g carbo., 0 g fiber, 1 g pro.
EXCHANGES: 1 Other Carbo., 2 Fat

POMEGRANATE MARTINIS

START TO FINISH: 10 MINUTES **MAKES:** 12 DRINKS

- 1 orange, cut into wedges (optional)
  Sugar (optional)
- 3 cups vodka or gin
- ¾ cup pomegranate syrup
- ⅓ cup (about 3 ounces) dry vermouth
  Ice cubes

1 If desired, rub orange wedges around rims of 12 martini glasses; dip rims in sugar. Set aside.

2 In a small pitcher combine vodka, pomegranate syrup, and vermouth. Place ice cubes in a cocktail shaker. For each drink, add ⅓ cup of the syrup mixture to the shaker; cover and shake until very cold. Strain liquid into one of the prepared glasses. If desired, garnish with *pomegranate seeds*.

ORANGE MARTINIS: Prepare as directed, except substitute frozen orange juice concentrate, thawed, for the syrup. Garnish with halved kumquats or fresh orange peel twists.

PER 3 OUNCES POMEGRANATE OR ORANGE VARIATION: 196 cal., 0 g total fat, 0 mg chol., 10 mg sodium, 16 g carbo., 0 g fiber, 1 g pro.
EXCHANGES: 1 Other Carbo., 3 Fat

APPLE MARTINIS: Prepare as directed, except substitute frozen apple juice concentrate, thawed, for pomegranate syrup. Garnish with thin apple slices.

PER 3 OUNCES: 176 cal., 0 g total fat, 0 mg chol., 5 mg sodium, 10 g carbo., 0 g fiber, 0 g pro.
EXCHANGES: ½ Other Carbo., 3 Fat

WHITE GRAPE SPRITZERS

PREP: 10 MINUTES **MAKES:** 4 SERVINGS

- 2 cups light white or red grape juice, chilled
- 2 cups sparkling wine or lemon-lime carbonated beverage, chilled

1 In each of four chilled wineglasses, combine ½ cup grape juice and ½ cup sparkling wine.

PER 8 OUNCES: 122 cal., 0 g total fat, 0 mg chol., 40 mg sodium, 13 g carbo., 0 g fiber, 0 g pro.
EXCHANGES: 1 Other Carbo., 1½ Fat

COLD IS KEY SHAKING THE INGREDIENTS VIGOROUSLY ALLOWS SMALL SHARDS OF ICE TO SPLINTER OFF FROM THE CUBES. THESE GLISTENING BITS HELP KEEP THE DRINK ULTRACOOL IN THE GLASS.

POMEGRANATE MARTINI
APPLE MARTINI
ORANGE MARTINI

SEVEN STYLISH BAR DRINKS

SOME LIKE THEIR COCKTAILS SWEET AND FRUITY; OTHERS WANT THEM BRISK AND SOUR; AND MARTINI LOVERS—IN A CLASS BY THEMSELVES—JUST WANT THEM STIFF AND COLD. KEEP THESE RECIPES IN YOUR REPERTOIRE AND YOU'LL BE COVERED NO MATTER WHOM YOU'RE HOSTING.

COSMOPOLITAN

In a cocktail shaker combine ¼ cup (2 ounces) vodka, 2 tablespoons (1 ounce) orange liqueur, 2 tablespoons (1 ounce) cranberry juice, and 1 tablespoon (½ ounce) lime juice. Add ice cubes; cover and shake until very cold. Strain liquid into a chilled glass. If desired, garnish with lime peel twist. Makes 1 serving.

MAI TAI

In a cocktail shaker combine ⅓ cup pineapple juice, 3 tablespoons (1½ ounces) rum, 3 tablespoons (1½ ounces) orange liqueur, 2 tablespoons (1 ounce) grenadine syrup, a dash lime juice, and a dash sugar. Add ice cubes; cover and shake until very cold. Strain liquid into a tall glass filled with crushed ice. If desired, garnish with fresh fruit (such as strawberries, kiwifruit, orange wedges) threaded on a long skewer. Makes 1 serving.

VODKA GIMLET

In a cocktail shaker combine 3 tablespoons (1½ ounces) vodka or gin and 1 tablespoon (½ ounce) bottled sweetened lime juice. Add ice cubes; cover and shake until very cold. Strain liquid into an ice-filled glass. If desired, garnish with a lime peel twist. Makes 1 serving.

SIDECAR

If desired, wet the rim of a chilled glass with water. Dip the rim into a dish of sugar to coat; set aside. In a cocktail shaker combine ¼ cup (2 ounces) brandy, 2 tablespoons (1 ounce) lemon juice, and 2 tablespoons (1 ounce) orange liqueur. Add ice cubes; cover and shake until very cold. Strain liquid into prepared glass filled with additional ice cubes. If desired, garnish with quartered lemon slices. Makes 1 serving.

WHISKEY SOUR

In a rocks glass combine ¼ cup (2 ounces) bourbon, 2 tablespoons (1 ounce) lime juice, 2 tablespoons (1 ounce) lemon juice, and 1 tablespoon sugar. Using a spoon, stir until combined and sugar is dissolved. Add ice cubes. If desired, garnish with an orange slice and a cherry. Makes 1 serving.

BLACKBERRY FIZZ

In a cocktail shaker combine 4 or 5 fresh or frozen blackberries, thawed; 1 tablespoon (½ ounce) lime juice; and 1 teaspoon superfine sugar. To muddle, gently crush berries with the back of a spoon. Add 3 tablespoons (1½ ounces) cognac or other brandy and ice cubes; cover and shake until very cold. Strain liquid into an ice-filled glass. Add 3 tablespoons (1½ ounces) chilled sparkling wine. Garnish with additional blackberries and, if desired, a mint sprig. Makes 1 serving.

MARTINI

Thread 2 or 3 green olives on a cocktail pick; set aside. In a cocktail shaker combine ¼ cup (2 ounces) gin or vodka and 1½ teaspoons (¼ ounce) dry vermouth. Add ice cubes; cover and shake until very cold. Strain liquid into a martini glass. Garnish with olives and/or a lemon peel twist. Makes 1 serving.

BREADS

CARAMEL-PECAN ROLLS, PAGE 117

BREADS

HOMEMADE BREADS ARE AMONG THE MOST GRATIFYING ITEMS YOU CAN BAKE. AND, YES, YOU CAN DO IT. THESE TIPS WILL HELP YOU GET THE HANG OF BREAD MAKING.

LEAVENER LOGIC

■ Active dry yeast (used in this book) feeds on sugar in the dough to make carbon dioxide. It works slowly and develops flavor in dough as breads rise. Store any opened yeast in the refrigerator; be sure to use before the expiration date.

■ Baking soda and baking powder work quickly and are used in quick breads and muffins. Baking soda reacts immediately with acidic ingredients, such as buttermilk, sour cream, brown sugar, and lemon juice, so be sure to bake batters with baking soda immediately. Do not substitute baking powder for baking soda or vice versa. Store both in a cool, dry place.

MEASURING THE FLOUR

Most flours are presifted, so sifting is not necessary. Before measuring, stir the flour in the container to loosen it. Over the container, lightly spoon the flour into a dry measuring cup until it overflows; use the flat side of a knife to level the flour even with the top of the cup (see photos, right). Don't shake or tap the cup or it will cause the flour to settle.

YEAST BREAD HINTS

■ Yeast bread dough needs to rise in a warm (80°F to 85°F), draft-free place. An unheated oven with a bowl of warm water on the rack below works well.

■ Place the dough in a greased bowl that's twice the size of the dough. Cover it with plastic wrap that's been sprayed with cooking spray or a towel.

■ Dough should double in size for its first rise. In its second rise, if it's in a pan, don't let the shaped dough rise above the top of the pan. It will rise more as it bakes due to "oven spring," a boost in rising caused by the oven's heat.

■ A baked loaf sounds hollow when tapped lightly with your fingers. If it's browning too fast but doesn't sound hollow, loosely tent the loaf with foil. Yeast breads containing sugar or butter often need this step.

■ Store yeast breads at room temperature because they become stale quickly when chilled. If the bread has cheese or meat in it, enjoy what you can the day it's baked and freeze the rest.

QUICK BREAD HINTS

GREASE PANS: Dip a brush in shortening; lightly coat the bottom and ½ to 1 inch up the sides of the pan, making sure to get into the pan's corners. Do not grease all the way up the sides because the batter needs to cling to the ungreased pan sides as it rises.

CHECK DONENESS: Peek at quick bread loaves 10 to 15 minutes before minimum baking time to see if they're browning too quickly. If they are, cover them loosely with foil.

REMOVE FROM PAN: Run a thin-bladed knife around the edges to loosen it, then turn it out onto a wire rack.

COOL AND STORE: For best flavor and easy slicing, let quick breads cool, wrap them in foil or plastic wrap, and store overnight at room temperature.

FREEZE FOR LATER: To freeze quick bread loaves, place cooled loaves in freezer containers or bags and freeze up to 3 months.

MIXED-GRAIN BREAD *(page 107)*

WHITE BREAD

PREP: 30 MINUTES **RISE:** 75 MINUTES
REST: 10 MINUTES **BAKE:** 35 MINUTES
OVEN: 375°F **MAKES:** 2 LOAVES (24 SLICES)

5¾ to 6¼ cups all-purpose flour
  1 package active dry yeast
2¼ cups milk or buttermilk
  2 tablespoons sugar
  1 tablespoon butter
1½ teaspoons salt

1 In a large mixing bowl combine 2½ cups of the flour and the yeast; set aside. In a saucepan heat and stir milk, sugar, butter, and salt just until warm (120°F to 130°F) and butter almost melts. Add milk mixture to flour mixture. Beat with an electric mixer on low speed for 30 seconds, scraping sides of bowl constantly. Beat on high speed for 3 minutes. Using a wooden spoon, stir in as much remaining flour as you can (see photo 1, below).

2 Turn dough out onto a lightly floured surface. Knead in enough of the remaining flour to make a moderately stiff dough that is smooth and elastic (6 to 8 minutes total; see photo 2, below). Shape dough into a ball. Place in a lightly greased bowl, turning once to grease surface of dough. Cover (see photo 3, below); let rise in a warm place until double in size (45 to 60 minutes).

3 Punch dough down (see photos 4 and 5, below). Turn dough onto a lightly floured surface; divide in half. Cover dough; let rest 10 minutes. Meanwhile, grease two 8×4×-inch loaf pans.

4 Shape each dough half into a loaf by patting or rolling (see photos 1 and 2, page 106). To shape dough by patting, gently pat and pinch each half of dough into a loaf shape, tucking edges underneath. To shape dough by rolling, on a lightly floured surface, roll each half of dough into a 12×8-inch rectangle. Tightly roll up, starting from a short side, sealing seams with fingertips.

PREPARING YEAST DOUGH, STEP-BY-STEP

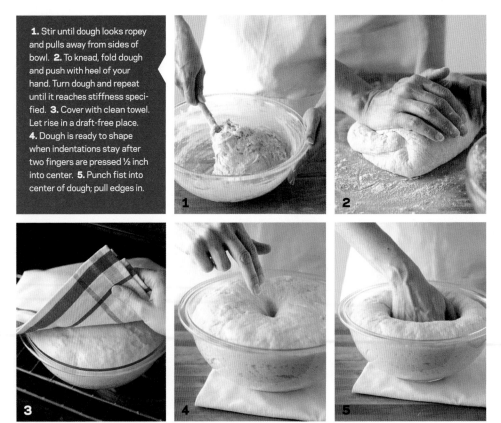

1. Stir until dough looks ropey and pulls away from sides of bowl. **2.** To knead, fold dough and push with heel of your hand. Turn dough and repeat until it reaches stiffness specified. **3.** Cover with clean towel. Let rise in a draft-free place. **4.** Dough is ready to shape when indentations stay after two fingers are pressed ½ inch into center. **5.** Punch fist into center of dough; pull edges in.

5 Place the shaped dough halves in the prepared pans, seam sides down. Cover and let rise in a warm place until nearly double in size (about 30 minutes).

6 Preheat oven to 375°F. Bake for 35 to 40 minutes or until bread sounds hollow when lightly tapped (if necessary, cover loosely with foil the last 5 to 10 minutes of baking to prevent overbrowning). Immediately remove bread from pans. Cool completely on wire racks.

WHOLE WHEAT BREAD: Prepare as directed, except decrease all-purpose flour to 3¾ to 4¼ cups and stir in 2 cups whole wheat flour after beating the mixture for 3 minutes in Step 1.

PER SLICE PLAIN OR WHOLE WHEAT VARIATION: 130 cal., 1 g total fat (1 g sat. fat, 0 g trans fat), 3 mg chol., 159 mg sodium, 25 g carbo., 1 g fiber, 4 g pro.
EXCHANGES: 1½ Starch

LOW FAT

POTATO BREAD

PREP: 55 MINUTES **RISE:** 90 MINUTES
REST: 10 MINUTES **BAKE:** 35 MINUTES
OVEN: 375°F **MAKES:** 2 LOAVES (24 SLICES)

- 1 large russet or long white potato (about 10 ounces)
- 2 cups water
- ¼ cup butter, cut up
- 1½ teaspoons salt
- 4½ to 4¾ cups all-purpose flour
- 2 packages active dry yeast
- 2 eggs
  All-purpose flour

1 Peel and cube potato. In a saucepan combine potato and the water. Bring to boiling; reduce heat. Simmer, covered, for 12 to 15 minutes or until very tender. Drain, reserving 1 cup of hot cooking liquid. Set liquid aside. Mash potato with a potato masher (should have 1 cup); set aside.

2 In a small bowl combine reserved cooking liquid, butter, and salt. Cool to 120°F to 130°F.

3 In a large mixing bowl combine 2 cups of the flour and the yeast. Add reserved cooking liquid mixture and the eggs. Beat with electric mixer on low to medium speed for 30 seconds, scraping sides of bowl constantly. Beat on high speed for 3 minutes. Using a wooden spoon, stir in mashed potato and as much of the remaining flour as you can (see photo 1, page 104).

4 Turn dough out onto a lightly floured surface. Knead in enough of the remaining flour to make a moderately stiff dough that is smooth and elastic (6 to 8 minutes total; see photo 2, page 104). Shape dough into a ball. Place in a lightly greased bowl, turning once to grease surface of dough. Cover (see photo 3, page 104); let rise in a warm place until doubled in size (1 to 1½ hours).

5 Punch dough down (see photos 4 and 5, page 104). Turn dough out onto lightly floured surface; divide in half. Cover dough; let rest for 10 minutes. Meanwhile, grease two 8×4×2-inch loaf pans.

6 Shape each dough half into a loaf by patting or rolling (see photos 1 and 2, page 106). Place loaves in prepared pans. Lightly sprinkle tops of loaves with additional flour. Cover; let rise until nearly double in size (30 to 40 minutes).

7 Preheat oven to 375°F. Bake for 35 to 40 minutes or until bread sounds hollow when lightly tapped. (If necessary, cover loosely with foil the last 15 minutes of baking to prevent overbrowning.) Cool on wire racks.

POTATO ROLLS: Prepare as directed through Step 5, except grease two large baking sheets. Divide each half of dough into 12 pieces. Shape pieces into balls. Lightly dip tops in flour. Arrange balls 1½ inches apart on prepared baking sheets. Bake for 20 to 25 minutes or until golden. Cool on wire racks. Makes 24 rolls.

PER SLICE OR ROLL: 119 cal., 3 g total fat (1 g sat. fat, 0 g trans fat), 23 mg chol., 167 mg sodium, 20 g carbo., 1 g fiber, 3 g pro.
EXCHANGES: 1 Starch, ½ Fat

THE RIGHT STIFFNESS
KNEAD THE DOUGH UNTIL IT IS THE STIFFNESS SPECIFIED IN THE RECIPE.

Each recipe offers approximate kneading times. The following terms are used to describe the stiffness you need to achieve.
SOFT DOUGH: Extremely sticky; used for breads that don't require kneading.
MODERATELY SOFT DOUGH: Slightly sticky but smooth; used for rich, sweet breads.
MODERATELY STIFF DOUGH: Slightly firm to the touch, not sticky; for nonsweet breads.
STIFF DOUGH: Firm to the touch; holds its shape after 8 to 10 minutes of kneading.

SHAPING THE DOUGH AND TESTING DONENESS, STEP-BY-STEP

1. To pat dough into a loaf shape, use your hands to gently pat and pinch it. Place, seam side down, in pan. **2.** To roll dough, roll dough out into a 12×8-inch rectangle. Tightly roll up the rectangle, starting from a short side. Pinch seam to seal. Place, seam side down, in pan. **3.** To test for doneness, tap loaf lightly on top with a finger. It should sound hollow when done.

GOLDEN WHEAT BREAD

PREP: 40 MINUTES **RISE:** 105 MINUTES
REST: 10 MINUTES **BAKE:** 55 MINUTES
OVEN: 350°F **MAKES:** 2 LOAVES (24 SLICES)

  2 packages active dry yeast
  ½ cup warm water (105°F to 115°F)
  2 cups milk
  ½ cup shortening
  ¾ cup packed brown sugar
  2 cups whole wheat flour
  1 egg, lightly beaten
1½ teaspoons salt
4¾ to 5¼ cups bread flour

1 In a small bowl dissolve yeast in the warm water; set aside. In a medium saucepan bring milk just to a simmer; remove from heat. Pour milk into a large mixing bowl. Whisk in shortening and brown sugar until shortening melts. Whisk in whole wheat flour. Cool to lukewarm (105°F to 115°F). Stir in yeast mixture, egg, and salt. Using a wooden spoon, stir in as much of the bread flour as you can (see photo 1, page 104).

2 Turn dough out onto a lightly floured surface. Knead in enough remaining bread flour to make a moderately stiff dough that is almost smooth and elastic (6 to 8 minutes total). Shape dough into a ball. Place in a lightly greased bowl; turn once to grease surface of dough. Cover (see photo 3, page 104); let rise in a warm place until double in size (1¼ to 1½ hours).

3 Punch dough down (see photos 4 and 5, page 104). Turn onto a lightly floured surface. Divide in half. Cover; let rest 10 minutes. Meanwhile, lightly grease two 9×5×3-inch loaf pans.

4 Shape each half into a loaf by patting or rolling (see photos 1 and 2, page 106). Place shaped dough halves in prepared pans. Cover; let rise in warm place until double in size (about 30 minutes).

5 Preheat oven to 350°F. Bake for 30 minutes; cover loosely with foil to prevent overbrowning. Bake about 25 minutes more or until an instant-read thermometer inserted into the center of the bread registers 210°F.* Immediately remove bread from pans. Cool on wire racks.

*NOTE: This bread will not sound hollow when tapped, so it is necessary to take an internal temperature reading to ensure that it is done.

PER SLICE: 210 cal., 5 g total fat (1 g sat. fat, 1 g trans fat), 10 mg chol., 160 mg sodium, 35 g carbo., 2 g fiber, 6 g pro.
EXCHANGES: 2 Starch, ½ Other Carbo., ½ Fat

MIXED-GRAIN BREAD (photo, page 103)

PREP: 30 MINUTES **RISE:** 90 MINUTES
REST: 10 MINUTES **BAKE:** 30 MINUTES
OVEN: 375°F **MAKES:** 2 LOAVES (24 SLICES)

3½ to 4 cups all-purpose flour
  2 packages active dry yeast
1½ cups milk
  ¾ cup water
  ½ cup cracked wheat
  ¼ cup cornmeal
  ¼ cup packed brown sugar
  3 tablespoons vegetable oil
  2 teaspoons salt
1½ cups whole wheat flour
  ½ cup rolled oats

1 In a large mixing bowl combine 2 cups all-purpose flour and the yeast; set aside. In a saucepan combine milk, ¾ cup water, cracked wheat, cornmeal, brown sugar, oil, and salt. Heat and stir over medium-low heat just until warm (120°F to 130°F). Add milk mixture to flour mixture. Beat with an electric mixer on low to medium speed 30 seconds, scraping sides of bowl. Beat on high speed for 3 minutes. Using a wooden spoon, stir in whole wheat flour, the ½ cup oats, and as much remaining all-purpose flour as you can.

2 Turn dough out onto a lightly floured surface. Knead in enough of the remaining all-purpose flour to make a moderately stiff dough that is almost smooth and elastic (6 to 8 minutes total). Shape dough into a ball. Place in a lightly greased bowl, turning to grease surface of dough. Cover; let rise in a warm place until double in size (about 1 hour).

3 Punch dough down (see photos 4 and 5, page 104). Turn onto a lightly floured surface. Divide in half. Cover; let rest 10 minutes. Meanwhile, lightly grease two 8×4×2-inch loaf pans.

4 Shape each half into a loaf by patting or rolling (see photos 1 and 2, page 106). Place shaped dough halves in prepared pans. Cover; let rise in warm place until double in size (about 30 minutes).

5 Preheat oven to 375°F. Brush loaf tops with additional water; sprinkle with additional rolled oats. Bake for 30 to 35 minutes or until bread sounds hollow when lightly tapped (see photo 3, page 106). Immediately remove bread from pans. Cool on wire racks.

PER SLICE: 157 cal., 3 g total fat (0 g sat. fat, 0 g trans fat), 1 mg chol., 203 mg sodium, 29 g carbo., 3 g fiber, 5 g pro.
EXCHANGES: 2 Starch

CARAWAY-RYE BREAD

PREP: 40 MINUTES **RISE:** 90 MINUTES
REST: 10 MINUTES **BAKE:** 30 MINUTES
OVEN: 375°F **MAKES:** 2 LOAVES (24 SLICES)

- 4 to 4½ cups bread flour
- 1 package active dry yeast
- 2 cups warm water (120°F to 130°F)
- ¼ cup packed brown sugar
- 2 tablespoons vegetable oil
- 1½ teaspoons salt
- 1½ cups rye flour
- 1 tablespoon caraway seeds
  Cornmeal
- 2 teaspoons milk

1 In a large mixing bowl stir together 2¾ cups of the bread flour and the yeast. Add the warm water, brown sugar, oil, and salt. Beat with an electric mixer on low speed for 30 seconds, scraping sides of bowl constantly. Beat on high speed for 3 minutes. Using a wooden spoon, stir in rye flour, caraway seeds, and as much of the remaining bread flour as you can (see photo 1, page 104).

2 Turn dough out onto a lightly floured surface. Knead in enough remaining bread flour to make a moderately stiff dough that is smooth and elastic (6 to 8 minutes total; see photo 2, page 104). Shape dough into a ball. Place in a lightly greased bowl, turning once to grease surface of dough. Cover (see photo 3, page 104); let rise in a warm place until double in size (about 1 hour).

3 Punch dough down (see photos 4 and 5, page 104). Turn dough out onto a lightly floured surface. Divide dough in half. Cover; let rest for

10 minutes. Meanwhile, lightly grease a baking sheet; sprinkle baking sheet with cornmeal.

4 Shape each dough half by gently pulling it into a ball, tucking edges under. Place dough rounds on prepared baking sheet. Flatten each round slightly to about 6 inches in diameter (see photo 1, below). (Or shape each dough half into a loaf shape by patting or rolling [see photos 1 and 2, page 106]. Place in two greased 8×4×2-inch loaf pans.) If desired, lightly score loaf tops with a sharp knife (see photo 2, below). Cover and let rise in a warm place until nearly double (30 to 45 minutes).

5 Preheat oven to 375°F. Brush loaf tops with milk. Bake for 30 to 35 minutes or until tops and sides are deep golden brown and bread sounds hollow when lightly tapped (see photo 3, page 106). Immediately remove from baking sheet (or pans). Cool on wire racks.

PEASANT RYE BREAD: Prepare as directed, except substitute ¼ cup yellow cornmeal and ¼ cup whole bran cereal for ½ cup rye flour.

PER SLICE FOR CARAWAY-RYE OR PEASANT RYE VARIATION: 126 cal., 2 g total fat (0 g sat. fat, 0 g trans fat), 0 mg chol., 148 mg sodium, 24 g carbo., 2 g fiber, 4 g pro. EXCHANGES: 1½ Starch

---

NO MIXER? GRAB A SPOON.
A WOODEN SPOON WORKS FOR BEATING DOUGH, BUT IT MIGHT TAKE MORE THAN 3 MINUTES AND REQUIRE THE MAXIMUM AMOUNT OF FLOUR WORKED IN.

SHAPING A ROUND LOAF, STEP-BY-STEP

1. Shape dough into a ball by gently pulling its edges and tucking them underneath the round until the top is smooth. After placing the shaped dough rounds on a prepared baking sheet, gently press them down with the palm of your hand until they are about 6 inches across. **2.** For a decorative finish, use a sharp knife to make shallow parallel cuts across tops of dough rounds.

MOCK SOURDOUGH BREAD

PREP: 45 MINUTES **RISE:** 75 MINUTES
REST: 10 MINUTES **BAKE:** 30 MINUTES
OVEN: 375°F **MAKES:** 2 LOAVES (24 SLICES)

- 6¾ to 7¼ cups all-purpose flour
- 1 package active dry yeast
- 1½ cups water
- 3 tablespoons sugar
- 3 tablespoons vegetable oil
- 2 teaspoons salt
- 1 6-ounce carton (⅔ cup) plain yogurt
- 2 tablespoons lemon juice

1 In a large mixing bowl combine 2½ cups of the flour and the yeast; set aside. In a saucepan heat and stir the water, sugar, oil, and salt just until warm (120°F to 130°F). Add water mixture to flour mixture along with the yogurt and lemon juice. Beat with an electric mixer on low speed for 30 seconds, scraping sides of bowl constantly. Beat on high speed for 3 minutes. Using a wooden spoon, stir in as much remaining flour as you can.

2 Turn dough out onto a lightly floured surface. Knead in enough remaining flour to make a moderately stiff dough that is smooth and elastic (6 to 8 minutes total; see photo 2, page 104). Shape dough into a ball. Place in a lightly greased bowl; turn once to grease surface. Cover; let rise in a warm place until double in size (45 to 60 minutes).

3 Punch dough down (see photos 4 and 5, page 104). Turn out onto a lightly floured surface. Divide in half. Cover; let rest 10 minutes. Meanwhile, lightly grease a baking sheet.

4 Shape each dough half by gently pulling it into a ball, tucking edges under. Place dough rounds on prepared baking sheet. Flatten each round slightly to about 6 inches in diameter (see photo 1, page 108). Using a sharp knife, make criss-cross slashes across loaf tops. Cover; let rise in a warm place until nearly double (about 30 minutes).

5 Preheat oven to 375°F. Bake for 30 to 35 minutes or until bread sounds hollow when lightly tapped. (An instant-read thermometer should register at least 200°F when inserted into centers of loaves.) If necessary, cover loosely with foil the last 10 minutes of baking to prevent over-browning. Immediately remove bread from baking sheet. Cool on wire racks.

PER SLICE: 155 cal., 2 g total fat (0 g sat. fat, 0 g trans fat), 0 mg chol., 200 mg sodium, 29 g carbo., 1 g fiber, 4 g pro.
EXCHANGES: 2 Starch

NO-KNEAD BREAD

PREP: 25 MINUTES **REST:** 4 TO 24 HOURS +
15 MINUTES **RISE:** 1 HOUR **BAKE:** 40 MINUTES
OVEN: 450°F **MAKES:** 1 LOAF (10 SLICES)

- 3 cups all-purpose flour
- 1¼ teaspoons salt
- ¼ teaspoon active dry yeast
- 1⅔ cups warm water (120°F to 130°F)
  All-purpose flour
  Yellow cornmeal

1 In a large bowl combine 3 cups flour, the salt, and yeast. Add the warm water. Stir until flour mixture is moistened (dough will be very sticky and soft). Cover; let rest at room temperature for 4 to 24 hours.

2 Generously sprinkle additional flour (3 to 4 tablespoons) on a large piece of parchment paper. Turn dough out onto floured paper. Sprinkle top of dough mixture lightly with additional flour (1 to 2 tablespoons); using a large spatula, gently fold dough over onto itself. Sprinkle lightly with additional flour (1 to 2 tablespoons). Cover; let rest for 15 minutes.

3 Grease a 5- to 6-quart Dutch oven or heavy pot with a diameter of 8½ to 9½ inches; sprinkle cornmeal over bottom and about 2 inches up the sides. Gently turn dough into prepared Dutch oven, using a spatula to help scrape dough off the paper (some dough may remain on the paper). Cover; let rise at room temperature until dough has risen by about 1 inch in the pan (1 to 2 hours).

4 Preheat oven to 450°F. Cover Dutch oven with a lid or foil; bake for 30 minutes. Uncover; bake for 10 to 15 minutes more or until top is golden brown. Immediately remove bread from pan. Cool completely on wire rack.

PER SLICE: 154 cal., 0 g total fat, 0 mg chol., 293 mg sodium, 32 g carbo., 1 g fiber, 4 g pro.
EXCHANGES: 2 Starch

KEEP THE YEAST ALIVE
USE AN INSTANT-READ THERMOMETER TO MAKE SURE LIQUID FOR BREAD IS NOT TOO HOT. IF IT'S TOO HOT, THE YEAST WILL BECOME INACTIVE—130°F IS THE MAX.

BEST BASIC CHALLAH

PREP: 60 MINUTES **RISE:** 90 MINUTES
REST: 10 MINUTES **BAKE:** 30 MINUTES
OVEN: 350°F **MAKES:** 3 LOAVES (36 SLICES)

- 1¾ cups warm water (105°F to 115°F)
- ½ cup honey
- 2 packages active dry yeast
- 4 eggs, lightly beaten
- ½ cup butter, melted and cooled
- 1 tablespoon salt
- 7½ to 8 cups bread flour or 8 to 8½ cups all-purpose flour
- 1 egg, lightly beaten
- 1 tablespoon water

1 In a large bowl stir together the 1¾ cups warm water, the honey, and yeast. Let stand about 10 minutes or until foamy. Using a wooden spoon, stir in the 4 eggs, the melted butter, and salt. Gradually stir in as much of the flour as you can.

2 Turn dough out onto a lightly floured surface. Knead in enough of the remaining flour to make a moderately soft dough that is smooth and elastic (5 to 7 minutes total; see photo 2, page 104). Shape dough into a ball. Place in a lightly greased bowl, turning once to grease surface of dough. Cover; let rise in a warm place until double in size (1 to 1½ hours).

3 Punch dough down (see photos 4 and 5, page 104). Turn dough out onto a lightly floured surface. Divide into six portions. Cover; let rest for 10 minutes. Meanwhile, lightly grease a large baking sheet; set aside.

4 Divide each portion into thirds (18 portions total). Gently roll each third into an 18-inch-long rope. Place three ropes on prepared baking sheet 1 inch apart; braid. Repeat with another three ropes to make another braid. Brush one side of a braid with *water*; lightly press the two braids together to make a double-braided loaf. Repeat with remaining portions of dough to make two more double-braided loaves. Cover and let rise in a warm place until nearly double in size (about 30 minutes).

5 Preheat oven to 350°F. In a small bowl combine the 1 egg and the 1 tablespoon water; brush over braids. Bake for 30 to 35 minutes or until loaves sound hollow when lightly tapped. Immediately remove loaves from baking sheet. Cool on wire racks.

CHOCOLATE CHALLAH: Prepare as directed, except substitute ⅔ cup packed brown sugar for the honey and stir ½ cup unsweetened cocoa powder and 2 teaspoons instant espresso coffee powder into 2 cups of the flour before adding to the yeast mixture (you will use less flour during kneading). To shape stacked loaves, divide dough into three portions. Remove one-fourth of the dough from each portion; divide each fourth into thirds (nine small portions total). Gently roll each third into a 15-inch-long rope. Braid three ropes at a time to make three small braids; cover and set aside. Divide the remaining three portions of dough into thirds (nine large portions total). Gently roll each third into an 18-inch-long rope. Braid three ropes at a time to make three large braids. For each stacked loaf, brush a large braid with some of the egg mixture; top with a small braid, pressing gently. Let rise as directed. Brush with the remaining egg mixture; bake as directed. Makes 3 loaves (36 slices).

GARLIC-HERB CHALLAH: Prepare as directed, except reduce honey to 2 tablespoons, use olive oil instead of melted butter, and add 4 cloves garlic, minced; 1 teaspoon dried basil, crushed; 1 teaspoon dried rosemary, crushed; and 1 teaspoon dried thyme, crushed, to the yeast mixture. To shape spiral loaves, divide dough into three portions. Divide each portion into thirds (nine portions total). Gently roll each third into a 24-inch-long rope. Braid three ropes at a time to make three braids; shape each into a spiral loaf. Let rise as directed. Instead of brushing with egg mixture, in a small bowl combine 3 tablespoons butter, melted; 1 teaspoon dried basil, crushed; 1 teaspoon dried thyme, crushed; 1 teaspoon dried rosemary, crushed; and 1 clove garlic, minced. Brush over loaves. Bake as directed. Makes 3 loaves (36 slices).

PER SLICE BASIC, CHOCOLATE, OR GARLIC-HERB VARIATIONS: 113 cal., 3 g total fat (1 g sat. fat, 0 g trans fat), 27 mg chol., 167 mg sodium, 19 g carbo., 1 g fiber, 3 g pro. EXCHANGES: 1 Starch, ½ Fat

---

LEFTOVER CHALLAH?
USE EXTRAS FOR FRENCH TOAST, BREAD PUDDING, OR STUFFING. IF YOU CAN'T USE IT RIGHT AWAY, FREEZE CHALLAH IN AIRTIGHT CONTAINERS.

BEST BASIC CHALLAH

A LIGHT TOUCH START WITH THE MINIMUM AMOUNT OF FLOUR GIVEN IN A RECIPE AND KNEAD IN JUST ENOUGH. AVOID USING MORE THAN THE MAXIMUM OR THE BREAD CAN BECOME HEAVY.

GARLIC-HERB CHALLAH

CHOCOLATE CHALLAH

10 TO TRY—FLAVORED BUTTERS

Start with ½ cup softened butter. **1. BLUE CHEESE:** Stir in 2 tablespoons crumbled blue cheese. **2. ORANGE-PEPPER:** Stir in 1 tablespoon frozen orange juice concentrate, thawed, and ½ teaspoon cracked black pepper. **3. MAPLE:** Whisk in ¼ cup maple syrup and ½ teaspoon ground cinnamon. **4. CITRUS:** Stir in 1 tablespoon powdered sugar and 1 teaspoon finely shredded orange or lemon peel. **5. NUT:** Stir in ½ cup finely chopped toasted almonds or walnuts and ¼ cup apricot preserves. **6. LEMON-DILL:** Stir in 2 tablespoons snipped fresh dill and 1 teaspoon lemon juice. **7. CHIPOTLE:** Stir in 1 teaspoon chopped chipotle pepper in adobo sauce and 1 tablespoon snipped fresh cilantro. **8. ONION-PARMESAN:** Stir in 2 tablespoons grated Parmesan and 1 tablespoon sliced green onion. **9. HONEY:** Whisk in ¼ cup honey. **10. HERB:** Stir in 2 teaspoons *each* snipped fresh thyme and marjoram or 1 tablespoon snipped fresh basil.

MULTIGRAIN ROLLS

PREP: 45 MINUTES **RISE:** 90 MINUTES
REST: 10 MINUTES **BAKE:** 12 MINUTES
OVEN: 375°F **MAKES:** 18 ROLLS

3¾ to 4¼ cups all-purpose flour
 2 packages active dry yeast
1½ cups milk
 ⅓ cup honey
 ¼ cup butter, cut up
 2 teaspoons salt
 2 eggs
 ⅔ cup whole wheat flour
 ½ cup rye flour
 ½ cup quick-cooking rolled oats
 ⅓ cup toasted wheat germ
 1 tablespoon cornmeal
 1 egg, lightly beaten

1 In a large mixing bowl combine 2 cups of the all-purpose flour and the yeast; set aside. In a saucepan heat and stir milk, honey, butter, and salt just until warm (120°F to 130°F) and butter almost melts. Add to flour mixture along with the 2 eggs. Beat with an electric mixer on medium speed for 30 seconds, scraping sides of bowl. Beat on high speed for 3 minutes. Using a wooden spoon, stir in whole wheat and rye flours, oats, the wheat germ, and cornmeal. Stir in as much of the remaining all-purpose flour as you can.

2 Turn dough out onto lightly floured surface. Knead in enough remaining all-purpose flour to make moderately stiff dough that is smooth and elastic (6 to 8 minutes total). Shape into a ball. Place in greased bowl; turn once to grease dough surface. Cover; let rise until double (1 to 1½ hours).

3 Punch dough down (see photos 4 and 5, page 104). Turn dough out onto a lightly floured sur-face. Divide dough into six portions. Cover; let rest 10 minutes. Meanwhile, lightly grease two large baking sheets. Lightly sprinkle baking sheets with additional cornmeal or quick-cooking rolled oats.

4 Divide each portion of dough into thirds. Shape each third into a ball by pulling dough and pinching underneath. Flatten and pull each ball to form a 4×2-inch oval. Place on prepared baking sheets. Using kitchen shears, make three slanted cuts about ¾ inch deep on both long sides of each oval, creating a feathered look. Cover; let rise in a warm place until nearly double in size (30 to 45 minutes).

5 Preheat oven to 375°F. In a bowl combine beaten egg with 1 tablespoon *water*. Brush rolls

with egg mixture. Sprinkle with *sesame seeds, poppy seeds,* and/or cornmeal. Bake for 12 to 15 minutes or until golden. Cool on wire racks.

PER ROLL: 211 cal., 5 g total fat (2 g sat. fat, 0 g trans fat), 44 mg chol., 298 mg sodium, 36 g carbo., 2 g fiber, 7 g pro.
EXCHANGES: 2½ Starch, ½ Fat

FRENCH BREAD

PREP: 40 MINUTES **RISE:** 95 MINUTES
REST: 10 MINUTES **BAKE:** 35 MINUTES
OVEN: 375°F **MAKES:** 2 LOAVES (28 SLICES)

5½ to 6 cups all-purpose flour
 2 packages active dry yeast
1½ teaspoons salt
 2 cups warm water (120°F to 130°F)
 1 egg white, lightly beaten
 1 tablespoon water

1 In a large bowl combine 2 cups of the flour, the yeast, and salt. Add 2 cups warm water. Beat with an electric mixer on low speed for 30 seconds, scraping bowl. Beat on high speed for 3 minutes. Stir in as much of the remaining flour as you can.

2 Turn dough out onto a lightly floured surface. Knead in enough remaining flour to make a stiff dough that is smooth and elastic (8 to 10 minutes total). Shape dough into a ball. Place in a greased bowl, turning to grease dough surface. Cover; let rise in a warm place until double (about 1 hour).

3 Punch dough down. Turn dough out onto a lightly floured surface; divide in half. Cover; let rest for 10 minutes. Meanwhile, lightly grease a baking sheet; sprinkle baking sheet with *cornmeal*.

4 Roll dough half into a 15×10-inch rectangle. Tightly roll up, starting from a long side; seal well. If desired, pinch and slightly pull to taper ends. Place, seam sides down, on prepared baking sheet. In a small bowl stir together egg white and the 1 tablespoon water. Brush some of the egg white mixture over loaf tops. Let rise until nearly double in size (35 to 45 minutes).

5 Preheat oven to 375°F. Using a sharp knife, make four ¼-inch-deep diagonal cuts across each loaf top. Bake 20 minutes. Brush again with egg white mixture. Bake for 15 to 20 minutes more or until bread sounds hollow when tapped. Immediately transfer bread to wire racks; cool.

PER SLICE: 92 cal., 0 g total fat, 0 mg chol., 128 mg sodium, 19 g carbo., 1 g fiber, 3 g pro.
EXCHANGES: 1 Starch

PULL-APART CORNMEAL DINNER ROLLS

PREP: 30 MINUTES **RISE:** 90 MINUTES
REST: 10 MINUTES **BAKE:** 12 MINUTES
OVEN: 400°F **MAKES:** 32 ROLLS

- 1 cup milk
- ¼ cup sugar
- ¼ cup butter, cut up
- ¼ cup yellow cornmeal
- 1 package active dry yeast
- ¼ cup warm water (105°F to 115°F)
- 1 egg, lightly beaten
- 3¾ to 4¼ cups all-purpose flour
- 2 tablespoons butter, melted
- 1 to 2 tablespoons yellow cornmeal

1 In a saucepan heat and stir milk, sugar, ¼ cup butter, ¼ cup cornmeal, and 1 teaspoon *salt* just until warm (105°F to 115°F). In a large bowl dissolve yeast in warm water. Add egg and warm milk mixture. Stir in enough flour to make a soft dough.

2 Turn dough out onto a lightly floured surface. Knead in enough of the remaining flour to make a moderately soft dough that is smooth and elastic (about 3 minutes total; see photo 2, page 104). Shape dough into a ball. Place in a lightly greased bowl, turning once to grease surface of dough. Cover (see photo 3, page 104); let rise in a warm place until double in size (about 1 hour).

3 Punch dough down (see photos 4 and 5, page 104). Turn dough out onto a lightly floured surface. Cover and let rest for 10 minutes. Meanwhile, grease a 15×10×1-inch baking pan.

4 Roll or pat dough into a 10×8-inch rectangle. Cut into 2½×1-inch strips. Arrange strips in prepared pan, leaving about ¼ inch between each strip. Cover; let rise in warm place until nearly double in size (about 30 minutes).

5 Preheat oven to 400°F. Brush rolls with melted butter. Sprinkle with 1 to 2 tablespoons cornmeal. Bake for 12 to 15 minutes or until golden. Cool slightly. Remove from pan and serve warm.

MAKE-AHEAD DIRECTIONS PREPARE THROUGH STEP 4, EXCEPT DO NOT LET ROLLS RISE. COVER; REFRIGERATE UP TO 24 HOURS. LET STAND AT ROOM TEMPERATURE FOR 30 MINUTES BEFORE BAKING.

PULL-APART CORNMEAL DINNER ROLLS

PARMESAN-HERB DINNER ROLLS: Prepare rolls as directed on page 114, except add ½ teaspoon dried rosemary, crushed, or 1 teaspoon dried thyme or oregano, crushed, to the saucepan with the milk mixture. Brush rolls with the butter; sprinkle with 2 tablespoons grated Parmesan cheese instead of the cornmeal. Bake as directed.

PER ROLL PLAIN OR PARMESAN VARIATION: 90 cal., 3 g total fat (2 g sat. fat, 0 g trans fat), 13 mg chol., 94 mg sodium, 14 g carbo., 1 g fiber, 2 g pro.
EXCHANGES: 1 Starch, ½ Fat

BEST EVER • LOW FAT

OVERNIGHT REFRIGERATOR ROLLS

PREP: 35 MINUTES **CHILL:** OVERNIGHT
REST: 10 MINUTES **RISE:** 45 MINUTES
BAKE: 12 MINUTES **OVEN:** 375°F **MAKES:** 24 ROLLS

- 1¼ cups warm water (105°F to 115°F)
- 1 package active dry yeast
- 4 to 4¼ cups all-purpose flour
- ⅓ cup butter, melted, or vegetable oil
- ⅓ cup sugar
- 1 teaspoon salt
- 1 egg
  Nonstick cooking spray
- 2 tablespoons butter, melted (optional)

1 In a large mixing bowl combine warm water and yeast. Stir to dissolve yeast. Add 1½ cups of the flour, ⅓ cup melted butter, the sugar, salt, and egg. Beat with an electric mixer on low speed for 1 minute, scraping sides of bowl constantly.

2 Using a wooden spoon, stir in enough of the remaining flour to make a soft dough that just starts to pull away from sides of bowl (dough will be slightly sticky). Coat a 3-quart covered container with cooking spray. Place dough in container; turn once to grease surface of dough. Cover and refrigerate overnight.

3 Punch dough down. Turn dough out onto a lightly floured surface. Divide dough in half. Cover; let rest for 10 minutes. Meanwhile, lightly grease a 13×9×2-inch baking pan or baking sheets.

4 Shape dough into 24 balls or desired rolls (be careful not to overwork dough; it becomes stickier the more you work with it) and place in prepared baking pan or 2 to 3 inches apart on baking sheets. Cover; let rise in a warm place until nearly double in size (about 45 minutes).

5 Preheat oven to 375°F. Bake for 12 to 15 minutes for individual rolls or about 20 minutes for pan rolls or until golden. Immediately remove rolls from pans. If desired, brush tops of rolls with melted butter. Serve warm.

BUTTERHORN ROLLS: On a lightly floured surface, roll each dough half into a 10-inch circle. If desired, brush with melted butter. Cut each dough circle into 12 wedges. To shape rolls, begin at wide end of each wedge and loosely roll toward the point. Place, point sides down, 2 to 3 inches apart on prepared baking sheets. Makes 24 rolls.

PARKER HOUSE ROLLS: On a lightly floured surface, roll each dough half until ¼ inch thick. Cut dough with a floured 2½-inch round cutter. Brush with melted butter. Using the dull edge of a table knife, make an off-center crease in each round. Fold each round along the crease. Press the folded edge firmly. Place, larger half up, 2 to 3 inches apart on prepared baking sheets. Makes 24 rolls.

PER ROLL PLAIN, BUTTERHORN, OR PARKER HOUSE VARIATIONS: 113 cal., 3 g total fat (2 g sat. fat, 0 g trans fat), 16 mg chol., 119 mg sodium, 19 g carbo., 1 g fiber, 3 g pro.
EXCHANGES: 1 Starch, ½ Fat

ROSETTES: Divide each dough half into 16 pieces. On a lightly floured surface, roll each piece into a 12-inch-long rope. Tie each rope in a loose knot, leaving two long ends. Tuck top end under the knot and bottom end into the top center. Place 2 to 3 inches apart on prepared baking sheets. Makes 32 rolls.

PER ROLL: 85 cal., 2 g total fat (1 g sat. fat, 0 g trans fat), 12 mg chol., 89 mg sodium, 14 g carbo., 0 g fiber, 2 g pro.
EXCHANGES: 1 Starch, ½ Fat

HAMBURGER OR FRANKFURTER BUNS: Divide dough into 12 pieces. Cover and let rest for 10 minutes. For hamburger buns, shape each piece into a ball, tucking edges under. Place on a greased baking sheet. Using your fingers, slightly flatten balls to 4 inches in diameter. For frankfurter buns, shape each portion into a roll about 5½ inches long, tapering ends. Place 2 to 3 inches apart on prepared baking sheets. Makes 12 buns.

PER BUN: 226 cal., 6 g total fat (3 g sat. fat, 0 g trans fat), 31 mg chol., 238 mg sodium, 38 g carbo., 1 g fiber, 5 g pro.
EXCHANGES: 2½ Starch, 1 Fat

MONKEY BREAD

PREP: 20 MINUTES **CHILL:** OVERNIGHT
BAKE: 40 MINUTES **OVEN:** 350°F
MAKES: 24 ROLLS

- 1 34.5-ounce package frozen cinnamon sweet roll dough or orange sweet roll dough (12 rolls)
- ½ cup chopped pecans
- ⅓ cup butter, melted
- ¾ cup sugar
- ¼ cup caramel-flavored ice cream topping

1 The night before, arrange frozen rolls about 2 inches apart on a large greased cookie sheet. Discard frosting packets or reserve for another use. Cover rolls with lightly greased plastic wrap. Refrigerate overnight to let dough thaw and begin to rise.

2 Preheat oven to 350°F. Generously grease a 10-inch fluted tube pan. Sprinkle ¼ cup of the pecans in the bottom of the pan.

3 Cut each roll in half. Dip each roll half into melted butter, then roll in sugar. Layer coated roll halves in the prepared pan. Drizzle with any remaining butter; sprinkle with any remaining sugar. Sprinkle the remaining ¼ cup pecans on top. Drizzle ice cream topping over all.

4 Place pan on a baking sheet. Bake for 40 to 45 minutes or until golden brown. Let stand for 1 minute. Invert onto a large serving platter. Spoon any topping and nuts that remain in pan onto rolls. Cool slightly. Serve warm.

PER ROLL: 171 cal., 6 g total fat (2 g sat. fat, 0 g trans fat), 7 mg chol., 150 mg sodium, 26 g carbo., 1 g fiber, 2 g pro. EXCHANGES: ½ Starch, 1½ Other Carbo., 1 Fat

BEST EVER

CINNAMON ROLLS

PREP: 45 MINUTES **RISE:** 75 MINUTES
REST: 10 MINUTES **BAKE:** 25 MINUTES
COOL: 10 MINUTES **OVEN:** 375°F **MAKES:** 12 ROLLS

- 4¼ to 4¾ cups all-purpose flour
- 1 package active dry yeast
- 1 cup milk
- 1 cup mashed cooked potato*
- ⅓ cup butter, cut up
- ⅓ cup granulated sugar
- 1 teaspoon salt
- 2 eggs
- ½ cup packed brown sugar
- 1 tablespoon ground cinnamon
- ¼ cup butter, softened
- 1 recipe Icing or Cream Cheese Icing (page 117)

1 In a large mixing bowl combine 1½ cups of the flour and the yeast; set aside. In a medium saucepan heat and stir milk, potato, ⅓ cup butter, granulated sugar, and salt just until warm (120°F to 130°F) and butter almost melts; add to flour mixture along with the eggs. Beat with an electric mixer on low to medium speed for 30 seconds, scraping sides of bowl constantly. Beat on high speed for 3 minutes. Using a wooden spoon, stir in as much of the remaining flour as you can.

2 Turn dough out onto a lightly floured surface. Knead in enough of the remaining flour to make a moderately soft dough that is smooth and elastic (3 to 5 minutes total). Shape dough into a ball. Place in a lightly greased bowl; turn once to grease surface of dough. Cover; let rise in a warm place until double in size (45 to 60 minutes).

3 Punch dough down. Turn out onto a lightly floured surface. Cover and let rest 10 minutes. Meanwhile, lightly grease a 13×9×2-inch baking pan; set aside. For filling, in a small bowl stir together brown sugar and cinnamon; set aside.

4 Roll dough into an 18×12-inch rectangle (see photo 1, page 117). Spread ¼ cup butter over dough (see photo 2, page 117) and sprinkle with filling, leaving about 1 inch unfilled along the long sides. Roll up rectangle, starting from a filled long side; pinch dough to seal seams (see photos 3 and 4, page 117). Slice rolled rectangle into 12 equal pieces (see photo 5, page 117). Arrange in prepared pan. Cover and let rise in a warm place until nearly double in size (about 30 minutes).

5 Preheat oven to 375°F. Bake 25 to 30 minutes or until golden. Cool in pan on wire rack for 10 minutes; remove from pan. Spread with Icing.

***MASHED COOKED POTATO:** Prick a 10-ounce unpeeled potato all over with a fork. Microwave on 100% power (high) for 5 to 7 minutes or until tender. Halve potato and scoop pulp out of skin into a small bowl; discard skin. Mash the potato pulp with a potato masher or an electric mixer on low speed. Measure 1 cup of mashed potatoes.

ICING: In a bowl stir together 1½ cups powdered sugar, ½ teaspoon vanilla, and enough milk (4 to 6 teaspoons) to reach drizzling consistency.

MAKE-AHEAD DIRECTIONS: Prepare as directed on page 116 through Step 4, except do not let rise after shaping. Cover loosely with oiled waxed paper, then with plastic wrap. Chill for 2 to 24 hours. Before baking, let chilled rolls stand, covered, for 30 minutes at room temperature. Uncover and bake as directed.

PER ROLL: 396 cal., 11 g total fat (6 g sat. fat, 0 g trans fat), 61 mg chol., 283 mg sodium, 68 g carbo., 2 g fiber, 7 g pro. EXCHANGES: 2 Starch, 2½ Other Carbo., 2 Fat

CREAM CHEESE ICING: In a medium bowl beat one 3-ounce package softened cream cheese with 2 tablespoons softened butter and 1 teaspoon vanilla. Gradually beat in 2½ cups powdered sugar until smooth. Beat in milk, 1 teaspoon at a time, to reach spreading consistency.

PER ROLL WITH CREAM CHEESE ICING: 475 cal., 15 g total fat (9 g sat. fat, 0 g trans fat), 74 mg chol., 319 mg sodium, 78 g carbo., 2 g fiber, 7 g pro. EXCHANGES: 2 Starch, 3 Other Carbo., 2½ Fat

CARAMEL-PECAN ROLLS: *(photo, page 101)* Prepare as directed on page 116 through Step 3. In a small saucepan combine ⅔ cup packed brown sugar, ¼ cup butter, and 2 tablespoons light-color corn syrup. Stir over medium heat until combined. Spread mixture in prepared pan. Sprinkle ⅔ cup toasted chopped pecans over butter mixture in pan; set aside. Continue with Step 4, placing rolls on top of pecan-sprinkled mixture in pan. After baking, immediately invert rolls onto a serving platter. Omit the icing.

PER ROLL: 463 cal., 19 g total fat (9 g sat. fat, 0 g trans fat), 71 mg chol., 314 mg sodium, 67 g carbo., 2 g fiber, 8 g pro. EXCHANGES: 2 Starch, 2½ Other Carbo., 3½ Fat

RAISIN-NUT ROLLS: Prepare as directed on page 116, except stir ½ cup golden raisins and/or ½ cup chopped toasted pecans into the filling.

PER ROLL: 416 cal., 11 g total fat (96 g sat. fat, 0 g trans fat), 61 mg chol., 284 mg sodium, 73 g carbo., 2 g fiber, 7 g pro. EXCHANGES: 2 Starch, 3 Other Carbo., 2 Fat

PREPARING CINNAMON ROLLS, STEP-BY-STEP

1. Roll dough from the center to the edges into a rectangle. **2.** Dab softened butter over top, then spread butter, leaving a ½- to 1-inch border at edges. **3.** Starting from a long side, firmly roll up dough, but not too tightly. **4.** Pinch the edge of the dough to the rolled dough to seal. **5.** Score roll to mark 12 rolls. Slide dental floss under roll at scores. Cross floss on top; pull until it cuts through.

ORANGE BOWKNOTS

Shape dough into a ball. Place in a lightly greased bowl, turning once to grease surface of dough. Cover (see photo 3, page 104); let rise in a warm place until double in size (about 1 hour).

3 Punch dough down (see photos 4 and 5, page 104). Turn out onto a lightly floured surface. Divide in half. Cover and let rest 10 minutes. Lightly grease two large baking sheets; set aside.

4 Roll each dough half into a 12×7-inch rectangle. Cut each rectangle into twelve 7-inch-long strips. Tie each strip loosely in a knot. Place knots 2 inches apart on prepared baking sheets. Cover; let rise in a warm place until nearly double in size (about 30 minutes).

5 Preheat oven to 375°F. Bake for 12 to 14 minutes or until golden. Immediately remove from baking sheets. Cool on wire racks. Drizzle with Orange Icing.

ORANGE ICING: In a medium bowl combine 1½ cups powdered sugar, 1½ teaspoons finely shredded orange peel, and enough orange juice (2 to 3 tablespoons) to reach drizzling consistency.

PER ROLL: 203 cal., 5 g total fat (3 g sat. fat, 0 g trans fat), 29 mg chol., 88 mg sodium, 35 g carbo., 1 g fiber, 4 g pro. EXCHANGES: 1½ Starch, ½ Other Carbo., 1 Fat

BEST EVER

ORANGE BOWKNOTS

PREP: 45 MINUTES **RISE:** 90 MINUTES
REST: 10 MINUTES **BAKE:** 12 MINUTES
OVEN: 375°F **MAKES:** 24 ROLLS

- 6 to 6½ cups all-purpose flour
- 1 package active dry yeast
- 1¼ cups milk
- ½ cup butter, cut up
- ⅓ cup sugar
- ½ teaspoon salt
- 2 eggs
- 2 tablespoons finely shredded orange peel
- ¼ cup orange juice
- 1 recipe Orange Icing

1 In a large mixing bowl combine 2 cups of the flour and the yeast; set aside. In a medium saucepan heat and stir the milk, butter, sugar, and salt just until warm (120°F to 130°F) and butter almost melts; add to flour mixture along with eggs. Beat with an electric mixer on low to medium speed for 30 seconds, scraping bowl. Beat on high speed for 3 minutes. Using a wooden spoon, stir in orange peel, orange juice, and as much of the remaining flour as you can.

2 Turn dough out onto a lightly floured surface. Knead in enough remaining flour to make a moderately soft dough that is smooth and elastic (3 to 5 minutes total; see photo 2, page 104).

EASY CINNAMON ROLLS

PREP: 25 MINUTES **RISE:** 60 MINUTES
BAKE: 25 MINUTES **COOL:** 5 MINUTES
OVEN: 375°F **MAKES:** 16 ROLLS

- ½ cup packed brown sugar
- 1 tablespoon ground cinnamon
- 2 16-ounce loaves frozen white bread dough or sweet roll dough, thawed
- 3 tablespoons butter, melted
- ¾ cup raisins (optional)
- 1 recipe Vanilla Icing (page 119)

1 Grease a 13×9×2-inch baking pan; set aside.

2 In a small bowl stir together brown sugar and cinnamon; set aside. On a lightly floured surface roll each loaf of dough into a 12×8-inch rectangle, stopping occasionally to let dough relax if needed. Brush with melted butter; sprinkle with brown sugar mixture. If desired, sprinkle with raisins.

3 Starting from a short side, roll up each dough rectangle. Pinch dough to seal seams. Slice each rolled rectangle into eight equal pieces. Arrange in prepared baking pan. Cover; let rise in a warm place until nearly double (about 1 hour).

4 Preheat oven to 375°F. Break any surface bubbles in rolls with a greased toothpick. Bake for 25 to 30 minutes or until rolls are golden and sound hollow when tapped. If necessary, cover rolls with foil the last 10 minutes of baking to prevent overbrowning. Cool in pan on a wire rack for 5 minutes; remove from pan. Drizzle with icing.

VANILLA ICING: In a small bowl stir together 1½ cups powdered sugar, ½ teaspoon vanilla, and enough milk (2 to 3 tablespoons) to reach drizzling consistency.

MAKE-AHEAD DIRECTIONS: Prepare as directed through Step 3. Cover with oiled waxed paper, then with plastic wrap. Chill for 2 hours or up to 24 hours. Before baking, let rolls stand, covered, for 1 hour at room temperature. Uncover and bake as directed.

PER ROLL: 235 cal., 4 g total fat (1 g sat. fat, 0 g trans fat), 6 mg chol., 284 mg sodium, 45 g carbo., 1 g fiber, 3 g pro. EXCHANGES: 1 Starch, 2 Other Carbo., ½ Fat

EASY CARAMEL-PECAN ROLLS: Prepare as directed, except generously grease the pan and line with parchment paper or nonstick foil. Stir together 1¼ cups powdered sugar and ⅓ cup whipping cream; pour evenly into prepared pan, spreading gently. Sprinkle 1 cup coarsely chopped pecans evenly over mixture. Continue as directed.

PER ROLL: 336 cal., 11 g total fat (3 g sat. fat, 0 g trans fat), 13 mg chol., 286 mg sodium, 55 g carbo., 1 g fiber, 4 g pro. EXCHANGES: 1 Starch, 2½ Other Carbo., 2 Fat

---

CHECKERBOARD ROLLS

DIP FROZEN ROLL DOUGH IN TOPPINGS FOR AN EYE-CATCHING SIDE.

In a shallow dish stir together 2 tablespoons *each* poppy seeds and sesame seeds and 1 teaspoon lemon-pepper seasoning. In a second dish stir together 2 tablespoons *each* yellow cornmeal and grated Parmesan cheese. Place 3 tablespoons melted butter in a third dish. Working quickly, roll 16 pieces (1.3 ounces each) frozen white roll dough in butter. Lightly coat eight rolls in poppy seed mixture and eight rolls in cornmeal mixture. Alternate rolls in a greased 9×9×2-inch pan. Cover with lightly greased plastic wrap; thaw in refrigerator for 8 to 24 hours. Before baking, let stand at room temperature for 45 minutes. Bake in a 375°F oven for 20 to 25 minutes or until golden. Makes 16 rolls.

QUICK FOCACCIA

PREP: 15 MINUTES **BAKE:** 18 MINUTES
COOL: 5 MINUTES **OVEN:** 400°F
MAKES: 16 SERVINGS

- 1 13.8-ounce package refrigerated pizza dough
- 1 to 2 tablespoons olive oil
- 2 cloves garlic, minced
- ½ cup pitted Kalamata or pitted ripe olives, halved or sliced (optional)
- 1 teaspoon snipped fresh rosemary or ½ teaspoon dried rosemary, crushed
- ½ teaspoon coarse salt or kosher salt
- ½ cup finely shredded Parmesan cheese (2 ounces)

1 Preheat oven to 400°F. On a greased large baking sheet unroll dough and stretch slightly.

2 Brush olive oil evenly over dough. Sprinkle with garlic, olives (if desired), rosemary, salt, and cheese. Bake for 18 to 20 minutes or until crisp and brown. Cool on a wire rack for 5 minutes. Cut into squares to serve.

TOMATO FOCACCIA: Place 2 cups halved grape tomatoes in a microwave-safe bowl. Microwave, uncovered, on 100% power (high) for 3 minutes, stirring once halfway through cooking. Drain tomatoes and let cool for 5 minutes. Prepare focaccia as directed, except substitute 1 tablespoon snipped fresh basil or ½ teaspoon dried basil, crushed, for the rosemary and add drained tomatoes with toppings before sprinkling with the cheese.

VEGETABLE FOCACCIA: Prepare as directed, except toss 1½ cups vegetables including sliced mushrooms, thinly sliced red onion, 1-inch pieces trimmed fresh asparagus, and/or drained and cut-up canned artichoke hearts with 1 tablespoon olive oil. Place on brushed focaccia crust with toppings before sprinkling with cheese.

PER SQUARE PLAIN, TOMATO, OR VEGETABLE VARIATIONS: 69 cal., 3 g total fat (1 g sat. fat, 0 g trans fat), 2 mg chol., 171 mg sodium, 9 g carbo., 0 g fiber, 2 g pro. EXCHANGES: ½ Starch, ½ Fat

GARLIC BREAD

PREP: 15 MINUTES **BAKE:** 12 MINUTES
OVEN: 400°F **MAKES:** 12 SERVINGS

  1 16-ounce loaf baguette-style French
    bread
  ½ cup butter, softened
  ½ teaspoon garlic salt

1 Preheat oven to 400°F. Using a serrated knife, cut bread in half horizontally.

2 In a small bowl stir together butter and garlic salt. Spread mixture on cut sides of bread halves. Reassemble loaf and wrap tightly in heavy foil.

3 Bake for 12 to 15 minutes or until heated through. (To broil, place bread on a baking sheet, spread sides up. Broil 4 to 5 inches from the heat for 3 to 4 minutes or until toasted.)

ROASTED GARLIC BREAD: Preheat oven to 425°F. With a sharp knife, cut ½ inch off the tops of two whole garlic bulbs to expose the ends of the individual cloves. Leaving garlic bulbs whole, remove any loose, papery outer layers. Place garlic bulbs in a shallow baking dish. Drizzle with 2 teaspoons olive oil. Cover with foil. Roast for 25 to 35 minutes or until garlic cloves are soft when gently squeezed. When cool enough to handle, squeeze garlic out of the bulbs. In a small bowl stir together ½ cup butter, softened, and the roasted garlic. Spread mixture on bread and bake or broil as directed.

PER SERVING PLAIN OR ROASTED VARIATION: 177 cal., 8 g total fat (5 g sat. fat, 0 g trans fat), 20 mg chol., 340 mg sodium, 21 g carbo., 1 g fiber, 5 g pro. EXCHANGES: 1½ Starch, 1½ Fat

HERBED GARLIC BREAD: In a food processor combine 6 cloves garlic, ¼ cup packed fresh basil leaves, 2 tablespoons fresh Italian parsley leaves, 1 tablespoon fresh oregano leaves, ¼ teaspoon salt, and ¼ teaspoon black pepper. Cover and pulse until chopped. Add ½ cup butter, softened, and 2 tablespoons olive oil. Cover and pulse until combined. Spread mixture on bread and bake or broil as directed.

PER SERVING: 200 cal., 11 g total fat (5 g sat. fat, 0 g trans fat), 20 mg chol., 349 mg sodium, 22 g carbo., 1 g fiber, 5 g pro. EXCHANGES: 1½ Starch, 2 Fat

CORN BREAD

PREP: 15 MINUTES **BAKE:** 20 MINUTES
OVEN: 400°F **MAKES:** 9 SERVINGS

  1 cup cornmeal
  ¾ cup all-purpose flour
  2 to 4 tablespoons sugar
  2½ teaspoons baking powder
  ½ teaspoon salt
  1 cup milk
  2 eggs
  ¼ cup butter, melted

1 Preheat oven to 400°F. Grease an 8×8×2-inch square or 9×1½-inch round baking pan; set aside. In a medium bowl stir together cornmeal, flour, sugar, baking powder, and salt; set aside.

2 In a bowl whisk together the milk, eggs, and butter. Add milk mixture all at once to cornmeal mixture. Stir just until moistened. Pour batter into prepared pan.

3 Bake about 20 minutes or until edges are golden brown. Cool slightly; serve warm.

STONE-GROUND CORN BREAD: Prepare as directed, except substitute ½ cup yellow cornmeal with ½ cup stone-ground yellow cornmeal.

PER SERVING PLAIN OR STONE-GROUND VARIATION: 173 cal., 7 g total fat (4 g sat. fat, 0 g trans fat), 63 mg chol., 298 mg sodium, 23 g carbo., 1 g fiber, 5 g pro. EXCHANGES: 1½ Other Carbo., 1 Fat

CORN MUFFINS: Prepare as directed, except spoon batter into 12 greased 2½-inch muffin cups, filling cups two-thirds full. Bake in a 400°F oven about 15 minutes or until edges are golden brown. Makes 12 muffins.

9-INCH CAST-IRON SKILLET: Prepare as directed, except place skillet in oven with unmelted butter; when butter melts, swirl pan to coat and pour butter into milk mixture. Continue as above, working quickly so batter goes into hot skillet. Bake as directed. Makes 12 wedges.

PER MUFFIN OR WEDGE: 130 cal., 6 g total fat (3 g sat. fat, 0 g trans fat), 47 mg chol., 224 mg sodium, 17 g carbo., 1 g fiber, 3 g pro. EXCHANGES: 1 Starch, 1 Fat

CORN STICKS: Prepare as directed, except generously grease corn stick pans; heat in preheated oven for 3 minutes. Carefully fill preheated pans two-thirds full. Bake in a 400°F oven for 12 to 15 minutes or until edges are golden brown. Makes about 20 corn sticks.

PER STICK: 78 cal., 3 g total fat (2 g sat. fat, 0 g trans fat), 28 mg chol., 134 mg sodium, 10 g carbo., 1 g fiber, 2 g pro. EXCHANGES: ½ Starch, ½ Fat

QUICK SEED BREAD

PREP: 20 MINUTES **BAKE:** 45 MINUTES
COOL: 10 MINUTES **STAND:** OVERNIGHT
OVEN: 350°F **MAKES:** 1 LOAF (14 SLICES)

- 1½ cups all-purpose flour
- ½ cup whole wheat flour
- ¾ cup packed brown sugar
- ½ cup dry-roasted sunflower kernels
- ⅓ cup flaxseed meal
- 2 tablespoons sesame seeds
- 2 tablespoons poppy seeds
- 1 teaspoon baking powder
- ½ teaspoon baking soda
- ½ teaspoon salt
- 1 egg
- 1¼ cups buttermilk or sour milk (see tip, page 19)
- ¼ cup vegetable oil
- 4 teaspoons sesame seeds, poppy seeds and/or dry-roasted sunflower kernels

1 Preheat oven to 350°F. Grease the bottom and ½ inch up sides of a 9×5×3-inch loaf pan (see photo, page 103); set aside.

2 In a large bowl stir together the flours, brown sugar, ½ cup sunflower kernels, flaxseed meal, the 2 tablespoons sesame seeds, the 2 tablespoons poppy seeds, baking powder, baking soda, and salt. Make a well in the center of the flour mixture; set aside. In a medium bowl beat egg with a fork; stir in buttermilk and oil. Add egg mixture all at once to flour mixture. Stir just until moistened (batter should be lumpy). Spread batter into prepared pan. Sprinkle with the 4 teaspoons seeds.

3 Bake for 45 to 55 minutes or until a wooden toothpick inserted near the center comes out clean. Cool in pan on a wire rack for 10 minutes. Remove from pan. Cool completely on wire rack. Wrap and store bread overnight before slicing.

PER SLICE: 216 cal., 10 g total fat (1 g sat. fat, 0 g trans fat), 16 mg chol., 180 mg sodium, 28 g carbo., 2 g fiber, 5 g pro. **EXCHANGES:** 2 Starch, 1½ Fat

*SOUR MILK TO MAKE 1¼ CUPS SOUR MILK, PLACE 4 TEASPOONS LEMON JUICE OR VINEGAR IN A GLASS MEASURING CUP. ADD ENOUGH MILK TO MAKE 1¼ CUPS TOTAL. LET STAND FOR 5 MINUTES.

QUICK SEED BREAD

CRANBERRY-NUT BREAD

MARBLING THE BATTER, STEP-BY-STEP

1. Pour the remaining half of the batter over the cinnamon mixture in the pan. **2.** To swirl the cinnamon mixture throughout the batter, use a thin metal spatula or table knife to cut down through the batter. Pull the batter up and over in a circular motion. Repeat a few times in different areas of the batter.

CINNAMON-NUT BREAD

PREP: 30 MINUTES **BAKE:** 55 MINUTES
COOL: 10 MINUTES **STAND:** OVERNIGHT
OVEN: 350°F **MAKES:** 1 LOAF (14 SLICES)

1⅓ cups sugar
½ cup finely chopped pecans or walnuts, toasted (see tip, page 20)
2 teaspoons ground cinnamon
2 cups all-purpose flour
1 teaspoon baking powder
½ teaspoon salt
1 egg
1 cup milk
⅓ cup vegetable oil

1 Preheat oven to 350°F. Grease and flour the bottom and ½ inch up the sides of a 9×5×3-inch loaf pan (see photo, page 103); set aside. In a small bowl stir together ⅓ cup of the sugar, the pecans, and cinnamon; set aside.

2 In a large bowl stir together the remaining 1 cup sugar, the flour, baking powder, and salt. In a medium bowl beat egg with a fork; stir in milk and oil. Add egg mixture all at once to flour mixture. Stir just until moistened (batter should be lumpy).

3 Spoon half of the batter into prepared pan. Sprinkle with half of the cinnamon mixture. Repeat with remaining batter and cinnamon mixture (see photo 1, page 122). Using a thin metal spatula or table knife, cut down through batter and pull up in a circular motion to marble the cinnamon mixture (see photo 2, page 122).

4 Bake for 55 to 60 minutes or until a wooden toothpick inserted near center comes out clean. Cool in pan on a wire rack for 10 minutes. Remove from pan. Cool completely on wire rack. Wrap and store overnight before slicing.

PER SLICE: 227 cal., 9 g total fat (1 g sat. fat, 0 g trans fat), 17 mg chol., 122 mg sodium, 35 g carbo., 1 g fiber, 3 g pro. EXCHANGES: ½ Starch, 1½ Other Carbo., 2 Fat

CRANBERRY-NUT BREAD: Prepare as directed, except fold 1 cup coarsely chopped cranberries into batter.

BLUEBERRY-NUT BREAD: Prepare as directed, except fold 1 cup fresh blueberries into batter.

PER SLICE CRANBERRY OR BLUEBERRY VARIATION: 233 cal., 9 g total fat (1 g sat. fat, 0 g trans fat), 17 mg chol., 122 mg sodium, 36 g carbo., 1 g fiber, 3 g pro. EXCHANGES: 1 Starch, 1½ Other Carbo., 2 Fat

BEST EVER

PUMPKIN BREAD

PREP: 20 MINUTES **BAKE:** 55 MINUTES
COOL: 10 MINUTES **STAND:** OVERNIGHT
OVEN: 350°F **MAKES:** 2 LOAVES (32 SLICES)

3 cups sugar
1 cup vegetable oil
4 eggs
3⅓ cups all-purpose flour
2 teaspoons baking soda
1½ teaspoons salt
1 teaspoon ground cinnamon
1 teaspoon ground nutmeg
1 15-ounce can pumpkin

1 Preheat oven to 350°F. Grease the bottom and ½ inch up sides of two 9×5×3-inch loaf pans; set aside. In an extra-large mixing bowl beat sugar and oil with an electric mixer on medium speed. Add eggs and beat well; set sugar mixture aside.

2 In a large bowl combine flour, baking soda, salt, cinnamon, and nutmeg. Alternately add flour mixture and ⅔ cup *water* to sugar mixture, beating on low speed after each addition just until combined. Beat in pumpkin. Spoon batter into prepared pans.

3 Bake for 55 to 60 minutes or until a wooden toothpick inserted near centers comes out clean. Cool in pans on a wire rack for 10 minutes. Remove from pans. Cool completely on wire rack. Wrap and store overnight before slicing.

PER SLICE: 195 cal., 8 g total fat (1 g sat. fat, 0 g trans fat), 26 mg chol., 198 mg sodium, 30 g carbo., 1 g fiber, 2 g pro. EXCHANGES: ½ Starch, 1½ Other Carbo., 1½ Fat

CREAM CHEESE RIBBON PUMPKIN BREAD: Prepare as directed in Step 1, except use three 8×4×2-inch pans. In a medium mixing bowl beat together half an 8-ounce package cream cheese, softened, and ¼ cup sugar with electric mixer on medium speed until combined. Beat in ½ cup dairy sour cream, 1 egg, and 1 tablespoon milk until combined. Stir in 3 tablespoons finely chopped crystallized ginger; set aside. Prepare batter as directed. Pour 1½ cups batter into each pan. Divide cream cheese mixture evenly among pans. Spoon remaining batter over cream cheese mixture; spread evenly. Bake 60 to 65 minutes or until cracks on tops of loaves appear dry. Cool as directed; wrap and refrigerate overnight before slicing. Let bread stand at room temperature for 1 hour before serving.

PER SLICE: 223 cal., 10 g total fat (2 g sat. fat, 0 g trans fat), 39 mg chol., 214 mg sodium, 32 g carbo., 1 g fiber, 3 g pro. EXCHANGES: ½ Starch, 1½ Other Carbo., 2 Fat

ZUCCHINI BREAD

PREP: 25 MINUTES **BAKE:** 55 MINUTES
COOL: 10 MINUTES **STAND:** OVERNIGHT
OVEN: 350°F **MAKES:** 2 LOAVES (28 SLICES)

     3 cups all-purpose flour
     1 tablespoon baking powder
  1½ teaspoons ground cinnamon
     1 teaspoon salt
     2 eggs, lightly beaten
     2 cups sugar
  2½ cups coarsely shredded, unpeeled
         zucchini
     1 cup vegetable oil
     2 teaspoons vanilla
     1 cup chopped walnuts or pecans (optional)
   ⅔ cup raisins (optional)

1 Preheat oven to 350°F. Grease bottom and
½ inch up sides of two 8×4×2-inch loaf pans (see
photo, page 103); set aside. In a large bowl stir
together flour, baking powder, cinnamon, and salt.
Make a well in center of flour mixture; set aside.

2 In a medium bowl combine eggs, sugar, shredded zucchini, oil, and vanilla. Add zucchini mixture
all at once to flour mixture. Stir just until moistened
(batter should be lumpy). If desired, fold in nuts and
raisins. Spoon batter into prepared pans.

3 Bake about 55 minutes or until a wooden
toothpick inserted near centers comes out clean.
Cool in pans on a wire rack for 10 minutes.
Remove from pans. Cool completely on wire rack.
Wrap and store overnight before slicing.

PER SLICE: 181 cal., 8 g total fat (1 g sat. fat, 0 g trans fat),
15 mg chol., 115 mg sodium, 25 g carbo., 1 g fiber, 2 g pro.
EXCHANGES: ½ Starch, 1 Other Carbo., 1½ Fat

PICK A QUICK BREAD PAN

To use a different size pan than specified in
a recipe, adjust the baking time. Remember
to fill the pan only two-thirds full. Bake any
leftover batter into muffins (see tip, page
126). Baking times are approximate.

Pan Size	Baking Time
9×5×3-inch loaf pan	55 to 75 min.
8×4×2-inch loaf pan	50 to 60 min.
7½×3½×2-inch loaf pans	40 to 45 min.
4½×2½×1½-inch loaf pans	30 to 35 min.
2½-inch muffin cups	15 to 18 min.

BEST EVER

BANANA BREAD

PREP: 25 MINUTES **BAKE:** 55 MINUTES
COOL: 10 MINUTES **STAND:** OVERNIGHT
OVEN: 350°F **MAKES:** 1 LOAF (16 SLICES)

     2 cups all-purpose flour
  1½ teaspoons baking powder
   ½ teaspoon baking soda
   ½ teaspoon ground cinnamon
   ¼ teaspoon salt
   ¼ teaspoon ground nutmeg
   ⅛ teaspoon ground ginger
     2 eggs, lightly beaten
  1½ cups mashed bananas (4 to 5 medium)
     1 cup sugar
   ½ cup vegetable oil or melted butter
   ¼ cup chopped walnuts
     1 recipe Streusel-Nut Topping (optional)

1 Preheat oven to 350°F. Grease bottom and
½ inch up the sides of one 9×5×3-inch or two
7½×3½×2-inch loaf pans (see photo, page 103);
set aside. In a large bowl combine flour, baking
powder, baking soda, cinnamon, salt, nutmeg,
and ginger. Make a well in center of flour mixture;
set aside.

2 In a medium bowl combine eggs, banana,
sugar, and oil. Add egg mixture all at once to flour
mixture. Stir just until moistened (batter should
be lumpy). Fold in walnuts. Spoon batter into
prepared pan(s). If desired, sprinkle Streusel-Nut
Topping over batter.

3 Bake for 55 to 60 minutes for 9×5×3-inch pan
or 40 to 45 minutes for 7½×3½×2-inch pans or
until a wooden toothpick inserted near center(s)
comes out clean. If necessary, cover loosely with
foil the last 15 minutes of baking to prevent overbrowning. Cool in pan(s) on a wire rack for
10 minutes. Remove from pan(s). Cool completely
on rack. Wrap and store overnight before slicing.

PER SLICE: 213 cal., 9 g total fat (1 g sat. fat, 0 g trans fat),
26 mg chol., 108 mg sodium, 32 g carbo., 1 g fiber, 3 g pro.
EXCHANGES: 1 Starch, 1 Other Carbo., 1½ Fat

STREUSEL-NUT TOPPING: In a bowl combine
¼ cup packed brown sugar and 3 tablespoons
all-purpose flour. Using a pastry blender, cut in
2 tablespoons butter until mixture resembles
coarse crumbs. Stir in ⅓ cup chopped walnuts.

MAKE-IT-MINE MUFFINS

VARY YOUR MUFFINS ACCORDING TO WHAT YOU CRAVE, WHAT'S IN SEASON, OR WHAT YOU HAPPEN TO HAVE ON HAND. FIRST DECIDE WHETHER YOU WANT A SWEET OR SAVORY TREAT, THEN CHOOSE YOUR INGREDIENTS ACCORDINGLY.

BASIC INGREDIENTS

PREP: 20 MINUTES
BAKE: 15 MINUTES
COOL: 5 MINUTES
OVEN: 400°F
MAKES: 12 MUFFINS

Flour
¼ cup granulated sugar or packed brown sugar
1½ teaspoons baking powder
½ teaspoon baking soda
¼ teaspoon salt
2 eggs, lightly beaten
Liquid
¾ cup buttermilk, sour milk (see tip, page 19), or milk
2 tablespoons butter, melted, or vegetable oil
Stir-In
Topping (optional)

FLOUR (PICK ONE)

2 cups all-purpose flour
1⅓ cups all-purpose flour and ¾ cup buckwheat flour
1½ cups all-purpose flour and ¾ cup quick-cooking oats
1 cup all-purpose flour and 1 cup yellow cornmeal
1 cup all-purpose flour and 1 cup rye flour
½ cup all-purpose flour and 1½ cups whole wheat flour

LIQUID (PICK ONE)

SAVORY OPTIONS

¾ cup ricotta cheese
¾ cup dairy sour cream
¾ cup plain yogurt
¾ cup finely shredded unpeeled zucchini

SWEET OPTIONS

¾ cup canned pumpkin
¾ cup applesauce
¾ cup lemon curd

STIR-IN (PICK ONE)

SAVORY OPTIONS

2 to 4 tablespoons thinly sliced green onions
2 to 4 tablespoons finely chopped sweet pepper
2 to 4 tablespoons crumbled crisp-cooked bacon
2 tablespoons grated Parmesan cheese

SWEET OPTIONS

¾ cup fresh or frozen blueberries
⅓ cup dried fruit (blueberries; raisins; chopped cranberries or cherries; snipped dates, apricots, or figs)

TOPPING (PICK ONE)

SAVORY OPTION

Chip Topping (right)

SWEET OPTION

Streusel Topping (right)

BASIC INSTRUCTIONS

1 Preheat oven to 400°F. Grease twelve 2½-inch muffin cups; set aside. In a medium bowl stir together the Flour, sugar, baking powder, baking soda, and salt. Make a well in center of flour mixture; set aside.

2 In a bowl combine eggs, Liquid, buttermilk, and butter. Add egg mixture all at once to flour mixture. Stir just until moistened (batter should be lumpy). Fold in Stir-In.

3 Spoon batter into prepared muffin cups, filling each half to two-thirds full. If desired, sprinkle Topping over batter in cups.

4 Bake for 15 to 18 minutes or until golden. Cool in muffin cups on a wire rack for 5 minutes. Remove from muffin cups; serve warm.

CHIP TOPPING: Crush 1 cup of your favorite flavored potato chips or dry cereal flakes; measure about ⅓ cup crushed.

STREUSEL TOPPING: In a small bowl stir together 3 tablespoons all-purpose flour, 3 tablespoons packed brown sugar, and ¼ teaspoon ground cinnamon or ground ginger. Cut in 2 tablespoons butter until mixture resembles coarse crumbs. If desired, stir in 2 tablespoons chopped nuts and 2 tablespoons coconut.

BRAN CEREAL MUFFINS

PREP: 15 MINUTES **BAKE:** 20 MINUTES
COOL: 5 MINUTES **OVEN:** 400°F **MAKES:** 24 MUFFINS

  1 cup boiling water
  3 cups whole bran cereal (not flakes)
2½ cups all-purpose flour
  ½ cup granulated sugar
  ½ cup packed brown sugar
  2 teaspoons baking powder
  1 teaspoon ground cinnamon (optional)
  ½ teaspoon baking soda
  ½ teaspoon salt
  2 eggs
  2 cups buttermilk
  ½ cup vegetable oil

1 Preheat oven to 400°F. Grease twenty-four 2½-inch muffin cups or line with paper bake cups; set aside. In a medium bowl pour boiling water over cereal. Stir to moisten cereal; set aside.

2 In another medium bowl combine flour, granulated sugar, brown sugar, baking powder, cinnamon (if desired), baking soda, and salt. In a large bowl combine eggs, buttermilk, and oil. Stir cereal and flour mixture into buttermilk mixture just until moistened.

3 Spoon batter into prepared muffin cups, filling each three-fourths full. Bake about 20 minutes or until a wooden toothpick inserted in centers comes out clean. Cool in muffin cups on a wire rack for 5 minutes. Remove from muffin cups; serve warm.

PER MUFFIN: 162 cal., 5 g total fat (1 g sat. fat, 0 g trans fat), 18 mg chol., 201 mg sodium, 29 g carbo., 5 g fiber, 3 g pro.
EXCHANGES: ½ Starch, 1½ Other Carbo., 1 Fat

PICK A MUFFIN PAN

Muffin cups come in various sizes. To make muffins in a size other than specified, prepare the batter as directed. Adjust baking time and temperature as indicated below. Baking times are approximate.

Pan Size	Time/Temperature
Mini (1¾-inch)	10 to 12 min./400°F
Standard (2½-inch)	15 to 18 min./400°F
Jumbo (3½-inch)	about 30 min./350°F
Muffin tops (3½-inch)	8 to 10 min./400°F

DOUBLE CHOCOLATE MUFFINS

PREP: 15 MINUTES **BAKE:** 18 MINUTES
COOL: 5 MINUTES **OVEN:** 375°F
MAKES: 12 MUFFINS

1¼ cups all-purpose flour
  ½ cup granulated sugar
  ⅓ cup packed brown sugar
  ¼ cup unsweetened cocoa powder
  2 teaspoons baking powder
  ¼ teaspoon baking soda
  ¼ teaspoon salt
  1 cup miniature semisweet chocolate
      pieces
  ½ cup vegetable oil
  ½ cup milk
  1 egg

1 Preheat oven to 375°F. Grease twelve 2½-inch muffin cups or line with paper bake cups; set aside. In a medium bowl combine flour, granulated sugar, brown sugar, cocoa powder, baking powder, baking soda, and salt. Stir in chocolate pieces. Make a well in center of flour mixture; set aside.

2 In a small bowl whisk together the oil, milk, and egg. Add oil mixture all at once to the flour mixture. Stir just until moistened.

3 Spoon batter into prepared muffin cups, filling each two-thirds full. Bake for 18 to 20 minutes or until edges are firm (tops will be slightly rounded). Cool in muffin cups on a wire rack for 5 minutes. Remove from muffin cups; serve warm.

PER MUFFIN: 295 cal., 15 g total fat (4 g sat. fat, 0 g trans fat), 19 mg chol., 148 mg sodium, 38 g carbo., 2 g fiber, 3 g pro.
EXCHANGES: 1 Starch, 1½ Other Carbo., 3 Fat

MIXING UP MUFFINS

AFTER ADDING THE LIQUIDS TO THE FLOUR MIXTURE, STIR JUST UNTIL THE DRY INGREDIENTS ARE MOIST. THE BATTER WILL LOOK LUMPY WITH LITTLE BITS OF FLOUR. DO NOT OVERMIX.

FLAKY BISCUITS

PREP: 15 MINUTES **BAKE:** 10 MINUTES
OVEN: 450°F **MAKES:** 12 BISCUITS

- 3 cups all-purpose flour
- 1 tablespoon baking powder*
- 1 tablespoon sugar
- 1 teaspoon salt
- ¾ teaspoon cream of tartar*
- ¾ cup butter, cut up, or ½ cup butter and
  ¼ cup shortening
- 1 cup milk

1 Preheat oven to 450°F. In a large bowl combine flour, baking powder, sugar, salt, and cream of tartar. Cut in butter until mixture resembles coarse crumbs (see photo 1, below). Make a well in the center of the flour mixture. Add milk all at once. Using a fork, stir just until mixture is moistened.

2 Turn dough out onto a lightly floured surface. Knead dough by folding and gently pressing it just until dough holds together. Pat or lightly roll dough until ¾ inch thick (see photo 2, below). Cut dough with a floured 2½-inch round cutter; reroll scraps as necessary; dip cutter into flour between cuts.

3 Place dough circles 1 inch apart on an ungreased baking sheet. Bake for 10 to 14 minutes or until golden. Remove biscuits from baking sheet and serve warm.

***NOTE:** If baking powder or cream of tartar is lumpy, sift it through a fine-mesh sieve.

DROP BISCUITS: Prepare as directed through Step 1, except increase the milk to 1¼ cups. Using a large spoon, drop dough into 12 mounds onto a greased baking sheet. Bake as directed. Makes 12 biscuits.

BUTTERMILK BISCUITS: Prepare as directed, except for rolled-dough biscuits, substitute 1¼ cups buttermilk or sour milk (see tip, page 19) for the 1 cup milk. For drop biscuits, substitute 1½ cups buttermilk or sour milk for the 1¼ cups milk.

MAKE-AHEAD DIRECTIONS: Biscuit dough can be made ahead and refrigerated for up to 3 days. Bake refrigerated dough for 20 to 22 minutes.

PER BISCUIT FOR PLAIN, DROP, OR BUTTERMILK VARIATIONS: 231 cal., 12 g total fat (8 g sat. fat, 0 g trans fat), 32 mg chol., 375 mg sodium, 26 g carbo., 1 g fiber, 4 g pro. EXCHANGES: 2 Starch, 2 Fat

PREPARING BISCUITS, STEP-BY-STEP

1. Use a pastry blender to cut butter into the flour mixture. Cut and combine until butter is uniform in size and mixture looks like coarse crumbs. **2.** On a lightly floured surface, use your hands to pat dough to the specified thickness. Measure thickness with a ruler. **3.** Lightly handling the dough will help you achieve irresistibly tender biscuits like these.

SCONES

PREP: 20 MINUTES **BAKE:** 12 MINUTES
OVEN: 400°F **MAKES:** 12 SCONES

2½ cups all-purpose flour
 2 tablespoons granulated sugar
 1 tablespoon baking powder
 ¼ teaspoon salt
 ⅓ cup butter, cut up
 2 eggs, beaten
 ¾ cup whipping cream
 ½ cup dried currants or snipped raisins
    Whipping cream or milk
    Coarse sugar

1 Preheat oven to 400°F. In a bowl combine flour, 2 tablespoons granulated sugar, baking powder, and salt. Cut in butter until mixture resembles coarse crumbs (see photo 1, page 127). Make a well in center of flour mixture; set aside.

2 In a medium bowl combine eggs, the ¾ cup whipping cream, and the currants. Add egg mixture all at once to flour mixture. Using a fork, stir just until moistened.

3 Turn dough out onto a lightly floured surface. Knead dough by folding and gently pressing it for 10 to 12 strokes or until dough is nearly smooth. Divide dough in half. Pat or lightly roll each dough half into a 6-inch circle. Cut each circle into six wedges.

4 Place dough wedges 2 inches apart on an ungreased baking sheet. Brush wedges with whipping cream and sprinkle with coarse sugar. Bake for 12 to 14 minutes or until golden. Remove scones from baking sheet; serve warm.

CHERRY SCONES: Prepare as directed, except omit the currants. In a small bowl pour enough boiling water over ½ cup snipped dried tart red cherries to cover. Let cherries stand for 5 minutes; drain well. Stir drained cherries and ¼ teaspoon almond extract in with egg mixture.

CHOCOLATE CHIP SCONES: Prepare as directed, except add ⅛ teaspoon ground cinnamon to the flour mixture and substitute ½ cup miniature semisweet chocolate pieces for the currants.

ORANGE SCONES: Prepare as directed, except omit the currants and stir in 1½ teaspoons finely shredded orange peel with egg mixture. Bake as directed. For icing, combine 1 cup powdered sugar, 1 tablespoon orange juice, and ¼ teaspoon vanilla; stir in additional orange juice,

1 teaspoon at a time, to reach a drizzling consistency. Drizzle over baked scones.

PER SCONE FOR PLAIN, CHERRY, CHOCOLATE CHIP, OR ORANGE VARIATIONS: 237 cal., 12 g total fat (7 g sat. fat, 0 g trans fat), 71 mg chol., 164 mg sodium, 28 g carbo., 1 g fiber, 4 g pro.
EXCHANGES: 1 Starch, 1 Other Carbo., 2 Fat

BACON AND CRACKED BLACK PEPPER BISCUITS

PREP: 25 MINUTES **BAKE:** 10 MINUTES
OVEN: 400°F **MAKES:** 10 TO 12 APPETIZERS

 9 slices thick-sliced bacon, crisp-cooked and drained
 2 cups all-purpose flour
 1 tablespoon sugar
2½ teaspoons baking powder
 1 teaspoon cracked black pepper
 ½ teaspoon salt
 6 tablespoons cold butter, cut up
 ½ cup half-and-half or light cream
 1 egg, lightly beaten
 ½ cup mayonnaise
 2 roma tomatoes, sliced
10 to 12 baby spinach or small lettuce leaves

1 Preheat oven to 400°F. Finely chop 3 slices bacon. Cut remaining bacon slices into quarters; set aside. In a large bowl combine flour, sugar, baking powder, pepper, and salt. Using a pastry blender, cut in butter until mixture resembles coarse crumbs (see photo 1, page 127). Stir in finely chopped bacon. Make a well in center of flour mixture; set aside. In a small bowl combine half-and-half and egg. Add all at once to flour mixture. Using a fork, stir just until moistened.

2 Turn dough out onto a lightly floured surface. Knead dough by folding and gently pressing it until dough is nearly smooth. Pat or lightly roll until ½ inch thick (see photo 2, page 127). Cut dough with a floured 2-inch round cutter; reroll scraps as necessary and dip cutter into flour between cuts.

3 Place dough circles 1 inch apart on an ungreased baking sheet. Bake for 10 to 12 minutes or until golden. Cool slightly.

4 To serve, split each biscuit. Spread bottoms of biscuits with mayonnaise. Top each with a tomato slice, a few spinach leaves, and two bacon pieces. Add biscuit tops.

PER APPETIZER: 321 cal., 22 g total fat (8 g sat. fat, 0 g trans fat), 57 mg chol., 564 mg sodium, 23 g carbo., 1 g fiber, 8 g pro.
EXCHANGES: 1½ Starch, ½ High-Fat Meat, 3½ Fat

BACON AND CRACKED BLACK PEPPER BISCUITS

PARTY BITES BISCUITS AND SCONES ARE GREAT FOR ENTERTAINING. SPLIT AND FILL WITH SANDWICH TOPPINGS FOR COCKTAIL PARTIES. SERVE WITH WHIPPED CREAM AND JAM FOR TEATIME GATHERINGS.

CHERRY SCONES

TOMATO-PESTO SCONES WITH KALAMATA OLIVES

4 Turn dough out onto a lightly floured surface. Knead dough by folding and gently pressing it for 10 to 12 strokes just until dough holds together. With floured hands, pat or lightly roll dough to a 9×6-inch rectangle on prepared baking sheet. Using a sharp knife, cut rectangle into nine to 15 diamond pieces (do not separate). Lightly press the 2 reserved tomatoes and a few *rosemary sprigs* into top of dough. Brush with olive oil. Bake for 12 to 14 minutes or until light brown. Gently pull or cut scones to separate. Serve warm.

PER SCONE: 208 cal., 9 g total fat (4 g sat. fat, 0 g trans fat), 39 mg chol., 595 mg sodium, 27 g carbo., 2 g fiber, 5 g pro. EXCHANGES: 2 Starch, 1½ Fat

POPOVERS

PREP: 10 MINUTES **BAKE:** 35 MINUTES
OVEN: 400°F **MAKES:** 6 POPOVERS

- 1 tablespoon shortening
- 2 eggs, lightly beaten
- 1 cup milk
- 1 tablespoon vegetable oil
- 1 cup all-purpose flour
- ½ teaspoon salt

1 Preheat oven to 400°F. Using ½ teaspoon shortening for each cup, grease the bottoms and sides of popover pan cups or six 6-ounce custard cups. Place custard cups in a 15×10×1-inch baking pan; set aside.

2 In a medium bowl use a wire whisk to beat eggs, milk, and oil until combined. Add flour and salt; beat until smooth.

3 Fill the prepared cups half full with batter. Bake about 35 minutes or until very firm.

4 Immediately after removing from oven, prick each popover to let steam escape. Turn off oven. For crisper popovers, return popovers to oven 5 to 10 minutes or until desired crispness is reached. Remove popovers from cups; serve immediately.

ASIAGO POPOVERS: Prepare as directed, except add 2 tablespoons grated Asiago or Parmesan cheese with the flour.

HERB POPOVERS: Prepare as directed, except stir 1 tablespoon finely snipped fresh dill or basil or ¾ teaspoon dried dillweed or basil, crushed, into batter before pouring it into cups or pans.

PER POPOVER FOR PLAIN, ASIAGO, OR HERB VARIATIONS: 158 cal., 7 g total fat (2 g sat. fat, 0 g trans fat), 74 mg chol., 234 mg sodium, 18 g carbo., 1 g fiber, 6 g pro. EXCHANGES: 1 Starch, 1 Fat

BEST EVER

TOMATO-PESTO SCONES WITH KALAMATA OLIVES

PREP: 25 MINUTES **BAKE:** 12 MINUTES
OVEN: 425°F **MAKES:** 9 TO 15 SCONES

- 1 cup dried tomatoes (not oil-packed)
- 2 cups all-purpose flour
- 1 0.5-ounce envelope pesto sauce mix
- 2 teaspoons baking powder
- ½ teaspoon baking soda
- ¼ cup butter, cut up
- ¾ cup milk
- 1 egg yolk
- ½ cup pitted Kalamata olives, coarsely chopped and drained
- 1 tablespoon snipped fresh rosemary
- 1 tablespoon olive oil

1 In a bowl pour boiling water over tomatoes to cover. Let stand 10 minutes; drain well. Remove 2 tomatoes and chop the rest; set aside.

2 Meanwhile, preheat oven to 425°F. Line a large baking sheet with parchment paper; set aside. In a large bowl combine flour, pesto sauce mix, baking powder, and baking soda. Using a pastry blender, cut in butter until mixture resembles coarse crumbs. Make a well in center of the flour mixture; set aside.

3 In a bowl combine milk and yolk. Add milk mixture all at once to flour mixture. Add chopped tomatoes, olives, and rosemary. Stir just until moistened.

BREAKFASTS & BRUNCHES

FRITTATA, PAGE 142

BREAKFASTS & BRUNCHES

GREAT MORNING MEALS ARE
A MUCH-LOVED HIGHLIGHT OF
HOME COOKING. THESE TIPS WILL
HELP YOU START YOUR DAYS IN
DELICIOUS STYLE.

COOKING BREAKFAST MEATS

PORK BACON: Follow the package directions for stovetop or microwave cooking. To bake, preheat oven to 400°F. Place bacon slices side by side on a rack in a foil-lined shallow baking pan with sides. Bake for 18 to 21 minutes or until bacon is crisp-cooked. Drain well on paper towels.

UNCOOKED SAUSAGE PATTIES: To fry, place ½-inch-thick patties in an unheated skillet and cook over medium-low heat about 12 minutes or until centers are no longer pink, turning once. Drain the sausage patties on paper towels. To bake, preheat oven to 400°F. Arrange ½-inch-thick sausage patties on a rack in a shallow baking pan with sides. Bake for 18 to 20 minutes or until centers are no longer pink and the internal temperature registers 160°F on an instant-read thermometer. Drain on paper towels.

UNCOOKED SAUSAGE LINKS: To fry, place links in an unheated skillet and cook over medium-low heat for 14 to 16 minutes or until centers are no longer pink, turning frequently to brown evenly. Drain on paper towels. To bake, preheat oven to 375°F. Place uncooked sausage links in a shallow baking pan with sides. Bake for 16 to 18 minutes or until centers are no longer pink, turning once. Drain on paper towels.

ALL ABOUT EGGS

Here's how to select, store, and handle these morning mainstays.

■ When purchasing eggs, select clean, fresh eggs from a refrigerated display case. Avoid eggs that are cracked or leaking; they might have become contaminated with harmful bacteria.

■ Keep eggs in their cartons and store on an inside shelf in the refrigerator for up to 5 weeks

after packing date. The packing date is represented by a number from 1 to 365 stamped on the carton, with 1 representing January 1 and 365 representing December 31.

■ When separating eggs, use an egg separator to avoid contaminating the yolk or white with any bacteria present on the shell. Avoid getting any eggshell in the raw eggs.

■ Wash your hands, utensils, and countertop after working with raw eggs.

■ Serve hot egg dishes promptly and chill leftovers quickly. Refrigerate cold dishes immediately after preparation.

■ For more information about handling eggs safely, call the U.S. Department of Agriculture Meat and Poultry Hotline at 888/674-6854.

STORING EGGS

Type of egg	Storage
Raw eggs in shell	Refrigerate up to 5 weeks; do not freeze.
Raw egg whites	Refrigerate, tightly covered, up to 4 days; freeze up to 1 year.
Raw whole egg yolks	Refrigerate in water, tightly covered, up to 2 days; do not freeze.
Hard-cooked eggs in shell	Refrigerate up to 7 days; do not freeze.

HOTCAKES (AND HOT WAFFLES)

When cooking for a crowd, you can keep finished pancakes and waffles warm while you're cooking the rest of the batch. Place the pancakes or waffles in a single layer on a baking sheet. Place the baking sheet in a preheated warm oven (200°F to 250°F) up to 15 or 20 minutes.

FREEZING COFFEE CAKES

Leftover coffee cake freezes well. Wrap in freezer wrap and freeze for up to 1 month. Thaw at room temperature for 1 hour. If desired, wrap in foil and reheat in a preheated 350°F oven for 10 to 15 minutes.

HARD-COOKED EGGS

START TO FINISH: 25 MINUTES
MAKES: 6 EGGS

    6 large eggs*
    Cold water

1 Place eggs in a single layer in a large saucepan (do not stack eggs). Add enough cold water to cover the eggs by 1 inch. Bring to a rapid boil over high heat (water will have large rapidly breaking bubbles). Remove from heat, cover, and let stand for 15 minutes; drain.

2 Run cold water over the eggs or place them in ice water until cool enough to handle; drain.

3 To peel eggs, gently tap each egg on the countertop. Roll the egg between the palms of your hands. Peel off eggshell, starting at the large end.

*NOTE: If you have extra-large eggs, let eggs stand in the boiled water for 18 minutes.

PER EGG: 78 cal., 5 g total fat (2 g sat. fat, 0 g trans fat), 212 mg chol., 62 mg sodium, 1 g carbo., 0 g fiber, 6 g pro. EXCHANGES: 1 Medium-Fat Meat

POACHED EGGS

START TO FINISH: 10 MINUTES
MAKES: 3 OR 4 EGGS

    4 cups water
    1 tablespoon vinegar
    3 or 4 eggs
    Salt and black pepper

1 Add water to a large skillet; add vinegar. Bring the vinegar mixture to boiling; reduce heat to simmering (bubbles should begin to break the surface of the water).

2 Break an egg into a cup and slip egg into the simmering water (see photo 1, below). Repeat with remaining eggs, allowing each egg an equal amount of space in the water-vinegar mixture.

3 Simmer eggs, uncovered, for 3 to 5 minutes or until whites are completely set and yolks begin to thicken but are not hard. Remove eggs (see photo 2, below). Season to taste with salt and pepper.

POACHING PAN DIRECTIONS: Lightly grease each cup of an egg-poaching pan. Place poaching cups into bottom pan over boiling water following manufacturer's directions; reduce heat to simmering. Break an egg into a measuring cup. Carefully slide egg into a poaching cup. Repeat with remaining eggs. Cover and cook for 4 to 6 minutes or until the whites are completely set and yolks begin to thicken but are not hard. Run a knife around edges to loosen eggs. Invert poacher cups to remove eggs.

MAKE-AHEAD DIRECTIONS: Prepare as directed. Place cooked eggs in a bowl of cold water. Cover and chill for up to 1 hour. To reheat eggs, in a saucepan bring water to simmering. Using a slotted spoon, slip eggs into the simmering water and heat about 2 minutes. Remove with a slotted spoon.

PER EGG: 73 cal., 5 g total fat (2 g sat. fat, 0 g trans fat), 212 mg chol., 273 mg sodium, 1 g carbo., 0 g fiber, 6 g pro. EXCHANGES: 1 Medium-Fat Meat

POACHED EGGS, STEP-BY-STEP

1. Break one egg at a time into a glass measuring cup, taking care not to break the yolk. Hold the lip of the cup as close to the simmering water-vinegar mixture as possible and slip egg into the water. **2.** When the eggs are cooked, use a slotted spoon to remove them from the water mixture, letting water drain away.

EGGS BENEDICT

START TO FINISH: 25 MINUTES **MAKES:** 4 SERVINGS

- 4 Poached Eggs (page 134)
- 1 recipe Mock Hollandaise Sauce
- 2 English muffins, split
- 4 slices Canadian-style bacon
  Cracked black pepper

1 Prepare Poached Eggs. Remove eggs from skillet with a slotted spoon and place them in a large pan of warm water to keep them warm. Prepare the Mock Hollandaise Sauce.

2 Preheat broiler. Place muffin halves, cut sides up, on a baking sheet. Broil 3 to 4 inches from the heat about 2 minutes or until brown. Top each muffin half with a slice of Canadian-style bacon; broil about 1 minute more or until bacon is heated.

3 To serve, top each bacon-topped muffin half with an egg. Spoon Mock Hollandaise Sauce over eggs. Sprinkle with pepper.

MOCK HOLLANDAISE SAUCE: In a small sauce-pan combine ⅓ cup dairy sour cream, ⅓ cup mayonnaise, 2 teaspoons lemon juice, and 1 teaspoon yellow mustard. Cook and stir over medium-low heat until warm. If desired, stir in a little milk to thin.

PORTOBELLO-MUSHROOM BENEDICT: Prepare as directed, except before poaching eggs in a large skillet cook four 3½- to 4-inch-diameter stemmed portobello mushroom caps in 1 table-spoon hot olive oil over medium-high heat about 6 minutes or until tender, turning once. Blot mushrooms with a paper towel. Slice mushrooms. Sprinkle lightly with salt and black pepper. Cover with foil to keep warm. Continue as directed, except substitute the mushroom caps for the Canadian-style bacon. Sprinkle with chopped, seeded tomato.

MAKE-AHEAD DIRECTIONS: Prepare Poached Eggs and toast English muffins as directed. Place muffin halves in a greased 8×8×2-inch baking pan. Top each muffin half with a slice of Canadian-style bacon and 1 cooked egg. Cover and chill for up to 24 hours. To serve, preheat oven to 350°F. Prepare 1 recipe Mock Hollandaise Sauce; spoon hot sauce over eggs. Bake, covered, about 30 minutes or until heated through.

PER SERVING PLAIN OR PORTOBELLO MUSHROOM VARIATION: 346 cal., 25 g total fat (7 g sat. fat, 0 g trans fat), 240 mg chol., 885 mg sodium, 14 g carbo., 1 g fiber, 14 g pro. EXCHANGES: 1 Starch, 1½ High-Fat Meat, 2½ Fat

SALMON BENEDICT: Prepare as directed, except spread 1 tablespoon softened tub-style cream cheese with herbs on each toasted English muffin half. Substitute 4 ounces thinly sliced smoked salmon (lox-style) for the Canadian-style bacon. If desired, stir 1 tablespoon drained capers and ½ teaspoon dried dillweed into Mock Hollandaise Sauce. If desired, sprinkle with additional dillweed.

PER SERVING: 391 cal., 30 g total fat (10 g sat. fat, 0 g trans fat), 248 mg chol., 1,161 mg sodium, 15 g carbo., 1 g fiber, 15 g pro. EXCHANGES: 1 Starch, 1½ High-Fat Meat, 3½ Fat

REUBEN BENEDICT: Prepare as directed, except substitute 4 slices marble rye or rye bread for the English muffins and thinly sliced corned beef for the Canadian-style bacon. Divide ½ cup rinsed and drained sauerkraut evenly over the corned beef. Stir ½ cup shredded Swiss cheese into the Mock Hollandaise Sauce.

PER SERVING: 461 cal., 34 g total fat (11 g sat. fat, 0 g trans fat), 269 mg chol., 1,160 mg sodium, 19 g carbo., 3 g fiber, 19 g pro. EXCHANGES: 1 Starch, 2 High-Fat Meat, 3½ Fat

FRIED EGGS

START TO FINISH: 10 MINUTES
MAKES: 4 EGGS

- 2 teaspoons butter or margarine, or nonstick cooking spray
- 4 eggs
  Salt (optional)
  Black pepper (optional)

1 In a large skillet melt butter over medium heat. (Or coat an unheated skillet with nonstick cooking spray.) Break eggs into skillet. If desired, sprinkle with salt and pepper. Reduce heat to low; cook eggs for 3 to 4 minutes or until whites are completely set and yolks start to thicken.

2 For fried eggs over easy or over hard, when the whites are completely set and the yolks start to thicken, turn the eggs and cook 30 seconds more (over easy) or 1 minute more (over hard).

STEAM-BASTED FRIED EGGS: Prepare as directed, except when egg edges turn white, add 1 to 2 teaspoons water. Cover skillet and cook eggs for 3 to 4 minutes or until yolks begin to thicken but are not hard.

PER EGG: 88 cal., 7 g total fat (3 g sat. fat, 0 g trans fat), 217 mg chol., 84 mg sodium, 0 g carbo., 0 g fiber, 6 g pro. EXCHANGES: 1 Medium-Fat Meat, ½ Fat

SCRAMBLED EGGS

START TO FINISH: 10 MINUTES
MAKES: 3 SERVINGS

    6 eggs
    ⅓ cup milk, half-and-half, or light cream
    ¼ teaspoon salt
       Dash black pepper
    1 tablespoon butter or margarine

1 In a bowl beat together eggs, milk, salt, and pepper with a rotary beater. In a large skillet melt butter over medium heat; pour in egg mixture. Cook over medium heat, without stirring, until mixture begins to set on bottom and around edges.

2 With a spatula or large spoon, lift and fold the partially cooked egg mixture so the uncooked portion flows underneath (see photo 1, page 138). Continue cooking over medium heat for 2 to 3 minutes or until egg mixture is cooked through but is still glossy and moist (see photo 2, page 138). Immediately remove from heat.

PER SERVING: 191 cal., 14 g total fat (6 g sat. fat, 0 g trans fat), 435 mg chol., 372 mg sodium, 2 g carbo., 0 g fiber, 14 g pro. EXCHANGES: 2 Medium-Fat Meat, 1 Fat

MEAT LOVER'S SCRAMBLED EGGS: Prepare as directed, except omit butter. In skillet cook and stir 3 slices bacon, chopped, and 4 ounces bulk pork sausage over medium heat until bacon is crisp and sausage is brown. Drain, reserving 1 tablespoon drippings in skillet. Set meat aside. Cook egg mixture in drippings. Sprinkle with bacon, sausage, and ⅓ cup chopped cooked ham or Polish sausage. Continue cooking as directed.

PER SERVING: 378 cal., 29 g total fat (10 g sat. fat, 0 g trans fat), 474 mg chol., 972 mg sodium, 3 g carbo., 0 g fiber, 25 g pro. EXCHANGES: 3½ Medium-Fat Meat, 2½ Fat

CHEESE-AND-ONION SCRAMBLED EGGS: Prepare as directed, except cook 1 sliced green onion in the butter for 30 seconds; add egg mixture and continue as directed. After eggs begin to set, fold in ½ cup shredded cheddar, mozzarella, or Monterey Jack cheese with jalapeño peppers (2 ounces).

PER SERVING: 268 cal., 21 g total fat (10 g sat. fat, 0 g trans fat), 455 mg chol., 490 mg sodium, 3 g carbo., 0 g fiber, 18 g pro. EXCHANGES: 2½ Medium-Fat Meat, 2 Fat

MUSHROOM SCRAMBLED EGGS: Prepare as directed, except increase the butter to 2 tablespoons. Cook 1½ cups sliced fresh mushrooms and 1 tablespoon chopped onion in the butter. Add 1 tablespoon snipped fresh parsley, ½ teaspoon dry mustard, and ¼ teaspoon Worcestershire sauce to beaten egg mixture. Add egg mixture to skillet and continue as directed.

PER SERVING: 239 cal., 18 g total fat (8 g sat. fat, 0 g trans fat), 446 mg chol., 407 mg sodium, 4 g carbo., 1 g fiber, 15 g pro. EXCHANGES: ½ Vegetable, 2 Medium-Fat Meat, 1½ Fat

DENVER SCRAMBLED EGGS: Prepare as directed, except omit salt and increase butter to 2 tablespoons. In the skillet cook 1 cup sliced fresh mushrooms, ⅓ cup diced cooked ham, ¼ cup chopped onion, and 2 tablespoons finely chopped green sweet pepper in the butter. Add egg mixture to skillet and continue as directed.

PER SERVING: 263 cal., 20 g total fat (9 g sat. fat, 0 g trans fat), 454 mg chol., 404 mg sodium, 5 g carbo., 1 g fiber, 17 g pro. EXCHANGES: ½ Vegetable, 2 Medium-Fat Meat, 2 Fat

LOW-FAT SCRAMBLED EGGS: Prepare as directed, except substitute 3 whole eggs and 5 egg whites for the 6 whole eggs. Substitute fat-free milk for the milk. Omit the butter and coat a nonstick skillet with nonstick cooking spray before cooking the egg mixture as directed.

PER SERVING: 107 cal., 5 g total fat (2 g sat. fat, 0 g trans fat), 212 mg chol., 367 mg sodium, 2 g carbo., 0 g fiber, 13 g pro. EXCHANGES: 2 Lean Meat

BREAKFAST BURRITOS: Prepare as directed, except omit the salt and butter. In the skillet cook 4 ounces bulk pork sausage, ¼ cup chopped onion, and 2 tablespoons finely chopped green sweet pepper over medium heat until meat is brown and vegetables are tender. Drain off fat. Add egg mixture to skillet with sausage mixture and continue as directed. To serve, warm four 10-inch flour tortillas. Place one-fourth of the egg mixture onto each tortilla just below the center. Divide ½ cup of Monterey Jack cheese (2 ounces) and ¼ cup bottled salsa among the tortillas. Fold bottom edge of each tortilla up and over the filling. Fold opposite sides in. Roll up from bottom. Serve with additional salsa. Makes 4 servings.

PER SERVING: 476 cal., 25 g total fat (10 g sat. fat, 0 g trans fat), 352 mg chol., 926 mg sodium, 40 g carbo., 4 g fiber, 24 g pro. EXCHANGES: 2½ Starch, 2½ Medium-Fat Meat, 2 Fat

BREAKFAST PIZZA

START TO FINISH: 45 MINUTES **OVEN:** 375°F
MAKES: 10 SLICES

    1 16-ounce loaf frozen whole wheat bread
       dough, thawed
    1 cup sliced zucchini, halved, and/or green
       or red sweet pepper pieces
    1 cup sliced fresh mushrooms

¼ teaspoon crushed red pepper (optional)

1 tablespoon vegetable oil

8 eggs

½ cup milk

1 tablespoon butter or margarine

1½ cups shredded cheddar and/or mozzarella cheese (6 ounces)

2 slices bacon, crisp-cooked, drained, and crumbled

Bottled salsa (optional)

1 Grease a 13-inch pizza pan; set aside. Preheat oven to 375°F. On a lightly floured surface roll bread dough into a 14-inch circle. If dough is difficult to roll out, stop and let it rest a few minutes. Transfer dough to prepared pan. Build up edges slightly. Prick dough generously with a fork. Bake for 15 to 20 minutes or until light brown.

2 Meanwhile, in a large skillet cook zucchini, mushrooms, and crushed red pepper (if desired) in hot oil about 5 minutes or until vegetables are almost tender. Remove zucchini mixture and drain.

3 In a medium bowl beat together eggs and milk. In the same skillet melt butter over medium heat; pour in egg mixture. Cook, without stirring, until mixture begins to set on the bottom and around edges. Using a large spatula, lift and fold partially cooked eggs so the uncooked portion flows underneath (see photo 1, page 138). Continue cooking over medium heat for 2 to 3 minutes or until egg mixture is cooked through but is still glossy and moist (see photo 2, page 138). Remove from heat.

4 Sprinkle half of the shredded cheese over the hot crust. Top with scrambled eggs, zucchini mixture, bacon, and remaining cheese. Bake for 5 to 8 minutes more or until cheese melts. Cut into 10 slices. If desired, serve with salsa.

PER SLICE: 283 cal., 15 g total fat (6 g sat. fat, 0 g trans fat), 193 mg chol., 465 mg sodium, 23 g carbo., 2 g fiber, 16 g pro. EXCHANGES: 1½ Starch, 1½ Lean Meat, 2 Fat

EVEN EASIER BREAKFAST PIZZA IF YOU LIKE, SUBSTITUTE A PACKAGE OF REFRIGERATED PIZZA DOUGH FOR THE BREAD DOUGH IN STEP 1. FOLLOW PACKAGE DIRECTIONS FOR BAKING.

BREAKFAST PIZZA

SPICY BRUNCH LASAGNA

PREP: 40 MINUTES **CHILL:** 8 TO 24 HOURS
STAND: 35 MINUTES **BAKE:** 60 MINUTES
OVEN: 350°F **MAKES:** 16 SERVINGS

1½ pounds bulk Italian sausage
 1 24-ounce carton cottage cheese
 ½ cup finely chopped green onions (4)
 ¼ cup snipped fresh chives
 ¼ cup finely shredded carrot
 18 eggs
 ⅓ cup milk
 2 tablespoons butter
 1 14-ounce jar purchased Alfredo sauce
 1 teaspoon dried Italian seasoning, crushed
 8 oven-ready lasagna noodles
 4 cups frozen shredded hash browns, thawed
 2 cups shredded mozzarella cheese

1 In a large skillet cook sausage until it browns. Drain off fat; set aside. In a bowl combine cottage cheese, onions, chives, and carrot; set aside.

2 In a very large bowl whisk together eggs, milk, ½ teaspoon *salt*, and ½ teaspoon *black pepper*. In a large skillet melt butter over medium heat; pour in egg mixture. Cook over medium heat, without stirring, until mixture begins to set on bottom and around the edges. Lift and fold partially cooked egg mixture so the uncooked portion flows underneath (see photo 1, below). Continue cooking over medium heat for 2 to 3 minutes or until egg mixture is cooked through but is still glossy and moist (see photo 2, below). Immediately remove from heat.

3 In a small bowl combine Alfredo sauce and seasoning. Spread about ½ cup sauce mixture over the bottom of a 3-quart rectangular baking dish. Layer half of the noodles in dish, overlapping as necessary. Top with half the remaining sauce, half the cottage cheese mixture, half the hash browns, half the scrambled egg mixture, and half the sausage (see photo 3, page 139). Sprinkle with half of the mozzarella cheese. Repeat layers (see photo 4, page 139). Cover dish tightly with plastic wrap. Chill for 8 hours or overnight.

4 Let lasagna stand at room temperature for 30 minutes before baking. Preheat oven to 350°F. Remove plastic wrap from baking dish and cover dish with foil. Bake for 45 minutes. Remove foil and bake 15 minutes more or until heated through. Let stand for 5 minutes before cutting into portions (see photo 5, page 139).

PER 3¼×2¼-INCH PIECE: 455 cal., 30 g total fat (13 g sat. fat, 0 g trans fat), 312 mg chol., 900 mg sodium, 20 g carbo., 1 g fiber, 26 g pro.
EXCHANGES: 1 Starch, 3 Medium-Fat Meat, 3 Fat

BEST EVER ▪ LOW FAT

FARMER'S CASSEROLE

PREP: 25 MINUTES **BAKE:** 40 MINUTES
STAND: 5 MINUTES **OVEN:** 350°F **MAKES:** 6 SERVINGS

 Nonstick cooking spray
 3 cups frozen shredded hash brown potatoes
 ¾ cup shredded Monterey Jack cheese with jalapeño peppers or shredded cheddar cheese (3 ounces)
 1 cup diced cooked ham, cooked breakfast sausage, or Canadian-style bacon

SPICY BRUNCH LASAGNA, STEP-BY-STEP

1. Use a spatula or large spoon to lift and fold the scrambled egg mixture. **2.** Avoid overcooking the eggs or they will be crumbly and dry. **3.** Distribute sausage evenly. **4.** Repeat with remaining half of ingredients, spreading hash browns evenly over cottage cheese mixture before eggs and sausage. **5.** Cut lasagna into serving-size pieces and transfer with spatula to plates.

¼ cup sliced green onions (2)

4 eggs, beaten, or 1 cup refrigerated or frozen egg product, thawed

1½ cups milk or one 12-ounce can evaporated milk or evaporated fat-free milk

⅛ teaspoon salt

⅛ teaspoon black pepper

1 Preheat oven to 350°F. Coat a 2-quart square baking dish with nonstick cooking spray. Arrange hash brown potatoes evenly in the dish. Sprinkle with cheese, ham, and green onions.

2 In a medium bowl combine eggs, milk, salt, and pepper. Pour egg mixture over layers in dish.

3 Bake, uncovered, for 40 to 45 minutes or until a knife inserted near the center comes out clean. Let stand 5 minutes before serving.

FARMER'S CASSEROLE FOR 12: Prepare as directed, except double all ingredients and use a 3-quart rectangular baking dish. Preheat oven to 350°F. Bake, uncovered, for 45 to 55 minutes or until a knife inserted near the center comes out clean. Let stand 5 minutes before serving. Makes 12 servings.

MAKE-AHEAD DIRECTIONS: Prepare as directed through Step 2. Cover and chill for up to 24 hours. Preheat oven to 350°F. Bake, uncovered, for 50 to 55 minutes or until a knife inserted near the center comes out clean. Let stand 5 minutes before serving.

PER 4×2½-INCH PIECE: 263 cal., 12 g total fat (6 g sat. fat, 0 g trans fat), 175 mg chol., 589 mg sodium, 22 g carbo., 2 g fiber, 17 g pro.
EXCHANGES: 1½ Starch, 2 Lean Meat, 1 Fat

OVERNIGHT BREAKFAST PIE

PREP: 20 MINUTES **CHILL:** 2 TO 24 HOURS
BAKE: 50 MINUTES **OVEN:** 325°F
MAKES: 6 TO 8 SERVINGS

8 slices bacon

½ cup panko (Japanese-style bread crumbs)

5 eggs

2½ cups frozen shredded hash brown potatoes

1 cup shredded Swiss cheese (4 ounces)

½ cup cottage cheese

⅓ cup milk

¼ cup chopped green onions (2)

½ teaspoon salt

¼ teaspoon black pepper

4 drops bottled hot pepper sauce

1 In a large skillet cook bacon over medium heat until crisp. Drain bacon on paper towels, reserving 1 tablespoon drippings in skillet. Crumble bacon; set aside. Stir bread crumbs into the reserved drippings. Transfer to a small bowl; cover and chill until needed.

2 Lightly grease a 9-inch pie plate; set aside. In a medium bowl beat eggs with a fork until foamy. Stir in crumbled bacon, potatoes, Swiss cheese, cottage cheese, milk, green onions, salt, pepper, and hot pepper sauce. Pour mixture into prepared pie plate. Cover and chill for 2 to 24 hours.

3 Preheat oven to 325°F. Sprinkle pie with bread crumb mixture. Bake, uncovered, about 50 minutes or until a knife inserted in the center comes out clean. Cut into six or eight wedges.

PER WEDGE: 324 cal., 17 g total fat (7 g sat. fat, 0 g trans fat), 210 mg chol., 640 mg sodium, 22 g carbo., 2 g fiber, 20 g pro.
EXCHANGES: 1½ Starch, 2 Medium-Fat Meat, 1 Fat

MAKE-IT-MINE EGG CASSEROLE

ROUND UP A HANDFUL OF YOUR FAVORITE INGREDIENTS AND YOU'LL BE 20 MINUTES AWAY FROM POPPING A COLORFUL CASSEROLE IN THE OVEN—OR INTO THE FRIDGE TO BAKE UP TO A DAY LATER.

BASIC INGREDIENTS

PREP: 20 MINUTES
BAKE: 45 MINUTES
STAND: 10 MINUTES **OVEN:** 325°F
MAKES: 6 SERVINGS

- 4 to 5 cups Bread Cubes*
- Meat
- Vegetable
- 4 to 6 ounces Shredded Cheese
- 4 eggs, lightly beaten
- 1½ cups Dairy
- Seasonings

BREAD CUBES (PICK ONE)

Baguette-style French bread
English muffins
Pumpernickel
Rye bread
Texas toast
White or wheat bread

MEAT (PICK ONE)

- 2 cups cubed cooked ham or cubed smoked turkey
- 1 6-ounce can lump crabmeat, drained and flaked
- 8 ounces cooked bulk pork sausage
- 6 slices bacon, crisp-cooked, drained, and crumbled
- 5 ounces chopped Canadian-style bacon

VEGETABLE (PICK ONE)

- ¾ cup chopped sweet peppers
- ½ cup canned sliced mushrooms
- 1½ cups blanched cut-up asparagus or broccoli florets
- 1 cup frozen hash brown potatoes
- 1 cup fresh or frozen chopped spinach (thawed and squeezed dry, if frozen)

SHREDDED CHEESE
(PICK ONE)

Cheddar
Italian-blend
Monterey Jack
Swiss

DAIRY (PICK ONE)

- Milk
- Half-and-half
- ½ cup dairy sour cream plus 1 cup milk

SEASONINGS (PICK ONE)

- 1 tablespoon Dijon-style or coarse-grain mustard
- 1 teaspoon dried dillweed
- ¼ cup sliced green onions
- 1 tablespoon snipped fresh Italian parsley or basil
- 1 teaspoon minced garlic

BASIC INSTRUCTIONS

1 Preheat oven to 325°F. Grease a 2-quart square baking dish. Spread half of the Bread Cubes in the dish. Add Meat, Vegetable, and Shredded Cheese. Top with the remaining Bread Cubes.

2 In a bowl whisk together eggs, Dairy, and Seasonings. Evenly pour over layers in dish.

3 Bake, uncovered, for 45 minutes or until a knife inserted near the center comes out clean. Let stand 10 minutes before serving.

MAKE-AHEAD DIRECTIONS:
Prepare as directed through Step 2. Cover and chill for 2 to 24 hours. Preheat oven to 350°F. Bake, uncovered, for 60 to 65 minutes or until a knife inserted near the center comes out clean. Let stand 10 minutes.

*CUTTING BREAD CUBES:
Stack several slices of bread. Cut into strips. While still stacked, cut crosswise into cubes.

CHILE RELLENOS CASSEROLE

PREP: 20 MINUTES **BAKE:** 15 MINUTES
STAND: 5 MINUTES **OVEN:** 450°F
MAKES: 4 SERVINGS

- 2 large fresh poblano chile peppers or fresh Anaheim chile peppers (8 ounces)
- 1½ cups shredded Monterey Jack cheese with jalapeño peppers or Mexican-style four-cheese blend (6 ounces)
- 3 eggs, lightly beaten
- ¼ cup milk
- ⅓ cup all-purpose flour
- ½ teaspoon baking powder
- ¼ teaspoon cayenne pepper
- ⅛ teaspoon salt
  Bottled salsa (optional)
  Dairy sour cream (optional)

1 Preheat oven to 450°F. Grease a 2-quart square baking dish; set aside. Quarter the peppers and remove seeds, stems, and veins (see tip, page 24). Immerse peppers into boiling water for 3 minutes; drain. Invert peppers onto paper towels to drain well. Place the peppers in prepared baking dish. Top with 1 cup of the cheese.

2 In a medium bowl combine eggs and milk. Add flour, baking powder, cayenne pepper, and salt. Beat until smooth with a rotary beater (or place in a food processor or blender; cover and process or blend until smooth). Pour egg mixture over peppers and cheese.

3 Bake, uncovered, about 15 minutes or until a knife inserted into the egg mixture comes out clean. Sprinkle with the remaining ½ cup cheese. Let stand about 5 minutes or until cheese melts. If desired, serve with salsa and sour cream.

PER SERVING: 296 cal., 18 g total fat (10 g sat. fat, 0 g trans fat), 205 mg chol., 450 mg sodium, 16 g carbo., 1 g fiber, 18 g pro.
EXCHANGES: 1 Starch, 2 Medium-Fat Meat, 1½ Fat

EASY HUEVOS RANCHEROS CASSEROLE

PREP: 15 MINUTES **BAKE:** 38 MINUTES
STAND: 10 MINUTES **OVEN:** 375°F
MAKES: 12 SERVINGS

  Nonstick cooking spray
- 1 32-ounce package frozen fried potato nuggets
- 12 eggs
- 1 cup milk

EASY HUEVOS RANCHEROS CASSEROLE

- 1½ teaspoons dried oregano, crushed
- 1½ teaspoons ground cumin
- ½ teaspoon chili powder
- ¼ teaspoon garlic powder
- 2 cups shredded Mexican-style four-cheese blend (8 ounces)
- 1 16-ounce jar thick and chunky salsa
  Snipped fresh cilantro
- 1 8-ounce carton dairy sour cream

1 Preheat oven to 375°F. Lightly coat a 3-quart rectangular baking dish with nonstick cooking spray. Arrange potato nuggets in dish.

2 In a large mixing bowl combine eggs, milk, oregano, cumin, chili powder, and garlic powder. Beat with a rotary beater or wire whisk until combined. Pour egg mixture over potato nuggets.

3 Bake, uncovered, for 35 to 40 minutes or until a knife inserted near center comes out clean. Sprinkle cheese evenly over egg mixture. Bake about 3 minutes more or until cheese melts. Let stand for 10 minutes before serving. Top with salsa and cilantro; serve with sour cream.

PER 3¼×3-INCH PIECE: 335 cal., 21 g total fat (9 g sat. fat, 0 g trans fat), 240 mg chol., 828 mg sodium, 25 g carbo., 2 g fiber, 14 g pro.
EXCHANGES: 1½ Starch, 1½ Medium-Fat Meat, 2½ Fat

FRITTATA (photo, page 131)

START TO FINISH: 25 MINUTES **MAKES:** 4 SERVINGS

- 8 eggs, lightly beaten
- 1 tablespoon snipped fresh basil or
  1 teaspoon dried basil, crushed
- ¼ teaspoon salt
- 2 tablespoons olive oil
- 1½ cups chopped fresh vegetables, such
  as summer squash, broccoli, roma
  tomatoes, and/or sweet peppers
- ⅓ cup thinly sliced green onions (3)
- ½ cup chopped cooked ham; chopped
  cooked kielbasa, chicken, or turkey; or
  crumbled cooked pork sausage
- ½ cup shredded cheddar, Monterey Jack, or
  Swiss cheese (2 ounces)

1 In a medium bowl combine eggs, basil, salt, and ¼ teaspoon *black pepper*; set aside. Heat oil in a large broilerproof skillet; add vegetables and green onions. Cook, uncovered, over medium heat about 5 minutes or until vegetables are crisp-tender, stirring occasionally. Stir in meat.

2 Pour egg mixture over vegetable mixture in skillet. Cook over medium heat. As mixture sets, run a spatula around edge of skillet, lifting egg mixture so uncooked portion flows underneath. Continue cooking and lifting edges until egg mixture is almost set (surface will be moist). Sprinkle with cheese.

3 Preheat broiler. Place skillet under the broiler, 4 to 5 inches from heat. Broil for 1 to 2 minutes or until top is just set and cheese melts. (Or preheat oven to 400°F; bake for 5 minutes until top is set.)

PER SERVING: 297 cal., 23 g total fat (8 g sat. fat, 0 g trans fat), 448 mg chol., 596 mg sodium, 4 g carbo., 1 g fiber, 20 g pro. EXCHANGES: 3 Medium-Fat Meat, 1½ Fat

SAUSAGE AND EGG ALFREDO SKILLET

START TO FINISH: 25 MINUTES
MAKES: 4 TO 6 SERVINGS

- Nonstick cooking spray
- 1 7-ounce package low-fat, reduced-sodium
  sausage links
- ¼ cup sliced green onions (2)
- 6 eggs, lightly beaten
- ½ cup purchased reduced-fat Alfredo sauce
- 1½ teaspoons yellow mustard
- ½ cup shredded American cheese (2 ounces)

1 Coat a large skillet with cooking spray. Cook sausage and onions over medium heat until sausage browns. Pour eggs over sausage mixture in skillet. As mixture sets, run a spatula around edge of skillet, lifting egg mixture so uncooked portion flows underneath. Continue cooking and lifting edges until egg mixture is almost set (surface will be moist). Remove from heat; cover and set aside.

2 In a small saucepan stir together Alfredo sauce and mustard. Heat until bubbly. Stir in cheese until it melts. Serve wedges with sauce.

PER SERVING: 313 cal., 21 g total fat (8 g sat. fat, 0 g trans fat), 354 mg chol., 805 mg sodium, 10 g carbo., 0 g fiber, 21 g pro. EXCHANGES: ½ Other Carbo., 3 Medium-Fat Meat, 1 Fat

FRENCH OMELET

START TO FINISH: 10 MINUTES **MAKES:** 1 SERVING

- 2 eggs
- 2 tablespoons water
- ⅛ teaspoon salt
- 1 tablespoon butter or margarine

1 In a bowl combine eggs, water, salt, and dash *black pepper*. Using a fork, beat until combined but not frothy. Heat an 8-inch nonstick skillet with flared sides over medium-high heat until skillet is hot. Melt butter in skillet. Add egg mixture; reduce heat to medium. Immediately begin stirring eggs gently but continuously with a wooden or plastic spatula until mixture resembles small pieces of cooked egg surrounded by liquid egg. Stop stirring. Cook 30 to 60 seconds or until egg is set.

2 With a spatula, lift and fold an edge of omelet about a third of the way toward center. Fold the opposite edge toward the center; transfer omelet to a warm plate. If making more than one omelet, cover with foil to keep warm while preparing more.

PER SERVING: 245 cal., 21 g total fat (10 g sat. fat, 0 g trans fat), 454 mg chol., 513 mg sodium, 1 g carbo., 0 g fiber, 13 g pro. EXCHANGES: 2 Medium-Fat Meat, 2 Fat

FILLED FRENCH OMELET: Prepare filling on page 143 before making omelet. For one omelet, if using fresh vegetables (⅓ to ½ cup chopped or sliced mushrooms, onion, sweet pepper, or potatoes), cook vegetables in 1 teaspoon butter or vegetable oil in skillet. If desired, add ⅛ to ¼ teaspoon herb to egg mixture. Use 2 to 3 tablespoons shredded cheese and ⅓ to ½ cup cooked meat. Spoon filling across center of omelet before Step 2. If desired, sprinkle top with extra cheese.

10 TO TRY— FILLED FRENCH OMELET

Start with Filled French Omelet, page 142. **1. POTATO-BACON:** Cook frozen diced hash brown potatoes and chopped bacon in oil. Add to omelet; add shredded cheddar cheese. **2. BEAN-FILLED:** Fill with black beans, salsa, and shredded Monterey Jack cheese. **3. SHRIMP-AVOCADO:** Fill with chopped cooked shrimp, chopped avocado, and snipped cilantro. **4. ARTICHOKE-OLIVE:** Add oregano to eggs; fill with chopped marinated artichoke hearts and sliced olives. **5. REUBEN:** Fill with chopped corned beef, Swiss cheese, and sauerkraut. **6. SPINACH-FETA:** Fill with shredded fresh spinach and crumbled feta cheese. **7. CHEESE-MUSHROOM:** Cook sliced fresh mushrooms in butter; add to omelet. Add shredded cheddar cheese. **8. DENVER:** Cook chopped green sweet pepper, onion, and basil in butter; stir in chopped cooked ham. **9. ITALIAN:** Fill with cooked Italian sausage, chopped roasted red sweet peppers, and shredded provolone cheese. **10. ASPARAGUS-HAM:** Add dill to eggs; fill with chopped cooked asparagus, cooked prosciutto or ham, and shaved Parmesan.

QUICHE LORRAINE

PREP: 30 MINUTES **BAKE:** 64 MINUTES
STAND: 10 MINUTES **OVEN:** 450°F/325°F
MAKES: 6 SERVINGS

- 1 recipe Pastry for Single-Crust Pie (page 444)
- 6 slices bacon or turkey bacon
- ½ cup chopped onion
- 5 eggs, lightly beaten
- 1¼ cups half-and-half or light cream
- ¼ teaspoon salt
  Dash ground nutmeg
- 1½ cups shredded Swiss cheese (6 ounces)
- 1 tablespoon all-purpose flour
  Chopped fresh tomato (optional)
  Snipped fresh parsley (optional)

1 Preheat oven to 450°F. Prepare pastry. Line the unpricked pastry shell with a double thickness of heavy foil. Bake for 8 minutes; remove foil. Bake for 6 to 8 minutes more or until pastry is golden. Remove from oven. Reduce oven temperature to 325°F. (Pie shell should still be hot when filling is added; do not partially bake pastry shell ahead of time.)

2 Meanwhile, in a very large skillet cook bacon until crisp (if using) or cook turkey bacon according to package directions. Drain, reserving 1 tablespoon drippings. Crumble bacon finely; set aside. Cook onion in reserved drippings over medium heat until tender but not brown; drain.

3 In a large bowl stir together eggs, half-and-half, salt, and nutmeg. Stir in crumbled bacon and onion. In a small bowl combine shredded cheese and flour. Add to egg mixture; mix well.

4 Pour egg mixture into the hot baked pastry shell. Bake in the 325°F oven for 50 to 55 minutes or until a knife inserted near the center comes out clean. If necessary, cover edge of crust with foil to prevent overbrowning. Let stand 10 minutes. Cut into six wedges. If desired, garnish with tomato and parsley before serving.

PER WEDGE: 560 cal., 39 g total fat (19 g sat. fat, 1 g trans fat), 252 mg chol., 668 mg sodium, 30 g carbo., 1 g fiber, 21 g pro. EXCHANGES: 2 Starch, 2 High-Fat Meat, 4 Fat

QUICHE LORRAINE WITH QUICK PASTRY:
Prepare as directed, except substitute half of a 15-ounce package rolled refrigerated unbaked piecrust for the pastry. Let stand according to package directions. Unroll and ease piecrust into a 9-inch pie plate, being careful not to stretch piecrust. Trim pastry to ½ inch beyond edge of pie plate. Fold under extra pastry. Crimp edge as desired. Do not prick pastry. Bake as directed.

PER WEDGE: 463 cal., 32 g total fat (15 g sat. fat, 0 g trans fat), 235 mg sodium, 563 mg sodium, 23 g carbo., 0 g fiber, 18 g pro. EXCHANGES: 1½ Starch, 2 High-Fat Meat, 3 Fat

SPINACH AND MUSHROOM QUICHE: Prepare as directed, except omit bacon. Cook the onion and 1½ cups sliced fresh mushrooms in 1 tablespoon hot vegetable oil until tender, stirring occasionally. Stir in 3 cups lightly packed coarsely chopped fresh spinach. Stir into egg mixture with cheese in Step 3.

PER WEDGE: 526 cal., 36 g total fat (17 g sat. fat, 1 g trans fat), 241 mg chol., 493 mg sodium, 31 g carbo., 2 g fiber, 19 g pro. EXCHANGES: 2 Starch, ½ Vegetable, 2 High-Fat Meat, 3 Fat

HAM SOUFFLÉ ROLL

PREP: 50 MINUTES **BAKE:** 65 MINUTES
CHILL: 2 TO 24 HOURS **OVEN:** 375°F/350°F
MAKES: 8 SERVINGS

- ¼ cup butter or margarine
- ½ cup all-purpose flour
- ⅛ teaspoon black pepper
- 2 cups milk
- 6 egg yolks, lightly beaten
- 6 egg whites
- ¼ teaspoon cream of tartar
- 6 ounces thinly sliced cooked ham
- 6 ounces thinly sliced Swiss or provolone cheese
- 1 recipe Parsley Sauce (page 145)
  Snipped fresh parsley (optional)

1 Preheat oven to 375°F. Line a 15×10×1-inch baking pan with foil; extend foil about 1 inch over edges of pan. Grease and lightly flour the foil.

2 In a medium saucepan melt butter. Stir in flour and pepper. Gradually stir in milk. Cook and stir until mixture is thickened and bubbly; cool slightly. Place egg yolks in a medium bowl; gradually stir in milk mixture (see photo 1, page 145). In a large bowl beat egg whites and cream of tartar with an electric mixer until stiff peaks form (tips stand straight). Fold some of the beaten egg whites into the egg yolk mixture. Fold egg yolk mixture into the remaining beaten egg whites (see photo 2, page 145). Spread in the prepared baking pan.

3 Bake about 20 minutes or until soufflé is puffed and a knife inserted in center comes out clean.

4 Meanwhile, place a long sheet of heavy foil (about 22×18 inches) on a large baking sheet. Generously grease the foil. After baking soufflé immediately loosen edges of soufflé from baking pan. Invert soufflé onto the foil-lined baking sheet. Carefully peel off foil (see photo 3, below).

5 Place ham and cheese slices in single layers on top of soufflé. Starting from a short side, use foil on baking sheet to lift and help roll up soufflé (see photo 4, below); don't roll the foil inside. Use the foil to lift soufflé roll onto another flat baking sheet. Cover soufflé with foil and chill for 2 to 24 hours. Prepare the Parsley Sauce; cover and chill sauce for up to 24 hours.

6 Before serving, preheat oven to 350°F. Bake soufflé roll, covered with the foil, about 45 minutes or until heated through. Meanwhile, shake sauce; transfer to a medium saucepan. Cook and stir over medium heat until thickened and bubbly. Cook and stir for 2 minutes more.

7 To serve, uncover soufflé roll. Transfer soufflé roll to a warm serving platter (see photo 5, below). If desired, spoon a little sauce over soufflé roll. Slice with a serrated knife; serve with the remaining sauce. If desired, garnish with snipped parsley.

PARSLEY SAUCE: In a blender or food processor combine ½ cup lightly packed fresh parsley sprigs; 2 shallots or green onions, cut up; and 1 teaspoon dried basil, crushed. Cover and blend or process until finely chopped. Add 1½ cups whipping cream, 1 tablespoon cornstarch, 1 tablespoon Dijon-style mustard, and ¼ teaspoon salt. Cover and blend or process for 10 to 20 seconds or until mixture is slightly thickened. (Be careful not to overblend or you will end up with butter.) Transfer mixture to a screw-top jar.

PER SERVING: 436 cal., 35 g total fat (20 g sat. fat, 0 g trans fat), 266 mg chol., 714 mg sodium, 14 g carbo., 1 g fiber, 18 g pro. EXCHANGES: 1 Starch, 2 High-Fat Meat, 3½ Fat

HAM SOUFFLÉ ROLL, STEP-BY-STEP

1. Gradually add some hot mixture to yolks to warm them; stir with a wire whisk. **2.** After folding some beaten whites into yolk mixture to lighten it, fold yolk mixture into remaining beaten whites. **3.** Avoid tearing soufflé when carefully pulling off foil that lined pan. **4.** Use one hand to guide the roll and the other to pull up on the foil. **5.** Carefully slide soufflé off baking sheet onto a platter.

CHEESE SOUFFLÉ

PREP: 50 MINUTES **BAKE:** 40 MINUTES
OVEN: 350°F **MAKES:** 4 SERVINGS

- 4 egg yolks
- 4 egg whites
- ¼ cup butter or margarine
- ¼ cup all-purpose flour
- ¼ teaspoon dry mustard
  Dash cayenne pepper
- 1 cup milk
- 2 cups shredded cheddar, Colby, Havarti, and/or process Swiss cheese (8 ounces)

1 Allow the egg yolks and egg whites to stand at room temperature for 30 minutes.

2 Preheat oven to 350°F. For cheese sauce, in a medium saucepan melt butter; stir in flour, dry mustard, and cayenne pepper. Add milk all at once. Cook and stir over medium heat until thickened and bubbly. Remove from heat. Add cheese, a little at a time, stirring until cheese melts. In a medium bowl beat egg yolks with a fork until combined. Slowly add cheese sauce to egg yolks, stirring constantly (see photo 1, page 145); cool slightly.

3 In a large mixing bowl beat egg whites with an electric mixer on medium to high speed until stiff peaks form (tips stand straight). Gently fold about 1 cup of the stiffly beaten egg whites into cheese sauce. Gradually pour cheese sauce over remaining stiffly beaten egg whites, folding to combine. Pour into an ungreased 2-quart soufflé dish.

4 Bake about 40 minutes or until a knife inserted near center comes out clean. Serve immediately.

PER SERVING: 459 cal., 36 g total fat (22 g sat. fat, 0 g trans fat), 305 mg chol., 521 mg sodium, 10 g carbo., 0 g fiber, 23 g pro. EXCHANGES: ½ Starch, 3 Medium-Fat Meat, 4 Fat

BUTTERMILK PANCAKES

START TO FINISH: 25 MINUTES
MAKES: 12 STANDARD-SIZE PANCAKES OR 40 MINI PANCAKES

- 1¾ cups all-purpose flour
- 2 tablespoons granulated sugar
- 2 teaspoons baking powder
- ½ teaspoon baking soda
- ¼ teaspoon salt
- 1 egg, lightly beaten
- 1½ cups buttermilk or sour milk (see tip, page 19)
- 3 tablespoons vegetable oil
  Desired fruit options (optional)*
  Butter (optional)
  Desired syrup (optional)

1 In a large bowl stir together flour, sugar, baking powder, baking soda, and salt. In another bowl use a fork to combine egg, buttermilk, and oil. Add egg mixture all at once to flour mixture. Stir just until moistened (batter should be slightly lumpy) (see photo 1, page 147). If desired, stir in fruit.

2 For standard-size pancakes, pour about ¼ cup batter onto a hot, lightly greased griddle or heavy skillet (see photo 2, page 147). Spread batter, if necessary. For dollar-size pancakes, use about 1 tablespoon batter. Cook over medium heat for 1 to 2 minutes on each side or until pancakes are golden brown. Turn over when surfaces are bubbly and edges are slightly dry (see photo 3, page 147). Serve warm. If desired, top with butter, syrup, and additional fruit.

PANCAKES: Prepare as directed, except substitute milk for buttermilk, increase baking powder to 1 tablespoon, and omit the baking soda.

WHOLE WHEAT PANCAKES: Prepare as directed, except substitute whole wheat flour for the all-purpose flour and packed brown sugar for the granulated sugar.

BUCKWHEAT PANCAKES: Prepare as directed, except use ¾ cup all-purpose flour and add 1 cup buckwheat flour.

CORNMEAL PANCAKES: Prepare as directed, except use 1¼ cups all-purpose flour and add ½ cup cornmeal.

BRAN PANCAKES: Prepare as directed, except use 1½ cups all-purpose flour and add ¼ cup oat bran, wheat bran, or toasted wheat germ.

PER STANDARD-SIZE BUTTERMILK, PLAIN, WHOLE WHEAT, BUCKWHEAT, CORNMEAL, OR BRAN VARIATIONS: 123 cal., 4 g total fat (1 g sat. fat, 0 g trans fat), 19 mg chol., 179 mg sodium, 18 g carbo., 0 g fiber, 3 g pro. EXCHANGES: 1 Starch, 1 Fat

*FRUIT OPTIONS: If desired, stir one of the following fruits into the pancake batter before pouring batter onto griddle: ½ cup chopped fresh apple, apricot, peach, nectarine, or pear; ½ cup fresh or frozen blueberries; or ¼ cup chopped dried apple, pear, apricot, raisins, currants, dates, cranberries, blueberries, cherries, or mixed fruit.

PREPARING BUTTERMILK PANCAKES, STEP-BY-STEP

1. When stirring the wet ingredients into flour mixture, the batter should be slightly lumpy. Do not overmix or the pancakes will be tough. **2.** Pour batter onto griddle or skillet, using a scoop or ¼-cup measuring cup. **3.** The pancakes are ready to turn when the top surfaces are bubbly and the edges look slightly dry.

CREPES

START TO FINISH: 40 MINUTES
MAKES: 16 TO 18 CREPES

- 2 eggs, beaten
- 1½ cups milk
- 1 cup all-purpose flour
- 1 tablespoon vegetable oil
- ¼ teaspoon salt

1 In a medium mixing bowl combine eggs, milk, flour, oil, and salt; whisk until smooth.

2 Heat a lightly greased 6-inch skillet over medium-high heat; remove from heat. Spoon in 2 tablespoons batter; lift and tilt skillet to spread batter evenly. Return to heat; cook for 1 to 2 minutes or until brown on one side only. (Or cook on a crepemaker according to manufacturer's directions.) Invert over paper towels; remove crepe. Repeat with remaining batter, greasing skillet occasionally. If crepes are browning too quickly, reduce heat to medium.

PER CREPE: 56 cal., 2 g total fat (1 g sat. fat, 0 g trans fat), 28 mg chol., 55 mg sodium, 7 g carbo., 0 g fiber, 2 g pro. EXCHANGES: ½ Starch, ½ Fat

PEANUT BUTTER-BANANA CREPES: Prepare as directed, except for each crepe spread unbrown side with 1 tablespoon peanut butter. Arrange ¼ of a sliced banana and 1 tablespoon raisins (if desired) along one edge of crepe. Drizzle with 1 teaspoon maple syrup; roll up from the filled edge.

PER CREPE: 194 cal., 10 g total fat (2 g sat. fat, 0 g trans fat), 28 mg chol., 129 mg sodium, 21 g carbo., 2 g fiber, 7 g pro. EXCHANGES: 1½ Starch, ½ High-Fat Meat, 1 Fat

STRAWBERRY-CREAM CHEESE CREPES:
Prepare as directed, except for each crepe spread unbrown side of a cooled crepe with 2 tablespoons whipped cream cheese. Arrange ¼ cup sliced fresh strawberries along one edge of crepe. Drizzle with 1 teaspoon honey; roll up from the filled edge.

PER CREPE: 149 cal., 8 g total fat (5 g sat. fat, 0 g trans fat), 48 mg chol., 145 mg sodium, 17 g carbo., 1 g fiber, 4 g pro. EXCHANGES: 1 Starch, 1½ Fat

WAFFLES

PREP: 15 MINUTES
BAKE: PER WAFFLE BAKER DIRECTIONS
MAKES: 12 TO 16 (4-INCH) WAFFLES

- 1¾ cups all-purpose flour
- 2 tablespoons sugar
- 1 tablespoon baking powder
- ¼ teaspoon salt
- 2 eggs
- 1¾ cups milk
- ½ cup vegetable oil or butter, melted
- 1 teaspoon vanilla

1 In a medium bowl stir together flour, sugar, baking powder, and salt. Make a well in the center of the flour mixture; set aside.

2 In another medium bowl beat eggs lightly; stir in milk, oil, and vanilla. Add egg mixture all at once to the flour mixture. Stir just until moistened (batter should be slightly lumpy).

3 Add batter to a preheated, lightly greased waffle baker according to manufacturer's directions (use a regular or Belgian waffle baker). Close lid quickly; do not open until done. Bake according to manufacturer's directions. When done, use a fork to lift waffle off grid. Repeat with remaining batter. Serve warm.

BUTTERMILK WAFFLES: Prepare as directed, except reduce baking powder to 1 teaspoon and add ½ teaspoon baking soda. Substitute 2 cups buttermilk or sour milk (see tip, page 19) for the milk.

CORNMEAL WAFFLES: Prepare as directed, except decrease flour to 1 cup and add 1 cup cornmeal to the flour mixture.

GINGERBREAD WAFFLES: Prepare as directed, except increase flour to 2 cups and omit the sugar. Add ½ teaspoon ground ginger, ½ teaspoon ground cinnamon, and ¼ teaspoon ground cloves to the flour mixture. Add 2 tablespoons molasses to the egg mixture.

PER WAFFLE PLAIN, BUTTERMILK, CORNMEAL, OR GINGERBREAD VARIATIONS: 185 cal., 11 g total fat (1 g sat. fat, 0 g trans fat), 38 mg chol., 135 mg sodium, 18 g carbo., 0 g fiber, 4 g pro. EXCHANGES: 1 Starch, 2 Fat

CHOCOLATE WAFFLES: Prepare as directed, except decrease flour to 1½ cups, increase sugar to ¼ cup, and add ⅓ cup unsweetened cocoa powder to the flour mixture. Fold ¼ cup miniature semisweet chocolate pieces into the batter. (You might need to lightly coat the waffle baker with nonstick cooking spray between each waffle to prevent waffle from sticking.)

PER WAFFLE: 216 cal., 12 g total fat (2 g sat. fat, 0 g trans fat), 38 mg chol., 136 mg sodium, 22 g carbo., 1 g fiber, 5 g pro. EXCHANGES: 1 Starch, ½ Other Carbo., 2 Fat

ADDITIONS: Fold one of the following into the batter: ½ cup raisins or finely snipped dried fruit;

½ cup fresh or frozen blueberries, raspberries, or blackberries; ½ cup finely chopped nuts (toasted, if desired); ½ cup chopped banana; ½ cup crumbled cooked bacon; ½ cup shredded cheddar cheese; or ¼ cup shredded coconut.

CARAMEL-PECAN FRENCH TOAST

PREP: 20 MINUTES **CHILL:** 2 TO 24 HOURS
BAKE: 30 MINUTES **STAND:** 10 MINUTES
OVEN: 350°F **MAKES:** 8 SERVINGS

CARAMEL-PECAN FRENCH TOAST

  1 cup packed brown sugar

  ½ cup butter

  2 tablespoons light-color corn syrup

  1 cup chopped pecans, toasted (see tip, page 20)

16 ½-inch slices French bread

  6 eggs, lightly beaten

1½ cups milk

  1 teaspoon vanilla

  1 tablespoon granulated sugar

1½ teaspoons ground cinnamon

  ¼ teaspoon ground nutmeg

    Raspberries, maple syrup, and/or chopped pecans, toasted (optional)

1 In a medium saucepan combine brown sugar, butter, and corn syrup. Cook and stir until butter melts and brown sugar dissolves. Pour into a 3-quart rectangular baking dish. Sprinkle with ½ cup of the pecans.

2 Arrange half of the bread slices in a single layer in the baking dish. Sprinkle with remaining ½ cup pecans; top with remaining bread slices.

3 In a medium bowl whisk together eggs, milk, and vanilla. Gradually pour egg mixture over bread; press lightly with the back of a large spoon to moisten bread. In a small bowl stir together granulated sugar, cinnamon, and nutmeg; sprinkle over bread. Cover and chill for 2 to 24 hours.

4 Preheat oven to 350°F. Bake, uncovered, for 30 to 40 minutes or until light brown. Let stand for 10 minutes before serving. To serve, invert French toast onto a large serving platter. If desired, serve with raspberries, maple syrup, and/or additional pecans.

PER 2 SLICES: 579 cal., 27 g total fat (10 g sat. fat, 0 g trans fat), 193 mg chol., 579 mg sodium, 72 g carbo., 3 g fiber, 15 g pro. EXCHANGES: 2 Starch, 3 Other Carbo., 1 Medium-Fat Meat, 4 Fat

FAST

FRENCH TOAST

PREP: 10 MINUTES **COOK:** 4 MINUTES PER SLICE
MAKES: 4 SERVINGS

4 eggs, lightly beaten

1 cup milk

2 tablespoons sugar

2 teaspoons vanilla

½ teaspoon finely shredded orange peel (optional)

½ teaspoon ground cinnamon (optional)

¼ teaspoon ground nutmeg (optional)

8 slices Texas toast, ½-inch slices country Italian bread, or rich egg bread (challah or brioche)

2 tablespoons butter or margarine

  Maple syrup (optional)

1 In a shallow bowl beat together eggs, milk, sugar, vanilla, and peel or spice (if desired). Dip bread into egg mixture, coating both sides (let soak in egg mixture about 10 seconds per side).

2 In a skillet or on a griddle melt 1 tablespoon of the butter over medium heat; add half of the bread slices and cook for 2 to 3 minutes on each side or until golden brown. Repeat with remaining butter and bread slices. Serve warm. If desired, serve with syrup.

PER 2 SLICES: 410 cal., 17 g total fat (7 g sat. fat, 0 g trans fat), 272 mg chol., 530 mg sodium, 48 g carbo., 2 g fiber, 16 g pro. EXCHANGES: 3 Starch, 1 Medium-Fat Meat, 2 Fat

CAKE DOUGHNUTS

PREP: 45 MINUTES **CHILL:** 2 TO 4 HOURS
COOK: 2 TO 3 MINUTES PER BATCH
MAKES: ABOUT 16 DOUGHNUTS AND HOLES

- 4 cups all-purpose flour
- 2 teaspoons baking powder
- ¼ teaspoon salt
- 2 eggs
- 1¼ cups granulated sugar
- 1 teaspoon vanilla
- ⅔ cup milk
- ¼ cup butter, melted
  Vegetable oil or shortening for deep-fat frying
  Powdered sugar, granulated sugar, Chocolate Glaze, or Powdered Sugar Icing (page 178)

1 In a medium bowl combine the flour, baking powder, and salt; set aside. In a large mixing bowl combine eggs, 1¼ cups granulated sugar, and the vanilla; beat with an electric mixer on medium speed for 3 minutes or until thick. In a small bowl combine the milk and melted butter.

2 Add flour mixture and milk mixture alternately to egg mixture, beating on low speed after each addition just until combined. Cover and chill dough for 2 to 4 hours.

3 On a well-floured surface roll dough to ½-inch thickness (do not stir in additional flour) (see photo 1, below). Cut dough with a floured 2 ½-inch doughnut cutter (see photo 2, below). Reroll dough as necessary.

4 Fry 2 or 3 doughnuts at a time in deep hot oil (365°F) for 2 to 3 minutes or until doughnuts are golden brown, turning once. Remove with a slotted spoon (see photo 3, page 151) and drain on paper towels. Repeat with remaining dough. Cool doughnuts slightly and coat with powdered sugar or granulated sugar, or dip tops in Chocolate Glaze (see photo 4, page 151) or Powdered Sugar Icing.

PER DOUGHNUT AND HOLE WITH POWDERED SUGAR: 342 cal., 18 g total fat (3 g sat. fat, 0 g trans fat), 35 mg chol., 100 mg sodium, 42 g carbo., 1 g fiber, 4 g pro.
EXCHANGES: 1 Starch, 2 Other Carbo., 3½ Fat

SPICED DOUGHNUTS: Prepare as directed, except add 1 teaspoon ground cinnamon, ½ teaspoon ground ginger, and ⅛ teaspoon ground cloves to the flour mixture and coat warm doughnuts in a mixture of ⅔ cup granulated sugar and ½ teaspoon ground cinnamon.

PER DOUGHNUT AND HOLE: 368 cal., 18 g total fat (3 g sat. fat, 0 g trans fat), 35 mg chol., 100 mg sodium, 49 mg carbo., 1 g fiber, 4 g pro.
EXCHANGES: 1 Starch, 2 Other Carbo., 3½ Fat

CHOCOLATE GLAZE: In a small saucepan melt 3 ounces unsweetened chocolate and 3 tablespoons butter over low heat. Remove from heat. Stir in 3 cups powdered sugar and 1½ teaspoons vanilla. Stir in 4 to 5 tablespoons warm water until glaze coats the back of a spoon.

TWO-BITE TREATS
REMOVE DOUGHNUT HOLES FROM THE CUTTER AND FRY THEM UP FOR TASTY SNACKS.

CAKE DOUGHNUTS, STEP-BY-STEP

1. Roll out dough on a generously floured surface so dough doesn't stick. **2.** Dip cutter into flour between cuts to prevent dough from sticking. **3.** Use a slotted spoon to turn and remove doughnuts; allow excess oil to drain into pan. **4.** If glazing doughnuts, dip tops halfway in glaze. Allow to dry on a rack. **5.** Frost or roll in powdered or granulated sugar; trim with sprinkles, if you like.

CHOCOLATE-PECAN COFFEE CAKE

PREP: 30 MINUTES **BAKE:** 55 MINUTES
COOL: 20 MINUTES **OVEN:** 325°F **MAKES:** 12 PIECES

- ½ cup butter, softened
- 1 cup granulated sugar
- 2 teaspoons baking powder
- ½ teaspoon baking soda
- ¼ teaspoon salt
- 2 eggs
- 1 teaspoon vanilla
- 2¼ cups all-purpose flour
- 1 8-ounce carton dairy sour cream
- 1 recipe Coconut-Pecan Topping

1 Preheat oven to 325°F. Grease and flour a 10-inch fluted tube pan; set aside. In a large mixing bowl beat butter with an electric mixer on medium to high speed for 30 seconds. Add the sugar, baking powder, baking soda, and salt. Beat until well combined, scraping sides of bowl occasionally. Add eggs, one at a time, beating well after each addition. Beat in vanilla. Alternately add flour and sour cream to butter mixture, beating on low speed after each addition just until combined.

2 Sprinkle half of the Coconut-Pecan Topping in the prepared pan. Spoon half of the cake batter in mounds over the coconut mixture. Carefully spread to an even layer. Sprinkle with remaining Coconut-Pecan Topping. Spoon on remaining cake batter and spread to an even layer.

3 Bake for 55 to 65 minutes or until a long wooden skewer inserted near the center comes out clean. Cool on a wire rack for 20 minutes. Invert cake and remove pan. Serve warm.

COCONUT-PECAN TOPPING: In a large bowl combine 1 cup all-purpose flour, 1 cup packed brown sugar, and 1 teaspoon ground cinnamon. Cut in ½ cup cold butter until mixture resembles coarse crumbs; stir in ¾ cup semisweet chocolate pieces, ½ cup flaked coconut, and ½ cup chopped pecans.

PER PIECE: 550 cal., 28 g total fat (16 g sat. fat, 0 g trans fat), 86 mg chol., 297 mg sodium, 71 g carbo., 2 g fiber, 6 g pro. EXCHANGES: 2 Starch, 3 Other Carbo., 5 Fat

NUN'S PUFFS

PREP: 25 MINUTES **COOL:** 5 MINUTES
BAKE: 30 MINUTES **OVEN:** 375°F **MAKES:** 12 PUFFS

- ½ cup butter
- 1 cup milk
- ¾ cup all-purpose flour
- 4 eggs
- 1 tablespoon sugar
- Honey (optional)

1 Preheat oven to 375°F. Generously grease twelve 2½-inch muffin cups, including edges and around tops; set aside. In a saucepan melt butter; add milk. Bring to boiling. Add flour all at once, stirring vigorously. Cook and stir until mixture forms a ball that does not separate. Remove from heat; cool 5 minutes. Add eggs, one at a time, beating 1 minute with spoon after each addition or until smooth. Divide dough evenly among prepared cups, filling about two-thirds full; sprinkle with sugar.

2 Bake about 30 minutes or until golden brown. Remove from pan; if desired, serve hot with honey.

PER PUFF: 134 cal., 10 g total fat (6 g sat. fat, 0 g trans fat), 92 mg chol., 86 mg sodium, 8 g carbo., 0 g fiber, 4 g pro. EXCHANGES: ½ Starch, ½ Medium-Fat Meat, 1½ Fat

FRUIT COFFEE CAKE

PREP: 35 MINUTES **BAKE:** 40 MINUTES
OVEN: 350°F **MAKES:** 9 PIECES

- 1½ to 2 cups sliced, peeled apricots or peaches; chopped, peeled apples; or blueberries or red raspberries
- ¼ cup sugar
- 2 tablespoons cornstarch
- 1½ cups all-purpose flour
- ¾ cup sugar
- ½ teaspoon baking powder
- ¼ teaspoon baking soda
- ¼ cup butter, cut up
- 1 egg, lightly beaten
- ½ cup buttermilk or sour milk (see tip, page 19)
- ½ teaspoon vanilla
- ¼ cup all-purpose flour
- ¼ cup sugar
- 2 tablespoons butter

1 For filling, in a medium saucepan combine fruit and ¼ cup *water*. Bring to boiling; reduce heat. Simmer (do not simmer raspberries), covered, about 5 minutes or until fruit is tender. Combine ¼ cup sugar and cornstarch; stir into fruit. Cook and stir over medium heat until thickened and bubbly. Cook and stir 2 minutes more; set filling aside.

2 Preheat oven to 350°F. In a medium bowl combine the 1½ cups flour, the ¾ cup sugar, baking powder, and baking soda. Using a pastry blender, cut in ¼ cup butter until mixture resembles coarse crumbs. Make a well in the center of the flour mixture; set aside.

3 In another bowl combine egg, buttermilk, and vanilla. Add egg mixture all at once to flour mixture. Stir just until moistened (batter should be lumpy). Spread half of the batter into an ungreased 8×8×2-inch baking pan. Spoon and gently spread filling over batter. Drop remaining batter in small mounds onto filling.

A COFFEE CAKE FOR ALL SEASONS VARY THIS TREAT ACCORDING TO WHICH FRUIT IS AT ITS FRESHEST BEST AT THE MARKET. TRY SPRING RHUBARB, SUMMER BERRIES, AND AUTUMN APPLES.

FRUIT COFFEE CAKE

4 In a small bowl stir together the ¼ cup flour and ¼ cup sugar. Cut in the 2 tablespoons butter until mixture resembles coarse crumbs. Sprinkle over coffee cake. Bake for 40 to 45 minutes or until golden. Serve warm.

RHUBARB-STRAWBERRY COFFEE CAKE:
Prepare as directed, except substitute ¾ cup fresh or frozen cut-up rhubarb and ¾ cup frozen unsweetened whole strawberries for the fruit.

LARGER-SIZE FRUIT COFFEE CAKE: Double
the recipe and use a 13×9×2-inch baking pan. Preheat oven to 350°F. Bake for 45 to 50 minutes.

PER PIECE FRUIT OR RHUBARB-STRAWBERRY VARIATION: 298 cal., 9 g total fat (5 g sat. fat, 0 g trans fat), 44 mg chol., 126 mg sodium, 52 g carbo., 1 g fiber, 4 g pro. EXCHANGES: 1½ Starch, 2 Other Carbo., 1½ Fat

BLUEBERRY BUCKLE

PREP: 20 MINUTES BAKE: 50 MINUTES
OVEN: 350°F MAKES: 9 PIECES

  2 cups all-purpose flour
2½ teaspoons baking powder
  ¼ teaspoon salt
  ½ cup shortening
  ¾ cup sugar
  1 egg
  ½ cup milk
  2 cups fresh or frozen blueberries
  ½ cup all-purpose flour
  ½ cup sugar
  ½ teaspoon ground cinnamon
  ¼ cup butter, cut up

1 Preheat oven to 350°F. Grease bottom and ½ inch up sides of a 9×9×2-inch or 8×8×2-inch baking pan; set aside. In a medium bowl combine 2 cups flour, baking powder, and salt; set aside.

2 In a medium mixing bowl beat shortening with an electric mixer on medium speed for 30 seconds. Add the ¾ cup sugar. Beat on medium to high speed until light and fluffy. Add egg; beat well. Alternately add flour mixture and milk to beaten egg mixture; beat until smooth after each addition.

3 Spread batter in prepared pan. Sprinkle with blueberries. In another bowl combine the ½ cup flour, the ½ cup sugar, and cinnamon. Using a pastry blender, cut in butter until mixture resembles coarse crumbs; sprinkle over blueberries. Bake for 50 to 60 minutes or until golden. Serve warm.

RASPBERRY BUCKLE: Prepare as directed,
except substitute fresh or frozen red raspberries for the blueberries.

PER PIECE BLUEBERRY OR RASPBERRY VARIATION: 411 cal., 17 g total fat (6 g sat. fat, 1 g trans fat), 38 mg chol., 182 mg sodium, 60 g carbo., 2 g fiber, 5 g pro. EXCHANGES: 2 Starch, 2 Other Carbo., 3 Fat

WHOLE GRAIN ▪ LOW FAT ▪ HEALTHY

STEEL-CUT OATMEAL

PREP: 10 MINUTES COOK: 25 MINUTES
MAKES: 6 SERVINGS

  4 cups water
  ½ teaspoon salt
1⅓ cups steel-cut oats
     Toppers (optional)

1 In a large saucepan bring water and salt to boiling. Stir in oats. Cover and simmer for 25 to 30 minutes or until oats are just tender and liquid is nearly absorbed. Serve warm in bowls. If desired, add Toppers.

MAKE-AHEAD DIRECTIONS: Prepare oatmeal as directed. Place cooked oatmeal in an airtight container and chill for up to 3 days. Place ⅔ cup chilled cooked oatmeal in a microwave-safe bowl. Microwave, covered with waxed paper, on 100% power (high) for 50 to 60 seconds or until heated, stirring once. Serve as directed.

SLOW COOKER OATMEAL: In a 3½- or 4-quart slow cooker combine 6 cups water, 2 cups steel-cut oats, and 1 teaspoon salt. Cover and cook on low-heat setting for 6 to 7 hours or on high-heat setting for 3 to 3½ hours. Serve as directed. Makes 9 servings.

PER ⅔ CUP STOVETOP OR SLOW COOKER VARIATION (WITHOUT TOPPERS): 142 cal., 3 g total fat (0 g sat. fat, 0 g trans fat), 0 mg chol., 199 mg sodium, 24 g carbo., 4 g fiber, 6 g pro. EXCHANGES: 1½ Starch, ½ Fat

TOPPERS: Top warm oatmeal with dried fruit (sweet cherries, raisins, tropical fruit bits, chopped dates, snipped apricots); chopped nuts (almonds, pecans, walnuts, hazelnuts); shredded or flaked coconut; brown sugar; maple syrup; and/or milk, half-and-half, or light cream.

WHY STEEL-CUT OATS?
FANS OF THIS CEREAL VARIETY APPRECIATE THEIR PLEASANTLY CHEWY TEXTURE.

GRANOLA

PREP: 15 MINUTES **BAKE:** 30 MINUTES
OVEN: 300°F **MAKES:** 14 SERVINGS

- 2 cups regular rolled oats
- 1 cup coarsely chopped slivered or sliced almonds, chopped walnuts, or chopped pecans
- ½ cup flaked coconut (optional)
- ½ cup dry-roasted sunflower kernels
- ¼ cup toasted wheat germ
- ¼ cup flaxseed meal
- ½ cup honey or maple-flavored syrup
- 2 tablespoons vegetable oil
- 2 teaspoons ground cinnamon (optional)
- 1 cup dried fruit (raisins, tart red cherries, blueberries, cranberries, and/or apricots, snipped) (optional)

1 Preheat oven to 300°F. Grease a 15×10×1-inch baking pan; set aside. In a large bowl combine the oats, nuts, coconut (if desired), sunflower kernels, wheat germ, and flaxseed meal. Stir together honey, oil, and cinnamon (if desired); stir into oat mixture. Spread evenly into prepared pan.

2 Bake for 30 to 35 minutes or until light brown, stirring after 20 minutes. Remove from oven. If desired, stir in dried fruit.

3 Spread on a large piece of foil to cool. Store at room temperature in an airtight container for up to 5 days. (Or place in freezer bags and freeze for up to 2 months.)

PER ½ CUP: 198 cal., 10 g total fat (1 g sat. fat, 0 g trans fat), 0 mg chol., 2 mg sodium, 24 g carbo., 4 g fiber, 6 g pro. EXCHANGES: 1½ Starch, 1½ Fat

CRANBERRY-ALMOND CEREAL MIX

PREP: 10 MINUTES **COOK:** 12 MINUTES
MAKES: 14 SERVINGS

- 1 cup regular rolled oats
- 1 cup quick-cooking barley
- 1 cup bulgur or cracked wheat
- 1 cup dried cranberries, raisins, and/or snipped dried apricots
- ¾ cup sliced almonds, toasted (see tip, page 20)
- ⅓ cup sugar
- 1 tablespoon ground cinnamon
- ¼ teaspoon salt
  Milk (optional)

1 In an airtight container stir together oats, barley, bulgur, cranberries, almonds, sugar, cinnamon, and salt. Cover; seal. Store at room temperature for up to 2 months or freeze for up to 6 months.

FOR TWO BREAKFAST SERVINGS: In a small saucepan bring 1⅓ cups *water* to boiling. Stir cereal mix before measuring; add ⅔ cup of the cereal mix to the boiling water. Reduce heat. Cover and simmer for 12 to 15 minutes or until cereal reaches desired consistency. If desired, serve with milk.

MICROWAVE DIRECTIONS: For one breakfast serving, in a microwave-safe 1-quart bowl combine ¾ cup water and ⅓ cup cereal mix. Microwave, uncovered, on 50% power (medium) for 8 to 11 minutes or until cereal reaches desired consistency, stirring once. Stir before serving. If desired, serve with milk.

PER ⅓ CUP MIX: 177 cal., 3 g total fat (0 g sat. fat, 0 g trans fat), 0 mg chol., 44 mg sodium, 35 g carbo., 5 g fiber, 4 g pro. EXCHANGES: 1 Starch, 1 Other Carbo., ½ Fat

FRUIT MUESLI

START TO FINISH: 10 MINUTES
MAKES: 12 SERVINGS

- 4 cups multigrain cereal with rolled rye, oats, barley, and wheat
- 1 cup regular rolled oats
- ¾ cup coarsely chopped almonds or pecans, toasted (see tip, page 20)
- 1 cup toasted wheat germ
- 1 7-ounce package mixed dried fruit bits
- ½ cup unsalted sunflower kernels
- ½ cup dried banana chips, coarsely crushed
  Milk or nonfat plain yogurt (optional)

1 In a large bowl stir together multigrain cereal, rolled oats, almonds, wheat germ, dried fruit bits, sunflower kernels, and banana chips. Cover tightly and chill for up to 4 weeks. If desired, serve with milk or yogurt.

PER ⅔ CUP: 293 cal., 10 g total fat (2 g sat. fat, 0 g trans fat), 0 mg chol., 13 mg sodium, 44 g carbo., 4 g fiber, 10 g pro. EXCHANGES: 3 Starch, 1½ Fat

OATS, MILLET, AND MORE
GRAINS CAN MAKE NOURISHING HOT CEREALS. SEE CHART, PAGE 83, FOR COOKING TIMES.

CAKES & FROSTINGS

CARROT CAKE, PAGE 167

CAKES & FROSTINGS

WITH THESE ESSENTIALS, YOU CAN CRAFT FLAWLESS CAKES—FROM SIMPLE TO SPECTACULAR.

THE BEST PAN FOR THE JOB

Pans come in a variety of materials. A superb all-around choice is the simple, sturdy, single-wall aluminum pan, with or without nonstick coating. Lightweight and a good conductor of heat, it ensures even baking and browning. Whichever pan you use, keep these maxims in mind.

■ Shiny baking pans reflect heat, producing cakes with delicate, golden crusts.

■ Dark- or dull-finish pans and glass dishes absorb heat, increasing browning. (If they brown your cakes too much, reduce oven temperature by 25°F; check doneness 3 to 5 minutes early.)

DON'T GET STUCK

Removing a cake from the pan is a make-or-break moment. Here are three ways to ensure your cake will slip out easily when the time comes.

■ Grease and lightly flour. Unless a recipe says otherwise, use a paper towel or pastry brush to evenly spread shortening or butter on bottom, sides, and corners of a pan. Sprinkle a little flour into the pan; tap so flour covers all greased surfaces. Tap out any extra flour into the sink. For chocolate cakes, consider using cocoa powder instead of flour.

■ Use nonstick spray. As an alternative to grease, apply nonstick cooking spray; flour as directed.

■ Line the pan. If a recipe calls for waxed or parchment paper, place the pan on the paper and trace around its base with a pencil. Cut just inside the traced line; line the bottom of a lightly greased pan with the paper, smoothing out any wrinkles or bubbles. Then, unless otherwise specified, grease and flour the lined pan as directed.

NICELY DONE!

Never underestimate the importance of the proper oven temperature to get your cake done just right.

■ Always fully preheat the oven before baking.

■ Use a reliable oven thermometer to ensure your oven is accurately calibrated.

DONENESS TESTS: Once the minimum baking time is reached, use the doneness test most appropriate for the type of cake you're baking.

■ For butter-style cakes (those with beaten butter and sugar in the batter): Insert a wooden toothpick near the center of the cake. If toothpick comes out with only a crumb or two on it, the cake is done. If there is any wet batter on it, bake the cake for a few minutes

more and test in a new spot with a clean toothpick.

■ For foam cakes (such as angel food, sponge, and chiffon): Touch the top lightly with your finger. If the top springs back, the cake is done.

NEAT TRICKS FOR FROSTING A CAKE

To keep the serving plate clean, tuck strips of waxed paper under the cake edges before frosting. Use a pastry brush to brush away loose crumbs from cake. Spread a thin coating of frosting over the sides and top to prevent crumbs from mixing with frosting. Frost as directed. After the cake is frosted, gently tug the waxed paper strips out from under the cake.

POPPY SEED CAKE, PAGE 169

WHITE CAKE

PREP: 55 MINUTES **BAKE:** 20 MINUTES
COOL: 60 MINUTES **OVEN:** 350°F
MAKES: 12 TO 16 SERVINGS

    4 egg whites
    2 cups all-purpose flour
    1 teaspoon baking powder
    ½ teaspoon baking soda
    ½ teaspoon salt
    ½ cup butter or shortening, softened
    1¾ cups sugar
    1 teaspoon vanilla
    1⅓ cups buttermilk or sour milk (page 19)

1 Allow egg whites to stand at room temperature for 30 minutes. Meanwhile, grease and lightly flour two 9×1½-inch or 8×1½-inch round cake pans or grease one 13×9×2-inch baking pan; set pan(s) aside. In a medium bowl stir together flour, baking powder, baking soda, and salt; set aside.

2 Preheat oven to 350°F. In a large mixing bowl beat butter with an electric mixer on medium to high speed for 30 seconds. Add sugar and vanilla (see photo 1, below); beat until combined. Add egg whites, one at a time, beating well after each addition. Alternately add flour mixture and buttermilk, beating on low speed after each addition just until combined (see photos 3 and 4, page 159). Spread batter in prepared pan(s) (see photo 5, page 159).

3 Bake for 20 to 25 minutes for 9-inch pans, 30 to 35 minutes for 8-inch pans or 13×9×2-inch pan, or until a wooden toothpick inserted near center(s) comes out clean. Cool in pans on wire racks for 10 minutes. Remove layers from pans;

cool thoroughly on racks. Or place 13×9×2-inch cake in pan on a wire rack; cool thoroughly. Frost with desired frosting (see pages 178 to 180).

PER SERVING: 275 cal., 8 g total fat (5 g sat. fat, 0 g trans fat), 21 mg chol., 271 mg sodium, 47 g carbo., 1 g fiber, 4 g pro. EXCHANGES: 1 Starch, 2 Other Carbo., 1½ Fat

YELLOW CAKE

PREP: 50 MINUTES **BAKE:** 20 MINUTES
COOL: 60 MINUTES **OVEN:** 375°F
MAKES: 12 TO 16 SERVINGS

    ¾ cup butter
    3 eggs
    2½ cups all-purpose flour
    2½ teaspoons baking powder
    ½ teaspoon salt
    1¾ cups sugar
    1½ teaspoons vanilla
    1¼ cups milk

1 Allow butter and eggs to stand at room temperature for 30 minutes. Meanwhile, grease and lightly flour two 9×1½-inch or 8×1½-inch round cake pans or grease one 13×9×2-inch baking pan; set pan(s) aside. In a medium bowl stir together flour, baking powder, and salt; set aside.

2 Preheat oven to 375°F. In a large mixing bowl beat butter with an electric mixer on medium to high speed for 30 seconds. Gradually add sugar, about ¼ cup at a time, beating on medium speed until well combined (see photo 1, below). Scrape sides of bowl; beat for 2 minutes more. Add eggs, one at a time, beating well after each addition (see photo 2, below). Beat in vanilla. Alternately add

PREPARING THE CAKE BATTER, STEP-BY-STEP

1. While beating butter, add sugar, ¼ cup at a time. Beat until light and fluffy. **2.** Add eggs, one at a time, beating after each until integrated. **3.** Alternate adding flour mixture and milk, approximately one-third of each at a time. Batter might look curdled. **4.** Add last third of the milk, beating on low until combined. **5.** Pour batter evenly between prepared pans; smooth tops before baking.

flour mixture and milk to butter mixture, beating on low speed after each addition just until combined (see photos 3 and 4, below). Spread batter into prepared pan(s) (see photo 5, below).

3 Bake for 20 to 25 minutes for 9-inch pans, 30 to 35 minutes for 8-inch pans, 25 to 30 minutes for 13×9×2-inch pan, or until a wooden toothpick inserted near center(s) comes out clean. Cool in pans on wire racks for 10 minutes. Remove layers from pans; cool thoroughly on wire racks. Or place 13×9×2-inch cake in pan on wire rack; cool. Frost with desired frosting (see pages 178 to 180).

PER SERVING:: 342 cal., 14 g total fat (8 g sat. fat, 0 g trans fat), 885 mg chol., 257 mg sodium, 51 g carbo., 1 g fiber, 5 g pro. EXCHANGES: 1½ Starch, 2 Other Carbo., 2½ Fat

BEST EVER

CHOCOLATE CAKE

PREP: 60 MINUTES **BAKE:** 35 MINUTES
COOL: 60 MINUTES **OVEN:** 350°F
MAKES: 12 TO 16 SERVINGS

- ¾ cup butter
- 3 eggs
- 2 cups all-purpose flour
- ¾ cup unsweetened cocoa powder
- 1 teaspoon baking soda
- ¾ teaspoon baking powder
- ½ teaspoon salt
- 2 cups sugar
- 2 teaspoons vanilla
- 1½ cups milk

1 Allow butter and eggs to stand at room temperature for 30 minutes. Meanwhile, lightly grease bottoms of two 8×8×2-inch square or 9×1½-inch round cake pans. Line bottoms of pans with waxed paper; grease and lightly flour pans. Or grease one 13×9×2-inch baking pan. Set pan(s) aside. In a medium bowl stir together flour, cocoa powder, baking soda, baking powder, and salt; set aside.

2 Preheat oven to 350°F. In a large mixing bowl beat butter with an electric mixer on medium to high speed for 30 seconds. Gradually add sugar, ¼ cup at a time, beating on medium speed until combined (see photo 1, page 158). Scrape sides of bowl; beat 2 minutes more. Add eggs, one at a time, beating well after each addition (see photo 2, page 158). Beat in vanilla. Alternately add flour mixture and milk, beating on low speed just until combined (see photos 3 and 4, below). Beat on medium to high speed for 20 seconds more. Spread into prepared pan(s) (see photo 5, below).

3 Bake for 35 to 40 minutes for 8-inch pans and 13×9×2-inch pan, 30 to 35 minutes for 9-inch pans, or until a wooden toothpick inserted near center(s) comes out clean. Cool layers in pans on wire racks for 10 minutes. Remove layers from pans; peel off waxed paper. Cool thoroughly on wire racks. Or place 13×9×2-inch cake in pan on a wire rack; cool thoroughly. Frost with desired frosting (see pages 178 to 180).

DEVIL'S FOOD CAKE: Prepare as directed, except omit baking powder and increase baking soda to 1¼ teaspoons.

PER SERVING PLAIN OR DEVIL'S FOOD VARIATION: 354 cal., 14 g total fat (9 g sat. fat, 0 g trans fat), 86 mg chol., 330 mg sodium, 54 g carbo., 2 g fiber, 6 g pro. EXCHANGES: 2 Starch, 1½ Other Carbo., 2½ Fat

3 **4** **5**

GERMAN CHOCOLATE CAKE

PREP: 60 MINUTES **BAKE:** 35 MINUTES
COOL: 60 MINUTES **OVEN:** 350°F
MAKES: 12 TO 16 SERVINGS

- 1 4-ounce package sweet baking chocolate, chopped
- 1½ cups milk
- ¾ cup butter
- 3 eggs
- 2 cups all-purpose flour
- 1 teaspoon baking soda
- ¾ teaspoon baking powder
- ½ teaspoon salt
- 1¾ cups sugar
- 2 teaspoons vanilla
- 1 recipe Coconut-Pecan Frosting

1 In a small saucepan combine chocolate and milk. Cook and stir over low heat until melted; set aside to cool.

2 Allow butter and eggs to stand at room temperature for 30 minutes. Meanwhile, lightly grease the bottoms of two 8×8×2-inch square or 9×1½-inch round cake pans. Line bottoms of pans with waxed paper; grease and lightly flour pans. Or grease one 13×9×2-inch baking pan. Set pan(s) aside. In a medium bowl stir together flour, baking soda, baking powder; and salt; set aside.

3 Preheat oven to 350°F. In a large mixing bowl beat butter with an electric mixer on medium to high speed for 30 seconds. Gradually add sugar, about ¼ cup at a time, beating on medium speed until well combined. Scrape sides of bowl; beat on medium speed for 2 minutes more. Add eggs, one at a time, beating well after each addition. Beat in vanilla. Alternately add flour mixture and chocolate mixture, beating on low speed after each addition just until combined. Beat on medium to high speed for 20 seconds more. Spread batter in prepared pan(s).

4 Bake for 35 to 40 minutes for 8-inch pans, 30 to 35 minutes for 9-inch pans, 40 to 45 minutes for 13×9×2-inch pan, or until a wooden toothpick inserted near the center(s) comes out clean. Cool layers in pans on wire racks for 10 minutes. Remove layers from pans; peel off waxed paper. Cool thoroughly on racks. Or place 13×9×2-inch cake in pan on a wire rack; cool thoroughly.

5 Spread Coconut-Pecan Frosting over the top of each layer; stack the layers on a cake plate. Or spread Coconut-Pecan Frosting over the top of the 13×9×2-inch cake.

COCONUT-PECAN FROSTING: In a medium saucepan lightly beat 2 eggs. Stir in two 5-ounce cans (1⅓ cups) evaporated milk, 1⅓ cups sugar, and ½ cup butter. Cook and stir over medium heat for 8 to 10 minutes or until thick and bubbly. Remove from heat; stir in 2⅔ cups flaked coconut and 1 cup chopped pecans. Cover and cool thoroughly before using to frost cake.

PER SERVING: 756 cal., 42 g total fat (24 g sat. fat, 0 g trans fat), 148 mg chol., 491 mg sodium, 90 g carbo., 4 g fiber, 11 g pro. EXCHANGES: 3½ Starch, 2½ Other Carbo., 8 Fat

BEST EVER

RED VELVET CAKE

PREP: 50 MINUTES **BAKE:** 25 MINUTES
COOL: 60 MINUTES **OVEN:** 350°F
MAKES: 16 SERVINGS

- 3 eggs
- ¾ cup butter
- 3 cups all-purpose flour
- 1 tablespoon unsweetened cocoa powder
- ¾ teaspoon salt
- 2¼ cups sugar
- 1 1-ounce bottle red food coloring (2 tablespoons)
- 1½ teaspoons vanilla
- 1½ cups buttermilk or sour milk (see tip, page 19)
- 1½ teaspoons baking soda
- 1½ teaspoons vinegar
- 1 recipe Buttercream Frosting

1 Allow eggs and butter to stand at room temperature for 30 minutes. Meanwhile, grease and lightly flour three 9×1½-inch or 8×1½-inch round cake pans. Or grease one 13×9×2-inch baking pan. Set pan(s) aside. In a medium bowl stir together flour, cocoa powder, and salt; set aside.

2 Preheat oven to 350°F. In a very large mixing bowl beat butter with an electric mixer on medium to high speed for 30 seconds. Gradually add sugar, about ¼ cup at time, beating on medium speed until well combined (see photo 1, page 158). Scrape sides of bowl; beat on medium speed for 2 minutes more. Add eggs, one at a time, beating well after each addition (see photo 2, page 158). Beat in red food coloring and vanilla. Alternately add flour mixture and buttermilk, beating on low speed after each addition just until combined (see photos 3 and 4, page 159). In a small bowl combine baking soda and vinegar; fold into batter. Spread batter into prepared pan(s).

3 Bake for 25 to 30 minutes for 8-inch pans, 20 to 25 minutes for 9-inch pans, 30 to 35 minutes for 13×9×2-inch pan, or until a wooden toothpick inserted near the center(s) comes out clean. Cool layers in pans on wire racks for 10 minutes. Remove layers from pans; cool thoroughly on wire racks. Or place 13×9×2-inch cake in pan on wire rack; cool thoroughly.

4 Prepare Buttercream Frosting (cut recipe in half if making 13×9×2-inch cake). Place one cake layer, bottom side up, on serving platter. Spread with one-third of the Buttercream Frosting. Top with second cake layer, bottom side up. Spread top with half of the remaining frosting. Top with third layer, rounded side up. Spread top with remaining frosting. If using 13×9×2-inch pan, spread frosting over cake in pan.

BUTTERCREAM FROSTING: In a medium saucepan whisk together 1½ cups sugar, 1½ cups milk, ⅓ cup all-purpose flour, and a dash salt. Cook and stir over medium heat until thickened and bubbly. Reduce heat; cook and stir for 1 minute more. Remove from heat; stir in 2 teaspoons vanilla. Cover and cool completely at room temperature. Transfer to a large mixing bowl. On medium speed of an electric mixer, gradually beat in 1½ cups softened butter until mixture is well combined and smooth, scraping sides of bowl occasionally. (Frosting might look curdled until all the butter is incorporated.)

PER SERVING: 546 cal., 28 g total fat (17 g sat. fat, 0 g trans fat), 112 mg chol., 467 mg sodium, 70 g carbo., 1 g fiber, 6 g pro. EXCHANGES: 2 Starch, 2½ Other Carbo., 5½ Fat

STRAWBERRY CAKE

PREP: 15 MINUTES **BAKE:** 30 MINUTES
COOL: 60 MINUTES **OVEN:** 350°F
MAKES: 15 SERVINGS

- 1 10-ounce package frozen halved strawberries in syrup or one 16-ounce container sliced strawberries in sugar, thawed
- 1 package 2-layer-size white cake mix
- ½ of an 8-ounce package cream cheese, softened
- ¼ cup butter, softened
- 1 teaspoon vanilla
- 4 cups powdered sugar
  Red food coloring (optional)

1 Preheat oven to 350°F. Grease a 13×9×2-inch baking pan; set pan aside. Drain strawberries,

STRAWBERRY CUPCAKES

reserving 3 tablespoons syrup for frosting. Add enough water to remaining syrup to equal ¾ cup. Prepare cake mix according to package directions, substituting the syrup-water mixture for the liquid called for on the package; stir in all of the strawberries. (Batter will be thick.) Spread batter in prepared pan.

2 Bake for 30 to 35 minutes or until a wooden toothpick inserted near the center comes out clean. Cool in pan on a wire rack.

3 For frosting, in a large mixing bowl beat cream cheese, butter, vanilla, and reserved syrup with an electric mixer on medium speed until light and fluffy. Gradually beat in powdered sugar. If desired, beat in 1 or 2 drops red food coloring. Spread frosting over cooled cake.

PER SERVING: 345 cal., 11 g total fat (4 g sat. fat, 0 g trans fat), 16 mg chol., 287 mg sodium, 63 g carbo., 0 g fiber, 3 g pro. EXCHANGES: 1 Starch, 3 Other Carbo., 2 Fat

STRAWBERRY CUPCAKES: Grease and flour twenty-four 2½-inch muffin cups or line with paper bake cups. Prepare batter as directed. Fill muffin cups two-thirds full with batter. Bake about 18 minutes or until a wooden toothpick inserted in centers comes out clean. Cool in cups on a wire rack 5 minutes. Remove from cups; cool completely on wire rack. Pipe or spread frosting on cupcakes. Makes 24 cupcakes.

PER CUPCAKE: 216 cal., 7 g total fat (3 g sat. fat, 0 g trans fat), 10 mg chol., 179 mg sodium, 40 g carbo., 0 g fiber, 2 g pro. EXCHANGES: 2½ Other Carbo., 1½ Fat

APPLE CAKE WITH BUTTERY CARAMEL SAUCE

PREP: 35 MINUTES **BAKE:** 45 MINUTES **COOL:**
45 MINUTES **OVEN:** 350°F **MAKES:** 16 SERVINGS

- 2 cups all-purpose flour
- 1 teaspoon baking powder
- ½ teaspoon salt
- ½ teaspoon ground nutmeg
- ½ teaspoon ground cinnamon
- ¼ teaspoon baking soda
- ½ cup butter, softened
- 2 cups sugar
- 2 eggs
- 6 cups chopped, unpeeled cooking apples
- 1 cup chopped walnuts
- 1 recipe Buttery Caramel Sauce

1 Preheat oven to 350°F. Grease a 13×9×2-inch baking pan; set pan aside. In a medium bowl stir together the flour, baking powder, salt, nutmeg, cinnamon, and baking soda; set aside.

2 In a large mixing bowl beat butter with an electric mixer on medium speed for 30 seconds. Gradually add sugar, ¼ cup at a time, beating on medium speed until well combined. Scrape sides of bowl; beat for 2 minutes more. Add eggs, one at a time, beating after each addition. Add flour mixture to butter mixture, beating on low speed just until combined. Fold in apples and walnuts. (Batter will be thick.) Spread batter into prepared pan.

3 Bake for 45 to 50 minutes or until a toothpick inserted near center comes out clean. Cool in pan for 45 minutes. Serve with Buttery Caramel Sauce.

BUTTERY CARAMEL SAUCE: In a small saucepan melt ⅓ cup butter over medium heat. Stir in ⅓ cup granulated sugar, ⅓ cup packed brown sugar, and ⅓ cup whipping cream. Bring to boiling, stirring constantly. Remove from heat; stir in ½ teaspoon vanilla. Serve warm.

PER SERVING: 369 cal., 17 g total fat (8 g sat. fat, 0 g trans fat), 59 mg chol., 188 mg sodium, 23 g carbo., 2 g fiber, 4 g pro. EXCHANGES: 1 Starch, 2½ Other Carbo., 3 Fat

EASY APPLE CAKE SPEED UP THIS QUICK, NO-PEEL APPLE CAKE BY SIMPLY HEATING UP SOME PURCHASED CARAMEL SAUCE—THE FINEST LIST BUTTER OR CREAM AS AN INGREDIENT.

APPLE CAKE WITH BUTTERY CARAMEL SAUCE

OATMEAL CAKE

PREP: 40 MINUTES **BAKE:** 30 MINUTES
BROIL: 3 MINUTES **COOL:** 30 MINUTES **OVEN:** 350°F
MAKES: 16 SERVINGS

- 2¼ cups water
- 1½ cups rolled oats
- ½ cup butter, cut up
- 3 eggs, lightly beaten
- 1½ cups packed brown sugar
- 1¼ cups whole wheat flour
- 1 cup all-purpose flour
- 1½ teaspoons baking soda
- 1½ teaspoons ground cinnamon
- ¾ teaspoon ground nutmeg
- ¾ teaspoon salt
- ½ cup butter
- 1⅓ cups packed brown sugar
- ½ cup half-and-half, light cream, or evaporated milk
- 2 cups flaked coconut
- 1 cup chopped pecans
- 1 teaspoon vanilla

1 Preheat oven to 350°F. Lightly grease the bottom of a 13×9×2-inch baking pan; set pan aside.

2 In a large saucepan bring water to boiling. Add oats and ½ cup butter. Reduce heat to low; cook for 5 minutes to soften the oats, stirring occasionally. Remove from heat; set aside.

3 In a large bowl stir together the eggs and the 1½ cups brown sugar; set aside. In a medium bowl stir together the flours, baking soda, cinnamon, nutmeg, and salt. Using a wooden spoon, stir oat mixture into egg mixture until combined. Fold in flour mixture just until moistened. (Batter will be thick.) Spread batter into prepared pan.

4 Bake for 30 to 35 minutes or until a wooden toothpick inserted near the center comes out clean. Transfer to a wire rack. Preheat broiler.

5 Meanwhile, in a medium saucepan melt ½ cup butter. Stir in the 1⅓ cups brown sugar and the half-and-half until combined. Remove from heat. Stir in coconut, pecans, and vanilla; mix well. Spoon coconut mixture over hot cake.

6 Broil 4 to 5 inches from the heat for 3 to 4 minutes or until topping is bubbly and begins to brown, watching closely. Cool in pan on a wire rack at least 30 minutes before serving.

PER SERVING: 481 cal., 24 g total fat (13 g sat. fat, 0 g trans fat), 73 mg chol., 378 mg sodium, 64 g carbo., 4 g fiber, 6 g pro.
EXCHANGES: 4 Other Carbo., 4 Fat

GINGERBREAD

PREP: 20 MINUTES **BAKE:** 20 MINUTES
COOL: 30 MINUTES **OVEN:** 325°F **MAKES:** 9 SERVINGS

- 1¼ cups all-purpose flour
- ¾ teaspoon ground ginger
- ½ teaspoon baking soda
- ½ teaspoon baking powder
- ½ teaspoon ground cinnamon
- ¼ teaspoon salt
- ¼ teaspoon ground cloves
- ¼ cup dairy sour cream
- 3 tablespoons strong brewed coffee, cooled, or milk
- ⅓ cup butter, softened
- ¼ cup packed brown sugar
- 1 egg
- ½ cup molasses
  Powdered sugar
  Sweetened Whipped Cream (page 287) (optional)

1 Preheat oven to 325°F. Lightly grease a 9×9×2-inch baking pan; set pan aside.

2 In a small bowl combine flour, ginger, baking soda, baking powder, cinnamon, salt, and cloves; set aside. In another small bowl whisk together sour cream and cooled coffee; set aside.

3 In a medium bowl beat butter and brown sugar with an electric mixer on medium speed until light and fluffy. Add egg, beating on medium speed until combined. Gradually add molasses, beating until smooth. Alternately add flour mixture and sour cream mixture, beating on low speed after each addition just until combined. Beat on high speed for 20 seconds more. Spread batter into prepared pan.

4 Bake for 20 to 25 minutes or until a wooden toothpick inserted near center comes out clean. (Cake might dip slightly in center.) Cool in pan on wire rack for 30 minutes. Sift powdered sugar over cake. If desired, serve with Whipped Cream.

PER SERVING: 224 cal., 9 g total fat (5 g sat. fat, 0 g trans fat), 44 mg chol., 217 mg sodium, 35 g carbo., 1 g fiber, 3 g pro.
EXCHANGES: 1 Starch, 1½ Other Carbo., 1½ Fat

TIP-TOP TREAT
SPRINKLE A LITTLE THINLY SLICED CANDIED GINGER OVER THE WHIPPED CREAM FOR EXTRA SPARKLE AND FLAVOR.

PINEAPPLE UPSIDE-DOWN CAKE

PREP: 25 MINUTES **BAKE:** 30 MINUTES
COOL: 35 MINUTES **OVEN:** 350°F
MAKES: 8 SERVINGS

- ¼ cup butter
- ½ cup packed brown sugar
- 1 8-ounce can pineapple tidbits, drained
- ½ cup chopped pecans, toasted (see tip, page 20)
- 1⅓ cups all-purpose flour
- ⅔ cup granulated sugar
- 2 teaspoons baking powder
- ¼ teaspoon salt
- ¼ teaspoon ground ginger
- ⅔ cup milk
- ¼ cup butter, softened
- 1 egg
- 1 teaspoon vanilla

1 Preheat oven to 350°F. Place ¼ cup butter in a 9×1½-inch round cake pan. Place pan in oven until butter melts. Stir in brown sugar. Arrange pineapple and pecans in pan; set aside.

2 In a medium mixing bowl stir together flour, granulated sugar, baking powder, salt, and ginger. Add milk, ¼ cup softened butter, the egg, and vanilla. Beat with an electric mixer on low speed until combined. Beat on medium speed for 1 minute. (Batter might still be lumpy.) Spread batter in prepared pan.

3 Bake for 30 to 35 minutes or until a toothpick inserted near center comes out clean. Cool in pan on wire rack 5 minutes. Loosen sides of cake; invert onto plate. Cool for 30 minutes; serve warm.

PER SERVING: 380 cal., 18 g total fat (8 g sat. fat, 0 g trans fat), 59 mg chol., 236 mg sodium, 53 g carbo., 1 g fiber, 4 g pro. EXCHANGES: 1 Starch, 2½ Other Carbo., 3½ Fat

BUSY-DAY CAKE

PREP: 25 MINUTES **BAKE:** 30 MINUTES **COOL:** 30 MINUTES **OVEN:** 350°F **MAKES:** 8 SERVINGS

- 1⅓ cups all-purpose flour
- ⅔ cup sugar
- 2 teaspoons baking powder
- ⅔ cup milk
- ¼ cup butter, softened
- 1 egg
- 1 teaspoon vanilla
- 3 cups assorted fresh berries

1 Preheat oven to 350°F. Grease and flour an 8×1½-inch round cake pan; set aside.

2 In a medium mixing bowl combine flour, sugar, and baking powder. Add milk, butter, egg, and vanilla. Beat with an electric mixer on low speed until combined. Beat on medium speed for 1 minute. Spread batter in prepared pan.

3 Bake about 30 minutes or until a wooden toothpick inserted near center comes out clean. Cool in pan on wire rack 10 minutes. Loosen sides of cake; invert onto plate. Cool 30 minutes; serve warm with berries and, if desired, *whipped cream.*

PER SERVING: 346 cal., 18 g total fat (11 g sat. fat, 0 g trans fat), 84 mg chol., 130 mg sodium, 42 g carbo., 2 g fiber, 5 g pro. EXCHANGES: 1½ Starch, 1½ Other Carbo., 3 Fat

CHOCOLATE CHIP-BANANA SNACK CAKE

PREP: 20 MINUTES **BAKE:** 25 MINUTES
COOL: 30 MINUTES **OVEN:** 350°F
MAKES: 9 SERVINGS

- 1 cup all-purpose flour
- ¾ teaspoon baking powder
- ½ teaspoon baking soda
- ¼ teaspoon salt
- ¼ cup butter, softened
- ¾ cup sugar
- 1 egg
- ⅓ cup mashed ripe banana (1)
- ½ teaspoon vanilla
- ⅓ cup buttermilk or sour milk (see tip, page 19)
- ⅓ cup miniature semisweet chocolate pieces
  Purchased fudge or caramel ice cream topping (optional)
  Banana slices (optional)

1 Preheat oven to 350°F. Grease an 8×8×2-inch baking pan; set aside. In a small bowl combine the flour, baking powder, soda, and salt; set aside.

2 In a medium mixing bowl beat butter with electric mixer on medium speed for 30 seconds. Add sugar, beating until combined. Beat in egg until well combined. Beat in banana and vanilla until combined. Alternately add flour mixture and buttermilk, beating on low speed after each addition just until combined. (Batter might appear slightly curdled.) Stir in chocolate pieces. Spread in prepared pan.

3 Bake for 25 to 30 minutes or until a wooden toothpick inserted near center comes out clean. Cool in pan on wire rack for 30 minutes. If desired, serve warm with fudge topping and banana slices.

PER SERVING: 232 cal., 8 g total fat (5 g sat. fat, 0 g trans fat), 37 mg chol., 219 mg sodium, 37 g carbo., 1 g fiber, 3 g pro. EXCHANGES: 1 Starch, 1½ Other Carbo., 1½ Fat

PINEAPPLE UPSIDE-DOWN CAKE

TOP IT OFF BUSY-DAY CAKE BECOMES A SPECIAL-DAY TREAT WITH WHIPPED CREAM AND BERRIES. OR TOP IT WITH YOUR FAVORITE ICE CREAM OR A DRIZZLE OF HONEY OR CARAMEL SAUCE.

BUSY-DAY CAKE

CHOCOLATE CHIP-BANANA SNACK CAKE

ITALIAN CREAM CAKE

PREP: 60 MINUTES **BAKE:** 35 MINUTES
COOL: 60 MINUTES **OVEN:** 350°F
MAKES: 16 SERVINGS

  5 eggs
  ½ cup butter
  2 cups all-purpose flour
  1 teaspoon baking soda
  ½ cup shortening
  2 cups sugar
  1 teaspoon vanilla
  1 cup buttermilk or sour milk (see tip, page 19)
  1 cup flaked coconut
  ½ cup finely chopped pecans, toasted
  1 recipe Cream Cheese Frosting (page 180)
  ¾ cup chopped pecans, toasted

1 Separate eggs. Allow egg yolks, egg whites, and butter to stand at room temperature for 30 minutes. Meanwhile, grease and flour three 8×1½-inch or 9×1½-inch round cake pans; set pans aside. In a medium bowl combine flour and baking soda; set aside.

2 Preheat oven to 350°F. In a very large mixing bowl beat butter and shortening with an electric mixer on medium to high speed for 30 seconds. Add sugar; beat until well combined. Add the egg yolks and vanilla; beat on medium speed until combined. Alternately add flour mixture and buttermilk to butter mixture, beating on low speed after each addition just until combined. Fold in coconut and the ½ cup finely chopped pecans.

3 Thoroughly wash the beaters. In a medium mixing bowl beat egg whites until stiff peaks form (tips stand straight; see photo 2, page 177). Fold about one-third of the egg whites into cake batter to lighten it. Fold in remaining whites. Spread batter evenly into prepared pans.

4 Bake about 35 minutes for 8-inch pans, about 25 minutes for 9-inch pans, or until a wooden toothpick inserted near centers comes out clean. Cool in pans on wire racks for 10 minutes. Remove layers from pans; cool thoroughly on wire racks.

5 Place one cake layer, bottom side up, on serving plate. Spread with about ½ cup of the Cream Cheese Frosting; sprinkle with ¼ cup pecans. Top

FROSTING A THREE-LAYER CAKE, STEP-BY-STEP

1. Place first cake layer, bottom side up, on a serving plate. Using a flat-bladed spatula, spread with about ½ cup frosting; add second layer, bottom side down. Spread with additional ½ cup frosting. **2.** Add third cake layer, bottom side up. Apply a thin coating of frosting to entire cake to seal crumbs, preventing them from mixing with frosting. **3.** Beginning with the sides and finishing with the top, evenly spread remaining frosting over cake, swirling and sculpting as you go.

with second cake layer, bottom side down. Spread with ½ cup more frosting (see photo 1, page 166) and sprinkle with ¼ cup nuts. Top with remaining layer, bottom side up; spread top and sides of cake with remaining frosting (see photos 2 and 3, page 166). Sprinkle remaining nuts around top edge of cake. Store cake in the refrigerator for up to 2 days.

PER SERVING: 644 cal., 33 g total fat (15 g sat. fat, 1 g trans fat), 112 mg chol., 262 mg sodium, 84 g carbo., 2 g fiber, 6 g pro. EXCHANGES: 2 Starch, 3½ Other Carbo., 6 Fat

BEST EVER

CARROT CAKE (photo, page 155)

PREP: 30 MINUTES BAKE: 35 MINUTES
COOL: 2 HOURS OVEN: 350°F
MAKES: 12 SERVINGS

- 4 eggs, lightly beaten
- 2 cups all-purpose flour
- 2 cups sugar
- 2 teaspoons baking powder
- 1 teaspoon ground cinnamon (optional)
- ½ teaspoon salt
- ½ teaspoon baking soda
- 3 cups finely shredded carrots (lightly packed)
- ¾ cup vegetable oil
- 1 recipe Cream Cheese Frosting (page 180)
- ½ cup finely chopped pecans, toasted (optional) (see tip, page 20)

1 Allow eggs to stand at room temperature for 30 minutes. Meanwhile, grease two 8×1½-inch round cake pans (see photo, page 157). Line bottoms of pans with waxed paper; grease the paper. Set pans aside.

2 Preheat oven to 350°F. In a large bowl stir together flour, sugar, baking powder, cinnamon (if desired), salt, and baking soda; set aside.

3 In another bowl combine eggs, carrots, and oil. Add egg mixture to flour mixture. Stir until combined. Spread batter evenly into prepared pans.

4 Bake for 35 to 40 minutes or until a wooden toothpick inserted near centers comes out clean. Cool layers in pans on wire racks for 10 minutes. Remove layers from pans; peel off waxed paper. Cool thoroughly on wire racks.

5 Frost with Cream Cheese Frosting. If desired, sprinkle chopped pecans over frosting. Cover and store cake in the refrigerator for up to 3 days.

PER SERVING: 711 cal., 30 g total fat (10 g sat. fat, 0 g trans fat), 112 mg chol., 350 mg sodium, 108 g carbo., 1 g fiber, 6 g pro. EXCHANGES: 2 Starch, 5 Other Carbo., 5½ Fat

CARAMEL-FROSTED HUMMINGBIRD CAKE

PREP: 65 MINUTES BAKE: 30 MINUTES
COOL: 2 HOURS OVEN: 350°F MAKES: 16 SERVINGS

- 3 eggs, lightly beaten
- 3 cups all-purpose flour
- 2 cups sugar
- 1 tablespoon baking powder
- 1 teaspoon salt
- ¼ teaspoon ground cloves
- 2 cups mashed ripe bananas (about 5)
- 1 cup vegetable oil
- 1½ teaspoons vanilla
- 2 cups shredded, peeled raw sweet potatoes
- 1 8-ounce can crushed pineapple (juice pack), drained
- 1 recipe Caramel Butter Frosting

1 Allow eggs to stand at room temperature for 30 minutes. Meanwhile, grease the bottoms of three 8×1½-inch or 9×1½-inch round cake pans. Line the bottoms of the pans with waxed paper; grease and lightly flour pans. Set pans aside.

2 Preheat oven to 350°F. In a large bowl stir together the flour, sugar, baking powder, salt, and cloves. Stir in the egg, bananas, oil, and vanilla just until combined. Fold in sweet potatoes and pineapple. Spread batter evenly in prepared pans.

3 Bake about 30 minutes or until a wooden toothpick inserted near the centers comes out clean. Cool layers in pans on wire racks for 10 minutes. Remove layers from pans; peel off waxed paper. Cool thoroughly on wire racks.

4 Prepare Caramel Butter Frosting. Place one cake layer, bottom side up, on serving plate. Spread with about ½ cup of the frosting. Top with second cake layer, bottom side down. Spread with ½ cup more frosting. Top with remaining layer, bottom side up; spread top and sides of cake with remaining frosting.

CARAMEL BUTTER FROSTING: In a large saucepan melt 1 cup butter; stir in 2 cups packed brown sugar. Bring to boiling over medium heat; stirring constantly. Cook and stir for 1 minute; remove from heat and cool for 5 minutes. Whisk in ½ cup milk until smooth. Whisk in 6 cups powdered sugar until smooth. Use immediately; frosting stiffens as it cools.

PER SERVING: 742 cal., 27 g total fat (9 g sat. fat, 0 g trans fat), 71 mg chol., 308 mg sodium, 125 g carbo., 2 g fiber, 4 g pro. EXCHANGES: 1 Starch, 7½ Other Carbo., 5 Fat

MAKE-IT-MINE SNACK CAKE

WHETHER YOU NEED SOMETHING TO TOTE TO POTLUCKS OR TO REWARD HUNGRY KIDS AFTER A WELL-PLAYED BALLGAME, HERE'S ONE SATISFYING CAKE RECIPE YOU CAN CUSTOMIZE IN COUNTLESS WAYS.

BASIC INGREDIENTS

PREP: 15 MINUTES
BAKE: 35 MINUTES **OVEN:** 350°F
MAKES: 12 SERVINGS

Flour
Sweetener
1 teaspoon baking soda
½ teaspoon baking powder
½ teaspoon salt
Liquid
⅔ cup vegetable oil
Flavoring
2 eggs
Sprinkle
Topper

FLOUR (PICK ONE)

3 cups all-purpose flour
3 cups cake flour
2 cups all-purpose flour plus 1 cup whole wheat flour
2 cups all-purpose flour plus 1 cup unsweetened cocoa powder

SWEETENER (PICK ONE)

2 cups granulated sugar
1 cup granulated sugar plus 1 cup packed brown sugar
1½ cups granulated sugar plus ½ cup honey
1½ cups granulated sugar plus ½ cup molasses

LIQUID (PICK ONE)

1½ cups milk
1 cup buttermilk plus ½ cup water
1 6-ounce carton plain yogurt plus ½ cup water
1 cup milk plus ½ cup orange juice

FLAVORING (PICK ONE)

2 teaspoons instant espresso powder or coffee crystals
1 teaspoon finely shredded citrus peel
1 teaspoon vanilla
½ teaspoon almond extract
½ teaspoon peppermint extract

SPRINKLE (PICK ONE)

½ cup semisweet, milk, or dark chocolate pieces; miniature semisweet chocolate pieces; or peanut butter pieces
½ cup flaked coconut
½ cup dried fruit (tart red cherries, raisins, apricots, or cranberries)
½ cup chopped toasted nuts (pecans, walnuts, hazelnuts, almonds, or macadamia nuts) (see tip, page 20)

TOPPER (PICK ONE)

Sift 2 teaspoons powdered sugar over top.
Sift 1 teaspoon cocoa powder mixed with 1 teaspoon powdered sugar over top.
Drizzle 2 ounces melted semisweet, milk, or dark chocolate over top.
Drizzle ½ cup powdered sugar mixed with 1 to 2 teaspoons milk over top.
Drizzle ½ cup powdered sugar mixed with 1 to 2 teaspoons citrus juice (orange, tangerine, lemon, or lime) over top.

BASIC INSTRUCTIONS

1 Preheat oven to 350°F. Grease a 13×9×2-inch baking pan; set aside. In a very large bowl stir together desired Flour, dry Sweetener, baking soda, baking powder, and salt. Add the Liquid, vegetable oil, liquid Sweetener (if using), and Flavoring. Beat with an electric mixer on low to medium speed until combined. Beat in eggs. Scrape sides of bowl; continue beating on medium speed for 2 minutes more. Spread batter in prepared pan.

2 Bake for 20 minutes. Top evenly with Sprinkle. Bake about 15 minutes more or until a wooden toothpick inserted near center comes out clean. Cool in pan on a wire rack. Add Topper.

SOUR CREAM POUND CAKE

PREP: 55 MINUTES **BAKE:** 60 MINUTES
COOL: 60 MINUTES **OVEN:** 325°F
MAKES: 10 SERVINGS

½ cup butter
3 eggs
½ cup dairy sour cream
1½ cups all-purpose flour
¼ teaspoon baking powder
⅛ teaspoon baking soda
1 cup sugar
½ teaspoon vanilla

1 Allow butter, eggs, and sour cream to stand at room temperature for 30 minutes. Meanwhile, grease and lightly flour a 9×5×3-inch loaf pan; set pan aside. In a medium bowl stir together flour, baking powder, and baking soda; set aside.

2 Preheat the oven to 325°F. In a large mixing bowl beat butter with an electric mixer on medium to high speed for 30 seconds. Gradually add sugar, beating about 10 minutes or until light and fluffy. Beat in vanilla. Add eggs, one at a time, beating 1 minute after each addition and scraping bowl frequently. Alternately add flour mixture and sour cream to butter mixture, beating on low to medium speed after each addition just until combined. Pour batter into prepared pan.

3 Bake for 60 to 75 minutes or until a wooden toothpick inserted near center comes out clean. Cool cake in pan on a wire rack for 10 minutes. Remove from pan; cool thoroughly on rack.

PER SERVING: 268 cal., 13 g total fat (7 g sat. fat, 0 g trans fat), 93 mg chol., 116 mg sodium, 35 g carbo., 1 g fiber, 4 g pro. **EXCHANGES:** 1 Starch, 1½ Other Carbo., 2½ Fat

BLUEBERRY POUND CAKE: Prepare as directed, except pour boiling water over ½ cup dried blueberries and let stand for 10 minutes; drain well. Fold berries into the batter.

PER SERVING: 296 cal., 13 g total fat (7 g sat. fat, 0 g trans fat), 93 mg chol., 116 mg sodium, 41 g carbo., 1 g fiber, 4 g pro. **EXCHANGES:** 1 Starch, 2 Other Carbo., 2½ Fat

BEST EVER

POPPY SEED CAKE *(photo, page 157)*

PREP: 15 MINUTES **BAKE:** 65 MINUTES
COOL: 60 MINUTES **OVEN:** 325°F
MAKES: 16 SERVINGS

3 cups all-purpose flour
2¼ cups sugar
1½ teaspoons baking powder
1½ teaspoons salt
3 eggs, lightly beaten
1½ cups milk
½ cup vegetable oil
½ cup butter, melted and cooled
4 teaspoons poppy seeds
1½ teaspoons vanilla
1½ teaspoons almond extract
1½ teaspoons butter flavoring
1 recipe Orange Glaze

1 Preheat oven to 325°F. Generously grease and flour a 10-inch fluted tube pan; set pan aside. In a large mixing bowl stir together flour, sugar, baking powder, and salt; set aside.

2 In a medium bowl combine eggs, milk, oil, butter, poppy seeds, vanilla, almond extract, and butter flavoring. Add egg mixture all at once to flour mixture. Beat with an electric mixer on medium to high speed for 2 minutes. Pour batter into prepared pan; spread evenly.

3 Bake about 65 minutes or until a wooden toothpick inserted near the center comes out clean. Cool in pan on a wire rack for 10 minutes. Remove cake from pan. Generously brush Orange Glaze over top and sides of warm cake. Cool thoroughly on wire rack.

ORANGE GLAZE: In a small saucepan combine ¾ cup sugar and ¼ cup orange juice. Heat and stir just until sugar dissolves. Remove from heat. Stir in ½ teaspoon vanilla and ½ teaspoon almond extract.

PER SERVING: 377 cal., 14 g total fat (5 g sat. fat, 0 g trans fat), 57 mg chol., 316 mg sodium, 58 g carbo., 1 g fiber, 5 g pro. **EXCHANGES:** 1½ Starch, 2½ Other Carbo., 2½ Fat

MAKE IT A CUPCAKE
TURN A RECIPE FOR ONE BIG CAKE INTO LOTS OF CUTE LITTLE CUPCAKES.

■ Choose a recipe for a butter-style cake (cake with a batter that starts with beating butter and sugar together). A two-layer cake usually makes 24 to 30 cupcakes.

■ Grease and flour muffin cups or line them with paper bake cups. Fill cups half to two-thirds full with batter.

■ Bake at the same temperature called for in the cake recipe, but reduce the baking time by one-third to one-half. Cool and frost with desired frosting.

PUMPKIN-CRANBERRY CAKE

PREP: 20 MINUTES **BAKE:** 60 MINUTES
COOL: 60 MINUTES **OVEN:** 350°F
MAKES: 12 TO 16 SERVINGS

- 2½ cups all-purpose flour
- 2 teaspoons baking soda
- 2 teaspoons ground cinnamon
- ½ teaspoon ground cloves
- ½ teaspoon ground nutmeg
- ¼ teaspoon salt
- 1 cup granulated sugar
- 1 cup packed brown sugar
- ¾ cup shortening
- 2 eggs
- 1 15-ounce can pumpkin
- 1 cup dried cranberries
- 1 cup chopped pistachio nuts or pecans
  Powdered sugar

1 Preheat oven to 350°F. Grease and flour a 10-inch fluted tube pan; set aside. In a medium bowl combine flour, baking soda, cinnamon, cloves, nutmeg, and salt; set aside.

2 In a very large mixing bowl beat granulated sugar, brown sugar, shortening, and eggs with an electric mixer on medium speed for 2 minutes, scraping sides of bowl occasionally. Alternately add flour mixture and pumpkin, beating on low speed after each addition just until combined. Fold in cranberries and pistachios. Pour batter into prepared pan; spread evenly.

3 Bake about 60 minutes or until a wooden toothpick inserted near the center comes out clean. If necessary, cover cake with foil during the last 10 minutes of baking to prevent overbrowning. Cool cake in pan on a wire rack for 10 minutes. Remove cake from pan; cool thoroughly on wire rack. Sprinkle with powdered sugar just before serving.

PER SERVING: 458 cal., 18 g total fat (4 g sat. fat, 2 g trans fat), 35 mg chol., 278 mg sodium, 70 g carbo., 4 g fiber, 6 g pro. EXCHANGES: 2 Starch, 2½ Other Carbo., 3 Fat

RHUBARB CAKE

PREP: 25 MINUTES **BAKE:** 40 MINUTES
COOL: 30 MINUTES **OVEN:** 350°F
MAKES: 15 SERVINGS

- ½ cup butter, softened
- 1½ cups packed brown sugar
- ¼ teaspoon salt
- 2 eggs

- 1 teaspoon vanilla
- 1 cup buttermilk or sour milk (see tip, page 19)
- 1 teaspoon baking soda
- 2 cups all-purpose flour
- 1½ cups sliced fresh rhubarb or chopped frozen unsweetened rhubarb
- ½ cup chopped pecans, toasted (see tip, page 20)
- ½ cup granulated sugar
- 1 teaspoon ground cinnamon
- 2 tablespoons butter

1 Preheat oven to 350°F. Grease and flour a 13×9×2-inch baking pan; set aside. In a large mixing bowl beat the ½ cup butter with an electric mixer on medium to high speed for 30 seconds. Add brown sugar and salt; beat until light and fluffy, scraping sides of bowl occasionally. Beat in eggs and vanilla until combined. In a small bowl combine buttermilk and baking soda. Alternately add flour and buttermilk mixture to butter mixture, beating on low speed after each addition just until combined. Fold in rhubarb and pecans. Spread batter into prepared pan.

2 In a small bowl combine granulated sugar and cinnamon. Using a fork, cut in the 2 tablespoons butter until mixture resembles coarse crumbs. Sprinkle sugar mixture evenly over batter.

3 Bake 40 to 45 minutes or until a wooden toothpick inserted in center comes out clean. Cool in pan on wire rack at least 30 minutes before serving.

PER SERVING: 283 cal., 11 g total fat (5 g sat. fat, 0 g trans fat), 49 mg chol., 211 mg sodium, 43 g carbo., 1 g fiber, 4 g pro. EXCHANGES: 1 Starch, 2 Other Carbo., 2 Fat

CARAMEL-NUT BROWNIE TORTE

PREP: 50 MINUTES **BAKE:** 45 MINUTES
STAND: 60 MINUTES **OVEN:** 350°F
MAKES: 16 SERVINGS

- 2 21- to 22.5-ounce packages brownie mix
- ½ cup butter
- 1 cup whipping cream
- ¾ cup packed light brown sugar
- 3 tablespoons light-color corn syrup
- 1 teaspoon vanilla
- 4 ounces semisweet chocolate, chopped
- ½ cup chopped pecans
- 1 cup pecan halves

1 Preheat oven to 350°F. Grease bottoms of two 9×1½-inch round cake pans. Line pans with waxed paper; grease and flour pans. Set pans aside.

2 Prepare each brownie mix according to package directions for fudgy brownies. Spread batter evenly into prepared pans. Bake about 45 minutes or until a wooden toothpick inserted near the centers comes out clean. Cool thoroughly in pans on a wire rack. Loosen edges and carefully remove layers from pans.

3 Meanwhile, for caramel, in a medium heavy saucepan combine butter, ½ cup of the whipping cream, the brown sugar, and corn syrup. Bring to boiling over medium-high heat, whisking occasionally. Reduce heat to medium. Boil gently for 3 minutes more. Stir in the vanilla. Transfer caramel to a bowl; cool thoroughly.

4 Meanwhile, in a small saucepan bring remaining ½ cup whipping cream just to boiling over medium-high heat. Remove from heat. Add chocolate (do not stir). Let stand 5 minutes. Stir until smooth. Cool about 15 minutes or until spreading consistency.

5 Place one cake layer, top side up, on a plate. Top with chocolate mixture, spreading evenly. Spoon ½ cup of the caramel over chocolate, spreading evenly. Sprinkle with chopped pecans. Add the second cake layer, top side up. Spoon the remaining caramel over top. Sprinkle with pecan halves. Let stand for 1 hour before serving. Using a long serrated knife, cut torte into wedges.

PER SERVING: 678 cal., 38 g total fat (13 g sat. fat, 0 g trans fat), 86 mg chol., 314 mg sodium, 78 g carbo., 1 g fiber, 7 g pro. EXCHANGES: 2 Starch, 3 Other Carbo., 7 Fat

LOVE CHOCOLATE?

IF YOU WISH, HEIGHTEN THIS CAKE'S CHOC-O-LISCIOUS INTENSITY BY USING CHOCO-LATE LABELED WITH 70% OR HIGHER CACAO CONTENT.

SWEET SIMPLICITY BOXED BROWNIE MIX NEVER TASTED SO GOOD! ANOTHER TIME TRY THE GOOEY, GANACHE-STYLE CHOCOLATE SAUCE OVER A PURCHASED POUND CAKE FOR AN EASY DESSERT.

CARAMEL-NUT BROWNIE TORTE

LEMONADE CAKE

PREP: 45 MINUTES **BAKE:** 30 MINUTES
COOL: 60 MINUTES **OVEN:** 350°F
MAKES: 15 SERVINGS

- ⅓ cup butter
- 3 eggs
- 2¼ cups all-purpose flour
- 1 teaspoon baking powder
- ½ teaspoon baking soda
- ½ teaspoon salt
- 1⅓ cups sugar
- ¼ cup frozen lemonade concentrate, thawed
- 1 teaspoon vanilla
- 1¼ cups buttermilk or sour milk (see tip, page 19)
  Yellow food coloring (optional)
- 1 recipe Lemon Butter Frosting
  Lemon peel strips (optional)

1 Allow butter and eggs to stand at room temperature for 30 minutes. Meanwhile, grease a 13×9×2-inch baking pan; set aside. In a medium bowl stir together flour, baking powder, baking soda, and salt; set aside.

2 Preheat oven to 350°F. In a large mixing bowl beat butter with an electric mixer on medium to high speed for 30 seconds. Gradually add sugar, about ¼ cup at a time, beating on medium speed until well combined. Scrape sides of bowl; beat for 2 minutes more. Add eggs, one at a time, beating well after each addition. Beat in lemonade concentrate and vanilla. Alternately add flour mixture and buttermilk, beating on low speed after each addition just until combined. If desired, stir in a few drops of yellow food coloring. Spread batter into prepared pan.

3 Bake for 30 to 35 minutes or until top springs back when lightly touched. Cool thoroughly in pan on a wire rack. Spread cake with Lemon Butter Frosting. If desired, garnish with strips of lemon peel.

LEMON BUTTER FROSTING: In a large mixing bowl beat ⅓ cup softened butter with an electric mixer on medium speed until smooth. Gradually add 1 cup powdered sugar, beating well. Beat in ⅓ cup frozen lemonade concentrate, thawed, and ½ teaspoon vanilla. Gradually beat in 3 cups additional powdered sugar. Beat in additional frozen lemonade concentrate, thawed (1 to 2 teaspoons), to reach spreading consistency.

PER SERVING: 380 cal., 10 g total fat (6 g sat. fat, 0 g trans fat), 65 mg chol., 238 mg sodium, 71 g carbo., 1 g fiber, 4 g pro. EXCHANGES: 1 Starch, 4 Other Carbo., 2 Fat

BUTTERSCOTCH MARBLE CAKE

PREP: 20 MINUTES **BAKE:** 55 MINUTES
COOL: 60 MINUTES **OVEN:** 350°F
MAKES: 12 SERVINGS

- 1 package 2-layer-size white cake mix
- 1 4-serving-size package butterscotch instant pudding and pie filling mix
- 4 eggs
- ¼ cup vegetable oil
- ½ cup chocolate-flavored syrup
- 2 ounces sweet baking chocolate, chopped
- 2 tablespoons butter
- ¾ cup powdered sugar
- 1 tablespoon hot water

1 Preheat oven to 350°F. Grease and flour a 10-inch fluted tube pan; set aside.

2 In a large mixing bowl combine cake mix, pudding mix, 1 cup *water*, the eggs, and oil. Beat with an electric mixer on low speed just until combined. Beat on medium speed for 2 minutes, scraping the sides of bowl occasionally.

3 Transfer 1½ cups of the batter to a medium bowl; stir in chocolate syrup. Pour light-color batter into prepared pan. Top with the chocolate batter. Using a table knife or thin metal spatula, gently cut through batters to swirl them together.

4 Bake for 55 to 60 minutes or until a wooden toothpick inserted near the center comes out clean. Cool in pan on a wire rack for 15 minutes. Remove cake from pan; cool.

5 For icing, in a small saucepan combine chocolate and the butter. Heat and stir over low heat until melted. Remove from heat. Stir in powdered sugar and the 1 tablespoon hot water. If necessary, stir in additional hot water, 1 teaspoon at a time, until icing reaches drizzling consistency. Drizzle icing over cake.

PER SERVING: 377 cal., 14 g total fat (4 g sat. fat, 0 g trans fat), 76 mg chol., 467 mg sodium, 60 g carbo., 1 g fiber, 5 g pro. EXCHANGES: 1½ Starch, 2½ Other Carbo., 2½ Fat

MISSISSIPPI MUD CAKE

PREP: 15 MINUTES **BAKE:** 30 MINUTES
STAND: 15 MINUTES **OVEN:** 350°F
MAKES: 12 TO 16 SERVINGS

- 1 package 2-layer-size chocolate cake mix
- 1¼ cups water
- ⅓ cup vegetable oil
- ⅓ cup creamy peanut butter
- 3 eggs

1 cup semisweet chocolate pieces

1 cup tiny marshmallows

1 16-ounce can chocolate fudge frosting

1 cup chopped peanuts

1 Preheat the oven to 350°F. Grease and lightly flour a 13×9×2-inch baking pan; set aside.

2 In a large mixing bowl combine cake mix, water, oil, peanut butter, and the eggs. Beat with an electric mixer on low speed just until combined. Beat on medium speed for 2 minutes. Fold in chocolate pieces. Spread batter into prepared pan.

3 Bake for 30 to 35 minutes or until a wooden toothpick inserted near center comes out clean. Sprinkle marshmallows over hot cake; let stand 15 minutes. Drop spoonfuls of frosting over cake and spread. Sprinkle with nuts.

PER SERVING: 592 cal., 31 g total fat (8 g sat. fat, 0 g trans fat), 53 mg chol., 484 mg sodium, 73 g carbo., 4 g fiber, 9 g pro. EXCHANGES: 3 Starch, 2 Other Carbo., 5½ Fat

LAYERED ICE CREAM CAKE

PREP: 30 MINUTES **BAKE:** 15 MINUTES
COOL: 60 MINUTES **FREEZE:** 4 TO 6 HOURS
STAND: 10 MINUTES **OVEN:** 350°F
MAKES: 16 SERVINGS

1 package 2-layer-size chocolate or white cake mix

½ gallon desired-flavor ice cream, softened

1 8-ounce package cream cheese, softened

½ cup powdered sugar

¼ cup milk

1 teaspoon vanilla

1 16-ounce container frozen whipped dessert topping, thawed

1 Preheat oven to 350°F. Grease and flour three 9×1½-inch round cake pans; set aside.* Prepare cake mix according to package directions. Spread batter evenly into prepared pans. Bake for 15 to 18 minutes or until tops spring back when lightly touched. Cool in pans on wire racks for 10 minutes. Remove layers from pans; cool on wire racks.

2 To assemble, place one cake layer on the bottom of a 9-inch springform pan (if necessary, trim to fit); add sides of pan (see photo 1, below). Spoon half of the ice cream onto cake layer in pan; spread evenly. Top with another cake layer. Spread remaining ice cream over cake layer in pan. Top with remaining cake layer (see photo 2, below). Cover with plastic wrap; freeze for 3 to 4 hours or until firm.

3 For frosting, in a large mixing bowl beat cream cheese, powdered sugar, milk, and vanilla with an electric mixer on medium to high speed until light and fluffy. Stir in a small amount of whipped topping to lighten. Fold in remaining whipped topping.

4 Remove plastic wrap from cake. Remove sides of pan. Using a wide spatula, transfer cake from pan bottom to serving plate. Spread top and sides of cake with frosting. Freeze, uncovered, for 1 to 2 hours or until firm. Cover with plastic wrap and freeze for up to 1 month. To serve, let stand at room temperature 10 to 15 minutes. Cut into wedges.

*NOTE: If you have only two round pans, chill one-third of the batter while two layers bake. After baking, wipe out one pan, repeat Step 1, spread chilled batter in pan, and bake as directed.

PER SERVING: 481 cal., 26 g total fat (14 g sat. fat, 0 g trans fat), 88 mg chol., 321 mg sodium, 55 g carbo., 1 g fiber, 6 g pro. EXCHANGES: 2 Starch, 1½ Other Carbo., 5 Fat

LAYERING THE ICE CREAM CAKE, STEP-BY-STEP

1. Place first cake layer on the bottom of the springform pan before adding the pan sides (this prevents cake from tearing). If necessary, trim to fit. Secure sides of pan.
2. Evenly spread half of the ice cream onto first cake layer. Top with another cake layer and remaining ice cream. Smooth surface of the ice cream before gently easing and pressing final cake layer into place.

CREAM-FILLED CAKE ROLL

PREP: 60 MINUTES **BAKE:** 12 MINUTES
COOL: 60 MINUTES **CHILL:** UP TO 6 HOURS
OVEN: 375°F **MAKES:** 10 SERVINGS

  4 eggs
  ½ cup all-purpose flour
  1 teaspoon baking powder
  ½ teaspoon vanilla
  ⅓ cup granulated sugar
  ½ cup granulated sugar
     Powdered sugar
  1 recipe desired filling

1 Separate eggs. Allow egg whites and yolks to stand at room temperature for 30 minutes. Meanwhile, grease a 15×10×1-inch baking pan. Line bottom of pan with waxed paper or parchment paper; grease paper. Set aside. In a medium bowl stir together flour and baking powder; set aside.

2 Preheat oven to 375°F. In a medium mixing bowl beat egg yolks and vanilla with an electric mixer on high speed about 5 minutes or until thick and lemon color. Gradually beat in the ⅓ cup granulated sugar, beating on high speed until sugar is almost dissolved.

3 Thoroughly wash beaters. In another bowl beat egg whites on medium speed until soft peaks form (tips curl; see photo 1, page 177). Gradually beat in the ½ cup granulated sugar, beating until stiff peaks form (tips stand straight). Fold egg yolk mixture into beaten egg whites. Sprinkle flour mixture over egg mixture; fold in gently just until combined. Spread batter evenly in prepared pan.

4 Bake for 12 to 15 minutes or until cake springs back when lightly touched. Immediately loosen edges of cake from pan and turn cake out onto a towel sprinkled with powdered sugar (see photo 1, page 175). Remove waxed paper. Roll towel and cake into a spiral, starting from a short side of the cake (see photo 2, page 175). Cool on a wire rack. Meanwhile, prepare desired filling.

5 Unroll cake; remove towel. Spread cake with desired filling to within 1 inch of edges (see photo 3, page 175). Roll up cake; trim ends. Cover; chill for up to 6 hours.

LEMON-CREAM FILLING: In a medium mixing bowl beat one 3-ounce package cream cheese, softened, with an electric mixer on medium speed until smooth. Beat in ¼ cup purchased lemon curd until combined. In another mixing bowl beat ½ cup whipping cream with the electric mixer on high speed until soft peaks form (tips curl); fold into cream cheese mixture. If desired, for icing, in a small bowl stir together ¾ cup powdered sugar, ½ teaspoon finely shredded lemon peel, and 1 tablespoon lemon juice; drizzle over filled cake.

PER SERVING: 219 cal., 10 g total fat (5 g sat. fat, 0 g trans fat), 116 mg chol., 90 mg sodium, 30 g carbo., 1 g fiber, 4 g pro.
EXCHANGES: 1 Starch, 1 Other Carbo., 2 Fat

STRAWBERRY-CREAM FILLING: In a medium mixing bowl beat ¾ cup whipping cream, 1 tablespoon sugar, and ½ teaspoon vanilla with an electric mixer on medium speed until soft peaks form (tips curl). Fold in 1 cup chopped strawberries or 1 cup fresh raspberries. Sprinkle filled cake with powdered sugar.

PER SERVING: 201 cal., 9 g total fat (5 g sat. fat, 0 g trans fat), 109 mg chol., 59 mg sodium, 28 g carbo., 0 g fiber, 4 g pro.
EXCHANGES: 1 Starch, 1 Other Carbo., 1½ Fat

SERVING AND STORING CAKE

TO ENJOY CAKES AT THEIR YUMMIEST BEST, FOLLOW THESE TIPS.

■ Allow cakes frosted with butter-type frosting to stand about an hour before slicing to let the frosting set.

■ Assemble cakes filled or frosted with whipped cream no more than 2 hours before serving to prevent them from becoming soggy.

■ Use a thin-bladed knife to cut cake. Run the knife under hot water and wipe dry before the first cut and between subsequent cuts.

■ Most cakes can be covered and stored at room temperature for 2 to 3 days. If you don't have a cake cover, invert a large bowl over the cake. Directly covering a cake with plastic wrap will mar the frosting.

■ If a cake filling or frosting contains whipped cream, cream cheese, or eggs, store the cake, covered, in the refrigerator.

■ To freeze cake, place the cooled, unfrosted layers on a baking sheet and freeze until firm. Transfer frozen layers to large freezer bags or wrap and seal in freezer wrap. Freeze for up to 4 months. Thaw before frosting.

■ Cakes that are served directly from pans can be covered and frozen in the pans. Frost these cakes after thawing.

CREAM-FILLED CAKE ROLL

MAKING A CAKE ROLL, STEP-BY-STEP

1. Dust a clean, lint-free towel with powdered sugar. Turn out cake onto prepared towel. Immediately peel waxed paper from the warm cake. **2.** Starting from a short side, roll towel and cake into a spiral. Let cake cool. **3.** Unroll cake, remove towel, and spread filling over cake, leaving a 1-inch border around the edges. The border will fill as you reroll the cake.

CHOCOLATE-ESPRESSO CHIFFON CAKE

PREP: 65 MINUTES **BAKE:** 60 MINUTES
COOL: 2 HOURS **OVEN:** 325°F
MAKES: 14 SERVINGS

- 8 eggs
- 2 cups all-purpose flour
- 1½ cups sugar
- 1 tablespoon baking powder
- 1 teaspoon salt
- 4 teaspoons instant espresso coffee powder or instant coffee crystals
- ¾ cup water
- ½ cup vegetable oil
- 1 teaspoon vanilla
- 3 ounces bittersweet chocolate, grated
- ½ teaspoon cream of tartar
- 1 recipe Espresso Whipped Cream

1 Separate eggs, discarding three of the yolks or saving them for another use. Allow egg yolks and egg whites to stand at room temperature for 30 minutes. Meanwhile, in large mixing bowl stir together flour, sugar, baking powder, and salt. Make a well in the center of the flour mixture. Dissolve espresso in the water; set aside.

2 Preheat oven to 325°F. Add the five egg yolks, dissolved espresso, oil, and vanilla to flour mixture. Beat with an electric mixer on low speed until combined. Beat on medium to high speed for 4 to 5 minutes or until smooth. Fold in grated chocolate.

3 Thoroughly wash beaters. In a very large mixing bowl beat egg whites and cream of tartar on medium speed until stiff peaks form (tips stand straight; see photo 2, page 177). Pour batter in thin stream over beaten egg whites; fold in gently. Pour into an ungreased 10-inch tube pan.

4 Bake for 60 to 70 minutes or until top springs back when lightly touched. Immediately invert cake; cool thoroughly in pan (see photo 5, page 177). Loosen sides of cake from pan; remove cake. Serve with Espresso Whipped Cream.

ESPRESSO WHIPPED CREAM: In a chilled mixing bowl combine 1 cup whipping cream, 1 tablespoons sugar, ½ to 1 teaspoon instant espresso coffee powder or instant coffee crystals, and ½ teaspoon vanilla. Beat with an electric mixer on medium speed until soft peaks form.

PER SERVING: 342 cal., 18 g total fat (7 g sat. fat, 0 g trans fat), 99 mg chol., 286 mg sodium, 41 g carbo., 1 g fiber, 6 g pro.
EXCHANGES: 2 Starch, ½ Other Carbo., 3 Fat

ANGEL FOOD ICE CREAM CAKE

PREP: 45 MINUTES **BAKE:** PER PACKAGE DIRECTIONS
COOL: PER PACKAGE DIRECTIONS
FREEZE: 6½ TO 24½ HOURS **OVEN:** 350°F
MAKES: 10 TO 12 SERVINGS

- 1 16-ounce package angel food cake mix
- 1¼ cups water
- 4 cups (2 pints) strawberry ice cream, softened
- 2 cups whipping cream
- ¼ cup sugar
- 1 teaspoon vanilla
- 1 cup small, whole strawberries

1 Prepare cake mix according to package directions using the 1¼ cups water. Pour batter into an ungreased 10-inch tube pan. Gently cut through batter to remove any large air pockets (see photo 4, page 177).

2 Bake angel food cake according to the package directions. Immediately invert cake; cool thoroughly in pan (see photo 5, page 177). Loosen sides of cake from pan; remove cake.

3 Using a serrated knife, carefully split the cake horizontally into thirds. Place the bottom layer and middle layer on freezer-safe platters; spread each layer with 2 cups softened ice cream. Freeze layers for 30 to 60 minutes or until ice cream is firm. Place the middle layer, ice cream side up, on top of the bottom layer. Top with the remaining cake layer. Cover with plastic wrap and freeze for 6 to 24 hours.

4 To serve, in chilled mixing bowl beat whipping cream, sugar, and vanilla with chilled beaters on medium speed of an electric mixer until soft peaks form.

5 Remove cake from freezer. Spread top and sides of frozen cake with whipped cream. Garnish with fresh strawberries. Serve immediately.

PER SERVING: 446 cal., 22 g total fat (14 g sat. fat, 0 g trans fat), 81 mg chol., 356 mg sodium, 57 g carbo., 1 g fiber, 6 g pro.
EXCHANGES: 1 Milk, 3 Other Carbo., 4 Fat

ORANGE ANGEL FOOD SHERBET CAKE:

Prepare as directed, except reduce water to 1 cup and add ¼ cup thawed orange juice concentrate with water. Add 2 teaspoons finely shredded orange peel to cake mix. Substitute orange, lime, or lemon sherbet for the strawberry ice cream. Garnish with orange, lemon, or lime peel strips instead of strawberries.

PER SERVING: 438 cal., 19 g total fat (12 g sat. fat, 0 g trans fat), 12 mg chol., 352 mg sodium, 63 g carbo., 5 g pro.
EXCHANGES: 1 Milk, 3½ Other Carbo., 3½ Fat

ANGEL FOOD CAKE

PREP: 50 MINUTES **BAKE:** 40 MINUTES
COOL: 2 HOURS **OVEN:** 350°F
MAKES: 12 SERVINGS

- 1½ cups egg whites (10 to 12 large)
- 1½ cups powdered sugar
- 1 cup sifted cake flour or all-purpose flour
- 1½ teaspoons cream of tartar
- 1 teaspoon vanilla
- 1 cup granulated sugar

1 In a very large mixing bowl allow egg whites to stand at room temperature for 30 minutes. Meanwhile, sift powdered sugar and flour together three times; set aside.

2 Adjust baking rack to the lowest position in oven. Preheat oven to 350°F. Add cream of tartar and vanilla to egg whites. Beat with an electric mixer on medium speed until soft peaks form (tips curl; see photo 1, below). Add granulated sugar, 2 tablespoons at a time, beating until stiff peaks form (tips stand straight; see photo 2, below).

3 Sift one-fourth of the flour mixture over the egg whites; fold in gently (see photo 3, below). Repeat, folding in remaining flour mixture by fourths. Pour into an ungreased 10-inch tube pan. Gently cut through batter to remove any large air pockets (see photo 4, below).

4 Bake on the lowest rack for 40 to 45 minutes or until top springs back when lightly touched. Immediately invert cake; cool thoroughly in pan (see photo 5, below). Loosen sides of cake from pan; remove cake from pan.

CHOCOLATE ANGEL FOOD CAKE: Prepare as directed, except sift ¼ cup unsweetened cocoa powder with the flour mixture.

PER SERVING PLAIN OR CHOCOLATE VARIATION:
172 cal., 0 g total fat, 0 mg chol., 51 mg sodium, 39 g carbo.,
0 g fiber, 4 g pro.
EXCHANGES: 2½ Other Carbo., ½ Lean Meat

ANGEL FOOD CAKE, STEP-BY-STEP

1. For soft peaks, tips of egg whites curl when beaters are lifted. **2.** For stiff peaks, tips of whites stand straight up. **3.** To fold in flour, cut down through whites with rubber spatula; scrape across bottom of bowl, bringing spatula up and over. **4.** To eliminate large bubbles, gently cut through batter in pan with a thin metal spatula. **5.** Cooling cake upside down sets its structure.

POWDERED SUGAR ICING

START TO FINISH: 10 MINUTES **MAKES:** ½ CUP

- 1 cup powdered sugar
- ¼ teaspoon vanilla
- 1 tablespoon milk or orange juice
  Milk

1 In a small bowl combine powdered sugar, vanilla, and 1 tablespoon milk. Stir in additional milk, 1 teaspoon at a time, until icing reaches drizzling consistency. (This makes enough to drizzle over one 10-inch tube cake.)

CHOCOLATE POWDERED SUGAR ICING:
Prepare as directed, except add 2 tablespoons unsweetened cocoa powder to the powdered sugar and use milk, not orange juice.

PER ½ OF RECIPE PLAIN OR CHOCOLATE VARIATION:
40 cal., 0 g total fat, 0 mg chol., 1 mg sodium, 10 g carbo.,
0 g fiber, 0 g pro.
EXCHANGES: ½ Other Carbo.

MERINGUE FROSTING

START TO FINISH: 25 MINUTES
MAKES: ABOUT 5 CUPS

- 1½ cups sugar
- ⅓ cup cold water
- 2 egg whites
- ¼ teaspoon cream of tartar
- 1 teaspoon vanilla

1 In a 3-quart top of a double boiler combine sugar, water, egg whites, and cream of tartar. Beat with an electric mixer on low speed for 30 seconds.

2 Place the pan over boiling water (upper pan should not touch the water). Cook, beating constantly with the electric mixer on high speed, for 10 to 13 minutes or until an instant-read thermometer registers 160°F when inserted in the mixture, stopping beaters and quickly scraping bottom and sides of pan every 5 minutes to prevent sticking. Remove pan from heat; add vanilla. Beat about 1 minute more or until frosting is fluffy and holds soft peaks. (This frosts tops and sides of two 8- or 9-inch cake layers or one 10-inch tube cake.) Store frosted cake in the refrigerator and serve the same day it is made.

PER ½ OF RECIPE: 101 cal., 0 g total fat, 0 mg chol., 9 mg
sodium, 25 g carbo., 0 g fiber, 1 g pro.
EXCHANGES: 1½ Other Carbo.

BUTTER FROSTING

START TO FINISH: 20 MINUTES
MAKES: ABOUT 4½ CUPS

- ¾ cup butter, softened
- 2 pounds powdered sugar (about 8 cups)
- ⅓ cup milk
- 2 teaspoons vanilla
  Milk
  Food coloring (optional)

1 In a very large mixing bowl beat butter with an electric mixer on medium speed until smooth. Gradually add 2 cups of the powdered sugar, beating well. Slowly beat in ⅓ cup milk and vanilla. Gradually beat in remaining sugar. Beat in enough additional milk to reach spreading consistency. If desired, tint with food coloring. (This frosts the tops and sides of two 8- or 9-inch layers. Halve the recipe to frost a 13×9×2-inch cake.)

PER ½ OF RECIPE: 401 cal., 12 g total fat (7 g sat. fat, 0 g trans
fat), 31 mg chol., 85 mg sodium, 76 g carbo., 0 g fiber, 0 g pro.
EXCHANGES: 5 Other Carbo., 2½ Fat

CREAMY WHITE FROSTING

START TO FINISH: 25 MINUTES
MAKES: ABOUT 3 CUPS

- 1 cup shortening
- 1½ teaspoons vanilla
- ½ teaspoon almond extract
- 1 pound powdered sugar (about 4 cups)
- 3 to 4 tablespoons milk

1 In a large mixing bowl beat shortening, vanilla, and almond extract with an electric mixer on medium speed for 30 seconds. Slowly add about half of the powdered sugar, beating well. Add 2 tablespoons of the milk. Gradually beat in remaining powdered sugar and enough remaining milk to reach spreading consistency. (This frosts the tops and sides of two 8- or 9-inch cake layers. Halve the recipe to frost a 13×9×2-inch cake.) You can freeze this frosting in a freezer container for up to 3 months; thaw at room temperature before using.

PER ½ OF RECIPE: 298 cal., 16 g total fat (4 g sat. fat, 2 g trans
fat), 0 mg chol., 2 mg sodium, 38 g carbo., 0 g fiber, 0 g pro.
EXCHANGES: 2½ Other Carbo., 3 Fat

10 TO TRY— BUTTER FROSTING

Start with Butter Frosting, page 178.

1. ALMOND: Substitute ½ teaspoon almond extract for the vanilla.

2. MILK CHOCOLATE: Melt 1 cup milk chocolate pieces and beat into butter before adding powdered sugar.

3. STRAWBERRY: Beat ⅓ cup strawberry jam into butter before adding powdered sugar.

4. SPICE: Add 1 to 2 teaspoons apple pie spice or pumpkin pie spice with the powdered sugar.

5. PEANUT BUTTER: Beat ½ cup peanut butter into butter before adding powdered sugar.

6. IRISH CREAM: Substitute Irish cream liqueur for the milk.

7. PEPPERMINT: Substitute ½ teaspoon peppermint extract for vanilla; if desired, tint with red food coloring.

8. DARK CHOCOLATE: Substitute ½ cup unsweetened cocoa powder for ½ cup of the powdered sugar.

9. COFFEE: Add 1 tablespoon instant espresso powder or coffee crystals, or substitute brewed coffee for the milk.

10. CITRUS: Substitute lemon or orange juice for the milk; add ½ teaspoon lemon or orange peel.

CREAM CHEESE FROSTING

START TO FINISH: 20 MINUTES **MAKES:** 3½ CUPS

    1 8-ounce package cream cheese, softened
    ½ cup butter, softened
    2 teaspoons vanilla
    5½ to 6 cups powdered sugar

1 In a large mixing bowl beat cream cheese, butter, and vanilla with an electric mixer on medium
speed until light and fluffy. Gradually beat in powdered sugar to reach spreading consistency. (This
frosts tops and sides of two 8- or 9-inch layers.
Halve the recipe to frost a 13×9×2-inch cake.)
Cover and store the frosted cake in refrigerator.

COCOA-CREAM CHEESE FROSTING: Prepare
as directed, except beat ½ cup unsweetened
cocoa powder into the cream cheese mixture and
reduce powdered sugar to 5 to 5½ cups.

PER ½ OF RECIPE PLAIN OR COCOA VARIATION:
348 cal., 14 g total fat (9 g sat. fat, 0 g trans fat), 41 mg chol.,
116 mg sodium, 56 g carbo., 0 g fiber, 1 g pro.
EXCHANGES: 3½ Other Carbo., 3 Fat

BROWNED BUTTER FROSTING

START TO FINISH: 20 MINUTES **MAKES:** 3 CUPS

    ¾ cup butter
    6 cups powdered sugar
    4 to 5 tablespoons milk
    2 teaspoons vanilla

1 In a small saucepan heat butter over low heat
until melted. Continue heating until butter turns a
light golden brown. Remove from heat. In a large
mixing bowl combine powdered sugar, 4 tablespoons of the milk, and the vanilla. Add browned
butter. Beat with an electric mixer on low speed
until combined. Beat on medium to high speed,
adding additional milk, if necessary, to reach
spreading consistency. (This frosts the tops and
sides of two 8- or 9-inch cake layers.)

PER ½ OF RECIPE: 340 cal., 12 g total fat (7 g sat. fat, 0 g trans
fat), 31 mg chol., 85 mg sodium, 60 g carbo., 0 g fiber, 0 g pro.
EXCHANGES: 4 Other Carbo., 2½ Fat

NO-COOK FUDGE FROSTING

START TO FINISH: 15 MINUTES **MAKES:** 4½ CUPS

    8 cups powdered sugar
    1 cup unsweetened cocoa powder
    1 cup butter, softened

    ⅔ cup boiling water
    2 teaspoons vanilla

1 In a large mixing bowl combine powdered sugar
and cocoa powder. Add butter, water, and vanilla.
Beat with an electric mixer on low speed until
combined. Beat 1 minute on medium speed. Cool
about 20 minutes or until spreading consistency.
If frosting is too thick, add *boiling water,* 1 tablespoon at a time, until spreading consistency.
(This frosts tops and sides of two 8- or 9-inch cake
layers. Halve the recipe for a 13×9×2-inch cake.)

PER ½ OF RECIPE: 447 cal., 16 g total fat (10 g sat. fat, 0 g trans
fat), 41 mg chol., 112 mg sodium, 79 g carbo., 2 g fiber, 1 g pro.
EXCHANGES: 5½ Other Carbo., 3 Fat

CHOCOLATE-SOUR CREAM FROSTING

START TO FINISH: 20 MINUTES **MAKES:** 4½ CUPS

    2 cups semisweet chocolate pieces
    ½ cup butter
    1 8-ounce carton dairy sour cream
    4½ cups powdered sugar

1 In a saucepan heat and stir chocolate and butter
over low heat until melted. Cool 5 minutes. Stir in
sour cream. Beat in powdered sugar with a wooden
spoon until smooth. (This frosts tops and sides of
two 8- or 9-inch cake layers. Halve the recipe for a
13×9×2-inch cake.) Refrigerate frosted cake.

CHOCOLATE-MINT SOUR CREAM FROSTING:
Prepare as directed, except stir in ½ teaspoon
mint extract with the sour cream.

PER ½ OF RECIPE PLAIN OR MINT VARIATION:
415 cal., 20 g total fat (12 g sat. fat, 0 g trans fat), 30 mg chol.,
73 mg sodium, 63 g carbo., 2 g fiber, 2 g pro.
EXCHANGES: 4 Other Carbo., 4 Fat

GANACHE

START TO FINISH: 35 MINUTES **MAKES:** 2 CUPS

    1 cup whipping cream
    12 ounces milk, semisweet, or bittersweet
        chocolate, chopped

1 In a medium saucepan bring cream just to
boiling over medium-high heat. Remove from
heat. Add chocolate (do not stir). Let stand for
5 minutes. Stir until smooth. Cool for 15 minutes.
(This frosts an 8- or 9-inch cake layer.)

PER ½ OF RECIPE: 220 cal., 16 g total fat (10 g sat. fat, 0 g trans
fat), 34 mg chol., 36 mg sodium, 17 g carbo., 0 g fiber, 3 g pro.
EXCHANGES: 1 Other Carbo., 3 Fat

CANDIES

TOFFEE BUTTER CRUNCH, PAGE 191

CANDIES

CANDY RECIPES RANGE FROM SUPER SIMPLE TO A LITTLE BIT TRICKY. ALL ARE WITHIN ANY COOK'S REACH WITH THE RIGHT EQUIPMENT, INGREDIENTS, AND KNOW-HOW.

EQUIPMENT

Using the right equipment helps ensure that your candy will be a success.

PAN SIZE: Recipes in this chapter include a recommended saucepan size. This is key. If your pan is too small, the candy mixture can boil over, causing dangerous spills. If it's too large, the mixture spreads too thinly and might not cover the thermometer bulb. Use high-quality, heavy saucepans.

THERMOMETER: While not all candies call for using a thermometer, many candies are much easier to make with a candy thermometer than without one. Choose a thermometer that's easy to read and clips to the side of the pan. Check the thermometer for accuracy each time you prepare candy. To do this, submerge the tip in boiling water for a few minutes. It should register 212°F (at sea level). If it registers above or below this temperature, add or subtract the number of degrees it is above or below 212°F from the temperature specified in the recipe and cook to that temperature.

SPOONS: Use long-handled wooden or high-heat-resistant spoons when stirring hot candy mixtures. Standard metal spoons become too hot to handle.

INGREDIENTS

■ Use exact ingredients specified in the recipe; for example, if the recipe calls for butter, don't substitute margarine.

PEANUT BRITTLE, PAGE 191

■ Measure and prepare all ingredients before you start. Candy making moves quickly; for example, once your peanut brittle mixture has reached the right temperature, you don't want to hunt down baking soda required in the next step.

■ Measure all ingredients accurately and do not halve or double candy recipes.

COOKING

Follow these tips to ensure success at key points in the candy-making process, from getting ready to cook to cooling down the mixture.

■ If a recipe calls for buttering the sides of the pan, do so to help prevent the mixture from boiling over.

■ When you combine the sugar with the other ingredients, make sure that sugar thoroughly dissolves as you bring the mixture to a boil.

■ When using a candy thermometer, clip the thermometer onto the pan after the sugar dissolves. Make sure the bulb or tip doesn't touch the bottom of the pan and that it's completely covered with the bubbling candy mixture—not just with foam.

■ Boil candy mixtures at a moderate, steady rate (bubbles should form over the entire surface of the mixture). If a recipe suggests a range-top heat setting, use this as a guide because the actual temperatures of heat settings vary among models.

■ When cooling candy, such as fudge, be sure the thermometer bulb is covered with the candy mixture for an accurate reading. If it isn't covered, carefully prop the saucepan with a folded hot pad.

STORAGE

Follow storage guidelines with each recipe. Avoid storing different types of candies in the same container. Candies can trade flavors, and one candy can change the consistency of another.

FUDGE

PREP: 15 MINUTES **COOK:** 20 MINUTES
COOL: 50 MINUTES
MAKES: ABOUT 1¼ POUNDS (32 PIECES)

- 2 cups sugar
- ¾ cup half-and-half or light cream
- 2 ounces unsweetened chocolate, cut up
- 1 teaspoon light-color corn syrup
- 2 tablespoons butter
- 1 teaspoon vanilla
- ½ cup chopped nuts (optional)

1 Line a 9×5×3-inch loaf pan with foil, extending foil over edges of pan. Butter foil; set pan aside.

2 Butter the sides of a 2-quart heavy saucepan. In the saucepan combine sugar, half-and-half, chocolate, corn syrup, and ⅛ teaspoon *salt*. Cook and stir over medium heat until mixture boils. Clip a candy thermometer to the side of the pan. Reduce heat to medium-low; continue boiling at a moderate, steady rate (see photo, page 183), stirring occasionally, until thermometer registers 236°F, soft-ball stage (20 to 25 minutes.) Adjust heat as necessary to maintain a steady boil.

3 Remove saucepan from heat. Add butter and vanilla, but do not stir. If necessary, tilt saucepan so the bulb of the thermometer is covered with the candy mixture. Cool, without stirring, to 110°F (50 to 60 minutes). Remove thermometer from saucepan. Beat mixture vigorously with a clean wooden spoon until candy just begins to thicken. If desired, add nuts. Continue beating until the fudge just starts to lose its gloss (6 to 8 minutes total).

4 Immediately spread fudge evenly in the prepared pan. Score into squares while warm. When fudge is firm, use foil to lift it out of pan. Cut fudge into squares (see photos 1 and 2, page 185). Store, tightly covered, at room temperature for up to 2 days or in the refrigerator for up to 1 month.

PER PIECE: 72 cal., 2 g total fat (1 g sat. fat, 0 g trans fat), 4 mg chol., 17 mg sodium, 13 g carbo., 0 g fiber, 0 g pro.
EXCHANGES: 1 Other Carbo., ½ Fat

CANNED MILK PRODUCTS
EVPORATED MILK IS WHOLE MILK WITH SOME OF THE WATER REMOVED; SWEETENED CONDENSED MILK ALSO HAS SUGAR ADDED.

EASY FUDGE

PREP: 45 MINUTES **CHILL:** 2 TO 3 HOURS
MAKES: ABOUT 5 POUNDS (96 PIECES)

- 4½ cups sugar
- 1 12-ounce can (1½ cups) evaporated milk
- ½ teaspoon salt
- 1 pound milk chocolate bars, chopped
- 1 12-ounce package (2 cups) semisweet chocolate pieces
- 1 7-ounce jar marshmallow creme
- 1 cup chopped walnuts or pecans (optional)
- 1 teaspoon vanilla

1 Line a 13×9×2-inch baking pan with foil, extending the foil over the edges of the pan. Butter the foil; set pan aside.

2 Butter the sides of a 3-quart heavy saucepan. In the saucepan combine sugar, evaporated milk, and salt. Cook and stir over medium-high heat until mixture boils. Reduce heat to medium; continue cooking and stirring for 10 minutes.

3 Remove the saucepan from heat. Add milk chocolate, chocolate pieces, marshmallow creme, nuts (if desired), and the vanilla. Stir until chocolate melts and mixture is combined. Beat by hand for 3 to 5 minutes or until mixture starts to become thicker.

4 Immediately pour fudge into the prepared pan; shake pan gently to spread fudge to edges of pan. Cover; chill for 2 to 3 hours or until firm. When fudge is firm, use foil to lift it out of pan. Cut fudge into squares (see photos 1 and 2, page 185). Store, tightly covered, at room temperature for up to 2 days or in the refrigerator for up to 1 month.

EASY MOCHA FUDGE: Prepare as directed, except stir 2 tablespoons instant espresso coffee powder or instant coffee crystals into the mixture with the vanilla.

PER PIECE PLAIN OR MOCHA VARIATION: 90 cal., 3 g total fat (2 g sat. fat, 0 g trans fat), 2 mg chol., 22 mg sodium, 16 g carbo., 0 g fiber, 1 g pro.
EXCHANGES: 1 Other Carbo., ½ Fat

EASY ROCKY ROAD FUDGE: Prepare as directed, except after spreading fudge in pan, sprinkle top with a mixture of 1 cup semisweet chocolate pieces, 1 cup tiny marshmallows, and ½ cup chopped walnuts, toasted (see tip, page 20). Press mixture lightly into fudge. Chill as directed.

PER PIECE: 105 cal., 4 g total fat (2 g sat. fat, 0 g trans fat), 2 mg chol., 23 mg sodium, 18 g carbo., 0 g fiber, 1 g pro.
EXCHANGES: 1 Other Carbo, 1 Fat

PEANUT BUTTER FUDGE

PREP: 15 MINUTES **COOK:** 12 MINUTES
STAND: 60 MINUTES
MAKES: ABOUT 1½ POUNDS (64 PIECES)

- 2 cups sugar
- 1 5-ounce can (⅔ cup) evaporated milk
- ½ cup butter
- ¾ cup peanut butter
- ½ of a 7-ounce jar marshmallow creme (about ¾ cup) or 2 cups tiny marshmallows
- ½ cup finely chopped peanuts (optional)
- ½ teaspoon vanilla

1 Line a 9×9×2-inch baking pan with foil, extending the foil over the edges of the pan. Butter the foil; set pan aside.

2 Butter the sides of a 1½- to 2-quart heavy saucepan. In saucepan combine sugar, milk, and butter. Cook and stir over medium-high heat until mixture boils. Reduce heat to medium; continue boiling at a moderate, steady rate for 12 minutes (see photo, page 183); stir occasionally.

3 Remove saucepan from heat. Add peanut butter, marshmallow creme, peanuts (if desired), and vanilla; stir until mixture is combined. Spread fudge evenly in the prepared pan. Let stand for 1 to 2 hours or until firm. When fudge is firm, use foil to lift it out of pan. Cut fudge into squares (see photos 1 and 2, below). Store fudge, tightly covered, at room temperature for up to 2 days or in the refrigerator for up to 1 month.

PER PIECE: 63 cal., 3 g total fat (1 g sat. fat, 0 g trans fat), 4 mg chol., 28 mg sodium, 8 g carbo., 0 g fiber, 1 g pro. EXCHANGES: ½ Other Carbo., ½ Fat

EASY WHITE FUDGE

PREP: 20 MINUTES **CHILL:** 2 HOURS
MAKES: ABOUT 2 POUNDS (64 PIECES)

- 3 cups white baking pieces
- 1 14-ounce can (1¼ cups) sweetened condensed milk
- 1 cup chopped pecans, almonds, or macadamia nuts
- 2 teaspoons finely shredded orange peel
- 1 teaspoon vanilla
  Coarsely chopped pecans, almonds, or macadamia nuts (optional)

1 Line an 8×8×2-inch or 9×9×2-inch baking pan with foil, extending the foil over the edges of the pan. Butter the foil; set pan aside.

2 In a 2-quart heavy saucepan cook and stir white baking pieces and sweetened condensed milk over low heat just until pieces melt and mixture is smooth. Remove saucepan from heat. Stir in 1 cup nuts, orange peel, and vanilla.

3 Spread fudge evenly in the prepared pan. If desired, sprinkle with additional nuts; press lightly into fudge. If desired, score into 1-inch pieces. Cover and chill about 2 hours or until firm.

4 When fudge is firm, use foil to lift it out of pan. Cut fudge into squares (see photos 1 and 2, below). Store fudge, tightly covered, at room temperature for up to 2 days or in the refrigerator for up to 1 month.

PER PIECE: 92 cal., 5 g total fat (3 g sat. fat, 0 g trans fat), 2 mg chol., 23 mg sodium, 10 g carbo., 0 g fiber, 1 g pro. EXCHANGES: ½ Other Carbo., 1 Fat

CUT FUDGE THE EASY WAY, STEP-BY-STEP

1. Lining the pan with foil makes it easy to remove the fudge from the pan. Grip the edges of the foil to remove the solid block of candy and place it on a cutting board. **2.** Use a long, thin-bladed sharp knife to cut the fudge. To make equal-size pieces, slice alongside a ruler to cut the fudge into long strips. Working with one strip at a time, cut the strips crosswise into rectangles or squares.

CANDY-BAR FUDGE

PREP: 15 MINUTES **COOK:** 7¼ MINUTES
CHILL: 2 TO 3 HOURS
MAKES: ABOUT 2¾ POUNDS (64 PIECES)

- ½ cup butter
- ⅓ cup unsweetened cocoa powder
- ¼ cup packed brown sugar
- ¼ cup milk
- 3½ cups powdered sugar
- 1 teaspoon vanilla
- 30 vanilla caramels, unwrapped
- 1 tablespoon water
- 2 cups peanuts
- ½ cup semisweet chocolate pieces
- ½ cup milk chocolate pieces

1 Line a 9×9×2-inch or 11×7×1½-inch baking pan with foil, extending the foil over the edges of the pan. Butter the foil; set pan aside.

2 In a large microwave-safe bowl microwave the butter, uncovered, on 100% power (high) for 1 to 1½ minutes or until butter melts. Stir in cocoa powder, brown sugar, and milk. Microwave, uncovered, on high for 1 to 1½ minutes or until mixture comes to a boil, stirring once. Stir again; microwave for 30 seconds more. Stir in powdered sugar and vanilla until smooth. Spread fudge in prepared pan.

3 In a medium microwave-safe bowl combine caramels and water. Microwave, uncovered, on 50% power (medium) for 2 to 2½ minutes or until caramels melt, stirring once. Stir in peanuts. Microwave, uncovered, on medium for 45 to 60 seconds more or until mixture softens. Gently and quickly spread caramel mixture over fudge layer in pan.

4 In a 2-cup microwave-safe glass measure or small bowl combine semisweet and milk chocolate pieces. Microwave, uncovered, on 50% power (medium) for 2 to 2½ minutes or until chocolate melts, stirring once or twice. Spread over caramel layer. Cover and chill for 2 to 3 hours or until firm. When fudge is firm, use foil to lift it out of pan. Cut fudge into pieces (see photos 1 and 2, page 185). Store, tightly covered, in the refrigerator for up to 3 weeks.

PER PIECE: 102 cal., 5 g total fat (2 g sat. fat, 0 g trans fat), 5 mg chol., 24 mg sodium, 14 g carbo., 1 g fiber, 2 g pro. EXCHANGES: 1 Other Carbo., 1 Fat

COOKIE TRUFFLES

PREP: 50 MINUTES **FREEZE:** 15 MINUTES
CHILL: 30 MINUTES **STAND:** 30 MINUTES
MAKES: ABOUT 50 TRUFFLES

- 1 12-ounce package semisweet chocolate pieces
- 1 8-ounce package cream cheese, cut up and softened
- 1 8-ounce package miniature chocolate sandwich cookies with white filling or 8 ounces regular-size chocolate sandwich cookies with white filling (20 cookies), finely chopped
- 2¼ cups milk chocolate pieces or semisweet chocolate pieces
- 2 tablespoons shortening

1 Line a tray or baking sheet with waxed paper; set aside. In a medium heavy saucepan heat and stir the 12 ounces semisweet chocolate pieces over low heat until chocolate melts. Remove from heat; stir in cream cheese until mixture is well combined (mixture will thicken). Stir in chopped cookies.* Use a small cookie scoop to drop mounds of mixture onto the prepared tray. Cover and freeze for 15 minutes or until firm.

2 In a small heavy saucepan combine the 2¼ cups milk chocolate pieces and shortening; stir over low heat until mixture melts and is smooth. Remove from heat.

3 Line a tray or baking sheet with waxed paper. Using a fork, dip balls into chocolate mixture, allowing excess chocolate to drip back into saucepan. Place dipped balls on prepared tray. Chill about 30 minutes or until firm. Store in a single layer in an airtight container in the refrigerator for up to 1 week or freeze for up to 1 month. Let stand at room temperature about 30 minutes before serving.

*NOTE: For smoother, rounder truffles, after stirring in the chopped cookies, chill the mixture for 30 to 60 minutes or until mixture is more firm.

PER TRUFFLE: 115 cal., 7 g total fat (4 g sat. fat, 0 g trans fat), 7 mg chol., 47 mg sodium, 12 g carbo., 1 g fiber, 1 g pro. EXCHANGES: 1 Other Carbo., 1½ Fat

MELTING CHOCOLATE
TO AVOID SCORCHING, USE A HEAVY SAUCEPAN OVER LOW HEAT OR A DOUBLE BOILER. THIS IS NO TIME TO MULTITASK! WATCH CAREFULLY; STIR OFTEN.

CLASSIC TRUFFLES

PREP: 60 MINUTES **CHILL:** 1½ TO 2 HOURS
MAKES: 25 TO 30 TRUFFLES

- 1 12-ounce package semisweet chocolate pieces or one 11.5-ounce package milk chocolate pieces
- ⅓ cup whipping cream
- 4 teaspoons cherry brandy, hazelnut or orange liqueur, or milk
- 3 tablespoons finely chopped candied cherries or candied orange peel

  Unsweetened cocoa powder; finely chopped nuts, toasted (see tip, page 20); and/or powdered sugar

1 In a medium heavy saucepan combine chocolate pieces and whipping cream. Cook and stir constantly over low heat until the chocolate melts. Remove saucepan from heat; cool slightly. Stir in cherry brandy. Beat the truffle mixture with an electric mixer on low speed until smooth. Stir in candied cherries. Chill for 1½ to 2 hours or until mixture is firm.

2 Line a tray or baking sheet with waxed paper. Shape the chilled chocolate mixture into ¾- to 1-inch balls. Roll balls in cocoa powder, finely chopped nuts, and/or powdered sugar; place on the prepared tray. Store in a single layer in an airtight container in the refrigerator for up to 2 weeks. Let stand at room temperature about 30 minutes before serving.

PER TRUFFLE: 85 cal., 5 g total fat (3 g sat. fat, 0 g trans fat), 4 mg chol., 3 mg sodium, 11 g carbo., 1 g fiber, 1 g pro.
EXCHANGES: 1 Other Carbo., 1 Fat

TOO MANY NUTS?
UNTOASTED NUTS KEEP EXCEEDINGLY WELL FROZEN IN FREEZER BAGS TO USE FOR SALAD AND SUNDAE TOPPERS.

MAKE TRUFFLES AMAZING SIMPLY CHANGE THE COATING YOU ROLL THEM IN. USE COCOA POWDER, POWDERED SUGAR, OR ANY KIND OF CHOPPED NUT YOU CRAVE, SUCH AS PISTACHIOS, CASHEWS, MACADAMIAS, OR PECANS.

CLASSIC TRUFFLES

MAKE-IT-MINE CANDY BARK

CANDY COATING + INGREDIENTS YOU LOVE = YOUR OWN CANDY MASTERPIECE. YOU CAN CREATE A ONE-OF-A-KIND TREAT EVERYONE WILL ADMIRE, YET NO ONE WILL SUSPECT HOW EASY IT WAS TO CONCOCT IN JUST THREE SIMPLE STEPS.

BASIC INGREDIENTS

PREP: 20 MINUTES
CHILL: 30 MINUTES **MAKES:**
ABOUT 1½ POUNDS (36 SERVINGS)

- 6 ounces (1 cup) chocolate-, vanilla-, or butterscotch-flavored candy coating, chopped
- 6 ounces (1 cup) Chocolate, chopped
- 1 tablespoon shortening
- 1 to 2 teaspoons Flavoring (optional)
- 1½ cups Stir-Ins
- 1 cup Toppings

CHOCOLATE (PICK ONE)

Milk chocolate

White baking chocolate

Semisweet chocolate

Dark chocolate

FLAVORING (PICK ONE)

Finely shredded citrus peel (orange, lemon, or lime)

Finely chopped candied orange peel

Finely chopped crystallized ginger

STIR-INS

Chopped chocolate sandwich cookies with white filling

Chopped peanut butter sandwich cookies with peanut butter filling

Chopped vanilla wafers

Flaked coconut, toasted

Toffee pieces

Chopped nuts, toasted (macadamia nuts, pecans, walnuts, hazelnuts, almonds) (see tip, page 20)

Chopped cocktail peanuts or cashews

Snipped dried fruit (cherries, raisins, cranberries, apricots)

TOPPINGS

Chopped chocolate-covered crisp peanut butter candy bar

Flaked coconut, toasted

Peanut butter-flavored pieces

Candy-coated peanut butter-flavored pieces

Chopped malted milk balls

Chopped chocolate-covered coffee beans

Chopped nuts, toasted (macadamia nuts, pecans, walnuts, hazelnuts, almonds) (see tip, page 20)

Chopped cocktail peanuts or cashews

Snipped dried fruit (cherries, raisins, cranberries, apricots)

BASIC INSTRUCTIONS

1 Line a large baking sheet with heavy foil; grease foil. Set aside.

2 In a large microwave-safe bowl combine candy coating, desired Chocolate, and shortening. Microwave, uncovered, on 100% power (high) for 1½ to 2 minutes or until chocolate melts, stirring every 30 seconds. If desired, add Flavoring. Add Stir-Ins; mix well. Pour onto prepared baking sheet. Spread about ¼ inch thick. Sprinkle Toppings over mixture; press lightly with back of spoon.

3 Chill candy about 30 minutes or until firm. Use foil to lift candy; carefully break into pieces. Store between layers of waxed paper in an airtight container. Refrigerate up to 2 weeks.

MARBLED BARK In Step 2 melt Chocolate with 2 teaspoons shortening about 1 minute; spread on baking sheet. Melt different-color candy coating about 1 minute; drop spoonfuls on chocolate. Swirl with spoon. Sprinkle with Toppings as above.

CHOCOLATE-COVERED CHERRIES

PREP: 75 MINUTES **CHILL:** 1 TO 4 HOURS
STAND: 3 HOURS **MAKES:** 40 CHERRIES

- 2 10-ounce jars maraschino cherries with stems (40 cherries)
- 3 tablespoons butter, softened
- 3 tablespoons light-color corn syrup
- 2 cups powdered sugar
- 8 ounces chocolate-flavored candy coating, cut up
- 8 ounces bittersweet or semisweet chocolate, cut up

1 Let cherries stand on paper towels for 2 hours to drain. Line baking sheet with waxed paper.

2 In a medium bowl combine butter and corn syrup; stir in powdered sugar. Knead until smooth (chill if mixture is too soft to handle). Shape about ¾ teaspoon mixture around each cherry. Place coated cherries, stem sides up, on prepared baking sheet. Chill for 1 to 4 hours or until firm.

3 In a medium heavy saucepan melt candy coating and chocolate over low heat, stirring constantly until smooth. Line another baking sheet with waxed paper. Holding cherries by stems, dip one at a time into melted mixture. If necessary, spoon mixture over cherries to cover and seal completely (to prevent juice from leaking). Let excess mixture drip off. Place coated cherries, stem sides up, on prepared baking sheet. Let cherries stand until coating is set (1 to 2 hours). Store, tightly covered, in the refrigerator for up to 1 month. (The longer the cherries are stored, the more the mixture around the cherries will soften and liquefy.)

PER CHERRY: 117 cal., 5 g total fat (3 g sat. fat, 0 g trans fat), 2 mg chol., 7 mg sodium, 19 g carbo., 1 g fiber, 0 g pro.
EXCHANGES: 1 Other Carbo., 1 Fat

CREAM CHEESE MINTS

PREP: 50 MINUTES **CHILL:** OVERNIGHT
MAKES: ABOUT 50 MINTS

- 1 3-ounce package cream cheese, softened
- ½ teaspoon peppermint extract
- 3 cups powdered sugar
  Few drops desired food coloring
  Granulated sugar

1 In a large bowl stir together cream cheese and extract. Gradually add powdered sugar, stirring until mixture is smooth. (Knead in the last of the powdered sugar with your hands.) Add food coloring; knead until food coloring is evenly distributed.

2 Form cream cheese mixture into ¾-inch balls. Roll each ball in granulated sugar; place on a waxed paper-lined tray. Flatten each ball with the bottom of a glass or with the tines of a fork. (Or sprinkle small candy molds lightly with sugar. Press ¾ to 1 teaspoon cream cheese mixture into each mold. Remove from molds.) Cover mints with paper towels; chill overnight. Transfer to an airtight container; store, covered, in the refrigerator for up to 2 weeks or freeze for up to 1 month.

PER MINT: 36 cal., 1 g total fat (0 g sat. fat, 0 g trans fat), 2 mg chol., 6 mg sodium, 8 g carbo., 0 g fiber, 0 g pro.
EXCHANGES: ½ Other Carbo.

PRALINES

PREP: 15 MINUTES **COOK:** 15 MINUTES
COOL: 20 MINUTES **STAND:** 2 HOURS
MAKES: ABOUT 30 PRALINES

- 1½ cups granulated sugar
- 1½ cups packed brown sugar
- 1 cup evaporated milk
- 2 tablespoons butter
- 2 tablespoons dark-color corn syrup
- ⅛ teaspoon salt
- 2 cups pecan halves, toasted (see tip, page 20)
- 1 teaspoon vanilla

1 Butter the sides of a 2-quart heavy saucepan. In saucepan combine granulated sugar, brown sugar, milk, butter, corn syrup, and salt. Cook and stir over medium-high heat until mixture boils. Clip a candy thermometer to side of pan. Reduce heat to medium-low; continue boiling at a moderate, steady rate (see photo, page 183), stirring occasionally, until the thermometer registers 236°F, soft-ball stage (15 to 20 minutes). Adjust heat as necessary to maintain a steady boil.

2 Remove saucepan from heat. Remove thermometer. Cool, without stirring, for 20 minutes. Line two baking sheets with waxed paper; set aside.

3 Stir in pecans and vanilla. Beat vigorously with a clean wooden spoon until mixture thickens but is still glossy (7 to 8 minutes). Working quickly, drop candy by spoonfuls onto prepared baking sheets (mixture will spread). Let stand about 2 hours or until firm. Store, tightly covered, in the refrigerator for up to 1 week.

PER PRALINE: 153 cal., 7 g total fat (1 g sat. fat, 0 g trans fat), 4 mg chol., 29 mg sodium, 24 g carbo., 1 g fiber, 1 g pro.
EXCHANGES: 1½ Other Carbo., 1½ Fat

TESTING CANDY MIXTURES

WHEN A CANDY THERMOMETER ISN'T AVAILABLE, THIS COLD-WATER TEST IS THE NEXT BEST THING.

EQUIPMENT

■ If candy-making intrigues you, invest in a candy thermometer. There's simply no more accurate way to determine the stages of the hot candy mixture. (See page 183 for information on how to use a candy thermometer.)

■ If you do not have a candy thermometer, use the cold-water test described here. All you need is a small bowl or cup and a spoon. You will want to use a wooden or high-heat-resistant spoon when stirring the mixture, but a kitchen spoon will work for the cold-water test.

COLD-WATER TEST

■ Fill the small bowl or cup with cold (but not icy) water. (When testing for thread stage [see photo 1, below], you will not need a bowl of water.)

■ Start testing candy mixtures shortly before they reach minimum cooking times.

■ To test, spoon a few drops hot candy mixture into the bowl of water. Using your fingers, attempt to form the candy mixture into a ball, then remove the ball from the water. For the soft-crack and hard-crack stages (see photos 5 and 6, below), the mixture won't form a ball but separates into threads.

■ Using the photos and captions below, you can determine the candy mixture's temperature by testing its firmness. If the mixture has not reached the desired stage, continue cooking and retesting, using fresh water at the same temperature you used in the previous test. Use a clean spoon each time.

1. THREAD STAGE *(230°F to 233°F)* When a teaspoon is dipped into the hot mixture in the pan then lifted out, the candy falls off the spoon in a 2-inch-long, fine, thin thread. **2. SOFT-BALL STAGE** *(234°F to 240°F)* When the ball of candy is removed from the cold water, it instantly flattens and runs over your finger. **3. FIRM-BALL STAGE** *(244°F to 248°F)* When the ball of candy is removed from the cold water, it is firm enough to hold its shape but quickly flattens. **4. HARD-BALL STAGE** *(250°F to 266°F)* When the ball of candy is removed from the cold water, it can be deformed by pressure, but it doesn't flatten until pressed. **5. SOFT-CRACK STAGE** *(270°F to 290°F)* When the hot mixture is dropped into the cold water, the candy separates into hard but pliable threads. **6. HARD-CRACK STAGE** *(295°F to 310°F)* When the hot mixture is dropped into the cold water, it separates into hard, brittle threads that snap easily and cannot be shaped into a ball.

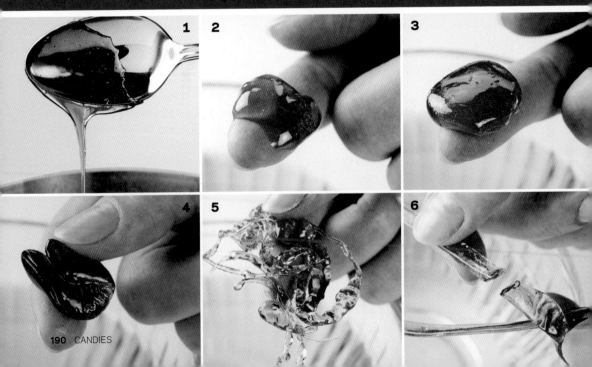

1 2 3 4 5 6

PEANUT BRITTLE (photo, page 183)

PREP: 10 MINUTES **COOK:** 45 MINUTES
MAKES: ABOUT 2¼ POUNDS (72 SERVINGS)

2 cups sugar
1 cup light-color corn syrup
½ cup water
¼ cup butter
2½ cups raw peanuts or raw cashews
1½ teaspoons baking soda, sifted

1 Butter two large baking sheets; set aside. Butter the sides of a 3-quart heavy saucepan. In saucepan combine sugar, corn syrup, water, and butter. Cook and stir over medium-high heat until mixture boils. Clip a candy thermometer to side of pan. Reduce heat to medium-low; continue boiling at a moderate, steady rate (see photo, page 183), stirring occasionally, until the thermometer registers 275°F, soft-crack stage (about 30 minutes). Adjust heat as necessary to maintain a steady boil.

2 Stir in raw nuts; continue cooking over medium-low heat, stirring frequently, until the thermometer registers 295°F, hard-crack stage (15 to 20 minutes more).

3 Remove saucepan from heat; remove thermometer. Quickly sprinkle baking soda over corn syrup mixture, stirring constantly. Immediately pour onto prepared baking sheets. Use two forks to lift and pull candy as it cools. Cool completely; break into pieces. Store, tightly covered, at room temperature for up to 1 week.

PER SERVING: 63 cal., 3 g total fat (1 g sat. fat, 0 g trans fat), 2 mg chol., 33 mg sodium, 8 g carbo., 0 g fiber, 1 g pro. EXCHANGES: ½ Other Carbo., ½ Fat

BEST EVER

TOFFEE BUTTER CRUNCH (photo, page 181)

PREP: 25 MINUTES **COOK:** 12 MINUTES
COOL: 4 MINUTES **STAND:** 3 HOURS
MAKES: 1¼ POUNDS (ABOUT 24 PIECES)

1 cup butter
1 cup sugar
3 tablespoons water
1 tablespoon light-color corn syrup
¾ cup milk chocolate pieces or semisweet chocolate pieces
½ to ¾ cup chopped nuts, such as almonds, pecans, walnuts, and/or cashews, toasted (see tip, page 20)

1 Line a 13×9×2-inch baking pan with foil, extending the foil over edges of pan; set pan aside.

2 In a 2-quart heavy saucepan melt butter over low heat. Stir in sugar, water, and corn syrup. Bring to boiling over medium-high heat, stirring until sugar is dissolved. Avoid splashing side of saucepan. Clip a candy thermometer to side of pan. Cook over medium heat, stirring frequently, until thermometer registers 290°F, soft-crack stage (about 12 minutes). Mixture should boil at a moderate, steady rate with bubbles over entire surface (see photo, page 183). Adjust heat as necessary to maintain a steady boil and watch temperature carefully during the last 5 minutes of cooking as temperature can increase quickly at the end. Remove from heat; remove thermometer.

3 Carefully pour corn syrup mixture into prepared pan; spread evenly. Cool 4 to 5 minutes or until top is just set. Sprinkle evenly with chocolate pieces; let stand for 2 minutes. Spread softened chocolate into an even layer over toffee layer. Sprinkle with nuts; lightly press into chocolate. Let stand at room temperature about 3 hours or until chocolate is set. Use foil to lift candy out of pan; break into pieces. Store with waxed paper between the layers in an airtight container at room temperature for up to 2 weeks.

PER PIECE: 141 cal., 10 g total fat (6 g sat. fat, 0 g trans fat), 22 mg chol., 59 mg sodium, 12 g carbo., 0 g fiber, 1 g pro. EXCHANGES: 1 Other Carbo., 2 Fat

PEANUT CLUSTERS

PREP: 20 MINUTES **CHILL:** 15 MINUTES
MAKES: ABOUT 48 PIECES

1 11.5-ounce package milk chocolate pieces or one 12-ounce package semisweet chocolate pieces
12 ounces vanilla-flavored candy coating, chopped
1 pound (3 cups) cocktail peanuts

1 Line a tray or baking sheet with waxed paper; set aside. In a medium heavy saucepan stir the milk chocolate and candy coating over low heat until chocolate melts and is smooth. Stir in peanuts. Drop from teaspoons onto prepared tray. Chill about 15 minutes or until set. Store, tightly covered, in the refrigerator for up to 1 week or freeze for up to 3 months.

PER PIECE: 133 cal., 9 g total fat (4 g sat. fat, 0 g trans fat), 1 mg chol., 23 mg sodium, 10 g carbo., 1 g fiber, 3 g pro. EXCHANGES: ½ Other Carbo., 2 Fat

PREPARING HOMEMADE MARSHMALLOWS, STEP-BY-STEP

1. Place marshmallow on a cutting surface sprinkled with powdered sugar mixture; carefully remove paper or plastic wrap. **2.** Use a long, thin-bladed, sharp knife to cut mixture into strips, then into squares. If knife sticks, sprinkle with powdered sugar mixture. **3.** Shake a portion of squares at a time with powdered sugar mixture in a plastic bag.

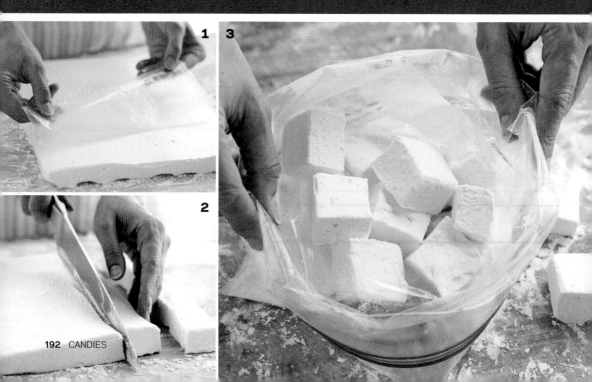

1

2

3

HOMEMADE MARSHMALLOWS

PREP: 30 MINUTES **COOK:** 12 MINUTES
CHILL: 5 HOURS **MAKES:** ABOUT 80 MARSHMALLOWS

    Nonstick cooking spray
  2 envelopes unflavored gelatin
     (4¼ teaspoons)
  ¾ cup cold water
  2 cups granulated sugar
  ⅔ cup light-color corn syrup
  ⅓ cup refrigerated egg white product or
     2 pasteurized liquid egg whites*
  1 tablespoon vanilla
  ¼ teaspoon salt
  ⅔ cup powdered sugar
  3 tablespoons cornstarch

1 Line a 13×9×2-inch baking pan with plastic wrap or line bottom of pan with waxed paper or parchment paper. Coat the plastic or paper with nonstick cooking spray; set pan aside.

2 In a large metal or heatproof bowl sprinkle gelatin over ½ cup of the cold water; set aside.

3 In a 2-quart heavy saucepan stir together remaining ¼ cup water, 1¾ cups of the granulated sugar, and corn syrup until combined. Bring to boiling over medium-high heat. Clip a candy thermometer to side of saucepan. Cook, without stirring, over medium-high heat until thermometer registers 260°F, hard-ball stage (12 to 15 minutes total). Remove from heat; pour over gelatin mixture in bowl and stir well to combine (mixture will foam and bubble up in the bowl).

4 Meanwhile, in a large mixing bowl beat egg whites, vanilla, and salt with an electric mixer on high speed until foamy. Gradually add remaining ¼ cup granulated sugar, 1 tablespoon at a time, until stiff peaks form (tips stand straight). With mixer running on high speed, gradually add gelatin mixture to egg white mixture, beating for 5 to 7 minutes or until thick (consistency of thick, pourable cake batter). Quickly and gently spread marshmallow mixture into prepared pan. Coat another piece of plastic wrap with nonstick spray; place, coated side down, over marshmallow mixture in pan. Chill at least 5 hours or until firm.

5 In a small bowl combine powdered sugar and cornstarch; sprinkle about one-fourth of the mixture evenly onto a large cutting board. Remove plastic wrap from top of marshmallows. Run a knife around edge of pan to loosen sides of marshmallow mixture and carefully invert onto the cutting board. Remove

plastic wrap or paper (see photo 1, page 192). Sprinkle top with some of the remaining powdered sugar mixture. Cut marshmallows into about 1-inch squares (see photo 2, page 192). If mixture sticks, coat knife with powdered sugar mixture. Place squares, about one-third at a time, in a large resealable plastic bag (see photo 3, page 192). Add remaining powdered sugar mixture; seal bag. Toss to coat all sides with powdered sugar mixture. Store marshmallows between sheets of waxed paper or parchment paper in an airtight container in refrigerator for up to 1 week or in freezer up to 1 month.

*NOTE: Buy a product that is only egg whites. If you can't find pasteurized egg whites, you can use regular eggs and pasteurize the whites following the tip on page 17.

ORANGE CREAM MARSHMALLOWS: Prepare as directed, except stir 1 envelope unsweetened orange-flavored soft drink mix into egg whites with the vanilla.

COCOA MARSHMALLOWS: Prepare as directed, except sift ¼ cup unsweetened cocoa powder over the stiffly beaten egg whites in Step 4. Gently fold cocoa powder into the egg whites with a large spatula before adding the hot gelatin mixture. Continue as directed in Step 4 adding the hot gelatin mixture and chilling. Reduce powdered sugar to ½ cup and add ¼ cup unsweetened cocoa powder to the powdered sugar-cornstarch mixture. Continue as directed in Step 5 to cut and coat the marshmallows.

PER PLAIN, ORANGE CREAM, OR COCOA VARIATIONS:
38 cal., 0 g total fat, 0 mg chol., 20 mg sodium, 9 g carbo., 0 g fiber, 0 g pro.
EXCHANGES: ½ Other Carbo.

COCONUT MARSHMALLOWS: Prepare as directed, except sprinkle 1½ cups toasted flaked coconut in the bottom of the 13×9×2-inch pan after coating with nonstick cooking spray. Add ¼ teaspoon coconut flavoring to the egg whites with the vanilla. Sprinkle top of marshmallow mixture in pan with an additional 1½ cups toasted flaked coconut. Cover and chill as directed in Step 4. Omit powdered sugar and cornstarch. Invert marshmallows onto a large cutting board. Cut into squares. Place several squares at a time in a large resealable plastic bag. Add 1¼ cups toasted flaked coconut. Seal bag and shake to coat all sides of marshmallows with coconut.

PER MARSHMALLOW: 62 cal., 2 g total fat (2 g sat. fat, 0 g trans fat), 0 mg chol., 37 mg sodium, 11 g carbo., 0 g fiber, 1 g pro.
EXCHANGES: 1 Other Carbo., ½ Fat

PEANUT BUTTER BALLS

PREP: 40 MINUTES **COOL:** 5 MINUTES
STAND: 10 MINUTES **MAKES:** ABOUT 40 CANDIES

- 1 cup peanut butter
- 6 tablespoons butter, softened
- 2 cups powdered sugar
- 12 ounces chocolate-flavored candy coating, cut up

1 Line a tray or baking sheet with waxed paper; set aside. In a large bowl stir together peanut butter and butter. Gradually add powdered sugar, stirring until combined. If necessary, knead with hands until smooth. Shape peanut butter mixture into 1-inch balls; place on the prepared tray. Set tray aside.

2 In a medium heavy saucepan melt candy coating over low heat, stirring constantly until smooth. Remove from heat and cool for 5 minutes. Using a fork, dip balls, one at a time, into coating, allowing excess coating to drip off. Return to waxed paper; let stand until coating is set (about 10 minutes). Store, tightly covered, in the refrigerator for up to 1 month or freeze for up to 3 months. If frozen, thaw at room temperature before serving.

CRISPY PEANUT BUTTER BALLS: Prepare as directed, except stir 1 cup crisp rice cereal into peanut butter mixture before shaping into balls.

PER CANDY PLAIN OR CRISPY VARIATION: 124 cal., 8 g total fat (4 g sat. fat, 0 g trans fat), 5 mg chol., 42 mg sodium, 13 g carbo., 0 g fiber, 2 g pro.
EXCHANGES: 1 Other Carbo., 1½ Fat

CARAMELS

PREP: 20 MINUTES **COOK:** 45 MINUTES
STAND: 2 HOURS **MAKES:** 64 OR 81 PIECES

- 1 cup chopped walnuts, toasted if desired (see tip, page 20) (optional)
- 1 cup butter
- 2¼ cups packed brown sugar
- 2 cups half-and-half or light cream
- 1 cup light-color corn syrup
- 1 teaspoon vanilla

1 Line an 8×8×2-inch or 9×9×2-inch baking pan with foil, extending foil over edges of pan. Butter the foil. If desired, sprinkle walnuts over bottom of pan. Set pan aside.

2 In a 3-quart heavy saucepan melt butter over low heat. Add brown sugar, half-and-half, and corn syrup; mix well. Cook and stir over medium-high heat until mixture boils. Clip a candy thermometer to the side of the pan. Reduce heat to medium;

continue boiling at a moderate, steady rate (see photo, page 183), stirring frequently, until the thermometer registers 248°F, firm-ball stage (45 to 60 minutes). Adjust heat as necessary to maintain a steady boil and watch temperature carefully during the last 10 to 15 minutes of cooking as temperature can increase quickly at end.

3 Remove saucepan from heat; remove thermometer. Stir in vanilla. Quickly pour mixture into prepared pan. Let stand about 2 hours or until firm. When firm, use foil to lift it out of pan. Use a buttered knife to cut into 1-inch squares. Wrap each piece in waxed paper or plastic wrap. Store at room temperature for up to 2 weeks.

SHORTCUT CARAMELS: Prepare as directed, except substitute one 14-ounce can (1¼ cups) sweetened condensed milk for the half-and-half. Bring mixture to boiling over medium heat instead of medium-high heat. This mixture will take less time to reach 248°F (about 20 to 25 minutes instead of 45 to 60 minutes).

PER PIECE REGULAR OR SHORTCUT VARIATION: 73 cal., 4 g total fat (2 g sat. fat, 0 g trans fat), 10 mg chol., 27 mg sodium, 10 g carbo., 0 g fiber, 0 g pro.
EXCHANGES: ½ Other Carbo., 1 Fat

BEST EVER

CARAMEL APPLES

PREP: 25 MINUTES **MAKES:** 6 APPLES

- 6 small tart apples
- 6 pop sticks or wooden skewers
- 1 14-ounce package vanilla caramels, unwrapped
- 2 tablespoons whipping cream, half-and-half, or light cream
  Desired trims (page 195) (optional)

1 Wash and dry apples; remove stems. Insert a pop stick into the stem end of each apple. Place apples on a buttered baking sheet.

2 In a medium saucepan combine caramels and whipping cream. Cook and stir over medium-low heat until caramels are completely melted, stirring constantly. Working quickly, dip each apple into hot caramel mixture; turn to coat (heat caramel mixture again over low heat if it becomes too thick to easily coat apples). If desired, dip in trims. Set on prepared baking sheet and let stand until set. For best results, serve the same day.

PER APPLE: 355 cal., 8 g total fat (4 g sat. fat, 0 g trans fat), 15 mg chol., 189 mg sodium, 67 g carbo., 3 g fiber, 4 g pro.
EXCHANGES: 1 Fruit, 3½ Other Carbo., 1½ Fat

10 TO TRY— CARAMEL APPLES

Start with Caramel Apples, page 194. **1. TOFFEE:** Stir ½ teaspoon pumpkin pie spice into caramel mixture; dip in chopped chocolate-covered English toffee bars. **2. CRANBERRY:** Dip in dried cranberries and chopped white baking chocolate; drizzle with melted white chocolate. **3. PRETZEL:** Dip in coarsely crushed pretzels. **4. CANDY:** Dip in miniature candy-coated milk chocolate pieces and chopped candy bar. **5. PEANUT BUTTER:** Melt peanut butter-flavored pieces and a little shortening over low heat. Dip in chopped peanuts; drizzle with mixture. **6. S'MORES:** Dip in honey graham cereal and tiny marshmallows; drizzle with melted chocolate. **7. GRANOLA:** Stir ½ teaspoon cinnamon into caramel mixture; dip in crushed granola. **8. HAWAIIAN:** Dip in toasted coconut and chopped macadamia nuts. **9. NUTTY:** Dip in chopped toasted pecans and/or walnuts. **10. CHOCOLATE TURTLE:** Dip in chopped toasted pecans and semisweet chocolate pieces; drizzle with melted chocolate.

POPCORN AND
CANDY BALLS

BEST EVER

CARAMEL CORN

PREP: 20 MINUTES **BAKE:** 20 MINUTES
OVEN: 300°F **MAKES:** 18 SERVINGS

- 14 cups popped popcorn
- 2 cups whole almonds and/or roasted, salted cashews (optional)
- 1½ cups packed brown sugar
- ¾ cup butter
- ⅓ cup light-color corn syrup
- ½ teaspoon baking soda
- ½ teaspoon vanilla

1 Preheat oven to 300°F. Remove all unpopped kernels from popped popcorn. Place popcorn and, if desired, nuts into a 17×12×2-inch roasting pan. Keep warm in oven while preparing caramel.

2 Butter a large piece of foil; set aside. For caramel, in a medium saucepan combine brown sugar, butter, and corn syrup. Cook and stir over medium heat until mixture boils. Continue boiling at a moderate, steady rate (see photo, page 183), without stirring, for 5 minutes more.

3 Remove saucepan from heat. Stir in baking soda and vanilla. Pour caramel over popcorn; stir gently to coat. Bake for 15 minutes. Stir mixture; bake for 5 minutes more. Spread caramel corn on prepared foil; cool. Store, tightly covered, at room temperature for up to 1 week.

PER 1 CUP: 171 cal., 8 g total fat (5 g sat. fat, 0 g trans fat), 20 mg chol., 97 mg sodium, 25 g carbo., 1 g fiber, 1 g pro.
EXCHANGES: ½ Starch, 1 Other Carbo., 1½ Fat

POPCORN AND CANDY BALLS

START TO FINISH: 45 MINUTES
OVEN: 300°F **MAKES:** 16 POPCORN BALLS

- 20 cups popped popcorn
- 1½ cups light-color corn syrup
- 1½ cups sugar
- 1 7-ounce jar marshmallow creme
- 2 tablespoons butter
- 1 teaspoon vanilla
- 1½ cups candy-coated milk chocolate pieces or candy-coated peanut butter-flavored pieces

1 Preheat oven to 300°F. Remove all unpopped kernels from popped popcorn. Place popcorn into a buttered 17×12×2-inch baking pan or roasting pan. Keep popcorn warm in oven while preparing marshmallow mixture.

2 In a large saucepan bring corn syrup and sugar to boiling over medium-high heat, stirring constantly. Remove from heat. Stir in marshmallow creme, butter, and vanilla until combined.

3 Pour marshmallow mixture over hot popcorn; stir gently to coat. Cool until popcorn mixture can be handled easily. Stir in chocolate pieces. With buttered hands, quickly shape mixture into 3-inch-diameter balls. Wrap each ball in plastic wrap. Store at room temperature for up to 1 week.

POPCORN CAKE: Turn out the popcorn mixture into a buttered 10-inch tube pan. Press gently into pan using a spatula or damp hands. Let stand about 30 minutes; remove popcorn mixture and cut into 16 slices.

PER BALL OR SLICE: 307 cal., 6 g total fat (4 g sat. fat, 0 g trans fat), 7 mg chol., 43 mg sodium, 63 g carbo., 2 g fiber, 2 g pro.
EXCHANGES: 1 Starch, 3 Other Carbo., 1 Fat

SLICK MEASURING TRICK

Syrup, honey, and molasses cling to the inside of a measuring cup, making it necessary to scrape out the liquid with a spatula. Skip that sticky step by  first spraying the empty measuring cup with nonstick cooking spray. The syrup, honey, or molasses will flow cleanly from the cup for a mess-free measure.

CANNING & FREEZING

STRAWBERRY-LEMON MARMALADE, PAGE 214

CANNING BASICS

CANNING IS MAKING A COMEBACK AS A NEW GENERATION DISCOVERS THE JOYS OF SERVING AND SHARING HOME-PRESERVED FOODS. FOLLOW THESE GUIDELINES FOR SAFE, DELICIOUS RESULTS.

EQUIPMENT

BOILING-WATER CANNER: In this chapter, we use only the boiling-water canner (see photo, below), not a pressure canner. A boiling-water (or water-bath) canner is used for fruits, jams, jellies, pickled vegetables, pickles, rel-

ishes, and tomatoes. It is a large pot that has a lid and a rack designed to hold canning jars. Any large cooking pot can be used if it has a rack, a tight-fitting lid, and enough depth for briskly boiling water to cover the jars by 1 inch.

A pressure canner must be used for vegetables and other low-acid foods. It is a large heavy pot that has a rack and a tight-fitting lid with a vent (or petcock), a dial or weighted-pressure gauge, and a safety fuse. It sometimes has a gasket. Pressure canners allow foods to be heated to 240°F and held at that temperature as long as necessary. When using a pressure canner, always refer to the manufacturer's instructions before beginning.

JARS: Use only standard canning jars. These are tempered to withstand the heat inside a canner, and their mouths are specially threaded to seal with canning lids.

Inspect all jars before using them; discard any that are cracked or have chipped rims.

LIDS: Use screw bands and flat metal lids that have a built-in sealing compound. Prepare them according to the manufacturer's directions. The flat lids are designed for one-time use only. Screw bands can be reused if they are not bent or rusty.

OTHER ESSENTIALS: Special kits can be purchased that include all the canning essentials in one box. Kits typically contain the following (see photo, above, from left): A jar lifter for removing hot jars from boiling water; a magnetic lid wand for retrieving sterilized lids from the hot water; a nonmetallic spatula (not pictured), which often has measuring increments for judging headspace (a ruler can be used instead); and a funnel for directing hot liquids into jars. In addition, you might want to have a food scale, food mill or sieve, and a colander. Wash any utensils that will directly touch the food with soap and warm water before beginning.

PICK A SIZE CANNING JARS COME IN MANY SIZES, FROM 4 OUNCES TO 1 QUART. THOSE WITH WIDE MOUTHS ARE PERFECT FOR PICKLES. USE THE SIZE AND STYLE CALLED FOR IN EACH RECIPE.

GENERAL CANNING STEPS

For a boiling-water canner, pack food into canning jars by the raw-pack (cold-pack) or hot-pack method. In raw packing, uncooked food is packed into the canning jar and covered with boiling water, juice, or syrup (see chart introduction, page 209, for syrup information). In hot packing, food is partially cooked, packed into jars, and covered with cooking liquid. The following guidelines apply to both methods.

1 Wash empty canning jars in hot, soapy water. Rinse thoroughly. Place jars in the boiling-water canner (or a separate large pot). Cover jars with hot water; bring to a simmer over medium heat. For food processed under 10 minutes, boil the jars 10 minutes and keep warm in simmering water until needed. Set screw bands aside; place lids in a separate saucepan. Cover with water; bring to a simmer over medium heat (do not boil).

2 If using a separate pot for sterilizing the jars, fill the boiling-water canner half full; bring to boiling. Heat additional water in another large pot (to top off water in the canner); keep it hot but not boiling.

3 Prepare only as much food as needed to fill the maximum number of jars your canner will hold at one time. Keep the work area clean.

4 Remove sterilized jars from the hot water (see photo 1, page 201); place hot jars on cloth towels to prevent them from slipping during packing.

5 Pack food into jars using a wide-mouth funnel (see photo 2, page 201), allowing for adequate headspace (see tip, right). Ladle boiling liquid over the food, leaving adequate headspace.

6 Release trapped air bubbles by gently working a sterilized nonmetal utensil (such as the one provided in a canning kit) down the jars' sides. Add liquid, if needed, to maintain necessary headspace.

7 Wipe jar rims with a clean, damp cloth (see photo 4, page 201); food on the rims prevents a perfect seal. Place prepared lids on jars; add screw bands; tighten according to the manufacturer's directions (see photos 5 and 6, page 201).

8 Set each jar into the rack in the canner as it is filled and sealed. Jars should not touch each other. Replace canner cover each time you add a jar.

9 When all jars have been added, ladle hot water from the extra pot into canner to cover jars by 1 inch (see photo 7, page 201).

10 Cover; heat to a full rolling boil. Begin processing time, following recipe procedures and timings exactly. (See tip, page 211, if necessary to adjust for altitude.) Keep water boiling gently during processing, adding additional boiling water if level drops. If water stops boiling when you add more, stop timing, turn up heat, and wait for a full boil before resuming counting.

11 At end of processing, remove jars (see photo 8, page 201); place them on a rack or on towels in a draft-free area to cool. Leave at least 1 inch of space between jars to allow air to circulate.

12 After jars are completely cooled (12 to 24 hours), press center of each lid to check the seal (see photo 9, page 201). If the dip in the lid holds, the jar is sealed. If the lid bounces up and down, the jar isn't sealed. Check unsealed jars for flaws. Contents can be refrigerated and used within 2 to 3 days, frozen, or reprocessed within 24 hours. To reprocess, use a clean, sterilized jar and a new lid; process for full length of time specified. Mark label so you can use any recanned jars first. If jars have lost liquid but are still sealed, the contents are safe. However, any food not covered by liquid will discolor, so use these jars first.

13 Wipe jars and lids. Remove, wash, and dry screw bands; store for future use. Label jars with contents and date; include batch number if you can more than a load a day (if a jar spoils, you can identify others from same batch). Store jars in cool (50°F to 70°F), dry, dark place. Use within 1 year.

CHECKING HEADSPACE

THE SPACE BETWEEN THE TOP OF THE FOOD AND THE CONTAINER RIM IS THE HEADSPACE. LEAVING THE CORRECT AMOUNT IS ESSENTIAL.

CANNING: Headspace allows a vacuum to form and the jar to seal. Use a ruler to make sure you have the amount specified in each recipe (see photo 3, page 201).

FREEZING: Headspace provides room for food to expand as it freezes. When using unsweetened (dry) pack, leave a ½-inch headspace unless otherwise directed. When using water, sugar, or syrup pack in freezer containers with wide tops, leave a ½-inch headspace for pints and a 1-inch headspace for quarts. For narrow-top containers, don't fill above the "shoulder."

BOILING-WATER CANNING, STEP-BY-STEP

Once you understand the hows and whys of canning, the process will become a smooth and seamless operation. Use the guidelines, page 200, and these photos as a primer. **1.** Sterilize your jars and lids separately in simmering water; remove hot jars from water with a jar lifter. **2.** Ladle prepared food into the jar using a clean wide-mouth funnel. **3.** Allow for the proper headspace according to each recipe; double-check space with a ruler. **4.** Use a clean, damp cloth to remove any liquid or food from the jar rims. **5.** Remove jar lids from hot water with a magnetized lid wand; place on the jars. **6.** Secure screw bands in place. **7.** Once all the jars are added to the rack in the canner, add enough additional hot water to cover jars by 1 inch. **8.** Remove jars from hot water; cool for 24 hours. **9.** Check the seal by pressing gently on the lids.

FREEZING BASICS

FREEZING IS AN EASY WAY TO ENJOY FRUITS AND VEGETABLES FROM GARDENS OR FARMERS' MARKETS WELL INTO THE WINTER.

For best results, use top-quality, garden-fresh produce and follow these guidelines.

EQUIPMENT

PANS AND UTENSILS: To freeze vegetables and fruits, you need a colander and a large pot or saucepan that has a wire basket. An accurate freezer thermometer will help you regulate your freezer temperature at 0°F or below.

JARS, CONTAINERS, AND WRAPS: A variety of freezer containers and materials are available. Choose moistureproof and vaporproof materials that are able to withstand temperatures of 0°F or below and capable of being tightly sealed. For liquid or semiliquid foods, use rigid plastic freezer containers, freezer bags, or wide-mouth jars designed for freezing. Regular jars seldom are tempered to withstand freezer temperatures. For solid or dry-pack foods, use freezer bags, heavy-duty foil, plastic wrap for the freezer, or laminated freezer wrap.

GENERAL FREEZING STEPS

1 For freezing, select fruits and vegetables that are at their peak of maturity. Hold produce in the refrigerator if it can't be frozen immediately. Rinse and drain small quantities through several changes of cold water. Lift fruits and vegetables out of the water; do not let them soak. Prepare cleaned produce for freezing as specified in the charts on pages 205, 209, 213, and 219.

2 Blanch vegetables (and fruits when directed) by scalding them in boiling water for specified time (see photo 1, below). This stops or slows enzymes that cause loss of flavor and color, and toughen the food. Do not blanch in the microwave because it might not inactivate some enzymes. Timings vary with vegetable type and size.

Blanching is a heat-and-cool process. First fill a large pot with water, using 1 gallon of water per 1 pound of prepared food. Heat to boiling. Add prepared food to the boiling water (or place it in a wire basket and lower it into the water); cover. Start timing immediately. Cook over high heat for the time specified in the charts. (Add 1 minute if you live 5,000 feet or higher above sea level.) Near the end of the time, fill your sink or a large container with ice water. As soon as the blanching time is complete, use a slotted spoon to remove the food from the boiling water (or lift the wire basket out of the water). Immediately plunge the food into the ice water. Chill for the same amount of time it was boiled; drain well.

3 Spoon the cooled, drained food into freezer containers or bags (see photo 3, page 203), leaving specified headspace

---

BLANCHING PRODUCE, STEP-BY-STEP

1. Place produce, a few pieces at a time, in a large pot of boiling water; cook for times specified in the charts. Remove and plunge into a bowl of ice water. **2.** When food is cool, remove from ice water and cut into small pieces (for corn, cut from cob as shown). **3.** Spoon produce into freezer-safe bags or containers. **4.** Squeeze air from bags and seal. **5.** Label each container with contents, amount, and date.

(see tip, page 200). Fruits often are frozen with added sugar or liquid for better texture and flavor. For more information, refer to the directions in the chart introduction on page 209. Here are the various packing methods referred to in the chart.

UNSWEETENED OR DRY PACK: Do not add sugar or liquid to fruit; simply pack in a container. This is best for small whole fruits, such as berries.

WATER PACK: Cover the fruit with water or unsweetened fruit juice. Do not use glass jars. Maintain the recommended headspace.

SUGAR PACK: Place a small amount of fruit in the container and sprinkle lightly with sugar; repeat layering. Cover and let stand about 15 minutes or until juicy; seal.

SYRUP PACK: Cover fruit with a syrup of sugar and water as directed in chart introductions on pages 209 and 213.

4 Wipe container rims (if using). Seal bags or containers according to manufacturer's directions, pressing out as much air as possible. If necessary, use freezer tape around lid edges for a tight seal.

5. Label each container or bag with its contents, amount, and date (see photo 5, below). Lay bags flat; add packages to the freezer in batches to make sure food freezes quickly. Leave space

FREEZER BAGS
RESEALABLE, FREEZER-SAFE BAGS ARE AN INEXPENSIVE WAY TO STORE PRODUCE.

between packages so air can circulate around them. When frozen solid, the packages can be placed closer together.

6 Use frozen fruits and vegetables within 8 to 10 months. Vegetables are best cooked from a frozen state without thawing them first. Thaw fruits in their containers either in the refrigerator or in a bowl of cool water.

VACUUM SEALERS
VACUUM SEALERS PROTECT FOODS BY REMOVING EXTRA AIR AND CREATING A TIGHT SEAL.

If you want to preserve your fruits, vegetables, and meats through long-term freezing, a vacuum sealer is an investment to consider. Conventional storage bags and containers trap air in the container with the food, which can cause damage from frost and freezer burn. Because the sealer sucks all the air out of the bag before creating a tight seal, the food in the bags is better protected against the elements. A vacuum sealer costs between $75 and $200 and requires purchase of special bags designed for this use. Besides preserving garden produce, this is a great tool to help you maximize the shelf life of other food items you buy in bulk at club stores or on sale.

3 **4** **5**

TOMATOES

ENJOY THE FLAVOR OF GARDEN-FRESH TOMATOES YEAR-ROUND WITH THE HELP OF YOUR FREEZER OR CANNER.

Although long touted as a vegetable, tomatoes—with their plentiful seeds and juicy pulp—are actually a fruit. Because of their high acidity, they can be canned just like other fruits with only a bit of added citrus juice or vinegar. You can process tomatoes whole, crushed, or halved, and the fresh flavors of summer will shine through your favorite recipes all year long. The creative joys of preserving summer's bounty come when you make recipes for pasta sauce and salsa. Or take it a step further and brew up tomato paste, chili sauce, barbecue sauce, ketchup, and more.

CHUNKY SALSA

PREP: 2 HOURS **COOK:** 100 MINUTES
PROCESS: 15 MINUTES **MAKES:** ABOUT 5 PINTS

- 8 pounds ripe tomatoes (about 16 medium)
- 2 cups seeded and chopped fresh Anaheim chile peppers (2 to 3) (see tip, page 24)
- ⅓ to ½ cup seeded and chopped fresh jalapeño chile peppers (2 large) (see tip, page 24)
- 2 cups chopped onions (2 large)
- ½ cup snipped fresh cilantro
- ½ cup lime juice
- ½ cup white vinegar
- ½ of a 6-ounce can tomato paste (⅓ cup)
- 5 cloves garlic, minced
- 1 teaspoon cumin seeds, toasted (see tip, page 47) and crushed
- 1 teaspoon salt
- 1 teaspoon black pepper

PICK OF THE CROP MOST TOMATOES CAN BE CANNED; HOWEVER, SOME HEIRLOOM VARIETIES ARE NOT THE BEST BECAUSE THEY RELEASE A LOT OF LIQUID. ROMA TOMATOES ARE GREAT FOR SAUCE.

1 If desired, peel tomatoes. Seed, core, and coarsely chop tomatoes (you should have about 15 cups). Place tomatoes in a large colander. Let drain 30 minutes.

2 Place drained tomatoes in a 7- to 8-quart stainless-steel, enamel, or nonstick heavy pot. Bring to boiling; reduce heat. Boil gently, uncovered, about 1½ hours or until desired consistency, stirring occasionally. Add chile peppers, onions, cilantro, lime juice, vinegar, tomato paste, garlic, crushed cumin, salt, and black pepper. Return mixture to boiling; reduce heat. Simmer, uncovered, for 10 minutes. Remove from heat.

3 Ladle hot salsa* into hot, sterilized pint canning jars, leaving a ½-inch headspace. Wipe jar rims; adjust lids. Process in a boiling-water canner for 15 minutes (start timing when water returns to boiling). Remove jars; cool on racks. (See "Canning Basics," pages 199–201.)

*TIP: If you have salsa that won't fill another pint jar, place extra salsa in an airtight container and chill up to 1 week.

PER 2 TABLESPOONS: 13 cal., 0 g total fat, 0 mg chol., 40 mg sodium, 3 g carbo., 1 g fiber, 1 g pro. EXCHANGES: ½ Other Carbo.

LOW FAT

FREEZER STEWED TOMATOES

PREP: 1 HOUR **MAKES:** ABOUT 3 QUARTS

- 8 pounds ripe firm tomatoes
- 1 cup chopped celery (2 stalks)
- ½ cup chopped onion (1 medium)
- ½ cup chopped green sweet pepper (1 small)
- 2 teaspoons sugar
- 2 teaspoons salt

1 Wash tomatoes; remove peels, stems, and cores. Chop tomatoes (you should have 17 cups).

2 Place chopped tomatoes in an 8- to 10-quart heavy pot. Add celery, onion, pepper, sugar, and salt to the pot. Bring to boiling; reduce heat. Simmer, covered, for 10 minutes, stirring frequently to prevent sticking.

3 Place pot of stewed tomatoes in a sink filled with ice water; let tomatoes cool, stirring frequently. Ladle tomatoes into wide-mouth freezer containers, leaving a ½-inch headspace. Seal and label; freeze for up to 10 months. (See "Freezing Basics," pages 202–203.)

PER ½ CUP: 37 cal., 0 g total fat, 0 mg chol., 246 mg sodium, 8 g carbo., 2 g fiber, 2 g pro. EXCHANGES: 1½ Vegetable

CANNING & FREEZING TOMATOES

Read "Canning Basics" and "Freezing Basics," pages 199–203. Allow 2½ to 3½ pounds unblemished tomatoes per quart. Wash tomatoes. To peel tomatoes, see photos 1 and 2, page 206.

Tomatoes	Preparation	Boiling-Water Canning	Freezing
Crushed	Wash and peel tomatoes. Cut into quarters; add enough to a large pan to cover bottom. Crush with a wooden spoon. Heat and stir until boiling. Slowly add remaining pieces, stirring constantly. Simmer for 5 minutes. Fill jars. Add bottled lemon juice* and salt.** Leave a ½-inch headspace.***	Process pints for 35 minutes and quarts for 45 minutes.	Set pan of tomatoes in ice water to cool. Fill containers, leaving a 1-inch headspace.***
Whole or halved, no added liquid	Wash and peel tomatoes; halve, if desired. Fill jars, pressing to fill spaces with juice. Add bottled lemon juice* and salt.** Leave a ½-inch headspace.***	Process pints and quarts for 85 minutes.	Fill freezer containers, leaving a 1-inch headspace.*** (Use only for cooking; freezing changes the texture.)
Whole or halved, water-pack	Wash and peel tomatoes; halve, if desired. Fill jars. Add bottled lemon juice* and salt.** Add boiling water, leaving a ½-inch headspace.*** Or heat tomatoes in saucepan with enough water to cover; simmer for 5 minutes. Fill jars with tomatoes and cooking liquid. Add bottled lemon juice* and salt.** Leave a ½-inch headspace.***	Process pints for 40 minutes and quarts for 45 minutes.	If heated, set pan of tomatoes in cold water to cool. Fill containers, leaving a 1-inch headspace.***

* Add 1 tablespoon bottled lemon juice for pints, 2 tablespoons for quarts.
**If desired, add salt: ¼ to ½ teaspoon for pints; ½ to 1 teaspoon for quarts.
***See tip, page 200.

ROASTED GARLIC PASTA SAUCE

PREP: 2½ HOURS **BAKE:** 40 MINUTES **OVEN:** 400°F
STAND: 15 MINUTES **COOK:** 60 MINUTES
PROCESS: 35 MINUTES **MAKES:** ABOUT 6 PINTS

- 6 bulbs garlic
- 3 tablespoons olive oil
- 4 medium red, yellow, and/or green sweet peppers, halved and seeded
- 12 pounds ripe tomatoes (about 25 tomatoes), peeled (see photos 1 and 2, below)
- 3 tablespoons packed brown sugar
- 2 tablespoons kosher salt or 4 teaspoons salt
- 1 tablespoon balsamic vinegar
- 1 teaspoon freshly ground black pepper
- 2 cups lightly packed fresh basil leaves, chopped
- 1 cup lightly packed assorted fresh herbs (such as oregano, thyme, parsley, Italian parsley, or basil), chopped
- 6 tablespoons lemon juice

1 Preheat oven to 400°F. Peel away the dry outer layers of skin from garlic bulbs, leaving skins and cloves intact. Cut off the pointed top portions (about ½ inch), leaving bulbs intact but exposing the individual cloves (see tip, page 603). Place the garlic bulbs, cut sides up, in a 1- to 1½-quart casserole. Drizzle with about 1 tablespoon of the olive oil. Cover casserole. Arrange peppers, cut sides down, on a foil-lined baking sheet; brush with remaining olive oil. Bake garlic and peppers for 40 to 45 minutes or until pepper skins are charred and cloves of garlic are soft. Cool garlic on a wire rack until cool enough to handle. Pull up sides of foil and pinch together to fully enclose the peppers. Let peppers stand 15 to 20 minutes or until cool enough to handle. When peppers are cool enough to handle, peel off skins and discard. Chop peppers; set aside.

2 Remove garlic cloves from papers by squeezing the bottoms of the bulbs. Place garlic cloves in a food processor. Cut peeled tomatoes into chunks and add some of the chunks to the food processor with garlic. Cover and process until chopped. Transfer chopped garlic and tomatoes to a 7- to 8-quart nonreactive heavy pot. Repeat chopping remaining tomatoes, in batches, in the food processor. Add all tomatoes to the pot.

3 Add brown sugar, salt, vinegar, and black pepper to the tomato mixture. Bring to boiling. Boil steadily, uncovered, for 50 minutes, stirring occasionally. Add chopped, peeled peppers to tomato mixture. Continue boiling for 10 to 20 minutes more or until mixture is reduced to about 11 cups and reaches desired sauce consistency, stirring occasionally. Remove from heat; stir in basil and assorted herbs.

4 Spoon 1 tablespoon lemon juice into each of six hot, sterilized pint canning jars. Ladle sauce into jars with lemon juice, leaving a ½-inch headspace. Wipe the jar rims; adjust lids. Process filled jars in a boiling-water canner for 35 minutes (start timing when water returns to boiling). Remove jars; cool on wire racks. (See "Canning Basics," pages 199–201.)

PER ½ CUP: 95 cal., 3 g total fat (0 g sat. fat, 0 g trans fat), 0 mg chol., 542 mg sodium, 17 g carbo., 4 g fiber, 3 g pro.
EXCHANGES: 1½ Vegetable, ½ Other Carbo., ½ Fat

PEELING TOMATOES, STEP-BY-STEP

1. To peel tomatoes, use a sharp knife to cut a shallow X on the bottom of each tomato. Immerse tomatoes, in batches, in boiling water to cover. Cook for 30 to 60 seconds or until tomato skins split open. **2.** Transfer tomatoes to a large bowl of ice water using a slotted spoon. When cool enough to handle, use a knife or your fingers to peel skin off tomatoes.

PASTA SAUCE FIX-UPS WHEN REHEATING THIS SAUCE TO SERVE, ADD ONE OR MORE OF THE FOLLOWING: COOKED MEATBALLS OR SAUSAGE, A SPLASH OF RED WINE, OR CHOPPED RIPE OLIVES, MUSHROOMS, ARTICHOKE HEARTS, OR GARDEN VEGETABLES.

APPLES, PEARS & STONEFRUIT

THE PARADE OF SUMMER AND FALL FRUITS KICKS CANNING AND FREEZING INTO HIGH GEAR.

Whether you pluck a bucket of these summer and fall beauties straight from the tree or find a hot deal on an extra-large bag at the supermarket, you can preserve them in all their glory. Whip up tasty canned applesauce, apple butter, and fruit cocktails, or freeze fruits lightly sweetened to create yummy pies and other baked goodies later. Note that the best types of apples for canning and freezing include Golden Delicious, Rome Beauty, and Jonathan. If your peaches and apricots aren't ripe when you purchase them, ripen them on the counter or in a paper bag. Avoid purchasing immature, rock-hard fruit that is out of season.

APPLESAUCE

PREP: 1 HOUR **COOK:** 25 MINUTES
PROCESS: 15 MINUTES **MAKES:** ABOUT 6 PINTS

- 8 pounds cooking apples, cored and quartered (24 cups)
- 2 cups water
- ¼ cup fresh lemon juice, strained
- ¾ to 1¼ cups granulated sugar

1 In an 8- to 10-quart heavy pot combine apples, water, and lemon juice. Bring to boiling; reduce heat. Simmer, covered, for 25 to 30 minutes until very tender, stirring often.

2 Press apples through a food mill or sieve. Return pulp to pot; discard skins. Stir in sugar to taste. If necessary, add ½ to 1 cup water for desired consistency. Bring to boiling.

3 Ladle hot applesauce into hot, sterilized pint canning jars, leaving a ½-inch headspace. Wipe jar rims and adjust lids. Process in a boiling-water canner for 15 minutes for pints (start timing when

CHOOSING APPLES MOST APPLES YOU USE FOR COOKING WILL WORK FOR CANNING AND FREEZING. AVOID SOFT APPLE VARIETIES—SUCH AS RED DELICIOUS—AND THOSE WITH BRUISES AND GOUGES.

water returns to boiling). Remove jars from hot water; cool on wire racks. (See "Canning Basics," pages 199–201.)

SPICED APPLESAUCE: Prepare as directed on page 208, except add 10 inches stick cinnamon and 1½ teaspoons apple pie spice in Step 1. Simmer as directed. Remove stick cinnamon and discard. Substitute ¾ cup packed brown sugar for the granulated sugar. Stir in enough additional brown sugar to taste (¼ to ¾ cup).

VERY BERRY APPLESAUCE: Prepare as directed on page 208, except replace 1 pound (4 cups) of the apples with 1 pound (4 cups) fresh or frozen thawed raspberries and/or strawberries, and decrease water to 1½ cups in Step 1.

PER ½ CUP PLAIN, SPICED, OR BERRY VARIATIONS: 81 cal., 0 g total fat, 0 mg chol., 1 mg sodium, 21 g carbo., 2 g fiber, 0 g pro.
EXCHANGES: 1 Fruit, ½ Other Carbo.

FREEZER DIRECTIONS: Place pot of applesauce in a sink filled with ice water; stir mixture to cool. Ladle into wide-mouth freezer containers, leaving ½-inch headspace. Seal and label; freeze for up to 8 months. (See "Freezing Basics," page 202–203.)

TAKE A CLOSE LOOK
ALWAYS EXAMINE HOME-CANNED JARS OF FOOD CAREFULLY TO SEE IF THE CONTENTS ARE MOLDY, MURKY, OR FOAMY. ALSO EXAMINE THE LID TO SEE IF IT IS SWOLLEN OR LEAKING. WHEN IN DOUBT, THROW IT OUT.

CANNING & FREEZING APPLES, PEARS, STONE FRUITS

Read "Canning Basics" and "Freezing Basics," pages 199–203. Wash fresh fruits with cool, clear tap water but do not soak them; drain. Follow preparation directions, below. If you choose to can or freeze fruits with syrup, select the syrup that best suits the fruit and your taste. Generally, heavier syrups are used with sour fruits, and lighter syrups are recommended for mild fruits. To prepare a syrup, place the following recommended amounts of sugar and water in a large saucepan. Heat until the sugar dissolves. Skim off foam, if necessary. Use the syrup hot for canned fruits and chilled for frozen fruits. Allow ½ to ⅔ cup syrup for each 2 cups fruit. For a very thin syrup, use 1 cup sugar and 4 cups water to yield about 4 cups syrup. For a thin syrup, use 1⅔ cups sugar and 4 cups water to yield about 4¼ cups syrup. For a medium syrup, use 2⅔ cups sugar and 4 cups water to yield about 4⅔ cups syrup. For a heavy syrup, use 4 cups sugar and 4 cups water to yield about 5¾ cups syrup.

Food	Preparation	Boiling-Water Canning, Raw Pack	Boiling-Water Canning, Hot Pack	Freezing
Apples, Pears	Allow 2 to 3 pounds per quart. For apples, select varieties that are crisp, not mealy, in texture. Peel and core; halve, quarter, or slice. Dip into ascorbic acid color keeper solution; drain.	Not recommended.	Simmer in syrup for 5 minutes, stirring occasionally. Fill jars with fruit and syrup, leaving a ½-inch headspace.* For apples, process pints and quarts for 20 minutes. For pears, process pints for 20 minutes and quarts for 25 minutes.	Use a syrup, sugar, or unsweetened pack (see Step 3, page 203), leaving the recommended headspace.*
Apricots, Nectarines, Peaches	Allow 2 to 3 pounds per quart. To peel peaches (peeling nectarines and apricots is not necessary), immerse in boiling water for 30 to 60 seconds or until skins start to split; remove and plunge into cold water. Halve and pit. If desired, slice. Treat with ascorbic acid color keeper solution; drain.	Fill jars, placing fruit cut sides down. Add boiling syrup or water, leaving a ½-inch headspace.* Process pints for 25 minutes and quarts for 30 minutes. Do not raw-pack apricots. (Note: Hot packing generally results in a better product.)	Add fruit to hot syrup; bring to boiling. Fill jars with fruit (placing cut sides down) and syrup, leaving a ½-inch headspace.* Process pints for 20 minutes and quarts for 25 minutes.	Use a syrup, sugar, or water pack (see Step 3, page 203), leaving the recommended headspace.*

*See tip, page 200.

APPLE BUTTER

PREP: 45 MINUTES **COOK:** 2 HOURS
PROCESS: 5 MINUTES **MAKES:** 6 HALF-PINTS

- 4½ pounds tart cooking apples, cored and quartered (about 14 medium)
- 3 cups apple cider or apple juice
- 2 cups granulated sugar
- 2 tablespoons fresh lemon juice, strained
- ½ teaspoon ground cinnamon

1 In an 8- to 10-quart heavy pot combine apples and cider. Bring to boiling; reduce heat. Simmer, covered, for 30 minutes, stirring occasionally. Press apple mixture through a food mill or sieve until you have 7½ cups. Return pulp to pot.

2 Stir in sugar, lemon juice, and cinnamon. Bring to boiling; reduce heat. Cook, uncovered, over very low heat for 1½ to 1¾ hours or until very thick and mixture mounds on a spoon, stirring often. Ladle hot apple butter into hot, sterilized half-pint canning jars, leaving a ¼-inch headspace. Wipe jar rims; adjust lids. Process filled jars in a boiling-water canner for 5 minutes (start timing when water returns to boiling). Remove jars from canner; cool on wire racks. (See "Canning Basics," pages 199–201.)

APPLE-PEAR BUTTER: Prepare recipe as directed, except substitute 2 pounds cored, quartered ripe pears for 2 pounds of the apples.

CARAMEL APPLE BUTTER: Prepare recipe as directed, except decrease granulated sugar to ½ cup and add 1½ cups packed brown sugar.

PER 1 TABLESPOON PLAIN, APPLE-PEAR, OR CARAMEL APPLE VARIATIONS: 28 cal., 0 g total fat, 0 mg chol., 0 mg sodium, 7 g carbo., 0 g fiber, 0 g pro.
EXCHANGES: ½ Other Carbo.

FREEZER DIRECTIONS: Place pot of apple butter in a sink filled with ice water; stir mixture to cool. Ladle into wide-mouth freezer containers, leaving a ½-inch headspace. Seal and label; freeze up to 10 months. Apple butter might darken on freezing. (See "Freezing Basics," page 202–203.)

APPLE BUTTER SERVE-ALONGS: SLATHER RICH APPLE BUTTER ON ENGLISH MUFFINS, TOAST, AND BAGELS. OR USE IN PLACE OF JAM, JELLY, OR PRESERVES.

APPLE BUTTER

MINTED PEARS

PREP: 45 MINUTES **COOK:** 5 MINUTES
PROCESS: 20 MINUTES **MAKES:** 7 PINTS

> 1 cup lightly packed fresh mint leaves
> 1 cup water
> 5⅔ cups water
> ¾ cup sugar
> 7 pounds pears (about 15 to 20)
> Ascorbic acid color keeper solution

1 In a small saucepan mash the mint leaves with the back of a spoon. Stir in the 1 cup water; heat to boiling. Remove from heat; let stand for 10 minutes. Strain liquid through a sieve, pressing on the mint leaves with the back of a spoon; discard leaves. Set mint-flavored water aside.

2 For syrup, in a 4- to 6-quart pot combine the 5⅔ cups water and sugar. Heat and stir until sugar dissolves. Add the mint-flavored water. Keep syrup hot, but do not boil.

3 Wash, peel, halve, and core pears; place pear halves in ascorbic acid color keeper solution as soon as peeled and cut. Drain pear halves; add to syrup. Heat to boiling. Boil, covered, for 5 minutes.

4 Using a slotted spoon, pack hot pear halves into hot, sterilized pint canning jars, leaving a ½-inch headspace. Cover with the hot syrup, leaving a ½-inch headspace. Wipe jar rims; adjust lids. Process filled pint jars in a boiling-water canner for 20 minutes (start timing when water returns to boiling). Remove jars from canner; cool on wire racks. (See "Canning Basics," pages 199–201.)

PER 2 PEAR HALVES: 163 cal., 1 g total fat (0 g sat. fat, 0 g trans fat), 0 mg chol., 3 mg sodium, 42 g carbo., 4 g fiber, 1 g pro. EXCHANGES: 2 Fruit, 1 Other Carbo.

ROSY FRUIT COCKTAIL

PREP: 60 MINUTES **PROCESS:** 20 MINUTES
MAKES: 9 PINTS

> 5¼ cups Light Syrup
> 1 2-pound pineapple
> 3 pounds peaches
> 3 pounds pears
> 1 pound dark sweet cherries
> 1 pound seedless green grapes

1 Prepare Light Syrup (measure 5¼ cups; might not use all of the syrup); keep hot but not boiling.

2 Wash fruit. Using a large sharp knife, slice off the bottom stem end and the green top of pineapple. Stand pineapple on one cut end and slice off the skin in wide strips from top to bottom; discard skin. To remove the eyes, cut diagonally around the fruit, following the pattern of the eyes and making narrow wedge-shape grooves into the pineapple. Cut away as little of the meat as possible. Cut pineapple in half lengthwise; place pieces cut sides down and cut lengthwise again. Cut off and discard center core from each quarter. Finely chop pineapple. Measure 3 cups pineapple. Peel, pit, and cut peaches into cubes. Measure 8½ cups peaches. Peel, core, and cut pears into cubes. Measure 6½ cups pears. Halve and pit cherries. Measure 2½ cups cherries. Remove stems from grapes. Measure 3 cups grapes.

3 In a 4- to 6-quart pot combine pineapple, peaches, pears, cherries, and grapes. Add hot syrup; heat to boiling. Pack hot fruit and syrup into hot, sterilized jars, leaving a ½-inch headspace. Wipe jar rims; adjust lids. Process filled jars in a boiling-water canner for 20 minutes for half-pints or pints (start timing when water returns to boiling). Remove jars from canner; cool on wire racks. (See "Canning Basics," pages 199–201.)

LIGHT SYRUP: In a large saucepan cook and stir 1¼ cups sugar, 5 cups water, and, if desired, one 3-inch stick of cinnamon over medium heat until sugar dissolves. Remove and discard cinnamon.

PER ½ CUP: 108 cal., 0 g total fat, 0 mg chol., 1 mg sodium, 27 g carbo., 2 g fiber, 1 g pro. EXCHANGES: 1 Fruit, 1 Other Carbo.

ALTITUDE ADJUSTMENTS

THE TIMINGS IN THESE RECIPES ARE FOR ALTITUDES UP TO 1,000 FEET ABOVE SEA LEVEL. WATER BOILS AT LOWER TEMPERATURES AT HIGHER ALTITUDES, SO FOLLOW THESE ADJUSTMENTS.

BLANCHING: Add 1 minute if you live 5,000 feet or more above sea level.

BOILING-WATER CANNING: Call your county extension service for detailed instructions.

JELLIES AND JAMS: Add 1 minute processing time for each additional 1,000 feet.

STERILIZING JARS: Boil jars an additional 1 minute for each additional 1,000 feet.

BERRIES, CHERRIES, GRAPES & RHUBARB

SWEET, TART, SOUR—THESE ARE THE FLAVORS OF THE SEASON. GROW YOUR OWN IN THE GARDEN OR VISIT A FARMER'S MARKET OR PICK-YOUR-OWN FARM.

Fresh berries, rhubarb, and grapes make exceptional jams, jellies, and preserves that are perfect for spreading on toast, sandwiches, and English muffins. But if you lack the time to prepare a recipe when they're fresh, you can freeze all of these fruits with little effort and use them in your cooking throughout the winter and spring. Imagine a fresh baked berry or cherry pie during the Christmas season.

LOW FAT

GRAPE JAM

PREP: 65 MINUTES **COOK:** 38 MINUTES
PROCESS: 5 MINUTES
MAKES: ABOUT 6 HALF-PINTS

> 3 to 3½ pounds Concord grapes
> 2 cups water
> 4½ cups sugar

1 Wash and stem grapes. Measure 8 cups. Remove skins from half of the grapes (see photo 1, below); set grape skins aside.

2 In an 8- to 10-quart heavy pot combine the skinned and unskinned grapes. Cover and cook 10 minutes or until very soft. Press grapes through a sieve or food mill (see photo 2, below); discard seeds and cooked skins. Measure 3 cups of strained pulp; return to pot. Stir in the uncooked grape skins and water. Cook, covered, for 10 minutes. Uncover; stir in sugar. Bring mixture to a full rolling boil, stirring often (see photo 3,

MAKING GRAPE JAM, STEP-BY-STEP

1. To remove skins, squeeze grape until the pulp pops out. **2.** Press cooked grapes through a sieve or food mill to remove skin and seeds. **3.** A full rolling boil occurs when the bubbles break the surface so rapidly you can't stir them down. **4.** When the mixture is ready, it will slide in sheets (rather than drips) from a metal spoon. **5.** Gently scoop the foam off the top with a spoon.

page 212). Boil, uncovered, for 18 to 24 minutes or until jam sheets off a metal spoon (see photo 4, page 212).

3 Remove pot from heat; quickly skim off foam with a metal spoon (see photo 5, page 212). Ladle at once into hot, sterilized half-pint canning jars, leaving a ¼-inch headspace. Wipe jar rims; adjust lids. Process in a boiling-water canner for 5 minutes (start timing when water returns to boiling). Remove jars; cool on racks until set. (See "Canning Basics," pages 199–201.)

PER TABLESPOON: 42 cal., 0 g total fat, 0 mg chol., 0 mg sodium, 11 g carbo., 0 g fiber, 0 g pro.
EXCHANGES: 1 Other Carbo.

JAMS AND JELLLIES
FOLLOW THESE TIPS AND YOUR JAMS AND JELLIES WILL BE SECOND TO NONE.

■ Add liquid or powdered pectin as called for; do not substitute one for the other.

■ Accurately measure the sugar called for in the recipe; it acts as a preservative, develops flavor, and aids in jelling.

■ Prepare only one batch at a time; do not double or triple recipes.

■ To prevent overboiling, fill pots no more than one-third full with jam or jelly mixture.

CANNING & FREEZING BERRIES, CHERRIES & RHUBARB

Read "Canning Basics" and "Freezing Basics," pages 199–203. Wash fresh fruits with cool, clear tap water but do not soak them; drain. Follow preparation directions, below. If you choose to can or freeze fruits with syrup, select the syrup that best suits the fruit and your taste. Generally, heavier syrups are used with sour fruits, and lighter syrups are recommended for mild fruits. To prepare a syrup, place the recommended amounts of sugar and water in a large saucepan (see chart introduction, page 209). Heat until the sugar dissolves. Skim off foam, if necessary. Use the syrup hot for canned fruits and chilled for frozen fruits. Allow ½ to ⅔ cup syrup for each 2 cups fruit.

Food	Preparation	Boiling-Water Canning, Raw Pack	Boiling-Water Canning, Hot Pack	Freezing
Berries	Allow 1 to 3 pounds per quart. Can or freeze blackberries, blueberries, currants, elderberries, gooseberries, huckle-berries, loganberries, and mulberries. Freeze (do not can) boysenberries, raspberries, and strawberries.	Fill jars with black-berries, loganberries, or mulberries. Shake down gently. Add boiling syrup, leaving a ½-inch headspace.* Process pints for 15 minutes and quarts for 20 minutes.	Simmer blueberries, currants, elderberries, gooseberries, and huckleberries in water for 30 seconds; drain. Fill jars with berries and hot syrup, leaving a ½-inch headspace.* Process pints and quarts for 15 minutes.	Slice strawberries, if desired. Use a syrup, sugar, or unsweetened pack (see Step 3, page 203), leaving the recommended headspace.*
Cherries	Allow 2 to 3 pounds per quart. If desired, treat with ascorbic acid color keeper solution; drain. If unpitted, prick skin on opposite sides to prevent splitting.	Fill jars, shaking down gently. Add boiling syrup or water, leaving a ½-inch headspace.* Process pints and quarts for 25 minutes.	Add cherries to hot syrup; bring to boiling. Fill jars with fruit and syrup, leaving a ½-inch headspace.* Process pints for 15 minutes and quarts for 20 minutes.	Use a syrup, sugar, or unsweetened pack (see Step 3, page 203), leaving the recommended headspace.*
Rhubarb	Allow 1½ pounds per quart. Discard leaves and woody ends. Cut into ½- to 1-inch pieces. Freeze for best quality.	Not recommended.	In a saucepan sprinkle ½ cup sugar over each 4 cups fruit; mix well. Let stand until juice appears. Bring slowly to boiling, stirring gently. Fill jars with hot fruit and juice, leaving a ½-inch headspace.* Process pints and quarts for 15 minutes.	Blanch for 1 minute; cool quickly and drain. Use a syrup or unsweetened pack (see Step 3, page 203) or use a sugar pack of ½ cup sugar to each 3 cups fruit, leaving the recommended headspace.*

*See tip, page 200.

RASPBERRY JAM

PREP: 35 MINUTES **PROCESS:** 5 MINUTES
MAKES: ABOUT 7 HALF-PINTS

12 cups fresh raspberries
1 1.75-ounce package regular powdered
  fruit pectin
½ teaspoon butter
7 cups sugar

1 In an 8-quart heavy pot crush berries; measure 5 cups crushed berries. Sieve half of the crushed berries (see photo 2, page 212). Stir in pectin and butter. Heat on high, stirring constantly, until mixture comes to a full rolling boil (see photo 3, page 212). Add sugar. Return to boiling; boil 1 minute, stirring constantly. Remove from heat; skim off foam with a metal spoon (see photo 5, page 212).

2 Ladle into hot, sterilized half-pint canning jars, leaving a ¼-inch headspace. Wipe rims; adjust lids. Process in a boiling-water canner for 5 minutes (start timing when water returns to boiling). Remove jars; cool on racks. (See "Canning Basics," pages 199–201.) Flip jars to distribute fruit.

STRAWBERRY JAM: Prepare as directed, except substitute the 12 cups raspberries with 3 quarts fresh hulled strawberries. Do not sieve.

PER 1 TABLESPOON RASPBERRY OR STRAWBERRY
VARIATION: 54 cal., 0 g total fat, 0 mg chol., 0 mg sodium,
14 g carbo., 0 g fiber, 0 g pro.
EXCHANGES: 1 Other Carbo.

ORANGE MARMALADE

PREP: 55 MINUTES **COOK:** 31 MINUTES
PROCESS: 5 MINUTES **STAND:** 2 WEEKS
MAKES: 6 HALF-PINTS

4 medium oranges
1 medium lemon
1½ cups water
⅛ teaspoon baking soda
5 cups sugar
½ of a 6-ounce package (1 foil pouch) liquid
  fruit pectin

1 Score orange and lemon peels into four lengthwise sections; remove peels. Scrape off white portions; discard. Cut peels into thin strips. In a saucepan bring peels, water, and baking soda to boiling. Cover; simmer for 20 minutes. Do not drain. Section fruits, reserving juices; discard seeds. Add fruits and juices to peels; return to boiling. Cover; simmer 10 minutes (should have 3 cups mixture).

2 In a 10-quart heavy pot combine fruit mixture and sugar. Bring to a full rolling boil (see photo 3, page 212), stirring constantly. Quickly stir in pectin. Return to a full rolling boil; boil for 1 minute, stirring constantly. Remove from heat; skim off foam with a metal spoon (see photo 5, page 212).

3 Ladle into hot, sterilized half-pint canning jars, leaving a ¼-inch headspace. Wipe jar rims; adjust lids. Process in a boiling-water canner for 5 minutes (start timing when water returns to boiling). Remove jars; cool on racks. Allow to set for 2 weeks before serving. (See "Canning Basics," pages 199–201.)

STRAWBERRY-LEMON MARMALADE: *(photo, page 197)* Prepare as directed, except omit oranges and increase to 2 lemons. Reduce water to ½ cup. Measure 3 cups hulled crushed strawberries. Stir into mixture with the lemon sections.

PER 1 TABLESPOON ORANGE OR STRAWBERRY-LEMON
VARIATION: 44 cal., 0 g total fat, 0 mg chol., 2 mg sodium,
11 g carbo., 0 g fiber, 0 g pro.
EXCHANGES: 1 Other Carbo.

STRAWBERRY FREEZER JAM

PREP: 35 MINUTES **STAND:** 10 MINUTES + 24 HOURS
MAKES: 5 HALF-PINTS*

4 cups strawberries
4 cups sugar
½ teaspoon finely shredded lemon peel
1 1.75-ounce package regular powdered
  fruit pectin
¾ cup water

1 Crush berries until you have 2 cups. Mix berries, sugar, and lemon peel. Let stand for 10 minutes, stirring occasionally. In a saucepan combine pectin and water. Bring to boiling over high heat; boil 1 minute, stirring constantly. Add to berry mixture; stir about 3 minutes or until sugar dissolves and mixture is not grainy.

2 Ladle into half-pint freezer containers, leaving a ½-inch headspace. Seal; label. Let stand at room temperature for 24 hours. Store up to 3 weeks in the refrigerator or for up to 1 year in the freezer. (See "Freezing Basics," pages 202–203.)

*****NOTE:** Yields vary for other flavors (page 215).

PER 1 TABLESPOON: 41 cal., 0 g total fat, 0 mg chol.,
0 mg sodium, 11 g carbo., 0 g fiber, 0 g pro.
EXCHANGES: 1 Other Carbo.

10 TO TRY— FREEZER JAMS

Start with Strawberry Freezer Jam, page 214. Prepare as directed, except replace strawberries with the following fruits for each variation. **1. RASPBERRY-ORANGE:** Measure 3 cups crushed raspberries. Increase sugar to 5¼ cups. Use orange peel for lemon peel. **2. STRAWBERRY-BRANDY:** Stir 3 tablespoons brandy into crushed berries with sugar. **3. CHERRY-BERRY:** Measure 1½ cups finely chopped tart red cherries. Add 1 cup crushed blueberries. Increase sugar to 4½ cups. **4. PEAR-BERRY:** Measure 3 cups finely chopped, peeled pear. Add 1 cup crushed raspberries. Increase sugar to 5 cups; add ¼ teaspoon anise flavoring. **5. TROPICAL:** Measure 3 cups crushed, peeled mango. Omit lemon peel; add ¼ cup pineapple juice. Increase sugar to 5 cups. **6. SPICED BLUEBERRY:** Measure 3 cups crushed blueberries. Increase sugar to 5¼ cups. Add 1 teaspoon ground cinnamon with sugar. **7. SPICED PEACH:** Measure 3 cups chopped, peeled peaches. Omit lemon peel; add 2 tablespoons lemon juice. Increase sugar to 4½ cups; add ½ teaspoon apple pie spice with sugar. **8. BERRY-RHUBARB:** Measure 1½ cups crushed strawberries. Add 1 cup finely chopped rhubarb. Increase sugar to 5 cups. **9. BLACKBERRY-LIME:** Measure 3 cups crushed blackberries. Increase sugar to 5¼ cups. Use lime peel for lemon peel. **10. APRICOT:** Measure 2½ cups finely chopped apricots. Omit lemon peel; add 2 tablespoons tangerine juice. Increase sugar to 5½ cups.

VEGETABLES

PICKLES, RELISHES, AND PEPPER JELLY—THEY'RE ALL PERFECT WAYS TO PRESERVE A BOUNTY OF GARDEN VEGGIES .

Vegetables are low-acid foods and cannot be canned with a water-bath canner unless they have plenty of extra acid—such as vinegar—in the recipe. The following recipes are all crafted to contain the adequate amount of acid, so be sure not to dilute the vinegar more than is recommended. When pickling with high levels of vinegar, use only stoneware, glass, enamel, stainless-steel, or nonstick pans and food-grade plastic containers and utensils. To can vegetables without pickling them, you must use a pressure canner and follow the manufacturer's directions closely. Alternately, you can freeze vegetables and enjoy them throughout the year. To freeze vegetables, see "Freezing Basics," pages 202–203.

LOW FAT

DILL PICKLES

PREP: 30 MINUTES **PROCESS:** 10 MINUTES
STAND: 1 WEEK **MAKES:** 6 PINTS

    3 pounds 4-inch pickling cucumbers*
       (about 36)
    3 cups water
    3 cups white vinegar
    ¼ cup pickling salt
    ¼ cup sugar
    6 to 12 heads fresh dill or 6 tablespoons
       dill seeds

1 Thoroughly rinse cucumbers. Remove stems and cut off a slice from each blossom end (see photo 1, below). In a large stainless-steel, enamel, or nonstick saucepan combine water, vinegar, pickling salt, and sugar. Bring mixture to boiling.

2 Pack cucumbers loosely into hot, sterilized pint canning jars, leaving a ½-inch headspace. Add 1 to 2 heads of dill or 1 tablespoon dill seeds to each jar (see photo 2, below). Pour hot vinegar mixture over cucumbers, leaving a ½-inch headspace (see photo 3, below). Discard any remaining hot vinegar mixture. Wipe jar rims and adjust lids.

MAKING DILL PICKLES, STEP-BY-STEP

1. Use a small knife to cut blossom end from each cucumber. **2.** Cut large cucumbers into spears; loosely pack cucumbers and spears in jars. Add herbs and seasonings to jar after adding cucumbers. **3.** Using a funnel, ladle vinegar mixture into jars, leaving a ½-inch headspace.

3 Process filled jars in a boiling-water canner for 10 minutes (start timing when water returns to boiling). Remove jars; cool on racks. (See "Canning Basics," pages 199-201.) Let stand 1 week.

DILL PICKLE RELISH: Prepare as directed, except use 3 to 3¼ pounds cucumbers. Seed and finely chop enough cucumbers to equal 8 cups. Reduce the water to 1½ cups and the vinegar to 1½ cups. Use a 4- to 5-quart pot. Stir chopped cucumbers into boiling vinegar mixture with 3 tablespoons dill seeds. Return to boiling. Cook, uncovered, for 5 minutes. Ladle into hot, clean pint canning jars, leaving a ½-inch headspace. Wipe the jar rims; adjust lids. Process in a boiling-water canner for 10 minutes. Remove jars; cool on wire racks. (See "Canning Basics," pages 199–201.) Makes 4 pints.

*NOTE: If pickling cucumbers are not available, cut regular cucumbers into 4-inch spears.

PER PICKLE OR 1 TABLESPOON DILL RELISH VARIATION: 10 cal., 0 g total fat, 0 mg chol., 389 mg sodium, 2 g carbo., 0 g fiber, 0 g pro.
EXCHANGES: Free

LOW FAT

BREAD AND BUTTER PICKLES

PREP: 40 MINUTES **CHILL:** 3 TO 12 HOURS
PROCESS: 10 MINUTES **MAKES:** 7 PINTS

- 16 cups (4 quarts) sliced medium cucumbers
- 8 medium white onions, sliced
- ⅓ cup pickling salt
- 3 cloves garlic, halved
  Crushed ice
- 4 cups sugar
- 3 cups cider vinegar
- 2 tablespoons mustard seeds
- 1½ teaspoons ground turmeric
- 1½ teaspoons celery seeds

1 In a 6- to 8-quart stainless-steel, enamel, or nonstick pot combine cucumbers, onions, pickling salt, and garlic. Add 2 inches crushed ice. Cover with lid and chill for 3 to 12 hours. Remove remaining ice. Drain mixture well; remove garlic.

2 In the pot combine sugar, vinegar, mustard seeds, turmeric, and celery seeds. Heat to boiling. Add cucumber mixture. Return to boiling.

3 Pack hot cucumber mixture and liquid into hot, sterilized pint canning jars, leaving a ½-inch headspace. Wipe jar rims; adjust lids. Process in a

boiling-water canner for 10 minutes (start timing when water returns to boiling). Remove jars; cool on racks. (See "Canning Basics," pages 199–201.)

PER ¼ CUP: 33 cal., 0 g total fat, 0 mg chol., 200 mg sodium, 9 g carbo., 0 g fiber, 0 g pro.
EXCHANGES: ½ Other Carbo.

LOW FAT

SWEET PICKLE RELISH

PREP: 60 MINUTES **STAND:** 2 HOURS
COOK: 10 MINUTES **PROCESS:** 10 MINUTES
MAKES: ABOUT 4 PINTS

- 6 cups finely chopped cucumbers,* seeded if desired
- 3 cups finely chopped green and/or red sweet peppers* (3 medium)
- 3 cups finely chopped onions* (6 medium)
- ¼ cup pickling salt
- 3 cups sugar
- 2 cups cider vinegar
- 1 tablespoon mustard seeds
- 2 teaspoons celery seeds
- ½ teaspoon ground turmeric

1 Combine cucumbers, sweet peppers, and onions in a very large bowl. Sprinkle with salt; add cold water to cover. Let stand at room temperature for 2 hours.

2 Drain vegetable mixture through a colander. Rinse; drain well. In an 8-quart heavy pot combine sugar, vinegar, mustard seeds, celery seeds, and turmeric. Heat to boiling. Add vegetables; return to boiling. Cook, uncovered, over medium-high heat for 10 minutes, stirring occasionally.

3 Ladle relish into hot, sterilized pint canning jars, leaving a ½-inch headspace. Wipe the jar rims; adjust lids. Process filled jars in a boiling-water canner for 10 minutes. Remove jars; cool on racks. (See "Canning Basics," pages 199-201.)

*NOTE: Use a food processor to chop vegetables in batches, if desired.

PER 1 TABLESPOON: 22 cal., 0 g total fat, 0 mg chol., 218 mg sodium, 5 g carbo., 0 g fiber, 0 g pro.
EXCHANGES: ½ Other Carbo.

ZUCCHINI RELISH

turmeric, and mustard seeds. Bring to boiling; reduce heat. Simmer, uncovered, for 3 minutes. Stir in drained vegetables and, if desired, green food coloring. Return to boiling; reduce heat. Simmer, uncovered, for 10 minutes.

3 Ladle relish into hot, sterilized half-pint canning jars, leaving a ½-inch headspace. Wipe the jar rims and adjust lids. Process jars in a boiling-water canner for 10 minutes (start timing when water returns to boiling). Remove jars; cool on a wire rack. (See "Canning Basics," pages 199–201.)

PER 1 TABLESPOON: 21 cal., 0 g total fat, 0 mg chol., 350 mg sodium, 5 g carbo., 0 g fiber, 0 g pro.
EXCHANGES: Free

LOW FAT

ZUCCHINI RELISH

PREP: 55 MINUTES **STAND:** 3 HOURS
COOK: 13 MINUTES **PROCESS:** 10 MINUTES
MAKES: 5 HALF-PINTS

     5 cups finely chopped zucchini
        (about 4 medium)
  1½ cups finely chopped onions (3 medium)
   ¾ cup finely chopped green sweet pepper
        (1 medium)
   ¾ cup finely chopped red sweet pepper
        (1 medium)
   ¼ cup pickling salt
  1¾ cups sugar
  1½ cups white vinegar
   ¼ cup water
     1 teaspoon celery seeds
     1 teaspoon ground turmeric
   ½ teaspoon mustard seeds
     1 or 2 drops green food coloring (optional)

1 In a nonreactive bowl combine zucchini, onions, and sweet peppers. Sprinkle the pickling salt evenly over the vegetables. Pour enough water (about 4 cups) over vegetables to cover. Cover bowl and let stand for 3 hours. Transfer zucchini mixture to a colander. Rinse with fresh water and drain mixture well.

2 In an 8- to 10-quart pot combine sugar, vinegar, the ¼ cup water, the celery seeds,

---

PICKLES AND RELISHES
THE RIGHT INGREDIENTS MAKE ALL THE DIFFERENCE.

CUCUMBERS: Pickling cucumbers will make crunchier pickles than table or slicing varieties. Select unwaxed cucumbers and use them as soon as possible after harvest. Otherwise, refrigerate cucumbers or spread them out in a cool, well-ventilated area. Wash them just before canning; remove the blossoms and slice off the blossom ends.
SALT: Use granulated pickling or canning salt as directed in recipes. Do not use table salt, which might cause the pickles to darken or make the brine cloudy.
VINEGAR: Cider vinegar is often used for pickles and relishes, but white vinegar can be used for a lighter-color product. Always use the vinegar specified in a recipe to ensure the proper acidity. Never dilute the vinegar more than is indicated in the recipe.
SPICES: Do not substitute ground spices, which might cause the product to be dark and cloudy, for whole spices.
WATER: Use soft or distilled water because hard water might prevent brined pickles from curing properly.

FREEZING VEGETABLES

Read "Freezing Basics," pages 202–203. Wash fresh vegetables with cool, clear tap water; scrub firm vegetables with a clean produce brush to remove any dirt.

Vegetable	Preparation	Freezing
Asparagus	Allow 2½ to 4½ pounds per quart. Wash; scrape off scales. Break off woody bases where spears snap easily; wash again. Sort by thickness. Leave whole or cut into 1-inch lengths.	Blanch small spears for 2 minutes, medium for 3 minutes, and large for 4 minutes; cool quickly by plunging into ice water; drain. Fill containers; shake down, leaving no headspace.
Beans: green, Italian, snap, or wax	Allow 1½ to 2½ pounds per quart. Wash; remove ends and strings. Leave whole or cut into 1-inch pieces.	Blanch for 3 minutes; cool quickly by plunging into ice water; drain. Fill containers; shake down, leaving a ½-inch headspace.*
Beets	Allow 3 pounds (without tops) per quart. Trim off beet tops, leaving 1 inch of stem and roots, to reduce bleeding of color. Scrub well.	Cook unpeeled beets in boiling water until tender. (Allow 25 to 30 minutes for small beets, 45 to 50 minutes for medium beets.) Cool quickly by plunging into ice water; drain. Peel; remove stem and roots. Cut into slices or cubes. Fill containers, leaving a ½-inch headspace.*
Carrots	Use 1- to 1¼-inch-diameter carrots (larger carrots might be too fibrous). Allow 2 to 3 pounds per quart. Wash, trim, peel, and rinse again. Leave tiny ones whole; slice or dice the remainder.	Blanch tiny whole carrots for 5 minutes and cut-up carrots for 2 minutes; cool quickly by plunging into ice water; drain. Pack tightly into containers, leaving a ½-inch headspace.*
Corn, whole kernel	Allow 4 to 5 pounds per quart. Remove husks. Scrub with a vegetable brush to remove silks. Wash and drain.	Cover ears with boiling water; return to boiling and boil 4 minutes. Cool by plunging into ice water; drain. Cut corn from cobs at two-thirds depth of kernels; do not scrape. Fill containers, leaving a ½-inch headspace.*
Peas: English or green	Allow 2 to 2½ pounds per pint. Wash, shell, rinse, and drain.	Blanch 1½ minutes; cool quickly by plunging into ice water; drain. Fill containers, shaking down and leaving a ½-inch headspace.*
Peppers, hot	Select firm jalapeño or other chile peppers; wash. Halve large peppers. Remove stems, seeds, and membranes (see tip, page 24). Place, cut sides down, on a foil-lined baking sheet. Bake in a 425°F oven for 20 to 25 minutes or until skins are bubbly and brown. Cover peppers or wrap in foil and let stand about 15 minutes or until cool. Pull the skin off gently and slowly using a paring knife.	Package in freezer containers, leaving no headspace.
Peppers, sweet	Select firm green, bright red, or yellow peppers; wash. Remove stems, seeds, and membranes. Place, cut sides down, on a foil-lined baking sheet. Bake in a 425°F oven for 20 to 25 minutes or until skins are bubbly and brown. Cover peppers or wrap in foil and let stand about 15 minutes or until cool. Pull the skin off gently and slowly using a paring knife.	Quarter large pepper pieces or cut into strips. Fill containers, leaving a ½-inch headspace.* Or spread peppers in a single layer on a baking sheet; freeze until firm. Fill container, shaking to pack closely and leaving no headspace.

*See tip, page 200.

PICKLED GARDEN VEGETABLES

3 In a large saucepan combine the 3 cups water, vinegar, sugar, salt, dill, crushed red pepper, and garlic. Bring to boiling. Pour over vegetables in jars, leaving a ½-inch headspace. Wipe jar rims; adjust lids. Process filled jars in a boiling-water canner for 5 minutes (start timing when water returns to boiling). Remove jars; cool on racks. (See "Canning Basics," pages 199–201.)

PER ¼ CUP: 14 cal., 0 g total fat, 0 mg chol., 71 mg sodium, 3 g carbo., 0 g fiber, 0 g pro.
EXCHANGES: Free

LOW FAT

PEPPER JELLY

PREP: 50 MINUTES **COOK:** 11 MINUTES
PROCESS: 5 MINUTES **MAKES:** 5 HALF-PINTS

  1½ cups cranberry juice (not low-calorie)
  1   cup vinegar
  3   to 4 fresh jalapeño chile peppers, halved
      lengthwise (see tip, page 24)
  5   cups sugar
  ½   of a 6-ounce package (1 foil pouch) liquid
      fruit pectin

1 In a medium stainless-steel, enamel, or nonstick saucepan combine cranberry juice, vinegar, and jalapeño peppers. Bring to boiling; reduce heat. Simmer, covered, for 10 minutes. Strain mixture through a sieve, pressing with the back of a spoon to remove all the liquid; measure 2 cups. Discard pulp and any excess liquid.

2 In a 5- to 6-quart heavy pot combine the 2 cups liquid and sugar. Bring to a full rolling boil over high heat, stirring constantly (see photo 3, page 212). Quickly stir in pectin. Return to a full rolling boil; boil for 1 minute, stirring constantly. Remove from heat. Quickly skim off foam with a metal spoon (see photo 5, page 212).

3 Ladle into hot, sterilized half-pint canning jars, leaving a ¼-inch headspace. Wipe jar rims; adjust lids. Process in a boiling-water canner for 5 minutes (start timing when water returns to boiling). Remove jars; cool on racks until set (2 to 3 days). (See "Canning Basics," pages 199–201.)

PER 1 TABLESPOON: 52 cal., 0 g total fat, 0 mg chol., 1 mg sodium, 13 g carbo., 0 g fiber, 0 g pro.
EXCHANGES: 1 Other Carbo.

LOW FAT

PICKLED GARDEN VEGETABLES

PREP: 90 MINUTES **MAKES:** 7 PINTS

  1   pound carrots, peeled
  1   pound fresh green beans, trimmed and cut
      into 2-inch pieces
  3   cups cauliflower florets
  3   green and/or red sweet peppers, cut into
      strips
  2   zucchini and/or yellow summer squash,
      halved lengthwise and sliced ½ inch
      thick, or 1 pound baby zucchini or yellow
      summer squash, halved
  2   onions, cut into wedges
  3   cups water
  3   cups white wine vinegar
  2   tablespoons sugar
  1   tablespoon pickling salt
  3   tablespoons snipped fresh dill
  ½   teaspoon crushed red pepper
  6   cloves garlic, minced

1 Halve any large carrots lengthwise. Using a crinkle cutter or knife, cut carrots into ¼-inch slices. In an 8-quart pot combine carrots, green beans, cauliflower, sweet peppers, zucchini, and onions. Add enough water to cover. Bring to boiling. Cook, uncovered, 3 minutes; drain.

2 Pack vegetables into hot, sterilized pint canning jars, leaving a ½-inch headspace; set aside.

CASSEROLES

BEEF STROGANOFF CASSEROLE, PAGE 228

CASSEROLES

MAKE YOUR CASSEROLES THE BEST THEY CAN BE WITH THE RIGHT EQUIPMENT AND SOME FREEZING AND SERVING KNOW-HOW.

EQUIPMENT

Casseroles and baking dishes can be made of glass, ceramic, stoneware, or enamel-coated cast iron. Here are the most versatile types of casserole bakeware and common sizes.

CASSEROLES: (1½-, 2-, and 3-quart) Usually round or oval, these casseroles often come with lids, which make them handy for storing leftovers. They have deeper sides than baking dishes.

SQUARE BAKING DISHES: Look for 8- or 9-inch square baking dishes.

RECTANGULAR BAKING DISHES: (2- and 3-quart) More shallow than casseroles, 11×7×1½ inches and 9×13 inches in size, respectively, these increase the dish's surface area.

AU GRATIN DISHES: (1½-, 2-, and 3-quart) These round or oval dishes are more shallow and offer more surface area than a casserole. Au gratin and rectangular baking dishes can generally be used interchangeably if the dish is of the volume specified in the recipe.

■ For best results, use the type and size of bakeware your recipe calls for. To check a dish's capacity, fill it with water, one quart at a time.

■ If you don't have the correct-size dish, use a larger dish. However, because the food will be more spread out, it will take less time to cook, so reduce your baking time by about 25 percent.

METAL PANS: In a pinch a metal pan can be used for a casserole or baking dish if the recipe includes no acidic ingredients, such as tomatoes and lemon. These can react with metal, causing the foods to discolor.

FREEZING FOR FUTURE MEALS

Most casseroles freeze beautifully. Simply follow these tips.

■ Make sure to use freezer-to-oven dishes. Line the dish with parchment paper, freezer paper or foil.

■ Prepare the casserole using the lined dish, but do not bake. Cover the dish with plastic freezer wrap or foil and freeze overnight. When frozen, lift out the paper- or foil-lined food and place it in a bag or container designed for freezer use (see photos, above). Freeze for up to 3 months.

■ To thaw and bake: Unwrap the casserole and place it in the original baking dish. Cover and thaw in the refrigerator for up to 2 days before baking. If you don't have time to thaw in the refrigerator, cover and heat the casserole in a 325°F oven for twice its normal baking time. To test for doneness, see tip, page 226.

LET IT STAND

Allowing a casserole to stand for several minutes after it comes out of the oven improves texture and flavor, and allows the food to firm and hold a cut edge. This is especially true with hot and cheesy dishes and layered casseroles.

TUNA NOODLE CASSEROLE, PAGE 236

TURKEY AND SWEET POTATO SHEPHERD'S PIE

PREP: 40 MINUTES **BAKE:** 20 MINUTES
OVEN: 375°F **MAKES:** 4 SERVINGS

- 1½ pounds sweet potatoes, peeled and cut into 2-inch pieces
- 2 cloves garlic, halved
- ¼ cup fat-free milk
- ½ teaspoon salt
- 12 ounces uncooked ground turkey breast
- ½ cup chopped onion (1 medium)
- 1¼ cups coarsely chopped zucchini (1 medium)
- 1 cup chopped carrots (2 medium)
- ½ cup frozen whole kernel yellow corn
- ¼ cup water
- 1 8-ounce can tomato sauce
- 2 tablespoons Worcestershire sauce
- 2 teaspoons snipped fresh sage or ½ teaspoon dried sage, crushed
- ⅛ teaspoon black pepper
  Snipped fresh sage (optional)

1 Preheat the oven to 375°F. In a medium saucepan cook sweet potatoes and garlic, covered, in enough lightly salted boiling water to cover for 15 to 20 minutes or until tender; drain. Mash with a potato masher or beat with an electric mixer on low speed. Gradually add milk and salt, mashing or beating to make potato mixture light and fluffy. Cover and keep warm.

2 Meanwhile, in a large skillet cook turkey and onion over medium heat until meat is brown, stirring to break up turkey as it cooks. Drain, if needed. Stir in zucchini, carrots, corn, and water. Bring to boiling; reduce heat. Simmer, covered, for 5 to 10 minutes or until vegetables are tender.

3 Add tomato sauce, Worcestershire sauce, sage, and pepper to turkey mixture; heat through. Spoon turkey mixture into a 1½-quart casserole or soufflé dish, spreading evenly. Spoon mashed potato mixture in mounds on turkey mixture.

4 Bake, uncovered, for 20 to 25 minutes or until heated through. If desired, sprinkle with additional fresh sage before serving.

PER 1½ CUPS: 268 cal., 1 g total fat (0 g sat. fat, 0 g trans fat), 42 mg chol., 824 mg sodium, 41 g carbo., 7 g fiber, 24 g pro. EXCHANGES: 1 Vegetable, 2½ Starch, 2 Lean Meat

ITALIAN POLENTA CASSEROLE

PREP: 45 MINUTES **BAKE:** 20 MINUTES
OVEN: 400°F **MAKES:** 8 SERVINGS

- 2½ cups chicken broth
- 3 tablespoons butter or margarine
- 2 cups milk
- 1½ cups quick-cooking polenta mix
- 1 3-ounce package cream cheese, cut up
- 1 cup shredded mozzarella or provolone cheese (4 ounces)
- ½ cup finely shredded or grated Parmesan cheese (2 ounces)
- 12 ounces sweet or hot bulk Italian sausage
- 1 cup fresh mushrooms, quartered
- 1 medium onion, cut into thin wedges
- 2 cloves garlic, minced
- 2 cups purchased pasta sauce

1 Preheat oven to 400°F. Lightly grease a 3-quart rectangular baking dish; set aside.

2 In a large saucepan bring broth and butter to boiling. Meanwhile, stir together milk and polenta. Add polenta mixture to boiling broth (see photo 1, page 225). Cook and stir until bubbly; cook and stir 3 to 5 minutes more or until very thick. Stir in cream cheese, ¾ cup of the mozzarella cheese, and ¼ cup of the Parmesan cheese until well mixed (see photo 2, page 225). Spread two-thirds of the polenta mixture in prepared dish; set aside.

3 In a large skillet cook sausage, mushrooms, onion, and garlic until meat is brown and onion is tender. Drain fat; discard. Stir pasta sauce into meat mixture; heat through. Spoon meat mixture over polenta in dish, spreading evenly. Spoon remaining polenta on sauce and sprinkle with remaining mozzarella and Parmesan cheeses (see photo 3, page 225).

4 Bake, uncovered, about 20 minutes or until heated through and top is lightly golden.

PER 1 CUP: 584 cal., 34 g total fat (18 g sat. fat, 0 g trans fat), 93 mg chol., 1,879 mg sodium, 36 g carbo., 4 g fiber, 31 g pro. EXCHANGES: 1 Vegetable, 2 Starch, 3 High-Fat Meat, 1½ Fat

KEEP IT GOLDEN
IF YOUR CASSEROLE IS GOLDEN ON TOP BEFORE IT'S DONE IN THE CENTER, COVER THE DISH LOOSELY WITH FOIL FOR THE REMAINING BAKING TIME.

PREPARING ITALIAN POLENTA CASSEROLE, STEP-BY-STEP

1. Slowly add the polenta mixture to the boiling broth in a steady stream, stirring constantly. **2.** Cook polenta slowly over low heat until very thick, stirring constantly. As soon as polenta thickens, add cheeses; continue stirring until the cheeses melt. **3.** Drop mixture from a spoon, scraping with a spatula to make small mounds on top of the meat mixture.

BAKED RISOTTO WITH SAUSAGE AND ARTICHOKES

PREP: 40 MINUTES **BAKE:** 70 MINUTES
STAND: 5 MINUTES **OVEN:** 350°F
MAKES: 6 TO 8 SERVINGS

- 1 pound bulk Italian sausage
- 1 cup chopped fennel bulb (1 medium)
- ½ cup chopped onion (1 medium)
- 2 cloves garlic, minced
- ¾ cup uncooked arborio or long grain rice
- 2 9-ounce packages frozen artichoke hearts, thawed, drained, and halved
- 1 cup coarsely shredded carrots (2 medium)
- 2 teaspoons snipped fresh thyme or ½ teaspoon dried thyme, crushed
- ½ teaspoon black pepper
- 2 cups chicken broth
- ⅓ cup dry white wine or chicken broth
- ½ cup panko (Japanese-style bread crumbs) or soft bread crumbs
- ¼ cup finely shredded Asiago or Parmesan cheese
- 1 tablespoon butter or margarine, melted
- ½ teaspoon finely shredded lemon peel

1 Preheat oven to 350°F. In a very large skillet cook and stir sausage, fennel, onion, and garlic over medium-high heat until vegetables are tender but not brown. Drain fat; discard. Add rice; cook and stir 1 minute more.

2 Add artichoke hearts, carrots, thyme, and pepper. Stir in broth and wine. Bring just to boiling. Transfer to a 2½-quart casserole. Bake, covered, about 60 minutes or until rice is tender; stir once.

3 Meanwhile, in a small bowl combine panko, cheese, butter, and lemon peel. Uncover casserole and top with crumb mixture. Bake, uncovered, for 10 minutes more. Let stand for 5 minutes before serving.

PER 1⅓ CUPS: 476 cal., 28 g total fat (11 g sat. fat, 0 g trans fat), 68 mg chol., 1,038 mg sodium, 36 g carbo., 8 g fiber, 17 g pro. EXCHANGES: 1½ Vegetable, 2 Starch, 1 High-Fat Meat, 3½ Fat

HOT-SPICED PORK AND RICE

PREP: 45 MINUTES **BAKE:** 60 MINUTES
STAND: 10 MINUTES **OVEN:** 375°F
MAKES: 6 SERVINGS

- 1 2- to 2¼-pound boneless pork shoulder roast
- 2 to 3 tablespoons vegetable oil
- 2 cups thinly sliced carrots (4 medium)
- 1 8-ounce can sliced water chestnuts, drained
- 1 cup yellow sweet pepper strips (1 medium)
- ½ cup chopped onion (1 medium)
- 1 cup uncooked long grain rice
- 1 14-ounce can reduced-sodium chicken broth
- ½ cup water
- ¼ cup soy sauce
- 2 tablespoons light-color corn syrup
- 2 tablespoons molasses
- 1 to 2 teaspoons chili paste
- 1 teaspoon five-spice powder
- ⅓ cup sliced green onions (3)

1 Preheat oven to 375°F. Trim fat from meat. Cut meat into ¾-inch cubes. In a very large skillet brown half of the meat at a time in 2 tablespoons hot oil. Transfer meat to a 3-quart rectangular baking dish. Add carrots, water chestnuts, and sweet pepper.

2 Add remaining tablespoon oil to skillet, if needed. Cook onion in hot oil until tender. Add uncooked rice to skillet; cook and stir for 1 minute. Stir in broth, water, soy sauce, corn syrup, molasses, chili paste, and five-spice powder. Cook and stir just until mixture comes to a boil. Remove from heat. Carefully add rice mixture to casserole; stir to combine. Cover dish with foil.

3 Bake about 60 minutes or until pork and rice are tender. Let stand, covered, for 10 minutes. Gently stir and sprinkle with green onions.

PER 2 CUPS: 439 cal., 14 g total fat (3 g sat. fat, 0 g trans fat), 91 mg chol., 980 mg sodium, 47 g carbo., 3 g fiber, 34 g pro. EXCHANGES: ½ Vegetable, 3 Starch, 3½ Lean Meat

---

CASSEROLE DONENESS TEST
TEST THE TEMPERATURE TO MAKE SURE IT'S AT ITS SAFEST, TASTIEST BEST.

For best flavor and food safety, a casserole needs to be heated to 160°F. When the casserole is bubbly around the edges, test by inserting an instant- read thermometer at an angle in the center, being careful not to touch the dish.

POTATO AND HAM BAKE

PREP: 25 MINUTES **BAKE:** 30 MINUTES
STAND: 5 MINUTES **OVEN:** 400°F
MAKES: 4 SERVINGS

- 1 pound Yukon gold potatoes, sliced
- 1 8-ounce tub light cream cheese spread with chive and onion
- ¾ cup milk
- ¼ cup finely shredded Parmesan cheese
- ¼ teaspoon black pepper
- 1 tablespoon snipped fresh tarragon or ½ teaspoon dried tarragon, crushed
- 8 ounces cooked boneless ham, cut into bite-size cubes
- 1 pound fresh asparagus spears, trimmed and cut into 2- to 3-inch pieces

1 Preheat oven to 400°F. Lightly grease a 1½-quart baking dish; set aside. In a medium saucepan cook potatoes, covered, in a small amount of lightly salted boiling water for 5 to 7 minutes or just until tender. Drain; transfer potatoes to a medium bowl and set aside.

2 For cheese sauce, in same saucepan combine cream cheese, milk, 2 tablespoons of the Parmesan cheese, and the pepper. Heat and whisk cream cheese mixture until smooth and cheese melts. Remove from heat and stir in tarragon.

3 Layer half of the potatoes, ham, asparagus, and cheese sauce in prepared baking dish. Repeat layers with remaining potatoes, ham, asparagus, and cheese sauce. Cover with foil.

4 Bake for 20 minutes. Remove foil; sprinkle with remaining Parmesan cheese. Return to oven and bake, uncovered, for 10 to 12 minutes more or until heated through. Let stand for 5 minutes.

PER SERVING: 346 cal., 16 g total fat (9 g sat. fat, 0 g trans fat), 67 mg chol., 1,162 mg sodium, 30 g carbo., 5 g fiber, 22 g pro.
EXCHANGES: 1 Vegetable, 1½ Starch, 2 Medium-Fat Meat, 1 Fat

SPECIAL SPUDS MOIST AND HIGH IN STARCH, YUKON GOLD WORK WELL FOR SCALLOPED POTATO DISHES BECAUSE THEY WON'T FALL APART. IF YOU WISH, YOU CAN SUBSTITUTE ROUND RED POTATOES.

POTATO AND HAM BAKE

BEEF STROGANOFF
CASEROLE *(photo, page 221)*
PREP: 35 MINUTES **BAKE:** 30 MINUTES
OVEN: 350°F **MAKES:** 6 SERVINGS

- 12 ounces packaged dried campanelle or penne pasta (4 cups)
- 1 17-ounce package refrigerated cooked beef roast au jus
- 2 large portobello mushrooms
- 1 medium sweet onion, cut into thin wedges
- 2 cloves garlic, minced
- 2 tablespoons butter or margarine
- 3 tablespoons all-purpose flour
- 2 tablespoons tomato paste
- 1 14-ounce can beef broth
- 1 tablespoon Worcestershire sauce
- 1 teaspoon smoked paprika or Spanish paprika
- ¼ teaspoon salt
- ¼ teaspoon black pepper
  Snipped fresh Italian parsley (optional)
- ½ cup dairy sour cream
- 1 tablespoon prepared horseradish
- 1 teaspoon snipped fresh dill or ¼ teaspoon dried dillweed

1 Preheat oven to 350°F. Cook pasta according to package directions; drain. Return pasta to hot saucepan; cover and keep warm. Place roast on a cutting board; reserve juices. Using two forks, pull meat apart into bite-size pieces; set aside.

2 Remove stems and gills from mushrooms; coarsely chop. (You should have about 4 cups.) In a very large skillet cook mushrooms, onion, and garlic in hot butter over medium heat for 4 to 5 minutes or until tender. Stir in flour and tomato paste. Add beef broth, reserved meat juices, Worcestershire sauce, paprika, salt, and pepper. Cook and stir until thickened and bubbly. Remove from heat.

3 Add pasta and beef to mushroom mixture in skillet; stir to combine. Transfer meat mixture to a 3-quart casserole or rectangular baking dish. Bake, covered, for 30 minutes or until heated through. If desired, sprinkle with parsley. In a small bowl combine sour cream, horseradish, and dill. Spoon some of the mixture over each serving.

PER 1½ CUPS: 450 cal., 14 g total fat (7 g sat. fat, 0 g trans fat), 61 mg chol., 770 mg sodium, 57 g carbo., 4 g fiber, 26 g pro. EXCHANGES: 1 Vegetable, 3½ Starch, 2 Medium-Fat Meat

EIGHT-LAYER CASSEROLE
PREP: 30 MINUTES **BAKE:** 55 MINUTES
STAND: 10 MINUTES **OVEN:** 350°F
MAKES: 8 SERVINGS

- 3 cups packaged dried medium noodles (6 ounces)
- 1 pound ground beef
- 2 8-ounce cans tomato sauce
- 1 teaspoon dried basil, crushed
- ½ teaspoon sugar
- ½ teaspoon garlic powder
- ¼ teaspoon salt
- ¼ teaspoon black pepper
- 1 8-ounce carton dairy sour cream
- 1 8-ounce package cream cheese, softened
- ½ cup milk
- ⅓ cup chopped onion (1 small)
- 1 10-ounce package frozen chopped spinach, cooked and well drained
- 1 cup shredded cheddar cheese (4 ounces)

1 Preheat oven to 350°F. Lightly grease a 2-quart casserole or square baking dish; set aside. Cook noodles according to package directions; drain and set aside.

2 Meanwhile, in a large skillet cook beef over medium heat until brown. Drain fat; discard. Stir tomato sauce, basil, sugar, garlic powder, salt, and pepper into skillet. Bring to boiling; reduce heat. Simmer, uncovered, for 5 minutes.

3 In a medium mixing bowl beat together sour cream and cream cheese with an electric mixer on medium speed until smooth. Stir in milk and onion.

4 In prepared casserole layer half each of the noodles (about 2 cups), meat mixture (about 1½ cups), and cream cheese mixture (about 1 cup), and all of the spinach. Top with remaining meat mixture and noodles. Cover and chill remaining cream cheese mixture until needed.

5 Cover casserole with lightly greased foil. Bake about 45 minutes or until heated through. Uncover; spread with remaining cream cheese mixture. Sprinkle with cheddar cheese. Bake, uncovered, 10 minutes more or until cheese melts. Let stand for 10 minutes before serving.

PER 1½ CUPS: 448 cal., 30 g total fat (16 g sat. fat, 1 g trans fat), 118 mg chol., 645 mg sodium, 24 g carbo., 3 g fiber, 22 g pro. EXCHANGES: ½ Vegetable, 1½ Starch, 2½ Medium-Fat Meat, 3 Fat

MAKE-IT-MINE NOODLE CASSEROLE

WHETHER YOU'RE SEEKING A SATISFYING WAY TO USE UP LEFTOVERS OR YOU WISH TO CREATE A ONE-OF-A-KIND HOUSE SPECIALTY, USE THIS MASTER PLAN TO DESIGN YOUR OWN CASSEROLE.

BASIC INGREDIENTS

PREP: 30 MINUTES
BAKE: 55 MINUTES **OVEN:** 350°F
MAKES: 6 SERVINGS

- 8 ounces packaged dried Pasta
- 1 pound Ground Meat or Chopped Ham or one 15-ounce can Beans, rinsed and drained
- 1 10.75-ounce can Condensed Soup
- 1½ cups Frozen Vegetable
- 1 cup Shredded Cheese
- ¾ cup milk
- ¼ cup Goodie
- 1 teaspoon Seasoning
- ½ cup Topper (optional)

PASTA (PICK ONE)
(Whole Grain or Regular)

Egg Noodles
Farfalle
Macaroni
Mostaccioli
Penne
Rotini

GROUND MEAT, CHOPPED HAM, OR BEANS (PICK ONE)

Bulk pork sausage
Chopped Ham
Ground beef
Ground turkey
Black beans
Kidney beans

CONDENSED SOUP
(PICK ONE)

Broccoli cheese
Cream of celery
Cream of chicken
Cream of mushroom
Creamy mushroom with roasted garlic
Tomato

FROZEN VEGETABLE
(PICK ONE)

Broccoli florets
Mixed vegetables
Peas
Peppers (yellow, green, and red) and onion stir-fry vegetables
Whole kernel corn

SHREDDED CHEESE
(PICK ONE)

Cheddar
Italian or Mexican blend
Monterey Jack or Monterey Jack with jalapeño peppers
Swiss

GOODIE (PICK ONE)

Bottled roasted red peppers, drained and chopped
Canned sliced mushrooms, drained
Canned sliced water chestnuts, drained
Ripe or green olives, sliced
Slivered almonds

SEASONING (PICK ONE)

Basil, dried, crushed
Cajun or Italian seasoning
Chili powder plus ¼ teaspoon ground cumin
Oregano, dried, crushed
Thyme, dried

TOPPER (PICK ONE)

Chow mein noodles
Corn or potato chips, crushed
Nuts, coarsely chopped
Panko (Japanese-style bread crumbs) or soft bread crumbs tossed with 2 tablespoons melted butter or margarine
Rich round crackers, crushed

BASIC INSTRUCTIONS

1 Preheat oven to 350°F. Grease a 2-quart casserole. In a large saucepan cook desired Pasta according to package directions. Drain; return to pan.

2 In a skillet cook Ground Meat until brown; drain. Stir Meat, Ham, or Beans; Soup; Vegetable; half of Cheese; milk; Goodie; and Seasoning into Pasta. Combine mixture well. Pour into dish. Sprinkle with remaining Cheese.

3 Bake, covered, for 45 minutes. Uncover; if desired, sprinkle with Topper. Bake, uncovered, for 10 to 15 minutes or until heated through.

BEEF-AND-BEAN ENCHILADA CASSEROLE

PREP: 25 MINUTES **BAKE:** 35 MINUTES
OVEN: 350°F **MAKES:** 6 SERVINGS

- 8 ounces ground beef
- ½ cup chopped onion (1 medium)
- 1 15-ounce can pinto beans, rinsed and drained
- 1 4-ounce can diced green chiles, undrained
- 1 teaspoon chili powder
- ½ teaspoon ground cumin
- 1 8-ounce carton dairy sour cream or light sour cream
- 2 tablespoons all-purpose flour
- ¼ teaspoon garlic powder
- 8 6-inch corn tortillas
- 1 10-ounce can enchilada sauce
- 1 cup shredded cheddar cheese (4 ounces)

1 Preheat oven to 350°F. Lightly grease a 2-quart rectangular baking dish; set aside. In a large skillet cook beef and onion until meat is brown and onion is tender. Drain fat; discard. Stir pinto beans, undrained chiles, chili powder, and cumin into meat mixture; set aside.

2 In a small bowl stir together sour cream, flour, and garlic powder until combined; set aside.

3 Arrange half the tortillas in bottom of prepared baking dish, cutting to fit if necessary (see photo 1, below). Top with half the meat mixture, sour cream mixture, and enchilada sauce (see photo 2, below). Repeat with remaining tortillas, meat mixture, sour cream mixture, and enchilada sauce.

4 Cover with foil. Bake about 30 minutes or until heated through. Remove foil; sprinkle casserole with cheese and bake 5 minutes more or until cheese melts.

MAKE-AHEAD DIRECTIONS: Prepare as directed through Step 3. Cover with plastic wrap and chill for up to 24 hours. Remove plastic wrap. Cover dish with foil. Bake in 350°F oven about 35 minutes or until heated through. Uncover; sprinkle with cheese. Return to oven and bake for 5 minutes more or until cheese melts.

PER SERVING: 408 cal., 22 g total fat (11 g sat. fat, 0 g trans fat), 65 mg chol., 668 mg sodium, 34 g carbo., 6 g fiber, 19 g pro.
EXCHANGES: 2 Starch, 2 Lean Meat, 3 Fat

EASY SPAGHETTI BAKE

PREP: 35 MINUTES **BAKE:** 30 MINUTES
OVEN: 350°F **MAKES:** 6 SERVINGS

- 8 ounces packaged dried thin spaghetti, broken in half
- 12 ounces lean ground beef
- 1½ cups chopped onions (3 medium)
- 1 cup chopped green sweet pepper (1 large)
- 1 clove garlic, minced
- 1 10.75-ounce can reduced-fat and reduced-sodium condensed cream of mushroom soup
- 1 10.75-ounce can reduced-fat and reduced-sodium condensed tomato soup
- 1⅓ cups water
- 2 cups shredded cheddar cheese (8 ounces)
- ½ teaspoon salt
- ½ teaspoon black pepper

BEEF-AND-BEAN ENCHILADA CASSEROLE , STEP-BY-STEP

1. Place 4 of the corn tortillas in the greased baking dish, overlapping as necessary to fit. (Lightly greasing the dish prevents the tortillas from sticking.) **2.** Arrange half of the meat mixture and sour cream mixture on top of the tortillas. Pour half of the sauce over top. Gently press down on the next layer of tortillas to help distribute the sauce evenly.

1 Preheat oven to 350°F. Lightly grease a 2-quart square baking dish; set aside. Cook spaghetti according to package directions; drain. Return to pan.

2 Meanwhile, in a large skillet cook beef, onions, sweet pepper, and garlic over medium heat until meat is brown and onion is tender. Drain fat; discard. Stir in mushroom soup, tomato soup, and water.

3 Bring to boiling; reduce heat. Simmer, uncovered, for 10 minutes, stirring occasionally. Stir in 1½ cups of the cheese, salt, and black pepper. Gently stir in cooked spaghetti.

4 Transfer mixture to prepared baking dish. Sprinkle with remaining cheese. Bake, uncovered, about 30 minutes or until heated through.

PER 1¼ CUPS: 504 cal., 23 g total fat (11 g sat. fat, 1 g trans fat), 80 mg chol., 871 mg sodium, 46 g carbo., 2 g fiber, 26 g pro. EXCHANGES: ½ Vegetable, 3 Starch, 2½ High-Fat Meat, 1½ Fat

BEST EVER

UPSIDE-DOWN PIZZA CASSEROLE

PREP: 20 MINUTES **BAKE:** 15 MINUTES
OVEN: 400°F **MAKES:** 5 SERVINGS

- 1½ pounds lean ground beef or bulk Italian sausage
- 1 15-ounce can Italian-style tomato sauce
- 1 4-ounce can sliced mushrooms, drained
- ¼ cup sliced pitted ripe olives (optional)
- 1 to 1½ cups shredded mozzarella cheese or four-cheese pizza blend (4 to 6 ounces)
- 1 10-ounce package refrigerated biscuits (10 biscuits)

1 Preheat oven to 400°F. In a large skillet cook beef until brown. Drain fat; discard. Stir in tomato sauce, mushrooms, and olives (if using). Heat through. Transfer meat mixture to a 2-quart rectangular baking dish. Sprinkle with cheese.

2 Flatten each biscuit with your hands. Arrange biscuits on top of cheese. Bake, uncovered, for 15 to 17 minutes or until biscuits are golden.

PER ABOUT 1 CUP MEAT MIXTURE + 2 BISCUITS: 565 cal., 33 g total fat (13 g sat. fat, 1 g trans fat), 105 mg chol., 1,351 mg sodium, 32 g carbo., 2 g fiber, 36 g pro. EXCHANGES: 2 Starch, 4½ Medium-Fat Meat, 1½ Fat

CHEESY ITALIAN MEATBALL CASSEROLE

PREP: 30 MINUTES **BAKE:** 45 MINUTES
OVEN: 350°F **MAKES:** 8 TO 10 SERVINGS

- 16 ounces packaged dried ziti or penne pasta
- 1 26-ounce jar tomato pasta sauce
- 1 16-ounce package frozen cooked Italian-style meatballs (32), thawed
- 1 15-ounce can Italian-style tomato sauce
- 1 15-ounce carton ricotta cheese
- ½ cup grated Parmesan cheese (2 ounces)
- 2 cups shredded mozzarella cheese (8 ounces)

1 Preheat oven to 350°F. Cook pasta according to package directions; drain. Return to pan. Stir in pasta sauce, meatballs, and tomato sauce. Transfer to a 3-quart rectangular baking dish. Cover dish with foil. Bake for 30 minutes.

2 Meanwhile, in a small bowl combine ricotta and Parmesan cheeses. Remove foil from baking dish and spoon ricotta mixture in mounds on top of pasta mixture. Cover loosely and bake about 10 minutes more or until heated through. Top with mozzarella cheese and bake, uncovered, about 5 minutes more or until cheese melts.

PER 2 CUPS: 636 cal., 30 g total fat (16 g sat. fat, 0 g trans fat), 91 mg chol., 1,371 mg sodium, 59 g carbo., 6 g fiber, 32 g pro. EXCHANGES: ½ Vegetable, 4 Starch, 2½ High-Fat Meat, 1 Fat

FAST FIXINGS

CASSEROLES ARE ALWAYS EASY. THESE TIME-SHAVERS MAKE THEM QUICK TOO.

■ Use prepeeled and precut vegetables, such as carrots, sweet peppers, and onions (found in the produce section).

■ Stock up on frozen vegetables. Smaller vegetables such as peas—or medleys of frozen diced vegetables—are recipe-ready, with no slicing or thawing needed before adding to casseroles. They're also nearly equal to fresh in quality and nutrition content.

■ Frozen precooked meatballs will stand in for ground beef in a pinch. Thaw, break them up with a fork, and add to a casserole.

CHEESEBURGER AND FRIES CASSEROLE

PREP: 20 MINUTES **BAKE:** 40 MINUTES
OVEN: 350°F **MAKES:** 6 SERVINGS

- 1½ pounds lean ground beef
- ¾ cup chopped green sweet pepper (1 medium)
- ½ cup chopped onion (1 medium)
- 2 cloves garlic, minced
- 1 14.5-ounce can diced tomatoes, undrained
- 1 6-ounce can tomato paste
- 1 10.75-ounce can condensed cheddar cheese soup
- ½ cup light dairy sour cream
- 4 cups frozen french-fried shoestring potatoes
- 1 teaspoon seasoned salt (optional)
- Assorted toppers (ketchup, pickle slices, yellow mustard, and/or chopped fresh tomato) (optional)

1 Preheat oven to 350°F. In a very large skillet cook beef, sweet pepper, onion, and garlic over medium heat until meat is brown and vegetables are tender. Drain fat; discard. Stir undrained tomatoes and tomato paste into beef mixture. Bring to boiling; reduce heat. Simmer, uncovered, for 5 minutes.

2 Spoon beef mixture into the bottom of an ungreased 2-quart rectangular baking dish. In a medium bowl stir together soup and sour cream; spread over meat mixture in baking dish. Sprinkle potatoes over top of soup mixture. If desired, sprinkle with seasoned salt.

3 Bake, uncovered, for 40 to 45 minutes or until heated through and potatoes are golden. If desired, serve with assorted toppers.

PER 1 CUP: 493 cal., 26 g total fat (10 g sat. fat, 1 g trans fat), 87 mg chol., 1,319 mg sodium, 46 g carbo., 5 g fiber, 28 g pro.
EXCHANGES: ½ Vegetable, 3 Starch, 2½ Medium-Fat Meat, 2 Fat

A PREP-FREE NIGHT! ASSEMBLE THIS CASSEROLE IN THE MORNING (OR EVEN THE NIGHT BEFORE) AND POP IT IN THE OVEN WHEN YOU GET HOME. JUST ADD ABOUT 15 MINUTES TO THE BAKE TIME.

CHEESEBURGER AND FRIES CASSEROLE

CHICKEN TETRAZZINI

PREP: 30 MINUTES **BAKE:** 15 MINUTES
OVEN: 350°F **MAKES:** 6 SERVINGS

- 8 ounces packaged dried spaghetti or linguine
- 2 cups sliced fresh mushrooms
- ½ cup sliced green onions (4)
- 2 tablespoons butter or margarine
- ¼ cup all-purpose flour
- ⅛ teaspoon black pepper
- ⅛ teaspoon ground nutmeg
- 1¼ cups chicken broth
- 1¼ cups half-and-half, light cream, or milk
- 2 cups chopped purchased roasted chicken (without skin), chopped cooked chicken, or chopped cooked turkey
- 2 tablespoons dry sherry or milk
- ¼ cup grated Parmesan cheese
- ¼ cup sliced almonds, toasted (see tip, page 20)
- 2 tablespoons snipped fresh parsley (optional)

1 Preheat oven to 350°F. Cook spaghetti according to package directions; drain.

2 Meanwhile, in a large saucepan cook mushrooms and green onions in hot butter over medium heat until tender. Stir in flour, pepper, and nutmeg. Add broth and half-and-half all at once. Cook and stir until thickened and bubbly. Stir in chicken, sherry, and half of the Parmesan cheese. Add cooked spaghetti; stir gently to coat.

3 Transfer pasta mixture to a 2-quart rectangular baking dish. Sprinkle with remaining Parmesan cheese and the almonds. Bake, uncovered, about 15 minutes or until heated through. If desired, sprinkle with snipped parsley before serving.

PER 1 CUP: 421 cal., 21 g total fat (9 g sat. fat, 0 g trans fat), 82 mg chol., 630 mg sodium, 38 g carbo., 2 g fiber, 21 g pro. EXCHANGES: ½ Vegetable, 2½ Starch, 2 Lean Meat, 2½ Fat

CHICKEN AND VEGETABLE TETRAZZINI:

Prepare as directed, except add 8 ounces fresh asparagus, trimmed and cut into 1-inch pieces, or 1½ cups small fresh broccoli florets to the pasta water during the last minute of cooking.

PER 1 CUP: 425 cal., 31 g total fat (9 g sat. fat, 0 g trans fat), 82 mg chol., 630 mg sodium, 39 g carbo., 3 g fiber, 22 g pro. EXCHANGES: 1 Vegetable, 2½ Starch, 2 Lean Meat, 2½ Fat

DILLED CHICKEN-ORZO CASSEROLE

PREP: 30 MINUTES **BAKE:** 35 MINUTES
OVEN: 350°F **MAKES:** 6 TO 8 SERVINGS

- 8 ounces packaged dried orzo pasta (1 cup)
- 1 2- to 2¼-pound purchased roasted chicken
- 2 tablespoons butter or margarine
- 2 tablespoons all-purpose flour
- 1 14-ounce can chicken broth
- 2 tablespoons capers, drained
- 2 tablespoons snipped fresh dill
- 1 tablespoon Dijon-style mustard
- 1 teaspoon finely shredded lemon peel
- 1 tablespoon lemon juice
- ½ teaspoon salt
- ¼ teaspoon black pepper
- 1 medium yellow summer squash, halved lengthwise and sliced (1¼ cups)
- 1 medium red sweet pepper, cut into bite-size strips (1 cup)
- ½ of a small red onion, thinly sliced
- ¼ cup pine nuts, toasted (see tip, page 20)
  Fresh dill (optional)

1 Preheat oven to 350°F. In a large saucepan cook pasta according to package directions. Drain pasta; return to pan. Meanwhile, remove chicken from bones, discarding skin and bones. Using two forks, coarsely shred chicken.

2 In a medium saucepan melt butter over medium heat. Stir in flour. Gradually stir in broth. Cook and stir until thickened and bubbly. Stir in capers, the 2 tablespoons dill, the mustard, lemon peel, lemon juice, salt, and pepper.

3 Stir shredded chicken, dill mixture, squash, sweet pepper, and onion into pasta in saucepan; combine well. Transfer mixture to an ungreased 3-quart rectangular baking dish. Cover with foil.

4 Bake about 35 minutes or until heated through. Sprinkle with pine nuts. If desired, garnish with additional fresh dill.

PER 1⅔ CUPS: 598 cal., 33 g total fat (11 g sat. fat, 0 g trans fat), 178 mg chol., 1,724 mg sodium, 37 g carbo., 3 g fiber, 42 g pro. EXCHANGES: ½ Vegetable, 2½ Starch, 5 Lean Meat, 3 Fat

CHICKEN CORDON BLEU

PREP: 50 MINUTES **BAKE:** 40 MINUTES
OVEN: 350°F **MAKES:** 6 SERVINGS

- 2 6-ounce packages uncooked long grain and wild rice mix
- 3 ounces Gruyère cheese (3×1½×1-inch block)
- 6 very thin slices Black Forest or country ham (about 3 ounces)
- 6 large skinless, boneless chicken breast halves
- ½ teaspoon salt
- ¼ teaspoon black pepper
- ⅓ cup all-purpose flour
- 2 eggs
- 2 tablespoons water
- 1½ cups panko (Japanese-style bread crumbs) or soft bread crumbs
- ¼ cup vegetable oil
- 2 tablespoons butter or margarine
- 2 cups sliced fresh mushrooms
- ¼ cup sliced green onions (2)
- 2 cloves garlic, minced
- 2 tablespoons all-purpose flour
- 2 cups half-and-half, light cream, or whole milk
- ½ cup shredded Gruyère cheese (2 ounces)
- 2 tablespoons dry sherry (optional)
  Salt

1 Preheat oven to 350°F. Prepare rice mixes according to package directions. Spread rice in a 3-quart rectangular baking dish; keep warm.

2 Cut cheese block into six 3×½×½-inch thick logs. Wrap a slice of ham around each cheese log. In the thickest side of each chicken breast half cut a horizontal slit to, but not through, the other side (see photo 1, below). Stuff ham-wrapped Gruyère into slit of chicken breast half (see photo 2, below). Secure with wooden toothpicks. Sprinkle chicken with the ½ teaspoon salt and the pepper.

3 In a shallow dish place the ⅓ cup flour. In a second dish lightly beat eggs and water. In a third shallow dish place panko. Coat the chicken with flour. Dip in egg mixture; coat with panko (see photo 3, page 235).

4 In a very large skillet cook half of the coated stuffed chicken in 2 tablespoons hot oil for 4 minutes or until golden, turning to brown all sides (see photo 4, page 235). Remove chicken from skillet. Repeat with remaining oil and chicken. Remove toothpicks. Place chicken on top of rice.

5 Meanwhile, for sauce, in a medium saucepan melt butter over medium heat. Add mushrooms, green onions, and garlic; cook until tender. Stir in 2 tablespoons flour. Gradually stir in half-and-half. Cook and stir until thickened and bubbly. Stir shredded cheese into sauce until cheese melts. If desired, stir in sherry. Season to taste with salt. Spoon sauce over chicken and rice (see photo 5, page 235). Cover dish with foil. Bake for 40 to 45 minutes or until chicken is no longer pink (170°F).

PER 1 CHICKEN BREAST + 1 CUP RICE + ⅓ CUP SAUCE: 836 cal., 35 g total fat (15 g sat. fat, 0 g trans fat), 243 mg chol., 1,518 mg sodium, 66 g carbo., 3 g fiber, 63 g pro.
EXCHANGES: 4½ Starch, 7 Lean Meat, 2 Fat

CHICKEN CORDON BLEU, STEP-BY-STEP

1. Cut a horizontal slit into the thickest side of chicken breast, slicing to, but not through, the other side. Note that breasts are easier to slice if slightly frozen. **2.** Stuff ham-wrapped Gruyère into the slit. Secure with wooden toothpicks.
3. Dredge egg-coated chicken in panko, coating all sides.
4. Cook chicken in the hot oil until golden. **5.** Top with sauce and bake.

1

2

CHICKEN ENCHILADAS

PREP: 30 MINUTES **BAKE:** 40 MINUTES
OVEN: 350°F **MAKES:** 6 SERVINGS

- ¼ cup slivered almonds, toasted (see tip, page 20)
- ¼ cup chopped onion
- 1 to 2 medium fresh jalapeño chile peppers, seeded and chopped (see tip, page 24) (optional)
- 2 tablespoons butter or margarine
- 1 4-ounce can diced green chiles, drained
- 1 3-ounce package cream cheese, softened
- 1 tablespoon milk
- 1 teaspoon ground cumin
- 3 cups chopped cooked chicken
- 12 7-inch flour tortillas or 6-inch corn tortillas
- 1 10.75-ounce can condensed cream of chicken or cream of mushroom soup
- 1 8-ounce carton dairy sour cream
- 1 cup milk
- ¾ cup shredded Monterey Jack or cheddar cheese (3 ounces)
- 2 tablespoons slivered almonds, toasted (see tip, page 20)

1 Preheat oven to 350°F. Grease a 3-quart rectangular baking dish; set aside. In a medium skillet cook the ¼ cup almonds, the onion, and jalapeño peppers (if using) in hot butter over medium heat until onion is tender. Remove skillet from heat. Stir in 1 tablespoon of the chiles; reserve remaining peppers for sauce.

2 In a medium bowl combine cream cheese, the 1 tablespoon milk, and cumin; add nut mixture and chicken. Stir until combined. Spoon about ¼ cup of the chicken mixture onto each tortilla near an edge; roll up. Place filled tortillas, seam sides down, in prepared baking dish; set aside.

3 For sauce, in a medium bowl combine soup, sour cream, 1 cup milk, and reserved chiles.* Pour soup mixture evenly over the tortillas in baking dish. Cover with foil.

4 Bake about 35 minutes or until heated through. Remove foil. Sprinkle enchiladas with cheese and the 2 tablespoons almonds. Bake about 5 minutes more or until cheese melts.

PER 2 ENCHILADAS: 660 cal., 38 g total fat (16 g sat. fat, 0 g trans fat), 127 mg chol., 1,140 mg sodium, 44 g carbo., 3 g fiber, 35 g pro. EXCHANGES: 3 Starch, 3½ Medium-Fat Meat, 3½ Fat

*NOTE: If you prefer a red sauce on your enchiladas, omit the soup, sour cream, 1 cup milk, and almonds. Stir the reserved chile peppers into 2½ cups homemade enchilada sauce or two 10-ounce cans enchilada sauce. Bake as directed.

LIGHTENED-UP CHICKEN ENCHILADAS:
Prepare as directed, except use fat-free or light cream cheese (4 ounces), reduced-sodium condensed soup, fat-free or light dairy sour cream, fat-free milk, and reduced-fat Monterey Jack cheese. Omit the 2 tablespoons slivered almonds. Top the baked enchiladas with ½ cup chopped tomato (1 medium).

PER 2 ENCHILADAS: 546 cal., 21 g total fat (8 g sat. fat, 0 g trans fat), 91 mg chol., 1,058 mg sodium, 51 g carbo., 4 g fiber, 37 g pro. EXCHANGES: 3½ Starch, 4 Lean Meat, 1½ Fat

TUNA NOODLE CASSEROLE (photo, page 223)

PREP: 30 MINUTES **BAKE:** 25 MINUTES
STAND: 5 MINUTES **OVEN:** 375°F
MAKES: 4 TO 6 SERVINGS

- 3 cups packaged dried wide noodles (about 5 ounces)
- ¾ cup chopped sweet red pepper (1 medium)
- 1 cup chopped celery (2 stalks)
- ¼ cup chopped onion
- ¼ cup butter or margarine
- ¼ cup all-purpose flour
- 1 to 2 tablespoons Dijon-style mustard
- ½ teaspoon salt
- ¼ teaspoon black pepper
- 2¼ cups milk
- 1 12-ounce can chunk white tuna (water pack), drained and broken into chunks; two 5-ounce pouches chunk light tuna in water, drained; or two 6-ounce cans skinless, boneless salmon, drained
- ½ cup panko (Japanese-style bread crumbs) or soft bread crumbs
- ¼ cup freshly grated Parmesan cheese
- 1 tablespoon snipped fresh parsley
- 1 tablespoon butter, melted

1 Preheat oven to 375°F. Lightly grease a 1½-quart casserole; set aside. In a large saucepan cook noodles according to package directions. Drain; return noodles to pan.

2 Meanwhile, for sauce, in a medium saucepan cook sweet pepper, celery, and onion in ¼ cup hot butter over medium heat for 8 to 10 minutes or until tender. Stir in flour, mustard, salt, and black pepper. Add milk all at once; cook and stir until slightly thickened and bubbly. Gently fold sauce and tuna into cooked noodles. Transfer noodle mixture to prepared casserole.

3 In a small bowl combine bread crumbs, cheese, parsley, and melted butter. Sprinkle crumb mixture over noodle mixture. Bake, uncovered, for 25 to 30 minutes or until heated through. Let stand 5 minutes before serving.

PER 1½ CUPS: 495 cal., 23 g total fat (12 g sat. fat, 0 g trans fat), 115 mg chol., 1,040 mg sodium, 42 g carbo., 3 g fiber, 33 g pro. EXCHANGES: ½ Vegetable, 2½ Starch, 3½ Lean Meat, 2 Fat

CHEESY TUNA NOODLE CASSEROLE: Prepare as directed, except add 1 cup cheddar cheese cubes (4 ounces) with the tuna.

PER 1½ CUPS: 609 cal., 31 g total fat (18 g sat. fat, 0 g trans fat), 145 mg chol., 1,216 mg sodium, 42 g carbo., 3 g fiber, 40 g pro. EXCHANGES: 2½ Starch, ½ Vegetable, 4½ Medium-Fat Meat, 2 Fat

MACARONI AND CHEESE

PREP: 25 MINUTES **BAKE:** 25 MINUTES
STAND: 10 MINUTES **OVEN:** 350°F
MAKES: 4 SERVINGS

- 2 cups packaged dried elbow macaroni (8 ounces)
- ½ cup chopped onion (1 medium)
- 2 tablespoons butter or margarine
- 2 tablespoons all-purpose flour
- ⅛ teaspoon black pepper
- 2½ cups milk
- 1½ cups shredded cheddar cheese (6 ounces)
- 1½ cups shredded American cheese (6 ounces)

1 Preheat oven to 350°F. Cook pasta according to package directions; drain. Set aside.

2 For cheese sauce, in a medium saucepan cook onion in hot butter until tender. Stir in flour and pepper. Add milk all at once. Cook and stir over medium heat until slightly thickened and bubbly. Add cheeses; stir until cheeses melt. Stir in pasta. Transfer pasta mixture to an ungreased 2-quart casserole.

3 Bake, uncovered, for 25 to 30 minutes or until bubbly. Let stand for 10 minutes before serving.

PER 1½ CUPS: 691 cal., 37 g total fat (23 g sat. fat, 0 g trans fat), 112 mg chol., 1,003 mg sodium, 56 g carbo., 2 g fiber, 33 g pro. EXCHANGES: 4 Starch, 3 High-Fat Meat, 2 Fat

SAUCEPAN MACARONI AND CHEESE: Prepare as directed, except reduce milk to 2 cups. After draining macaroni, immediately return to saucepan. Pour cheese sauce over top; stir to coat macaroni with sauce. Cook over low heat for 2 to 3 minutes or until heated through, stirring frequently. Let stand for 10 minutes before serving.

PER 1½ CUPS: 676 cal., 36 g total fat (23 g sat. fat, 0 g trans fat), 110 mg chol., 991 mg sodium, 54 g carbo., 2 g fiber, 32 g pro. EXCHANGES: 3½ Starch, 3 High-Fat Meat, 2 Fat

CHOOSE A CHEESE
IN THE ABOVE RECIPE YOU CAN SUBSTITUTE ANY MELTING CHEESE, SUCH AS PROVOLONE, MOZZARELLA, OR FONTINA, FOR THE AMERICAN CHEESE.

10 TO TRY—
MAC 'N' CHEESE

Start with Macaroni and Cheese, page 236.

1. PESTO: Add 2 tablespoons purchased basil pesto to pasta mixture. Before baking, top with mixture of ¾ cup soft bread crumbs and 2 tablespoons melted butter.

2. VEGGIE: Add 2½ cups fresh broccoli florets and/or thinly sliced carrots to pasta water the last 5 minutes of cooking.

3. GREEK-STYLE: Add ½ cup pitted, halved Kalamata olives to pasta mixture. After baking, top with crumbled feta cheese and oregano. **4. MEAT LOVER'S:** Add 1½ cups crumbled cooked sausage to pasta mixture. After baking, top with chopped red sweet pepper and basil.

5. BLUE CHEESE-GARLIC: Cook 4 cloves garlic, minced, with onion. Substitute ½ cup crumbled blue cheese for ½ cup of cheddar.

6. SMOKY APPLE: Use smoked cheddar cheese. Add 4 slices crisp-cooked, crumbled bacon to pasta mixture. After baking, top with thinly sliced apple and cheese.

7. TUNA: Stir two 3-ounce pouches tuna into pasta mixture. Before baking, top with fish-shape crackers. **8. CRUMB-TOPPED:** Before baking, top with mixture of 1½ cups cornflakes, 3 tablespoons melted butter, and 1 tablespoon snipped fresh parsley.

9. STUFFING-TOPPED: Add 1½ cups shredded roasted chicken and 1 teaspoon dried thyme to pasta mixture. Before baking, top with crushed herb-seasoned stuffing mix. **10. CHILI-STYLE:** Stir one 15-ounce can chili beans in chili gravy into pasta mixture. Before baking, top with crushed corn chips.

MEDITERRANEAN PASTA GRATIN

cheese lightly browns. Let stand 5 minutes before serving. Sprinkle each serving with basil.

*NOTE: To soften extra-firm tomatoes, add them to some of the hot pasta cooking water and let stand for 5 minutes. Drain well and add to the pasta mixture as directed.

PER 1 CUP: 379 cal., 19 g total fat (7 g sat. fat, 0 g trans fat), 33 mg chol., 485 mg sodium, 33 g carbo., 5 g fiber, 18 g pro. EXCHANGES: 1 Vegetable, 2 Starch, 1½ Medium-Fat Meat, 2 Fat

BEST EVER • LOW FAT

THREE-BEAN TAMALE PIE

PREP: 30 MINUTES **BAKE:** 20 MINUTES
OVEN: 400°F **MAKES:** 8 SERVINGS

- 1 cup chopped green sweet pepper (1 large)
- ½ cup chopped onion (1 medium)
- 3 cloves garlic, minced
- 1 tablespoon vegetable oil
- 1 15- to 16-ounce can kidney beans, rinsed, drained, and slightly mashed
- 1 15- to 16-ounce can pinto beans, rinsed, drained, and slightly mashed
- 1 15-ounce can black beans, rinsed, drained, and slightly mashed
- 1 11.5-ounce can (1⅓ cups) vegetable juice
- 1 4-ounce can diced green chile peppers, undrained
- 1¼ teaspoons chili powder
- ¾ teaspoon ground cumin
- 1 8½-ounce package corn muffin mix
- ½ cup shredded cheddar cheese (2 ounces)
- ¼ cup snipped fresh cilantro or parsley
  Salsa and/or dairy sour cream (optional)

1 Preheat oven to 400°F. Grease a 3-quart rectangular baking dish; set aside.

2 In a large skillet cook sweet pepper, onion, and garlic in hot oil until tender. Stir in kidney, pinto, and black beans; vegetable juice; undrained chile peppers; chili powder; and cumin. Heat bean mixture through and spoon into prepared dish.

3 Prepare corn muffin mix according to package directions; add cheese and cilantro to batter, stirring just until combined. Evenly spoon corn muffin mixture on top of bean mixture. Bake, uncovered, for 20 to 25 minutes or until golden. If desired, serve with salsa and/or sour cream.

PER ⅔ CUP: 313 cal., 8 g total fat (3 g sat. fat, 0 g trans fat), 8 mg chol., 994 mg sodium, 52 g carbo., 12 g fiber, 14 g pro. EXCHANGES: 3½ Starch, ½ Lean Meat, ½ Fat

WHOLE GRAIN

MEDITERRANEAN PASTA GRATIN

PREP: 30 MINUTES **BAKE:** 30 MINUTES
STAND: 5 MINUTES **OVEN:** 375°F
MAKES: 6 SERVINGS

- 2½ cups packaged dried multigrain or whole grain penne pasta (8 ounces)
- 4 cups packaged fresh baby spinach
- 2 cups fresh cremini mushrooms, quartered
- ½ cup coarsely chopped oil-packed dried tomatoes*
- ¼ cup chopped, pitted Kalamata olives
- ½ cup purchased basil pesto
- 2 tablespoons balsamic vinegar
- 1 4-inch ball (about 8 ounces) fresh mozzarella cheese, thinly sliced
- ½ cup shredded fresh basil

1 Preheat oven to 375°F. Lightly grease a 1½-quart au gratin dish; set aside. In a large pot cook pasta in lightly salted boiling water according to package directions, adding spinach and mushrooms for the last 1 minute of cooking. Drain pasta mixture; return to pot.

2 Stir dried tomatoes and olives into pasta mixture. Add pesto and vinegar; toss gently to coat. Transfer pasta mixture to prepared dish. Cover dish with foil. Bake for 20 to 25 minutes or until heated through. Remove from oven. Uncover dish and top pasta mixture with cheese slices. Return dish to oven; bake 10 minutes more or until

CONVENIENCE COOKING

SIMPLE STROMBOLI, PAGE 246

CONVENIENCE COOKING

NOURISHING MEALS AT HOME CAN BE A MEANINGFUL PART OF ANY DAY—EVEN THE BUSIEST—WHEN YOU COMBINE THESE SHORTCUT STRATEGIES WITH THE QUICK RECIPES IN THIS CHAPTER.

FAST SUPERMARKET FIXES

To save time in the kitchen, start at the supermarket with ingredients that can speed up your cooking.

SHORTCUT INGREDIENTS: It's amazing how much prep time can be eliminated thanks to convenience products such as grated cheese, pasta sauces, frozen meatballs, bread shells, presliced mushrooms, bottled roasted sweet peppers, prepared salsas, sauce mixes, and seasoning blends.

READY-MADE ENTRÉES: Refrigerated main dishes, such as pot roast and meat loaf, give you a head start on dinner. Freshen them with a handful of well-chosen ingredients—see the two pot roast recipes, page 242, for creative, quick meals.

DELI SOLUTIONS: A good supermarket deli lets you tap into the "make some/buy some" strategy.

■ Prepare the main dish and serve purchased deli salads to effortlessly round out the meal.

■ Pick up a roasted chicken to serve for one night's dinner. Use leftovers for another meal—find ideas on pages 248, 251, and 252.

■ Turn your favorite deli salad into a main dish by adding chopped cooked meat, such as turkey, ham, or roast beef, leftover from another meal.

MEATS THAT KEEP LONGER: Avoid a time-eating trip to the store by stocking up on a supply of meats with long shelf lives, such as pepperoni, kielbasa, and cooked corned beef. Kielbasa takes just minutes to heat. Pepperoni can be tossed with pasta or tucked into omelets, and you can use cooked corned beef in reuben sandwiches or add it to casseroles.

ON THE HOME FRONT

If you find yourself heading to the drive-through or calling for takeout more often than you really want, consider these tips instead.

■ Sizzle up a double batch. Leftover grilled meats taste great in salads or sandwiches, or tossed with pasta and prepared pasta sauce.

■ Save every last leftover. A cup of chili and some leftover stew here and there might not look like a lot, but they can add up to a satisfying meal on nights when everyone's eating in shifts. Reheat and serve them over corn bread, couscous, or baked potatoes to make them into a meal. Keep little cans of veggies around for sides.

■ Toss together some tacos. Leftover chicken, pork roast, steak, or seafood—just about anything—tucks tastily into or on top of tortillas for satisfying tacos and quesadillas. Keep a few extra ingredients on hand, such as salsa, olives, roasted sweet peppers, and favorite cheeses. For good go-withs, stash a few cans of refried beans and a box or two of Spanish rice mix in the cupboard.

■ Serve swift sides. When a main dish is all you have the time or energy to cook, reach for the easiest serve-alongs on the shelf. Couscous, angel hair pasta, pouches of cooked rice, and refrigerated mashed potatoes top the list.

■ Bring on the bruschetta. Well-topped toasts can morph a soup or salad into a full meal. Simply toast French bread slices, rub with garlic, and brush on olive oil. Top with whatever you have handy, such as pesto, cheese, bottled roasted sweet peppers, olives, and/or fresh herbs. Slip the topped toasts under the broiler to warm and/or melt the toppings.

SKILLET POT ROAST WITH MUSHROOMS AND CHERRIES

START TO FINISH: 30 MINUTES
MAKES: 4 TO 6 SERVINGS

- 1 12-ounce package frozen unsweetened pitted dark sweet cherries
- 1 8-ounce package fresh mushrooms, halved (3 cups)
- 1 medium red sweet pepper, cut into bite-size strips
- 1 cup chopped onion (1 large)
- 2 teaspoons dried sage or thyme, crushed
- 1 tablespoon olive or vegetable oil
- 2 16- or 17-ounce packages refrigerated cooked beef pot roast with juices
- 2 tablespoons balsamic vinegar

1 Place frozen cherries in colander. Run cold water over cherries to partially thaw. Set aside; drain well.

2 In a very large skillet cook mushrooms, sweet pepper, onion, and 1 teaspoon of the sage in hot oil about 7 minutes or until tender. Add the beef pot roast and juices, balsamic vinegar, and the cherries to the skillet. Bring mixture to boiling; reduce heat. Simmer, uncovered, about 10 minutes or until mixture heats through and the juices thicken slightly, stirring occasionally. Stir in remaining 1 teaspoon sage.

PER SERVING: 451 cal., 18 g total fat (7 g sat. fat, 0 g trans fat), 120 mg chol., 727 mg sodium, 27 g carbo., 4 g fiber, 49 g pro. EXCHANGES: 1 Vegetable, 1 Fruit, ½ Starch, 6 Lean Meat

---

BEST EVER ▪ FAST ▪ LOW FAT

PICANTE POT ROAST

START TO FINISH: 20 MINUTES
MAKES: 4 SERVINGS

- 1 16- or 17-ounce package refrigerated cooked beef pot roast with juices
- 1½ cups sliced fresh mushrooms
- 1 cup bottled picante sauce
- 1 14-ounce can chicken broth
- 1 cup couscous
- 2 tablespoons snipped fresh cilantro
  Dairy sour cream (optional)
  Chopped fresh tomato (optional)
  Sliced avocado (optional)

1 Transfer the juices from the pot roast package to a large skillet. Stir mushrooms and picante sauce into juices in skillet.

2 Cut pot roast into 1- to 1½-inch pieces; add to skillet. Bring to boiling; reduce heat. Simmer, covered, for 10 minutes.

3 Meanwhile, in a medium saucepan bring broth to boiling. Stir in couscous; cover and remove from heat. Let stand about 5 minutes or until liquid absorbs. Fluff couscous with a fork. Stir in cilantro.

4 Spoon pot roast mixture over couscous mixture. If desired, serve with sour cream, tomato, and/or avocado.

PER ¾ CUP MIXTURE + ¾ CUP COUSCOUS: 370 cal., 9 g total fat (3 g sat. fat, 0 g trans fat), 61 mg chol., 1,268 mg sodium, 44 g carbo., 3 g fiber, 31 g pro. EXCHANGES: 3 Starch, 3 Lean Meat, ½ Fat

---

SPEEDY BEEF STIR-FRY

START TO FINISH: 30 MINUTES
MAKES: 4 SERVINGS

- 1 8.8-ounce pouch cooked long grain rice
- 1 pound boneless beef top loin steak, trimmed of fat and cut into thin strips (see photos, page 244)
- 2 tablespoons vegetable oil
- 1 16-ounce package frozen broccoli stir-fry vegetable blend
- ½ cup orange juice
- 1 tablespoon soy sauce
- 2 teaspoons cornstarch
- 1 teaspoon ground ginger
- ¼ teaspoon crushed red pepper
- ¼ teaspoon salt
  Sliced almonds, toasted (see tip, page 20) (optional)

1 Heat rice according to package directions; set aside. In a large skillet cook beef strips in 1 tablespoon hot oil over medium-high heat until brown; remove from skillet. Add stir-fry vegetables and remaining oil to skillet. Cook until tender. Drain any excess liquid; discard.

2 In a small bowl combine orange juice, soy sauce, cornstarch, ginger, crushed pepper, and salt. Return meat to skillet. Add orange juice mixture to skillet; cook and stir until thick and bubbly. Serve over rice. If desired, sprinkle with almonds.

PER 1 CUP MIXTURE + ABOUT ⅓ CUP RICE: 472 cal., 26 g total fat (8 g sat. fat, 0 g trans fat), 65 mg chol., 504 mg sodium, 31 g carbo., 4 g fiber, 28 g pro. EXCHANGES: 1½ Vegetable, 1½ Starch, 3 Lean Meat, 3 Fat

SKILLET POT ROAST WITH MUSHROOMS AND CHERRIES

TWO FLASHES IN THE PAN ASIAN STIR-FRIES TOP THE LIST OF ALL-TIME-QUICKEST MEALS. BUT POT ROAST? YES—IT, TOO, CAN BE SPEEDY WHEN YOU START WITH A PRECOOKED PRODUCT.

SPEEDY BEEF STIR-FRY

ASIAN BEEF SALAD

START TO FINISH: 25 MINUTES
MAKES: 4 SERVINGS

- 1 9- to 10-ounce package chopped hearts of romaine
- 12 ounces beef top loin steak (about ¾ inch thick) or beef strips cut for stir-fry
- ¼ teaspoon salt
- ¼ teaspoon black pepper
- 1 tablespoon vegetable oil
- 1 medium red sweet pepper, cut into strips
- ¾ cup coarsely shredded fresh carrots
- ½ cup chopped green onions (4)
- ½ cup chopped dry-roasted peanuts
- ½ cup bottled sesame-ginger salad dressing

1 Divide romaine among four plates, set aside. Trim fat from steak; thinly slice steak into bite-size strips (see photos 1 and 2, below). (If using beef strips for stir-fry, cut any large pieces into bite-size strips.) Season meat with salt and pepper.

2 In a large skillet cook meat strips in hot oil over medium-high heat for 4 to 5 minutes or until brown. Add sweet pepper and carrots; cook and stir for 1 minute more. Remove skillet from heat; stir in green onions. Spoon meat mixture over romaine on each plate. Sprinkle with peanuts. Drizzle with dressing. Serve immediately.

PER 1 CUP: 474 cal., 35 g total fat (8 g sat. fat, 0 g trans fat), 48 mg chol., 512 mg sodium, 18 g carbo., 5 g fiber, 23 g pro.
EXCHANGES: 2 Vegetable, ½ Other Carbo., 2½ Lean Meat, 5½ Fat

CHILI BURGERS

START TO FINISH: 30 MINUTES
MAKES: 4 SERVINGS

- 4 4-ounce purchased uncooked ground beef or turkey patties
- ½ teaspoon salt
  Dash black pepper
- 1 tablespoon vegetable oil
- ¼ cup chopped onion (1 small)
- 1 clove garlic, minced
- 1 15-ounce can chili with beans
- 1 14.5-ounce can diced tomatoes, undrained
- 4 slices Texas toast, toasted
- ½ cup shredded cheddar cheese (2 ounces)

1 Sprinkle patties with salt and pepper. Heat a very large skillet over medium-high heat. Add patties; reduce heat to medium. Cook, uncovered, for 6 to 8 minutes or until juices run clear (160°F for beef; 165°F for turkey), turning once. Remove patties from skillet and keep warm. Drain fat from skillet; discard. Carefully wipe out skillet.

2 Add oil to skillet. Return skillet to heat. Add onion and garlic; cook over medium heat until tender. Stir in chili and undrained tomatoes. Bring to boiling; reduce heat. Simmer, uncovered, for 5 to 10 minutes or until desired consistency, stirring occasionally.

3 To serve, place patties on top of toast. Spoon chili mixture over top. Sprinkle with cheese.

PER SERVING: 676 cal., 43 g total fat (16 g sat. fat, 0 g trans fat), 172 mg chol., 1,419 mg sodium, 39 g carbo., 5 g fiber, 36 g pro.
EXCHANGES: 1 Vegetable, 2 Starch, 4 Medium-Fat Meat, 4 Fat

PREPARING MEAT FOR STIR-FRYING, STEP-BY-STEP

1. Using kitchen shears, trim away fat along the edges of the meat. **2.** For a more tender stir-fry, thinly slice the meat across the grain into bite-size pieces. To slice raw meat easily, pop it into the freezer for 10 to 15 minutes; this firms up the meat, making it easier to slice and to control the thickness of the slices.

TEX-MEX SKILLET

START TO FINISH: 20 MINUTES
MAKES: 4 SERVINGS

- 8 ounces ground pork
- 4 ounces bulk chorizo sausage or lean ground beef
- 1 10-ounce can diced tomatoes and green chiles
- 1 cup frozen whole kernel corn
- ¾ cup water
- ½ cup chopped red sweet pepper
- 1 cup uncooked instant rice
- ½ cup shredded cheddar cheese or Monterey Jack cheese (2 ounces)
- Flour tortillas, warmed (optional)
- Dairy sour cream (optional)

1 In a large skillet cook pork and sausage until meat is brown. Drain fat; discard. Stir in undrained tomatoes, corn, water, and sweet pepper. Bring mixture to boiling.

2 Stir uncooked rice into skillet. Remove skillet from heat. Top with cheese. Cover and let stand about 5 minutes or until rice is tender. If desired, serve meat mixture in flour tortillas and top with sour cream.

PER 1 CUP: 484 cal., 28 g total fat (12 g sat. fat, 0 g trans fat), 81 mg chol., 671 mg sodium, 34 g carbo., 2 g fiber, 24 g pro. EXCHANGES: ½ Vegetable, 2 Starch, 2½ Medium-Fat Meat, 3 Fat

PORK WITH NOODLES AND CABBAGE

START TO FINISH: 30 MINUTES
MAKES: 4 SERVINGS

- 3 cups packaged dried noodles (6 ounces) or one 10.5-ounce package dried spaetzle
- 3 tablespoons butter or margarine
- 1 tablespoon chopped fresh parsley
- ¼ teaspoon salt
- ¼ teaspoon black pepper
- 2 tablespoons packed brown sugar
- 2 tablespoons water
- 2 tablespoons cider vinegar
- 3 cups shredded red or green cabbage (half of a 1½-pound head)
- 1 17-ounce package refrigerated cooked pork roast au jus

1 Cook noodles according to package directions; drain. In a large skillet cook drained noodles in 2 tablespoons of the butter over medium heat about 3 minutes or until heated through, gently stirring occasionally. Stir in parsley. Season with ⅛ teaspoon each of salt and pepper. Remove from skillet; keep warm.

2 In same skillet combine brown sugar, water, vinegar, and remaining butter. Bring to boiling over medium heat, stirring to dissolve brown sugar. Add cabbage. Return to boiling; reduce heat. Cook, covered, for 5 minutes or until cabbage is crisp-tender. Season with remaining salt and pepper.

3 Meanwhile, heat pork roast according to package directions. Serve pork with noodles and cabbage.

PER 1 CUP EACH PORK, NOODLES, AND CABBAGE: 565 cal., 17 g total fat (8 g sat. fat, 0 g trans fat), 152 mg chol., 1,453 mg sodium, 64 g carbo., 4 g fiber, 37 g pro. EXCHANGES: 1 Vegetable, 4 Starch, 3 Lean Meat, 1 Fat

PORK MEDALLIONS WITH LEMON-DILL GREEN BEANS

START TO FINISH: 20 MINUTES
MAKES: 4 SERVINGS

- 1 1.7-pound package honey-mustard marinated pork tenderloin
- 1 tablespoon butter or margarine
- 1 9-ounce package frozen French-cut green beans, thawed
- 1 teaspoon dried dillweed
- 1 teaspoon lemon juice

1 Cut pork tenderloin into ¼-inch slices. In a very large skillet cook pork in hot butter over medium heat for 4 to 6 minutes or until juices run clear, turning once. Remove meat from skillet; reserve drippings. Keep warm.

2 Add green beans and dillweed to drippings in skillet. Cook and stir for 3 to 4 minutes or until beans are tender. Stir in lemon juice. Transfer beans to a serving platter. Arrange pork slices on top of green beans.

PER SERVING: 189 cal., 8 g total fat (4 g sat. fat, 0 g trans fat), 53 mg chol., 531 mg sodium, 8 g carbo., 2 g fiber, 21 g pro. EXCHANGES: ½ Vegetable, ½ Other Carbo., 3 Lean Meat

QUICK MU SHU PORK

START TO FINISH: 20 MINUTES
MAKES: 4 SERVINGS

- 12 ounces boneless pork top loin chops, cut into thin strips
- 1 tablespoon vegetable oil
- 1 8-ounce package sliced fresh mushrooms
- ½ cup bias-sliced green onions (4)
- 4 cups packaged shredded cabbage with carrot (coleslaw mix)
- 2 tablespoons soy sauce
- 1 teaspoon toasted sesame oil
- ⅛ teaspoon crushed red pepper
- 8 7- to 8-inch flour tortillas, warmed
- ¼ cup bottled hoisin or plum sauce

1 In a large skillet cook pork strips in hot oil over medium-high heat for 4 to 5 minutes or until no longer pink. Remove meat from skillet.

2 Add mushrooms and green onions to skillet; cook about 3 minutes or until tender. Add coleslaw mix; cook about 1 minute or until mixture wilts. Return meat to skillet. Add soy sauce, sesame oil, and crushed pepper; heat through. Serve pork mixture with tortillas and hoisin sauce.

PER SERVING: 400 cal., 13 g total fat (3 g sat. fat, 0 g trans fat), 57 mg chol., 1,066 mg sodium, 43 g carbo., 4 g fiber, 27 g pro. EXCHANGES: 1½ Vegetable, 2½ Starch, 4 Lean Meat

EASY BARBECUED PORK PIZZA

PREP: 15 MINUTES **BAKE:** 12 MINUTES
OVEN: 425°F **MAKES:** 8 SERVINGS

- 1 17- to 18-ounce tub refrigerated barbecue sauce with shredded pork (2 cups)
- 2 medium red and/or yellow sweet peppers, cut into thin strips
- 1 medium onion, cut into thin wedges
- 1 tablespoon vegetable oil
- 1 12-inch packaged prebaked pizza crust
- 1 cup shredded Monterey Jack cheese (4 ounces)

1 Preheat oven to 425°F. Heat shredded pork according to package directions. Meanwhile, in a large skillet cook sweet pepper and onion in hot oil over medium-high heat about 5 minutes or until crisp-tender.

2 Place pizza crust on an ungreased baking sheet. Spoon shredded pork over crust, spreading evenly. Top with sweet pepper and onion mixture. Sprinkle with cheese. Bake about 12 minutes or until cheese melts and crust edge turns light brown.

PER SERVING: 319 cal., 11 g total fat (3 g sat. fat, 0 g trans fat), 33 mg chol., 862 mg sodium, 39 g carbo., 1 g fiber, 17 g pro. EXCHANGES: 2½ Starch

SIMPLE STROMBOLI (photo, page 239)

PREP: 20 MINUTES **BAKE:** 30 MINUTES
STAND: 10 MINUTES **OVEN:** 375°F
MAKES: 4 TO 6 SERVINGS

- 2 teaspoons olive oil
- 1 tablespoon cornmeal
- 1 13.8-ounce package refrigerated pizza dough
- 4 ounces thinly sliced cooked ham
- 1 cup shredded mozzarella cheese (4 ounces)
- 1 cup fresh prewashed baby spinach or torn spinach
- 4 ounces thinly sliced cooked turkey
- ¼ cup Kalamata olives, pitted and chopped
- ⅓ cup chopped red, green, or yellow sweet pepper
- 1 egg, lightly beaten

1 Preheat oven to 375°F. Lightly brush a baking sheet with olive oil and sprinkle with cornmeal; set aside. On a lightly floured surface carefully stretch or roll pizza dough into a 13×10-inch rectangle. Arrange ham slices on dough about ½ inch from edges. Sprinkle with half the cheese. Layer spinach and turkey on cheese. Top with remaining cheese, olives, and sweet pepper. Roll up dough, starting from a long side. Pinch dough to seal the seam and ends.

2 Place loaf, seam side down, on prepared baking sheet. Brush with egg. Using a sharp knife, cut slits in top for steam to escape. Bake about 30 minutes or until golden brown. Let stand for 10 minutes. To serve, slice loaf into serving-size pieces.

PER SERVING: 422 cal., 18 g total fat (6 g sat. fat, 0 g trans fat), 188 mg chol., 1,335 mg sodium, 43 g carbo., 3 g fiber, 23 g pro. EXCHANGES: 3 Starch, 2 Medium-Fat Meat, 1 Fat

MAKE-IT-MINE POTPIE

WHETHER YOU GO GOURMET WITH CHICKEN, BABY VEGGIES, AND PUFF PASTRY OR KEEP IT DOWN HOME WITH GROUND BEEF, STEW VEGGIES, AND BISCUITS, YOU'RE JUST 25 MINUTES FROM POPPING A WARMING POTPIE IN THE OVEN.

BASIC INGREDIENTS

PREP: 25 MINUTES
BAKE: 22 MINUTES
STAND: 20 MINUTES **OVEN:** 400°F
MAKES: 6 SERVINGS

- 1 pound Ground Meat or 2 cups Cooked Meat
- 1 9- to 10-ounce package Frozen Vegetables (about 2 cups)
- 1 10½- to 10¾-ounce can condensed soup Base or 1¼ cups gravy or pasta sauce Base
- 1 teaspoon Seasoning
- ½ cup water (optional)
- ½ cup Cheese (optional)

  Topper

  Milk

  Grated Parmesan cheese (optional)

GROUND MEAT OR COOKED MEAT (PICK ONE)

Ground beef

Ground pork, bulk pork sausage, or Italian sausage

Cooked chicken

Cooked turkey

FROZEN VEGETABLES
(PICK ONE)

Baby mixed beans and carrots

Mixed vegetables

Peas and carrots

Peas and pearl onions

Stew vegetables

BASE (PICK ONE)

Condensed soup (cream of celery, chicken, mushroom, onion, or potato)

Canned or jarred gravy (beef, brown with mushrooms, chicken, country-style, golden pork, mushroom, or turkey)

Bottled Alfredo pasta sauce

SEASONING (PICK ONE)

Chili powder

Curry powder

Dried dillweed

Dried tarragon, crushed

Dried thyme, crushed

Ground chipotle chile pepper

Italian seasoning

CHEESE (PICK ONE)

Cheddar, Monterey Jack, or Mozzarella cheese

TOPPER (PICK ONE)

- ½ of a 17.3-ounce package frozen puff pastry sheets (1 sheet)
- ½ of a 15-ounce package rolled refrigerated unbaked piecrust (1)
- 1 7.5-ounce package refrigerated biscuits (10)
- 1 8-ounce package refrigerated crescent rolls (8)

BASIC INSTRUCTIONS

1 Preheat oven to 400°F. If using Ground Meat, in a large skillet cook meat until no longer pink. Drain fat; discard. In large skillet combine Ground or Cooked Meat, Frozen Vegetables, Base, and Seasoning. Bring meat mixture to boiling. Add water, if needed, for desired consistency. If desired, stir in Cheese. Transfer meat mixture to a 2-quart round casserole or baking dish.

2 For Topper, if using pastry sheet or piecrust, unfold pastry sheet or unroll piecrust. On a lightly floured surface roll pastry sheet or piecrust to 1 inch beyond edge of casserole. Place pastry on top of casserole. Trim pastry evenly with casserole edge, leaving 1 inch excess pastry. Fold excess pastry under, even with casserole edge. Press pastry along edges to seal.

3 If using biscuits or crescent rolls, quarter individual pieces and arrange over filling.

4 Brush Topper lightly with milk and, if desired, sprinkle with additional Seasoning or grated Parmesan cheese.

5 Bake, uncovered, for 22 to 25 minutes or until golden brown and bubbly. Let stand for 20 minutes before serving.

VERMICELLI WITH SAUSAGE AND SPINACH

START TO FINISH: 25 MINUTES
MAKES: 4 TO 6 SERVINGS

- 1 pound cooked smoked sausage, halved lengthwise and cut into ½-inch slices
- ¾ cup chopped onion (1 large)
- 2 large cloves garlic, chopped
- 2 teaspoons olive oil
- 2 14-ounce cans reduced-sodium chicken broth
- ¼ cup water
- 8 ounces packaged dried vermicelli or angel hair pasta, broken in half
- 1 9-ounce package fresh prewashed baby spinach
- ¼ teaspoon black pepper
- ⅓ cup whipping cream

1 In a 4-quart Dutch oven cook sausage, onion, and garlic in hot oil over medium-high heat until sausage is lightly browned and onion is tender.

2 Add broth and water to Dutch oven; bring to boiling. Add pasta; cook for 3 minutes, stirring frequently. Add spinach and pepper; cook about 1 minute more or until spinach wilts. Stir in cream. Serve immediately.

PER 1¾ CUPS: 689 cal., 43 g total fat (16 g sat. fat, 0 g trans fat), 97 mg chol., 1,470 mg sodium, 50 g carbo., 4 g fiber, 26 g pro. EXCHANGES: 1 Vegetable, 3 Starch, 2 High-Fat Meat, 5 Fat

LOVE THOSE LEFTOVERS

THESE TIPS WILL TRANSFORM ONE NIGHT'S EXTRAS INTO A FRESH MEAL.

■ Cook up a pasta. Use the recipe above as a guideline, omitting the smoked sausage. Stir in reheated leftover cooked meat when you add the spinach.

■ Toss up a salad. Add roasted meat to fresh lettuces, vegetables, a sprinkling of cheese, and your favorite salad dressing.

■ Stir up a soup. Cook pasta in beef or chicken broth until tender, adding frozen vegetables the last few minutes of cooking time. Add leftover meat; heat through.

■ Fashion some French bread sandwiches. Sliced lengthwise, the long loaves are great for piling with leftover meat and topping with cheeses. Run under the broiler for terrifically tasty open-face sandwiches.

QUICK CHICKEN TACOS

START TO FINISH: 20 MINUTES **MAKES:** 10 TACOS

- 1 16-ounce can refried beans
- 2 6-ounce packages refrigerated cooked chicken breast strips, cut into bite-size pieces
- 1 10.5-ounce package 6-inch flour tortillas (10)
- 2 cups shredded Mexican-style four-cheese blend (8 ounces)
- 2 cups packaged shredded greens or iceberg lettuce
- ¾ cup chopped tomato (1 large)
- ½ cup bottled salsa
- ½ cup dairy sour cream
  Lime wedges

1 In a saucepan cook refried beans over medium heat until heated through, stirring occasionally.

2 Meanwhile, heat chicken breast strips according to package directions. Spread about 2 tablespoons refried beans on each tortilla. Top with chicken, cheese, lettuce, and tomato. Fold tortillas over filling. Serve with salsa, sour cream, and lime wedges.

PER TACO: 286 cal., 13 g total fat (7 g sat. fat, 0 g trans fat), 50 mg chol., 959 mg sodium, 25 g carbo., 4 g fiber, 18 g pro. EXCHANGES: 1½ Starch, 2 Lean Meat, 1 Fat

BUFFALO CHICKEN PIZZAS

START TO FINISH: 20 MINUTES **OVEN:** 450°F
MAKES: 4 SERVINGS

- 4 pita bread rounds
- ¼ cup bottled blue cheese salad dressing
- 1 9-ounce package refrigerated Southwest-flavor cooked chicken breast strips, cut into bite-size pieces
- 2 stalks celery, cut into thin strips
- 4 tablespoons blue cheese crumbles
  Bottled hot pepper sauce or Buffalo chicken wing sauce (optional)

1 Preheat oven to 450°F. Place pita rounds on baking sheet. Brush with blue cheese dressing. Top with chicken and celery strips.

2 Bake, uncovered, about 10 minutes or until heated through and pitas are crisp. Transfer to plates. Sprinkle with blue cheese crumbles. If desired, pass hot pepper sauce.

PER PIZZA: 353 cal., 13 g total fat (4 g sat. fat, 0 g trans fat), 52 mg chol., 1,171 mg sodium, 36 g carbo., 2 g fiber, 22 g pro. EXCHANGES: 2½ Starch, 2 Lean Meat, 1 Fat

VERMICELLI WITH SAUSAGE AND SPINACH

MEAL STARTERS KEEP PASTA, TORTILLAS, AND PITA BREADS ON HAND FOR QUICK DINNERS. START WITH THESE RECIPES AND IMPROVISE YOUR WAY TO MANY GOOD MEALS IN THE FUTURE.

QUICK CHICKEN TACOS

BUFFALO CHICKEN PIZZAS

COOK ONCE, EAT TWICE

MAKE A DOUBLE BATCH OF FAMILY-FRIENDLY CHICKEN STRIPS. THEN WATCH THEM GET DEVOURED THE NEXT NIGHT IN A COLORFUL SALAD WITH KID-PLEASING RANCH DRESSING.

TONIGHT

CRUNCHY CHICKEN STRIPS

PREP: 25 MINUTES **BAKE:** 10 MINUTES
OVEN: 425°F **MAKES:** 2 MEALS (4 SERVINGS EACH)

    Nonstick cooking spray
7 cups bite-size cheddar fish-shape crackers or 14 cups pretzels (14 ounces)
1½ cups bottled buttermilk ranch salad dressing
2 pounds chicken breast tenderloins
    Bottled buttermilk ranch salad dressing (optional)

1 Preheat oven to 425°F. Line two 15×10×1-inch baking pans with foil. Lightly coat foil with cooking spray; set aside.

2 Crush crackers* (you should have 5 cups); transfer to a shallow dish. In another shallow dish place the 1½ cups ranch dressing. Dip chicken tenderloins into dressing, allowing excess to drip off; dip into cracker crumbs to coat. Arrange chicken in prepared pans. Lightly coat chicken with cooking spray.

3 Bake, uncovered, for 10 to 15 minutes or until chicken is no longer pink (170°F), rotating pans halfway through baking. If desired, serve half of the chicken strips with additional ranch dressing.

4 Cool remaining chicken strips for 20 minutes. Place in an airtight container; cover and chill for up to 3 days or freeze for up to 1 month. To reheat strips, preheat oven to 400°F. Arrange chilled or frozen strips in a single layer on a baking sheet. Bake, uncovered, until heated through (allow 15 minutes for chilled and 20 minutes for frozen strips).

PER SERVING: 582 cal., 35 g total fat (7 g sat. fat, 0 g trans fat), 90 mg chol., 765 mg sodium, 34 g carbo., 1 g fiber, 33 g pro.
EXCHANGES: 2 Starch, 4 Lean Meat, 6 Fat

TOMORROW

RANCH-STYLE CHICKEN SALAD

START TO FINISH: 20 MINUTES
MAKES: 4 TO 6 SERVINGS

½ recipe Crunchy Chicken Strips or one 10-ounce package frozen breaded chicken breast strips
1 10-ounce package torn mixed salad greens
½ cup halved cherry tomatoes
½ cup red, yellow, and/or green sweet pepper strips (½ medium)
¼ cup sliced red onion
2 slices precooked bacon, heated according to package directions and crumbled
½ cup bottled ranch salad dressing

1 Heat chicken strips according to recipe or package directions. Arrange greens on salad plates. Top with chicken strips, tomatoes, sweet peppers, onion, and bacon. Drizzle with dressing.

PER SERVING: 765 cal., 52 g total fat (9 g sat. fat, 0 g trans fat), 94 mg chol., 1,178 mg sodium, 41 g carbo., 3 g fiber, 35 g pro.
EXCHANGES: 2 Vegetable, 2 Starch, 4 Lean Meat, 9 Fat

*NO-FUSS CRUMBS: Place the crackers in a resealable plastic bag and crush with a rolling pin; empty the bag and discard bag.

PESTO PENNE WITH ROASTED CHICKEN

START TO FINISH: 25 MINUTES
MAKES: 4 SERVINGS

- 8 ounces packaged dried penne, mostaccioli, or bow tie pasta (about 3 cups)
- 2 cups fresh broccoli florets
- 1 7-ounce container purchased basil pesto (about ¾ cup)
- 2½ cups bite-size slices of purchased roasted chicken, refrigerated cooked chicken breast strips, or bite-size slices of left-over cooked chicken (about 12 ounces)
- 1 cup bottled roasted red sweet peppers, drained and cut into strips
- ¼ cup finely shredded Parmesan cheese
- ½ teaspoon black pepper
   Finely shredded Parmesan cheese (optional)

1 In a 4-quart Dutch oven cook pasta according to package directions, adding broccoli the last 2 minutes of cooking. Drain, reserving ½ cup of the pasta water. Return drained pasta and broccoli to Dutch oven.

2 In a small bowl combine reserved pasta water and pesto. Add pesto mixture, chicken, and sweet peppers to Dutch oven; toss to combine. Heat through. Remove Dutch oven from heat; add the ¼ cup Parmesan cheese and black pepper; toss to combine. If desired, serve with additional cheese.

PER 2 CUPS: 657 cal., 36 g total fat (9 g sat. fat, 0 g trans fat), 95 mg chol., 1,025 mg sodium, 54 g carbo., 6 g fiber, 32 g pro. EXCHANGES: ½ Vegetable, 3½ Starch, 3 Lean Meat, 4½ Fat

SALSA-SAUCED TURKEY AND SWEET POTATOES

START TO FINISH: 40 MINUTES
MAKES: 4 SERVINGS

- 1 pound sweet potatoes
- 2 turkey breast tenderloins (1 to 1¼ pounds)
- ½ teaspoon salt
- ¼ teaspoon black pepper
- 1 tablespoon vegetable oil
- 1 cup bottled chunky salsa
- ¼ cup orange juice
   Snipped fresh cilantro or parsley (optional)

1 Peel sweet potatoes; cut into 1-inch pieces. In a saucepan cook potatoes, covered, in enough boiling water to cover for 10 to 12 minutes or until potatoes are just tender; drain.

2 Meanwhile, cut turkey crosswise into ½-inch slices. Sprinkle with salt and pepper. In a large nonstick skillet cook turkey in hot oil over medium-high heat for 6 to 8 minutes or until turkey is no longer pink, turning to brown evenly.

3 Add sweet potatoes, salsa, and orange juice to skillet. Cook until heated through, stirring gently. If desired, sprinkle with cilantro.

PER 1¼ CUPS: 251 cal., 4 g total fat (1 g sat. fat, 0 g trans fat), 70 mg chol., 775 mg sodium, 22 g carbo., 7 g fiber, 30 g pro. EXCHANGES: 1½ Starch, 3½ Lean Meat

CAESAR SALAD TURKEY ON CROSTINI

PREP: 15 MINUTES **BROIL:** 14 MINUTES
MAKES: 4 SERVINGS

- 4 4-ounce purchased uncooked ground turkey or beef patties
- ¼ teaspoon salt
- ¼ teaspoon black pepper
- 8 ½-inch slices sourdough bread
- ½ cup bottled Caesar salad dressing
- 4 cups packaged Mediterranean-blend torn mixed salad greens
- ½ cup bottled roasted red sweet peppers, drained and cut into thin strips
- ¼ cup shredded Parmesan cheese (2 ounces)

1 Preheat broiler. Sprinkle patties with salt and pepper. Place patties on unheated rack of a broiler pan. Broil 3 to 4 inches from heat for 12 to 14 minutes or until no longer pink (165°F for turkey; 160°F for beef), turning once. Remove from pan; keep warm.

2 Using 2 tablespoons of the dressing, brush both sides of bread slices. Place bread slices on broiler pan. Broil about 4 inches from heat for 1 to 2 minutes per side or until lightly toasted.

3 To serve, toss greens with remaining dressing. Top each of 4 bread slices with greens mixture. Add a burger and sweet pepper strips; sprinkle with Parmesan cheese. Top with remaining bread slices.

PER SANDWICH: 506 cal., 29 g total fat (6 g sat. fat, 0 g trans fat), 105 mg chol., 986 mg sodium, 32 g carbo., 3 g fiber, 29 g pro. EXCHANGES: ½ Vegetable, 2 Starch, 3 Lean Meat, 3½ Fat

TWO-BEAN CHILI WITH AVOCADO

START TO FINISH: 40 MINUTES **MAKES:** 4 SERVINGS

- 1 cup chopped onion (1 large)
- 2 teaspoons dried oregano, crushed
- 2 teaspoons olive oil
- 2 14.5-ounce cans diced tomatoes, undrained
- 1 15-ounce can black or kidney beans, rinsed and drained
- 1 15-ounce can pinto beans, rinsed and drained
- ½ cup bottled salsa
- 1 medium ripe avocado, halved, seeded, peeled, and diced
- ¼ cup snipped fresh cilantro

1 In a large saucepan cook onion and oregano in hot oil over medium-high heat for 3 to 5 minutes or until onion is tender, stirring occasionally. Stir in undrained tomatoes, beans, salsa, and ½ cup *water*. Bring to boiling; reduce heat. Simmer, covered, for 25 minutes, stirring occasionally. Top servings with avocado and cilantro.

PER 1¾ CUPS: 302 cal., 9 g total fat (1 g sat. fat, 0 g trans fat), 0 mg chol., 1,182 mg sodium, 49 g carbo., 17 g fiber, 15 g pro. EXCHANGES: 3 Starch, 1 Lean Meat, 1 Fat

MEDITERRANEAN-STYLE SHRIMP QUESADILLAS

START TO FINISH: 20 MINUTES
MAKES: 4 SERVINGS

- 4 8-inch vegetable tortillas
  Nonstick cooking spray
- ½ a 7-ounce carton garlic or roasted red pepper hummus (⅓ cup)
- 6 ounces peeled, deveined cooked shrimp
- 1 6-ounce jar marinated artichoke hearts, drained and coarsely chopped
- 1 4-ounce package crumbled feta cheese

1 Coat one side of each tortilla with cooking spray. Place tortillas, sprayed sides down, on work surface; spread with hummus. Top half of each tortilla with shrimp, artichokes, and cheese. Fold tortillas in half, pressing gently.

2 Heat large nonstick skillet or griddle over medium heat for 1 minute. Cook quesadillas, two at a time, for 4 to 6 minutes or until browned and heated through, turning once.

PER SERVING: 448 cal., 20 g total fat (7 g sat. fat, 0 g trans fat), 108 mg chol., 1,098 mg sodium, 42 g carbo., 4 g fiber, 21 g pro. EXCHANGES: 3 Starch, 1½ Lean Meat, 2½ Fat

20-MINUTE NOODLE BOWLS

START TO FINISH: 20 MINUTES **MAKES:** 4 SERVINGS

- 1 14-ounce can reduced-sodium chicken broth or lower-sodium beef broth
- ½ cup bottled peanut sauce
- 2 cups frozen stir-fry or mixed vegetables
- 2 3-ounce packages ramen noodles (any flavor), broken

1 In a large saucepan combine broth and peanut sauce. Bring to boiling. Stir in frozen vegetables and noodles (discard seasoning packet). Return to boiling; reduce heat. Simmer, covered, for 3 minutes or until noodles and vegetables are tender. Divide noodles and broth among four bowls.

PER SERVING: 293 cal., 12 g total fat (7 g sat. fat, 0 g trans fat), 0 mg chol., 532 mg sodium, 39 g carbo., 3 g fiber, 8 g pro. EXCHANGES: ½ Vegetable, 2½ Starch, 2 Fat

CHICKEN FIVE WAYS

TURN DELI-ROASTED CHICKEN INTO A VARIETY OF GREAT-TASTING MEALS.

TUCKED INTO FAJITAS: Saute thin slices of red sweet pepper and onion in vegetable oil. Toss in strips of chicken and heat through. Serve mixture in warm tortillas with salsa and sour cream.
SAUCED IN A PASTA: Combine chicken strips with roasted red sweet pepper strips and sauteed sliced mushrooms. Add Alfredo sauce; heat through. Serve over hot cooked pasta; top with grated Parmesan cheese.
CURRIED IN A CROISSANT: Combine cubed chicken with sliced celery and chopped apple. For dressing, combine mayonnaise with honey-Dijon mustard and curry powder to taste. Toss dressing with chicken mixture. Serve in a croissant.
PERCHED ON A NO-COOK PIZZA: Spread ranch-style salad dressing over prepared pizza bread shell. Top with assorted greens, shredded chicken, sliced green onions, sliced olives, chopped tomato, and freshly shredded Parmesan cheese.
FOLDED INTO A FIRST-RATE OMELET: Top the French Omelet, page 142, with warmed chicken and, if you like, fresh herbs, grated cheese, tapenade, and/or salsa.

10 TO TRY—
NOODLE BOWLS

Start with 20-Minute Noodle Bowls, page 252. **1. SOUTHWEST:** Substitute salsa for peanut sauce and frozen sweet peppers and onions for vegetables. Top with corn chips. **2. SHRIMP:** Add 1 teaspoon grated fresh ginger to broth mixture. Stir in cooked shrimp; heat through. **3. BEEF AND BROCCOLI:** Use beef broth and frozen broccoli for broth and vegetables. Stir in cooked roast beef strips; heat through. **4. SWEET-AND-SOUR:** Substitute sweet-and-sour sauce for peanut sauce. Stir in breaded chicken strips; heat through. **5. TERIYAKI:** Substitute ¼ cup each teriyaki sauce and water for peanut sauce. Top with cashews. **6. ALFREDO:** Substitute Alfredo sauce for peanut sauce. Use chicken broth and frozen peas for broth and vegetables. Stir in cubed cooked chicken; heat through. Top with bacon. **7. MEXICAN:** Substitute salsa for peanut sauce. Stir in cooked chorizo sausage; heat through. **8. THAI-CURRY VEGETABLE:** Add ½ cup unsweetened coconut milk and 1 teaspoon curry powder to broth. Top with peanuts. **9. ITALIAN:** Substitute pasta sauce for peanut sauce and chopped zucchini, fresh spinach, and frozen Italian-cut green beans for vegetables. Stir in cooked meatballs; heat through. **10. TOFU-SESAME:** Omit peanut sauce; stir in ¼ cup each hoisin sauce and water, 1 teaspoon toasted sesame oil, and 1 cup cubed tofu; heat through. Top with toasted sesame seeds.

SHORTCUT SHRIMP RISOTTO

CURRIED TUNA ON BISCUITS

START TO FINISH: 20 MINUTES
MAKES: 4 SERVINGS

  3 tablespoons butter or margarine

  3 tablespoons all-purpose flour

  2 to 3 teaspoons curry powder

  ¼ teaspoon salt

  2 cups milk

  1 12-ounce can chunk white tuna, drained

  1 cup frozen peas

  ½ cup purchased coarsely shredded fresh
     carrot

  4 baked biscuits

1 In a large saucepan melt butter over medium heat. Stir in flour, curry powder, and salt. Cook and stir for 30 seconds. Add milk all at once. Cook and stir until thick and bubbly; cook and stir 1 minute more. Stir in tuna, peas, and carrot; cook and stir until heated through.

2 Meanwhile, heat biscuits according to package directions. Serve tuna mixture over split biscuits.

PER 1½ CUPS: 494 cal., 23 g total fat (10 g sat. fat, 0 g trans fat), 68 mg chol., 1,244 mg sodium, 39 g carbo., 3 g fiber, 31 g pro. EXCHANGES: 2½ Starch, 3½ Lean Meat, 2 Fat

PIZZA-STYLE FISH STICKS

PREP: 15 MINUTES **BAKE:** 20 MINUTES
OVEN: 425°F **MAKES:** 4 SERVINGS

  1 11- to 12-ounce package (18) frozen
     baked breaded fish sticks

  1 8-ounce can pizza sauce

  1 cup shredded provolone or mozzarella
     cheese (4 ounces)

  2 tablespoons shredded fresh basil
     (optional)

1 Preheat oven to 425°F. Arrange fish in a 2-quart square or rectangular baking dish. Spoon sauce over fish; Sprinkle with cheese. Bake, uncovered, about 20 minutes or until heated through. If desired, sprinkle with basil.

PER SERVING: 258 cal., 11 g total fat (5 g sat. fat, 0 g trans fat), 38 mg chol., 801 mg sodium, 22 g carbo., 0 g fiber, 16 g pro. EXCHANGES: 1½ Starch, 1½ Lean Meat, 1 Fat

CURRY ANYTIME
KEEP THE CURRY SAUCE, ABOVE RIGHT, IN MIND FOR ALL KINDS OF MEALS. SWITCH HARD-COOKED EGGS OR CHICKEN FOR THE TUNA; USE TOAST INSTEAD OF BISCUITS.

SHORTCUT SHRIMP RISOTTO

START TO FINISH: 30 MINUTES
MAKES: 4 SERVINGS

  2 14-ounce cans reduced-sodium chicken
     broth

 1⅓ cups arborio rice or short grain white rice

  ½ cup chopped onion (1 medium)

  1 tablespoon snipped fresh basil or
     ¾ teaspoon dried basil, crushed

  1 10- to 12-ounce package frozen peeled,
     cooked shrimp, thawed

 1½ cups frozen peas

  ¼ cup grated Parmesan cheese

1 In a large saucepan combine broth, rice, onion, and dried basil, if using. Bring mixture to boiling; reduce heat. Cover and simmer for 18 minutes.

2 Stir in shrimp and peas. Cover and cook for 3 minutes more (do not lift lid). Stir in fresh basil, if using. Sprinkle each serving with cheese.

PER 1½ CUPS: 305 cal., 3 g total fat (1 g sat. fat, 0 g trans fat), 143 mg chol., 821 mg sodium, 45 g carbo., 3 g fiber, 25 g pro. EXCHANGES: ½ Vegetable, 3 Starch, 2 Lean Meat

COOKIES & BARS

CHOCO-CARAMEL THUMBPRINTS, PAGE 265

COOKIES & BARS

FOLLOW THESE TIPS TO MAKE YOUR COOKIES INTO PERFECT PACKAGES OF PLEASURE THE FIRST AND EVERY TIME YOU BAKE THEM.

SHEET SMARTS

A quality cookie sheet in top-notch condition can make all the difference. Here are a few tips.

■ Replace cookie sheets that have become warped or dark from years of baked-on grease.

■ Purchase shiny, heavy-gauge cookie sheets that have very low or no sides.

■ Choose cookie sheets that fit easily in your oven, allowing 1 to 2 inches of space all around the pan.

■ Avoid dark-color cookie sheets, which can cause cookies to overbrown.

■ Use jelly-roll pans (four-sided, 15×10×1-inch baking pans) for bar cookies only. Their 1-inch sides prevent other types of cookies from browning evenly.

BUTTER BASICS

Nothing beats the flavor, richness, and texture butter adds to cookies—substitute another ingredient only if the option is offered. Make sure the butter you use has softened to room temperature. It should have lost its chill and be spreadable; 30 minutes should do the trick. Never use melted butter unless specifically called for.

SAVVY STORAGE

Proper storage keeps cookies fresh and appetizing.

■ Cool cookies completely before storing.

■ Layer cookies between waxed paper and use storage containers with tight-fitting lids.

■ Store cookies or bars that have creamy or delicate toppings in a single layer.

■ Avoid storing crisp cookies and soft cookies in the same container—one type can change the consistency of another.

■ Store cookies and bars at room temperature for up to 3 days or in the refrigerator as specified in the recipe.

FREEZE WITH EASE

Most cookies will freeze well if you keep these tips in mind.

■ Freeze unfrosted, unfilled, and undrizzled cookies and bars layered between waxed paper in airtight containers up to 3 months.

■ To thaw, leave the cookies in their storage containers and place the containers in the refrigerator or on the countertop. Frost or fill cookies after they have completely thawed.

■ Most cookie doughs, with the exceptions of bar batters and meringue and macaroon doughs, can be frozen for up to 6 months. Thaw in the refrigerator.

COOKIE PACKAGING

Use these tips to send cookies in the mail.

■ Choose crisp or firm cookies, such as sliced, drop, and bar cookies. Avoid sending moist, frosted, and filled ones.

■ Wrap cookies in plastic wrap back-to-back.

■ Line a sturdy cardboard box with bubble wrap and pack cookies in layers of tissue paper. Be sure to fill the box completely so the cookies do not shift. Mark "perishable" on box.

SUGAR COOKIE CUTOUTS, PAGE 272

CHOCOLATE CHIP COOKIES

PREP: 40 MINUTES **BAKE:** 8 MINUTES PER BATCH
OVEN: 375°F **MAKES:** ABOUT 60 COOKIES

- ½ cup butter, softened
- ½ cup shortening or vegetable oil
- 1 cup packed brown sugar
- ½ cup granulated sugar
- ½ teaspoon baking soda
- ½ teaspoon salt
- 2 eggs
- 1 teaspoon vanilla
- 2¾ cups all-purpose flour
- 1 12-ounce package (2 cups) semisweet chocolate pieces or miniature candy-coated semisweet chocolate pieces
- 1½ cups chopped walnuts, pecans, or hazelnuts (filberts), toasted (see tip, page 20) if desired (optional)

1 Preheat oven to 375°F. In a large mixing bowl beat butter and shortening with an electric mixer on medium to high speed for 30 seconds. Add the brown sugar, granulated sugar, baking soda, and salt. Beat until mixture is combined, scraping sides of bowl occasionally. Beat in eggs and vanilla until combined. Beat in as much of the flour as you can with the mixer. Stir in any remaining flour. Stir in chocolate pieces and, if desired, nuts.

2 Drop dough by rounded teaspoons 2 inches apart onto ungreased cookie sheets (see photos 1 and 2, below). Bake for 8 to 9 minutes or until edges are just light brown. Cool on cookie sheet for 2 minutes. Transfer to wire racks and let cool.

PER COOKIE: 99 cal., 5 g total fat (2 g sat. fat, 0 g trans fat), 11 mg chol., 45 mg sodium, 13 g carbo., 0 g fiber, 1 g pro.
EXCHANGES: 1 Other Carbo., 1 Fat

CHOCOLATE CHIP COOKIE BARS: Prepare as directed, except press dough into a lightly greased 15×10×1-inch baking pan. Bake for 15 to 20 minutes or until golden. Cool on a wire rack. Cut into bars. Makes 48 bars.

PER BAR: 124 cal., 3 g total fat (3 g sat. fat, 0 g trans fat), 14 mg chol., 56 mg sodium, 17 g carbo., 1 g fiber, g pro.
EXCHANGES: 1 Other Carbo., 1 Fat

BIG CHOCOLATE CHIP COOKIES: Prepare as directed, except use a ¼-cup measure or scoop to drop mounds of dough about 4 inches apart onto ungreased cookie sheets. If desired, flatten dough mounds to circles about ¾ inch thick. Bake for 10 to 12 minutes or until edges are light brown. Cool on cookie sheet on wire rack for 2 minutes. Transfer cookies to wire racks and let cool. Makes about 18 cookies.

PER COOKIE: 331 cal., 17 g total fat (8 g sat. fat, 1 g trans fat), 37 mg chol., 150 mg sodium, 44 g carbo., 2 g fiber, 4 g pro.
EXCHANGES: 3 Other Carbo., 3½ Fat

MACADAMIA NUT AND WHITE CHOCOLATE CHIP COOKIES: Prepare as directed, except substitute white baking pieces for the semisweet chocolate pieces. Stir in one 3½-ounce jar macadamia nuts, chopped, with the white baking pieces.

PER COOKIE: 116 cal., 6 g total fat (3 g sat. fat, 0 g trans fat), 11 mg chol., 57 mg sodium, 14 g carbo., 0 g fiber, 1 g pro.
EXCHANGES: 1 Other Carbo., 1 Fat

TWO WAYS TO DROP COOKIE DOUGH, STEP-BY-STEP

1. Fill a spoon with cookie dough and use another spoon to push the dough onto the cookie sheet. Note that when a cookie recipe calls for dropping dough from a teaspoon or tablespoon, it is referring to flatware spoons rather than measuring spoons. **2.** Use a small cookie scoop—available at kitchenware stores—to ensure uniform size and shape for every cookie in the batch.

MAKE-IT-MINE OATMEAL COOKIES

WHAT'S THE BEST RECIPE FOR OATMEAL COOKIES? THE ONE THAT'S MADE WITH INGREDIENTS YOU LIKE THE MOST! START WITH THE BASICS AND MIX IT UP WITH TASTY OPTIONS FOR YOUR OWN ONE-OF-A-KIND COOKIE.

BASIC INGREDIENTS

PREP: 30 MINUTES
BAKE: 8 TO 12 MINUTES PER BATCH
OVEN: 350°F
MAKES: 72 TEASPOON-SIZE, 36 TABLESPOON-SIZE, 24 COOKIE SCOOP-SIZE, 18 ¼-CUP-SIZE

    Fat
    Sugar
1 teaspoon baking soda
    Spice
½ teaspoon salt
2 eggs
    Flavoring
    Flour
3 cups regular or quick-cooking rolled oats
1 cup Stir-In (optional)

FAT (PICK ONE)

1 cup butter
½ cup butter plus ½ cup shortening
½ cup butter plus ½ cup peanut butter

SUGAR (PICK ONE)

1 cup packed brown sugar plus ½ cup granulated sugar
1½ cups packed brown sugar
1 cup granulated sugar plus ½ cup molasses (add ¼ cup additional all-purpose flour)
1 cup granulated sugar plus ½ cup honey

SPICE (PICK ONE)

1 teaspoon ground cinnamon, pumpkin pie spice, or apple pie spice
½ teaspoon ground allspice

FLAVORING (PICK ONE)

1 teaspoon vanilla
½ teaspoon coconut flavoring
½ teaspoon maple flavoring

FLOUR (PICK ONE)

1½ cups all-purpose flour
¾ cup all-purpose flour plus ¾ cup whole wheat flour
1 cup all-purpose flour plus ½ cup oat bran
1¼ cups all-purpose flour plus ¼ cup toasted wheat germ

STIR-IN (PICK ONE)

Raisins
Semisweet or milk chocolate pieces
Mixed dried fruit bits or dried tart red cherries
White baking pieces
Butterscotch-flavored baking pieces
Peanut butter-flavored baking pieces
Flaked coconut

BASIC INSTRUCTIONS

1 Preheat oven to 350°F. In a large mixing bowl beat Fat with an electric mixer on medium to high speed for 30 seconds. Add desired Sugar, baking soda, Spice, and salt. Beat until combined, scraping sides of bowl. Beat in eggs and Flavoring. Beat in as much of the Flour as you can with the mixer. Stir in any remaining Flour and the oats. If desired, add Stir-In.*

2 Drop dough by rounded teaspoons or tablespoons (see photos 1 and 2, page 258) or by a ¼-cup measure or cookie scoop 2 to 3 inches apart onto ungreased cookie sheets. Bake for 8 to 10 minutes for rounded teaspoons or tablespoons or 12 to 14 minutes for ¼ cup or cookie-scoop portions or until light brown and centers appear set. Cool on cookie sheets 2 minutes. Transfer to wire racks to cool completely.

*TIP: Instead of using just one optional Stir-In, you can use two or even three. Just be sure the total amount of the Stir-In equals 1 cup.

TRIPLE-CHOCOLATE COOKIES

PREP: 40 MINUTES **COOL:** 10 MINUTES
STAND: 20 MINUTES **BAKE:** 9 MINUTES PER BATCH
OVEN: 350°F **MAKES:** ABOUT 60 COOKIES

- 7 ounces bittersweet chocolate, chopped
- 5 ounces unsweetened chocolate, chopped
- ½ cup butter
- ⅓ cup all-purpose flour
- ¼ teaspoon baking powder
- ¼ teaspoon salt
- 1 cup granulated sugar
- ¾ cup packed brown sugar
- 4 eggs
- ¼ cup finely chopped pecans, toasted (see tip, page 20)
- 1 recipe Chocolate Drizzle

1 In a 2-quart saucepan combine chocolates and butter. Heat and stir over low heat until melted and smooth. Remove from heat. Let cool for 10 minutes. In a small bowl, stir together flour, baking powder, and salt; set aside.

2 In a large mixing bowl combine sugars and eggs. Beat with an electric mixer on medium to high speed for 2 to 3 minutes or until color lightens slightly. Beat in melted chocolate mixture. Add flour mixture to chocolate mixture; beat until combined. Stir in pecans (see photo 1, below). Cover surface of cookie dough with plastic wrap. Let stand for 20 minutes (dough thickens as it stands).

3 Preheat oven to 350°F. Line cookie sheets with parchment paper or foil. Drop dough by rounded teaspoons 2 inches apart on prepared cookie sheets (see photo 2, below). Bake about 9 minutes or just until tops are set. Cool on cookie sheet for 1 minute. Transfer to wire racks and let cool. Spoon Chocolate Drizzle over cookies (see photo 3, below).

CHOCOLATE DRIZZLE: In a small saucepan heat and stir 1 cup semisweet chocolate pieces with 4 teaspoons shortening over low heat until melted and smooth. Remove from heat.

PER COOKIE: 92 cal., 6 g total fat (3 g sat. fat, 0 g trans fat), 18 mg chol., 19 mg sodium, 11 g carbo., 1 g fiber, 1 g pro.
EXCHANGES: 2½ Other Carbo., 4 Fat

TRIPLE-CHOCOLATE COOKIES, STEP-BY-STEP

1. Using a wooden spoon, gently stir in the chopped pecans. Note that before standing, the dough has a batterlike consistency. **2.** After standing, the dough is thick enough to scoop. **3.** For easy cleanup, place the cooling rack over parchment or waxed paper. To drizzle, dip a spoon into the melted chocolate and move it over the cookies as it streams off the spoon.

SOUR CREAM-CHOCOLATE DROPS

PREP: 25 MINUTES **BAKE:** 8 MINUTES PER BATCH
OVEN: 350°F **MAKES:** ABOUT 42 COOKIES

- ½ cup butter, softened
- 1 cup packed brown sugar
- ½ teaspoon baking soda
- 1 egg
- 1 teaspoon vanilla
- 2 ounces unsweetened chocolate, melted and cooled
- 1 8-ounce carton dairy sour cream
- 2 cups all-purpose flour
- 1 recipe Chocolate Buttercream Frosting

1 Preheat oven to 350°F. In a large mixing bowl beat butter with an electric mixer on medium speed for 30 seconds. Add brown sugar, baking soda, and ¼ teaspoon *salt*. Beat until combined, scraping sides of bowl. Beat in egg and vanilla. Add melted chocolate; beat until combined. Beat in sour cream. Beat in as much of the flour as you can with the mixer. Stir in any remaining flour.

2 Drop dough by rounded teaspoons 2 inches apart onto an ungreased cookie sheet (see photos 1 and 2, page 258). Bake for 8 to 10 minutes or until edges are firm. Transfer to a wire rack; let cool. Frost with Chocolate Buttercream Frosting.

CHOCOLATE BUTTERCREAM FROSTING: Beat ¼ cup butter until fluffy. Gradually add 1 cup powdered sugar and ⅓ cup unsweetened cocoa powder, beating well. Slowly beat in 3 table-spoons half-and-half and 1 teaspoon vanilla. Gradually beat in 1½ cups powdered sugar. If necessary, beat in additional half-and-half to make a spreading consistency.

PER COOKIE: 120 cal., 5 g total fat (3 g sat. fat, 0 g trans fat), 17 mg chol., 60 mg sodium, 18 g carbo., 1 g fiber, 1 g pro. EXCHANGES: 1 Other Carbo., 1 Fat

FROSTED MAPLE DROPS

PREP: 30 MINUTES **BAKE:** 8 MINUTES PER BATCH
OVEN: 350°F **MAKES:** ABOUT 96 COOKIES

- 1 cup butter, softened
- 1 cup packed brown sugar
- 1 teaspoon baking soda
- ⅛ teaspoon salt
- 1 cup pure maple syrup
- 1 egg
- 1 teaspoon vanilla
- 4 cups all-purpose flour
- 1 recipe Maple Frosting

1 Preheat oven to 350°F. Lightly grease cookie sheets; set aside. In a mixing bowl beat butter with an electric mixer on medium to high speed for 30 seconds. Add brown sugar, baking soda, and salt. Beat until combined, scraping bowl occasionally. Add maple syrup, egg, and vanilla; beat until combined. Beat in as much of the flour as you can. Stir in any remaining flour.

2 Drop dough by rounded teaspoons 2 inches apart onto prepared cookie sheet (see photos 1 and 2, page 258); flatten slightly. Bake for 8 to 10 minutes or until tops are set. Transfer cookies to a wire rack; cool.

MAPLE FROSTING: In a medium bowl whisk together ½ cup evaporated milk, 6 tablespoons melted butter, and 1 teaspoon maple flavoring until combined. Gradually stir in 3 to 4 cups pow-dered sugar until mixture is icing consistency. Spread tops of cooled cookies with icing.

PER COOKIE: 77 cal., 3 g total fat (2 g sat. fat, 0 g trans fat), 10 mg chol., 38 mg sodium, 12 g carbo., 0 g fiber, 1 g pro. EXCHANGES: 1 Other Carbo., ½ Fat

BEST EVER ▪ LOW FAT

COCONUT MACAROONS

PREP: 30 MINUTES **BAKE:** 20 MINUTES
OVEN: 325°F **MAKES:** ABOUT 60 COOKIES

- 4 egg whites
- 1 teaspoon vanilla
- ¼ teaspoon cream of tartar
- ⅛ teaspoon salt
- 1⅓ cups sugar
- 1 14-ounce package flaked coconut (5⅓ cups)

1 Preheat oven to 325°F. Line cookie sheets with parchment paper; set aside. In a very large mixing bowl beat egg whites, vanilla, cream of tartar, and salt on high speed until soft peaks form (tips curl). Gradually add sugar, about 1 tablespoon at a time, beating until stiff peaks form (tips stand straight). Fold in coconut, half at a time.

2 Drop mixture from a teaspoon 1 inch apart into small mounds on prepared cookie sheets.* Bake for 20 to 25 minutes or until bottoms are light brown. Cool on wire racks.

*NOTE: If you cannot use all cookie mixture at once, cover and chill while first batch bakes.

PER COOKIE: 49 cal., 2 g total fat (2 g sat. fat, 0 g trans fat), 0 mg chol., 7 g carbo., 0 g fiber, 1 g pro. EXCHANGES: ½ Other Carbo., ½ Fat

MELT-IN-YOUR-MOUTH SUGAR COOKIES

PREP: 35 MINUTES **BAKE:** 12 MINUTES PER BATCH
OVEN: 300°F **MAKES:** ABOUT 48 COOKIES

½ cup butter, softened

½ cup shortening

2 cups sugar

1 teaspoon baking soda

1 teaspoon cream of tartar

⅛ teaspoon salt

3 egg yolks

½ teaspoon vanilla

1¾ cups all-purpose flour

1 Preheat oven to 300°F. In a large mixing bowl beat butter and shortening with an electric mixer on medium to high speed for 30 seconds. Add sugar, baking soda, cream of tartar, and salt. Beat mixture until combined, scraping sides of bowl occasionally. Beat in egg yolks and vanilla. Beat in as much of the flour as you can with the mixer. Stir in any remaining flour.

2 Shape dough into 1-inch balls. Place balls 2 inches apart on ungreased cookie sheets.

3 Bake for 12 to 14 minutes or until edges are set; do not let edges brown. Cool cookies on cookie sheet for 2 minutes. Transfer to wire racks and let cool.

PER COOKIE: 88 cal., 4 g total fat (2 g sat. fat, 0 g trans fat), 18 mg chol., 47 mg sodium, 12 g carbo., 0 g fiber, 1 g pro.
EXCHANGES: 1 Other Carbo., 1 Fat

SNICKERDOODLES

PREP: 35 MINUTES **CHILL:** 60 MINUTES
BAKE: 10 MINUTES PER BATCH **OVEN:** 375°F
MAKES: ABOUT 48 COOKIES

1 cup butter, softened

1½ cups sugar

1 teaspoon baking soda

1 teaspoon cream of tartar

¼ teaspoon salt

2 eggs

1 teaspoon vanilla

3 cups all-purpose flour

¼ cup sugar

2 teaspoons ground cinnamon

1 In a large mixing bowl beat butter with an electric mixer on medium to high speed for 30 seconds. Add the 1½ cups sugar, baking soda, cream of tartar, and salt. Beat until combined, scraping sides of bowl occasionally. Beat in eggs and vanilla until combined. Beat in as much of the flour as you can with the mixer. Stir in any remaining flour. Cover and chill dough about 60 minutes or until easy to handle.

2 Preheat oven to 375°F. In a small bowl combine the ¼ cup sugar and the cinnamon. Shape dough into 1¼-inch balls. Roll balls in sugar mixture to coat. Place 2 inches apart on ungreased cookie sheets.

3 Bake for 10 to 12 minutes or until bottoms are light brown. Transfer cookies to wire racks and let cool.

PER COOKIE: 94 cal., 4 g total fat (3 g sat. fat, 0 g trans fat), 19 mg chol., 69 mg sodium, 13 g carbo., 0 g fiber, 1 g pro.
EXCHANGES: 1 Other Carbo., 1 Fat

BEST EVER

SANDIES

PREP: 35 MINUTES **CHILL:** 30 MINUTES
BAKE: 15 MINUTES PER BATCH **OVEN:** 325°F
MAKES: ABOUT 55 COOKIES

1 cup butter, softened

½ cup powdered sugar

1 tablespoon water

1 teaspoon vanilla

2 cups all-purpose flour

1½ cups finely chopped pecans, toasted (see tip, page 20)

1 cup powdered sugar

1 In a large mixing bowl beat butter with an electric mixer on medium to high speed for 30 seconds. Add the ½ cup powdered sugar. Beat until combined, scraping sides of bowl occasionally. Beat in water and vanilla until combined. Beat in as much of the flour as you can with the mixer. Stir in any remaining flour and the pecans. Cover and chill for 30 to 60 minutes or until firm enough to shape.

2 Preheat oven to 325°F. Shape dough into 1-inch balls or 2×½-inch logs. Place 1 inch apart on ungreased cookie sheets. Bake about 15 minutes or until bottoms are light brown. Transfer to wire racks and let cool. Place the 1 cup powdered sugar in a large plastic bag. Add cooled cookies in batches to bag. Gently shake to coat.

PER COOKIE: 80 cal., 6 g total fat (2 g sat. fat, 0 g trans fat), 9 mg chol., 24 mg sodium, 7 g carbo., 0 g fiber, 1 g pro.
EXCHANGES: ½ Other Carbo., 1 Fat

PEANUT BUTTER COOKIES

PREP: 35 MINUTES **CHILL:** 60 MINUTES
BAKE: 7 MINUTES PER BATCH **OVEN:** 375°F
MAKES: ABOUT 56 COOKIES

- 1 cup peanut butter
- ½ cup butter, softened
- ½ cup shortening
- 1 cup granulated sugar
- 1 cup packed brown sugar or ½ cup honey
- 1 teaspoon baking soda
- 1 teaspoon baking powder
- 2 eggs
- 1 teaspoon vanilla
- 2½ cups all-purpose flour

1 In a large mixing bowl beat peanut butter, butter, and shortening with an electric mixer for 30 seconds. Add sugars, baking soda, and baking powder. Beat until combined, scraping sides of bowl. Beat in eggs and vanilla until combined. Beat in as much of the flour as you can. Stir in any remaining flour. Cover and chill dough about 60 minutes or until easy to handle.

2 Preheat oven to 375°F. Shape dough into 1¼-inch balls. Roll in additional granulated sugar to coat. Place 2 inches apart on ungreased cookie sheets. Flatten by making crisscross marks with the tines of a fork. Bake for 7 to 9 minutes or until bottoms are light brown. Let cool on cookie sheet for 1 minute. Transfer cookies to a wire rack and let cool.

PER COOKIE: 114 cal., 6 g total fat (2 g sat. fat, 0 g trans fat), 12 mg chol., 63 mg sodium, 14 g carbo., 0 g fiber, 2 g pro. EXCHANGES: 1 Other Carbo., 1 Fat

PEANUT BUTTER BLOSSOMS

PREP: 25 MINUTES **BAKE:** 10 MINUTES PER BATCH
OVEN: 350°F **MAKES:** ABOUT 54 COOKIES

- ½ cup shortening
- ½ cup peanut butter
- ½ cup granulated sugar
- ½ cup packed brown sugar
- 1 teaspoon baking powder
- ⅛ teaspoon baking soda
- 1 egg
- 2 tablespoons milk
- 1 teaspoon vanilla
- 1¾ cups all-purpose flour
- ¼ cup granulated sugar
  Milk chocolate kisses or stars

1 Preheat oven to 350°F. In a large mixing bowl beat shortening and peanut butter with an electric mixer on medium to high speed for 30 seconds. Add the ½ cup granulated sugar, brown sugar, baking powder, and baking soda. Beat until combined, scraping sides of bowl occasionally. Beat in egg, milk, and vanilla until combined. Beat in as much of the flour as you can with the mixer. Stir in any remaining flour.

2 Shape dough into 1-inch balls. Roll balls in the ¼ cup granulated sugar. Place 2 inches apart on an ungreased cookie sheet. Bake for 10 to 12 minutes or until edges are firm and bottoms are light brown. Immediately press a chocolate kiss into each cookie's center. Transfer cookies to a wire rack and let cool.

PER COOKIE: 96 cal., 5 g total fat (2 g sat. fat, 0 g trans fat), 5 mg chol., 27 mg sodium, 11 g carbo., 0 g fiber, 2 g pro. EXCHANGES: 1 Other Carbo., 1 Fat

GINGER COOKIES

PREP: 40 MINUTES **BAKE:** 8 MINUTES PER BATCH
OVEN: 350°F **MAKES:** ABOUT 120 COOKIES

- 4½ cups all-purpose flour
- 4 teaspoons ground ginger
- 2 teaspoons baking soda
- 1½ teaspoons ground cinnamon
- 1 teaspoon ground cloves
- 1½ cups shortening
- 2 cups sugar
- 2 eggs
- ½ cup molasses
- ¾ cup sugar

1 Preheat oven to 350°F. In a bowl stir together flour, ginger, baking soda, cinnamon, cloves, and ¼ teaspoon *salt;* set aside. In a large mixing bowl beat shortening on low speed for 30 seconds. Add the 2 cups sugar. Beat until combined, scraping sides of bowl. Beat in eggs and molasses until combined. Beat in as much of the flour mixture as you can. Stir in any remaining flour mixture.

2 Shape dough into 1-inch balls. Roll balls in the ¾ cup sugar. Place 1½ inches apart on an ungreased cookie sheet. Bake for 8 to 9 minutes or until bottoms are light brown and tops are puffed (do not overbake). Cool on cookie sheet 1 minute. Transfer to a wire rack and let cool.

PER COOKIE: 62 cal., 3 g total fat (1 g sat. fat, 0 g trans fat), 4 mg chol., 28 mg sodium, 9 g carbo., 0 g fiber, 1 g pro. EXCHANGES: ½ Other Carbo., ½ Fat

CHOCOLATE CRINKLES

PREP: 35 MINUTES **COOL:** 15 MINUTES
CHILL: 2 HOURS **BAKE:** 10 MINUTES PER BATCH
OVEN: 375°F **MAKES:** ABOUT 60 COOKIES

- 4 ounces unsweetened chocolate
- ½ cup shortening
- 3 eggs, lightly beaten
- 2 cups granulated sugar
- 2 teaspoons baking powder
- 2 teaspoons vanilla
- ¼ teaspoon salt
- 2 cups all-purpose flour
- ⅔ cup powdered sugar

1 In a small saucepan combine chocolate and shortening. Cook and stir over low heat until melted and smooth. Cool 15 minutes.

2 In a large bowl combine eggs, granulated sugar, baking powder, vanilla, and salt. Add chocolate mixture. Gradually add flour, stirring until thoroughly combined. Cover dough; chill about 2 hours or until easy to handle.

3 Preheat oven to 375°F. Lightly grease cookie sheets; set aside. Shape dough into 1-inch balls. Roll in powdered sugar to coat generously. Place 2 inches apart on prepared cookie sheets. Bake about 10 minutes or until edges are just set. Transfer cookies to wire racks and let cool.

PER COOKIE: 74 cal., 3 g total fat (1 g sat. fat, 0 g trans fat), 11 mg chol., 22 mg sodium, 12 g carbo., 0 g fiber, 1 g pro. EXCHANGES: 1 Other Carbo., ½ Fat

BURIED-CHERRY COOKIES

PREP: 30 MINUTES **BAKE:** 10 MINUTES PER BATCH
OVEN: 350°F **MAKES:** 42 TO 48 COOKIES

- 1 10-ounce jar maraschino cherries
- ½ cup butter, softened
- 1 cup sugar
- ¼ teaspoon baking powder
- ¼ teaspoon baking soda
- ¼ teaspoon salt
- 1 egg
- 1½ teaspoons vanilla
- ½ cup unsweetened cocoa powder
- 1½ cups all-purpose flour
- 1 cup semisweet chocolate pieces*
- ½ cup sweetened condensed milk

1 Preheat oven to 350°F. Drain cherries, reserving juice. Halve any large cherries. In a medium mixing bowl beat butter with an electric mixer on medium to high speed for 30 seconds. Add the sugar, baking powder, baking soda, and salt. Beat until combined, scraping sides of bowl occasionally. Beat in egg and vanilla until combined. Beat in cocoa powder and as much of the flour as you can with the mixer. Stir in any remaining flour.

2 Shape dough into 1-inch balls (see photos 1 and 2, below). Place balls about 2 inches apart on an ungreased cookie sheet. Press your thumb into the center of each ball (see photo 3, page 265). Place a cherry in each center (see photo 4, page 265).

3 For frosting, in a small saucepan heat and stir chocolate pieces and sweetened condensed milk over low heat until melted and smooth. Stir in 4 teaspoons reserved cherry juice. (If necessary,

BLONDIE BURIED-CHERRY COOKIES, STEP-BY-STEP

1. To make the balls uniform in size, pat dough into a 6×7-inch rectangle on a lightly floured surface. Cut into 42 equal-size squares. Roll the squares into balls. **2.** Or scoop dough using a small cookie scoop, then roll into balls. **3.** Gently press your thumb into each dough ball. **4.** Place a cherry into each indentation. **5.** Top each ball with frosting, spreading to completely cover the cherry.

frosting may be thinned with additional cherry juice.) Spoon 1 teaspoon frosting over each cherry, spreading to cover (see photo 5, below).

4 Bake about 10 minutes or until edges are firm. Cool on cookie sheet for 1 minute. Transfer cookies to a wire rack and let cool.

*NOTE: Do not substitute imitation chocolate pieces for semisweet chocolate pieces.

BLONDIE BURIED-CHERRY COOKIES: Prepare as directed, except increase baking powder to ½ teaspoon and omit baking soda. Substitute almond extract for the vanilla, omit the cocoa powder, and increase flour to 2 cups.

PER COOKIE REGULAR OR BLONDIE VARIATION: 101 cal., 4 g total fat (2 g sat. fat, 0 g trans fat), 12 mg chol., 46 mg sodium, 16 g carbo., 1 g fiber, 1 g pro.
EXCHANGES: 1 Other Carbo., 1 Fat

BEST EVER

CHOCO-CARAMEL THUMBPRINTS
(photo, page 255)

PREP: 40 MINUTES **CHILL:** 2 HOURS
BAKE: 10 MINUTES PER BATCH **OVEN:** 350°F
MAKES: ABOUT 32 COOKIES

> 1 egg
> ½ cup butter, softened
> ⅔ cup sugar
> 2 tablespoons milk
> 1 teaspoon vanilla
> 1 cup all-purpose flour
> ⅓ cup unsweetened cocoa powder
> 16 vanilla caramels, unwrapped
> 3 tablespoons whipping cream

> 1¼ cups finely chopped pecans
> ½ cup semisweet chocolate pieces
> 1 teaspoon shortening

1 Separate egg; place yolk and white in separate bowls. Cover and chill egg white until needed. In a mixing bowl beat butter 30 seconds. Add sugar and beat well. Beat in egg yolk, milk, and vanilla.

2 Combine flour, cocoa powder, and ¼ teaspoon *salt*. Add flour mixture to butter mixture; beat until well combined. Wrap cookie dough in plastic wrap and chill about 2 hours or until easy to handle.

3 Preheat oven to 350°F. Lightly grease two cookie sheets; set aside. In a small saucepan heat and stir caramels and whipping cream over low heat until mixture is smooth; set aside.

4 Lightly beat reserved egg white. Shape dough into 1-inch balls. Roll balls in egg white, then in pecans to coat. Place balls 1 inch apart on prepared cookie sheets. Press your thumb into the center of each ball (see photo 3, below).

5 Bake about 10 minutes or until edges are firm. If cookie centers puff during baking, re-press with the back of a small spoon. Spoon or pipe melted caramel mixture into indentations of cookies. (If necessary, reheat caramel mixture to keep it spooning consistency.) Transfer cookies to wire racks; cool.

6 In another saucepan heat and stir chocolate pieces and shortening over low heat until melted and smooth; cool slightly. Drizzle chocolate mixture over tops of cookies; let stand until set.

PER COOKIE: 127 cal., 8 g total fat (3 g sat. fat, 0 g trans fat), 17 mg chol., 54 mg sodium, 14 g carbo., 1 g fiber, 2 g pro.
EXCHANGES: 1 Other Carbo., 1½ Fat

3

4

5

JAM THUMBPRINTS

PREP: 25 MINUTES **CHILL:** 60 MINUTES
BAKE: 10 MINUTES PER BATCH **OVEN:** 375°F
MAKES: ABOUT 30 COOKIES

- ⅔ cup butter, softened
- ½ cup sugar
- 2 egg yolks
- 1 teaspoon vanilla
- 1½ cups all-purpose flour
- 2 egg whites, lightly beaten
- 1 cup finely chopped walnuts, hazelnuts, or pecans
- ⅓ to ½ cup jam or preserves, chocolate-hazelnut spread, and/or desired-flavor fruit curd

1 In a large mixing bowl beat butter with an electric mixer on medium to high speed for 30 seconds. Add sugar. Beat until combined, scraping sides of bowl occasionally. Beat in egg yolks and vanilla until combined. Beat in as much of the flour as you can with the mixer. Stir in any remaining flour. Cover and chill dough about 60 minutes or until easy to handle.

2 Preheat oven to 375°F. Grease cookie sheets; set aside. Shape dough into 1-inch balls. Roll balls in egg whites, then in nuts. Place 1 inch apart on prepared cookie sheets. Press your thumb into the center of each ball. Bake for 10 to 12 minutes or until bottoms are light brown. If cookie centers puff during baking, re-press with the back of a measuring teaspoon. Transfer to a wire rack; let cool. Just before serving, fill the centers with jam.

PER COOKIE: 112 cal., 7 g total fat (3 g sat. fat, 0 g trans fat), 25 mg chol., 35 mg sodium, 11 g carbo., 0 g fiber, 2 g pro. EXCHANGES: 1 Other Carbo., 1½ Fat

BEST EVER

PECAN TASSIES

PREP: 30 MINUTES **BAKE:** 25 MINUTES
COOL: 5 MINUTES **OVEN:** 325°F
MAKES: 24 TASSIES

- ½ cup butter, softened
- 1 3-ounce package cream cheese, softened
- 1 cup all-purpose flour
- 1 egg, lightly beaten
- ¾ cup packed brown sugar
- 1 tablespoon butter, melted
- ⅔ cup coarsely chopped pecans

1 Preheat oven to 325°F. For pastry, in a mixing bowl beat the ½ cup butter and cream cheese until combined. Stir in the flour. Shape dough into 24 balls. Press each ball into the bottoms and up the sides of 24 ungreased 1¾-inch muffin cups.

2 For pecan filling, in a bowl stir together egg, brown sugar, and the 1 tablespoon melted butter. Stir in pecans. Spoon about 1 heaping teaspoon of filling into each pastry-lined cup. Bake for 25 to 30 minutes or until pastry is golden and filling is puffed. Cool tassies in pan on wire rack for 5 minutes. Carefully transfer to a wire rack and let cool.

PER TASSIE: 119 cal., 8 g total fat (4 g sat. fat, 0 g trans fat), 24 mg chol., 47 mg sodium, 11 g carbo., 0 g fiber, 1 g pro. EXCHANGES: 1 Other Carbo., 1½ Fat

ROCKY ROAD TASSIES

PREP: 40 MINUTES **CHILL:** 30 MINUTES
BAKE: 21 MINUTES **COOL:** 5 MINUTES **OVEN:** 325°F
MAKES: 24 TASSIES

- ½ cup butter, softened
- 1 3-ounce package cream cheese, softened
- 1 cup all-purpose flour
- ½ cup miniature semisweet chocolate pieces
- 2 tablespoons butter
- ⅓ cup sugar
- 1 egg
- 1 teaspoon vanilla
- ¼ cup chopped pecans, toasted (see tip, page 20)
- 2 tablespoons miniature semisweet chocolate pieces
- 24 tiny marshmallows

1 Preheat oven to 325°F. In a medium bowl combine ½ cup butter and cream cheese. Beat with an electric mixer on medium speed until mixture is combined. Add flour. Beat on low speed just until combined.

2 Shape dough into 24 balls. Press each ball evenly into the bottoms and up the sides of 24 ungreased 1¾-inch muffin cups; set aside.

3 In a small saucepan heat and stir the ½ cup chocolate pieces and the 2 tablespoons butter over low heat until melted and smooth. Remove from heat. Whisk in sugar, egg, and vanilla. Spoon chocolate mixture into the pastry-lined cups.

4 Bake for 20 to 25 minutes or until pastry is golden and filling is puffed. Quickly top tassies with pecans, the 2 tablespoons chocolate pieces, and the marshmallows. Bake for 1 to 2 minutes more or until marshmallows are softened. Cool tassies in pan on wire rack for 5 minutes. Run a thin knife or thin metal spatula around the edge of each tassie and carefully remove from the muffin cup. Transfer tassies to a wire rack; let cool.

PER TASSIE: 137 cal., 9 g total fat (5 g sat. fat, 0 g trans fat), 25 mg chol., 51 mg sodium, 13 g carbo., 0 g fiber, 2 g pro. EXCHANGES: 1 Other Carbo., 2 Fat

LOW FAT

STAR MINT MERINGUES

PREP: 20 MINUTES **BAKE:** 90 MINUTES
OVEN: 200°F **MAKES:** ABOUT 24 COOKIES

  3 egg whites
  ¼ teaspoon cream of tartar
  ¼ teaspoon peppermint extract
  ⅛ teaspoon salt
  ¾ cup sugar
     Red paste food coloring

1 Preheat oven to 200°F. Line a cookie sheet with parchment paper; set aside. In a large mixing bowl combine egg whites, cream of tartar, peppermint extract, and salt. Beat with an electric mixer on medium speed until soft peaks form (tips curl). Gradually add sugar, about 1 tablespoon at a time, beating on high speed until stiff peaks form (tips stand straight).

2 With a clean small paintbrush, brush stripes of red paste food coloring on the inside of a pastry bag fitted with a ½-inch open star tip (see photo 1, below). Carefully transfer meringue into the bag. Pipe 2-inch stars 1 inch apart onto prepared cookie sheet (see photo 2, below).

3 Bake for 90 minutes or until meringues appear dry and are firm when lightly touched (see photo 3, below). Transfer cookies to a wire rack; let cool.

PER COOKIE: 27 cal., 0 g total fat, 0 mg chol., 19 mg sodium, 6 g carbo., 0 g fiber, 0 g pro. EXCHANGES: ½ Other Carbo.

STAR MINT MERINGUES, STEP-BY-STEP

1. Fit a disposable piping bag with a ½-inch open star tip. Use a clean small brush to paint stripes of paste food coloring inside bag. **2.** To pipe stars, use one hand to apply pressure at top of bag, forcing meringue to the tip. Use your other hand to guide the tip. **3.** To check doneness, gently touch the meringues. They should be dry and firm to the touch.

SPRITZ

PREP: 25 MINUTES **BAKE:** 8 MINUTES PER BATCH
OVEN: 375°F **MAKES:** ABOUT 84 COOKIES

- 1½ cups butter, softened
- 1 cup granulated sugar
- 1 teaspoon baking powder
- 1 egg
- 1 teaspoon vanilla
- ¼ teaspoon almond extract (optional)
- 3½ cups all-purpose flour
  - Colored sugar (optional)
- 1 recipe Powdered Sugar Icing (page 280) (optional)

1 Preheat oven to 375°F. In a large mixing bowl beat butter with an electric mixer on medium to high speed for 30 seconds. Add granulated sugar and baking powder. Beat until combined, scraping sides of bowl occasionally. Beat in egg, vanilla, and, if desired, almond extract until combined. Beat in as much of the flour as you can with the mixer. Stir in any remaining flour.

2 Force unchilled dough through a cookie press onto an ungreased cookie sheet. If desired, sprinkle cookies with colored sugar. Bake for 8 to 10 minutes or until edges are firm but not brown. Transfer to a wire rack and let cool. If desired, drizzle cookies with Powdered Sugar Icing.

CHOCOLATE SPRITZ: Prepare as directed, except reduce flour to 3¼ cups and add ¼ cup unsweetened cocoa powder with the sugar.

PER COOKIE REGULAR OR CHOCOLATE VARIATION:
58 cal., 3 g total fat (2 g sat. fat, 0 g trans fat), 11 mg chol., 27 mg sodium, 6 g carbo., 0 g fiber, 1 g pro.
EXCHANGES: ½ Starch, ½ Fat

LOW FAT

ALMOND BISCOTTI

PREP: 25 MINUTES **BAKE:** 45 MINUTES
COOL: 15 MINUTES **OVEN:** 325°F
MAKES: ABOUT 84 COOKIES

- 2¾ cups all-purpose flour
- 1½ teaspoons baking powder
- 1 teaspoon salt
- 1½ cups sugar
- 2 eggs
- 2 egg yolks
- 6 tablespoons butter, melted
- 1½ teaspoons finely shredded orange or lemon peel (optional)
- 1 cup coarsely chopped almonds, hazelnuts, pistachios, or cashews

1 Preheat oven to 325°F. Lightly grease two cookie sheets; set aside. In a large bowl combine flour, baking powder, salt, and sugar. Make a well in the center of the flour mixture. Place eggs and egg yolks in the well and stir into the flour mixture. Add butter and, if desired, orange peel; stir until dough starts to form a ball. Stir in nuts (dough will be crumbly). Use your hands to knead the dough until it comes together.

2 Turn the dough out onto a lightly floured surface; divide into three equal portions. Shape each portion into a 14-inch-long roll (see photo 1, below). Place rolls about 3 inches apart on prepared cookie sheets; flatten rolls slightly until about 1½ inches wide (see photo 2, below). Bake for 25 to 30 minutes or until firm and light brown. Remove from oven and place cookie sheets on wire racks; cool 15 minutes.

ALMOND BISCOTTI, STEP-BY-STEP

1. Using your hands, roll each portion of dough into a 14-inch-long roll. **2.** Transfer the rolls to the prepared cookie sheets, placing one roll on one sheet and two rolls, 3 inches apart, on the other sheet. Flatten the rolls, gently patting with your fingers, until each is about 1½ inches wide.

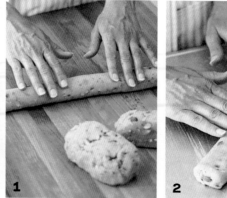

3 Transfer rolls to cutting board. Use a serrated knife to cut each roll diagonally into ½-inch slices. Place slices, cut sides down, on cookie sheets. Bake for 10 minutes. Turn slices over; bake 10 to 15 minutes more or until crisp and golden brown. Transfer to wire racks; cool.

PER COOKIE: 45 cal., 2 g total fat (1 g sat. fat, 0 g trans fat), 12 mg chol., 40 mg sodium, 7 g carbo., 0 g fiber, 1 g pro. EXCHANGES: ½ Other Carbo., ½ Fat

CHOCOLATE BISCOTTI

PREP: 30 MINUTES BAKE: 35 MINUTES
COOL: 60 MINUTES OVEN: 375°F/325°F
MAKES: ABOUT 24 COOKIES

   ½ cup butter, softened
   ⅔ cup sugar
   ¼ cup unsweetened cocoa powder
   2 teaspoons baking powder
   2 eggs
   1¾ cups all-purpose flour
   2 cups bittersweet or semisweet chocolate
       pieces
   2 teaspoons shortening

1 Preheat oven to 375°F. Lightly grease a cookie sheet; set aside. In a large mixing bowl beat butter with an electric mixer on medium to high speed for 30 seconds. Add sugar, cocoa powder, and baking powder. Beat until combined, scraping sides of bowl occasionally. Beat in eggs until combined. Beat in as much of the flour as you can with the mixer. Stir in any remaining flour. Stir in 1 cup of the chocolate pieces.

2 Divide dough in half. Shape each half into a 9-inch-long roll. Place rolls about 3 inches apart on prepared cookie sheet; flatten slightly until about 2 inches wide.

3 Bake for 20 to 25 minutes or until a wooden toothpick inserted near center comes out clean. Cool on cookie sheet for 60 minutes. (For easier slicing, wrap cooled rolls in plastic wrap and let stand over night at room temperature.)

4 Preheat oven to 325°F. Use a serrated knife to cut each roll diagonally into ½-inch slices. Place slices, cut sides down, on an ungreased cookie sheet. Bake for 8 minutes. Turn slices over and bake for 7 to 9 minutes more or until dry and crisp. Transfer to a wire rack; let cool.

5 Microwave remaining 1 cup chocolate pieces and shortening, uncovered, in a small microwave-safe bowl on 50% power (medium) for 1 to

2 minutes or until melted and smooth, stirring twice. Dip one long side of each cookie into the melted chocolate; let excess drip back into bowl. Place cookies on waxed paper; let stand until set.

PER COOKIE: 173 cal., 10 g total fat (6 g sat. fat, 0 g trans fat), 28 mg chol., 40 mg sodium, 21 g carbo., 2 g fiber, 2 g pro. EXCHANGES: 1½ Other Carbo., 2 Fat

BEST EVER

BROWN SUGAR-HAZELNUT ROUNDS

PREP: 25 MINUTES CHILL: 6 HOURS
BAKE: 7 MINUTES PER BATCH OVEN: 375°F
MAKES: ABOUT 60 COOKIES

   ½ cup butter, softened
   ½ cup shortening
   1¼ cups packed brown sugar
   ½ teaspoon baking soda
   ¼ teaspoon salt
   1 egg
   1 teaspoon vanilla
   2½ cups all-purpose flour
   ¾ cup ground hazelnuts (filberts) or pecans,
       toasted (see tip, page 20)
   1 recipe Browned Butter Icing (optional)

1 In a large mixing bowl beat butter and shortening with an electric mixer on medium to high speed for 30 seconds. Add brown sugar, baking soda, and salt. Beat until combined, scraping sides of bowl occasionally. Beat in egg and vanilla until combined. Beat in as much of the flour as you can. Stir in any remaining flour. Stir in nuts.

2 Divide dough in half. Shape each half into a 10-inch-long roll. Wrap in plastic wrap or waxed paper. Chill 6 hours or until firm enough to slice.

3 Preheat oven to 375°F. Use a serrated knife to cut rolls into ¼-inch slices (see photo 3, page 270). Place slices 1 inch apart on ungreased cookie sheets. Bake for 7 to 8 minutes or until edges are light brown. Transfer cookies to wire racks; cool. If desired, drizzle with Browned Butter Icing.

PER COOKIE: 77 cal., 4 g total fat (1 g sat. fat, 0 g trans fat), 8 mg chol., 34 mg sodium, 9 g carbo., 0 g fiber, 1 g pro. EXCHANGES: ½ Other Carbo., 1 Fat

BROWNED BUTTER ICING: In a small saucepan heat 2 tablespoons butter over medium heat until butter turns the color of light brown sugar, stirring frequently. Remove from heat. Slowly beat in 1½ cups powdered sugar, 1 teaspoon vanilla, and enough milk (1 to 2 tablespoons) to make a drizzling consistency.

CHOCOLATE-MINT PINWHEELS

PREPARING CHOCOLATE-MINT PINWHEELS, STEP-BY-STEP

1. Use the waxed paper and your hand to carefully invert chocolate dough rectangle onto peppermint dough rectangle.
2. Starting from a long side, roll up dough using bottom layer of waxed paper to help lift and guide the roll. **3.** Using a sharp, thin-bladed knife, cut across dough to make ¼-inch-thick slices. Rotate roll while cutting to prevent flattening.

CHOCOLATE-MINT PINWHEELS

PREP: 40 MINUTES **CHILL:** 2 HOURS
BAKE: 6 MINUTES PER BATCH **OVEN:** 375°F
MAKES: ABOUT 72 COOKIES

- 1 cup butter, softened
- 1 cup granulated sugar
- 1 teaspoon baking powder
- ¼ teaspoon salt
- 1 egg
- 1 teaspoon vanilla
- 2¼ cups all-purpose flour
- 2 ounces semisweet chocolate, melted and slightly cooled
- 1 4.67-ounce package layered chocolate-mint candies, finely chopped (1 cup)
- ¼ teaspoon peppermint extract

1 In a large mixing bowl beat butter with an electric mixer on medium to high speed for 30 seconds. Add granulated sugar, baking powder, and salt. Beat until mixture is combined, scraping sides of bowl. Beat in egg and vanilla until combined. Beat in as much flour as you can with the mixer. Stir in any remaining flour.

2 Divide dough in half. Stir melted chocolate into one dough portion. Stir chopped mint candies and peppermint extract into remaining dough portion. Divide each dough portion in half. Cover dough and chill for at least 1 hour or until easy to handle.

3 Roll each peppermint dough portion into a 9½×6-inch rectangle on waxed paper. Roll each chocolate dough portion into a 9½×6-inch rectangle on waxed paper. Invert one chocolate dough rectangle on top of one peppermint dough rectangle; remove top layer of waxed paper (see photo 1, page 270). Roll up dough (see photo 2, page 270). Pinch dough edges to seal; wrap in plastic wrap. Repeat with remaining chocolate and peppermint dough rectangles. Chill dough rolls for 1 to 2 hours or until very firm.

4 Preheat oven to 375°F. Lightly grease cookie sheets; set aside. Unwrap dough rolls; reshape, if necessary. Cut dough rolls crosswise into ¼-inch-thick slices (see photo 3, page 270). Place slices 2 inches apart on prepared cookie sheets.

5 Bake in preheated oven for 6 to 8 minutes or until edges are firm and just starting to brown. Transfer cookies to wire racks and let cool.

PER COOKIE: 65 cal., 4 g total fat (2 g sat. fat, 0 g trans fat), 10 mg chol., 32 mg sodium, 8 g carbo., 0 g fiber, 1 g pro.
EXCHANGES: ½ Other Carbo., 1 Fat

DATE PINWHEELS

PREP: 40 MINUTES **CHILL:** 60 MINUTES
FREEZE: 2 HOURS **BAKE:** 8 MINUTES PER BATCH
OVEN: 375°F **MAKES:** ABOUT 64 COOKIES

- 1 8-ounce package (1⅓ cups) pitted whole dates, finely snipped
- ½ cup water
- ⅓ cup granulated sugar
- 2 tablespoons lemon juice
- ½ teaspoon vanilla
- ½ cup butter, softened
- ½ cup shortening
- ½ cup granulated sugar
- ½ cup packed brown sugar
- ½ teaspoon baking soda
- ¼ teaspoon salt
- 1 egg
- 2 tablespoons milk
- 1 teaspoon vanilla
- 3 cups all-purpose flour

1 For filling, in a medium saucepan combine dates, water, and the ⅓ cup granulated sugar. Bring to boiling; reduce heat. Cook and stir about 2 minutes or until thick. Stir in lemon juice and the ½ teaspoon vanilla; cool.

2 In a large mixing bowl beat butter and shortening with an electric mixer on medium to high speed for 30 seconds. Add the ½ cup granulated sugar, the brown sugar, baking soda, and salt. Beat until combined, scraping sides of bowl occasionally. Beat in egg, milk, and the 1 teaspoon vanilla until combined. Beat in as much of the flour as you can with the mixer. Stir in any remaining flour. Divide dough in half. Cover; chill dough about 60 minutes or until easy to handle.

3 Roll half of the dough between pieces of waxed paper into a 12×10-inch rectangle. Spread with half of the filling; roll up dough (see photo 2, page 270). Moisten edges; pinch to seal. Wrap in plastic wrap. Repeat with remaining dough and filling. Freeze 2 to 24 hours.

4 Preheat oven to 375°F. Grease cookie sheets; set aside. Use a serrated knife to cut rolls into ¼-inch-thick slices. Place slices 1 inch apart on prepared cookie sheets. Bake for 8 to 10 minutes or until bottoms are light brown. Cool on cookie sheet 1 minute. Transfer to a wire rack; let cool.

PER COOKIE: 76 cal., 3 g total fat (1 g sat. fat, 0 g trans fat), 7 mg chol., 32 mg sodium, 12 g carbo., 0 g fiber, 1 g pro.
EXCHANGES: 1 Other Carbo., ½ Fat

SUGAR COOKIE CUTOUTS *(photo, page 257)*

PREP: 40 MINUTES **CHILL:** 30 MINUTES
BAKE: 7 MINUTES PER BATCH **OVEN:** 375°F
MAKES: 36 TO 48 COOKIES

- ⅔ cup butter, softened
- ¾ cup granulated sugar
- 1 teaspoon baking powder
- ¼ teaspoon salt
- 1 egg
- 1 tablespoon milk
- 1 teaspoon vanilla
- 2 cups all-purpose flour
- 1 recipe Powdered Sugar Icing (page 280) (optional)

1 In a large mixing bowl beat butter on medium to high speed for 30 seconds. Add granulated sugar, baking powder, and salt. Beat until combined, scraping sides of bowl occasionally. Beat in egg, milk, and vanilla until combined. Beat in as much of the flour as you can with the mixer. Stir in any remaining flour. Divide dough in half. Cover and chill dough about 30 minutes or until easy to handle.

2 Preheat oven to 375°F. On a floured surface, roll half the dough at a time to ⅛- to ¼-inch thickness. Using a 2½-inch cookie cutter, cut into desired shapes. Place 1 inch apart on ungreased cookie sheets.

3 Bake for 7 to 10 minutes or until edges are firm and bottoms are very light brown. Transfer cookies to wire racks and let cool. If desired, frost with Powdered Sugar Icing.

PER COOKIE: 74 cal., 4 g total fat (2 g sat. fat, 0 g trans fat), 15 mg chol., 49 mg sodium, 10 g carbo., 0 g fiber, 1 g pro.
EXCHANGES: ½ Other Carbo., 1 Fat

STICKING SOLUTIONS
RATHER THAN GREASING THE COOKIE SHEET, YOU CAN LINE IT WITH PARCHMENT PAPER OR A SILICONE BAKING MAT.

GINGERBREAD CUTOUTS

PREP: 35 MINUTES **CHILL:** 3 HOURS
BAKE: 5 MINUTES PER BATCH **OVEN:** 375°F
MAKES: 36 TO 48 COOKIES

- ½ cup shortening
- ½ cup granulated sugar
- 1 teaspoon baking powder
- 1 teaspoon ground ginger
- ½ teaspoon baking soda
- ½ teaspoon ground cinnamon
- ½ teaspoon ground cloves
- ½ cup molasses
- 1 egg
- 1 tablespoon vinegar
- 2½ cups all-purpose flour
- 1 recipe Powdered Sugar Icing (page 280) (optional)
- Decorative candies (optional)

1 In a large mixing bowl beat shortening with an electric mixer on medium to high speed for 30 seconds. Add granulated sugar, baking powder, ginger, baking soda, cinnamon, and cloves. Beat until combined, scraping sides of bowl occasionally. Beat in molasses, egg, and vinegar until combined. Beat in as much of the flour as you can with the mixer. Stir in any remaining flour. Divide dough in half. Cover and chill dough about 3 hours or until easy to handle.

2 Preheat oven to 375°F. Grease a cookie sheet; set aside. On a lightly floured surface, roll half of the dough at a time to ⅛ inch thick. Using a 2½-inch cookie cutter, cut into desired shapes. Place 1 inch apart on prepared cookie sheet.

3 Bake for 5 to 6 minutes or until bottoms are light brown. Cool on cookie sheet for 1 minute. Transfer cookies to a wire rack and let cool. If desired, decorate cookies with Powdered Sugar Icing and candies.

PER COOKIE: 82 cal., 3 g total fat (1 g sat. fat, 0 g trans fat), 6 mg chol., 28 mg sodium, 13 g carbo., 0 g fiber, 1 g pro.
EXCHANGES: 1 Other Carbo., ½ Fat

SHORTBREAD

PREP: 15 MINUTES **BAKE:** 25 MINUTES
COOL: 5 MINUTES **OVEN:** 325°F
MAKES: 16 WEDGES

1¼ cups all-purpose flour
3 tablespoons sugar
½ cup butter

1 Preheat oven to 325°F. In a medium bowl combine flour and sugar. Using a pastry blender, cut in butter until mixture resembles fine crumbs and starts to cling (see photo 1, below). Form the mixture into a ball and knead until smooth (see photo 2, below).

2 To make shortbread wedges, on an ungreased cookie sheet pat or roll the dough into an 8-inch circle (see photo 3, below). Make a scalloped edge (see photo 4, below). Cut circle into 16 wedges (see photo 5, below). Leave wedges in the circle. Bake for 25 to 30 minutes or until bottom just starts

to brown and center is set. Cut circle into wedges again while warm. Cool on cookie sheet 5 minutes. Transfer to a wire rack and let cool.

BUTTER-PECAN SHORTBREAD: Prepare as directed, except substitute brown sugar for the sugar. After cutting in butter, stir in 2 tablespoons finely chopped pecans. Sprinkle mixture with ½ teaspoon vanilla before kneading.

CRANBERRY SHORTBREAD: Prepare as directed, except after cutting in butter stir in ⅓ cup snipped dried cranberries.

SPICED SHORTBREAD: Prepare as directed, except substitute brown sugar for the sugar and stir ½ teaspoon ground cinnamon, ¼ teaspoon ground ginger, and ⅛ teaspoon ground cloves into the flour mixture.

PER WEDGE REGULAR, BUTTER-PECAN, CRANBERRY, OR SPICED VARIATIONS: 96 cal., 6 g total fat (4 g sat. fat, 0 g trans fat), 15 mg chol., 41 mg sodium, 10 g carbo., 0 g fiber, 1 g pro.
EXCHANGES: ½ Other Carbo., 1½ Fat

SHORTBREAD, STEP-BY-STEP

1. Cut the butter into the flour mixture just until the dough starts to cling. **2.** Knead until dough is smooth. **3.** Use your fingers to pat dough into an 8-inch circle. **4.** Make a scalloped edge by pinching the upper edge of the dough with your thumb and forefinger while pressing into the pinched dough with your other forefinger. **5.** Cut slices into wedges before baking for easy slicing after baking.

STRAWBERRY SHORTBREAD

PREP: 45 MINUTES **FREEZE:** 1 HOUR
BAKE: 12 MINUTES PER BATCH
OVEN: 325°F **MAKES:** ABOUT 54 2-INCH COOKIES OR
108 1½-INCH COOKIES

- 2 tablespoons strawberry preserves
- 1 cup butter, softened
- ½ teaspoon almond extract
- 2⅔ cups all-purpose flour
- ½ cup granulated sugar
- ⅛ teaspoon salt
- 1 recipe Powdered Sugar Icing (page 280)
  Coarse sugar (optional)

1 Snip any large pieces of fruit in the preserves. In a large bowl beat preserves, butter, and almond extract until well combined. Transfer mixture to a sheet of plastic wrap; shape into a 6-inch roll. Wrap and freeze for 1 to 2 hours or until firm.

2 Preheat oven to 325°F. In a large bowl stir together flour, granulated sugar, and salt. Add butter mixture. Cut butter mixture into flour mixture with a pastry blender until mixture resembles fine crumbs and starts to cling (see photo 1, page 273). Knead dough until smooth; form dough into a ball. (Dough will eventually come together during kneading from the warmth of your hands) [see photo 2, page 273].

3 Divide dough in half. Roll each portion of dough to ¼-inch thickness on a lightly floured surface. Cut out dough rounds or squares with a scalloped-edge 1½- or 2-inch cookie cutter. Place cutouts 1 inch apart on ungreased cookie sheets.

4 Bake for 12 to 14 minutes for 1½-inch cookies or 14 to 16 minutes for 2-inch cookies or until edges just start to brown. Transfer cookies to wire racks and cool completely. Drizzle tops with Powdered Sugar Icing. If desired, sprinkle with coarse sugar. Let stand until icing is set.

PER 2-INCH COOKIE: 84 cal., 4 g total fat (2 g sat. fat, 0 g trans fat), 9 mg chol., 31 mg sodium, 12 g carbo., 0 g fiber, 1 g pro.
EXCHANGES: 1 Other Carbo., 1 Fat

BERRY UP ADD STRAWBERRY FLAVOR TO POWDERED SUGAR ICING (PAGE 280) BY INCREASING POWDERED SUGAR TO 2 CUPS AND ADDING 2 TABLESPOONS MELTED STRAWBERRY PRESERVES.

STRAWBERRY SHORTBREAD

LEMONY GLAZED SHORTBREAD BARS

PREP: 40 MINUTES **BAKE:** 40 MINUTES
OVEN: 300°F **MAKES:** 32 BARS

   3 cups all-purpose flour
   ⅓ cup cornstarch
 1¼ cups powdered sugar
   ¼ cup finely shredded lemon peel
      (5 to 6 lemons)
 1½ cups butter, softened
   1 tablespoon lemon juice
   ½ teaspoon vanilla
      Lemony Glaze

1 Preheat oven to 300°F. Line a 13×9×2-inch baking pan with foil, extending foil 2 inches over edges of the pan (see photo 1, page 278). Lightly grease foil; set aside.

2 In a bowl combine flour and cornstarch; set aside. In another bowl combine powdered sugar and lemon peel. Pressing against side of bowl with a wooden spoon, work lemon peel into powdered sugar until sugar is yellow and fragrant; set aside.

3 In a large mixing bowl beat butter, lemon juice, ½ teaspoon *salt,* and vanilla with an electric mixer on medium speed until combined. Gradually beat in powdered sugar mixture. Stir in flour mixture.

4 With lightly floured fingers, press dough evenly into the prepared pan. Bake about 40 minutes or until pale golden in color and edges begin to brown. Remove from oven. Immediately spoon Lemony Glaze over top, gently spreading to evenly distribute glaze. Cool completely. Use foil to lift uncut bars out of pan. Cut into bars.

LEMONY GLAZE: Whisk together 2½ cups powdered sugar, 2 teaspoons finely shredded lemon peel, 3 tablespoons lemon juice, 1 tablespoon light-color corn syrup, and ½ teaspoon vanilla.

PER BAR: 181 cal., 9 g total fat (5 g sat. fat, 0 g trans fat), 23 mg chol., 98 mg sodium, 25 g carbo., 0 g fiber, 1 g pro.
EXCHANGES: 1½ Other Carbo., 2 Fat

PECAN PIE BARS

PREP: 25 MINUTES **BAKE:** 40 MINUTES
OVEN: 350°F **MAKES:** 24 BARS

 1¼ cups all-purpose flour
   ½ cup powdered sugar
   ¼ teaspoon salt
   ½ cup butter, cut up
   2 eggs, lightly beaten

   1 cup chopped pecans
   ½ cup packed brown sugar
   ½ cup light-colored corn syrup
   2 tablespoons butter, melted
   1 teaspoon vanilla

1 Preheat oven to 350°F. For crust, in a medium bowl combine flour, powdered sugar, and salt. Cut in the ½ cup butter until mixture resembles coarse crumbs. Pat crumb mixture into an ungreased 11×7×1½-inch baking pan. Bake for 20 minutes or until light brown.

2 Meanwhile, for filling, in a medium bowl stir together eggs, pecans, ½ cup brown sugar, the corn syrup, 2 tablespoons melted butter, and vanilla. Pour over the baked crust, spreading evenly.

3 Bake about 20 minutes more or until the filling is set. Cool completely in pan on a wire rack. Cut into bars. Cover and store in the refrigerator.

PER BAR: 132 cal., 9 g total fat (3 g sat. fat, 0 g trans fat), 30 mg chol., 67 mg sodium, 13 g carbo., 1 g fiber, 2 g pro.
EXCHANGES: 1 Other Carbo., 2 Fat

BLONDIES

PREP: 20 MINUTES **BAKE:** 25 MINUTES
OVEN: 350°F **MAKES:** 36 BARS

   2 cups packed brown sugar
   ⅔ cup butter, cut up
   2 eggs
   2 teaspoons vanilla
   2 cups all-purpose flour
   1 teaspoon baking powder
   ¼ teaspoon baking soda
 1½ cups chopped almonds or pecans

1 Preheat oven to 350°F. Grease a 13×9×2-inch baking pan; set aside. In a medium saucepan heat brown sugar and butter over medium heat until butter melts and mixture is smooth, stirring constantly. Cool slightly. Stir in eggs, one at a time; stir in vanilla. Stir in flour, baking powder, and baking soda.

2 Spread batter in prepared baking pan. Sprinkle with almonds. Bake for 25 to 30 minutes or until a wooden toothpick inserted near center comes out clean. Cool slightly in pan on a wire rack. Cut into bars while warm.

PER BAR: 129 cal., 6 g total fat (2 g sat. fat, 0 g trans fat), 21 mg chol., 47 mg sodium, 18 g carbo., 1 g fiber, 2 g pro.
EXCHANGES: 1 Other Carbo., 1 Fat

10 TO TRY—BROWNIES

Start with Fudgy Brownies, page 277. **1. CARAMEL-PECAN:** Use pecans. Top unfrosted brownies with pecans; drizzle with caramel topping. **2. FRUIT:** Top frosted brownies with strawberries, bananas, peanuts, and whipped cream. **3. COFFEE:** Dissolve 1 teaspoon instant espresso powder in 2 teaspoons hot water; add with ½ teaspoon ground cinnamon along with eggs. To frosting, add ½ teaspoon instant espresso powder to chocolate. Top with chocolate-covered espresso beans. **4. MALTED:** Stir ¼ cup malted milk powder in with flour. Frost; top with malted milk balls. **5. ROCKY ROAD:** Top frosted brownies with walnuts and marshmallows. **6. COCONUT-ALMOND:** Use almonds. Frost; top with chopped macaroons. **7. RASPBERRY:** Spread baked brownies with ⅔ cup raspberry preserves. Frost; top with raspberries. **8. MINT:** Add ½ teaspoon mint extract with vanilla. Frost; top with chocolate-mint candies. **9. PEANUT BUTTER:** Fold ¾ cup chopped chocolate-covered peanut butter cups into batter. Frost; top with additional peanut butter cups. **10. DOUBLE CHOCOLATE:** Fold ¾ cup white chocolate baking pieces into batter. Frost; top with chocolate curls.

FUDGY BROWNIES

PREP: 20 MINUTES **BAKE:** 30 MINUTES
COOL: 15 MINUTES **OVEN:** 350°F
MAKES: 16 BROWNIES

- ½ cup butter
- 3 ounces unsweetened chocolate, coarsely chopped
- 1 cup sugar
- 2 eggs
- 1 teaspoon vanilla
- ⅔ cup all-purpose flour
- ¼ teaspoon baking soda
- ½ cup chopped nuts (optional)
- 1 recipe Chocolate-Cream Cheese Frosting (optional)

1 In a medium saucepan heat and stir butter and unsweetened chocolate over low heat until smooth; set aside to cool. Preheat oven to 350°F. Line an 8×8×2-inch baking pan with foil, leaving about 1 inch of the foil extending over the edges of the pan (see photo, page 278). Grease foil; set pan aside.

2 Stir the sugar into the cooled chocolate mixture. Add the eggs, one at a time, beating with a wooden spoon just until combined. Stir in vanilla. In a small bowl stir together the flour and baking soda. Add flour mixture to chocolate mixture; stir just until combined. If desired, stir in nuts. Spread the batter evenly in the prepared pan.

3 Bake for 30 minutes. Cool in pan on a wire rack. If desired, spread Chocolate-Cream Cheese Frosting over cooled brownies. Use foil to lift uncut brownies out of pan. Place on cutting board; cut into brownies.

PER BROWNIE: 157 cal., 10 g total fat (6 g sat. fat, 0 g trans fat), 43 mg chol., 90 mg sodium, 18 g carbo., 1 g fiber, 2 g pro. EXCHANGES: 1 Other Carbo., 2 Fat

CHOCOLATE-CREAM CHEESE FROSTING: In a small saucepan heat and stir 1 cup semisweet chocolate pieces over low heat until melted and smooth. Remove from heat; let cool. In a medium bowl stir together two 3-ounce packages softened cream cheese and ½ cup powdered sugar. Stir in melted chocolate until smooth.

CHOCOLATE-BUTTERMILK BROWNIES

PREP: 30 MINUTES **BAKE:** 25 MINUTES
COOL: 60 MINUTES **OVEN:** 350°F
MAKES: 24 BROWNIES

- 2 cups all-purpose flour
- 2 cups sugar
- 1 teaspoon baking soda
- ¼ teaspoon salt
- 1 cup butter
- ⅓ cup unsweetened cocoa powder
- 2 eggs
- ½ cup buttermilk or sour milk (see tip, page 19)
- 1½ teaspoons vanilla
- 1 recipe Chocolate-Buttermilk Frosting

1 Preheat oven to 350°F. Grease a 15×10×1-inch or a 13×9×2-inch baking pan; set aside. In a medium bowl stir together flour, sugar, baking soda, and salt; set aside.

2 In a medium saucepan combine butter, cocoa powder, and 1 cup *water*. Bring mixture just to boiling, stirring constantly. Remove from heat. Add the cocoa mixture to flour mixture and beat with an electric mixer on medium to high speed until thoroughly combined. Add eggs, buttermilk, and vanilla. Beat for 1 minute (batter will be thin). Pour batter into the prepared pan.

3 Bake about 25 minutes for the 15×10×1-inch pan, 35 minutes for the 13×9×2-inch pan, or until a wooden toothpick inserted in the middle comes out clean.

4 Pour warm Chocolate-Buttermilk Frosting over brownies, spreading evenly. Cool in pan on wire rack for 60 minutes. Cut into brownies.

CHOCOLATE-BUTTERMILK FROSTING: In a medium saucepan combine ¼ cup butter, 3 tablespoons unsweetened cocoa powder, and 3 tablespoons buttermilk. Bring to boiling. Remove from heat. Add 2¼ cups powdered sugar and ½ teaspoon vanilla. Beat until smooth. If desired, stir in ¾ cup coarsely chopped toasted pecans.

CHOCOLATE-CINNAMON-BUTTERMILK BROWNIES: Prepare as directed, except add 1 teaspoon ground cinnamon to the flour mixture.

PER BROWNIE REGULAR OR CINNAMON VARIATION: 245 cal., 10 g total fat (6 g sat. fat, 0 g trans fat), 43 mg chol., 158 mg sodium, 37 g carbo., 1 g fiber, 2 g pro. EXCHANGES: 2½ Other Carbo., 2 Fat

CHOCOLATE REVEL BARS

PREP: 30 MINUTES **BAKE:** 25 MINUTES
OVEN: 350°F **MAKES:** 60 BARS

- 1 cup butter, softened
- 2 cups packed brown sugar
- 1 teaspoon baking soda
- 2 eggs
- 2 teaspoons vanilla
- 2½ cups all-purpose flour
- 3 cups quick-cooking rolled oats
- 1½ cups semisweet chocolate pieces
- 1 14-ounce can (1¼ cups) sweetened condensed milk
- ½ cup chopped walnuts or pecans
- 2 teaspoons vanilla

1 Preheat oven to 350°F. Set aside 2 tablespoons of the butter. In a large mixing bowl beat remaining butter with an electric mixer on medium to high speed for 30 seconds. Add the brown sugar and baking soda. Beat until combined, scraping sides of bowl occasionally. Beat in eggs and 2 teaspoons vanilla until combined. Beat in as much of the flour as you can with the mixer. Stir in any remaining flour. Stir in the rolled oats.

2 For filling, in a medium saucepan combine the reserved 2 tablespoons butter, the chocolate pieces, and sweetened condensed milk. Cook over low heat until chocolate melts, stirring occasionally. Remove from heat. Stir in the nuts and 2 teaspoons vanilla.

3 Press two-thirds (about 3⅓ cups) of the rolled oats mixture into the bottom of an ungreased 15×10×1-inch baking pan. Spread filling evenly over the oats mixture. Dot remaining rolled oats mixture on filling (see photo 2, below).

4 Bake for about 25 minutes or until top is light brown (chocolate filling will still look moist). Cool pan on a wire rack. Cut into bars.

PEANUT BUTTER-CHOCOLATE REVEL BARS:
Prepare as directed, except substitute ½ cup peanut butter for the 2 tablespoons butter when making the chocolate filling and substitute peanuts for the walnuts or pecans.

PER BAR CHOCOLATE OR PEANUT BUTTER VARIATION:
145 cal., 6 g total fat (3 g sat. fat, 0 g trans fat), 17 mg chol., 56 mg sodium, 21 g carbo., 1 g fiber, 2 g pro.
EXCHANGES: 1½ Other Carbo., 1 Fat

OATMEAL-CARAMEL BARS

PREP: 25 MINUTES **BAKE:** 22 MINUTES
OVEN: 350°F **MAKES:** 60 BARS

- 1 cup butter, softened
- 2 cups packed brown sugar
- 2 eggs
- 2 teaspoons vanilla
- 1 teaspoon baking soda
- 2½ cups all-purpose flour
- 3 cups quick-cooking rolled oats
- 1 cup miniature semisweet chocolate pieces
- ½ cup chopped walnuts or pecans
- 30 vanilla caramels (9 ounces), unwrapped
- 3 tablespoons milk

1 Preheat oven to 350°F. Line a 15×10×1-inch baking pan with foil, leaving about 1 inch of foil

OATMEAL-CARAMEL BARS, STEP-BY-STEP

1. To line the pan with foil: Turn pan upside down and shape the foil over the outside, extending foil about 1 inch past the pan's edges. Place the shaped foil inside the pan, as shown.
2. After drizzling caramel mixture over chocolate and nuts, use a spoon and a small spatula or table knife to drop remaining oats mixture over the surface of the caramel. You do not need to spread it.

extending over the edges of the pan (see photo 1, page 278); set aside.

2 In a large mixing bowl beat butter with an electric mixer on medium to high speed for 30 seconds. Add the brown sugar. Beat until combined, scraping sides of bowl occasionally. Add eggs, vanilla, and baking soda; beat until combined. Beat or stir in the flour. Stir in the oats. Press two-thirds of the oats mixture (about 3⅓ cups) evenly into the bottom of the prepared pan. Sprinkle with chocolate pieces and nuts.

3 In a medium saucepan heat and stir the caramels and milk over low heat until melted and smooth. Drizzle caramel mixture over chocolate and nuts. Drop the remaining oats mixture by teaspoons over the caramel (see photo 2, page 278).

4 Bake for 22 to 25 minutes or until top is light brown. Cool in pan on a wire rack. Use foil to lift uncut bars out of pan. Place on cutting board; cut into bars.

PER BAR: 139 cal., 6 g total fat (3 g sat. fat, 0 g trans fat), 16 mg chol., 60 mg sodium, 21 g carbo., 1 g fiber, 2 g pro. EXCHANGES: 1½ Other Carbo., 1 Fat

BANANA BARS

PREP: 30 MINUTES **BAKE:** 25 MINUTES **OVEN:** 350°F **MAKES:** 36 BARS

⅓ cup butter, softened
1⅓ cups sugar
1½ teaspoons baking powder
½ teaspoon baking soda
¼ teaspoon salt
1 egg
1 cup mashed bananas (2 to 3 medium)
½ cup dairy sour cream
1 teaspoon vanilla
2 cups all-purpose flour
1 cup chopped pecans or walnuts, toasted (see tip, page 20)
1 recipe Cream Cheese Frosting (page 180)

1 Preheat oven to 350°F. Lightly grease a 15×10×1-inch baking pan; set aside. In a large mixing bowl beat butter with an electric mixer on medium to high speed for 30 seconds. Add sugar, baking powder, baking soda, and salt; beat until combined, scraping sides of bowl occasionally. Beat in the egg, mashed bananas, sour cream, and vanilla until combined. Beat or stir in the flour. Stir

in pecans. Pour the batter into the prepared baking pan, spreading evenly.

2 Bake for about 25 minutes or until a wooden toothpick inserted near center comes out clean. Cool completely in pan on a wire rack. Frost with Cream Cheese Frosting. Cut into bars.

PER BAR: 228 cal., 10 g total fat (5 g sat. fat, 0 g trans fat), 28 mg chol., 105 mg sodium, 34 g carbo., 1 g fiber, 2 g pro. EXCHANGES: 2 Other Carbo., 2 Fat

BEST EVER

PUMPKIN BARS

PREP: 25 MINUTES **BAKE:** 20 MINUTES **COOL:** 2 HOURS **OVEN:** 350°F **MAKES:** 36 BARS

2 cups all-purpose flour
1½ cups sugar
2 teaspoons baking powder
2 teaspoons ground cinnamon
1 teaspoon baking soda
½ teaspoon salt
¼ teaspoon ground cloves
4 eggs, lightly beaten
1 15-ounce can pumpkin
1 cup vegetable oil
2½ cups Cream Cheese Frosting (page 180)

1 Preheat oven to 350°F. In a large bowl stir together the flour, sugar, baking powder, cinnamon, baking soda, salt, and cloves. Stir in the eggs, pumpkin, and oil until combined. Pour batter into an ungreased 15×10×1-inch baking pan, spreading evenly.

2 Bake for 20 to 25 minutes or until a wooden toothpick inserted near the center comes out clean. Cool in pan on a wire rack 2 hours. Spread with Cream Cheese Frosting. Cut into bars. Store bars in the refrigerator.

APPLESAUCE BARS: Prepare as directed, except substitute one 15-ounce jar (1¾ cups) applesauce for the pumpkin.

PER BAR PUMPKIN OR APPLESAUCE VARIATION: 243 cal., 11 g total fat (3 g sat. fat, 0 g trans fat), 37 mg chol., 135 mg sodium, 34 g carbo., 1 g fiber, 2 g pro. EXCHANGES: 2 Other Carbo., 2 Fat

BLUEBERRY SWIRL CHEESECAKE BARS

PREP: 25 MINUTES **BAKE:** 40 MINUTES
COOL: 60 MINUTES **CHILL:** 60 MINUTES
OVEN: 350°F **MAKES:** 36 BARS

    2 tablespoons granulated sugar
    2 teaspoons cornstarch
    1 cup fresh or frozen blueberries
    ¼ cup orange juice
    2 cups all-purpose flour
    ½ cup powdered sugar
    1 cup butter, cut up
    1 8-ounce package cream cheese, softened
    ½ cup granulated sugar
    1 tablespoon all-purpose flour
    2 eggs, lightly beaten
    1 teaspoon vanilla
       Powdered sugar (optional)

1 Preheat oven to 350°F. Line a 13×9×2-inch baking pan with foil, extending foil over the edges of the pan; set baking pan aside.

2 In a small saucepan stir together the 2 tablespoons sugar and the cornstarch. Stir in blueberries and orange juice. Cook and stir over medium heat until thickened and bubbly. Remove from heat and set aside.

3 For crust, in a large mixing bowl stir together the 2 cups flour and the ½ cup powdered sugar. Cut in butter until fine crumbs form and mixture starts to cling together (mixture will still be crumbly). Pat mixture firmly into prepared pan. Bake for 20 minutes.

4 Meanwhile, in a medium bowl beat cream cheese, the ½ cup granulated sugar, and the 1 tablespoon flour until smooth. Beat in eggs and vanilla until combined. Pour over hot baked crust, spreading evenly. Spoon blueberry mixture in small mounds over the cheese layer. Use a thin metal spatula or table knife to marble the mixtures.

5 Bake about 20 minutes more or until center is set. Remove and cool in pan on a wire rack for 60 minutes. Cover and chill at least 60 minutes. Use foil to lift uncut bars out of pan. Cut into bars. Store in an airtight container in the refrigerator for up to 2 days. If desired, sift bars with powdered sugar just before serving.

PER BAR: 120 cal., 8 g total fat (5 g sat. fat, 0 g trans fat), 32 mg chol., 61 mg sodium, 12 g carbo., 0 g fiber, 2 g pro.
EXCHANGES: 1 Other Carbo., 1½ Fat

BEST EVER

CHERRY KUCHEN BARS

PREP: 25 MINUTES **BAKE:** 42 MINUTES
COOL: 10 MINUTES **OVEN:** 350°F
MAKES: 32 BARS

    ½ cup butter, softened
    ½ cup shortening
   1¾ cups sugar
   1½ teaspoons baking powder
    ½ teaspoon salt
    3 eggs
    1 teaspoon vanilla
    3 cups all-purpose flour
    1 21-ounce can cherry pie filling*
    1 recipe Powdered Sugar Icing

1 Preheat oven to 350°F. In a large mixing bowl beat butter and shortening with an electric mixer on medium speed for 30 seconds. Add sugar, baking powder, and salt. Beat until well combined, scraping sides of bowl occasionally. Beat in eggs and vanilla. Beat in as much of the flour as you can with the mixer. Stir in any remaining flour. Reserve 1½ cups of the dough. Spread remaining dough in the bottom of an ungreased 15×10×1-inch baking pan.

2 Bake for 12 minutes. Spread pie filling over crust in pan. Spoon reserved dough into small mounds on top of pie filling.

3 Bake about 30 minutes more or until top is light brown. Cool in pan on a wire rack for 10 minutes. Drizzle top with Powdered Sugar Icing. Cool completely. Cut into bars to serve.

*NOTE: You can substitute your favorite flavor of pie filling for the cherry pie filling.

POWDERED SUGAR ICING: In a small bowl combine 1½ cups powdered sugar, ¼ teaspoon vanilla or almond extract, and enough milk (3 to 4 teaspoons) to make a smooth drizzling consistency.

PER BAR: 189 cal., 6 g total fat (3 g sat. fat, 0 g trans fat), 27 mg chol., 84 mg sodium, 31 g carbo., 0 g fiber, 2 g pro.
EXCHANGES: 2 Other Carbo., 1½ Fat

JUST A DROP WILL DO
WHEN MAKING POWDERED SUGAR ICING, ADD THE LIQUID BIT BY BIT. ICING CAN GO FROM TOO STIFF TO TOO RUNNY IN JUST A FEW DROPS.

HANDLE WITH CARE TO AVOID TEARING OR BREAKING BAKED BARS, REMOVE THEM FROM THE PAN WITH A SPATULA THAT'S SMALLER THAN THE BARS.

LEMON BARS

PREP: 25 MINUTES **BAKE:** 33 MINUTES
OVEN: 350°F **MAKES:** 36 BARS

- 2 cups all-purpose flour
- ½ cup powdered sugar
- 2 tablespoons cornstarch
- ¼ teaspoon salt
- ¾ cup butter, cut up
- 4 eggs, lightly beaten
- 1½ cups granulated sugar
- 3 tablespoons all-purpose flour
- 1 teaspoon finely shredded lemon peel
- ¾ cup lemon juice
- ¼ cup half-and-half, light cream, or milk
  Powdered sugar

1 Preheat oven to 350°F. Line a 13x9x2-inch baking pan with foil, extending the foil over the edges (see photo 1, page 278.) Grease foil; set aside. In a large bowl combine the 2 cups flour, the ½ cup powdered sugar, the cornstarch, and salt. Using a pastry blender, cut in butter until mixture resembles coarse crumbs. Press mixture into the bottom of prepared pan. Bake for 18 to 20 minutes or until edges are light brown.

2 Meanwhile, for filling, in a bowl stir together eggs, the granulated sugar, the 3 tablespoons flour, the lemon peel, lemon juice, and half-and-half. Pour filling over hot crust. Bake for 15 to 20 minutes more or until center is set. Cool completely in pan on a wire rack. Use foil to lift uncut bars out of pan. Cut into bars. Just before serving, sift powdered sugar over tops. Cover and store in the refrigerator.

RASPBERRY/BLUEBERRY LEMON BARS:
Prepare as directed, except sprinkle 1½ cups fresh raspberries or blueberries evenly over filling before second baking. Bake for 20 to 25 minutes or until center is set.

PER BAR REGULAR OR RASPBERRY/BLUEBERRY VARIATION: 115 cal., 5 g total fat (3 g sat. fat, 0 g trans fat), 34 mg chol., 52 mg sodium, 17 g carbo., 0 g fiber, 2 g pro. EXCHANGES: 1 Other Carbo., 1 Fat

DANISH PASTRY APPLE BARS

PREP: 30 MINUTES **BAKE:** 50 MINUTES
OVEN: 375°F **MAKES:** 32 BARS

- 2½ cups all-purpose flour
- 1 teaspoon salt
- 1 cup shortening
- 1 egg yolk
  Milk
- 1 cup cornflakes
- 8 cups tart cooking apples, peeled, cored, and sliced (8 to 10)
- ¾ to 1 cup granulated sugar
- 1 teaspoon ground cinnamon
- 1 egg white, lightly beaten
- 1 cup powdered sugar
- 3 to 4 teaspoons milk

1 Preheat oven to 375°F. In a large bowl combine flour and salt. Use a pastry blender to cut in shortening until the mixture resembles coarse

BAR COOKIE YIELDS—MORE OR LESS

Although you should heed the pan sizes called for in each recipe, the number of bars you cut from a pan is up to you. To go up or down on the yield, make more or fewer horizontal and crosswise cuts using the guide below. Note that smaller is better when bars are especially rich.

Baking Pan Size	Number of Cuts		Approximate Size of Bar	Number of Bars
	Lengthwise	Crosswise		
13×9×2-inch	2	7	3×1⅝-inch	24
	3	7	2¼×1⅝-inch	32
	5	5	1½×2⅛-inch	36
	7	4	1⅛×2⅝-inch	40
	7	5	1⅛×2⅛-inch	48
15×10×1-inch	3	8	2½×1¾-inch	36
	3	11	2½×1¼-inch	48
	3	14	2½×1-inch	60
	7	7	1¼×1⅞-inch	64
	7	8	1¼×1¾-inch	72

crumbs. In a liquid measuring cup beat egg yolk lightly. Add enough milk to make ⅔ cup liquid. Stir well to combine. Stir milk mixture into flour mixture with a fork until combined (dough will be slightly sticky). Divide mixture in half.

2 On a well-floured surface, roll half of the dough into a 17×12-inch rectangle. Fold dough crosswise into thirds. Transfer to a 15×10×1-inch baking pan and unfold dough, pressing to fit into the bottom and up sides of the pan. Sprinkle with cornflakes. Top evenly with apples. In a small bowl combine granulated sugar and cinnamon. Sprinkle mixture over apples. Roll remaining dough to a 15×10-inch rectangle. Fold dough crosswise into thirds. Place on top of apples and unfold dough. Crimp edges or use the tines of a fork to seal. Cut slits in the top. Brush top with beaten egg white.

3 Bake about 50 minutes or until light brown and apples are tender, covering with foil after the first 25 minutes of baking time to prevent pastry from overbrowning.

4 In a small bowl combine powdered sugar and 3 to 4 teaspoons milk to make a drizzling consistency. Drizzle over warm bars. Let cool completely on a wire rack. Cut into bars.

PER BAR: 155 cal., 6 g total fat (2 g sat. fat, 1 g trans fat), 7 mg chol., 83 mg sodium, 23 g carbo., 1 g fiber, 2 g pro. EXCHANGES: 1½ Other Carbo., 1 Fat

EASY MONSTER COOKIE BARS

PREP: 15 MINUTES **BAKE:** 20 MINUTES
OVEN: 350°F **MAKES:** 16 TO 20 BARS

 1 16.5-ounce roll refrigerated peanut butter cookie dough
 ¾ cup rolled oats
 1 cup candy-coated milk chocolate pieces
 ½ cup semisweet chocolate pieces
 ½ cup chopped peanuts (optional)

1 Preheat oven to 350°F. Line a 9×9×2-inch baking pan with foil, extending foil over edges of pan (see photo 1, page 278). Lightly grease foil; set aside. Break up cookie dough into a large bowl. Stir in oats. Stir in milk chocolate pieces, semisweet chocolate pieces, and nuts (if desired).

2 Pat mixture into prepared baking pan. Bake about 20 minutes or until light brown. Cool in pan on a wire rack. Use foil to lift uncut bars out of pan. Cut into bars.

PER BAR: 241 cal., 12 g total fat (4 g sat. fat, 0 g trans fat), 9 mg chol., 123 mg sodium, 31 g carbo., 2 g fiber, 4 g pro. EXCHANGES: 2 Other Carbo., 2½ Fat

FIVE-LAYER BARS

PREP: 10 MINUTES **BAKE:** 37 MINUTES
OVEN: 350°F **MAKES:** 30 BARS

 2 13-ounce packages soft coconut macaroon cookies (32 cookies)
 ¾ cup sweetened condensed milk
 ¾ cup semisweet chocolate pieces
 ¾ cup raisins or dried cranberries
 1 cup coarsely chopped peanuts

1 Preheat oven to 350°F. Arrange cookies in the bottom of a greased 13×9×2-inch baking pan. Press cookies together to form a crust. Bake for 12 minutes. Drizzle crust evenly with condensed milk. Sprinkle with chocolate pieces, raisins, and peanuts. Bake about 25 minutes or until edges are light brown. Cool in pan on a wire rack. Cut into bars.

PER BAR: 181 cal., 7 g total fat (4 g sat. fat, 0 g trans fat), 3 mg chol., 86 mg sodium, 28 g carbo., 1 g fiber, 3 g pro. EXCHANGES: 2 Other Carbo., 1½ Fat

FRUIT FORWARD
LEFTOVER RAISINS AND OTHER DRIED FRUITS CAN BE WRAPPED IN AIRTIGHT PACKAGING AND STORED IN THE FREEZER FOR UP TO 6 MONTHS.

YUMMY NO-BAKE BARS

PREP: 30 MINUTES **CHILL:** 60 MINUTES
MAKES: 64 BARS

- 1 cup granulated sugar
- 1 cup light-color corn syrup
- 2 cups peanut butter
- 3 cups crisp rice cereal
- 3 cups cornflakes
- ¾ cup butter
- 4 cups powdered sugar
- 2 4-serving-size packages vanilla instant pudding and pie filling mix
- ¼ cup milk
- 1 12-ounce package (2 cups) semisweet chocolate pieces
- ½ cup butter

1 Line a 15×10×1-inch baking pan with foil, extending the foil over the edges of the pan (see photo 1, page 278); set aside.

2 In a large saucepan combine granulated sugar and corn syrup; heat and stir just until mixture boils around edges. Heat and stir for 1 minute more. Remove from heat. Stir in peanut butter until melted. Use a wooden spoon to stir in rice cereal and cornflakes until coated. Press mixture into the bottom of prepared pan.

3 For pudding layer, in a medium saucepan melt the ¾ cup butter. Stir in powdered sugar, pudding mix, and milk. Spread pudding mixture over cereal layer; set aside.

4 For frosting, in a small saucepan heat and stir chocolate pieces and the ½ cup butter over low heat until melted and smooth. Spread frosting over pudding layer. Loosely cover and chill about 60 minutes or until set. To serve, use foil to lift uncut bars out of pan. Place on a cutting board; cut into bars. Store in the refrigerator.

PER BAR: 175 cal., 9 g total fat (4 g sat. fat, 0 g trans fat), 10 mg chol., 133 mg sodium, 23 g carbo., 1 g fiber, 2 g pro.
EXCHANGES: 1½ Other Carbo., 2 Fat

A CLEAN CUT FOR SMOOTH, SMUDGE-FREE SIDES TO YOUR BARS, HOLD A THIN-BLADED KNIFE UNDER RUNNING HOT WATER; WIPE THE BLADE DRY AND CUT THE BARS. REPEAT AS NECESSARY.

YUMMY NO-BAKE BARS

DESSERTS

MIXED-BERRY SHORTCAKES, PAGE 290

DESSERTS

MAKE LIFE SWEETER WITH THESE TIPS FOR BETTER ENDINGS AND ADVICE ON KEEPING GOODIES ON HAND IN THE FREEZER.

FINISHING FLOURISHES

Add extra pleasure to your desserts with these tasty touches.

CANDIED NUTS: Line a baking sheet with foil; butter the foil. Set pan aside. Spread 3 cups pecan halves or whole almonds in a shallow baking pan. Bake in a preheated 325°F oven for 10 minutes, stirring once. Meanwhile, heat ½ cup sugar in a medium heavy skillet over medium-high heat, shaking skillet occasionally to heat sugar evenly. Do not stir. Heat until some of the sugar melts (it should look syrupy); begin to stir only the melted sugar to keep it from overbrowning. Stir in remaining sugar as it melts. Reduce heat to medium-low; continue to cook until all the sugar is melted and golden, about 5 minutes. Add 2 tablespoons butter to melted sugar in skillet, stirring until butter melts and mixture is combined. Remove from heat. Stir in ½ teaspoon vanilla.

Add warm nuts to skillet, stirring to coat. Pour nut mixture onto the prepared baking sheet. Cool completely. Break apart. Makes about 4⅓ cups.

SWEETENED WHIPPED CREAM: In a chilled mixing bowl add 1 cup whipping cream, 2 tablespoons sugar, and ½ teaspoon vanilla. Beat with an electric mixer on medium speed until soft peaks form. If desired, add one of the following ingredients with the vanilla: 2 tablespoons unsweetened cocoa powder plus 1 tablespoon additional sugar; 2 tablespoons amaretto, coffee, hazelnut, orange, or praline liqueur; ½ teaspoon finely shredded citrus peel; or ¼ teaspoon ground cinnamon, nutmeg, or ginger.

CHOCOLATE GARNISHES: For shavings, make short strokes with a vegetable peeler across a solid piece of chocolate. For curls, draw a vegetable peeler across the narrow side of a chocolate bar (milk chocolate works best). To grate chocolate, rub a solid piece of chocolate across either the fine or the coarse side of a grater.

TO FREEZE OR NOT TO FREEZE

Some desserts freeze fabulously, making them terrific make-ahead options for entertaining (or allowing you to stash leftovers to savor later). Other desserts need to be enjoyed soon after they're made. Here are a few guidelines.

■ Puddings and custard desserts, such as flan and panna cotta, do not freeze well. Refrigerate leftovers up to 2 days.

■ Cheesecakes rank among the best desserts to freeze. Wrap in freezer wrap; freeze a whole cheesecake up to 1 month and pieces up to 2 weeks. Thaw in the refrigerator.

■ The crumb topping for fruit crisps freezes well. Next time you make a crisp, consider preparing a double batch of the topping; place extra in a freezer bag and freeze up to 1 month. When ready, prepare fruit as directed in the recipe and top with frozen crisp topping; bake—you might need to add a few minutes to the baking time.

■ Freeze unfilled cream puffs up to 1 month. To thaw, place frozen cream puffs in a 350°F oven about 7 minutes or until crisp. Cool before filling.

■ Unfrosted fruit or nut-filled pastries such as baklava, turnovers, and strudel generally freeze well for up to 1 month.

■ Freeze unfilled meringue shells up to 6 months.

PEACH TURNOVERS, PAGE 290

APPLE CRISP

PREP: 25 MINUTES **BAKE:** 35 MINUTES
OVEN: 375°F **MAKES:** 6 SERVINGS

- 6 cups sliced, peeled cooking apples
- 3 to 4 tablespoons granulated sugar
- ½ cup regular rolled oats
- ½ cup packed brown sugar
- ¼ cup all-purpose flour
- ¼ teaspoon ground cinnamon, ginger, or nutmeg
- ¼ cup butter
- ¼ cup chopped nuts or flaked coconut
  Vanilla ice cream (optional)

1 Preheat oven to 375°F. In a large bowl combine apples and granulated sugar. Transfer to a 1½- to 2-quart square baking dish; set aside.

2 For topping, in a medium bowl combine the oats, brown sugar, flour, and cinnamon. Cut in butter until mixture resembles coarse crumbs. Stir in nuts. Sprinkle topping over apple mixture.

3 Bake for 35 to 40 minutes or until apples are tender and topping is golden. If desired, serve warm with ice cream.

PER ½ CUP: 298 cal., 12 g total fat (5 g sat. fat, 0 g trans fat), 20 mg chol., 60 mg sodium, 49 g carbo., 3 g fiber, 3 g pro. EXCHANGES: 1 Fruit, 2 Starch, 2 Fat

PEACH OR CHERRY CRISP: Prepare as directed, except substitute 6 cups sliced, peeled ripe peaches or fresh pitted tart red cherries (or two 16-ounce packages frozen unsweetened peach slices or frozen unsweetened pitted tart red cherries) for the apples. For the filling, increase granulated sugar to ½ cup and add 3 tablespoons all-purpose flour. If using frozen fruit, bake for 50 to 60 minutes or until filling is bubbly across entire surface (if necessary, cover with foil the last 10 minutes to prevent overbrowning).

RHUBARB CRISP: Prepare as directed, except substitute 6 cups fresh sliced rhubarb or two 16-ounce packages frozen unsweetened sliced rhubarb for the apples. For the filling, increase granulated sugar to ¾ cup and add 3 tablespoons all-purpose flour. If using frozen fruit, bake for 50 to 60 minutes or until filling is bubbly across entire surface (if necessary, cover with foil the last 10 minutes to prevent overbrowning).

PER ½ CUP PEACH, CHERRY, OR RHUBARB VARIATIONS: 358 cal., 12 g total fat (5 g sat. fat, 0 g trans fat), 20 mg chol., 65 mg sodium, 62 g carbo., 4 g fiber, 4 g pro. EXCHANGES: 3 Starch, 1 Fruit, ½ Other Carbo., 2 Fat

MIXED-FRUIT CLAFOUTI

PREP: 30 MINUTES **BAKE:** 50 MINUTES
COOL: 15 MINUTES **OVEN:** 375°F
MAKES: 8 SERVINGS

- 1 teaspoon butter
- ⅔ cup whipping cream
- ⅓ cup milk
- 3 eggs
- ⅓ cup all-purpose flour
- ¼ cup granulated sugar
- 2 tablespoons butter, melted
- 1 teaspoon vanilla
- ¼ teaspoon almond extract (optional)
- ⅛ teaspoon salt
- 3 cups mixed fruit, such as fresh or frozen sliced plums and/or peaches, thawed, and frozen sweet cherries, thawed
- 1 tablespoon powdered sugar

1 Preheat oven to 375°F. Butter a 9-inch pie plate or eight 6- to 8-ounce custard cups or ramekins with the 1 teaspoon butter; set aside.

2 In a medium mixing bowl combine whipping cream, milk, eggs, flour, granulated sugar, melted butter, vanilla, almond extract (if desired), and salt. Beat with an electric mixer on low speed until smooth. Arrange mixed fruit in prepared pie plate or custard cups. Pour cream mixture over fruit. If using custard cups, place on a baking sheet.

3 Bake for 50 to 55 minutes for pie plate, 25 to 30 minutes for custard cups, or until puffed and light brown. Cool for 15 to 20 minutes on a wire rack. Sift powdered sugar over top(s). Serve warm.

MIXED-BERRY CLAFOUTI: Prepare as directed, except substitute 3 cups mixed berries, such as blueberries, raspberries, and/or sliced strawberries for the mixed fruit.

PER SERVING REGULAR OR BERRY VARIATION: 204 cal., 13 g total fat (7 g sat. fat, 0 g trans fat), 116 mg chol., 98 mg sodium, 19 g carbo., 1 g fiber, 4 g pro. EXCHANGES: ½ Fruit, ½ Starch, ½ Lean Meat, 2½ Fat

CHERRY COBBLER

PREP: 40 MINUTES **BAKE:** 20 MINUTES **COOL:** 60 MINUTES **OVEN:** 400°F **MAKES:** 6 SERVINGS

- 1 cup all-purpose flour
- 2 tablespoons sugar
- 1½ teaspoons baking powder
- ¼ teaspoon salt
- ½ teaspoon ground cinnamon (optional)
- ¼ cup butter, cut up

- 6 cups fresh or frozen unsweetened pitted tart red cherries (2 pounds)
- 1 cup sugar
- 3 tablespoons cornstarch
- 1 egg
- ¼ cup milk
- 2 teaspoons sugar (optional)
- ⅛ teaspoon ground cinnamon (optional)

1 Preheat oven to 400°F. For biscuit topper, in a medium bowl stir together flour, the 2 tablespoons sugar, baking powder, salt, and ½ teaspoon cinnamon (if desired). Cut in butter until mixture resembles coarse crumbs; set aside.

2 For filling, in a large saucepan combine cherries, the 1 cup sugar, and cornstarch. Cook over medium heat until cherries release juices, stirring occasionally. Continue to cook, stirring constantly, over medium heat until thickened and bubbly. Keep the filling hot.

3 In a small bowl stir together egg and milk. Add to flour mixture, stirring just to moisten (see photo 1, below). Transfer hot filling to a 2-quart square baking dish. Using a spoon, immediately drop batter into six mounds on top of filling (see photo 2, below). If desired, combine the 2 teaspoons sugar with ⅛ teaspoon cinnamon; sprinkle over biscuits.

4 Bake for 20 to 25 minutes or until biscuits are golden. Cool in pan on a wire rack for 60 minutes.

PER BISCUIT + ½ CUP FILLING: 400 cal., 9 g total fat (5 g sat. fat, 0 g trans fat), 56 mg chol., 233 mg sodium, 77 g carbo., 3 g fiber, 5 g pro.
EXCHANGES: 1 Fruit, 2 Starch, 2 Other Carbo., 1½ Fat

BLUEBERRY COBBLER: Prepare as directed, except, for filling, substitute 6 cups fresh or frozen blueberries for the cherries, decrease sugar to ¾ cup, and decrease cornstarch to 2 tablespoons.

PER BISCUIT + ½ CUP FILLING: 367 cal., 9 g total fat (5 g sat. fat, 0 g trans fat), 56 mg chol., 229 mg sodium, 69 g carbo., 4 g fiber, 5 g pro.
EXCHANGES: 2 Starch, 1 Fruit, 1½ Other Carbo., 1½ Fat

RHUBARB COBBLER: Prepare as directed, except, for filling, substitute 6 cups fresh or frozen unsweetened sliced rhubarb for cherries; decrease cornstarch to 2 tablespoons.

PER BISCUIT + ½ CUP FILLING: 350 cal., 9 g total fat (5 g sat. fat, 0 g trans fat), 56 mg chol., 228 mg sodium, 64 g carbo., 3 g fiber, 5 g pro.
EXCHANGES: 2 Starch, 1 Fruit, 1 Other Carbo., 1½ Fat

MAKING COBBLER, STEP-BY-STEP

1. Using a fork, stir the dry and wet ingredients just until the dry ingredients are moistened. Do not overmix or the biscuits will be tough. **2.** Drop same-size spoonfuls of batter onto hot filling, spacing them equally on filling.

CHERRY COBBLER

STRAWBERRY SHORTCAKES

PREP: 30 MINUTES **BAKE:** 12 MINUTES
OVEN: 400°F **MAKES:** 8 SHORTCAKES

- 1½ cups all-purpose flour
- ¼ cup sugar
- 1 teaspoon baking powder
- ¼ teaspoon baking soda
- ¼ teaspoon salt
- ⅓ cup cold butter, cut up
- 1 egg, lightly beaten
- ½ cup dairy sour cream
- 2 tablespoons milk
- 5 cups sliced strawberries
- 3 tablespoons sugar
- 1 recipe Whipped Cream (page 287)

1 Preheat oven to 400°F. Lightly grease a baking sheet; set aside. In a medium bowl combine flour, the ¼ cup sugar, baking powder, baking soda, and salt. Using a pastry blender, cut in butter until mixture resembles coarse crumbs. Combine egg, sour cream, and milk. Add to flour mixture, stirring with a fork just until moistened.

2 Drop dough into eight mounds onto prepared baking sheet. Bake for 12 to 15 minutes or until golden. Transfer to a wire rack; let cool.

3 Meanwhile, combine 4 cups of the strawberries and the 3 tablespoons sugar. Using a potato masher, mash berries slightly. To serve, split shortcakes in half; fill with mashed strawberries and Whipped Cream. Top with remaining strawberries.

WHOLE SHORTCAKE: Prepare as directed, except spread all dough into a greased 8×1½-inch round baking pan. Bake for 18 to 20 minutes or until a wooden toothpick inserted near center comes out clean. Cool in pan 10 minutes. Remove from pan; cool completely. To serve, split in half horizontally. Spoon half the Whipped Cream and berries over bottom. Replace top. Top with remaining berries and cream. Cut into eight wedges.

PER INDIVIDUAL SHORTCAKE OR WEDGE OF WHOLE VARIATION: 375 cal., 22 g total fat (13 g sat. fat, 0 g trans fat), 94 mg chol., 229 mg sodium, 40 g carbo., 2 g fiber, 5 g pro. EXCHANGES: ½ Fruit, 2 Starch, 4 Fat

MIXED-BERRY OR MIXED-FRUIT SHORTCAKES:
(photo, page 285) Prepare as directed, except substitute 5 cups mixed berries or fruit (blueberries or raspberries; sliced peaches, nectarines, bananas; or grapes) for strawberries. Do not mash fruit.

PER SHORTCAKE: 392 cal., 22 g total fat (13 g sat. fat, 0 g trans fat), 94 mg chol., 229 mg sodium, 45 g carbo., 4 g fiber, 5 g pro. EXCHANGES: 2 Starch, ½ Fruit, ½ Other Carbo., 4 Fat

PEACH TURNOVERS *(photo, page 287)*

PREP: 25 MINUTES **BAKE:** 15 MINUTES
OVEN: 400°F **MAKES:** 4 TURNOVERS

- 2 tablespoons granulated sugar
- 1 tablespoon all-purpose flour
- ⅛ teaspoon ground cinnamon
- 1⅓ cups chopped peach or nectarine or chopped peeled apple (1 large)
- ½ of a 17.3-ounce package frozen puff pastry sheets (1 sheet), thawed
- 3 to 4 teaspoons milk
- ¾ cup powdered sugar
- 1 tablespoon butter, softened
- ½ teaspoon vanilla

1 Preheat oven to 400°F. Line a large baking sheet with parchment paper; set aside. In a small bowl stir together granulated sugar, flour, and cinnamon. Add peach; toss to coat.

2 Unfold pastry. Cut pastry into four squares. Brush edges of squares with some milk. Evenly spoon peach mixture onto centers of squares. Fold one corner of a square over filling to opposite corner. Press edges with tines of a fork to seal. Place turnover on prepared baking sheet. Repeat with remaining dough squares. Prick tops of turnovers several times with a fork. Brush with additional milk and, if desired, sprinkle with *coarse sugar*.

3 Bake for 15 to 18 minutes or until puffed and golden brown. Cool on baking sheet on a wire rack.

4 Meanwhile, stir together powdered sugar, butter, vanilla, and dash *salt*. Add enough milk to make thin icing. Drizzle over warm turnovers.

PER TURNOVER: 507 cal., 27 g total fat (8 g sat. fat, 0 g trans fat), 8 mg chol., 213 mg sodium, 63 g carbo., 2 g fiber, 5 g pro. EXCHANGES: 2 Starch, 2 Other Carbo., 5 Fat

APPLE DUMPLINGS

PREP: 45 MINUTES **BAKE:** 55 MINUTES
OVEN: 350°F **MAKES:** 6 DUMPLINGS

- 2 cups water
- 1¼ cups sugar
- ½ teaspoon ground cinnamon
- ¼ cup butter, cut up
- 2 cups all-purpose flour
- ½ teaspoon salt
- ⅔ cup shortening
- ⅓ to ½ cup half-and-half or whole milk
- 2 tablespoons chopped raisins

2 tablespoons chopped walnuts
1 tablespoon honey
2 tablespoons sugar
½ teaspoon ground cinnamon
6 small cooking apples (about 1½ pounds)
2 tablespoons butter

1 Preheat oven to 350°F. For sauce, in a medium saucepan combine the water, the 1¼ cups sugar, and ½ teaspoon cinnamon. Bring to boiling; reduce heat. Simmer, uncovered, for 5 minutes. Add the ¼ cup butter; set aside.

2 Meanwhile, for pastry, in a medium bowl combine flour and salt. Using a pastry blender, cut in shortening until pieces are pea size. Sprinkle 1 tablespoon of the half-and-half over part of the mixture; gently toss with a fork. Push moistened dough to the side of the bowl. Repeat moistening dough, using 1 tablespoon of the half-and-half at a time, until all of the dough is moistened. Form dough into a ball. On a lightly floured surface, roll dough to an 18×12-inch rectangle. Cut into six 6-inch squares (see photos 1 and 2, below).

3 In a small bowl combine raisins, walnuts, and honey. In another bowl stir together 2 tablespoons sugar and ½ teaspoon cinnamon; set aside.

4 Core and peel apples (see photo 3, below). Place an apple on each pastry square. Fill apples with raisin mixture. Sprinkle with sugar-cinnamon mixture; dot each with 1 teaspoon butter (see photo 4, below). Moisten edges of pastry squares with water; gather corners around apples (see photo 5, below). Pinch to seal. Place dumplings in a 13×9×2-inch baking pan. Heat sauce to boiling; pour over dumplings. Bake, uncovered, for 55 to 60 minutes or until apples are tender and pastry is golden. Spoon sauce over warm dumplings.

PER DUMPLING: 736 cal., 37 g total fat (14 g sat. fat, 3 g trans fat), 35 mg chol., 286 mg sodium, 99 g carbo., 4 g fiber, 6 g pro. EXCHANGES: 1 Fruit, 5½ Other Carbo., 6 Fat

ASSEMBLING APPLE DUMPLINGS, STEP-BY-STEP

1. Using a rolling pin, roll dough from the center out into an 18×12-inch rectangle. **2.** A pizza cutter makes it easy to cut the rectangle into 6-inch squares. **3.** Using an apple corer, twist and remove each apple's core. **4.** After filling the apples with the raisin mixture, top them with a small piece of butter. **5.** Gather the corners of dough squares at the apple tops; pinch to form a tight seal.

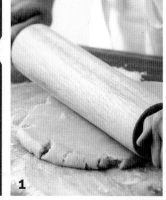

CRANBERRY STRUDEL ROLLS

PREP: 30 MINUTES **BAKE:** 15 MINUTES
OVEN: 375°F **MAKES:** 12 ROLLS

- 1 cup fresh or frozen cranberries
- ⅓ cup water
- ⅔ cup finely chopped, peeled apple (1 small)
- ¼ cup golden raisins
- ¼ cup finely chopped walnuts
- ⅓ cup granulated sugar
- ½ teaspoon ground cinnamon
- ½ teaspoon finely shredded orange peel
- 10 sheets frozen phyllo dough (14×9-inch rectangles), thawed
- ¼ cup butter, melted
  Powdered sugar

1 Preheat oven to 375°F. Line a baking sheet with parchment paper or foil; set aside. In a small saucepan combine cranberries and water. Bring to boiling; reduce heat. Simmer, uncovered, about 3 minutes or until cranberries pop. Drain cranberries; discard liquid. Return cranberries to pan.

2 Add apple, raisins, and nuts to cranberries in saucepan. Add granulated sugar, cinnamon, and orange peel. Toss gently until mixed; set aside.

3 Unroll phyllo dough. Layer five phyllo sheets on work surface, brushing each sheet lightly with some melted butter. Repeat with remaining phyllo sheets and melted butter to form a second stack. Cut each phyllo stack crosswise into thirds, then lengthwise in half to form 12 squares total.

4 Spoon a rounded tablespoon of the cranberry mixture near bottom edge of a phyllo square. Fold bottom edge over mixture; fold in sides. Roll up around filling. Place on prepared baking sheet. Repeat with remaining phyllo and cranberry mixture. Brush tops with remaining melted butter.

5 Bake for 15 to 18 minutes or until golden. (Rolls might leak slightly during baking.) Transfer to a wire rack; cool completely. Before serving, sift powdered sugar over tops.

PER ROLL: 140 cal., 6 g total fat (3 g sat. fat, 0 g trans fat), 10 mg chol., 105 mg sodium, 19 g carbo., 1 g fiber, 2 g pro.
EXCHANGES: 1 Starch, 1 Fat

BAKLAVA

PREP: 45 MINUTES **BAKE:** 35 MINUTES
OVEN: 325°F **MAKES:** 32 TO 48 PIECES

- 3 cups walnuts, finely chopped
- 1½ cups sugar
- 1 teaspoon ground cinnamon
- ¾ cup butter, melted
- ½ of a 16-ounce package frozen phyllo dough (14×9-inch rectangles), thawed
- ¾ cup water
- 3 tablespoons honey
- ½ teaspoon finely shredded lemon peel
- 1 tablespoon lemon juice
- 2 inches stick cinnamon

1 Preheat oven to 325°F. In a large bowl stir together walnuts, ½ cup of the sugar, and the ground cinnamon; set aside.

2 Brush the bottom of a 13×9×2-inch baking pan with some melted butter. Unroll phyllo dough. Layer 5 or 6 phyllo sheets in the prepared baking pan, brushing each sheet generously with

ASSEMBLING BAKLAVA, STEP-BY-STEP

1. Each phyllo layer will consist of five or six sheets. **2.** As you layer, brush each sheet to the edges with some of the butter. **3.** After layering first set of sheets, sprinkle about 1 cup of the nut mixture evenly over top sheet. **4.** Before baking, use a sharp knife to cut through all layers into desired shapes. **5.** Pour syrup evenly over the still warm baked baklava in the pan. Cool completely.

some melted butter (see photos 1 and 2, below). Sprinkle with about 1 cup nut mixture (see photo 3, below). Repeat layering phyllo and sprinkling with nut mixture two more times, brushing each sheet with butter.

3 Layer the remaining phyllo sheets on top of filling, brushing each sheet with more butter. Drizzle with any remaining butter. Using a sharp knife, cut stacked layers into 32 to 48 diamond-, rectangle-, or square-shape pieces (see photo 4, below).

4 Bake for 35 to 45 minutes or until golden. Cool slightly in pan on a wire rack.

5 Meanwhile, in a saucepan stir together the remaining sugar, the water, honey, lemon peel, lemon juice, and stick cinnamon. Bring to boiling; reduce heat. Simmer, uncovered, for 20 minutes. Remove cinnamon. Pour syrup over warm baklava in pan (see photo 5, below). Cool completely.

PER PIECE: 174 cal., 12 g total fat (4 g sat. fat, 0 g trans fat), 11 mg chol., 65 mg sodium, 16 g carbo., 1 g fiber, 2 g pro. EXCHANGES: 1 Other Carbo., 2½ Fat

PHYLLO DOUGH KNOW-HOW
THOUGH IT MAKES IMPRESSIVE DESSERTS, THE DOUGH IS EASY TO HANDLE.

■ Thaw as directed on package.

■ Once unwrapped, phyllo dries out quickly and crumbles. As you work, keep the opened stack of dough covered with plastic wrap or a damp paper towel to prevent drying.

■ Brush each sheet you layer with melted butter or olive oil. Tightly rewrap any leftover sheets; return them to the freezer.

FRUIT PIZZA
PREP: 30 MINUTES **BAKE:** 12 MINUTES
OVEN: 375°F **MAKES:** 20 TRIANGLES

- 1 recipe Sugar Cookie Cutouts dough (page 272) or 1½ 16.5-ounce rolls refrigerated sugar cookie dough
- 1 8-ounce package cream cheese, softened
- ½ cup sugar
- 1 teaspoon vanilla
- 4 cups sliced or halved fresh strawberries; halved seedless red and/or green grapes; fresh blueberries or fresh raspberries; sliced kiwifruits; canned mandarin orange sections, drained; and/or fresh nectarine slices
- ¼ cup apricot or seedless raspberry jam, or orange marmalade, melted

1 Preheat oven to 375°F. Pat dough into the bottom of an ungreased 15×10×1-inch baking pan. Bake for 12 to 14 minutes or until light golden brown (dough may puff while baking but will fall as it cools). Cool completely in pan on a wire rack.

2 In a medium bowl beat cream cheese with an electric mixer on medium to high speed for 30 seconds. Add sugar and vanilla; beat until fluffy. Spread cheese mixture over cooled crust. Arrange fruit on top. Brush or drizzle with jam. Serve immediately or cover and chill for up to 24 hours. To serve, cut into triangles.

PER TRIANGLE: 219 cal., 10 g total fat (6 g sat. fat, 0 g trans fat), 39 mg chol., 127 mg sodium, 29 g carbo., 1 g fiber, 3 g pro. EXCHANGES: 1 Starch, 1 Other Carbo., 2 Fat

MERINGUE SHELLS WITH FRUIT

PREP: 45 MINUTES **BAKE:** 35 MINUTES
STAND: 60 MINUTES **OVEN:** 300°F
MAKES: 6 MERINGUES

- 2 egg whites
- ½ teaspoon vanilla
- ⅛ teaspoon cream of tartar
- ½ cup sugar
- 1 recipe Fluffy Lemon Filling or 1½ to 2 cups Lemon Curd (page 308), purchased lemon curd, or vanilla or lemon yogurt or pudding
- 2 to 3 cups assorted whole or cut-up fresh fruit

1 Allow egg whites to stand at room temperature for 30 minutes. Line a large baking sheet with parchment paper or foil. Draw six 3- to 3½-inch circles 3 inches apart on the paper or foil; set aside.

2 Preheat oven to 300°F. For meringue, in a medium mixing bowl beat egg whites, vanilla, and cream of tartar with electric mixer on medium speed until soft peaks form (tips curl; see photo 1, page 177). Add sugar, 1 tablespoon at a time, beating on high speed until stiff peaks form (tips stand straight; see photo 2, page 177) and sugar is almost dissolved (5 to 6 minutes).

3 Spoon or pipe meringue over circles on paper; build up sides to form shells. Bake for 35 minutes. Turn off oven; let meringues dry in oven with door closed for 60 minutes. Lift meringues off paper. Transfer to a wire rack; cool completely.

4 Meanwhile, make Fluffy Lemon Filling. To serve, spoon lemon filling into cooled shells. Arrange fruit on top of filling. Serve immediately.

FLUFFY LEMON FILLING: In a medium bowl stir together one 10-ounce jar purchased lemon curd and ½ of an 8-ounce carton frozen whipped topping, thawed.

MAKE-AHEAD DIRECTIONS: Carefully wrap meringue shells in foil. Freeze for up to 6 months.

PER MERINGUE + ¼ CUP FLUFFY LEMON FILLING + ⅓ CUP FRUIT: 293 cal., 6 g total fat (4 g sat. fat, 0 g trans fat), 35 mg chol., 54 mg sodium, 30 g carbo., 6 g fiber, 2 g pro. EXCHANGES: ½ Fruit, 3½ Other Carbo., 1 Fat

---

IT'S MERINGUE TIME
HUMIDITY MAKES MERINGUES STICKY, SO IT'S BEST TO BAKE THEM ON A DRY DAY.

SWIRLED CHOCOLATE AND PEANUT BUTTER SOUFFLÉ

PREP: 35 MINUTES **BAKE:** 45 MINUTES
OVEN: 350°F **MAKES:** 6 TO 8 SERVINGS

- 2 ounces bittersweet or semisweet chocolate, chopped
- 3 tablespoons butter
- ¼ cup all-purpose flour
- 1¼ cups half-and-half, light cream, or milk
- ¼ cup creamy peanut butter
- 4 egg yolks
- 6 egg whites
- ⅓ cup sugar

1 Preheat oven to 350°F. Butter sides of a 2-quart soufflé dish. For a collar on the soufflé dish, measure enough foil to wrap around the dish top; add 3 inches. Fold the foil into thirds lengthwise. Lightly grease one side with *butter*; sprinkle with *sugar*. Place foil, sugar side in, around the outside of the dish so the foil extends about 2 inches above the dish. Tape ends of foil together. Sprinkle inside dish with sugar; set aside.

2 In a small saucepan cook and stir chocolate over low heat until chocolate melts; set aside. In a medium saucepan melt the 3 tablespoons butter. Stir in flour; gradually stir in half-and-half. Cook and stir over medium heat until thickened and bubbly. Remove from heat. Stir half of the hot cream mixture into melted chocolate; set aside.

3 Stir peanut butter into the remaining hot cream mixture in the saucepan. In a medium bowl beat 2 of the egg yolks with a fork just until combined. Gradually stir the peanut butter mixture into the egg yolks; set aside.

4 In another medium bowl lightly beat the remaining 2 egg yolks. Gradually stir the chocolate mixture into the egg yolks; set aside. In a large bowl beat egg whites with an electric mixer on medium to high speed until soft peaks form (tips curl; see photo 1, page 177). Gradually add the ⅓ cup sugar, 1 tablespoon at a time, beating until stiff peaks form (tips stand straight).

5 Gently fold half of the beaten egg whites into the peanut butter mixture. Transfer peanut butter mixture to the prepared soufflé dish. Gently fold the remaining beaten egg whites into the chocolate mixture. Spoon chocolate mixture over peanut butter mixture in soufflé dish. Using a table knife or thin spatula, gently swirl chocolate mixture into peanut butter mixture to marble.

6 Bake for 45 to 50 minutes or until a knife inserted near the center comes out clean. Serve immediately. To serve, insert two forks back to back in soufflé; gently pull apart into wedges.

PER SERVING: 366 cal., 26 g total fat (13 g sat. fat, 0 g trans fat), 179 mg chol., 184 mg sodium, 27 g carbo., 2 g fiber, 11 g pro. EXCHANGES: 1 Starch, 1 Other Carbo., 1 High-Fat Meat, 3½ Fat

BEST EVER

BREAD PUDDING

PREP: 30 MINUTES **BAKE:** 50 MINUTES
OVEN: 350°F **MAKES:** 8 SERVINGS

  4 cups dried white or cinnamon-swirl bread cubes* (6 to 7 slices)
  ⅓ cup raisins or dried cranberries
  2 eggs, lightly beaten
  2 cups milk
  ¼ cup butter, melted
  ½ cup sugar
  1 teaspoon ground cinnamon
  ½ teaspoon ground nutmeg
  1 teaspoon vanilla
  1 recipe Caramel Sauce (page 546) or Bourbon Sauce (page 546) (optional)

1 Preheat oven to 350°F. Grease a 1½-quart casserole; set aside. In a large bowl combine bread cubes and raisins.

2 In a medium bowl combine eggs, milk, melted butter, sugar, cinnamon, nutmeg, and vanilla. Stir into bread mixture. Pour into prepared casserole.

3 Bake, uncovered, for 50 to 55 minutes or until puffed and a knife inserted near the center comes out clean. Cool slightly. If desired, serve with Caramel Sauce.

PEAR-GINGER BREAD PUDDING: Prepare as directed, except substitute snipped dried pears for raisins, 1 tablespoon finely chopped crystallized ginger for cinnamon, and 1 teaspoon finely shredded orange peel for nutmeg.

PER ¾ CUP PLAIN OR PEAR-GINGER VARIATION: 219 cal., 9 g total fat (5 g sat. fat, 0 g trans fat), 73 mg chol., 212 mg sodium, 30 g carbo., 1 g fiber, 5 g pro. EXCHANGES: 1 Starch, 1 Other Carbo., 2 Fat

CHOCOLATE CHIP BREAD PUDDING: Prepare as directed, except substitute semisweet chocolate pieces for raisins and chocolate milk for the milk. Omit nutmeg; add ½ cup chopped pecans, toasted. Omit sauce. If desired, serve with ice cream.

PER ¾ CUP: 299 cal., 16 g total fat (7 g sat. fat; 0 g trans fat), 73 mg chol., 228 mg sodium, 36 g carbo., 2 g fiber, 6 g pro. EXCHANGES: 1½ Starch, 1 Other Carbo., 3 Fat

*TO DRY BREAD CUBES: CUT BREAD INTO ½-INCH CUBES. SPREAD IN A 15×10×1-INCH BAKING PAN; BAKE IN A 300°F OVEN FOR 10 TO 15 MINUTES OR UNTIL DRY, STIRRING TWICE.

BREAD PUDDING

MERINGUE SHELLS WITH FRUIT

BROWNIE PUDDING CAKE

PREP: 15 MINUTES **BAKE:** 40 MINUTES
COOL: 45 MINUTES **OVEN:** 350°F
MAKES: 6 TO 8 SERVINGS

- 1 cup all-purpose flour
- ¾ cup granulated sugar
- 2 tablespoons unsweetened cocoa powder
- 2 teaspoons baking powder
- ¼ teaspoon salt
- ½ cup milk
- 2 tablespoons vegetable oil
- 1 teaspoon vanilla
- ½ cup chopped walnuts
- ¾ cup packed brown sugar
- ¼ cup unsweetened cocoa powder
- 1½ cups boiling water
  Vanilla ice cream (optional)

1 Preheat oven to 350°F. Grease an 8×8×2-inch baking pan; set aside. In a medium bowl stir together the flour, granulated sugar, the 2 tablespoons cocoa powder, baking powder, and salt. Stir in milk, oil, and vanilla. Stir in walnuts.

2 Pour batter into prepared baking pan. In a small bowl stir together the brown sugar and the ¼ cup cocoa powder. Stir in the boiling water. Slowly pour brown sugar mixture over batter.

3 Bake for 40 minutes. Transfer to a wire rack and cool for 45 to 60 minutes. Serve warm. Spoon cake into dessert bowls; spoon pudding from bottom of the pan over cake. If desired, serve with vanilla ice cream.

PER ½ CUP: 406 cal., 12 g total fat (2 g sat. fat, 0 g trans fat), 2 mg chol., 237 mg sodium, 74 g carbo., 3 g fiber, 5 g pro. EXCHANGES: 2 Starch, 3 Other Carbo., 2 Fat

BEST EVER

MOLTEN CHOCOLATE CAKES

PREP: 30 MINUTES **COOL:** 15 MINUTES
CHILL: 2 HOURS **BAKE:** 15 MINUTES
STAND: 10 MINUTES **OVEN:** 375°F
MAKES: 8 CAKES

- 1¼ cups semisweet chocolate pieces
- ½ cup whipping cream
- 1 tablespoon butter
- ¾ cup semisweet chocolate pieces
- ½ cup butter
- 4 eggs
- ½ cup sugar
- ½ cup all-purpose flour
  Fresh raspberries
  Vanilla ice cream (optional)

1 Generously butter eight 6-ounce ramekins or custard cups. For filling, in a small saucepan combine the 1¼ cups chocolate pieces, whipping cream, and the 1 tablespoon butter. Cook and stir over low heat until chocolate melts and mixture is smooth. Remove from heat. Cool for 15 minutes, stirring occasionally. Cover and chill about 2 hours or until it reaches a fudgelike consistency.

2 Preheat oven to 375°F. In a saucepan combine the ¾ cup chocolate pieces and the ½ cup butter. Cook and stir over low heat until chocolate melts and mixture is smooth; cool slightly.

3 In a large mixing bowl beat eggs and sugar with an electric mixer on medium to high speed for 5 minutes. Beat in flour and cooled chocolate mixture. Spoon enough batter into each ramekin to measure 1 inch in depth.

4 Form chilled filling into eight portions. Working quickly, use your hands to roll each portion into a ball. Place a ball of filling on top of the batter in each ramekin; do not allow the filling to touch the sides of the ramekins. Spoon remaining batter into the ramekins.

5 Bake for 15 minutes. Remove from oven; let stand for 10 minutes. Using a knife, loosen cakes from sides of ramekins. Invert onto dessert plates. Serve immediately with raspberries. If desired, serve with small scoops of vanilla ice cream.

MAKE-AHEAD DIRECTIONS: Prepare as directed through Step 4. Cover; chill until ready to bake or up to 4 hours. Let stand at room temperature for 30 minutes before baking as directed.

PER CAKE: 490 cal., 34 g total fat (20 g sat. fat, 0 g trans fat), 161 mg chol., 138 mg sodium, 47 g carbo., 3 g fiber, 6 g pro. EXCHANGES: 2 Starch, 1 Other Carbo., 6½ Fat

PECAN UPSIDE-DOWN BABY CAKES

PREP: 20 MINUTES **BAKE:** 25 MINUTES
COOL: 5 MINUTES **OVEN:** 350°F **MAKES:** 12 CAKES

- 2½ cups all-purpose flour
- 1 teaspoon baking powder
- ½ teaspoon baking soda
- ½ teaspoon salt
- ⅔ cup packed brown sugar
- ½ cup butter
- ⅓ cup honey

1½ cups coarsely chopped pecans
1 teaspoon finely shredded orange peel
3 eggs
2 cups granulated sugar
1 cup vegetable oil
1 8-ounce carton dairy sour cream
2 teaspoons vanilla

1 Preheat oven to 350°F. Lightly grease twelve 3½-inch (jumbo) muffin cups; set aside. In a medium bowl stir together flour, baking powder, baking soda, and salt; set aside.

2 In a medium saucepan combine brown sugar, butter, and honey. Cook and stir over medium heat about 2 minutes or until smooth; remove from heat. Stir in pecans and orange peel; set aside.

3 In a large mixing bowl combine eggs and granulated sugar. Beat with an electric mixer on medium to high speed about 3 minutes or until mixture is thick and lemon color. Add oil,

sour cream, and vanilla; beat until combined. Gradually add the flour mixture, beating on low speed until smooth.

4 Place 2 tablespoons of the pecan mixture in the bottom of each prepared muffin cup. Spoon a heaping ⅓ cup of the batter into each cup. Place muffin pans on a foil-lined large baking sheet.

5 Bake for 25 to 30 minutes or until a wooden toothpick inserted in the centers comes out clean. Cool in pans on a wire rack for 5 minutes. Using a sharp knife or thin spatula, loosen cakes from sides of muffin cups. Invert onto wire rack. Spoon any pecan mixture remaining in the muffin cups onto cakes. Serve warm or cool.

PER CAKE: 679 cal., 41 g total fat (10 g sat. fat, 0 g trans fat), 83 mg chol., 271 mg sodium, 76 g carbo., 2 g fiber, 6 g pro. EXCHANGES: 2 Starch, 3 Other Carbo., 8 Fat

MULTIPURPOSE PAN THIS MOIST, GOOEY DESSERT CALLS ON A MUFFIN PAN WITH JUMBO-SIZE CUPS. FOR MORE WAYS TO USE THIS SPECIALTY BAKEWARE, SEE PAGE 126.

PECAN UPSIDE-DOWN
BABY CAKES

CRÈME BRÛLÉE

PREP: 10 MINUTES **BAKE:** 30 MINUTES
CHILL: 1 TO 8 HOURS **STAND:** 20 MINUTES
OVEN: 325°F **MAKES:** 6 SERVINGS

1¾ cups half-and-half or light cream
5 egg yolks, lightly beaten
⅓ cup sugar
1 teaspoon vanilla
⅛ teaspoon salt
¼ cup sugar

1 Preheat oven to 325°F. In a small heavy saucepan heat half-and-half over medium-low heat just until bubbly. Remove from heat; set aside.

2 Meanwhile, in a medium bowl combine egg yolks, the ⅓ cup sugar, the vanilla, and salt. Beat with a wire whisk just until combined. Slowly whisk the hot half-and-half into the custard.

3 Place six 4-ounce ramekins or 6-ounce custard cups in a 3-quart rectangular baking dish. Divide custard evenly among ramekins. Place baking dish on oven rack. Pour enough boiling water into the baking dish to reach halfway up sides of ramekins.

4 Bake for 30 to 40 minutes or until a knife inserted near centers comes out clean (centers will shake slightly). Remove ramekins from water; cool on a wire rack. Cover; chill for 1 to 8 hours.

5 Before serving, let custards stand at room temperature for 20 minutes. Meanwhile, in a medium heavy skillet heat the ¼ cup sugar over medium-high heat until sugar begins to melt, shaking skillet occasionally to heat sugar evenly (see photo 1, below). Do not stir. Once sugar starts to

melt, reduce heat to low and cook about 5 minutes or until all sugar melts and is golden, stirring as needed with a wooden spoon (see photo 2, below).

6 Quickly drizzle the caramelized sugar over custards. (If sugar hardens in the skillet, return to heat; stir until melted.) Serve immediately.

AMARETTO CRÈME BRÛLÉE: Prepare as directed, except stir 2 tablespoons amaretto or coffee liqueur into the custard mixture in Step 2.

PER SERVING PLAIN OR AMARETTO VARIATION:
214 cal., 12 g total fat (6 g sat. fat, 0 g trans fat), 201 mg chol., 84 mg sodium, 23 g carbo., 0 g fiber, 4 g pro.
EXCHANGES: 1½ Other Carbo., ½ Medium-Fat Meat, 1½ Fat

CARAMEL FLANS

PREP: 25 MINUTES **STAND:** 10 MINUTES
BAKE: 30 MINUTES **OVEN:** 325°F **MAKES:** 4 FLANS

⅓ cup sugar
3 eggs, lightly beaten
1½ cups half-and-half
⅓ cup sugar
1 teaspoon vanilla
Ground nutmeg (optional)

1 To caramelize sugar, in a medium heavy skillet heat ⅓ cup sugar over medium-high heat until it begins to melt, shaking the skillet occasionally; do not stir (see photo 1, below). When the sugar starts to melt, reduce heat to low and cook about 5 minutes or until all of the sugar melts and is golden, stirring as needed with a wooden spoon (see photo 2, below). Immediately divide caramelized sugar among four 6-ounce custard cups; tilt cups to coat bottoms. Let stand for 10 minutes.

MAKING CARAMELIZED SUGAR, STEP-BY-STEP

1. Spread sugar in an even layer in a heavy skillet. Shake the skillet occasionally for even melting, but don't stir it until the sugar starts to melt.
2. When sugar starts to melt, stir it occasionally with a wooden spoon, gradually incorporating the unmelted sugar into the melted sugar until all is melted and golden brown. Reduce heat if syrup browns too rapidly before all sugar melts.

2 Meanwhile, preheat oven to 325°F. Combine eggs, half-and-half, ⅓ cup sugar, and vanilla. Beat until well combined but not foamy. Place custard cups in a 2-quart square baking dish. Divide egg mixture among custard cups. If desired, sprinkle with ground nutmeg. Place baking dish on oven rack. Pour boiling water into baking dish around custard cups to a depth of 1 inch. Bake for 30 to 40 minutes or until a knife inserted near centers comes out clean.

3 Remove custard cups from water. Cool slightly on a wire rack and unmold. (Or cool completely in cups. Cover; chill until serving time.) Using a sharp knife, loosen flan from sides of cups. Invert a plate over each cup; turn plate and cup over together. Remove cups.

PER FLAN: 304 cal., 14 g total fat (8 g sat. fat, 0 g trans fat), 192 mg chol., 89 mg sodium, 38 g carbo., 0 g fiber, 7 g pro. EXCHANGES: 2½ Other Carbo., 1 High-Fat Meat, 1 Fat

VANILLA PANNA COTTA

PREP: 20 MINUTES **STAND:** 5 MINUTES
CHILL: 4 TO 24 HOURS **MAKES:** 8 SERVINGS

> 1 envelope unflavored gelatin
> ¼ cup water
> ½ cup sugar
> 2 cups whipping cream
> 1¼ cups dairy sour cream
> 1½ teaspoons vanilla
>   Blueberries, raspberries, or strawberries
> 8 fresh mint sprigs

1 Place eight 4- to 6-ounce ramekins or custard cups in a shallow baking pan; set aside. In a small bowl sprinkle gelatin over the water. Do not stir. Let stand for 5 minutes.

2 Meanwhile, in a medium saucepan combine sugar and ½ cup of the whipping cream. Heat over medium heat until hot but not boiling. Add gelatin; stir until gelatin dissolves. Remove from heat. Whisk in sour cream until smooth. Stir in remaining whipping cream and the vanilla. Pour into cups. Cover and chill for 4 to 24 hours or until set.

3 To serve, immerse bottom halves of cups in hot water for 10 seconds. Using a sharp knife, loosen panna cotta from sides of cups. Invert a plate over each cup; turn plate and cup over together. Remove cups. Serve with berries and mint sprigs.

PER SERVING: 325 cal., 28 g total fat (17 g sat. fat, 0 g trans fat), 98 mg chol., 49 mg sodium, 17 g carbo., 0 g fiber, 3 g pro. EXCHANGES: 1 Other Carbo., ½ High-Fat Meat, 5 Fat

COCONUT PANNA COTTA: Prepare as directed, except substitute one 14-ounce can unsweetened coconut milk for the whipping cream, increase the sour cream to 1½ cups, and substitute 1 teaspoon coconut extract for the vanilla.

PER SERVING: 237 cal., 19 g total fat (15 g sat. fat, 0 g trans fat), 19 mg chol., 38 mg sodium, 16 g carbo., 1 g fiber, 3 g pro. EXCHANGES: 1 Other Carbo., ½ High-Fat Meat, 3 Fat

ESPRESSO PANNA COTTA: Prepare as directed, except add 2 tablespoons instant espresso coffee powder with sugar. Serve with Hot Fudge Sauce (page 545).

PER SERVING: 461 cal., 39 g total fat (24 g sat. fat, 0 g trans fat), 119 mg chol., 59 mg sodium, 28 g carbo., 1 g fiber, 4 g pro. Exchanges: 2 Other Carbo., ½ High-Fat Meat, 7 Fat

CREAMY RICE PUDDING

PREP: 20 MINUTES **COOK:** 25 MINUTES
MAKES: 3 CUPS

> 1 cup water
> ¾ cup milk
> ¼ teaspoon salt
> ½ cup arborio or long grain rice
> 1 teaspoon butter
> 1 cup half-and-half or light cream
> ½ of a vanilla bean, halved lengthwise, or 1 teaspoon vanilla
> 2 egg yolks
> ⅓ cup sugar

1 In a saucepan heat water, milk, and salt over medium heat until nearly boiling. Stir in rice and butter. Bring to boiling; reduce heat. Cover; simmer over very low heat 25 to 30 minutes or until thick and nearly all liquid is gone, stirring every 5 minutes at end of cooking. Transfer to a bowl.

2 Meanwhile, place half-and-half in a small saucepan. Using a paring knife, scrape seeds from inside of vanilla bean (if using); add seeds to the cream. Heat just to boiling. In a medium bowl whisk together yolks and sugar. Gradually whisk in hot half-and-half; return all to saucepan. Cook and stir over medium-low heat for 3 to 5 minutes or until sauce thickens and coats the back of a spoon (see photo 1, page 306).

3 Stir sauce and vanilla (if using) into rice in bowl; serve warm. Or cover and chill for several hours or overnight. If desired, just before serving, stir in additional *half-and-half* until desired consistency.

PER ½ CUP: 189 cal., 7 g total fat (4 g sat. fat, 0 g trans fat), 89 mg chol., 134 mg sodium, 27 g carbo., 0 g fiber, 4 g pro. EXCHANGES: 1 Starch, 1 Other Carbo., 1 Fat

CREAM PUFFS

PREP: 25 MINUTES **COOL:** 10 MINUTES
BAKE: 30 MINUTES **OVEN:** 400°F
MAKES: 12 CREAM PUFFS

- 1 cup water
- ½ cup butter
- ⅛ teaspoon salt
- 1 cup all-purpose flour
- 4 eggs
- 3 cups whipped cream, pudding, or ice cream

1 Preheat oven to 400°F. Grease a baking sheet. In a saucepan combine the water, butter, and salt. Bring to boiling. Immediately add flour all at once; stir vigorously. Cook and stir until mixture forms a ball (see photo 1, below). Remove from heat. Cool for 10 minutes. Add eggs, one at a time, beating well after each addition (see photo 2, below).

2 Drop 12 heaping tablespoons of dough onto prepared baking sheet. Bake for 30 to 35 minutes or until golden brown and firm. Transfer to a wire rack; let cool.

3 Just before serving, cut tops from puffs; remove soft dough from inside. Fill with whipped cream. Replace tops.

PER CREAM PUFF: 233 cal., 21 g total fat (12 g sat. fat, 0 g trans fat), 132 mg chol., 114 mg sodium, 9 g carbo., 0 g fiber, 4 g pro. EXCHANGES: ½ Starch, ½ High-Fat Meat, 3½ Fat

MINI PUFFS: Prepare as directed, except drop dough by rounded teaspoons 2 inches apart onto greased baking sheets. Bake, one sheet at a time, in a preheated 400°F oven for 25 minutes (keep remaining dough covered while the first batch bakes). Cool, split, and fill as directed. Makes about 30 mini puffs.

PER MINI PUFF: 93 cal., 8 g total fat (5 g sat. fat, 0 g trans fat), 53 mg chol., 4 g carbo., 46 mg sodium, 0 g fiber, 2 g pro. EXCHANGES: 2 Fat

---

CHEESECAKE CHAT
HERE ARE TWO TIPS FOR MAKING THIS SPECTACULAR DESSERT.

■ Always use a springform pan to make a cheesecake. Removing the cheesecake from any other type of pan is nearly impossible.

■ For extra-creamy results, consider baking the cheesecake in a water bath: Prepare crust as directed. Place crust-lined springform pan on a double layer of 18×12-inch heavy-duty foil. Bring edges of foil up and mold around sides of pan to form a watertight seal. Prepare filling; pour into prepared pan. Place pan in a roasting pan. Pour enough boiling water into roasting pan to reach halfway up sides of the springform pan (see photo, right). Bake for 60 minutes. When done, cake edges will jiggle slightly when the pan is gently shaken. Turn oven off; allow cheese-

cake to sit in oven for 60 minutes (cheesecake will continue to set up during standing time in oven). Carefully remove springform pan from water bath. Remove foil from pan. Cool and chill as directed on page 301.

MAKING CREAM PUFF DOUGH, STEP-BY-STEP

1. Using a wooden spoon, vigorously stir dough in saucepan over heat until it forms a ball that doesn't separate.
2. Remove the pan from the heat. Let dough cool for 10 minutes. Beat in eggs, one at a time. Beat until the dough is smooth before adding the next egg.

MAKE-IT-MINE CHEESECAKE

RASPBERRY-ALMOND CHEESECAKE, ANYONE? HOW ABOUT A MOCHA VERSION WITH A TOUCH OF ORANGE? WITH THIS MASTER RECIPE, YOU CAN DISCOVER YOUR OWN COMBINATION FOR A ONE-OF-A-KIND DELIGHT.

BASIC INGREDIENTS

PREP: 30 MINUTES
BAKE: 40 MINUTES
COOL: 45 MINUTES
CHILL: 4 HOURS **OVEN:** 350°F
MAKES: 12 SERVINGS

- 1¾ cups Crumbs, crushed
- ¼ cup finely chopped Nuts
- 1 tablespoon sugar
- ½ teaspoon Spice (optional)
- ½ cup butter, melted
    Dairy
    Sweetener
- 2 tablespoons all-purpose flour
- 1 teaspoon Flavoring
- ¼ cup Liquid
- 3 eggs, lightly beaten
    Stir-In/Swirl-In

CRUMBS (PICK ONE)

Chocolate sandwich cookies (use 3 tablespoons butter, melted)
Gingersnaps
Graham crackers
Vanilla wafers

NUTS (PICK ONE)

Almonds, pecans, and/or walnuts
Macadamia nuts

SPICE (PICK ONE)

Ground allspice, cinnamon, or ginger
Apple pie or pumpkin pie spice

DAIRY (PICK ONE)

Three 8-ounce packages cream cheese, softened
Two 8-ounce packages cream cheese, softened, plus one 8-ounce carton dairy sour cream (omit Liquid)
Two 8-ounce packages cream cheese, softened, plus two 6-ounce cartons plain low-fat yogurt (omit Liquid)
Two 8-ounce packages cream cheese, softened, plus 1 cup canned pumpkin (omit Liquid)

SWEETENER (PICK ONE)

- 1 cup granulated sugar
- ½ cup granulated sugar plus ½ cup brown sugar

FLAVORING (PICK ONE)

Peppermint or almond extract
Shredded lemon or orange peel
Vanilla

LIQUID (PICK ONE)

Brewed coffee
Milk
Orange or pineapple juice

STIR-IN (PICK ONE)

- 1 cup milk chocolate pieces
- 3 ounces chopped white baking chocolate
- 1 cup blueberries

SWIRL-IN (PICK ONE)

- 4 ounces semisweet chocolate melted with 2 tablespoons cream
- 1 cup raspberries, pureed and sieved

BASIC INSTRUCTIONS

1 Preheat oven to 350°F. For crust, in a bowl combine desired Crumbs, Nuts, the 1 tablespoon sugar, and Spice (if desired). Stir in melted butter. Press the crumb mixture onto the bottom and about 1½ inches up the sides of a 9-inch springform pan; set aside.

2 For filling, in a large mixing bowl beat the Dairy, Sweetener, flour, and Flavoring with an electric mixer until combined. Beat in Liquid until smooth. Stir in eggs and Stir-In.

3 Pour filling into crust-lined pan. Dot with Swirl-In, if using; use a thin metal spatula to marble. Place pan in a shallow baking pan (see optional water bath, page 300). Bake for 40 to 50 minutes or until a 2½-inch area around outside edge appears set when gently shaken.

4 Cool in pan on a wire rack for 15 minutes. Using a small sharp knife, loosen the crust from sides of pan; cool for 30 minutes. Remove sides of pan; cool cheesecake completely on rack. Cover and chill at least 4 hours before serving.

PUMPKIN CHOCOLATE CHEESECAKE SQUARES

PREP: 25 MINUTES **BAKE:** 55 MINUTES
COOL: 90 MINUTES · **CHILL:** 3 TO 24 HOURS
OVEN: 325°F **MAKES:** 24 TO 36 SQUARES

- 1 recipe Graham Cracker Crust
- 2 8-ounce packages cream cheese, softened
- 1¾ cups sugar
- 3 eggs
- 1 cup canned pumpkin
- ½ teaspoon pumpkin pie spice
- ½ teaspoon vanilla
- ¼ teaspoon salt
- 6 ounces semisweet chocolate, chopped, or 1 cup semisweet chocolate pieces
- 2 tablespoons butter
- 1¼ cups dairy sour cream
- ¼ cup sugar

   Grated fresh nutmeg or grated semisweet chocolate

1 Preheat oven to 325°F. Prepare Graham Cracker Crust; set aside. In a large mixing bowl beat cream cheese and 1¾ cups sugar with an electric mixer on medium speed until smooth. Add eggs, one at a time, beating on low speed after each addition just until combined. Beat in pumpkin, pumpkin pie spice, vanilla, and salt on low speed just until combined. Pour 1¼ cups of the pumpkin mixture into a medium bowl. Set both bowls aside.

2 In a small heavy saucepan heat chocolate and butter over low heat until melted, stirring frequently. Whisk the melted chocolate mixture into the 1¼ cups pumpkin mixture. Carefully spread the chocolate mixture evenly over Graham Cracker Crust.

3 Bake for 15 minutes. Remove from oven. Carefully pour remaining pumpkin mixture over baked chocolate layer, spreading evenly. Bake for 40 to 45 minutes more or until puffed and center is set. Cool in pan on a wire rack for 30 minutes.

4 Meanwhile, stir together sour cream and the ¼ cup sugar. Gently spread the sour cream mixture over top of cheesecake. Cool completely. Cover and chill for 3 to 24 hours before cutting. Sprinkle with nutmeg just before serving. Cut into desired-size squares.

GRAHAM CRACKER CRUST: Lightly grease a 13×9×2-inch baking pan. In a medium bowl combine 1¼ cups graham cracker crumbs and ¼ cup sugar. Add ⅓ cup melted butter; mix well. Press crumb mixture evenly over bottom of prepared pan.

PER SQUARE: 256 cal., 15 g total fat (9 g sat. fat, 0 g trans fat), 62 mg chol., 151 mg sodium, 28 g carbo., 1 g fiber, 3 g pro. EXCHANGES: 1 Starch, 1 Other Carbo., 3 Fat

VANILLA PUDDING

PREP: 10 MINUTES **COOK:** 20 MINUTES
MAKES: ABOUT 3 CUPS

- ¾ cup sugar
- 3 tablespoons cornstarch
- 3 cups milk
- 4 egg yolks, lightly beaten
- 1 tablespoon butter
- 1½ teaspoons vanilla

1 In a medium heavy saucepan combine sugar and cornstarch. Stir in milk. Cook and stir over medium heat until thickened and bubbly. Cook and stir 2 minutes more. Remove from heat. Gradually stir 1 cup of the milk mixture into egg yolks.

2 Add egg mixture to milk mixture in saucepan. Bring to a gentle boil; reduce heat. Cook and stir for 2 minutes more. Remove from heat. Stir in butter and vanilla. Pour pudding into a bowl. Cover surface of pudding with plastic wrap. Cool slightly and serve warm, or chill. (Do not stir during chilling.)

CHOCOLATE PUDDING: Prepare as directed, except add ⅓ cup unsweetened cocoa powder with the sugar. (For the most intense chocolate flavor, use Dutch-process cocoa.) Decrease cornstarch to 2 tablespoons and milk to 2⅔ cups.

PER ABOUT ¾ CUP VANILLA OR CHOCOLATE VARIATION: 363 cal., 13 g total fat (7 g sat. fat, 0 g trans fat), 236 mg chol., 102 mg sodium, 52 g carbo., 0 g fiber, 9 g pro. EXCHANGES: 1 Milk, 2½ Other Carbo., 2½ Fat

TIRAMISU

PREP: 45 MINUTES **CHILL:** 4 TO 24 HOURS
MAKES: 16 SERVINGS

- ½ cup sugar
- ½ cup water
- 2 tablespoons instant espresso coffee powder
- 1 tablespoon amaretto
- 1 tablespoon hazelnut liqueur
- 2 8-ounce cartons mascarpone cheese
- ¼ cup sugar

1 teaspoon vanilla
1½ cups whipping cream
3 tablespoons sugar
½ cup water
3 tablespoons dried egg whites*
⅓ cup sugar
2 3-ounce packages ladyfingers, split
2 tablespoons unsweetened cocoa powder

1 For syrup, in a small saucepan combine the ½ cup sugar, ½ cup water, and the espresso powder. Bring to boiling over medium heat, stirring to dissolve sugar. Boil gently, uncovered, for 1 minute. Remove from heat. Stir in amaretto and hazelnut liqueur; cool.

2 In a medium bowl stir together mascarpone, the ¼ cup sugar, and vanilla. In a chilled large mixing bowl combine whipping cream and the 3 tablespoons sugar. Beat with an electric mixer on medium speed until soft peaks form. Fold ½ cup whipped cream mixture into mascarpone mixture to lighten; set both mixtures aside.

3 Clean beaters thoroughly. In another large mixing bowl beat the ½ cup water and dried egg whites with an electric mixer on medium speed until soft peaks form (tips curl). Gradually beat in the ⅓ cup sugar, 1 tablespoon at a time, until stiff peaks form (tips stand straight).

4 Arrange half of the ladyfinger halves in the bottom of a 9×9×2-inch baking pan. Brush with half of the syrup (see photo 1, below). Spread with half of the mascarpone mixture. Spread with half of the egg white mixture (see photo 2, below). Top with half of the whipped cream mixture, spreading evenly. Sift half of the cocoa powder over the whipped cream layer. Repeat layers once, except do not sift remaining cocoa powder over top.

5 Cover and chill for 4 to 24 hours. Uncover and sift remaining cocoa powder over the top just before serving (see photo 3, below).

*NOTE: Dried egg whites are a safe alternative to raw whites. Find them in the grocer's baking aisle.

PER SERVING: 316 cal., 22 g total fat (13 g sat. fat, 0 g trans fat), 90 mg chol., 57 mg sodium, 26 g carbo., 0 g fiber, 9 g pro. EXCHANGES: 1 Starch, 1 Other Carbo., 1 High-Fat Meat, 2½ Fat

ASSEMBLING TIRAMISU, STEP-BY-STEP

1. Brush ladyfingers evenly with coffee syrup. **2.** To evenly spread egg white mixture over mascarpone mixture, start by spooning mounds of the egg white mixture over the mascarpone mixture. Use an offset spatula to spread the egg white mixture evenly. **3.** Just before serving, dust the top of the tiramisu with cocoa powder.

ENGLISH TRIFLE

PREP: 30 MINUTES **CHILL:** 2 TO 24 HOURS
MAKES: 8 SERVINGS

- 1 4-serving-size package instant vanilla pudding and pie filling mix
- 1¾ cups milk
- ½ cup dairy sour cream
- 6 cups 1-inch cubes pound cake*
- 6 tablespoons raspberry liqueur, orange liqueur, or orange juice
- 3 cups fresh berries (raspberries, blueberries, and/or sliced strawberries)
- ¼ cup sliced toasted almonds (see tip, page 20)
- ½ cup whipping cream
- 1 tablespoon powdered sugar
- 1 tablespoon raspberry liqueur, orange liqueur, or orange juice

1 In a medium bowl whisk together the pudding mix, milk, and sour cream for 2 minutes or until smooth and mixture starts to thicken; set aside.

2 Arrange one-third of the cake cubes in the bottom of a 2-quart clear serving bowl. Drizzle with 2 tablespoons of the liqueur. Top with 1 cup of the berries. Spread ⅔ cup pudding mixture over berries. Top with 1 tablespoon of the almonds. Repeat layers twice. Cover and chill for 2 to 24 hours.

3 To serve, in a medium mixing bowl beat whipping cream, powdered sugar, and the 1 tablespoon

liqueur with an electric mixer on medium speed until soft peaks form (tips curl). Spread over top of trifle. Arrange additional berries over whipped cream and sprinkle with remaining almonds.

*NOTE: One 10.75-ounce frozen pound cake, thawed, yields 6 cups of 1-inch cubes.

PER SERVING: 378 cal., 18 g total fat (10 g sat. fat, 0 g trans fat), 115 mg chol., 266 mg sodium, 45 g carbo., 4 g fiber, 6 g pro. EXCHANGES: ½ Fruit, 1 Starch, 1½ Other Carbo., 3½ Fat

FAST

BLUEBERRY-LEMON PARFAIT

START TO FINISH: 25 MINUTES **MAKES:** 6 PARFAITS

- 1 8-ounce package cream cheese, softened
- ¼ cup sugar
- ½ cup Lemon Curd (page 308) or purchased lemon curd
- 1 cup whipping cream
- 1 teaspoon vanilla
- 1½ cups crumbled purchased soft molasses cookies or coarsely crushed gingersnaps (about 6 ounces)
- 2 cups fresh blueberries
  Fresh blueberries and/or halved or crumbled purchased soft molasses cookies, or coarsely crushed gingersnaps

1 In a large mixing bowl beat cream cheese and sugar with an electric mixer on medium speed until fluffy. Beat in lemon curd until combined; set aside.

2 Clean beaters thoroughly. In a medium mixing bowl beat whipping cream and vanilla with an electric mixer on medium speed until soft peaks form (tips curl). Fold whipping cream mixture into cream cheese mixture.

3 Spoon one-third of the cream cheese mixture evenly into the bottom of six parfait or dessert glasses. Top with half of the cookies and half of the berries. Repeat layers. Top with remaining cream mixture. Garnish with additional berries and/or halved or crushed cookies.

PER PARFAIT: 535 cal., 33 g total fat (18 g sat. fat, 1 g trans fat), 123 mg chol., 321 mg sodium, 59 g carbo., 4 g fiber, 5 g pro. EXCHANGES: ½ Fruit, 1 Starch, 2½ Other Carbo., 6½ Fat

A SPOT OF SHERRY?
CREAM SHERRY IS A CLASSIC TRIFLE FLAVORING—SUBSTITUTE IT FOR THE LIQUEUR, BUT USE JUST 3 TABLESPOONS.

ORANGE SHERBET

PREP: 20 MINUTES
FREEZE: PER MANUFACTURER'S DIRECTIONS
RIPEN: 4 HOURS (OPTIONAL) **MAKES:** 6 CUPS

1½ cups sugar
1 envelope unflavored gelatin
1 teaspoon finely shredded orange peel
3¾ cups orange juice
1 cup milk

1 In a medium saucepan combine sugar and gelatin. Stir in 2 cups of the orange juice. Cook and stir until sugar and gelatin dissolve. Remove from heat. Stir in remaining orange juice, the orange peel, milk, and a few drops *orange food coloring* (if desired). (Mixture might appear curdled.)

2 Transfer mixture to a 4-quart ice cream freezer; freeze according to manufacturer's directions.* If desired, ripen 4 hours (see tip, page 306).

*NOTE: If you don't have an ice cream freezer, transfer mixture to a 13×9×2-inch pan. Cover; freeze 2 to 3 hours or until almost firm. Break mixture into small chunks; transfer to a large mixing bowl. Beat with an electric mixer until smooth but not melted. Return to pan. Cover; freeze until firm.

LEMON SHERBET: In a saucepan combine sugar and gelatin as in Step 1. Stir in 1½ cups water. Cook and stir until sugar and gelatin dissolve. Remove from heat. Stir in 1½ cups cold water, 1 cup milk, 1 teaspoon finely shredded lemon peel, and ¾ cup lemon juice. Continue as directed.

PER ½ CUP ORANGE OR LEMON VARIATION: 150 cal., 1 g total fat (0 g sat. fat, 0 g trans fat), 2 mg chol., 14 mg sodium, 34 g carbo., 0 g fiber, 3 g pro.
EXCHANGES: 2 Other Carbo., ½ Very Lean Meat

RASPBERRY SORBET

PREP: 20 MINUTES **CHILL:** 60 MINUTES
FREEZE: 10 HOURS **STAND:** 5 MINUTES
MAKES: 3 CUPS

1 cup sugar
1 cup water
2 tablespoons lemon juice
3 cups fresh raspberries
2 tablespoons orange juice

1 For syrup, in a medium saucepan heat and stir the sugar and water over medium heat until just simmering, stirring to dissolve sugar. Remove from heat; stir in lemon juice. Transfer to a medium bowl; cover and chill completely.

2 Place raspberries and orange juice in a food processor or blender. Cover and process until smooth. Press mixture through a fine-mesh sieve; discard seeds. Stir puree into chilled syrup.

3 Pour raspberry mixture into a 2-quart square baking dish. Cover; freeze 4 hours or until firm. Break up mixture with a fork; place in food processor or blender, half at a time if necessary. Cover and process for 30 to 60 seconds or until smooth. Spoon back into the same dish; cover and freeze for 6 to 8 hours or until firm. To serve, let stand at room temperature for 5 minutes before scooping.

PER ⅓ CUP: 110 cal., 0 g total fat, 0 mg chol., 1 mg sodium, 28 g carbo., 3 g fiber, 1 g pro.
EXCHANGES: ½ Fruit, 1½ Other Carbo.

MANGO SORBET: Prepare as directed, except substitute cut-up, peeled mango for raspberries. Omit pressing through sieve. Makes 4 cups.

PER ⅓ CUP: 94 cal., 0 g total fat, 0 mg chol., 1 mg sodium, 24 g carbo., 1 g fiber, 0 g pro.
EXCHANGES: 1½ Other Carbo.

BUTTERSCOTCH CRUNCH SQUARES

PREP: 40 MINUTES **BAKE:** 10 MINUTES
FREEZE: 6 HOURS **STAND:** 5 MINUTES **OVEN:** 400°F
MAKES: 12 SQUARES

1 cup all-purpose flour
¼ cup quick-cooking rolled oats
¼ cup packed brown sugar
½ cup butter
½ cup chopped pecans or walnuts
½ cup butterscotch-flavored ice cream topping
½ gallon butter brickle or vanilla ice cream

1 Preheat oven to 400°F. In a medium bowl combine flour, oats, and sugar. Cut in butter until mixture resembles coarse crumbs. Stir in nuts. Pat nut mixture lightly into an ungreased 13×9×2-inch baking pan. Bake 10 to 15 minutes or until golden. While still warm, stir nut mixture to crumble; cool.

2 Spread half the crumbs in a 9×9×2-inch pan; drizzle half of the ice cream topping over crumbs in pan. Place ice cream in a chilled bowl; stir to soften. Spread ice cream evenly over crumbs in pan. Top with remaining topping and crumbs. Cover; freeze 6 hours or until firm. Let stand at room temperature 5 to 10 minutes before serving.

PER SQUARE: 404 cal., 25 g total fat (11 g sat. fat, 0 g trans fat), 47 mg chol., 239 mg sodium, 43 g carbo., 1 g fiber, 4 g pro.
EXCHANGES: 1 Starch, 2 Other Carbo., 5 Fat

EASY VANILLA ICE CREAM

PREP: 5 MINUTES
FREEZE: PER MANUFACTURER'S DIRECTIONS
RIPEN: 4 HOURS (OPTIONAL) **MAKES:** 8 CUPS

4 cups half-and-half, light cream, or milk

1½ cups sugar

1 tablespoon vanilla

2 cups whipping cream

1 In a large bowl combine half-and-half, sugar, and vanilla. Stir until sugar dissolves. Stir in whipping cream. Freeze cream mixture in a 4- to 5-quart ice cream freezer according to the manufacturer's directions. If desired, ripen for at least 4 hours (see tip, below).

PER ½ CUP: 206 cal., 14 g total fat (9 g sat. fat, 0 g trans fat), 51 mg chol., 29 mg sodium, 18 g carbo., 0 g fiber, 2 g pro. EXCHANGES: 1 Other Carbo., 3 Fat

---

BEST WHEN RIPE

RIPEN (OR HARDEN) ICE CREAM EASILY.

■ For a traditional ice cream freezer, after churning remove lid and dasher. Cover the top with foil. Plug the lid hole with a cloth; replace lid on can and fill the outer freezer bucket with ice and rock salt (enough to cover top of the freezer can) in a ratio of 4 cups ice to 1 cup rock salt. Let stand at room temperature about 4 hours.

■ For an ice cream freezer with an insulated freezer bowl, transfer the ice cream to a freezer container, cover, and store in the freezer for at least 4 hours.

CLASSIC VANILLA ICE CREAM

PREP: 50 MINUTES **CHILL:** 4 TO 24 HOURS
FREEZE: PER TO MANUFACTURER'S DIRECTIONS
RIPEN: 4 HOURS (OPTIONAL) **MAKES:** 6 CUPS

2 cups whole milk

8 egg yolks

¾ cup sugar

2 cups whipping cream

2 tablespoons vanilla

1 teaspoon kosher salt or ½ teaspoon salt
   Kosher or rock salt and crushed ice
   (for hand-crank or electric ice cream
   freezers)

1 In a medium heavy saucepan whisk together milk, egg yolks, and sugar. Cook over medium heat, stirring constantly with a heatproof rubber scraper, until custard coats the back of the scraper (see photo 1, below).

2 Strain custard through a fine-mesh sieve into a bowl placed in a larger bowl of ice water (see photo 2, below). Stir custard until cooled. Stir in whipping cream, vanilla, and the 1 teaspoon kosher salt. Cover and chill for 4 to 24 hours.

3 Freeze chilled mixture in a 4- to 5-quart ice cream freezer according to the manufacturer's directions. If desired, ripen for at least 4 hours (see tip, left).

PER ½ CUP: 253 cal., 19 g total fat (11 g sat. fat, 0 g trans fat), 199 mg chol., 198 mg sodium, 16 g carbo., 0 g fiber, 4 g pro. EXCHANGES: 1 Other Carbo., ½ High-Fat Meat, 3 Fat

---

MAKING ICE CREAM CUSTARD, STEP-BY-STEP

1. To check the custard for doneness, swipe a finger across the scraper. When the custard is done, the line made by your finger will remain without the custard running back together.
2. Place a bowl in a large bowl of ice. (The ice will help cool the custard quickly.) Strain the custard into the bowl through a fine-mesh sieve to catch any bits of egg that might have overcooked in the custard.

10 TO TRY—ICE CREAM

Start with Classic Vanilla Ice Cream, page 306. **1. DOUBLE VANILLA:** Scrape seeds from 1 halved vanilla bean; stir in before freezing. **2. CHOCOLATE-ALMOND:** Use ½ cup sugar; stir in one 16-ounce can chocolate-flavored syrup and ½ cup chopped toasted almonds before freezing. **3. STRAWBERRY:** Puree 4 cups strawberries; stir in before freezing. **4. CHOCOLATE CHIP:** Stir in 1 cup mini chocolate pieces after freezing. **5. PEPPERMINT:** Stir in 1 cup chopped layered chocolate-mint candies; swirl in ⅓ cup hot fudge topping after freezing. **6. COOKIES AND CREAM:** Stir in 1 cup coarsely chopped cookies after freezing. **7. COFFEE:** Halve salt; dissolve 2 tablespoons instant coffee crystals in cream and stir in 1 cup chopped chocolate before freezing. **8. PEANUT BUTTER:** Stir in 1 cup chopped chocolate-covered peanut butter cups after freezing. **9. TOASTED PECAN:** Stir in 1 cup coarsely chopped toasted pecans; swirl in ½ cup caramel ice cream topping after freezing. **10. PEACH:** Puree 4 cups peaches; stir in before freezing.

CHOCOLATE FONDUE

MOCHA FONDUE: Prepare as directed, except substitute ⅓ cup strong brewed coffee for milk.

PER ¼ CUP: 301 cal., 13 g total fat (8 g sat. fat, 0 g trans fat), 17 mg chol., 63 mg sodium, 43 g carbo., 2 g fiber, 6 g pro. EXCHANGES: ½ Milk, 2½ Other Carbo., 2½ Fat

WHITE CHOCOLATE FONDUE: Prepare as directed, except substitute white baking chocolate for semisweet chocolate and add one 7-ounce jar marshmallow creme to the saucepan with the chocolate. Reduce milk to 2 tablespoons. After fondue is smooth and melted, stir in ¼ cup crème de cacao or amaretto.

PER ¼ CUP: 428 cal., 14 g total fat (9 g sat. fat, 0 g trans fat), 22 mg chol., 115 mg sodium, 67 g carbo., 0 g fiber, 9 g pro. EXCHANGES: ½ Milk, 4 Other Carbo., 3 Fat

LEMON CURD

PREP: 5 MINUTES **COOK:** 8 MINUTES
CHILL: 60 MINUTES **MAKES:** 2 CUPS

- 1 cup sugar
- 2 tablespoons cornstarch
- 3 teaspoons finely shredded lemon peel
- 6 tablespoons lemon juice
- 6 tablespoons water
- 6 egg yolks, lightly beaten
- ½ cup butter, cut up

1 In a medium saucepan stir together sugar and cornstarch. Stir in lemon peel, lemon juice, and water. Cook and stir over medium heat until thickened and bubbly.

2 Stir half of the lemon mixture into the egg yolks. Return egg mixture to the saucepan. Cook, stirring constantly, over medium heat until mixture comes to a gentle boil. Cook and stir for 2 minutes more. Remove from heat. Add butter pieces, stirring until melted. Remove from heat. Transfer to a bowl. Cover surface with plastic wrap. Chill for at least 60 minutes.

MAKE-AHEAD DIRECTIONS: Cover and store prepared curd in refrigerator for up to 1 week or transfer to a freezer container and freeze for up to 2 months. Thaw in refrigerator before serving.

PER 2 TABLESPOONS: 125 cal., 7 g total fat (4 g sat. fat, 0 g trans fat), 94 mg chol., 44 mg sodium, 14 g carbo., 0 g fiber, 1 g pro. EXCHANGES: 1 Other Carbo., 1½ Fat

ORANGE CURD: Prepare as directed, except decrease sugar to ¾ cup; substitute orange peel for the lemon peel and ¾ cup orange juice for the lemon juice and water. Makes about 1½ cups.

PER 2 TABLESPOONS: 156 cal., 10 g total fat (6 g sat. fat, 0 g trans fat), 125 mg chol., 59 mg sodium, 16 g carbo., 0 g fiber, 2 g pro. EXCHANGES: 1 Other Carbo., 2 Fat

FAST

CHOCOLATE FONDUE

PREP: 15 MINUTES **MAKES:** 2 CUPS

- 8 ounces semisweet chocolate, chopped
- 1 14-ounce can (1¼ cups) sweetened condensed milk
- ⅓ cup milk
   Assorted dippers, such as angel food or pound cake cubes, brownie squares, marshmallows, whole strawberries, banana slices, pineapple chunks, or dried apricots

1 In a medium heavy saucepan heat and stir chocolate over low heat until melted. Stir in sweetened condensed milk and milk; heat through. Transfer to a fondue pot; keep warm.

2 Serve fondue with dippers. Swirl pieces as you dip. If the fondue thickens, stir in additional milk.

CHOCOLATE-LIQUEUR FONDUE: Prepare as directed, except stir 2 to 4 tablespoons amaretto or orange, hazelnut, or cherry liqueur into mixture after heating.

PER ¼ CUP REGULAR OR CHOCOLATE-LIQUEUR VARIATION: 306 cal., 14 g total fat (8 g sat. fat, 0 g trans fat), 18 mg chol., 67 mg sodium, 44 g carbo., 2 g fiber, 6 g pro. EXCHANGES: ½ Milk, 2½ Other Carbo., 3 Fat

CHOCOLATE-PEANUT FONDUE: Prepare as directed, except stir ½ cup creamy peanut butter in with the milk.

PER ¼ CUP: 400 cal., 22 g total fat (10 g sat. fat, 0 g trans fat), 18 mg chol., 141 mg sodium, 47 g carbo., 3 g fiber, 10 g pro. EXCHANGES: ½ Milk, 2½ Other Carbo., 1 High-Fat Meat, 2½ Fat

FISH & SHELLFISH

THAI-STYLE FISH AND
VEGETABLES, PAGE 317

FISH & SHELLFISH

THE TRICK TO COOKING GREAT SEAFOOD IS TO BUY IT AT ITS BEST AND AVOID OVERCOOKING. READ HERE AND PAGES 330-332 FOR PURCHASING AND PREPARING TIPS.

COMMON FISH FORMS

DRAWN: Whole fish with internal organs removed; the scales might or might not be removed.
DRESSED: Ready-to-cook fish with organs, scales, gills, and fins removed.
PAN DRESSED: Dressed fish with the heads and tails removed.
STEAK: A ready-to-cook crosscut slice from a large dressed fish; usually ½ to 1 inch thick.
FILLET: A ready-to-cook boneless piece of fish cut from the side and away from the backbone; it might or might not be skinned.

SELECTING FRESH FISH

Look for fish with the following characteristics.

■ Clear, bright, bulging eyes with black pupils

■ Shiny, taut, bright skin

■ Red gills that are not slippery

■ Flesh that feels firm, elastic, and tight to the bone

■ Moist, cleanly cut fillets and steaks.

Avoid fish that have the following characteristics.

■ Strong "fishy" odor

■ Dull, bloody, or sunken eyes

■ Fading skin with bruises, red spots, or browning or yellowing flesh edges

■ Ragged cuts in fillets and steaks

TO STORE: Plan to cook fresh fish the same day you buy it. If that's not possible, wrap fish loosely in plastic wrap and store in the coldest part of your refrigerator; use within 2 days. If not using fresh fish within 2 days, wrap it tightly in moisture- and vapor-proof wrap and store it in the freezer (set at 0°F or lower) for up to 3 months. Leftover cooked fish can be covered and chilled up to 2 days.

TESTING FISH FOR DONENESS

The delicate texture of fish makes it easy to overcook. To test for doneness, insert a fork into the fish and gently twist. The fish is done as soon as it begins to flake. Be sure to check at the minimum cooking time.

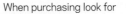

LIVE CRABS AND LOBSTERS

When purchasing look for

■ Hard shells (except for soft-shell crabs)

■ Vigorous activity; the lobster's or crab's legs should move when the body is touched

■ Lobster tail that curls under body when lifted

TO STORE: Lobsters should be cooked live. Ideally, live lobsters and crabs should be cooked on the day they are purchased. Otherwise, place them on in a shallow pan or large bowl and refrigerate them covered with a damp towel. Or place them on damp newspapers in an insulated cooler half filled with ice. Cook within 1 day.

LIVE CLAMS, MUSSELS, AND OYSTERS

When purchasing, look for

■ Tightly closed shells. Mussels might gape slightly but should close when tapped; oysters should always be tightly closed.

■ Clean, unbroken, moist shells

■ Fresh scent, not a strong fishy odor

TO STORE: Refrigerate live clams, mussels, and oysters covered with a moist cloth in an open container for 1 to 2 days.

SHUCKED CLAMS, OYSTERS, AND SCALLOPS

When purchasing, look for

■ Plump meats in clear liquor (juices) without shell particles or grit; the liquor should not exceed 10 percent of total volume

■ Fresh ocean scent (not sour or sulfurlike)

■ Scallops that are firm and moist, retaining their shape when touched

TWO TYPES OF SCALLOPS: There are many species of scallops in the sea, but you'll find two general categories at the market. Sea scallops are about 1½ inches in diameter; on average, there are 20 to 30 per pound. Bay scallops are about ½ inch in diameter and average from 70 to 100 per pound. Be sure to use the type of scallop called for in each recipe, because cooking times differ between the two.

TO STORE: Refrigerate shucked clams, oysters, and scallops, covered, in the liquor for up to 2 days or freeze for up to 3 months.

SHRIMP

When purchasing, look for

■ Firm meat

■ Translucent, moist shells without black spots

■ Fresh scent (not an ammonia odor, which indicates spoilage)

RAW, COOKED, AND CANNED EQUIVALENTS: Twelve ounces raw shrimp in the shell equals 8 ounces raw shelled shrimp, one 4.5-ounce can shrimp, or 1 cup cooked shelled shrimp.

TO STORE: Refrigerate shrimp in a covered container for up to 2 days. Keep frozen shrimp in freezer for up to 6 months.

GUIDE TO SHRIMP SIZE

Raw unshelled shrimp, available fresh or frozen, is sold by the pound. Use this list as a reference for market names and number of shrimp per pound.

Market Name	Number Per Pound
Colossal	Fewer than 15
Extra Jumbo	16 to 20
Jumbo	21 to 25
Extra Large	26 to 30
Large	31 to 40
Medium	41 to 50
Small	51 to 60
Extra Small	61 to 70

THAWING FISH AND SHELLFISH

For the best flavor and for food safety, thaw fish or shellfish gradually by placing the unopened package in a container in the refrigerator. A 1-pound package will thaw in 1 to 2 days. If you must thaw seafood quickly, place it in a resealable plastic bag and immerse in cold water; or microwave on the defrost setting until it is pliable but still icy. Fish and shellfish thawed in the microwave must be cooked immediately after thawing because some spots may become warm and begin to cook.

QUESTIONS ABOUT FOOD SAFETY?

Call the U.S. Food and Drug Administration's Center for Food Safety and Applied Nutrition Safe Food Information Line, 888/723-3366, weekdays from 10 a.m. to 4 p.m. (Eastern Standard Time).

Because most fish and shellfish contain small amounts of mercury, pregnant women and young children should monitor the fish they eat and restrict the amount. For more information, check out the website at *fda.gov/Food/ResourcesForYou/Consumers/ucm110591.htm*.

CRISPY OVEN-FRIED FISH

PREP: 20 MINUTES
BAKE: 4 TO 6 MINUTES PER ½-INCH THICKNESS
OVEN: 450°F **MAKES:** 4 SERVINGS

- 1 pound fresh or frozen skinless fish fillets, ½ to ¾ inch thick
- ¼ cup milk
- ⅓ cup all-purpose flour
- ⅓ cup fine dry bread crumbs
- ¼ cup grated Parmesan cheese
- ½ teaspoon dried dillweed
- ⅛ teaspoon black pepper
- 2 tablespoons butter, melted

1 Thaw fish, if frozen. Rinse fish; pat dry with paper towels. Cut into four serving-size pieces, if necessary. Measure thickness of fish; set aside.

2 Preheat oven to 450°F. Place milk in a shallow dish. Place flour in a second shallow dish. In a third shallow dish combine bread crumbs, Parmesan cheese, dillweed, and pepper. Add melted butter; stir until combined.

3 Dip fish fillets in milk; coat with flour. Dip again in milk; dip in crumb mixture to coat all sides. Place fish on a greased baking sheet. Bake, uncovered, for 4 to 6 minutes per ½-inch thickness or until fish begins to flake when tested with a fork.

PER FILLET: 212 cal., 8 g total fat (5 g sat. fat, 0 g trans fat), 67 mg chol., 218 mg sodium, 10 g carbo., 0 g fiber, 24 g pro. EXCHANGES: ½ Starch, 3 Lean Meat, 1 Fat

PAN-FRIED FISH

PREP: 10 MINUTES **COOK:** 6 MINUTES PER BATCH
OVEN: 300°F **MAKES:** 4 SERVINGS

- 1 pound fresh or frozen skinless fish fillets, ½ to ¾ inch thick
- 1 egg, lightly beaten
- ⅔ cup cornmeal or fine dry bread crumbs
- ½ teaspoon salt
  Dash black pepper
  Vegetable oil or shortening for frying

1 Thaw fish, if frozen. Rinse fish; pat dry with paper towels. Cut into four serving-size pieces. In a shallow dish mix egg and 2 tablespoons *water*. In another shallow dish mix cornmeal, salt, and black pepper. Dip fish into egg mixture; coat fish with cornmeal mixture (see photo 1, below).

2 Preheat oven to 300°F. In a large skillet heat ¼ inch oil. Add half of the fish in a single layer; fry on one side until golden. Turn carefully (see photo 2, below). Fry until second side is golden and fish begins to flake when tested with a fork. Allow 3 to 4 minutes per side. Drain on paper towels. Keep warm in the oven while frying remaining fish.

PER FILLET: 255 cal., 13 g total fat (2 g sat. fat, 0 g trans fat), 101 mg chol., 230 mg sodium, 12 g carbo., 1 g fiber, 23 g pro. EXCHANGES: 1 Starch, 3 Lean Meat, 1 Fat

POTATO CHIP PAN-FRIED FISH: Prepare as above, except substitute 1⅓ cups finely crushed potato chips (about 4 cups chips) or saltine crackers for the cornmeal and omit salt.

PER FILLET: 278 cal., 17 g total fat (3 g sat. fat, 0 g trans fat), 101 mg chol., 153 mg sodium, 7 g carbo., 1 g fiber, 23 g pro. EXCHANGES: ½ Starch, 3 Lean Meat, 2 Fat

PAN-FRIED FISH, STEP-BY-STEP

1. Dip each egg-coated fish piece in the cornmeal mixture and press gently to help the cornmeal mixture adhere to the fish; turn the piece over and repeat to coat the second side. **2.** Once the first side is golden, flip the fish over using a large metal spatula and a fork to steady the fish. When turning the fish, be careful to avoid splattering fat. Cook until the second side is golden.

FISH AND CHIPS

START TO FINISH: 60 MINUTES **OVEN:** 300°F
MAKES: 4 SERVINGS

- 1 pound fresh or frozen skinless fish fillets, about ½ inch thick
- 1¼ pounds medium potatoes (about 4)
  Vegetable oil or shortening for deep-fat frying
- 1 cup all-purpose flour
- ½ cup beer
- 1 egg
- ¼ teaspoon baking powder
- ¼ teaspoon salt
- ¼ teaspoon black pepper
  Coarse salt
- 1 recipe Tartar Sauce (page 543) (optional)
  Malt vinegar or cider vinegar (optional)

1 Thaw fish, if frozen. Preheat oven to 300°F. Cut fish into 3×2-inch pieces. Rinse fish; pat dry with paper towels. Cover and chill until needed.

2 For chips, cut the potatoes lengthwise into ½-inch-wide wedges. Pat dry with paper towels. In a 3-quart saucepan or deep-fat fryer heat 2 inches of vegetable oil to 375°F. Fry potatoes, one-fourth at a time, for 4 to 6 minutes or until tender and light brown. Remove potatoes; drain on paper towels. Transfer potatoes to a wire rack set on a baking sheet, arranging them in a single layer. Keep warm in oven.

3 Meanwhile, place ½ cup of the flour in a shallow dish. For batter, in a medium bowl combine remaining ½ cup flour, the beer, egg, baking powder, ¼ teaspoon salt, and the pepper. Beat with a rotary beater or wire whisk until smooth. Dip fish into the flour in dish, turning to coat all sides; shake off excess flour. Dip fish into batter, turning to coat all sides.

4 Fry fish, two or three pieces at a time, in the hot (375°F) oil for 3 to 4 minutes or until coating is golden brown and fish begins to flake when tested with a fork, turning once. Remove fish and drain on paper towels. Transfer fish to a second baking sheet; keep warm in oven while frying remaining fish. Sprinkle fish and chips with coarse salt. If desired, serve with Tartar Sauce or vinegar.

PER 3 OUNCES FISH + 8 POTATO WEDGES: 552 cal., 29 g total fat (4 g sat. faf, 0 g trans fat), 101 mg chol., 449 mg sodium, 43 g carbo., 4 g fiber, 27 g pro. EXCHANGES: 3 Starch, 3 Lean Meat, 4 Fat

HUSH PUPPIES

PREP: 15 MINUTES **COOK:** 3 MINUTES PER BATCH
MAKES: 14 TO 18 HUSH PUPPIES

- 1 cup cornmeal
- ¼ cup all-purpose flour
- 2 teaspoons sugar
- ¾ teaspoon baking powder
- ¼ teaspoon baking soda
- 1 egg, beaten
- ½ cup buttermilk or sour milk (see tip, page 19)
- ¼ cup sliced green onions (2)
  Vegetable oil or shortening for deep-fat frying

1 In a medium bowl mix cornmeal, flour, sugar, baking powder, baking soda, and ½ teaspoon *salt*. Make a well in center of flour mixture. In another bowl mix egg, buttermilk, and green onions. Add egg mixture all at once to flour mixture. Stir just until moistened (batter should be lumpy).

2 In a 3-quart saucepan or deep-fat fryer heat 2 inches oil to 375°F. For each hush puppy, drop a rounded tablespoon of batter into hot oil. Fry, three or four at a time, 3 minutes or until golden, turning once. Drain on paper towels. Serve warm.

PER HUSH PUPPY: 85 cal., 5 g total fat (1 g sat. fat, 0 g trans fat), 15 mg chol., 136 mg sodium, 10 g carbo., 1 g fiber, 2 g pro. EXCHANGES: ½ Starch, 1 Fat

NUT-CRUSTED CATFISH

START TO FINISH: 25 MINUTES
MAKES: 4 SERVINGS

- 4 fresh or frozen catfish fillets, about ½ inch thick (about 1½ pounds)
- 1 egg, lightly beaten
- ¼ cup milk
- 2 cups cornflakes, finely crushed
- ¼ cup finely chopped black walnuts, walnuts, pecans, hazelnuts, or almonds
- 1 tablespoon butter
- ¼ cup pure maple syrup
- ¼ cup butter, cut up and softened

1 Thaw fish, if frozen. Rinse fish; pat dry. Sprinkle fish with *salt* and *black pepper;* set aside.

2 In a shallow dish combine egg and milk. In a second shallow dish combine cornflakes and nuts. Dip fish into egg mixture, allowing excess to drip off. Dip fish into crumb mixture; coat all sides.

3 In a large skillet melt the 1 tablespoon butter. Cook fish, half at a time, in hot butter for 4 to 6 minutes or until golden and fish begins to flake when tested with a fork, turning once.

4 For sauce, in a small saucepan bring maple syrup to boiling. Remove from heat; whisk in the ¼ cup butter until combined. Serve with fish.

PER 1 FILLET + 2 TABLESPOONS SAUCE: 505 cal., 32 g total fat (13 g sat. fat, 0 g trans fat), 171 mg chol., 437 mg sodium, 24 g carbo., 1 g fiber, 30 g pro.
EXCHANGES: 1½ Other Carbo., 4 Lean Meat, 4½ Fat

FAST • LOW FAT

SESAME-CRUSTED COD

START TO FINISH: 30 MINUTES
MAKES: 4 SERVINGS

- 1 pound fresh or frozen cod fillets, ¾ inch thick
- 3 tablespoons butter or margarine, melted
- 2 tablespoons sesame seeds
- 12 ounces fresh tender young green beans
- 1 medium orange, halved and sliced
- 3 cloves garlic, thinly sliced

1 Thaw fish, if frozen. Rinse fish; pat dry. Cut into four serving-size pieces, if necessary. Place fish on the unheated rack of a broiler pan. Sprinkle fish lightly with *salt* and *black pepper.*

2 Preheat broiler. Combine butter and sesame seeds. Measure 1 tablespoon; set aside. Brush fish with half of remaining mixture. Broil 5 to 6 inches from heat 4 minutes; turn fish. Brush with remaining mixture. Broil 5 to 6 minutes more or until fish begins to flake when tested with fork.

3 Meanwhile, in covered very large skillet cook beans and orange in reserved butter mixture over medium-high heat for 2 minutes. Add garlic; cook, uncovered, for 5 to 6 minutes more or until beans are crisp-tender, stirring often. Serve with fish.

PER 3 OUNCES FISH + ¾ CUP BEANS: 240 cal., 12 g total fat (6 g sat. fat, 0 g trans fat), 71 mg chol., 274 mg sodium, 12 g carbo., 4 g fiber, 23 g pro.
EXCHANGES: 1 Vegetable, ½ Fruit, 3 Lean Meat, ½ Fat

LOVE SESAME? ANOTHER TIME TRY USING THE BUTTER-SESAME SEED MIXTURE TO FLAVOR BROCCOLI OR ASPARAGUS. SAUTE COOKED VEGGIES IN THE MIXTURE UNTIL SEEDS ARE LIGHT BROWN.

SESAME-CRUSTED COD

MAKE-IT-MINE FISH

CRUMB-TOPPED BAKED FISH IS A QUICK AND HEALTHFUL, FAMILY-PLEASING ENTRÉE. NOW YOU CAN MAKE IT JUST THE WAY YOUR FAMILY LIKES IT, WITH EVERYONE'S FAVORITE FISH, SEASONINGS, AND TOPPINGS.

BASIC INGREDIENTS

PREP: 20 MINUTES
BAKE: 12 MINUTES **OVEN:** 425°F
MAKES: 4 TO 6 SERVINGS

- 1½ pounds fresh or frozen skinless Fish Fillets
- 2 eggs or egg whites, lightly beaten
- 1 tablespoon milk or water
- 1 cup Crumb Topping
  Seasoning Combo
  Nonstick cooking spray
  Topping

FISH FILLETS (PICK ONE)

Catfish
Grouper
Red snapper
Salmon
Tilapia

CRUMB TOPPING

(PICK ONE)

- 1 cup crushed Italian-seasoned or garlic croutons
- 1 cup panko (Japanese-style bread crumbs)
- 1 cup crushed saltine crackers
- 1 cup crushed rich round crackers
- ½ cup shredded coconut and ½ cup panko (Japanese-style bread crumbs)

SEASONING COMBO

(PICK ONE)

- 1 teaspoon curry powder, ¼ teaspoon salt, and ¼ teaspoon garlic salt
- 1 teaspoon dried Italian seasoning, ½ teaspoon salt, and ¼ teaspoon black pepper
- 1 tablespoon dried ranch salad dressing mix and 1 teaspoon finely shredded lemon peel
- 1 tablespoon chopped fresh cilantro and 2 teaspoons taco seasoning mix

TOPPING (PICK ONE)

Honey
Tartar sauce
Honey-barbecue sauce
Purchased basil pesto
Lemon wedges and horseradish sauce
- ¼ cup dairy sour cream, ¼ cup mayonnaise, and ½ teaspoon grated fresh ginger
- ½ cup ranch dressing and 1 tablespoon finely chopped chipotle chile pepper in adobo sauce

BASIC INSTRUCTIONS

1 Thaw desired Fish Fillets, if frozen. Preheat oven to 425°F. Line a large baking sheet with foil. Lightly grease foil; set aside.

2 Rinse fish; pat dry with paper towels. Cut fish into four to six serving-size pieces, if necessary. In a shallow dish combine eggs and milk. In a second shallow dish combine Crumb Topping and Seasoning Combo. Dip fish into egg mixture; coat fish with crumb mixture. Place fish on prepared baking sheet. Coat fish with nonstick cooking spray.

3 Bake in for 12 to 15 minutes or until fish begins to flake when tested with a fork. Serve fish with Topping.

THAI-STYLE FISH
AND VEGETABLES *(photo, page 309)*

START TO FINISH: 25 MINUTES
MAKES: 4 SERVINGS

- 4 4- to 6-ounce fresh or frozen skinless cod, tilapia, or other fish fillets, about ½ inch thick
- 1 red sweet pepper, cut into thin bite-size strips
- 1 cup fresh green beans or thin asparagus spears, trimmed and cut into 2-inch pieces
- 1 medium carrot, cut into thin bite-size strips
- ¼ teaspoon salt
- ⅛ teaspoon black pepper
- ¾ cup canned unsweetened light coconut milk
- 2 teaspoons lime juice
- 2 teaspoons fish sauce or soy sauce
- 1 teaspoon grated fresh ginger or ½ teaspoon ground ginger
- ⅛ to ¼ teaspoon crushed red pepper
- 2 tablespoons chopped peanuts
- 1 tablespoon snipped fresh cilantro

1 Thaw fish, if frozen. Rinse fish; pat dry with paper towels.

2 Fill a very large skillet with water to a depth of 1 inch. Bring water to boiling; reduce heat. Arrange sweet pepper, green beans, and carrot in a steamer basket. Place fish on top of vegetables. Sprinkle fish and vegetables with salt and black pepper. Place steamer over simmering water. Cover and simmer gently for 6 to 8 minutes or until fish begins to flake when tested with a fork.

3 Meanwhile, for sauce, in a small saucepan combine coconut milk, lime juice, fish sauce, ginger, and crushed red pepper. Bring to boiling; reduce heat. Boil gently, uncovered, for 2 to 3 minutes or until slightly thickened.

4 Remove fish and vegetables from steamer basket and arrange on dinner plates. Drizzle with sauce; sprinkle with peanuts and cilantro.

PER FILLET + ¾ CUP VEGETABLES: 173 cal., 5 g total fat (2 g sat. fat, 0 g trans fat), 48 mg chol., 557 mg sodium, 8 g carbo., 2 g fiber, 23 g pro.
EXCHANGES: 1 Vegetable, 3 Lean Meat

TILAPIA VERACRUZ

START TO FINISH: 25 MINUTES
MAKES: 4 SERVINGS

- 4 6- to 8-ounce fresh or frozen skinless tilapia, red snapper, mahi mahi, or other fish fillets, about 1 inch thick
- 1 tablespoon olive oil
- 1 small onion, cut into thin wedges
- 1 jalapeño chile pepper, seeded and finely chopped (see tip, page 24) (optional)
- 1 clove garlic, minced
- 1 14.5-ounce can diced tomatoes, undrained
- 1 cup sliced fresh cremini or button mushrooms
- ¾ cup pimiento-stuffed olives, coarsely chopped
- 1 tablespoon snipped fresh oregano or ½ teaspoon dried oregano, crushed
- ¼ teaspoon salt
- ⅛ teaspoon black pepper
- 2 cups hot cooked rice

1 Thaw fish, if frozen. Rinse fish; pat dry with paper towels. Set fish aside.

2 For sauce, in a very large skillet heat olive oil over medium heat. Add onion, chile pepper (if desired), and garlic; cook and stir for 2 to 3 minutes or until onion is tender. Add undrained tomatoes, mushrooms, olives, oregano, salt, and black pepper. Bring to boiling.

3 Gently place fish in sauce in skillet, spooning sauce over fish. Return to boiling; reduce heat. Simmer, covered, for 8 to 10 minutes or until fish begins to flake when tested with a fork. Using a wide spatula, carefully lift fish from skillet to a serving dish. Spoon sauce over fish. Serve with hot cooked rice.

PER FILLET + ½ CUP SAUCE + ½ CUP RICE: 363 cal., 10 g total fat (2 g sat. fat, 0 g trans fat), 84 mg chol., 1,111 mg sodium, 31 g carbo., 3 g fiber, 38 g pro.
EXCHANGES: 1 Vegetable, 1½ Starch, 4½ Lean Meat, ½ Fat

SHRIMP VERACRUZ

FOR SHRIMP VERACRUZ, PRE-PARE SAUCE AND SUBSTITUTE 1 POUND COOKED SHELLED AND DEVEINED SHRIMP FOR FISH; HEAT THROUGH.

TILAPIA WITH ALMOND BUTTER

START TO FINISH: 20 MINUTES
MAKES: 4 SERVINGS

- 4 6- to 8-ounce fresh or frozen skinless tilapia fillets or other fish fillets
- 3 cups snow pea pods, trimmed
  Sea salt and black pepper
- 1 teaspoon all-purpose flour
- 1 tablespoon olive oil
- 2 tablespoons butter
- ¼ cup sliced almonds

1 Thaw fish, if frozen. In a covered large saucepan cook snow peas in a small amount of lightly salted boiling water for 2 minutes. Drain and set aside.

2 Rinse fish; pat dry with paper towels. Measure thickness of fish. Season fish on one side with salt and pepper; sprinkle with flour. In a very large nonstick skillet heat olive oil over medium-high heat. Add fish to skillet, flour sides up. Cook for 4 to 6 minutes per ½-inch thickness of fish or until fish begins to flake when tested with a fork, turning once. Place snow peas and fish on serving plates.

3 For almond butter, in the same skillet melt butter over medium heat. Stir in almonds. Cook for 30 to 60 seconds or until nuts are lightly toasted (do not let butter burn). Spoon almond butter over fish fillets.

PER FILLET + ¾ CUP PEAS: 298 cal., 15 g total fat (6 g sat. fat, 0 g trans fat), 100 mg chol., 231 mg sodium, 5 g carbo., 2 g fiber, 37 g pro.
EXCHANGES: 1 Vegetable, 5 Lean Meat, 1 Fat

RED SNAPPER WITH CARROTS AND FENNEL

PREP: 25 MINUTES **BAKE:** 12 MINUTES
OVEN: 450°F **MAKES:** 4 SERVINGS

- 1 pound fresh or frozen skinless red snapper, grouper, or ocean perch fillets, about ½ inch thick
  Salt and black pepper
- 1 tablespoon olive oil
- 2 cups sliced fennel bulb (1 large)
- 1 cup chopped onion (1 large)
- 1 cup chopped carrots (2 medium)
- 2 cloves garlic, minced
- ¼ cup dry white wine or chicken broth
- 2 tablespoons snipped fresh dill
- ¼ teaspoon salt
- ¼ teaspoon black pepper

1 Thaw fish, if frozen. Rinse fish; pat dry with paper towels. Sprinkle fish lightly with salt and pepper; set aside.

2 Preheat oven to 450°F. In a large skillet heat olive oil over medium heat. Add fennel, onion, carrots, and garlic to hot oil; cook for 7 to 9 minutes or until vegetables are tender and light brown. Remove from heat. Stir in wine, dill, the ¼ teaspoon salt, and the ¼ teaspoon pepper.

3 Reserve ¼ cup of the vegetable mixture; spoon remaining vegetable mixture into a 2-quart square baking dish. Place fish on top of vegetables, tucking under any thin edges. Spoon reserved vegetable mixture on top of fish.

4 Bake, uncovered, about 12 minutes or until fish begins to flake when tested with a fork. To serve, transfer fish and vegetables to serving plates. If desired, garnish with additional fresh dill.

PER 3 OUNCES FISH + 1 CUP VEGETABLES: 199 cal., 5 g total fat (1 g sat. fat, 0 g trans fat), 41 mg chol., 410 mg sodium, 11 g carbo., 3 g fiber, 25 g pro.
EXCHANGES: 1 Vegetable, 3 Lean Meat, ½ Fat

FISH TACOS

START TO FINISH: 20 MINUTES **OVEN:** 450°F
MAKES: 4 SERVINGS

- 12 ounces fresh or frozen skinless fish fillets
- 1 tablespoon olive oil
- ¼ teaspoon salt
- ¼ teaspoon ground cumin
- ⅛ teaspoon garlic powder
- 1½ cups shredded lettuce
- 1 medium tomato, seeded and chopped
- 8 corn taco shells, warmed according to package directions
- ½ cup bottled salsa

1 Thaw fish, if frozen. Preheat oven to 450°F. Rinse fish; pat dry with paper towels. Cut fish crosswise into ¾-inch slices. Place fish in a single layer in a greased shallow baking pan. Combine olive oil, salt, cumin, and garlic powder. Brush over fish. Bake for 4 to 6 minutes or until fish begins to flake when tested with a fork.

2 To serve, spoon lettuce and tomato into each taco shell; add fish slices and top with salsa.

PER 2 TACOS: 322 cal., 19 g total fat (3 g sat. fat, 0 g trans fat), 44 mg chol., 353 mg sodium, 21 g carbo., 3 g fiber, 17 g pro.
EXCHANGES: ½ Vegetable, 1 Starch, 2 Lean Meat, 3½ Fat

Start with Fish Tacos, page 318. **1. CRUNCHY:** Add baked onion rings or shoestring french fried potatoes and malt vinegar. **2. BLT:** Add shredded lettuce, crisp-cooked bacon, tomato, and mayonnaise. **3. SPINACH:** Add fresh spinach, caramelized onions (sliced onions cooked in olive oil over medium heat for 10 minutes or until brown and tender), and provolone cheese. **4. CAESAR:** Add shredded romaine lettuce, bottled Caesar salad dressing, and finely shredded Parmesan cheese. **5. ASIAN:** Add broccoli slaw, toasted sliced almonds, and bottled Asian vinaigrette. **6. CHIPOTLE:** Add sweet pepper strips and mayonnaise mixed with a chopped chipotle pepper. **7. CAPRESE:** Add basil, cubed tomato, cubed mozzarella cheese, and balsamic vinaigrette. **8. SLAW:** Add coleslaw mix combined with mayonnaise and lime juice. **9. FRUITY:** Add fresh fruit salsa made with kiwifruit, red onion, strawberries, and mango. **10. SALSA:** Add a combination of black beans, tomato, corn, chopped jalapeño chile pepper (see tip, page 24), and cilantro.

FISH IN PARCHMENT

PREP: 20 MINUTES **BAKE:** 12 MINUTES
OVEN: 400°F **MAKES:** 4 SERVINGS

- 1½ pounds fresh or frozen skinless halibut, red snapper, or other whitefish fillets, about ¾ inch thick
- ¼ cup reduced-sodium chicken broth
- 2 tablespoons bottled hoisin sauce
- 2 tablespoons reduced-sodium soy sauce
- 1 tablespoon sugar
- 2 teaspoons cornstarch
- 2 teaspoons Asian chili garlic sauce (optional)
- 2 teaspoons toasted sesame oil
- 1 teaspoon grated fresh ginger
- 1 clove garlic, minced
- 4 12-inch squares parchment paper
- 3 green onions, cut into thin strips
- 1 carrot, cut into thin strips
  Hot cooked rice (optional)

1 Thaw fish, if frozen. Rinse fish; pat dry with paper towels. Cut fish into four serving-size pieces, if necessary. Set fish aside.

2 In a small saucepan combine chicken broth, hoisin sauce, soy sauce, sugar, cornstarch, Asian chili sauce (if desired), sesame oil, ginger, and garlic. Cook and stir until thickened and bubbly; cook and stir for 1 minute more. Remove from heat.

3 Preheat oven to 400°F. Place one portion of fish in the middle of a parchment square. Top with 2 tablespoons of the sauce and one-fourth of the green onions and carrot. Bring up two opposite sides of parchment (see photo 1, below) and fold

several times over fish. Fold ends of parchment (see photo 2, below). Repeat to make three more packets. Place packets in a shallow baking pan.

4 Bake for 12 to 15 minutes or until fish begins to flake when tested with a fork (open a packet to check doneness). If desired, serve with rice.

PER PACKET: 261 cal., 6 g total fat (1 g sat. fat, 0 g trans fat), 54 mg chol., 533 mg sodium, 12 g carbo., 1 g fiber, 37 g pro.
EXCHANGES: ½ Vegetable, ½ Other Carbo., 5 Lean Meat

SESAME-TERIYAKI SEA BASS

START TO FINISH: 25 MINUTES
MAKES: 4 SERVINGS

- 4 4-ounce fresh or frozen skinless sea bass, rockfish, or other fish fillets, ½ to ¾ inch thick
- ¼ teaspoon black pepper
- 3 tablespoons soy sauce
- ¼ cup sweet rice wine (mirin)
- 2 teaspoons honey
- 2 teaspoons vegetable oil
- 2 teaspoons sesame seeds and/or black sesame seeds, toasted (see tip, page 20)

1 Thaw fish, if frozen. Rinse fish; pat dry with paper towels. Measure thickness of fish. Sprinkle fish with pepper; set aside.

2 For glaze, in a small saucepan combine soy sauce, rice wine, and honey. Bring to boiling; reduce heat. Simmer, uncovered, about 10 minutes or until glaze is slightly thickened and reduced to ⅓ cup; set aside.

PREPARING FISH PACKETS, STEP-BY-STEP

1. Place a piece of fish in the center of a parchment square. Top with sauce, green onions, and carrots. Lift up two opposite sides of the parchment and bring together over fish. Fold several times, but leave space for steam to build.
2. Fold the two ends of parchment over. Fold the parchment one or two more times to seal packet but leave space for steam to build.

1

2

3 Meanwhile, in a large nonstick skillet heat oil over medium heat. Add fish fillets; cook in hot oil until fish is golden and begins to flake when tested with a fork, turning once. Allow 4 to 6 minutes per ½-inch thickness. Drain on paper towels.

4 To serve, transfer fish to a serving platter. Drizzle glaze over fish. Sprinkle with sesame seeds.

PER FILLET: 181 cal., 5 g total fat (1 g sat. fat, 0 g trans fat), 46 mg chol., 968 mg sodium, 11 g carbo., 0 g fiber, 22 g pro. EXCHANGES: ½ Other Carbo., 3 Lean Meat, ½ Fat

FAST • LOW FAT • HEALTHY

BROILED TUNA WITH ROSEMARY

START TO FINISH: 20 MINUTES
MAKES: 4 SERVINGS

- 4 4-ounce fresh or frozen tuna or salmon steaks, cut ½ to 1 inch thick
- 2 teaspoons olive oil
- 2 teaspoons lemon juice
- ⅛ teaspoon salt
- ⅛ teaspoon black pepper
- 2 teaspoons snipped fresh rosemary or tarragon or 1 teaspoon dried rosemary or tarragon, crushed
- 2 cloves garlic, minced
- 1 tablespoon capers, rinsed and drained

1 Thaw fish, if frozen. Rinse fish; pat dry with paper towels. Measure thickness of fish. Brush fish with oil and lemon juice; sprinkle with salt and pepper. Sprinkle rosemary and garlic on fish; rub in with your fingers.

2 Preheat broiler. Place fish on the greased unheated rack of a broiler pan. Broil 4 inches from heat or until fish flakes easily when tested with a fork. Allow for 4 to 6 minutes per ½-inch thickness of fish, turning once if fish is 1 inch thick or more. Transfer fish to dinner plates; top with capers.

PER STEAK: 145 cal., 3 g total fat (1 g sat. fat, 0 g trans fat), 51 mg chol., 179 mg sodium, 1 g carbo., 0 g fiber, 27 g pro. EXCHANGES: 4 Lean Meat

CITRUS-MARINATED FISH

PREP: 25 MINUTES
COOK: 4 TO 6 MINUTES PER ½-INCH THICKNESS
MARINATE: 15 MINUTES **MAKES:** 4 SERVINGS

- 4 6- to 8-ounce fresh or frozen skinless salmon, swordfish, or halibut fillets, ¾ to 1 inch thick
- ¼ cup finely chopped green onions (2)
- ¼ cup lime or lemon juice
- 3 tablespoons snipped fresh cilantro, basil, or Italian parsley
- 2 tablespoons olive oil
- ½ teaspoon salt
- ½ teaspoon ground cumin
- ⅛ teaspoon cayenne pepper
- 2 cloves garlic, minced
   Lime or lemon wedges (optional)

1 Thaw fish, if frozen. Rinse fish; pat dry with paper towels. Measure thickness of fish. Place fish in a shallow dish; set aside. In a small bowl combine green onions, lime juice, 2 tablespoons of the cilantro, the olive oil, salt, cumin, cayenne pepper, and garlic. Pour half of the lime juice mixture over the fish; turn fish to coat. Marinate for 15 minutes. Set the remaining lime juice mixture aside.

2 Meanwhile, heat a lightly greased grill pan over medium-high heat. Transfer fish to the hot grill pan, allowing excess marinade to drip off fish. Discard any remaining marinade in dish. Cook until fish begins to flake when tested with a fork. Allow 4 to 6 minutes per ½-inch thickness of fish, turning once and brushing with reserved lime juice mixture halfway through cooking. Discard any remaining lime juice mixture. Sprinkle with the remaining 1 tablespoon cilantro. If desired, serve with lime wedges.

PER FILLET: 403 cal., 28 g total fat (6 g sat. fat, 0 g trans fat), 92 mg chol., 247 mg sodium, 2 g carbo., 0 g fiber, 35 g pro. EXCHANGES: 5 Lean Meat, 4 Fat

---

SERVING SIZES

USE THESE AMOUNTS AS A GUIDELINE FOR HOW MUCH FISH OR SHELLFISH TO PURCHASE PER PERSON.

- ■ 12 ounces to 1 pound whole fish
- ■ 8 ounces drawn or dressed fish
- ■ 4 to 5 ounces of steaks or fillets
- ■ 1 pound of live crabs
- ■ 3 to 4 ounces shelled shrimp
- ■ One 1- to 1½-pound whole lobster, one 8-ounce lobster tail, or 4 to 5 ounces cooked lobster meat

POACHED SALMON WITH CITRUS SALAD

START TO FINISH: 25 MINUTES
MAKES: 4 SERVINGS

- 4 4-ounce fresh or frozen skinless salmon, cod, or haddock fillets, about 1 inch thick
- 1 lime
- 6 oranges (navel, blood, Cara Cara) and/or tangerines
- ¼ cup olive oil
- 1 teaspoon sugar
  Salt and black pepper
- 2 tablespoons vegetable oil
- 6 wonton wrappers, cut into ½-inch strips
- 1 7-ounce bunch watercress, trimmed, or 4 cups arugula or baby spinach

1 Thaw fish, if frozen. Rinse fish; pat dry with paper towels. Finely shred 1 teaspoon peel from lime; set aside. Squeeze juice from the lime and 2 of the oranges; combine lime and orange juice. Measure ¼ cup juice for dressing and set aside. Pour the remaining juice into a large nonstick skillet; add ½ cup *water* and the lime peel. Bring to boiling. Add salmon; reduce heat to medium. Simmer, covered, for 8 to 12 minutes or until fish begins to flake when tested with a fork.

2 Meanwhile, for dressing, in a small bowl whisk together the reserved ¼ cup juice, olive oil, and sugar; season to taste with salt and pepper.

3 For wonton strips, in another large skillet heat oil over medium-high heat. Add wonton strips; cook about 1 to 2 minutes or until crisp, stirring often.

4 Peel and section or slice remaining oranges; arrange oranges, watercress, and salmon on dinner plates. Drizzle with dressing. Pass wonton strips.

PER FILLET + 1½ CUPS SALAD: 553 cal., 36 g total fat (6 g sat. fat, 0 g trans fat), 63 mg chol., 303 mg sodium, 32 g carbo., 5 g fiber, 27 g pro.
EXCHANGES: ½ Vegetable, 1½ Fruit, ½ Starch, 3½ Lean Meat, 5½ Fat

---

FLASH-FROZEN FISH
FISH THAT'S PROCESSED AND FROZEN IMMEDIATELY AFTER IT'S BEEN CAUGHT CAN OFFER TERRIFIC FLAVOR. LOOK FOR FLASH-FROZEN FISH IN VACUUM-SEALED PACKAGING.

WEEKNIGHT SALMON CAKES

PREP: 20 MINUTES **BROIL:** 14 MINUTES
MAKES: 4 SERVINGS

- 1 pound fresh or frozen skinless salmon fillet(s)
- ¾ cup soft bread crumbs
- 1 egg white
- ¼ cup thinly sliced green onions (2)
- 2 tablespoons chopped roasted red sweet pepper
- 1 tablespoon snipped fresh basil
- ¼ teaspoon salt
- ¼ cup mayonnaise
- ½ teaspoon smoked paprika or dash cayenne pepper
- ⅛ teaspoon black pepper

1 Thaw fish, if frozen. Rinse fish; pat dry with paper towels. In a food processor or blender combine half of the salmon, the bread crumbs, egg white, green onions, roasted pepper, basil, and salt. Process or blend until combined. Chop the remaining salmon into ½-inch pieces. In a medium bowl combine salmon mixture and chopped salmon (mixture will be soft). Shape salmon mixture into four ¾-inch-thick cakes.

2 Preheat broiler. Arrange cakes on a greased foil-lined baking sheet. Broil 4 to 5 inches from heat for 14 to 18 minutes or until done (160°F), turning once halfway through broiling time.

3 Meanwhile, in a small bowl combine mayonnaise, paprika, and black pepper. Serve salmon cakes with mayonnaise mixture.

GRILLING DIRECTIONS: For a charcoal grill, grill salmon cakes on the well-greased rack of an uncovered grill directly over medium coals for 14 to 18 minutes or until done (160°F), turning once. (For a gas grill, preheat grill. Reduce heat to medium. Place cakes on well-greased grill rack over heat. Cover; grill as directed.)

PER CAKE: 359 cal., 26 g total fat (5 g sat. fat, 0 g trans fat), 67 mg chol., 345 mg sodium, 4 g carbo., 1 g fiber, 25 g pro.
EXCHANGES: 3½ Lean Meat, 4½ Fat

SALMON BURGERS: Prepare salmon cakes and mayonnaise mixture as directed. Serve cakes on 4 whole wheat hamburger buns with mayonnaise mixture, shredded spinach, and/or sliced tomato.

PER BURGER: 475 cal., 27 g total fat (5 g sat. fat, 0 g trans fat), 67 mg chol., 562 mg sodium, 26 g carbo., 3 g fiber, 29 g pro.
EXCHANGES: ½ Vegetable, 1½ Starch, 3½ Lean Meat, 4 Fat

COOK ONCE, EAT TWICE

SAVOR FLAVORFUL ROASTED SALMON ONE NIGHT. THE NEXT, TOSS THE LEFTOVER SALMON WITH FETTUCCINE AND A CREAMY SAUCE FOR A QUICK ONE-DISH MEAL.

TONIGHT

SALMON WITH ROASTED TOMATOES AND SHALLOTS

PREP: 20 MINUTES **ROAST:** 30 MINUTES
OVEN: 400°F **MAKES:** 4 SERVINGS + RESERVES

- 2 pounds fresh or frozen salmon fillet(s), skinned if desired
- 3 cups grape tomatoes
- 2 shallots, thinly sliced
- 4 teaspoons snipped fresh oregano or 1 teaspoon dried oregano, crushed
- 1 tablespoon olive oil
- ½ teaspoon salt
- ½ teaspoon black pepper
- 4 cloves garlic, minced

1 Thaw fish, if frozen. Rinse fish; pat dry with paper towels. Preheat oven to 400°F. In a greased 13×9×2-inch baking pan, toss together tomatoes, shallots, oregano, olive oil, ¼ teaspoon of the salt, ¼ teaspoon of the pepper, and the garlic.

2 Roast, uncovered, for 15 minutes. Place fish, skin sides down, on top of tomato mixture. Sprinkle fish with remaining ¼ teaspoon salt and remaining ¼ teaspoon pepper. Roast, uncovered, for 15 to 18 minutes or until fish begins to flake when tested with a fork. Using two large pancake turners, transfer salmon to cutting board.

3 If desired, remove and discard skin. Reserve half of the cooked salmon for Salmon Pasta Toss.* Serve remaining salmon with tomato mixture.

*TO STORE: Place the reserved cooked salmon in an airtight container. Cover; store in the refrigerator up to 3 days or freeze up to 3 months.

PER 3 OUNCES SALMON + ¾ CUP TOMATO MIXTURE: 304 cal., 19 g total fat (4 g sat. fat, 0 g trans fat), 62 mg chol., 294 mg sodium, 9 g carbo., 2 g fiber, 25 g pro.
EXCHANGES: 1 Vegetable, 3 Lean Meat, 3 Fat

TOMORROW

SALMON PASTA TOSS

START TO FINISH: 25 MINUTES
MAKES: 6 SERVINGS

- 1 0.5-ounce envelope pesto mix
- 3 tablespoons olive oil
- 12 ounces dried fettuccine
- 1 16-ounce jar dried-tomato Alfredo sauce
- 1 14.5-ounce can diced tomatoes with basil, oregano, and garlic, undrained
- 1 7-ounce jar roasted red sweet peppers, drained and coarsely chopped (1 cup)
- ½ cup finely shredded Parmesan cheese (2 ounces)
- ⅓ cup milk
- ½ of the cooked salmon from Salmon with Roasted Tomatoes and Shallots

1 In a small bowl stir together pesto mix and olive oil; set aside.

2 Meanwhile, in a large pot cook fettuccine according to package directions. Drain well; return to pot. Stir in pesto mixture, Alfredo sauce, undrained tomatoes, sweet pepper, ¼ cup of the Parmesan cheese, and the milk. Heat through.

3 Break salmon into large chunks; gently fold into pasta mixture. Heat through. Transfer to a serving bowl. Sprinkle with the ¼ cup remaining Parmesan cheese.

PER 1½ CUPS: 561 cal., 24 g total fat (6 g sat. fat, 0 g trans fat), 59 mg chol., 1,166 mg sodium, 56 g carbo., 3 g fiber, 29 g pro.
EXCHANGES: 1 Vegetable, 3½ Starch, 2½ Lean Meat, 2 Fat

SALMON-VEGETABLE BAKE

PREP: 30 MINUTES **BAKE:** 30 MINUTES
OVEN: 350°F **MAKES:** 4 SERVINGS

  1 pound fresh or frozen skinless salmon,
       cod, or arctic char fillets, about ¾ inch
       thick
  2 cups thinly sliced carrots (4 medium)
  2 cups sliced fresh mushrooms
  ½ cup sliced green onions (4)
  2 teaspoons finely shredded orange peel
  1 tablespoon snipped fresh oregano or
       1 teaspoon dried oregano, crushed
  ¼ teaspoon salt
  ¼ teaspoon black pepper
  4 cloves garlic, halved
  4 teaspoons olive oil
       Salt and black pepper
  2 medium oranges, thinly sliced
  4 sprigs fresh oregano (optional)

1 Thaw fish, if frozen. Rinse fish; pat dry with
paper towels. Cut into four serving-size pieces,
if necessary; set aside. In a small saucepan cook
carrots, covered, in a small amount of boiling
water for 2 minutes. Drain and set aside. Tear off
four 24-inch pieces of 18-inch-wide heavy foil.
Fold each in half to make four 18×12-inch pieces.

2 In a large bowl combine carrots, mushrooms,
green onions, orange peel, oregano, the
¼ teaspoon salt, the ¼ teaspoon pepper, and
garlic; toss gently.

3 Preheat oven to 350°F. Divide vegetables
among the four pieces of foil, placing vegetables
in center of each piece. Place one fish piece on top
of each vegetable portion. Drizzle 1 teaspoon of
the oil over each fish piece. Sprinkle lightly with
additional salt and pepper; top with orange slices.
Bring together two opposite foil edges and seal
with a double fold. Fold remaining edges together
to completely enclose the food, allowing space for
steam to build. Place the foil packets in a single
layer in a 15×10×1-inch baking pan.

4 Bake about 30 minutes or until carrots are
tender and fish begins to flake when tested with
a fork (open a packet to check doneness). Open
packets carefully to allow steam to escape. To
serve, transfer the packets to dinner plates. If
desired, garnish with fresh oregano sprigs.

PER FILLET: 351 cal., 20 g total fat (4 g sat. fat, 0 g trans fat),
62 mg chol., 405 mg sodium, 18 g carbo., 4 g fiber, 26 g pro.
EXCHANGES: 1 Vegetable, ½ Fruit, 3½ Lean Meat, 3½ Fat

GREEK LEEKS AND SHRIMP STIR-FRY

START TO FINISH: 30 MINUTES
MAKES: 4 SERVINGS

  1¼ pounds fresh or frozen peeled, deveined
         medium shrimp (see tip, page 433)
  ⅓   cup lemon juice
  1   tablespoon cornstarch
  ¾   teaspoon bouquet garni seasoning or
         dried oregano, crushed
  1   cup couscous
  ½   teaspoon dried oregano, crushed
  ¼   teaspoon salt
  1   tablespoon olive oil
  1⅓ cups thinly sliced leeks
  ½   cup crumbled feta cheese (2 ounces)

1 Thaw shrimp, if frozen. Rinse shrimp and pat
dry with paper towels; set aside.

2 In a small bowl combine ⅔ cup *water,* the
lemon juice, cornstarch, and ¼ teaspoon of the
bouquet garni seasoning; set aside.

3 In a small bowl combine couscous, oregano,
salt, and the remaining ½ teaspoon bouquet garni
seasoning. Pour 1½ cups boiling water over
couscous. Cover and let stand for 5 minutes.

4 Meanwhile, in a wok or very large skillet heat
oil over medium-high heat. Add leeks; cook and stir
for 2 to 3 minutes or until tender. Remove leeks
from wok; set aside. Stir lemon juice mixture; add
to wok. Bring to boiling. Add shrimp; cook for
2 to 3 minutes or until shrimp are opaque. Stir in
cooked leeks and ¼ cup of the feta cheese.

5 To serve, fluff couscous mixture with a fork.
Transfer couscous mixture to a serving platter.
Spoon shrimp mixture over couscous; sprinkle
with the remaining ¼ cup feta cheese.

PER 1 CUP SHRIMP MIXTURE + ½ CUP COUSCOUS:
433 cal., 10 g total fat (4 g sat. fat, 0 g trans fat), 232 mg chol.,
548 mg sodium, 45 g carbo., 3 g fiber, 38 g pro.
EXCHANGES: 3 Starch, 4 Lean Meat

NO LEEKS? NO PROBLEM.
IN A PINCH, SUBSTITUTE ¾ CUP
CHOPPED YELLOW ONION AND
¼ CUP SLICED GREEN ONIONS
FOR THE LEEKS CALLED FOR IN
THE ABOVE RECIPE.

SALMON-VEGETABLE BAKE

THE OTHER PINK FISH ARCTIC CHAR IS A GOOD STAND-IN FOR SALMON. PALE ORANGE-PINK TO BRIGHT RED IN COLOR, CHAR BOASTS A FLAVOR THAT'S SIMILAR TO A CROSS BETWEEN TROUT AND SALMON.

GREEK LEEKS AND SHRIMP STIR-FRY

SHRIMP SCAMPI

START TO FINISH: 20 MINUTES
MAKES: 4 SERVINGS

  1½ pounds fresh or frozen large shrimp
    8 ounces dried angel hair pasta
    ¼ cup butter, melted
    ¼ cup olive oil
    6 cloves garlic, minced
    ¼ teaspoon salt
    ⅛ teaspoon crushed red pepper
    2 tablespoons snipped fresh parsley
    1 teaspoon finely shredded lemon peel
      Lemon wedges (optional)

1 Thaw shrimp, if frozen. Peel and devein shrimp, leaving the tails intact if desired (see photo, page 433). Rinse shrimp; pat dry with paper towels; set shrimp aside.

2 In a large pot cook pasta according to package directions; drain. Return pasta to pot.

3 Meanwhile, in a large skillet heat butter, olive oil, and garlic over medium-high heat. Add shrimp, salt, and crushed red pepper to skillet. Cook and stir about 3 minutes or until shrimp are opaque. Stir in parsley and lemon peel. Add shrimp mixture to pasta in pot; toss to combine. If desired, serve shrimp mixture with lemon wedges.

PER 1¾ CUPS: 574 cal., 28 g total fat (10 g sat. fat, 0 g trans fat), 224 mg chol., 390 mg sodium, 45 g carbo., 1 g fiber, 33 g pro. EXCHANGES: 3 Starch, 3½ Lean Meat, 4 Fat

BOILED LOBSTER

PREP: 15 MINUTES **COOK:** 15 MINUTES
MAKES: 2 SERVINGS

    8 quarts water
    ½ cup coarse kosher salt or salt
    2 1- to 1½-pound live lobsters
    1 recipe Clarified Butter

1 In a 20-quart or larger kettle bring water and salt to boiling. Grasp lobsters just behind the eyes; rinse under cold running water. Quickly plunge lobsters head first into the boiling water. Cover and return to boiling. Boil for 15 minutes adjusting heat as necessary to maintain a steady boil. Drain lobsters; remove any bands on large claws.

2 When cool enough to handle, place each lobster on its back. Separate the tail from the body (see photo 1, below). Cut through tail membrane to expose meat (see photo 2, below). Remove and discard the black vein running through tail. Remove meat from tail. Twist large claws away from body (see photo 3, page 327). Using a nutcracker, break open claws (see photo 4, page 327). Remove meat from the claws. Crack the shell on remaining part of the body; remove meat with a small fork. Discard the green tomalley (liver) and the coral roe (found in female lobsters). Serve with Clarified Butter.

CLARIFIED BUTTER: Melt ¼ cup butter over very low heat without stirring; cool slightly. Strain through sieve lined with 100-percent-cotton cheesecloth (see photo 5, page 327).

PER LOBSTER + 2 TABLESPOONS BUTTER: 293 cal., 24 g total fat (15 g sat. fat, 0 g trans fat), 156 mg chol., 2,343 mg sodium, 1 g carbo., 0 g fiber, 19 g pro. EXCHANGES: 3 Lean Meat, 3½ Fat

REMOVING MEAT FROM LOBSTER, STEP-BY-STEP

1. Remove the tail by twisting the tail and body in opposite directions. **2.** Cut the membrane from the tail to expose the meat. **3.** Twist the large claws where they join the body to remove them. **4.** Break open the large claws with a nutcracker. **5.** For clarified butter, pour melted butter through a sieve lined with several layers of cheesecloth to strain out the milky white solids.

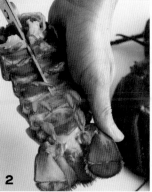

LOBSTER TAILS WITH CHILI BUTTER

PREP: 15 MINUTES **BROIL:** 12 MINUTES
MAKES: 4 SERVINGS

- 4 8-ounce fresh or frozen lobster tails
- ¼ cup butter
- 1 teaspoon finely shredded orange peel
- ½ teaspoon chili powder
- 1 clove garlic, minced
- 2 recipes Clarified Butter (page 326) (optional)

1 Thaw lobster tails, if frozen. Preheat broiler. Butterfly lobster tails by using kitchen shears to cut lengthwise through centers of hard top shells and meat, cutting to but not through bottoms of shells. Spread halves of tails apart. Place tails, meat sides up, on unheated rack of a broiler pan.

2 In saucepan melt butter. Add orange peel, chili powder, and garlic; heat 30 seconds or until garlic is tender. Brush over lobster meat. Broil 4 inches from heat for 12 to 14 minutes or until lobster is opaque. If desired, serve with Clarified Butter.

LOBSTER TAILS WITH LEMON-CHIVE BUTTER: Prepare as directed, except use lemon peel for orange peel. Omit chili powder and garlic. Stir in 2 tablespoons snipped fresh chives with butter.

LOBSTER TAILS WITH BASIL BUTTER: Prepare as directed, except omit orange peel and chili powder. Stir in 2 tablespoons snipped fresh basil after cooking garlic.

PER TAIL WITH CHILI, LEMON-CHIVE, OR BASIL BUTTER VARIATIONS: 149 cal., 12 g total fat (7 g sat. fat, 0 g trans fat), 78 mg chol., 211 mg sodium, 1 g carbo., 0 g fiber, 10 g pro.
EXCHANGES: 1½ Lean Meat, 2 Fat

SCALLOPS WITH DILL SAUCE

PREP: 20 MINUTES **BROIL:** 8 MINUTES
MAKES: 4 SERVINGS

- 1 pound fresh or frozen sea scallops
- 3 tablespoons butter, melted
- ¼ teaspoon black pepper
- ⅛ teaspoon paprika
- 1 recipe Dill Sauce
  Lemon wedges (optional)

1 Thaw scallops, if frozen. Rinse scallops; pat dry with paper towels. Halve any large scallops. Thread scallops onto four 8- to 10-inch skewers, leaving a ¼-inch space between pieces. Preheat broiler. Place skewers on the greased unheated rack of a broiler pan.

2 In a small bowl stir together melted butter, pepper, and paprika. Brush half of the butter mixture over scallops. Broil about 4 inches from the heat for 8 to 10 minutes or until scallops are opaque, turning and brushing with the remaining butter mixture halfway through broiling.

3 Serve scallops with Dill Sauce and, if desired, lemon wedges.

DILL SAUCE: In a small bowl stir together ⅔ cup mayonnaise, 1 tablespoon finely chopped onion, 2 teaspoons lemon juice, and 1½ teaspoons snipped fresh dill or ½ teaspoon dried dillweed.

PER KABOB + 3 TABLESPOONS SAUCE: 446 cal., 39 g total fat (11 g sat. fat, 0 g trans fat), 74 mg chol., 418 mg sodium, 3 g carbo., 0 g fiber, 19 g pro.
EXCHANGES: 3 Lean Meat, 7 Fat

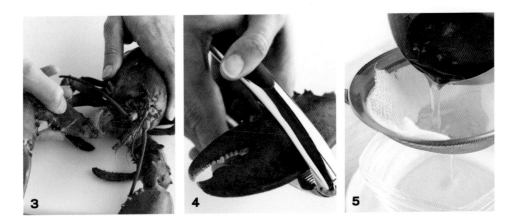

SEARED SCALLOPS WITH GINGER SAUCE

START TO FINISH: 15 MINUTES
MAKES: 4 SERVINGS

- 1 pound fresh or frozen sea scallops
- 4 teaspoons butter
- ⅓ cup chicken broth
- ¼ cup frozen pineapple-orange juice concentrate, thawed
- 1 teaspoon grated fresh ginger

1 Thaw scallops, if frozen. Rinse scallops; pat dry with paper towels. In a large skillet melt butter over medium-high heat. Add scallops to skillet. Cook for 2 to 3 minutes or until scallops are opaque, stirring frequently. Remove scallops from skillet; keep warm.

2 For sauce, add chicken broth, juice concentrate, and ginger to skillet. Bring to boiling. Boil, uncovered, until sauce is reduced by about half. Spoon over scallops.

PER 3 OUNCES SCALLOPS + 1 TABLESPOON SAUCE: 168 cal., 5 g total fat (3 g sat. fat, 0 g trans fat), 48 mg chol., 262 mg sodium, 11 g carbo., 0 g fiber, 19 g pro. EXCHANGES: ½ Fruit, 3 Lean Meat

OYSTERS AU GRATIN

PREP: 30 MINUTES **BAKE:** 10 MINUTES
OVEN: 400°F **MAKES:** 4 SERVINGS

- 2 pints shucked oysters (page 330)
- 3 tablespoons butter
- 1 cup sliced fresh mushrooms
- 1 clove garlic, minced
- 2 tablespoons all-purpose flour
- ¾ cup milk
- ¼ cup dry white wine
- 2 tablespoons snipped fresh parsley
- ½ teaspoon Worcestershire sauce
- 1 cup soft bread crumbs
- ¼ cup grated Parmesan cheese
- 1 tablespoon butter, melted

1 Preheat oven to 400°F. Rinse oysters; pat dry with paper towels. In a large skillet melt 1 tablespoon of the butter over medium heat. Add oysters; cook and stir for 3 to 4 minutes or until oyster edges curl; drain. Spread oysters in a 1- to 1½-quart au gratin dish.

2 For sauce, in the same skillet melt the remaining 2 tablespoons butter over medium heat. Add mushrooms and garlic; cook until tender. Stir in flour. Add milk all at once. Cook and stir until thickened and bubbly. Stir in wine, parsley, and Worcestershire sauce. Spoon over oysters. In a small bowl toss together bread crumbs, Parmesan cheese, and 1 tablespoon melted butter. Sprinkle over oyster mixture. Bake about 10 minutes or until crumbs are golden brown.

PER 1 CUP: 478 cal., 26 g total fat (11 g sat. fat, 0 g trans fat), 216 mg chol., 793 mg sodium, 23 g carbo., 1 g fiber, 33 g pro. EXCHANGES: 1½ Starch, 4 Lean Meat, 4 Fat

CRAB CAKES

PREP: 40 MINUTES **COOK:** 6 MINUTES PER BATCH
CHILL: 60 MINUTES **MAKES:** 4 SERVINGS

- 2 tablespoons chopped green onion (1)
- 1 tablespoon butter
- 1 tablespoon all-purpose flour
- ¼ teaspoon seafood seasoning
- ⅛ teaspoon black pepper
- ½ cup milk
- 1 6- to 8-ounce package frozen lump crabmeat, thawed, or one 6-ounce can crabmeat, drained, flaked, and cartilage removed
- 2 tablespoons panko (Japanese-style bread crumbs) or fine dry bread crumbs
- ¼ cup all-purpose flour
- 1 egg
- 1 teaspoon water
- ¾ cup panko (Japanese-style bread crumbs) or fine dry bread crumbs
- 2 tablespoons vegetable oil
- ¼ cup Mustard Chutney

1 In a small saucepan cook onion in hot butter until tender. Stir in the 1 tablespoon flour, seafood seasoning, and pepper. Add milk all at once. Cook and stir until thickened and bubbly. Transfer to a medium bowl. Cover and chill about 60 minutes or until cold.

2 Stir crabmeat and the 2 tablespoons panko into chilled sauce. Place the ¼ cup flour in a shallow dish. In a second shallow dish beat together egg and water. Place the ¾ cup panko in a third shallow dish.

3 Form about 2 tablespoons of the crab mixture into a small patty. Dip patty into flour. Carefully turn to coat. Dip in egg mixture, then in bread crumbs. Set on a sheet of waxed paper. Repeat with remaining crab mixture, flour, egg mixture, and crumbs.

4 In a large skillet heat oil over medium heat. Add crab cakes, half at a time. Cook about 3 minutes on each side or until golden brown and heated through. Serve with Mustard Chutney.

MUSTARD CHUTNEY: Stir together ½ cup purchased chutney (snip any large pieces), 1½ teaspoons Dijon-style mustard, and 1 teaspoon lemon juice. Cover and chill leftovers.

PER 2 CAKES AND 1 TABLESPOON CHUTNEY: 328 cal., 13 g total fat (3 g sat. fat, 0 g trans fat), 85 mg chol., 849 mg sodium, 36 g carbo., 1 g fiber, 14 g pro. EXCHANGES: 1½ Starch, 1 Other Carbo., 1½ Lean Meat, 2 Fat

FAST • LOW FAT

STEAMED CRAB LEGS

START TO FINISH: 15 MINUTES
MAKES: 4 SERVINGS

- 4 4- to 8-ounce fresh or frozen crab legs (see photo 1, below)
- ¼ cup butter, melted
- 1 tablespoon snipped fresh basil or fresh Italian parsley
- ½ teaspoon finely shredded lemon peel
- 1 tablespoon lemon juice

1 Thaw crab legs, if frozen. Place crab legs in a steamer basket in a very large skillet. If necessary, bend crab legs at joints to fit in steamer basket (see photo 2, below). Add water to skillet to just below the basket. Bring to boiling. Cover; steam for 5 to 6 minutes or until heated through.

2 For butter sauce, stir together butter, basil, lemon peel, and lemon juice.

3 To remove the meat, twist legs at joints (see photo 3, below) or split shell using kitchen shears (see photo 4, below). Peel back shell (see photo 5, below); remove meat. Serve with butter sauce.

BOILED CRAB LEGS: Thaw crab legs, if frozen. Place crab legs in a large pot of boiling salted water. Return to boiling. Cook, uncovered, for 4 to 5 minutes or until heated through.

PER 4 OUNCES MEAT: 157 cal., 12 g total fat (7 g sat. fat, 0 g trans fat), 58 mg chol., 622 mg sodium, 0 g carbo., 0 g fiber, 12 g pro. EXCHANGES: 2 Lean Meat, 1½ Fat

STEAMING AND CRACKING CRAB LEGS, STEP-BY-STEP

1. Crab legs range in size from 4 to 8 ounces. **2.** Bend the legs at the joints to fit in the steamer basket. Steam until heated through. **3.** To remove the meat, twist the legs at the joint. Often you can pull the meat from the shell as you twist. **4.** You can also use kitchen shears to cut through the shell. **5.** Pull the shell apart. Use a seafood fork to remove the meat.

PREPARING AND COOKING SHELLFISH

When you purchase shellfish at its top-quality best, you don't have to do a lot to make it taste great—simply follow these guidelines. If you like, serve with one of the sauces on pages 538-543.

Shellfish Type	Amount Per Serving	Preparing	Cooking
Clams	6 clams in the shell	Scrub live clams under cold running water. For 24 clams in shells, in an 8-quart pot combine 4 quarts cold water and ⅓ cup salt. Add clams and soak for 15 minutes; drain and rinse. Discard water. Repeat.	For 24 clams in shells, add ½ inch water to an 8-quart pot; bring to boiling. Place clams in a steamer basket. Steam, covered, for 5 to 7 minutes or until clams open. Discard any that do not open.
Crabs, hard-shell	1 pound live crabs	Grasp live crabs from behind, firmly holding the back two legs on each side. Rinse under cold running water.	To boil 3 pounds live hard-shell blue crabs, in a 12- to 16-quart pot bring 8 quarts water and 2 teaspoons salt to boiling. Add crabs. Simmer, covered, for 10 minutes or until crabs turn pink; drain. (To crack and clean a crab, see page 331.)
Crawfish	1 pound live crawfish	Rinse live crawfish under cold running water. For 4 pounds crawfish, in a 12- to 16-quart pot combine 8 quarts cold water and ⅓ cup salt. Add crawfish. Soak for 15 minutes; rinse and drain.	For 4 pounds live crawfish, in a 12- to 16-quart pot bring 8 quarts water and 2 teaspoons salt to boiling. Add crawfish. Simmer, covered, 5 to 8 minutes or until shells turn red; drain.
Lobster tails (To boil a live lobster, see page 326.)	One 8-ounce frozen lobster tail	Thaw frozen lobster tails in the refrigerator.	For four 8-ounce lobster tails, in a 3-quart saucepan bring 6 cups water and 1½ teaspoons salt to boiling; add tails. Simmer, uncovered, for 8 to 12 minutes or until shells turn bright red and meat is tender; drain.
Mussels	12 mussels in shells	Scrub live mussels under cold running water. Using your fingers, pull out the beards that are visible between the shells. For 24 mussels, soak as for clams, above.	For 24 mussels, add ½ inch water to an 8-quart pot; bring to boiling. Place mussels in a steamer basket. Steam, covered, for 5 to 7 minutes or until shells open. Discard any that do not open.
Oysters	6 oysters in shells	Scrub live oysters under cold running water. For easier shucking, chill. To shuck, hold oyster in heavy towel or mitt. Carefully insert oyster knife tip into hinge between shells. Move blade along inside of upper shell to free muscle; twist knife to pry shell open. Slide knife under oyster to cut muscle from bottom shell.	For 2 pints shucked oysters, rinse oysters; pat dry with paper towels. In large skillet cook and stir oysters in 1 tablespoon hot butter over medium heat for 3 to 4 minutes or until oyster edges curl; drain.
Shrimp	6 ounces shrimp in shells or 3 to 4 ounces peeled, deveined shrimp	To peel, open shell down the underside. Starting at head end, pull back the shell. Gently pull on the tail to remove. Use a sharp knife to remove the black vein that runs along center of back. Rinse under cold running water.	For 1 pound shrimp, in a 3-quart saucepan bring 4 cups water and 1 teaspoon salt to a boil. Add shrimp. Simmer, uncovered, 1 to 3 minutes or until shrimp turn opaque, stirring occasionally. Rinse under cold running water, drain, and chill (if desired).

CRACKING AND CLEANING COOKED CRAB

As any crab lover will tell you, the reward of cracking and cleaning hard-shell crabs, such as the Atlantic blue crab or the Pacific Dungeness (shown below), is well worth the effort. Follow these steps to get every last morsel of the rich, sweet-tasting meat, which is amazing simply dipped in butter. Or chill the meat and use it as an opulent extra in anything from salads and gazpacho to deviled eggs.

1. Turn the cooked, cooled crab on its back. Using your thumb, fold back the tail flap (apron), twist off, and discard.

3. Discard the crab's internal organs, mouth, and appendages at the front; rinse crab. Using a small knife, remove the spongy gills from each side of the top of the crab.

2. Holding the crab with the top shell in one hand, grasp the bottom shell at the point where the apron was removed. Pull the top shell away from the body of the crab and discard.

4. Twist off the claws and legs. Use a nutcracker to crack each joint; pick out the meat. Cut the crab body into quarters. Use a small fork to remove the meat.

COOKING FISH

Minutes count when cooking fish. To best estimate minimum cooking time, weigh dressed fish or use a ruler to measure the thickness of fillets and steaks before cooking. Properly cooked fish is opaque, flakes when tested with a fork, and comes away from the bones readily; the juices should be a milky white. If you like, serve with one of the sauces on page 538–543.

Cooking Method	Preparation	Fresh or Thawed Fillets or Steaks	Dressed
Bake	Place in a single layer in a greased shallow baking pan. For fillets, tuck under any thin edges. Brush with olive oil or melted butter.	Bake, uncovered, in a 450°F oven for 4 to 6 minutes per ½-inch thickness fish.	Bake, uncovered, in a 350°F oven for 6 to 9 minutes per 8 ounces.
Broil	Preheat broiler. Place fish on greased unheated rack of a broiler pan. For fillets, tuck under any thin edges. Brush with olive oil or melted butter.	Broil 4 inches from the heat for 4 to 6 minutes per ½-inch thickness. If fish is 1 inch or more thick, turn once halfway through broiling time.	Not recommended.
Grill	See Direct-Grilling and Indirect-Grilling Fish charts, page 375.		
Microwave	Arrange fish in a single layer in a shallow baking dish. For fillets, tuck under any thin edges. Cover with vented plastic wrap.	Cook on 100% power (high). For 8 ounces of ½-inch-thick fillets, allow 1½ to 2 minutes. For 1 pound of ½-inch-thick fillets, allow 2½ to 4 minutes. For 1 pound of ¾- to 1-inch-thick steaks, allow 3 to 5 minutes.	Not recommended.
Poach	Add 1½ cups water, broth, or wine to a large skillet. Bring to boiling. Add fish. Return to boiling; reduce heat.	Simmer, uncovered, for 4 to 6 minutes per ½-inch thickness.	Simmer, covered, for 6 to 9 minutes per 8 ounces.

GUIDE TO FISH TYPES

There are many fish in the sea—as well as in lakes and rivers—and they range greatly in flavor and texture. This chart describes the varieties that most often make their way to the market and offers appropriate substitutes for when you can't find a fish that's called for in a recipe.

Types	Market Forms	Texture	Flavor	Substitutions
FRESHWATER FISH				
Catfish	Whole, fillets, steaks	Firm	Mild	Grouper, rockfish, sea bass, tilapia
Lake trout (North American char)	Whole, fillets, steaks	Slightly firm	Moderate	Pike, sea trout, whitefish
Rainbow trout	Fillets	Slightly firm	Delicate	Salmon, sea trout
Tilapia	Whole, dressed, fillets	Slightly firm	Delicate	Catfish, flounder, orange roughy
Whitefish	Whole, fillets	Moderately firm	Delicate	Cod, lake trout, salmon, sea bass
SALTWATER FISH				
Atlantic ocean perch (redfish)	Whole, fillets	Slightly firm	Mild	Orange roughy, rockfish, snapper
Cod	Fillets, steaks	Moderately firm	Delicate	Flounder, haddock, pollack
Flounder	Whole, fillets	Fine	Delicate to mild	Cod, orange roughy, sea trout, sole, whitefish, whiting
Grouper	Whole, dressed, fillets	Moderately firm	Mild	Mahi mahi, sea bass
Haddock	Fillets	Moderately firm	Delicate	Cod, grouper, halibut, lake trout, sole, whitefish, whiting
Halibut	Fillets, steaks	Firm	Delicate	Cod, grouper, red snapper, sea bass
Mackerel	Whole	Delicate	Pronounced	Mahi mahi, swordfish, tuna
Mahi mahi (dolphinfish)	Whole, fillets	Firm	Mild to moderate	Grouper, orange roughy, red snapper
Orange roughy	Fillets	Moderately firm	Delicate	Cod, flounder, haddock, ocean perch, sea bass, sole
Red snapper	Whole, fillets	Moderately firm	Mild to moderate	Grouper, lake trout, ocean perch, rockfish, whitefish
Rockfish	Whole, fillets	Slightly firm	Mild to moderate	Cod, grouper, ocean perch, red snapper
Salmon	Whole, fillets, steaks	Moderately firm	Mild to moderate	Rainbow trout, swordfish, tuna, arctic char
Shark (mako)	Fillets, steaks	Firm, dense	Moderate	Swordfish, tuna
Sole	Fillets	Fine	Delicate	Flounder, haddock, halibut, pollack
Swordfish	Loins, steaks	Firm, dense	Mild to moderate	Halibut, shark, tuna
Tuna	Loins, steaks	Firm	Mild to moderate	Mackerel, salmon, shark, swordfish

GRILLING

KANSAS CITY PORK SPARERIBS, PAGE 350

GRILLING

NO SECRET HANDSHAKES ARE
NEEDED TO JOIN THE CLUB OF
EXPERT GRILLERS. HERE'S WHAT
YOU REALLY NEED TO KNOW.

The instructions here and on page 336 are for
grilling using charcoal and gas grills. To learn about
smoking, see page 361. For information on using
a turkey fryer, turn to page 365.

DIRECT VERSUS INDIRECT COOKING

Choose direct or indirect cooking depending on
the foods you plan to cook.

DIRECT COOKING: This method works best for
foods that cook in 30 minutes or less; these
include tender, thin, and small foods such as
burgers, steaks, chops, boneless chicken pieces,
brats or frankfurters, and vegetables. With direct
cooking, food cooks on the grill rack directly
over the heat sources, with or without the grill lid
closed (check the grill manufacturer's directions).
For even cooking, turn foods only once during the
cooking time.

INDIRECT COOKING: Recommended for large
roasts, ribs, whole birds, and whole fish, this method positions the food on the grill rack away from
or to the side of the heat source, with grill cover
closed. Heat inside the grill reflects off the lid and
other interior surfaces, cooking the food from all
sides and eliminating the need to turn the food.

COOKING WITH GAS

Gas grills are clean, convenient, and easy to control.

■ To light a gas grill, open the lid. Turn the gas
valve to "on" and ignite grill as directed by the
manufacturer. Turn burners on high. Close the lid
and preheat the grill (usually with all burners on
high for 10 to 15 minutes).

■ For indirect-cooking method, turn off burners
directly below where you place the food. Adjust
burner controls to needed temperature.

GRILLING WITH A CHARCOAL GRILL

Charcoal grills require more work than gas grills,
but their fans love the smoky flavors they bring
to food. Here's how to handle one.

■ About 25 to 30 minutes prior to cooking,
remove the grill cover and rack and open all vents.

■ For direct cooking, use enough briquettes
to cover the charcoal grate completely with one
layer. Pile these briquettes into a pyramid in the
center of the grate.

■ For indirect cooking, the number of briquettes
you need to use is based on your grill size. Refer to
the following chart.

SETUP FOR INDIRECT COOKING

Grill diameter in inches	Briquettes needed to start	Briquettes to add for longer cooking
26 ¾	60	18
22 ½	50	16
18 ½	32	10

■ Apply fire starter, use an electric starter, or
place briquettes in a chimney starter. (If using a
liquid starter, wait 1 minute before igniting fire.)
Let the fire burn for 25 to 30 minutes or until the
coals are covered with a light coating of gray ash.

■ For direct cooking, use long-handled tongs to
spread coals evenly across the bottom of the grill,
covering an area 3 inches larger on all sides of the
food you are cooking.

■ For indirect cooking, arrange coals to one side
of the grill; place the drip pan on the other side. Or
place the drip pan in the center; arrange the coals
into two equal piles on two sides of the pan.

■ Install grill rack and check temperature of coals
using a built-in or separate flat grill thermometer.
Or use the hand test (see chart, page 336).

HAND TEST

To judge how hot your grill is, carefully place the palm of your hand just above the grill rack and count the number of seconds you can hold it in that position. (For example, "One, I love grilling; two, I love grilling," and so on.) Note that when grilling indirectly, hot coals will provide medium-hot heat and medium-hot coals will provide medium heat.

Time	Thermometer	Temperature	Visual
2 seconds	400°F to 450°F	Hot (high)	Coals glowing and lightly covered with gray ash
3 seconds	375°F to 400°F	Medium-high	
4 seconds	350°F to 375°F	Medium	Coals glowing through a layer of ash
5 seconds	325°F to 350°F	Medium-low	
6 seconds	300°F to 325°F	Low	Coals burning down and covered with thick layer of ash

ADJUSTING THE HEAT

Weather conditions can affect the coal temperature, and not everyone judges coal temperature alike. Therefore, use timings given with each recipe as a guideline and watch all foods on the grill closely. Here's what to do when the temperature isn't quite right.

CHARCOAL GRILLS: If the coals are too hot, raise the grill rack, spread the coals apart, close the air vents halfway, or remove some briquettes. If the coals are too cool, use long-handled tongs to tap ashes off the burning coals, move coals together, add briquettes, lower the rack, or open vents.

GAS OR ELECTRIC GRILLS: Adjust burners to higher or lower settings as needed.

SAFETY PRECAUTIONS

Because grilling is cooking with fire, it requires its own set of safety rules.

■ Use charcoal or gas grills outside only—never in a garage, porch, or enclosed area.

■ Don't use lighter fluid, an electric starter, or a chimney starter with instant-lighting briquettes.

■ Never leave a grill unattended or try to move it while it's in use or still hot.

■ Periodically test your gas grill for leaks and clean the venturi tubes regularly according to the manufacturer's directions.

■ Allow coals to burn completely and ashes to cool for 24 hours before disposing of them.

■ Let the grill cool completely before covering or storing it.

REINING IN THOSE FLARE-UPS

Fat and meat juices dripping onto the source of the heat can cause flare-ups, making your meat taste charred. Here's how to handle or avoid them.

■ On a charcoal grill, raise the grill rack, cover the grill, space the hot coals farther apart, or remove a few coals. As a last resort, remove food from grill and mist the fire with water from a spray bottle. When the flame subsides, return food to the grill.

■ To prevent flare-ups on a gas grill, clean after each use as directed below.

KEEP IT CLEAN

For best results, clean your grill after each use.

CLEANING CHARCOAL GRILLS: Let the coals die down and the grill rack cool slightly. Brush off any debris using a brass-bristle grill brush or crumpled aluminum foil. For a more thorough cleaning, wash the grill rack using mild soap and a steel wool pad.

CLEANING GAS GRILLS: Burn off any residue by covering the grill and turning the grill on high until smoke subsides (about 10 to 15 minutes). Turn it off and allow it to cool slightly; brush the grill rack with a brass-bristle grill brush or crumpled aluminum foil.

MAKE-IT-MINE BURGERS

SIZZLE UP ALL KINDS OF BURGERS, FROM SATISFYINGLY STRAIGHTFORWARD TO DASHINGLY EXOTIC. AND THERE'S NO NEED TO WAIT FOR GRILLING SEASON THANKS TO THE BROILING INSTRUCTIONS BELOW.

BASIC INGREDIENTS

Meat
Liquid (optional)
Seasoning
⅓ to ½ cup Stuffing (optional)
Bread
Spread* and/or Toppers**
(optional)

MEAT (PICK ONE)

1½ pounds ground beef
1½ pounds ground pork
1½ pounds ground lamb
1 pound ground beef plus
   8 ounces ground Italian
   sausage
1½ pounds ground turkey
   (use a Liquid; brush
   burgers lightly with
   vegetable oil before
   grilling; cook turkey
   burgers to 165°F)

LIQUID (PICK ONE)

2 tablespoons apricot
   preserves (snip large
   pieces)
2 tablespoons barbecue
   sauce
2 tablespoons chutney
   (snip large pieces)
1 egg, lightly beaten
1 egg white, lightly beaten
2 tablespoons milk
2 tablespoons steak sauce

SEASONING (PICK ONE)

½ teaspoon dried basil,
   crushed
1 teaspoon chili powder
2 cloves garlic, minced
2 tablespoons finely
   chopped onion
½ teaspoon salt plus
   ¼ teaspoon black
   pepper
1 teaspoon steak
   seasoning
2 teaspoons
   Worcestershire sauce
   or soy sauce

STUFFING (PICK ONE)

Crisp-cooked, crumbled bacon
Crumbed feta or blue cheese
Shredded provolone,
   mozzarella, smoked cheddar,
   cheddar, or Monterey Jack
   cheese
Cooked sliced fresh mushrooms
Chopped roasted red sweet
   peppers

BREAD (PICK ONE)

4 kaiser rolls, split
4 onion rolls, split
4 white or whole wheat
   hamburger buns
2 white or whole wheat
   pita bread rounds,
   halved

BASIC INSTRUCTIONS

1 Combine Meat, Liquid (if desired), and Seasoning; mix well. Shape meat mixture into four ¾-inch-thick patties. (To stuff, divide mixture into eight portions; shape into ¼-inch-thick patties. Place Stuffing on centers of four patties. Top with remaining patties; pinch edges to seal.)

2 For a charcoal grill, grill stuffed or unstuffed patties on the rack of an uncovered grill directly over medium coals for 14 to 18 minutes or until done (160°F to 165°F), turning once halfway through grilling. (For a gas grill, preheat grill. Reduce heat to medium. Place patties on grill rack over heat. Cover; grill as directed.)

3 Serve burgers on Bread with Spread and Toppers.

*SPREAD: mayonnaise, ketchup, yellow mustard, Dijon-style mustard, basil pesto, barbecue sauce

**TOPPERS: cheese slices, tomato slices, onion slices, caramelized onion, pickle slices, cooked bacon, roasted peppers, fresh basil leaves, spinach leaves, and/or lettuce leaves

BROILED BURGERS: Shape the patties as directed. Preheat broiler. Place patties on the unheated rack of a broiler pan. Broil 3 to 4 inches from heat for 12 to 14 minutes or until done (160°F to 165°F), turning once.

SPICY SOY-MARINATED FLANK STEAK

PREP: 25 MINUTES **MARINATE:** 2 TO 4 HOURS
GRILL: 17 MINUTES **STAND:** 5 MINUTES
MAKES: 4 SERVINGS

- 1 1¼- to 1½-pound beef flank steak
- 1 recipe Spicy Soy Marinade
- 1 3-ounce package ramen noodles (any flavor)
- 1 cup thin bite-size carrot strips
- 1 cup lengthwise-sliced sugar snap peas
- ¼ cup loosely packed fresh cilantro leaves
- 2 tablespoons sliced almonds, toasted (see tip, page 20)

1 Trim fat from steak. Score both sides of steak in a diamond pattern (see photo 1, below). Place steak in a large resealable plastic bag set in a shallow dish. Reserve 3 tablespoons of the Spicy Soy Marinade for noodles. Pour remaining marinade over steak in bag (see photo 2, below); seal bag. Turn to coat steak. Marinate in the refrigerator for 2 to 4 hours, turning bag occasionally.

2 Drain steak, discarding marinade. For a charcoal grill, grill steak on the rack of an uncovered grill directly over medium coals for 17 to 21 minutes for medium doneness (160°F), turning once halfway through grilling. (For a gas grill, preheat grill. Reduce heat to medium. Place steak on grill rack over heat. Cover and grill as directed.) Let steak stand for 5 minutes. Thinly slice steak diagonally across the grain into bite-size pieces.

3 Prepare ramen noodles according to package directions, omitting the seasoning packet. (Discard seasoning packet.) Drain noodles. If desired, snip noodles into short pieces. In a large bowl combine noodles, steak, the 3 tablespoons reserved marinade, carrots, sugar snap peas, and cilantro. Toss to mix. Sprinkle with almonds.

SPICY SOY MARINADE: In a small bowl combine ¼ cup soy sauce, 2 tablespoons rice vinegar, 2 tablespoons vegetable oil, 1 teaspoon finely shredded lime peel, 2 tablespoons lime juice, 1 tablespoon grated fresh ginger, 1 teaspoon Asian chili sauce, 1 teaspoon toasted sesame oil (if desired), ¼ teaspoon salt, ¼ teaspoon black pepper, and 2 cloves garlic, minced.

PER ¾ CUP: 373 cal., 16 g total fat (5 g sat. fat, 0 g trans fat), 47 mg chol., 741 mg sodium, 20 g carbo., 3 g fiber, 35 g pro. EXCHANGES: ½ Vegetable, 1 Starch, 4½ Lean Meat, ½ Fat

FAST

CHIPOTLE STEAK AND TOMATOES

PREP: 10 MINUTES **GRILL:** 10 MINUTES
STAND: 5 MINUTES **MAKES:** 4 SERVINGS

- 2 beef shoulder petite tenders or beef ribeye steaks, cut 1 inch thick (12 to 16 ounces)
- 1 canned chipotle pepper in adobo sauce, finely chopped, plus 2 teaspoons adobo sauce
- ¼ cup olive oil
- ¼ cup vinegar
- 3 medium tomatoes, thickly sliced (1 pound)
- 2 medium avocados, halved, seeded, peeled, and sliced
- ½ of a small red onion, very thinly sliced

MARINATING FLANK STEAK, STEP-BY-STEP

1. Score the steak with a sharp knife, making shallow diagonal cuts at 1-inch intervals. Make intersecting diagonal cuts in the opposite direction to form a diamond pattern. Turn steak over and score the second side.
2. Place the meat in a plastic bag and place bag in a shallow dish. Pour the marinade over the meat and seal the bag. Turn the bag a few times to coat all sides of steak with marinade.

1 Sprinkle steaks lightly with *salt* and *black pepper*. Spread the 2 teaspoons adobo sauce over steaks. For a charcoal grill, grill steaks on the rack of an uncovered grill directly over medium coals. Allow 10 to 12 minutes for medium rare (145°F) and 12 to 15 minutes for medium (160°F). (For gas grill, preheat grill. Reduce heat to medium. ace steaks on the grill rack over heat. Cover and [?]l as directed.) Let steaks stand for 5 minutes.

[?]or dressing, in a screw-top jar combine the [?]tle pepper, oil, and vinegar. Cover; shake well.

[?] serve, slice steaks and arrange on dinner [?]s with tomato and avocado slices. Top with [?]i slices; drizzle with dressing.

[?] STEAK + ¾ CUP VEGETABLES: 379 cal., 29 g total fat [?]at. fat, 0 g trans fat), 48 mg chol., 223 mg sodium, 11 g carbo., [?]iber, 20 g pro.
[?]HANGES: 1 Vegetable, ½ Other Carbo., 2½ Lean Meat, [?]Fat

FLAT-IRON STEAK WITH AVOCADO BUTTER

PREP: 20 MINUTES **GRILL:** 7 MINUTES
STAND: 5 MINUTES **MAKES:** 6 SERVINGS

- 6 beef shoulder top blade (flat-iron) steaks or boneless ribeye steaks, cut 1 inch thick
- 1 tablespoon olive oil
- 1 tablespoon herbes de Provence, crushed
- ½ teaspoon salt
- ½ teaspoon freshly ground black pepper
- 1 recipe Avocado Butter

1 Brush steaks with the olive oil. For rub, combine herbes de Provence, salt, and pepper. Rub over both sides of each steak. If desired, cover and chill steaks for up to 24 hours.

2 For a charcoal grill, grill steaks on the rack of an uncovered grill directly over medium coals to desired doneness, turning once halfway through grilling. Allow 7 to 9 minutes for medium rare (145°F) and 10 to 12 minutes for medium (160°F). (For a gas grill, preheat grill. Reduce heat to medium. Place steaks on the grill rack over heat. Cover and grill as directed.) Let steaks stand for 5 minutes. Serve steaks with Avocado Butter.

AVOCADO BUTTER: Halve, seed, peel, and chop 1 ripe avocado. In a medium bowl combine the chopped avocado, ¼ cup softened butter, 3 tablespoons lime juice, 2 tablespoons snipped fresh chervil or parsley, 1 tablespoon snipped fresh tarragon, ¼ teaspoon salt, and, if desired, ⅛ teaspoon cayenne pepper. Using a fork, gently mash the ingredients together until thoroughly combined (if desired, leave mixture somewhat chunky). Chill until almost firm.

PER 1 STEAK + 3 TABLESPOONS AVOCADO BUTTER: 369 cal., 25 g total fat (10 g sat. fat, 0 g trans fat), 109 mg chol., 463 mg sodium, 3 g carbo., 2 g fiber, 33 g pro.
EXCHANGES: 4½ Lean Meat, 2½ Fat

STEAK WITH SQUASH AND ARUGULA

PREP: 30 MINUTES **STAND:** 25 MINUTES
GRILL: 8 MINUTES **MAKES:** 4 SERVINGS

- ¼ cup white wine vinegar
- ½ teaspoon kosher or sea salt or ¼ teaspoon salt
- 2 cloves garlic, minced
- ¼ cup olive oil
- 1 medium yellow summer squash or zucchini, very thinly sliced
- 1 cup baby pattypan squash, halved
- 1 cup yellow or red pear or cherry tomatoes, halved
- ¼ cup finely chopped yellow sweet pepper
- 4 boneless beef ribeye steaks, cut 1 inch thick (2½ to 3 pounds)
- 5 cups loosely packed arugula or baby spinach
- 2 tablespoons snipped fresh Italian parsley

1 In a large bowl combine vinegar, the ½ teaspoon salt, and the garlic. Cover and let stand at room temperature for 20 minutes. Whisk in olive oil. Add summer squash, pattypan squash, tomato halves, and sweet pepper. Toss gently; set aside.

2 Lightly sprinkle steaks with *black pepper* and additional salt. For a charcoal grill, grill steaks on the rack of an uncovered grill directly over medium coals to desired doneness, turning once halfway through grilling. Allow 8 to 12 minutes for medium rare (145°F) or 10 to 15 minutes for medium (160°F). (For a gas grill, preheat grill. Reduce heat to medium. Place steaks on grill rack over heat. Cover; grill as directed.) Let steaks stand for 5 minutes.

3 Add arugula and parsley to squash mixture; toss to mix. Serve vegetable mixture with steaks.

PER STEAK + 1¼ CUPS VEGETABLES: 602 cal., 36 g total fat (10 g sat. fat, 0 g trans fat), 165 mg chol., 511 mg sodium, 6 g carbo., 1 g fiber, 59 g pro.
EXCHANGES: 1½ Vegetable, 8 Lean Meat, 2½ Fat

ROSEMARY PORTERHOUSE STEAKS WITH OLIVE MAYO

PREP: 25 MINUTES **GRILL:** 10 MINUTES
STAND: 5 MINUTES **MAKES:** 4 TO 6 SERVINGS

- ½ cup mayonnaise
- 2 tablespoons chopped pitted Kalamata olives
- 1 tablespoon snipped fresh dill
- 1 clove garlic, minced
- 2 porterhouse steaks, cut 1 to 1¼ inches thick (about 1 pound each)
- 1 tablespoon olive oil
- 1 tablespoon snipped fresh rosemary
- ¾ teaspoon kosher salt or salt
- ½ teaspoon freshly ground black pepper
  Snipped fresh rosemary (optional)
- 1 recipe Herbed Potatoes and Squash* (page 360) (optional)

1 For olive mayo, in a small bowl stir together mayonnaise, olives, dill, and garlic. Cover and chill until serving time.

2 Brush steaks with oil. Combine the 1 tablespoon rosemary, salt, and pepper; rub on steaks.

3 For a charcoal grill, grill steaks on the rack of an uncovered grill directly over medium coals to desired doneness, turning once halfway through grilling. Allow 10 to 12 minutes for medium rare (145°F) and 12 to 15 minutes for medium (160°F), turning once halfway through grilling. (For a gas grill, preheat grill. Reduce heat to medium-high. Cover and grill as directed.) Let steaks stand for 5 minutes.

4 If desired, sprinkle steaks with additional fresh rosemary; cut steaks into serving portions. Serve with olive mayo and, if desired, Herbed Potatoes and Squash.

*****NOTE:** If your grill is too small to grill the potatoes and steaks at the same time, grill potatoes first and cover with foil while grilling steaks.

PER 6 OUNCES STEAK + 3 TABLESPOONS OLIVE MAYO: 589 cal., 46 g total fat (11 g sat. fat, 0 g trans fat), 112 mg chol., 667 mg sodium, 1 g carbo., 0 g fiber, 40 g pro. EXCHANGES: 5½ Lean Meat, 6 Fat

GARLICKY GRILLED BEEF KABOBS

PREP: 20 MINUTES **STAND:** 60 MINUTES
GRILL: 10 MINUTES **MAKES:** 6 SERVINGS

- ¼ cup coarse-grain Dijon-style mustard
- 2 tablespoons red wine vinegar
- 2 tablespoons soy sauce
- 2 tablespoons honey
- 2 teaspoons snipped fresh rosemary
- 2 teaspoons smoked paprika
- ¼ teaspoon salt
- ¼ teaspoon black pepper
  Dash cayenne pepper
- 4 cloves garlic, minced
- 2 pounds beef tenderloin roast

1 In a small bowl whisk together mustard, vinegar, soy sauce, honey, rosemary, paprika, salt, black pepper, cayenne pepper, and garlic. Cover and let stand at room temperature for at least 60 minutes to blend flavors.

2 Trim fat from meat. Cut meat into 1½-inch pieces. Transfer meat to a large bowl. Spoon half of the mustard mixture over meat; toss gently to coat. On six 10-inch skewers thread meat, leaving a ¼-inch space between pieces.

3 For a charcoal grill, grill kabobs on the rack of an uncovered grill directly over medium coals for 10 to 12 minutes or until meat reaches desired doneness, turning once and brushing with the remaining mustard mixture halfway through grilling. (For a gas grill, preheat grill. Reduce heat to medium. Place kabobs on grill rack over heat. Cover and grill as directed.)

PER KABOB: 414 cal., 28 g total fat (11 g sat. fat, 0 g trans fat), 100 mg chol., 752 mg sodium, 7 g carbo., 0 g fiber, 30 g pro. EXCHANGES: ½ Other Carbo., 4 Lean Meat, 3 Fat

FRESH ROSEMARY LEAVES
TO USE FRESH ROSEMARY, REMOVE LEAVES FROM THE WOODY STEM BY RUBBING YOUR THUMB AND INDEX FINGER DOWN THE STEM FROM THE TOP TO THE SNIPPED END. SNIP OR CHOP THE LEAVES.

COOK ONCE, EAT TWICE

TEX-MEX SPICES LIVEN UP BEEF TENDERLOIN FOR THE THE FIRST MEAL. FOR THE NEXT MEAL, LEFTOVERS GET A LUSCIOUS NEW LEASE ON LIFE IN A HOT SAUCY SANDWICH.

TONIGHT

SPICE-RUBBED BEEF TENDERLOIN

PREP: 15 MINUTES **GRILL:** 60 MINUTES
STAND: 15 MINUTES
MAKES: 6 SERVINGS + RESERVES

- 1 tablespoon chili powder
- 1 tablespoon ground coriander
- 1 tablespoon packed brown sugar
- 1 teaspoon paprika
- 1 teaspoon dry mustard
- 1 teaspoon salt
- ½ teaspoon garlic powder
- ¼ teaspoon cayenne pepper
- 1 3- to 4-pound center-cut beef tenderloin roast

1 For rub, in a small bowl combine chili powder, coriander, brown sugar, paprika, dry mustard, salt, garlic powder, and cayenne pepper. Sprinkle rub over roast and rub in with your fingers.

2 For a charcoal grill, arrange hot coals around a drip pan. Test for medium-high heat above the pan. Place roast on grill rack over drip pan. Cover and grill for 60 to 75 minutes for medium rare (135°F). (For a gas grill, preheat grill. Reduce heat to medium-high. Adjust for indirect cooking. Grill as directed, except place roast on a rack in a shallow roasting pan.) Remove meat from grill. Cover meat with foil; let stand for 15 minutes. Temperature of meat after standing should be 145°F.

3 Cut roast into slices; serve warm. Transfer half of the slices to an airtight storage container; cover and chill for up to 3 days or freeze for up to 1 month (thaw overnight in the refrigerator before using.) Use in Mop Sauce Beef Sandwiches.

PER 4 OUNCES: 193 cal., 10 g total fat (4 g sat. fat, 0 g trans fat), 70 mg chol., 253 mg sodium, 2 g carbo., 0 g fiber, 24 g pro.
EXCHANGES: 3½ Lean Meat

TOMORROW

MOP SAUCE BEEF SANDWICHES

PREP: 15 MINUTES **COOK:** 30 MINUTES
GRILL: 5 MINUTES **MAKES:** 6 SANDWICHES

- 1 cup strong brewed coffee
- 1 cup ketchup
- ½ cup Worcestershire sauce
- ¼ cup butter or margarine
- 1 tablespoon sugar
- ½ to 1 teaspoon black pepper
- ½ teaspoon salt
- ½ recipe Spice-Rubbed Beef Tenderloin
- 6 French-style rolls, unsliced
- 6 ounces cheddar or Monterey Jack cheese, thinly sliced

1 In a large saucepan combine coffee, ketchup, Worcestershire sauce, butter, sugar, pepper, and salt. Bring to boiling, stirring occasionally; reduce heat. Simmer, uncovered, for 30 minutes, stirring frequently. Reserve ½ cup of the sauce. Add beef to remaining sauce in saucepan; heat through.

2 Cut ½ inch from top of each roll. Hollow out the rolls (reserve bread tops, if desired, and/or save bread scraps for another use). Add beef to the rolls and spoon reserved sauce over each. Top with cheese and, if desired, reserved bread tops.

3 For a charcoal grill, arrange medium-hot coals around the outer edge of the grill. Test for medium heat above center of grill. Place rolls on the grill rack in the center of the grill. Cover and grill for 5 to 10 minutes or until cheese melts. (For a gas grill, preheat grill. Reduce heat to medium. Adjust heat for indirect cooking. Add rolls to grill rack over burner that is off. Cover and grill as directed.)

PER SANDWICH: 549 cal., 28 g total fat (15 g sat. fat, 0 g trans fat), 120 mg chol., 1,615 mg sodium, 37 g carbo., 2 g fiber, 35 g pro.
EXCHANGES: 2 Starch, ½ Other Carbo., 4 Lean Meat, 3 Fat

LAMB CHOPS AND BEANS WITH CHILE BUTTER

PREP: 25 MINUTES **GRILL:** 12 MINUTES
CHILL: 1 TO 24 HOURS **MAKES:** 4 SERVINGS

- 8 lamb loin chops, cut 1 inch thick
  Salt and black pepper
- 1 15-ounce can cannellini (white kidney) beans or pinto beans, rinsed and drained
- ½ cup chopped celery (1 stalk)
- ¼ cup chopped green onions (2)
- 1 recipe Chile Butter
- 1 tablespoon lime juice
  Lime wedges (optional)

1 Trim fat from chops. Sprinkle chops lightly with salt and pepper. For a charcoal grill, grill chops on the rack of an uncovered grill directly over medium coals until desired doneness, turning once halfway through grilling. Allow 12 to 14 minutes for medium rare (145°F) and 15 to 17 minutes for medium (160°F). (For a gas grill, preheat grill. Reduce heat to medium. Place chops on grill rack over heat. Cover and grill as directed.)

2 Meanwhile, in a medium saucepan combine beans, celery, green onion, and 2 tablespoons of the Chile Butter. Cook over medium heat until heated through, stirring occasionally. Stir in lime juice. To serve, top each lamb chop with a slice of Chile Butter and serve with bean mixture. If desired, garnish with lime wedges.

CHILE BUTTER: In a small bowl stir together ½ cup softened butter; ¼ cup snipped fresh cilantro; 2 fresh jalapeño chile peppers, seeded and finely chopped (see tip, page 24); 1 teaspoon chili powder; and 1 clove garlic, minced. Place on waxed paper; form into a log. Wrap well; chill for 1 hour or overnight. Store in refrigerator for up to 2 weeks or freeze for up to 1 month.

PER 2 CHOPS + ½ CUP BEANS: 445 cal., 30 g total fat (17 g sat. fat, 0 g trans fat), 141 mg chol., 565 mg sodium, 17 g carbo., 6 g fiber, 32 g pro.
EXCHANGES: 1 Starch, 4 Lean Meat, 3½ Fat

LEMON-HERB LAMB AND VEGETABLE KABOBS

PREP: 45 MINUTES **MARINATE:** 1 TO 4 HOURS
GRILL: 12 MINUTES **MAKES:** 4 SERVINGS

- ⅓ cup red wine vinegar
- ⅓ cup lemon juice
- ⅓ cup olive oil
- 1 tablespoon snipped fresh rosemary
- ½ teaspoon salt
- ¼ teaspoon black pepper
- 1 to 1¼ pounds boneless leg of lamb, cut into 1½-inch pieces
- 1 small eggplant (about 1 pound), cut into 1-inch pieces
- 1 medium zucchini or yellow summer squash, cut into 1-inch pieces
- ½ cup cherry tomatoes
- 2 tablespoons olive oil
- 1 cup couscous
- ¼ cup crumbled feta cheese (1 ounce)

1 For marinade, in a small bowl stir together vinegar, lemon juice, the ⅓ cup olive oil, rosemary, salt, and pepper; reserve ½ cup of the marinade. Place lamb in a large resealable plastic bag set in a shallow dish. Pour the remaining marinade over meat. Seal bag; marinate in the refrigerator for 1 to 4 hours, turning bag occasionally.

2 Drain meat, discarding marinade. Thread meat onto four 12-inch skewers, leaving a ¼-inch space between pieces. Thread eggplant, zucchini, and tomatoes onto separate 12-inch skewers, leaving a ¼-inch space between pieces. (You will need about seven skewers for the vegetables.) Brush vegetables with the 2 tablespoons olive oil.

3 For a charcoal grill, grill kabobs on the rack of an uncovered grill directly over medium coals. Grill tomatoes for 3 to 4 minutes or just until softened, turning occasionally. Grill lamb, zucchini, and eggplant for 12 to 14 minutes or until lamb is desired doneness and vegetables are tender, turning occasionally. Remove kabobs from the grill as they are done. (For a gas grill, preheat grill. Reduce heat to medium. Place kabobs on grill rack over heat. Cover and grill as directed.)

4 Meanwhile, cook couscous according to package directions. Remove vegetables from skewers and place in a large bowl. Add couscous and the reserved ½ cup marinade to vegetables. Toss to mix. Serve lamb kabobs with couscous mixture; sprinkle with feta cheese.

PER 4 OUNCES MEAT + 1¼ CUPS COUSCOUS MIXTURE: 518 cal., 23 g total fat (5 g sat. fat, 0 g trans fat), 81 mg chol., 308 mg sodium, 45 g carbo., 6 g fiber, 32 g pro.
EXCHANGES: 1 Vegetable, 2½ Starch, 3 Lean Meat, 2½ Fat

PORK SKEWERS WITH FIVE-SPICE HOISIN SAUCE

PREP: 30 MINUTES **GRILL:** 12 MINUTES
MAKES: 6 KABOBS

    1 egg, lightly beaten
    ⅓ cup finely chopped water chestnuts
    ¼ cup fine dry bread crumbs
    2 teaspoons grated fresh ginger
    ½ teaspoon garlic salt
    ¼ teaspoon black pepper
    1 pound ground pork
    1 cup 1-inch pieces red, yellow, and/or
       green sweet pepper
    1 small red onion, cut into wedges
    1 recipe Five-Spice Hoisin Sauce
       Bottled plum sauce

1 In a large bowl combine egg, water chestnuts, bread crumbs, ginger, garlic salt, and pepper. Add ground pork; mix well. Shape pork mixture into eighteen 1¼- to 1½-inch meatballs.

2 On six long metal skewers alternately thread meatballs, sweet pepper pieces, and onion wedges, leaving a ¼-inch space between pieces.

3 For a charcoal grill, arrange medium-hot coals around a drip pan. Test for medium heat above the pan. Place skewers on a well-greased grill rack over pan. Cover and grill for 12 to 15 minutes or until meatballs are no longer pink and juices run clear (160°F), turning and occasionally brushing kabobs with Five-Spice Hoisin Sauce. (For a gas grill, preheat grill. Reduce heat to medium. Adjust for indirect cooking. Grill as directed.) Serve kabobs with plum sauce.

FIVE-SPICE HOISIN SAUCE: In a small bowl stir together 3 tablespoons bottled hoisin sauce, 1 tablespoon orange juice, ¼ teaspoon five-spice powder, and dash crushed red pepper.

PER KABOB: 301 cal., 18 g total fat (6 g sat. fat, 0 g trans fat), 90 mg chol., 401 mg sodium, 20 g carbo., 2 g fiber, 15 g pro.
EXCHANGES: 1 Other Carbo., 2 Lean Meat, 2½ Fat

MEATBALL MASTERY WHEN SHAPING THE MEATBALLS FOR THE SKEWERS, AVOID OVERMIXING THE MEAT MIXTURE AND BE SURE THE MEATBALLS ARE PACKED FIRM ENOUGH TO HOLD THEIR SHAPE.

PORK SKEWERS WITH FIVE-SPICE
HOISIN SAUCE

GRILLED PIZZA

On a lightly floured surface roll out each dough portion to a thin circle that measures 8 to 10 inches in diameter.

4 Line a baking sheet with waxed paper or parchment paper. Stack pizza dough rounds on baking sheet, separating rounds with waxed paper or parchment paper. Wrap and freeze dough for at least 2 hours* or until very firm. Use as directed in Grilled Pizza (below).

*NOTE: For longer storage, transfer pizza dough crusts to 2-gallon freezer bags. Seal bags and freeze for up to 1 month.

PER ½ OF A PIZZA CRUST: 255 cal., 6 g total fat (1 g sat. fat, 0 g trans fat), 0 mg chol., 149 mg sodium, 44 g carbo., 2 g fiber, 6 g pro.
EXCHANGES: 3 Starch, ½ Fat

GRILLED PIZZA

PREP: 30 MINUTES GRILL: 6 MINUTES
MAKES: FOUR 8- TO 10-INCH PIZZAS (8 SERVINGS)

- 12 ounces uncooked fresh hot or mild Italian sausage links, cut into ½-inch pieces
- 2 cups sliced fresh mushrooms, chopped sweet pepper, and/or thin onion wedges (optional)
- 1 recipe Homemade Pizza Crusts for Grilled Pizza
  Olive oil
- 1 8-ounce can pizza sauce
- 2 cups shredded mozzarella or provolone cheese (8 ounces)

1 In a large skillet cook sausage and vegetables until sausage is brown; drain off fat. Pat sausage and vegetables with paper towels to remove additional fat.

2 Remove Homemade Pizza Crusts from freezer; discard waxed paper. Do not thaw. Brush crusts with olive oil.

3 For a charcoal grill, carefully slide two of the pizza dough rounds, oiled sides down, onto the lightly oiled rack of an uncovered grill directly over medium-hot coals. Grill for 1 to 2 minutes or until dough is puffed in some places and starting to become firm. Working quickly, carefully brush tops with olive oil. Using tongs, carefully turn the crusts over and transfer to the back of a baking sheet. For each pizza, spread a crust with one-fourth of the pizza sauce. Sprinkle with one-fourth of the cheese. Top with one-fourth of the sausage mixture. Transfer the pizzas from the baking sheet to the grill rack. Grill about 2 minutes more or until

HOMEMADE PIZZA CRUSTS FOR GRILLED PIZZA

PREP: 30 MINUTES RISE: 45 MINUTES
REST: 10 MINUTES FREEZE: 2 HOURS
MAKES: 4 PIZZA CRUST ROUNDS

- 3¼ cups all-purpose flour
- ¼ cup whole wheat or all-purpose flour
- 2 packages active dry yeast
- 1 cup warm water (120°F to 130°F)
- 3 tablespoons olive oil
- 1 tablespoon honey
- ½ teaspoon salt

1 In a food processor combine all-purpose flour, whole wheat flour, and yeast. In a small bowl combine water, olive oil, honey, and salt. With the processor running, pour water mixture through feed tube in a steady stream. Process until dough forms a mass and clears side of the bowl.

2 Turn dough out onto a lightly floured surface. Knead about 5 minutes or until smooth and elastic, adding additional flour as needed to keep dough from sticking. Shape into a ball. Place in a lightly greased bowl, turning once. Cover; let rise in a warm place until double in size (45 to 60 minutes).

3 Punch dough down. Turn dough out onto a lightly floured surface. Cut dough into four equal portions with a serrated knife. Cover; let rest for 10 minutes. Pat each piece of dough into a disk.

cheese melts and crust is crisp. Remove pizzas from grill. (For a gas grill, preheat grill. Reduce heat to medium-hot. Place dough circles on grill rack over heat. Cover and grill as directed.)

4 Repeat with the remaining two pizza crusts and toppings. Transfer pizzas to a cutting board; serve immediately.

PER ½ PIZZA: 528 cal., 29 g total fat (10 g sat. fat, 0 g trans fat), 48 mg chol., 702 mg sodium, 48 g carbo., 3 g fiber, 20 g pro. EXCHANGES: 3 Starch, 1½ High-Fat Meat, 3 Fat

BARBECUE CHICKEN PIZZA: Prepare as directed, except substitute 12 ounces skinless, boneless chicken breast halves or boneless pork loin chops, cut into thin bite-size strips, for the sausage and 1 cup bottled barbecue sauce for the pizza sauce.

PER ½ PIZZA WITH CHICKEN: 459 cal., 16 g total fat (5 g sat. fat, 0 g trans fat), 40 mg chol., 716 mg sodium 57 g carbo., 2 g fiber, 23 g pro. EXCHANGES: 3 Starch. 1 Other Carbo., 2 Lean Meat, 1½ Fat

FAST

BRATS WITH MANGO RELISH

START TO FINISH: 20 MINUTES
MAKES: 4 SANDWICHES

- 1 large fresh mango, halved, seeded, and peeled
- 1 small red onion, cut into ½-inch slices
- 3 tablespoons vegetable oil
- 4 cooked smoked bratwurst (12 ounces)
- 2 hearts of romaine lettuce, halved
- 4 hoagie buns, bratwurst buns, or other crusty rolls, split
- ½ teaspoon Jamaican jerk seasoning
  Salt and black pepper

1 Brush mango and onion with 1 tablespoon of the oil.

2 For a charcoal gill, grill mango halves, onion slices, and bratwurst directly over medium coals about 8 minutes or until mango and brats are brown and heated through and onion is crisp-tender, turning once halfway through grilling. Set aside mango, onion, and brats. Lightly brush romaine with 1 tablespoon of the oil. Grill romaine for 1 to 2 minutes or until light brown and wilted, turning once. Lightly toast buns for 1 to 2 minutes on grill. (For a gas grill, preheat grill. Reduce heat to medium. Place mango, onion, and bratwurst on grill rack over heat. Cover and grill as directed.)

3 For mango relish, chop grilled mango and onion. In a medium bowl combine mango, onion, the remaining 1 tablespoon oil, and the jerk seasoning. Season with salt and pepper. Serve brats in buns with relish and romaine on the side.

PER SANDWICH: 671 cal., 38 g total fat (10 g sat. fat, 0 g trans fat), 50 mg chol., 1,397 mg sodium, 67 g carbo., 5 g fiber, 18 g pro. EXCHANGES: 1 Vegetable, 4 Starch, 1 High-Fat Meat, 5 Fat

LOW FAT

ISLAND SPICED PORK CHOPS

PREP: 15 MINUTES **MARINATE:** 4 TO 24 HOURS
GRILL: 11 MINUTES **MAKES:** 4 SERVINGS

- 4 pork rib chops, cut ¾ inch thick (about 1¾ pounds)
- ¼ cup lime juice
- 1 tablespoon chili powder
- 1 tablespoon olive oil
- 2 teaspoons ground cumin
- 1 teaspoon ground cinnamon
- ½ teaspoon bottled hot pepper sauce
- ¼ teaspoon salt
- 2 cloves garlic, minced
  Papaya slices (optional)

1 Trim fat from chops. Place chops in a large resealable plastic bag set in a shallow dish. For marinade, in a small bowl stir together lime juice, chili powder, olive oil, cumin, cinnamon, hot pepper sauce, salt, and garlic. Pour marinade over chops in bag; seal bag. Marinate in the refrigerator for 4 to 24 hours, turning bag occasionally. Drain chops, discarding marinade.

2 For a charcoal grill, grill chops on the rack of an uncovered grill directly over medium coals for 11 to 14 minutes or until chops are slightly pink in center and juices run clear (160°F), turning once halfway through grilling. (For a gas grill, preheat grill. Reduce heat to medium. Place chops on grill rack over heat. Cover and grill as directed.) If desired, serve with mango.

PER CHOP: 285 cal., 10 g total fat (3 g sat. fat, 0 g trans fat), 136 mg chol., 201 mg sodium, 2 g carbo., 1 g fiber, 43 g pro. EXCHANGES: 6 Lean Meat, 1 Fat

FRUITS ON THE SIDE
IF YOU CAN'T FIND PAPAYA TO SERVE ALONGSIDE THE CHOPS (ABOVE), TRY SLICED MANGO OR CHOPPED FRESH PINEAPPLE.

MEDITERRANEAN STUFFED CHOPS

PREP: 30 MINUTES **GRILL:** 35 MINUTES
MAKES: 4 SERVINGS

- 2 tablespoons olive oil
- 1 cup coarsely chopped fresh mushrooms
- ½ cup chopped onion (1 medium)
- 1 teaspoon dried oregano, crushed
- ¼ teaspoon salt
- ⅛ teaspoon black pepper
- 1 cup coarsely chopped fresh spinach
- ¼ cup chopped Kalamata olives
- ¼ cup panko (Japanese-style bread crumbs)
- 4 pork loin chops or pork rib chops, cut 1¼ to 1½ inches thick
- ¼ cup crumbled feta cheese

1 For stuffing, in a large skillet heat 1 tablespoon of the olive oil over medium heat. Add mushrooms and onion; cook until onion is tender. Remove skillet from heat; stir in oregano, the ¼ teaspoon salt, and the ⅛ teaspoon pepper. Add spinach, olives, and bread crumbs; toss gently to combine.

2 Trim fat from chops. Make a pocket in each chop by cutting horizontally from fat side almost to the bone (see photo 1, below). Spoon one-fourth of the stuffing into each pocket (see photo 2, below). Secure openings with wooden toothpicks. Brush chops with remaining 1 tablespoon oil; sprinkle chops lightly with salt and black pepper.

3 For a charcoal grill, arrange medium-hot coals around a drip pan. Test for medium heat above the pan. Place chops on grill rack over pan. Cover and grill for 35 to 40 minutes or until chops are slightly pink in center (160°F), turning once halfway through grilling. (For a gas grill, preheat grill. Reduce heat to medium. Adjust for indirect cooking. Place chops on grill rack over the burner that is turned off. Grill as directed.) To serve, sprinkle chops with feta cheese.

PER STUFFED CHOP: 600 cal., 50 g total fat (16 g sat. fat, 0 g trans fat), 128 mg chol., 525 mg sodium, 7 g carbo., 1 g fiber, 29 g pro. EXCHANGES: ½ Starch, 4 Lean Meat, 7½ Fat

GRILLED PLANTAINS AND SWEET POTATOES

PREP: 15 MINUTES **GRILL:** 12 MINUTES
MAKES: 4 TO 6 SERVINGS

Bias-slice 2 to 3 peeled ripe plantains into ½-inch slices or cut four to six ½-inch slices from a peeled, cored pineapple. Cut 2 medium sweet potatoes into ½- to ¾-inch slices. Brush vegetables and fruit and 6 to 8 green banana peppers with vegetable oil; sprinkle with salt and black pepper. For a charcoal grill, grill potatoes directly over medium coals for 6 minutes. Turn potatoes. Add plantains or pineapple and banana peppers to grill rack. Grill for 6 to 8 minutes more or until sweet potato and plantain centers are soft and pineapple and banana peppers are heated through, turning once. (For a gas grill, preheat grill. Reduce heat to medium. Place sweet potatoes on grill rack over heat. Cover and grill as above, adding plantains or pineapple and banana peppers as directed.) Serve warm.

PER SERVING: 244 cal., 7 g total fat (1 g sat. fat, 0 g trans fat), 0 mg chol., 194 mg sodium, 45 g carbo., 6 g fiber, 3 g pro. EXCHANGES: 3 Starch, 1 Fat

STUFFING CHOPS, STEP-BY-STEP

1. To cut pockets in chops, insert the tip of a sharp utility knife horizontally into the fat side of the chop. Work the knife to cut the meat in half, cutting almost to the bone.
2. Lift up the top flap of meat. Spoon the stuffing into the pocket, spreading it as evenly as you can. Insert wooden toothpicks to hold the cut side closed during grilling.

1

2

COOK ONCE, EAT TWICE

FEATURE THE CARIBBEAN FLAVORS OF SUNNY CITRUS IN A GRILLED PORK ROAST. THE NEXT NIGHT, TUCK THE TENDER MEAT INTO AN IRRESISTIBLY JUICY CUBAN-STYLE SANDWICH.

TONIGHT

CUBAN-STYLE PORK ROAST

PREP: 15 MINUTES **MARINATE:** 3 TO 6 HOURS
GRILL: 45 MINUTES **STAND:** 15 MINUTES
MAKES: 4 TO 6 SERVINGS + RESERVES

- 1 1½- to 2-pound boneless pork top loin roast (single loin)
- ½ cup orange juice
- 3 tablespoons lemon juice
- 1 tablespoon soy sauce
- 1 teaspoon dried oregano, crushed
- 4 cloves garlic, minced
- 1 recipe Grilled Plantains and Sweet Potatoes (page 346) (optional)

1 Trim fat from pork. Place pork in a resealable plastic bag set in shallow dish. For marinade, whisk together orange juice, lemon juice, soy sauce, oregano, ½ teaspoon *salt,* ¼ teaspoon *black pepper,* and garlic. Pour marinade over pork; seal bag. Marinate in refrigerator for 3 to 6 hours, turning bag occasionally. Drain pork, discarding marinade.

2 For charcoal grill, arrange medium-hot coals around a drip pan. Test for medium heat above pan. Place pork, fat side up, on grill rack over pan. Cover; grill 45 to 60 minutes or until thermometer registers 150°F. (For a gas grill, preheat grill. Reduce heat to medium. Adjust for indirect cooking. Place pork on grill rack over burner that is turned off; grill as directed.) Remove pork. Cover; let for stand for 15 minutes. Temperature of meat after standing should be 160°F. Transfer one-fourth of the roast to airtight container. Cover; chill for up to 3 days or freeze for up to 1 month. Use in Cuban Panini with Quick Pickle. Slice remaining pork. If desired, serve with Grilled Plantains and Sweet Potatoes.

PER 4 OUNCES: 217 cal., 11 g total fat (4 g sat. fat, 0 g trans fat), 82 mg chol., 162 mg sodium, 1 g carbo., 0 g fiber, 27 g pro.
EXCHANGES: 4 Lean Meat

TOMORROW

CUBAN PANINI WITH QUICK PICKLE

PREP: 20 MINUTES **GRILL:** 6 MINUTES
MAKES: 2 SERVINGS

- 1 cup thinly sliced cucumber
- ¼ cup thinly sliced red onion
- 1 tablespoon lime juice
- 1 teaspoon snipped fresh oregano
- 1 teaspoon sugar
- 1 1-pound loaf country-style bread
- 4 ounces sliced Swiss cheese
- 6 ounces thinly sliced Cuban-Style Pork Roast
- 2 tablespoons olive oil

1 For quick pickle, in a bowl combine cucumber, onion, lime juice, oregano, and sugar; set aside.

2 Cut two ¾-inch slices from the bread. (Reserve remaining bread for another use.) Top one slice with half of the cheese and all the pork. Using a slotted spoon, place quick pickle on pork. Top with remaining cheese and second bread slice. Brush both sides of sandwich with olive oil.

3 For a charcoal grill, arrange medium-hot coals around the edge of grill. Test for medium heat in center of grill. Place sandwich on grill rack in the center of the grill. Place a baking sheet on top of the sandwich and weight it with two bricks. Cover; grill for 6 to 8 minutes or until bread is golden brown, turning once halfway through grilling. (For a gas grill, preheat grill. Reduce heat to medium. Adjust for indirect cooking. Wait for 2 minutes to allow the grill rack to cool slightly. Place sandwich on the side that burner is turned off. Grill as directed.) To serve, cut sandwich in half.

PER ½ SANDWICH: 574 cal., 38 g total fat (14 g sat. fat, 0 g trans fat), 102 mg chol., 386 mg sodium, 24 g carbo., 2 g fiber, 36 g pro.
EXCHANGES: 2 Starch, 4 Lean Meat, 5 Fat

MOJO PORK FAJITAS WITH ORANGE-AVOCADO SALSA

PREP: 45 MINUTES **MARINATE:** 8 TO 24 HOURS
GRILL: 30 MINUTES **STAND:** 10 MINUTES
MAKES: 4 SERVINGS (2 FAJITAS EACH)

- ⅓ cup olive oil
- ¼ cup chopped onion
- ⅓ cup lime juice
- ⅓ cup orange juice
- 1 teaspoon ground cumin
- 1 teaspoon dried oregano, crushed
- 1 tablespoon minced garlic (6 cloves)
- 1 1-pound pork tenderloin
- 2 large red sweet peppers, quartered lengthwise and seeded
- 2 medium onions, cut into thick slices
- 8 8-inch flour tortillas, warmed*
- 1 recipe Orange-Avocado Salsa
- ¼ cup dairy sour cream
  Fresh cilantro leaves (optional)
  Lime wedges (optional)

1 For marinade, in a small bowl combine olive oil, the ¼ cup chopped onion, lime juice, orange juice, cumin, oregano, and garlic. Trim fat from meat. Place meat in a large resealable plastic bag set in a shallow dish. Pour marinade over meat; seal bag. Marinate in the refrigerator for 8 to 24 hours, turning bag occasionally.

2 Drain meat, reserving marinade. Brush sweet pepper quarters and onion slices with some of the marinade; discard the remaining marinade.

3 For a charcoal grill, arrange hot coals around a drip pan. Test for medium-hot heat above the pan. Place meat on the grill rack over drip pan. Place pepper quarters and onion slices on the grill directly over coals. Cover and grill for 10 to 12 minutes for onions and 8 to 10 minutes for peppers or until vegetables are crisp-tender, turning occasionally. Remove vegetables from grill; keep warm. Cover grill and grill meat for 20 to 25 minutes more or until thermometer registers 155°F. (For a gas grill, preheat grill. Reduce heat to medium-high. Adjust for indirect cooking. Grill vegetables and meat as directed.)

4 Remove meat from grill. Cover with foil and let stand for 10 minutes. (The temperature of the meat after standing should be 160°F.) Meanwhile, if desired or if skin of peppers is too charred, peel skin from peppers. Cut peppers into thin strips and chop onions. Slice meat. Serve meat and vegetables on warm tortillas with Orange-Avocado Salsa and sour cream. If desired, sprinkle with cilantro and serve lime wedges.

ORANGE-AVOCADO SALSA: In a medium bowl combine 2 medium oranges, peeled, sectioned, and chopped; 1 ripe large avocado, halved, seeded, peeled, and chopped; ¼ cup chopped red onion; ¼ cup snipped fresh cilantro; 2 tablespoons lime juice; ½ to 1 teaspoon bottled hot pepper sauce; and ¼ teaspoon salt. If desired, cover and chill for up to 4 hours.

*NOTE: Wrap tortillas tightly in foil. Place on edge of grill rack for 10 minutes, turning once.

PER 2 FAJITAS: 736 cal., 32 g total fat (6 g sat. fat, 0 g trans fat), 80 mg chol., 729 mg sodium, 79 g carbo., 8 g fiber, 36 g pro. EXCHANGES: 1 Vegetable, 5 Starch, 2½ Lean Meat, 4 Fat

MOJO CHICKEN FAJITAS: Prepare as directed, except substitute 1 pound skinless, boneless chicken breast halves for the pork. Marinate chicken for 2 to 4 hours. For a charcoal grill, grill chicken on the rack of an uncovered grill directly over medium coals for 12 to 15 minutes or until tender and no longer pink (170°F). Place pepper quarters and onion slices on grill rack with chicken and grill as directed. (For a gas grill, preheat grill. Reduce heat to medium. Add chicken to grill rack. Place pepper quarters and onion slices on grill rack. Cover and grill as directed.)

PER 2 FAJITAS: 724 cal., 29 g fat (5 g sat. fat, 0 g trans fat), 72 mg chol., 744 mg sodium, 79 g carbo., 8 g fiber, 39 g pro. EXCHANGES: 1 Vegetable, 5 Starch, 3 Lean Meat, 3 Fat

BASIC RUB

PREP: 5 MINUTES **MAKES:** ABOUT ¼ CUP

- 1 tablespoon paprika
- 1 tablespoon onion powder
- 1½ teaspoons cracked black pepper
- 1½ teaspoons garlic powder
- 1 teaspoon salt
- 1 teaspoon dry mustard
- 1 teaspoon ground ginger
- ½ teaspoon ground allspice

1 In a small bowl stir together paprika, onion powder, pepper, garlic powder, salt, mustard, ginger, and allspice.

2 To use, sprinkle rub over meat, poultry, or fish; rub in with your fingers. Grill as directed (see pages 370 to 375).

PER TEASPOON: 7 cal., 0 g fat 0, 0 mg chol., 195 mg sodium, 1 g carbo., 0 g fiber, 0 g pro. EXCHANGES: Free

10 TO TRY—RUBS

Start with Basic Rub, page 348. **1. AU POIVRE:** Omit onion powder, ginger, and allspice. Add 1½ teaspoons each cracked white peppercorns and cracked pink peppercorns. **2. MEDITERRANEAN:** Omit ginger and allspice. Add 1½ teaspoons dried oregano and 1 teaspoon each dried mint and finely shredded lemon peel. **3. SMOKY:** Substitute smoked paprika for paprika. Omit ginger and allspice. Add 1 teaspoon ground chipotle chile pepper. **4. MOLE:** Substitute chili powder for paprika. Omit ginger and allspice. Add 1 tablespoon grated semisweet chocolate and 1 teaspoon finely shredded orange peel. **5. ASIAN:** Omit paprika. Substitute five-spice powder for allspice. Add 1 tablespoon sesame seeds and 1 teaspoon crushed red pepper. **6. CAJUN:** Omit the ginger and allspice. Add 2 teaspoons Cajun seasoning. **7. WESTERN:** Substitute smoked salt for salt. Omit ginger. Add 1 tablespoon instant coffee crystals and 1 tablespoon brown sugar. **8. BARBECUE:** Substitute chili powder for paprika. Omit ginger and allspice. Add 1 tablespoon brown sugar, 2 teaspoons ground cumin, and ¼ teaspoon ground cloves. **9. INDIAN:** Add 2 tablespoons finely chopped pistachios, 1 tablespoon curry powder, and 1 teaspoon crushed red pepper. **10. HERB:** Omit ginger and allspice. Add 1 teaspoon each dried rosemary, dried thyme, and dried oregano.

KANSAS CITY PORK SPARERIBS

(photo, page 333)

PREP: 20 MINUTES **GRILL:** 90 MINUTES
MAKES: 4 SERVINGS

- 4 pounds meaty pork spareribs or loin back ribs
- 1 tablespoon packed brown sugar
- 1 tablespoon garlic pepper
- 1 tablespoon paprika
- 1½ teaspoons chili powder
- 1 teaspoon salt
- ½ teaspoon celery seeds
- ¼ cup cider vinegar
- 4 cups hickory, oak, or apple wood chips
- 1 recipe Kansas City Barbecue Sauce

1 Trim fat from ribs. For rub, in a small bowl stir together brown sugar, garlic pepper, paprika, chili powder, salt, and celery seeds. Brush ribs with vinegar. Sprinkle rub evenly over both sides of ribs; rub in with your fingers.

2 For a charcoal grill, arrange medium-hot coals around a drip pan. Test for medium heat above pan. Sprinkle some of the wood chips over coals. If desired, place ribs in a rib rack. Place ribs, bone sides down, on the grill rack over drip pan. Cover and grill for 90 to 105 minutes or until ribs are tender. Add more coals and wood chips as needed to maintain temperature and smoke. (For a gas grill, preheat grill. Reduce heat to medium. Adjust for indirect cooking. Add wood chips according to manufacturer's directions. Place ribs in roasting pan; place pan on grill rack over burner that is off. Grill as directed.) Serve ribs with Kansas City Barbecue Sauce.

KANSAS CITY BARBECUE SAUCE: In a medium saucepan cook ½ cup finely chopped onion and 2 cloves garlic, minced, in 1 tablespoon hot olive oil until onion is tender. Stir in ¾ cup apple juice, ½ of a 6-ounce can (⅓ cup) tomato paste, ¼ cup vinegar, 2 tablespoons packed brown sugar, 2 tablespoons molasses, 1 tablespoon paprika, 1 tablespoon Worcestershire sauce, 1 teaspoon salt, and ½ teaspoon black pepper. Bring to boiling; reduce heat. Simmer, uncovered, about 30 minutes or until sauce reaches desired consistency, stirring occasionally. Stir in 1 tablespoon prepared horseradish.

PER ¼ RIBS + ⅓ CUP SAUCE: 1,059 cal., 72 g total fat (23 g sat. fat, 1 g trans fat), 247 mg chol., 1,713 mg sodium, 40 g carbo., 6 g fiber, 53 g pro.
EXCHANGES: 2½ Other Carbo., 7½ High-Fat Meat, 2½ Fat

SOUTHWEST STUFFED CHICKEN BREASTS WITH BLACK BEAN SALAD

PREP: 30 MINUTES **CHILL:** 2 TO 8 HOURS
GRIILL: 15 MINUTES **MAKES:** 8 SERVINGS

- 8 skinless, boneless chicken breast halves
- 1 cup shredded Monterey Jack cheese (4 ounces)
- 1 4-ounce can diced green chiles, undrained
- 3 tablespoons chopped green onions
- 1 teaspoon ground cumin
- 2 cloves garlic, minced
- 1 tablespoon olive oil
- ½ teaspoon salt
- ⅛ to ¼ teaspoon crushed red pepper
- 1 recipe Black Bean Salad

1 Make a pocket in each chicken breast half by cutting horizontally from the thickest side almost to the opposite side.

2 For stuffing, in a medium bowl combine cheese, undrained chiles, green onions, cumin, and garlic. Divide stuffing among pockets in chicken. If necessary, secure the openings with wooden toothpicks. Brush chicken with olive oil and sprinkle with salt and crushed red pepper.

3 For a charcoal grill, arrange medium-hot coals around a drip pan. Test for medium heat above pan. Place chicken on the greased grill rack over pan. Cover and grill 15 to 18 minutes or until chicken is no longer pink (170°F), turning once halfway through grilling. (For a gas grill, preheat grill. Reduce heat to medium. Adjust for indirect cooking. Place chicken on grill rack over burner that is turned off. Cover and grill as directed.)

4 To serve, remove and discard any toothpicks. Serve chicken with Black Bean Salad.

BLACK BEAN SALAD: In a large bowl combine one 15-ounce can black beans, rinsed and drained; 1 medium avocado, seeded, peeled, and chopped; ¾ cup chopped yellow sweet pepper; ⅓ cup chopped roma tomato; ¼ cup chopped red onion; ¼ cup snipped fresh cilantro; 2 tablespoons lime juice; 1 tablespoon olive oil; 1 fresh jalapeño chile pepper, seeded and chopped (see tip, page 24); 1 clove garlic, minced; ¼ teaspoon salt; and ¼ teaspoon black pepper. Cover and chill for 2 to 8 hours.

PER CHICKEN BREAST HALF + ½ CUP SALAD: 316 cal., 12 g total fat (4 g sat. fat, 0 g trans fat), 95 mg chol., 563 mg sodium, 12 g carbo., 5 g fiber, 40 g pro.
EXCHANGES: ½ Vegetable, ½ Starch, 5½ Lean Meat, 1 Fat

ORANGE CHICKEN KABOBS

PREP: 30 MINUTES **MARINATE:** 1 TO 4 HOURS
GRILL: 10 MINUTES **MAKES:** 8 SERVINGS

  6 skinless, boneless chicken breast halves
  ½ teaspoon salt
  ¼ teaspoon black pepper
  ¾ cup orange marmalade
  ½ cup chicken broth
  1 tablespoon finely shredded lemon peel
  ¼ cup lemon juice
  ¼ cup honey
  ¼ cup coarse-grain Dijon-style mustard
  3 tablespoons light mayonnaise
  1 tablespoon sesame seeds, toasted (see tip, page 20)
     Sliced green onions (optional)

1 Cut each chicken breast half lengthwise into four or five strips. Sprinkle chicken with salt and pepper. Place chicken in a large resealable plastic bag set in a shallow dish; set aside.

2 For marinade, in a medium bowl whisk together orange marmalade, chicken broth, lemon peel, and lemon juice. Pour over chicken in bag. Turn to coat chicken. Marinate in the refrigerator for 1 to 4 hours, turning bag occasionally.

3 For dipping sauce, in a small bowl stir together honey, mustard, mayonnaise, and sesame seeds. Cover and chill until ready to serve.

4 Drain chicken, discarding marinade. Thread chicken strips, accordion-style, onto skewers.

5 For a charcoal grill, grill kabobs on the rack of an uncovered grill directly over medium coals for 10 to 12 minutes or until chicken is no longer pink, turning occasionally to cook evenly. (For a gas grill, preheat grill. Reduce heat to medium. Place kabobs on grill rack over heat. Cover and grill as directed.) Serve chicken with dipping sauce. If desired, sprinkle with green onions.

PER 4 OUNCES CHICKEN + 2 TABLESPOONS SAUCE: 224 cal., 4 g total fat (1 g sat. fat, 0 g trans fat), 76 mg chol., 473 mg sodium, 15 g carbo., 0 g fiber, 30 g pro. EXCHANGES: 1 Other Carbo., 4½ Lean Meat

SESAME SECRETS
KEEP A KEEN EYE ON SESAME SEEDS AS YOU TOAST THEM. THE SEEDS QUICKLY GO FROM GORGEOUSLY GOLDEN TO SORROWFULLY SCORCHED.

FROM TAME TO TANTALIZING MILD CHICKEN BREASTS SOAK UP WINDFALLS OF LIVELY FLAVORS FROM MARINADES. FOR TENDER, MOIST RESULTS, DO NOT EXCEED MAXIMUM MARINATING TIMES.

ORANGE CHICKEN KABOBS

SOUTHWEST STUFFED CHICKEN BREASTS WITH BLACK BEAN SALAD

ALL-AMERICAN BARBECUED CHICKEN

PREP: 30 MINUTES **MARINATE:** 4 TO 6 HOURS
GRILL: 50 MINUTES **MAKES:** 4 TO 6 SERVINGS

- 3 to 3½ pounds meaty chicken pieces (breast halves, thighs, and drumsticks)
- 3 tablespoons lemon juice
- 1 tablespoon vegetable oil
- 1 teaspoon salt
- ½ teaspoon black pepper
- 1 clove garlic, minced
- 1 cup Balsamic BBQ Sauce (page 540)

1 Place chicken in a large resealable plastic bag set in a shallow dish. For marinade, stir together lemon juice, oil, salt, pepper, and garlic. Pour over chicken; seal bag. Marinate in the refrigerator for 4 to 6 hours, turning bag occasionally.

2 Drain chicken, discarding marinade. For a charcoal grill, arrange medium-hot coals around a drip pan. Test for medium heat above the pan. Place chicken, bone sides down, on grill rack over drip pan. Cover and grill for 50 to 60 minutes or until chicken is no longer pink (170°F for breast halves; 180°F for thighs and drumsticks), brushing with half of the Balsamic BBQ Sauce during the last 15 minutes of grilling. (For a gas grill, preheat grill. Reduce heat to medium. Adjust for indirect cooking. Place chicken pieces on grill rack over burner that is off. Grill as directed.) To serve, pass the remaining sauce with the chicken.

PER 2 PIECES: 630 cal., 37 g total fat (10 g sat. fat, 0 g trans fat), 173 mg chol., 900 mg sodium, 26 g carbo., 1 g fiber, 44 g pro. EXCHANGES: 2 Other Carbo., 6 Lean Meat, 3½ Fat

CHICKEN FOR A CROWD
YOU CAN EASILY DOUBLE OR TRIPLE THE RECIPE FOR THIS BACKYARD FAVORITE.

TIMING IS EVERYTHING BRUSH FOODS WITH BARBECUE SAUCE TOWARD THE END OF GRILLING. IF YOU ADD THE SAUCE TOO SOON, IT MIGHT BURN, BRINGING A CHARRED FLAVOR TO THE FOOD.

ALL-AMERICAN BARBECUED CHICKEN

GINGER-PEACH-GLAZED CHICKEN

PREP: 15 MINUTES **GRILL:** 50 MINUTES
MAKES: 4 SERVINGS

- 2½ to 3 pounds meaty chicken pieces (breast halves, thighs, and drumsticks)
  Salt and coarsely ground black pepper
- ½ cup peach preserves
- 1 tablespoon white wine vinegar
- 1 tablespoon prepared horseradish
- 1 teaspoon freshly grated ginger
- ½ teaspoon salt
- ½ teaspoon coarsely ground black pepper

1 If desired, skin chicken. Sprinkle chicken lightly with salt and pepper. For a charcoal grill, arrange preheated coals around a drip pan. Test for medium heat above the pan. Place chicken on grill rack above pan. Cover and grill for 40 minutes. (For a gas grill, preheat grill. Reduce heat to medium. Adjust for indirect cooking. Place chicken on grill rack over burner that is off. Grill as directed.)

2 Meanwhile, for glaze, place peach preserves in a small microwave-safe bowl; snip any large pieces. Stir in vinegar, horseradish, ginger, ½ teaspoon salt, and ½ teaspoon pepper. Microwave, uncovered, on 100% power (high) for 30 to 60 seconds or until preserves are melted, stirring once.

3 Brush glaze over chicken pieces. Cover and grill for 10 to 20 minutes more or until chicken is no longer pink (170°F for breast halves, 180°F for thighs and drumsticks), brushing occasionally with glaze. Spoon any remaining glaze over chicken.

PER 2 PIECES: 436 cal., 16 g total fat (4 g sat. fat, 0 g trans fat), 130 mg chol., 575 mg sodium, 28 g carbo., 1 g fiber, 42 g pro. EXCHANGES: 2 Other Carbo., 6 Lean Meat

BEST EVER

BEER-CAN CHICKEN

PREP: 25 MINUTES **GRILL:** 75 MINUTES
STAND: 10 MINUTES **MAKES:** 4 TO 6 SERVINGS

- 2 teaspoons salt
- 2 teaspoons packed brown sugar
- 2 teaspoons paprika
- 1 teaspoon dry mustard
- ½ teaspoon dried thyme, crushed
- ½ teaspoon black pepper
- ¼ teaspoon garlic powder
- 1 12-ounce can beer
- 1 3½- to 4-pound whole broiler-fryer chicken
- 2 tablespoons butter or margarine, softened
- 1 lemon wedge

1 For rub, in a small bowl combine salt, brown sugar, paprika, dry mustard, thyme, pepper, and garlic powder. Discard about half of the beer from the can. Add 1 teaspoon of the rub mixture to the half-empty can (beer will foam up).

2 Remove neck and giblets from chicken; reserve for another use or discard. Rinse the chicken body cavity; pat dry with paper towels. Sprinkle 1 teaspoon of the rub inside the body cavity. Add the softened butter to the remaining rub mixture in bowl; mix well. Rub butter mixture over the outside of the chicken.

3 Hold the chicken upright with the opening of the body cavity at the bottom and lower it onto the beer can so the can fits into the cavity. Pull the chicken legs forward so the bird rests on its legs and the can. Twist wing tips behind back. Stuff the lemon wedge in the neck cavity to seal in steam.*

4 For a charcoal grill, arrange medium-hot coals around a drip pan. Test for medium heat above pan. Stand chicken upright on grill rack over drip pan. Cover and grill for 75 to 105 minutes or until chicken is no longer pink (180°F in thigh muscle). If necessary, tent chicken with foil to prevent overbrowning. (For a gas grill, preheat grill. Reduce heat to medium. Adjust for indirect cooking. Place chicken on grill rack as directed over burner that is turned off. If necessary, remove upper grill racks so chicken will stand upright. Grill as directed.) With hot pads or oven mitts, carefully remove chicken from grill, holding by the can. Cover with foil; let stand for 10 minutes. To pull the can from the chicken, use a hot pad to grasp the can and heavy tongs to carefully remove the chicken.

*NOTE: To grill the chicken without the beer can, prepare chicken as directed. Place the chicken, breast side up, on grill rack directly over drip pan. Cover and grill as directed.

PER ¼ CHICKEN: 670 cal., 47 g total fat (15 g sat. fat, 0 g trans fat), 218 mg chol., 1,399 mg sodium, 6 g carbo., 2 g fiber, 51 g pro. EXCHANGES: ½ Other Carbo., 7½ Lean Meat, 5 Fat

NEW ENGLAND GRILLED TURKEY

PREP: 40 MINUTES **MARINATE:** 12 TO 24 HOURS
GRILL: 2½ HOURS **STAND:** 15 MINUTES
MAKES: 8 TO 12 SERVINGS

     4 cups hot water
  1¼ cups kosher salt
     1 cup pure maple syrup
     1 6-ounce can apple juice concentrate,
         thawed
   16 cups cold water
    ¼ teaspoon whole black peppercorns
     4 whole cloves
     3 cloves garlic, crushed
     1 8- to 10-pound whole turkey
    ½ cup butter, softened
     1 teaspoon ground sage
         Salt and black pepper
     1 recipe Gingered Cranberry Sauce

1 For brine, in a deep pot combine hot water, the
1¼ cups kosher salt, maple syrup, and juice concentrate. Stir until salt dissolves. Add cold water,
peppercorns, cloves, and garlic. Remove neck and
giblets from turkey; reserve for another use or
discard. Rinse turkey cavity. Add turkey to brine
and weight it to keep it covered by brine. Cover;
marinate in refrigerator 12 to 24 hours.

2 Drain turkey, discarding brine; pat dry. In a
small bowl combine butter and sage; set aside.
Starting at the neck on one side of the breast, slip
your fingers between skin and meat, loosening the
skin as you work toward the tail end. Once your
entire hand is under the skin, free the skin around
the thigh and leg area up to, but not around, the
tip of the drumstick. Repeat on the other side of
the breast. Rub sage butter under the skin directly
on meat. Skewer neck skin to the back. Twist
wing tips behind back. Sprinkle surface and cavity
of turkey with salt and pepper. Tuck drumsticks
under band of skin or tie to tail. Insert a meat
thermometer into center of an inside thigh muscle.

3 For a charcoal grill, arrange medium-hot coals
around a drip pan. Test for medium heat above the
pan. Place turkey in a foil pan on grill rack over drip
pan. Cover; grill for 2½ to 3 hours or until thermometer registers 180°F and turkey is no longer
pink, adding fresh coals every 45 to 60 minutes
and cutting band of skin or string the last hour of
grilling. (For a gas grill, preheat grill; reduce heat to
medium. Adjust for indirect cooking. Place turkey
in foil pan on rack over burner that is turned off.

Grill as directed.) Remove turkey from grill. Cover
with foil; let stand for 15 minutes before carving.
Serve with Gingered Cranberry Sauce.

GINGERED CRANBERRY SAUCE: In a medium
saucepan combine 1 cup sugar and 1 cup water.
Bring to boiling, stirring to dissolve sugar. Boil
rapidly for 5 minutes. Add 2 cups fresh cranberries, ½ cup snipped dried apples, 1½ teaspoons
grated fresh ginger, and 1 teaspoon finely shredded lemon peel. Return to boiling; reduce heat.
Boil gently, uncovered, over medium heat for
3 to 4 minutes or until cranberry skins pop,
stirring occasionally. Remove from heat. Serve
warm or chilled.

PER 4 OUNCES TURKEY + ⅓ CUP SAUCE: 330 cal., 10 g
total fat (4 g sat. fat, 0 g trans fat), 111 mg chol., 463 mg sodium,
33 g carbo., 2 g fiber, 28 g pro.
EXCHANGES: ½ Fruit, 1½ Other Carbo., 4 Lean Meat, 1 Fat

BUFFALO-STYLE TURKEY WRAPS

PREP: 35 MINUTES **MARINATE:** 2 TO 3 HOURS
GRILL: 12 MINUTES **MAKES:** 6 WRAPS

     2 turkey breast tenderloins (1 to
         1½ pounds)
     3 tablespoons bottled hot pepper sauce
     2 tablespoons vegetable oil
     2 teaspoons paprika
    ¼ teaspoon salt
    ¼ teaspoon cayenne pepper
     6 10-inch flour tortillas
  1½ cups thin carrot strips (3 medium)
  1½ cups thinly bias-sliced celery (3 stalks)
     3 cups shredded lettuce
     1 recipe Blue Cheese Sauce (page 355)

1 Cut each turkey tenderloin in half horizontally
to make 4 steaks. Place turkey steaks in a resealable plastic bag set in a shallow dish. For marinade, in a small bowl combine hot pepper sauce,
oil, paprika, salt, and cayenne pepper. Pour over
turkey in bag; seal bag. Marinate in the refrigerator for 2 to 3 hours, turning bag occasionally.

2 Drain turkey steaks, discarding marinade. For a
charcoal grill, grill turkey on the rack of an uncovered grill directly over medium coals for 12 to
15 minutes or until no longer pink (170°F), turning
once halfway through grilling. Wrap tortillas tightly
in foil. Place on grill rack; heat for 10 minutes,
turning once. (For a gas grill, preheat grill. Reduce
heat to medium. Place turkey and wrapped tortillas on grill rack over heat. Cover; grill as directed.)

3 Thinly slice turkey. Divide sliced turkey, carrots, celery, and lettuce among the warm tortillas. Top with Blue Cheese Sauce. Roll up tortillas tightly; serve immediately.

BLUE CHEESE SAUCE: In a blender or food processor combine ½ cup dairy sour cream; ¼ cup mayonnaise; ¼ cup crumbled blue cheese; 1 tablespoon lemon juice; 1 clove garlic, cut up; and ⅛ teaspoon salt. Cover and blend or process until nearly smooth.

PER WRAP: 377 cal., 19 g total fat (5 g sat. fat, 0 g trans fat), 63 mg chol., 513 mg sodium, 28 g carbo., 3 g fiber, 24 g pro. EXCHANGES: ½ Vegetable, 2 Starch, 2½ Lean Meat, 3 Fat

LOW FAT

TANDOORI-STYLE TURKEY KABOBS

PREP: 30 MINUTES **MARINATE:** 4 TO 24 HOURS
CHILL: 1 TO 4 HOURS **GRILL:** 14 MINUTES
MAKES: 4 SERVINGS

1½ pounds turkey tenderloins, cut into 1½-inch cubes
¾ cup plain low-fat yogurt
2 teaspoons finely shredded lime peel
3 tablespoons lime juice
½ of a fresh serrano chile pepper, seeded and finely chopped (see tip, page 24)
1 tablespoon grated fresh ginger
2 teaspoons paprika
1 teaspoon ground cumin
½ teaspoon ground coriander
½ teaspoon ground cardamom
¼ teaspoon cayenne pepper
6 cloves garlic, minced

1 recipe Carrot-Radish Salad
   Lime wedges (optional)

1 Place turkey in a large resealable plastic bag set in a shallow dish. For marinade, in a small bowl stir together yogurt, lime peel, lime juice, serrano pepper, ginger, paprika, cumin, coriander, cardamom, cayenne, and garlic. Pour over turkey in bag; seal bag. Marinate in refrigerator 4 to 24 hours.

2 If using wooden skewers, soak skewers in water for at least 30 minutes (see photo 1, below). Drain turkey, discarding marinade. Thread turkey onto skewers, leaving a ¼-inch space between pieces (see photo 2, below).

3 For charcoal grill, grill kabobs on rack of an uncovered grill directly over medium coals for 14 to 16 minutes or until turkey is no longer pink (170°F). (For a gas grill, preheat grill. Reduce heat to medium. Place kabobs on rack over heat. Cover and grill as directed.) Serve immediately with Carrot-Radish Salad and, if desired, lime wedges.

CARROT-RADISH SALAD: In a medium bowl stir together 1½ cups shredded carrots (3 medium); ½ cup shredded radishes; ½ cup golden raisins; and ¼ cup bias-sliced green onions (2). In a small bowl stir together ⅓ cup plain low-fat yogurt, ¼ teaspoon finely shredded lime peel, 1 tablespoon lime juice, 1 tablespoon honey, and ¼ teaspoon ground coriander. Stir yogurt mixture into carrot mixture. Cover and chill for 1 to 4 hours. Stir well before serving.

PER 5 OUNCES TURKEY + ⅔ CUP SALAD: 346 cal., 3 g total fat (1 g sat. fat, 0 g trans fat), 109 mg chol., 170 mg sodium, 34 g carbo., 3 g fiber, 47 g pro. EXCHANGES: 1 Vegetable, 2 Other Carbo., 6½ Lean Meat

ASSEMBLING TURKEY KABOBS, STEP-BY-STEP

1. Soak wooden skewers in water to keep them from scorching during grilling. Use a rectangular baking dish filled with about an inch of water. Soak the skewers for at least 30 minutes. **2.** Thread five or six turkey pieces onto each skewer, leaving about ¼ inch between the pieces. The space between the pieces ensures that the turkey will cook evenly.

THAI-STYLE SEA BASS

SECONDS COUNT GRILLED FISH CAN GO FROM SPARKLINGLY MOIST TO OVERCOOKED IN A MATTER OF SECONDS. STAY CLOSE BY THE GRILL AND CHECK FOR DONENESS AT THE MINIMUM GRILLING TIME.

GRILLED SALMON AND ASPARAGUS WITH
GARDEN MAYONNAISE

THAI-STYLE SEA BASS

PREP: 25 MINUTES **MARINATE:** 60 MINUTES
GRILL: 4 TO 6 MINUTES PER ½-INCH THICKNESS
MAKES: 4 SERVINGS

- 4 5- to 6-ounce fresh or frozen skinless sea bass fillets
- ¼ teaspoon salt
- ½ cup lime juice
- 2 tablespoons fish sauce or soy sauce
- 1 tablespoon toasted sesame oil
- 1 teaspoon sugar
- 1 teaspoon grated fresh ginger
- ¼ teaspoon crushed red pepper
- 1 tablespoon minced fresh garlic (6 cloves)
- 2 cups hot cooked rice noodles or rice
  Snipped fresh cilantro (optional)

1 Thaw fish, if frozen. Rinse fish; pat dry with paper towels. Measure thickness of fish. Sprinkle fish with salt. Place fish in a large resealable plastic bag set in a shallow dish; set aside.

2 In a small bowl stir together lime juice, fish sauce, sesame oil, sugar, ginger, crushed red pepper, and garlic. Pour half of the marinade over fish in bag; seal bag. Marinate in the refrigerator for 60 minutes, turning bag occasionally. Chill remaining lime juice mixture.

3 Drain fish, discarding marinade. For a charcoal grill, place fish on the greased rack of an uncovered grill directly over medium coals. Grill for 4 to 6 minutes per ½-inch thickness of fish or until fish begins to flake easily when tested with a fork. (For a gas grill, preheat grill. Reduce heat to medium. Place fish on greased grill rack over heat. Cover and grill as directed.)

4 Serve fish with rice noodles. Drizzle the remaining lime juice mixture over fish and noodles. If desired, sprinkle with cilantro.

PER FILLET + ½ CUP NOODLES: 270 cal., 6 g total fat (1 g sat. fat, 0 g trans fat), 58 mg chol., 781 mg sodium, 26 g carbo., 1 g fiber, 28 g pro.
EXCHANGES: 2 Starch, 3 Lean Meat

SEA BASS SUBSTITUTES
SEA BASS IS A LEAN TO MODERATELY FAT FISH, MAKING IT A GOOD CHOICE FOR GRILLING. IF IT'S NOT AVAILABLE, TRY ORANGE ROUGHY, GROUPER, OR RED SNAPPER.

GRILLED SALMON AND ASPARAGUS WITH GARDEN MAYONNAISE

PREP: 10 MINUTES **GRILL:** 8 MINUTES
MAKES: 4 SERVINGS

- 4 6- to 8-ounce fresh or frozen skinless salmon fillets, about 1 inch thick
- 1 pound asparagus spears
- 1 tablespoon olive oil
  Sea salt or salt
  Freshly ground black pepper
- ½ cup finely chopped celery (1 stalk)
- ⅓ cup mayonnaise
- ¼ cup thinly sliced green onions (2)
- 1 tablespoon lemon juice
- 2 teaspoons snipped fresh tarragon or
  ½ teaspoon dried tarragon, crushed
  Lemon wedges (optional)

1 Thaw fish, if frozen. Rinse fish; pat dry with paper towels. Snap off and discard woody bases from asparagus. Brush both sides of fish and asparagus lightly with olive oil. Sprinkle fish and asparagus with sea salt and pepper.

2 For a charcoal grill, place fish on the greased rack of an uncovered grill directly over medium coals. Place asparagus on grill rack next to salmon. Grill for 8 to 12 minutes or until fish begins to flake when tested with a fork and asparagus is tender, turning fish once halfway through grilling and turning asparagus occasionally. (For a gas grill, preheat grill. Reduce heat to medium. Place fish and asparagus on a greased grill rack over heat. Cover and grill as directed.)

3 Meanwhile, for garden mayonnaise, in a small bowl combine celery, mayonnaise, green onions, lemon juice, and tarragon. Chill until serving time.

4 To serve, arrange fish and asparagus on four dinner plates. Top fish with garden mayonnaise. If desired, serve with lemon wedges.

BROILER METHOD: Prepare as directed, except preheat broiler. Place salmon and asparagus on the unheated greased rack of a broiler pan. Broil 4 to 5 inches from the heat for 8 to 12 minutes or until fish begins to flake when tested with a fork and asparagus is tender, turning fish once and turning asparagus occasionally.

PER FILLET + 5 ASPARAGUS SPEARS + ¼ CUP MAYONNAISE: 545 cal., 41 g total fat (8 g sat. fat, 0 g trans fat), 100 mg chol., 314 mg sodium, 6 g carbo., 3 g fiber, 37 g pro.
EXCHANGES: 1 Vegetable, 5 Lean Meat, 5 Fat

GRILLED HALIBUT WITH CORN AND PEPPER RELISH

PREP: 45 MINUTES **GRILL:** 8 MINUTES
MAKES: 4 SERVINGS (PLUS 2 CUPS LEFTOVER RELISH)

- 4 5- to 6-ounce fresh or frozen halibut fillets, about 1 inch thick
  Kosher salt
  Freshly ground black pepper
- 4 tablespoons snipped fresh Italian parsley
- 3 tablespoons olive oil
- 1 tablespoon snipped fresh oregano
- 1½ cups fresh or frozen corn kernels
- 2 cups finely chopped red and/or green sweet peppers (2 large)
- ¼ teaspoon kosher salt
- ⅛ teaspoon cayenne pepper
- 2 cloves garlic, minced
- ½ cup chopped tomato (1 medium)
- ¼ cup finely chopped red onion
- 1 tablespoon white wine vinegar

1 Thaw fish, if frozen. Rinse fish; pat dry with paper towels. Sprinkle both sides of fish with kosher salt and black pepper. In a small bowl combine 1 table-spoon of the parsley, 1 tablespoon of the olive oil, and oregano. Rub over both sides of fish; set aside.

2 In a large skillet heat 1 tablespoon of the remaining oil over medium-high heat. Add corn; cook about 4 minutes or until corn begins to brown, stirring often. Add sweet peppers; cook and stir 2 minutes more. Stir in the ¼ teaspoon kosher salt, cayenne pepper, and the garlic. Cook and stir for 1 minute more. Remove from heat.

3 For a charcoal grill, place fish on the greased rack of an uncovered grill directly over medium coals. Grill for 8 to 12 minutes or until fish begins to flake when tested with a fork, turning once half-way through grilling. (For a gas grill, preheat grill. Reduce heat to medium. Place fish on greased grill rack over heat. Cover and grill as directed.)

4 Meanwhile, for relish, in a medium bowl combine corn mixture, tomato, red onion, vinegar, the remaining 3 tablespoons parsley, and the remaining 1 tablespoon olive oil; toss to mix.

5 To serve, place fillets on four dinner plates. Top each fillet with ½ cup relish. Cover and chill the remaining 2 cups relish for up to 3 days.

PER FILLET + ½ CUP RELISH: 289 cal., 14 g total fat (2 g sat. fat, 0 g trans fat), 45 mg chol., 263 mg sodium, 10 g carbo., 2 g fiber, 31 g pro.
EXCHANGES: ½ Vegetable, ½ Starch, 4 Lean Meat, 2 Fat

GRILLED PROSCIUTTO-STUFFED TROUT

PREP: 20 MINUTES **GRILL:** 6 MINUTES
MAKES: 4 SERVINGS

- 4 8- to 10-ounce fresh or frozen pan-dressed trout (see page 311)
- 1 tablespoon olive oil
- ¼ teaspoon salt
- ⅛ teaspoon black pepper
- 1 ounce prosciutto, chopped, or 2 slices bacon, crisp-cooked and crumbled
- 2 oil-packed dried tomatoes, patted dry and chopped
- 1 tablespoon snipped fresh Italian parsley
- ½ teaspoon finely shredded lemon peel
  Lemon wedges (optional)

1 Thaw trout, if frozen. Rinse trout; pat dry with paper towels. Brush the outside and inside of each trout with olive oil. Sprinkle inside of trout with salt and pepper. In a small bowl combine prosciutto, tomatoes, parsley, and lemon peel. Divide mixture among the cavities of each trout.

2 For a charcoal grill, place trout in a well-greased grill basket. Place trout on the rack of an uncovered grill directly over medium coals. Grill for 6 to 9 minutes or until trout begins to flake when tested with a fork, turning basket once halfway through grilling. (For a gas grill, preheat grill. Reduce heat to medium. Place trout in a well-greased grill basket. Place basket on grill rack over heat. Cover and grill as directed.) If desired, serve with lemon wedges.

PER TROUT: 174 cal., 11 g total fat (1 g sat. fat, 0 g trans fat), 46 mg chol., 317 mg sodium, 0 g carbo., 0 g fiber, 18 g pro.
EXCHANGES: 2½ Lean Meat, 1 Fat

SCALLOPS WITH GARLICKY TOMATILLO SALSA

PREP: 35 MINUTES **CHILL:** 30 MINUTES
GRILL: 2 MINUTES **MAKES:** 4 SERVINGS

- 16 fresh or frozen sea scallops (1½ to 2 pounds)
- 1 tablespoon olive oil
- ½ teaspoon ground ancho chile pepper
- ½ teaspoon smoked paprika
- 1 11- to 12-ounce can tomatillos, rinsed and drained
- ⅓ cup coarsely chopped red onion
- ⅓ cup lightly packed fresh cilantro

1 small fresh jalapeño chile pepper, seeded
   and cut up (see tip, page 24)
1 tablespoon lime juice
¾ teaspoon ground cumin
¼ teaspoon salt
4 large cloves garlic, halved
1 cup crumbled queso fresco (4 ounces)

1 Thaw scallops, if frozen. Rinse scallops with cold water; pat dry with paper towels. On two 10- to 12-inch skewers that are parallel to each other thread four of the scallops, leaving a ¼-inch space between each scallop. Repeat with the remaining scallops to make four sets of skewered scallops. Brush scallops with olive oil; sprinkle with ancho chile pepper and smoked paprika. Place on a tray; cover and chill for 30 minutes.

2 Meanwhile, for salsa, in a food processor or blender combine drained tomatillos, onion, cilantro, jalapeño pepper, lime juice, cumin, salt, and garlic. Cover and process or blend until mixture reaches consistency of a chunky sauce.

3 For a charcoal grill, place skewers on the rack of an uncovered grill directly over medium-hot coals for 2 to 3 minutes or until scallops turn opaque, turning once halfway through grilling. (For a gas grill, preheat grill. Reduce heat to medium-high. Place skewers on grill rack over heat. Cover and grill as directed.)

4 To serve, spoon salsa onto four serving plates. Top with skewers; sprinkle with queso fresco.

PER 4 SCALLOPS + ⅓ CUP SALSA: 303 cal., 8 g total fat (2 g sat. fat, 0 g trans fat), 100 mg chol., 1,228 mg sodium, 11 g carbo., 2 g fiber, 43 g pro.
EXCHANGES: ½ Vegetable, ½ Other Carbo., 6 Lean Meat, ½ Fat

LEMON SHRIMP AND BREAD SALAD

PREP: 30 MINUTES **MARINATE:** 60 MINUTES
GRILL: 17 MINUTES **STAND:** 20 MINUTES
MAKES: 4 TO 6 SERVINGS

1 pound fresh or frozen large shrimp
3 tablespoons olive oil
1 teaspoon lemon-pepper seasoning
2 large pita bread rounds
2 yellow sweet peppers, quartered
   lengthwise and seeded
1 cup chopped tomatoes (2 medium)
½ cup chopped English cucumber
¼ cup sliced radishes
¼ cup sliced green onions (2)
¼ cup bottled red wine vinaigrette

LEMON SHRIMP AND BREAD SALAD

1 Thaw shrimp, if frozen. Peel and devein shrimp (page 433). Rinse shrimp; pat dry. Place shrimp in a medium bowl. For marinade, stir together 2 tablespoons of the olive oil and the lemon-pepper seasoning. Toss shrimp with marinade. Cover and marinate in the refrigerator for 60 minutes, stirring occasionally. Thread shrimp on four long metal skewers, leaving a ¼-inch space between shrimp. Lightly brush pita bread and sweet pepper quarters with the remaining 1 tablespoon olive oil.

2 For a charcoal grill, grill sweet pepper quarters, cut sides up, on rack of an uncovered grill directly over medium-hot coals about 10 minutes or until pepper skins are blistered. Wrap peppers in foil and let stand for 20 minutes. Meanwhile, grill shrimp for 5 to 8 minutes or until shrimp turn opaque, turning once. Grill pita bread for 2 to 4 minutes or until lightly toasted, turning once. (For a gas grill, preheat grill. Reduce heat to medium-hot. Place peppers, cut sides up, and shrimp and bread on grill rack over heat. Cover; grill as directed.)

3 Peel and coarsely chop peppers. Cut pita into 1-inch pieces. Remove shrimp from skewers. In a bowl combine grilled peppers, bread, and shrimp. Stir in tomatoes, cucumber, radishes, and onions. Drizzle with vinaigrette. Toss gently to coat. Season with *salt* and *black pepper*. Serve immediately.

PER 2 CUPS: 376 cal., 17 g total fat (2 g sat. fat, 0 g trans fat), 172 mg chol., 802 mg sodium, 28 g carbo., 2 g fiber, 27 g pro.
EXCHANGES: 1 Vegetable, 1½ Starch, 3 Lean Meat, 2½ Fat

CORN ON THE COB WITH HERB BUTTER

PREP: 20 MINUTES **SOAK:** 60 MINUTES
GRILL: 25 MINUTES **MAKES:** 6 SERVINGS

    6 fresh ears corn (with husks)
    1 recipe Herb Butter
       Salt and black pepper

1 Place ears of corn with husks and silks intact in two very large bowls, two 13×9×2-inch pans, or a clean sink. Cover with water; soak corn for 60 minutes; drain.

2 For a charcoal grill, grill corn on the rack of an uncovered grill directly over medium coals for 25 to 30 minutes or until corn kernels are tender, turning and rearranging ears occasionally. (For a gas grill, preheat grill. Reduce heat to medium. Place corn on grill rack over heat. Cover and grill as directed.)

3 Cool slightly. Peel back cornhusks and silks. Serve with Herb Butter and salt and pepper.

HERB BUTTER: In a small bowl stir together 6 tablespoons softened butter and 2 tablespoons snipped fresh basil, cilantro, or thyme until combined. Serve immediately or cover and store in refrigerator for up to 1 week. Let chilled butter stand at room temperature for about 30 minutes or until spreadable before using.

PER EAR + 1 TABLESPOON HERB BUTTER: 180 cal., 13 g total fat (7 g sat. fat, 0 g trans fat), 31 mg chol., 192 mg sodium, 17 g carbo., 2 g fiber, 3 g pro.
EXCHANGES: 1 Starch, 2½ Fat

WHITE CHEDDAR AND NEW POTATOES HOBO PACK

PREP: 15 MINUTES **GRILL:** 35 MINUTES
STAND: 2 MINUTES **MAKES:** 4 SERVINGS

       Nonstick cooking spray
    1 pound fingerling, new red, or tiny
       yellow-flesh potatoes, halved
    ¼ cup chopped onion
    1 teaspoon snipped fresh thyme
    ¼ teaspoon salt
    ¼ teaspoon black pepper
    ¼ cup shredded white cheddar cheese
       (1 ounce)

1 Fold a 36×18-inch piece of heavy foil in half to make an 18-inch square. Coat foil with nonstick cooking spray. Place potatoes and onion in center of foil. Sprinkle with thyme, salt, and pepper. Bring up two opposite edges of foil; seal with a double fold. Fold remaining edges to completely enclose vegetables, leaving space for steam to build.

2 For a charcoal grill, grill packet on the rack of an uncovered grill directly over medium coals for 35 to 40 minutes or until potatoes are tender, turning packet occasionally. (For a gas grill, preheat grill. Reduce heat to medium. Place packet on a grill rack over heat. Cover and grill as directed.)

3 Carefully open packet; sprinkle potatoes with cheese. Loosely pinch packet together; let stand about 2 minutes or until cheese melts.

PER ¾ CUP: 120 cal., 2 g total fat (2 g sat. fat, 0 g trans fat), 7 mg chol., 197 mg sodium, 21 g carbo., 3 g fiber, 4 g pro.
EXCHANGES: 1½ Starch

HERBED POTATOES AND SQUASH

PREP: 20 MINUTES **GRILL:** 25 MINUTES
MAKES: 4 TO 6 SERVINGS

    2 tablespoons olive oil
    2 teaspoons snipped fresh rosemary or
       ½ teaspoon dried rosemary, crushed
    ½ teaspoon salt
    1 pound red and/or white tiny new potatoes,
       halved
    2 small yellow summer squash, cut into
       thick slices (about 2 cups)
       Snipped fresh rosemary (optional)

1 In a large bowl stir together olive oil, the 2 teaspoons rosemary, and the salt. Add potatoes; toss to coat potatoes with oil mixture.

2 For a charcoal grill, arrange medium-hot coals around a drip pan. Place a grill wok, basket, or foil pan on rack above drip pan; heat wok for 5 minutes. Add potatoes to wok; cover and grill for 10 minutes, stirring once. Add squash; cover and grill about 15 minutes more or until potatoes are tender, stirring once. (For a gas grill, preheat grill. Reduce heat to medium. Adjust for indirect cooking. Place grill wok, basket, or foil pan on rack over burner that is off. Cover grill and heat for 5 minutes. Add potatoes to wok; add squash to wok. Grill as directed.) Transfer to serving dish. If desired, sprinkle with fresh rosemary.

PER 1¼ CUPS: 147 cal., 7 g total fat (1 g sat. fat, 0 g trans fat), 0 mg chol., 249 mg sodium, 20 g carbo., 3 g fiber, 3 g pro.
EXCHANGES: ½ Vegetable, 1 Starch, 1 Fat

SMOKING ESSENTIALS

SMOKING IS ALL ABOUT "LOW AND SLOW." FOODS COOK AT TEMPERATURES BETWEEN 180°F AND 220°F, WITH COOKING TIMES UP TO THREE TIMES THAT OF GRILLING. THE RESULTS ARE LEGENDARY.

GENERAL SMOKING TIPS

Vertical water smokers are the most common type of smoker—follow manufacturer's directions for using. If you don't have a smoker, use your charcoal or gas grill. These hints help make for moist, smoke-imbued foods.

■ Maintain temperatures by adding 8 to 10 briquettes every 45 to 60 minutes. Do not add instant-start charcoal briquettes during the cooking process.

■ Keep the water pan filled to the recommended level, replenishing as needed with hot tap water. The water helps keep the temperature steady and adds moisture to keep meats tender.

■ Resist the temptation to peek. Heat and smoke escape each time you open the lid.

■ Start with a small amount of wood (about four chunks) to see how you like the flavor. Add more as desired to maintain smoke as you cook. Don't overdo it, though, and don't add wood after the first half of smoking. Adding wood too late in the process can impart a bitter flavor to food.

USING A CHARCOAL GRILL FOR SMOKING

When using a charcoal grill to smoke foods, follow the tips at left, as well as these steps.

1 Using long-handled tongs, arrange hot ash-covered coals around a foil pan that's filled with 1 inch of hot water.

2 Add the wood chips or chunks to coals.

3 Place food on grill rack above water pan and cover grill.

4 Check food, temperature, and water pan every 45 to 60 minutes. Add briquettes as needed.

USING A GAS GRILL FOR SMOKING

For a gas grill, follow these steps in addition to the relevant points under "General Smoking Tips."

1 Use wood chips, rather than chunks.

2 If your gas grill is equipped with a smoker box attachment, before firing up the grill, fill the pan on the attachment with hot water. Place wood chips in the compartment following manufacturer's instructions. If you don't have the attachment, place wood chips in a foil pan; cover pan with foil and poke 10 holes in the foil. Before lighting the grill, place the pan on the flavorizer bars (beneath the grate) in a corner of the grill. You do not need a water pan for cooking times less than 2 hours. For longer cooking, fill a foil pan with 1 inch hot water; place on the grate over a lit burner.

3 Place food on grill rack over unlit burner; cover.

4 Check food, temperature, and water pan every 45 to 60 minutes. Do not replenish wood chips.

FOOD AND WOOD PAIRINGS

Smoke only foods that can handle an assertive smoke flavor. These include beef, lamb, pork, poultry, oily fish, and game.

Wood type	Characteristics	Pair with
Alder	Delicate	Fish, pork, and poultry
Apple or cherry	Delicate, slightly sweet and fruity	Veal, pork, and poultry
Hickory	Strong and hearty, smoky	Beef brisket, ribs, pork chops, and game
Mesquite	Light, sweet	Most meats
Oak	Assertive but versatile	Beef, pork, and poultry
Pecan	Similar to hickory but more subtle	Pork, poultry, and fish

SPICY-AND-SASSY BEEF RIBS

PREP: 30 MINUTES **CHILL:** 8 TO 24 HOURS
SMOKE: 2½ HOURS **MAKES:** 4 SERVINGS

- 4 pounds beef back ribs (about 8 ribs)
- 1 tablespoon garlic salt
- 1 tablespoon paprika
- 1 tablespoon finely cracked mixed peppercorns or 1½ teaspoons coarsely ground black pepper
- ½ teaspoon onion powder
- ½ teaspoon ground cumin
- ½ teaspoon dried thyme, crushed
- ¼ teaspoon ground coriander
- ⅛ teaspoon cayenne pepper
- ⅛ teaspoon ground cardamom
- 8 to 10 mesquite or hickory wood chunks
- 1 recipe Mustard Dipping Sauce

1 Trim fat from ribs. For rub, in a small bowl combine garlic salt, paprika, peppercorns, onion powder, cumin, thyme, coriander, cayenne pepper, and cardamom. Sprinkle the rub evenly over ribs; rub in with your fingers. Wrap meat tightly in plastic wrap; chill for 8 to 24 hours.

2 In a smoker arrange preheated coals, wood chunks, and water pan according to the manufacturer's directions. Pour water into pan. Place ribs, bone sides down, on the grill rack over water pan. Cover and smoke for 2½ to 3 hours or until tender. Add additional coals and water as needed to maintain temperature and moisture. Serve ribs with Mustard Dipping Sauce.

MUSTARD DIPPING SAUCE: In a small saucepan whisk together ⅓ cup Dijon-style mustard, ¼ cup honey, ¼ cup apple juice, 4 teaspoons packed brown sugar, 1 tablespoon cider vinegar, and ⅛ teaspoon salt. Bring to boiling; reduce heat. Simmer, uncovered, for 3 minutes. Serve warm or chilled.

PER 2 RIBS + ¼ CUP SAUCE: 1,272 cal., 89 g total fat (34 g sat. fat, 0 g trans fat), 302 mg chol., 1,488 mg sodium, 25 g carbo., 1 g fiber, 84 g pro.
EXCHANGES: 1½ Other Carbo., 12 Medium-Fat Meat, 6 Fat

SMOKED BEEF BRISKET

PREP: 45 MINUTES **CHILL:** 8 TO 24 HOURS
SMOKE: 8 HOURS **STAND:** 15 MINUTES
MAKES: 10 TO 12 SERVINGS + LEFTOVERS

- 2 tablespoons paprika
- 1 tablespoon chili powder
- 1 teaspoon ground coriander
- 1 teaspoon ground cumin
- 1 teaspoon sugar
- 1 teaspoon salt
- ½ teaspoon black pepper
- ½ teaspoon curry powder
- ½ teaspoon dry mustard
- ½ teaspoon cayenne pepper
- ½ teaspoon dried thyme, crushed
- 2 cups bottled barbecue sauce
- 1 10- to 12-pound fresh beef brisket
- 8 to 10 mesquite or hickory wood chunks

1 For rub, in a bowl combine paprika, chili powder, coriander, cumin, sugar, salt, black pepper, curry powder, mustard, cayenne, and thyme. Stir 1 tablespoon of the rub mixture into barbecue sauce; cover and chill. Do not trim fat from brisket. Sprinkle brisket with remaining rub mixture. Wrap meat tightly in plastic wrap; chill for 8 to 24 hours.

2 In smoker arrange preheated coals, half of the wood chunks, and water pan according to manufacturer's directions. Pour water into pan. Place brisket, fat side up, on grill rack over water pan. Cover; smoke for 8 to 10 hours or until a fork can easily be inserted into meat. Add additional coals and water as needed to maintain temperature and moisture. Add additional wood chips as needed during the first 3 hours. (Too much smoke can give a bitter taste to smoked meat.)

3 Remove brisket from smoker. Cover; let stand for 15 minutes. Meanwhile, in a small saucepan heat barbecue sauce over low heat. Trim away crusty outer layer from brisket. Starting at the widest end, cut along the seam of fat running through the meat, slicing the meat in half horizontally. Trim away excess fat. Slice each section across the grain. Serve with hot barbecue sauce.

PER 4 OUNCES + ¼ CUP SAUCE: 443 cal., 34 g total fat (14 g sat. fat, 0 g trans fat), 121 mg chol., 356 mg sodium, 7 g carbo., 1 g fiber, 27 g pro.
EXCHANGES: 1 Other Carbo., 4 Medium-Fat Meat, 3 Fat

PULLED PORK SHOULDER

PREP: 15 MINUTES **SMOKE:** 4 HOURS
STAND: 15 MINUTES
MAKES: 14 TO 18 SANDWICHES

- 1 tablespoon paprika
- 1 tablespoon black pepper
- 2 teaspoons salt
- 2 teaspoons chili powder
- 2 teaspoons ground cumin
- 2 teaspoons packed brown sugar
- 1 teaspoon granulated sugar
- 1 teaspoon cayenne pepper
- 1 5- to 5½-pound boneless pork shoulder roast
- 6 to 8 hickory wood chunks or 3 cups hickory wood chips
- 1 recipe Vinegar Barbecue Sauce
- 14 to 18 hamburger buns
  Bottled hot pepper sauce (optional)

1 For rub, in a small bowl stir together paprika, black pepper, salt, chili powder, cumin, brown sugar, granulated sugar, and cayenne pepper. Sprinkle rub evenly over meat; rub in with your fingers.

2 In a smoker arrange preheated coals, wood chunks, and water pan according to the manufacturer's directions. Pour water into pan. Place meat on the grill rack over water pan. Cover and smoke for 4 to 5 hours or until meat is very tender. Add additional coals and water as needed to maintain temperature and moisture. Do not add wood after the first 2 hours of smoking. (Too much smoke can give a bitter taste to smoked meat.)

3 Remove meat from smoker. Cover meat with foil; let stand for 15 minutes. Cut meat into thick pieces (see photo 1, below). Using two forks, gently pull the meat into long thin shreds (see photo 2, below). Place pulled pork in a large bowl. Add about 1½ cups of the Vinegar Barbecue Sauce. Stir until slightly moist, adding sauce if necessary.

4 To serve, pile meat mixture onto buns. If desired, sprinkle with hot pepper sauce. Serve with remaining sauce.

VINEGAR BARBECUE SAUCE: In a clean 1-quart jar with a screw-top lid combine 3 cups cider vinegar, ⅓ cup granulated sugar, 1 tablespoon dry mustard, 2 to 3 teaspoons crushed red pepper, 2 teaspoons bottled hot pepper sauce, 1½ teaspoons salt, and 1½ teaspoons black pepper. Cover and shake well.

MAKE-AHEAD DIRECTIONS: Prepare as directed through Step 4. Cover and chill pork for up to 3 days. Reheat in a large pot over medium heat, stirring occasionally.

PER SANDWICH: 390 cal., 17 g total fat (6 g sat. fat, 0 g trans fat), 76 mg chol., 875 mg sodium, 29 g carbo., 2 g fiber, 26 g pro. EXCHANGES: 2 Starch, 3 Medium-Fat Meat

PASS THE COLESLAW
ON THE SIDE OR IN A BUN, COLESLAW IS THE CONDIMENT OF CHOICE FOR PULLED PORK SANDWICHES.

PULLING SMOKED PORK, STEP-BY-STEP

1. To shred the pork, first use a sharp carving knife to cut the smoked roast into large pieces. **2.** Insert two forks into a piece of meat and pull in opposite directions. The meat will easily form shreds that are perfect for a sandwich filling.

MAPLE-SMOKED SALMON FILLET

until juices run clear (170°F for breasts; 180°F for thighs and drumsticks). Add additional coals and water to maintain temperature and moisture.

PER 2 PIECES: 363 cal., 26 g total fat (7 g sat. fat, 0 g trans fat), 116 mg chol., 507 mg sodium, 3 g carbo., 0 g fiber, 29 g pro. EXCHANGES: 4 Lean Meat, 3 Fat

MAPLE-SMOKED SALMON FILLET

PREP: 15 MINUTES **MARINATE:** 60 MINUTES
SMOKE: 50 MINUTES **MAKES:** 4 SERVINGS

> 1 2-pound fresh or frozen salmon fillet (with skin), about 1 inch thick
> 6 to 8 alder or apple wood chunks
> ½ cup pure maple syrup
> 2 tablespoons water
> 1 tablespoon coarsely cracked mixed peppercorns
> ¼ teaspoon salt
> 2 tablespoons pure maple syrup

1 Thaw salmon, if frozen. Rinse fish; pat dry with paper towels. Place fish in a large resealable plastic bag set in a baking dish. For marinade, in a small bowl combine the ½ cup maple syrup, the water, peppercorns, and salt. Pour marinade over fish; seal bag. Marinate in refrigerator 60 minutes, turning bag occasionally.

2 Drain fish, discarding marinade. Lightly sprinkle salmon with additional salt.

3 In a smoker arrange preheated coals, wood chunks, and water pan according to the manufacturer's directions. Pour water into pan. Place salmon, skin side down, on grill rack over water pan. Cover and smoke for 45 to 60 minutes or until fish begins to flake when tested with a fork. Brush salmon with the 2 tablespoons maple syrup. Cover and smoke for 5 minutes more.

4 To serve, cut salmon into four equal pieces, cutting to, but not through, the skin. Carefully slip a metal spatula between the fish and skin, lifting fish away from skin. Transfer to four dinner plates.

PER SERVING: 516 cal., 30 g total fat (7 g sat. fat, 0 g trans fat), 123 mg chol., 310 mg sodium, 12 g carbo., 0 g fiber, 46 g pro. EXCHANGES: 1 Other Carbo., 6½ Lean Meat, 2 Fat

JERK-STYLE SMOKED CHICKEN

PREP: 15 MINUTES **MARINATE:** 1 TO 4 HOURS
SMOKE: 90 MINUTES **MAKES:** 6 SERVINGS

> 3 pounds meaty chicken pieces (breasts, thighs, and drumsticks)
> ½ cup tomato juice
> ⅓ cup finely chopped onion (1 small)
> 2 tablespoons water
> 2 tablespoons lime juice
> 1 tablespoon vegetable oil
> 1 tablespoon Pickapeppa sauce (optional)
> ½ teaspoon salt
> 4 cloves garlic, minced
> 6 to 8 fruit wood chunks
> 1 to 2 tablespoons Jamaican jerk seasoning

1 If desired, remove skin from chicken. Place chicken in a resealable plastic bag set in a deep dish. For marinade, in a small bowl combine tomato juice, onion, water, lime juice, oil, Pickapeppa sauce (if desired), salt, and garlic. Pour over chicken; seal bag. Marinate in the refrigerator for 1 to 4 hours, turning bag occasionally.

2 Drain chicken, discarding marinade. Rub jerk seasoning evenly over chicken.

3 In a smoker arrange preheated coals, wood chunks, and water pan according to the manufacturer's directions. Pour water into pan. Place chicken, bone sides down, on grill rack over water pan. Cover and smoke for 1½ to 2 hours or

TURKEY FRYER ESSENTIALS

COOKING WITH A TURKEY FRYER HAS JOINED THE RANKS OF GRILLING AND SMOKING AS ALL-TIME FAVORITE BACKYARD PURSUITS.

No matter what you're sizzling up in that fryer, follow instructions closely and never take shortcuts when it comes to safety.

SETUP AND TAKEDOWN

■ Read and follow the manufacturer's directions.

■ Never operate a turkey fryer indoors or in a garage or other attached structure. Do not cook on a wooden deck, which might catch fire.

■ Position the fryer on a level dirt or grassy area. You can also place the fryer on a concrete surface. To avoid grease stains, place a layer of sand under and around the fryer. The sand absorbs any oil that spills and easily cleans up when finished.

■ Check the level of fuel in your propane tank. You will need about 1½ hours of fuel for deep-frying a turkey—half for bringing the oil up to temperature and half for the actual cooking.

■ Do not cover the pot when deep-frying.

■ Choose an oil with a high smoke point such as peanut, corn, canola, soybean, safflower, or cottonseed oil.

■ Do not overfill the fryer with oil.

■ Never leave hot oil unattended. The oil stays hot for hours after you turn off the burner, so allow it to cool in a safe place.

■ Keep children and pets away from the frying area.

EQUIPMENT

■ Wear heat-resistant gloves, long sleeves, and an apron to protect yourself from splattering oil.

■ Use long-handled tongs, meat forks, slotted fry spoons, and/or a fry basket to add and remove foods from fryer.

■ When frying poultry and meat, an instant-read meat thermometer is a handy tool to determine when the food is done.

■ Have plates, platters, and paper towels handy.

■ Keep a fire extinguisher close at hand.

■ Make sure there is 5 to 6 inches from surface of the oil to the rim of the pot. This space is needed because the oil will bubble up during cooking.

■ Once the oil reaches the appropriate temperature, turn off the burner before slowly lowering the food into the hot oil. Relight the burner after the food is in the pot and turn it off again when you're ready to remove the food.

■ Monitor the oil temperature by using a deep-frying thermometer.

■ Allow the oil to completely cool after use. To discard, return cooled oil to the original container.

■ If you plan to reuse the oil, strain it through 100%-cotton cheesecloth and store in a covered container in the refrigerator. You can reuse oil once or twice within 1 month only if the food cooked in the oil didn't burn.

CALCULATING FRYING TIME

Use this chart to estimate frying times for foods. After the minimum cooking time remove the food from the fryer and check the internal temperature with an instant-read meat thermometer. See page 368 for additional tips.

Food	Time	Oil temperature*
Turkey, whole	3 minutes per pound	350°F
Turkey breast with bone (about 5 to 6 pounds)	45 to 55 minutes	350°F
Turkey legs (2 legs, 10 ounces each)	about 20 minutes	350°F
Chicken, whole (about 3½ to 4 pounds)	25 to 30 minutes	350°F
Cornish hens (2 hens, 1¼ pounds each)	15 to 18 minutes	350°F
Duck, whole (4 to 6 pounds)	40 to 60 minutes	350°F

*To maintain recommended temperatures, oil must be 10°F hotter before food is added.

MOZZARELLA CHEESE STICKS

PREP: 20 MINUTES **FREEZE:** 1 TO 48 HOURS
FRY: 2 MINUTES PER BATCH **MAKES:** 12 STICKS

- ¾ cup all-purpose flour
- ½ teaspoon salt
- ½ teaspoon black pepper
- 2 eggs, lightly beaten
- 2 tablespoons water
- 12 mozzarella cheese sticks or one 16-ounce block mozzarella cheese, cut into twelve 4×½-inch sticks
- 1 cup fine dry Italian bread crumbs
  Peanut oil or other vegetable oil
- ¾ cup marinara sauce

1 In a shallow dish combine flour, salt, and pepper. In another shallow dish combine eggs and water. Dip cheese sticks in egg mixture, then coat with flour mixture. Dip cheese sticks again in egg mixture (see photo 1, below); coat with bread crumbs (see photo 2, below). Place on a baking sheet. Cover; freeze for 1 hour or up to 2 days.*

2 In a turkey fryer preheat oil to 350°F. Preheat basket in hot oil. Fry cheese sticks, half at a time, in basket for 2 to 2 ½ minutes or until crisp and golden. Do not crowd. Be cautious of splattering oil. Maintain oil temperature around 350°F. Remove cheese sticks from hot oil; drain on wire racks (see photo 3, below). In a small saucepan heat marinara sauce over medium heat. Serve cheese sticks with hot marinara sauce.

*NOTE: If the cheese sticks are frozen for 1 to 2 days, let stand at room temperature for 15 minutes before frying.

PER STICK + 1 TABLESPOON SAUCE: 254 cal., 16 g total fat (6 g sat. fat, 0 g trans fat), 65 mg chol., 592 mg sodium, 15 g carbo., 1 g fiber, 12 g pro.
EXCHANGES: 1 Starch, 1 High-Fat Meat, 1½ Fat

SWEET-AND-SAVORY POTATO CHIPS

PREP: 25 MINUTES **SOAK:** 10 MINUTES
FRY: 3 MINUTES PER BATCH
MAKES: 12 TO 16 SERVINGS

- Peanut oil or other vegetable oil
- 3 medium sweet potatoes (1 pound)
- 3 medium baking potatoes (1 pound)
- Coarse salt

FRYING MOZZARELLA STICKS, STEP-BY-STEP

1. Dip cheese sticks in the egg mixture, coating all sides. Roll the sticks in the flour mixture, then dip again in the egg mixture. **2.** Sprinkle some of the bread crumbs over the top and turn the cheese sticks to be sure all sides are well coated. **3.** When the cheese sticks are golden, use tongs to remove to a wire rack to drain and cool slightly.

1 In a turkey fryer preheat oil to 350°F. Peel potatoes; cut into very thin slices (about 1/16 inch thick).* Place potato slices in a large bowl of ice water; soak for 10 minutes. Drain potato slices; pat dry with paper towels.

2 Fry potato slices, half at a time, in the basket for 3 to 5 minutes or until crisp and golden. Do not crowd. Be cautious of splattering oil. Maintain oil temperature around 350°F. Remove potato slices from the hot oil; drain on wire racks.

3 Sprinkle with salt. If desired, fry chips up to 2 days ahead and store in an airtight container.

*NOTE: A mandoline, a special slicing tool, makes quick work of slicing thin, even potato slices. Look for a mandoline at a kitchen specialty shop.

PER 3/4 CUP: 101 cal., 5 g total fat (1 g sat. fat, 0 g trans fat), 0 mg chol., 103 mg sodium, 14 g carbo., 2 g fiber, 1 g pro. EXCHANGES: 1 Starch, 1 Fat

PORK CHOPS ON A STICK

PREP: 15 MINUTES **MARINATE:** 60 MINUTES
FRY: 5 MINUTES PER BATCH **MAKES:** 8 SERVINGS

　　8　6-ounce boneless pork loin chops, about
　　　　1 inch thick
　　½　cup bottled Italian salad dressing
　　　　Peanut oil or other vegetable oil
　　8　8×¼-inch wooden skewers or dowels
　　　　Honey mustard or bottled barbecue sauce

1 Place chops in a resealable plastic bag set in a shallow dish. Pour salad dressing over chops; seal bag. Marinate in the refrigerator for 60 minutes, turning bag occasionally.

2 Meanwhile, in a turkey fryer preheat oil to 350°F. Drain chops, discarding marinade. Insert a wooden skewer into a short side of each chop. Place skewers, half at a time, in fry basket for 5 to 7 minutes or until chops are done (160°F). (To test for doneness, carefully remove one chop from the hot oil. Insert an instant-read meat thermometer horizontally into chop.) Be cautious of splattering oil. Maintain oil temperature around 350°F. Remove chops from hot oil and drain on wire racks. Serve chops with honey mustard.

PER CHOP: 346 cal., 19 g total fat (5 g sat. fat, 0 g trans fat), 93 mg chol., 213 mg sodium, 2 g carbo., 0 g fiber, 37 g pro. EXCHANGES: 5 Lean Meat, 1 Fat

FRIED CHICKEN TENDERS

PREP: 35 MINUTES **FRY:** 5 MINUTES PER BATCH
MAKES: 10 TO 12 SERVINGS (3 PIECES EACH)

　　3　pounds fresh or frozen chicken breast
　　　　tenders (about 30 to 36)
　　　　Peanut oil or other vegetable oil
　　4　cups all-purpose flour
　　2　teaspoons garlic salt
　　1　teaspoon black pepper
　　3　cups buttermilk
　　1　recipe Cayenne-Butter Sauce (optional)
　　　　Bottled ranch or blue cheese salad
　　　　dressing, or Creamy Parmesan Dressing
　　　　(page 500) (optional)

1 Thaw chicken, if frozen. In a turkey fryer preheat oil to 365°F. Preheat basket in hot oil.

2 Meanwhile, in a large bowl stir together flour, garlic salt, and pepper; transfer half of the mixture to another bowl. Pour buttermilk into a medium bowl. Dip chicken in buttermilk, allowing excess to drip off. Dip in flour mixture to coat (when flour mixture in first bowl clumps too much, discard and use remaining flour mixture in second bowl).

3 Preheat oven to 200°F. Fry chicken tenders, one-fourth at a time, in the basket about 5 minutes or until golden brown and chicken is no longer pink. Be cautious of splattering oil. Maintain oil temperature around 365°F. Keep fried chicken warm on a baking sheet in oven while frying remaining chicken.

4 If desired, serve chicken with Cayenne-Butter Sauce and/or salad dressing.

CAYENNE-BUTTER SAUCE: In a blender combine 1 cup bottled cayenne pepper sauce and ⅔ cup melted butter. Cover and blend about 1 minute or until slightly thickened.

PER 3 PIECES + 2 TABLESPOONS SAUCE: 648 cal., 35 g total fat (6 g sat. fat, 0 g trans fat), 82 mg chol., 359 mg sodium, 42 g carbo., 1 g fiber, 39 g pro. EXCHANGES: 3 Starch, 4 Lean Meat, 5½ Fat

---

APPETIZER OR MAIN EVENT
SERVE CRISP FRIED CHICKEN TENDERS AS AN APPETIZER. OR SERVE WITH BARBECUE OR SWEET-AND-SOUR SAUCE FOR A KID-PLEASING MAIN DISH.

TIPS FOR TURKEY FRYING
DEEP-FRYING A TURKEY TAKES SOME KNOW-HOW AND PRECAUTIONS.

■ Select turkeys that weigh 12 pounds or less. If you need to serve more people, consider frying two smaller turkeys.

■ Never fry a turkey that is too big for the fryer pot. The pot must be big enough to hold the turkey and enough oil to completely cover the turkey (up to 5 gallons).

■ To determine the amount of oil needed, place the unwrapped frozen turkey in the empty fryer pot; fill the pot with enough water to cover the bird by 1 to 2 inches. Remove the bird and mark the waterline. This is the level of oil you will need. Dry the pot thoroughly before adding oil.

■ Rinse the body cavity of the thawed turkey; thoroughly pat dry both the inside and outside of the turkey with paper towels.

■ Make sure equipment is dry before frying. All food that goes into the fryer must be blotted dry to avoid splattering oil.

■ Do not stuff the turkey.

■ Remove all plastic parts from turkey, including tie that holds legs and pop-up timer.

■ Check the internal temperature of turkey for doneness by inserting an instant-read thermometer into the meaty part of a thigh. The thermometer should register 180°F. If the turkey has not reached 180°F, remove the thermometer and slowly lower the turkey back into the oil. Fry 3 to 5 minutes more and check temperature again.

CAJUN DEEP-FRIED TURKEY

PREP: 30 MINUTES **FRY:** 24 MINUTES
STAND: 15 MINUTES **MAKES:** 10 TO 12 SERVINGS

  1 8- to 10-pound turkey
     Peanut oil or other vegetable oil
1½ teaspoons salt
1½ teaspoons sweet paprika
 ¾ teaspoon dried thyme, crushed
 ¾ teaspoon black pepper
 ½ teaspoon garlic powder
 ½ teaspoon onion powder
 ¼ teaspoon cayenne pepper

1 Remove the neck and giblets from the turkey. Rinse the turkey body cavity; pat dry with paper towels. If present, remove and discard the plastic leg holder and pop-up timer. In a turkey fryer preheat oil to 350°F.

2 For rub, in a small bowl combine salt, paprika, thyme, black pepper, garlic powder, onion powder, and cayenne pepper. Slip your fingers between turkey skin and meat to loosen the skin over the breast and leg areas. Lift skin and spread some of the rub directly over breast, thigh, and drumstick meat. Season cavity with any remaining rub. Tuck the ends of the drumsticks under the band of skin across the tail or tie legs to tail with 100%-cotton kitchen string. Twist wing tips under back.

3 Place turkey, breast side up, in turkey rack. Use the grab hook to slowly lower turkey into hot oil. Be cautious of splattering oil. Maintain oil temperature around 350°F. Fry turkey for 24 to 30 minutes (3 minutes per pound). Remove turkey from hot oil to check doneness by inserting an instant-read meat thermometer into the meaty part of the thigh. Turkey is done when thermometer registers 180°F (see last tip, left).

4 Remove turkey from hot oil; drain on wire rack. Let stand for 15 minutes before carving.

PER 4 OUNCES: 255 cal., 15 g total fat (3 g sat. fat, 0 g trans fat), 100 mg chol., 231 mg sodium, 0 g carbo., 0 g fiber, 28 g pro. EXCHANGES: 4 Lean Meat, ½ Fat

GLAZED CHICKEN

PREP: 30 MINUTES **FRY:** 40 MINUTES
STAND: 15 MINUTES **MAKES:** 6 TO 8 SERVINGS

     Peanut oil or other vegetable oil
  1 5- to 6-pound whole roasting chicken
  1 recipe Maple-Mustard Glaze or Chipotle-Raspberry Glaze (page 369)

1 In a turkey fryer preheat oil to 350°F. Remove neck and giblets from chicken. Weigh chicken to determine cooking time. Rinse inside of chicken; pat dry with paper towels. Skewer neck skin to back. Tie legs to tail with 100%-cotton kitchen string. Twist wing tips under back.

2 Place the chicken, breast side up, in the basket. Slowly lower the basket into the hot oil. Be cautious of splattering oil. Maintain the oil temperature around 350°F. Fry chicken for 40 to 48 minutes (8 minutes per pound).

3 Remove chicken from hot oil to check doneness. Insert an instant-read meat thermometer into the meaty part of the thigh. Chicken is done when thermometer registers 180°F (see tips, page 368). Remove chicken from hot oil; drain on wire rack. Spoon Maple-Mustard Glaze or Chipotle-Raspberry Glaze over hot chicken. Let chicken stand for 15 minutes before carving.

MAPLE-MUSTARD GLAZE: In a small saucepan combine ¼ cup pure maple syrup, 3 tablespoons butter, 2 tablespoons frozen orange juice concentrate, 2 tablespoons coarse-grain brown mustard, and ¼ to ½ teaspoon cayenne pepper. Bring to boiling; reduce heat. Simmer, uncovered, for 2 to 3 minutes. Remove saucepan from heat; stir in ¼ cup finely chopped toasted pecans (see tip, page 20) and 1 to 1½ teaspoons finely shredded orange peel.

PER ⅙ CHICKEN WITH MUSTARD GLAZE: 764 cal., 57 g total fat (17 g sat. fat, 0 g trans fat), 208 mg chol., 342 mg sodium, 12 g carbo., 1 g fiber, 48 g pro.
EXCHANGES: 1 Other Carbo., 7 Lean Meat, 7 Fat

CHIPOTLE-RASPBERRY GLAZE: In a medium saucepan stir together 1½ cups seedless raspberry preserves; 2 tablespoons white vinegar; 2 or 3 whole chipotle peppers in adobo sauce, drained and chopped; and 3 cloves garlic, minced. Bring to boiling; reduce heat. Simmer, uncovered, for 5 minutes.

PER ⅙ CHICKEN WITH CHIPOTLE-RASPBERRY GLAZE: 859 cal., 48 g total fat (13 g sat. fat, 0 g trans fat), 193 mg chol., 214 mg sodium, 56 g carbo., 1 g fiber, 48 g pro.
EXCHANGES: 4 Other Carbo., 7 Lean Meat, 5½ Fat

OPTIONS GALORE
ANOTHER TIME TRY THIS CHICKEN WITH PURCHASED BARBECUE SAUCE, AN ASIAN-STYLE SAUCE, OR APRICOT-CHERRY GLAZE ON PAGE 405.

PASS THE SAUCE, PLEASE POUR JUST ENOUGH GLAZE OVER THE CHICKEN TO LIGHTLY COAT IT. POUR THE REMAINING GLAZE INTO A SMALL BOWL OR GRAVY BOAT AND PASS WITH THE CHICKEN.

GLAZED CHICKEN WITH MAPLE-MUSTARD GLAZE

SHRIMP AND VEGETABLE TEMPURA

PREP: 25 MINUTES FRY: 3 MINUTES PER BATCH
MAKES: 4 SERVINGS

- 12 large fresh or frozen shrimp in shells (about 6 ounces)
- Peanut oil or other vegetable oil
- 1½ cups all-purpose flour
- 1½ teaspoons salt
- 1 teaspoon black pepper
- ½ teaspoon cayenne pepper
- 1 12-ounce can beer
- 3 medium red, yellow, and/or orange sweet peppers, cut into ½-inch rings
- 3 cups broccoli florets
- 1 recipe Soy Dipping Sauce

1 Thaw shrimp, if frozen. Peel and devein shrimp (see page 433). If desired, remove the tails. Rinse shrimp and pat dry with paper towels.

2 In a turkey fryer preheat oil to 350°F. For batter, in a large bowl combine flour, salt, black pepper, and cayenne pepper. Slowly whisk in beer until batter is smooth. Dip shrimp, sweet peppers, and broccoli into batter; let excess drip off.

3 Fry shrimp and vegetables, five or six pieces at a time, for 3 to 4 minutes or until crisp and golden. Do not crowd. Be cautious of splattering oil. Maintain oil temperature around 350°F. Remove shrimp and vegetables from hot oil; drain on wire racks. Serve shrimp and vegetables with Soy Dipping Sauce.

SOY DIPPING SAUCE: In a small bowl combine ¼ cup reduced-sodium soy sauce, 3 tablespoons rice vinegar, 2 tablespoons honey, 1 tablespoon thinly sliced green onion, and 2 teaspoons lime juice. Stir until honey dissolves.

PER 3 SHRIMP + ½ CUP VEGETABLES + 3 TABLESPOONS SAUCE: 473 cal., 15 g total fat (3 g sat. fat, 0 g trans fat), 65 mg chol., 1,533 mg sodium, 60 g carbo., 5 g fiber, 18 g pro. EXCHANGES: 1½ Vegetable, 3½ Starch, 1 Lean Meat, 2 Fat

DIRECT-GRILLING POULTRY

If desired, remove skin from poultry. For a charcoal grill, place poultry on grill rack, bone side(s) up, directly over medium coals (see page 336). Grill, uncovered, for time given below or until the proper temperature is reached and meat is no longer pink, turning once halfway through grilling. (For a gas grill, preheat grill. Reduce heat to medium. Place poultry on grill rack, bone side(s) down, over heat. Cover and grill.)

Test for doneness using a meat thermometer (use an instant-read thermometer to test small portions). Thermometer should register 180°F, except in breast meat where thermometer should register 170°F. If desired, during last 5 to 10 minutes of grilling, brush often with a sauce.

Type of Bird	Weight	Grilling Temperature	Approximate Direct-Grilling Time*	Doneness
CHICKEN				
Chicken breast half, skinned and boned	4 to 5 ounces	Medium	12 to 15 minutes	170°F
Chicken, broiler-fryer, half or quarters	1½- to 1¾-pound half or 12- to 14-ounce quarters	Medium	40 to 50 minutes	180°F
Chicken thigh, skinned and boned	4 to 5 ounces	Medium	12 to 15 minutes	180°F
Meaty chicken pieces (breast halves, thighs, and drumsticks)	2½ to 3 pounds total	Medium	35 to 45 minutes	180°F
TURKEY				
Turkey breast tenderloin	8 to 10 ounces (¾ to 1 inch thick)	Medium	16 to 20 minutes	170°F

*All cooking times are based on poultry removed directly from refrigerator.

INDIRECT-GRILLING POULTRY

For a charcoal grill, arrange medium-hot coals around a drip pan. Test for medium heat above drip pan (see page 336). Place poultry on grill rack over drip pan (if whole, place breast side up and do not stuff). Cover; grill for the time given below or until poultry is no longer pink (180°F for most cuts, 170°F for breast meat), adding more charcoal as necessary. Or if desired, place whole birds on a rack in a roasting pan and omit the drip pan. (For a gas grill, preheat grill. Reduce heat to medium. Adjust heat for indirect cooking [see page 335].) Test for doneness using a meat or instant-read thermometer. For whole birds, insert meat thermometer into center of the inside thigh muscle, away from bone (see page 467). (Poultry sizes vary; use times as a general guide.)

Type of Bird	Weight	Grilling Temperature	Approximate Indirect-Grilling Time*	Doneness
CHICKEN				
Chicken breast half, skinned and boned	4 to 5 ounces	Medium	15 to 18 minutes	170°F
Chicken, broiler-fryer, half	1½ to 1¾ pounds	Medium	1 to 1¼ hours	180°F
Chicken, broiler-fryer, quarters	12 to 14 ounces each	Medium	50 to 60 minutes	180°F
Chicken thigh, skinned and boned	4 to 5 ounces	Medium	15 to 18 minutes	180°F
Chicken, whole	2½ to 3 pounds 3½ to 4 pounds 4½ to 5 pounds	Medium Medium Medium	1 to 1¼ hours 1¼ to 1¾ hours 1¾ to 2 hours	180°F 180°F 180°F
Meaty chicken pieces (breast halves, thighs, and drumsticks)	2½ to 3 pounds total	Medium	50 to 60 minutes	180°F
GAME				
Cornish game hen, halved lengthwise	10 to 12 ounces each	Medium	40 to 50 minutes	180°F
Cornish game hen, whole	1¼ to 1½ pounds	Medium	50 to 60 minutes	180°F
Pheasant, quartered	8 to 12 ounces each	Medium	50 to 60 minutes	180°F
Pheasant, whole	2 to 3 pounds	Medium	1 to 1½ hours	180°F
Quail, semiboneless	3 to 4 ounces	Medium	15 to 20 minutes	180°F
Squab	12 to 16 ounces	Medium	¾ to 1 hour	180°F
TURKEY				
Turkey breast, half	2 to 2½ pounds	Medium	1¼ to 2 hours	170°F
Turkey breast tenderloin	8 to 10 ounces (¾ to 1 inch thick)	Medium	25 to 30 minutes	170°F
Turkey breast tenderloin steak	4 to 6 ounces	Medium	15 to 18 minutes	170°F
Turkey breast, whole	4 to 6 pounds 6 to 8 pounds	Medium Medium	1¾ to 2¼ hours 2½ to 3½ hours	170°F 170°F
Turkey drumstick	½ to 1 pound	Medium	¾ to 1¼ hours	180°F
Turkey thigh	1 to 1½ pounds	Medium	50 to 60 minutes	180°F
Turkey, whole	6 to 8 pounds 8 to 12 pounds 12 to 16 pounds	Medium Medium Medium	1¾ to 2¼ hours 2½ to 3½ hours 3 to 4 hours	180°F 180°F 180°F

*All cooking times are based on poultry removed directly from refrigerator.

INDIRECT-GRILLING MEAT

For a charcoal grill, arrange medium-hot coals around a drip pan. Test for medium heat above drip pan, unless chart says otherwise. Place meat, fat side up, on grill rack over drip pan. Cover and grill for the time given below or to desired temperature, adding more charcoal to maintain heat as necessary. (For a gas grill, preheat grill. Reduce heat to medium. Adjust heat for indirect cooking [see page 335].) To test for doneness, insert a meat thermometer (see tip, page 383), using an instant-read thermometer to test small portions. Thermometer should register temperature listed under Final Grilling Temperature. Remove meat from grill. For larger cuts, such as roasts, cover with foil and let stand 15 minutes before slicing. The meat's temperature will rise 10°F during the time it stands. For thinner cuts, such as steaks, cover and let stand 5 minutes.

Cut	Thickness/Weight	Approximate Indirect-Grilling Time*	Final Grilling Temperature (when to remove from grill)
BEEF			
Boneless top sirloin steak	1 inch	22 to 26 minutes	145°F medium rare
	1 inch	26 to 30 minutes	160°F medium
	1½ inches	32 to 36 minutes	145°F medium rare
	1½ inches	36 to 40 minutes	160°F medium
Boneless tri-tip roast (bottom sirloin)	1½ to 2 pounds	35 to 40 minutes	135°F (145°F medium rare after standing)
	1½ to 2 pounds	40 to 45 minutes	150°F (160°F medium after standing)
Flank steak	1¼ to 1¾ pounds	23 to 28 minutes	160°F medium
Rib roast (chine bone removed) (medium-low heat)	4 to 6 pounds	2 to 2¾ hours	135°F (145°F medium rare after standing)
	4 to 6 pounds	2½ to 3¼ hours	150°F (160°F medium after standing)
Ribeye roast (medium-low heat)	4 to 6 pounds	1¼ to 1¾ hours	135°F (145°F medium rare after standing)
	4 to 6 pounds	1½ to 2¼ hours	150°F (160°F medium after standing)
Steak (porterhouse, rib, ribeye, shoulder top blade [flat-iron], T-bone, tenderloin, top loin [strip])	1 inch	16 to 20 minutes	145°F medium rare
	1 inch	20 to 24 minutes	160°F medium
	1½ inches	22 to 25 minutes	145°F medium rare
	1½ inches	25 to 28 minutes	160°F medium
Tenderloin roast (medium-high heat)	2 to 3 pounds	¾ to 1 hour	135°F (145°F medium rare after standing)
	4 to 5 pounds	1 to 1¼ hours	135°F (145°F medium rare after standing)
GROUND MEAT			
Patties (beef, lamb, pork, or veal)	½ inch	15 to 18 minutes	160°F medium
	¾ inch	20 to 24 minutes	160°F medium
LAMB			
Boneless leg roast (medium-low heat)	3 to 4 pounds	1½ to 2¼ hours	135°F (145°F medium rare after standing)
	3 to 4 pounds	1¾ to 2½ hours	150°F (160°F medium after standing)
	4 to 6 pounds	1¾ to 2½ hours	135°F (145°F medium rare after standing)
	4 to 6 pounds	2 to 2¾ hours	150°F (160°F medium after standing)
Boneless sirloin roast (medium-low heat)	1½ to 2 pounds	1 to 1¼ hours	135°F (145°F medium rare after standing)
	1½ to 2 pounds	1¼ to 1½ hours	150°F (160°F medium after standing)
Chop (loin or rib)	1 inch	16 to 18 minutes	145°F medium rare
	1 inch	18 to 20 minutes	160°F medium
Leg of lamb (with bone) (medium-low heat)	5 to 7 pounds	1¾ to 2¼ hours	135°F (145°F medium rare after standing)
	5 to 7 pounds	2¼ to 2¾ hours	150°F (160°F medium after standing)

*All cooking times are based on meat removed directly from refrigerator.

Cut	Thickness/Weight	Approximate Indirect-Grilling Time*	Final Grilling Temperature (when to remove from grill)
PORK			
Boneless top loin roast (medium-low heat)	2 to 3 pounds (single loin)	1 to 1½ hours	150°F (160°F medium after standing)
	3 to 5 pounds (double loin, tied)	1½ to 2¼ hours	150°F (160°F medium after standing)
Chop (boneless top loin)	¾ to 1 inch	20 to 24 minutes	160°F medium
	1¼ to 1½ inch	30 to 35 minutes	160°F medium
Chop (loin or rib)	¾ to 1 inch	22 to 25 minutes	160°F medium
	1¼ to 1½ inch	35 to 40 minutes	160°F medium
Country-style ribs		1½ to 2 hours	Tender
Ham, cooked (boneless) (medium-low heat)	3 to 5 pounds	1¼ to 2 hours	140°F
	6 to 8 pounds	2 to 2¾ hours	140°F
Ham steak, cooked (medium-high heat)	1 inch	20 to 24 minutes	140°F
Loin back ribs or spareribs		1½ to 1¾ hours	Tender
Loin center rib roast (backbone loosened) (medium-low heat)	3 to 4 pounds	1¼ to 2 hours	150°F (160°F medium after standing)
	4 to 6 pounds	2 to 2¾ hours	150°F (160°F medium after standing)
Sausages, uncooked (bratwurst, Polish, or Italian sausage links)	about 4 per pound	20 to 30 minutes	160°F medium
Smoked shoulder picnic (with bone), cooked (medium-low heat)	4 to 6 pounds	1½ to 2¼ hours	140°F heated through
Tenderloin (medium-high heat)	¾ to 1 pound	30 to 35 minutes	155°F (160°F medium after standing)
VEAL			
Chop (loin or rib)	1 inch	19 to 23 minutes	160°F medium

*All cooking times are based on meat removed directly from refrigerator.

DIRECT-GRILLING MEAT

For a charcoal grill, place meat on grill rack directly over medium coals (see page 335). Grill, uncovered, for the time given below or to desired doneness, turning once halfway through grilling. (For a gas grill, preheat grill. Reduce heat to medium. Place meat on grill rack over heat. Cover the grill.) Test for doneness using a meat thermometer. For steaks, cover and let stand for 5 minutes.

Cut	Thickness/Weight	Grilling Temperature	Approximate Direct-Grilling Time*	Doneness
BEEF				
Boneless steak (top loin [strip], ribeye, shoulder top blade [flat-iron], shoulder petite tenders, shoulder center [ranch], chuck eye, tenderloin)	1 inch 1 inch 1½ inches 1½ inches	Medium Medium Medium Medium	10 to 12 minutes 12 to 15 minutes 15 to 19 minutes 18 to 23 minutes	145°F medium rare 160°F medium 145°F medium rare 160°F medium
Boneless top sirloin steak	1 inch 1 inch 1½ inches 1½ inches	Medium Medium Medium Medium	14 to 18 minutes 18 to 22 minutes 20 to 24 minutes 24 to 28 minutes	145°F medium rare 160°F medium 145°F medium rare 160°F medium
Boneless tri-tip steak (bottom sirloin)	¾ inch ¾ inch 1 inch 1 inch	Medium Medium Medium Medium	9 to 11 minutes 11 to 13 minutes 13 to 15 minutes 15 to 17 minutes	145°F medium rare 160°F medium 145°F medium rare 160°F medium
Flank steak	1¼ to 1¾ pounds	Medium	17 to 21 minutes	160°F medium
Steak with bone (porterhouse, T-bone, rib)	1 inch 1 inch 1½ inches 1½ inches	Medium Medium Medium Medium	10 to 13 minutes 12 to 15 minutes 18 to 21 minutes 22 to 25 minutes	145°F medium rare 160°F medium 145°F medium rare 160°F medium
GROUND MEAT				
Patties (beef, lamb, pork, or veal)	½ inch ¾ inch	Medium Medium	10 to 13 minutes 14 to 18 minutes	160°F medium 160°F medium
LAMB				
Chop (loin or rib)	1 inch 1 inch	Medium Medium	12 to 14 minutes 15 to 17 minutes	145°F medium rare 160°F medium
Chop (sirloin)	¾ to 1 inch	Medium	14 to 17 minutes	160°F medium
MISCELLANEOUS				
Kabobs (beef or lamb)	1-inch cubes	Medium	8 to 12 minutes	160°F medium
Kabobs (pork or veal)	1-inch cubes	Medium	10 to 14 minutes)	160°F medium
Sausages, cooked (frankfurters, smoked bratwurst, etc.)		Medium	3 to 7 minutes	Heated through
PORK				
Chop (boneless top loin)	¾ to 1 inch 1¼ to 1½ inches	Medium Medium	7 to 9 minutes 14 to 18 minutes	160°F medium 160°F medium
Chop with bone (loin or rib)	¾ to 1 inch 1¼ to 1½ inches	Medium Medium	11 to 13 minutes 16 to 20 minutes	160°F medium 160°F medium
VEAL				
Chop (loin or rib)	1 inch	Medium	12 to 15 minutes	160°F medium

*All cooking times are based on meat removed directly from refrigerator.

DIRECT-GRILLING FISH AND SEAFOOD

Thaw fish or seafood, if frozen. Rinse fish or seafood; pat dry. Place fish fillets in a well-greased grill basket. For fish steaks and whole fish, grease the grill rack. Thread scallops or shrimp on skewers, leaving a ¼-inch space between pieces. For a charcoal grill, place fish on the grill rack directly over medium coals (see page 336). Grill, uncovered, for the time given below or until fish begins to flake when tested with a fork (seafood should look opaque), turning once halfway through grilling. (For a gas grill, preheat grill. Reduce heat to medium. Place fish on grill rack over heat. Cover the grill.) If desired, brush with olive oil or melted butter after turning.

Form of Fish	Thickness, Weight, or Size	Grilling Temperature	Approximate Direct-Grilling Time*	Doneness
Dressed whole fish	½ to 1½ pounds	Medium	6 to 9 minutes per 8 ounces	Flakes
Fillets, steaks, cubes (for kabobs)	½ to 1 inch thick	Medium	4 to 6 minutes per ½-inch thickness	Flakes
Lobster tails	6 ounces 8 ounces	Medium Medium	10 to 12 minutes 12 to 15 minutes	Opaque Opaque
Sea scallops (for kabobs)	12 to 15 per pound	Medium	5 to 8 minutes	Opaque
Shrimp (for kabobs)	20 per pound 12 to 15 per pound	Medium Medium	5 to 8 minutes 7 to 9 minutes	Opaque Opaque

*All cooking times are based on fish or seafood removed directly from refrigerator.

INDIRECT-GRILLING FISH AND SEAFOOD

Thaw fish or seafood, if frozen. Rinse fish or seafood; pat dry. Place fish fillets in a well-greased grill basket. For fish steaks and whole fish, grease the grill rack. Thread scallops or shrimp on skewers, leaving a ¼-inch space between pieces. For a charcoal grill, arrange medium-hot coals around drip pan. Test for medium heat above the pan (see page 336). Place fish on grill rack over drip pan. Cover and grill for the time given below or until fish begins to flake when tested with a fork (seafood should look opaque), turning once halfway through grilling if desired. (For a gas grill, preheat grill. Reduce heat to medium. Adjust heat for indirect cooking [see page 335].) If desired, brush with olive oil or melted butter halfway through grilling.

Form of Fish	Thickness, Weight, or Size	Grilling Temperature	Approximate Indirect-Grilling Time*	Doneness
Dressed fish	½ to 1½ pounds	Medium	15 to 20 minutes per 8 ounces	Flakes
Fillets, steaks, cubes (for kabobs)	½ to 1 inch thick	Medium	7 to 9 minutes per ½-inch thickness	Flakes
Sea scallops (for kabobs)	12 to 15 per pound	Medium	11 to 14 minutes	Opaque
Shrimp (for kabobs)	20 per pound 12 to 15 per pound	Medium Medium	8 to 10 minutes 9 to 11 minutes	Opaque Opaque

*All cooking times are based on fish or seafood removed directly from refrigerator.

DIRECT-GRILLING VEGETABLES

Before grilling, rinse, trim, cut up, and precook vegetables as directed below under Preparation. To precook vegetables, bring a small amount of water to boiling in a saucepan; add desired vegetable and simmer, covered, for the time specified in the chart; drain well. Generously brush vegetables with olive oil or melted butter or margarine before grilling to prevent vegetables from sticking to the grill rack. Place vegetables on a piece of heavy foil or directly on the grill rack. (If putting vegetables directly on grill rack, place them perpendicular to wires of the rack so they won't fall into the coals.) For a charcoal grill, place vegetables on rack directly over medium coals (see page 336). Grill, uncovered, for the time given below or until crisp-tender, turning occasionally. (For a gas grill, preheat grill. Reduce heat to medium. Place vegetables on grill rack directly over heat. Cover the grill.) Monitor the grilling closely so vegetables don't char.

Vegetable	Preparation	Precooking Time	Approximate Direct-Grilling Time
Asparagus	Snap off and discard tough bases of stems.	Do not precook.	7 to 10 minutes
Baby carrots, fresh	Cut off carrot tops. Wash and peel carrots.	3 to 5 minutes	3 to 5 minutes
Corn on the cob	Place corn with husks and silks intact in bowl or pan. Cover with water. Soak 1 hour; drain.	Do not precook.	25 to 30 minutes
Eggplant	Cut off top and blossom ends. Cut eggplant crosswise into 1-inch slices.	Do not precook.	8 minutes
Fennel	Snip off feathery leaves. Cut off stems.	10 minutes; then cut into 6 to 8 wedges	8 minutes
Mushrooms, portobello	Remove stems and scrape out gills. Grill; turn halfway through grilling.	Do not precook.	10 to 12 minutes
New potatoes	Halve potatoes.	10 minutes or until almost tender	10 to 12 minutes
Onions, white, yellow, or red	Peel and cut into 1-inch crosswise slices. Grill; turn halfway through grilling.	Do not precook.	10 minutes
Potatoes, baking	Scrub potatoes; prick with a fork. Wrap individually in a double thickness of foil.	Do not precook.	1 to 1½ hours
Sweet peppers	Remove stems. Halve peppers lengthwise. Remove seeds and membranes. Cut into 1-inch-wide strips.	Do not precook.	8 to 10 minutes
Tomatoes	Remove cores; cut in half crosswise.	Do not precook.	5 minutes
Zucchini or yellow summer squash	Wash; cut off ends. Quarter lengthwise.	Do not precook.	5 to 6 minutes

MEAT

BEEF AND SWEET POTATO PAN ROAST, PAGE 384

MEAT

MEATS ARE THE ANCHOR TO MANY SATISFYING MEALS. THESE TIPS WILL HELP YOU BUY AND KEEP MEATS AT THEIR BEST.

BUYING MEAT

WHAT TO LOOK FOR: When buying beef, veal, pork, and lamb, the meat should have good color and appear moist but not wet. Any cut edges should be even, not ragged. When buying packaged meats, avoid those with tears or with liquid in the bottom of the tray. The meat should feel firm and cold to the touch.

HOW MUCH TO BUY: Count on purchasing 3 to 4 ounces per serving for boneless roasts, steaks, and ground meat. For steaks and roasts with bones, each pound should yield two to three servings. For bony cuts such as ribs, each pound yields one or two servings.

GUIDE TO BEEF STEAKS

The names of meat cuts vary among shops and regions. Here is a quick reference:

Standard Name	Other Names You Might See
Flank steak	London broil
Ribeye steak	Delmonico steak
Round tip steak	Top sirloin steak
Tenderloin steak	Filet mignon
Top loin steak	Strip steak, Kansas City steak, New York strip steak
Top sirloin steak (boneless)	Boneless sirloin butt steak
Tri-tip steak	Triangle steak

HANDLING MEAT SAFELY

Cooks should know and follow guidelines for the safe handling of meat and poultry. See page 467.

STORING MEAT

REFRIGERATING TIMELINE: Store meat in the coldest part of the refrigerator as soon as possible after purchase. Use fresh ground and cubed meat within 2 days; use roasts, steaks, and chops within 3 days.

TO FREEZE MEATS: If you do not plan to use meats within the guidelines given above, you should freeze them. If you plan to use the meat within a week, you can freeze it in the transparent film-wrapped supermarket package. For longer storage, overwrap the meat with moisture- and vapor-proof wrap, such as freezer paper or heavy foil, or place in food-safe freezer bags. Label and date the package. Freeze the meat quickly and maintain freezer temperature at 0°F or below.

FREEZING TIMELINE: For best quality, freeze uncooked roasts, steaks, and chops no longer than 12 months, uncooked ground meat up to 4 months, and cooked meat up to 3 months.

TO THAW MEAT: Thaw meat in the refrigerator on a plate or in a pan to catch any juices. Never thaw meat on the counter at room temperature.

THE ROASTING PAN DEFINED

To roast meat and poultry, you need a pan specifically designed for roasting—a large, sturdy shallow pan with a rack. The pan's sides should be 2 to 3 inches high to allow the heat to circulate around the meat. The rack keeps the meat above the juices and allows the heat to circulate below the roast. If you don't have a roasting pan, you can place a wire rack in a 13×9×2-inch baking pan.

BEEF CUTS AND HOW TO COOK THEM

A surefire way to enjoy beef at its best is to use the cooking method that best suits each cut. These pages help you do just that. The photos show the cuts that are the most widely available at supermarkets, along with the most recommended ways for cooking them. They correspond to the drawing, which shows where the cuts come from on the animal.

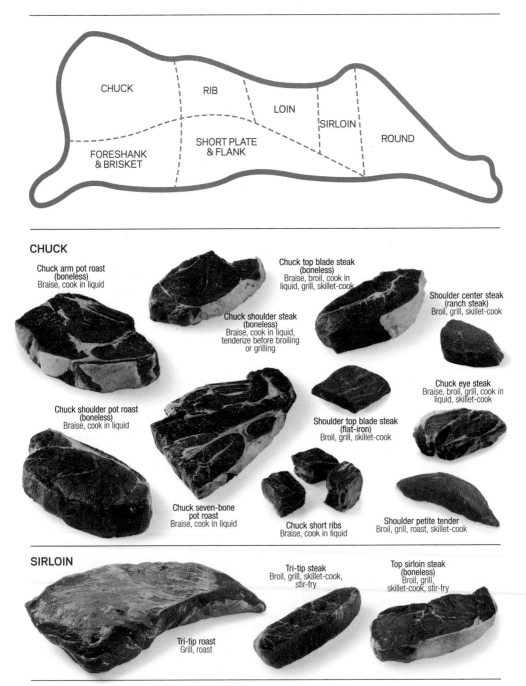

CHUCK

RIB

LOIN

SIRLOIN

ROUND

FORESHANK & BRISKET

SHORT PLATE & FLANK

CHUCK

Chuck arm pot roast (boneless)
Braise, cook in liquid

Chuck top blade steak (boneless)
Braise, broil, cook in liquid, grill, skillet-cook

Shoulder center steak (ranch steak)
Broil, grill, skillet-cook

Chuck shoulder steak (boneless)
Braise, cook in liquid, tenderize before broiling or grilling

Chuck eye steak
Braise, broil, grill, cook in liquid, skillet-cook

Chuck shoulder pot roast (boneless)
Braise, cook in liquid

Shoulder top blade steak (flat-iron)
Broil, grill, skillet-cook

Chuck seven-bone pot roast
Braise, cook in liquid

Chuck short ribs
Braise, cook in liquid

Shoulder petite tender
Broil, grill, roast, skillet-cook

SIRLOIN

Tri-tip steak
Broil, grill, skillet-cook, stir-fry

Top sirloin steak (boneless)
Broil, grill, skillet-cook, stir-fry

Tri-tip roast
Grill, roast

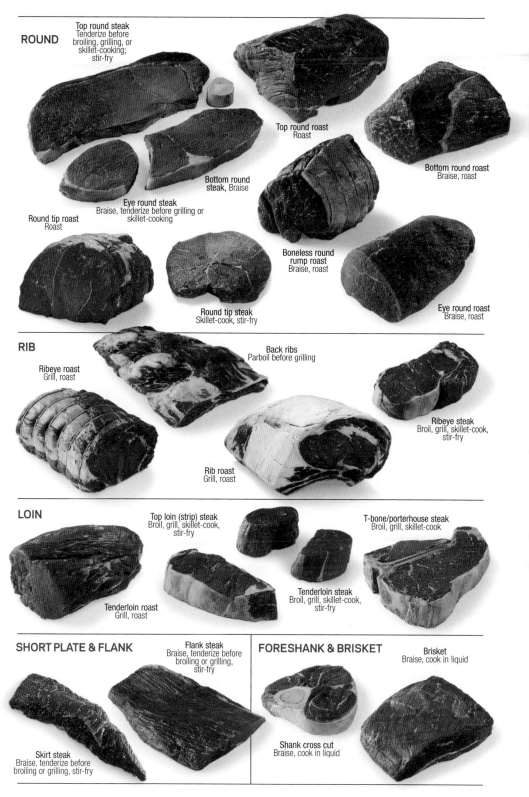

ROUND

Top round steak
Tenderize before broiling, grilling, or skillet-cooking; stir-fry

Top round roast
Roast

Bottom round roast
Braise, roast

Bottom round steak, Braise

Eye round steak
Braise, tenderize before grilling or skillet-cooking

Round tip roast
Roast

Boneless round rump roast
Braise, roast

Eye round roast
Braise, roast

Round tip steak
Skillet-cook, stir-fry

RIB

Ribeye roast
Grill, roast

Back ribs
Parboil before grilling

Ribeye steak
Broil, grill, skillet-cook, stir-fry

Rib roast
Grill, roast

LOIN

Top loin (strip) steak
Broil, grill, skillet-cook, stir-fry

T-bone/porterhouse steak
Broil, grill, skillet-cook

Tenderloin steak
Broil, grill, skillet-cook, stir-fry

Tenderloin roast
Grill, roast

SHORT PLATE & FLANK

Flank steak
Braise, tenderize before broiling or grilling, stir-fry

Skirt steak
Braise, tenderize before broiling or grilling, stir-fry

FORESHANK & BRISKET

Brisket
Braise, cook in liquid

Shank cross cut
Braise, cook in liquid

STANDING RIB ROAST

PREP: 10 MINUTES **ROAST:** 1¾ HOURS
STAND: 15 MINUTES **OVEN:** 350°F/450°F
MAKES: 12 TO 16 SERVINGS

- 1 4- to 6-pound beef rib roast
    Kosher salt and freshly ground
    black pepper
- 2 to 3 cloves garlic, slivered
- 1 recipe Oven-Browned Potatoes or
    Yorkshire Pudding
- 1 recipe Horseradish Sauce (page 542)
    (optional)

1 Preheat oven to 350°F. Sprinkle meat with salt and pepper. Cut shallow slits all over meat (see photo 1, below); insert garlic slivers into slits (see photo 2, below). Place meat, fat side up, in a 15½×10½×2-inch roasting pan. Insert an oven-going meat thermometer into center of roast (see tip, page 383). The thermometer should not touch bone.

2 Roast, uncovered, for 1¾ to 2¼ hours or until meat thermometer registers 135°F for medium rare. Add Oven-Browned Potatoes (if using) to the pan 30 to 40 minutes before the roast is done (temperature of meat should be about 100°F). Cover roast with foil; let stand for 15 minutes. Temperature of meat after standing should be 145°F. (For medium, roast for 2¼ to 2¾ hours or until meat thermometer registers 150°F. Cover with foil; let stand for 15 minutes. Temperature of meat after standing should be 160°F.)

3 While roast stands, prepare Yorkshire Pudding (if using). Slice meat. Serve with potatoes, pudding and, if desired, Horseradish Sauce.

PER 4 OUNCES MEAT: 348 cal., 25 g total fat (10 g sat. fat, 0 g trans fat), 98 mg chol., 188 mg sodium, 0 g carbo., 0 g fiber, 28 g pro.
EXCHANGES: 4 Medium-Fat Meat, 1 Fat

OVEN-BROWNED POTATOES: Halve or quarter 3 pounds assorted small potatoes (tiny new, fingerling, or yellow). Cook potatoes and 1 large onion, cut into thin wedges, in boiling salted water for 10 minutes; drain. Toss hot potatoes and onion with 2 tablespoons olive oil and ½ teaspoon kosher salt. About 30 to 40 minutes before roast is done (the roast temperature should be about 100°F), arrange potatoes and onion around roast.

PER 1 CUP: 113 cal., 2 g total fat (0 g sat. fat, 0 g trans fat), 0 mg chol., 136 mg sodium, 21 g carbo., 3 g fiber, 2 g pro.
EXCHANGES: 1½ Starch

YORKSHIRE PUDDING: After removing the meat from the oven, increase the oven temperature to 450°F. Measure pan drippings. If necessary, add enough vegetable oil to drippings to equal ¼ cup; return to pan. In a large mixing bowl combine 4 eggs and 2 cups milk. Add 2 cups all-purpose flour and ½ teaspoon salt. Beat with an electric mixer or rotary beater until smooth. Stir into drippings in roasting pan. Bake, uncovered, for 20 to 25 minutes or until puffy and golden. Cut into 12 squares. Serve immediately.

PER SQUARE: 160 cal., 7 g total fat (2 g sat. fat, 0 g trans fat), 74 mg chol., 137 mg sodium, 18 g carbo., 1 g fiber, 6 g pro.
EXCHANGES: 1 Starch, 1½ Fat

STUDDING ROAST WITH GARLIC, STEP-BY-STEP

1. Using the tip of a small sharp knife, poke several slits randomly over the roast. Make the cuts about 1 inch deep. **2.** Cut each garlic clove lengthwise into six to eight slivers. Insert the garlic slivers into the slits.

STEAK WITH CREAMY ONION SAUCE

START TO FINISH: 40 MINUTES **MAKES:** 4 SERVINGS

- 1 tablespoon butter
- 1 cup coarsely chopped sweet onion (such as Maui or Walla Walla) (1 large)
- ½ cup light dairy sour cream
- 1 tablespoon capers, drained
- 4 beef ribeye steaks, cut about 1 inch thick
- 2 teaspoons Montreal steak seasoning

1 For sauce, in a large skillet melt butter over medium-low heat. Add onion; cook, covered, for 13 to 15 minutes or until onion is tender, stirring occasionally. Uncover; increase heat to medium-high. Cook and stir for 3 to 5 minutes or until onion is golden. Reduce heat to medium-low. Stir in sour cream, capers, and ½ teaspoon of the Montreal steak seasoning. Cook until heated through (do not boil); set sauce aside.

2 Meanwhile, preheat broiler. Trim fat from steaks. Sprinkle steaks with the remaining 1½ teaspoons seasoning. Place steaks on the unheated rack of a broiler pan. Broil steaks 3 to 4 inches from the heat for 12 to 14 minutes for medium rare (145°F) or 15 to 18 minutes for medium (160°F), turning once halfway through broiling. Cover steaks with foil; let stand for 5 minutes before serving.

3 Transfer steaks to serving plates. Spoon some of the sauce over steaks. Pass remaining sauce.

PER STEAK + ½ CUP SAUCE: 348 cal., 20 g total fat (9 g sat. fat, 0 g trans fat), 116 mg chol., 550 mg sodium, 6 g carbo., 1 g fiber, 36 g pro.
EXCHANGES: ½ Other Carbo., 5 Lean Meat, 1 Fat

MUSTARD-CRUSTED BEEF TENDERLOIN

PREP: 20 MINUTES **ROAST:** 35 MINUTES
STAND: 15 MINUTES **OVEN:** 425°F
MAKES: 4 SERVINGS

- ¼ cup coarse-grain mustard
- 2 teaspoons honey
- 1 teaspoon black pepper
- ¾ teaspoon dry mustard
- ½ teaspoon salt
- ½ teaspoon finely shredded orange peel
- ½ teaspoon finely shredded lemon peel
- 1 tablespoon olive oil
- 1 1-pound beef tenderloin roast

1 Preheat oven to 425°F. In a small bowl stir together coarse-grain mustard, honey, pepper, dry mustard, salt, orange peel, and lemon peel; set aside.

2 In a large heavy skillet heat olive oil over medium-high heat. Quickly brown roast on all sides in hot oil. Place roast on a rack set in a shallow roasting pan. Spread mustard mixture over top and sides of roast. Insert an oven-going meat thermometer into center of roast.

3 Roast, uncovered, for 35 to 45 minutes or until the meat thermometer registers 140°F. Cover meat with foil; let stand for 15 minutes before slicing. The temperature of the meat after standing should be 145°F.

PER 3 OUNCES: 339 cal., 24 g total fat (9 g sat. fat, 0 g trans fat), 75 mg chol., 708 mg sodium, 3 g carbo., 0 g fiber, 22 g pro.
EXCHANGES: 3 Medium-Fat Meat, 2 Fat

THERMOMETER CHOICES
CHOOSE A MODEL THAT'S APPROPRIATE FOR THE MEAT YOU ARE COOKING.

Be sure to insert the thermometer into the meat so that it is not touching fat, bone, or the pan.

1 DIAL OVEN-GOING THERMOMETER: Use for roasts and larger cuts of meat; insert it into the meat before cooking.

2 PROBE THERMOMETER: Also for larger cuts, this model has a probe you insert into the meat before cooking. It's wired to a digital display that remains outside of the oven, allowing you to check the temperature of the meat

without opening the oven door.

3 INSTANT-READ THERMOMETER: This is used to check both larger and smaller cuts of meat toward the end of cooking time. These are not meant to be left in foods during cooking (unless the model you have is specifically designed to do so). For thin meats, such as burgers, steaks, and chops, insert into the side of the cut as shown.

STEAK WITH PAN SAUCE

START TO FINISH: 25 MINUTES **MAKES:** 2 SERVINGS

  2 beef steaks, such as top loin, ribeye, or
       tenderloin, cut about ¾ inch thick
  5 tablespoons cold unsalted butter
  ⅓ cup dry red wine or apple juice
  ¼ cup reduced-sodium beef broth
  2 tablespoons finely chopped shallots or
       1 clove garlic, minced
  1 tablespoon whipping cream
       (no substitutes)

1 Trim fat from steaks. Heat a large skillet over
medium-high heat (if possible, do not use a nonstick skillet). Add 1 tablespoon butter; reduce heat
to medium. Cook steaks about 3 minutes per side
or until medium rare (145°F). Cover steaks with
foil; let stand for 5 minutes while preparing sauce.

2 Drain fat from skillet. Add wine, broth, and
shallots to hot skillet. Cook and stir over medium
heat, scraping up browned bits in bottom of skillet
(see photo 1, below). Cook over medium heat for
3 to 4 minutes or until liquid is reduced to about
2 tablespoons. Reduce heat to medium-low.

3 Stir in whipping cream; stir in the remaining
4 tablespoons butter, 1 tablespoon at a time (see
photo 2, below), whisking until butter melts and
sauce thickens slightly. Season to taste with *salt*
and *white pepper*. Serve sauce over steak (see
photo 3, below).

NOTE: See page 537 for additional flavor
variations for pan sauces.

PER STEAK + 2 TABLESPOONS SAUCE: 668 cal., 57 g total
fat (30 g sat. fat, 0 g trans fat), 182 mg chol., 283 mg sodium,
3 g carbo., 0 g fiber, 28 g pro.
EXCHANGES: 4 Medium-Fat Meat, 7½ Fat

BEEF AND SWEET POTATO
PAN ROAST *(photo, page 377)*

PREP: 25 MINUTES **ROAST:** 30 MINUTES
STAND: 10 MINUTES **OVEN:** 425°F
MAKES: 6 SERVINGS

  1 tablespoon dried Italian seasoning,
       crushed
  1 tablespoon bottled roasted minced garlic
  ½ teaspoon crushed red pepper

PREPARING PAN SAUCE, STEP-BY-STEP

1. After adding the wine, broth, and shallots, stir with a wire whisk, scraping the bottom of the skillet to incorporate
flavorful browned bits. **2.** When adding the 1 tablespoon butter, whisk until it melts. Continue to add and whisk in butter.
3. Place steaks on serving plates with the spinach. With a large metal spoon, drape the sauce over each steak.

3 tablespoons olive oil

2 pounds medium orange and/or white sweet potatoes, cut into 1-inch wedges

4 6- to 8-ounce beef shoulder petite tenders or 1½ to 2 pounds beef tenderloin

1 cup cherry tomatoes

1 recipe Chopped Parsley Topping

1 Preheat oven to 425°F. In a small bowl combine Italian seasoning, garlic, 1 teaspoon *salt,* and crushed red pepper. Stir in olive oil. Divide seasoning mixture between two large resealable plastic bags. Place sweet potatoes in one bag; shake to coat potatoes. Spread potatoes in a single layer in a greased shallow roasting pan. Roast, uncovered, for 15 minutes.

2 Meanwhile, place beef tenders in the remaining bag. Shake to coat meat with seasoning mixture. In a very large skillet brown beef tenders over medium-high heat, turning to brown evenly. Stir sweet potatoes in roasting pan and push to edges of pan. Place beef tenders in center of pan. Roast, uncovered, for 5 minutes. Add tomatoes; roast for 10 to 15 minutes more or until a thermometer inserted into the thickest parts of tenders registers 145°F for medium rare or 160°F for medium. Cover with foil; let stand for 10 minutes before slicing. Serve with Chopped Parsley Topping.

CHOPPED PARSLEY TOPPING: In a small bowl stir together ¼ cup snipped fresh parsley; 2 teaspoons finely shredded orange peel; 2 cloves garlic, minced; and ⅛ teaspoon salt.

PER ½ TENDER + 1 CUP SWEET POTATOES: 365 cal., 14 g total fat (3 g sat. fat, 0 g trans fat), 65 mg chol., 589 mg sodium, 33 g carbo., 5 g fiber, 26 g pro.
EXCHANGES: 2 Starch, 3 Lean Meat, ½ Fat

FAST • LOW FAT

FLAT-IRON STEAK WITH BBQ BEANS

START TO FINISH: 20 MINUTES **MAKES:** 4 SERVINGS

2 boneless beef shoulder top blade (flat-iron) steaks, halved (1 to 1¼ pounds)

2 teaspoons fajita seasoning

1 15-ounce can black beans, rinsed and drained

⅓ cup bottled barbecue sauce

2 to 3 medium tomatoes, sliced

1 Lightly grease a grill pan; preheat the pan over medium-high heat. Trim fat from steaks. Sprinkle steaks with fajita seasoning. Place the steaks on the grill pan; grill for 8 to 12 minutes for medium rare (145°F) or 12 to 15 minutes for medium (160°F). Remove steaks from pan. Cover with foil; let stand for 5 minutes.

2 Meanwhile, in a microwave-safe medium bowl stir together drained beans and barbecue sauce. Cover loosely with plastic wrap. Microwave on 100% power (high) about 3 minutes or until heated through, stirring once.

3 Serve steaks with beans, sliced tomatoes, and, if desired, *pickled jalapeño chile pepper slices.*

PER ½ STEAK + ⅓ CUP BEANS: 305 cal., 11 g total fat (4 g sat. fat, 0 g trans fat), 74 mg chol., 678 mg sodium, 25 g carbo., 6 g fiber, 29 g pro.
EXCHANGES: 1 Starch, ½ Other Carbo., 3½ Lean Meat

FAST

BEEF STROGANOFF

START TO FINISH: 30 MINUTES
MAKES: 4 SERVINGS

12 ounces boneless beef sirloin steak

1 8-ounce carton dairy sour cream

2 tablespoons all-purpose flour

½ cup water

2 teaspoons instant beef bouillon granules

¼ teaspoon black pepper

2 tablespoons butter or margarine

2 cups sliced mixed fresh mushrooms (such as button, cremini, and/or stemmed shiitake)

½ cup chopped onion (1 medium)

1 clove garlic, minced

2 cups hot cooked noodles

1 If desired, partially freeze beef for easier slicing. Trim fat from meat. Thinly slice meat across the grain into bite-size strips. In a small bowl stir together sour cream and flour. Stir in the water, bouillon granules, and pepper; set aside.

2 In a large skillet melt butter over medium-high heat. Add meat, mushrooms, onion, and garlic; cook and stir about 5 minutes or until meat is desired doneness. Drain off fat.

3 Stir the sour cream mixture into the meat mixture in skillet. Cook and stir until thickened and bubbly. Cook and stir for 1 minute more. Serve meat mixture over noodles.

PER ABOUT 1 CUP MIXTURE + ½ CUP NOODLES: 486 cal., 30 g total fat (15 g sat. fat, 0 g trans fat), 108 mg chol., 573 mg sodium, 30 g carbo., 2 g fiber, 24 g pro.
EXCHANGES: ½ Vegetable, 2 Starch, 2½ Medium-Fat Meat, 3 Fat

COOK ONCE, EAT TWICE

SPICE UP ROAST BEEF WITH THE FLAVORFUL SOUTHWESTERN RUB. THE NEXT NIGHT THE PEPPERY BEEF ENLIVENS A REFRESHING SALAD.

TONIGHT

SOUTHWESTERN TRI-TIP ROAST

PREP: 20 MINUTES **ROAST:** 30 MINUTES
STAND: 15 MINUTES **OVEN:** 425°F
MAKES: 4 SERVINGS+ RESERVES

- 1 1¾- to 2-pound boneless beef tri-tip roast (bottom sirloin)
- 1 recipe Southwestern Rub
- 1 8-ounce pouch cooked seasoned black beans
    Dairy sour cream, snipped fresh cilantro, and lime wedges (optional)

1 Preheat oven to 425°F. Trim fat from roast. Sprinkle Southwestern Rub over meat; rub over surface of meat. Place roast on rack in a shallow roasting pan. Roast, uncovered, for 30 to 35 minutes or until meat thermometer inserted in center of roast registers 135°F. Cover with foil; let stand 15 minutes. Temperature of meat after standing should be 145°F. (For medium, roast 40 to 45 minutes or until thermometer registers 150°F. Cover with foil; let stand 15 minutes. Temperature of meat after standing should be 160°F.)

2 Prepare black beans according to package directions. Slice meat. Transfer half of the beef to container. Cover and chill for up to 3 days; use in Southwestern Salad Plates. Serve remaining meat with cooked beans and, if desired, dairy sour cream, snipped fresh cilantro, and lime wedges.

SOUTHWESTERN RUB: Combine 1½ teaspoons chili powder; 1½ teaspoons paprika; 1 teaspoon packed brown sugar; 1 teaspoon ground cumin; ½ teaspoon garlic powder; ½ teaspoon dried thyme, crushed; ½ teaspoon black pepper; ¼ teaspoon salt; and ⅛ teaspoon cayenne pepper.

PER 4 OUNCES MEAT + ½ CUP BEANS: 228 cal., 9 g total fat (3 g sat. fat, 0 g trans fat), 64 mg chol., 261 mg sodium, 11 g carbo., 4 g fiber, 24 g pro.
EXCHANGES: 1 Starch, 3 Lean Meat

TOMORROW

SOUTHWESTERN SALAD PLATES

START TO FINISH: 20 MINUTES **MAKES:** 4 SERVINGS

- 6 cups torn mixed salad greens
- 1 cup purchased corn relish
- ½ recipe Southwestern Tri-Tip Roast, sliced
- 1 cup halved cherry or grape tomatoes
- ½ of a small red onion, thinly sliced
    Snipped fresh rosemary (optional)
    Soft breadsticks (optional)

1 Arrange greens on four chilled dinner plates. Top with half of the corn relish. Arrange beef, tomato halves, and onion on top. Spoon remaining corn relish over all. If desired, sprinkle with rosemary and serve with breadsticks.

PER SERVING: 274 cal., 9 g total fat (3 g sat. fat, 0 g trans fat), 64 mg chol., 483 mg sodium, 26 g carbo., 2 g fiber, 22 g pro.
EXCHANGES: 1½ Vegetable, 1 Starch, 3 Lean Meat

TRY A TRI-TIP

KEEP THIS VERSATILE CUT IN MIND FOR OTHER BUDGET-FRIENDLY DINNERS.

A tri-tip beef roast is an economical cut of meat that comes from the sirloin section. This lean cut of meat is a good choice for roasting and grilling. You can also cut it into steaks or into cubes for kabobs. Because it contains so little fat, be sure not to cook it past medium doneness (150°F).

BEEF AND NOODLES

PREP: 25 MINUTES **COOK:** 100 MINUTES
MAKES: 4 SERVINGS

- 1 pound lean beef stew meat, trimmed and cut into ¾-inch cubes
- ¼ cup all-purpose flour
- 1 tablespoon vegetable oil
- ½ cup chopped onion (1 medium)
- 2 cloves garlic, minced
- 3 cups beef broth
- 1 teaspoon dried thyme or basil, crushed
- 8 ounces frozen egg noodles
- 2 tablespoons snipped fresh parsley

1 Toss meat with flour to coat. In a large saucepan brown half of the meat in hot oil. Remove meat from pan. Brown remaining meat with the onion and garlic, adding more oil if necessary. Drain off fat. Return meat to saucepan. Stir in broth, thyme, and ¼ teaspoon *black pepper*. Bring to boiling; reduce heat. Simmer, covered, for 75 to 90 minutes or until meat is tender.

2 Stir in noodles. Bring to boiling; reduce heat. Cook, uncovered, for 25 to 30 minutes or until noodles are tender, stirring occasionally. Sprinkle with parsley.

PER 1½ CUPS: 416 cal., 15 g total fat (4 g sat. fat, 0 g trans fat), 139 mg chol., 905 mg sodium, 35 g carbo., 2 g fiber, 33 g pro. EXCHANGES: 2 Starch, 4 Lean Meat

SHORT RIBS WITH GREMOLATA

PREP: 30 MINUTES **BAKE:** 2 HOURS
OVEN: 350°F **MAKES:** 6 SERVINGS

- 3 pounds bone-in beef short ribs
- 1 tablespoon olive oil
- 1½ cups finely chopped carrots (3 medium)
- 6 cloves garlic, minced
- 1 14-ounce can beef broth
- ½ cup dry red wine or beef broth
- 1 teaspoon dried thyme, crushed
- 1 bay leaf
- 2 cups frozen small whole onions
- 1 tablespoon Dijon-style mustard
- 1 tablespoon prepared horseradish
- 1 recipe Gremolata

1 Preheat oven to 350°F. Trim fat from ribs; sprinkle with ½ teaspoon *salt* and ¼ teaspoon *black pepper*. In a 4- to 5-quart oven-going Dutch oven brown ribs on all sides in hot oil. Remove ribs

and set aside. Discard all but 1 tablespoon drippings in Dutch oven. Reduce heat to medium-low. Add carrots and garlic to drippings. Cook and stir about 10 minutes or just until carrots are tender.

2 Return ribs to pan. Add broth, wine, thyme, bay leaf, and ¼ teaspoon *salt*. Bring to boiling. Cover Dutch oven. Transfer Dutch oven to oven. Bake about 2 hours or until ribs are very tender, adding onions the last 30 minutes of baking.

3 Transfer ribs to deep platter; keep warm. Skim fat from cooking liquid; discard bay leaf and any bones. If sauce is too thin, bring to boiling and cook, uncovered, about 5 minutes to reduce to about 2½ cups. Whisk in mustard and horseradish. Pour sauce over ribs. Top with Gremolata.

GREMOLATA: Mix 2 tablespoons snipped fresh Italian parsley; 2 cloves garlic, minced; and 2 teaspoons finely shredded orange peel.

PER 4 OUNCES MEAT + ½ CUP SAUCE: 717 cal., 62 g total fat (26 g sat. fat, 0 g trans fat), 126 mg chol., 714 mg sodium, 8 g carbo., 1 g fiber, 25 g pro. EXCHANGES: ½ Vegetable, ½ Starch, 3 High-Fat Meat, 7½ Fat

STEAKS WITH TOMATO SAUCE

PREP: 15 MINUTES **COOK:** 30 MINUTES
MAKES: 4 SERVINGS

- 4 5-ounce or two 10-ounce beef cubed steaks
- 2 tablespoons vegetable oil
- 1 cup sliced fresh mushrooms
- ½ cup chopped onion (1 medium)
- 1 clove garlic, minced
- 1 14.5-ounce can diced tomatoes with basil, garlic, and oregano
- 1 10.75-ounce can reduced-fat and reduced-sodium condensed cream of mushroom soup
- 3 cups hot cooked noodles

1 If using 10-ounce steaks, cut in half. In a very large skillet brown steaks on both sides in hot oil. Remove meat from skillet. Add mushrooms, onion, and garlic; cook until onion is tender.

2 Stir in undrained tomatoes and soup. Return meat to skillet. Bring to boiling; reduce heat. Simmer, covered, about 30 minutes or until meat is tender. Serve with noodles.

PER 4 OUNCES STEAK + ¾ CUP SAUCE + ¾ CUP NOODLES: 595 cal., 27 g total fat (8 g sat. fat, 0 g trans fat), 120 mg chol., 926 mg sodium, 48 g carbo., 2 g fiber, 38 g pro. EXCHANGES: 1 Vegetable, 3 Starch, 4 Lean Meat, 2½ Fat

SWEET-AND-SPICY EDAMAME-BEEF STIR-FRY

PREP: 20 MINUTES **COOK:** 10 MINUTES
MAKES: 4 SERVINGS

- 8 ounces beef sirloin steak
- 4 teaspoons canola or vegetable oil
- 2 teaspoons finely chopped fresh ginger
- 2 cups fresh broccoli florets
- 1 cup red and/or yellow sweet pepper strips
- 1 cup frozen shelled sweet soybeans (edamame)
- 3 tablespoons bottled hoisin sauce
- 2 tablespoons rice vinegar
- 1 teaspoon red chili paste
- 2 cups hot cooked brown or white rice

1 If desired, partially freeze beef for easier slicing. Trim fat from meat. Thinly slice meat across the grain into bite-size strips. Set beef aside.

2 In a nonstick wok or large skillet heat 2 teaspoons of the oil over medium-high heat. Add ginger; cook and stir for 15 seconds. Add broccoli and sweet pepper to wok. Cook and stir about 4 minutes or until crisp-tender. Remove vegetables from wok.

3 Add the remaining 2 teaspoons oil to wok. Add beef and soybeans; cook and stir about 2 minutes or until beef is desired doneness. Return vegetables to wok.

4 In a small bowl combine hoisin, vinegar, and chili paste. Add to beef mixture, tossing to coat. Heat through. Serve over rice.

PER ¾ CUP BEEF MIXTURE + ½ CUP RICE: 340 cal., 11 g total fat (2 g sat. fat, 0 g trans fat), 24 mg chol., 262 mg sodium, 38 g carbo., 6 g fiber, 22 g pro.
EXCHANGES: 1 Vegetable, 2 Starch, 2 Lean Meat, 1 Fat

READY, SET, GO STIR-FRYING IS A QUICK-MOVING METHOD OF COOKING. HAVE YOUR INGREDIENTS PREPPED AND MEASURED BEFORE YOU TURN ON THE HEAT.

SWEET-AND-SPICY EDAMAME-BEEF STIR-FRY

SWISS STEAK

PREP: 25 MINUTES **COOK:** 75 MINUTES
MAKES: 4 SERVINGS

- 2 tablespoons all-purpose flour
- 1 teaspoon smoked paprika or sweet paprika
- ¼ teaspoon salt
- ¼ teaspoon black pepper
- 4 5-ounce beef cubed steaks or two 10-ounce beef cubed steaks
- 1 tablespoon vegetable oil
- 1 14.5-ounce can diced tomatoes with basil, garlic, and oregano, undrained
- ¼ cup water
- 1 small onion, sliced and separated into rings
- ½ cup sliced celery (1 stalk)
- ½ cup sliced carrot (1 medium)
  Mashed Potatoes (page 607)

1 In a shallow dish combine flour, paprika, salt, and pepper. If using 10-ounce steaks, cut each steak in half. Coat meat with flour mixture.

2 In a large skillet heat oil over medium-high heat. Add meat; brown meat on both sides in hot oil. Add undrained tomatoes, water, onion, celery, and carrot. Bring to boiling; reduce heat. Simmer, covered, about 75 minutes or until meat is tender. Serve meat and vegetable mixture with hot mashed potatoes.

OVEN DIRECTIONS: Preheat the oven to 350°F. Prepare and brown meat in skillet as directed. Transfer meat to a 2-quart square baking dish. In the same skillet combine undrained tomatoes, water, onion, celery, and carrot. Bring to boiling, scraping up any browned bits from bottom of skillet. Pour over meat. Bake, covered, about 1 hour or until meat is tender. Serve as directed.

PER 4 OUNCES MEAT + ⅔ CUP VEGETABLES AND SAUCE + ¾ CUP MASHED POTATOES: 421 cal., 15 g total fat (5 g sat. fat, 0 g trans fat), 59 mg chol., 1,099 mg sodium, 33 g carbo., 3 g fiber, 36 g pro.
EXCHANGES: 1 Vegetable, 2 Starch, 4 Lean Meat, ½ Fat

SMOKED PAPRIKA
SMOKED PAPRIKA RANGES FROM MILD TO HOT AND GIVES FOOD A MORE INTENSE FLAVOR THAN REGULAR PAPRIKA.

CHICKEN FRIED STEAK

PREP: 20 MINUTES **COOK:** 85 MINUTES
MAKES: 4 SERVINGS

- 4 5-ounce beef cubed steaks or two 10-ounce beef cubed steaks
- ¾ teaspoon salt
- ¼ teaspoon black pepper
- ¼ cup all-purpose flour
- 1 egg, lightly beaten
- 1 tablespoon milk
- ¾ cup seasoned fine dry bread crumbs
- 3 tablespoons vegetable oil
- 2 tablespoons water
- 1 small onion, halved, sliced, and separated into rings
- 2 tablespoons all-purpose flour
- 1½ cups milk
  Black pepper (optional)

1 If using 10-ounce steaks, cut each steak in half. Sprinkle meat with ½ teaspoon of the salt and the ¼ teaspoon pepper.

2 Place the ¼ cup flour in a shallow dish. In a second shallow dish combine egg and the 1 table-spoon milk. In a third dish place bread crumbs. Dip meat pieces into the flour, then into egg mixture. Coat with the bread crumbs.

3 In a very large skillet heat oil over medium-high heat. Cook meat, half at time, in hot oil over medium-high heat about 8 minutes or until brown, turning once. (Add more oil, if necessary.) Return all of the meat to the skillet. Add water. Reduce heat to medium-low. Cook, covered, about 40 minutes more or until meat is tender, carefully turning meat with a spatula after 20 minutes. Transfer meat to a serving platter, reserving drippings in skillet. Keep warm.

4 For gravy, add onion to reserved drippings in skillet; cook until tender. (Add more oil, if necessary.) Stir in the 2 tablespoons flour and the remaining ¼ teaspoon salt. Gradually stir in the 1½ cups milk. Cook and stir over medium heat until thickened and bubbly. Cook and stir for 1 minute more. If desired, season to taste with additional pepper. Serve gravy with meat.

PER 4 OUNCES BEEF + ⅓ CUP GRAVY: 483 cal., 20 g total fat (5 g sat. fat, 0 g trans fat), 139 mg chol., 976 mg sodium, 31 g carbo., 2 g fiber, 42 g pro.
EXCHANGES: 2 Starch 5 Lean Meat, 1 Fat

MAKE-IT-MINE POT ROAST

THERE ARE THOUSANDS OF RECIPES FOR POT ROAST IN THE WORLD, BUT NONE WILL BE BETTER THAN THE ONE YOU MAKE WITH EXACTLY THE INGREDIENTS YOUR FAMILY LIKES BEST.

BASIC INGREDIENTS

PREP: 30 MINUTES
COOK: 105 MINUTES
MAKES: 6 TO 8 SERVINGS

- 1 2½- to 3-pound beef chuck arm pot roast, beef chuck shoulder pot roast, or beef chuck seven-bone pot roast
- Salt and black pepper
- 2 tablespoons vegetable oil
- ¾ cup Liquid
- 1 tablespoon Liquid Seasoning
- 1 teaspoon Dried Herb, crushed
- ½ teaspoon salt
- 1 pound Potatoes
- 1 pound Vegetables, cut into 1- to 2-inch pieces
- ½ cup cold water
- ¼ cup all-purpose flour

LIQUID (PICK ONE)

Apple juice
Beef broth
Cranberry juice
Tomato juice
½ cup beef broth plus ¼ cup dry red wine
Water

LIQUID SEASONING
(PICK ONE)

Barbecue sauce
Dijon-style mustard
Soy sauce
Steak sauce
Worcestershire sauce

DRIED HERB (PICK ONE)

Basil
Herbes de Provence
Italian seasoning
Oregano
Thyme

POTATOES (PICK ONE)

Fingerling
Red
Russet
Sweet
Tiny new
Yellow

VEGETABLES
(PICK ONE OR MORE)

Peeled butternut squash
Peeled carrots or parsnips
Celery
Trimmed fennel bulb
Sliced leeks or shallots
Mushrooms
Onion wedges or peeled pearl onions
Peeled turnips or rutabaga

BASIC INSTRUCTIONS

1 Trim fat from meat. Sprinkle meat with salt and pepper. In a 4- to 6-quart Dutch oven brown roast on all sides in hot oil. Drain off fat. Combine desired Liquid, Liquid Seasoning, Dried Herb, and ½ teaspoon salt. Pour over roast. Bring to boiling; reduce heat. Simmer, covered, 1 hour.

2 If using new potatoes, peel a strip of skin from centers. If using medium-size or sweet potatoes, peel and quarter. Add Potatoes and Vegetables to Dutch oven. Return to boiling; reduce heat. Simmer, covered, 45 to 60 minutes or until tender. Remove meat and vegetables, reserving juices in Dutch oven. Keep warm.

3 For gravy, if necessary, add enough water to juices to equal 1½ cups. Return to Dutch oven. Stir together cold water and flour until smooth. Stir into juices in pan. Cook and stir until thickened and bubbly. Cook and stir for 1 minute more. If desired, season with black pepper. Serve gravy with meat and vegetables.

OVEN DIRECTIONS: Preheat oven to 325°F. Prepare as directed through Step 1. Bake, covered, for 1 hour. Prepare potatoes as directed. Add vegetables to pan with meat. Cover; bake 45 to 60 minutes more or until tender. Prepare gravy in a saucepan as directed in Step 3.

FAJITAS

PREP: 15 MINUTES **CHILL:** 30 MINUTES
COOK: 6 MINUTES **MAKES:** 4 TO 6 SERVINGS

- 12 ounces beef skirt or flank steak, cut into thin bite-size strips
- 1 recipe Homemade Fajita Seasoning
- 1 cup thin strips red or green sweet pepper
- ½ cup thinly sliced onion
- 2 tablespoons vegetable oil
- ¾ cup chopped tomato (1 medium)
- 1 tablespoon lime juice
- 4 to six 8-inch flour tortillas, warmed

1 Sprinkle beef with 2 teaspoons of the Homemade Fajita Seasoning; toss to coat. Cover and chill for 30 minutes.

2 In a very large skillet cook pepper, onion, and remaining seasoning in 1 tablespoon oil until tender. Remove from skillet. Add remaining 1 tablespoon oil and meat to skillet. Cook and stir for 2 to 3 minutes until desired doneness. Return pepper mixture to skillet. Stir in tomato. Cook until heated through. Remove from heat; stir in lime juice. To serve, fill warmed tortillas with beef mixture. If desired, top with *guacamole, salsa,* and *dairy sour cream.* Roll up tortillas.

HOMEMADE FAJITA SEASONING: Mix 1½ teaspoons ground cumin; ½ teaspoon dried oregano, crushed; ¼ teaspoon salt; ¼ teaspoon cayenne pepper; ¼ teaspoon black pepper; ⅛ teaspoon garlic powder; and ⅛ teaspoon onion powder.

PER TORTILLA + ¾ CUP BEEF MIXTURE: 356 cal., 21 g total fat (6 g sat. fat, 0 g trans fat), 51 mg chol., 326 mg sodium, 21 g carbo., 2 g fiber, 20 g pro.
EXCHANGES: 1 Vegetable, 1 Starch, 2 Lean Meat, 3 Fat

SUPER BURRITOS

PREP: 40 MINUTES **BAKE:** 10 MINUTES
OVEN: 350°F **MAKES:** 8 BURRITOS

- 1 pound lean ground beef
- 1 cup chopped onion (1 large)
- ½ cup chopped green sweet pepper (1 small)
- 1 clove garlic, minced
- 1 tablespoon medium or hot chili powder
- ¼ teaspoon ground cumin
- 1 cup cooked rice
- 1 4-ounce can diced green chiles, drained
- 8 10-inch flour tortillas, warmed
- 1½ cups shredded Monterey Jack cheese
- 1 cup chopped tomato (1 large)
- 2 cups shredded lettuce
- 1 recipe Guacamole (page 46)

1 Preheat oven to 350°F. In a skillet cook beef, onion, sweet pepper, and garlic until meat browns. Drain off fat. Stir in chili powder, cumin, ¼ cup *water,* and ¼ teaspoon *salt.* Cook 5 minutes or until most of the water has evaporated. Remove from heat. Add rice and chiles.

2 Spoon ½ cup beef mixture onto each tortilla. Top with cheese and tomato. Fold bottom edges of tortillas over filling (see photo 1, below). Fold in opposite sides and roll up (see photo 2, below). Secure with wooden toothpicks. Arrange burritos, seam sides down, on baking sheet. Bake for 10 to 12 minutes or until hot. Serve burritos on lettuce with Guacamole.

PER BURRITO: 449 cal., 25 g total fat (9 g sat. fat, 1 g trans fat), 63 mg chol., 528 mg sodium, 37 g carbo., 5 g fiber, 21 g pro.
EXCHANGES: ½ Vegetable, 2½ Starch, 2 Lean Meat, 3 Fat

FOLDING BURRITOS, STEP-BY-STEP

1. Spread about ½ cup of filling on a warmed tortilla so it's just below the center. Top the filling with cheese and tomato. Fold the bottom of the tortilla up and over the filling. **2.** Fold the ends of the tortilla in and over the filling. Roll up from the bottom, completely enclosing the filling. Secure with wooden toothpicks.

BALSAMIC-GLAZED FLANK STEAK WITH FALL FRUIT SALSA

START TO FINISH: 40 MINUTES
MAKES: 4 SERVINGS

- 1 pound beef flank steak
  Salt and black pepper
- 3 tablespoons balsamic vinegar
- 1⅓ cups chopped red and/or green apples (2 medium)
- 1 cup chopped pear (1 medium)
- ¼ cup dried cranberries
- 2 teaspoons sugar
- ¼ teaspoon ground cinnamon

1 Preheat broiler. Trim fat from steak. Score both sides of steak in a diamond pattern by making shallow diagonal cuts at 1-inch intervals. Sprinkle both sides lightly with salt and pepper. Place steak on the unheated rack of a broiler pan. Broil 3 to 4 inches from heat for 16 minutes, turning once. Brush both sides of steak with 1 tablespoon of the balsamic vinegar; broil for 1 to 5 minutes more or until medium doneness (160°F). Cover with foil; let steak stand for 5 minutes before slicing.

2 Meanwhile, for salsa, in a medium bowl combine apples, pear, cranberries, the remaining 2 tablespoons balsamic vinegar, the sugar, and cinnamon. Thinly slice steak; serve with salsa.

PER 3 OUNCES STEAK + ⅔ CUP SALSA: 261 cal., 8 g total fat (3 g sat. fat, 0 g trans fat), 40 mg chol., 210 mg sodium, 22 g carbo., 3 g fiber, 24 g pro.
EXCHANGES: 1 Fruit, ½ Other Carbo., 3½ Lean Meat

WINE-BRAISED BRISKET WITH ONIONS

PREP: 30 MINUTES **MARINATE:** 12 TO 24 HOURS
BAKE: 3 HOURS **STAND:** 15 MINUTES **OVEN:** 325°F
MAKES: 6 TO 8 SERVINGS + LEFTOVERS

- 1 3- to 3½-pound boneless beef brisket
- ½ teaspoon kosher salt
- ½ teaspoon freshly ground black pepper
- 1½ cups dry red wine
- 1 14-ounce can beef broth
- 2 large red onions, sliced
- ½ teaspoon dried thyme, crushed
- 1 bay leaf
- 6 cloves garlic, minced
- 10 ounces fresh mushrooms, quartered
- 2 tablespoons snipped fresh Italian parsley
  Mashed Potatoes (page 607) (optional)

WEIGHING IN ON FLANK STEAK MOST FLANK STEAKS WEIGH 2 POUNDS. IF YOU BUY A 2-POUND FLANK STEAK FOR THE ABOVE RECIPE, CUT IT IN HALF AND FREEZE THE EXTRA POUND FOR LATER.

BALSAMIC-GLAZED FLANK STEAK WITH FALL FRUIT SALSA

WINE-BRAISED BRISKET WITH ONIONS

1 One night before cooking brisket, pat brisket dry with paper towels. Sprinkle meat with ½ teaspoon salt and ½ teaspoon pepper. Transfer to a stainless-steel, enamel, or nonstick 6- to 8-quart Dutch oven; add wine, broth, onions, thyme, bay leaf, and garlic. Cover with lid; marinate in refrigerator overnight.

2 Preheat oven to 325°F. Place Dutch oven with meat over high heat; bring to boiling. Cover Dutch oven and transfer to oven. Bake for 1 hour; stir in mushrooms. Cover and bake for 2 to 2½ hours more or until meat is tender. Remove Dutch oven from oven; uncover. Let stand for 15 minutes.

3 Transfer the brisket to a cutting board; slice the meat across the grain. For sauce, skim fat from cooking liquid. Discard bay leaf. Bring to boiling; reduce heat. Simmer, uncovered, until desired consistency. Stir in parsley. Season with additional salt and pepper. Serve with meat.

SLOW COOKER DIRECTIONS: Trim fat from meat. Sprinkle meat with ½ teaspoon salt and ½ teaspoon pepper. If necessary, cut brisket to fit into a 5- to 6-quart slow cooker. Place meat in removeable liner of slow cooker. Pour wine and broth evenly over brisket. Top with onions, thyme, bay leaf, garlic, and mushrooms. Cover and marinate in refrigerator overnight. Remove from refrigerator. Place liner in slow cooker. Cover and cook on low-heat setting for 10 to 12 hours or on high-heat setting for 5 to 6 hours. Carefully remove brisket from slow cooker; slice across the grain. If desired, transfer cooking liquid to a large saucepan. Discard bay leaf. Bring to boiling; reduce heat. Simmer, uncovered, until desired consistency. Serve brisket with sauce.

PER 3½ OUNCES MEAT + ⅔ CUP VEGETABLES + ⅓ CUP SAUCE: 222 cal., 9 g total fat (3 g sat. fat, 0 g trans fat), 120 mg chol., 337 mg sodium, 5 g carbo., 1 g fiber, 25 g pro.
EXCHANGES: 1 Vegetable, 3½ Lean Meat

NEW ENGLAND BOILED DINNER

PREP: 20 MINUTES **COOK:** 2 HOURS + 25 MINUTES
MAKES: 6 SERVINGS

  1 2- to 2½-pound corned beef brisket
  1 teaspoon whole black peppercorns*
  2 bay leaves*
12 ounces tiny new potatoes, quartered
  6 medium carrots and/or parsnips, peeled and quartered
  1 medium onion, cut into 6 wedges
  1 small cabbage, cut into 6 wedges

1 Trim fat from meat. Place meat in a 5- to 6-quart Dutch oven; add juices and spices from package of corned beef. (*Add peppercorns and bay leaves only if your brisket does not come with spice packet.) Add enough water to cover meat. Bring to boiling; reduce heat. Simmer, covered, about 2 hours or until almost tender.

2 Add potatoes, carrots, and onion to meat in Dutch oven. Return to boiling; reduce heat. Simmer, covered, for 10 minutes. Add cabbage. Cover and cook for 15 to 20 minutes more or until tender. Discard bay leaves (if using). Thinly slice meat across grain. Transfer meat and vegetables to serving platter; discard cooking liquid. If desired, season with *salt* and *black pepper* and serve with *prepared horseradish.*

PER ABOUT 3½ OUNCES BEEF + 1 CUP VEGETABLES: 401 cal., 23 g total fat (7 g sat. fat, 0 g trans fat), 82 mg chol., 1,904 mg sodium, 24 g carbo., 6 g fiber, 25 g pro.
EXCHANGES: 2 Vegetable, 1 Starch, 2½ Medium-Fat Meat, 2 Fat

FAST

VEAL CHOPS WITH TOMATO SAUCE

START TO FINISH: 30 MINUTES **MAKES:** 4 SERVINGS

1 tablespoon olive oil
4 veal loin chops, cut ½ to ¾ inch thick (about 1¾ pounds)
¼ cup chicken broth
¼ cup dry white wine or chicken broth
1 14.5-ounce can diced tomatoes, undrained
2 tablespoons whipping cream
2 teaspoons snipped fresh thyme
1 teaspoon finely shredded lemon peel

1 In a very large skillet heat olive oil over medium-high heat. Reduce heat to medium. Add chops to skillet. Sprinkle with ¼ teaspoon *salt* and ¼ teaspoon *black pepper.* Cook, uncovered, for 10 to 14 minutes or until done (160°F), turning once. Remove to a serving platter; cover with foil to keep warm while making sauce.

2 Add broth and wine to skillet, stirring to scrape up browned bits. Bring to boiling; boil gently, uncovered, 3 minutes or until reduced by half. Stir in undrained tomatoes. Boil gently for 5 minutes. Stir in cream, thyme, and lemon peel. Heat through. Spoon sauce over chops.

PER CHOP + ⅓ CUP SAUCE: 320 cal., 13 g total fat (4 g sat. fat, 0 g trans fat), 169 mg chol., 594 mg sodium, 6 g carbo., 2 g fiber, 41 g pro.
EXCHANGES: ½ Vegetable, 5½ Lean Meat

VEAL PICCATA

START TO FINISH: 35 MINUTES **MAKES:** 4 SERVINGS

- ⅓ cup all-purpose flour
- ½ teaspoon salt
- ¼ teaspoon black pepper
- 1 pound veal cutlets (thinly sliced boneless veal)
- 2 tablespoons olive oil
- ¾ cup dry white wine or chicken broth
- ⅓ cup chicken broth
- 3 tablespoons lemon juice
- 3 tablespoons butter
- 2 tablespoons drained capers
- ¼ cup finely shredded Parmesan cheese (1 ounce)
- 2 tablespoons snipped fresh Italian parsley
  Hot cooked spaghetti (optional)

1 In a shallow dish combine flour, salt, and pepper. Cut veal into eight serving-size pieces. If necessary, use a meat mallet to pound veal to ⅛-inch thickness. Coat veal with flour mixture.

2 In a very large skillet heat oil over medium-high heat. Add veal slices, half at a time, to skillet. Cook about 4 minutes or until no longer pink, turning once. Remove from skillet to a serving dish; cover to keep warm while cooking remaining slices.

3 Remove skillet from heat. Add wine and chicken broth. Return skillet to heat. Bring to boiling; reduce heat. Simmer, uncovered, for 6 minutes. Stir in lemon juice, butter, and capers. Stir until butter melts. Spoon sauce over veal in dish. Sprinkle with Parmesan cheese and parsley. If desired, serve with spaghetti.

PER 3 OUNCES VEAL + 3 TABLESPOONS SAUCE: 369 cal., 21 g total fat (8 g sat. fat, 0 g trans fat), 117 mg chol., 751 mg sodium, 11 g carbo., 1 g fiber, 26 g pro.
EXCHANGES: 1 Starch, 3½ Lean Meat, 2 Fat

CHICKEN PICCATA: Prepare as directed, except use 4 small skinless, boneless chicken breast halves (1 to 1¼ pounds). Cut each chicken breast half in half crosswise. Place each chicken piece between two pieces of plastic wrap. Use the flat side of a meat mallet to lightly pound each piece to about ⅛-inch thickness, working from center to edges. Remove plastic wrap. Coat chicken with flour mixture and continue as directed.

PER 3 OUNCES CHICKEN + 3 TABLESPOONS SAUCE: 362 cal., 18 g total fat (8 g sat. fat, 0 g trans fat), 92 mg chol., 722 mg sodium, 11 g carbo., 1 g fiber, 30 g pro.
EXCHANGES: 1 Starch, 4 Very Lean Meat, 2½ Fat

MEAT LOAF

PREP: 15 MINUTES **BAKE:** 75 MINUTES
STAND: 10 MINUTES **OVEN:** 350°F
MAKES: 8 SERVINGS

- 2 eggs, beaten
- ½ cup seasoned fine dry bread crumbs
- ½ cup finely chopped fresh mushrooms
- ½ cup shredded carrot (1 medium)
- ⅓ cup chopped onion (1 small)
- 3 tablespoons ketchup
- 1 tablespoon Dijon-style mustard
- 1 tablespoon Worcestershire sauce
- 2 cloves garlic, minced
- 2 pounds ground beef sirloin*
- ½ cup ketchup
- ¼ cup packed brown sugar
- 2 teaspoons Dijon-style mustard

1 Preheat oven to 350°F. In a large bowl combine eggs, bread crumbs, mushrooms, carrot, onion, the 3 tablespoons ketchup, the 1 table-spoon mustard, Worcestershire sauce, and garlic.

2 Add ground beef; mix well. In a 3-quart rectangular baking dish, lightly pat the mixture into a 9×5-inch loaf. For glaze, in a small bowl combine the ½ cup ketchup, brown sugar, and the 2 teaspoons mustard; set aside.

3 Bake meat loaf for 75 to 90 minutes or until internal temperature reaches 160°F, spooning glaze over meat loaf during the last 10 minutes of baking.

4 Let the meat loaf stand for 10 minutes. Using two spatulas, transfer loaf to a serving platter; cut into eight slices.

*NOTE: If desired, use a mixture of ground beef, ground sweet Italian sausage, ground pork, ground veal, and/or ground uncooked turkey.

PER SERVING: 330 cal., 16 g total fat (6 g sat. fat, 0 g trans fat), 106 mg chol., 589 mg sodium, 19 g carbo., 1 g fiber, 26 g pro.
EXCHANGES: 1 Starch, 3 Lean Meat, 1½ Fat

MIXED-MEAT MEAT LOAF
IF USING GROUND VEAL IN THE MIXTURE, ALSO USE SOME GROUND SAUSAGE OR PORK TO ADD FLAVOR AND SUCCULENCE.

10 TO TRY—
MEAT LOAF GLAZES

Start with Meat Loaf, page 394, except replace the glaze with one of the following mixtures. **1. SWEET-AND-SOUR:** ½ cup sweet-and-sour sauce and ¼ cup drained canned crushed pineapple. **2. PIZZA:** ½ cup pizza sauce and 1 tablespoon snipped fresh basil. **3. SPICY-SWEET:** ½ cup peach preserves, 2 teaspoons garlic chili paste, and 2 teaspoons grated fresh ginger. **4. SESAME:** ½ cup bottled stir-fry sauce and 1 teaspoon sesame seeds. **5. THAI:** ½ cup Thai peanut sauce and 1 to 2 tablespoons chopped peanuts. **6. TEX-MEX:** ½ cup fresh or bottled salsa. **7. ITALIAN:** ½ cup marinara sauce and 2 tablespoons balsamic vinegar. **8. CRANBERRY-TOMATO:** ½ cup ketchup and ¼ cup whole cranberry sauce. **9. SPICY BARBECUE:** ½ cup barbecue sauce and 5 or 6 fresh jalapeño chile pepper slices (see tip, page 24). **10. APRICOT-MUSTARD:** ½ cup apricot preserves and 2 tablespoons Dijon-style mustard.

PORK CUTS AND HOW TO COOK THEM

A surefire way to enjoy pork at its best is to use the cooking method that best suits each cut. These pages help you do just that. The photos show the cuts that are the most widely available at supermarkets, along with the most recommended ways for cooking them. They correspond to the drawing, which shows where the cuts come from on the animal.

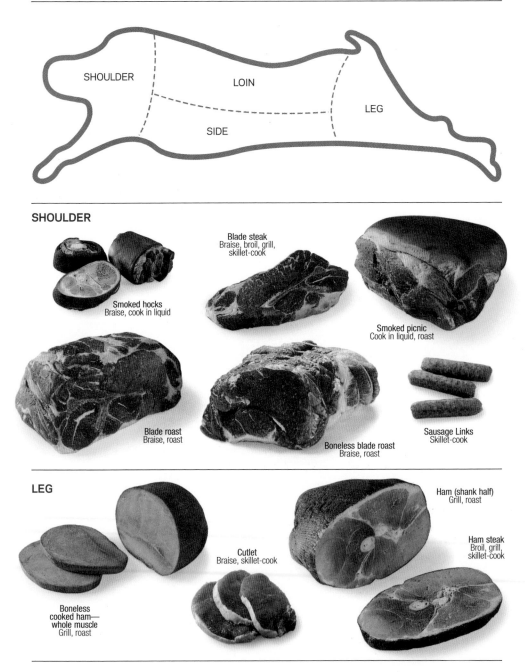

SHOULDER   LOIN   LEG   SIDE

SHOULDER

Smoked hocks
Braise, cook in liquid

Blade steak
Braise, broil, grill, skillet-cook

Smoked picnic
Cook in liquid, roast

Blade roast
Braise, roast

Boneless blade roast
Braise, roast

Sausage Links
Skillet-cook

LEG

Boneless cooked ham—whole muscle
Grill, roast

Cutlet
Braise, skillet-cook

Ham (shank half)
Grill, roast

Ham steak
Broil, grill, skillet-cook

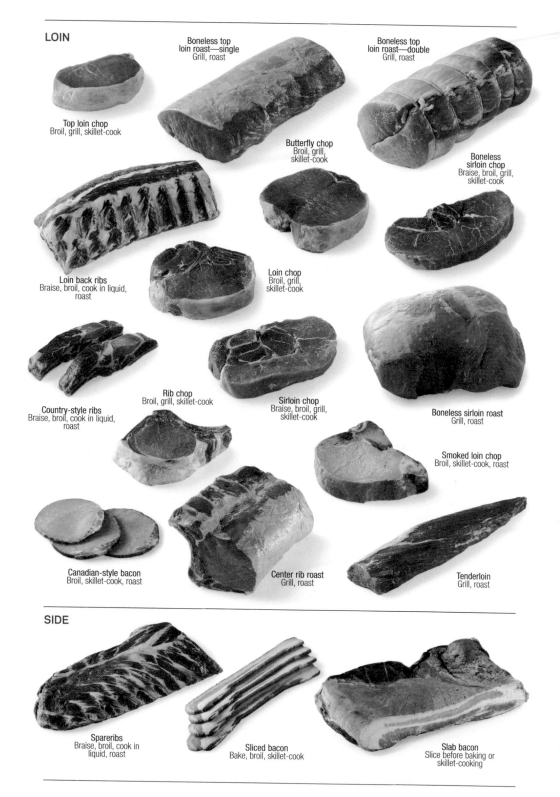

LOIN

Top loin chop
Broil, grill, skillet-cook

Boneless top loin roast—single
Grill, roast

Boneless top loin roast—double
Grill, roast

Butterfly chop
Broil, grill, skillet-cook

Boneless sirloin chop
Braise, broil, grill, skillet-cook

Loin back ribs
Braise, broil, cook in liquid, roast

Loin chop
Broil, grill, skillet-cook

Country-style ribs
Braise, broil, cook in liquid, roast

Rib chop
Broil, grill, skillet-cook

Sirloin chop
Braise, broil, grill, skillet-cook

Boneless sirloin roast
Grill, roast

Smoked loin chop
Broil, skillet-cook, roast

Canadian-style bacon
Broil, skillet-cook, roast

Center rib roast
Grill, roast

Tenderloin
Grill, roast

SIDE

Spareribs
Braise, broil, cook in liquid, roast

Sliced bacon
Bake, broil, skillet-cook

Slab bacon
Slice before baking or skillet-cooking

PORK ROAST WITH CHERRY AND WILD RICE STUFFING

PREP: 60 MINUTES **ROAST:** 1¾ HOURS
STAND: 15 MINUTES **OVEN:** 325°F
MAKES: 8 TO 10 SERVINGS

- 1 recipe Cherry and Wild Rice Stuffing (page 399)
- 1 3-pound boneless pork top loin roast (single loin)
   Snipped fresh thyme
- 2 tablespoons all-purpose flour

1 Prepare Cherry and Wild Rice Stuffing. Trim fat from pork. Butterfly the meat by making a lengthwise cut down the center of the meat, cutting to within ½ inch of the other side (see photo 1, below). Spread open. Place knife in the V of the cut. Cut horizontally to the cut surface and away from the center cut to within ½ inch of the other side of the meat (see photo 2, below). Repeat on opposite side of the V. Spread meat open. Cover the roast with plastic wrap. Working from center (thicker part) to edges, pound with a meat mallet until ½ to ¾ inch thick (see photo 3, below). Remove plastic wrap. Set meat aside.

2 Preheat oven to 325°F. Spread the stuffing over roast (see photo 4, below). Roll meat into a spiral, starting from a short side. Tie with heavy 100%-cotton kitchen string (photo 5, below). Place roast on a rack in a shallow roasting pan. Sprinkle with *salt, freshly ground black pepper,* and thyme. Insert an oven-going meat thermometer into center of roast. Roast, uncovered, for 1¾ to 2¼ hours or until thermometer registers 155°F, covering ends of meat after 45 minutes to prevent stuffing from drying out. Remove roast to serving platter. Cover loosely with foil; let stand for 15 minutes before carving. (Temperature of the meat after standing should be 160°F.)

3 For pan gravy, add 1 cup *water* to pan, using a wire whisk to stir and scrape up browned bits. In a

STUFFING PORK ROAST, STEP-BY-STEP

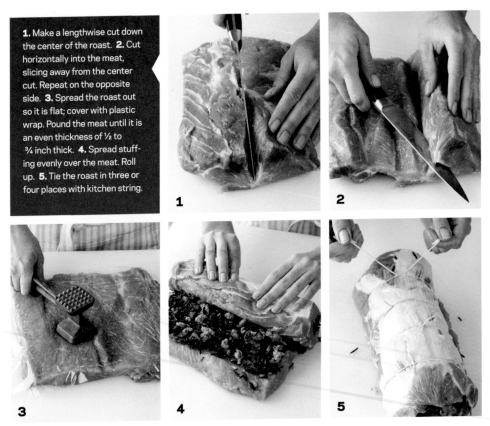

1. Make a lengthwise cut down the center of the roast. **2.** Cut horizontally into the meat, slicing away from the center cut. Repeat on the opposite side. **3.** Spread the roast out so it is flat; cover with plastic wrap. Pound the meat until it is an even thickness of ½ to ¾ inch thick. **4.** Spread stuffing evenly over the meat. Roll up. **5.** Tie the roast in three or four places with kitchen string.

1

2

3

4

5

small saucepan whisk together ⅓ cup cold *water* and flour. Whisk in pan juices. Cook and stir over medium heat until thickened and bubbly. Cook and stir for 1 minute. Season with additional salt and black pepper. Slice roast; serve with gravy.

CHERRY AND WILD RICE STUFFING: Rinse ⅓ cup wild rice under cold running water until clean; drain. In small saucepan combine the rice; 1¼ cups water; 2 teaspoons snipped fresh rosemary or ½ teaspoon dried rosemary, crushed; and ½ teaspoon salt. Bring to boiling; reduce heat. Simmer, covered, for 40 to 45 minutes or until tender. Remove from heat. Stir in ¾ cup coarsely chopped dried cherries or cranberries. In a large skillet cook 6 ounces bulk pork sausage and ½ cup chopped onion over medium heat until sausage is brown. Drain off fat. Stir in 1 tablespoon snipped fresh parsley; 1 teaspoon snipped fresh thyme or ¼ teaspoon dried thyme, crushed; and ¼ teaspoon black pepper. If necessary, drain the rice mixture. Stir cooked rice mixture into sausage mixture.

PER 5 OUNCES MEAT + ⅓ CUP STUFFING + 2 TABLESPOONS PAN GRAVY: 353 cal., 10 g total fat (4 g sat. fat, 0 g trans fat), 121 mg chol., 392 mg sodium, 19 g carbo., 1 g fiber, 43 g pro.
EXCHANGES: 1 Starch, 5½ Lean Meat, 1 Fat

LOW FAT

PORK WITH HOT PEAR RELISH

PREP: 30 MINUTES **ROAST:** 75 MINUTES
STAND: 15 MINUTES **OVEN:** 350°F
MAKES: 8 SERVINGS

- 1 tablespoon olive oil
- 1 cup finely chopped sweet onion (1 large)
- ¾ cup finely chopped red sweet pepper
- 1 fresh jalapeño chile pepper, seeded and finely chopped (see tip, page 24)
- 2 cups chopped, peeled pears (2 medium)
- ½ cup sugar
- ½ cup white balsamic vinegar
- 1 teaspoon dry mustard
- ¼ teaspoon salt
- 1 2- to 2½-pound boneless pork top loin roast (single loin)

1 For pear relish, in a large skillet heat oil over medium heat. Add onion, sweet pepper, and jalapeño pepper; cook and stir for 2 minutes. Stir in pears, sugar, vinegar, mustard, and salt. Bring to boiling over medium-high heat, stirring occasionally; reduce heat. Simmer, uncovered, about 10 minutes or until pears are soft and transparent.

2 Meanwhile, preheat oven to 350°F. Place pork on a rack in a shallow roasting pan. Sprinkle with additional salt and *black pepper.* Insert an oven-going meat thermometer into center of roast. Roast, uncovered, for 60 minutes. Top with ½ cup of the pear relish. Roast for 15 to 30 minutes more or until thermometer registers 150°F.

3 Remove roast from oven. Cover with foil and let stand for 15 minutes. Temperature of the meat after standing should be 160°F. Slice meat and serve with remaining pear relish.

PER 4 OUNCES MEAT + ¼ CUP RELISH: 309 cal., 11 g total fat (3 g sat. fat, 0 g trans fat), 73 mg chol., 167 mg sodium, 25 g carbo., 2 g fiber, 25 g pro.
EXCHANGES: 1½ Other Carbo., 3½ Lean Meat

HEALTHY

CASHEW PORK AND VEGETABLES

START TO FINISH: 45 MINUTES **MAKES:** 4 SERVINGS

- ¼ cup orange juice
- 2 tablespoons bottled hoisin sauce
- ½ teaspoon ground ginger
- ⅛ teaspoon crushed red pepper (optional)
- 1 tablespoon vegetable oil
- 3 medium carrots, bias-sliced (1½ cups)
- 2 cups fresh pea pods, strings and tips removed
- ¼ cup sliced green onions (2)
- 1 pound lean boneless pork, cut into thin bite-size strips
- 2 cups hot cooked rice
- ½ cup cashews or peanuts

1 For sauce, stir together orange juice, hoisin sauce, ginger, and, if desired, crushed red pepper; set aside.

2 Pour oil into a wok or large skillet. (Add more oil as necessary during cooking.) Preheat over medium-high heat. Stir in carrots. Cook and stir for 2 minutes. Add pea pods and green onions. Cook and stir for 2 to 3 minutes or until vegetables are crisp-tender. Remove vegetables from wok.

3 Add half of the pork strips to hot wok. Cook and stir for 2 to 3 minutes or until no pink remains; remove from pan. Repeat with remaining strips. Return all meat and vegetables to wok. Stir sauce; add to center of wok. Cook and stir until heated through. Stir in rice until coated. Top with nuts.

PER 2 CUPS: 439 cal., 17 g total fat (3 g sat. fat, 0 g trans fat), 60 mg chol., 204 mg sodium, 41 g carbo., 4 g fiber, 32 g pro.
EXCHANGES: 1 Vegetable, 2½ Starch, 3 Lean Meat, 1 Fat

COOK ONCE, EAT TWICE

SERVE A LUSCIOUSLY SAUCED, CRUMB-TOPPED ROAST FOR A LEISURELY WEEKEND DINNER. TUCK THE LEFTOVERS INTO A STYLISH SANDWICH FOR A QUICK WEEKNIGHT SUPPER.

TONIGHT

GARLIC AND THYME ROASTED PORK

PREP: 25 MINUTES **ROAST:** 35 MINUTES
STAND: 10 MINUTES **OVEN:** 425°F
MAKES: 4 SERVINGS + RESERVES

- 2 1-pound pork tenderloins
- ½ cup panko (Japanese-style bread crumbs)
- ¼ cup bottled roasted garlic
- 3 tablespoons snipped fresh thyme
- 1 pound tiny new potatoes, quartered
- 4 medium carrots, quartered
- 2 fennel bulbs, trimmed and cut into wedges
- 3 tablespoons olive oil
- ½ cup apple juice

1 Preheat oven to 425°F. Place tenderloins on rack in roasting pan. Combine crumbs, garlic, and 2 tablespoons of the thyme. Spread over tenderloins. Sprinkle with *kosher salt* and *black pepper*.

2 Combine potatoes, carrots, fennel, oil, the remaining 1 tablespoon thyme, 1 teaspoon *kosher salt,* and ¼ teaspoon *black pepper.* Arrange vegetable mixture in a single layer around meat.

3 Roast, uncovered, for 35 to 40 minutes or until thermometer registers 155°F. Remove meat from pan. Cover; let stand for 10 minutes. Temperature of the meat after standing should be 160°F.

4 Use a slotted spoon to remove vegetables from the pan. Stir apple juice into pan. Cook and stir over medium heat, scraping up any of the browned bits. Return vegetables to pan; toss to mix.

5 Serve one tenderloin with vegetable mixture. Cover and chill remaining tenderloin for Roast Pork, Fig, and Goat Cheese Sandwiches.

PER 3 OUNCES MEAT + 1 CUP VEGETABLE MIXTURE: 418 cal., 13 g total fat (2 g sat. fat, 0 g trans fat), 74 mg chol., 797 mg sodium, 46 g carbo., 8 g fiber, 30 g pro.
EXCHANGES: 1½ Vegetable, 2½ Starch, 3 Lean Meat, 1½ Fat

TOMORROW

ROAST PORK, FIG, AND GOAT CHEESE SANDWICHES

START TO FINISH: 10 MINUTES
MAKES: 4 SANDWICHES

- 8 ½-inch slices crusty bread (lightly toasted, if desired)
- 2 tablespoons butter or margarine, softened
- 2 teaspoons spicy Dijon-style mustard
  Reserved roasted pork from Garlic and Thyme Roasted Pork, sliced
- ½ cup fig, apricot, plum, or tomato preserves
- 2 ounces goat cheese (chèvre)
  Baby spinach, arugula, or watercress

1 Spread the bread slices with butter. Spread four of the bread slices with mustard. Top with sliced pork, preserves, goat cheese, and spinach. Top with the remaining bread slices. Cut each sandwich in half.

PER SANDWICH: 708 cal., 20 g total fat (8 g sat. fat, 0 g trans fat), 77 mg chol., 1,201 mg sodium, 99 g carbo., 9 g fiber, 33 g pro.
EXCHANGES: ½ Vegetable, 2 Starch, 4½ Other Carbo., 3½ Lean Meat, 1½ Fat

GOAT CHEESE OPTIONS
YOU CAN USE A SPREADABLE SOFT GOAT CHEESE FOR THESE FRUITY SANDWICHES. OR SLICE OR CRUMBLE A SEMISOFT (SEMI-RIPENED) GOAT CHEESE.

PORK MEDALLIONS WITH FENNEL AND PANCETTA

START TO FINISH: 30 MINUTES **MAKES:** 4 SERVINGS

- 12 ounces pork tenderloin
- ¼ cup all-purpose flour
  Dash salt
  Dash black pepper
- 2 tablespoons olive oil
- 2 ounces pancetta (Italian bacon) or bacon, finely chopped
- 2 fennel bulbs,* trimmed and cut crosswise into ¼-inch slices
- 1 small onion, thinly sliced
- 2 cloves garlic, minced
- 2 tablespoons lemon juice
- ½ cup whipping cream
- 2 tablespoons snipped fresh Italian parsley

1 Trim fat from pork. Cut pork crosswise into 1-inch slices. Place each slice between two pieces of plastic wrap. Use the flat side of a meat mallet to lightly pound pork to ¼-inch thickness. Discard plastic wrap.

2 In a shallow dish combine flour, salt, and pepper. Dip pork slices into flour mixture to coat. In a large heavy skillet heat oil over medium-high heat. Cook pork, half at a time, in hot oil for 2 to 3 minutes or until meat is slightly pink in center, turning once. (Add more oil during cooking, if necessary.) Remove meat from skillet; set aside.

3 In the same skillet cook pancetta over medium-high heat until crisp. Add fennel, onion, and garlic; cook for 3 to 5 minutes or until crisp-tender. Add lemon juice; stir in whipping cream. Bring to boiling; return meat to skillet. Cook until meat is heated through and sauce is slightly thickened.

4 Transfer meat to a serving platter. Spoon vegetable mixture and sauce over meat. Sprinkle with parsley.

*****NOTE:** Choose fennel bulbs that are smooth and firm, without cracks or brown spots. The stalks should be crisp, and the leaves should be bright green and fresh-looking.

PER 2½ OUNCES MEAT + ½ CUP VEGETABLES: 382 cal., 24 g total fat (10 g sat. fat, 0 g trans fat), 106 mg chol., 416 mg sodium, 18 g carbo., 4 g fiber, 23 g pro.
EXCHANGES: ½ Vegetable, 1 Starch, 3 Lean Meat, 3 Fat

THAI PORK AND VEGETABLE CURRY

START TO FINISH: 30 MINUTES **MAKES:** 4 SERVINGS

- 1⅓ cups uncooked jasmine rice (about 9 ounces)
- 12 ounces pork tenderloin or lean boneless pork
  Salt and black pepper
- 2 tablespoons vegetable oil
- 8 ounces green beans,* bias-sliced into 1½-inch pieces (2 cups)
- 1 red sweet pepper, cut into thin bite-size strips
- 2 green onions, bias-sliced into ¼-inch pieces
- 1 14-ounce can unsweetened coconut milk
- 4 teaspoons bottled curry paste
- 1 teaspoon sugar
- ⅛ teaspoon crushed red pepper
- 1 lime, cut into wedges

1 Cook rice according to package directions; drain. Keep warm.

2 Meanwhile, thinly slice pork into bite-size strips. Sprinkle with salt and pepper. In a large nonstick skillet heat 1 tablespoon of the oil over medium-high heat. Add pork; cook and stir about 4 minutes or until no pink remains. Remove meat from skillet.

3 Add the remaining 1 tablespoon oil to skillet. Add green beans; cook and stir for 3 minutes. Add sweet pepper and green onions; cook and stir about 2 minutes more or until vegetables are crisp-tender. Remove vegetables from skillet. Add coconut milk, curry paste, sugar, and crushed red pepper to skillet. Bring mixture to boiling; reduce heat. Simmer, uncovered, about 2 minutes or until mixture is slightly thickened. Stir in pork and vegetables; heat through. Serve over hot cooked rice with lime wedges.

*****NOTE:** A 9-ounce package of frozen cut green beans, thawed, can be substituted for the fresh beans. Add them to the skillet along with the sweet pepper and green onions; cook as directed.

PER 1 CUP PORK MIXTURE + 1 CUP RICE: 490 cal., 16 g total fat (5 g sat. fat, 0 g trans fat), 47 mg chol., 593 mg sodium, 63 g carbo., 3 g fiber, 23 g pro.
EXCHANGES: 1 Vegetable, 2 Starch, 2 Other Carbo., 2 Lean Meat, 1½ Fat

PORK POT ROAST IN CIDER

PREP: 15 MINUTES **COOK:** 90 MINUTES
MAKES: 4 SERVINGS

  2 tablespoons vegetable oil
  1 1½- to 2-pound boneless pork blade roast or sirloin roast
1¼ cups apple cider or apple juice
  2 teaspoons instant beef bouillon granules
  ½ teaspoon dry mustard
  ¼ teaspoon black pepper
  3 medium red potatoes or round white potatoes, peeled (if desired) and quartered
  3 medium carrots, cut into 2-inch pieces
  3 medium parsnips, peeled and cut into 2-inch pieces
  1 large onion, cut into wedges
  ¼ cup all-purpose flour

1 Trim fat from meat. In a 4- to 6-quart Dutch oven heat oil over medium-high heat. Brown roast on all sides in hot oil. Drain off fat. In a medium bowl stir together apple cider, bouillon granules, mustard, and pepper. Pour over meat. Bring to boiling; reduce heat. Simmer, covered, for 60 minutes.

2 Add potatoes, carrots, parsnips, and onion. Simmer, covered, for 30 to 40 minutes more or until meat and vegetables are tender. Transfer meat and vegetables to a serving platter, reserving juices in Dutch oven. Keep warm.

3 For gravy, measure juices; skim fat. If necessary, add enough *water* to juices to equal 1½ cups. Return to Dutch oven. Stir ⅓ cup *cold water* into flour. Stir into juices in pan. Cook and stir over medium heat until thickened and bubbly. Cook and stir for 1 minute more. To serve, slice meat and serve with vegetables and gravy.

SLOW COOKER DIRECTIONS: Prepare meat as directed in Step 1. Place vegetables in a 3½- or 4-quart slow cooker. Cut meat to fit, if necessary; place on top of vegetables. Stir together apple cider, bouillon granules, mustard, and pepper. Pour over meat and vegetables in cooker. Cover and cook on low-heat setting for 8 to 10 hours or on high-heat setting for 4 to 5 hours or until tender. Transfer meat and vegetables to a serving platter; keep warm. Prepare gravy in a medium saucepan on the stovetop as in Step 3.

PER 5 OUNCES PORK + ABOUT ½ CUP GRAVY: 765 cal., 49 g total fat (15 g sat. fat, 0 g trans fat), 123 mg chol., 573 mg sodium, 50 g carbo., 6 g fiber, 32 g pro.
EXCHANGES: 2 Vegetable, 2½ Starch, 3 Medium-Fat Meat, 6½ Fat

FAST ▪ LOW FAT

PORK CHOPS WITH BLACK BEAN SALSA *(photo, page 379)*

START TO FINISH: 25 MINUTES **MAKES:** 4 SERVINGS

  4 pork loin chops, cut 1¼ inches thick (about 3 pounds)
  1 teaspoon Jamaican jerk or Cajun seasoning
  ⅛ teaspoon black pepper
  ¾ cup canned black beans, rinsed and drained (½ of a 15-ounce can)
  ⅔ cup corn relish
1½ teaspoons lime juice
  ¼ teaspoon ground cumin
    Dairy sour cream (optional)

1 Preheat broiler. Trim fat from chops. Rub Jamaican jerk seasoning and pepper onto both sides of chops. Place pork chops on the unheated rack of a broiler pan. Broil 3 to 4 inches from the heat for 16 to 20 minutes or until 160°F, turning once halfway through broiling.

2 Meanwhile, for salsa, in a small bowl combine black beans, corn relish, lime juice, and cumin. Serve chops with salsa and, if desired, sour cream.

PER CHOP + ⅓ CUP SALSA: 442 cal., 9 g total fat (3 g sat. fat, 0 g trans fat), 185 mg chol., 457 mg sodium, 20 g carbo., 2 g fiber, 66 g pro.
EXCHANGES: 1 Starch, 9 Lean Meat

FAST

OVEN-FRIED PORK CHOPS

PREP: 10 MINUTES **BAKE:** 20 MINUTES
OVEN: 425°F **MAKES:** 4 SERVINGS

  4 pork loin chops, cut ¾ inch thick
  2 tablespoons butter, melted
  1 egg, beaten
  2 tablespoons milk
  ¼ teaspoon black pepper
  1 cup herb-seasoned stuffing mix, finely crushed

1 Preheat oven to 425°F. Trim fat from meat. Pour butter into a 13×9×2-inch baking pan, tilting pan to coat the bottom. In a shallow dish combine egg, milk, and pepper. Place stuffing mix in another shallow dish. Dip chops into the egg mixture. Coat both sides with stuffing mix. Place chops in the prepared pan.

2 Bake, uncovered, for 10 minutes. Turn chops. Bake for 10 to 15 minutes more or until 160°F and juices run clear.

PER CHOP: 327 cal., 14 g total fat (6 g sat. fat, 0 g trans fat), 147 mg chol., 383 mg sodium, 13 g carbo., 2 g fiber, 35 g pro. EXCHANGES: 1 Starch, 4½ Lean Meat, 2 Fat

PESTO-STUFFED PORK CHOPS

PREP: 20 MINUTES **BAKE:** 35 MINUTES
OVEN: 375°F **MAKES:** 4 SERVINGS

- 3 tablespoons crumbled feta cheese
- 2 tablespoons refrigerated basil pesto
- 1 tablespoon pine nuts, toasted (see tip, page 20)
- 4 pork loin chops or boneless pork loin chops, cut 1¼ inches thick
- 1 teaspoon freshly ground black pepper
- 1 teaspoon dried oregano, crushed
- ¼ teaspoon crushed red pepper
- ¼ teaspoon dried thyme, crushed
- 2 cloves garlic, minced
- 1 tablespoon balsamic vinegar

1 Preheat oven to 375°F. For filling, in a small bowl stir together feta cheese, pesto, and pine nuts; set aside.

2 Trim fat from meat. Make a pocket in each chop by cutting horizontally from fat side almost to bone or opposite side. Spoon filling into pockets. Secure the openings with wooden toothpicks.

3 For rub, in a small bowl combine black pepper, oregano, crushed red pepper, thyme, and garlic. Rub evenly onto all sides of meat. Place chops on a rack in a shallow roasting pan. Bake for 35 to 45 minutes or until chops are 160°F and juices run clear. Brush vinegar onto chops the last 5 minutes of baking. Discard toothpicks before serving.

PER CHOP: 415 cal., 20 g total fat (7 g sat. fat, 0 g trans fat), 133 mg chol., 228 mg sodium, 3 g carbo., 0 g fiber, 52 g pro. EXCHANGES: 7½ Lean Meat

CHOPS FOR STUFFING USE EITHER BONE-IN OR BONELESS CHOPS TO STUFF AS LONG AS THEY ARE AT LEAST 1¼ INCHES THICK. FOR THICKER CHOPS, EXTEND THE COOKING TIME A FEW MINUTES.

PESTO-STUFFED PORK CHOPS

OVEN-BARBECUED RIBS

PREP: 25 MINUTES **BAKE:** 90 MINUTES
OVEN: 350°F **MAKES:** 4 SERVINGS

  3 to 4 pounds pork loin back ribs
  ¾ cup ketchup
  ¾ cup water
  2 tablespoons vinegar
  2 tablespoons Worcestershire sauce
  1 teaspoon paprika
  1 teaspoon chili powder
  ½ teaspoon black pepper
  ¼ teaspoon salt
  ¼ to ½ teaspoon cayenne pepper
  1 cup finely chopped onion (1 large)

1 Preheat oven to 350°F. If desired, cut ribs into serving-size pieces. Place the ribs, bone sides down, in a large shallow roasting pan. Bake, covered, for 60 minutes. Carefully drain off fat in roasting pan.

2 Meanwhile, for sauce, in a medium bowl combine ketchup, water, vinegar, Worcestershire sauce, paprika, chili powder, black pepper, salt, and cayenne pepper. Stir in onion. Pour sauce over ribs. Bake, uncovered, for 30 minutes more or until ribs are tender, basting once with sauce. Pass sauce with ribs.

PER ¼ RIBS + ¼ CUP SAUCE: 675 cal., 50 g total fat (18 g sat. fat, 0 g trans fat), 171 mg chol., 915 mg sodium, 18 g carbo., 2 g fiber, 36 g pro.
EXCHANGES: 5 High-Fat Meat, 2 Fat

OVEN-ROASTED ASIAN-STYLE PORK RIBS

PREP: 45 MINUTES **BAKE:** 15 MINUTES
OVEN: 350°F **MAKES:** 4 SERVINGS

  3 pounds pork loin back ribs or pork
     spareribs
  3 tablespoons pineapple, peach, or
     apricot preserves
  ⅓ cup ketchup
  2 tablespoons soy sauce
  1 teaspoon grated fresh ginger or
     ¼ teaspoon ground ginger
  1 clove garlic, minced

1 Cut ribs into serving-size pieces. Place ribs in a 4- to 6-quart Dutch oven. Add enough water to cover. Bring to boiling; reduce heat. Simmer, covered, for 25 to 30 minutes or until tender; drain.

2 Meanwhile, for sauce, cut up any large pieces of fruit in the preserves. In a small bowl stir

together preserves, ketchup, soy sauce, ginger, and garlic.

3 Preheat oven to 350°F. Brush some of the sauce over both sides of the ribs. Place ribs, bone sides down, in a shallow roasting pan. Bake, uncovered, for 15 to 20 minutes or until glazed and heated through. Brush ribs with the remaining sauce before serving.

PER ¼ RIBS + 2 TABLESPOONS SAUCE: 662 cal., 50 g total fat (18 g sat. fat, 0 g trans fat), 171 mg chol., 893 mg sodium, 16 g carbo., 0 g fiber, 35 g pro.
EXCHANGES: 1 Other Carbo., 5 High-Fat Meat, 2 Fat

HONEY-AND-APPLE RIBS

PREP: 30 MINUTES **BAKE:** 105 MINUTES
OVEN: 350°F **MAKES:** 4 SERVINGS

  3 pounds bone-in pork country-style ribs
  1 tablespoon vegetable oil
  ½ cup chopped onion (1 medium)
  2 cloves garlic, minced
  ¾ cup bottled chili sauce
  ½ cup apple juice or apple cider
  ¼ cup honey
  2 tablespoons Worcestershire sauce
  ½ teaspoon dry mustard

1 Preheat oven to 350°F. Place ribs, bone sides down, in a shallow roasting pan. Bake, uncovered, for 60 minutes. Drain off fat in pan.

2 Meanwhile, for sauce, in a medium saucepan heat oil over medium heat. Add onion and garlic; cook and stir until tender. Stir in chili sauce, apple juice, honey, Worcestershire sauce, and dry mustard. Bring to boiling; reduce heat. Simmer, uncovered, for 20 minutes (about 1½ cups sauce).

3 Spoon ⅓ cup of the sauce over the ribs. Bake, covered, for 45 to 60 minutes more or until tender, turning ribs and spooning ⅓ cup more of the sauce over ribs after 25 minutes. Heat remaining sauce until warm; pass with ribs.

PER ¼ RIBS + 2 TABLESPOONS SAUCE: 590 cal., 30 g total fat (10 g sat. fat, 0 g trans fat), 163 mg chol., 828 mg sodium, 34 g carbo., 3 g fiber, 44 g pro.
EXCHANGES: 2 Other Carbo., 6½ Medium-Fat Meat

GINGER ON HAND
GINGER FREEZES WELL. PLACE UNPEELED GINGER IN FREEZER BAG; PEEL AND GRATE AS NEEDED IN FROZEN STATE.

SMOKED CHOPS WITH DILL SAUCE

PREP: 10 MINUTES **BROIL:** 9 MINUTES
MAKES: 6 SERVINGS

 6 smoked pork loin chops, cut 1 inch thick

 3 tablespoons packed brown sugar

 3 tablespoons cider vinegar or white
     wine vinegar

 ½ cup Dijon-style mustard

 3 tablespoons olive oil

 ½ teaspoon dried dillweed
     Dash black pepper

1 Preheat broiler. Place chops on the unheated rack of a broiler pan. Broil 3 to 4 inches from the heat for 9 to 12 minutes or until heated through, turning once halfway through broiling.

2 Meanwhile, for sauce, in a small bowl stir together brown sugar and vinegar until sugar is dissolved. Using a wire whisk, beat in mustard, olive oil, dillweed, and pepper until well combined. To serve, spoon some of the sauce over chops. Pass remaining sauce.

PER CHOP + 2 TABLESPOONS SAUCE: 208 cal., 11 g total fat (2 g sat. fat, 0 g trans fat), 45 mg chol., 1,453 mg sodium, 7 g carbo., 0 g fiber, 15 g pro.
EXCHANGES: ½ Other Carbo., 2 Lean Meat, 1 Fat

GLAZED HAM

PREP: 15 MINUTES **BAKE:** 1½ HOURS
OVEN: 325°F **MAKES:** 16 TO 20 SERVINGS

 1 5- to 6-pound cooked ham (rump half or
     shank portion)

 24 whole cloves (optional)

 1 recipe Orange Glaze

 1 recipe Mint and Lemon Sprinkle (optional)

1 Preheat oven to 325°F. Score ham by making diagonal cuts in a diamond pattern. If desired, stud ham with cloves. Place ham on a rack in a shallow roasting pan. Insert an oven-going meat thermometer into center of ham (see tip, page 383). The thermometer should not touch the bone.

2 Bake for 1½ to 2¼ hours or until thermometer registers 140°F. Brush ham with some of the desired glaze during the last 20 minutes of baking. Serve with remaining glaze and, if desired, Mint and Lemon Sprinkle.

ORANGE GLAZE: In a medium saucepan combine 2 teaspoons finely shredded orange peel, 1 cup orange juice, ½ cup packed brown sugar, 4 tea-

SMOKED CHOPS WITH DILL SAUCE

spoons cornstarch, and 1½ teaspoons dry mustard. Cook and stir until bubbly. Cook and stir for 2 minutes more.

PER 3 OUNCES MEAT + ABOUT 1 TABLESPOON ORANGE GLAZE: 156 cal., 7 g total fat (1 g sat. fat, 0 g trans fat), 62 mg chol., 984 mg sodium, 7 g carbo., 0 g fiber, 16 g pro.
EXCHANGES: ½ Vegetable, 2½ Lean Meat

PEACH-PINEAPPLE GLAZE: Cook and stir one 8-ounce can crushed pineapple, ½ cup peach preserves, 2 tablespoons vinegar, and ½ teaspoon ground ginger until hot.

PER 3 OUNCES MEAT + ABOUT 1 TABLESPOON GLAZE: 156 cal., 6 g total fat (1 g sat. fat, 0 g trans fat), 62 mg chol., 985 mg sodium, 7 g carbo., 0 g fiber, 16 g pro.
EXCHANGES: ½ Other Carbo., 2½ Lean Meat

APRICOT-CHERRY GLAZE: In a bowl stir together ½ cup apricot preserves, ½ cup cherry preserves, and 1 tablespoon lemon juice.

PER 3 OUNCES MEAT + ABOUT 1 TABLESPOON GLAZE: 183 cal., 6 g total fat (1 g sat. fat, 0 g trans fat), 62 mg chol., 989 mg sodium, 14 g carbo., 0 g fiber, 16 g pro.
EXCHANGES: 1 Other Carbo., 2½ Lean Meat

STOUT GLAZE: In a saucepan combine ½ cup Irish stout beer or apple cider, ¼ cup honey, and ¼ cup butter. Bring to boiling; reduce heat. Simmer, uncovered, for 10 minutes.

PER 3 OUNCES MEAT + 2 TEASPOONS GLAZE: 166 cal., 9 g total fat (3 g sat. fat, 0 g trans fat), 69 mg chol., 1,001 mg sodium, 4 g carbo., 0 g fiber, 16 g pro.
EXCHANGES: 2½ Lean Meat, ½ Fat

MINT AND LEMON SPRINKLE: In a bowl combine ½ cup snipped fresh mint, 1 tablespoon finely shredded lemon peel, and 2 cloves garlic, minced.

APPLE BUTTER-GLAZED HAM

START TO FINISH: 20 MINUTES
MAKES: 4 SERVINGS

  2 medium sweet potatoes, peeled and cut
    into 1-inch cubes
 12 ounces Brussels sprouts, trimmed and
    halved
  2 tablespoons butter or margarine
  1 to 1¼ pounds sliced cooked ham, about
    ¼ inch thick
  ½ cup apple butter
  2 tablespoons cider vinegar
    Baguette slices (optional)

1 In a large saucepan cook sweet potatoes and
Brussels sprouts in lightly salted boiling water for
8 or 10 minutes or just until tender; drain.

2 Meanwhile, in a very large skillet melt butter
over medium-high heat. Add ham; cook for 4 to
5 minutes, turning occasionally. Remove ham
from skillet. Place ham and vegetables on serving
plates; cover to keep warm. Stir apple butter and
vinegar into the skillet; heat through. Serve with
ham, vegetables, and, if desired, baguette slices.
Season to taste with *salt* and *black pepper*.

PER 4 OUNCES HAM + ¾ CUP VEGETABLES: 513 cal.,
16 g total fat (7 g sat. fat, 0 g trans fat), 80 mg chol., 1,664 mg
sodium, 70 g carbo., 8 g fiber, 23 g pro.
EXCHANGES: 1 Vegetable, 2 Starch, 2½ Other Carbo., 2 Medium-
Fat Meat, 1 Fat

HAM BALLS IN BARBECUE SAUCE

PREP: 20 MINUTES **BAKE:** 45 MINUTES
OVEN: 350°F **MAKES:** 6 SERVINGS

  2 eggs, beaten
 1½ cups soft bread crumbs (2 slices)
  ½ cup finely chopped onion (1 medium)
  2 tablespoons milk
  1 teaspoon dry mustard
  ¼ teaspoon black pepper
 12 ounces ground cooked ham
 12 ounces ground pork or ground beef
  ¾ cup packed brown sugar
  ½ cup ketchup
  2 tablespoons vinegar
  1 teaspoon dry mustard

1 Preheat oven to 350°F. Lightly grease a
2-quart rectangular baking dish; set aside. In a
large bowl combine eggs, bread crumbs, onion,
milk, 1 teaspoon mustard, and the pepper. Add
ground ham and ground pork; mix well. Shape
meat mixture into 12 balls, using about ⅓ cup
mixture for each. Place ham balls in the prepared
baking dish.

2 In a small bowl combine brown sugar, ketchup,
vinegar, and 1 teaspoon mustard. Stir until the
brown sugar dissolves. Pour ketchup mixture
over meatballs.

3 Bake, uncovered, about 45 minutes or until
done (160°F).

PER 2 HAM BALLS: 429 cal., 19 g total fat (7 g sat. fat,
0 g trans fat), 144 mg chol., 1,104 mg sodium, 42 g carbo.,
1 g fiber, 23 g pro.
EXCHANGES: 1 Starch, 2 Other Carbo., 3 Medium-Fat Meat,
½ Fat

KIELBASA AND KRAUT SKILLET

START TO FINISH: 25 MINUTES
MAKES: 4 SERVINGS

  1 pound cooked kielbasa, bias-sliced into
    2-inch pieces
  1 small red onion, thinly sliced
  1 15-ounce can sauerkraut, undrained
  1 tablespoon coarse-grain brown mustard
  ¼ to ½ teaspoon caraway seeds
  ¼ teaspoon salt
  ¼ teaspoon black pepper

1 In a large skillet cook kielbasa and onion over
medium heat just until onion is tender, turning sausage to brown evenly. Stir in undrained sauerkraut,
mustard, caraway seeds, salt, and pepper. Cook,
covered, over medium heat about 10 minutes or
until heated through.

PER CUP: 392 cal., 34 g total fat (16 g sat. fat, 0 g trans fat),
50 mg chol., 1,755 mg sodium, 6 g carbo., 2 g fiber, 14 g pro.
EXCHANGES: ½ Starch, 2 High-Fat Meat, 3½ Fat

KIELBASA AND ORZO

START TO FINISH: 20 MINUTES
MAKES: 4 SERVINGS

  1 tablespoon vegetable oil
  1 pound cooked kielbasa, halved lengthwise
    and cut into 2-inch lengths
  1 cup dried orzo (rosamarina)
  1 14-ounce can beef broth
  ½ cup water
  1 teaspoon dried Italian seasoning, crushed

2½ cups coarsely chopped zucchini
(2 medium)

⅓ cup 1-inch pieces green onions and/
or finely chopped red sweet pepper
(optional)

Salt and black pepper

1 In a large skillet heat oil over medium-high heat. Add kielbasa; cook about 2 minutes or until kielbasa browns; stir in orzo. Cook and stir for 1 minute.

2 Stir in beef broth, water, and Italian seasoning. Bring to boiling; reduce heat. Simmer, covered, about 8 minutes or until orzo is tender, adding the zucchini for the last 4 minutes of cooking, and stirring occasionally. If desired, stir in green onions. Season to taste with salt and pepper.

PER 1½ CUPS: 589 cal., 38 g total fat (16 g sat. fat, 0 g trans fat), 50 mg chol., 1,373 mg sodium, 39 g carbo., 2 g fiber, 21 g pro. EXCHANGES: ½ Vegetable, 2½ Starch, 2 High-Fat Meat, 4 Fat

FAST

CORN DOGS

PREP: 25 MINUTES **COOK:** 2 TO 3 MINUTES PER BATCH
OVEN: 200°F **MAKES:** 10 TO 12 CORN DOGS

1 cup all-purpose flour

⅔ cup yellow cornmeal

2 tablespoons sugar

1½ teaspoons baking powder

½ teaspoon dry mustard

¼ teaspoon salt

1 tablespoon shortening

1 egg, lightly beaten

¾ cup milk

10 to 12 wooden skewers

10 to 12 frankfurters, smoked frankfurters, or cheese-filled frankfurters (1¼ pounds)

Vegetable oil for frying (about 8 cups)

Ketchup and/or yellow mustard (optional)

1 Preheat oven to 200°F. For batter, in a large bowl stir together flour, cornmeal, sugar, baking powder, dry mustard, and salt. Using a pastry blender, cut in shortening until mixture resembles fine crumbs. In a small bowl combine egg and milk. Add egg mixture to flour mixture; mix well.

2 Insert the wooden skewers into ends of frankfurters. Pour vegetable oil into a very large skillet to a depth of 1 inch; heat oil over medium-high heat to 365°F.

3 Coat frankfurters with batter (if batter is too thick, add 1 to 2 tablespoons additional milk). Spoon and spread batter over franks (see photo 1, below).

4 Arrange batter-coated franks, three at a time, in hot oil. Turn franks with tongs after 10 seconds of cooking to prevent batter from sliding off (see photo 2, below). Cook 2 to 3 minutes or until golden brown, turning again halfway through cooking. Drain corn dogs on paper towels; transfer to a baking sheet and keep warm in oven while frying remaining franks. Serve hot and, if desired, with ketchup and yellow mustard.

PER CORN DOG: 315 cal., 22 g total fat (6 g sat. fat, 0 g trans fat), 45 mg chol., 632 mg sodium, 21 g carbo., 1 g fiber, 8 g pro. EXCHANGES: 1½ Starch, ½ Medium-Fat Meat, 3½ Fat

MAKING CORN DOGS, STEP-BY-STEP

1. Holding a frankfurter by the skewer, spoon some of the batter over the frank. Use the back of the spoon to spread the batter and coat the frank in an even thickness of batter.
2. Using tongs to grab the skewer, turn the corn dog after 10 seconds of cooking. This prevents the batter from slipping off the frankfurter and ensures even cooking.

LAMB CUTS AND HOW TO COOK THEM

This page helps you identify lamb cuts and offers recommended ways to cook them. The photos show cuts available at markets. They correspond to the drawing, which shows where the cuts come from on the animal.

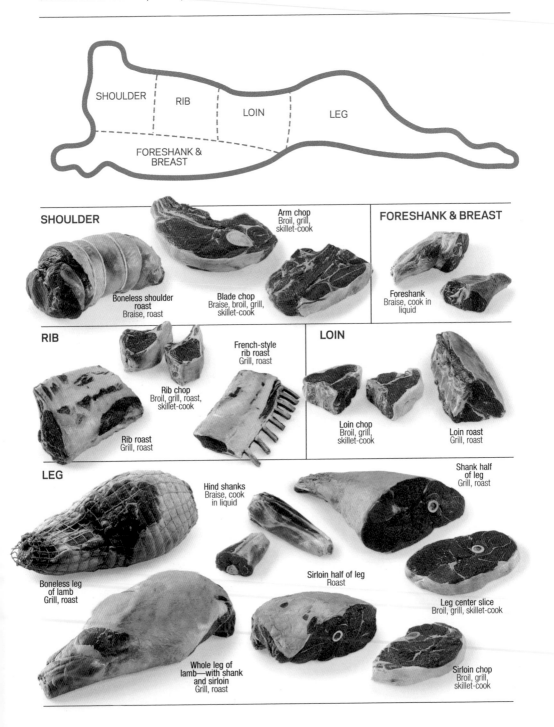

SHOULDER RIB LOIN LEG

FORESHANK & BREAST

SHOULDER

Arm chop
Broil, grill,
skillet-cook

Boneless shoulder
roast
Braise, roast

Blade chop
Braise, broil, grill,
skillet-cook

FORESHANK & BREAST

Foreshank
Braise, cook in
liquid

RIB

French-style
rib roast
Grill, roast

Rib chop
Broil, grill, roast,
skillet-cook

Rib roast
Grill, roast

LOIN

Loin chop
Broil, grill,
skillet-cook

Loin roast
Grill, roast

LEG

Hind shanks
Braise, cook
in liquid

Shank half
of leg
Grill, roast

Boneless leg
of lamb
Grill, roast

Sirloin half of leg
Roast

Leg center slice
Broil, grill, skillet-cook

Whole leg of
lamb—with shank
and sirloin
Grill, roast

Sirloin chop
Broil, grill,
skillet-cook

HERB-RUBBED LEG OF LAMB

PREP: 30 MINUTES **ROAST:** 1¾ HOURS
STAND: 15 MINUTES **OVEN:** 325°F
MAKES: 12 TO 16 SERVINGS

- 1 5- to 7-pound whole leg of lamb (with bone)
  - Lemon juice
- 2 tablespoons snipped fresh parsley
- 1 tablespoon snipped fresh mint or basil or 1 teaspoon dried mint or basil, crushed
- 1 tablespoon snipped fresh rosemary or ½ teaspoon dried rosemary, crushed
- ½ teaspoon onion salt
- ¼ teaspoon black pepper
- 1 or 2 cloves garlic, slivered
  - Mint jelly (optional)
- 1 recipe Creamy Mustard Sauce (page 539) (optional)

1 Preheat oven to 325°F. Trim fat from meat. Cut ½-inch-wide slits about 1 inch deep into roast. Drizzle lemon juice over meat's surface and into slits. Stir together parsley, mint, rosemary, onion salt, and pepper. Rub parsley mixture onto meat and into slits. Insert garlic slivers into slits.

2 Place meat, fat side up, on a rack in a shallow roasting pan. Insert an oven-going meat thermometer into center of roast (see tip, page 383). The thermometer should not touch the bone. Roast, uncovered, for 1¾ to 2¼ hours or until meat thermometer registers 135°F for medium rare. Remove from oven. Cover with foil and let stand for 15 minutes. Temperature of the meat after standing should be 145°F. (For medium, roast for 2¼ to 2¾ hours or until meat thermometer registers 150°F. Remove from oven. Cover and let stand for 15 minutes. Temperature of the meat after standing should be 160°F.) If desired, serve with mint jelly and Creamy Mustard Sauce.

PER 4½ OUNCES: 311 cal., 21 g total fat (9 g sat. fat, 0 g trans fat), 100 mg chol., 151 mg sodium, 1 g carbo., 0 g fiber, 27 g pro. EXCHANGES: 4 Medium-Fat Meat

HERB-RUBBED BONELESS LEG OF LAMB:

Substitute a 5- to 6-pound boneless leg of lamb roast for the bone-in roast. Prepare meat as directed. Insert meat thermometer and roast in the preheated 325°F oven for 2 to 2½ hours for medium-rare doneness or 2½ to 3 hours for medium doneness. Continue as directed.

PER 5 OUNCES MEAT: 397 cal., 27 g total fat (12 g sat. fat, 0 g trans fat), 129 mg chol., 175 mg sodium, 1 g carbo., 0 g fiber, 35 g pro. EXCHANGES: 5 Medium-Fat Meat

ROASTED LAMB WITH OLIVE TAPENADE

PREP: 30 MINUTES **ROAST:** 1¾ HOURS
STAND: 15 MINUTES **OVEN:** 325°F
MAKES: 8 SERVINGS

- 1 cup pitted Kalamata olives
- 1 tablespoon snipped fresh Italian parsley
- 1 tablespoon olive oil
- 1 teaspoon finely shredded lemon peel
- 2 teaspoons lemon juice
- 1 teaspoon snipped fresh rosemary
- 1 teaspoon snipped fresh thyme
- ¼ teaspoon freshly ground black pepper
- 2 cloves garlic, minced
- 1 3½- to 4-pound boneless leg of lamb, rolled and tied
- ⅓ cup dry red wine
- 1 teaspoon kosher salt
- 1 teaspoon freshly ground black pepper

1 Preheat oven to 325°F. For tapenade, in a food processor combine olives, parsley, oil, lemon peel, lemon juice, rosemary, thyme, the ¼ teaspoon pepper, and garlic. Cover and process until finely chopped, stopping to scrape down sides of the food processor as necessary; set aside.

2 Preheat oven to 325°F. Untie and unroll roast; trim fat. If necessary, place meat, boned side up, between two pieces of plastic wrap; pound meat with a meat mallet to an even thickness. Spread tapenade over cut surface of meat. Roll up; tie securely with 100%-cotton kitchen string.

3 Place roast, seam side down, on a rack in a shallow roasting pan. In a small bowl combine wine, salt, and the 1 teaspoon pepper. Roast meat, uncovered, for 1¾ to 2¼ hours or until thermometer inserted into the center of the roast (see tip, page 383) registers 135°F (medium rare), basting with red wine mixture several times until the last 10 minutes of roasting. Discard any remaining wine mixture.

4 Remove roast from oven. Cover with foil and let stand for 15 minutes before slicing. Temperature of the meat after standing should be 145°F. Remove string and slice meat.

PER 5 OUNCES MEAT + 1½ TABLESPOONS TAPENADE: 320 cal., 14 g total fat (4 g sat. fat, 0 g trans fat), 127 mg chol., 591 mg sodium, 2 g carbo., 1 g fiber, 41 g pro. EXCHANGES: 6 Lean Meat

ROAST RACK OF LAMB

PREP: 20 MINUTES **ROAST:** 45 MINUTES
STAND: 15 MINUTES **OVEN:** 325°F
MAKES: 6 SERVINGS

- 2 1- to 1½-pound lamb rib roasts (6 to 8 ribs each), with or without backbone
- 3 tablespoons Dijon-style mustard
- 3 tablespoons lemon juice
- 1 tablespoon snipped fresh rosemary or thyme
- ½ teaspoon salt
- ¾ cup soft bread crumbs (1 slice)
- 1 tablespoon butter or margarine, melted
- 1 recipe Peach-Ginger Chutney

1 Preheat oven to 325°F. Trim fat from meat. Stir together mustard, lemon juice, rosemary, and salt. Rub onto meat. In a small bowl toss together crumbs and melted butter. Sprinkle onto meat.

2 Place meat on a rack in a shallow roasting pan, arranging roasts to stand upright (see photo 1, below). Insert oven-going meat thermometer into one roast (see tip, page 383). Thermometer should not touch the bone. Roast, uncovered, for 45 to 60 minutes or until meat thermometer registers 135°F for medium rare. Cover with foil; let stand for 15 minutes. Temperature of meat after standing should be 145°F. (For medium, roast for 1 to 1½ hours or until thermometer registers 150°F. Cover; let stand for 15 minutes. Temperature of meat after standing should be 160°F.) To carve, slice between ribs (see photo 2, below). Serve with Peach-Ginger Chutney.

PEACH-GINGER CHUTNEY: In a medium saucepan stir together ½ cup packed brown sugar, ½ cup dried tart red cherries, ⅓ cup vinegar, ¼ cup chopped onion, 1 teaspoon grated fresh ginger, and ¼ teaspoon crushed red pepper. Bring to boiling; reduce heat. Simmer, uncovered, for 15 minutes, stirring occasionally. Stir in 3 cups chopped, peeled fresh peaches or frozen, thawed peach slices. Let cool.

PER 2 RIBS + ⅓ CUP CHUTNEY: 304 cal., 8 g total fat (3 g sat. fat, 0 g trans fat), 48 mg chol., 480 mg sodium, 42 g carbo., 2 g fiber, 14 g pro.
EXCHANGES: 1 Starch, 2 Other Carbo., 1½ Lean Meat, ½ Fat

SPICY APRICOT LAMB CHOPS

PREP: 20 MINUTES **BROIL:** 10 MINUTES
MAKES: 4 SERVINGS

- 8 lamb rib chops, cut 1 inch thick
- 1 tablespoon packed brown sugar
- 1 teaspoon garlic salt
- 1 teaspoon chili powder
- 1 teaspoon paprika
- ½ teaspoon dried oregano, crushed
- ¼ teaspoon ground cinnamon
- ¼ teaspoon ground allspice
- ¼ teaspoon black pepper
- ¼ cup apricot preserves

1 Preheat broiler. Trim fat from chops. In a small bowl combine brown sugar, garlic salt, chili powder, paprika, oregano, cinnamon, allspice, and black pepper. Sprinkle spice mixture on all sides of the chops; rub in with your fingers.

2 Place chops on the unheated rack of a broiler pan. Broil 4 to 5 inches from the heat for 10 to

ROASTING AND CARVING RACK OF LAMB, STEP-BY-STEP

1. Place roasts on a rack in roasting pan. Stand roasts on long ends with ribs on top. Lean roasts against each other, fitting the ribs of one roast between ribs of the second roast. **2.** To carve roasts, place one roast on a cutting board and slice between ribs. Repeat with the second roast. Allow two rib portions per serving.

15 minutes for medium (160°F), turning the chops and brushing with preserves once halfway through broiling.

PER 2 CHOPS: 311 cal., 8 g total fat (3 g sat. fat, 0 g trans fat), 119 mg chol., 345 mg sodium, 18 g carbo., 1 g fiber, 39 g pro. EXCHANGES: 1 Other Carbo., 5½ Very Lean Meat, ½ Fat

FAST

MEDITERRANEAN LAMB SKILLET

START TO FINISH: 25 MINUTES
MAKES: 4 SERVINGS

½ cup dried orzo (rosamarina)
8 lamb rib chops, cut 1 inch thick
   Salt and black pepper
2 teaspoons olive oil
3 cloves garlic, minced
1 14.5-ounce can diced tomatoes with basil, garlic, and oregano, undrained
1 tablespoon balsamic vinegar
2 teaspoons snipped fresh rosemary
⅓ cup halved, pitted Kalamata olives
2 tablespoons pine nuts, toasted (see tip, page 20)
   Fresh rosemary sprigs (optional)

1 Cook orzo according to package directions; drain and keep warm. Meanwhile, trim fat from chops. Sprinkle chops with salt and pepper. In a large skillet heat olive oil over medium heat. Add chops; cook in hot oil for 9 to 11 minutes for medium (160°F), turning once halfway through cooking. Remove chops from skillet; keep warm.

2 Stir garlic into drippings in skillet. Cook and stir for 1 minute. Stir in undrained tomatoes, vinegar, and snipped rosemary. Bring to boiling; reduce heat. Simmer, uncovered, for 5 minutes. Stir in orzo and olives. Spoon orzo mixture onto four dinner plates; arrange two chops on each plate. Sprinkle with pine nuts and, if desired, top with rosemary sprigs.

PER 2 CHOPS + ¾ CUP ORZO MIXTURE: 678 cal., 51 g total fat (20 g sat. fat, 0 g trans fat), 105 mg chol., 886 mg sodium, 28 g carbo., 2 g fiber, 27 g pro. EXCHANGES: ½ Vegetable, 1½ Starch, 3 Medium-Fat Meat, 7 Fat

A SPECIAL CUT
THINK AHEAD IF YOU'RE MAKING A DISH FEATURING LAMB SHANKS. YOU MIGHT NEED TO SPECIAL-ORDER THEM.

BEST EVER • LOW FAT

LAMB SHANKS WITH BEANS

PREP: 30 MINUTES STAND: 60 MINUTES
COOK: 2¼ HOURS + 10 MINUTES MAKES: 6 SERVINGS

1¼ cups dried navy beans
4 cups water
1 tablespoon vegetable oil
4 meaty lamb shanks (about 4 pounds), cut into 3- to 4-inch pieces, or meaty veal shank cross cuts (about 3 pounds)
1 medium onion, sliced and separated into rings
2 cloves garlic, minced
2 cups chicken broth
1 teaspoon dried thyme, crushed
½ teaspoon salt
¼ teaspoon black pepper
1 14.5-ounce can diced tomatoes, undrained

1 Rinse beans. In a 4- to 6-quart Dutch oven combine the beans and the water. Bring to boiling; reduce heat. Simmer, uncovered, for 2 minutes. Remove from heat. Do not drain. Cover and let stand for 60 minutes. (Or add water to cover beans. Cover and let stand overnight.)

2 Drain and rinse beans. In the same pan heat the oil over medium heat. Add lamb shanks and brown on all sides; remove from pan. Add onion and garlic to the same pan; cook until tender. Stir in beans, chicken broth, thyme, salt, and pepper. Add shanks. Bring to boiling; reduce heat. Simmer, covered, for 2 to 2½ hours or until meat and beans are tender. (If necessary, add more chicken broth to keep mixture moist.)

3 Remove meat from pan; cool slightly. When cool enough to handle, cut meat off bones and coarsely chop. Discard fat and bones. Skim fat from the top of the bean mixture. Stir in the meat and undrained tomatoes. Bring to boiling; reduce heat. Simmer, covered, for 10 to 15 minutes or until heated through and flavors are blended.

PER 1½ CUPS MEAT-BEAN MIXTURE: 430 cal., 10 g total fat (2 g sat. fat, 0 g trans fat), 132 mg chol., 785 mg sodium, 31 g carbo., 12 g fiber, 53 g pro. EXCHANGES: ½ Vegetable, 2 Starch, 6½ Lean Meat, ½ Fat

LATINO BISON BURGERS
WITH TOMATILLO SALSA

65 minutes more or until meat thermometer registers 135°F (medium rare). Cover with foil and let stand for 15 minutes. Temperature of the meat after standing should be 145°F. Thinly slice meat across the grain to serve.

PER 4 OUNCES: 238 cal., 8 g total fat (2 g sat. fat, 0 g trans fat), 121 mg chol., 573 mg sodium, 2 g carbo., 1 g fiber, 37 g pro. EXCHANGES: 5 Lean Meat

LATINO BISON BURGERS WITH TOMATILLO SALSA

PREP: 40 MINUTES **BROIL:** 12 MINUTES
MAKES: 4 BURGERS

- 1½ pounds ground bison (buffalo)
- 2 teaspoons chili powder
- 1 teaspoon ground cumin
- ½ teaspoon onion powder
- ½ teaspoon garlic powder
- ½ teaspoon salt
- 6 medium tomatillos, husked, rinsed, and chopped (12 ounces)
- 1 large yellow sweet pepper, chopped
- 2 tablespoons snipped fresh cilantro
- 2 tablespoons lime juice
- 1 tablespoon honey
- 1 medium fresh jalapeño chile pepper, seeded and finely chopped (see tip, page 24)
- 6 cloves garlic, minced
- 4 1-ounce slices Monterey Jack cheese
  Corn or flour tortillas, warmed (optional)
- 1 large tomato, sliced
- 1 cup shredded fresh spinach

1 In a bowl combine bison, chili powder, cumin, onion powder, garlic powder, and salt; mix well. Shape into four ¾-inch-thick oval-shape patties.

2 For salsa, in another large bowl combine tomatillos, sweet pepper, cilantro, lime juice, honey, jalapeño pepper, and garlic; set aside.

3 Preheat broiler. Place patties on the unheated rack of a broiler pan. Broil 3 to 4 inches from the heat for 12 to 14 minutes or until done (160°F), turning once halfway through broiling. Add cheese to burgers the last 1 minute of broiling.

4 If desired, serve on tortillas. Top with tomatillo salsa, tomato slices, and spinach. Cover and chill any remaining salsa for up to 3 days.

PER BURGER: 559 cal., 37 g total fat (17 g sat. fat, 0 g trans fat), 144 mg chol., 581 mg sodium, 16 g carbo., 3 g fiber, 41 g pro. EXCHANGES: 1 Vegetable, ½ Other Carbo., 5½ Medium-Fat Meat, 1 Fat

LOW FAT

HERB-RUBBED BISON SIRLOIN TIP ROAST

PREP: 20 MINUTES **ROAST:** 75 MINUTES
STAND: 15 MINUTES **OVEN:** 375°F/300°F
MAKES: 8 SERVINGS

- 1 tablespoon paprika
- 2 teaspoons kosher salt or sea salt, or 1 teaspoon salt
- 1 teaspoon garlic powder
- ½ teaspoon dried oregano, crushed
- ½ teaspoon dried thyme, crushed
- ½ teaspoon black pepper
- ½ teaspoon onion powder
- ½ teaspoon cayenne pepper
- 2 tablespoons olive oil
- 1 3- to 3½-pound boneless bison (buffalo) sirloin tip roast

1 Preheat oven to 375°F. In a small bowl combine paprika, salt, garlic powder, oregano, thyme, black pepper, onion powder, and cayenne pepper. Stir in oil until well combined; set aside. Trim fat from roast. Spread oil mixture over meat.

2 Place meat on a rack in a shallow roasting pan. Insert an oven-going meat thermometer into center of roast (see tip, page 383).

3 Roast, uncovered, for 15 minutes. Reduce oven temperature to 300°F. Roast for 60 to

BROILING MEAT

Preheat broiler. Place meat on the unheated rack of a broiler pan. For cuts less than 1½ inches thick, broil 3 to 4 inches from the heat. For 1½-inch-thick cuts, broil 4 to 5 inches from the heat. Broil for the time listed or until done, turning meat over after half of the broiling time. For steaks, cover and let stand for 5 minutes.

Cut	Thickness/Weight	Approximate Time*	Doneness
BEEF			
Boneless steak (chuck eye, shoulder center [ranch], ribeye, shoulder top blade [flat-iron], tenderloin, top loin)	1 inch 1 inch 1½ inches 1½ inches	12 to 14 minutes 15 to 18 minutes 18 to 21 minutes 22 to 27 minutes	145°F medium rare 160°F medium 145°F medium rare 160°F medium
Boneless top sirloin steak	1 inch 1 inch 1½ inches 1½ inches	15 to 17 minutes 20 to 22 minutes 25 to 27 minutes 30 to 32 minutes	145°F medium rare 160°F medium 145°F medium rare 160°F medium
Boneless tri-tip steak (bottom sirloin)	¾ inch ¾ inch 1 inch 1 inch	6 to 7 minutes 8 to 9 minutes 9 to 10 minutes 11 to 12 minutes	145°F medium rare 160°F medium 145°F medium rare 160°F medium
Flank steak	1¼ to 1¾ pounds	17 to 21 minutes	160°F medium
Steak with bone (porterhouse, rib, T-bone)	1 inch 1 inch 1½ inches 1½ inches	12 to 15 minutes 15 to 20 minutes 20 to 25 minutes 25 to 30 minutes	145°F medium rare 160°F medium 145°F medium rare 160°F medium
GROUND MEAT			
Patties (beef, lamb, pork, or veal)	½ inch ¾ inch	10 to 12 minutes 12 to 14 minutes	160°F medium 160°F medium
LAMB			
Chop (loin or rib)	1 inch	10 to 15 minutes	160°F medium
Chop (sirloin)	1 inch	12 to 15 minutes	160°F medium
PORK			
Chop (boneless top loin)	¾ to 1 inch 1¼ to 1½ inches	9 to 11 minutes 15 to 18 minutes	160°F medium 160°F medium
Chop with bone (loin or rib)	¾ to 1 inch 1¼ to 1½ inches	9 to 12 minutes 16 to 20 minutes	160°F medium 160°F medium
Chop with bone (sirloin)	¾ to 1 inch	10 to 13 minutes	160°F medium
Ham steak, cooked	1 inch	12 to 15 minutes	140°F heated through
SAUSAGES			
Frankfurters and sausage links, cooked		3 to 7 minutes	140°F heated through
VEAL			
Chop (loin or rib)	¾ to 1 inch 1½ inches	14 to 16 minutes 21 to 25 minutes	160°F medium 160°F medium

*All cooking times are based on meat removed directly from refrigerator.

ROASTING MEAT

Place meat, fat side up, on a rack in a shallow roasting pan. (Roasts with a bone do not need a rack.) Insert a meat thermometer (see tip, page 383). Do not add water or liquid, and do not cover. Roast in a 325°F oven (unless chart says otherwise) for the time listed and until the thermometer registers the temperature under Final Roasting Temperature. Remove the meat from the oven; cover with foil and let it stand 15 minutes before carving. The meat's temperature will rise 10°F during the time it stands.

Cut	Weight	Approximate Roasting Time*	Final Roasting Temperature (when to remove from oven)
BEEF			
Boneless tri-tip roast (bottom sirloin) Roast at 425°F.	1½ to 2 pounds	30 to 35 minutes 40 to 45 minutes	135°F (145°F medium rare after standing) 150°F (160°F medium after standing)
Eye round roast Roasting past medium rare is not recommended.	2 to 3 pounds	1½ to 1¾ hours	135°F (145°F medium rare after standing)
Ribeye roast Roast at 350°F.	3 to 4 pounds 4 to 6 pounds 6 to 8 pounds	1½ to 1¾ hours 1¾ to 2 hours 1¾ to 2 hours 2 to 2½ hours 2 to 2¼ hours 2½ to 2¾ hours	135°F (145°F medium rare after standing) 150°F (160°F medium after standing) 135°F (145°F medium rare after standing) 150°F (160°F medium after standing) 135°F (145°F medium rare after standing) 150°F (160°F medium after standing)
Rib roast (chine bone removed) Roast at 350°F.	4 to 6 pounds 6 to 8 pounds 8 to 10 pounds**	1¾ to 2¼ hours 2¼ to 2¾ hours 2¼ to 2½ hours 2¾ to 3 hours 2½ to 3 hours 3 to 3½ hours	135°F (145°F medium rare after standing) 150°F (160°F medium after standing) 135°F (145°F medium rare after standing) 150°F (160°F medium after standing) 135°F (145°F medium rare after standing) 150°F (160°F medium after standing)
Round tip roast	3 to 4 pounds 4 to 6 pounds 6 to 8 pounds	1¾ to 2 hours 2¼ to 2½ hours 2 to 2½ hours 2½ to 3 hours 2½ to 3 hours 3 to 3½ hours	135°F (145°F medium rare after standing) 150°F (160°F medium after standing) 135°F (145°F medium rare after standing) 150°F (160°F medium after standing) 135°F (145°F medium rare after standing) 150°F (160°F medium after standing)
Tenderloin roast Roast at 425°F	2 to 3 pounds 4 to 5 pounds	35 to 40 minutes 45 to 50 minutes 50 to 60 minutes 60 to 70 minutes	135°F (145°F medium rare after standing) 150°F (160°F medium after standing) 135°F (145°F medium rare after standing) 150°F (160°F medium after standing)
Top round roast Roasting past medium rare is not recommended.	4 to 6 pounds 6 to 8 pounds	1¾ to 2½ hours 2½ to 3 hours	135°F (145°F medium rare after standing) 135°F (145°F medium rare after standing)
LAMB			
Boneless leg of lamb	4 to 5 pounds 5 to 6 pounds	1¾ to 2¼ hours 2 to 2½ hours 2 to 2½ hours 2½ to 3 hours	135°F (145°F medium rare after standing) 150°F (160°F medium after standing) 135°F (145°F medium rare after standing) 150°F (160°F medium after standing)
Boneless shoulder roast	3 to 4 pounds 4 to 5 pounds	1½ to 2 hours 1¾ to 2¼ hours 2 to 2½ hours 2¼ to 3 hours	135°F (145°F medium rare after standing) 150°F (160°F medium after standing) 135°F (145°F medium rare after standing) 150°F (160°F medium after standing)

*All cooking times are based on meat removed directly from refrigerator.
**Roasts weighing more than 8 pounds should be loosely covered with foil halfway through roasting.

Cut	Weight	Approximate Roasting Time*	Final Roasting Temperature (when to remove from oven)
LAMB *(continued)*			
Boneless sirloin roast	1½ to 2 pounds	1 to 1¼ hours 1¼ to 1½ hours	135°F (145°F medium rare after standing) 150°F (160°F medium after standing)
Leg of lamb (with bone)	5 to 7 pounds 7 to 8 pounds	1¾ to 2¼ hours 2¼ to 2¾ hours 2¼ to 2¾ hours 2½ to 3 hours	135°F (145°F medium rare after standing) 150°F (160°F medium after standing) 135°F (145°F medium rare after standing) 150°F (160°F medium after standing)
Leg of lamb, shank half (with bone)	3 to 4 pounds	1¾ to 2¼ hours 2 to 2½ hours	135°F (145°F medium rare after standing) 150°F (160°F medium after standing)
Leg of lamb, sirloin half (with bone)	3 to 4 pounds	1½ to 2 hours 1¾ to 2¼ hours	135°F (145°F medium rare after standing) 150°F (160°F medium after standing)
PORK			
Boneless sirloin roast	1½ to 2 pounds	¾ to 1¼ hours	150°F (160°F medium after standing)
Boneless top loin roast (double loin)	3 to 4 pounds 4 to 5 pounds	1½ to 2¼ hours 2 to 2½ hours	150°F (160°F medium after standing) 150°F (160°F medium after standing)
Boneless top loin roast (single loin)	2 to 3 pounds	1¼ to 1¾ hours	150°F (160°F medium after standing)
Loin center rib roast (backbone loosened)	3 to 4 pounds 4 to 6 pounds	1¼ to 1¾ hours 1¾ to 2½ hours	150°F (160°F medium after standing) 150°F (160°F medium after standing)
Loin back ribs or spareribs		1½ to 1¾ hours	Tender
Country-style ribs Roast at 350°F		1½ to 2 hours	Tender
Crown roast	6 to 8 pounds	2½ to 3¼ hours	150°F (160°F medium after standing)
Tenderloin Roast at 425°F	¾ to 1 pound	25 to 35 minutes	155°F (160°F medium after standing)
Ham, cooked (boneless)	1½ to 3 pounds 3 to 5 pounds 6 to 8 pounds 8 to 10 pounds**	¾ to 1¼ hours 1 to 1¾ hours 1¾ to 2½ hours 2¼ to 2¾ hours	140°F 140°F 140°F 140°F
Ham, cooked (with bone) (half or whole)	6 to 8 pounds 14 to 16 pounds**	1½ to 2¼ hours 2¾ to 3¾ hours	140°F 140°F
Ham, cook before eating (with bone)	3 to 5 pounds 7 to 8 pounds 14 to 16 pounds**	1¾ to 3 hours 2½ to 3¼ hours 4 to 5¼ hours	150°F (160°F medium after standing) 150°F (160°F medium after standing) 150°F (160°F medium after standing)
Smoked shoulder picnic, cooked (with bone)	4 to 6 pounds	1¼ to 2 hours	140°F
VEAL			
Loin roast (with bone)	3 to 4 pounds	1¾ to 2¼ hours	150°F (160°F medium after standing)
Rib roast (chine bone removed)	4 to 5 pounds	1½ to 2¼ hours	150°F (160°F medium after standing)

*All cooking times are based on meat removed directly from refrigerator.
**Roasts weighing more than 8 pounds should be loosely covered with foil halfway through roasting.

SKILLET-COOKING MEAT

Select a heavy skillet that is the correct size for the amount of meat you are cooking. (If the skillet is too large, the pan juices can burn.) Lightly coat the skillet with nonstick cooking spray. (Or use a heavy nonstick skillet.) Preheat skillet over medium-high heat until very hot. Add meat. Do not add any liquid and do not cover the skillet. Reduce heat to medium and cook for the time listed or until done, turning meat occasionally. If meat browns too quickly, reduce heat to medium-low.

Cut	Thickness	Approximate Cooking Time*	Doneness
BEEF			
Boneless chuck eye steak	¾ inch 1 inch	9 to 11 minutes 12 to 15 minutes	145°F med. rare to 160°F medium 145°F med. rare to 160°F medium
Boneless top sirloin steak	¾ inch 1 inch	10 to 13 minutes 15 to 20 minutes	145°F med. rare to 160°F medium 145°F med. rare to 160°F medium
Boneless tri-tip steak (bottom sirloin)	¾ inch 1 inch	6 to 9 minutes 9 to 12 minutes	145°F med. rare to 160°F medium 145°F med. rare to 160°F medium
Cubed steak	½ inch	5 to 8 minutes	160°F medium
Porterhouse or T-bone steak	¾ inch 1 inch	11 to 13 minutes 14 to 17 minutes	145°F med. rare to 160°F medium 145°F med. rare to 160°F medium
Ribeye steak	¾ inch 1 inch	8 to 10 minutes 12 to 15 minutes	145°F med. rare to 160°F medium 145°F med. rare to 160°F medium
Shoulder center steak (ranch steak)	¾ inch 1 inch	9 to 12 minutes (turn twice) 13 to 16 minutes (turn twice)	145°F med. rare to 160°F medium 145°F med. rare to 160°F medium
Shoulder top blade steak (flat-iron)	6 to 8 ounces	13 to 15 minutes (turn twice)	145°F med. rare to 160°F medium
Tenderloin steak	¾ inch 1 inch	7 to 9 minutes 10 to 13 minutes	145°F med. rare to 160°F medium 145°F med. rare to 160°F medium
Top loin steak	¾ inch 1 inch	10 to 12 minutes 12 to 15 minutes	145°F med. rare to 160°F medium 145°F med. rare to 160°F medium
GROUND MEAT			
Patties (beef, lamb, pork, or veal)	½ inch ¾ inch	9 to 12 minutes 12 to 15 minutes	160°F medium 160°F medium
LAMB			
Chop (loin or rib)	1 inch	9 to 11 minutes	160°F medium
PORK			
Canadian-style bacon	¼ inch	3 to 4 minutes	heated through
Chop (loin or rib) (with bone or boneless)	¾ to 1 inch	8 to 12 minutes	160°F medium
Cutlet	¼ inch	3 to 4 minutes	no longer pink
Ham slice, cooked	½ inch	9 to 11 minutes	140°F heated through
VEAL			
Chop (loin or rib)	¾ to 1 inch	10 to 14 minutes	160°F medium
Cutlet	⅛ inch ¼ inch	2 to 3 minutes 4 to 6 minutes	no longer pink no longer pink

*All cooking times are based on meat removed directly from refrigerator.

PASTA

PASTA WITH BOLOGNESE SAUCE, PAGE 426

PASTA

FEW FOODS ARE AS FAST, EASY, AND VERSATILE AS PASTA. THESE HINTS WILL HELP YOU MAKE IT INTO MEALS YOUR FAMILY WILL LOVE.

FRESH OR DRIED?

Most pasta comes in fresh and dried forms, and each has its advantages. For example, sometimes you'll appreciate the light egg flavor and tender, delicate texture of fresh homemade pasta; other times you may prefer the simpler flavor (and convenience) of dried. Here's an overview of each.

FRESH PASTA: Make your own from scratch (see recipe, page 422) or purchase fresh ready-made pasta, which can be found in the refrigerated section of grocery stores.

■ Choose fresh pasta with consistent color throughout that looks dry without appearing brittle and crumbly.

■ Plan on 3 ounces for each main-dish serving and 1½ to 2 ounces for each side-dish serving. To substitute fresh pasta for dried in a recipe, use 6 to 8 ounces fresh for each 4 ounces dried. Follow package directions for cooking times.

■ Store unopened packages of fresh pasta in the refrigerator for up to 2 weeks or in the freezer for up to a month.

DRIED PASTA: Found in boxes or bags at the super-market, this is the most readily available form.

■ Plan on 2 ounces cooked pasta for each main-dish serving and 1 to 1½ ounces for each side-dish serving. In most cases, 8 ounces uncooked dried pasta will equal 4 main-dish servings (4 cups). An exception is uncooked egg noodles: 8 ounces dried egg noodles uncooked yields 2½ cups cooked.

■ Store in a cool, dry place for up to 1 year.

MATCHING SAUCES AND PASTAS

Pasta comes in scores of shapes, lengths, and thicknesses. When it comes to matching pasta with sauce, it's hard to go wrong. However, these are some particularly good pairings.

■ Heavy meat and tomato sauces are well suited to long, thick noodles, such as fettuccine.

■ Light, thin sauces work well with thin, delicate pastas, such as angel hair and thin spaghetti.

■ Sauces that are chunky, with lots of pieces (such as Hamburger Pasta Skillet, page 426), go well with short, thick pastas with holes or ridges, such as penne, rigatoni, and campanelle.

COOKING DRIED PASTA

To cook dried pasta, follow package directions, as cooking times vary by brand. Whichever brand you buy, keep the following concepts in mind.

USE PLENTY OF WATER: In general, count on about 3 quarts of water for 4 to 8 ounces of pasta.

NO OIL NEEDED: If you use plenty of water and stir the pasta occasionally during cooking, you won't need to add oil to the water to prevent the pasta from sticking together. Adding oil prevents the sauce from adhering to the pasta.

GO FOR AL DENTE: To bring out pasta's full, nutty flavor, cook it just until it has a firm, chewy texture known as al dente (Italian for "to the tooth"). Test near the end of cooking time by giving it a taste. When done, drain the cooked pasta in a colander and shake well to remove excess water.

TO RINSE OR NOT TO RINSE: Rinsing removes a light coating of starch that helps the sauce and seasonings cling; therefore, do not rinse pasta unless it will be baked or served cool in a salad.

SERVE ASAP: Pasta continues to cook after draining, so try to serve immediately. Or follow the instructions on page 426 to keep pasta warm.

PASTA

Capellini

Bow ties (farfalle)

Spaghetti

Campanelle

Small bow ties
(farfallini)

Gnocchi

Penne

Mostaccioli

Manicotti

Orzo (rosamarina)

Linguine

Couscous

Rotini

Small shell
macaroni

Fusilli

Fine egg noodles

Medium shell
macaroni

Jumbo shell macaroni

Medium egg noodles

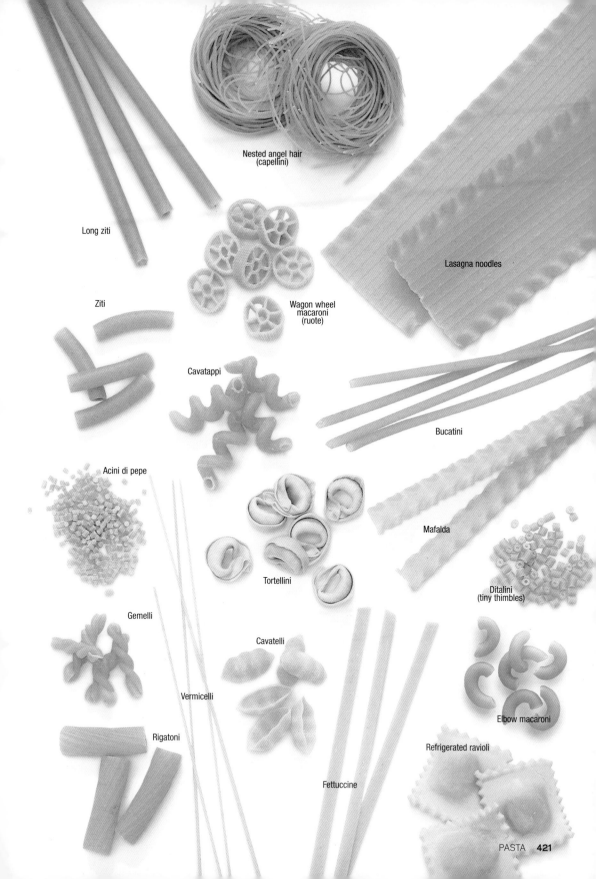

Nested angel hair
(capellini)

Long ziti

Lasagna noodles

Ziti

Wagon wheel
macaroni
(ruote)

Cavatappi

Bucatini

Acini di pepe

Mafalda

Tortellini

Ditalini
(tiny thimbles)

Gemelli

Cavatelli

Vermicelli

Elbow macaroni

Rigatoni

Refrigerated ravioli

Fettuccine

PASTA   **421**

HOMEMADE PASTA

PREP: 60 MINUTES **COOK:** SEE CHART, PAGE 423
MAKES: 5 SERVINGS

- 2⅓ cups all-purpose flour
- ½ teaspoon salt
- 2 eggs, lightly beaten
- ⅓ cup water
- 1 teaspoon vegetable or olive oil
  All-purpose flour

1 In a large bowl stir together 2 cups of the flour and the salt. Make a well in the center of the flour mixture. In a small bowl combine eggs, water, and oil. Add egg mixture to flour mixture; stir to combine.

2 Sprinkle a clean kneading surface with remaining ⅓ cup flour. Turn dough out onto floured surface. Knead until smooth and elastic (8 to 10 minutes total). Cover and let dough rest for 10 minutes. Divide the dough into four equal portions.

3 On a lightly floured surface roll each portion into a 12-inch square about 1/16 inch thick. Lightly dust both sides of squares with additional flour. Let stand, uncovered, about 20 minutes; cut as desired. If using a pasta machine, pass each portion through machine per manufacturer's directions (see photo 1, below) until dough is 1/16 inch thick, dusting dough with flour as needed. Let stand; cut as desired.

4 To serve pasta immediately, cook according to the chart, page 423; drain.

5 To store cut pasta, spread it on a wire cooling rack (see photo 2, below) or hang it from a pasta-drying rack or clothes hanger. Let dry up to 2 hours. Place in airtight container and chill for up to 3 days.

Or dry pasta for at least 1 hour; place in freezer bag or freezer container and freeze up to 8 months.

FOOD PROCESSOR DIRECTIONS: Place steel blade in food processor. Add all of the flour, salt, and eggs to food processor. Cover; process until mixture forms fine crumbs, about the consistency of cornmeal. With processor running, slowly pour the water and oil through the feed tube. Continue processing just until dough forms a ball. Transfer dough to a lightly floured surface. Cover; let dough rest for 10 minutes. Divide dough into four equal portions. Continue as directed in Step 3.

BOW TIE PASTA: Cut rolled dough to 2×1-inch rectangles. Pinch centers to form bow tie shapes.

MAKE-AHEAD TIP: Prepare pasta dough through Step 2; wrap in plastic wrap. Transfer dough to an airtight container; freeze for up to 3 months. Thaw completely in refrigerator; continue with Step 3.

HERBED PASTA: Prepare as directed, except stir 2 tablespoons snipped fresh basil, thyme, or sage or 1 teaspoon dried basil, thyme, or sage, crushed, into the flour mixture before adding liquid.

PER 1 CUP COOKED PASTA: 255 cal., 3 g total fat (1 g sat. fat, 0 g trans fat), 85 mg chol., 262 mg sodium, 46 g carbo., 2 g fiber, 8 g pro. EXCHANGES: 3 Starch

SPINACH PASTA: Prepare as directed, except increase flour to 2¾ cups and reduce water to ¼ cup. Stir ¼ cup cooked spinach, well drained and finely chopped, into water mixture before adding to flour mixture.

PER 1 CUP COOKED SPINACH PASTA VARIATION: 294 cal., 4 g total fat (1 g sat. fat, 0 g trans fat), 85 mg chol., 269 mg sodium, 54 g carbo., 2 g fiber, 10 g pro. EXCHANGES: 3½ Starch

---

HOMEMADE PASTA, STEP-BY-STEP

1. Use a pasta machine according to the manufacturer's directions to knead the pasta dough and form a thinly rolled pasta sheet. Attach the noodle-cutting attachment to the machine and feed the sheet through, cutting the noodles. **2.** Lift and separate the freshly cut noodles and space them out on a cooling rack to keep them from sticking together while drying.

HOMEMADE EGG NOODLES: Prepare Homemade Pasta as directed, except reduce flour to 2 to 2¼ cups, using 1¾ cups in Step 1 and the remaining flour in Step 2; substitute 2 egg yolks and 1 whole egg for the 2 eggs. To shape noodles, roll each dough portion into a 12×9-inch rectangle or pass through pasta machine until ¹⁄₁₆ inch thick. Dust both sides of dough portions with additional flour. After standing, loosely roll dough into a spiral; cut crosswise into ¼-inch-wide strips. Unroll strips to separate; cut strips into 2- to 3-inch lengths. Cook immediately according to chart, below; drain. Or continue as in Step 5 to store.

PER 1 CUP COOKED PASTA: 231 cal., 4 g total fat (1 g sat. fat, 0 g trans fat), 126 mg chol., 251 mg sodium, 40 g carbo., 1 g fiber, 8 g pro. EXCHANGES: 2½ Starch, ½ Fat

MEAT-FILLED RAVIOLI: Prepare Meat Filling; set aside. Prepare Homemade Pasta dough. To shape ravioli, cut rolled dough into 2-inch-wide strips. Leaving a ½-inch margin around the edges, place about 1 teaspoon filling at 1-inch intervals on one strip of dough. Using a pastry brush or your finger, moisten the dough with water around the mounds of filling. Lay a second strip of dough over the first. Using the side of your hand, press the pasta around each mound of filling so the two moistened strips of dough stick together. With a fluted pastry wheel or sharp knife, cut the pasta between the mounds of filling to separate into uniform-size individual ravioli.

MEAT FILLING: In a medium skillet cook 4 ounces each ground beef and bulk Italian sausage over medium heat until no longer pink; drain fat. In a small bowl stir together ½ cup ricotta cheese, ½ cup shredded mozzarella cheese, ¼ cup grated Parmesan cheese, and ½ teaspoon dried Italian seasoning. Stir in meat mixture.

PER 1 CUP COOKED PASTA: 483 cal., 22 g total fat (9 g sat. fat, 0 g trans fat), 140 mg chol., 601 mg sodium, 47 g carbo., 2 g fiber, 23 g pro. EXCHANGES: 3 Starch, 2 Medium-Fat Meat, 2 Fat

CHEESE-FILLED TORTELLINI: Prepare Cheese Filling; set aside. Prepare Homemade Pasta dough. To shape tortellini, cut rolled dough into circles with a 1½-inch round cutter, cutting out as many circles from rolled dough as possible. Gather scraps and reroll with remaining dough. Fill by placing ¼ teaspoon Cheese Filling in the center of each circle. To seal, fold the circle in half to make a half-moon. Press edges of dough together with fingers, moistening with water if necessary. Place index finger against the fold; bend tortellini around your finger, bringing the outer two corners

together. Press one corner over the other, moistening with water if necessary. Pinch the ends firmly together to secure. Let dry a few minutes before cooking.

CHEESE FILLING: Toast ½ cup walnuts and/or pine nuts (see tip, page 20). Place toasted nuts in a blender or food processor; cover and blend or process until finely chopped. With machine running, slowly add 1 tablespoon olive oil, blending mixture until smooth. In a small bowl stir together the nut mixture, ½ cup ricotta cheese, 1 tablespoon grated Parmesan cheese, and ½ teaspoon dried basil, crushed.

PER 1 CUP COOKED PASTA: 402 cal., 17 g total fat (0 g sat. fat, 0 g trans fat), 98 mg chol., 299 mg sodium, 48 g carbo., 2 g fiber, 14 g pro. EXCHANGES: 3 Starch, 1 High-Fat Meat, 1½ Fat

COOKING HOMEMADE PASTA
COOKING FRESH PASTA IS AS EASY AS BOILING WATER. HERE'S HOW TO DO IT.

Fill a large pot with water (allow 3 quarts of water for 4 to 8 ounces pasta). Bring water to boiling. If desired, add 1 teaspoon salt. Add pasta a little at a time so the water does not stop boiling. This also helps keep the pasta from sticking together. Reduce heat slightly and boil, uncovered, stirring occasionally, for the time specified below or until the pasta is al dente. (For tip on testing pasta for doneness, see page 419.) Test often for doneness near the end of the cooking time. Drain in a colander, giving it a good shake to remove all the water.

Homemade Pasta	Cooking Time
Bow ties	2 to 3 minutes
Egg noodles	1½ to 2 minutes
Fettuccine	1½ to 2 minutes
Lasagna	2 to 3 minutes
Linguine	1½ to 2 minutes
Ravioli	7 to 9 minutes
Tortellini	7 to 9 minutes

Allow 1 to 2 minutes more for dried or frozen pasta.

PASTA WITH MARINARA SAUCE

PREP: 20 MINUTES **COOK:** 55 MINUTES
MAKES: 8 TO 10 SERVINGS

- 2 tablespoons olive oil
- 1 cup finely chopped onion (1 large)
- ½ cup finely chopped carrot (1 medium)
- ½ cup finely chopped celery (1 stalk)
- 3 cloves garlic, minced
- 2 15-ounce cans tomato sauce
- 1 tablespoon tomato paste
- 1 cup water
- 1 cup dry red wine or cranberry juice
- 3 tablespoons snipped fresh Italian parsley
- 2 tablespoons snipped fresh basil
- 1 tablespoon dried Italian seasoning
- 2 to 3 teaspoons sugar
- ¼ teaspoon crushed red pepper (optional)
- 3 bay leaves
- ½ teaspoon salt
- ¼ teaspoon black pepper
- 16 ounces packaged dried pasta, such as spaghetti or linguine
  Freshly grated Parmesan cheese

1 In a large saucepan heat oil over medium heat. Add onion, carrot, celery, and garlic. Cook, uncovered, for 10 minutes or until vegetables are very tender but not brown, stirring occasionally.

2 Stir in tomato sauce, tomato paste, water, wine, parsley, basil, Italian seasoning, sugar, crushed red pepper (if desired), bay leaves, salt, and black pepper.

3 Bring sauce to boiling; reduce heat. Simmer sauce, uncovered, for 45 minutes, stirring occasionally, or until desired consistency.

4 In a large pot cook pasta according to package directions; drain. Remove and discard bay leaves from sauce. Serve sauce over pasta. Sprinkle each serving with Parmesan cheese.

MAKE-AHEAD DIRECTIONS: Place sauce in freezer containers. Seal and freeze for up to 3 months. To use, thaw sauce overnight in the refrigerator. Transfer to saucepan; heat through.

PER 1 CUP COOKED PASTA + ⅔ CUP SAUCE: 234 cal., 6 g total fat (2 g sat. fat, 0 g trans fat), 4 mg chol., 786 mg sodium, 54 g carbo., 4 g fiber, 11 g pro.
EXCHANGES: 1 Vegetable, 3 Starch, ½ Fat

PASTA WITH MARINARA MEAT SAUCE: Prepare as directed, except omit oil. In a large saucepan cook 12 ounces ground beef or bulk pork sausage with the onion, carrot, celery, and garlic until meat is brown; drain. Continue as directed in Step 2.

PER 1 CUP COOKED PASTA + ¾ CUP SAUCE: 395 cal., 9 g total fat (4 g sat. fat, 0 g trans fat), 33 mg chol., 814 mg sodium, 54 g carbo., 4 g fiber, 19 g pro.
EXCHANGES: 3 Starch, 1 Vegetable, 1 Medium-Fat Meat, ½ Fat

PASTA WITH MARINARA MEATBALL SAUCE:
Prepare sauce as directed. Meanwhile, in a large bowl combine 2 eggs, lightly beaten; ⅓ cup soft bread crumbs; ¼ cup finely shredded Parmesan cheese; ¼ cup snipped fresh parsley; ¼ cup finely chopped onion; 1 teaspoon salt; ½ teaspoon crushed red pepper; and 1 clove garlic, minced. Add 1 pound lean ground beef and 8 ounces ground pork; mix well. Shape mixture into 18 meatballs, about 2 tablespoons per meatball. In a very large skillet heat 1 tablespoon olive oil over medium heat. Add meatballs; cook about 10 minutes or until brown and cooked through (160°F), turning occasionally. Drain off fat. Stir meatballs into sauce. Serve as directed in Step 4.

PER 1 CUP COOKED PASTA + ⅔ CUP SAUCE + 2 MEATBALLS : 581 cal., 24 g total fat (8 g sat. fat, 1 g trans fat), 118 mg chol., 1,204 mg sodium, 56 g carbo., 4 g fiber, 29 g pro.
EXCHANGES: 3½ Starch, 1 Vegetable, 2½ Lean Meat, 2½ Fat

FREEZER-READY MEATBALLS

MAKE A DOUBLE BATCH OF MEATBALLS, AS DIRECTED ABOVE, AND FREEZE SOME FOR LATER MEALS.

■ To freeze, place cooked meatballs in a single layer on a baking sheet. Freeze them overnight and repack in resealable freezer bags. Label with the date and return to the freezer. Use within 2 months.

■ To use, thaw meatballs in the refrigerator or microwave oven. Serve meatballs whole in soups and sandwiches or sliced on top of pizza. Or simply add them to your favorite pasta sauce and serve over pasta for a quick, classic spaghetti and meatball dinner.

10 TO TRY—
SPAGHETTI TOPPERS

Start with Pasta with Marinara Sauce, page 424. **1.** Shredded cheddar cheese, chopped onion, and red beans. **2.** Shredded Parmesan cheese, snipped Italian parsley, and lemon peel. **3.** Roasted red sweet peppers and Asiago cheese shavings. **4.** Sliced or slivered Kalamata olives, crumbled feta cheese, and snipped fresh oregano. **5.** Sauteed leeks and mushrooms with chopped toasted almonds. **6.** Crumbled blue cheese and toasted pine nuts (see tip, page 20). **7.** Roasted grape tomatoes,* slices of fresh mozzarella cheese, and snipped fresh basil. **8.** Slices of cooked Italian sausage links and grated Parmesan or shredded smoked cheddar cheese. **9.** Shredded fresh spinach and crumbled crisp-cooked bacon. **10.** Long shreds or ribbons of slightly cooked carrots, zucchini, and/or yellow summer squash.

*Note: Toss the tomatoes with olive oil and roast in a 425°F oven for 5 to 10 minutes or until skins split.

PASTA WITH BOLOGNESE SAUCE

(Photo, page 417)

PREP: 40 MINUTES **COOK:** 30 MINUTES
MAKES: 6 SERVINGS

- 1 pound bulk sweet Italian sausage or ground beef
- 1 cup chopped onion (1 large)
- ½ cup finely chopped carrot (1 medium)
- ½ cup chopped green sweet pepper (½ large)
- ¼ cup chopped celery (½ stalk)
- 4 cloves garlic, minced
- 2 pounds roma tomatoes, peeled (if desired), seeded, and chopped (about 4 cups), or two 14.5-ounce cans diced tomatoes, undrained
- 1 6-ounce can tomato paste
- ½ cup dry red wine or beef broth
- 2 tablespoons snipped fresh basil or 1½ teaspoons dried basil, crushed
- 1 tablespoon snipped fresh oregano or 1 teaspoon dried oregano, crushed
- 2 teaspoons snipped fresh marjoram or ½ teaspoon dried marjoram, crushed
- ½ teaspoon salt
- ¼ teaspoon black pepper
- ¼ cup whipping cream
- 2 tablespoons snipped fresh Italian parsley
- 12 ounces packaged dried pasta, such as spaghetti, linguine, or penne

1 In a large pot cook sausage, onion, carrot, sweet pepper, celery, and garlic until meat is brown and onion is tender; drain.

2 Stir in tomatoes, tomato paste, wine, dried herbs (if using), salt, and black pepper. Bring to boiling; reduce heat. Simmer, covered, for 30 minutes, stirring occasionally. If necessary, uncover and simmer for 10 minutes more or until desired consistency, stirring occasionally. Stir in whipping cream, parsley, and fresh herbs (if using); heat mixture through.

3 In a large saucepan cook pasta according to package directions; drain. Serve sauce over hot pasta.

PER ¾ CUP COOKED PASTA + 1 CUP SAUCE: 570 cal., 22 g total fat (10 g sat. fat, 0 g trans fat), 66 mg chol., 652 mg sodium, 60 g carbo., 6 g fiber, 22 g pro.
EXCHANGES: 1 Vegetable, 3½ Starch, 1½ Medium-Fat Meat, 2½ Fat

HAMBURGER PASTA SKILLET

START TO FINISH: 35 MINUTES
MAKES: 4 SERVINGS

- 8 ounces packaged dried campanelle or penne pasta (3 cups)
- 8 ounces lean ground beef or bulk hot or sweet Italian sausage
- 1 medium onion, cut into thin wedges
- 1 26-ounce jar garlic pasta sauce
- ⅔ cup bottled roasted red sweet peppers, cut into bite-size strips
- ¼ cup pitted Kalamata olives, quartered
- 1 cup shredded Italian-blend cheese

1 In a large saucepan cook pasta according to package directions; drain.

2 In a large skillet cook ground beef and onion until meat is brown and onion is tender; drain fat. Stir in pasta sauce, roasted peppers, and olives. Bring to boiling. Stir in pasta to coat. Top with cheese.

PER 1½ CUPS: 512 cal., 18 g total fat (7 g sat. fat, 1 g trans fat), 59 mg chol., 1,215 mg sodium, 59 g carbo., 8 g fiber, 28 g pro.
EXCHANGES: 1 Vegetable, 3½ Starch, 2½ Lean Meat, 1½ Fat

KEEPING PASTA WARM

FOR BEST FLAVOR AND TEXTURE, SERVE PASTA IMMEDIATELY AFTER COOKING.

If your pasta should get done before your sauce, here's how to keep it warm.

■ Return the drained cooked pasta to the warm cooking pan. Stir in a little butter or olive oil to help prevent it from sticking together. Cover and let the pasta stand no more than 15 minutes.

■ Fill a serving bowl with hot water and let it stand for a few minutes. Empty and dry the bowl. Add the hot pasta and cover. Serve the pasta within 5 minutes.

SPAGHETTI WITH ITALIAN SAUSAGE AND SPINACH

START TO FINISH: 35 MINUTES
MAKES: 8 SERVINGS

- 1 19- to 20-ounce package uncooked mild or hot Italian sausage links, cut into 1-inch pieces
- 2 medium yellow or green sweet peppers, cut into bite-size strips
- 1 small sweet onion, cut into wedges
- 1 14- to 16-ounce package dried multigrain, whole wheat, or regular spaghetti
- 1 teaspoon crushed red pepper
- ¼ teaspoon salt
- ½ cup chicken broth
- 6 cups packaged fresh baby spinach
- 2 to 3 ounces Asiago cheese, shaved
  Additional crushed red pepper (optional)

1 In a very large skillet cook sausage for 15 minutes or until no longer pink, turning occasionally. Add sweet peppers and onion to skillet. Cook for 5 minutes more or until vegetables are tender, stirring occasionally.

2 Meanwhile, in a large pot cook pasta according to package directions with crushed red pepper added to water. Reserve 1 cup pasta-cooking water. Drain pasta; return to pan.

3 Toss sausage mixture and salt with spaghetti in pan. Stir in chicken broth and enough reserved pasta water to thin. Add spinach; toss just until combined and spinach is slightly wilted. Sprinkle each serving with Asiago cheese and, if desired, additional crushed red pepper.

PER 1½ CUPS: 466 cal., 24 g total fat (9 g sat. fat, 0 g trans fat), 59 mg chol., 738 mg sodium, 40 g carbo., 5 g fiber, 21 g pro. EXCHANGES: 1½ Vegetable, 2 Starch, 2 Medium-Fat Meat, 2½ Fat

WHOLE GRAIN OPTIONS MAKE YOUR PASTA DISHES MORE HEALTHFUL BY USING WHOLE GRAIN PASTA. TO TRANSITION YOUR FAMILY'S TASTEBUDS TO WHOLE GRAIN, START WITH EQUAL PARTS WHOLE GRAIN PASTA AND REFINED (REGULAR) PASTA. COOK ACCORDING TO PACKAGE DIRECTIONS.

TOO MUCH PASTA? COOKED PASTA CAN BE REFRIGERATED UP TO 2 DAYS, SEALED IN AN AIRTIGHT CONTAINER. REHEAT THE PASTA IN A SAUCE OR CLEAR BROTH.

HAMBURGER PASTA SKILLET

SPAGHETTI WITH ITALIAN SAUSAGE AND SPINACH

WHITE BEAN AND SAUSAGE RIGATONI

START TO FINISH: 20 MINUTES
MAKES: 4 SERVINGS

- 8 ounces packaged dried rigatoni (2 cups)
- 1 15-ounce can cannellini (white kidney) beans, Great Northern beans, or navy beans, rinsed and drained
- 1 14.5-ounce can Italian-style stewed tomatoes, undrained
- 8 ounces cooked smoked turkey sausage, halved lengthwise and cut into ½-inch slices
- ⅓ cup snipped fresh basil or 1 tablespoon dried basil, crushed
- ¼ cup shredded Asiago or Parmesan cheese

1 In a large saucepan cook pasta according to package directions. Drain; return pasta to pan. In another large saucepan combine beans, undrained tomatoes, sausage, and dried basil (if using). Cook and stir until heated through. Add bean mixture and fresh basil (if using) to pasta; stir to combine. To serve, sprinkle each serving with cheese.

PER 2 CUPS: 419 cal., 9 g total fat (3 g sat. fat, 0 g trans fat), 45 mg chol., 992 mg sodium, 65 g carbo., 8 g fiber, 24 g pro. EXCHANGES: ½ Vegetable, 4 Starch, 1½ Lean Meat

CHICKEN PAD THAI

PREP: 35 MINUTES **COOK:** 12 MINUTES
MAKES: 4 SERVINGS

- 8 ounces packaged dried rice noodles (Vietnamese banh pho or Thai sen-mee)
- ¼ cup salted peanuts, finely chopped
- ½ teaspoon grated lime peel
- 3 tablespoons fish sauce
- 2 tablespoons fresh lime juice
- 2 tablespoons packed brown sugar
- 4½ teaspoons rice vinegar
- 1 tablespoon Asian chili sauce with garlic
- 1 pound boneless, skinless chicken breasts, cut into bite-size strips
- 1 tablespoon finely chopped garlic
- 3 tablespoons vegetable oil
- 1 egg, lightly beaten
- 1 cup fresh bean sprouts
- ⅓ cup sliced green onions (3)
- 2 tablespoons snipped fresh cilantro

1 Place noodles in a large bowl. Add enough hot tap water to cover. Let stand for 10 to 15 minutes or until pliable but not soft; drain well.

2 For peanut topping, combine peanuts and lime peel; set aside. In a small bowl combine fish sauce, lime juice, brown sugar, rice vinegar, and chili sauce; stir until smooth. Set aside.

3 In a very large nonstick skillet cook chicken and garlic in 1 tablespoon of oil over medium-high heat for 6 minutes or until chicken is tender and no pink remains. Transfer chicken to a bowl. Add egg to the hot skillet and cook for 30 seconds. Turn egg with spatula and cook for 30 to 60 seconds more just until set. Remove and chop egg; set aside.

4 In same skillet heat remaining oil over medium-high heat for 30 seconds. Add drained noodles and sprouts; stir-fry for 2 minutes. Add fish sauce mixture and chicken; cook 1 to 2 minutes or until heated through. Divide mixture among four plates. Sprinkle each serving with egg and peanut topping. Garnish with green onions and cilantro.

PER 1¼ CUPS: 557 cal., 18 g total fat (2 g sat. fat, 0 g trans fat), 119 mg chol., 945 mg sodium, 62 g carbo., 3 g fiber, 34 g pro. EXCHANGES: 4 Starch, 3 Lean Meat, 2½ Fat

FARFALLE WITH MUSHROOMS AND SPINACH

START TO FINISH: 20 MINUTES
MAKES: 4 SERVINGS

- 12 ounces packaged dried farfalle (bow tie pasta) (about 5½ cups)
- 2 tablespoons olive oil
- 1 cup chopped onion (1 large)
- 2 cups sliced portobello or other fresh mushrooms
- 4 cloves garlic, minced
- 8 cups thinly sliced fresh spinach
- 2 teaspoons snipped fresh thyme
- ¼ teaspoon black pepper
- ¼ cup shredded Parmesan cheese

1 In a 4-quart pot cook pasta according to package directions; drain.

2 Meanwhile, in a very large skillet heat oil over medium heat. Add onion, mushrooms, and garlic; cook and stir for 2 to 3 minutes or until mushrooms are nearly tender. Stir in spinach, thyme, and pepper; cook 1 minute or until heated through and spinach is slightly wilted. Stir in cooked pasta; toss gently to mix. Sprinkle with cheese.

PER 1¾ CUPS: 451 cal., 11 g total fat (2 g sat. fat, 0 g trans fat), 4 mg chol., 131 mg sodium, 74 g carbo., 5 g fiber, 17 g pro. EXCHANGES: 2 Vegetable, 4 Starch, 1½ Fat

FETTUCCINE ALLA CARBONARA

START TO FINISH: 35 MINUTES
MAKES: 6 SERVINGS

- 16 ounces packaged dried fettuccine
- 8 slices bacon
- 4 ounces sliced prosciutto
- 2 tablespoons finely chopped onion
- ¾ cup unsalted butter
- ⅓ cup dry white wine
- ½ cup whipping cream
- ½ cup milk
- ½ cup grated Parmesan cheese
- 1 tablespoon snipped fresh parsley
   Black pepper

1 In a large pot cook pasta according to package directions; drain. Return pasta to pan; keep warm.

2 Meanwhile, for sauce, in a large skillet cook bacon over medium heat until crisp. Drain well on paper towels; coarsely crumble bacon and set aside. Chop the prosciutto into ½-inch pieces; set aside.

3 In a medium saucepan cook onion in hot butter over medium heat for 4 minutes or until tender. Add prosciutto. Cook and stir over medium heat for 3 minutes. Remove pan from heat. Carefully add wine.

4 Return saucepan to heat and bring mixture to boiling. Boil gently, uncovered, for 5 minutes. Stir in the bacon, cream, and milk; bring to boiling. Boil gently, uncovered, for 5 minutes.

5 Stir in ¼ cup of the Parmesan cheese and the parsley. Immediately pour sauce over pasta, stirring gently to coat. Sprinkle each serving with remaining cheese. Season to taste with pepper. Serve immediately.

PER 1⅓ CUPS: 722 cal., 43 g total fat (22 g sat. fat, 0 g trans fat), 108 mg chol., 705 mg sodium, 59 g carbo., 3 g fiber, 22 g pro. **EXCHANGES:** 4 Starch, 1½ High-Fat Meat, 5½ Fat

DISTINCTIVE ITALIAN FLAVOR PROSCIUTTO, A SALT-CURED, AIR-DRIED HAM, ADDS A SWEET, COMPLEX FLAVOR TO FETTUCCINE ALLA CARBONARA. IN A PINCH, USE CHOPPED THINLY SLICED HAM.

FETTUCCINE ALLA CARBONARA

FETTUCCINE ALFREDO (photo, page 419)

START TO FINISH: 35 MINUTES **MAKES:** 4 SERVINGS

- 8 ounces packaged dried fettuccine
- 2 cloves garlic, minced
- 2 tablespoons butter
- 1 cup whipping cream
- ½ teaspoon salt
- ⅛ teaspoon black pepper
- ½ cup grated Parmesan cheese
  Grated or finely shredded Parmesan cheese (optional)

1 In a large saucepan cook pasta according to package directions; drain.

2 Meanwhile, in a large saucepan cook garlic in hot butter over medium-high heat for 1 minute. Add cream, salt, and pepper. Bring to boiling; reduce heat. Boil gently, uncovered, about 3 minutes or until mixture begins to thicken. Remove from heat and stir in ½ cup Parmesan cheese. Drain pasta. Add pasta to hot sauce. Toss to combine. If desired, sprinkle each serving with additional cheese.

PER 1¼ CUPS: 514 cal., 32 g total fat (19 g sat. fat, 0 g trans fat), 107 mg chol., 511 mg sodium, 45 g carbo., 2 g fiber, 13 g pro. EXCHANGES: 3 Starch, ½ High-Fat Meat, 5 Fat

LEMONY FETTUCCINE ALFREDO WITH SHRIMP AND PEAS: Prepare as directed, except add 8 ounces peeled, deveined uncooked shrimp (see photos 1–3, page 433) and 1 cup frozen peas to pasta the last 1 minute of cooking. Stir 1 teaspoon finely shredded lemon peel and 1 tablespoon lemon juice into sauce before adding pasta.

PER 1¼ CUPS: 603 cal., 33 g total fat (20 g sat. fat, 0 g trans fat), 192 mg chol., 634 mg sodium, 51 g carbo., 4 g fiber, 26 g pro. EXCHANGES: 3½ Starch, 2 Lean Meat, 5 Fat

SHIITAKE FETTUCCINE ALFREDO: Prepare as directed, except cook 1½ cups sliced fresh shiitake (stems removed) or button mushrooms in the hot butter for 4 to 5 minutes or until tender before adding the cream, salt, and pepper.

PER 1¼ CUPS: 544 cal., 32 g total fat (19 g sat. fat, 0 g trans fat), 106 mg chol., 513 mg sodium, 53 g carbo., 3 g fiber, 13 g pro. EXCHANGES: 3 Starch, ½ Vegetable, ½ Meat, 5 Fat

FAST

SALMON AND ASPARAGUS-SAUCED PASTA

START TO FINISH: 25 MINUTES **MAKES:** 4 SERVINGS

- 1 pound fresh asparagus spears
- 8 ounces packaged dried cavatappi or penne pasta (2⅔ cups)
- 1 small red or yellow sweet pepper, cut into bite-size strips
- ½ cup chopped onion (1 medium)
- 1 tablespoon butter or margarine
- 1 10-ounce container refrigerated Alfredo pasta sauce
- ¼ cup milk
- 3 ounces lox-style smoked salmon, coarsely chopped
- 2 teaspoons snipped fresh tarragon or ½ teaspoon dried tarragon, crushed

1 Snap off and discard woody bases from asparagus. If desired, scrape off scales. Bias-slice asparagus into 2-inch pieces (you should have about 3 cups).

2 In a large saucepan cook pasta according to package directions, except add asparagus the last 3 minutes of cooking. Drain; keep warm.

3 Meanwhile, for sauce, in a medium saucepan cook and stir sweet pepper and onion in hot butter over medium heat until tender. Stir in Alfredo sauce, milk, and ¼ teaspoon *black pepper;* heat through. Gently stir in salmon and tarragon; heat through. Add to pasta mixture.

PER 2 CUPS: 446 cal., 18 g total fat (11 g sat. fat, 0 g trans fat), 54 mg chol., 910 mg sodium, 53 g carbo., 4 g fiber, 18 g pro. EXCHANGES: 1½ Vegetable, 3 Starch, 1 Lean Meat, 2½ Fat

GREAT GRATING CHEESES

FOR TOSSING INTO PASTA AND SPRINKLING OVER FINISHED DISHES, TRY THESE CLASSIC GRATING CHEESES.

To enjoy these cheeses at their freshest, full-flavored best, grate them as needed just before adding to recipes.

PARMIGIANO-REGGIANO: A granular texture and bold, snappy flavor are hallmarks of this time-honored cheese. Also try it thinly shaved in salads.

PECORINO ROMANO: This granular sheep's-milk cheese brings a sharp, peppery flavor to dishes.

AGED ASIAGO: Choose this one for its nutty, pleasantly salty flavor.

COOK ONCE, EAT TWICE

TONIGHT YOU'RE 30 MINUTES FROM A FRESH AND COLORFUL PASTA TOSS. TOMORROW YOU CAN HAVE A LIVELY MEDITERRANEAN-STYLE SALAD READY IN JUST 15.

TONIGHT

PASTA MARGHERITA

START TO FINISH: 30 MINUTES
MAKES: 4 SERVINGS + RESERVES

- 16 ounces packaged dried plain and/or spinach-flavored angel hair pasta or spaghetti
- ¼ cup olive oil
- 1 medium onion, cut into thin wedges
- 4 cloves garlic, minced
- 10 roma tomatoes, chopped
- 1 teaspoon salt
- ½ teaspoon crushed red pepper
- 8 ounces tiny fresh mozzarella balls (pearls) or 1-inch fresh mozzarella balls, quartered
- ½ cup shredded fresh basil
  Finely shredded Parmesan cheese

1 In a large pot cook pasta according to package directions; drain. Return pasta to pot; keep warm.

2 Meanwhile, in a very large skillet heat oil over medium heat. Add onion and garlic. Cook and stir about 4 minutes or until onion is tender. Stir in tomatoes, salt, and crushed red pepper. Cook and stir for 2 to 3 minutes or until tomatoes soften.

3 Add tomato mixture to pasta; toss to coat. Add mozzarella cheese and basil; toss to coat. Remove half of the mixture to a storage container; cover and chill for up to 24 hours and use in Chicken and Spinach Pasta Salad. Serve remaining mixture topped with Parmesan cheese.

PER 1½ CUPS: 388 cal., 15 g total fat (6 g sat. fat, 0 g trans fat), 22 mg chol., 428 mg sodium, 48 g carbo., 3 g fiber, 15 g pro.
EXCHANGES: 1 Vegetable, 3 Starch, ½ High-Fat Meat, 1½ Fat

TOMORROW

CHICKEN AND SPINACH PASTA SALAD

START TO FINISH: 15 MINUTES
MAKES: 6 TO 8 SERVINGS

- ½ recipe Pasta Margherita, chilled (about 7 cups)
- 2 cups shredded cooked chicken
- 4 cups baby spinach and/or arugula
- ½ cup halved Kalamata olives
- 2 tablespoons olive oil
- 2 tablespoons red wine vinegar
- ¼ teaspoon salt
- ¼ teaspoon black pepper
- 1 ounce Parmesan cheese, shaved (optional)

1 In a very large bowl toss together Pasta Margherita, chicken, spinach, and olives. In a small bowl whisk together olive oil, vinegar, salt, and pepper. Drizzle oil mixture over pasta mixture; toss to coat.* Serve chilled. If desired, top with shaved Parmesan cheese.

PER 2 CUPS: 410 cal., 19 g total fat (5 g sat. fat, 0 g trans fat), 56 mg chol., 636 mg sodium, 34 g carbo., 3 g fiber, 24 g pro.
EXCHANGES: 1 Vegetable, 2 Starch, 2½ Lean Meat, 2 Fat

FUSILLI WITH GARLIC PESTO AND PECORINO

START TO FINISH: 35 MINUTES
MAKES: 6 TO 8 SERVINGS

15 cloves garlic, peeled
⅓ cup lightly packed fresh basil leaves
16 ounces packaged dried fusilli or gemelli pasta
½ cup olive oil
⅓ cup pine nuts, toasted (see tip, page 20)
2 tablespoons finely shredded Pecorino Romano cheese (½ ounce)
¾ teaspoon sea salt
⅛ teaspoon black pepper
1 cup small fresh basil leaves
¼ cup finely shredded Pecorino Romano cheese (1 ounce)

1 In a large pot cook garlic cloves in a large amount of boiling *salted water* for 8 minutes. Using a slotted spoon, transfer garlic to a blender or food processor. Add the ⅓ cup basil leaves to the boiling water and cook for 5 seconds; remove with slotted spoon and drain well on paper towels. (Do not drain boiling water.) Add basil to blender.

2 Add pasta to boiling water and cook according to package directions. Before draining pasta, remove ½ cup of cooking water; set aside. Drain pasta; return to pot.

3 Meanwhile, for pesto, add oil, 2 tablespoons of the pine nuts, the 2 tablespoons cheese, salt, and pepper to blender or food processor. Cover; blend or process until nearly smooth (pesto will be thin).

4 Add pesto to cooked pasta; toss gently to coat. If necessary, toss in enough of the reserved cooking water to help coat the pasta evenly with pesto. Transfer pasta mixture to a serving bowl. Sprinkle with the 1 cup basil leaves, the ¼ cup cheese, and the remaining pine nuts. Serve immediately.

PER 1 CUP: 518 cal., 25 g total fat (4 g sat. fat, 0 g trans fat), 5 mg chol., 264 mg sodium, 61 g carbo., 3 g fiber, 14 g pro. EXCHANGES: 4 Starch, 4½ Fat

---

NO SCALE NEEDED

TO MEASURE PASTAS SUCH AS FETTUCCINE AND SPAGHETTI, HOLD THE DRIED PASTA IN A BUNDLE. A 1½-INCH-DIAMETER BUNCH WEIGHS 8 OUNCES.

PASTA WITH WHITE CLAM SAUCE

START TO FINISH: 30 MINUTES **MAKES:** 4 SERVINGS

10 ounces packaged dried linguine or fettuccine
2 6.5-ounce cans chopped or minced clams
About 2 cups half-and-half, light cream, or whole milk
½ cup chopped onion (1 medium)
2 cloves garlic, minced
2 tablespoons butter or margarine
¼ cup all-purpose flour
2 teaspoons snipped fresh oregano or ½ teaspoon dried oregano, crushed
¼ teaspoon salt
⅛ teaspoon black pepper
¼ cup snipped fresh parsley
¼ cup dry white wine, nonalcoholic dry white wine, or chicken broth
¼ cup finely shredded or grated Parmesan cheese (1 ounce)

1 In a large saucepan cook pasta according to package directions. Drain; keep warm. Meanwhile, drain canned clams, reserving the juice from one of the cans (you should have about ½ cup). Add enough half-and-half to reserved clam juice to equal 2½ cups liquid. Set clams and clam juice mixture aside.

2 In a medium saucepan cook onion and garlic in hot butter over medium heat until tender but not brown. Stir in flour, dried oregano (if using), salt, and pepper. Add clam juice mixture all at once. Cook and stir until thickened and bubbly. Cook and stir for 1 minute more. Stir in drained clams, fresh oregano (if using), parsley, and wine. Heat through. Serve over hot pasta. Sprinkle with Parmesan cheese.

PER 1½ CUPS: 680 cal., 24 g total fat (14 g sat. fat, 0 g trans fat), 125 mg chol., 430 mg sodium, 72 g carbo., 3 g fiber, 40 g pro. EXCHANGES: 5 Starch, 3½ Lean Meat, 1½ Fat

SEAFOOD PASTA

PREP: 30 MINUTES **SOAK:** 45 MINUTES
COOK: 20 MINUTES **MAKES:** 6 SERVINGS

1 pound fresh or frozen medium shrimp in shells
12 fresh mussels
12 fresh small littleneck clams
9 quarts water
9 tablespoons salt
12 ounces dried linguine or fettuccine

1 tablespoon olive oil
1 6.5-ounce can minced clams, drained
1 cup dry white wine
2 to 3 cloves garlic, minced
1 8-ounce bottle clam juice
¼ cup butter
1 teaspoon finely shredded lemon peel
2 tablespoons lemon juice
¼ to ½ teaspoon crushed red pepper
¼ cup snipped fresh Italian parsley
  Salt

1 Thaw shrimp, if frozen. Peel and devein shrimp, leaving tails intact (see photos 1–3, below). Rinse shrimp; pat dry with paper towels. Cover and chill shrimp until ready to use.

2 Scrub mussels and clams under cold running water. Using your fingers, pull out any beards visible between mussel shells; discard. In a very large bowl combine 3 quarts of the water and 3 tablespoons of the salt. Add mussels and clams; soak for 15 minutes. Drain and rinse thoroughly; drain. Repeat two more times with fresh water and salt. Drain and rinse mussels and clams thoroughly.

3 Meanwhile, cook pasta according to package directions. Drain; keep warm.

4 In a large pot heat oil over medium-high heat. Add the shrimp and minced clams. Cook and stir about 3 minutes or until shrimp are opaque. Remove shrimp and clams; set aside.

5 Remove pan from heat. Add wine and garlic to pot. Return to heat. Bring to boiling; reduce heat and simmer, uncovered, 5 minutes or until reduced by half (measures about ½ cup). Add mussels and clams, the clam juice, butter, lemon peel, lemon juice, and crushed red pepper. Bring to boiling; reduce heat. Cook, covered, for 5 to 9 minutes or until mussels and clams open, discarding any unopened shells. Stir in drained pasta and the shrimp mixture; heat through.

6 To serve, spoon pasta mixture onto a large serving platter, making sure most shellfish are on top. Sprinkle with parsley. Season to taste with salt.

PER 1½ CUPS: 497 cal., 13 g total fat (6 g sat. fat, 0 g trans fat), 171 mg chol., 839 mg sodium, 48 g carbo., 2 g fiber, 40 g pro. EXCHANGES: 3 Starch, 4½ Lean Meat, 1½ Fat

PEELING AND DEVEINING SHRIMP, STEP-BY-STEP

1. Open shell lengthwise down the body on its belly side. Starting at the head end, peel back and remove the shell. Gently pull on tail to remove it or leave it intact. **2.** Use a sharp knife to make a shallow slit along the back from the head to the tail end, exposing black vein. **3.** Place the knife's tip under the vein and lift it out; rinse shrimp under cold water.

SHRIMP PASTA DIAVOLO

START TO FINISH: 20 MINUTES **MAKES:** 4 SERVINGS

- 1 9-ounce package refrigerated linguine
- 12 ounces medium fresh shrimp, peeled and deveined (see photos 1–3, page 433)
- 1 medium onion, cut into thin wedges
- 3 cloves garlic, minced
- ¼ teaspoon crushed red pepper
- 2 tablespoons olive oil
- 1 14.5-ounce can diced tomatoes, undrained
- ½ cup torn fresh basil
- 2 cups fresh baby spinach
- ½ cup finely shredded Parmesan cheese (2 ounces)

1 In a large saucepan cook pasta according to package directions. Drain pasta and return to pan; set aside. Rinse shrimp; pat dry.

2 Meanwhile, in a large skillet cook onion, garlic, and crushed red pepper in hot oil until tender. Stir in tomatoes. Bring to boiling; reduce heat. Simmer, uncovered, for 3 minutes. Add shrimp to skillet; cover and simmer for 3 minutes or until shrimp are opaque. Add shrimp mixture to pasta. Stir in basil and spinach. Top each serving with Parmesan cheese.

PER 2 CUPS: 412 cal., 13 g total fat (4 g sat. fat, 0 g trans fat), 204 mg chol., 528 mg sodium, 44 g carbo., 4 g fiber, 30 g pro. EXCHANGES: 1 Vegetable, 2½ Starch, 3 Lean Meat, ½ Fat

GORGONZOLA-SAUCED TORTELLINI WITH ARTICHOKES

START TO FINISH: 30 MINUTES
MAKES: 4 SERVINGS

- 1 9-ounce package refrigerated spinach cheese or three-cheese tortellini
- 8 ounces bulk sweet or hot Italian sausage
- 1½ cups fresh cremini, stemmed shiitake, or button mushrooms, sliced (6 ounces)
- 1 small onion, cut into thin wedges
- 2 ounces Gorgonzola cheese, crumbled (½ cup)
- 1 14.5-ounce can diced tomatoes with basil, garlic, and oregano, drained
- 1 6-ounce jar marinated artichoke hearts, drained and quartered
- 1 tablespoon finely shredded Parmesan cheese
- 2 tablespoons thinly sliced fresh basil

1 In a large saucepan cook tortellini according to package instructions; drain.

2 Meanwhile, in a 3-quart saucepan cook sausage, mushrooms, and onion until sausage is no longer pink and onion is tender, breaking up sausage with a wooden spoon. Drain fat; discard.

3 Add Gorgonzola cheese; cook and stir over low heat until cheese melts. Gently stir in tortellini, drained tomatoes, and artichokes; heat through. Top with Parmesan cheese and basil.

PER 1½ CUPS: 464 cal., 24 g total fat (11 g sat. fat, 0 g trans fat), 71 mg chol., 1,384 mg sodium, 37 g carbo., 3 g fiber, 23 g pro. EXCHANGES: ½ Vegetable, 2½ Starch, 2 High-Fat Meat, 1 Fat

MEATBALL PIE

PREP: 30 MINUTES **COOK:** 20 MINUTES
BAKE: 60 MINUTES **STAND:** 15 MINUTES
OVEN: 350°F **MAKES:** 8 TO 10 SERVINGS

- 3 eggs, lightly beaten
- ⅔ cup grated Parmesan cheese
- 8 ounces packaged dried bucatini pasta or spaghetti
- 3 cups thinly sliced sweet onions (2 large)
- 2 tablespoons butter or margarine
- 1 cup ricotta cheese
- 2 tablespoons snipped fresh basil or 2 teaspoons dried basil, crushed
- ¼ teaspoon black pepper
- 1 24- to 26-ounce jar purchased tomato and basil pasta sauce or marinara sauce or 2½ cups Marinara Sauce (page 424)
- 1½ cups shredded mozzarella cheese (6 ounces)
- 1 pound frozen cooked Italian meatballs, thawed
  Small fresh basil leaves
  Shaved Parmesan cheese

1 Grease a 10-inch springform pan. Line pan with parchment paper or foil (see photo 1, page 435). Grease parchment or foil; set pan aside. Or grease a 2-quart square baking dish.

2 For pasta crust, in a small bowl stir together two of the eggs and grated Parmesan cheese; set aside. In a large saucepan cook pasta according to package directions. Drain pasta; return to saucepan. Add egg mixture; toss to coat. Press pasta mixture into prepared springform pan, building up sides slightly (see photo 2, page 435); set aside.

3 Meanwhile, in a large skillet cook onions, covered, in hot butter over medium-low heat about 15 minutes or until onions are tender and lightly browned, stirring occasionally. Uncover; increase heat to medium. Cook about 5 minutes more or until onions are golden brown, stirring occasionally. Remove from heat; cool slightly.

4 Preheat oven to 350°F. In a small bowl stir together the remaining egg, ricotta cheese, 2 tablespoons basil, and pepper. Spread ricotta cheese mixture over pasta crust. Top with caramelized onions (see photo 3, below). Place springform pan on a large pizza pan or baking sheet (if using a baking dish, place directly on the oven rack). Bake for 15 minutes. Spoon ¾ cup of the pasta sauce over layers in pan. Sprinkle with ½ cup of the mozzarella cheese.

5 Toss meatballs with ¾ cup of the pasta sauce and ½ cup of the mozzarella cheese. Arrange

meatball mixture over layers in pan, forming a mound (see photo 4, below). Top with ½ cup of the remaining pasta sauce.

6 Tent pie lightly with foil. Bake for 45 to 50 minutes or until heated through. Sprinkle with remaining mozzarella cheese. Let stand, uncovered, on a wire rack for 15 minutes. Lift pie out of pan. Using a serrated knife, cut pie into wedges (see photo 5, below). Garnish with small basil leaves and shaved Parmesan cheese before serving. Heat and pass remaining pasta sauce.

PER WEDGE: 542 cal., 29 g total fat (15 g sat. fat, 0 g trans fat), 157 mg chol., 1,029 mg sodium, 41 g carbo., 5 g fiber, 29 g pro. EXCHANGES: ½ Vegetable, 2½ Starch, 3 Medium-Fat Meat, 2½ Fat

---

MAKE A FREEZER-READY MEAL PREPARE A DOUBLE BATCH OF THE MEATBALL PIE AND FREEZE ONE FOR UP TO 2 MONTHS.

LAYERING THE MEATBALL PIE, STEP-BY-STEP

1. Line springform pan with parchment paper to prevent pie from sticking. **2.** Place noodles on top of parchment paper in pan; build up edges slightly. **3.** Arrange cooked onion mixture over ricotta layer in pan. **4.** Spoon meatball mixture over prepared layers in pan. **5.** After baking, be sure to let the pie stand 15 minutes to allow it to set up. Lift pie out of pan and cut into wedges.

1

2

3

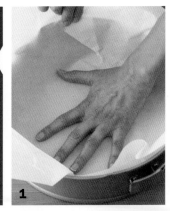

4

5

RAVIOLI SKILLET LASAGNA

START TO FINISH: 25 MINUTES **MAKES:** 4 SERVINGS

- 2 cups chunk-style spaghetti sauce
- ½ cup water
- 4 cups packaged fresh baby spinach
- 1 pound frozen meat- or cheese-filled ravioli (4½ cups)
- 1 egg, lightly beaten
- ½ of a 15-ounce carton ricotta cheese
- ¼ cup grated Romano or Parmesan cheese
  Grated Romano or Parmesan cheese

1 In a large skillet combine spaghetti sauce and water. Bring to boiling. Stir in spinach until it wilts. Stir in the ravioli. Return to boiling; reduce heat. Cover and cook mixture over medium heat about 5 minutes or until ravioli are nearly tender, stirring once to prevent sticking.

2 In a medium bowl combine egg, ricotta cheese, and ¼ cup Romano cheese. Spoon ricotta mixture over ravioli mixture in large mounds. Cover and cook over medium-low heat about 10 minutes or until ricotta is set and pasta is just tender. Sprinkle each serving with additional grated cheese.

PER 1¾ CUPS: 490 cal., 21 g total fat (10 g sat. fat, 0 g trans fat), 146 mg chol., 1,061 mg sodium, 53 g carbo., 7 g fiber, 23 g pro. EXCHANGES: 1 Vegetable, 3 Starch, 1½ Medium-Fat Meat, 2 Fat

MILE-HIGH LASAGNA PIE

PREP: 50 MINUTES **BAKE:** 60 MINUTES
STAND: 15 MINUTES **OVEN:** 375°F
MAKES: 10 SERVINGS

- 16 dried whole wheat or whole grain lasagna noodles
- 2 tablespoons olive oil
- 1½ cups finely chopped carrots (3 medium)
- 2 cups finely chopped zucchini (1 medium)
- 4 cloves garlic, minced
- 3 cups sliced fresh button mushrooms (8 ounces)
- 2 6-ounce packages fresh baby spinach
- 2 tablespoons snipped fresh basil
- 1 egg, lightly beaten
- 1 15-ounce container ricotta cheese
- ⅓ cup finely shredded Parmesan cheese
- ½ teaspoon salt
- ¼ teaspoon black pepper
- 1 26-ounce jar tomato and basil pasta sauce (2½ cups)
- 2 cups shredded fontina or mozzarella cheese (8 ounces)
  Rosemary sprigs (optional)

1 Preheat oven to 375°F. In a large saucepan cook noodles according to package directions. Drain noodles; rinse with cold water. Drain well; set aside.

2 Meanwhile, in a large skillet heat 1 tablespoon of the olive oil over medium-high heat. Add carrots, zucchini, and half of the garlic. Cook and stir about 5 minutes or until crisp-tender. Transfer vegetables to a bowl. Add the remaining oil to the same skillet and heat over medium-high heat. Add mushrooms and remaining garlic. Cook and stir about 5 minutes or until tender. Gradually add spinach. Cook and stir until spinach is wilted, 1 to 2 minutes. Remove from skillet with a slotted spoon; stir in 2 tablespoons basil. Set aside.

3 In a small bowl, stir together egg, ricotta cheese, Parmesan cheese, salt, and pepper; set aside.

4 To assemble pie, in the bottom of a 9×3-inch springform pan spread ½ cup of the pasta sauce. Arrange 3 to 4 of the cooked noodles over the sauce, trimming and overlapping as necessary to cover sauce with one layer (see photo 1, page 437). Top with half of the mushroom mixture. Spoon half of the ricotta cheese mixture over mushroom mixture. Top with another layer of noodles. Spread with 1 cup remaining pasta sauce. Top with all of the carrot mixture. Sprinkle with half the fontina cheese. Top with another layer of noodles. Layer with remaining mushroom mixture and remaining ricotta cheese mixture. Top with another layer of noodles and remaining sauce (might have extra noodles). Gently press down pie with back of spatula (see photo 2, page 437).

5 Place springform pan on a foil-lined baking sheet. Bake about 60 minutes or until heated through, topping with remaining fontina cheese for the last 15 minutes of baking. Cover and let stand on a wire rack for 15 minutes before serving. Cut around outside edges of pie and carefully remove the pan ring (see photos 3 and 4, page 437). To serve, cut lasagna into wedges. If desired, garnish with rosemary sprigs.

PER WEDGE: 463 cal., 23 g total fat (12 g sat. fat, 0 g trans fat), 82 mg chol., 965 mg sodium, 38 g carbo., 8 g fiber, 28 g pro. EXCHANGES: 2 Vegetable, 2 Starch, 2½ Medium-Fat Meat, 1½ Fat

BUILDING THE LASAGNA PIE, STEP-BY-STEP

1. Allow lasagna noodles to overlap in pan for a firm base; trim noodles to fit the pan. **2.** Using back of spatula, gently press down pie before baking. **3.** After baking, cut around outside edges of pie to loosen the ring. **4.** Remove the ring.

MAKE-IT-MINE LASAGNA

WITH THIS EASY-TO-FOLLOW FORMULA, YOU CAN GO GOURMET WITH GOAT CHEESE AND PANCETTA OR KEEP IT CLASSIC WITH MOZZARELLA AND SAUSAGE—AND THERE ARE PLENTY OF OPTIONS IN BETWEEN.

BASIC INGREDIENTS

PREP: 45 MINUTES
COOK: 15 MINUTES
BAKE: 40 MINUTES
STAND: 10 MINUTES **OVEN:** 375°F
MAKES: 8 SERVINGS

  Noodles
12 ounces Meat
 1 cup chopped onion
 2 cloves garlic, minced
  Tomatoes
  Seasoning
 1 egg, lightly beaten
  Dairy
¼ cup grated Parmesan cheese
 1 cup bottled roasted red sweet peppers, drained and cut into strips (optional)
 8 ounces Cheese
  Grated Parmesan cheese (optional)

NOODLES (PICK ONE)

 6 dried lasagna noodles
 6 dried whole wheat lasagna noodles

MEAT (PICK ONE)

12 ounces ground beef or pork sausage or ground uncooked Italian sausage or turkey
 8 ounces Italian sausage plus 4 ounces chopped pancetta or bacon

TOMATOES (PICK ONE)

 1 14.5-ounce can diced tomatoes, undrained, plus one 8-ounce can tomato sauce and ¼ cup tomato paste
 2 cups purchased pasta sauce

SEASONING (PICK ONE)

 1 tablespoon dried Italian seasoning, crushed
 2 tablespoons snipped fresh basil or 2 teaspoons dried basil, crushed

DAIRY (PICK ONE)

 1 15-ounce container regular or light ricotta cheese
 2 cups cream-style cottage cheese, drained
 1 cup bottled Alfredo pasta sauce

CHEESE (PICK ONE)

Shredded mozzarella, provolone, Monterey Jack, fontina, and/or Italian-blend cheese
Crumbled goat cheese
Sliced fresh mozzarella cheese

BASIC INSTRUCTIONS

1 Cook Noodles according to package directions or until tender but still firm. Drain noodles; rinse with cold water. Drain well and set aside.

2 Meanwhile, for sauce, in a large saucepan cook desired Meat, onion, and garlic until meat is brown, stirring to break up meat as it cooks. Drain off fat.

3 Stir Tomatoes and Seasoning into meat mixture. Bring to boiling; reduce heat. Simmer, uncovered, for 15 minutes, stirring occasionally.

4 Preheat oven to 375°F. For cheese filling, combine egg, Dairy, and ¼ cup Parmesan cheese; set aside.

5 Spread about ½ cup of the meat sauce over the bottom of a 2-quart rectangular baking dish. Layer half of the Noodles in the bottom of the dish, trimming or overlapping as necessary to fit. Spread with half of the cheese filling. Top with half of the remaining meat sauce, half of the roasted sweet peppers (if desired), and half of the Cheese. Repeat layers. If desired, sprinkle additional Parmesan cheese over top.

6 Place baking dish on a baking sheet. Bake, uncovered, for 40 to 45 minutes or until heated through. Let stand for 10 minutes before serving.

STUFFED MANICOTTI

PREP: 30 MINUTES **BAKE:** 35 MINUTES
OVEN: 350°F **MAKES:** 6 SERVINGS

12 packaged dried manicotti
8 ounces lean ground beef
8 ounces bulk Italian sausage
½ of a 15-ounce carton ricotta cheese (about 1 cup)
2 cups shredded mozzarella cheese (8 ounces)
½ cup finely shredded Parmesan cheese
1½ teaspoons dried Italian seasoning, crushed
3 cups Marinara Sauce (page 424)

1 Preheat oven to 350°F. Cook pasta according to package directions; drain. Place pasta in a single layer on a sheet of greased foil.

2 Meanwhile, in a large skillet cook ground beef and Italian sausage over medium heat until brown. Drain fat; discard. In a medium bowl combine ricotta cheese, 1 cup of the mozzarella cheese, Parmesan cheese, and Italian seasoning. Stir in cooked meat mixture. Using a small spoon, fill pasta with meat mixture. Arrange filled pasta in an ungreased 3-quart rectangular baking dish. Pour marinara sauce over pasta. Sprinkle with remaining 1 cup mozzarella cheese.

3 Bake, covered, for 25 minutes. Uncover and bake about 10 minutes more or until mixture heats through and cheese melts.

PER SERVING: 646 cal., 36 g total fat (16 g sat. fat, 0 g trans fat), 109 mg chol., 1,203 mg sodium, 44 g carbo., 3 g fiber, 34 g pro. EXCHANGES: ½ Vegetable, 3 Starch, 3½ Medium-Fat Meat, 3 Fat

VEGGIE-STUFFED PASTA SHELLS

START TO FINISH: 40 MINUTES **MAKES:** 4 SERVINGS

12 packaged dried jumbo shell macaroni
1½ cups purchased coarsely shredded fresh carrots
1⅓ cups shredded zucchini (1 medium)
½ cup finely chopped onion (1 medium)
2 tablespoons olive oil
1 10-ounce package frozen chopped spinach, thawed and well drained
½ of a 15-ounce carton ricotta cheese
1½ cups shredded Italian-blend cheese (6 ounces)
¼ teaspoon salt
⅛ teaspoon cayenne pepper
1 14- to 16-ounce jar pasta sauce

1 Cook pasta according to package directions; drain. Rinse pasta with cold water; drain again.

2 Meanwhile, in a large skillet cook carrots, zucchini, and onion in hot oil over medium-high heat for 3 to 5 minutes or until tender. Stir in spinach; cook and stir for 1 minute. Transfer to a bowl.

3 Stir ricotta cheese, 1 cup of the Italian-blend cheese, salt, and cayenne pepper into vegetable mixture. Spoon a rounded 2 tablespoons cheese mixture into each pasta shell (see photo 1, below). Spoon pasta sauce into skillet; place filled shells in sauce (see photo 2, below). Heat shells and sauce, covered, over medium heat for 10 minutes or until heated through. Sprinkle with remaining cheese.

PER SERVING: 538 cal., 26 g total fat (11 g sat. fat, 0 g trans fat), 57 mg chol., 891 mg sodium, 52 g carbo., 6 g fiber, 27 g pro. EXCHANGES: 2 Vegetable, 3 Starch, 2 Medium-Fat Meat, 2½ Fat

---

VEGGIE-STUFFED PASTA SHELLS, STEP-BY-STEP

1. Use a flatware tablespoon to fill each of the cooked jumbo shells with the vegetable mixture, using 2 rounded tablespoons for each shell.
2. Place filled jumbo shells in sauce in skillet and cook over medium heat until heated through. You might need to gently lift and rearrange the shells with a large spoon during cooking to keep them from sticking to the pan.

BAKED ZITI WITH THREE CHEESES

4 Bake, covered, for 35 to 40 minutes or until heated through. Uncover; sprinkle with remaining cheese. Bake 5 minutes more or until cheese melts.

PER 1¼ CUPS: 468 cal., 20 g total fat (10 g sat. fat, 0 g trans fat), 52 mg chol., 903 mg sodium, 46 g carbo., 5 g fiber, 21 g pro. EXCHANGES: ½ Vegetable, 3 Starch, 1½ High-Fat Meat, 1 Fat

BAKED ZITI WITH THREE CHEESES

PREP: 30 MINUTES **BAKE:** 30 MINUTES
OVEN: 425°F **MAKES:** 6 SERVINGS

- 12 ounces packaged dried ziti or penne pasta (4 cups)
- 1 14.5-ounce can fire-roasted crushed tomatoes or one 14.5-ounce can diced tomatoes, undrained
- 1 cup chopped onion (2 medium)
- 12 cloves garlic, minced
- 2 tablespoons olive oil
- ½ cup dry white wine
- 2 cups whipping cream
- 1 cup shredded Parmesan cheese (4 ounces)
- ¾ cup crumbled Gorgonzola or other blue cheese (3 ounces)
- ½ cup shredded fontina cheese (2 ounces)
- ¾ teaspoon salt
- ¼ teaspoon black pepper

1 Preheat oven to 425°F. In a large saucepan cook pasta according to package directions; drain. Place in an ungreased 3-quart rectangular baking dish; stir in undrained tomatoes. Set aside.

2 Meanwhile, in a large saucepan cook onion and garlic in hot oil over medium heat just until tender. Carefully stir in wine and cook about 3 minutes or until liquid reduces by half. Add cream; heat to boiling. Boil gently, uncovered, about 5 minutes or until mixture thickens slightly, stirring frequently. Remove from heat. Stir in Parmesan cheese, ½ cup of the Gorgonzola cheese, the fontina cheese, salt, and pepper.

3 Pour cheese mixture over pasta. Bake, covered, for 30 to 35 minutes or until sauce is bubbly. Stir pasta to coat. Sprinkle with remaining Gorgonzola cheese.

PER 2 CUPS: 741 cal., 48 g total fat (28 g sat. fat, 0 g trans fat), 141 mg chol., 970 mg sodium, 53 g carbo., 3 g fiber, 24 g pro. EXCHANGES: ½ Vegetable, 3 Starch, 2 High-Fat Meat, 5½ Fat

BEST EVER

BAKED CAVATELLI

PREP: 20 MINUTES **BAKE:** 40 MINUTES
OVEN: 375°F **MAKES:** 6 SERVINGS

- 7 ounces packaged dried cavatelli or medium shell macaroni (1¾ cups)
- 12 ounces bulk Italian sausage or ground beef
- ¾ cup chopped onion (1 large)
- ½ cup chopped green sweet pepper (optional)
- 2 cloves garlic, minced
- 1 26-ounce jar tomato and basil pasta sauce
- 1¼ cups shredded mozzarella cheese (5 ounces)
- ¼ cup sliced pitted ripe olives (optional)
- ¼ teaspoon black pepper

1 Preheat oven to 375°F. Cook pasta according to package directions. Drain; set aside.

2 Meanwhile, in a large skillet cook sausage, onion, sweet pepper (if desired), and garlic until sausage is brown. Drain fat; discard.

3 In a large bowl stir together pasta sauce, 1 cup of the mozzarella cheese, the olives (if desired), and black pepper. Add cooked pasta and drained sausage mixture. Stir gently to combine. Spoon mixture into a 2-quart casserole.

PIES & TARTS

CRUMB-TOPPED FRUIT PIE, PAGE 447

PIES & TARTS

ONCE YOU'VE MASTERED A FEW
BASICS, BAKING ONE OF THESE
YEARNED-FOR DESSERTS IS AS
EASY AS—WELL, PIE!

THE ART OF THE PASTRY

You needn't be a pastry chef—or a grandmother—
to pull off gorgeous homemade crusts. Yes,
making piecrusts is an art, but one that becomes
second nature with know-how and practice.

USE EXACT MEASURES: Too much flour or water
will make a crust tough, and too much shortening
will make it crumbly. Also the water must be
ice-cold, to keep the shortening and butter from
melting. Those bits of fat help separate the pastry into layers as it bakes—that's how your pastry
gets flaky.

GO EASY ON THE FLOUR:
Rolling the dough on top of a
pastry cloth helps you avoid
using excess flour, which
can make a pastry tough. If
desired, you can also cover
your rolling pin with a cotton

stockinette designed for pastry making; lightly
flour both the cloth and stockinette. When rolling
the dough, work it as little as possible, because too
much rolling also can make the pastry tough.

TRI-BERRY PIE, PAGE 450

THE COVER-UP: To protect
the crimped edge from
overbrowning, fold a 12-inch
square of foil into quarters.
Cut off 3½ inches from the
folded corners; unfold. There
will be a 7-inch hole in center.

Loosely mold foil over edge of the pie before baking.
Or use purchased pie shields to protect crust.

PLATES AND PANS

Always use the size of pie plate or tart pan called
for in a recipe. Here is the equipment you'll need.

PIE PLATES: These can be made of glass, ceramic,
stoneware, aluminum, or tin; the recipes in this
chapter call for a 9-inch plate.

TART PANS: The fluted sides of these pans make
your tarts pretty; the removable bottoms make it
easy to transfer tarts to serving plates. They come
in a variety of sizes, including 4-inch individual
tartlet pans.

MASTERING MERINGUES

Follow these tips for airy, sweet meringues.

■ Allow egg whites to stand at room temperature
30 minutes to bring more volume to the meringue.

■ Use a large bowl made of copper, stainless
steel, or glass, and make sure the bowls, beaters, and any other utensils are very clean and dry
before using them. Oil or grease residue prevents
whites from beating properly. Also be sure no yolk
gets into the whites when separating the eggs.

■ Prevent shrinkage of baked meringue by beating egg whites until stiff peaks form (tips stand
straight; see photo 2, page 177) and sealing the
meringue to the crust's edge when spreading it
over the filling (see photo 2, page 453).

■ Prevent beading—small beads of moisture that
can form on the surface of the baked meringue—
by not overbaking the meringue.

■ Prevent weeping—the water layer that can
form between the meringue and filling—by spooning the meringue over the filling while it's still hot
(see photo 1, page 453).

PASTRY FOR DOUBLE-CRUST PIE

START TO FINISH: 15 MINUTES
MAKES: 2 PIECRUSTS (8 SERVINGS)

- 2½ cups all-purpose flour
- 1 teaspoon salt
- ½ cup shortening
- ¼ cup butter, cut up, or shortening
- ½ to ⅔ cup ice water

1 In a large bowl stir together flour and salt. Using a pastry blender, cut in shortening and butter until pieces are pea size (see photo 1, below).

2 Sprinkle 1 tablespoon of the water over part of the flour mixture; toss with a fork. Push moistened pastry to side of bowl. Repeat moistening flour mixture, 1 tablespoon of the water at a time, until flour mixture is moistened. Gather flour mixture into a ball, kneading gently until it holds together. Divide pastry in half; form halves into balls.

3 On a lightly floured surface use your hands to slightly flatten one pastry ball. Roll pastry from center to edges into a circle 12 inches in diameter (see photo 2, below).

4 Wrap pastry circle around rolling pin. Unroll pastry into a 9-inch pie plate (see photo 3, page 445). Ease pastry into plate without stretching it. Transfer desired filling to pastry-lined pie plate. Trim pastry even with pie plate rim (see photo 4, page 445).

5 Roll remaining ball into a 12-inch-diameter circle. Using a sharp knife, cut slits in pastry. Place pastry circle on filling; trim to ½ inch beyond edge of plate. Fold top pastry edge under bottom pastry (see photo 5, page 445). Crimp edge as desired (see page 446). Bake as directed in recipes.

NUT PASTRY: Prepare as directed, except substitute ¼ cup ground toasted pecans or almonds for ¼ cup of the flour.

PASTRY FOR QUICK LATTICE-TOP PIE: Prepare as directed, except trim bottom pastry to ½ inch beyond edge of pie plate. Roll out remaining pastry and cut into ½-inch-wide strips. Transfer desired filling to pastry-lined pie plate. Place half of the pastry strips on filling 1 inch apart. Give pie a quarter turn; arrange remaining strips perpendicular to the first half of strips on filling (see photos 1–3, page 451). Press strip ends into bottom pastry on rim. Fold bottom pastry over strip ends; seal and crimp edge (see page 446). Bake as directed in recipes.

PER SERVING PLAIN, NUT, OR LATTICE VARIATIONS: 303 cal., 18 g total fat (7 g sat. fat, 2 g trans fat), 15 mg chol., 333 mg sodium, 30 g carbo., 1 g fiber, 4 g pro.
EXCHANGES: 2 Starch, 3 Fat

PASTRY FOR SINGLE-CRUST PIE

START TO FINISH: 15 MINUTES
MAKES: 1 PIECRUST (8 SERVINGS)

- 1½ cups all-purpose flour
- ½ teaspoon salt
- ¼ cup shortening
- ¼ cup butter, cut up, or shortening
- ¼ to ⅓ cup ice water

PREPARING PIE PASTRY, STEP-BY-STEP

1. With pastry blender, cut in shortening and butter until the pieces are pea size. **2.** Place pastry ball on a lightly floured surface. Roll from center out until circle is 12 inches across. **3.** Wrap pastry around rolling pin; unroll it over the plate. Do not stretch it or it might shrink. **4.** For double-crust pie, trim bottom pastry even with plate's edge. **5.** Fold top pastry edge under bottom pastry; crimp.

1 In a medium bowl stir together flour and salt. Using pastry blender, cut in shortening and butter until pieces are pea size (see photo 1, page 444).

2 Sprinkle 1 tablespoon of the water over part of the flour mixture; toss with a fork. Push moistened pastry to side of bowl. Repeat moistening flour mixture, using 1 tablespoon of the water at a time, until flour mixture is moistened. Gather flour mixture into a ball, kneading gently until it holds together.

3 On a lightly floured surface use your hands to slightly flatten pastry. Roll pastry from center to edges into a circle about 12 inches in diameter (see photo 2, page 444).

4 Wrap pastry circle around the rolling pin. Unroll into a 9-inch pie plate (see photo 3, below). Ease pastry into pie plate without stretching it.

5 Trim pastry to ½ inch beyond edge of pie plate. Fold under extra pastry even with the plate's edge. Crimp edge as desired (see page 446). Do not prick pastry. Fill and bake as directed in recipes.

PER SERVING: 191 cal., 12 g total fat (5 g sat. fat, 1 g trans fat), 15 mg chol., 187 mg sodium, 18 g carbo., 1 g fiber, 2 g pro. EXCHANGES: 1 Starch, 2½ Fat

BAKED PASTRY SHELL: Preheat oven to 450°F. Prepare as directed, except prick bottom and sides of pastry with a fork. Line pastry with a double thickness of foil. Bake for 8 minutes. Remove foil. Bake for 6 to 8 minutes more or until golden. Cool on a wire rack.

BAKED PASTRY TART SHELL: Preheat oven to 450°F. Prepare as directed through Step 3. Wrap pastry around rolling pin. Unroll it into a 10-inch tart pan with a removable bottom. Ease pastry into pan without stretching it. Press pastry into fluted sides of tart pan and trim edges. Prick pastry with a fork. Line pastry with a double thickness of foil. Bake for 8 minutes. Remove foil. Bake for 6 to 8 minutes more or until golden. Cool on a wire rack.

RICH TART PASTRY

PREP: 15 MINUTES CHILL: 30 TO 60 MINUTES
MAKES: 1 TART CRUST (8 SERVINGS)

- 1¼ cups all-purpose flour
- ¼ cup sugar
- ½ cup cold butter, cut up
- 2 egg yolks, lightly beaten
- 1 tablespoon ice water

1 In a medium bowl stir together flour and sugar. Using a pastry blender, cut in butter until pieces are pea size (see photo 1, page 444). In a small bowl stir together egg yolks and water. Gradually stir egg yolk mixture into flour mixture. Using your fingers, gently knead the dough just until a ball forms. Cover pastry with plastic wrap and chill for 30 to 60 minutes or until dough is easy to handle.

2 On a floured surface slightly flatten the pastry. Roll pastry from center to edges into a circle 12 inches in diameter (see photo 2, page 444).

3 Wrap pastry circle around rolling pin. Unroll it into a 10-inch tart pan with a removable bottom. Ease pastry into pan without stretching it. Press pastry into fluted sides of pan; trim edges. Do not prick pastry. Fill and bake as directed in recipes.

PER SERVING: 211 cal., 13 g total fat (8 g sat. fat, 0 g trans fat), 83 mg chol., 84 mg sodium, 21 g carbo., 1 g fiber, 3 g pro. EXCHANGES: 1½ Starch, 2½ Fat

CREATIVE CRIMPING

HOW YOU FINISH YOUR PASTRY EDGES ADDS A CERTAIN HOMESPUN GRACE TO YOUR CREATIONS. HERE ARE A FEW IDEAS FOR CRAFTING ENTICING EDGES.

SMALL SHAPES

Trim the pastry even with the pie plate edge. With a cookie cutter, cut small circles (or other small shapes) from additional rolled-out pastry or scraps. Brush the edge of the pastry in the pie plate lightly with water. Place the circles (or other shapes) around the pastry edge, overlapping them slightly, and gently press.

THE WEAVE

Trim the pastry even with the edge of the pie plate. Cut the pastry at ½- to 1-inch intervals. Fold every other section in toward the center. If desired, angle every two sections toward each other at the inside of the pie.

SPOON FINISH

Trim the pastry even with the edge of the pie plate. Use a spoon to press a design into edge. Other utensils, such as a fork, can be used to make simple decorative edges.

CLASSIC FLUTE

Fold under the pastry edge as directed. Place one of your thumbs against the inside edge of the pastry. Using the thumb and index finger of your other hand, press the pastry from the outside into your first thumb to form a crimp. Continue around the edge. You can leave the flutes straight or slant them slightly toward the inside edge of the pie plate.

SMALL SHAPES

THE WEAVE

SPOON FINISH

CLASSIC FLUTE

OIL PASTRY FOR SINGLE-CRUST PIE

START TO FINISH: 10 MINUTES
MAKES: 1 PIECRUST (8 SERVINGS)

1⅓ cups all-purpose flour

¼ teaspoon salt

¼ cup vegetable oil

3 to 4 tablespoons milk

1 In a medium bowl stir together flour and salt. Add oil and 3 tablespoons milk all at once to flour. Stir lightly with a fork until combined. If necessary, stir in 1 tablespoon more milk to moisten (pastry will appear crumbly). Form pastry into a ball.

2 On a lightly floured surface use your hands to slightly flatten pastry ball. Roll dough from center to edges into a circle about 12 inches in diameter (press any cracks back together). Ease pastry circle into a 9-inch pie plate without stretching it (see photo 3, page 445). Trim pastry to ½ inch beyond edge of pie plate. Fold under extra pastry. Crimp edge as desired (see page 446). Do not prick pastry. Fill and bake as directed in recipes.

BAKED OIL PASTRY SHELL: Preheat oven to 450°F. Prepare as directed, except prick bottom and sides of pastry with a fork. Line pastry with a double thickness of foil. Bake for 8 minutes. Remove foil. Bake 5 to 6 minutes more or until crust is golden. Cool on a wire rack.

PER SERVING: 139 cal., 7 g total fat (1 g sat. fat, 0 g trans fat), 0 mg chol., 75 mg sodium, 16 g carbo., 1 g fiber, 2 g pro. EXCHANGES: 1 Starch, 1 Fat

GRAHAM CRACKER CRUST

PREP: 10 MINUTES **BAKE:** 5 MINUTES **OVEN:** 375°F
MAKES: 1 PIECRUST (8 SERVINGS)

Nonstick cooking spray

⅓ cup butter

¼ cup sugar

1¼ cups finely crushed graham crackers (about 18)

1 Preheat oven to 375°F. Lightly coat a 9-inch pie plate with cooking spray; set aside. Melt butter; stir in sugar. Add crackers; toss to mix. Spread in pie plate; press evenly onto bottom and sides. Bake 5 minutes or until edges are light brown. Cool completely on a wire rack. Fill as directed in recipes.

GINGERSNAP CRUST: Prepare as directed, except omit sugar and substitute 1¼ cups finely crushed crisp gingersnaps (20 to 22) for graham crackers.

VANILLA WAFER CRUST: Prepare as directed, except omit sugar and substitute 1½ cups finely crushed vanilla wafers (about 44) for graham crackers.

CHOCOLATE WAFER CRUST: Prepare as directed, except omit sugar; substitute 1½ cups finely crushed chocolate wafers (about 25) for graham crackers. Do not bake; chill 1 hour or until firm.

PER SERVING GRAHAM CRACKER, GINGERSNAP, VANILLA WAFER, OR CHOCOLATE WAFER VARIATIONS: 159 cal., 9 g total fat (5 g sat. fat, 0 g trans fat), 20 mg chol., 180 mg sodium, 17 g carbo., 0 g fiber, 2 g pro. EXCHANGES: 1 Starch, 1½ Fat

CRUMB-TOPPED FRUIT PIE (photo, page 441)

PREP: 35 MINUTES **BAKE:** 65 MINUTES
OVEN: 375°F **MAKES:** 8 SLICES

1 recipe Pastry for Single-Crust Pie (page 444)

⅔ cup rolled oats

⅔ cup all-purpose flour

½ cup packed brown sugar

¼ teaspoon salt

¼ teaspoon ground cinnamon

6 tablespoons butter

1 recipe Fruit-Pie Filling (see chart, page 448)

1 Preheat oven to 375°F. Prepare and roll out Pastry for Single-Crust Pie. Line a 9-inch pie plate with the pastry circle and trim. Crimp edge as desired (see page 446); set aside.

2 In a medium bowl stir together the oats, flour, brown sugar, salt, and cinnamon. Using a pastry blender, cut in butter until mixture resembles coarse crumbs; set aside.

3 In a large bowl prepare desired Fruit-Pie Filling, first combining the sugar and starch in the amounts specified for desired fruit. Add desired fruit. Gently toss fruit until coated. (If using frozen fruit, let mixture stand for 30 to 45 minutes or until fruit is partially thawed but still icy.)

4 Transfer fruit filling to the pastry-lined pie plate. Sprinkle oats mixture over filling.

5 To prevent overbrowning, cover edge of pie with foil. Bake 30 minutes (50 minutes for frozen fruit). Remove foil. Bake for 35 to 40 minutes more or until fruit is tender and topping is golden. (If necessary, loosely cover top of pie with foil the last 10 to 15 minutes.) Cool on a wire rack.

PER SLICE APPLE VARIATION: 504 cal., 22 g total fat (11 g sat. fat, 1 g trans fat), 38 mg chol., 325 mg sodium, 73 g carbo., 3 g fiber, 6 g pro. EXCHANGES: 1 Fruit, 2 Starch, 2 Other Carbo., 4 Fat

DOUBLE-CRUST FRUIT PIE

PREP: 30 MINUTES **BAKE:** 65 MINUTES
OVEN: 375°F **MAKES:** 8 SLICES

> 1 recipe Pastry for Double-Crust Pie
> (page 444)
> 1 recipe Fruit-Pie Filling (see chart, below)
> Milk (optional)
> Sugar (optional)

1 Preheat oven to 375°F. Prepare and roll out Pastry for Double-Crust Pie. Line a 9-inch pie plate with a pastry circle; set aside.

2 In a very large bowl prepare desired Fruit-Pie Filling, first combining the sugar and starch in amounts specified for desired fruit. Add the desired fruit; gently toss fruit until coated. (If using frozen fruit, let mixture stand for 30 to 45 minutes or until the fruit is partially thawed but still icy.)

3 Transfer fruit filling to the pastry-lined pie plate. Trim bottom pastry to edge of pie plate. Cut slits in remaining pastry circle; place on filling and seal. Crimp edge as desired (see page 446).

4 If desired, brush top pastry with milk and sprinkle with additional sugar. To prevent overbrowning, cover edge of pie with foil (see page 443). Place a foil-lined baking sheet on the rack below the pie in oven. Bake pie for 30 minutes (50 minutes for frozen fruit). Remove foil. Bake for 35 to 40 minutes more or until fruit is tender and filling is bubbly. (If necessary, loosely cover top of pie with foil the last 10 to 15 minutes.) Cool on a wire rack.

PER SLICE APPLE VARIATION: 399 cal., 18 g total fat (7 g sat. fat, 2 g trans fat), 15 mg chol., 333 mg sodium, 54 g carbo., 2 g fiber, 5 g pro.
EXCHANGES: 1 Fruit, 2 Starch, ½ Other Carbo., 3½ Fat

FRUIT-PIE FILLINGS

From rhubarb and berries in spring and summer to apples and pears in fall and winter, your homemade pies can march to the beat of what's fresh and in season. You can even bridge the seasons using frozen fruit. Simply choose a fruit; adjust the sugar amount according to the fruit's sweetness and adjust the starch amount according to its juiciness.* This chart shows you how.

Fruit	Amount of Fruit	Sugar	Starch
Apples, peeled, cored, and thinly sliced	6 cups	½ to ¾ cup	2 tablespoons all-purpose flour
Blackberries	6 cups	1 to 1¼ cups	⅓ cup all-purpose flour or 3 tablespoons quick-cooking tapioca or cornstarch
Blueberries	6 cups	1 to 1¼ cups	¼ cup all-purpose flour or 2 tablespoons quick-cooking tapioca or cornstarch
Cherries, tart, red, and pitted	6 cups	1¼ to 1½ cups	⅓ cup all-purpose flour or 3 tablespoons quick-cooking tapioca or cornstarch
Gooseberries, stemmed	6 cups	1¼ to 1½ cups	⅓ cup all-purpose flour or 3 tablespoons quick-cooking tapioca or cornstarch
Nectarines, pitted and thinly sliced	6 cups	½ to 1 cup	3 tablespoons all-purpose flour or 4½ teaspoons quick-cooking tapioca or cornstarch
Peaches, peeled, pitted, and thinly sliced	6 cups	½ to 1 cup	3 tablespoons all-purpose flour or 4½ teaspoons quick-cooking tapioca or cornstarch
Pears, peeled, cored, and thinly sliced	6 cups	⅓ to ½ cup	3 tablespoons all-purpose flour
Raspberries	6 cups	¾ to 1 cup	¼ cup all-purpose flour or 2 tablespoons quick-cooking tapioca or cornstarch
Rhubarb, cut into 1-inch pieces	6 cups	1¼ to 1½ cups	½ cup all-purpose flour or ¼ cup quick-cooking tapioca or cornstarch

*For added flavor, add one of the following to the filling with the sugar and starch: ½ teaspoon finely shredded lemon peel, ¼ to ½ teaspoon ground cinnamon or ground ginger, ¼ teaspoon ground allspice, or ⅛ teaspoon ground nutmeg. Or add ¼ teaspoon almond extract to the filling with the fruit.

APPLE-PEAR PRALINE PIE

PREP: 50 MINUTES **BAKE:** 82 MINUTES
COOL: 4 HOURS **OVEN:** 375°F **MAKES:** 8 SLICES

- 1 recipe Nut Pastry (page 444)
- ¾ cup granulated sugar
- ¼ cup all-purpose flour
- ½ teaspoon ground nutmeg
- ½ teaspoon ground cinnamon
  Dash salt
- 3 cups thinly sliced, peeled tart apples
- 3 cups thinly sliced, peeled pears
- 2 tablespoons butter, cut up
- ¼ cup butter
- ½ cup packed brown sugar
- 2 tablespoons milk, half-and-half,
  or light cream
- ½ cup chopped pecans

1 Preheat oven to 375°F. Prepare and roll out Nut Pastry. Line 9-inch pie plate with pastry circle.

2 In a large bowl stir together granulated sugar, flour, nutmeg, cinnamon, and salt. Add apples and pears; gently toss until coated. Transfer apple mixture to pastry-lined plate. Dot with 2 tablespoons butter. Trim bottom pastry to edge of pie plate. Cut slits in remaining pastry circle; place on filling and seal. Crimp edge as desired (see page 446).

3 To prevent overbrowning, cover edge of pie with foil. Place a foil-lined baking sheet on the rack below the pie in oven. Bake pie for 50 minutes. Remove foil. Bake for 30 to 40 minutes more or until filling is bubbly. Transfer to a wire rack.

4 In a small saucepan melt the ¼ cup butter over medium heat. Gradually stir in brown sugar and milk. Cook and stir until mixture comes to a boil. Carefully spoon over baked pie; sprinkle with pecans. Return pie to oven; bake for 2 to 3 minutes or until topping bubbles. Cool on a wire rack.

PER SLICE: 636 cal., 34 g total fat (13 g sat. fat, 2 g trans fat), 38 mg chol., 419 mg sodium, 79 g carbo., 5 g fiber, 6 g pro.
EXCHANGES: 1 Fruit, 2 Starch, 2 Other Carbo., 6½ Fat

THE APPLE OF YOUR PIE GRANNY SMITH AND CORTLAND ARE GOOD CHOICES FOR THE TART APPLES CALLED FOR IN THIS PIE. NO NEED TO PEEL THEM—THEY'RE SLICED SO THINLY, IT WON'T MATTER.

APPLE-PEAR PRALINE PIE

TRI-BERRY PIE *(photo, page 443)*

PREP: 30 MINUTES **BAKE:** 65 MINUTES **OVEN:** 375°F
MAKES: 8 SLICES

- ½ to ¾ cup sugar
- 3 tablespoons cornstarch
- 2 cups fresh or frozen red raspberries
- 1½ cups fresh or frozen blueberries
- 1½ cups fresh or frozen blackberries
- 1 recipe Pastry for Quick Lattice-Top Pie (page 444)

1 For filling, in a large bowl stir together sugar and cornstarch. Add raspberries, blueberries, and blackberries. Gently toss berries until coated. (If using frozen fruit, let mixture stand for 45 minutes or until fruit is partially thawed but still icy.)

2 Preheat oven to 375°F. Prepare and roll out Pastry for Quick Lattice-Top Pie. Line a 9-inch pie plate with a pastry circle.

3 Stir berry mixture. Transfer berry mixture to the pastry-lined pie plate. Trim bottom pastry to ½ inch beyond edge of pie plate. Continue as directed for Pastry for Quick Lattice-Top Pie (see photos 1–3, page 451).

4 To prevent overbrowning, cover edge of pie with foil (see page 443). Place a foil-lined baking sheet on the rack below pie in the oven. Bake for 30 minutes (50 minutes for frozen fruit). Remove foil. Bake for 35 to 40 minutes more or until filling is bubbly. Cool on a wire rack.

PER SLICE: 406 cal., 19 g total fat (7 g sat. fat, 2 g trans fat), 15 mg chol., 334 mg sodium, 55 g carbo., 5 g fiber, 5 g pro. EXCHANGES: ½ Fruit, 2 Starch, 1 Other Carbo., 3½ Fat

LATTICE-TOP CRANBERRY RELISH PIE

PREP: 35 MINUTES **BAKE:** 60 MINUTES
COOL: 30 MINUTES **OVEN:** 375°F **MAKES:** 8 SLICES

- ½ cup dried cranberries
- ½ cup golden raisins
- 2 teaspoons finely shredded orange peel
- ½ cup orange juice
- 1 12-ounce package fresh cranberries or frozen cranberries, thawed
- 1 cup sugar
- ¼ cup all-purpose flour
- 1 recipe Pastry for Quick Lattice-Top Pie (page 444)
- 1 egg, lightly beaten
- 1 tablespoon sugar

1 For filling, in a small saucepan combine dried cranberries, raisins, and orange juice; bring to boiling over medium heat. Remove from heat; cover and let stand 10 minutes. Transfer cranberry mixture to a large bowl; stir in fresh cranberries, the 1 cup sugar, the orange peel, and flour.

2 Preheat oven to 375°F. Prepare and roll out Pastry for Quick Lattice-Top Pie. Line a 9-inch pie plate with a pastry circle.

3 Transfer cranberry mixture to the pastry-lined plate. Trim bottom pastry to ½ inch beyond edge of plate. Continue as directed for Pastry for Quick Lattice-Top Pie (see photos 1–3, page 451). Brush with beaten egg; sprinkle with 1 tablespoon sugar.

4 To prevent overbrowning, cover edge of pie with foil (see page 443). Bake for 30 minutes. Remove foil. Bake pie for 30 to 35 minutes more or until filling is bubbly and pastry is golden. Cool on a wire rack for 30 minutes before cutting.

PER SLICE: 511 cal., 19 g total fat (7 g sat. fat, 2 g trans fat), 42 mg chol., 344 mg sodium, 81 g carbo., 4 g fiber, 6 g pro. EXCHANGES: 1 Fruit, 2 Starch, 2½ Other Carbo., 3½ Fat

FRESH STRAWBERRY PIE

PREP: 35 MINUTES **COOL:** 10 MINUTES
CHILL: 1 TO 3 HOURS **MAKES:** 8 SLICES

- 1 recipe Baked Pastry Shell (page 445)
- 9 cups medium fresh strawberries, hulled and halved
- ½ cup water
- ⅔ cup sugar
- 2 tablespoons cornstarch

1 Prepare Baked Pastry Shell; set aside.

2 For strawberry glaze, in a blender or food processor combine 1½ cups of the strawberries and the water. Cover and blend or process until smooth. In a medium saucepan combine sugar and cornstarch; stir in blended strawberry mixture. Cook and stir over medium heat until mixture is thickened and bubbly. Cook and stir 2 minutes more. If desired, stir in *red food coloring*. Remove from heat; cool for 10 minutes without stirring.

3 In a large bowl combine remaining strawberries and the strawberry glaze; toss gently to coat. Transfer strawberry mixture to the cooled pie shell. Chill pie for at least 1 hour or up to 3 hours (after 3 hours, bottom of crust starts to soften).

PER SLICE: 316 cal., 12 g total fat (5 g sat. fat, 1 g trans fat), 15 mg chol., 189 mg sodium, 49 g carbo., 4 g fiber, 4 g pro. EXCHANGES: 1 Fruit, 1 Starch, 1 Other Carbo., 2½ Fat

LATTICE-TOP CRANBERRY
RELISH PIE

ASSEMBLING A QUICK LATTICE-TOP PIE, STEP-BY-STEP

1. Place half of the pastry strips over the filling parallel to each other and 1 inch apart. **2.** Place the remaining pastry strips at 1-inch intervals perpendicular to the first strips. **3.** Before crimping the edge, roll the bottom pastry up over the ends of the pastry strips to seal. If desired, brush lightly with *milk* and sprinkle with sugar.

STRAWBERRY-RHUBARB PIE

PREP: 25 MINUTES **BAKE:** 50 MINUTES
STAND: 15 MINUTES **OVEN:** 375°F **MAKES:** 8 SLICES

1¼ cups sugar

3 tablespoons quick-cooking tapioca

¼ teaspoon salt

¼ teaspoon ground nutmeg

1 pound fresh rhubarb, cut into 1-inch
   pieces (3 cups), or one 16-ounce
   package frozen cut rhubarb

3 cups sliced fresh strawberries

1 recipe Pastry for Double-Crust Pie
   (page 444)

1 For filling, in a large bowl stir together sugar,
tapioca, salt, and nutmeg. Add rhubarb and strawberries; gently toss until coated. Let rhubarb mixture stand for 15 minutes, stirring occasionally. (If
using frozen rhubarb, let stand 45 minutes.)

2 Preheat oven to 375°F. Prepare and roll out
Pastry for Double-Crust Pie. Line 9-inch pie plate
with pastry circle (see photo 3, page 445).

3 Stir rhubarb mixture; transfer to pastry-lined
pie plate (see photo 4, page 445). Trim bottom
pastry to edge of the pie plate. Cut slits in remaining pastry; place on filling and seal. Crimp edge as
desired (see page 446).

4 To prevent overbrowning, cover edge of pie with
foil (see page 443). Place a foil-lined baking sheet
on rack below pie in oven. Bake pie 25 minutes.
Remove foil; bake 25 to 30 minutes more or until
filling bubbles and crust is golden (45 to 50 minutes
more if using frozen rhubarb). Cool on wire rack.

PER SLICE: 467 cal., 18 g total fat (7 g sat. fat, 2 g trans fat),
15 mg chol., 408 mg sodium, 71 g carbo., 3 g fiber, 5 g pro.
EXCHANGES: 1 Fruit, 2 Starch, 2 Other Carbo., 3 Fat

BLACK RASPBERRY CREAM PIE

PREP: 10 MINUTES **FREEZE:** 4 TO 24 HOURS
STAND: 5 MINUTES **MAKES:** 8 SLICES

1 recipe Graham Cracker Crust (page 447)

1 cup whipping cream

1 8-ounce package cream cheese, softened

1 10-ounce jar seedless black raspberry
   spreadable fruit
   Fresh black raspberries (optional)

1 Prepare Graham Cracker Crust; set aside.

2 In a medium mixing bowl beat whipping cream
with electric mixer on medium to high speed until
stiff peaks form; set aside.

3 In a large mixing bowl beat cream cheese with
an electric mixer on medium speed until smooth.
Add spreadable fruit; beat until combined. Fold in
whipped cream. Spoon cream mixture into crust.

4 Cover and freeze pie for 4 to 24 hours or until
firm. To serve, place pie plate on a warm, damp
cloth and let stand for 5 minutes before cutting
to loosen crust from bottom of plate. If desired,
garnish with fresh black raspberries.

PER SLICE: 438 cal., 30 g total fat (18 g sat. fat, 0 g trans fat),
93 mg chol., 282 mg sodium, 39 g carbo., 0 g fiber, 4 g pro.
EXCHANGES: 1 Starch, 1½ Other Carbo., 6 Fat

WHIPPED KEY LIME PIE

PREP: 20 MINUTES **FREEZE:** 2 TO 4 HOURS
MAKES: 8 SLICES

1 recipe Graham Cracker Crust (page 447)

1 14-ounce can (1¼ cups) sweetened
   condensed milk

1 teaspoon finely shredded Key lime peel
   or lime peel

½ cup Key lime juice or lime juice

2 cups whipping cream
   Shredded Key lime or lime peel (optional)

1 Prepare Graham Cracker Crust; set aside.

2 For filling, in a medium bowl combine sweetened condensed milk, 1 teaspoon lime peel, and
the lime juice; set aside. In a medium mixing bowl
beat 1 cup of the whipping cream with an electric
mixer on medium speed until soft peaks form. Fold
the whipped cream into lime mixture. Spoon filling
into crust. Cover and freeze for 2 to 4 hours or
until firm. Chill the remaining whipping cream.

3 To serve, remove pie from freezer. In a medium
mixing bowl beat remaining chilled whipping cream
with an electric mixer on medium to high speed
until soft peaks form. Spread whipped cream over
filling. If desired, sprinkle with additional lime peel.

PER SLICE: 529 cal., 36 g total fat (22 g sat. fat, 0 g trans fat),
119 mg chol., 266 mg sodium, 47 g carbo., 1 g fiber, 7 g pro.
EXCHANGES: 2 Starch, 1 Other Carbo., 7 Fat

NO KEY LIMES?
REGULAR LIMES MAKE A GREAT PIE TOO. JUST MAKE SURE THE JUICE IS FRESH, NOT BOTTLED.

VANILLA CREAM PIE

PREP: 50 MINUTES **BAKE:** 30 MINUTES
COOL: 60 MINUTES **CHILL:** 3 TO 6 HOURS
OVEN: 325°F **MAKES:** 8 SLICES

1 recipe Baked Pastry Shell (page 445)
4 eggs
1 recipe Meringue for Pie (page 455)
¾ cup sugar
3 tablespoons cornstarch
2½ cups half-and-half, light cream, or milk
1 tablespoon butter
1½ teaspoons vanilla

1 Prepare Baked Pastry Shell. Separate egg yolks from whites. Set aside yolks for filling and whites for Meringue for Pie.

2 Preheat oven to 325°F. For filling, in a saucepan combine sugar and cornstarch. Gradually stir in half-and-half. Cook and stir over medium-high heat until thickened and bubbly; reduce heat. Cook and stir 2 minutes more. Remove from heat. Slightly beat egg yolks with a fork. Gradually stir about 1 cup of the hot filling into yolks. Add yolk mixture to saucepan. Bring to a gentle boil, stirring constantly; reduce heat. Cook and stir 2 minutes more. Remove from heat. Stir in butter and vanilla. Keep filling warm. Prepare Meringue for Pie.

3 Pour warm filling into Baked Pastry Shell. Spread meringue over warm filling; seal to edge (see photos 1 and 2, below). Bake for 30 minutes. Cool on wire rack for 60 minutes. Chill for 3 to 6 hours before serving; cover for longer storage.

PER SLICE: 483 cal., 25 g total fat (12 g sat. fat, 1 g trans fat), 152 mg chol., 291 mg sodium, 56 g carbo., 1 g fiber, 10 g pro. EXCHANGES: 1 Starch, 3 Other Carbo., 1 Lean Meat, 4½ Fat

COCONUT CREAM PIE: Prepare as directed, except stir in 1 cup flaked coconut with butter and vanilla. Sprinkle an additional ⅓ cup flaked coconut over meringue before baking.

PER SLICE: 576 cal., 31 g total fat (18 g sat. fat, 1 g trans fat), 153 mg chol., 344 mg sodium, 64 g carbo., 2 g fiber, 11 g pro. EXCHANGES: 1 Starch, 3 Other Carbo., 1 Lean Meat, 6 Fat

BANANA CREAM PIE: Prepare as directed, except, before adding filling arrange 3 medium bananas, sliced (about 2¼ cups), over bottom of the pastry shell.

PER SLICE: 522 cal., 25 g total fat (12 g sat. fat, 1 g trans fat), 152 mg chol., 291 mg sodium, 66 g carbo., 2 g fiber, 10 g pro. EXCHANGES: 1 Starch, ½ Fruit, 3 Other Carbo., 1 Lean Meat, 4½ Fat

DARK CHOCOLATE CREAM PIE: Prepare as directed, except increase the sugar to 1 cup. Stir in 3 ounces chopped unsweetened chocolate with the half-and-half.

PER SLICE: 560 cal., 30 g total fat (16 g sat. fat, 1 g trans fat), 153 mg chol., 293 mg sodium, 65 g carbo., 2 g fiber, 11 g pro. EXCHANGES: 1 Starch, 3 Other Carbo., 1 Lean Meat, 5½ Fat

SOUR CREAM-RAISIN PIE: Prepare as directed, except decrease the sugar to ⅔ cup and increase the cornstarch to ¼ cup. Fold in 1 cup raisins and ½ cup dairy sour cream with the butter and vanilla. Heat filling mixture through but do not boil.

PER SLICE: 556 cal., 27 g total fat (14 g sat. fat, 1 g trans fat), 159 mg chol., 302 mg sodium, 69 g carbo., 1 g fiber, 10 g pro. EXCHANGES: 1 Starch, 3½ Other Carbo., 1 Lean Meat, 5 Fat

---

TOPPING PIE WITH MERINGUE, STEP-BY-STEP

1. Spoon the meringue over the warm filling, mounding it high in the center. The hot filling helps the meringue cook all the way through, minimizing weeping (the watery layer that can form between the meringue and filling layers). **2.** Use a spatula to gently spread the meringue to edges of the crust to seal it. This helps prevent the meringue from shrinking after the pie bakes and cools.

LEMON MERINGUE PIE

PREP: 25 MINUTES **BAKE:** 30 MINUTES
COOL: 60 MINUTES **CHILL:** 5 TO 6 HOURS
OVEN: 325°F **MAKES:** 8 SLICES

  1 recipe Baked Pastry Shell (page 445)
  5 eggs
  1 recipe Five-Egg White Meringue (page 455)
  2 cups sugar
  ⅓ cup cornstarch
  2 teaspoons finely shredded lemon peel
       (optional)
  1 cup water
  ¾ cup lemon juice
  ⅓ cup butter, cut up

1 Prepare Baked Pastry Shell; set aside.
Separate egg yolks from whites. Set aside yolks
for filling and whites for Five-Egg White Meringue.

2 Preheat oven to 325°F. For filling, in a medium
saucepan stir together sugar and cornstarch. Stir
in lemon peel (if desired), the water, and lemon
juice. Cook and stir over medium heat until
thickened and bubbly. Remove from heat.

3 Lightly beat egg yolks with a fork. Gradually
stir half of the hot lemon mixture into yolks. Return
egg yolk mixture to saucepan. Bring to a gentle
boil; reduce heat. Cook and stir for 2 minutes
more. Remove from heat. Stir in butter pieces until
melted. Cover filling and keep warm.

4 Prepare Five-Egg White Meringue. Pour the
warm filling into Baked Pastry Shell. Immediately
spread meringue over filling; seal to the edge
of the pastry (see photos 1 and 2, page 453).
Using the back of a spoon, add high peaks to the
meringue. Bake for 30 minutes. Cool on a wire
rack for 60 minutes. Chill for 5 to 6 hours before
serving; cover pie for longer storage.

PER SLICE: 623 cal., 23 g total fat (11 g sat. fat, 1 g trans fat),
167 mg chol., 283 mg sodium, 101 g carbo., 1 g fiber, 7 g pro.
EXCHANGES: 1 Starch, 6 Other Carbo., ½ Lean Meat, 4 Fat

A PERFECT CUT BEFORE CUTTING EACH SLICE FROM A MERINGUE-
TOPPED PIE, DIP THE KNIFE IN WATER AND DO NOT DRY IT OFF. THIS
PREVENTS THE MERINGUE FROM STICKING TO THE KNIFE.

MERINGUE FOR PIE

PREP: 15 MINUTES **STAND:** 30 MINUTES
MAKES: 8 SERVINGS (ENOUGH TO TOP ONE 9-INCH PIE)

4 egg whites
1 teaspoon vanilla
½ teaspoon cream of tartar
½ cup sugar

1 Allow egg whites to stand at room temperature for 30 minutes. In a mixing bowl combine whites, vanilla, and cream of tartar. Beat with electric mixer on medium speed about 1 minute or until soft peaks form (tips curl; see photo 1, page 177).

2 Gradually add sugar, 1 tablespoon at a time, beating on high speed about 5 minutes or until mixture forms stiff, glossy peaks (tips stand straight; see photo 2, page 177) and sugar dissolves (rub a small amount between two fingers; it should feel completely smooth).

3 Immediately spread meringue over hot pie filling, sealing to edge of pastry (see photo 2, page 453). Bake as directed in recipes.

PER SERVING: 59 cal., 0 g total fat, 0 mg chol., 28 mg sodium, 13 g carbo., 0 g fiber, 2 g pro.
EXCHANGES: 1 Other Carbo.

FIVE-EGG WHITE MERINGUE: Prepare as directed, except use 5 egg whites and 1 cup sugar. In Step 2, beat about 6 minutes or until stiff peaks form. Continue as directed in Step 3.

PER SERVING: 109 cal., 0 g total fat, 0 mg chol., 34 mg sodium, 26 g carbo., 0 g fiber, 2 g pro.
EXCHANGES: 1½ Other Carbo.

BEST EVER

PUMPKIN PIE

PREP: 30 MINUTES **BAKE:** 60 MINUTES
COOL: 60 MINUTES **OVEN:** 400°F **MAKES:** 8 SLICES

1 recipe Pastry for Single-Crust Pie (page 444)
1 15-ounce can pumpkin
¾ cup packed brown sugar
1¼ teaspoons ground cinnamon
1 teaspoon ground ginger
½ teaspoon salt
¼ teaspoon ground cloves
¼ teaspoon finely shredded orange peel (optional)
4 eggs, lightly beaten
1½ cups half-and-half or light cream

1 Preheat oven to 400°F. Prepare and roll out Pastry for Single-Crust Pie. Line a 9-inch pie plate with pastry circle and trim. Crimp edge as desired (see page 446). Do not prick pastry. Line pastry with a double thickness of foil. Bake for 15 minutes. Remove foil.

2 Meanwhile, in a large bowl combine pumpkin, brown sugar, cinnamon, ginger, salt, cloves, and (if desired) orange peel. Add eggs; beat lightly with a fork until combined. Gradually add half-and-half; stir just until combined.

3 Place the partially baked piecrust on the oven rack. Carefully pour pumpkin mixture into pastry shell. To prevent overbrowning, cover edge of pie with foil (see page 443). Bake for 20 minutes. Remove foil. Bake for 25 to 30 minutes more or until a knife inserted near center comes out clean. Cool on a wire rack. Cover and chill within 2 hours.

PER SLICE: 449 cal., 25 g total fat (13 g sat. fat, 1 g trans fat), 158 mg chol., 400 mg sodium, 49 g carbo., 3 g fiber, 8 g pro.
EXCHANGES: 1 Starch, 2 Other Carbo., ½ Lean Meat, 4½ Fat

SWEET POTATO PIE

PREP: 30 MINUTES **BAKE:** 35 MINUTES
COOL: 30 MINUTES **OVEN:** 375°F **MAKES:** 8 SLICES

1 recipe Baked Pastry Shell (page 445)
2 cups mashed cooked sweet potatoes or one 17.2-ounce can sweet potatoes, drained and mashed
½ cup sugar
½ teaspoon ground cinnamon
¼ teaspoon ground allspice
¼ teaspoon ground nutmeg
⅛ teaspoon salt
3 eggs, lightly beaten
1 cup buttermilk or dairy sour cream

1 Prepare Baked Pastry Shell; set aside. Preheat oven to 375°F. For filling, in a large bowl stir together sweet potatoes, sugar, cinnamon, allspice, nutmeg, and salt. Add eggs; beat lightly with a fork just until combined. Gradually stir in buttermilk until thoroughly combined.

2 Place Baked Pastry Shell on the oven rack. Carefully pour filling into pastry shell. Bake for 35 to 40 minutes or until knife inserted near the center comes out clean. Cool on a wire rack for at least 30 minutes. Cover and chill within 2 hours.

PER SLICE: 342 cal., 14 g total fat (6 g sat. fat, 1 g trans fat), 96 mg chol., 303 mg sodium, 47 g carbo., 3 g fiber, 7 g pro.
EXCHANGES: 2 Starch, 1 Other Carbo., 2½ Fat

PECAN PIE

PREP: 25 MINUTES **BAKE:** 45 MINUTES
OVEN: 350°F **MAKES:** 8 SLICES

- 1 recipe Pastry for Single-Crust Pie (page 444)
- 3 eggs, lightly beaten
- 1 cup light-color corn syrup
- ⅔ cup sugar
- ⅓ cup butter or margarine, melted
- 1 teaspoon vanilla
- 1¼ cups pecan halves or chopped macadamia nuts

1 Preheat oven to 350°F. Prepare and roll out Pastry for Single-Crust Pie. Line a 9-inch pie plate with the pastry circle and trim. Crimp edge as desired (see page 446).

2 For filling, in a medium bowl combine eggs, corn syrup, sugar, butter, and vanilla; mix well. Stir in pecan halves.

3 Place the pastry-lined pie plate on the oven rack. Carefully pour filling into the pastry shell. To prevent overbrowning, cover edge of pie with foil (see page 443). Bake for 25 minutes. Remove foil. Bake for 20 to 25 minutes more or until a knife inserted near the center comes out clean. Cool on a wire rack. Cover and chill within 2 hours.

PER SLICE: 532 cal., 34 g total fat (12 g sat. fat, 1 g trans fat), 115 mg chol., 281 mg sodium, 54 g carbo., 2 g fiber, 6 g pro.
EXCHANGES: 1 Starch, 2½ Other Carbo., ½ High-Fat Meat, 6 Fat

CHOCOLATE PECAN PIE: Prepare as directed, except before adding the filling to the pastry-lined pie plate pat ½ cup semisweet chocolate pieces onto the bottom of pastry.

PER SLICE: 584 cal., 37 g total fat (14 g sat. fat, 1 g trans fat), 115 mg chol., 283 mg sodium, 61 g carbo., 3 g fiber, 7 g pro.
EXCHANGES: 1 Starch, 3 Other Carbo., ½ High-Fat Meat, 6½ Fat

BEST EVER

SNICKERDOODLE PIE

PREP: 40 MINUTES **BAKE:** 45 MINUTES
COOL: 30 MINUTES **OVEN:** 350°F **MAKES:** 10 SLICES

- 1 recipe Pastry for Single-Crust Pie (page 444)
- 1 tablespoon granulated sugar, raw sugar, or coarse sugar
- ¾ teaspoon ground cinnamon
- 2 teaspoons butter, melted
- ½ cup packed brown sugar
- ¼ cup butter
- 3 tablespoons water
- 2 tablespoons light-color corn syrup
- 1½ teaspoons vanilla
- ¼ cup butter, softened
- ½ cup granulated sugar
- ¼ cup powdered sugar
- 1 teaspoon baking powder
- ½ teaspoon salt
- ¼ teaspoon cream of tartar
- 1 egg
- ½ cup milk
- 1¼ cups all-purpose flour

1 Preheat oven to 350°F. Prepare pastry and roll out Pastry for a Single-Crust Pie. Line 9-inch pie plate with the pastry circle and trim. Crimp edge as desired (see page 446). Combine the 1 tablespoon sugar and ½ teaspoon of the cinnamon. Brush the 2 teaspoons melted butter over crust. Sprinkle with 1 teaspoon cinnamon-sugar mixture; set aside.

2 For syrup, in a small saucepan combine brown sugar, ¼ cup butter, the water, corn syrup, and the remaining ¼ teaspoon cinnamon. Bring to boiling over medium heat, stirring to dissolve sugar. Boil gently for 2 minutes. Remove from heat. Stir in ½ teaspoon of the vanilla; set aside.

3 For filling, in a large mixing bowl beat ¼ cup softened butter with an electric mixer on medium speed for 30 seconds. Beat in ½ cup granulated sugar, the powdered sugar, baking powder, salt, and cream of tartar until well combined. Beat in egg and remaining 1 teaspoon vanilla. Gradually beat in milk until combined. Beat in flour. Spread evenly in pastry-lined pie plate. Slowly pour syrup over filling in pie plate. Sprinkle with remaining cinnamon-sugar mixture.

4 To prevent overbrowning, cover edge of pie with foil (see page 443). Bake for 25 minutes. Remove foil; bake about 20 minutes more or until top is puffed and golden brown and a toothpick inserted near center comes out clean. Cool on a wire rack for at least 30 minutes.

PER SLICE: 423 cal., 20 g total fat (11 g sat. fat, 1 g trans fat), 61 mg chol., 380 mg sodium, 55 g carbo., 1 g fiber, 5 g pro.
EXCHANGES: 2 Starch, 1½ Other Carbo., 3½ Fat

PRESSED FOR TIME?
PURCHASED ROLLED UNBAKED REFRIGERATED PIECRUSTS ARE THE NEXT BEST THING TO HOMEMADE.

BROWNIE WALNUT PIE

PREP: 40 MINUTES **COOL:** 20 MINUTES
BAKE: 50 MINUTES **OVEN:** 350°F **MAKES:** 8 SLICES

- ½ cup butter
- 3 ounces unsweetened chocolate, cut up
- 1 recipe Pastry for Single-Crust Pie (page 444)
- 3 eggs, lightly beaten
- 1½ cups sugar
- ½ cup all-purpose flour
- 1 teaspoon vanilla
- 1 cup chopped walnuts
- 1 recipe Hot Fudge Sauce (page 545); fresh fruit, such as raspberries, sliced strawberries, or sliced peaches; vanilla ice cream; and/or chopped walnuts (optional)

1 For filling, in a small heavy saucepan melt butter and chocolate over low heat, stirring frequently. Remove from heat; cool for 20 minutes.

2 Preheat oven to 350°F. Prepare and roll out Pastry for Single-Crust Pie. Line a 9-inch pie plate with the pastry circle and trim. Crimp edge as desired (see page 446).

3 For filling, in a medium bowl combine eggs, sugar, flour, and vanilla; stir in the chocolate mixture and nuts.

4 Pour filling into a pastry-lined pie plate. Bake for 50 to 55 minutes or until a knife inserted near the center comes out clean. Cool on a wire rack. If desired, serve with Hot Fudge Sauce, fresh fruit, vanilla ice cream, and/or chopped walnuts.

PER SLICE: 645 cal., 41 g total fat (17 g sat. fat, 1 g trans fat), 125 mg chol., 298 mg sodium, 67 g carbo., 4 g fiber, 9 g pro.
EXCHANGES: 2½ Starch, 2 Other Carbo., 7½ Fat

BROWNIE CHIP PIE: Prepare as directed, except substitute 1 cup semisweet chocolate pieces, chocolate-mint pieces, or raspberry-flavored pieces for the walnuts.

PER SLICE: 653 cal., 37 g total fat (20 g sat. fat, 1 g trans fat), 125 mg chol., 300 mg sodium, 79 g carbo., 4 g fiber, 8 g pro.
EXCHANGES: 2½ Starch, 2½ Other Carbo., 7 Fat

CUSTARD PIE

PREP: 25 MINUTES **BAKE:** 52 MINUTES
COOL: 60 MINUTES **OVEN:** 450°F/350°F
MAKES: 8 SLICES

- 1 recipe Pastry for Single-Crust Pie (page 444)
- 4 eggs
- ½ cup sugar
- 2 teaspoons vanilla

BROWNIE WALNUT PIE

- ⅛ teaspoon salt
- ⅛ teaspoon ground nutmeg
- 2 cups half-and-half, light cream, or whole milk

1 Preheat oven to 450°F. Prepare and roll out Pastry for Single-Crust Pie. Line a 9-inch pie plate with pastry circle and trim. Crimp edge as desired (see page 446). Line pastry with a double thickness of foil. Bake for 8 minutes. Remove foil. Bake for 4 to 5 minutes more or until set and dry. Remove from oven; reduce the oven temperature to 350°F.

2 Meanwhile, for filling, in a medium bowl lightly beat eggs with a fork. Stir in sugar, vanilla, salt, and nutmeg. Gradually stir in half-and-half until mixture is thoroughly combined.

3 Place the partially baked pastry-lined pie plate on the oven rack. Carefully pour filling into pastry shell. To prevent overbrowning, cover edge of pie with foil (see page 443). Bake for 25 minutes. Remove foil. Bake for 15 to 20 minutes or until a knife inserted near the center comes out clean. To serve warm, cool on a wire rack for at least 60 minutes. Cover and chill within 2 hours. For longer storage, cover and chill for 2 days.

PER SLICE: 357 cal., 21 g total fat (10 g sat. fat, 1 g trans fat), 143 mg chol., 283 mg sodium, 33 g carbo., 1 g fiber, 7 g pro.
EXCHANGES: 1 Starch, 1 Other Carbo., ½ Lean Meat, 4 Fat

FRENCH SILK PIE

PREP: 40 MINUTES **CHILL:** 5 TO 24 HOURS
MAKES: 8 SLICES

- 1 recipe Baked Pastry Shell (page 445)
- 1 cup whipping cream
- 1 cup semisweet chocolate pieces (6 ounces)
- ⅓ cup butter
- ⅓ cup sugar
- 2 egg yolks, lightly beaten
- 3 tablespoons crème de cacao or whipping cream
- 1 cup whipped cream

1 Prepare Baked Pastry Shell; set aside. In a medium heavy saucepan combine 1 cup whipping cream, chocolate pieces, butter, and sugar. Cook over low heat, stirring constantly, until chocolate is melted (about 10 minutes). Remove from heat. Gradually stir half of the hot mixture into beaten egg yolks. Return egg mixture to chocolate mixture in pan. Cook over medium-low heat, stirring constantly, until mixture is slightly thickened and begins to bubble (about 5 minutes). Remove from heat. (Mixture might appear slightly curdled.) Stir in crème de cacao. Place the saucepan in a bowl of ice water, stirring occasionally, until the mixture stiffens and becomes hard to stir (about 20 minutes).

2 Transfer the chocolate mixture to a medium mixing bowl. Beat chocolate mixture with an electric mixer on medium to high speed for 2 to 3 minutes or until light and fluffy. Spread filling in the Baked Pastry Shell. Cover and chill for 5 to 24 hours. To serve, top with whipped cream.

PER SLICE: 583 cal., 44 g total fat (25 g sat. fat, 1 g trans fat), 150 mg chol., 263 mg sodium, 44 g carbo., 2 g fiber, 7 g pro. EXCHANGES: ½ Milk, 1 Starch, 1½ Other Carbo., 8½ Fat

STRAWBERRY ICE CREAM PIE

PREP: 20 MINUTES **FREEZE:** 4 HOURS
STAND: 10 MINUTES **MAKES:** 8 SLICES

- 2 pints (4 cups) strawberry ice cream
- ½ cup sliced almonds, toasted (see tip, page 20) (optional)
- 1 purchased graham cracker crumb pie shell* or 1 recipe Graham Cracker Crust (page 447)
- ¾ cup hot fudge ice cream topping, warmed
  Whole strawberries (optional)

Whipped cream (optional)
Sliced almonds, toasted (see tip, page 20) (optional)

1 In a chilled bowl stir ice cream until softened but not melted. If desired, stir in ½ cup almonds. Spoon ice cream mixture into pie shell, spreading evenly. Cover; freeze about 4 hours or until firm.

2 To serve, let pie stand at room temperature for 10 to 15 minutes before cutting. Top slices with hot fudge topping and (if desired) strawberries, whipped cream, and additional toasted almonds.

*****NOTE:** Brushing the crust with egg white and prebaking it makes it easier to cut. Preheat oven to 375°F. Brush pie shell with a lightly beaten egg white and bake 5 minutes. Cool completely on a wire rack before filling.

PER SLICE: 323 cal., 14 g total fat (7 g sat. fat, 0 g trans fat), 15 mg chol., 193 mg sodium, 44 g carbo., 0 g fiber, 4 g pro. EXCHANGES: 1 Starch, 2 Other Carbo., 2½ Fat

CARAMEL-BUTTER PECAN ICE CREAM PIE: Prepare as directed, except use butter pecan ice cream. Omit almonds, hot fudge topping, and strawberries. Drizzle slices with caramel ice cream topping. If desired, top with whipped cream and chopped toasted pecans.

PER SLICE: 340 cal., 16 g total fat (6 g sat. fat, 0 g trans fat), 20 mg chol., 304 mg sodium, 48 g carbo., 0 g fiber, 3 g pro. EXCHANGES: 1 Starch, 2 Other Carbo., 3 Fat

PEPPERMINT-STICK ICE CREAM PIE: Prepare as directed, except use peppermint ice cream and a purchased chocolate-flavored crumb pie shell.* Omit almonds, strawberries, and whipped cream. Top slices with the hot fudge topping. If desired, sprinkle with crushed peppermint candies.

PER SLICE: 345 cal., 15 g total fat (9 g sat. fat, 0 g trans fat), 30 mg chol., 269 mg sodium, 47 g carbo., 0 g fiber, 5 g pro. EXCHANGES: 1 Starch, 2 Other Carbo., 3 Fat

S'MORES ICE CREAM PIE: Prepare as directed, except use chocolate ice cream. Omit almonds and strawberries. Stir 1 cup tiny marshmallows into ice cream. Spoon ice cream mixture into a purchased graham cracker crumb or chocolate-flavored crumb pie shell.* Sprinkle slices with additional marshmallows. Drizzle with hot fudge topping. If desired, top with whipped cream and chopped honey-roasted peanuts.

PER SLICE: 376 cal., 16 g total fat (9 g sat. fat, 0 g trans fat), 22 mg chol., 219 mg sodium, 54 g carbo., 1 g fiber, 5 g pro. EXCHANGES: 1 Starch, 2½ Other Carbo., 3 Fat

COUNTRY PEACH TART

PREP: 30 MINUTES **BAKE:** 50 MINUTES
COOL: 30 MINUTES **OVEN:** 375°F **MAKES:** 8 SLICES

- 1 recipe Pastry for Single-Crust Pie (page 444)
- ¼ cup sugar
- 4 teaspoons all-purpose flour
- ¼ teaspoon ground nutmeg, cinnamon, or ginger
- 3 cups sliced, peeled peaches or nectarines (about 1¼ pounds)
- 1 tablespoon lemon juice
- 1 tablespoon sliced almonds
  Milk

1 Preheat oven to 375°F. Prepare pastry for Single-Crust Pie through Step 2. On a large piece of lightly floured parchment paper roll pastry into a 13-inch circle. Slide paper with pastry onto a baking sheet; set aside.

2 For filling, in a large bowl stir together ¼ cup sugar, the flour, and nutmeg. Add peaches and lemon juice; toss until coated. Mound filling in center of pastry, leaving the outer 2 inches uncovered (see photo 1, below). Fold uncovered pastry up over filling, pleating as necessary and using paper to lift pastry border (see photo 2, below). Sprinkle filling with sliced almonds (see photo 3, below). Lightly brush pastry top and sides with milk and sprinkle with additional sugar.

3 Bake for 50 to 55 minutes or until filling is bubbly and crust is golden. If necessary to prevent overbrowning, cover edge of tart with foil the last 5 to 10 minutes of baking. Cool for 30 minutes on the baking sheet on a wire rack.

PER SLICE: 253 cal., 13 g total fat (5 g sat. fat, 1 g trans fat), 15 mg chol., 188 mg sodium, 32 g carbo., 2 g fiber, 3 g pro. EXCHANGES: ½ Fruit, 1 Starch, ½ Other Carbo., 2½ Fat

COUNTRY PEAR TART: Prepare as directed, except increase sugar to ⅓ cup and substitute 4 cups sliced, peeled pears (1½ pounds) for the peaches; substitute 1 tablespoon finely chopped crystallized ginger or ¼ teaspoon ground ginger and ¼ teaspoon ground cinnamon for the nutmeg. Assemble tart as directed, except dot the filling with 1 tablespoon butter.

PER SLICE: 293 cal., 15 g total fat (5 g sat. fat, 1 g trans fat), 15 mg chol., 189 mg sodium, 43 g carbo., 3 g fiber, 3 g pro. EXCHANGES: ½ Fruit, 1 Starch, 1½ Other Carbo., 2½ Fat

PREPARING COUNTRY PEACH TART, STEP-BY-STEP

1. Spoon the filling in the center of the pastry circle. Leave a 2-inch pastry border around the filling. **2.** Gently fold the pastry edge over the filling. Pleat the pastry as necessary to keep it flat against the fruit, using the parchment to lift the pastry. **3.** Sprinkle the sliced almonds evenly over the filling.

FRESH FRUIT AND CREAM TARTS

PREP: 40 MINUTES **BAKE:** 13 MINUTES
CHILL: 4 HOURS **OVEN:** 450°F **MAKES:** 8 TARTS

- 1 recipe Pastry Cream
- 1 recipe Rich Tart Pastry (page 445)
- 2 cups fresh fruit, such as sliced strawberries; raspberries; blackberries; peeled, sliced papaya; and/or peeled, sliced kiwifruit

1 Prepare and chill Pastry Cream. Preheat oven to 450°F. Prepare Rich Tart Pastry through Step 1; divide pastry into eight portions. On a floured surface use your hands to slightly flatten each portion. Roll pastry from center to edges into circles about 5 inches in diameter. Transfer each pastry circle to a 4-inch tart pan with a removable bottom. Press pastry into fluted sides of tart pans; trim edges. Prick bottoms and sides of pastry shells. Line pastry shells with a double thickness of foil. Place on a large baking sheet. Bake for 8 minutes. Remove foil. Bake for 5 to 6 minutes more or until pastry shells are golden. Cool on a wire rack.

2 To serve, divide the chilled Pastry Cream among the baked pastry shells. Arrange fresh fruit on top of each tart.* Remove sides of tart pans.

PASTRY CREAM: In a heavy saucepan combine ½ cup sugar, 4 teaspoons cornstarch, and ¼ teaspoon salt. Gradually stir in 2 cups half-and-half. If desired, add 1 vanilla bean, split lengthwise. Cook and stir over medium heat until thickened and bubbly. Cook and stir 1 minute more. Gradually stir half of the hot mixture into 4 beaten egg yolks. Return yolk mixture to pan. Bring to a boil; reduce heat. Cook and stir 2 minutes. Remove from heat. Strain Pastry Cream into a bowl. If not using vanilla bean, stir in 1 teaspoon vanilla. Place Pastry Cream bowl in a bowl of ice water; let stand 5 minutes, stirring occasionally. Cover surface with plastic wrap. Chill for 4 hours or until cold; do not stir. Makes 2 cups.

WHOLE FRESH FRUIT AND CREAM TART:
Prepare Rich Tart Pastry as directed, except roll out Rich Tart Pastry as on page 444 and transfer pastry circle to a 10-inch tart pan with a removable bottom. Press pastry into fluted sides of tart pan and trim edges. Prick pastry. Bake and cool as directed. To serve, fill cooled shell with Pastry Cream and top with fruit.* Makes 8 slices.

*NOTE: Finished tarts can be chilled up to 4 hours.

PER TART OR 1 SLICE WHOLE TART VARIATION: 383 cal., 22 g total fat (13 g sat. fat, 0 g trans fat), 210 mg chol., 186 mg sodium, 41 g carbo., 1 g fiber, 6 g pro.
EXCHANGES: 1 Starch, 2 Other Carbo., ½ Lean Meat, 4 Fat

THE ART OF THE TART TOP CREAM TARTS WITH A COLORFUL ARRAY OF FRUITS. BAKE THE CHERRY-ALMOND TART IN A RECTANGULAR FLUTED TART PAN TO BRING EVEN MORE BEAUTY TO THE DESSERT.

FRESH FRUIT AND CREAM TARTS

CHERRY-ALMOND TART

CHERRY-ALMOND TART

PREP: 45 MINUTES **BAKE:** 50 MINUTES
COOL: 15 MINUTES **OVEN:** 350°F
MAKES: 12 SLICES

- 1 recipe Nut Pastry (page 444)
- 2 12-ounce jars cherry preserves
- 1 egg yolk
- 1 teaspoon water
- ¼ cup sliced almonds

1 Preheat oven to 350°F. Lightly grease a 13×4-inch fluted rectangular tart pan or a 9- or 9½-inch fluted round or square tart pan with a removable bottom; set aside.

2 Prepare Nut Pastry as directed through Step 2. Press half of the pastry onto the bottom and up the sides of the prepared tart pan. Bake for 15 to 20 minutes or until crust is light brown.

3 Meanwhile, on a lightly floured surface roll the remaining pastry into a 13×10-inch oval. Using a fluted pastry wheel or pizza cutter, cut pastry crosswise into ¾- to 1-inch-wide strips.

4 Spread preserves evenly over hot crust. Arrange pastry strips on top of preserves in a lattice design, leaving about ¾ inch between each strip.

5 In a small bowl combine egg yolk and water; brush some of the mixture on pastry strips. Place tart on a baking sheet. Bake for 15 minutes. Remove from oven. Brush lattice strips with additional egg yolk mixture and sprinkle with sliced almonds. Bake about 20 minutes more or until top is golden brown.

6 Cool in pan on a wire rack for 15 minutes. Using a small sharp knife, gently loosen edge of crust from sides of pan; cool completely. Remove sides from tart pan.

PER SLICE: 381 cal., 15 g total fat (5 g sat. fat, 1 g trans fat), 28 mg chol., 241 mg sodium, 58 g carbo., 2 g fiber, 4 g pro. EXCHANGES: 1½ Starch, 2½ Other Carbo., 2½ Fat

NUT AND CHOCOLATE CHIP TART

PREP: 30 MINUTES **BAKE:** 40 MINUTES
OVEN: 350°F **MAKES:** 10 TO 12 SLICES

- 1 recipe Pastry for Single-Crust Pie (page 444)
- 3 eggs
- 1 cup light-color corn syrup
- ½ cup packed brown sugar
- ⅓ cup butter, melted and cooled
- 1 teaspoon vanilla
- 1 cup coarsely chopped salted mixed nuts
- ½ cup miniature semisweet chocolate pieces
- ⅓ cup miniature semisweet chocolate pieces (optional)
- 1 tablespoon shortening (optional)

1 Preheat oven to 350°F. Prepare and roll out Pastry for Single-Crust Pie. Transfer the pastry to an 11-inch tart pan with a removable bottom. Press pastry into fluted sides of tart pan and trim edges. Do not prick pastry.

2 For filling, in a large bowl beat eggs lightly with a fork. Stir in corn syrup. Add brown sugar, melted butter, and vanilla, stirring until sugar dissolves. Stir in nuts and the ½ cup chocolate pieces. Place pastry-lined tart pan on a baking sheet; place baking sheet on the oven rack. Carefully pour filling into tart pan. Bake about 40 minutes or until a knife inserted near the center comes out clean. Cool on a wire rack.

3 If desired, in a small heavy saucepan melt the ⅓ cup chocolate pieces and shortening over very low heat. Immediately remove from heat; stir until smooth. Cool slightly. Drizzle over tart. Let stand until chocolate is set. To serve, remove sides from tart pan and cut tart into slices. Cover and chill any remaining tart for up to 2 days.

PER SLICE: 454 cal., 26 g total fat (11 g sat. fat, 1 g trans fat), 92 mg chol., 272 mg sodium, 71 g carbo., 1 g fiber, 7 g pro. EXCHANGES: 1 Starch, 4 Other Carbo., ½ High-Fat Meat, 4 Fat

---

STORING PIES AND TARTS
KEEP YOUR CREATIONS AT THEIR BEST.

■ Do not freeze cream pies and tarts, or those that include eggs in the filling, such as custard or pecan pies, or the Nut and Chocolate Chip Tart (left). To store, lightly cover in plastic wrap; refrigerate up to 2 days.

■ To freeze a baked fruit pie: Let it cool completely. Place it in a freezer bag; seal, label, and freeze for up to 4 months. To serve, thaw at room temperature.

■ To freeze an unbaked fruit pie: Before assembling treat light-color fruit with ascorbic acid color keeper. Assemble pie in a metal pie pan. Place in a freezer bag; seal, label, and freeze for up to 4 months. To bake, unwrap frozen pie; cover with foil. Bake in a preheated 450°F oven 15 minutes. Reduce temperature to 375°F; bake for 15 minutes. Uncover; bake for 55 to 60 minutes more or until filling is bubbly and crust is golden.

BUTTERSCOTCH-PECAN TART

PREP: 30 MINUTES **BAKE:** 15 MINUTES
OVEN: 400°F/350°F **MAKES:** 12 SLICES

  1 recipe Rich Tart Pastry (page 445)
  3 cups pecan halves
1¼ cups Creamy Butterscotch Sauce
  ⅔ cup semisweet chocolate pieces
  ⅓ cup butterscotch-flavored pieces
     Whipped cream (optional)
     Chocolate curls (see tip, page 287)
     (optional)

1 Preheat oven to 400°F. Prepare Rich Tart
Pastry; roll it into an 11-inch circle. Transfer the
pastry circle to a 9-inch tart pan with a removable
bottom. Press pastry into fluted sides of tart pan
and trim edges. Line the pastry shell with a double
thickness of foil. Bake for 10 minutes. Remove
foil. Bake for 5 to 6 minutes more or until light
brown. Cool slightly on a wire rack. Reduce oven
temperature to 350°F.

2 For filling, toast pecans (see tip, page 20).
Meanwhile, prepare Creamy Butterscotch Sauce.
Transfer 1¼ cups of the butterscotch sauce to
a medium heatproof bowl. Stir in warm pecans,
chocolate pieces, and butterscotch-flavored
pieces, stirring until pieces melt. Pour filling into
pastry shell.

3 Bake about 15 minutes or until filling edges
are bubbly; cool on a wire rack. Remove sides
from tart pan. If desired, serve with remaining
Butterscotch Sauce, whipped cream, and/or
chocolate curls.

CREAMY BUTTERSCOTCH SAUCE: In a
medium heavy saucepan melt ½ cup butter over
low heat, stirring often. Increase heat to medium.
Stir in ⅔ cup granulated sugar, ⅔ cup packed
dark brown sugar, ¾ cup light-color corn syrup,
2 tablespoons water, and ¼ teaspoon salt.
Bring to boiling, stirring constantly; reduce heat.
Simmer, uncovered, for 5 minutes, stirring often.
Remove from the heat. Carefully stir in ¾ cup
whipping cream and 2 teaspoons vanilla. Cover
and chill any remaining sauce for up to 2 weeks.

PER SLICE: 546 cal., 39 g total fat (14 g sat. fat, 0 g trans fat),
76 mg chol., 127 mg sodium, 48 g carbo., 4 g fiber, 5 g pro.
EXCHANGES: 1½ Starch, 1½ Other Carbo., 7½ Fat

BROWNED BUTTER TART

PREP: 40 MINUTES **BAKE:** 25 MINUTES
COOL: 60 MINUTES **OVEN:** 350°F **MAKES:** 12 SLICES

  1 recipe Rich Tart Pastry (page 445)
  3 eggs
1¼ cups sugar
  ½ cup all-purpose flour
  1 vanilla bean, split lengthwise, or
     1 teaspoon vanilla
  ¾ cup butter
  3 cups assorted mixed berries or assorted
     cut-up fresh fruit
     Whipped cream (optional)

1 Preheat oven to 350°F. Prepare Rich Tart
Pastry; roll it into a 12-inch circle. Transfer pastry
circle to a 10-inch tart pan with a removable
bottom. Press pastry into fluted sides of tart pan
and trim edges. Set aside.

2 For filling, in a large bowl lightly beat the eggs
with a fork. Stir in sugar, flour, and (if using) liquid
vanilla; set aside.

3 In a medium heavy saucepan combine the
vanilla bean (if using) and butter. Cook over
medium-high heat until the butter turns the color
of light brown sugar. Remove from heat. Remove
and discard vanilla bean. Slowly add the browned
butter to the egg mixture, stirring until combined.
Pour filling into the pastry-lined tart pan.

4 Bake for 25 to 30 minutes or until the top is
crisp and golden. To serve warm, cool in pan on a
wire rack for 60 minutes.

5 To serve, remove sides from tart pan. Serve
with assorted mixed berries and (if desired)
whipped cream. Cover and chill within 2 hours.

PER SLICE: 371 cal., 21 g total fat (13 g sat. fat, 0 g trans fat),
139 mg chol., 156 mg sodium, 41 g carbo., 3 g fiber, 4 g pro.
EXCHANGES: 1½ Starch, 1½ Other Carbo., 4 Fat

HANDLE WITH CARE
IF YOUR TART PANS ARE MADE
OF TINNED STEEL, MAKE SURE
THEY ARE COMPLETELY DRY
BEFORE STORING THEM SO
THEY DON'T RUST.

10 TO TRY—MINI TARTS

Start with one 2-ounce box baked mini phyllo dough shells (15). **1. HONEY-NUT:** Fill shells with chopped nuts; drizzle with honey. **2. ICE CREAM:** Spoon desired ice cream into shells. **3. PEACH-ALMOND:** Fill shells with diced peaches; top with sliced almonds. **4. CHOCOLATE-RASPBERRY:** Melt ¾ cup semisweet chocolate pieces with ⅓ cup sweetened condensed milk; fill shells. Top with raspberries. **5. HAZELNUT:** Fill shells with chocolate-hazelnut spread; top with whole hazelnuts. **6. LEMON:** Fill shells with lemon curd; top with whipped cream and lemon peel. **7. CHEESECAKE:** Prepare cheesecake dessert mix; fill shells. Top with phyllo crumbs. **8. CARAMEL APPLE:** Fill shells with diced apple. Drizzle with caramel topping; top with chopped nuts. **9. FLUFFY FRUIT:** Spoon whipped cream into shells; top with berries. **10. PEANUT BUTTER S'MORE:** Fill shells with marshmallow creme; top with peanut butter and mini chocolate pieces.

GANACHE-GLAZED PEANUT BUTTER TART

PREP: 30 MINUTES **BAKE:** 10 MINUTES
COOL: 10 MINUTES **CHILL:** 4 TO 24 HOURS
STAND: 10 MINUTES **OVEN:** 350°F
MAKES: 16 SLICES

- 1 cup crushed chocolate wafer cookies
- 3 tablespoons sugar
- 3 tablespoons butter, melted
- 1½ cups half-and-half or light cream
- 2 tablespoons all-purpose flour
- ¼ teaspoon salt
- 3 egg yolks
- ⅓ cup sugar
- ½ cup creamy peanut butter
- 1 teaspoon vanilla
- 4 ounces bittersweet chocolate, chopped
- 5 tablespoons butter, cut into small pieces
- 1 tablespoon light-color corn syrup

1 Preheat oven to 350°F. For crust, in a medium bowl combine crushed chocolate cookies and the 3 tablespoons sugar. Stir in the melted butter. Press chocolate mixture onto the bottom of a 9-inch tart pan with a removable bottom. Bake about 10 minutes or until set. Cool on a wire rack.

2 For filling, in a medium saucepan combine half-and-half, flour, and salt. Cook over medium heat until simmering, stirring frequently.

3 In a small bowl combine the egg yolks and the ⅓ cup sugar. Gradually whisk hot half-and-half mixture into egg yolk mixture. Return egg yolk mixture to saucepan. Cook and stir over medium heat until mixture is thickened and bubbly. Remove from heat. Whisk in peanut butter and vanilla until combined. Pour filling into crust, spreading evenly. Cover and chill for 3 hours.

4 For ganache, in a small saucepan combine chocolate and the 5 tablespoons butter. Cook and stir over low heat until melted. Remove from heat. Stir in corn syrup; cool for 10 minutes.

5 Pour ganache over filling; tilt pan to allow ganache to flow evenly over tart (see photo 1, below). Cover and chill for 1 to 24 hours.

6 Let stand at room temperature for 10 minutes before serving. Using a small sharp knife, gently loosen edge of tart from sides of pan; remove sides from tart pan. To cut, dip a sharp knife in hot water; dry the knife. Quickly score the top of the tart with warm knife (see photo 2, below). Cut tart along score marks.

PER SLICE: 235 cal., 17 g total fat (8 g sat. fat, 0 g trans fat), 63 mg chol., 166 mg sodium, 19 g carbo., 1 g fiber, 4 g pro.
EXCHANGES: 1 Starch, 3½ Fat

GANACHE PANACHE

THIS RICH CHOCOLATE ICING MUST BE SPREAD WHEN IT'S WARM TO ENSURE A SMOOTH SURFACE. ONCE COOLED, IT CREATES A FIRM, CANDYLIKE COATING FOR TARTS OR CAKES.

PREPARING GANACHE GLAZE, STEP-BY-STEP

1. After pouring ganache over filling, quickly and gently tilt the pan in all directions to completely cover the top of the tart with ganache. This will give a nice smooth surface to the ganache. **2.** To cut the tart without cracking the ganache, dip a sharp knife in hot water to warm it. Dry it and quickly score the top of the tart. Dip and dry the knife between scores. Cleanly cut the scored tart.

POULTRY

HERB-ROASTED CHICKEN AND VEGETABLES, PAGE 468

POULTRY

THERE ARE MANY GREAT WAYS TO ENJOY POULTRY. BEFORE YOU DIVE IN, REVIEW A FEW BASICS.

BUYING POULTRY

Here's information you'll often find on the label.

■ "Sell by" date: This tells you not to buy the package after a particular date.

■ "Use by" date: If there is no "sell by" date, a "use by" date indicates when raw poultry should be cooked or frozen. Precooked poultry will have a "use by" date.

■ Note other information such as Nutrition Facts and handling and cooking tips.

STORING AND THAWING POULTRY

Store raw poultry in its original package in the coldest part of the refrigerator; cook within 2 days of purchase. For longer storage, freeze poultry in its original package up to 2 months at 0°F. To freeze longer, wrap package with foil. Whole poultry will keep up to 1 year and cut-up pieces up to 9 months. Never freeze stuffed poultry.

Never thaw poultry at room temperature. Thaw it in the refrigerator in a dish to catch any drips. Allow at least 9 hours for parts and 24 hours per 5 pounds for whole birds.

For quicker thawing, use the defrost setting on your microwave oven and be sure to cook the poultry immediately after thawing. For whole birds that don't fit in the microwave, place the poultry in an airtight plastic bag in a sink full of cold water. Allow 30 minutes per pound, changing water every 30 minutes.

SAFE HANDLING OF POULTRY AND MEAT

■ Set aside a cutting board to use exclusively for raw poultry, raw meat, and other foods that will be cooked. Have another cutting board for breads and foods that will not be cooked.

■ Wash work surfaces and utensils in hot, soapy water before and right after handling poultry and meat to prevent the spread of bacteria. Never partially cook poultry and meat, refrigerate, and finish cooking later as bacteria may grow.

■ Discard used marinades. If you wish to use some of the marinade for basting, set aside a little bit of it before adding it to poultry and meat.

■ Serve cooked poultry and meat immediately; refrigerate leftovers within 2 hours.

■ Rinsing poultry and meat is not necessary. The less you handle it the better. However, you will want to rinse cavities of whole birds that will be stuffed; drain well and pat dry with paper towels.

IS IT DONE?

A thermometer is the most accurate way to check doneness. For poultry, dark meat is done at 180°F, white meat at 170°F, and ground poultry at 165°F. For whole birds, it's important to insert the thermometer into the thickest part of the thigh muscle without touching bone. If you don't have a thermometer, check doneness by piercing the thickest part of the thigh with a fork. The meat should be tender and no longer pink in the center, and juices should run clear. (For meat, refer to the charts on pages 414 to 416 for safe internal temperatures.)

BUTTERMILK-BRINED
FRIED CHICKEN, PAGE 468

HERB-ROASTED CHICKEN (photo, page 465)

PREP: 20 MINUTES ROAST: 75 MINUTES
STAND: 10 MINUTES OVEN: 375°F
MAKES: 4 SERVINGS

- 1 3½- to 4-pound whole broiler chicken
- 2 tablespoons butter or margarine, melted
- 2 cloves garlic, minced
- 1 teaspoon dried basil, crushed
- ½ teaspoon ground sage
- ½ teaspoon dried thyme, crushed
- ¼ teaspoon salt
- ¼ teaspoon lemon-pepper seasoning or black pepper

1 Preheat oven to 375°F. Rinse chicken body cavity; pat dry with paper towels. Skewer neck skin to back (see photo 2, page 486); tie legs to tail (see photo 3, page 487). Twist wing tips under back (see photo 4, page 487). Place chicken, breast side up, on a rack in a shallow roasting pan. Brush with melted butter; rub with garlic.

2 In a small bowl stir together basil, sage, thyme, salt, and lemon-pepper seasoning; rub onto chicken. If desired, insert a meat thermometer into center of an inside thigh muscle (see photo 5, page 487). (Thermometer should not touch bone.)

3 Roast, uncovered, for 75 to 90 minutes or until drumsticks move easily in sockets and chicken is no longer pink (180°F). Remove chicken from oven. Cover; let stand 10 minutes before carving.

PER 4 OUNCES CHICKEN: 619 cal., 45 g total fat (15 g sat. fat, 0 g trans fat), 216 mg chol., 406 mg sodium, 1 g carbo., 0 g fiber, 50 g pro.
EXCHANGES: 7 Medium-Fat Meat, 2 Fat

HERB-ROASTED CHICKEN AND VEGETABLES:

Prepare as directed, except before roasting chicken in a large saucepan cook 1 pound red potatoes, quartered (halved, if small); 3 carrots, halved lengthwise and cut into 1-inch pieces; and 1 medium turnip, peeled and cut into 1½-inch pieces in lightly salted boiling water for 5 minutes; drain. In a large bowl combine drained vegetables and 1 medium onion, cut into 1-inch chunks. Toss vegetables with. 2 tablespoons melted butter or margarine, ¼ teaspoon salt, and ¼ teaspoon black pepper. Arrange vegetable mixture around chicken in pan. Roast as directed, stirring vegetables once or twice during roasting.

PER 4 OUNCES CHICKEN + ⅔ CUP VEGETABLES: 796 cal., 51 g total fat (19 g sat. fat, 0 g trans fat), 232 mg chol., 797 mg sodium, 29 g carbo., 5 g fiber, 54 g pro.
EXCHANGES: 1½ Starch, 7 Medium-Fat Meat, 1 Vegetable, 3 Fat

BUTTERMILK-BRINED FRIED CHICKEN (photo, page 467)

PREP: 30 MINUTES CHILL: 2 TO 4 HOURS
COOK: 12 MINUTES PER BATCH MAKES: 6 SERVINGS

- 3 cups buttermilk
- ⅓ cup kosher salt
- 2 tablespoons sugar
- 2½ to 3 pounds meaty chicken pieces (breast halves, thighs, and drumsticks)
- 2 cups all-purpose flour
- ¼ teaspoon salt
- ¼ teaspoon black pepper
- ¾ cup buttermilk
    Vegetable oil

1 For brine, in a resealable plastic bag set in a bowl combine the 3 cups buttermilk, the kosher salt, and sugar. Using a chef's knife, cut chicken breasts in half crosswise. Add all chicken pieces to the brine; seal bag. Chill for 2 to 4 hours; remove chicken from brine. Drain chicken; pat dry with paper towels. Discard brine.

2 In a large bowl combine flour, salt, and pepper. Place the ¾ cup buttermilk in a shallow dish. Coat chicken with flour mixture, dip in the buttermilk, and coat again with flour mixture.

3 Meanwhile, in a deep, heavy pot or a deep-fat fryer, heat 1½ inches oil to 350°F. Using tongs, carefully add a few pieces of chicken to hot oil. (Oil temperature will drop; maintain temperature at 325°F.) Fry chicken for 12 to 15 minutes or until chicken is no longer pink (170°F for breasts; 180°F for thighs and drum-sticks) and coating is golden, turning once. Drain on a wire rack or paper towels. If desired, keep fried chicken warm in a preheated 300°F oven while frying remaining chicken pieces.

SPICY BUTTERMILK-BRINED FRIED CHICKEN:

Prepare as directed, except add 1½ teaspoons cayenne pepper to the flour mixture.

PER 3 OUNCES CHICKEN PLAIN OR SPICY VARIATION: 618 cal., 36 g total fat (7 g sat. fat, 0 g trans fat), 110 mg chol., 1,701 mg sodium, 37 g carbo., 1 g fiber, 36 g pro.
EXCHANGES: 2½ Starch, 4 Medium-Fat Meat, 2½ Fat

WHY BRINE?

BRINING WAS AN ANCIENT WAY TO PRESERVE FOODS. NOW WE USE BRINES TO MAKE FOODS MOIST AND FLAVORFUL.

FRIED CHICKEN WITH CREAMY GRAVY

PREP: 20 MINUTES **COOK:** 45 MINUTES
MAKES: 6 SERVINGS

- 1 egg, lightly beaten
- 3 tablespoons milk
- 1 cup finely crushed saltine crackers
- 1 teaspoon dried thyme, crushed
- ½ teaspoon paprika
- 2½ to 3 pounds meaty chicken pieces (breast halves, thighs, and drumsticks)
- 2 to 3 tablespoons vegetable oil
- 1 cup milk
- 1 recipe Creamy Gravy

1 In a small bowl combine the egg and the 3 tablespoons milk. In a shallow bowl combine crushed crackers, thyme, paprika, ½ teaspoon *salt,* and ⅛ teaspoon *black pepper*. Dip chicken pieces, one at a time, in egg mixture; roll in cracker mixture to coat.

2 In a very large skillet brown chicken in hot oil over medium heat for 10 to 15 minutes, turning occasionally; drain well.

3 Add the 1 cup milk to skillet. Heat just to boiling. Reduce heat to medium-low; cover tightly. Cook for 30 minutes. Uncover; cook for 5 to 10 minutes more or until chicken is no longer pink (170°F for breasts; 180°F for thighs and drumsticks). Remove chicken, reserving drippings for gravy. Cover chicken; keep warm.

CREAMY GRAVY: In a screw-top jar combine ¾ cup milk, 1 tablespoon all-purpose flour, ¼ teaspoon salt, and ⅛ teaspoon black pepper; cover and shake well. Add to drippings in skillet. Stir in 1 cup milk. Cook over medium heat, stirring constantly, until thickened and bubbly. Cook and stir for 1 minute more. (If desired, stir in additional milk to make desired consistency.)

PER 3 OUNCES CHICKEN + ⅓ CUP GRAVY: 448 cal., 25 g total fat (7 g sat. fat, 0 g trans fat), 152 mg chol., 590 mg sodium, 17 g carbo., 1 g fiber, 36 g pro. EXCHANGES: ½ Milk, ½ Starch, 4 Medium-Fat Meat, 1½ Fat

SKIN IF DESIRED FOR ANY OF THE FRIED CHICKEN RECIPES, YOU CAN REMOVE THE SKIN BEFORE COATING THE PIECES. FOR OTHER RECIPES, REMOVE THE SKIN BEFORE OR AFTER COOKING.

FRIED CHICKEN WITH CREAMY GRAVY

OVEN-FRIED CHICKEN

PREP: 20 MINUTES **BAKE:** 45 MINUTES
OVEN: 375°F **MAKES:** 4 TO 6 SERVINGS

- 1 egg, lightly beaten
- 3 tablespoons milk
- 1¼ cups crushed cornflakes or finely crushed rich round crackers (about 35 crackers)
- 1 teaspoon dried thyme, crushed
- ½ teaspoon paprika
- ¼ teaspoon salt
- ⅛ teaspoon black pepper
- 2 tablespoons butter or margarine, melted
- 2½ to 3 pounds meaty chicken pieces (breast halves, thighs, and drumsticks)

1 Preheat oven to 375°F. In a small bowl combine egg and milk. For coating, in a shallow dish combine crushed cornflakes, thyme, paprika, salt, and pepper; stir in melted butter. Set aside. Skin chicken (see photos 1 and 2, below). Dip chicken pieces, one at a time, into egg mixture; coat with crumb mixture.

2 In a greased 15×10×1-inch baking pan arrange chicken, bone sides down, so the pieces aren't touching. Sprinkle chicken pieces with any remaining crumb mixture so they are well coated.

3 Bake, uncovered, for 45 to 55 minutes or until chicken is no longer pink (170°F for breasts; 180°F for thighs and drumsticks). Do not turn chicken pieces while baking.

PER 5 OUNCES CHICKEN: 373 cal., 11 g total fat (5 g sat. fat, 0 g trans fat), 187 mg chol., 522 mg sodium, 23 g carbo., 0 g fiber, 43 g pro.
EXCHANGES: 1½ Starch, 5½ Lean Meat, 1 Fat

OVEN-FRIED PARMESAN CHICKEN: Prepare as directed, except omit thyme and salt and reduce crushed cornflakes to ½ cup. For coating, combine cornflakes; ½ cup grated Parmesan cheese; 1 teaspoon dried oregano, crushed; the paprika; and pepper. Stir in melted butter.

PER 5 OUNCES CHICKEN: 355 cal., 14 g total fat (7 g sat. fat, 0 g trans fat), 195 mg chol., 398 mg sodium, 10 g carbo., 0 g fiber, 45 g pro.
EXCHANGES: ½ Starch, 6 Lean Meat, 1½ Fat

OVEN-BARBECUED CHICKEN

PREP: 25 MINUTES **BAKE:** 45 MINUTES
OVEN: 375°F **MAKES:** 6 SERVINGS

- 4 pounds meaty chicken pieces (breast halves, thighs, and drumsticks)
- 1 cup finely chopped onion
- 1 tablespoon minced garlic
- 2 tablespoons kosher salt
- ¼ cup butter or margarine
- 1 tablespoon paprika
- 1 tablespoon chili powder
- 1½ teaspoons crushed red pepper
- 1 cup cider vinegar
- 1 cup packed dark brown sugar
- 2 tablespoons Worcestershire sauce
- 1 cup tomato paste
- ¼ cup molasses

1 Preheat oven to 375°F. Skin chicken (see photos 1 and 2, below). Arrange chicken, bone sides up, in a foil-lined 15×10×1-inch baking pan. Bake for 35 minutes.

REMOVING SKIN FROM DRUMSTICKS, STEP-BY-STEP

1. To remove skin from chicken pieces, use a paper towel to grip the skin and pull it away from the meat. For drumsticks, start at the meaty end and pull downward toward the bony end. **2.** Use kitchen shears to cut the skin at the joint. Wash the shears in hot, soapy water when you are finished.

2 Meanwhile, for sauce, in a large saucepan cook onion, garlic, and salt in butter over medium-low heat for 10 to 15 minutes or until tender, stirring occasionally. Add paprika, chili powder, crushed red pepper, and ½ teaspoon *black pepper;* cook and stir 1 minute. Add 1½ cups *water,* vinegar, brown sugar, and Worcestershire sauce; bring to boiling. Whisk in tomato paste and molasses until smooth. Boil gently, uncovered, for 15 to 20 minutes or until sauce is thickened and reduced to about 4 cups, stirring occasionally.

3 Turn chicken bone sides down. Brush 1 cup of the sauce over chicken. Bake for 10 to 20 minutes more or until chicken is no longer pink (170°F for breasts; 180°F for thighs and drumsticks). Reheat some of the remaining sauce; pass with the chicken. Store any remaining sauce in an airtight container in the refrigerator for up to 1 week.

PER 4 OUNCES CHICKEN + ¼ CUP SAUCE: 420 cal., 10 g total fat (4 g sat. fat, 0 g trans fat), 142 mg chol., 1,724 mg sodium, 40 g carbo., 2 g fiber, 41 g pro. EXCHANGES: 2½ Other Carbo., 6 Lean Meat, ½ Fat

CHICKEN AND DUMPLINGS

PREP: 30 MINUTES **COOK:** 47 MINUTES
MAKES: 6 SERVINGS

- 2½ to 3 pounds meaty chicken pieces (breast halves, thighs, and drumsticks), skinned
- 1 medium onion, cut into wedges
- ½ teaspoon dried sage or marjoram, crushed
- 1 bay leaf
- 1 cup sliced celery (2 stalks)
- 1 cup thinly sliced carrots (2 medium)
- 1 cup sliced fresh mushrooms
- 1 recipe Dumplings
- ¼ cup all-purpose flour

1 In a 4-quart pot combine chicken, onion, sage, bay leaf, 3 cups *water,* ¾ teaspoon *salt,* and ¼ teaspoon *black pepper.* Bring to boiling; reduce heat. Simmer, covered, for 25 minutes. Add celery, carrots, and mushrooms. Return to boiling; reduce heat. Simmer, covered, about 10 minutes more or until vegetables are tender and chicken is no longer pink (170°F for breasts; 180°F for thighs and drumsticks). Discard bay leaf. Arrange chicken on top of vegetables in pot.

2 Spoon Dumpling batter into six mounds on top of the chicken. (Do not spoon batter into the liquid.) Return to boiling; reduce heat. Simmer,

covered, for 12 to 15 minutes or until a wooden toothpick inserted into dumplings comes out clean. Do not lift lid while simmering. With a slotted spoon transfer chicken, dumplings, and vegetables to a bowl; keep warm.

3 For gravy, measure 2 cups cooking liquid. Skim fat from liquid (see photo 1, page 488); discard fat. Pour liquid into pot. Stir ½ cup *cold water* into the flour; stir into liquid in pot. Cook and stir over medium heat until mixture is thickened and bubbly. Cook and stir for 1 minute more. Serve gravy over chicken, vegetables, and dumplings in bowls.

DUMPLINGS: In a medium bowl combine 1 cup all-purpose flour, 1 teaspoon baking powder, and ½ teaspoon salt. Cut in 2 tablespoons shortening until mixture resembles coarse crumbs. Add ½ cup buttermilk, stirring just until moistened.

PER 3 OUNCES CHICKEN + ½ CUP VEGETABLE MIXTURE + 1 DUMPLING: 296 cal., 6 g total fat (2 g sat. fat, 1 g trans fat), 72 mg chol., 644 mg sodium, 26 g carbo., 2 g fiber, 33 g pro. EXCHANGES: ½ Vegetable, 1½ Starch, 2½ Lean Meat, 1 Fat

CHICKEN AND NOODLES

PREP: 30 MINUTES **COOK:** 60 MINUTES
MAKES: 6 SERVINGS

- 1 3- to 3½-pound broiler-fryer chicken
- 5 cups chicken broth
- 1 recipe Homemade Noodles (page 423) or one 12-ounce package frozen noodles
- 2 tablespoons all-purpose flour

1 In a 4- to 5-quart pot combine chicken, 4 cups of the broth, ½ teaspoon *salt,* and ¼ teaspoon *black pepper.* Bring to boiling; reduce heat. Simmer, covered, for 40 to 45 minutes or until chicken is very tender. Remove chicken from pot; cool slightly. Remove meat from bones; discard skin and bones. Chop chicken; set aside.

2 Strain broth; return to pot. Skim fat from broth. Bring to boiling. Add noodles; boil gently, uncovered, for 15 minutes, stirring occasionally. In a screw-top jar combine the remaining 1 cup broth and the flour; cover and shake until smooth. Stir into noodle mixture. Cook and stir until thickened and bubbly. Stir in chicken. Cook 5 minutes more or until heated through, stirring occasionally. If necessary, stir in additional broth. If desired, serve with Mashed Potatoes (page 607).

PER 1 CUP: 358 cal., 7 g total fat (2 g sat. fat, 0 g trans fat), 183 mg chol., 1,270 mg sodium, 39 g carbo., 1 g fiber, 31 g pro. EXCHANGES: 2½ Starch, 3 Lean Meat, ½ Fat

MAKE-IT-MINE SKILLET CHICKEN

PUT THIS SIMPLE AND SATISFYINGLY SAUCY DISH IN YOUR RECIPE ROTATION AND YOU'LL NEVER RUN OUT OF WAYS TO SERVE MEATY, INEXPENSIVE CHICKEN PIECES. THE OPTIONS ARE SO VARIED, YOU COULD SERVE IT TWICE IN THE SAME WEEK.

BASIC INGREDIENTS

PREP: 30 MINUTES
COOK: 50 MINUTES
MAKES: 4 TO 6 SERVINGS

- ¼ cup all-purpose flour
- 1 teaspoon Seasoning
- ½ teaspoon salt
- ¼ teaspoon black pepper
- 1 3- to 3½-pound broiler-fryer chicken, cut up and skinned, or 3 to 3½ pounds meaty chicken pieces, skinned
- 2 tablespoons vegetable oil
- ½ cup chopped onion (1 medium)
- 2 cloves garlic, minced
  Liquid
  Sauce
- 2 teaspoons cornstarch
- 2 pounds Vegetables
  Hot cooked Pasta

SEASONING (PICK ONE)

Chili powder
Dry ranch salad dressing mix
Dried thyme, oregano, or basil, crushed
Garlic powder
Paprika

LIQUID (PICK ONE)

- ¾ cup chicken broth
- 1 15-ounce can tomato sauce
- ½ cup chicken broth plus ¼ cup wine
- 1 10.75-ounce can condensed cream of mushroom or chicken soup plus ½ cup milk

SAUCE (PICK ONE)

- ⅓ cup dairy sour cream, whipping cream, or milk
- ⅓ cup pasta sauce
- ¼ cup chicken broth plus 1 tablespoon Dijon-style mustard
- ¼ cup chicken broth plus 1 tablespoon soy sauce or hoisin sauce

VEGETABLES
(PICK ONE OR MORE)

Cut fresh asparagus
Cooked halved baby carrots
Broccoli or cauliflower florets
Quartered mushrooms
Sweet pepper strips

PASTA (PICK ONE)

Bow ties
Egg noodles
Penne
Rotini

BASIC INSTRUCTIONS

1 In a plastic or paper bag combine flour, Seasoning, salt, and pepper. Add chicken, a few pieces at a time; close bag and shake to coat well.

2 In a very large skillet cook chicken pieces in hot oil over medium heat about 10 minutes or until chicken browns, turning to brown evenly. Remove chicken from skillet. If necessary, add 1 tablespoon additional vegetable oil to skillet.

3 Add the chopped onion and garlic to skillet. Cook and stir for 4 to 5 minutes or until onion is tender. Carefully stir in Liquid. Return chicken to skillet.

4 Bring to boiling; reduce heat. Simmer, covered, for 30 minutes.

5 In a measuring cup combine the Sauce ingredients and cornstarch; stir into chicken mixture. Add Vegetables.

6 Return to boiling; reduce heat. Simmer, covered, for 5 to 10 minutes more or until vegetables are crisp-tender. Serve with Pasta.

COQ AU VIN

PREP: 35 MINUTES **COOK:** 50 MINUTES
MAKES: 6 SERVINGS

2½ to 3 pounds meaty chicken pieces (breast halves, thighs, and drumsticks)

2 tablespoons vegetable oil

Salt and black pepper

12 to 18 pearl onions or shallots, peeled

1¼ cups Pinot Noir or Burgundy

1 cup whole fresh mushrooms

1 cup thinly sliced carrots (2 medium)

¼ cup chicken broth or water

1 tablespoon snipped fresh parsley

1½ teaspoons snipped fresh marjoram or
  ½ teaspoon dried marjoram, crushed

1½ teaspoons snipped fresh thyme or
  ½ teaspoon dried thyme, crushed

1 bay leaf

2 cloves garlic, minced

2 tablespoons all-purpose flour

2 tablespoons butter or margarine, softened

2 slices bacon, crisp-cooked, drained, and crumbled

Snipped fresh parsley (optional)

Hot cooked noodles (optional)

1 Skin chicken. In a large skillet cook chicken in hot oil over medium heat about 15 minutes or until chicken browns, turning to brown evenly. Drain fat. Sprinkle chicken with salt and pepper. Add onions, wine, mushrooms, carrots, broth, the 1 tablespoon parsley, dried marjoram (if using), dried thyme (if using), bay leaf, and garlic. Bring to boiling; reduce heat. Simmer, covered, for 35 to 40 minutes or until chicken is no longer pink (170°F for breasts; 180°F for thighs and drumsticks). If using, add fresh marjoram and thyme. Discard bay leaf. Transfer chicken and vegetables to a serving platter; keep warm.

2 In a small bowl stir together flour and softened butter to make a smooth paste. Stir into wine mixture in skillet. Cook and stir until thickened and bubbly. Cook and stir for 1 minute more. Season to taste with additional salt and pepper.

3 Pour sauce over chicken and vegetables. Sprinkle with bacon. If desired, top with additional parsley and serve with hot cooked noodles.

PER 3 OUNCES CHICKEN + ½ CUP VEGETABLE MIXTURE: 288 cal., 12 g total fat (4 g sat. fat, 0 g trans fat), 92 mg chol., 311 mg sodium, 7 g carbo., 1 g fiber, 28 g pro. EXCHANGES: ½ Vegetable, 4 Lean Meat, 2 Fat

DRUMSTICKS WITH MINTY RICE AND PEAS

PREP: 25 MINUTES **COOK:** 60 MINUTES
MAKES: 4 SERVINGS

8 chicken drumsticks, skinned if desired

½ teaspoon salt

3 tablespoons butter or margarine

1 tablespoon olive or vegetable oil

1 cup chopped onion (1 large)

1 shallot, finely chopped

2 cloves garlic, minced

1 teaspoon dried thyme, crushed

¼ teaspoon freshly ground black pepper

1¼ cups reduced-sodium chicken broth

1 tablespoon butter or margarine (optional)

1 recipe Minty Rice and Peas

1 Sprinkle chicken with salt. In a very large skillet heat butter and oil over medium heat until butter melts. Add chicken; cook for 10 minutes, turning often. Remove chicken, reserving butter and oil in skillet. Set chicken aside.

2 Add onion, shallot, and garlic to skillet. Cook and stir about 5 minutes or until onion is tender, scraping up browned bits.

3 Return chicken to pan. Sprinkle with thyme and pepper. Add broth. Bring to boiling; reduce heat. Simmer, covered, for 35 to 40 minutes or until tender and no longer pink (180°F), spooning juices over chicken occasionally. Remove chicken to a serving platter; keep warm. (If chicken is skinned, add 1 tablespoon butter or margarine to onion mixture.) Simmer onion mixture in pan, uncovered, for 10 minutes, stirring occasionally.

4 To serve, spoon onion mixture over chicken and serve with Minty Rice and Peas.

MINTY RICE AND PEAS: In a medium saucepan combine 2½ cups water, 1 cup uncooked jasmine or long grain rice, 1 tablespoon butter or margarine, and ¼ teaspoon salt. Bring to boiling; reduce heat. Simmer, covered, for 15 to 18 minutes or until rice is tender and most of the liquid is absorbed. Stir in 1½ cups frozen peas, 2 tablespoons sliced green onion, and 2 tablespoons snipped fresh mint or 1 teaspoon dried thyme, crushed. Cover; let stand for 5 minutes. Stir before serving.

PER 2 DRUMSTICKS + 1 CUP RICE MIXTURE: 596 cal., 27 g total fat (11 g sat. fat, 0 g trans fat), 149 mg chol., 915 mg sodium, 50 g carbo., 3 g fiber, 35 g pro. EXCHANGES: 3 Starch, 3½ Medium-Fat Meat, 2 Fat

COOK ONCE, EAT TWICE

WHO DOESN'T LOVE CHICKEN CACCIATORE? EVERYONE WILL FALL IN LOVE WITH IT ALL OVER AGAIN WHEN YOU TRANSFORM LEFTOVERS INTO A ZESTY SAUCE FOR POLENTA.

TONIGHT

CHICKEN CACCIATORE

PREP: 30 MINUTES **COOK:** 50 MINUTES
MAKES: 4 SERVINGS + RESERVES

- 4 pounds meaty chicken pieces (breast halves, thighs, and drumsticks), skinned
- 2 tablespoons olive oil
- 2 cups sliced fresh mushrooms
- 1 large onion, sliced
- 3 cloves garlic, minced
- 1 28-ounce can diced tomatoes, undrained
- ¾ cup dry white wine or chicken broth
- 1 6-ounce can tomato paste
- 2 teaspoons sugar
- 2 teaspoons dried Italian seasoning, crushed
- 2 cups hot cooked fettuccine or linguine

1 In a very large skillet brown chicken in hot oil over medium heat about 15 minutes, turning to brown all sides. Remove chicken, reserving drippings in skillet. Set chicken aside.

2 Add mushrooms, onion, and garlic to skillet. Cook and stir for 5 minutes. Return chicken to skillet. Combine undrained tomatoes, wine, tomato paste, sugar, Italian seasoning, ½ teaspoon *salt,* and ¼ teaspoon *black pepper.* Pour over chicken in skillet. Bring to boiling; reduce heat. Simmer, covered, for 30 to 35 minutes or until chicken is no longer pink (170°F for breasts; 180°F for thighs and drumsticks), turning once.

3 Remove half of the chicken and sauce mixture to a storage container. Cover and chill for up to 3 days, use in Chicken and Mushroom Polenta. Serve remaining chicken over pasta.

PER 3 OUNCES CHICKEN + ½ CUP VEGETABLES + ½ CUP PASTA: 372 cal., 8 g total fat (1 g sat. fat, 0 g trans fat), 96 mg chol., 597 mg sodium, 35 g carbo., 4 g fiber, 37 g pro.
EXCHANGES: 1½ Vegetable, 2 Starch, 4 Lean Meat

TOMORROW

CHICKEN AND MUSHROOM POLENTA

START TO FINISH: 35 MINUTES
MAKES: 4 TO 6 SERVINGS

- 1 recipe Polenta (page 78)
- ½ cup shredded fontina cheese (2 ounces)
- ½ recipe Chicken Cacciatore
- 1 tablespoon olive oil
- 1 medium zucchini, halved lengthwise and sliced
- 4 ounces cremini mushrooms, quartered
- 1 medium red sweet pepper, cut into bite-size strips

1 Prepare Polenta as directed, except stir in cheese after cooking; cover and keep warm.

2 Meanwhile, remove Chicken Cacciatore from sauce; set sauce aside. Remove meat from bones; discard bones. Chop chicken meat into bite-size pieces; set aside.

3 In a large skillet heat olive oil over medium-high heat. Add zucchini, mushrooms, and sweet pepper. Cook and stir for 3 to 4 minutes or until vegetables are tender. Stir in chicken and reserved sauce. Bring to boiling; reduce heat. Simmer, uncovered, for 5 minutes. Serve chicken mixture over polenta.

PER 1¾ CUPS CHICKEN MIXTURE + ¾ CUP POLENTA: 554 cal., 20 g total fat (7 g sat. fat, 0 g trans fat), 129 mg chol., 1,417 mg sodium, 46 g carbo., 6 g fiber, 44 g pro.
EXCHANGES: 2½ Vegetable, 2 Starch, 4½ Medium-Fat Meat

CHICKEN LO MEIN

PREP: 15 MINUTES **STAND:** 20 MINUTES
COOK: 10 MINUTES **MAKES:** 6 SERVINGS

- 12 ounces skinless, boneless chicken breast halves, beef sirloin steak, or lean boneless pork
- 6 tablespoons reduced-sodium soy sauce
- 1 tablespoon rice vinegar
- 4 teaspoons sugar
- 10 ounces dried Chinese egg noodles or linguine
- ⅓ cup reduced-sodium chicken broth
- 2 teaspoons cornstarch
- 1 tablespoon vegetable oil
- 1 tablespoon sesame oil
- 4 cloves garlic, minced
- ½ cup shredded carrot (1 medium)
- 1 cup chopped bok choy
- 4 green onions, cut into 2-inch thin strips

1 Cut chicken into thin bite-size strips. In a medium bowl combine 2 tablespoons of the soy sauce, the rice vinegar, and 2 teaspoons of the sugar. Add chicken; toss to coat. Let stand at room temperature for 20 minutes or cover and chill for 1 hour. Cook noodles according to package directions until tender; drain. Rinse with cold water; drain well. Set noodles aside. For sauce, in a small bowl stir together broth, the remaining 4 tablespoons soy sauce, the remaining 2 teaspoons sugar, and the cornstarch. Set aside.

2 Pour vegetable oil and sesame oil into a wok or large nonstick skillet. Heat over medium-high heat. Add garlic; cook and stir for 30 seconds. Add carrot; cook and stir for 2 minutes. Add bok choy and green onions; cook and stir for 2 minutes more. Remove vegetables from wok.

3 Drain chicken; discarding marinade. Add chicken to wok (add more oil if necessary); cook and stir for 3 to 4 minutes or until no longer pink. Push chicken from center of wok. Stir sauce and add to center of wok. Cook and stir until thickened and bubbly. Add the cooked noodles and vegetables. Using two spatulas or wooden spoons, lightly toss the mixture until combined and heated through. Transfer to a serving platter. Serve immediately.

PER 1⅓ CUPS: 326 cal., 7 g total fat (1 g sat. fat, 0 g trans fat), 73 mg chol., 615 mg sodium, 42 g carbo., 2 g fiber, 22 g pro. EXCHANGES: 2½ Starch, 2 Lean Meat, 1 Fat

SHRIMP LO MEIN: Prepare as directed, except substitute 1 pound fresh or frozen shrimp in shells for the chicken. Thaw shrimp, if frozen. Peel and devein shrimp. Rinse shrimp; pat dry with paper towels. In Step 3 cook shrimp about 3 minutes or until opaque.

PER 1⅓ CUPS: 324 cal., 8 g total fat (1 g sat. fat, 0 g trans fat), 126 mg chol., 657 mg sodium, 43 g carbo., 2 g fiber, 21 g pro. EXCHANGES: 2½ starch, 2 Lean Meat, 1 Fat

GARLIC CHICKEN STIR-FRY

PREP: 25 MINUTES **MARINATE:** 30 MINUTES
COOK: 4 MINUTES **MAKES:** 4 SERVINGS

- 12 ounces skinless, boneless chicken breast halves
- 1 cup water
- 3 tablespoons reduced-sodium soy sauce
- 1 tablespoon rice vinegar or white wine vinegar
- 1 tablespoon cornstarch
- 2 tablespoons vegetable oil
- 10 green onions, cut into 1-inch pieces
- 1 cup thinly sliced fresh mushrooms
- 12 cloves garlic, peeled and finely chopped
- ½ cup sliced water chestnuts
- 2 cups hot cooked rice

1 Cut chicken into ½-inch pieces. Place chicken in a resealable plastic bag set in a shallow dish. For marinade, stir together water, soy sauce, and vinegar. Pour over chicken; seal bag. Marinate in the refrigerator for 30 minutes. Drain chicken, reserving the marinade. Stir cornstarch into reserved marinade; set aside.

2 Pour oil into a wok or large skillet. (If necessary, add more oil during cooking.) Heat over medium-high heat. Add green onions, mushrooms, and garlic to wok; cook and stir for 1 to 2 minutes or until tender. Remove vegetables from wok.

3 Add chicken to wok; cook and stir for 3 to 4 minutes or until no longer pink. Push chicken from center of wok. Stir marinade mixture; add to center of wok. Cook and stir until thickened and bubbly. Return cooked vegetables to wok. Add water chestnuts. Cook and stir about 1 minute more or until heated through. Serve with rice.

PER 1 CUP MIXTURE + ½ CUP RICE: 311 cal., 8 g total fat (1 g sat. fat, 0 g trans fat), 49 mg chol., 755 mg sodium, 35 g carbo., 2 g fiber, 25 g pro. EXCHANGES: ½ Vegetable, 2 Starch, 2½ Lean Meat, 1½ Fat

THAI CHICKEN STIR-FRY

WHITE MEAT OR DARK? WHEN A RECIPE CALLS FOR MEATY CHICKEN PIECES, USE ALL BREAST HALVES, ALL THIGHS, ALL DRUMSTICKS, OR ANY COMBINATION OF THOSE PIECES.

CHICKEN WITH BLACK
BEANS AND RICE

THAI CHICKEN STIR-FRY

START TO FINISH: 35 MINUTES
MAKES: 4 SERVINGS

- 1 pound skinless, boneless chicken breast halves
- ¼ cup rice wine
- 3 tablespoons reduced-sodium soy sauce
- 2 tablespoons water
- 1 tablespoon fish sauce (optional)
- 1½ teaspoons cornstarch
- ½ teaspoon crushed red pepper
- 1 tablespoon vegetable oil
- 1 teaspoon grated fresh ginger
- 2 cloves garlic, minced
- 1½ cups bias-sliced carrots (3 medium)
- 2 cups fresh pea pods, tips and strings removed, or one 6-ounce package frozen pea pods, thawed
- 4 green onions, bias-sliced into 1-inch pieces
- ⅓ cup dry-roasted peanuts
- 2 cups hot cooked rice
  Chopped dry-roasted peanuts (optional)

1 Cut chicken into 1-inch pieces; set aside.

2 For sauce, stir together rice wine, soy sauce, water, fish sauce (if desired), cornstarch, and crushed red pepper; set aside.

3 Pour oil into a wok or large skillet. (If necessary, add more oil during cooking.) Heat over medium-high heat. Add ginger and garlic to wok; cook and stir for 15 seconds. Add carrots; cook and stir for 2 minutes. Add pea pods and green onions; cook and stir for 2 to 3 minutes more or until vegetables are crisp-tender. Remove vegetables from wok.

4 Add half of the chicken to hot wok. Cook and stir for 3 to 4 minutes or until chicken is no longer pink. Remove from wok. Repeat with remaining chicken. Return all chicken to wok. Push chicken from center of wok. Stir sauce; add to center of wok. Cook and stir until thickened and bubbly. Return vegetables to wok. Stir in the ⅓ cup peanuts. Cook and stir for 1 to 2 minutes more or until heated through. Serve with rice. If desired, sprinkle with additional chopped peanuts.

PER 1 CUP MIXTURE + ½ CUP RICE: 406 cal., 11 g total fat (2 g sat. fat, 0 g trans fat), 66 mg chol., 1,020 mg sodium, 43 g carbo., 3 g fiber, 34 g pro.
EXCHANGES: 1 Vegetable, 2½ Starch, 3½ Lean Meat, ½ Fat

CHICKEN WITH BLACK BEANS AND RICE

PREP: 20 MINUTES **COOK:** 45 MINUTES
MAKES: 6 SERVINGS

- ¼ cup all-purpose flour
- 1½ teaspoons chili powder
- ¼ teaspoon salt
- ¼ teaspoon black pepper
- 2½ to 3 pounds meaty chicken pieces (breast halves, thighs, and drumsticks)
- 2 tablespoons vegetable oil
- 1 15-ounce can black beans, rinsed and drained
- 1 14.5-ounce can diced tomatoes with onion and green pepper, undrained
- 1 cup tomato juice
- 1 cup frozen whole kernel corn
- ⅔ cup uncooked long grain rice
- ½ cup water
- ¼ teaspoon salt
- ⅛ to ¼ teaspoon cayenne pepper
- 2 cloves garlic, minced

1 In a large resealable plastic bag combine flour, 1 teaspoon of the chili powder, ¼ teaspoon salt, and black pepper. Add chicken pieces, half at a time. Seal bag; shake to coat.

2 In a very large skillet heat oil over medium heat. Add chicken; cook about 10 minutes or until brown on all sides, turning occasionally. Remove chicken from skillet; set aside. Discard drippings.

3 Add beans, undrained tomatoes, tomato juice, corn, uncooked rice, water, ¼ teaspoon salt, the remaining ½ teaspoon chili powder, the cayenne pepper, and garlic to the skillet. Bring to boiling. Arrange chicken pieces on top of rice mixture. Reduce heat to medium-low. Cook, covered, for 35 to 40 minutes or until chicken is no longer pink (170°F for breasts; 180°F for thighs and drumsticks) and rice is tender.

PER 3 OUNCES CHICKEN + ⅔ CUP RICE MIXTURE: 508 cal., 22 g total fat (5 g sat. fat, 0 g trans fat), 107 mg chol., 830 mg sodium, 43 g carbo., 6 g fiber, 38 g pro.
EXCHANGES: 1 Vegetable, 2½ Starch, 4 Medium-Fat Meat

ANYTHING-GOES THAI STIR-FRY
ALSO TRY GREEN BEANS, SWEET PEPPERS, AND OTHER VEGETABLES YOU ENJOY—JUST COOK UNTIL CRISP-TENDER.

CHICKEN PARMIGIANA

PREP: 30 MINUTES **COOK:** 25 MINUTES
MAKES: 4 SERVINGS

- 1 tablespoon butter or margarine
- ⅓ cup chopped onion (1 small)
- 1 clove garlic, minced
- 1 14.5-ounce can diced tomatoes, undrained
- ½ teaspoon sugar
- ¼ cup snipped fresh basil
- 4 skinless, boneless chicken breast halves
- ⅓ cup seasoned fine dry bread crumbs
- 4 tablespoons grated Parmesan cheese
- ½ teaspoon dried oregano, crushed
- 1 egg, lightly beaten
- 2 tablespoons milk
- 3 tablespoons olive oil or vegetable oil
- ¼ cup shredded mozzarella cheese (1 ounce)

1 For sauce, in a medium saucepan melt butter over medium heat. Add onion and garlic; cook until tender. Carefully stir in undrained tomatoes, sugar, ⅛ teaspoon *salt,* and dash *black pepper.* Bring to boiling; reduce heat. Simmer, uncovered, about 10 minutes or to desired consistency, stirring occasionally. Stir in basil. Set aside; keep warm.

2 Meanwhile, place each chicken breast half between two pieces of plastic wrap. Using the flat side of a meat mallet, pound chicken lightly to about ¼ inch thick (see photo 2, page 481). Discard plastic wrap.

3 In a shallow bowl stir together bread crumbs, 3 tablespoons of the Parmesan cheese, and the oregano. In a second bowl stir together the egg and milk. Dip chicken into egg mixture and into crumb mixture to coat.

4 In a very large skillet cook chicken in hot oil over medium heat for 2 to 3 minutes on each side or until golden. Transfer chicken to platter.

5 Spoon sauce over chicken. Top with mozzarella cheese and the remaining 1 tablespoon Parmesan cheese. Let stand 2 minutes or until cheese melts.

PER 3 OUNCES CHICKEN + ⅓ CUP SAUCE: 398 cal., 19 g total fat (6 g sat. fat, 0 g trans fat), 151 mg chol., 761 mg sodium, 15 g carbo., 2 g fiber, 41 g pro.
EXCHANGES: 1 Vegetable, ½ Starch, 4½ Lean Meat, 3 Fat

VEAL PARMIGIANA: Prepare as directed, except substitute 1 pound boneless veal sirloin steak or boneless veal leg round steak, cut ½ inch thick, for the chicken breast halves. Cut meat into four serving-size pieces and pound to ¼ inch thick.

PER 3 OUNCES VEAL + ⅓ CUP SAUCE: 366 cal., 20 g total fat (6 g sat. fat, 0 g trans fat), 159 mg chol., 760 mg sodium, 15 g carbo., 2 g fiber, 31 g pro.
EXCHANGES: 1 Vegetable, ½ Starch, 4 Lean Meat, 3 Fat

CREAMY TOMATO CHICKEN PARMIGIANA:
Prepare as directed, except after simmering the sauce to desired consistency slowly add 3 tablespoons whipping cream, half-and-half, or light cream, stirring constantly. Cook and stir for 3 minutes more; stir in the basil.

PER 3 OUNCES CHICKEN + ⅓ CUP SAUCE: 437 cal., 23 g total fat (8 g sat. fat, 0 g trans fat), 167 mg chol., 766 mg sodium, 15 g carbo., 2 g fiber, 41 g pro.
EXCHANGES: 1 Vegetable, ½ Starch, 4½ Lean Meat, 3½ Fat

CHICKEN WITH PAN SAUCE

START TO FINISH: 35 MINUTES
MAKES: 4 SERVINGS

- 4 skinless, boneless chicken breast halves
- 5 tablespoons cold butter
- ⅔ cup dry white wine or chicken broth
- ½ cup chicken broth
- ¼ cup finely chopped shallot or onion
- 2 tablespoons whipping cream (no substitutes)

1 Place each chicken breast half between two pieces of plastic wrap. Using the flat side of a meat mallet, pound chicken lightly to about ¼ inch thick (see photo 2, page 481). Discard plastic wrap. Sprinkle chicken with ¼ teaspoon *salt* and ¼ teaspoon *black pepper.*

2 In a very large skillet melt 1 tablespoon of the butter over medium-high heat. Reduce heat to medium. Add chicken to skillet. Cook chicken for 6 to 8 minutes or until no longer pink, turning once. Transfer chicken to a platter; cover with foil to keep warm. Remove skillet from heat.

3 Add wine, broth, and shallot to the hot skillet. Return skillet to heat. Cook and stir to scrape up the browned bits from the bottom of the pan. Bring to boiling. Boil gently, uncovered, about 10 minutes or until liquid is reduced to ¼ cup. Reduce heat to medium-low.

4 Stir in cream. Add remaining 4 tablespoons butter, 1 tablespoon at a time, stirring until butter melts after each addition. Sauce should be slightly thickened. Season to taste with additional *salt* and *black pepper.* Serve sauce over chicken.

PER BREAST HALF + 2 TABLESPOONS SAUCE: 351 cal., 19 g total fat (11 g sat. fat, 0 g trans fat), 131 mg chol., 466 mg sodium, 3 g carbo., 0 g fiber, 33 g pro.
EXCHANGES: 5 Lean Meat, 3 Fat

10 TO TRY—SAUCES

Start with Chicken with Pan Sauce, page 478. Prepare as directed, except for desired addition.

1. LEEK: Add ½ cup sliced leek to skillet with shallot. **2. PARMESAN:** Stir 2 tablespoons grated Parmesan into sauce. **3. MUSHROOM-TOMATO:** Add 1 cup sliced fresh mushrooms to skillet with shallot and stir 2 tablespoons snipped drained oil-packed dried tomatoes into sauce. **4. LEMON:** Stir 2 teaspoons lemon juice and 2 teaspoons snipped fresh thyme, chervil, or parsley into sauce. **5. BALSAMIC-CAPER:** Stir 2 teaspoons balsamic vinegar and 2 teaspoons drained capers into sauce. **6. BACON:** Stir 3 slices crumbled cooked bacon into sauce. **7. ALMOND:** Stir 2 tablespoons toasted sliced almonds into sauce. **8. BASIL:** Stir 1 tablespoon snipped fresh basil into sauce. **9. MUSTARD:** Stir 1 tablespoon snipped fresh Italian parsley and 2 teaspoons Dijon-style mustard into sauce. **10. CILANTRO:** Stir 1 tablespoon snipped fresh cilantro and ½ teaspoon finely chopped chipotle chile pepper in adobo sauce into sauce.

CHEESE-STUFFED CHICKEN BREASTS

PREP: 20 MINUTES **COOK:** 18 MINUTES
MAKES: 4 SERVINGS

- 4 skinless, boneless chicken breast halves
- ½ of an 8-ounce tub cream cheese
- 2 tablespoons purchased dried tomato pesto
- ¾ cup panko (Japanese-style bread crumbs)
- 1 tablespoon grated Parmesan cheese
- ½ teaspoon dried basil, crushed
- ⅛ teaspoon garlic powder
- ⅛ teaspoon black pepper
- ¼ cup milk
- 1 tablespoon olive oil or vegetable oil
- 1 tablespoon butter or margarine

1 Using a sharp knife, cut a pocket in each chicken breast by cutting horizontally through the thickest portion to, but not through, the opposite side. In a small bowl combine cream cheese and pesto. Spoon a rounded tablespoon of the cheese mixture into each pocket; set aside.

2 In a shallow bowl combine panko, Parmesan cheese, basil, garlic powder, and pepper. Place milk in a second shallow bowl. Dip stuffed chicken in milk to moisten and in panko mixture to coat.

3 In a large skillet heat oil and butter over medium heat. Add chicken. Cook for 18 to 20 minutes or until chicken is no longer pink (170°F) and golden brown, turning once.

PER SERVING: 389 cal., 21 g total fat (9 g sat. fat, 0 g trans fat), 124 mg chol., 299 mg sodium, 11 g carbo., 1 g fiber, 38 g pro. EXCHANGES: ½ Starch, 5 Lean Meat, 2½ Fat

---

LOW FAT

BAKED CHICKEN CHILES RELLENOS

PREP: 45 MINUTES **BAKE:** 30 MINUTES
OVEN: 375°F **MAKES:** 6 SERVINGS

- 6 skinless, boneless chicken breast halves
- ⅓ cup all-purpose flour
- 3 tablespoons cornmeal
- ¼ teaspoon salt
- ¼ teaspoon cayenne pepper
- 1 egg, lightly beaten
- 1 tablespoon water
- 1 4-ounce can whole green chiles or whole jalapeño peppers, rinsed, stemmed, seeded, and halved lengthwise (6 pieces total) (see tip, page 24)
- 2 ounces Monterey Jack cheese, cut into six 2×½-inch sticks
- 2 tablespoons snipped fresh cilantro or fresh parsley
- ¼ teaspoon black pepper
- 2 tablespoons butter or margarine, melted
- 1 8-ounce jar green or red salsa

1 Place each chicken breast half between two pieces of plastic wrap. Using the flat side of a meat mallet, pound chicken lightly into rectangles, ¼ to ½ inch thick (see photo 2, page 481). Discard plastic wrap.

2 Preheat oven to 375°F. Line a shallow baking pan with foil; set aside. In a shallow bowl combine flour, cornmeal, salt, and cayenne pepper. In a second shallow bowl combine egg and water.

3 Place a chile pepper half on each chicken piece near an edge. Place a stick of cheese on each chile pepper. Sprinkle with cilantro and black pepper. Fold in side edges; roll up from edge with cheese and chile pepper (see photo 3, page 481). Secure with wooden toothpicks.

4 Dip chicken rolls into egg mixture to coat; coat all sides with cornmeal mixture. Place rolls, seam sides down, in prepared baking pan. Brush with melted butter.

5 Bake, uncovered, for 30 to 35 minutes or until chicken is no longer pink (170°F). Remove toothpicks. Meanwhile, heat salsa; serve over chicken.

PER SERVING: 299 cal., 10 g total fat (5 g sat. fat, 0 g trans fat), 141 mg chol., 396 mg sodium, 11 g carbo., 1 g fiber, 40 g pro. EXCHANGES: ½ Starch, 5½ Lean Meat, ½ Fat

---

CHICKEN KIEV

PREP: 20 MINUTES **CHILL:** 1 TO 24 HOURS
COOK: 5 MINUTES **BAKE:** 15 MINUTES
OVEN: 400°F **MAKES:** 4 SERVINGS

- 1 tablespoon chopped green onion
- 1 tablespoon snipped fresh parsley
- 1 clove garlic, minced
- ½ of a ¼-pound stick of butter, chilled
- 1 egg, lightly beaten
- 1 tablespoon water
- ¼ cup all-purpose flour
- ½ cup fine dry bread crumbs
- 4 skinless, boneless chicken breast halves
  Salt and black pepper
- 1 tablespoon butter
- 1 tablespoon vegetable oil

1 In a small bowl combine green onion, parsley, and garlic; set aside. Cut chilled butter into four 2×½-inch sticks (see photo 1, below). In a shallow bowl stir together egg and water. Place flour in a second shallow bowl. Place bread crumbs in a third shallow bowl. Set all three bowls aside.

2 Place each chicken breast half between two pieces of plastic wrap. Using the flat side of a meat mallet, pound chicken lightly into rectangles ¼ to ½ inch thick (see photo 2, below). Discard plastic wrap. Sprinkle chicken with salt and pepper. Divide green onion mixture among chicken pieces. Place a butter stick in center of each chicken piece. Fold in side edges; roll up from bottom edge (see photo 3, below).

3 Coat rolls with flour. Dip in egg mixture; coat with crumbs. Dip in egg mixture again; coat with additional crumbs (see photo 4, below). Coat ends well. Place chicken in 2-quart rectangular baking dish. Cover; chill for 1 to 24 hours.

4 Preheat oven to 400°F. In a large skillet melt the 1 tablespoon butter over medium-high heat; add oil. Add chilled chicken rolls, seam sides down. Cook about 5 minutes or until golden brown, turning to brown on all sides (see photo 5, below). Return rolls to baking dish. Bake, uncovered, for 15 to 18 minutes or until chicken is no longer pink (170°F). Spoon any drippings over rolls.

PER SERVING: 416 cal., 22 g total fat (11 g sat. fat, 0 g trans fat), 173 mg chol., 450 mg sodium, 17 g carbo., 1 g fiber, 37 g pro. EXCHANGES: 1 Starch, 4½ Lean Meat, 3 Fat

CHEESY CHICKEN ROLLS: Prepare as directed, except substitute 2½×½-inch sticks of Gruyère or cheddar cheese for the butter. If using Gruyère cheese, substitute 2 teaspoons snipped fresh tarragon for the parsley. If using cheddar cheese, substitute 2 teaspoons snipped fresh thyme for the parsley.

PER SERVING: 420 cal., 18 g total fat (9 g sat. fat, 0 g trans fat), 169 mg chol., 563 mg sodium, 17 g carbo., 1 g fiber, 44 g pro. EXCHANGES: 1 Starch, 4½ Lean Meat, 1 High Fat Meat, 1 Fat

CHICKEN KIEV, STEP-BY-STEP

1. Cut the half stick of butter lengthwise into four pieces. **2.** Starting from center, lightly pound chicken pieces with the flat side of a meat mallet. **3.** To enclose butter, fold in the side edges. Roll up chicken from bottom edge. **4.** Completely cover chicken, including the ends, with the crumb mixture. **5.** Cook chicken until golden, turning to brown evenly. Place rolls in baking dish.

COCONUT CHICKEN
WITH PINEAPPLE-MANGO SALSA

3 Meanwhile, for salsa, in a medium bowl combine pineapple, mango, cilantro (if desired), lime juice, and the remaining ¼ teaspoon salt. Serve with chicken.

PER 3 OUNCES CHICKEN + ⅓ CUP SALSA: 393 cal., 18 g total fat (12 g sat. fat, 0 g trans fat), 110 mg chol., 461 mg sodium, 31 g carbo., 4 g fiber, 27 g pro. EXCHANGES: 1 Fruit, 1 Other Carbo., 4 Lean Meat, 2 Fat

CHICKEN WITH TOMATOES AND SPINACH

PREP: 20 MINUTES **COOK:** 15 MINUTES
MAKES: 4 SERVINGS

- ¼ cup buttermilk
- ½ cup all-purpose flour
- ½ teaspoon salt
- ½ teaspoon black pepper
- 4 skinless, boneless chicken breast halves
- 3 tablespoons vegetable oil
- 2 cups grape tomatoes or cherry tomatoes
- 1 tablespoon packed brown sugar
- 1 9-ounce package fresh spinach
  Salt and black pepper
- 1 recipe Polenta (see recipe, page 78) (optional)

1 Pour buttermilk into a shallow bowl. In a second shallow bowl combine flour, the ½ teaspoon salt, and the ½ teaspoon pepper. Dip chicken into buttermilk and into flour mixture, turning to coat both sides.

2 In a very large skillet heat oil over medium-high heat. Add chicken; cook for 15 to 20 minutes or until no longer pink (170°F), turning chicken halfway through cooking. Reduce heat to medium if chicken is browning too quickly.

3 Meanwhile, pierce tomatoes with a sharp knife. Place tomatoes in a microwave-safe medium bowl; sprinkle with brown sugar. Cover loosely with plastic wrap. Microwave on 100% power (high) about 3 minutes or until skins burst and tomatoes are soft, stirring once; set aside.

4 Remove chicken from skillet; keep warm. Add spinach to drippings in skillet; cook and stir about 1 minute or just until wilted. Season with additional salt and pepper. Serve chicken with wilted spinach, tomato mixture, and, if desired, Polenta.

PER CHICKEN PIECE + ½ CUP SPINACH, + ⅓ CUP TOMATOES: 354 cal., 13 g total fat (1 g sat. fat, 0 g trans fat), 528 mg sodium, 83 mg chol., 22 g carbo., 3 g fiber, 38 g pro. EXCHANGES: 1½ Vegetable, 1 Starch, 4½ Lean Meat, 1½ Fat

FAST

COCONUT CHICKEN WITH PINEAPPLE-MANGO SALSA

START TO FINISH: 30 MINUTES **OVEN:** 400°F
MAKES: 4 SERVINGS

- 1 egg, lightly beaten
- 1 tablespoon vegetable oil
- ½ teaspoon salt
- ⅛ teaspoon cayenne pepper
- 1¼ cups flaked coconut
- 14 to 16 ounces chicken breast tenderloins
- 1 8-ounce can pineapple tidbits (juice pack), drained
- 1 cup chopped refrigerated mango slices (about 10 slices)
- 2 tablespoons snipped fresh cilantro (optional)
- 1 tablespoon lime juice
- ¼ teaspoon salt

1 Preheat oven to 400°F. Line a large baking sheet with foil; lightly grease foil. Set pan aside.

2 In a shallow bowl whisk together egg, oil, ¼ teaspoon of the salt, and the cayenne pepper. Spread coconut in a second shallow bowl. Dip each chicken piece in egg mixture, allowing excess to drip off. Coat chicken pieces with coconut. Arrange chicken on the prepared baking sheet. Bake for 10 to 12 minutes or until chicken is no longer pink (170°F).

CITRUS-HERB-MARINATED CHICKEN

PREP: 20 MINUTES **MARINATE:** 2 TO 4 HOURS
BROIL: 12 MINUTES **MAKES:** 4 SERVINGS

- 4 skinless, boneless chicken breast halves
- ⅓ cup lemon juice or orange juice
- 1 tablespoon honey
- 1 tablespoon olive oil
- 1 tablespoon snipped fresh thyme or
    1 teaspoon dried thyme, crushed
- 2 teaspoons snipped fresh rosemary or
    ½ teaspoon dried rosemary, crushed
- 2 tablespoons finely chopped shallot
- 1 clove garlic, minced
- ½ teaspoon salt
- ¼ teaspoon freshly ground black pepper
    Lemon or orange wedges (optional)

1 Place chicken breast halves in a resealable plastic bag set in a shallow bowl. For marinade, stir together lemon juice, honey, oil, thyme, rosemary, shallot, garlic, salt, and pepper. Pour over chicken; seal the bag. Marinate in the refrigerator for 2 to 4 hours, turning the bag occasionally.

2 Preheat broiler. Drain chicken, reserving marinade. Place chicken on the unheated rack of a broiler pan. Broil 4 to 5 inches from the heat about 6 minutes or until light brown.

3 Turn chicken and brush lightly with reserved marinade. Discard remaining marinade. Broil for 6 to 9 minutes more or until chicken is no longer pink (170°F). If desired, serve with lemon wedges.

PER PIECE: 212 cal., 5 g total fat (1 g sat. fat, 0 g trans fat), 82 mg chol., 366 mg sodium, 7 g carbo., 0 g fiber, 33 g pro.
EXCHANGES: ½ Other Carbo., 3½ Lean Meat, ½ Fat

CHICKEN WITH PARMESAN RICE

PREP: 25 MINUTES **COOK:** 20 MINUTES
STAND: 5 MINUTES **MAKES:** 6 SERVINGS

- 6 skinless, boneless chicken breast halves
- 2 tablespoons olive oil or vegetable oil
- 2 cloves garlic, minced
- 1⅓ cups uncooked long grain rice
- 1 8- to 9-ounce package frozen artichoke
    hearts, thawed and quartered
- 1½ cups fresh mushrooms, quartered
- ½ cup sliced green onions (4)
- 2 14-ounce cans reduced-sodium
    chicken broth
- 2 teaspoons finely shredded lemon peel

- 1 tablespoon lemon juice
- ½ cup finely shredded Parmesan cheese
- ¼ teaspoon cayenne pepper

1 Sprinkle chicken with *salt* and *black pepper*. In a very large skillet brown chicken in hot oil for 2 minutes per side; remove from skillet.

2 Add garlic and rice to skillet; cook and stir for 1 minute. Stir in artichokes, mushrooms, and green onions. Add broth, lemon peel, lemon juice, ¼ cup of the cheese, and cayenne pepper. Bring to boiling. Top with chicken. Reduce heat. Cook, covered, for 20 to 25 minutes or until chicken is no longer pink (170°F) and rice is tender. Remove from heat; let stand for 5 minutes. Sprinkle with the remaining ¼ cup cheese.

PER BREAST HALF + 1 CUP RICE MIXTURE: 434 cal., 10 g total fat (3 g sat. fat, 0 g trans fat), 96 mg chol., 635 mg sodium, 39 g carbo., 3 g fiber, 45 g pro.
EXCHANGES: ½ Vegetable, 2½ Starch, 5 Lean Meat, ½ Fat

KALAMATA LEMON CHICKEN

PREP: 10 MINUTES **BAKE:** 35 MINUTES
OVEN: 400°F **MAKES:** 4 SERVINGS

- 1 tablespoon olive oil
- 1 to 1¼ pounds skinless, boneless
    chicken thighs
- 1 14-ounce can chicken broth
- ⅔ cup dried orzo
- ½ cup drained pitted Kalamata olives
- ½ of a lemon, cut into wedges or chunks
- 1 tablespoon lemon juice
- 1 teaspoon dried Greek seasoning or dried
    oregano, crushed
    Hot chicken broth (optional)
    Fresh snipped oregano (optional)

1 Preheat oven to 400°F. In a 4-quart Dutch oven heat oil over medium-high heat. Add chicken; cook about 5 minutes or until brown, turning once. Stir in broth, orzo, olives, lemon wedges, lemon juice, Greek seasoning, ¼ teaspoon *salt*, and ¼ teaspoon *black pepper*. Transfer mixture to a 2-quart rectangular baking dish.

2 Bake, covered, about 35 minutes or until chicken is tender and no longer pink (180°F). If desired, serve in shallow bowls with additional hot broth and top with fresh oregano.

PER 3 OUNCES CHICKEN + ½ CUP ORZO: 304 cal., 10 g total fat (2 g sat. fat, 0 g trans fat), 95 mg chol., 830 mg sodium, 25 g carbo., 2 g fiber, 27 g pro.
EXCHANGES: 1½ Starch, 3 Lean Meat, 1 Fat

CHICKEN BURRITOS

PREP: 20 MINUTES **BAKE:** 40 MINUTES
OVEN: 350°F **MAKES:** 8 BURRITOS

- 8 8- to 10-inch flour tortillas
- 1½ cups shredded cooked chicken, turkey, beef, or pork
- 1 cup bottled salsa
- 1 3⅛-ounce can jalapeño-flavored bean dip
- 1 teaspoon fajita seasoning
- 8 ounces Monterey Jack cheese or cheddar cheese, cut into eight 5×½-inch sticks
     Shredded lettuce (optional)
     Dairy sour cream (optional)
     Bottled salsa (optional)

1 Preheat oven to 350°F. Wrap tortillas in foil; heat in oven about 10 minutes or until warm.

2 Meanwhile, in a large bowl stir together chicken, 1 cup salsa, bean dip, and fajita seasoning.

3 To assemble, place ⅓ cup chicken mixture onto each tortilla near the edge. Top chicken mixture with a stick of cheese. Fold in sides of tortilla; roll up, starting from edge with the filling (see photos 1 and 2, page 391). Place filled tortillas, seam sides down, in a greased 3-quart rectangular baking dish. Bake, uncovered, about 30 minutes or until heated through. If desired, serve with lettuce, sour cream, and additional salsa.

PER BURRITO: 267 cal., 13 g total fat (7 g sat. fat, 0 g trans fat), 49 mg chol., 589 mg sodium, 19 g carbo., 1 g fiber, 18 g pro. EXCHANGES: 1 Starch, 2 Lean Meat, 2 Fat

TURKEY MEAT LOAF

PREP: 30 MINUTES **BAKE:** 60 MINUTES
STAND: 10 MINUTES **OVEN:** 350°F
MAKES: 6 SERVINGS

- 1 tablespoon olive oil
- 1 cup finely chopped fresh mushrooms
- ¾ cup finely chopped onion (1 large)
- ½ cup finely chopped green sweet pepper
- 3 cloves garlic, minced
- 1 cup soft bread crumbs
- ¼ cup ketchup
- 1 egg, lightly beaten
- ½ teaspoon salt
- ¼ teaspoon black pepper
- 1½ pounds uncooked ground turkey or chicken
- ½ cup ketchup
- 2 tablespoons apricot preserves

1 Preheat oven to 350°F. Line a 13×9×2-inch baking pan with foil; set aside. In a large skillet heat oil over medium heat. Add mushrooms, onion, sweet pepper, and garlic; cook about 5 minutes or until tender.

2 In a large bowl combine the cooked vegetables, bread crumbs, the ¼ cup ketchup, the egg, salt, and black pepper. Add ground turkey; mix well. In the prepared pan, lightly pat turkey mixture into a 9×5-inch loaf. Bake for 45 minutes.

3 Meanwhile, in a small bowl stir together the ½ cup ketchup and the preserves. Spoon over turkey loaf. Bake for 15 to 25 minutes more or until juices run clear and thermometer inserted in center of loaf registers 165°F.

4 Let meat loaf stand for 10 minutes. Using two spatulas, transfer loaf to a serving platter.

PER SLICE: 279 cal., 13 g total fat (3 g sat. fat, 0 g trans fat), 125 mg chol., 686 mg sodium, 18 g carbo., 1 g fiber, 23 g pro. EXCHANGES: 1 Other Carbo., 3 Medium-Fat Meat

FAST ▪ LOW FAT

TURKEY AND POTATOES IN PAPRIKA SAUCE

START TO FINISH: 30 MINUTES
MAKES: 4 SERVINGS

- 1 pound tiny new potatoes, halved
- 1 medium onion, cut into thin wedges
- 1 tablespoon vegetable oil
- 1 pound turkey breast tenderloins or skinless, boneless chicken breast halves, cut into ¾-inch cubes
     Salt and black pepper
- ⅔ cup light dairy sour cream
- 2 tablespoons milk
- 1 tablespoon all-purpose flour
- 1 teaspoon smoked paprika or paprika
- ¼ teaspoon salt
- ⅛ teaspoon black pepper

1 In a covered large saucepan cook potato halves and onion in enough boiling lightly salted water to cover about 20 minutes or until tender.

2 Meanwhile, in a large skillet heat oil over medium-high heat. Sprinkle turkey lightly with salt and pepper. Cook turkey in hot oil for 4 to 6 minutes or until brown and no longer pink inside, stirring occasionally.

3 Drain potato mixture; add to turkey in skillet. In a small bowl stir together sour cream, milk, flour, paprika, ¼ teaspoon salt, and ⅛ teaspoon pepper. Add sour cream mixture to skillet. Cook and stir just until bubbly; cook and stir 1 minute more.

PER 1 CUP: 303 cal., 8 g total fat (3 g sat. fat, 0 g trans fat), 82 mg chol., 380 mg sodium, 25 g carbo., 3 g fiber, 32 g pro. EXCHANGES: 1½ Starch, 4 Lean Meat, 1 Fat

BEST EVER ▪ FAST ▪ LOW FAT

ZESTY SKILLET TURKEY

START TO FINISH: 30 MINUTES
MAKES: 4 SERVINGS

    2 turkey breast tenderloins
    1 tablespoon olive oil
    1 cup bottled salsa
    ¼ cup raisins
    1 tablespoon honey
    ½ teaspoon ground cumin
    ¼ teaspoon ground cinnamon
    1 cup water
    ¼ teaspoon salt

    ¾ cup couscous
    ¼ cup slivered almonds, toasted (see tip, page 20)

1 Cut each turkey tenderloin in half horizontally. In a large skillet heat oil over medium-high heat. Add turkey pieces; cook in hot oil about 2 minutes per side or until brown.

2 In a medium bowl stir together salsa, raisins, honey, cumin, and cinnamon. Add salsa mixture to skillet. Bring to boiling; reduce heat. Simmer, covered, for 10 to 12 minutes or until turkey is no longer pink (170°F).

3 Meanwhile, in a medium saucepan bring water and salt to boiling. Stir in couscous. Cover; remove from heat. Let stand for 5 minutes. Fluff with a fork before serving. Serve turkey and salsa mixture over couscous; sprinkle with almonds.

PER PIECE + ⅓ CUP SAUCE + ½ CUP COUSCOUS: 447 cal., 8 g total fat (1 g sat. fat, 0 g trans fat), 105 mg chol., 598 mg sodium, 44 g carbo., 4 g fiber, 49 g pro. EXCHANGES: ½ Fruit, 2½ Starch, 5½ Lean Meat

LOVE TURKEY? TWO TURKEY TENDERLOINS HALVED LENGTHWISE CAN BE SUBSTITUTED FOR FOUR SKINLESS, BONELESS CHICKEN BREAST HALVES IN MOST RECIPES.

ZESTY SKILLET TURKEY

ROAST TURKEY

PREP: 15 MINUTES **ROAST:** 2¾ HOURS
STAND: 15 MINUTES **OVEN:** 325°F
MAKES: 12 TO 14 SERVINGS

- 1 8- to 10-pound turkey
  Stuffing (optional)
  Vegetable oil
- 1 recipe Currant Glaze (optional)

1 Preheat oven to 325°F. Rinse the turkey body cavity; pat dry with paper towels. If desired, sprinkle body cavity with *salt*. If desired, spoon stuffing loosely into neck and body cavities (see photo 1, below). Skewer neck skin to back (see photo 2, below). Tuck drumstick ends under band of skin across the tail, if available. If there is no band of skin, tie drumsticks securely to the tail (see photo 3, page 487). Twist wing tips under back (see photo 4, page 487).

2 Place turkey, breast side up, on a rack in a shallow roasting pan. Brush with oil. If desired, insert an oven-going meat thermometer into the center of an inside thigh muscle (see photo 5, page 487). The thermometer should not touch bone. Cover turkey loosely with foil.

3 Roast for 2¼ hours. Remove foil; cut band of skin or string between drumsticks so thighs will cook evenly. Roast for 30 to 45 minutes more (1 to 1¼ hours if stuffed) or until the thermometer registers 180°F; if stuffed, the center of the stuffing should register 165°F. (The juices should run clear and drumsticks should move easily in their sockets.) If desired, during the last 15 minutes of roasting, brush turkey twice with Currant

Glaze. Remove turkey from oven. Cover with foil; let stand for 15 to 20 minutes before carving. Transfer turkey to a cutting board. Carve turkey.

PER 7 OUNCES TURKEY: 319 cal., 11 g total fat (3 g sat. fat, 0 g trans fat), 183 mg chol., 99 mg sodium, 0 g carbo., 0 g fiber, 51 g pro.
EXCHANGES: 7 Lean Meat

CURRANT GLAZE: In a small saucepan combine ½ cup red currant or plum jelly, 1 tablespoon lemon juice, 1 teaspoon dry mustard, 1 teaspoon Worcestershire sauce, and ¼ teaspoon black pepper. Heat and stir until jelly melts.

CLASSIC GIBLET STUFFING

PREP: 35 MINUTES **COOK:** 80 MINUTES
BAKE: 35 MINUTES **OVEN:** 325°F
MAKES: 10 TO 12 SERVINGS

- Turkey giblets
- ½ cup butter or margarine
- 1 cup finely chopped celery (2 stalks)
- ½ cup chopped onion (1 medium)
- 1 tablespoon snipped fresh sage or
  1 teaspoon ground sage
- 8 cups dry bread cubes
- 1 to 1¼ cups chicken broth, water, or giblet cooking broth

1 Rinse giblets. Refrigerate liver until needed. In a small saucepan cook remaining giblets, covered, in enough boiling water to cover for 1 hour. Add liver. Simmer, covered, for 20 to 30 minutes more or until tender. Drain and chop giblets; set aside.

2 Preheat oven to 325°F. In the same saucepan melt butter over medium heat. Add celery and onion; cook until tender but not brown. Remove

ROASTING TURKEY, STEP-BY-STEP

1. Spoon the stuffing into body cavity and neck cavity.
2. Fasten the neck skin to the body with a turkey skewer.
3. Tie the drumsticks together. Fasten the drumsticks to the tail if present. **4.** Bend the wings so they rest beneath the turkey. **5.** Insert the thermometer into the center of an inside thigh muscle. Do not let the thermometer stem touch either the bone or the pan.

1

2

from heat. Stir in giblets, sage, ¼ teaspoon *black pepper,* and ⅛ teaspoon *salt.* Place the bread cubes in an extra-large bowl; add onion mixture. Drizzle with enough broth to moisten, tossing lightly to combine. Transfer bread mixture to a 2-quart casserole.*

3 Bake, covered, for 35 to 40 minutes or until heated through.

*NOTE: Or use bread mixture to stuff an 8- to 10-pound turkey.

PER ¾ CUP: 190 cal., 11 g total fat (6 g sat. fat, 0 g trans fat), 73 mg chol., 418 mg sodium, 17 g carbo., 1 g fiber, 6 g pro. EXCHANGES: 1 Starch, 2 Fat

OYSTER STUFFING: Prepare as directed, except omit the giblets and use a medium saucepan. Add 1 pint shucked oysters, drained and chopped, to the cooked vegetables. Cook and stir for 2 minutes more. Stir in seasonings. Reduce broth to ¼ cup.

PER ¾ CUP: 189 cal., 11 g total fat (6 g sat. fat, 0 g trans fat), 42 mg chol., 368 mg sodium, 18 g carbo., 1 g fiber, 5 g pro. EXCHANGES: 1 Lean Meat, 2 Fat

CHESTNUT STUFFING: Prepare as directed, except omit the giblets. Preheat oven to 400°F. With a knife, cut an X in the shells of 1 pound fresh chestnuts (3 cups). Spread chestnuts on a large baking sheet. Roast chestnuts for 15 minutes; cool. Peel and coarsely chop chestnuts. (Or use one 8-ounce jar or one 10-ounce can whole, peeled chestnuts, drained and chopped.) Add chestnuts with seasonings. Use ¾ cup to 1 cup broth.

PER ¾ CUP: 238 cal., 11 g total fat (6 g sat. fat, 0 g trans fat), 25 mg chol., 380 mg sodium, 32 g carbo., 2 g fiber, 4 g pro. EXCHANGES: 2 Starch, 2 Fat

SAUSAGE STUFFING

PREP: 30 MINUTES **BAKE:** 30 MINUTES
OVEN: 325°F **MAKES:** 10 TO 12 SERVINGS

- 12 ounces bulk pork sausage
- ½ cup butter or margarine
- ¾ cup finely chopped onion (1 large)
- ½ cup chopped green sweet pepper (1 small)
- ½ cup chopped celery (1 stalk)
- 5 cups dry white bread cubes
- 4½ cups crumbled corn bread
- 1 teaspoon poultry seasoning
- ⅛ teaspoon black pepper
- ¾ cup chopped pecans, toasted (see tip, page 20) (optional)
- 1¼ to 1½ cups chicken broth

1 Preheat oven to 325°F. In a large skillet brown sausage over medium heat; drain well. Remove sausage from skillet; set aside. In the same skillet melt butter over medium heat. Add onion, sweet pepper, and celery; cook until tender. Set vegetable mixture aside.

2 In an extra-large bowl combine bread cubes and corn bread. Add sausage, vegetable mixture, poultry seasoning, black pepper, and, if desired, pecans. Drizzle with enough broth to moisten, tossing lightly to combine. Transfer stuffing to a 2-quart casserole.* Bake, covered, for 30 to 45 minutes or until heated through.

*NOTE: Or use bread mixture to stuff an 8- to 10-pound turkey. Reduce broth to ¾ to 1 cup.

PER ¾ CUP: 316 cal., 21 g total fat (9 g sat. fat, 0 g trans fat), 61 mg chol., 712 mg sodium, 23 g carbo., 1 g fiber, 9 g pro. EXCHANGES: 1½ Starch, 1 High-Fat Meat, 2 Fat

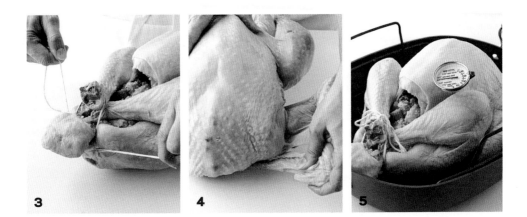

3   **4**   **5**

PAN GRAVY

START TO FINISH: 15 MINUTES **MAKES:** 2 CUPS

Pan drippings from roasted chicken
or turkey
¼ cup all-purpose flour
Chicken broth

1 After roasting, transfer roasted poultry to a
serving platter. Pour pan drippings into a large
measuring cup. Scrape the browned bits from the
pan into the cup. Skim and reserve fat from the
drippings (see photo 1, below).

2 Pour ¼ cup of the fat* into a medium saucepan
(discard remaining fat). Stir in flour. Add enough
broth to remaining drippings in the measuring cup
to equal 2 cups. Add broth mixture all at once to
flour mixture in saucepan (see photo 2, below).
Cook and stir over medium heat until thickened
and bubbly (see photo 3, below). Cook and stir
1 minute more. Season with *salt* and *black pepper*.

***NOTE:** If there is no fat, use ¼ cup melted butter.

PER ¼ CUP: 76 cal., 7 g total fat (2 g sat. fat, 0 g trans fat),
7 mg chol., 313 mg sodium, 3 g carbo., 0 g fiber, 1 g pro.
EXCHANGES: 1½ Fat

GIBLET GRAVY

PREP: 15 MINUTES **COOK:** 80 MINUTES
MAKES: 2½ CUPS

Whole turkey or chicken
4 ounces turkey or chicken giblets, including
the neck, rinsed
1 stalk celery with leaves, cut up
½ small onion, cut up
Pan drippings from roasted turkey or
chicken
¼ cup all-purpose flour

1 Roast poultry according to directions on page
493. Refrigerate liver until needed. In a medium
saucepan combine remaining giblets, neck, celery,
onion, and enough lightly salted boiling water
to cover. Bring to boiling; reduce heat. Simmer,
covered, 60 minutes. Add liver. Simmer, covered,
for 20 to 30 minutes for turkey (5 to 10 minutes
for chicken) or until tender. Remove giblets;
finely chop. Discard neck. Strain broth. Discard
vegetables. Cover and chill while poultry roasts.

2 Transfer roast poultry to platter; pour drippings
into large measuring cup. Skim and reserve fat

MAKING GRAVY, STEP-BY-STEP

1. To skim fat off roast poultry or meat drippings, pour the drippings into a glass measuring cup. Tip the measure and use
a metal spoon to carefully remove the clear fat that rises to the top; reserve fat. **2.** Add the drippings and broth mixture
to the flour mixture. Stir with a wooden spoon until the mixture is smooth. **3.** Cook over medium heat, stirring constantly,
until bubbles appear on the surface. Cook and stir for 1 minute more to cook the floury flavor out of the gravy.

from drippings (see photo 1, page 488). Pour ¼ cup of the fat* into a medium saucepan (discard remaining fat). Stir in flour, ¼ teaspoon *salt*, and ⅛ teaspoon *black pepper.*

3 Add enough reserved broth to remaining drippings in the measuring cup to equal 2 cups. Add broth mixture all at once to flour mixture in the saucepan (see photo 2, page 488). Cook and stir over medium heat until thickened and bubbly. Cook and stir for 1 minute more (see photo 3, page 488). Stir in chopped giblets. Heat through.

*NOTE: If there is no fat, use ¼ cup melted butter.

PER ¼ CUP: 72 cal., 6 g total fat (2 g sat. fat, 0 g trans fat), 37 mg chol., 186 mg sodium, 3 g carbo., 0 g fiber, 3 g pro.
EXCHANGES: ½ Medium-Fat Meat, 1 Fat

BEST EVER

CITRUS-MARINATED TURKEY BREAST

PREP: 30 MINUTES **MARINATE:** 8 TO 24 HOURS
ROAST: 75 MINUTES **STAND:** 10 MINUTES
OVEN: 350°F **MAKES:** 10 TO 12 SERVINGS

- 2 3- to 3½-pound turkey breast halves with bones
- 2 cups lightly packed fresh cilantro leaves
- 1⅓ cups orange juice
- ½ cup lemon juice
- 12 cloves garlic, halved
- 1 fresh jalapeño chile pepper, seeded and cut up (see tip, page 24)
- 2 teaspoons salt
- 2 teaspoons ground cumin
- ½ teaspoon freshly ground black pepper
- 1½ cups olive oil

1 Using a sharp knife, cut several slits in turkey breast halves. Place breast halves, skin sides down, in a very large resealable plastic bag set in a baking dish; set aside.

2 For cilantro sauce, in a food processor combine cilantro, orange juice, lemon juice, garlic, jalapeño pepper, salt, cumin, and black pepper. Cover and process until almost smooth. With processor running, add oil in thin stream. Measure 2 cups sauce; cover and chill until serving. Pour remaining sauce over turkey breast halves; marinate in the refrigerator for 8 to 24 hours, turning occasionally.

3 Preheat oven to 350°F. Remove turkey from marinade; discard marinade. Place turkey, bone sides down, on greased rack in greased roasting pan. Insert an oven-going meat thermometer into thickest part of one of the turkey breast halves, without touching bone. Roast, uncovered, for 1¼ to 1½ hours or until thermometer registers 170°F and juices run clear. If necessary, cover with foil to prevent overbrowning. Let stand, covered with foil, for 10 to 15 minutes before slicing. Stir reserved sauce; pass with turkey.

PER 7 OUNCES TURKEY: 685 cal., 49 g total fat (9 g sat. fat, 0 g trans fat), 158 mg chol., 577 mg sodium, 6 g carbo., 0 g fiber, 54 g pro.
EXCHANGES: ½ Other Carbo., 7½ Lean Meat, 7 Fat

HONEY-MUSTARD TURKEY BREAST: Omit marinating turkey and cilantro sauce. Combine ½ cup honey, 3 tablespoons Dijon-style mustard, 2 tablespoons Worcestershire-style marinade for chicken, and 2 tablespoons melted butter. Brush on turkey the last 15 minutes of roasting.

PER 7 OUNCES TURKEY: 450 cal., 18 g total fat (6 g sat. fat, 0 g trans fat), 164 mg chol., 281 mg sodium, 14 g carbo., 0 g fiber, 54 g pro.
EXCHANGES: 1 Other Carbo., 7½ Lean Meat, 1 Fat

PESTO TURKEY BREAST: Combine two 7-ounce containers refrigerated basil pesto, ⅓ cup finely snipped fresh sage, ¼ cup finely chopped toasted walnuts, and ½ teaspoon black pepper. Set aside half of the pesto mixture. Starting at breast bone, slip your fingers between skin and meat to loosen skin, leaving skin attached at top. Rub about two-thirds of the remaining pesto mixture under the skin over the meat. Rub remaining pesto mixture over skin. Insert oven-going meat thermometer into thickest part of breast, without touching bone. Roast as directed. Cover with foil the last 30 to 45 minutes to prevent overbrowning. Let stand, covered with foil, for 10 to 15 minutes before slicing. Serve with reserved pesto mixture.

PER 7 OUNCES TURKEY: 587 cal., 36 g total fat (8 g sat. fat, 0 g trans fat), 171 mg chol., 454 mg sodium, 5 g carbo., 2 g fiber, 59 g pro.
EXCHANGES: 8 Lean Meat, 5 Fat

MAPLE BARBECUE-GLAZED TURKEY BREAST: Omit marinating turkey and cilantro sauce. In a small saucepan stir together ½ cup pure maple syrup, 2 tablespoons bottled chili sauce, 2 tablespoons cider vinegar, 1 tablespoon Worcestershire sauce, ½ teaspoon dry mustard, and ¼ teaspoon black pepper. Heat and stir until slightly thickened. Brush on turkey the last 15 minutes of roasting.

PER 7 OUNCES TURKEY: 422 cal., 16 g total fat (4 g sat. fat, 0 g trans fat), 158 mg chol., 223 mg sodium, 12 g carbo., 0 g fiber, 54 g pro.
EXCHANGES: 1 Other Carbo., 7½ Lean Meat, ½ Fat

MAPLE-BRINED TURKEY

PREP: 30 MINUTES **CHILL:** 12 TO 24 HOURS
ROAST: 75 MINUTES **OVEN:** 325°F
MAKES: 8 TO 10 SERVINGS

- 1 cup maple syrup
- ¾ cup kosher salt
- 1 6-ounce can apple juice concentrate, thawed
- 4 whole cloves
- ¼ teaspoon whole black peppercorns
- 3 cloves garlic, minced
- 6 to 8 pounds meaty turkey pieces (breast halves with bones, drumsticks, and/or thighs)

1 In a large deep container* combine 4 cups *hot water,* maple syrup, salt, and juice concentrate; stir until salt dissolves. Add 6 cups *cold water,* cloves, peppercorns, and garlic. Add turkey. Cover and chill in refrigerator for 12 to 24 hours.

2 Preheat oven to 325°F. Remove turkey from brine; discard brine. Pat turkey pieces dry. Place turkey pieces, meaty sides up, in a 15×10×1-inch baking pan, making sure pieces do not touch.

3 Roast, uncovered, for 75 to 90 minutes or until no pink remains (170°F for breast halves; 180°F for drumsticks and thighs).

*NOTE: Use a container that will allow turkey pieces to be submerged in the brine.

PER SERVING: 441 cal., 20 g total fat (6 g sat. fat, 0 g trans fat), 188 mg chol., 1,222 mg sodium, 4 g carbo., 0 g fiber, 57 g pro. EXCHANGES: 8 Lean Meat, 2 Fat

CRIMSON HOLIDAY HENS

PREP: 20 MINUTES **COOK:** 20 MINUTES
ROAST: 60 MINUTES **OVEN:** 375°F
MAKES: 4 SERVINGS

- 2 cloves garlic
- 3 tablespoons sliced or chopped shallot
- 1 tablespoon butter or margarine
- ¾ cup red cherry preserves (with whole cherries)
- ¼ cup red wine vinegar
- ¼ teaspoon ground allspice
- ⅛ teaspoon ground cloves
- 2 24-ounce Cornish game hens
- 1 tablespoon olive oil
- ¼ teaspoon salt
- ⅛ teaspoon black pepper

1 Preheat oven to 375°F. Mince 1 clove garlic. In saucepan cook minced garlic and shallot in butter until tender. Stir in preserves, vinegar, allspice, and cloves. Boil gently, uncovered, about 20 minutes or until desired consistency. Halve remaining clove garlic. Rub each hen with halved garlic clove. Tie drumsticks to tail (see photo 3, page 487). Brush hens with oil; sprinkle with the salt and pepper. Place hens, breast sides up, on rack in shallow roasting pan. Twist wing tips under back (see photo 4, page 487).

2 Roast, uncovered, for 60 to 75 minutes or until juices run clear and thermometer inserted into the thigh of each hen registers 180°F (the thermometer should not touch bone), brushing hens with glaze the last 15 minutes of roasting time.

3 Use kitchen shears to carefully cut hens in half lengthwise. Spoon any remaining glaze over hens.

APRICOT-GLAZED HOLIDAY HENS: Prepare as directed, except substitute apricot preserves for the cherry preserves, white wine vinegar for the red wine vinegar, and ¼ teaspoon ground cinnamon for the allspice; omit the cloves.

PER ½ HEN + ¼ CUP GLAZE FOR CRIMSON OR APRICOT VARIATION: 632 cal., 33 g total fat (10 g sat. fat, 0 g trans fat), 215 mg chol., 288 mg sodium, 43 g carbo., 1 g fiber, 36 g pro. EXCHANGES: 3 Other Carbo., 5 Medium-Fat Meat, 1½ Fat

ORANGE-GINGER DUCK

PREP: 25 MINUTES **MARINATE:** 4 TO 24 HOURS
COOK: 35 MINUTES **ROAST:** 12 MINUTES
OVEN: 350°F **MAKES:** 6 SERVINGS

- 6 boneless duck breast halves (with skin)
- 1 tablespoon finely shredded orange peel
- 1 cup orange juice
- 1 cup dry white wine
- 6 tablespoons honey
- 4 tablespoons grated fresh ginger
- 1 tablespoon olive oil
- ¼ cup chicken broth
- 1 tablespoon soy sauce
- 3 cups hot cooked rice

1 Trim fat from breast halves (do not remove the skin). Score skin in a diamond pattern (see photo 1, page 491). Place duck in a resealable plastic bag set in a bowl. For marinade, mix orange peel, orange juice, ½ cup of the wine, 4 tablespoons of the honey, and 3 tablespoons of the ginger. Pour over duck in bag; seal. Marinate in the refrigerator for 4 to 24 hours, turning bag occasionally.

2 Remove duck from marinade; reserve marinade. In a large saucepan bring marinade and remaining ½ cup wine to boiling; reduce heat. Boil gently, uncovered, for 20 to 25 minutes or until reduced to 1¼ cups.

3 Preheat oven to 350°F. Heat very large ovenproof skillet over medium heat. Place duck pieces in hot skillet, skin sides down; cook for 5 minutes. Turn duck over and cook for 5 minutes more or until duck browns (see photo 2, below). Drain off fat. Place the skillet in oven; roast for 12 to 18 minutes or until thermometer registers 155°F.

4 Meanwhile, for glaze, add remaining honey and ginger, broth, and soy sauce to reduced marinade. Return to boiling. Boil gently, uncovered, about 15 minutes or until reduced to ⅔ cup, stirring often. Season with *salt* and *black pepper*. Slice duck and arrange on rice; spoon glaze over duck.

PER BREAST HALF + ½ CUP RICE + 2 TABLESPOONS GLAZE: 628 cal., 29 g total fat (9 g sat. fat, 0 g trans fat), 155 mg chol., 701 mg sodium, 46 g carbo., 1 g fiber, 37 g pro. EXCHANGES: 1½ Starch, 1½ Other Carbo., 4½ Medium-Fat Meat, 1½ Fat

PAN-SEARED DUCK WITH APPLES

PREP: 15 MINUTES **COOK:** 15 MINUTES
ROAST: 12 MINUTES **STAND:** 10 MINUTES
OVEN: 350°F **MAKES:** 4 SERVINGS

- 4 boneless duck breast halves (with skin)
- ¼ cup butter or margarine
- 4 Golden Delicious or Gala apples, sliced
- ⅓ cup balsamic vinegar
- ¼ cup apple juice
- 4 cups broccoli rabe or kale

1 Preheat oven to 350°F. Trim excess fat from duck (do not remove skin). Score the skin in a diamond pattern (see photo 1, below). Sprinkle duck with *black pepper*.

2 Heat a very large ovenproof skillet over medium heat. Place duck pieces in hot skillet, skin sides down; cook for 5 minutes. Turn duck over and cook for 5 minutes more or until duck browns (see photo 2, below). Drain off fat. Place the skillet in oven; roast for 12 to 18 minutes or until thermometer registers 155°F.

3 Meanwhile, in a large skillet melt butter over medium heat. Add apples; cook for 10 minutes or until tender, stirring frequently. Season apples with *salt* and additional *pepper*; remove apples from skillet. Set aside and keep warm.

4 Remove duck from skillet; cover and let stand for 10 minutes (the temperature of the duck will rise 5°F during standing time). For sauce, reserve 1 tablespoon drippings in skillet used to cook the duck; discard remaining drippings. Add vinegar and apple juice to drippings in skillet, scraping up browned bits. Return skillet to stovetop. Bring to boiling over medium-high heat. Cook for 3 to 5 minutes or until liquid is reduced by half.

5 In a large saucepan bring 4 cups water to boiling. Add broccoli rabe and cook for 1 minute. Drain in colander. To serve, arrange duck breasts, broccoli rabe, and apples on a serving platter. Drizzle with sauce.

PER BREAST HALF + ½ CUP SAUCE + ½ CUP BROCCOLI RABE: 620 cal., 38 g total fat (16 g sat. fat, 0 g trans fat), 185 mg chol., 332 mg sodium, 33 g carbo., 5 g fiber, 36 g pro. EXCHANGES: 1 Vegetable, 1½ Fruit, 5 Medium-Fat Meat, 3 Fat

PAN-SEARING DUCK BREASTS, STEP-BY-STEP

1. Use a large sharp knife to cut through the skin but not into the meat. Make parallel cuts about ½ inch apart; cut in the opposite direction to make a diamond pattern. **2.** Place the duck in the hot skillet, fat sides down. The duck will release enough fat to brown and crisp the skin. Cook until the skin browns and crisps before turning.

ROAST DUCKLING WITH MAPLE-CIDER GLAZE

PREP: 30 MINUTES **ROAST:** 1½ TO 2 HOURS
STAND: 15 MINUTES **OVEN:** 350°F
MAKES: 4 SERVINGS

- 1 4- to 6-pound domestic duckling
- 2 cups apple cider
- 1 tablespoon snipped fresh sage
- 1 tablespoon maple or maple-flavored syrup
  Chicken broth (optional)
- ¼ cup apple cider or apple juice
- 1 tablespoon brandy
- 1½ teaspoons cornstarch
- 1½ teaspoons snipped fresh sage
- 1 recipe Cranberry-Fig Chutney

1 Preheat oven to 350°F. Rinse duckling body cavity; pat dry. Skewer neck skin to back; tie legs to tail. Twist wing tips under back. Place, breast side up, on rack in shallow roasting pan. Prick skin generously. Sprinkle with *salt* and *black pepper*.

2 Roast duck, uncovered, for 1½ to 2 hours or until the drumsticks move easily in their sockets (180°F). Juices might still appear pink.

3 Meanwhile, for glaze, in a medium saucepan bring 2 cups cider to boiling. Boil for 10 to 15 minutes or until reduced to ⅓ cup (mixture will be thin and syrupy). Remove from heat. Stir in the 1 tablespoon sage and maple syrup. Brush glaze over duck the last 30 minutes of roasting. Cover and let stand for 15 minutes before carving.

4 For sauce, reserve drippings from the roasting pan. Skim and discard fat from drippings. Strain drippings through a fine-mesh sieve. If necessary, add enough broth to drippings to equal ¾ cup. Place drippings in small saucepan. Combine the ¼ cup cider, brandy, and cornstarch; add to drippings in saucepan. Cook and stir until thickened and bubbly. Cook and stir for 2 minutes more. Stir in the 1½ teaspoons snipped sage; season to taste with *salt* and *black pepper*. Serve duck with sauce and Cranberry-Fig Chutney. If desired, garnish with *apple slices* and fresh *sage leaves*.

CRANBERRY-FIG CHUTNEY: In a saucepan stir together 1 cup fresh cranberries; 1 cup chopped, peeled apple; ½ cup apple cider or apple juice; ¼ cup snipped dried figs; 2 tablespoons packed brown sugar; and ⅛ teaspoon ground ginger. Bring to boiling; reduce heat. Simmer, uncovered, about 10 minutes or until slightly thickened (chutney will thicken as it cools).

PER 4 OUNCES DUCK + ½ CUP CHUTNEY: 299 cal., 9 g total fat (4 g sat. fat, 0 g trans fat), 119 mg chol., 420 mg sodium, 21 g carbo., 0 g fiber, 28 g pro. EXCHANGES: ½ Fruit, 1½ Other Carbo., 4 Lean Meat

PHEASANT BREAST SUPREME

PREP: 25 MINUTES **COOK:** 30 MINUTES
MAKES: 4 SERVINGS

- 4 skinless, boneless pheasant breast halves
- ¼ cup all-purpose flour
- 5 tablespoons butter or margarine
- 1½ cups sliced fresh mushrooms
- ¼ cup finely chopped shallots
- ¼ cup finely chopped celery
- ¼ cup cream sherry or chicken broth
- 2 tablespoons lemon juice
- ½ cup chicken broth
- 1 cup whipping cream
- ¼ cup dairy sour cream
- 2 cloves garlic, minced
- 6 cups torn fresh spinach
- ¼ cup sliced almonds, toasted (see tip, page 20)

1 Place each breast half between two pieces of plastic wrap. Using flat side of meat mallet, pound pheasant lightly until about ¼ inch thick. Combine flour and ⅛ teaspoon each *salt* and *black pepper*. Coat pheasant on both sides with flour mixture.

2 In a large skillet cook pheasant, half at a time, in 2 tablespoons butter over medium-high heat for 3 to 4 minutes until no longer pink (170°F), turning occasionally. Remove from skillet; keep warm.

3 In same skillet cook mushrooms, shallots, and celery in 1 tablespoon butter until tender, stirring often. Remove from heat. Carefully add sherry and lemon juice, stirring to scrape up browned bits. Add ½ cup broth to skillet. Bring to boiling; reduce heat. Cook over medium-high heat for 6 to 8 minutes or until most of the liquid evaporates (should have about 2 tablespoons), stirring often. Whisk in whipping cream and sour cream. Cook, whisking constantly, over medium heat until mixture is reduced to about 1¼ cups. Return pheasant to skillet; heat through.

4 In a very large skillet cook garlic in 2 tablespoons butter for 1 minute. Add spinach. Cook and toss just until wilted. Serve pheasant with sauce over spinach. Sprinkle with almonds.

PER SERVING: 622 cal., 46 g total fat (26 g sat. fat, 0 g trans fat), 193 mg chol., 402 mg sodium, 16 g carbo., 2 g fiber, 34 g pro. EXCHANGES: 2 Vegetable, ½ Starch, 4 Medium-Fat Meat, 5 Fat

ROASTING POULTRY

Because birds vary in size and shape, use times as general guides. For stuffed birds, see page 486.

1 If desired, thoroughly rinse a whole bird's body and neck cavities. Pat dry with paper towels. If desired, sprinkle the body cavity with salt.

2 If desired, place quartered onions and celery in body cavity. Pull neck skin to back and fasten with skewer. If a band of skin crosses tail, tuck drumsticks under band. If there is no band, tie drumsticks to tail. Twist wing tips under back.

3 Place bird, breast side up, on a rack in a shallow roasting pan; brush with vegetable oil and, if desired, sprinkle with a crushed dried herb, such as thyme or oregano. (When cooking a domestic duckling or goose, prick skin generously all over and omit oil.) For large birds, insert a meat thermometer into center of one of the inside thigh muscles. Thermometer should not touch the bone.

4 Cover Cornish hen, pheasant, and whole turkey with foil, leaving air space between bird and foil. Lightly press foil to ends of drumsticks and neck to enclose bird. Leave other poultry uncovered.

5 Roast in an uncovered pan. Two-thirds through roasting time cut band of skin or string between drumsticks. Uncover large birds last 45 minutes of roasting; uncover small birds last 30 minutes of roasting. Continue roasting until meat thermometer registers 180°F in thigh muscle (check temperature of thigh in several places) or until drumsticks move easily in sockets and juices run clear. (For a whole or half turkey breast, thermometer should register 170°F.) Remove bird from oven; cover. Allow whole birds and turkey portions to stand for 15 minutes before carving.

Type of Bird	Weight	Oven Temperature	Roasting Time
CHICKEN			
Capon	5 to 7 pounds	325°F	1¾ to 2½ hours
Meaty pieces (breast halves, drumsticks, and thighs with bone)	2½ to 3 pounds	375°F	45 to 55 minutes
Whole	2½ to 3 pounds 3½ to 4 pounds 4½ to 5 pounds	375°F 375°F 375°F	1 to 1¼ hours 1¼ to 1¾ hours 1½ to 2 hours
GAME			
Cornish game hen	1¼ to 1½ pounds	375°F	1 to 1¼ hours
Duckling, domestic	4 to 6 pounds	350°F	1½ to 2 hours
Goose, domestic	7 to 8 pounds 8 to 10 pounds	350°F 350°F	2 to 2½ hours 2½ to 3 hours
Pheasant	2 to 3 pounds	350°F	1¼ to 1½ hours
TURKEY			
Boneless whole	2½ to 3½ pounds 4 to 6 pounds	325°F 325°F	2 to 2½ hours 2½ to 3½ hours
Breast, whole	4 to 6 pounds 6 to 8 pounds	325°F 325°F	1½ to 2¼ hours 2¼ to 3¼ hours
Drumstick	1 to 1½ pounds	325°F	1¼ to 1¾ hours
Thigh	1½ to 1¾ pounds	325°F	1½ to 1¾ hours
Whole (unstuffed)*	8 to 12 pounds 12 to 14 pounds 14 to 18 pounds 18 to 20 pounds 20 to 24 pounds	325°F 325°F 325°F 325°F 325°F	2¾ to 3 hours 3 to 3¾ hours 3¾ to 4¼ hours 4¼ to 4½ hours 4½ to 5 hours

*Stuffed birds generally require 15 to 45 minutes more roasting time than unstuffed birds. Always verify doneness temperatures of poultry and center of stuffing (165°F) with a meat thermometer.

BROILING POULTRY

If desired, remove poultry skin; sprinkle with salt and black pepper. Preheat broiler for 5 to 10 minutes. Arrange poultry on the unheated rack of broiler pan with the bone side(s) up. If desired, brush poultry with vegetable oil. Place pan under broiler so surface of the poultry is 4 to 5 inches from the heat; chicken and Cornish game hen halves should be 5 to 6 inches from the heat. Turn pieces over when brown on one side, usually after half of the broiling time. Chicken halves and quarters and meaty pieces should be turned after 20 minutes. Brush again with oil. The poultry is done when the meat is no longer pink and the juices run clear (180°F for thighs and drumsticks; 170°F for breast meat; 160°F for duck breast). If desired, brush with a sauce the last 5 minutes of cooking.

Type of Bird	Thickness/Weight	Broiling Time
CHICKEN		
Broiler-fryer, half	1¼ to 1½ pounds	28 to 32 minutes
Broiler-fryer, quarter	10 to 12 ounces	28 to 32 minutes
Kabobs (boneless breast, cut into 2½-inch strips and threaded loosely onto skewers)		8 to 10 minutes
Meaty pieces (breast halves, drumsticks, and thighs with bone)	2½ to 3 pounds	25 to 35 minutes
Skinless, boneless breast halves	4 to 5 ounces	12 to 15 minutes
GAME		
Cornish game hen, half	10 to 12 ounces	25 to 35 minutes
Boneless duck breast, skin removed	6 to 8 ounces	14 to 16 minutes
TURKEY		
Breast cutlet	2 ounces	6 to 8 minutes
Breast tenderloin steaks (to make ½-inch-thick steaks, cut turkey tenderloin in half horizontally)	4 to 6 ounces	8 to 10 minutes

SKILLET-COOKING POULTRY

Select a heavy skillet that is the right size for the amount of poultry being cooked. (If the skillet is too large, pan juices can burn. If it's too small, poultry will steam instead of brown.) If the skillet is not nonstick, lightly coat it with nonstick cooking spray or 2 to 3 teaspoons of oil. Preheat skillet over medium-high heat until hot. Add poultry. Do not add any liquid and do not cover the skillet. Reduce heat to medium; cook for the time given or until done, turning poultry occasionally. (If poultry browns too quickly, reduce heat to medium-low.) Poultry is done when the meat is no longer pink and the juices run clear (180°F for thighs; 170°F for breast meat).

Type of Bird	Thickness/Weight	Approximate Cooking Time
CHICKEN		
Breast tenders	1 to 2 ounces	6 to 8 minutes
Skinless, boneless breast halves	3 to 5 ounces	8 to 12 minutes
Skinless, boneless thighs	3 to 4 ounces	14 to 18 minutes
TURKEY		
Breast tenderloin steaks	4 to 6 ounces	15 to 18 minutes

SALADS & DRESSINGS

BISTRO SALAD, PAGE 517

SALADS & DRESSINGS

WHETHER YOUR SALAD IS A
FIRST COURSE, A SIDE, OR THE
MAIN ATTRACTION OF THE MEAL,
HERE'S HOW TO MAKE IT SPARKLE.

PREPARING SALAD GREENS

Use these tips to showcase greens at their crispest and cleanest—and tastiest.

■ Select greens that appear fresh and have no brown, bruised, or wilted leaves.

■ To wash greens, remove and discard the root end; separate the leaves. Gently move the leaves around in a large bowl or sink filled with cold water for about 30 seconds. Remove the leaves, gently shaking them to remove any dirt or debris. Repeat this process, using fresh water each time, until the water remains clear.

■ To dry the greens, use a salad spinner or pat each leaf dry with paper towels.

■ When you are ready to use the greens, tear them into bite-size pieces.

■ Store washed and dried greens in the refrigerator in a resealable plastic bag lined with paper towels or in a fabric produce bag.

■ Packaged prewashed greens are a realistic choice when you don't have time to prep greens yourself. Because these packages are specifically designed to allow the greens to breathe, store any undressed leftovers in the original bag.

BISTRO SALAD, PAGE 517

HOMEMADE DRESSINGS

French, honey mustard, creamy Parmesan—these are classic dressings you've seen countless times on store shelves and restaurant menus. Yet nothing beats a homemade version. Many start with oil and vinegar; this guide to some of the available varieties can help you mix and match.

SALAD OILS

NUT OILS: Almond, hazelnut, and walnut oils can add rich flavor to dressings. Highly perishable, they should be stored in the refrigerator.

OLIVE OIL: Choose pure olive oil for a milder flavor; extra-virgin olive oil when you want the flavor of the oil to shine through. Store in a cool, dark place.

VEGETABLE OIL: With their neutral taste, vegetable oils, such as canola, safflower, and sunflower, bring body to a dressing without impacting the flavor of the other ingredients in the dressing or salad. Store at room temperature.

VINEGARS

CIDER VINEGAR: This tartly acidic vinegar is most often used for dressing cabbage and other hearty vegetables, but can also be used for dressing greens. When a recipe simply calls for vinegar, cider vinegar works just fine.

DISTILLED WHITE VINEGAR: Mainly used for pickling, this is the sharpest of all vinegars. For something more subtle, substitute white wine vinegar.

FLAVORED VINEGARS: Infused with herbs, nuts, or fruits, these vinegars bring a subtle taste of the flavoring ingredient to the dressing.

RICE VINEGAR: Made from fermented rice, this vinegar is mild in flavor; its subtle sweetness provides an especially enticing contrast to spicy or bitter greens.

WINE VINEGAR: These are time-honored choices for classic vinaigrettes. Balsamic vinegar is a wine vinegar that's been aged in barrels, which imbues it with a dark color and sweetly pungent flavor.

GIVE IT A SHAKE

One key step in making a vinaigrette is to thoroughly combine the oil and vinegar into one smooth mixture. An easy way to do this is to use a screw-top jar. Combine the ingredients in the jar, then shake and serve.

SALAD GREENS

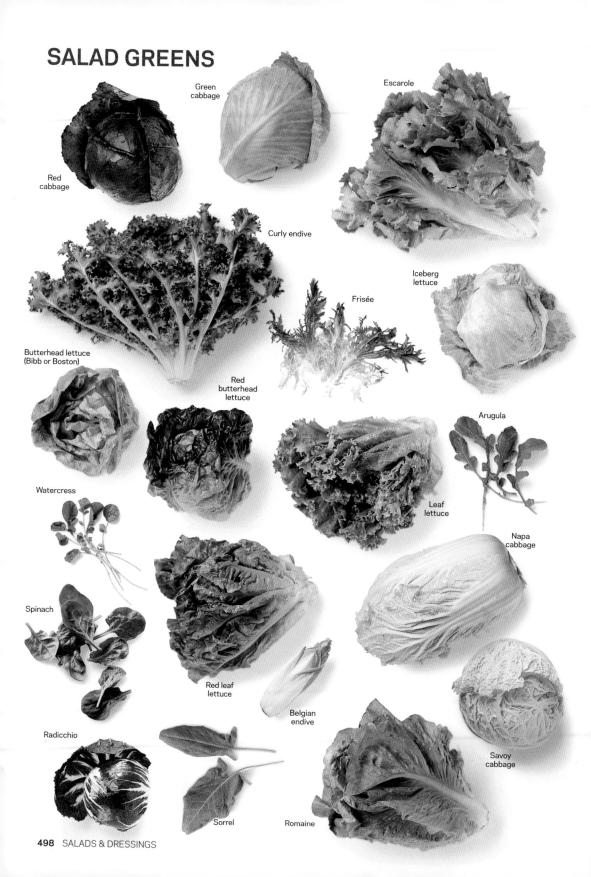

Green cabbage

Escarole

Red cabbage

Curly endive

Iceberg lettuce

Frisée

Butterhead lettuce (Bibb or Boston)

Red butterhead lettuce

Arugula

Watercress

Leaf lettuce

Napa cabbage

Spinach

Red leaf lettuce

Radicchio

Belgian endive

Savoy cabbage

Sorrel

Romaine

GUIDE TO SALAD GREENS

Type	Weight at Purchase	Amount after Preparation	Preparation and Storage*
Arugula	1 ounce	1 cup torn	Rinse thoroughly in cold water to remove all sand; pat dry. Refrigerate in plastic bag for up to 2 days.
Cabbage	2 pounds (1 head)	12 cups shredded or 10 cups coarsely chopped	Refrigerate in plastic bag for up to 5 days. Rinse in cold water just before using; pat dry.
Cabbage, napa	2 pounds (1 head)	12 cups sliced stems and shredded leaves	Cut off bottom core. Rinse in cold water; pat dry. Refrigerate in plastic bag for up to 3 days.
Cabbage, savoy	1¾ pounds (1 head)	12 cups coarsely shredded	Refrigerate in plastic bag for up to 5 days. Rinse in cold water just before using; pat dry.
Endive, Belgian	4 ounces (1 head)	20 leaves	Cut off bottom core. Rinse in cold water; pat dry. Refrigerate in plastic bag and use within 1 day.
Endive, curly	12 ounces (1 head)	14 cups torn	Rinse in cold water; pat dry. Refrigerate, tightly wrapped, for up to 3 days.
Escarole	8 ounces (1 head)	7 cups torn	Rinse in cold water; pat dry. Refrigerate, tightly wrapped, for up to 3 days.
Frisée	8 ounces	7 cups torn	Rinse in cold water; pat dry. Refrigerate in plastic bag for up to 3 days.
Lettuce, butterhead (Bibb or Boston)	8 ounces (1 head)	6 cups torn	Cut off bottom core. Rinse in cold water; pat dry. Refrigerate in plastic bag for up to 3 days.
Lettuce, iceberg	1¼ pounds (1 head)	10 cups torn or 12 cups shredded	Remove core. Rinse (core side up) under cold running water; invert to drain. Refrigerate in plastic bag for up to 5 days.
Lettuce, leaf	12 ounces (1 head)	10 cups torn	Cut off bottom core. Rinse in cold water; pat dry. Refrigerate in plastic bag for up to 3 days.
Radicchio	8 ounces (1 head)	5½ cups torn	Rinse in cold water; pat dry. Refrigerate in plastic bag for up to 1 week.
Romaine	1 pound (1 head)	10 cups torn	Cut off bottom core. Rinse leaves in cold water; pat dry. Refrigerate in plastic bag for up to 5 days. Before using, remove fibrous rib from each leaf.
Sorrel	1 ounce	1 cup torn	Rinse in cold water; pat dry. Refrigerate in plastic bag for up to 3 days.
Spinach	1 pound	12 cups torn, stems removed	Rinse thoroughly in cold water to remove all sand; pat dry. Refrigerate in plastic bag for up to 3 days.
Watercress	4 ounces	2⅓ cups, stems removed	Rinse in cold water. Wrap in damp paper towels; refrigerate in plastic bag for up to 2 days.

*Line a resealable plastic bag with paper towels. For more information, see "Preparing Salad Greens," page 497.

CHOOSING GREENS

VARY THE GREENS YOU CHOOSE DEPENDING ON YOUR TASTES AND HOW THEY WILL BEST COMPLEMENT THE OTHER INGREDIENTS IN THE SALAD. FOLLOW THESE GUIDELINES.

■ Crunchy, mild-flavor greens, such as iceberg, romaine, and spinach, stand up admirably to thick and/or creamy dressings.

■ Soft and mild butterhead and red- or green-leaf lettuces are winning choices when you want the other salad ingredients, such as in-season fruits and vegetables, to stand out.

■ Spicy and bitter greens, such as endive, radicchio, watercress, arugula, and frisée, make terrific choices when you want the flavor of the greens themselves to be a starring component of the salad.

■ Rough, sturdy cabbages are best shredded. Perfect in coleslaw, they can also be added to green salads in smaller amounts for extra flavor and texture.

BUTTERMILK DRESSING

PREP: 10 MINUTES **CHILL:** 30 MINUTES
MAKES: 1¼ CUPS

- ¾ cup buttermilk
- ½ cup mayonnaise
- 1 tablespoon snipped fresh Italian parsley
- ¼ teaspoon onion powder
- ¼ teaspoon dry mustard
- ¼ teaspoon black pepper
- 1 clove garlic, minced
  Buttermilk (optional)

1 In a small bowl stir together the ¾ cup buttermilk, mayonnaise, parsley, onion powder, mustard, pepper, and garlic. If necessary, add additional buttermilk until dressing reaches desired consistency.

2 Cover and chill dressing for 30 minutes before serving. Cover and store in the refrigerator for up to 1 week. Stir or shake well before using.

PEPPERCORN-BUTTERMILK DRESSING: Prepare as directed, except omit black pepper and stir in ½ teaspoon cracked black pepper.

PER 1 TABLESPOON PLAIN OR PEPPERCORN VARIATION: 44 cal., 4 g total fat (1 g sat. fat, 0 g trans fat), 2 mg chol., 40 mg sodium, 1 g carbo., 0 g fiber, 0 g pro. EXCHANGES: 1 Fat

BLUE CHEESE DRESSING

START TO FINISH: 10 MINUTES
MAKES: ABOUT 1¼ CUPS

- ½ cup plain yogurt or dairy sour cream
- ¼ cup cottage cheese
- ¼ cup mayonnaise
- ¾ to 1 cup crumbled blue cheese
  (3 to 4 ounces)
- ¼ teaspoon salt
- ¼ teaspoon cracked black pepper
- 1 to 2 tablespoons milk (optional)

1 In a blender or food processor combine yogurt, cottage cheese, mayonnaise, ¼ cup of the crumbled blue cheese, salt, and pepper. Cover and blend or process until smooth. Stir in remaining blue cheese. If necessary, stir in milk until dressing reaches desired consistency. Serve immediately or cover and store in the refrigerator for up to 2 weeks. Stir before using.

PER 1 TABLESPOON: 44 cal., 4 g total fat (2 g sat. fat, 0 g trans fat), 6 mg chol., 127 mg sodium, 1 g carbo., 0 g fiber, 2 g pro. EXCHANGES: 1 Fat

CREAMY PARMESAN DRESSING

START TO FINISH: 10 MINUTES
MAKES: ABOUT 1 CUP

- ½ cup mayonnaise
- ¼ cup grated Parmesan cheese
- ¼ cup buttermilk
- 3 cloves garlic, minced
- 1 tablespoon snipped fresh Italian parsley
  Buttermilk (optional)

1 In a small bowl stir together mayonnaise, cheese, the ¼ cup buttermilk, garlic, and parsley. Cover; store in the refrigerator for up to 1 week. Stir before using. If necessary, add additional buttermilk if dressing thickens during chilling.

PER 1 TABLESPOON: 58 cal., 6 g total fat (1 g sat. fat, 0 g trans fat), 4 mg chol., 61 mg sodium, 0 g carbo., 0 g fiber, 1 g pro. EXCHANGES: 1 Fat

CREAMY ITALIAN DRESSING

START TO FINISH: 15 MINUTES
MAKES: ABOUT 1 CUP

- ¾ cup mayonnaise
- ¼ cup dairy sour cream
- 2 teaspoons white wine vinegar
- 1 clove garlic, minced
- ½ teaspoon dried Italian seasoning
- ¼ teaspoon dry mustard
- 1 to 2 tablespoons milk (optional)

1 In a small bowl stir together mayonnaise, sour cream, vinegar, garlic, Italian seasoning, mustard, and ⅛ teaspoon *salt*. Serve immediately or cover and store in the refrigerator for up to 1 week. Before serving, if necessary, stir in milk until dressing reaches desired consistency.

CREAMY GARLIC DRESSING: Prepare as directed, except add 2 additional cloves garlic, minced.

PER 1 TABLESPOON PLAIN OR GARLIC VARIATION: 82 cal., 9 g total fat (2 g sat. fat, 0 g trans fat), 5 mg chol., 77 mg sodium, 0 g carbo., 0 g fiber, 0 g pro. EXCHANGES: 2 Fat

CREAMY FRENCH DRESSING

START TO FINISH: 15 MINUTES
MAKES: ABOUT 2 CUPS

- ⅓ cup water
- ⅓ cup vinegar
- 2 tablespoons sugar

1 tablespoon lemon juice

2 teaspoons paprika

1 teaspoon salt

1 teaspoon dry mustard

1 teaspoon black pepper

1 teaspoon Worcestershire sauce

1 clove garlic, quartered

1⅓ cups vegetable oil or olive oil

1 In a blender combine the water, vinegar, sugar, lemon juice, paprika, salt, mustard, pepper, Worcestershire sauce, and garlic. Cover and blend until combined. With blender running, slowly add oil in a thin, steady stream (dressing will thicken as oil is added). Serve immediately or cover and store in the refrigerator for up to 2 weeks. Stir before serving.

PER 1 TABLESPOON: 85 cal., 9 g total fat (1 g sat. fat, 0 g trans fat), 0 mg chol., 75 mg sodium, 1 g carbo., 0 g fiber, 0 g pro. EXCHANGES: 2 Fat

FAST

THOUSAND ISLAND DRESSING

START TO FINISH: 15 MINUTES **MAKES:** 1½ CUPS

1 cup mayonnaise

¼ cup bottled chili sauce

2 tablespoons sweet pickle relish

2 tablespoons finely chopped sweet pepper

2 tablespoons finely chopped onion

1 teaspoon Worcestershire sauce

1 to 2 tablespoons milk (optional)

1 In a small bowl combine mayonnaise and chili sauce. Stir in relish, sweet pepper, onion, and Worcestershire sauce. Serve immediately or cover and store in the refrigerator for up to 1 week. Before serving, if necessary, stir in milk until dressing reaches desired consistency.

PER 1 TABLESPOON: 71 cal., 7 g total fat (1 g sat. fat, 0 g trans fat), 3 mg chol., 93 mg sodium, 1 g carbo., 0 g fiber, 0 g pro. EXCHANGES: 1½ Fat

BEST WHEN MADE AHEAD IF POSSIBLE, PREPARE MAYONNAISE-BASED DRESSINGS THE DAY BEFORE YOU WANT TO USE THEM. THIS ALLOWS TIME FOR THE FLAVORS TO BLEND AND INTENSIFY.

CREAMY PARMESAN DRESSING

CREAMY FRENCH DRESSING

BLUE CHEESE DRESSING

HONEY-MUSTARD DRESSING

START TO FINISH: 10 MINUTES
MAKES: ABOUT 1 CUP

- ¼ cup stone-ground mustard
- ¼ cup olive oil or vegetable oil
- ¼ cup lemon juice
- ¼ cup honey
- 2 cloves garlic, minced

1 In a screw-top jar combine mustard, oil, lemon juice, honey, and garlic. Cover and shake well. Serve immediately or cover and store in the refrigerator for up to 1 week. Stir or shake well before using.

PER 1 TABLESPOON: 51 cal., 4 g total fat (0 g sat. fat, 0 g trans fat), 0 mg chol., 51 mg sodium, 5 g carbo., 0 g fiber, 0 g pro. EXCHANGES: 1 Fat

ORANGE-POPPY SEED DRESSING

START TO FINISH: 15 MINUTES **MAKES:** ⅔ CUP

- 2 tablespoons honey
- 1½ teaspoons finely shredded orange peel
- 2 tablespoons orange juice
- 2 tablespoons vinegar
- 1 tablespoon finely chopped onion
- ⅛ teaspoon salt
  Dash black pepper
- ⅓ cup vegetable oil
- 1 teaspoon poppy seeds

1 In a small food processor or blender combine honey, orange peel, orange juice, vinegar, onion, salt, and pepper. Cover and process or blend until combined. With processor or blender running, slowly add oil in a steady stream until mixture is thickened. Stir in poppy seeds. Serve immediately or cover and store in the refrigerator for up to 1 week. Stir or shake well before using.

PER 1 TABLESPOON: 81 cal., 7 g total fat (1 g sat. fat, 0 g trans fat), 0 mg chol., 30 mg sodium, 4 g carbo., 0 g fiber, 0 g pro. EXCHANGES: 1½ Fat

FRESH HERB VINAIGRETTE

START TO FINISH: 10 MINUTES
MAKES: ABOUT ¾ CUP

- ⅓ cup olive oil or vegetable oil
- ⅓ cup white or red wine vinegar, rice vinegar, or cider vinegar
- 1 tablespoon snipped fresh thyme, oregano, or basil, or ½ teaspoon dried thyme, oregano, or basil, crushed
- 1 to 2 teaspoons sugar
- ¼ teaspoon dry mustard
- 1 clove garlic, minced
- ⅛ teaspoon black pepper

1 In a screw-top jar combine oil, vinegar, herb, sugar, mustard, garlic, and pepper. Cover and shake well. Serve immediately or cover and store in refrigerator for up to 3 days if using fresh herbs. If using dried herbs, store in refrigerator for up to 1 week. Stir or shake well before using.

BALSAMIC VINAIGRETTE: Prepare as directed, except use regular or white balsamic vinegar.

GINGER VINAIGRETTE: Prepare as directed, except use rice vinegar; use 1 teaspoon grated fresh ginger instead of herb and substitute 2 teaspoons honey for sugar. Add 2 teaspoons soy sauce.

RASPBERRY VINAIGRETTE: Prepare as directed, except use raspberry or red wine vinegar, omit the sugar, and add 3 tablespoons seedless raspberry preserves.

PER 1 TABLESPOON PLAIN, BALSAMIC, GINGER, OR RASPBERRY VARIATIONS: 57 cal., 6 g total fat (1 g sat. fat, 0 g trans fat), 0 mg chol., 1 mg sodium, 1 g carbo., 0 g fiber, 0 g pro. EXCHANGES: 1½ Fat

CHEF'S SALAD

START TO FINISH: 30 MINUTES
MAKES: 4 MAIN-DISH SERVINGS

- 4 cups torn iceberg or leaf lettuce
- 4 cups torn romaine or fresh spinach
- 4 ounces cooked ham, chicken, turkey, or beef, cut into bite-size strips (1 cup)
- 4 ounces Swiss, cheddar, American, or provolone cheese, cut into bite-size strips (1 cup)
- 2 Hard-Cooked Eggs, sliced (page 134)
- 2 medium tomatoes, cut into wedges, or 8 cherry tomatoes, halved
- 1 small green or red sweet pepper, cut into bite-size strips (½ cup)
- 1 cup Parmesan Croutons (page 506) or purchased croutons
- ½ cup Creamy French Dressing (page 500), Buttermilk Dressing (page 500), Creamy Italian Dressing (page 500), or other salad dressing

1 In a large bowl toss together greens. Divide among four large salad plates. Arrange meat, cheese, eggs, tomatoes, and sweet pepper strips on top of the greens. Sprinkle with croutons. Drizzle desired salad dressing over all; pass any remaining dressing.

PER 2 CUPS: 494 cal., 38 g total fat (12 g sat. fat, 0 g trans fat), 165 mg chol., 775 mg sodium, 19 g carbo., 4 g fiber, 20 g pro. EXCHANGES: 2 Vegetable, ½ Starch, 2 Lean Meat, 6½ Fat

ITALIAN CHEF'S SALAD: Use 2 ounces chicken and mozzarella cheese. Omit eggs. Add 2 ounces sliced pepperoni; one 6-ounce jar marinated artichoke heart quarters, drained; and ¼ cup sliced ripe olives. For dressing, use Creamy Italian Dressing or bottled Italian vinaigrette.

PER 2 CUPS: 473 cal., 34 g total fat (13 g sat. fat, 1 g trans fat), 67 mg chol., 1,184 mg sodium, 22 g carbo., 3 g fiber, 18 g pro. EXCHANGES: 1 Starch, 2 Vegetable, 1½ Lean Meat, 6 Fat

BEST EVER

TACO SALAD

PREP: 30 MINUTES **BAKE:** 15 MINUTES
COOK: 10 MINUTES **OVEN:** 350°F
MAKES: 6 MAIN-DISH SERVINGS

- 6 purchased taco salad shells or 1 recipe Tortilla Shells
- 8 ounces lean ground beef or uncooked ground turkey
- 3 cloves garlic, minced
- 1 15-ounce can dark red kidney beans or black beans, rinsed and drained
- 1 cup bottled salsa
- ¾ cup frozen whole kernel corn (optional)
- 6 cups shredded leaf or iceberg lettuce

- 1 cup chopped tomatoes (2 medium)
- 1 cup chopped green sweet pepper (1 large)
- ½ cup thinly sliced green onions (4)
- 1 cup chopped avocado (1 medium)
- ¾ cup shredded sharp cheddar cheese (3 ounces)
  Dairy sour cream and bottled salsa (optional)

1 Prepare taco salad shells according to package directions; set aside. In a medium saucepan cook ground beef and garlic until beef is brown. Drain off fat. Stir in beans, 1 cup salsa, and thawed corn (if desired). Bring to boiling; reduce heat. Simmer, covered, for 10 minutes.

2 Meanwhile, in a very large bowl combine lettuce, tomatoes, sweet pepper, and green onions. To serve, divide lettuce mixture among the shells. Top each serving with some of the meat mixture and avocado. Sprinkle with cheese. If desired, serve with sour cream and additional salsa.

TORTILLA SHELLS: Preheat oven to 350°F. Lightly brush one side of six 9- or 10-inch flour tortillas with vegetable oil or lightly coat with nonstick cooking spray. Coat six small oven-safe bowls with nonstick cooking spray. Press tortillas, coated sides up, into prepared bowls; place a ball of foil in each tortilla cup (see photo 1, below). Bake about 15 minutes or until light brown. Remove foil; let cool. Remove cups from bowls (see photo 2, below). Serve immediately or store in an airtight container for up to 5 days.

PER SALAD: 345 cal., 17 g total fat (6 g sat. fat, 1 g trans fat), 41 mg chol., 553 mg sodium, 34 g carbo., 9 g fiber, 20 g pro. EXCHANGES: 1½ Vegetable, ½ Starch, 2½ Lean Meat, 2 Fat

MAKING TORTILLA SHELLS, STEP-BY-STEP

1. Carefully fit each tortilla into an oven-safe bowl, pleating the edges as needed to fit. Form large pieces of foil into balls and place them inside each tortilla to hold it in place.
2. After the tortillas turn light brown, remove the foil and allow the shells to cool before removing them from the bowls.

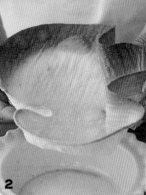

CRISPY CHOPPED CHICKEN SALAD

PREP: 45 MINUTES **BAKE:** 8 MINUTES
COOK: 8 MINUTES **OVEN:** 400°F
MAKES: 6 MAIN-DISH SERVINGS

- 6 thin slices prosciutto (about 4 ounces)
- ½ cup olive oil
- 4 skinless, boneless chicken breast halves
  Salt and black pepper
  Paprika
- 2 lemons
- 2 tablespoons finely chopped shallot (1)
- 2½ cups chopped zucchini (2 medium)
- ¾ cup chopped red sweet pepper (1 medium)
- ¾ cup chopped yellow sweet pepper (1 medium)
- ⅔ cup thinly sliced, peeled carrots (2 small)
- ¼ cup chopped red onion
- 5 ounces blue cheese, crumbled
  Romaine lettuce leaves

1 Preheat oven to 400°F. Place prosciutto in single layer on a large baking sheet. Bake for 8 to 10 minutes or until crisp; set aside.

2 In large nonstick skillet heat 1 tablespoon of the olive oil over medium heat. Sprinkle chicken with salt, black pepper, and paprika; add to skillet. Cook for 8 to 10 minutes or until chicken is no longer pink (170°F), turning once. Cool; slice.

3 For dressing, finely shred peel from one lemon; squeeze both lemons to make ⅓ cup juice. In a small bowl whisk together remaining olive oil, lemon juice, shredded peel, and shallot. Season to taste with salt and pepper; set aside.

4 In a large bowl combine sliced chicken, zucchini, sweet pepper, carrots, and onion. Toss with dressing. Add blue cheese.

5 Line salad bowls with romaine. Spoon in chicken mixture. Top with prosciutto.

PER 1½ CUPS: 434 cal., 28 g total fat (8 g sat. fat, 0 g trans fat), 86 mg chol., 923 mg sodium, 14 g carbo., 5 g fiber, 35 g pro. EXCHANGES: 1 Vegetable, ½ Starch, 4½ Lean Meat, 3 Fat

CHICKEN SALAD

PREP: 20 MINUTES **CHILL:** 1 TO 4 HOURS
MAKES: 4 MAIN-DISH SERVINGS

- 8 ounces chopped cooked chicken or turkey (2 cups)
- ½ cup chopped celery (1 stalk)
- ¼ cup thinly sliced green onions (2)
- ⅓ to ½ cup mayonnaise
- 1 teaspoon snipped fresh basil or ¼ teaspoon dried basil, crushed
- ¼ teaspoon salt
- ½ teaspoon finely shredded lemon peel (optional)
  Bread slices or mixed salad greens (optional)

1 In a medium bowl combine chicken, celery, and green onions. For dressing, in a small bowl stir together mayonnaise, basil, salt, and lemon peel (if desired). Pour dressing over chicken mixture and toss gently to coat. Cover and chill for 1 to 4 hours. If desired, serve on bread or over salad greens.

PER 1 CUP: 245 cal., 19 g total fat (3 g sat. fat, 0 g trans fat), 57 mg chol., 315 mg sodium, 4 g carbo., 1 g fiber, 16 g pro. EXCHANGES: 1 Vegetable, 2 Lean Meat, 2½ Fat

TUNA OR SALMON SALAD

PREP: 20 MINUTES **CHILL:** 1 TO 24 HOURS
MAKES: 4 MAIN-DISH SERVINGS

- 1 12-ounce can solid white tuna or two 5-ounce cans skinless, boneless pink salmon, drained and flaked
- ½ cup celery, chopped (1 stalk)
- ¼ cup thinly sliced green onions (2)
- 3 tablespoons chopped sweet pickles
- ½ cup mayonnaise
- 1 tablespoon lemon juice
- 2 teaspoons snipped fresh dill or ½ teaspoon dried dillweed
  Bread slices or mixed salad greens (optional)

1 In a medium bowl combine tuna, celery, green onions, and chopped sweet pickles. For dressing, in a small bowl stir together mayonnaise, lemon juice, and dill. Add to tuna mixture; toss to coat. Cover and chill for 1 to 24 hours before serving. If desired, serve as a sandwich filling on bread slices or over salad greens.

CAJUN TUNA OR SALMON SALAD: Prepare as directed, except omit celery, sweet pickle, and dill. Add ½ cup chopped green sweet pepper, 2 tablespoons drained capers, 1 tablespoon Creole or stone-ground mustard, ½ teaspoon Cajun seasoning, and several dashes bottled hot pepper sauce. If desired, serve with additional bottled hot pepper sauce.

PER ½ CUP PLAIN OR CAJUN VARIATION: 321 cal., 25 g total fat (5 g sat. fat, 0 g trans fat), 46 mg chol., 518 mg sodium, 3 g carbo., 0 g fiber, 20 g pro. EXCHANGES: 3 Lean Meat, 3½ Fat

10 TO TRY— CHICKEN SALAD

Start with Chicken Salad, page 504.

1. BUFFALO: Omit basil. Stir in ½ cup crumbled blue cheese and ¼ to ½ teaspoon hot pepper sauce. **2. HAWAIIAN:** Stir in ½ cup chopped pineapple. Before serving, stir in ¼ cup chopped macadamia nuts. **3. MEDITERRANEAN:** Omit celery. Stir in ½ cup chopped marinated artichoke hearts and ¼ cup crumbled feta cheese. **4. GRAPE-NUT:** Stir in ¾ cup chopped seedless grapes. Before serving, stir in ⅓ cup chopped toasted walnuts. **5. BACON-EGG-TOMATO:** Stir in 2 Hard-Cooked Eggs (page 134), chopped. Before serving, stir in ½ cup chopped cherry tomatoes. Top with crumbled crisp-cooked bacon. **6. CHILI:** Omit basil and lemon peel. Stir in 1 to 2 teaspoons chili powder. Top with toasted pumpkin seeds. **7. CASHEW-CURRY:** Stir in 1 to 2 teaspoons curry powder. Before serving, stir in 2 tablespoons chopped roasted cashews. **8. CUCUMBER-MELON:** Before serving, stir in ½ cup chopped cucumber. Serve on melon wedges. **9. CILANTRO-LIME:** Omit basil and lemon peel. Stir in 1 tablespoon snipped cilantro and ½ teaspoon shredded lime peel. Top with toasted sesame seeds and cilantro. **10. APPLE:** Stir in ¾ cup chopped apple. Before serving, stir in ⅓ cup chopped toasted pecans.

SALAD NIÇOISE

PREP: 40 MINUTES **CHILL:** 2 TO 24 HOURS
MAKES: 4 MAIN-DISH SERVINGS

- 8 ounces fresh green beans (2 cups)
- 12 ounces tiny new potatoes, scrubbed and sliced (8)
- 1 recipe Niçoise Dressing or ½ cup bottled balsamic vinaigrette salad dressing
  Spring greens and/or baby lettuce
- 1½ cups flaked cooked tuna or salmon (8 ounces) or one 9.25-ounce can chunk white tuna (water pack), drained and broken into chunks
- 2 medium tomatoes, cut into wedges
- 2 Hard-Cooked Eggs, sliced, halved, or quartered (page 134)
- ½ cup niçoise or Kalamata olives
- ¼ cup thinly sliced green onions (2)
- 4 anchovy fillets, drained, rinsed, and patted dry (optional)

1 Wash green beans; remove ends and strings. In a large saucepan cook green beans and potatoes, covered, in a small amount of lightly salted boiling water about 10 minutes or just until tender. Drain; place vegetables in a medium bowl. Cover and chill for 2 to 24 hours.

2 Prepare Niçoise Dressing. To serve, line four salad plates with lettuce leaves. Arrange chilled vegetables, tuna, tomatoes, eggs, and olives on lettuce-lined plates. Sprinkle each serving with green onions. If desired, top each salad with an anchovy fillet. Shake dressing; drizzle over salads.

NIÇOISE DRESSING: In a screw-top jar combine ¼ cup olive oil or vegetable oil; ¼ cup white wine vinegar or vinegar; 1 teaspoon honey; 1 teaspoon snipped fresh tarragon or ¼ teaspoon dried tarragon, crushed; 1 teaspoon Dijon-style mustard; ¼ teaspoon salt; and dash black pepper. Cover and shake well.

PER 2 CUPS: 473 cal., 28 g total fat (5 g sat. fat, 0 g trans fat), 134 mg chol., 512 mg sodium, 32 g carbo., 7 g fiber, 25 g pro. EXCHANGES: 2 Vegetable, 1½ Starch, 2½ Lean Meat, 4 Fat

BEST EVER

CAESAR SALAD

PREP: 30 MINUTES **BAKE:** 20 MINUTES
OVEN: 300°F **MAKES:** 6 SIDE-DISH SERVINGS

- 3 cloves garlic
- 3 anchovy fillets
- 2 tablespoons lemon juice
- ¼ cup olive oil
- 1 teaspoon Dijon-style mustard
- ½ teaspoon sugar
- 1 Hard-Cooked Egg yolk (page 134)
- 1 clove garlic, halved
- 10 cups torn romaine lettuce leaves
- 1 recipe Parmesan Croutons or 2 cups purchased garlic Parmesan croutons
- ¼ cup grated Parmesan cheese or ½ cup Parmesan curls
  Anchovy fillets, halved lengthwise (optional)
  Freshly ground black pepper

1 For dressing, in a blender combine the 3 garlic cloves, the 3 anchovy fillets, and lemon juice. Cover and blend until mixture is nearly smooth, stopping to scrape down sides as needed. Add oil, mustard, sugar, and cooked egg yolk. Cover and blend or process until smooth. Use immediately or cover and chill up to 24 hours.

2 To serve, rub inside of a wooden salad bowl with cut edges of halved garlic clove; discard garlic clove. Add romaine and croutons to bowl. Pour dressing over salad; toss lightly to coat. Sprinkle Parmesan cheese over top; toss gently. If desired, add additional anchovy fillets. To serve, divide salad among salad plates; sprinkle pepper over each salad.

PARMESAN CROUTONS: Preheat oven to 300°F. Cut four ¾-inch-thick slices Italian or French bread into 1-inch cubes (about 3½ cups); set aside. In a small saucepan melt ¼ cup butter. Remove from heat. Transfer to a large bowl. Stir in 3 tablespoons grated Parmesan cheese and 2 finely minced garlic cloves. Add bread cubes, stirring until cubes are coated with butter mixture. Spread bread cubes in a single layer in a shallow baking pan or on a baking sheet. Bake for 10 minutes; stir. Bake about 10 minutes more or until bread cubes are crisp and golden. Cool completely; store in an airtight container for up to 24 hours.

PER 1⅔ CUPS: 261 cal., 20 g total fat (8 g sat. fat, 0 g trans fat), 62 mg chol., 362 mg sodium, 15 g carbo., 2 g fiber, 6 g pro. EXCHANGES: 1 Vegetable, ½ Starch, ½ Medium-Fat Meat, 3½ Fat

CHICKEN CAESAR SALAD: Prepare as directed, except add 2 cups chopped cooked chicken with the romaine. Makes 6 main-dish servings.

PER 2 CUPS: 350 cal., 15 g total fat (9 g sat. fat, 0 g trans fat), 104 mg chol., 402 mg sodium, 15 g carbo., 2 g fiber, 20 g pro. EXCHANGES: ½ Starch, 1 Vegetable, 2½ Lean Meat, 3 Fat

POTATO AND SQUASH SALAD

PREP: 25 MINUTES **COOK:** 8 MINUTES
MAKES: 8 TO 10 SIDE-DISH SERVINGS

- 2 cups cubed, peeled sweet and/or white potatoes (2 medium)
- 1 1¼- to 1½-pound butternut squash, peeled, halved, seeded, and cubed (about 4 cups)
- ½ cup chopped red sweet pepper
- ½ of a small onion, cut into thin wedges
- 2 cloves garlic, minced
- ¼ cup olive oil
- 1 tablespoon packed brown sugar
- 1 teaspoon snipped fresh thyme
- 1 teaspoon snipped fresh basil
- ½ teaspoon salt
- ¼ teaspoon crushed red pepper
- ¼ teaspoon black pepper
- 5 cups spinach leaves
  Snipped fresh thyme (optional)

1 In a large skillet combine sweet potatoes and squash. Pour 1 cup water over all. Bring mixture to boiling; reduce heat. Simmer, covered, about 8 minutes or until vegetables are tender. Drain mixture; set aside.

2 In the same large skillet cook the sweet pepper, onion, and garlic in hot olive oil over medium heat for 5 minutes until the onion is tender, stirring occasionally. Stir in the brown sugar until combined. Remove from heat and stir in the 1 teaspoon thyme, basil, salt, crushed red pepper, and black pepper.

3 Carefully stir in the potato mixture. Place spinach in salad bowl or on a platter. Top with warm potato mixture. If desired, sprinkle with additional snipped fresh thyme. (Or let potato mixture stand at room temperature up to 2 hours before serving over spinach.)

PER ½ CUP: 135 cal., 7 g total fat (1 g sat. fat, 0 g trans fat), 0 mg chol., 182 mg sodium, 18 g carbo., 3 g fiber, 2 g pro. EXCHANGES: 1 Vegetable, 1 Starch, 1 Fat

SELECTING SWEET POTATOES
LOOK FOR SMALL TO MEDIUM SWEET POTATOES WITH SMOOTH, UNBLEMISHED SKINS. THEY TEND TO SPOIL QUICKLY, SO STORE THEM IN A COOL, DARK PLACE AND USE WITHIN 1 WEEK.

MAKE-AHEAD NIÇOISE PREPARE THE HARD-COOKED EGGS, GREEN BEANS, AND POTATOES IN ADVANCE. CHILL UNTIL SERVING TIME, THEN ARRANGE ON A PLATTER TO SERVE.

SALAD NIÇOISE

POTATO AND SQUASH SALAD

WILTED SPINACH SALAD

START TO FINISH: 25 MINUTES
MAKES: 4 SIDE-DISH SERVINGS

- 8 cups fresh baby spinach or torn spinach (5 ounces)
- 1 cup sliced fresh mushrooms
- ¼ cup thinly sliced green onions (2)
  Dash black pepper (optional)
- 3 slices bacon
  Vegetable oil (optional)
- ¼ cup vinegar
- 2 teaspoons sugar
- ½ teaspoon dry mustard
- 1 Hard-Cooked Egg, chopped (page 134)

1 In a large bowl combine spinach, mushrooms, and green onions. If desired, sprinkle with pepper; set aside.

2 For dressing, in a very large skillet cook bacon until crisp. Remove bacon; reserve 2 tablespoons drippings in skillet (add vegetable oil, if necessary). (If desired, substitute 2 tablespoons vegetable oil for bacon drippings.) Crumble bacon; set aside. Stir vinegar, sugar, and dry mustard into drippings. Bring to boiling; remove from heat. Add the spinach mixture. Toss mixture in skillet for 30 to 60 seconds or just until spinach wilts.

3 Transfer spinach mixture to a serving dish. Add crumbled bacon and chopped egg; toss to combine. Serve salad immediately.

PER 1 CUP: 157 cal., 11 g total fat (4 g sat. fat, 0 g trans fat), 66 mg chol., 253 mg sodium, 8 g carbo., 3 g fiber, 7 g pro. EXCHANGES: 2 Vegetable, ½ High-Fat Meat, 1½ Fat

WILTED GARDEN GREENS SALAD: Prepare recipe as directed, except omit the spinach and use 8 cups arugula or torn leaf lettuce (5 ounces). Omit Hard-Cooked Egg.

PER 2 CUPS: 121 cal., 10 g total fat (3 g sat. fat, 0 g trans fat), 13 mg chol., 162 mg sodium, 5 g carbo., 1 g fiber, 4 g pro. EXCHANGES: 2 Vegetable, 2 Fat

GREEK SALAD

START TO FINISH: 15 MINUTES
MAKES: 6 SIDE-DISH SERVINGS

- 6 cups torn mixed salad greens or romaine lettuce leaves
- 2 medium tomatoes, cut into wedges, or 8 cherry tomatoes, halved
- 1 small cucumber, halved lengthwise and thinly sliced
- 1 small red onion, cut into thin wedges
- ½ cup pitted Kalamata olives
- ½ cup crumbled feta cheese (2 ounces)
- 1 recipe Greek Vinaigrette
- 2 small pita bread rounds, cut into wedges (optional)

1 In a salad bowl combine salad greens, tomatoes, cucumber, onion, olives, and crumbled cheese. Add Greek Vinaigrette; toss to coat. If desired, serve with pita bread wedges.

GREEK VINAIGRETTE: In a screw-top jar combine 2 tablespoons olive oil; 2 tablespoons lemon juice; 2 teaspoons snipped fresh oregano or ½ teaspoon dried oregano, crushed; ⅛ teaspoon salt; and ⅛ teaspoon black pepper. Cover and shake well.

PER 2¼ CUPS: 109 cal., 8 g total fat (2 g sat. fat, 0 g trans fat), 8 mg chol., 289 mg sodium, 7 g carbo., 2 g fiber, 3 g pro. EXCHANGES: 1½ Vegetable, 1½ Fat

CHOPPED SALAD

START TO FINISH: 30 MINUTES
MAKES: 8 SIDE-DISH SERVINGS

- 6 ounces romaine and/or iceberg lettuce
- 2 ounces arugula or spinach
- 12 ounces tomatoes (3 small)
- 1 large yellow or red sweet pepper
- 1 medium red onion
- 4 ounces ricotta salata or feta cheese, cut into ¾-inch cubes
- 1 15-ounce can garbanzo beans (chickpeas), rinsed and drained
- 4 ounces salami, cut into ¾-inch cubes (optional)
- ½ cup pitted Kalamata olives, halved
- ½ cup olive oil
- 3 tablespoons white wine vinegar
- 1 tablespoon Dijon-style mustard
- ½ teaspoon salt
- ¼ teaspoon black pepper

1 Chop romaine, arugula, tomatoes, sweet pepper, and onion into ¾-inch pieces. On a large platter arrange greens, tomatoes, peppers, onion, cheese, beans, salami (if desired), and olives; set aside.

2 For dressing, in a small bowl whisk together oil, vinegar, mustard, salt, and black pepper. Serve with greens mixture.

PER 2 CUPS: 264 cal., 19 g total fat (4 g sat. fat, 0 g trans fat), 13 mg chol., 609 mg sodium, 19 g carbo., 4 g fiber, 6 g pro. EXCHANGES: 2 Vegetable, ½ Starch, 4 Fat

WILTED SPINACH SALAD

PEP UP WITH PEPPER IF YOU'RE LOOKING TO ADD EXTRA KICK TO THESE RECIPES, TRY USING PEPPERED BACON IN THE WILTED SPINACH SALAD AND PEPPERED SALAMI IN THE CHOPPED SALAD.

CHOPPED SALAD

CREAMY COLESLAW

PREP: 20 MINUTES **CHILL:** 2 TO 24 HOURS
MAKES: 6 SIDE-DISH SERVINGS

- ½ cup mayonnaise
- 1 tablespoon vinegar
- 1 to 2 teaspoons sugar
- ½ teaspoon celery seeds
- ¼ teaspoon salt
- 4 cups shredded green and/or red cabbage*
  (see photos 1 and 2, below)
- 1 cup shredded carrots (2 medium)*
- ¼ cup thinly sliced green onions (2)

1 For dressing, in a large bowl stir together mayonnaise, vinegar, sugar, celery seeds, and salt. Add cabbage, carrots, and onions. Toss to coat. Cover; chill for 2 to 24 hours. Stir before serving.

*NOTE: If desired, substitute 5 cups packaged shredded cabbage with carrot (coleslaw mix) for cabbage and carrots.

PER ¾ CUP: 159 cal., 15 g total fat (3 g sat. fat, 0 g trans fat), 7 mg chol., 220 mg sodium, 6 g carbo., 2 g fiber, 1 g pro.
EXCHANGES: 1 Vegetable, 3 Fat

VINAIGRETTE COLESLAW

PREP: 20 MINUTES **CHILL:** 2 TO 24 HOURS
MAKES: 6 SIDE-DISH SERVINGS

- 3 tablespoons cider vinegar
- 2 tablespoons sugar
- 2 tablespoons vegetable oil
- ½ teaspoon celery or caraway seeds
  (optional)
- ¼ teaspoon salt
- ¼ teaspoon dry mustard
- ⅛ to ¼ teaspoon black pepper
- 4 cups shredded green and/or red cabbage*
  (see photos 1 and 2, below)
- 1 cup shredded carrots* (2 medium)
- ¼ cup thinly sliced green onions (2)

1 For vinaigrette, in a screw-top jar combine vinegar, sugar, oil, celery seeds (if desired), salt, mustard, and pepper. Cover and shake well. In a large bowl combine cabbage, carrots, and green onions. Pour vinaigrette over cabbage mixture. Toss lightly to coat. Cover and chill for 2 to 24 hours.

*NOTE: If desired, substitute 5 cups packaged shredded cabbage with carrot (coleslaw mix) for cabbage and carrots.

PER ¾ CUP: 79 cal., 5 g total fat (0 g sat. fat, 0 g trans fat), 0 mg chol., 120 mg sodium, 10 g carbo., 2 g fiber, 1 g pro.
EXCHANGES: ½ Vegetable, ½ Other Carbo., 1 Fat

SESAME NOODLE SLAW

PREP: 20 MINUTES **BAKE:** 15 MINUTES
CHILL: 30 MINUTES TO 4 HOURS **OVEN:** 300°F
MAKES: 8 SIDE-DISH SERVINGS

- ½ cup sliced almonds
- 2 tablespoons sesame seeds
- ⅓ cup vegetable oil
- 3 tablespoons rice vinegar or cider vinegar
- 2 tablespoons reduced-sodium soy sauce
- 1 3-ounce package chicken-flavored ramen noodles

SHREDDING CABBAGE, STEP-BY-STEP

1. Using a large chef's knife, cut cabbage head into wedges; remove and discard the core from each wedge. **2.** Thinly slice the cored cabbage wedge across the grain of the leaves.

1 tablespoon sugar

¼ teaspoon black pepper

½ of a medium head cabbage, cored and shredded (about 6 cups) (see photos 1 and 2, page 510); 6 cups packaged shredded cabbage with carrot (coleslaw mix); or 6 cups packaged shredded broccoli (broccoli slaw mix)

⅓ to ½ cup thinly sliced green onions (3 or 4)

⅓ cup golden raisins or raisins (optional)

1 Preheat oven to 300°F. Spread almonds and sesame seeds in a shallow baking pan. Bake for 15 to 20 minutes or until toasted, stirring once; cool.

2 Meanwhile, for dressing, in a screw-top jar combine oil, vinegar, soy sauce, seasoning packet from noodles, sugar, and pepper. Cover and shake well.

3 In a large bowl combine almonds and sesame seeds, cabbage, green onions, and, if desired, raisins. Break noodles into small pieces; add to salad.

4 Add dressing; toss gently to coat. Cover and chill for 30 minutes to 4 hours.

PER 1 CUP: 205 cal., 16 g total fat (1 g sat. fat, 0 g trans fat), 0 mg chol., 349 mg sodium, 14 g carbo., 3 g fiber, 4 g pro. EXCHANGES: 1 Starch, 3 Fat

SESAME CHICKEN AND NOODLE SLAW:
Prepare as directed, except layer 1½ cups chopped cooked chicken with the cabbage and onions. Makes 4 main-dish servings.

PER 1¼ CUPS: 510 cal., 28 g total fat (3 g sat. fat, 0 g trans fat), 47 mg chol., 744 mg sodium, 28 g carbo., 5 g fiber, 23 g pro. EXCHANGES: 2 Starch, 2½ Lean Meat, 5 Fat

FAST

ZESTY THREE-BEAN SALAD

PREP: 25 MINUTES **CHILL:** UP TO 24 HOURS
MAKES: 10 SIDE-DISH SERVINGS

2 cups frozen sweet soybeans (edamame)

1 15-ounce can kidney beans, rinsed and drained

1 15-ounce can garbanzo beans (chickpeas), rinsed and drained

½ cup thinly sliced red onion

½ cup chopped fresh cilantro

¼ cup olive oil

1 teaspoon finely shredded lime peel

¼ cup lime juice

½ teaspoon salt

1 Prepare soybeans according to package directions. Drain in colander and rinse with cold water.

2 In a large bowl combine cooked soybeans, kidney beans, garbanzo beans, onion, and cilantro.

3 For dressing, in a small bowl whisk together olive oil, lime peel, lime juice, and salt. Pour over bean mixture and toss to coat. Cover and chill for up to 24 hours. Stir well before serving.

PER ½ CUP: 174 cal., 8 g total fat (1 g sat. fat, 0 g trans fat), 0 mg chol., 317 mg sodium, 21 g carbo., 6 g fiber, 9 g pro. EXCHANGES: 1½ Starch, ½ Very Lean Meat, 1 Fat

CREAMY BROCCOLI SALAD

PREP: 20 MINUTES **CHILL:** 2 TO 24 HOURS
MAKES: 12 TO 16 SIDE-DISH SERVINGS

1 cup mayonnaise

½ cup raisins

¼ cup finely chopped red onion

3 tablespoons sugar

2 tablespoons vinegar

7 cups chopped broccoli florets

½ cup shelled sunflower kernals

8 slices bacon, crisp-cooked, drained, and crumbled

1 In a large bowl combine mayonnaise, raisins, onion, sugar, and vinegar. Add broccoli and stir to coat. Cover and chill for 2 hours to 24 hours. Before serving, stir in sunflower seeds and bacon.

PER ½ CUP: 247 cal., 20 g total fat (4 g sat. fat, 0 g trans fat), 13 mg chol., 242 mg sodium, 13 g carbo., 2 g fiber, 5 g pro. EXCHANGES: ½ Vegetable, ½ Other Carbo., ½ High-Fat Meat, 3 Fat

ENJOY EDAMAME

EDAMAME, ALSO CALLED SWEET OR GREEN SOYBEANS, MAKE GREAT ADDITIONS TO SALADS.

Fresh edamame beans can be found in specialty markets. They are typically sold frozen, in and out  of the pod, in 1 pound bags. Frozen shelled edamame are a great timesaver; prepare according to package directions. Edamame are easy to digest and very high in protein, fiber, zinc, calcium, iron, and B vitamins.

BROCCOLI-CAULIFLOWER-RAISIN SALAD

START TO FINISH: 30 MINUTES
MAKES: 10 SIDE-DISH SERVINGS

- 6 cups broccoli florets (see photo 1, below)
- 3 cups cauliflower florets
- ½ cup golden raisins
- ⅓ cup walnut pieces, toasted (see tip, page 20)
- ¼ cup olive oil or canola oil
- ¼ cup cider vinegar
- 1 teaspoon honey or sugar
- ½ teaspoon dried basil, crushed
- ½ teaspoon black pepper
- ¼ teaspoon crushed red pepper (optional)

1 In a saucepan bring 2 inches of water to boiling. Add broccoli, return to boiling. Cook, covered, for 2 minutes or until broccoli is crisp-tender and bright green; drain. Rinse with cold water; drain well.

2 In the same saucepan cook cauliflower in water as directed in Step 1.

3 In 2- to 2½-quart bowl layer half the cauliflower, raisins, broccoli, and walnuts. Repeat layers (see photo 2, below). Cover and chill. In a screw-top jar combine olive oil, vinegar, 1 teaspoon *salt*, the honey, basil, black pepper, and red pepper (if desired). Cover tightly; shake well. Add dressing just before serving; toss to coat.

PER ⅔ CUP: 128 cal., 8 g total fat (1 g sat. fat, 0 g trans fat), 0 mg chol., 29 mg sodium, 13 g carbo., 3 g fiber, 3 g pro.
EXCHANGES: 1 Vegetable, 3½ Other Carbo., 1½ Fat

FIESTA CORN SALAD

START TO FINISH: 30 MINUTES
MAKES: 16 SIDE-DISH SERVINGS

- 4 cups fresh or frozen whole kernel corn
- 1 cup frozen shelled sweet soybeans (edamame)
- 1 small red onion, cut into thin wedges
- ¼ cup snipped fresh cilantro
- 1 fresh jalapeño chile pepper, seeded and finely chopped*
- 2 tablespoons olive oil
- ½ teaspoon finely shredded lime peel
- 3 tablespoons lime juice
- 1 teaspoon cumin seeds, toasted**
- 1 teaspoon salt
- 2 cloves garlic, minced
- ¼ teaspoon chili powder
- 2 cups cherry or grape tomatoes, halved
  Fresh cilantro (optional)

1 In a large saucepan cook corn and soybeans, covered, in enough boiling water to cover for 2 minutes; drain. Rinse with cold water and drain again.

2 In a large bowl stir together corn, soybeans, red onion, snipped cilantro, and jalapeño pepper.

3 In a screw-top jar combine olive oil, lime peel, lime juice, cumin seeds, salt, garlic, and chili powder. Cover and shake well.

4 Pour dressing over corn mixture, tossing gently to coat. Gently stir in tomatoes. If desired, garnish with additional cilantro. Serve immediately. (Or cover and chill for up to 24 hours, stirring in

BROCCOLI-CAULIFLOWER-RAISIN SALAD, STEP-BY-STEP

1. For 6 cups broccoli florets, start with 1¾ pounds whole stalks. Remove florets by cutting above the thick stalk at the base of the stem of each floret. Halve larger florets. For cauliflower florets, remove the woody stem and break the head into florets; a 1½- to 2-pound head yields 3 cups florets.
2. Arrange layers of cauliflower, raisins, broccoli, and walnuts in the serving dish.

tomatoes just before serving; let stand for 30 minutes before serving.)

*NOTE: Because chile peppers contain volatile oils that can burn your skin and eyes, avoid direct contact with them as much as possible. When working with chile peppers, wear plastic or rubber gloves. If your bare hands do touch the peppers, wash your hands and nails well with soap and warm water.

**NOTE: To toast cumin seeds, place seeds in a small skillet over medium heat. Heat about 2 minutes or until aromatic, shaking skillet often.

FIESTA CORN AND RICE SALAD: Prepare salad as directed, except add 2 cups cooked long grain rice to the salad. Makes 20 (½-cup) servings.

PER ½ CUP PLAIN OR RICE VARIATION: 75 cal., 3 g total fat (0 g sat. fat, 0 g trans fat), 0 mg chol., 150 mg sodium, 12 g carbo., 2 g fiber, 3 g pro.
EXCHANGES: 1 Starch, ½ Fat

LOW FAT

CREAMY CUCUMBERS

PREP: 15 MINUTES CHILL: 4 HOURS TO 3 DAYS
MAKES: 6 SIDE-DISH SERVINGS

- ½ cup dairy sour cream or plain yogurt
- 1 tablespoon vinegar
- ½ teaspoon salt
- ¼ teaspoon dried dillweed
  Dash black pepper
- 1 large cucumber, peeled (if desired), halved lengthwise, and thinly sliced (3 cups)
- ⅓ cup thinly sliced onion (about half of 1 small)

1 In a medium bowl combine sour cream, vinegar, salt, dillweed, and pepper. Add cucumber and onion; toss to coat. Cover and chill for 4 hours or up to 3 days, stirring occasionally. Stir before serving.

PER ½ CUP: 45 cal., 3 g total fat (2 g sat. fat, 0 g trans fat), 8 mg chol., 209 mg sodium, 4 g carbo., 0 g fiber, 1 g pro.
EXCHANGES: ½ Vegetable, ½ Fat

PEELING CUCUMBERS
PEEL CUCUMBERS FOR MORE DELICATE SALADS. CUT OFF ROUNDED ENDS AND USE A VEGETABLE PEELER TO REMOVE PEEL FROM TOP TO BOTTOM.

LOW FAT ▪ HEALTHY

GINGER-SPICED CUCUMBERS

PREP: 20 MINUTES CHILL: 60 MINUTES
MAKES: 8 SIDE-DISH SERVINGS

- ⅓ cup seasoned rice vinegar
- ⅓ cup apple juice or mirin (sweet cooking rice wine)
- ⅓ cup packed brown sugar
- 1 tablespoon grated fresh ginger (optional)
- 2 large cucumbers (10 to 12 ounces each), peeled (if desired) and thinly sliced
- ½ cup thinly sliced quartered red onion

1 In a medium bowl combine rice vinegar, apple juice, brown sugar, and ginger (if desired). Stir in cucumbers and onion slices to coat. Cover and chill for at least 1 hour or up to 3 days, stirring occasionally. Serve with a slotted spoon.

PER ½ CUP: 62 cal., 0 g total fat, 0 mg chol., 6 mg sodium, 15 g carbo., 1 g fiber, 1 g pro.
EXCHANGES: 1 Vegetable, ½ Other Carbo.

PEA SALAD

PREP: 20 MINUTES CHILL: 4 TO 24 HOURS
MAKES: 6 TO 8 SIDE-DISH SERVINGS

- 1 16-ounce package frozen peas
- 4 ounces cheddar cheese, cut into ½-inch cubes
- ½ cup chopped celery
- ½ cup mayonnaise
- ½ cup dairy sour cream
- 1 small red onion, finely chopped
- 1 teaspoon snipped fresh dill or ¼ teaspoon dried dillweed (optional)
- ¼ teaspoon salt
- ¼ teaspoon black pepper
- 2 slices bacon, crisp-cooked, drained, and crumbled

1 Place the peas in a colander and run under cold water just until thawed but still cold; drain well.

2 In a medium bowl stir together peas, cheese, and celery. In a small bowl stir together mayonnaise, sour cream, onion, dill (if desired), salt, and pepper. Add to pea mixture. Stir to combine.

3 Cover and chill for 4 hours to 24 hours. Just before serving, top with bacon.

PER ½ CUP: 321 cal., 25 g total fat (9 g sat. fat, 0 g trans fat), 38 mg chol., 566 mg sodium, 12 g carbo., 4 g fiber, 10 g pro.
EXCHANGES: 1 Starch, 1 High-Fat Meat, 3 Fat

CLASSIC POTATO SALAD

PREP: 40 MINUTES **CHILL:** 6 TO 24 HOURS
MAKES: 12 SIDE-DISH SERVINGS

- 2 pounds potatoes (6 medium)
- ¼ teaspoon salt
- 1¼ cups mayonnaise
- 1 tablespoon yellow mustard
- ½ teaspoon salt
- ¼ teaspoon black pepper
- 1 cup thinly sliced celery (2 stalks)
- ⅓ cup chopped onion (1 small)
- ½ cup chopped sweet or dill pickles or sweet or dill pickle relish
- 6 Hard-Cooked Eggs, coarsely chopped (page 134)

  Lettuce leaves (optional)

  Paprika (optional)

1 In a large saucepan place potatoes, the ¼ teaspoon salt, and enough water to cover. Bring to boiling; reduce heat. Simmer, covered, for 20 to 25 minutes or just until tender. Drain well; let cool slightly. If desired, peel the potatoes. Cube the potatoes.

2 Meanwhile, for dressing, in a large bowl stir together mayonnaise, mustard, the ½ teaspoon salt, and pepper.

3 Stir in the celery, onion, and pickles. Add potatoes and eggs. Toss lightly to coat. Cover and chill for 6 to 24 hours.

4 To serve, if desired, line a salad bowl with lettuce leaves. Transfer potato salad to the bowl. If desired, sprinkle with paprika.

PER ½ CUP: 276 cal., 21 g total fat (4 g sat. fat, 0 g trans fat), 114 mg chol., 358 mg sodium, 16 g carbo., 2 g fiber, 5 g pro. EXCHANGES: 1 Starch, ½ Lean Meat, 3½ Fat

FRESH TOMATO SALAD

START TO FINISH: 20 MINUTES
MAKES: 6 SIDE-DISH SERVINGS

- 5 roma tomatoes, sliced
- ½ cup tiny fresh mozzarella balls or 1-inch mozzarella balls, quartered
- ¼ cup sliced pitted olives (pimiento-stuffed, Kalamata, or ripe)
- 3 tablespoons olive oil
- 3 tablespoons white wine vinegar
- 2 cloves garlic, minced
- ¼ teaspoon salt
- ⅛ teaspoon black pepper
- 2 tablespoons snipped fresh basil

1 Arrange tomato slices on a plate or serving platter. Scatter mozzarella and olives over tomatoes. For dressing, in a screw-top jar combine the oil, vinegar, garlic, salt, and pepper. Cover and shake well to combine. Drizzle over tomatoes. Sprinkle basil over tomatoes.

PER ⅔ CUP: 113 cal., 10 g total fat (2 g sat. fat, 0 g trans fat), 7 mg chol., 242 mg sodium, 4 g carbo., 1 g fiber, 3 g pro. EXCHANGES: ½ Vegetable, 2 Fat

LAYERED VEGETABLE SALAD

PREP: 35 MINUTES **CHILL:** 4 TO 24 HOURS
MAKES: 8 TO 10 SIDE-DISH SERVINGS

- 6 cups torn mixed salad greens
- 1 15-ounce can garbanzo beans (chickpeas), rinsed and drained, or one 10-ounce package frozen peas, thawed
- 1 cup cherry or grape tomatoes, quartered or halved
- 1 cup small broccoli florets
- 1 cup chopped yellow and/or red sweet pepper (1 large)
- 6 ounces diced cooked chicken or ham (1 cup) (optional)
- ¼ cup thinly sliced green onions (2)
- 3 ounces smoked cheddar cheese or cheddar cheese, shredded (¾ cup)
- 1 cup mayonnaise
- 1 8-ounce carton dairy sour cream
- 2 tablespoons snipped fresh dill or 2 teaspoons dried dillweed
- ⅛ teaspoon black pepper

1 Place 3 cups of the mixed greens in the bottom of a 3-quart clear salad bowl. Layer in the following order: garbanzo beans, tomatoes, broccoli, sweet pepper, remaining greens, chicken (if desired), green onions, and cheese.

2 For dressing, stir together mayonnaise, sour cream, dill, and black pepper. Spoon dressing over salad. Cover tightly with plastic wrap. Chill for 4 to 24 hours before serving.

PER 1¼ CUPS: 405 cal., 34 g total fat (10 g sat. fat, 0 g trans fat), 55 mg chol., 429 mg sodium, 13 g carbo., 4 g fiber, 13 g pro. EXCHANGES: 2 Vegetable, 1 Lean Meat, 6½ Fat

MAKE-IT-MINE PASTA SALAD

A PASTA SALAD IS A GREAT WAY TO FEED
A CROWD. YOUR VERSION WILL REALLY
STAND OUT ON THE PICNIC OR POTLUCK
TABLE WHEN YOU USE INGREDIENTS YOUR
FAMILY AND FRIENDS LIKE BEST.

BASIC INGREDIENTS

PREP: 40 MINUTES
CHILL: OVERNIGHT PLUS 4 HOURS
MAKES: 16 (¾-CUP) SERVINGS

- 3 cups Dried Pasta
- 2 tablespoons olive oil
- 1 tablespoon lemon juice
- 2 teaspoons seasoned salt
- 3 to 4 cups Vegetable
- 8 ounces cubed Cheese
- 1 cup Tomato
- 1 cup cubed Cooked Meat (optional)
- ½ cup chopped red onion or sliced green onions (4)
- ½ cup Olives (optional)
  Snipped Fresh Herb
- 1½ cups bottled Salad Dressing

DRIED PASTA (PICK ONE)

Bow ties
Cavatelli
Gemelli
Medium shells
Mostaccioli
Penne
Rotini
Wagon wheels

VEGETABLE
(PICK ONE OR MORE)

Fresh broccoli florets
Fresh green beans, trimmed
  and cut into 1- to 2-inch
  pieces (cook in boiling water
  5 minutes; drain and cool)
Frozen peas, thawed
Frozen whole kernel corn,
  thawed
Red, green, and/or yellow
  sweet peppers, cut into strips
Thinly sliced carrots
Yellow summer squash or
  zucchini, halved lengthwise
  and sliced

CHEESE (PICK ONE)

Cheddar
Monterey Jack
Monterey Jack with jalapeño
  peppers
Provolone
Smoked cheddar
Swiss

TOMATO (PICK ONE)

Chopped tomato
Halved cherry tomatoes
Halved grape tomatoes

COOKED MEAT (PICK ONE)

Cooked ham
Salami
Pepperoni
Turkey or chicken

OLIVES (PICK ONE)

Halved pitted Kalamata
Sliced pimiento-stuffed green
Sliced pitted ripe black

FRESH HERB (PICK ONE)

- 2 tablespoons basil,
  oregano, or dill
- 1 tablespoon rosemary or
  thyme

SALAD DRESSING
(PICK ONE)

Balsamic vinaigrette
Caesar
Creamy garlic
Creamy Parmesan
Italian (creamy or
  vinaigrette-style)
Ranch
Vinaigrette

BASIC INSTRUCTIONS

1 Cook desired Dried Pasta
according to package directions;
drain. Rinse with cold water;
drain. In a very large bowl whisk
together olive oil, lemon juice,
and salt. Add pasta; toss to coat.
Cover and chill overnight.

2 Add Vegetable, Cheese,
Tomato, Meat (if desired), onion,
Olives (if desired), and Herb to
pasta. Add Salad Dressing; toss.
Cover; chill 4 to 24 hours.

CURRIED WILD RICE SALAD

PREP: 20 MINUTES **COOK:** 40 MINUTES
CHILL: 4 TO 24 HOURS **STAND:** 30 MINUTES
MAKES: 10 SIDE-DISH SERVINGS

- 3 cups water
- ⅔ cup uncooked wild rice, rinsed and drained
- ⅔ cup uncooked brown rice
- ½ of a 10-ounce package frozen peas, thawed (1 cup)
- ¾ cup chopped red or yellow sweet pepper (1 medium)
- ¼ cup thinly sliced green onions (2)
- ¼ cup currants or raisins
- 3 tablespoons canola oil
- 1 teaspoon finely shredded orange peel
- 3 tablespoons orange juice
- 1 tablespoon honey
- 1 teaspoon curry powder
- ½ cup chopped honey-roasted peanuts (optional)

1 In a medium saucepan combine the water, wild rice, and brown rice. Bring to boiling; reduce heat. Simmer, covered, about 40 minutes or until rice is tender; drain, if necessary.

2 Transfer rice to a large bowl and let cool to room temperature. Add peas, sweet pepper, green onions, and currants to rice mixture.

3 In a screw-top jar combine oil, orange peel, orange juice, honey, curry powder, and ½ teaspoon *salt*. Cover and shake well.

4 Pour dressing over rice mixture in bowl. Gently toss to combine. Cover and chill for 4 to 24 hours.

5 Let salad stand at room temperature for 30 minutes before serving. If desired, sprinkle with chopped peanuts just before serving.

PER ½ CUP: 155 cal., 5 g total fat (0 g sat. fat, 0 g trans fat), 0 mg chol., 153 mg sodium, 25 g carbo., 2 g fiber, 4 g pro.
EXCHANGES: 1½ Starch, 1 Fat

CURRY POWDER PRIMER CURRY POWDER IS MADE WITH UP TO 20 HERBS AND SPICES. BECAUSE IT LOSES FLAVOR QUICKLY, BUY IT IN SMALL AMOUNTS AND STORE IT FOR NO LONGER THAN 2 MONTHS.

CURRIED WILD RICE SALAD

BISTRO SALAD (photos, pages 495 and 497)

START TO FINISH: 25 MINUTES
MAKES: 8 SIDE-DISH SERVINGS

- 10 cups mesclun, torn romaine lettuce, butterhead lettuce and/or spinach
- 3 cups red and/or green pears, cored and thinly sliced; sliced strawberries; and/or blueberries
- ¼ cup olive oil
- ¼ cup balsamic vinegar
- 1 tablespoon snipped fresh thyme, oregano, or basil, or ½ teaspoon dried thyme, oregano, or basil, crushed
- 1 teaspoon sugar
- 1 clove garlic, minced
- ¼ teaspoon dry mustard or 1 teaspoon Dijon-style mustard
- ⅛ teaspoon black pepper
- ½ cup broken walnuts, toasted (see tip, page 20) or ½ cup Candied Nuts (page 287)
- ½ cup crumbled blue or feta cheese (2 ounces)

1 In a large salad bowl place mesclun and fruit. Toss lightly to combine.

2 For dressing, in a screw-top jar combine oil, vinegar, herbs, sugar, garlic, mustard, and pepper. Cover and shake well. Pour dressing over salad; toss lightly to coat.

3 Divide evenly among salad plates. Sprinkle each serving with nuts and cheese.

PER 1⅓ CUPS: 188 cal., 14 g total fat (3 g sat. fat, 0 g trans fat), 6 mg chol., 125 mg sodium, 14 g carbo., 3 g fiber, 4 g pro.
EXCHANGES: 1 Vegetable, ½ Fruit, 3 Fat

BEET AND APPLE SALAD

PREP: 35 MINUTES **COOK:** 40 MINUTES
CHILL: 2 TO 24 HOURS
MAKES: 8 SIDE-DISH SERVINGS

- 3 medium beets (about 1 pound total); one 16-ounce can julienne beets, rinsed and drained; or two 8-ounce packages refrigerated cooked whole baby beets, cut into bite-size strips
- ¼ cup vegetable oil
- ¼ cup white wine vinegar
- 2 teaspoons finely shredded orange peel
- 3 tablespoons orange juice
- ¼ cup sliced green onions (2)
- 2 tablespoons snipped fresh mint or 2 teaspoons dried mint, crushed
- 1 teaspoon honey
- ⅛ teaspoon salt
- 6 cups torn romaine lettuce
- 1⅓ cups coarsely chopped tart green apples (2 medium)

1 If using whole beets, in a large saucepan combine beets and enough water to cover. Bring to boiling; reduce heat. Simmer, covered, for 40 to 50 minutes or until tender; drain. Cool slightly; slip off skins* and cut into thin bite-size strips.

2 Meanwhile, for dressing, in a screw-top jar combine vegetable oil, vinegar, orange peel, orange juice, green onions, mint, honey, and salt. Cover and shake well.

3 In a medium bowl combine beet strips and ¼ cup of the dressing. Cover and chill the beet mixture and the remaining dressing for 2 to 24 hours.

4 To serve, in a large bowl combine torn romaine and chopped apples. Toss lettuce and apple mixture with the remaining dressing. Arrange on a large platter. Using a slotted spoon, spoon beet mixture over lettuce mixture on platter.

***NOTE:** Wear plastic gloves when removing skins from beets to prevent your hands from turning red.

PER 1¼ CUPS: 113 cal., 7 g total fat (1 g sat. fat, 0 g trans fat), 0 mg chol., 64 mg sodium, 12 g carbo., 3 g fiber, 1 g pro.
EXCHANGES: 1 Vegetable, ½ Other Carbo., 1½ Fat

MELON AND BERRIES SALAD

PREP: 20 MINUTES **CHILL:** UP TO 24 HOURS
MAKES: 4 TO 6 SIDE-DISH SERVINGS

- 2 cups chilled cantaloupe cubes or balls
- 2 cups chilled honeydew melon cubes or balls
- 1 tablespoon honey
- 1 teaspoon fresh lime juice
- 1 tablespoon snipped fresh mint
- 1 cup fresh blueberries and/or red raspberries

1 In a medium bowl combine cantaloupe and honeydew melon. Drizzle honey and lime juice over melon; toss to mix. Cover; chill for up to 24 hours.

2 Just before serving, add mint and toss gently to mix. Sprinkle with fresh berries.

PER 1 CUP: 97 cal., 0 g total fat, 0 mg chol., 30 mg sodium, 24 g carbo., 2 g fiber, 1 g pro.
EXCHANGES: 1 Fruit, ½ Other Carbo.

STRAWBERRY PRETZEL SALAD

STRAWBERRY PRETZEL SALAD

PREP: 30 MINUTES **BAKE:** 10 MINUTES
CHILL: 4 TO 24 HOURS **OVEN:** 350°F
MAKES: 24 SIDE-DISH SERVINGS

- 2 cups finely crushed pretzels
- ⅓ cup sugar
- ¾ cup butter, melted
- 1 8-ounce package cream cheese, softened
- 1 cup sugar
- 1 8-ounce container frozen whipped dessert topping, thawed
- 2 10-ounce packages frozen strawberries in syrup, thawed
- 2 3-ounce packages strawberry-flavored gelatin
- 2 cups boiling water

1 Preheat oven to 350°F. In a medium bowl combine crushed pretzels and the ⅓ cup sugar. Add melted butter and stir well to combine. Press onto bottom of a 13×9×2-inch baking pan. Bake for 10 minutes. Let cool on a wire rack.

2 In a large mixing bowl beat the cream cheese and 1 cup sugar with an electric mixer on medium speed until well combined. Fold in the whipped dessert topping until combined. Spread over cooled crust.

3 In another large bowl combine strawberries and syrup, gelatin, and boiling water. Stir about 2 minutes or until gelatin is dissolved. Carefully pour over the cream cheese layer. Cover and chill for 4 hours or until set or up to 24 hours. Cut into 24 squares to serve.

PER SQUARE: 255 cal., 11 g total fat (7 g sat. fat, 0 g trans fat), 26 mg chol., 275 mg sodium, 36 g carbo., 1 g fiber, 3 g pro.
EXCHANGES: 1½ Starch, 1 Other Carbo., 2 Fat

ONE HEARTY WALDORF
IF YOU LIKE, TURN YOUR WALDORF INTO A MAIN-DISH SALAD BY ADDING CHOPPED COOKED TURKEY OR CHICKEN. STIR IN COOKED WILD RICE TO MAKE IT EVEN MORE HEARTY. ADD A LITTLE EXTRA MAYO AS NEEDED.

WALDORF SALAD

PREP: 20 MINUTES
MAKES: 8 TO 10 SIDE-DISH SERVINGS

- 4 cups chopped apples and/or pears
- 4 teaspoons lemon juice
- ½ cup chopped celery
- ½ cup chopped walnuts or pecans, toasted (see tip, page 20)
- ½ cup raisins, snipped pitted whole dates, or dried tart cherries
- ½ cup seedless green grapes, halved
- ⅔ cup mayonnaise

1 In a medium bowl toss apples and/or pears with lemon juice. Stir in celery, nuts, raisins, and grapes. Stir in mayonnaise until combined. Serve immediately or cover and chill for up to 8 hours.

PER ½ CUP: 245 cal., 20 g total fat (3 g sat. fat, 0 g trans fat), 7 mg chol., 107 mg sodium, 18 g carbo., 2 g fiber, 2 g pro.
EXCHANGES: 1 Fruit, 4 Fat

FLUFFY WALDORF SALAD: Prepare as directed, except substitute 1½ cups frozen whipped dessert topping, thawed, for the mayonnaise. Stir in 1 cup tiny marshmallows. Serve immediately or cover and chill for up to 8 hours.

PER ¾ CUP: 174 cal., 7 g total fat (3 g sat. fat, 0 g trans fat), 0 mg chol., 16 mg sodium, 27 g carbo., 2 g fiber, 2 g pro.
EXCHANGES: 1 Fruit, 1½ Other Carbo., 1½ Fat

SANDWICHES & PIZZAS

BBQ RANCH CHICKEN SANDWICHES, PAGE 528

SANDWICHES & PIZZAS

SANDWICHES ARE MORE ABOUT CHOOSING GOOD INGREDIENTS THAN ABOUT MASTERING TRICKY TECHNIQUES. HERE'S SOME SANDWICH SAVVY TO GET YOU STARTED.

BREAD

From white and wheat to rye, pumpernickel, and more, sliced bread is tailor-made for making sandwiches. However, if you want to shake up your sandwich routine, look for other kinds, too, including baguettes (long, cylindrical French bread), bolillos (crusty Mexican sandwich rolls), croissants, ciabatta (crusty Italian bread that's perfect for panini), and tortillas for wraps.

FREEZING BREAD: Most yeast breads and rolls freeze extremely well. Transfer to freezer bags and freeze for up to 3 months. Thaw at room temperature. Unless a recipe or package directions state otherwise, do not refrigerate yeast breads—they grow stale in that temperature zone.

TO TOAST SANDWICH BUNS: Toasting sandwich buns helps the bread stand up to the filling while adding a little crunch to the meal. The easiest way to toast rolls and hoagie buns is in a toaster oven; however, you can also use your broiler. Place the rolls and buns, cut sides up, on the unheated rack of a broiler pan and broil 4 to 5 inches from heat for 1 to 2 minutes or until golden brown.

MEAT

Just about any cooked meat that can be sliced, chopped, shredded, or ground can be tucked into a sandwich. Select the best quality of meat.

CHEESE

Choose a cheese depending on how it will be used.

MELTERS: For hot sandwiches, good melting cheeses include American, cheddar, Monterey Jack, Monterey Jack with jalapeño peppers, Colby-Jack, mozzarella, provolone, Muenster, Swiss, Gruyère, and fontina.

STACKERS: For cold, stacked sandwiches, choose a semisoft cheese that slices easily and is moist and pliable. Most melting cheeses will work fine in a cold sandwich (they're best sliced thin). Also try Brie, fresh mozzarella, and Havarti.

CRUMBLERS: Some cheeses, such as a few goat cheeses and most blue and feta cheeses, cannot be sliced; however, they'll pack plenty of flavor crumbled in pita-pocket or wrap-style sandwiches.

CONDIMENTS AND MORE

Many a masterful sandwich is all in the details.

■ A slather of something on the bread not only adds flavor and moisture, but it also does the all-important work of binding the bread and ingredients together. Mustard and mayonnaise are must-haves; also consider chutney, tapenade, pesto, cranberry sauce, apricot jam, and hummus.

■ For a more healthful alternative to mayonnaise, combine minced garlic with olive oil and brush onto bread rolls.

■ Add color, flavor, and crunch to sandwiches with a variety of extras, including thinly sliced cucumbers, radishes, sweet and hot peppers, and red onion; lettuces, from mild greens like spinach to spicy arugula and watercress; and pickles and relishes. Fruits can also add much to sandwiches, from sliced grapes in a chicken salad to thinly sliced apple or pear on top of a turkey sandwich.

SLOPPY JOES

START TO FINISH: 25 MINUTES
MAKES: 6 SANDWICHES

- 1 pound lean ground beef or ground pork
- ½ cup chopped onion (1 medium)
- ½ cup chopped green sweet pepper (1 small)
- 1 8-ounce can tomato sauce
- 2 tablespoons water
- 1 to 1½ teaspoons chili powder
- 1 teaspoon Worcestershire sauce
- ½ teaspoon garlic salt
  Dash bottled hot pepper sauce
- 6 kaiser rolls or hamburger buns, split and toasted

1 In a large skillet cook meat, onion, and sweet pepper until meat is brown and vegetables are tender; drain off fat. Stir in tomato sauce, water, chili powder, Worcestershire sauce, garlic salt, and hot pepper sauce. Bring to boiling; reduce heat. Simmer, uncovered, for 5 minutes. Serve on toasted rolls.

PER SANDWICH: 349 cal., 14 g total fat (5 g sat. fat, 1 g trans fat), 51 mg chol., 628 mg sodium, 34 g carbo., 2 g fiber, 20 g pro. EXCHANGES: 2 Starch, 2 Medium-Fat Meat, 1 Fat

PIZZA JOES: Prepare as directed, except substitute one 14-ounce jar pizza sauce for the tomato sauce and water; omit chili powder, Worcestershire sauce, garlic salt, and hot pepper sauce. Add ½ cup chopped pepperoni. Serve on toasted rolls with 6 ounces sliced mozzarella cheese.

PER SANDWICH: 501 cal., 25 g total fat (10 g sat. fat, 1 g trans fat), 82 mg chol., 983 mg sodium, 38 g carbo., 2 g fiber, 30 g pro. EXCHANGES: 2½ Starch, 3½ Medium-Fat Meat, 1 Fat

TEX-MEX JOES: Prepare as directed, except add ½ cup fresh or frozen whole kernel corn and 1 tablespoon chopped chipotle chile in adobo sauce with the tomato sauce. Serve on toasted rolls with 6 ounces sliced cheddar cheese.

PER SANDWICH: 476 cal., 23 g total fat (11 g sat. fat, 1 g trans fat), 81 mg chol., 816 mg sodium, 38 g carbo., 3 g fiber, 28 g pro. EXCHANGES: 2½ Starch, 3 Medium-Fat Meat, 1 Fat

VEGGIE JOES: Prepare as directed, except omit ground beef. Cook onion and sweet pepper in 1 tablespoon hot olive oil over medium heat until tender. Add 2 cups cooked brown rice; one 15- to 16-ounce can kidney beans, rinsed and drained; and ½ cup shredded carrot (1 medium) with the tomato sauce.

PER SANDWICH: 338 cal., 6 g total fat (1 g sat. fat, 1 g trans fat), 0 mg chol., 705 mg sodium, 62 g carbo., 8 g fiber, 13 g pro. EXCHANGES: 4 Starch, ½ Fat

ANYTHING GOES USE THE WRAPS RECIPE ON PAGE 523 AS A TEMPLATE AND FILL WITH ANY MEATS AND CHEESES YOU LIKE, SUCH AS TURKEY FOR THE BEEF OR GOAT CHEESE FOR THE BLUE.

TEX-MEX JOES

BEEF AND BLUE CHEESE WRAPS

FRENCH DIP SANDWICHES

START TO FINISH: 30 MINUTES
MAKES: 4 SANDWICHES

- 1 large onion, sliced and separated into rings (2 cups)
- 1 clove garlic, minced
- 1 tablespoon butter or margarine
- 1 14-ounce can beef broth
- ½ teaspoon dried thyme, marjoram, or oregano, crushed
- ¼ teaspoon black pepper
- 12 ounces thinly sliced cooked roast beef
- 4 French-style rolls, split

1 In a large saucepan cook onion and garlic in hot butter until tender. Stir in broth, thyme, and pepper. Bring to boiling; reduce heat. Simmer, uncovered, for 10 minutes. Add beef. Return to boiling; reduce heat. Simmer, uncovered, about 5 minutes more or until beef is heated through.

2 If desired, toast rolls. Remove meat and onion from broth mixture. Arrange on rolls. If desired, serve with dishes of broth mixture for dipping.

PER SANDWICH: 346 cal., 10 g total fat (4 g sat. fat, 0 g trans fat), 80 mg chol., 662 mg sodium, 27 g carbo., 3 g fiber, 35 g pro. EXCHANGES: 2 Starch, 4 Lean Meat

FRENCH DIP SANDWICHES WITH CHEESE AND VEGGIES: Prepare as directed, except use a large skillet. Add 1 cup sliced fresh mushrooms and 1 cup green sweet pepper strips with the broth and seasonings. Continue cooking as directed. Preheat broiler. Place vegetables and beef on bottom halves of rolls. Place a slice of provolone cheese on each sandwich. Place on broiler pan; broil about 4 inches from heat about 1 minute or until cheese melts. Add tops of rolls and serve as directed.

PER SANDWICH: 458 cal., 18 g total fat (9 g sat. fat, 0 g trans fat), 99 mg chol., 913 mg sodium, 30 g carbo., 4 g fiber, 43 g pro. EXCHANGES: ½ Vegetable, 2 Starch, 5 Lean Meat, 1 Fat

BEEF AND BLUE CHEESE WRAPS

START TO FINISH: 20 MINUTES **MAKES:** 4 WRAPS

- 3 tablespoons mayonnaise
- 1 teaspoon dried thyme, crushed
- 2 tablespoons yellow mustard
- 4 8-inch flour tortillas
- 12 ounces thinly sliced cooked roast beef

- 1 12-ounce jar roasted red sweet peppers, drained
- ⅓ cup crumbled blue cheese (1½ ounces)
- 4 cups mixed greens
   Olive oil (optional)
   Crumbled blue cheese (optional)

1 In a bowl stir together mayonnaise and thyme. Set aside 1 tablespoon mayonnaise mixture. Stir mustard into remaining mayonnaise mixture.

2 Spread mustard mixture evenly over tortillas. Top evenly with roast beef, sweet peppers, and blue cheese. Roll up tortillas; brush with reserved 1 tablespoon mayonnaise mixture.

3 In a large skillet cook wraps over medium heat about 2 minutes per side or until light brown. Cut wraps in half. Divide greens among salad dishes. If desired, drizzle olive oil and sprinkle additional blue cheese over greens; serve with halved wraps.

PER WRAP: 330 cal., 17 g total fat (5 g sat. fat, 0 g trans fat), 53 mg chol., 1,375 mg sodium, 23 g carbo., 3 g fiber, 21 g pro. EXCHANGES: 1½ Vegetable, 1 Starch, 2½ Medium-Fat Meat, ½ Fat

REUBEN SANDWICHES

PREP: 10 MINUTES **COOK:** 8 MINUTES
MAKES: 4 SANDWICHES

- 3 tablespoons butter or margarine, softened
- 8 slices dark rye or pumpernickel bread
- 3 tablespoons bottled Thousand Island or Russian salad dressing
- 6 ounces thinly sliced cooked corned beef
- 4 slices Swiss cheese (3 ounces)
- 1 cup sauerkraut, well drained

1 Spread butter on one side of each bread slice and salad dressing on the other. With the buttered sides down, top 4 bread slices with meat, cheese, and sauerkraut. Top with remaining bread slices, dressing sides down.

2 Preheat a large skillet over medium heat. Reduce heat to medium low. Cook two of the sandwiches at a time over medium-low heat for 4 to 6 minutes or until the bread is toasted and the cheese melts, turning once. Repeat with remaining sandwiches.

PER SANDWICH: 404 cal., 22 g total fat (10 g sat. fat, 0 g trans fat), 64 mg chol., 2,508 mg sodium, 34 g carbo., 8 g fiber, 20 g pro. EXCHANGES: 2 Starch, 2 Medium-Fat Meat, 2 Fat

PORK TENDERLOIN SANDWICHES

PREP: 20 MINUTES **COOK:** 6 MINUTES
MAKES: 4 SANDWICHES

- 1 pound pork tenderloin
- ¼ cup all-purpose flour
- ¼ teaspoon garlic salt
- ¼ teaspoon black pepper
- 1 egg
- 1 tablespoon milk
- ½ cup seasoned fine dry bread crumbs
- 2 tablespoons vegetable oil
- 4 large hamburger buns or kaiser rolls, split and toasted

  Ketchup, mustard, onion slices, and/or dill pickle slices

1 Trim fat from meat. Cut meat crosswise into four pieces (see photo 1, below). Place each piece between two pieces of plastic wrap. Use the flat side of a meat mallet to pound the pork lightly to about ¼ inch thick (see photos 2 and 3, below). Remove plastic wrap.

2 In a shallow bowl combine flour, garlic salt, and black pepper. In an another shallow bowl whisk together egg and milk. In a third bowl place bread crumbs. Dip pork into flour mixture to coat. Dip into egg mixture; coat with bread crumbs.

3 In a large heavy skillet cook pork in hot oil over medium heat for 6 to 8 minutes or until brown and meat is slightly pink in center, turning once (see photos 4 and 5, below).*

4 Serve tenderloins on warm buns with ketchup, mustard, onion slices, and/or dill pickle slices.

*NOTE: If necessary, cook two tenderloin slices at a time. Keep warm on a baking sheet in a pre-heated 300°F oven until all four are done. Add additional oil to pan if needed.

PER SANDWICH: 424 cal., 13 g total fat (3 g sat. fat, 0 g trans fat), 127 mg chol., 776 mg sodium, 42 g carbo., 2 g fiber, 33 g pro. EXCHANGES: 2½ Starch, 3½ Lean Meat, 1½ Fat

MAKING PORK TENDERLOINS, STEP-BY-STEP

1. Cut tenderloin crosswise into four equal pieces. **2.** Working from center to edges, pound pork pieces into an even ¼-inch thickness. **3.** To make pieces rounder, fold any long edges toward the center and pound again until even. **4.** You might have to brown pork in two batches (two at a time). **5.** Cook until slices are brown and a little pink in the middle. Cut into a slice to check doneness.

THAI PORK WRAPS

START TO FINISH: 30 MINUTES **OVEN:** 350°F
MAKES: 6 WRAPS

- 6 8- to 10-inch vegetable-flavored flour tortillas or plain flour tortillas
- ½ teaspoon garlic salt
- ¼ to ½ teaspoon black pepper
- 12 ounces pork tenderloin, cut into 1-inch strips
- 1 tablespoon vegetable oil
- 4 cups packaged shredded broccoli (broccoli slaw mix)
- 1 medium red onion, cut into thin wedges
- 1 teaspoon grated fresh ginger
- 1 recipe Peanut Sauce

1 Preheat oven to 350°F. Wrap tortillas in foil. Bake about 10 minutes or until warm. Meanwhile, in a medium bowl combine garlic salt and pepper. Add pork, tossing to coat.

2 In a large skillet cook and stir pork in hot oil over medium-high heat for 4 to 6 minutes or until no longer pink. (Reduce heat, if necessary, to prevent overbrowning.) Remove pork from skillet; keep warm. Add broccoli, onion, and ginger to skillet. Cook and stir for 4 to 6 minutes or until vegetables are crisp-tender. Remove from heat.

3 Spread Peanut Sauce evenly over tortillas. Top evenly with pork strips and vegetable mixture. Roll up tortillas, securing with wooden toothpicks as needed. Serve immediately.

PEANUT SAUCE: In a small saucepan combine ¼ cup creamy peanut butter, 3 tablespoons water, 1 tablespoon sugar, 2 teaspoons soy sauce, and 1 clove garlic, minced. Heat over medium-low heat, whisking constantly, until smooth and warm. Use immediately or keep warm over very low heat, stirring occasionally.

THAI CHICKEN WRAPS: Prepare as directed, except substitute 12 ounces skinless, boneless chicken breast strips for the pork.

PER WRAP PORK OR CHICKEN VARIATION: 383 cal., 13 g total fat (3 g sat. fat, 0 g trans fat), 37 mg chol., 661 mg sodium, 44 g carbo., 5 g fiber, 22 g pro.
EXCHANGES: 1 Vegetable, 2½ Starch, 2 Lean Meat, ½ High-Fat Meat, ½ Fat

ITALIAN SAUSAGE GRINDERS

PREP: 25 MINUTES **COOK:** 30 MINUTES
BROIL: 2 MINUTES **MAKES:** 4 SANDWICHES

- 1 pound bulk hot or sweet Italian sausage
- 1 14.5-ounce can fire-roasted diced tomatoes
- 1 14.5-ounce can crushed tomatoes
- 2 cloves garlic, minced
- 1 teaspoon balsamic vinegar
- 1 teaspoon dried basil, crushed
- ½ teaspoon dried oregano, crushed
- ¼ teaspoon salt
- ¼ teaspoon crushed red pepper
- 1 small yellow onion, sliced
- 1 small green sweet pepper, seeded and cut into strips
- 2 tablespoons olive oil
- 4 French-style rolls or hoagie buns, split
- 4 slices provolone cheese

1 In a large saucepan cook the sausage over medium heat until no longer pink; drain off fat. Stir in undrained diced tomatoes, undrained crushed tomatoes, the garlic, vinegar, basil, oregano, salt, and crushed red pepper. Bring to boiling; reduce heat. Simmer, uncovered, for 30 minutes or until thickened.

2 Meanwhile, in a large skillet cook onion and sweet pepper in the hot oil over medium heat until tender. Set aside and keep warm.

3 Preheat broiler. Place split rolls on a baking sheet. If desired, toast rolls. Spoon the meat mixture evenly on bottom halves of rolls. Top with onion mixture. Top with cheese slices. Broil 4 to 5 inches from the heat for 2 to 3 minutes or until the cheese melts and bubbles. Add tops of rolls.

BAKING DIRECTIONS: Prepare as directed, but do not broil. Preheat oven to 325°F. Wrap sandwiches with foil. Bake about 15 minutes or until heated through.

PER SANDWICH: 735 cal., 48 g total fat (21 g sat. fat, 0 g trans fat), 96 mg chol., 2,121 mg sodium, 38 g carbo., 4 g fiber, 37 g pro.
EXCHANGES: 1½ Vegetable, 2 Starch, 4 High-Fat Meat, 3 Fat

PICKLED PEPPER SAUSAGE GRINDERS:
Prepare as directed, except omit onion, sweet pepper, and olive oil. Top meat mixture evenly with ½ cup bottled roasted red sweet peppers, drained, and ½ cup bottled sliced banana or pepperoncini peppers, drained.

PER SANDWICH: 672 cal., 41 g total fat (21 g sat. fat, 0 g trans fat), 96 mg chol., 2,339 mg sodium, 37 g carbo., 3 g fiber, 37 g pro.
EXCHANGES: 1½ Vegetable, 2 Starch, 4 High-Fat Meat, 1½ Fat

BEER-BRAISED BRATS

PREP: 15 MINUTES **COOK:** 25 MINUTES
MAKES: 5 SANDWICHES

- ½ cup thinly sliced onion
- 2 tablespoons butter
- 1 12-ounce bottle dark German beer
- 1 tablespoon packed brown sugar
- 1 tablespoon vinegar
- ½ teaspoon caraway seeds
- ½ teaspoon dried thyme, crushed
- ½ teaspoon Worcestershire sauce
- 5 uncooked bratwurst links (1¼ pounds total)
- 5 hoagie buns, bratwursts buns, or other crusty rolls, split and toasted
- 1 recipe Easy Cranberry-Pickle Relish

1 In a large saucepan, cook and stir onion in hot butter over medium heat about 5 minutes or until tender. Add beer, brown sugar, vinegar, caraway seeds, thyme, and Worcestershire sauce. Bring to boiling; reduce heat. Add bratwursts. Cover and simmer for 10 minutes.

2 Remove bratwursts from cooking liquid; keep liquid warm. In a grill pan or skillet cook bratwursts over medium heat about 10 minutes or until brown and an instant-read thermometer inserted into bratwursts registers 160°F, turning occasionally. If desired, return bratwursts to cooking liquid to keep warm until serving time.

3 To serve, place grilled bratwursts in buns. Using a slotted spoon, top bratwursts with some of the cooked onion slices and Easy Cranberry-Pickle Relish.

EASY CRANBERRY-PICKLE RELISH: In a small bowl stir together ½ cup canned whole cranberry sauce and ¼ cup sweet pickle relish.

PER SANDWICH: 600 cal., 26 g total fat (12 g sat. fat, 0 g trans fat), 53 mg chol., 1,267 mg sodium, 69 g carbo., 3 g fiber, 23 g pro. EXCHANGES: 4½ Starch, 2 High-Fat Meat, 1 Fat

BERRY GOOD LEFTOVERS
REFRIGERATE EXTRA CANNED CRANBERRY SAUCE IN AN AIR-TIGHT CONTAINER. STORE UP TO 2 WEEKS AND USE IN OTHER SANDWICHES—TRY IT WITH TURKEY AND HAVARTI CHEESE.

BACON, SPINACH, AND TOMATO SALSA WRAPS

START TO FINISH: 25 MINUTES **MAKES:** 4 WRAPS

- 1¾ cups coarsely chopped, seeded tomatoes (2 large)
- ¼ cup finely chopped red onion
- ¼ cup snipped fresh cilantro
- 1 tablespoon finely chopped fresh jalapeño chile pepper (see tip, page 24)
- 1 tablespoon lime juice
- ¼ teaspoon kosher salt or salt
- 8 slices bacon or turkey bacon
- ¼ cup mayonnaise or light mayonnaise
- 4 10-inch vegetable-flavored flour tortillas or plain flour tortillas
- 2 cups fresh baby spinach

1 For tomato salsa, in a medium bowl stir together tomatoes, onion, cilantro, and jalapeño pepper. Stir in lime juice and salt; set aside.

2 Cook bacon according to package directions; drain well on paper towels. Cut the bacon into large pieces.

3 Spread mayonnaise evenly over tortillas; top with spinach. Using a slotted spoon, scoop salsa evenly over spinach. Top with bacon. Roll up tortillas. Cut each wrap in half.

PER WRAP: 465 cal., 23 g total fat (5 g sat. fat, 0 g trans fat), 23 mg chol., 1,050 mg sodium, 48 g carbo., 5 g fiber, 15 g pro. EXCHANGES: 1 Vegetable, 3 Starch, 1 High-Fat Meat, 2 Fat

NEW ORLEANS-STYLE MUFFULETTA

PREP: 10 MINUTES **CHILL:** 4 TO 24 HOURS
MAKES: 6 SANDWICHES

- ½ cup coarsely chopped pitted ripe olives
- ½ cup chopped pimiento-stuffed green olives
- 1 tablespoon snipped fresh parsley
- 2 teaspoons lemon juice
- ½ teaspoon dried oregano, crushed
- 1 tablespoon olive oil
- 1 clove garlic, minced
- 1 16-ounce loaf ciabatta or unsliced French bread
- 6 lettuce leaves
- 3 ounces thinly sliced salami, pepperoni, or summer sausage
- 3 ounces thinly sliced cooked ham or turkey

6 ounces thinly sliced provolone, Swiss, or mozzarella cheese

1 or 2 medium tomatoes, thinly sliced

⅛ teaspoon coarsely ground black pepper

1 For olive relish, in a small bowl combine the ripe olives, green olives, parsley, lemon juice, and oregano. Cover and chill for 4 to 24 hours.

2 Stir together olive oil and garlic. Split the bread loaf horizontally and hollow out the inside of the top half, leaving a ¾-inch-thick shell.

3 Brush the bottom bread half with olive oil mixture. Top with lettuce, meats, cheese, and tomatoes; sprinkle with pepper. Stir olive relish; mound on top of tomato. Add top of the bread. To serve, cut into six portions.*

*NOTE: For easiest slicing, use a serrated knife to gently saw through the sandwich.

PER SANDWICH: 398 cal., 19 g total fat (8 g sat. fat, 0 g trans fat), 43 mg chol., 1,219 mg sodium, 39 g carbo., 2 g fiber, 20 g pro.
EXCHANGES: ½ Vegetable, 2½ Starch, 2 Medium-Fat Meat, 1 Fat

ITALIAN-STYLE MUFFULETTA: Prepare as directed, except omit the ripe and green olives, the parsley, lemon juice, and oregano. Drain a 16-ounce jar of pickled mixed vegetables, reserving the liquid. Chop the vegetables, removing any pepperoncini stems if present. In a medium bowl stir together the chopped vegetables; 2 tablespoons of the reserved liquid; ¼ cup chopped pimiento-stuffed green olives and/or pitted ripe olives; 1 clove garlic, minced; and 1 tablespoon olive oil. Assemble sandwich as directed, spooning the pickled vegetable mixture on top of the tomatoes.

PER SANDWICH: 409 cal., 19 g total fat (8 g sat. fat, 0 g trans fat), 43 mg chol., 2,008 mg sodium, 41 g carbo., 2 g fiber, 20 g pro.
EXCHANGES: 1 Vegetable, 2½ Starch, 2 Medium-Fat Meat, 1 Fat

MUFFULETTA MASTERY IT'S WORTH HEADING TO A SPECIALTY MARKET FOR QUALITY BREAD, MEATS, AND CHEESES TO MAKE THIS CLASSIC NEW ORLEANS SANDWICH REALLY STAND OUT.

NEW ORLEANS-STYLE MUFFULETTA

HAM SALAD SANDWICHES

PREP: 15 MINUTES **CHILL:** 1 TO 4 HOURS
MAKES: 4 SANDWICHES

2½ cups cubed cooked ham (10 ounces)
½ cup finely chopped celery (1 stalk)
¼ cup thinly sliced green onions (2)
½ cup mayonnaise
4 teaspoons sweet pickle relish
8 slices bread
Lettuce leaves

1 Place ham cubes, celery, onions, mayonnaise, and relish in a food processor. Cover and process until creamy and finely chopped. Transfer to a small bowl. Cover and chill for 1 to 4 hours. Spread ham salad evenly on 4 slices of bread. Top with lettuce and the remaining bread slices.

PER SANDWICH: 416 cal., 26 g total fat (5 g sat. fat, 0 g trans fat), 41 mg chol., 1,708 mg sodium, 28 g carbo., 2 g fiber, 18 g pro. EXCHANGES: 2 Starch, 2 Lean Meat, 3½ Fat

FAST

BBQ RANCH CHICKEN SANDWICHES

(photo, page 519)

PREP: 15 MINUTES **BAKE:** 7 MINUTES **OVEN:** 450°F
MAKES: 4 SANDWICHES

1 10-ounce (12-inch) Italian thin-crust bread shell
Nonstick cooking spray
1½ cups shredded Colby-Jack cheese (6 ounces)
1 cup shredded cooked chicken
2 tablespoons barbecue sauce
6 slices packaged ready-to-serve cooked bacon
1½ cups shredded lettuce
2 tablespoons finely chopped sweet onion
1 tablespoon bottled ranch salad dressing
1 medium tomato, sliced

1 Preheat oven to 450°F. Place bread shell on baking sheet, bottom side up. Coat bread shell with nonstick cooking spray. With pizza cutter, cut shell in half. Sprinkle cheese evenly over bread halves. In a small bowl combine chicken and barbecue sauce. Top one bread half with chicken mixture and bacon slices.

2 Bake for 7 to 9 minutes or until cheese melts and bacon is crisp. Cool on baking sheet for 2 minutes. Meanwhile, in a small bowl combine lettuce, onion, and ranch salad dressing.

3 To serve, cut each half into four wedges (eight wedges total). Spoon lettuce mixture evenly over wedges with chicken. Top with tomato slices. Invert remaining wedges over toppings.

PER SANDWICH: 608 cal., 27 g total fat (11 g sat. fat, 0 g trans fat), 86 mg chol., 1,196 mg sodium, 56 g carbo., 1 g fiber, 35 g pro. EXCHANGES: ½ Vegetable, 3½ Starch, 3 Medium-Fat Meat, 2 Fat

CHICKEN ENCHILADA WRAPS

PREP: 25 MINUTES **CHILL:** UP TO 24 HOURS
MAKES: 6 WRAPS

2 skinless, boneless chicken breast halves
1 tablespoon butter
1 teaspoon chili powder
½ teaspoon ground cumin
1 clove garlic, minced
Dash cayenne pepper
1 3-ounce package cream cheese, softened
½ cup shredded sharp cheddar cheese (2 ounces)
¼ cup dairy sour cream
1 10-ounce can diced tomatoes and green chile peppers, drained
¼ cup thinly sliced green onions (2)
2 tablespoons snipped fresh cilantro
6 8-inch flour tortillas
12 leaves Boston, Bibb, or green leaf lettuce
Cucumber slices, avocado slices, or tomato slices (optional)

1 Finely chop chicken. In a large skillet cook chicken in hot butter over medium heat until chicken is no longer pink. Stir in chili powder, cumin, garlic, and cayenne pepper. Cook and stir for 1 minute more; cool slightly.

2 In a medium mixing bowl combine cream cheese, cheddar cheese, and sour cream; beat on low to medium speed of an electric mixer until creamy. Fold in chicken mixture, tomatoes, green onions, and cilantro. Cover and chill for up to 24 hours.

3 Spread chicken mixture evenly over tortillas. Top evenly with lettuce and, if desired, cucumber, avocado, or tomato slices. Roll up tortillas.

PER WRAP: 289 cal., 15 g total fat (8 g sat. fat, 0 g trans fat), 68 mg chol., 466 mg sodium, 20 g carbo., 2 g fiber, 19 g pro. EXCHANGES: 1 Vegetable, 1 Starch, 2 Lean Meat, 2 Fat

EGG SALAD SANDWICHES

START TO FINISH: 15 MINUTES
MAKES: 4 SANDWICHES

- 8 Hard-Cooked Eggs (page 134), chopped
- ¼ cup finely chopped green onions (2)
- ¼ cup mayonnaise
- 1 tablespoon yellow mustard
- 1 tablespoon pickle relish (optional)
- 1 teaspoon snipped fresh dill, tarragon, or chives (optional)
- ¼ teaspoon salt
- ⅛ teaspoon black pepper
- 8 slices bread or 4 small croissants, split

1 In a large bowl combine chopped eggs and green onions. Stir in mayonnaise, mustard, pickle relish (if desired), dill (if desired), salt, and pepper. Spread egg salad evenly on 4 slices of bread. Top with *lettuce* and remaining bread slices.

PER SANDWICH: 394 cal., 23 g total fat (6 g sat. fat, 0 g trans fat), 429 mg chol., 729 mg sodium, 27 g carbo., 2 g fiber, 17 g pro.
EXCHANGES: 2 Starch, 2 Medium-Fat Meat, 2 Fat

CALIFORNIA-STYLE EGG SALAD SANDWICHES:
Prepare as directed, except omit the mustard and pickle relish. Stir 1 avocado, halved, seeded, peeled, and chopped, and 2 slices crisp-cooked bacon, crumbled, into egg mixture. Substitute tomato slices for the lettuce.

PER SANDWICH: 471 cal., 30 g total fat (7 g sat. fat, 0 g trans fat), 433 mg chol., 782 mg sodium, 31 g carbo., 4 g fiber, 19 g pro.
EXCHANGES: 2 Starch, 2 Medium-Fat Meat, 3½ Fat

GREEK-STYLE EGG SALAD SANDWICHES:
Prepare as directed, except omit the mustard, pickle relish, and dill. Stir 1 cup crumbled feta cheese, ½ cup finely chopped, seeded tomato, and ¼ cup sliced pitted ripe olives into egg mixture.

PER SANDWICH: 504 cal., 32 g total fat (11 g sat. fat, 0 g trans fat), 462 mg chol., 1,180 mg sodium, 30 g carbo., 2 g fiber, 22 g pro.
EXCHANGES: 2 Starch, 2½ Medium-Fat Meat, 3 Fat

INFINITELY ADAPTABLE IF YOU LIKE, TOP YOUR EGG SALAD WITH SLICED RADISHES OR THINLY SLICED RED SWEET PEPPER RINGS FOR EXTRA COLOR AND CRUNCH.

EGG SALAD SANDWICHES

10 TO TRY—PANINI

Start with Panini, page 531;p.
1. APRICOT-TURKEY: Sliced roasted turkey or chicken, apricot preserves, Havarti or Brie cheese, and leaf lettuce. **2. HAM AND APPLE:** Thinly sliced cooked ham, sliced Taleggio or Brie cheese, and thinly sliced apple or pear. **3. BARBECUE:** Barbecued shredded pork or chicken, smoked Gouda cheese, and dill pickle slices. **4. CHICKEN-BACON:** Shredded smoked chicken, crisp-cooked bacon, corn relish, and shredded romaine. **5. SOUTHWEST CHICKEN:** Shredded rotisserie chicken, guacamole, sliced tomato, and Monterey Jack cheese with jalapeño peppers. **6. MEAT LOAF:** Sliced leftover meat loaf, thinly sliced onion, dill pickle slices, provolone or mozzarella cheese, arugula, and Dijon-style mustard. **7. ITALIAN BEEF:** Sliced rare roast beef, mild giardiniera mix, and Colby-Jack cheese. **8. CRANBERRY-TURKEY:** Sliced roasted turkey, cranberry chutney, Muenster cheese, and arugula or fresh spinach. **9. ROAST BEEF:** Sliced rare roast beef, sliced red onion, sliced horseradish cheese, and baby lettuce. **10. VEGGIE:** Thinly sliced cucumber, thinly sliced tomato, thinly sliced onion, fresh spinach, sliced provolone, and creamy ranch dressing.

PANINI

START TO FINISH: 20 MINUTES
MAKES: 4 SANDWICHES

Filling (page 530)

8 slices French, sourdough, multigrain, or
   Italian bread, sliced ¾ inch thick

2 tablespoons olive oil or butter, softened

1 Preheat a covered indoor grill, panini press,
grill pan, or large skillet. Layer desired amount
of Filling ingredients on four slices of bread. Top
with the remaining bread slices. Brush outsides of
sandwiches with olive oil or spread with butter.

2 Place sandwiches (half at a time, if necessary)
in grill. Cover and cook about 6 minutes or
until cheese melts (or until heated through)
and bread is crisp. (If using a grill pan or skillet,
place sandwiches on grill pan or skillet. Weight
sandwiches down and grill about 2 minutes or until
bread is toasted. Turn sandwiches over, weight
them down, and grill until second side is toasted.)
(See tip, below.)

NO PANINI PRESS NEEDED

GET THE PACKED-TIGHT APPEAL OF THIS
SANDWICH WITH YOUR SKILLETS.

Although you can buy a
panini press designed
to cook these pressed,
grilled sandwiches, they
can easily be made with-
out one. Here's how.

■ Assemble and oil or
butter the sandwiches as directed; place in
the heated skillet.

■ Weight the sandwiches down by placing a
large skillet on top of the sandwiches; add a
few unopened cans of food to the top skillet.
(If you use a heavy cast-iron skillet, you might
not need to use the cans for weight.)

■ Grill about 2 minutes; turn. Replace skillet and weights; cook 2 minutes more or until
sandwiches are golden and heated through.

■ Panini cooked with this method will not
have the sandwich's classic grilled ridges—
but they will have all the crisp, melty goodness that's so loved in these treats.

PORTOBELLO FOCACCIA SANDWICHES

START TO FINISH: 30 MINUTES
MAKES: 4 SANDWICHES

1 12-inch round garlic Italian flatbread
   (focaccia)

4 large portobello mushroom caps, stems
   and gills removed

2 tablespoons olive oil

2 tablespoons balsamic vinegar

¼ cup purchased basil pesto

2 to 4 tablespoons mayonnaise

⅛ teaspoon ground black pepper

1 cup bottled roasted red sweet pepper
   strips, drained (optional)

3 ounces fontina cheese, thinly sliced

2 cups arugula or fresh spinach

1 Preheat broiler. Split focaccia in half horizontally. Place bread halves, cut sides up, on a large
baking sheet. Broil 4 to 5 inches from the heat for
3 to 4 minutes or until lightly toasted. Cool bread
halves slightly.

2 Arrange mushroom caps on unheated rack of
broiler pan. In a small bowl whisk together oil and
vinegar. Brush over both sides of mushroom caps.
Broil 4 to 5 inches from the heat for 8 to 10 minutes or until tender, turning once halfway through
broiling time; cool slightly.

3 Meanwhile, spread cut side of the bottom
bread half with pesto. Spread cut side of top
bread half with mayonnaise. Sprinkle mayonnaise
with black pepper.

4 Transfer mushrooms to a cutting board. Cut
each mushroom into quarters; arrange quarters
on top of pesto. If desired, top with roasted red
pepper strips. Top with cheese. If desired, return
to broiler and broil about 1 minute or until cheese
melts. Add arugula and top bread half, cut side
down. Cut into four sandwiches.

PER SANDWICH: 572 cal., 31 g total fat (10 g sat. fat, 0 g trans
fat), 31 mg chol., 308 mg sodium, 57 g carbo., 6 g fiber, 21 g pro.
EXCHANGES: 1½ Vegetable, 3 Starch, 1 High-Fat Meat, 4 Fat

DELUXE GRILLED CHEESE SANDWICHES

START TO FINISH: 20 MINUTES
MAKES: 6 SANDWICHES

- 1 1-pound loaf unsliced bakery white bread
- 6 slices cheddar cheese
- 6 slices Swiss cheese
- 2 tablespoons mayonnaise (optional)
- 1 tablespoon desired mustard (optional)
- 3 tablespoons olive oil
- 3 tablespoons butter (optional)

1 Slice bread ½ inch thick (you should have 12 slices; reserve end slices for another use). Top six of the bread slices with cheese slices.* If desired, spread remaining bread slices evenly with mayonnaise and mustard; place on top of cheese, spread sides down. Brush both sides of each sandwich with olive oil.

2 Heat a large skillet or griddle over medium heat. Add 1 tablespoon of the butter, if using; heat until butter melts. Add two sandwiches to skillet. Cook for 2 minutes or until bottoms are golden. Turn sandwiches over; cook for 2 to 3 minutes more or until bottoms are golden and cheese melts. (Adjust heat as necessary to prevent over-browning.) Repeat with remaining sandwiches.

*NOTE: If desired, add cooked bacon slices, cooked ham slices, tomato slices, or apple slices to sandwiches before grilling. Serve with purchased chutney or ketchup.

PER SANDWICH: 483 cal., 27 g total fat (12 g sat. fat, 0 g trans fat), 56 mg chol., 745 mg sodium, 40 g carbo., 2 g fiber, 20 g pro. EXCHANGES: 2½ Starch, 2 High-Fat Meat, 1½ Fat

FISH SANDWICHES WITH SPICY TARTAR SAUCE

START TO FINISH: 20 MINUTES
MAKES: 4 SANDWICHES

- 4 frozen breaded or battered fish fillets
- ¼ cup mayonnaise
- 1 tablespoon dill or sweet pickle relish
- 1 tablespoon finely chopped onion
- 1 teaspoon Creole mustard or spicy brown mustard
- ¼ teaspoon bottled hot pepper sauce
- 4 hamburger buns, split and toasted
- 1 cup shredded iceberg lettuce
- ¼ cup shredded carrot

1 Bake fish according to package directions. Meanwhile, in a small bowl stir together mayonnaise, relish, onion, mustard, and hot pepper sauce. Divide fish fillets among buns. Top with mayonnaise mixture, lettuce, and carrot.

PER SANDWICH: 359 cal., 21 g total fat (4 g sat. fat, 0 g trans fat), 18 mg chol., 558 mg sodium, 31 g carbo., 1 g fiber, 9 g pro. EXCHANGES: 2 Starch, 1 Lean Meat, 3½ Fat

CATFISH PO'BOYS

START TO FINISH: 20 MINUTES
MAKES: 4 SANDWICHES

- 1 to 1¼ pounds catfish fillets
  Salt and ground black pepper
- ½ cup fine dry bread crumbs
- 2 tablespoons olive oil
- 4 hoagie buns, split and toasted
- 2 medium red and/or yellow sweet peppers, cored and sliced in rings
- 1 cup shredded Monterey Jack cheese with jalapeño peppers (4 ounces)
- 1 cup purchased deli coleslaw
  Bottled hot pepper sauce (optional)
  Small hot peppers (optional)

1 Cut catfish fillets into 3-inch pieces. Season catfish fillets lightly with salt and pepper. Dredge fillets in bread crumbs to coat. In a very large skillet cook catfish in hot oil over medium heat for 6 to 8 minutes or until golden brown and fish flakes easily when tested with a fork, turning fillets over once.

2 Divide catfish among hoagie buns. Top with sweet pepper rings, cheese, and coleslaw. If desired, pass hot pepper sauce and serve with small hot peppers.

PER SANDWICH: 679 cal., 29 g total fat (10 g sat. fat, 0 g trans fat), 85 mg chol., 1,025 mg sodium, 68 g carbo., 4 g fiber, 35 g pro. EXCHANGES: 1 Vegetable, 4 Starch, 3 Medium-Fat Meat, 2 Fat

EUROPEAN ANGLE
FOR BOLDER FLAVOR, SUBSTITUTE IMPORTED GRUYÈRE FOR THE SWISS CHEESE IN THE DELUXE GRILLED CHEESE SANDWICH.

MAKE-IT-MINE PIZZA

PIZZA HAS ALWAYS BEEN ABOUT CHOOS-
ING THE TOPPINGS YOU LOVE. NOW YOU
CAN CHOOSE THE CRUST (PURCHASED
OR HOMEMADE) AND THE SAUCE (PESTO,
PASTA, ALFREDO, OR BARBECUE) TO SUIT
YOUR TASTES—AND YOUR SCHEDULE.

BASIC INGREDIENTS

PREP: 30 MINUTES
BAKE: ACCORDING TO RECIPE
OR PACKAGE DIRECTIONS
MAKES: 8 SERVINGS

Crust
Sauce (optional)
Olive oil (optional)
Meat (optional)
1 to 2 cups Vegetables
(optional)
2 cups Cheese (8 ounces)
Crushed red pepper
(optional)

CRUST (PICK ONE)

1 recipe Pizza Dough (page
534)
2 10-ounce (12-inch)
Italian bread shells
2 packages pizza crust
mix, prepared according
to package directions
2 13.8-ounce packages
refrigerated pizza dough

SAUCE (PICK ONE)

1 cup Alfredo pasta sauce
1 cup barbecue sauce
½ cup basil pesto
1 cup pasta sauce
1 cup pizza sauce

MEAT (PICK ONE)

8 ounces sliced Canadian-
style bacon
1 cup shredded cooked
chicken
1 cup diced cooked ham
3.5 ounces sliced pepperoni
4 ounces thinly sliced
prosciutto
8 ounces bulk Italian
sausage or ground beef,
cooked and drained

VEGETABLES
(PICK ONE OR MORE)

Red or yellow onion slivers
Sliced pitted ripe olives or
green olives
Sliced fresh cremini, button, or
shiitake mushrooms
Chopped green sweet pepper
Thinly sliced roma tomatoes
Quartered artichoke hearts
Roasted red sweet pepper
strips
Chopped fresh spinach
Thinly sliced cooked red
potatoes

CHEESE (PICK ONE)

Fontina, shredded
Fresh mozzarella, sliced
Mozzarella, shredded
Italian cheese blend, shredded
Parmesan, shredded
Smoked cheddar, shredded
Asiago, grated
Blue cheese, crumbled
Chèvre (goat cheese), crumbled
Feta, crumbled

BASIC INSTRUCTIONS

1 Prepare desired Crust. If
desired, spread Sauce onto hot
crust or lightly brush with olive
oil. If desired, top with Meat and
Vegetables. Top with Cheese.
Bake as directed for Pan Pizza or
Thin-Crust Pizzas (page 534) or
according to package directions.
If desired, sprinkle with crushed
red pepper.

PIZZA DOUGH

PREP: 20 MINUTES **STAND:** 10 MINUTES
BAKE: 20 MINUTES **OVEN:** 400°F OR 425°F
MAKES: 1 PAN PIZZA OR 2 THIN-CRUST PIZZAS

- 2½ to 3 cups all-purpose flour
- 1 package active dry yeast
- ½ teaspoon salt
- 1 cup warm water (120°F to 130°F)
- 2 tablespoons vegetable oil or olive oil

1 In a large mixing bowl combine 1¼ cups of the flour, the yeast, and salt; add warm water and oil. Beat with an electric mixer on low speed for 30 seconds, scraping sides of bowl. Beat on high speed 3 minutes. Using a wooden spoon, stir in as much of the remaining flour as you can.

2 Turn dough out onto a lightly floured surface. Knead in enough of the remaining flour to make a moderately stiff dough that is smooth and elastic (6 to 8 minutes total). Divide dough in half (unless making Pan Pizza). Cover; let rest for 10 minutes. Use dough to make Pan Pizza or Thin-Crust Pizzas. Top as desired for Make-It-Mine Pizza (page 533). Bake as directed.

WHOLE WHEAT PIZZA DOUGH: Prepare as directed, except use only the 1¼ cups all-purpose flour mixed with the yeast and salt. Using a wooden spoon, stir in as much of 1¼ to 1¾ cups whole wheat flour as you can. Knead in remaining whole wheat flour to make a moderately stiff dough that is smooth and elastic (6 to 8 minutes total). Continue as directed for Pan Pizza or Thin-Crust Pizzas.

PAN PIZZA: Lightly grease a 15×10×1-inch baking pan. If desired, sprinkle with *cornmeal*. On a lightly floured surface roll all of the dough into a 15×10-inch rectangle. Transfer to prepared pan. Build up edges slightly. Cover and let rise in a warm place until nearly double (30 to 45 minutes). Preheat oven to 400°F. Prick bottom of crust with a fork. Bake crust for 10 to 15 minutes or until light brown. Spread pizza sauce onto hot crust and top with desired meat, vegetables, and cheese (page 533). Bake for 10 to 12 minutes more or until bubbly. Cut into eight wedges.

THIN-CRUST PIZZAS: Preheat oven to 425°F. Grease two 12-inch pizza pans or large baking sheets. If desired, sprinkle with *cornmeal*. On a lightly floured surface roll each dough portion into a 13-inch circle (see photo 1, below). Transfer to pans (see photo 2, below). Build up edges slightly. Prick bottoms of crusts with a fork.* Do not let rise. Bake crusts about 12 minutes or until light brown. Spread pizza sauce onto hot crust and top with desired meat, vegetables, and cheese (page 533). Bake for 10 to 12 minutes more or until bubbly. Cut each pizza into eight wedges.

*NOTE: To bake pizzas on a baking stone, place cold stone in a cold oven. Preheat oven as directed. Roll pizza dough as directed; prick dough all over with a fork. Gently slide the pizza crust onto hot baking stone using a pizza peel or baking sheet with no edges. Bake crust about 12 minutes or until light brown. Using the peel or baking sheet, remove the crust from the oven; top as desired and return to oven. Bake for 10 to 12 minutes more or until bubbly.

WORKING WITH PIZZA DOUGH, STEP-BY-STEP

1. Use a rolling pin or your fingers to roll or push the dough from the center to the edges into a 13-inch circle. If the dough springs back when working with it, let it rest for 5 minutes, then continue rolling. **2.** Transfer the dough circle to a baking sheet that, if desired, has been dusted with cornmeal. The cornmeal makes it easy to remove the finished pizza from the sheet and adds texture to the crust.

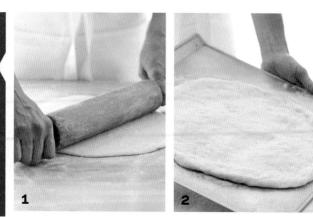

1

2

SAUCES & RELISHES

RASPBERRY-CRANBERRY SAUCE, PAGE 542

SAUCES

IT'S AMAZING HOW MUCH FLAVOR AND FINESSE A SAUCE BRINGS TO A MEAL. LUCKILY, MOST ARE SIMPLE TO MAKE—ESPECIALLY WHEN YOU KEY INTO THE BASICS.

PAN SAUCES

With a pan sauce in your recipe rotation, you'll never lack inspiration for a simple yet thoroughly enjoyable meal. Start with the Steak with Pan Sauce, page 384, and the Chicken with Pan Sauce, page 478, and follow these tips.

■ Get all your ingredients measured and ready to go before you start cooking. Once you start the sauce, the steps move quickly.

■ Choose the optimum size of pan. If your pan is too small, meat won't brown nicely; if it's too large, the drippings will burn—and you need good drippings to flavor the sauce. Cook meat as directed.

■ Remove and cover the meat with aluminum foil while making the sauce. The standing time allows the juices to distribute throughout the meat, making for tender and moist results.

■ After you've removed the meat from the pan, add the liquid ingredients as directed and stir to loosen up the flavorful browned bits left behind by the meat. This is known as deglazing a pan.

■ Finish the sauce as directed. If the sauce is too thick, whisk in a little more broth.

■ Once you master basic pan sauce, you can create many variations by adding ingredients that are fresh, in season, or on hand. See the tip, right, for some flavoring ideas.

FLOUR-THICKENED SAUCES

Some sauces, such as the Cheese Sauce, page 538, start with cooking the flour and fat together to thicken the finished sauce. For smooth, lump-free results, follow these tips.

■ Use a wooden spoon to cook and stir the flour into the melted butter until the mixture is evenly combined and lump-free.

■ Slowly add all the milk to the cooked flour-butter mixture. Stir constantly with a whisk to evenly blend the mixture with the milk.

■ Cook and stir the sauce over medium heat until the mixture bubbles across the entire surface. Cook and stir the sauce 1 minute more—this removes the floury taste from the sauce.

■ Finish the sauce as directed in the recipe.

TRICKY SAUCES

Hollandaise, Béarnaise, and Beurre Blanc, pages 538–539, require a little extra care. Be sure to cook them as specified in the recipe (in a double boiler over gently boiling water for the Hollandaise and Béarnaise; in a pan over medium-low heat to finish the Beurre Blanc). Excessive heat can cause the sauces to separate or curdle. Serve these sauces as soon as they're ready because they often separate upon reheating.

VARIATIONS ON PAN SAUCE

NEXT TIME YOU MAKE A PAN SAUCE, TRY ADDING OTHER INGREDIENTS TO THE BASIC FORMULA. A FEW IDEAS:

HERB SAUCE: Stir in 1 teaspoon snipped fresh herb, such as thyme, oregano, sage, tarragon, or parsley, with the shallot.
SAUCE DIJONNAISE: Stir in ½ teaspoon Dijon-style mustard with the shallot.
BALSAMIC SAUCE: Stir ½ teaspoon balsamic vinegar into the finished sauce.
CAPER SAUCE: Stir ½ teaspoon capers into the finished sauce.

CHEESE SAUCE

START TO FINISH: 15 MINUTES **MAKES:** 2 CUPS

- 2 tablespoons butter
- 2 tablespoons all-purpose flour
  Dash black pepper
- 1½ cups milk
- 1½ cups shredded American or Swiss cheese (6 ounces) or ½ cup crumbled blue cheese (2 ounces)

1 In a small saucepan melt butter over medium heat. Stir in flour and pepper. Stir in milk. Cook and stir over medium heat until thickened and bubbly. Cook and stir for 1 minute more.

2 Reduce heat to low. Add cheese; stir until cheese melts. Serve with vegetables.

PER 2 TABLESPOONS: 68 cal., 5 g total fat (3 g sat. fat, 0 g trans fat), 16 mg chol., 178 mg sodium, 2 g carbo., 0 g fiber, 3 g pro. EXCHANGES: 1½ Fat

CURRY SAUCE: Prepare as directed, except cook 1 teaspoon curry powder in melted butter 1 minute before adding flour. Add ¼ teaspoon salt with flour. Omit cheese. Stir 2 tablespoons snipped chutney into sauce. Serve with poultry or fish.

HERB-GARLIC SAUCE: Prepare as directed, except cook 2 cloves garlic, minced, in the melted butter for 30 seconds. Stir in ½ teaspoon caraway seeds or celery seeds or crushed dried basil, oregano, or sage and ¼ teaspoon salt with the flour. Omit cheese. Serve with vegetables or poultry.

PER 2 TABLESPOONS CURRY OR HERB-GARLIC VARIATION: 44 cal., 3 g total fat (2 g sat. fat, 0 g trans fat), 8 mg chol., 96 mg sodium, 4 g carbo., 0 g fiber, 1 g pro. EXCHANGES: ½ Fat

HOLLANDAISE SAUCE

START TO FINISH: 15 MINUTES **MAKES:** ¾ CUP

- 3 egg yolks, lightly beaten
- 1 tablespoon lemon juice
- 1 tablespoon water
- ½ cup butter (1 stick), cut into thirds, softened
  Salt
  White or black pepper

1 In the top of a double boiler combine egg yolks, lemon juice, and water. Add a piece of the butter (see photo 1, below). Place over gently boiling water (upper pan should not touch water). Cook, stirring rapidly with a whisk (see photo 2, below), until butter melts and sauce begins to thicken (see photo 3, page 539). (Sauce might appear to curdle at this point but will smooth out when remaining butter is added.)

2 Add the remaining butter, a piece at a time, stirring constantly until melted (see photo 4, page 539). Continue to cook and stir for 2 to 2½ minutes more or until sauce thickens (see photo 5, page 539). Immediately remove from heat. If sauce is too thick or curdles, immediately whisk in 1 to 2 tablespoons *hot water*. Season to taste with salt and pepper. Serve with cooked vegetables, poultry, fish, or eggs.

PER 2 TABLESPOONS: 163 cal., 18 g total fat (11 g sat. fat, 0 g trans fat), 146 mg chol., 210 mg sodium, 1 g carbo., 0 g fiber, 2 g pro. EXCHANGES: 3½ Fat

MAKING HOLLANDAISE SAUCE, STEP-BY-STEP

1. Combine first three ingredients and first third of the butter away from heat in the top of a double boiler. **2.** Use a whisk to stir quickly so the sauce cooks evenly. **3.** After adding the first third of butter, cook and stir until sauce thinly coats a spoon. **4.** Melt each third of butter completely before adding more or the sauce will cool down too much. **5.** Thickened sauce will "drape" off the spoon.

BÉARNAISE SAUCE

START TO FINISH: 15 MINUTES
MAKES: ABOUT 1½ CUPS

- 5 tablespoons white wine vinegar
- 1½ teaspoons finely chopped shallot
- 1½ teaspoons snipped fresh tarragon or ¼ teaspoon dried tarragon, crushed
- ¼ teaspoon snipped fresh chervil or dash dried chervil, crushed (optional)
- ⅛ teaspoon white or black pepper
- 6 egg yolks, lightly beaten
- 2 tablespoons water
- ¾ cup butter (1½ sticks), cut into thirds, softened

1 In a small saucepan stir together vinegar, shallot, tarragon, chervil (if desired), and pepper. Bring to boiling. Boil gently, uncovered, about 2 minutes or until reduced by about half.

2 Place the egg yolks and water in the top of a double boiler. Whisk in vinegar mixture. Add a piece of butter. Place over gently boiling water (upper pan should not touch water). Cook, whisking rapidly, until butter melts and sauce begins to thicken. Add the remaining butter, one piece at a time, whisking until melted. Cook and stir for 1½ to 2 minutes more or until sauce thickens (an instant-read thermometer inserted in sauce should register 160°F). Immediately remove from heat. If sauce is too thick or curdles, immediately whisk in 1 to 2 tablespoons *hot water*. Serve with beef, pork, or poultry.

PER 2 TABLESPOONS: 131 cal., 14 g total fat (8 g sat. fat, 0 g trans fat), 135 mg chol., 86 mg sodium, 0 g carbo., 0 g fiber, 1 g pro. EXCHANGES: 3 Fat

BEURRE BLANC

START TO FINISH: 20 MINUTES
MAKES: 1 CUP (UNSTRAINED)

- ¼ cup dry white wine
- 2 tablespoons finely chopped shallot (1 medium)
- 1 tablespoon white wine vinegar
- 2 tablespoons whipping cream
- ¾ cup cold unsalted butter (1½ sticks), cut into 2-tablespoon pieces
  Salt and white pepper

1 In a small stainless-steel saucepan (aluminum can react with the vinegar and cause curdling) combine wine, shallot, and vinegar. Bring to boiling; reduce heat to medium. Boil gently, uncovered, for 7 to 9 minutes or until almost all of the liquid evaporates. Stir in the cream. Bring to boiling and cook about 1 minute to reduce the cream slightly. Reduce heat to medium-low.

2 Using a wire whisk, stir in the butter, a piece at a time, allowing each piece to melt before adding the next. Allow about 8 minutes. If desired, strain sauce. Season to taste with salt and white pepper. Serve over fish or vegetables.

LEMONY BEURRE BLANC: Prepare as directed, except substitute lemon juice for the vinegar. If desired, garnish with finely shredded lemon peel.

CREAMY MUSTARD SAUCE: Prepare as directed, except whisk in 2 teaspoons Dijon-style mustard before serving.

PER 2 TABLESPOONS PLAIN, LEMONY, OR MUSTARD VARIATIONS: 174 cal., 19 g total fat (12 g sat. fat, 0 g trans fat), 51 mg chol., 41 mg sodium, 1 g carbo., 0 g fiber, 0 g pro. EXCHANGES: 4 Fat

BORDELAISE SAUCE

START TO FINISH: 40 MINUTES **MAKES:** ABOUT 1 CUP

1¼ cups reduced-sodium beef broth

¾ cup dry red wine

2 tablespoons finely chopped shallot or onion

3 tablespoons butter or margarine, softened

1 tablespoon all-purpose flour

¼ teaspoon salt

1 tablespoon snipped fresh parsley (optional)

1 In a medium saucepan combine broth, wine, and shallot. Bring to boiling; reduce heat. Simmer, uncovered, skimming surface often with a spoon, for 25 to 30 minutes or until reduced to 1 cup.

2 With a fork, in a small bowl stir together butter and flour. Whisk butter mixture into wine mixture, 1 teaspoon at a time, whisking constantly (mixture will thicken). Cook and stir for 1 minute more. Stir in salt and, if desired, parsley. Serve with beef or lamb.

PER 2 TABLESPOONS: 64 cal., 4 g total fat (3 g sat. fat, 0 g trans fat), 11 mg chol., 173 mg sodium, 2 g carbo., 0 g fiber, 1 g pro. EXCHANGES: 1 Fat

FAST ▪ LOW FAT

SAUCE PROVENÇAL

START TO FINISH: 25 MINUTES **MAKES:** 1¾ CUPS

¼ cup finely chopped onion

1 clove garlic, minced

2 tablespoons olive oil

¼ cup dry white wine

¼ cup chicken broth

1½ cups chopped, peeled, seeded tomatoes (3 medium)

1 tablespoon snipped fresh parsley

2 teaspoons snipped fresh thyme

¼ teaspoon salt

1 In a medium saucepan cook onion and garlic in hot oil over medium-high heat until tender but not brown. Stir in the wine and broth. Bring to boiling; reduce heat. Boil gently, uncovered, about 8 minutes or until reduced to ¼ cup. Stir in tomatoes, parsley, thyme, and salt; heat through. Serve over fish, chicken, couscous, or pasta.

PER 2 TABLESPOONS: 26 cal., 2 g total fat (0 g sat. fat, 0 g trans fat), 0 mg chol., 60 mg sodium, 1 g carbo., 0 g fiber, 0 g pro. EXCHANGES: ½ Fat

BEST EVER ▪ LOW FAT

BALSAMIC BBQ SAUCE

PREP: 10 MINUTES **COOK:** 45 MINUTES **MAKES:** 2 CUPS

1 cup lager beer

1 cup ketchup

½ cup packed brown sugar

⅓ cup white balsamic vinegar

6 cloves garlic, minced

1 tablespoon honey

1 teaspoon ground cumin

1 teaspoon Asian chile sauce (optional)

1 teaspoon chili powder

½ teaspoon black pepper

1 In a medium saucepan combine beer, ketchup, brown sugar, vinegar, garlic, honey, cumin, chile sauce (if desired), chili powder, and pepper. Bring to boiling; reduce heat. Simmer, uncovered, for 45 minutes to 1 hour or until mixture reaches desired consistency, stirring frequently. (Cover and chill any leftovers for up to 1 week. Before serving, warm sauce in saucepan.)

PER 2 TABLESPOONS: 60 cal., 0 g total fat, 0 mg chol., 172 mg sodium, 14 g carbo., 0 g fiber, 0 g pro. EXCHANGES: 1 Other Carbo.

CHIMICHURRI SAUCE

PREP: 15 MINUTES **CHILL:** 2 HOURS **MAKES:** ⅔ CUP

1¼ cups packed fresh Italian parsley leaves

¼ cup olive oil

2 tablespoons fresh oregano or basil leaves

1 shallot, peeled

3 to 4 cloves garlic, peeled

2 tablespoons cider vinegar or red wine vinegar

1 tablespoon lemon juice

½ teaspoon salt

¼ to ½ teaspoon crushed red pepper

1 In a food processor or blender combine parsley, oil, oregano, shallot, garlic, vinegar, lemon juice, salt, and crushed red pepper. Cover and process or blend just until chopped and a few herb leaves are still visible. Cover and chill for 2 hours before serving. (Transfer any leftovers to a storage container. Store in the refrigerator for up to 1 week. Before serving, let stand for 30 minutes at room temperature.)

PER TABLESPOON: 53 cal., 5 g total fat (1 g sat. fat, 0 g trans fat), 0 mg chol., 114 mg sodium, 2 g carbo., 0 g fiber, 0 g pro. EXCHANGES: 1 Fat

ROMESCO SAUCE

START TO FINISH: 20 MINUTES **MAKES:** 2 CUPS

- 4 medium roma tomatoes, peeled, seeded, and cut up
- ⅔ cup bottled roasted red sweet peppers, cut up
- 1 ¾-inch slice country-style bread, toasted and torn into pieces (2 ounces)
- ½ cup blanched whole almonds, toasted
- ¼ cup sherry vinegar or red wine vinegar
- 4 cloves garlic, smashed
- 1 tablespoon snipped fresh Italian parsley
- 1 teaspoon smoked paprika
- ½ teaspoon ground ancho chile pepper
- ⅛ teaspoon cayenne pepper
- ¼ to ⅓ cup olive oil
  Salt

1 In a food processor combine tomatoes, roasted red sweet peppers, bread pieces, almonds, vinegar, garlic, parsley, paprika, ancho chile pepper, and cayenne. Cover and process until combined. With the motor running, add the olive oil through the opening in the lid in a thin, steady stream until combined and mixture is finely chopped. Season to taste with salt. Serve immediately. (Transfer any leftovers to a storage container. Store in the refrigerator for up to 1 week. Before serving, let stand for 30 minutes at room temperature.) Serve with fish, poultry, beef, pork, or vegetables.

PER 2 TABLESPOONS: 76 cal., 6 g total fat (1 g sat. fat, 0 g trans fat), 0 mg chol., 61 mg sodium, 5 g carbo., 1 g fiber, 2 g pro. EXCHANGES: 1½ Fat

COCKTAIL SAUCE

START TO FINISH: 10 MINUTES **MAKES:** ABOUT 1 CUP

- ¾ cup bottled chili sauce
- 2 tablespoons lemon juice
- 2 tablespoons thinly sliced green onion (1)
- 1 tablespoon prepared horseradish
- 2 teaspoons Worcestershire sauce
  Several dashes bottled hot pepper sauce

1 In a small bowl stir together chili sauce, lemon juice, green onion, horseradish, Worcestershire sauce, and hot pepper sauce. Serve immediately or transfer to a storage container; cover and chill for up to 2 weeks. Serve with fish or seafood.

PER 2 TABLESPOONS: 34 cal., 0 g total fat, 0 mg chol., 740 mg sodium, 9 g carbo., 0 g fiber, 0 g pro. EXCHANGES: ½ Other Carbo.

CHANGE UP YOUR CHIMICHURRI THOUGH OREGANO IS CLASSIC IN THIS ARGENTINEAN SAUCE (PAGE 540), YOU CAN SUBSTITUTE OTHER HERBS, SUCH AS CHIVES OR CILANTRO, FRESH FROM YOUR GARDEN.

CHIMICHURRI SAUCE

ROMESCO SAUCE

SWEET-AND-SOUR SAUCE

START TO FINISH: 20 MINUTES **MAKES:** 1 CUP

- ½ cup packed brown sugar
- 4 teaspoons cornstarch
- ⅓ cup chicken broth
- ⅓ cup red wine vinegar
- ¼ cup finely chopped green sweet pepper
- 2 tablespoons chopped pimiento
- 2 tablespoons soy sauce
- 1½ teaspoons minced fresh ginger
- 1 clove garlic, minced
- ⅛ to ¼ teaspoon crushed red pepper

1 In a saucepan stir together brown sugar and cornstarch. Stir in broth, vinegar, green pepper, pimiento, soy sauce, ginger, garlic, and crushed red pepper. Cook and stir until thickened and bubbly. Cook and stir 2 minutes more. Serve warm with egg rolls and wontons or use in recipes calling for sweet-and-sour sauce. (Cover and chill any leftovers up to 3 days. Before serving, warm sauce.)

PER 2 TABLESPOONS: 65 cal., 0 g total fat, 0 mg chol., 298 mg sodium, 16 g carbo., 0 g fiber, 0 g pro.
EXCHANGES: 1 Other Carbo.

HORSERADISH SAUCE

PREP: 5 MINUTES **CHILL:** 60 MINUTES **MAKES:** 1 CUP

- 1 8-ounce carton dairy sour cream
- 3 tablespoons prepared horseradish
- ⅛ teaspoon salt

1 In a bowl stir together sour cream, horseradish, and salt. Cover and chill for at least 60 minutes before serving. Serve with beef or pork.

MUSTARD-HORSERADISH SAUCE: Prepare as directed, except stir in 2 tablespoons chopped green onion (1) and 2 tablespoons Dijon-style mustard. Makes 1⅓ cups.

PER TABLESPOON PLAIN OR MUSTARD VARIATION:
57 cal., 6 g total fat (3 g sat. fat, 0 g trans fat), 15 mg chol.,
77 mg sodium, 1 g carbo., 0 g fiber, 1 g pro.
EXCHANGES: 1 Fat

RASPBERRY-CRANBERRY SAUCE

(photo, page 535)

START TO FINISH: 20 MINUTES
MAKES: ABOUT 2 CUPS

- 2 cups fresh or frozen cranberries
- ½ cup golden raisins
- 1 cup sugar
- ¼ cup dry red wine or cranberry juice
- ½ teaspoon ground ginger
- 1 cup fresh or frozen raspberries
- 1 teaspoon finely shredded orange peel
- ½ cup chopped pecans (optional)

1 In a medium saucepan combine cranberries and raisins. Stir in sugar, wine, and ginger. Cook and stir over medium heat until sugar dissolves. Cook, uncovered, about 5 minutes more or until cranberries pop and mixture thickens slightly, stirring occasionally. Remove from heat.

2 Stir in raspberries, orange peel, and, if desired, pecans. Cool slightly. Serve warm or at room temperature. (Cover and chill any leftovers for up to 3 days. Before serving, let stand for 30 minutes at room temperature.)

PER ¼ CUP: 153 cal., 0 g total fat, 0 mg chol., 4 mg sodium, 38 g carbo., 3 g fiber, 1 g pro.
EXCHANGES: 1 Fruit, 1 Other Carbo.

TZATZIKI SAUCE

START TO FINISH: 15 MINUTES **MAKES:** 1¼ CUPS

- 1 6-ounce carton plain Greek or regular yogurt
- 1 cup shredded, seeded cucumber
- 1 tablespoon lemon juice
- 1 tablespoon olive oil
- 1 tablespoon snipped fresh mint
- 1 clove garlic, minced
- ¼ teaspoon salt

1 In a small bowl stir together yogurt, cucumber, lemon juice, oil, mint, garlic, and salt. Serve immediately or cover and chill for up to 4 hours.

PER 2 TABLESPOONS: 35 cal., 3 g total fat (1 g sat. fat, 0 g trans fat), 6 mg chol., 66 mg sodium, 2 g carbo., 0 g fiber, 1 g pro.
EXCHANGES: ½ Fat

TZATZIKI SAUCE

THIS GO-TO FOR GYROS SANDWICHES GOES WITH MANY OTHER FOODS TOO.

This classic Greek sauce is creamy and refreshing (thanks to the yogurt and cucumber) yet pleasantly zippy (thanks to the garlic and lemon juice). It offers a cooling counterbalance to boldly spiced broiled and grilled meats and fish. In a pinch substitute white wine vinegar for the lemon juice.

EASY AÏOLI

PREP: 10 MINUTES **CHILL:** 60 MINUTES
MAKES: ⅔ CUP

- ⅓ cup mayonnaise
- 3 cloves garlic, minced
- 1 teaspoon water
- ½ teaspoon lemon juice
- ⅛ teaspoon kosher salt or salt
- ¼ cup olive oil

1 In a medium bowl combine the mayonnaise and garlic. Whisk in the water, lemon juice, and salt until the mixture is smooth. Slowly whisk in the olive oil until combined and smooth. Cover and chill for at least 60 minutes before serving. Serve with vegetables, shellfish, or beef.

PER TABLESPOON: 96 cal., 11 g total fat (2 g sat. fat, 0 g trans fat), 2 mg chol., 60 mg sodium, 0 g carbo., 0 g fiber, 0 g pro. EXCHANGES: 2 Fat

TARTAR SAUCE

BEST EVER • LOW FAT • HEALTHY

SWEET MANGO CHUTNEY

PREP: 25 MINUTES **COOK:** 25 MINUTES
CHILL: 8 HOURS **MAKES:** ABOUT 2 CUPS

- 2 mangoes, seeded, peeled, and chopped (2 cups)
- 1 medium pear or tart apple, peeled, cored, and chopped (1 cup)
- ½ cup chopped leek or onion (1 medium)
- ½ cup honey
- ⅓ cup rice vinegar, dry white wine, or white balsamic vinegar
- 1 tablespoon orange juice
- 2 cloves garlic, minced
- ¼ teaspoon salt
- ¼ teaspoon crushed red pepper
- ¼ teaspoon ground ginger

1 In a large saucepan stir together the mangoes, pear, leek, honey, vinegar, orange juice, garlic, salt, crushed red pepper, and ginger. Bring to boiling; reduce heat. Simmer, uncovered, about 25 minutes or until mixture reaches desired consistency, stirring occasionally. Remove from heat; cool.

2 Transfer the chutney to a tightly covered container and chill for at least 8 hours before serving. (Cover and chill any leftovers for up to 1 week. Before serving, let stand for 30 minutes at room temperature.)

PER ¼ CUP: 120 cal., 0 g total fat, 0 mg chol., 77 mg sodium, 31 g carbo., 2 g fiber, 1 g pro. EXCHANGES: ½ Fruit, 1½ Other Carbo.

BEST EVER

TARTAR SAUCE

PREP: 10 MINUTES **CHILL:** 2 HOURS
MAKES: 1 CUP

- ¾ cup mayonnaise
- ¼ cup sweet or dill pickle relish
- 2 tablespoons finely chopped onion
- 1 tablespoon snipped fresh dill or 1 teaspoon dried dillweed
- 1 teaspoon lemon juice
- 2 teaspoons capers, drained (optional)

1 In a small bowl stir together mayonnaise, pickle relish, onion, dill, lemon juice, and, if desired, capers. Cover and chill for at least 2 hours before serving. Serve with fish or seafood. (Cover and chill any leftovers for up to 1 week.)

PER 2 TABLESPOONS: 161 cal., 17 g total fat (3 g sat. fat, 0 g trans fat), 8 mg chol., 173 mg sodium, 3 g carbo., 0 g fiber, 0 g pro. EXCHANGES: 3½ Fat

LOW-FAT TARTAR SAUCE: Prepare as directed, except substitute ½ cup light mayonnaise and ¼ cup plain low-fat yogurt for the ¾ cup mayonnaise.

PER 2 TABLESPOONS: 64 cal., 5 g total fat (1 g sat. fat, 0 g trans fat), 6 mg chol., 167 mg sodium, 5 g carbo., 0 g fiber, 1 g pro. EXCHANGES: 1 Fat

ZESTY FRUIT RELISH

PREP: 25 MINUTES **CHILL:** 4 TO 24 HOURS
MAKES: ABOUT 3 CUPS

- 2 cups chopped fresh cranberries
    (8 ounces)
- ¾ cup finely chopped, peeled pear (1 small)
- ½ cup finely chopped, peeled apple (1 small)
- ½ cup finely chopped, peeled, seeded
    orange (1 medium)
- 2 tablespoons finely chopped shallot
    (1 medium)
- 2 tablespoons thinly sliced green onion (1)
- 1 to 2 fresh jalapeño chile peppers, seeded
    and finely chopped (see tip, page 24)
- ⅓ cup sugar
- 1 tablespoon lime juice
- 1 tablespoon white wine vinegar
- ½ teaspoon salt

1 In a medium nonreactive bowl stir together
cranberries, pear, apple, orange, shallot, green
onion, and jalapeño pepper. Stir in the sugar, lime
juice, vinegar, and salt. Cover and chill for 4 to
24 hours before serving. Stir before serving.
Serve with ham, poultry, or pork.

PER ¼ CUP: 44 cal., 0 g total fat, 0 mg chol., 98 mg sodium,
11 g carbo., 1 g fiber, 0 g pro.
EXCHANGES: ½ Other Carbo.

RASPBERRY SAUCE

PREP: 20 MINUTES **CHILL:** 60 MINUTES
MAKES: ABOUT 1 CUP

- 3 cups fresh or frozen raspberries
- ⅓ cup sugar
- 1 teaspoon cornstarch

1 Thaw berries, if frozen. Do not drain. Place half
of the berries in a food processor or blender. Cover
and process or blend until berries are smooth.
Press berries through a fine-mesh sieve; discard
seeds. Repeat with remaining berries. (You should
have about 1¼ cups sieved puree.)

2 In a small saucepan stir together sugar and
cornstarch. Add raspberry puree. Cook and stir
over medium heat until thickened and bubbly.
Cook and stir for 2 minutes more. Transfer to a
small bowl. Cover and chill for at least 60 minutes
before serving. Serve over angel food cake,

cheesecake, or ice cream. (Cover and chill any
leftovers for up to 1 week.)

PER 2 TABLESPOONS: 130 cal., 0 g total fat, 0 mg chol., 1 mg
sodium, 33 g carbo., 4 g fiber, 1 g pro.
EXCHANGES: 2 Other Carbo.

STRAWBERRY SAUCE: Prepare as directed,
except substitute 3 cups fresh strawberries or
one 16-ounce package frozen unsweetened whole
strawberries, thawed, for the raspberries and do
not sieve. Use a medium saucepan and reduce
sugar to ¼ cup. (You should have 1¾ to 2 cups
puree.) Makes about 2 cups.

PER 2 TABLESPOONS: 21 cal., 0 g total fat, 0 mg chol.,
0 mg sodium, 5 g carbo., 1 g fiber, 0 g pro.
EXCHANGES: Free

RHUBARB SAUCE

START TO FINISH: 20 MINUTES **MAKES:** 2 CUPS

- 3 cups sliced fresh* or frozen rhubarb
- ½ to ⅔ cup sugar
- ¼ cup water
- 1 strip orange peel (optional)
- 1 to 2 drops red food coloring (optional)

1 Thaw rhubarb, if frozen; set aside. In a
medium saucepan stir together sugar, water,
and, if desired, orange peel. Bring to boiling; stir
in rhubarb. Return to boiling; reduce heat. Cover
and simmer for 5 to 6 minutes or until rhubarb is
tender. Remove the orange peel, if using. If using
fresh rhubarb, stir in food coloring if desired.
Serve warm over cake or ice cream. (Cover and
chill any leftovers for up to 3 days.)

*NOTE: You will need about 1 pound of fresh
rhubarb to make 3 cups sliced fruit.

PER 2 TABLESPOONS: 29 cal., 0 g total fat, 0 mg chol., 1 mg
sodium, 7 g carbo., 0 g fiber, 0 g pro.
EXCHANGES: ½ Other Carbo.

CHERRY SAUCE

START TO FINISH: 15 MINUTES **MAKES:** 2 CUPS

- ½ cup sugar
- 2 tablespoons cornstarch
- ½ cup water
- 2 cups fresh or frozen pitted tart cherries
- 1 tablespoon orange or cherry liqueur,
    cherry brandy, or orange juice
- 1 to 2 drops red food coloring (optional)

1 In a medium saucepan stir together sugar and cornstarch; stir in water. Add cherries. Cook and stir over medium heat until thickened and bubbly. Cook and stir for 2 minutes more. Remove from heat.

2 Stir in liqueur and, if desired, food coloring. Serve warm or cooled to room temperature. (Cover and chill any leftovers for up to 3 days.)

PER 2 TABLESPOONS: 40 cal., 0 g total fat, 0 mg chol., 1 mg sodium, 10 g carbo., 0 g fiber, 0 g pro.
EXCHANGES: ½ Other Carbo.

BEST EVER ▪ FAST

HOT FUDGE SAUCE

START TO FINISH: 15 MINUTES **MAKES:** 1½ CUPS

¾ cup semisweet chocolate pieces

¼ cup butter

⅔ cup sugar

1 5-ounce can evaporated milk (⅔ cup)

1 In a small heavy saucepan melt chocolate and butter over medium heat. Add the sugar; gradually stir in the evaporated milk until sugar dissolves

(see photo 1, below). Bring to boiling; reduce heat. Boil gently over low heat for 8 minutes, stirring frequently (see photo 2, below). Remove from heat; cool slightly. Serve warm over ice cream. (Cover and chill any leftovers for up to 3 days.)

PER 2 TABLESPOONS: 145 cal., 8 g total fat (5 g sat. fat, 0 g trans fat), 14 mg chol., 41 mg sodium, 19 g carbo., 1 g fiber, 1 g pro.
EXCHANGES: 1 Other Carbo., 1½ Fat

PEANUT BUTTER FUDGE SAUCE: Prepare as directed, except after gently boiling for 8 minutes, stir in ¼ cup peanut butter. Makes 1¾ cups.

PER 2 TABLESPOONS: 151 cal., 9 g total fat (5 g sat. fat, 0 g trans fat), 12 mg chol., 56 mg sodium, 17 g carbo., 1 g fiber, 2 g pro.
EXCHANGES: 1 Other Carbo.; 2 Fat

HAZELNUT-MOCHA SAUCE: Prepare as directed, except stir in ¼ cup chocolate-hazelnut spread with the semisweet pieces and butter. After removing sauce from heat, stir in 2 tablespoons coffee-flavored liqueur or strong coffee. Makes 2 cups.

PER 2 TABLESPOONS: 181 cal., 9 g total fat (5 g sat. fat, 0 g trans fat), 14 mg chol., 46 mg sodium, 23 g carbo., 1 g fiber, 2 g pro.
EXCHANGES: 1½ Other Carbo, 2 Fat

PREPARING HOT FUDGE SAUCE, STEP-BY-STEP

1. Using a whisk, slowly incorporate the evaporated milk. Keep stirring until the sugar dissolves, scraping the sides of the pan for thorough blending. **2.** Stir the sauce frequently while it boils to prevent it from scorching at the bottom.

CARAMEL SAUCE

PREP: 20 MINUTES **COOL:** 15 MINUTES
MAKES: 1½ CUPS

½ cup whipping cream
½ cup butter (1 stick)
¾ cup packed brown sugar
2 tablespoons light-color corn syrup
1 teaspoon vanilla

1 In a medium heavy saucepan stir together whipping cream, butter, brown sugar, and corn syrup. Bring to boiling over medium-high heat, whisking occasionally; reduce heat to medium. Boil gently for 3 minutes more. Remove from heat; stir in vanilla. Let cool for 15 minutes. (Cover and chill any leftovers for up to 2 weeks. Before serving, let stand at room temperature for 1 hour.)

PER 2 TABLESPOONS: 166 cal., 11 g total fat (7 g sat. fat, 0 g trans fat), 34 mg chol., 65 mg sodium, 16 g carbo., 0 g fiber, 0 g pro. EXCHANGES: 1 Other Carbo., 2 Fat

CUSTARD SAUCE

PREP: 15 MINUTES **CHILL:** 2 HOURS
MAKES: ABOUT 2 CUPS

5 egg yolks, lightly beaten
1½ cups whole milk
¼ cup sugar
1½ teaspoons vanilla

1 In a medium heavy saucepan combine egg yolks, milk, and sugar. Cook and stir continuously with a heatproof rubber scraper over medium heat until sauce thickens and just coats the back of the scraper (see photo 1, page 306). Remove from heat. Stir in vanilla. Cool custard mixture by placing the saucepan in a large bowl of ice water for 1 to 2 minutes, stirring constantly.

2 Pour custard sauce into a bowl. Cover the surface with plastic wrap to prevent a skin from forming. Chill for at least 2 hours before serving. Do not stir. Serve over fresh fruit, baked fruit tarts, or dessert soufflés. (Cover and chill any leftovers for up to 3 days.)

CHOCOLATE CUSTARD SAUCE: Prepare as directed, except add ¼ cup unsweetened Dutch-process cocoa powder or unsweetened cocoa powder and, if desired, a dash ground cinnamon with the sugar. (If necessary, use a whisk to combine ingredients.)

BRANDIED CUSTARD SAUCE: Prepare as directed, except add 1 to 2 tablespoons brandy or desired liqueur (such as cinnamon, orange, amaretto, or raspberry) after removing from heat.

PER 2 TABLESPOONS PLAIN, CHOCOLATE, OR BRANDIED VARIATIONS: 44 cal., 2 g total fat (1 g sat. fat, 0 g trans fat), 68 mg chol., 12 mg sodium, 4 g carbo., 0 g fiber, 2 g pro. EXCHANGES: ½ Fat

VANILLA SAUCE

START TO FINISH: 10 MINUTES **MAKES:** 1¼ CUPS

½ cup sugar
1 tablespoon cornstarch
1 cup boiling water
2 tablespoons butter
1 teaspoon vanilla paste or vanilla
Dash salt

1 In a medium saucepan stir together sugar and cornstarch. Slowly stir in water. Bring to boiling over medium heat; reduce heat. Boil gently for 5 minutes; remove from heat. Stir in butter, vanilla, and salt. Serve over gingerbread, apple dumplings, or your favorite berry pie. (Cover and chill any leftovers for up to 3 days.)

PER 2 TABLESPOONS: 64 cal., 2 g total fat (1 g sat. fat, 0 g trans fat), 6 mg chol., 31 mg sodium, 11 g carbo., 0 g fiber, 0 g pro. EXCHANGES: ½ Other Carbo., ½ Fat

BOURBON SAUCE

PREP: 10 MINUTES **COOL:** 5 MINUTES **MAKES:** ¾ CUP

¼ cup butter, cut up
½ cup sugar
1 egg yolk, lightly beaten
2 tablespoons water
2 tablespoons bourbon

1 In a small saucepan melt the butter. Stir in the sugar, egg yolk, and water. Cook and stir over medium heat for 6 to 8 minutes or until mixture thickens and just boils. Remove from heat. Stir in bourbon; cool slightly. Serve warm over bread pudding or ice cream.

PER 2 TABLESPOONS: 153 cal., 8 g total fat (5 g sat. fat, 0 g trans fat), 55 mg chol., 56 mg sodium, 17 g carbo., 0 g fiber, 1 g pro. EXCHANGES: 1 Other Carbo., 2 Fat

SLOW COOKER RECIPES

CHICKEN AND NOODLES WITH VEGETABLES, PAGE 564

SLOW COOKER RECIPES

FROM PARTY DIPS TO FAMILY MEALS, SLOW-COOKING GIVES YOU SATISFYING RESULTS WITH FIX-NOW/SAVOR-LATER EASE.

COOKER CHOICES

Slow cookers range in size from 1 to 7 quarts. One-quart models generally provide one heat setting (low) and are best for making dips or meals for one or two. The most popular family sizes range from 3 to 6 quarts. In addition, some models offer specialized designs and features.

OVAL-SHAPE COOKERS: These models provide more space in the crockery insert, allowing you to cook larger cuts of meat, such as brisket and ribs.

TIGHT-FITTING, SEE-THROUGH LIDS: These let you view the food as it cooks without lifting the lid, which allows heat to escape.

REMOVABLE INSERTS OR LINERS: These should have large, sturdy handles to make it easier (and safer) to remove them from the base and to clean. A stovetop-safe insert lets you brown meat and slow-cook it in one pan. Before washing the ceramic liner, let it cool to room temperature so it doesn't crack when it comes in contact with water.

A PROGRAMMABLE TIMER: This allows you to set the cooker to start while you're out. (Note that the cooker should be set to start within 2 hours of filling.) Some timers can be programmed to cook on high for a set time, then switch to low. Newer programmable models automatically switch to a warm-heat setting once the food is cooked, which holds food at a safe temperature of 165°F.

WRAPAROUND HEATING ELEMENTS: Cookers with heating elements on the sides heat more evenly than those with the heating element below the food container. Recipes in this chapter require cookers with wraparound heating elements.

DISPOSABLE PLASTIC BAG LINERS: Allowing for easy cleanup with no soaking or scrubbing, these fit most oval or round slow cookers with capacities of 3 to 6.5 quarts. Look for the liners where plastic storage bags are sold.

TIPS FOR SLOW-COOKED SUCCESS:

■ Always thaw frozen meat and poultry before cooking. If you're in a time crunch, use your microwave oven to thaw these foods.

■ Trim excess fat from meat and skin poultry before cooking. Skim fat from cooking juices before serving (see tip, page 557).

■ Take time to brown the meat before placing it in the cooker. Browning, which adds color and flavor, requires little fat when you use a nonstick skillet coated with nonstick cooking spray.

■ Fill the cooker at least half full and no more than two-thirds full.

■ Don't peek. Every time you lift the slow cooker lid, you release heat and add 30 minutes to the cooking time. If you need to lift the lid to stir in ingredients during cooking time, do so quickly.

■ If you omit an ingredient because of family preferences, replace it with an equal amount of another ingredient. For example, if you decide to eliminate three parsnips in a pot roast recipe, replace them with three carrots.

■ Allow your meals to cook as long as the recipe specifies for the most tender, juicy results.

■ A touch of fresh herbs at the end of cooking will brighten the flavor and freshen the look of your finished dish.

RED BEANS AND RICE, PAGE 559

PREPPING AHEAD

Here are a few ways to get a jump start on prepping slow-cooked meals.

■ Chop vegetables and refrigerate in separate covered containers.

■ Assemble, cover, and chill liquid ingredients or sauces in separate covered containers.

■ Brown ground meat, ground poultry, and ground sausage the night before, making sure they're fully cooked before covering and refrigerating. (Do not brown other meats, such as chicken, beef, or pork cubes, or roasts; it is unsafe to partially cook meats and refrigerate for later cooking.)

SAFETY POINTERS

■ If you're concerned that your slow cooker is not heating properly, test it. Fill it half to two-thirds with cool tap water. Heat it on the low-heat setting, covered, for 2 to 3 hours; check the water temperature with an accurate food thermometer. It should be about 185°F. If it's not, replace your slow cooker with a new one.

■ One of the nice things about slow-cooking is that many recipes make big batches, allowing you to freeze leftovers to reheat on busy days. Immediately after the meal, transfer leftover food to freezer containers and freeze up to 6 months. To serve, thaw the food in the refrigerator before reheating it on the stovetop or in the microwave.

■ Don't cook a whole chicken in the slow cooker because it will remain in the bacterial "danger zone" too long (that's the temperature where bacteria grow the fastest).

MEET THE MEATS

These less tender (and less expensive) cuts of meat are ideal for long, slow, moist cooking.

BEEF: Arm pot roast, blade steak, brisket, chuck pot roast, chuck short ribs, flank steak, round steak, rump roast, shank cross cuts, shoulder steak, stew meat.

PORK: Blade roast, boneless pork shoulder roast (butt roast), country-style ribs, sirloin chops, sirloin roast, smoked pork hocks.

CHICKEN AND TURKEY: Breast halves (bone-in), drumsticks, thighs (bone-in or boneless).

SLOW-COOKING LONGTIME FAVORITES

Some of your family's favorite recipes might be good candidates for slow-cooked meals. To adapt them, follow these guidelines.

■ Choose recipes that feature one of the less-tender cuts (see "Meet the Meats," above), then find a recipe in this chapter similar to yours and use it as a guide for quantities, piece sizes, liquid levels, and cooking times.

■ Unless your dish contains long grain rice, reduce the liquids in the recipe you are adapting by about half.

■ Trim the meat, cut it to the right size for a slow cooker, and, if desired, brown it.

■ Cut vegetables into bite-size pieces; place them at the bottom of the slow cooker so they'll cook evenly and completely.

ENHANCE THE FLAVOR OF MEAT DISHES BY ADDING BROTH, WINE, OR JUICE FOR THE LIQUID.

SPINACH-ARTICHOKE DIP

PREP: 25 MINUTES **COOK:** 3 TO 4 HOURS (LOW)
MAKES: 6 CUPS

- 4 slices bacon, cooked and drained
- 1 cup coarsely chopped sweet onion
- 2 14-ounce cans artichoke hearts, drained and coarsely chopped
- 1 10-ounce package frozen chopped spinach, thawed and well drained
- 1 cup chopped red sweet pepper (1 large)
- 1 cup light mayonnaise
- 1 8-ounce package cream cheese, cut up
- 4 ounces blue cheese, crumbled
- 3 cloves garlic, minced
- ½ teaspoon dry mustard

1 Crumble bacon; chill until ready to use. Cook onion in 1 tablespoon bacon drippings about 5 minutes or until tender.

2 In a 3½- or 4-quart slow cooker stir together onion and remaining ingredients. Cover; cook on low-heat setting for 3 to 4 hours or until heated through. Add bacon. Serve with assorted *crackers*.

PER ¼ CUP: 112 cal., 9 g total fat (4 g sat. fat, 0 g trans fat), 19 mg chol., 323 mg sodium, 4 g carbo., 1 g fiber, 3 g pro. EXCHANGES: 2 Fat

CRAB AND HORSERADISH DIP

PREP: 20 MINUTES **COOK:** 2 TO 3 HOURS (LOW)
MAKES: 2½ CUPS

- 1 8-ounce package cream cheese, softened
- 1¼ cups shredded Havarti cheese (5 ounces)
- ⅓ cup dairy sour cream
- ¼ cup mayonnaise
- 1 cup cooked crabmeat or one 6-ounce can crabmeat, drained, flaked, and cartilage removed
- 1 cup shredded fresh baby spinach leaves
- ⅓ cup thinly sliced green onions (3)
- 1 tablespoon snipped fresh chives
- 2 teaspoons prepared horseradish

1 Combine cream cheese, 1 cup Havarti cheese, sour cream, and mayonnaise; beat until well mixed. Stir in crabmeat and spinach. Transfer to 1½-quart slow cooker. Cover; cook on low-heat setting 2 to 3 hours. Sprinkle with remaining Havarti cheese, green onions, chives, and horseradish. Serve with toasted *flat bread, bagel chips,* or *crostini.*

PER ¼ CUP: 204 cal., 18 g total fat (9 g sat. fat, 0 g trans fat), 52 mg chol., 387 mg sodium, 2 g carbo., 0 g fiber, 8 g pro. EXCHANGES: 1 Medium-Fat Meat, 3 Fat

CRAB AND HORSERADISH DIP

FLAMIN' CAJUN RIBLETS

PREP: 20 MINUTES
COOK: 5 TO 6 HOURS (LOW) OR 2½ TO 3 HOURS (HIGH)
MAKES: 12 APPETIZER SERVINGS

- 3 pounds pork loin back ribs, cut in half crosswise*
- 1 tablespoon Cajun seasoning
- 1 cup bottled chili sauce
- ½ cup finely chopped onion (1 medium)
- 1 fresh serrano chile pepper, seeded and finely chopped (see tip, page 24)
- 2 tablespoons quick-cooking tapioca, crushed
- 1 teaspoon finely shredded lemon peel
- 1 tablespoon lemon juice
- 1 to 2 teaspoons bottled hot pepper sauce

1 Sprinkle ribs with Cajun seasoning; rub in with your fingers. Cut ribs into single-rib portions; place in a 3½- or 4-quart slow cooker.

2 Combine chili sauce, onion, serrano pepper, tapioca, lemon peel, lemon juice, and hot pepper sauce. Pour sauce over ribs. Cover; cook on low-heat setting 5 to 6 hours or on high-heat setting 2½ to 3 hours. Keep warm on warm- or low-heat setting up to 2 hours. (Remove any bare bones.)

*NOTE: Ask your butcher to cut the ribs in half crosswise.

PER 2 RIBLETS: 233 cal., 16 g total fat (6 g sat. fat, 0 g trans fat), 56 mg chol., 739 mg sodium, 10 g carbo., 0 g fiber, 12 g pro. EXCHANGES: ½ Other Carbo., ½ High-Fat Meat

10 TO TRY—SAUSAGE & MEATBALL SAUCES

Start with Sausage and Meatball Bites, page 553. **1. FIVE-SPICE:** Omit cranberry sauce and mustard; add 1 cup sweet-and-sour sauce and ½ teaspoon five-spice powder to cooker before adding meat. **2. ITALIAN:** Omit cranberry sauce and mustard; add 1½ cups marinara sauce and ⅓ cup grated Parmesan cheese to cooker before adding meat. **3. MANGO-CHIPOTLE:** Add 1 to 2 teaspoons chopped chipotle peppers in adobo sauce and ½ cup chopped mango to cranberry mixture. **4. SPICY:** Add 1 small finely chopped, seeded jalapeño pepper (see tip, page 24) to cranberry mixture. **5. ORANGE:** Add one 11-ounce can mandarin orange sections (drained) and ½ cup orange marmalade to cranberry mixture. **6. APRICOT:** Add ½ cup apricot preserves and ½ cup snipped dried apricots to cranberry mixture. **7. JERK:** Omit cranberry sauce and mustard; add one 8-ounce can crushed pineapple (undrained), ½ cup barbecue sauce, and 1 teaspoon Jamaican jerk seasoning to cooker before adding meat. **8. MAPLE:** Add 1 tablespoon maple syrup to cranberry mixture. **9. BARBECUE:** Omit cranberry sauce and mustard; add 1¼ cups barbecue sauce and 1 tablespoon honey to cooker before adding meat. **10. POLYNESIAN:** Omit cranberry sauce and mustard; add ⅔ cup pineapple preserves, ¼ cup honey, 2 tablespoons lemon juice, and 1 teaspoon ground ginger to cooker before adding meat.

SAUSAGE AND MEATBALL BITES

PREP: 10 MINUTES
COOK: 4 TO 5 HOURS (LOW) OR 2 TO 2½ HOURS (HIGH)
MAKES: 12 TO 16 APPETIZER SERVINGS

- 1 14-ounce can whole cranberry sauce
- 1 tablespoon Dijon-style mustard
- 1 16-ounce package frozen cooked meatballs
- 1 16-ounce package small cooked smoked sausage links

1 In a 3½- or 4-quart slow cooker combine cranberry sauce and mustard. Stir in meatballs and sausage. Cover and cook on low-heat setting for 4 to 5 hours or on high-heat setting for 2 to 2½ hours. Serve immediately. Keep warm on warm- or low-heat setting up to 1 hour. Serve with picks.

PER ⅓ CUP: 283 cal., 20 g total fat (8 g sat. fat, 0 g trans fat), 37 mg chol., 713 mg sodium, 16 g carbo., 1 g fiber, 10 g pro.
EXCHANGES: 1 Other Carbo., 2 High-Fat Meat

BEST EVER ▪ WHOLE GRAIN

APRICOT-PECAN STUFFING

PREP: 25 MINUTES **COOK:** 3½ TO 4 HOURS (LOW)
MAKES: 12 SIDE-DISH SERVINGS

- 1 cup sliced leeks (3 medium)
- 1 cup chopped onion (1 large)
- 6 tablespoons butter or margarine
- 2 medium apples, peeled (if desired), cored, and chopped (2 cups)
- 1 cup chopped pecans
- ¾ cup snipped dried apricots
- 1 teaspoon dried thyme, crushed
- ½ teaspoon salt
- ½ teaspoon ground nutmeg
- ⅛ teaspoon black pepper
- 12 cups dry whole wheat or white bread cubes (see tip, page 295)
- 1 14-ounce can chicken broth
  Nonstick cooking spray

1 In a large skillet cook leeks and onion in hot butter over medium heat for 5 minutes or until tender, stirring frequently. Stir in apples, pecans, apricots, thyme, salt, nutmeg, and pepper. Cook for 3 minutes more, stirring occasionally. In a very large bowl combine apple mixture and bread cubes. Drizzle broth over bread mixture to moisten, tossing gently. Lightly coat a 5- to

6-quart slow cooker with cooking spray. Transfer bread mixture to prepared cooker. Cover and cook on low-heat setting for 3½ to 4 hours.

PER 1 CUP: 254 cal., 14 g total fat (5 g sat. fat, 0 g trans fat), 16 mg chol., 450 mg sodium, 29 g carbo., 5 g fiber, 7 g pro.
EXCHANGES: ½ Fruit, 1½ Starch, 2 Fat

LOW FAT

ORANGE-SAGE SWEET POTATOES WITH BACON

PREP: 25 MINUTES
COOK: 5 TO 6 HOURS (LOW) OR 2½ TO 3 HOURS (HIGH)
MAKES: 10 TO 12 SIDE-DISH SERVINGS

- 4 pounds sweet potatoes, peeled and cut into ¼-inch-thick slices (about 10 cups)
- ¼ cup frozen orange juice concentrate, thawed
- ¼ cup water
- 3 tablespoons packed brown sugar
- 1½ teaspoons salt
- ½ teaspoon dried leaf sage, crushed
- ½ teaspoon dried thyme, crushed
- 2 tablespoons butter or margarine, cut up
- 4 slices bacon, crisp-cooked and crumbled

1 Place sweet potato slices in a 5- to 6-quart slow cooker. In a small bowl stir together orange juice concentrate, water, brown sugar, salt, sage, and thyme. Pour over sweet potato slices; toss to coat. Dot with butter.

2 Cover and cook on low-heat setting for 5 to 6 hours or on high-heat setting for 2½ to 3 hours. Before serving, stir to coat with orange juice mixture and sprinkle with bacon.

PER 1 CUP: 177 cal., 4 g total fat (2 g sat. fat, 0 g trans fat), 10 mg chol., 512 mg sodium, 33 g carbo., 4 g fiber, 3 g pro.
EXCHANGES: 2 Starch, ½ Fat

LEFTOVER PRECAUTIONS
DO NOT LEAVE LEFTOVERS IN THE SLOW COOKER TO COOL DOWN; TRANSFER WARM LEFTOVERS TO CONTAINERS AND REFRIGERATE OR FREEZE PROMPTLY. ALSO, NEVER REHEAT LEFTOVERS IN THE SLOW COOKER.

HERBED WILD RICE

PREP: 25 MINUTES
COOK: 6 TO 7 HOURS (LOW) OR 3 TO 3½ HOURS (HIGH)
MAKES: 12 TO 14 SIDE-DISH SERVINGS

- 2 cups fresh button mushrooms, quartered
- 1 cup sliced carrots (2 medium)
- 1½ cups chopped onions (3 medium)
- 1 cup uncooked wild rice, rinsed and drained
- 1 cup uncooked brown rice
- 1 teaspoon dried basil, crushed
- ½ teaspoon dried thyme, crushed
- ½ teaspoon dried rosemary, crushed
- ¼ teaspoon black pepper
- 4 cloves garlic, minced
- 1 tablespoon butter or margarine
- 1 14.5-ounce can diced tomatoes, undrained
- 2 14-ounce cans vegetable or chicken broth

1 In a 3½- or 4-quart slow cooker combine mushrooms, carrots, onions, wild rice, brown rice, basil, thyme, rosemary, pepper, garlic, and butter. Pour undrained tomatoes and broth over the mixture in cooker.

2 Cover and cook on low-heat setting for 6 to 7 hours or on high-heat setting for 3 to 3½ hours. Stir mixture before serving.

PER 1 CUP: 141 cal., 2 g total fat (1 g sat. fat, 0 g trans fat), 3 mg chol., 345 mg sodium, 28 g carbo., 3 g fiber, 4 g pro.
EXCHANGES: ½ Vegetable, 1½ Starch

EASY CHEESY POTATOES

PREP: 20 MINUTES **COOK:** 5 TO 6 HOURS (LOW)
STAND: 10 MINUTES **MAKES:** 12 SIDE-DISH SERVINGS

- Nonstick cooking spray
- 1 28-ounce package frozen diced hash brown potatoes with onion and peppers, thawed
- 1 10.75-ounce can condensed cream of chicken with herbs soup
- 4 ounces smoked Gouda cheese, shredded (1 cup)
- 4 ounces American cheese slices, torn into 1-inch pieces
- ¾ cup milk
- ¼ cup thinly sliced leek or green onions
- ½ teaspoon black pepper
- 1 8-ounce package cream cheese, cut into cubes
- 4 strips bacon, crisp-cooked and crumbled
- Sliced green onions (optional)

1 Coat a 3½- or 4-quart slow cooker with cooking spray. Combine thawed potatoes, condensed soup, Gouda and American cheeses, milk, leek, and pepper in cooker.

2 Cover and cook on low-heat setting for 5 to 6 hours. Stir in cream cheese; cover and let stand for 10 minutes.

3 Just before serving, stir mixture. Sprinkle with bacon and, if desired, green onions.

PER ½ CUP: 219 cal., 14 g total fat (8 g sat. fat, 0 g trans fat), 44 mg chol., 626 mg sodium, 16 g carbo., 2 g fiber, 8 g pro.
EXCHANGES: 1 Starch, 1 Other Carbo., 1 High-Fat Meat, 1 Fat

SLOW-ROASTED ROOT VEGETABLES

PREP: 30 MINUTES **COOK:** 3 TO 4 HOURS (HIGH)
MAKES: 12 SIDE-DISH SERVINGS

- 1 pound butternut squash, peeled and cut into 2-inch pieces
- 8 ounces tiny new potatoes, halved
- 8 ounces beets, peeled and cut into 1-inch pieces
- 8 ounces turnips or rutabagas, peeled and cut into 1-inch pieces
- 1 cup packaged peeled fresh baby carrots
- 1 small red onion, cut into ½-inch wedges
- 8 cloves garlic, peeled
- 2 tablespoons olive oil
- ½ teaspoon salt
- ½ teaspoon black pepper
- Chopped fresh parsley

1 In a very large bowl combine squash, potatoes, beets, turnips, carrots, onion, and garlic. Drizzle with olive oil and toss to coat. Sprinkle with salt and pepper. Place squash mixture in a 3½- or 4-quart slow cooker.

2 Cover and cook on high-heat setting for 3 to 4 hours or until vegetables are tender when pierced with a fork. Sprinkle with parsley.

PER ½ CUP: 73 cal., 2 g total fat (0 g sat. fat, 0 g trans fat), 0 mg chol., 135 mg sodium, 12 g carbo., 2 g fiber, 1 g pro.
EXCHANGES: ½ Vegetable, ½ Starch, ½ Fat

FOR UNIFORM DONENESS
CUT MEAT AND VEGETABLES INTO THE SIZE OF PIECES SPECIFIED IN THE RECIPE.

HERBED WILD RICE

SIDES TO SERVE A CROWD FOR HOLIDAYS, CONSIDER USING YOUR
SLOW COOKER TO PREPARE THE SIDE DISHES. DOING SO FREES UP
OVEN AND STOVETOP SPACE FOR COOKING OTHER FOODS.

EASY CHEESY POTATOES

SLOW-ROASTED ROOT
VEGETABLES

SO-EASY PEPPER STEAK

PREP: 15 MINUTES
COOK: 9 TO 10 HOURS (LOW) OR 4½ TO 5 HOURS (HIGH)
MAKES: 6 MAIN-DISH SERVINGS

- 1 2-pound boneless beef round steak, cut ¾ to 1 inch thick
- 1 14.5-ounce can Cajun-, Mexican-, or Italian-style stewed tomatoes, undrained
- ⅓ cup tomato paste
- ½ teaspoon bottled hot pepper sauce (optional)
- 1 16-ounce package frozen pepper stir-fry vegetables (yellow, green, and red sweet peppers and onion)
- 4 cups hot cooked whole wheat pasta (optional)

1 Trim fat from steak. Cut steak into six serving-size pieces. Sprinkle meat with ½ teaspoon *salt* and ¼ teaspoon *black pepper*. Place in a 3½- or 4-quart slow cooker. Combine undrained tomatoes, tomato paste, and, if desired, hot pepper sauce. Pour over meat in cooker. Top with frozen vegetables. Cover and cook on low-heat setting for 9 to 10 hours or on high-heat setting for 4½ to 5 hours. If desired, serve with hot cooked pasta.

PER SERVING: 258 cal., 6 g total fat (2 g sat. fat, 0 g trans fat), 83 mg chol., 644 mg sodium, 12 g carbo., 2 g fiber, 37 g pro.
EXCHANGES: 1½ Vegetable, 4½ Lean Meat

BUSY-DAY BEEF-VEGETABLE SOUP

PREP: 20 MINUTES
COOK: 8 TO 10 HOURS (LOW) OR 4 TO 5 HOURS (HIGH)
MAKES: 4 MAIN-DISH SERVINGS

- 1 pound boneless beef chuck roast, trimmed and cut into bite-size pieces
- 3 medium carrots, cut into ½-inch-thick slices
- 2 small potatoes, peeled (if desired) and cut into ½-inch cubes
- ½ cup chopped onion (1 medium)
- ½ teaspoon dried thyme, crushed
- 1 bay leaf
- 2 14.5-ounce cans diced tomatoes, undrained
- ½ cup frozen peas

1 In a 3½- or 4-quart slow cooker combine beef, carrots, potatoes, and onion. Sprinkle with thyme and ½ teaspoon *salt*. Add bay leaf. Pour undrained tomatoes and 1 cup *water* over mixture in cooker.

2 Cover and cook on low-heat setting for 8 to 10 hours or on high-heat setting for 4 to 5 hours. Discard bay leaf. Stir in frozen peas.

PER ABOUT 2 CUPS: 279 cal., 8 g total fat (3 g sat. fat, 0 g trans fat), 72 mg chol., 860 mg sodium, 26 g carbo., 7 g fiber, 26 g pro.
EXCHANGES: 1½ Vegetable, 1 Starch, 3 Lean Meat

PEPPERY ITALIAN BEEF SANDWICHES

PREP: 30 MINUTES
COOK: 10 HOURS (LOW) OR 5 TO 6 HOURS (HIGH)
MAKES: 8 MAIN-DISH SERVINGS

- 1 2½- to 3-pound boneless beef chuck pot roast
- 4 teaspoons garlic-pepper seasoning
- 1 tablespoon vegetable oil
- 1 14-ounce can beef broth
- 1 0.7-ounce envelope Italian dry salad dressing mix
- 1 teaspoon onion salt
- 1 teaspoon dried oregano, crushed
- 1 teaspoon dried basil, crushed
- 1 teaspoon dried parsley
- 1 12- to 16-ounce jar pepperoncini salad peppers, drained
- 8 hoagie buns or kaiser rolls, split and toasted
- 2 cups shredded mozzarella cheese (8 ounces)

1 Trim fat from meat. Coat meat with garlic-pepper seasoning. In a Dutch oven brown meat on all sides in hot oil.

2 If necessary, cut meat in half to fit into a 3½- or 4-quart slow cooker. Place meat in cooker. In a medium bowl whisk together beef broth, dressing mix, onion salt, oregano, basil, and parsley. Pour over meat in cooker. Top with peppers.

3 Cover and cook on low-heat setting for 10 hours or on high-heat setting for 5 to 6 hours. Transfer meat to a cutting board. Using two forks, pull meat apart into shreds. Remove peppers from cooking liquid; transfer to a bowl. Skim fat from cooking liquid; transfer cooking liquid to a bowl.

4 To serve, spoon some shredded meat on the bottom halves of buns. Sprinkle with cheese. If desired, spoon desired amount of cooking liquid over top. Top with peppers and bun tops.

PER SANDWICH: 579 cal., 21 g total fat (8 g sat. fat, 0 g trans fat), 105 mg chol., 2,390 mg sodium, 54 g carbo., 2 g fiber, 42 g pro.
EXCHANGES: 3½ Starch, 4½ Medium-Fat Meat

BEEF CHILI MAC

PREP: 25 MINUTES
COOK: 4 TO 6 HOURS (LOW) OR 2 TO 3 HOURS (HIGH)
MAKES: 6 MAIN-DISH SERVINGS

1½ pounds ground beef
1 cup chopped onion (1 large)
3 cloves garlic, minced
1 15-ounce can chili beans in chili gravy
1 14.5-ounce can diced tomatoes and
    green chiles, undrained
1 cup beef broth
¾ cup chopped green sweet pepper
2 teaspoons chili powder
1 teaspoon ground cumin
¼ teaspoon salt
8 ounces dried cavatappi or macaroni,
    cooked according to package directions
    Tortilla chips or corn chips
    Shredded cheddar cheese (optional)

1 In a large skillet cook ground beef, onion, and garlic over medium heat until meat browns and onion is tender. Drain fat; discard.

2 In a 3½- or 4-quart slow cooker combine meat mixture, undrained chili beans, undrained tomatoes and green chiles, broth, sweet pepper, chili powder, cumin, and salt.

3 Cover and cook on low-heat setting for 4 to 6 hours or on high-heat setting for 2 to 3 hours. Stir in cooked pasta. Serve with tortilla chips. If desired, top with cheese.

PER 1½ CUPS: 559 cal., 22 g total fat (7 g sat. fat, 1 g trans fat), 77 mg chol., 871 mg sodium, 57 g carbo., 8 g fiber, 33 g pro.
EXCHANGES: 1 Vegetable, 3½ Starch, 3 Medium-Fat Meat, ½ Fat

BEER-BRAISED BEEF SHORT RIBS

PREP: 20 MINUTES
COOK: 11 TO 12 HOURS (LOW) OR 5½ TO 6 HOURS (HIGH)
MAKES: 4 TO 6 MAIN-DISH SERVINGS

5 pounds beef short ribs
1 14-ounce can beef broth
1 12-ounce can dark beer
1 medium onion, cut into thin wedges
¼ cup molasses
2 tablespoons balsamic vinegar
1 teaspoon dried thyme, crushed
1 teaspoon bottled hot pepper sauce
½ teaspoon salt
    Mashed potatoes or hot buttered noodles
    (optional)
    Fresh thyme leaves (optional)

1 Place ribs in a 5- to 6-quart slow cooker. Add broth, beer, onion, molasses, vinegar, thyme, hot pepper sauce, and salt.

2 Cover and cook on low-heat setting for 11 to 12 hours or on high-heat setting for 5½ to 6 hours.

3 Using a slotted spoon, transfer ribs to platter (see photo 1, below); cover to keep warm. Skim fat from cooking liquid (see photo 2, below). Serve cooking liquid with ribs for dipping. If desired, serve ribs with mashed potatoes and garnish with thyme leaves.

PER SERVING: 491 cal., 19 g total fat (8 g sat. fat, 0 g trans fat), 132 mg chol., 822 mg sodium, 24 g carbo., 0 g fiber, 46 g pro.
EXCHANGES: 1½ Other Carbo., 6 Medium-Fat Meat

REMOVING MEAT AND SKIMMING FAT, STEP-BY-STEP

1. Use a long-handled slotted spoon to gently drain the short ribs and transfer them to a platter. **2.** To skim the fat off the meat drippings, pour the drippings into a glass measure. Use a large metal spoon to carefully remove the clear fat that rises to the top. Skimming off the fat creates a less-greasy mixture with more concentrated flavor.

COOK ONCE, EAT TWICE

COME HOME TO A COMFORT-FOOD FAVORITE: TENDER, SUCCULENT BEEF BRISKET. ANOTHER NIGHT SAVOR THE LEFTOVERS IN A CHEESY CHUTNEY-BEEF PANINI.

TONIGHT

BARBECUED BRISKET

PREP: 15 MINUTES
COOK: 12 TO 14 HOURS (LOW) OR 6 TO 7 HOURS (HIGH)
MAKES: 6 MAIN-DISH SERVINGS + RESERVES

- 1 4- to 4½-pound fresh beef brisket
  Black pepper
- 1 16-ounce package peeled fresh baby carrots
- 2 stalks celery, cut into ½-inch-thick slices
- 1½ cups bottled smoke-flavored barbecue sauce
- 2 tablespoons quick-cooking tapioca, crushed
- 2 tablespoons Dijon-style mustard
- 1 tablespoon Worcestershire sauce
- 4 cups mashed potatoes or hot cooked noodles

1 Trim fat from brisket. If necessary, cut brisket in half to fit into a 5- to 6-quart slow cooker. Season brisket with pepper. In the cooker combine carrots and celery. Place brisket on vegetables. In a small bowl combine barbecue sauce, tapioca, mustard, and Worcestershire sauce; pour over brisket.

2 Cover and cook on low-heat setting for 12 to 14 hours or on high-heat setting for 6 to 7 hours.

3 Transfer brisket to cutting board; cut in half. Thinly slice half of brisket across the grain. Skim fat from cooking liquid. Serve cooking liquid with sliced brisket, vegetables, and mashed potatoes.

4 Slice remaining half of brisket. Place slices in an airtight container; cover and chill for up to 24 hours or freeze for up to 1 month; use in Chutney-Beef Panini.

PER SERVING: 441 cal., 7 g total fat (3 g sat. fat, 0 g trans fat), 65 mg chol., 1,580 mg sodium, 54 g carbo., 5 g fiber, 37 g pro. EXCHANGES: 1 Vegetable, 1½ Starch, 2 Other Carbo., 4½ Lean Meat

TOMORROW

CHUTNEY-BEEF PANINI

PREP: 10 MINUTES **COOK:** 5 MINUTES PER BATCH
MAKES: 6 MAIN-DISH SERVINGS

- ½ recipe Barbecued Brisket or
  1 pound deli-style cooked beef
- ½ cup mango chutney
- 12 slices whole wheat bread
- 6 slices provolone cheese (6 ounces)
  Olive oil or melted butter

1 Thaw brisket, if frozen. Finely snip chutney. Spread evenly on one side of each bread slice. Arrange brisket slices on six of the bread slices. Top with provolone cheese. Cover with remaining bread slices, chutney sides down. Lightly brush bread with olive oil.

2 Preheat an indoor grill or a panini grill according to manufacturer's directions, or griddle or skillet over medium heat. Place sandwiches, a few at a time, on hot grill, griddle, or skillet. If using a covered indoor grill, close lid and grill for 5 to 6 minutes or until bread toasts and cheese melts. (If using an uncovered indoor grill, griddle, or skillet, place a heavy plate on top of the sandwiches [see photo, page 531]). Cook for 2 to 3 minutes or until bottoms toast. Carefully remove plate, turn sandwiches over, and top with the plate. Cook for 2 to 3 minutes more or until bread toasts and cheese melts.)

PER SANDWICH: 508 cal., 20 g total fat (8 g sat. fat, 0 g trans fat), 82 mg chol., 770 mg sodium, 33 g carbo., 3 g fiber, 46 g pro. EXCHANGES: 2 Starch, 5½ Lean Meat, 2 Fat

SPAGHETTI SAUCE ITALIANO

PREP: 25 MINUTES
COOK: 8 TO 10 HOURS (LOW) OR 4 TO 5 HOURS (HIGH)
MAKES: 6 TO 8 MAIN-DISH SERVINGS

- 1 pound bulk Italian sausage or ground beef
- 1 cup chopped onion (1 large)
- 2 cloves garlic, minced
- 2 14.5-ounce cans diced tomatoes, undrained
- 1 6-ounce can tomato paste
- 2 4-ounce cans mushroom stems and pieces, drained
- 1 bay leaf
- 2 teaspoons dried Italian seasoning, crushed
- 1 cup chopped green sweet pepper (1 large)
- 12 to 16 ounces hot cooked spaghetti
  Finely shredded or grated Parmesan cheese (optional)

1 In a large skillet cook sausage, onion, and garlic over medium heat until meat browns. Drain fat; discard. In a 3½- or 4-quart slow cooker combine undrained tomatoes, tomato paste, mushrooms, bay leaf, Italian seasoning, ½ teaspoon *salt,* and ¼ teaspoon *black pepper.* Add meat mixture. Cover and cook on low-heat setting for 8 to 10 hours or on high-heat setting for 4 to 5 hours. Stir in sweet pepper. Discard bay leaf. Serve meat mixture over hot cooked spaghetti. If desired, sprinkle with Parmesan cheese.

PER 1 CUP SAUCE + 1 CUP SPAGHETTI: 553 cal., 23 g total fat (10 g sat. fat, 0 g trans fat), 51 mg chol., 1,506 mg sodium, 62 g carbo., 6 g fiber, 27 g pro.
EXCHANGES: 1 Vegetable, 3½ Starch, 2½ High-Fat Meat

BEST EVER • LOW FAT

SPICY PULLED PORK

PREP: 15 MINUTES
COOK: 8 TO 10 HOURS (LOW) OR 4 TO 5 HOURS (HIGH)
MAKES: 8 MAIN-DISH SERVINGS

- 2 to 2½ pounds boneless pork shoulder
- 1 large sweet onion, cut into thin wedges
- 1 18- to 20-ounce bottle hot-style barbecue sauce (about 1¾ cups)
- 1 cup Dr. Pepper carbonated beverage (not diet)
- 8 hamburger buns, toasted

1 Trim fat from meat. If necessary, cut meat to fit in a 3½- or 4-quart slow cooker. Sprinkle meat with *salt* and *black pepper.* Place onion wedges in cooker. Top with meat. Combine barbecue sauce and carbonated beverage; pour mixture over meat. Cover and cook on low-heat setting for 8 to 10 hours or on high-heat setting for 4 to 5 hours.

2 Transfer meat to a cutting board. Using forks, shred meat; place in bowl. Remove onions from cooker; add to meat. Skim fat from cooking liquid; add enough liquid to meat mixture to moisten. Divide meat mixture among buns.

PER SANDWICH: 378 cal., 8 g total fat (3 g sat. fat, 0 g trans fat), 73 mg chol., 1,355 mg sodium, 45 g carbo., 1 g fiber, 27 g pro.
EXCHANGES: 2 Starch, 1 Other Carbo., 3 Lean Meat, ½ Fat

RED BEANS AND RICE *(photo, page 549)*

PREP: 30 MINUTES **STAND:** 1 HOUR
COOK: 9 TO 10 HOURS (LOW) OR 4½ TO 5 HOURS (HIGH) + 30 MINUTES (HIGH) **MAKES:** 6 MAIN-DISH SERVINGS

- 1 cup dry red kidney beans
- 1 smoked pork hock
- 12 ounces andouille sausage or cooked kielbasa, cut into ½-inch pieces
- 2½ cups reduced-sodium chicken broth
- ½ cup chopped onion (1 medium)
- ½ cup chopped celery (1 stalk)
- 1 tablespoon tomato paste
- 2 cloves garlic, minced
- ½ teaspoon dried thyme, crushed
- ½ teaspoon dried oregano, crushed
- ⅛ to ¼ teaspoon cayenne pepper
- 1 8.8-ounce pouch cooked long grain rice
- ½ cup chopped red or yellow sweet pepper

1 Rinse beans; drain. In a large saucepan combine beans and 6 cups water. Bring to boiling; reduce heat. Simmer, uncovered, for 10 minutes. Remove from heat. Cover; let stand 1 hour. Drain and rinse beans.

2 In a 3½- or 4-quart slow cooker combine beans, pork hock, sausage, broth, onion, celery, tomato paste, garlic, thyme, oregano, and cayenne pepper. Cover; cook on low-heat setting 9 to 10 hours or on high-heat setting 4½ to 5 hours.

3 Remove pork hock; cool. Cut meat off bone; cut meat into bite-size pieces. Discard bone. Stir meat, rice, and sweet pepper into bean mixture in cooker. If using low-heat setting, turn cooker to high-heat setting. Cover; cook for 30 minutes more or until heated through.

PER 1⅓ CUPS: 429 cal., 22 g total fat (9 g sat. fat, 0 g trans fat), 40 mg chol., 766 mg sodium, 37 g carbo., 6 g fiber, 21 g pro.
EXCHANGES: 2½ Starch, 2½ High-Fat Meat

MAKE-IT-MINE ONE-POT MEAL

IF YOU'VE EVER LOOKED AT A CUT OF MEAT AND WONDERED HOW TO COOK IT IN A SLOW COOKER, THIS RECIPE IS FOR YOU! ADAPT THE MEATS AND INGREDIENTS YOU LIKE BEST FOR A DISH YOU'LL LOVE.

BASIC INGREDIENTS

PREP: 25 MINUTES
COOK: 8 TO 10 HOURS (LOW) OR 4 TO 5 HOURS (HIGH)
MAKES: 6 SERVINGS

- 2½ to 3 pounds Meat
- 1½ to 2 pounds Vegetable
- 1½ teaspoons Seasoning
- ½ teaspoon salt
- ¼ teaspoon black pepper
  Liquid
  Side (optional)

MEAT (PICK ONE)

Beef chuck or bottom round roast

Chicken thighs and/or drumsticks (skinned)

Lamb shoulder roast

Pork shoulder or sirloin roast

VEGETABLE (PICK ONE)

Brussels sprouts, halved*

Carrots, peeled and cut into 2-inch pieces

Frozen stew vegetables*

Mushrooms, whole button

Onion wedges

Potatoes (russet, red, or peeled sweet), cut into 2-inch pieces

Sweet pepper, cut into thick slices

Zucchini, cut into slices*

*NOTE: Add to cooker during last hour of cooking.

SEASONING (PICK ONE)

Chili powder

Dried basil, crushed

Dried Italian seasoning, crushed

Dried oregano, crushed

Dried thyme, crushed

Salt-free seasoning blend

Steak seasoning

LIQUID (PICK ONE)

- 1 cup chicken or beef broth
- 1 10.75-ounce can condensed soup: tomato, cream of chicken, cream of mushroom, or cream of celery
- ½ cup dry red or white wine* plus ½ cup chicken or beef broth
- 1 cup tomato juice
- 1 8-ounce can tomato sauce

*NOTE: For superior flavor, choose a wine that you like to drink.

SIDE (PICK ONE)

Hot cooked pasta (couscous, gnocchi, noodles, or spaetzle)

Hot cooked rice (white, brown, or long grain)

Mashed potatoes

BASIC INSTRUCTIONS

1 Trim any fat from desired Meat. If necessary, cut meat in half to fit into a 4- to 6-quart slow cooker.* Place Vegetable in slow cooker. Sprinkle with half the Seasoning. Top with meat. Sprinkle with remaining Seasoning, salt, and pepper. Pour Liquid over top.

2 Cover and cook on low-heat setting for 8 to 10 hours or on high-heat setting for 4 to 5 hours. If desired, serve with a Side and Gravy.

GRAVY: If desired, make gravy with the cooking liquid. Remove meat and vegetables from cooker using a slotted spoon. Strain cooking liquid into a 4-cup glass measure. If necessary, add enough chicken or beef broth to equal 3 cups total. Pour into a medium saucepan. In a small bowl combine ⅓ cup all-purpose flour and ⅓ cup water until very smooth. Stir into cooking liquid. Cook and stir over medium heat until thickened and bubbly. Cook and stir for 1 minute more.

*NOTE: When filling your slow cooker, make sure it is half to two-thirds full before you turn it on. Adjust the ingredient amounts as needed.

PORK CARNITAS WITH SWEET CORN POLENTA

PREP: 25 MINUTES
COOK: 8 TO 10 HOURS (LOW) OR 4 TO 5 HOURS (HIGH)
MAKES: 10 TO 12 MAIN-DISH SERVINGS

1½ teaspoons garlic powder
1 teaspoon salt
¾ teaspoon dried oregano, crushed
¾ teaspoon ground coriander
¾ teaspoon ground ancho chile pepper
¼ teaspoon ground cinnamon
1 5-pound boneless pork shoulder roast
2 tablespoons vegetable oil
2 bay leaves
1 cup chicken broth
1 recipe Sweet Corn Polenta
  Snipped fresh oregano (optional)

1 In a large bowl combine garlic powder, salt, dried oregano, coriander, ground chile pepper, and cinnamon; set aside.

2 Trim fat from meat. Cut meat into 2-inch pieces. Add meat to spice mixture; toss gently to coat.

3 In a large skillet heat oil over medium-high heat. Cook meat, one-third at a time, in hot oil until brown. Using a slotted spoon, transfer meat to a 4- or 4½-quart slow cooker. Add bay leaves. Pour broth over meat.

4 Cover and cook on low-heat setting for 8 to 10 hours or on high-heat setting for 4 to 5 hours. Remove bay leaves. Serve meat and cooking liquid with Sweet Corn Polenta. If desired, sprinkle with fresh oregano.

SWEET CORN POLENTA: In a large saucepan combine 4 cups chicken broth; two 12-ounce cans evaporated milk; two 4-ounce cans diced green chiles, undrained; 2 teaspoons dried oregano, crushed; 2 teaspoons garlic powder; and 1 teaspoon salt. Bring to boiling. Gradually add 2 cups quick-cooking polenta mix or coarse cornmeal, stirring constantly. Reduce heat to low. Cook, uncovered, for 5 to 10 minutes or until thickened. Stir in 2 cups frozen whole kernel corn and, if desired, 1½ cups shredded Monterey Jack cheese (6 ounces). Remove from heat. Let stand for 5 minutes before serving.

PER SERVING: 674 cal., 22 g total fat (8 g sat. fat, 0 g trans fat), 168 mg chol., 1,270 mg sodium, 59 g carbo., 7 g fiber, 56 g pro. EXCHANGES: ½ Milk, 3½ Starch, 6 Lean Meat, 1½ Fat

LOW FAT

LAMB SHANKS WITH HERBED POTATOES

PREP: 35 MINUTES
COOK: 10 TO 11 HOURS (LOW) OR 5 TO 5½ HOURS (HIGH)
MAKES: 4 MAIN-DISH SERVINGS

1 tablespoon Dijon-style mustard
1 tablespoon olive oil
½ teaspoon salt
¼ teaspoon black pepper
4 to 5 pounds meaty lamb shanks (3 to 4 shanks)
1½ pounds round red potatoes or Yukon gold potatoes, cut into 2-inch pieces
8 cloves garlic, peeled
1 teaspoon snipped fresh thyme or ½ teaspoon dried thyme, crushed
1 teaspoon snipped fresh rosemary or ½ teaspoon dried rosemary, crushed
1 teaspoon snipped fresh sage or ½ teaspoon dried sage, crushed
⅓ cup chicken broth
½ cup chopped tomato
1 tablespoon snipped fresh parsley

1 In a small bowl combine mustard, olive oil, ½ teaspoon salt, and ¼ teaspoon pepper. Brush mixture onto lamb shanks.

2 Place potatoes and garlic cloves in a 5- to 6-quart slow cooker. Sprinkle with thyme, rosemary, and sage. Top with lamb shanks. Pour broth over all in cooker.

3 Cover and cook on low-heat setting for 10 to 11 hours or on high-heat setting for 5 to 5½ hours.

4 Remove lamb shanks from cooker. Skim excess fat from cooking liquid (see photo 2, page 557); season to taste with additional salt and black pepper. Serve lamb shanks with potatoes and cooking juices. Sprinkle with tomato and parsley.

PER SERVING: 444 cal., 11 g total fat (3 g sat. fat, 0 g trans fat), 148 mg chol., 859 mg sodium, 33 g carbo., 4 g fiber, 51 g pro. EXCHANGES: 2 Starch, 6½ Lean Meat

A WINDFALL OF GARLIC
DON'T BE ALARMED BY THE AMOUNT OF GARLIC ADDED TO THIS LAMB RECIPE; IT BECOMES SWEET AND MELLOW WITH THE LONG COOKING.

CHICKEN WITH CREAMY CHIVE SAUCE

PREP: 15 MINUTES **COOK:** 4 TO 5 HOURS (LOW)
MAKES: 6 MAIN-DISH SERVINGS

- 6 skinless, boneless chicken breast halves (about 1¾ pounds)
- ¼ cup butter or margarine
- 1 0.7-ounce envelope Italian dry salad dressing mix
- 1 10.75-ounce can condensed golden mushroom soup
- ½ cup dry white wine
- ½ of an 8-ounce tub cream cheese with chives and onion
  Hot cooked whole wheat pasta (optional)
  Snipped fresh chives (optional)

1 Place chicken in a 3½- or 4-quart slow cooker. In a medium saucepan melt the butter over medium heat. Stir in the dressing mix. Stir in mushroom soup, wine, and cream cheese until combined. Pour over the chicken in cooker.

2 Cover and cook on low-heat setting for 4 to 5 hours. Serve chicken with sauce. If desired, serve with pasta and sprinkle with chives.

PER SERVING: 329 cal., 17 g total fat (9 g sat. fat, 0 g trans fat), 119 mg chol., 1,101 mg sodium, 7 g carbo., 0 g fiber, 33 g pro. EXCHANGES: ½ Starch, 4½ Lean Meat, 2 Fat

LOW FAT

JAMBALAYA

PREP: 30 MINUTES **COOK:** 6 TO 8 HOURS (LOW) OR
3 TO 4 HOURS (HIGH) + 30 MINUTES (HIGH)
MAKES: 6 MAIN-DISH SERVINGS

- 6 skinless, boneless chicken thighs (1½ pounds)
- 4 ounces cooked ham
- 1 cup chopped onion (1 large)
- 1 cup thinly sliced celery (2 stalks)
- 1 14.5-ounce can fire-roasted diced tomatoes,* undrained
- 1 cup chicken broth
- 2 tablespoons tomato paste
- 2 tablespoons quick-cooking tapioca, crushed
- 1 tablespoon Worcestershire sauce
- 1 tablespoon lemon juice
- 1 fresh serrano chile pepper, seeded and finely chopped (see tip, page 24)
- 3 cloves garlic, minced
- ½ teaspoon dried thyme, crushed

- ½ teaspoon dried oregano, crushed
- ¼ teaspoon salt
- ¼ teaspoon cayenne pepper
- 8 ounces medium fresh shrimp, peeled and deveined
- ½ cup yellow sweet pepper, chopped (1 small)
- 2 cups frozen cut okra (optional)
- 1 14.8-ounce pouch cooked long grain rice

1 Cut chicken and ham into bite-size pieces. In a 3½- or 4-quart slow cooker combine chicken, ham, onion, and celery. Stir in undrained tomatoes, broth, tomato paste, tapioca, Worcestershire sauce, lemon juice, serrano pepper, garlic, thyme, oregano, salt, and cayenne pepper.

2 Cover; cook on low-heat setting for 6 to 8 hours or on high-heat setting for 3 to 4 hours.

3 If using low-heat setting, turn cooker to high-heat setting. Stir in shrimp, sweet pepper, and, if desired, okra. Cover and cook about 30 minutes more or until shrimp turn opaque.

4 Prepare rice according to package directions; serve with jambalaya.

*NOTE: If you can't find fire-roasted diced tomatoes, use plain diced tomatoes and add ¼ teaspoon liquid smoke.

PER 1 CUP CHICKEN MIXTURE + ½ CUP RICE: 365 cal., 7 g total fat (1 g sat. fat, 0 g trans fat), 160 mg chol., 941 mg sodium, 35 g carbo., 2 g fiber, 37 g pro. EXCHANGES: 1½ Vegetable, 2 Starch, 4 Lean Meat

---

SIZING IT UP

HERE'S HOW TO ADAPT A RECIPE TO COOK IN A LARGER COOKER.

Most slow cookers with programmable features come in larger sizes than those called for in standard slow cooker recipes. When using these larger cookers, you'll need to adjust the recipe by increasing the amounts. For the best results, increase everything—from the meat and vegetables to the liquid and seasonings—proportionately. Be sure that the cooker is half to just two-thirds full. Cook the food for the same amount of time as you would in a smaller cooker.

ITALIAN BRAISED CHICKEN WITH FENNEL AND CANNELLINI

PREP: 30 MINUTES
COOK: 5 TO 6 HOURS (LOW) OR 2½ TO 3 HOURS (HIGH)
MAKES: 6 SERVINGS

- 2 to 2½ pounds chicken drumsticks and/or thighs, skinned
- 1 15-ounce can cannellini (white kidney) beans, rinsed and drained
- 1 fennel bulb, cored and cut into thin wedges
- 1 medium yellow sweet pepper, seeded and cut into 1-inch pieces
- 1 medium onion, cut into thin wedges
- 3 cloves garlic, minced
- 1 teaspoon snipped fresh rosemary or ½ teaspoon dried rosemary, crushed
- 1 teaspoon snipped fresh oregano or ½ teaspoon dried oregano, crushed
- ¼ teaspoon crushed red pepper
- 1 14.5-ounce can diced tomatoes, undrained
- ½ cup dry white wine or reduced-sodium chicken broth
- ¼ cup tomato paste
- ¼ cup shaved Parmesan cheese
- 1 tablespoon snipped fresh Italian parsley

1 Sprinkle chicken pieces with ¼ teaspoon each of *salt* and *black pepper.* Place chicken in a 3½- or 4-quart slow cooker. Top with beans, fennel, sweet pepper, onion, garlic, rosemary, oregano, and crushed red pepper. In a medium bowl combine tomatoes, white wine, tomato paste, and ½ teaspoon *salt;* pour over mixture in cooker.

2 Cover and cook on low-heat setting for 5 to 6 hours or on high-heat setting for 2½ to 3 hours.

3 Sprinkle each serving with Parmesan cheese and parsley.

PER SERVING: 223 cal., 4 g total fat (1 g sat. fat, 0 g trans fat), 68 mg chol., 762 mg sodium, 23 g carbo., 7 g fiber, 25 g pro. EXCHANGES: 1½ Vegetable, 1 Starch, 2½ Lean Meat

GO FOR A GREMOLATA ADD 1 CLOVE GARLIC, MINCED, AND ½ TEASPOON FINELY SHREDDED LEMON PEEL TO THE PARSLEY TO MAKE A FRESH, FANTASTIC GREMOLATA TOPPER FOR THIS DISH.

ITALIAN BRAISED CHICKEN WITH FENNEL AND CANNELLINI

TURKEY AND DUMPLINGS

from bones; discard bones. Shred or chop meat; stir into mixture in cooker.

3 To serve, in a large serving bowl stir together chicken mixture and noodles.

PER 2½ CUPS: 388 cal., 8 g total fat (2 g sat. fat, 0 g trans fat), 122 mg chol., 928 mg sodium, 48 g carbo., 5 g fiber, 31 g pro.
EXCHANGES: ½ Vegetable, 3 Starch, 3 Lean Meat

LOW FAT

TURKEY AND DUMPLINGS

PREP: 20 MINUTES **COOK:** 6 TO 7 HOURS (LOW) OR 3 TO 3½ HOURS (HIGH) + 45 MINUTES (HIGH)
STAND: 15 MINUTES **MAKES:** 6 MAIN-DISH SERVINGS

- 1½ cups thinly sliced carrots (3 medium)
- 1½ cups thinly sliced celery (3 stalks)
- 1 medium onion, cut in very thin wedges
- 1¼ pounds turkey breast tenderloin, cut into ¾-inch cubes
- 1 14-ounce can reduced-sodium chicken broth
- 1 10.75-ounce can condensed cream of chicken soup
- 2 teaspoons dried sage, crushed
- 1 cup all-purpose flour
- 1 teaspoon baking powder
- 2 tablespoons shortening
- ½ cup milk
- ¼ cup all-purpose flour

1 In a 3½- or 4-quart slow cooker combine carrots, celery, and onion; stir in turkey. Reserve ½ cup of broth. Combine remaining broth, soup, sage, and ¼ teaspoon *black pepper*; stir into cooker. Cover; cook on low-heat setting 6 to 7 hours or on high-heat setting for 3 to 3½ hours.

2 For dumplings, stir together 1 cup flour, baking powder, and ½ teaspoon *salt*. Use a pastry blender to cut in shortening until mixture resembles coarse crumbs. Add milk and stir just until moistened.

3 If using low-heat setting, turn cooker to high-heat setting. In a small bowl whisk together reserved ½ cup broth and the ¼ cup flour; stir into mixture in cooker. Drop dumpling dough by small spoonfuls on top of mixture in cooker. Cover and cook for 45 minutes more. Remove ceramic liner from cooker or turn off cooker. Let stand, covered, for 15 minutes before serving.

PER 1½ CUPS: 320 cal., 8 g total fat (2 g sat. fat, 1 g trans fat), 64 mg chol., 809 mg sodium, 30 g carbo., 2 g fiber, 29 g pro.
EXCHANGES: ½ Vegetable, 1½ Starch, 3 Lean Meat, 1 Fat

BEST EVER • LOW FAT

CHICKEN AND NOODLES WITH VEGETABLES *(photo, page 547)*

PREP: 30 MINUTES
COOK: 8 TO 9 HOURS (LOW) OR 4 TO 4½ HOURS (HIGH)
MAKES: 6 MAIN-DISH SERVINGS

- 2 cups sliced carrots (4 medium)
- 1½ cups chopped onions (3 medium)
- 1 cup sliced celery (2 stalks)
- 1 bay leaf
- 4 medium chicken legs (drumstick-thigh portion) (about 2½ pounds total), skinned
- 2 10.75-ounce cans reduced-fat and reduced-sodium condensed cream of chicken soup
- 1 teaspoon dried thyme, crushed
- 8 ounces dried wide noodles (about 4 cups)
- 1 cup frozen peas

1 In a 3½- or 4-quart slow cooker stir together carrots, onions, celery, and bay leaf. Place chicken on top of vegetables. Stir together soup, ½ cup *water*, thyme, 1 teaspoon *salt*, and ¼ teaspoon *black pepper*. Pour over chicken in cooker. Cover and cook on low-heat setting for 8 to 9 hours or on high-heat setting for 4 to 4½ hours.

2 Remove chicken from slow cooker; cool slightly. Discard bay leaf. Cook noodles according to package directions; drain. Meanwhile, stir frozen peas into mixture in cooker. Remove chicken

SOUPS & STEWS

MINESTRONE, PAGE 584

SOUPS & STEWS

FROM WARM, HEARTY CHOWDERS TO SUMMERY GAZPACHO, MANY OF THE WORLD'S MOST BELOVED DISHES ARE SERVED UP IN A BOWL. HERE'S SOME KNOW-HOW.

TAKE STOCK

When you have the time, call on made-from-scratch broth to add extra homemade goodness to your soup recipes. When time is not on your side, these are the best options.

CANNED BROTH: Use straight from the can or carton, unless it's a condensed broth, which you should dilute according to the label directions. Canned broths can be high in sodium; either pick a low-sodium version or adjust the salt in the recipe.

CHICKEN OR BEEF BASE: This pastelike ingredient comes in a jar and must be refrigerated after opening. When reconstituted in water, it makes a flavorful broth for recipes.

PERFECTLY PUREED

Some soups need to be pureed, and a handheld immersion blender provides an easy, safe, mess-free way to do this right in the pan (see photo 2, page 588). If using a traditional blender, follow these precautions.

■ Cool the hot mixture slightly before blending.

■ Fill container no more than half full and make sure the blender lid is on tight.

■ Remove the round plastic piece in the center of the lid and hold a kitchen towel over the opening to allow steam to escape during blending.

■ Blend on low speed to avoid an eruption.

SOUPS AND STEWS ON HAND

Soups and stews can often be made in larger batches—simply double a recipe that makes four to six servings and you'll likely have leftovers. The good news is they generally keep well. In fact, some even improve after a day in the fridge—extra time allows flavors to meld. Follow these pointers to keep leftovers at their best.

■ Cool soup or stew before freezing or refrigerating. Place the pot in a sink of ice water and stir the soup so it cools quickly.

■ For short-term storage, divide the cooled soup or stew among shallow containers. Cover and refrigerate for up to 3 days.

■ For long-term storage, divide the cooled soup or stew among shallow freezer-safe containers. Leave about ½ inch space between the top of the soup or stew and the rim of its container. This will provide  room for the food to expand while it freezes without breaking the container or causing the lid to pop off. Freeze soups and stews up to 3 months.

■ Avoid freezing soups and stews thickened with cornstarch or flour; freezing causes them to lose their thickening capacity.

THAWING AND REHEATING LEFTOVERS

Here's how to bring leftovers safely to the table.

■ If soup or stew has been frozen, thaw it for one to two days in the refrigerator before reheating.

■ You can also thaw soup or stew in the microwave on 50% power (medium). Pop the soup or stew out of the freezer container into a microwave-safe dish. Cover the dish with a microwave-safe lid or plastic wrap and loosen or vent the lid, or wrap to prevent spattering. Stir soup or stew once or twice as it thaws.

■ Heat thawed soup or stew on the stovetop, using medium-high heat for broth-based soups and medium heat for purees or stews. Stir often to keep it from burning; watch bean, potato, and flour-thickened mixtures closely.

■ For food safety, soups and stews should be brought to a rolling boil before serving.

BEEF BROTH

PREP: 30 MINUTES **ROAST:** 30 MINUTES
COOK: 3½ HOURS **OVEN:** 450°F
MAKES: 6 TO 7 CUPS

  4 pounds meaty beef soup bones (beef
       shank crosscuts or short ribs)
  ½ cup water
  3 carrots, cut up
  2 medium onions, unpeeled and cut up
  2 stalks celery with leaves, cut up
  1 tablespoon dried basil or thyme, crushed
1½ teaspoons salt
 10 whole black peppercorns
  8 sprigs fresh parsley
  4 bay leaves
  2 cloves garlic, unpeeled and halved
  8 cups water

1 Preheat oven to 450°F. Place soup bones in a
large, shallow roasting pan. Roast about
30 minutes or until brown, turning once.

2 Place soup bones in a large pot. Pour the
½ cup water into the roasting pan and scrape up
browned bits; add water mixture to large pot. Stir
in carrots, onions, celery, basil, salt, peppercorns,
parsley, bay leaves, and garlic. Add the 8 cups
water. Bring to boiling; reduce heat. Simmer,
covered, for 3½ hours. Remove soup bones from
broth; set aside.

3 Strain broth (see photo 2, below). Discard
vegetables and seasonings.

4 If using broth while hot, skim fat (see photos
3 and 4, page 569). If storing broth for later use,
chill in bowl for 6 hours; lift off fat (see photo
5, page 569). Place broth in a container. Cover
and chill up to 3 days or freeze up to 6 months.

5 If desired, when bones are cool enough to
handle, remove meat. Chop meat; discard bones.
Place meat in a container. Cover and chill for up to
3 days or freeze for up to 3 months.

SLOW COOKER DIRECTIONS: Prepare as directed,
except use 2 small onions and 7½ cups water total.
Roast soup bones as directed. Place bones in a
4- to 6-quart slow cooker. Pour the ½ cup water
into the roasting pan and scrape up browned bits;
add water mixture to slow cooker. Stir in carrots,
onions, celery, basil, salt, peppercorns, parsley,
bay leaves, and garlic. Add 7 cups water. Cover;
cook on low-heat setting for 10 to 12 hours or on
high-heat setting for 5 to 6 hours. Remove soup
bones from broth; set aside. Continue as directed.

PER 1 CUP: 17 cal., 0 g total fat, 3 mg chol., 595 mg sodium,
2 g carbo., 1 g fiber, 14 g pro.
EXCHANGES: Free

CHICKEN BROTH

PREP: 25 MINUTES **COOK:** 2½ HOURS
MAKES: ABOUT 5½ CUPS

  3 pounds bony chicken pieces (wings, backs,
       and/or necks)
  3 stalks celery with leaves, cut up
  2 carrots, cut up
  1 large onion, unpeeled and cut up
  1 teaspoon salt
  1 teaspoon dried thyme, sage, or basil,
       crushed

MAKING HOMEMADE BROTH, STEP-BY-STEP

1. Cut wings to expose more bones; this gives the broth a richer flavor. **2.** Strain broth in a sieve or colander lined with two layers of 100-percent-cotton cheesecloth. **3.** Use a fat-separating pitcher. Let fat rise to the top, then pour broth from the spout. **4.** Or use a spoon to skim away fat floating on the surface. **5.** You can also chill broth and lift off the fat layer with a spoon.

1

2

½ teaspoon whole black peppercorns or
  ¼ teaspoon black pepper
4 sprigs fresh parsley
2 bay leaves
2 garlic cloves, unpeeled and halved
6 cups cold water

1 If using wings, cut each wing at joints into three pieces (see photo 1, page 568). Place chicken pieces in a large pot. Add celery, carrots, onion, salt, thyme, peppercorns, parsley, bay leaves, and garlic. Add water. Bring to boiling; reduce heat. Simmer, covered, for 2½ hours. Remove chicken pieces from broth; set aside.

2 Strain broth (see photo 2, page 568). Discard vegetables and seasonings.

3 If using broth while hot, skim fat (see photos 3 and 4, below). If storing, chill 6 hours; lift off fat (see photo 5, below). Place broth in a container. Cover; chill up to 3 days or freeze up to 6 months.

4 If desired, when chicken is cool enough to handle, remove meat. Chop meat; discard bones. Place meat in a container. Cover and chill for up to 3 days or freeze for up to 6 months.

SLOW COOKER DIRECTIONS: Place chicken pieces in a 4- to 6-quart slow cooker. Add remaining ingredients and 6 cups water. Cover; cook on low-heat setting for 10 to 12 hours or on high-heat setting for 5 to 6 hours. Remove chicken; set aside. Continue as directed.

PER 1 CUP: 11 cal., 0 g total fat, 3 mg chol., 411 mg sodium, 1 g carbo., 0 g fiber, 1 g pro.
EXCHANGES: Free

LOW FAT

BARLEY-BEEF SOUP

PREP: 25 MINUTES **COOK:** 105 MINUTES
MAKES: 8 MAIN-DISH SERVINGS

12 ounces beef or lamb stew meat, cut into
   1-inch cubes
1 tablespoon vegetable oil
4 14-ounce cans beef broth (about 7 cups)
1 cup chopped onion (1 large)
½ cup chopped celery (1 stalk)
1 teaspoon dried oregano or basil, crushed
¼ teaspoon black pepper
2 cloves garlic, minced
1 bay leaf
1 cup frozen mixed vegetables
1 14.5-ounce can diced tomatoes,
   undrained
1 cup ½-inch slices peeled parsnip or
   ½-inch cubes peeled potato
⅔ cup quick-cooking barley

1 In a large pot brown meat in hot oil. Stir in broth, onion, celery, oregano, pepper, garlic, and bay leaf. Bring to boiling; reduce heat. Simmer, covered, for 90 minutes for beef (45 minutes for lamb).

2 Stir in frozen vegetables, undrained tomatoes, parsnip, and barley. Return to boiling; reduce heat. Simmer, covered, about 15 minutes more or until meat and vegetables are tender. Discard bay leaf.

PER 1⅓ CUPS: 188 cal., 5 g total fat (1 g sat. fat, 0 g trans fat), 20 mg chol., 880 mg sodium, 23 g carbo., 5 g fiber, 14 g pro.
EXCHANGES: 1 Vegetable, 1 Starch, 1½ Lean Meat

BEEF BOURGUIGNONNE

PREP: 40 MINUTES **COOK:** 70 MINUTES
MAKES: 6 MAIN-DISH SERVINGS

- 1 pound boneless beef chuck roast, cut into ¾-inch cubes
- 2 tablespoons vegetable oil
- 1 cup chopped onion (1 large)
- 1 clove garlic, minced
- 1½ cups Burgundy wine
- ¾ cup beef broth
- 1 teaspoon dried thyme, crushed
- ¾ teaspoon dried marjoram, crushed
- 2 bay leaves
- 3 cups whole fresh mushrooms
- 4 medium carrots, cut into ¾-inch pieces
- 8 ounces pearl onions or 2 cups frozen small whole onions
- 2 tablespoons all-purpose flour
- ¼ cup water
- 3 cups hot cooked noodles or mashed potatoes
- 2 slices bacon, crisp-cooked, drained, and crumbled
- 1 tablespoon snipped fresh parsley

1 In a large pot cook half of meat in 1 tablespoon hot oil until meat is brown; remove meat from pan. Add remaining oil and meat, chopped onion, and garlic to pot. Cook until meat is brown and onion is tender. Drain fat. Return all meat to pot.

2 Stir in wine, broth, thyme, marjoram, bay leaves, ½ teaspoon *salt,* and ¼ teaspoon *black pepper.* Bring to boiling; reduce heat. Simmer, covered, about 45 minutes, stirring occasionally. Add mushrooms, carrots, and pearl onions. Return to boiling; reduce heat. Simmer, covered, for 25 to 30 minutes more or until vegetables are tender, stirring occasionally. Discard bay leaves.

3 Combine flour and water; stir into meat mixture. Cook and stir until thickened and bubbly. Cook and stir for 1 minute more. Serve with noodles. Top with bacon and parsley.

SLOW COOKER DIRECTIONS: Brown meat, chopped onion, and garlic as directed. In a 3½- or 4-quart slow cooker layer mushrooms, carrots, and pearl onions. Sprinkle with 3 tablespoons quick-cooking tapioca. Place meat mixture on vegetables. Add thyme, marjoram, bay leaves, salt, and pepper. Pour 1¼ cups wine and ½ cup beef broth over meat. Cover; cook on low-heat setting for 10 to 12 hours or on high-heat setting for 5 to 6 hours or until tender. Discard bay leaves. Continue as directed.

PER 1 CUP: 430 cal., 19 g total fat (6 g sat. fat, 0 g trans fat), 66 mg chol., 444 mg sodium, 35 g carbo., 4 g fiber, 19 g pro. EXCHANGES: 1½ Vegetable, 2 Starch, 1½ Medium-Fat Meat, 2 Fat

OLD-FASHIONED BEEF STEW

PREP: 20 MINUTES **COOK:** 90 MINUTES
MAKES: 5 MAIN-DISH SERVINGS

- 2 tablespoons all-purpose flour
- 12 ounces beef stew meat, cut into ¾-inch cubes
- 2 tablespoons vegetable oil
- 3 cups vegetable juice
- 1 cup beef broth
- 1 medium onion, cut into thin wedges
- 1 tablespoon Worcestershire sauce
- 1 teaspoon dried oregano, crushed
- ½ teaspoon dried marjoram, crushed
- ¼ teaspoon black pepper
- 1 bay leaf
- 3 cups cubed potatoes (about 3 medium)
- 1½ cups frozen cut green beans
- 1 cup frozen whole kernel corn
- 1 cup sliced carrots (2 medium)

1 Place flour in a plastic bag. Add meat cubes, a few at a time, shaking to coat. In a large saucepan or pot brown meat in hot oil; drain fat. Stir in vegetable juice, broth, onion, Worcestershire sauce, oregano, marjoram, pepper, and bay leaf. Bring to boiling; reduce heat. Simmer, covered, for 60 to 75 minutes or until meat is nearly tender.

2 Stir in potatoes, beans, corn, and carrots. Return to boiling; reduce heat. Simmer, covered, about 30 minutes more or until meat and vegetables are tender. Discard bay leaf.

SLOW COOKER DIRECTIONS: Prepare and brown meat as directed. In a 3½- or 4-quart slow cooker layer meat, onion, potatoes, beans, corn, and carrots. Combine 2 cups vegetable juice, the broth, Worcestershire sauce, oregano, marjoram, pepper, and bay leaf. Pour over meat and vegetables in slow cooker. Cover; cook on low-heat setting for 10 to 12 hours or on high-heat setting for 5 to 6 hours or until meat and vegetables are tender.

PER 1⅓ CUPS: 362 cal., 17 g total fat (5 g sat. fat, 0 g trans fat), 39 mg chol., 664 mg sodium, 39 g carbo., 6 g fiber, 16 g pro. EXCHANGES: 1½ Vegetable, 2 Starch, 1½ Medium-Fat Meat, 2 Fat

ALL-AMERICAN CHEESEBURGER SOUP

PREP: 20 MINUTES **COOK:** 20 MINUTES
MAKES: 6 MAIN-DISH SERVINGS

- 1 pound ground beef
- ½ cup chopped onion (1 medium)
- ½ cup chopped celery (1 stalk)
- 2 cloves garlic, minced
- 2 tablespoons all-purpose flour
- 2 14-ounce cans lower-sodium beef broth
- 2 medium potatoes, scrubbed and chopped
- 1 14.5-ounce can diced tomatoes, drained
- 1 8-ounce package shredded cheddar and American cheese blend (2 cups)
- 1 6-ounce can tomato paste
- ¼ cup ketchup
- 2 tablespoons Dijon-style mustard
- 1 cup whole milk
- 6 cocktail buns or brown-and-serve rolls, split and toasted*

Assorted condiments (pickles, onions, lettuce, mustard, and/or ketchup) (optional)

1 In a large pot cook beef, onion, celery, and garlic over medium heat until meat browns and vegetables are tender; drain fat. Sprinkle flour on beef mixture; cook and stir about 2 minutes. Stir in broth and potatoes. Bring to boiling, stirring occasionally. Reduce heat. Simmer, covered, for 10 minutes or until potatoes are tender.

2 Stir in tomatoes, cheese, tomato paste, ketchup, and mustard. Cook and stir until soup comes to a gentle boil. Stir in milk; heat through. Serve with toasted buns and top with condiments.

*NOTE: To toast buns, preheat the broiler. Place, split sides up, on a broiler pan. Brush with 1 tablespoon melted butter. Broil 4 to 5 inches from heat about 1 minute or until golden.

PER 1½ CUPS: 528 cal., 27 g total fat (13 g sat. fat, 1 g trans fat), 94 mg chol., 1,461 mg sodium, 39 g carbo., 4 g fiber, 32 g pro. EXCHANGES: ½ Vegetable, 2½ Starch, 3½ Medium-Fat Meat, 1½ Fat

TOP IT YOUR WAY ANY TOPPING YOU ENJOY ON A CHEESEBURGER WILL TASTE GREAT IN THIS SOUP. ALSO TRY BACON, GUACAMOLE, JALAPEÑO PEPPERS, CHOPPED TOMATO, AND OTHER FAVES.

KANSAS CITY STEAK SOUP

PREP: 15 MINUTES **COOK:** 21 MINUTES
MAKES: 6 MAIN-DISH SERVINGS

- 1½ pounds lean ground beef (sirloin)
- 1 cup chopped onion (1 large)
- 1 cup sliced celery (2 stalks)
- 2 14-ounce cans lower-sodium beef broth
- 1 28-ounce can diced tomatoes, undrained
- 1 10-ounce package frozen mixed vegetables
- 2 tablespoons steak sauce
- 2 teaspoons Worcestershire sauce
- ¼ cup all-purpose flour

1 In a large pot cook beef, onion, and celery over medium heat until meat is brown and vegetables are tender. Drain; return to pot. Add 1 can of broth, undrained tomatoes, frozen vegetables, steak sauce, Worcestershire sauce, and ¼ teaspoon each *salt* and *black pepper*. Bring to boiling; reduce heat. Simmer, covered, about 20 minutes.

2 Whisk together remaining can of broth and the flour. Add to pot. Cook and stir until thickened and bubbly. Cook and stir for 1 minute more.

PER 2 CUPS: 306 cal., 12 g total fat (5 g sat. fat, 1 g trans fat), 74 mg chol., 747 mg sodium, 21 g carbo., 4 g fiber, 27 g pro. EXCHANGES: 1 Vegetable, 1 Starch, 3 Lean Meat, ½ Fat

LAMB STEW WITH PASTA

PREP: 25 MINUTES **COOK:** 60 MINUTES
MAKES: 4 MAIN-DISH SERVINGS

- 1 pound lean boneless lamb, cut into 1-inch cubes, or beef stew meat
- 1 medium onion, sliced and separated into rings
- 2 tablespoons vegetable oil
- ¼ cup snipped dried tomatoes
- 1 teaspoon dried Italian seasoning, crushed
- 2 cups sliced fresh mushrooms
- 1 9-ounce package frozen cut green beans
- 1 cup thinly sliced carrots (2 medium)
- ¾ cup dried medium bow tie pasta
- 1 15-ounce can tomato sauce

1 In a large saucepan cook lamb and onion in hot oil until meat is brown. Stir 3½ cups *water*, dried tomatoes, Italian seasoning, and ¼ teaspoon each *salt* and *pepper* into saucepan. Bring to boiling; reduce heat. Simmer, covered, about 45 minutes (75 minutes for beef) or until meat is nearly tender.

2 Stir mushrooms, beans, carrots, and pasta into meat mixture. Return to boiling; reduce heat. Simmer, covered, for 15 minutes more or until pasta is tender. Add tomato sauce; heat through.

PER 1¾ CUPS: 315 cal., 12 g total fat (2 g sat. fat, 0 g trans fat), 71 mg chol., 806 mg sodium, 24 g carbo., 5 g fiber, 29 g pro. EXCHANGES: 2 Vegetable, 1 Starch, 3 Lean Meat, ½ Fat

LAMB CASSOULET

PREP: 30 MINUTES **STAND:** 60 MINUTES
COOK: 90 MINUTES **MAKES:** 6 MAIN-DISH SERVINGS

- 2 cups dry navy beans
- 1 pound lean boneless lamb, cut into 1-inch cubes
- 1 tablespoon vegetable oil
- 1 cup chopped carrots (2 medium)
- ½ cup chopped green sweet pepper
- ½ cup chopped onion (1 medium)
- 1 tablespoon instant beef bouillon granules
- 1 tablespoon Worcestershire sauce
- 2 teaspoons snipped fresh thyme or 1 teaspoon dried thyme, crushed
- 3 cloves garlic, minced
- 2 bay leaves
- 8 ounces skinless, boneless chicken thighs, cut into 1-inch pieces
- 1 14.5-ounce can diced tomatoes, undrained

1 Rinse beans. In a large pot combine beans and 8 cups water. Bring to boiling; reduce heat. Simmer, uncovered, for 2 minutes. Remove from heat. Cover and let stand for 60 minutes. Drain and rinse beans. Wipe pot dry.

2 In the same pot, brown lamb, half at a time, in hot oil; drain. Return all lamb to pot. Add beans, carrots, sweet pepper, onion, bouillon granules, Worcestershire sauce, dried thyme (if using), garlic, and bay leaves. Add 4 cups fresh *water*. Bring to boiling; reduce heat. Simmer, covered, for 60 to 90 minutes or until beans are tender.

3 Add chicken, undrained tomatoes, ½ teaspoon *salt*, and fresh thyme (if using). Return to boiling; reduce heat. Simmer, uncovered, for 30 minutes more. Discard bay leaves. Skim fat, if necessary. Season to taste with *salt* and *black pepper*.

PER 1⅔ CUPS: 417 cal., 8 g total fat (2 g sat. fat, 0 g trans fat), 79 mg chol., 899 mg sodium, 49 g carbo., 18 g fiber, 39 g pro. EXCHANGES: 1 Vegetable, 3 Starch, 4 Lean Meat, ½ Fat

KANSAS CITY STEAK SOUP

FOR A BETTER TOMORROW STEWS SUCH AS LAMB CASSOULET ARE PERFECT MAKE-AHEAD FARE—THEIR FLAVORS LUSCIOUSLY MELD AFTER A DAY IN THE FRIDGE. SEE PAGE 567 FOR STORAGE TIPS.

LAMB CASSOULET

MAKE-IT-MINE CHILI

WITH SO MANY POSSIBILITIES FOR MAKING GREAT CHILI, WHY LIMIT YOURSELF TO THE USUAL FORMULA? WITH THIS RECIPE YOU CAN MIX AND MATCH YOUR WAY TO YOUR OWN ONE-BOWL WONDER.

BASIC INGREDIENTS

PREP: 25 MINUTES
COOK: 20 MINUTES
MAKES: 8 MAIN-DISH SERVINGS

- 1½ pounds Meat
- 3 cups Chopped Vegetables
- 4 cloves garlic, minced
- 1 tablespoon vegetable oil
- 2 15- to 16-ounce cans Beans, rinsed and drained
- 2 14.5-ounce cans diced tomatoes, undrained
- 1 15-ounce can tomato sauce
- 1 cup Liquid
- 2 tablespoons chili powder, ancho chili powder, or 1 teaspoon ground chipotle chile pepper
- 1 teaspoon Dried Herb, crushed
- ½ teaspoon Pepper
  Toppers

MEAT (PICK ONE)

Ground beef or pork

Beef shoulder top blade steak (flat-iron) or pork shoulder, cut into ¾-inch cubes

Beef stew meat

CHOPPED VEGETABLES

(PICK ONE)

Carrots or celery
Onions or potatoes
Sweet peppers

BEANS (PICK ONE)

Black
Cannellini (white kidney)
Garbanzo (chickpeas)
Pinto
Red kidney

LIQUID (PICK ONE)

Apple juice
Beef or chicken broth
Beer
Water

DRIED HERB (PICK ONE)

Basil
Italian seasoning
Oregano
Thyme

PEPPER (PICK ONE)

Black pepper
Cayenne pepper
Crushed red pepper
1 tablespoon finely chopped chipotle chile peppers in adobo sauce

TOPPERS

(PICK ONE OR MORE)

Dairy sour cream
Guacamole
Shredded cheddar or Monterey Jack cheese
Sliced jalapeño chile peppers

BASIC INSTRUCTIONS

1 In a large pot cook Meat, Chopped Vegetables, and garlic in hot oil until meat is brown and vegetables are tender. Drain fat (see photo, below). Stir in Beans, undrained tomatoes, tomato sauce, Liquid, chili powder, Dried Herb, and Pepper. Bring to boiling; reduce heat. Simmer, covered, for 20 minutes for ground meat (60 minutes for cubed meat) or until meat is tender, stirring occasionally. Serve with Toppers.

SLOW COOKER DIRECTIONS: Cook Meat, Vegetables, and garlic as directed. Drain fat. In a 4- to 5-quart slow cooker combine meat mixture, Beans, tomatoes, tomato sauce, ½ cup Liquid, chili powder, Dried Herb, and Pepper. Cover; cook on low-heat setting for 8 to 10 hours or on high-heat setting for 4 to 5 hours. Serve with Toppers.

HAM AND BEAN SOUP

PREP: 45 MINUTES **STAND:** 60 MINUTES
COOK: 60 MINUTES **MAKES:** 4 MAIN-DISH SERVINGS

- 1 cup dried navy beans
- 1 to 1½ pounds meaty smoked pork hocks or one 1- to 1½-pound meaty ham bone
- 1 tablespoon butter or margarine
- 1½ cups sliced celery (3 stalks)
- 1½ cups chopped onions (3 medium)
- ¾ teaspoon dried thyme, crushed
- 1 bay leaf

1 Rinse beans. In a large pot combine beans and 4 cups water. Bring to boiling; reduce heat. Simmer, uncovered, for 2 minutes. Remove from heat. Cover and let stand for 60 minutes. (Or place beans in water in pot. Cover and let soak in a cool place for 6 to 8 hours or overnight.) Drain and rinse beans. Wipe pot dry.

2 In same pot brown pork hocks on all sides in hot butter over medium heat (see photo 1, below). Add celery and onions to pot. Cook and stir until softened. Stir in beans, thyme, ¼ teaspoon *salt,* ¼ teaspoon *black pepper,* bay leaf, and 4 cups fresh *water.* Bring to boiling; reduce heat. Simmer, covered, for 60 to 90 minutes or until beans are tender. Remove pork hocks. When cool enough to handle, cut meat off bones; coarsely chop meat (see photo 2, below). Discard bones and bay leaf. Slightly mash beans in pot.

3 Stir in chopped meat; heat through. Season to taste with additional *salt* and *pepper.*

PER 1¾ CUPS: 267 cal., 5 g total fat (3 g sat. fat, 0 g trans fat), 26 mg chol., 750 mg sodium, 37 g carbo., 14 g fiber, 18 g pro. EXCHANGES: 2½ Starch, 1½ Lean Meat

SPLIT PEA SOUP

PREP: 20 MINUTES **COOK:** 80 MINUTES
MAKES: 4 MAIN-DISH SERVINGS

- 1½ cups dry split peas, rinsed and drained
- 1 14-ounce can reduced-sodium chicken broth
- 1 to 1½ pounds meaty smoked pork hocks or one 1- to 1½-pound meaty ham bone
- ¼ teaspoon dried marjoram, crushed
- 1 bay leaf
- ½ cup chopped carrot (1 medium)
- ½ cup chopped celery (1 stalk)
- ½ cup chopped onion (1 medium)

1 In a large saucepan combine 2¾ cups *water,* split peas, broth, pork hocks, marjoram, bay leaf, and dash *black pepper.* Bring to boiling; reduce heat. Simmer, covered, for 60 minutes, stirring occasionally. Remove pork hocks.

2 When cool enough to handle, cut meat off bones; coarsely chop meat (see photo 2, below). Discard bones. Return meat to saucepan. Stir in carrot, celery, and onion. Return to boiling; reduce heat. Simmer, covered, for 20 to 30 minutes more or until vegetables are tender. Discard bay leaf.

SLOW COOKER DIRECTIONS: In a 3½- or 4-quart slow cooker combine split peas, pork hocks, marjoram, pepper, bay leaf, carrot, celery, and onion. Pour water and broth over all. Cover; cook on low-heat setting for 8 to 10 hours or on high-heat setting 4 to 5 hours. Discard bay leaf. Remove hocks, cut off meat, and add to soup.

PER 1½ CUPS: 307 cal., 3 g total fat (1 g sat. fat, 0 g trans fat), 19 mg chol., 676 mg sodium, 47 g carbo., 19 g fiber, 25 g pro. EXCHANGES: ½ Vegetable, 3 Starch, 2½ Very Lean Meat

PREPARING PORK HOCKS, STEP-BY-STEP

1. When preparing the hocks for Ham and Bean Soup, brown the meat over medium heat (butter can burn at higher temperatures). Browning adds flavor to the meat as well as browned bits to the pan that will lend richness to the finished soup. **2.** For both of the above recipes, use a sturdy knife to cut the ham off the bones; discard bones and coarsely chop the meat.

COOK ONCE, EAT TWICE

ENJOY A WARMLY SPICED PORK STEW, THEN TURN IT INTO SOMETHING ENTIRELY NEW WITH GOODIES SUCH AS COUSCOUS, SPINACH, HERBS, YOGURT, AND GOAT CHEESE.

TONIGHT

CURRIED PORK AND APPLE STEW

PREP: 25 MINUTES **COOK:** 60 MINUTES
MAKES: 4 MAIN-DISH SERVINGS

- 4 pounds boneless pork shoulder
- 4 medium green tart cooking apples
- 2 tablespoons vegetable oil
- 2 medium onions, cut into thin wedges
- 1 teaspoon curry powder
- 1 teaspoon ground coriander
- ½ teaspoon ground cumin
- 2 14-ounce cans chicken broth
- 2 cups packaged peeled baby carrots, halved lengthwise
- 1 2-pound butternut squash, peeled, seeded, and cubed (3 cups)
    Dairy sour cream

1 Trim fat from pork; cut into 1-inch cubes. Peel, core, and chop two apples. In a large pot brown pork, half at a time, in hot oil; drain. Return all pork to pot; add chopped apples, onions, curry powder, coriander, and cumin. Cook and stir for 2 minutes. Add broth, ½ teaspoon *salt,* and ¼ teaspoon *black pepper*. Bring to boiling; reduce heat. Simmer, covered, for 30 minutes, stirring occasionally.

2 Add carrots to pot. Return to boiling; reduce heat. Simmer, covered, for 20 minutes, stirring occasionally. Meanwhile, cut remaining apples into ¼-inch-thick wedges; add to pot along with squash. Cook, covered, for 10 to 12 minutes more or until pork and vegetables are tender. Remove half of mixture from pot; cool quickly in ice bath and transfer to a container. Cover and chill up to 3 days, use it in Mediterranean Pork and Couscous. Serve remaining mixture; top with sour cream.

PER 1½ CUPS: 510 cal., 23 g total fat (7 g sat. fat, 0 g trans fat), 159 mg chol., 752 mg sodium, 30 g carbo., 6 g fiber, 47 g pro.
EXCHANGES: 1 Vegetable, ½ Fruit, 1 Starch, 6 Lean Meat, 1 Fat

TOMORROW

MEDITERRANEAN PORK AND COUSCOUS

START TO FINISH: 25 MINUTES
MAKES: 4 TO 6 MAIN-DISH SERVINGS

- ½ recipe Curried Pork and Apple Stew (6 cups)
- ½ cup raisins
- 1½ cups water
- 1 cup couscous
- ½ cup plain yogurt
- 1 tablespoon snipped fresh Italian parsley
- ¼ teaspoon finely shredded orange peel
- ¼ teaspoon salt
- ⅛ teaspoon black pepper
- ½ cup sliced almonds, toasted (see tip, page 20)
- 1 cup shredded fresh spinach
- 2 ounces goat cheese, crumbled (optional)

1 Place stew in a large skillet. Stir in raisins. Bring to boiling; reduce heat. Simmer, uncovered, about 12 minutes or until slightly thickened, stirring occasionally. Meanwhile, in a medium saucepan bring the water to boiling. Stir in couscous. Remove from heat and set aside.

2 For yogurt sauce, in a small bowl stir together yogurt, parsley, orange peel, salt, and pepper.

3 Stir almonds into stew mixture. Fluff couscous with a fork. Divide couscous among shallow bowls. Top with stew mixture, yogurt sauce, spinach, and goat cheese (if desired).

PER 1⅓ CUPS: 802 cal., 27 g total fat (7 g sat. fat, 0 g trans fat), 155 mg chol., 925 mg sodium, 85 g carbo., 10 g fiber, 57 g pro.
EXCHANGES: 1 Vegetable, 1 Fruit, 4½ Starch, 6 Lean Meat, 1 Fat

LENTIL AND SAUSAGE SOUP

PREP: 20 MINUTES **COOK:** 30 MINUTES
MAKES: 6 MAIN-DISH SERVINGS

- 1 medium fennel bulb, trimmed, cored, and thinly sliced
- 1 cup thinly sliced carrots (2 medium)
- ½ cup chopped onion (1 medium)
- 2 cloves garlic, minced
- 1 tablespoon olive oil
- 2 uncooked sweet or hot Italian sausage links, sliced
- 2 14-ounce cans reduced-sodium chicken broth or 3½ cups chicken broth
- 1 14.5-ounce can diced tomatoes with basil, garlic, and oregano, undrained
- 1 cup brown lentils, rinsed and drained
- ⅛ teaspoon crushed red pepper

1 In a large saucepan cook fennel, carrots, onion, and garlic in hot oil over medium-high heat about 5 minutes or until tender. Add sausage and cook for 2 to 3 minutes more or until sausage browns.

2 Stir in broth, undrained tomatoes, lentils, and crushed red pepper. Bring to boiling; reduce heat. Simmer, covered, for 30 to 35 minutes or until vegetables and lentils are tender.

PER 1 CUP: 238 cal., 5 g total fat (1 g sat. fat, 0 g trans fat), 9 mg chol., 866 mg sodium, 33 g carbo., 12 g fiber, 16 g pro. EXCHANGES: ½ Vegetable, 2 Starch, 1 Medium-Fat Meat

WILD RICE AND TURKEY SOUP

PREP: 25 MINUTES **COOK:** 20 MINUTES
MAKES: 6 MAIN-DISH SERVINGS

- 1 6.2-ounce package quick-cooking long grain and wild rice mix
- 2 tablespoons butter or margarine
- 4 ounces fresh shiitake mushrooms, stems removed and sliced (about 1½ cups)
- 1 cup sliced celery (2 stalks)
- 2 14-ounce cans reduced-sodium chicken broth or 3½ cups chicken broth
- ¼ teaspoon black pepper
- 2 cups chopped smoked turkey or chopped cooked turkey or chicken (about 10 ounces)
- 1 cup whipping cream
- 2 tablespoons dry sherry (optional)

1 Prepare the rice mix (using the seasoning packet) according to package directions, except omit any butter or margarine.

2 In a large saucepan melt butter over medium heat. Add mushrooms and celery. Cook about 5 minutes or until vegetables are almost tender and most of the mushroom liquid evaporates, stirring occasionally. Add chicken broth and pepper. Bring to boiling; reduce heat. Simmer, covered, for 5 minutes. Stir in cooked rice mixture, turkey, whipping cream, and dry sherry (if desired). Heat through.

PER 1⅓ CUPS: 347 cal., 21 g total fat (12 g sat. fat, 0 g trans fat), 90 mg chol., 1,301 mg sodium, 28 g carbo., 1 g fiber, 15 g pro. EXCHANGES: 2 Starch, 1½ Lean Meat, 3 Fat

BEST EVER ▪ LOW FAT

CHICKEN NOODLE-VEGETABLE SOUP

PREP: 30 MINUTES **COOK:** 35 MINUTES
MAKES: 6 MAIN-DISH SERVINGS

- 2 14-ounce cans chicken broth
- 1 cup water
- 1 10.75-ounce can condensed cream of chicken soup
- ½ teaspoon dried thyme, crushed
- ⅛ teaspoon salt
- ⅛ teaspoon black pepper
- 2 medium chicken legs with thigh portions (1¼ pounds total), skinned
- 1 cup sliced carrots (2 medium)
- ¾ cup chopped onion
- ½ cup sliced celery (1 stalk)
- 1 bay leaf
- 4 ounces dried wide noodles (about 2 cups)
- ½ cup frozen peas

1 In a large pot combine chicken broth, water, soup, thyme, salt, and pepper. Add chicken legs, carrots, onion, celery, and bay leaf. Bring to boiling; reduce heat. Simmer, covered, for 30 to 40 minutes or until chicken is no longer pink and vegetables are tender.

2 Remove chicken from pot; cool slightly. Discard bay leaf. Return broth mixture to boiling; add noodles and frozen peas. Cook for 5 to 7 minutes or until noodles are tender, stirring occasionally. Remove chicken from bones; discard bones. Shred or chop meat; stir into soup. Heat through.

PER 1⅓ CUPS: 223 cal., 7 g total fat (2 g sat. fat, 0 g trans fat), 64 mg chol., 1,063 mg sodium, 24 g carbo., 2 g fiber, 16 g pro. EXCHANGES: ½ Vegetable, 1½ Starch, 1½ Lean Meat, ½ Fat

LOW FAT

MEXICAN CHICKEN-TORTILLA SOUP

(photo, page 567)

PREP: 25 MINUTES **COOK:** 35 MINUTES
BAKE: 10 MINUTES **OVEN:** 375°F
MAKES: 4 MAIN-DISH SERVINGS

- 2 medium chicken breast halves (with bone) (about 1¼ pounds total)
- 1 14-ounce can reduced-sodium chicken broth
- ½ cup chopped onion (1 medium)
- 1 clove garlic, minced
- ½ teaspoon ground cumin
- 1 tablespoon cooking oil
- 1 14.5-ounce can no-salt-added diced tomatoes, undrained
- 1 8-ounce can tomato sauce
- 1 4-ounce can whole green chiles, rinsed, seeded, and cut into thin bite-size strips (see tip, page 24)
- ¼ cup snipped fresh cilantro or parsley
- 1 tablespoon snipped fresh oregano or 1 teaspoon dried oregano, crushed
- 4 6-inch corn tortillas
- ½ cup shredded cheddar or Monterey Jack cheese (2 ounces)

1 In a large saucepan or pot combine chicken, chicken broth, and 1¾ cups *water*. Bring to boiling; reduce heat. Simmer, covered, about 15 minutes or until chicken is tender and no longer pink. Remove chicken. When cool enough to handle, skin, bone, and finely shred chicken; set aside. Discard skin and bones. Strain broth (see photo 2, page 568). Skim fat from broth (see photos 3 and 4, page 569) and set broth aside.

2 In the same saucepan or pot cook onion, garlic, and cumin in hot oil until onion is tender. Stir in strained broth, undrained tomatoes, tomato sauce, chiles, cilantro, and oregano. Bring to boiling; reduce heat. Simmer, covered, for 20 minutes. Stir in chicken; heat through.

3 Meanwhile, preheat oven to 375°F. Cut tortillas in half. Cut each half crosswise into ½-inch-wide strips. Place tortilla strips on a baking sheet. Bake about 10 minutes or until crisp.

4 Ladle soup into bowls. Sprinkle each serving with shredded cheese and top with tortilla strips. Serve immediately.

PER 1½ CUPS: 313 cal., 11 g total fat (4 g sat. fat, 0 g trans fat), 71 mg chol., 836 mg sodium, 24 g carbo., 5 g fiber, 30 g pro. EXCHANGES: 1 Vegetable, 1½ Starch, 3½ Lean Meat, 1 Fat

FAST

SOUTHWESTERN WHITE CHILI

START TO FINISH: 30 MINUTES
MAKES: 8 MAIN-DISH SERVINGS

- 1 cup chopped onion (1 large)
- 4 cloves garlic, minced
- 1 tablespoon olive oil
- 2 teaspoons ground cumin
- 1 teaspoon dried oregano, crushed
- ¼ teaspoon cayenne pepper
- 3 15.5-ounce cans great Northern beans, rinsed and drained
- 2 4.5-ounce cans diced green chiles or chopped jalapeño peppers
- 4 cups chicken stock or broth or reduced-sodium chicken broth
- 3 cups chopped cooked chicken
- 2 cups shredded Monterey Jack cheese (8 ounces)
  Dairy sour cream (optional)
  Canned diced green chiles or chopped jalapeño peppers (optional)

1 In a large pot cook onion and garlic in hot oil until onion is tender.

2 Stir in cumin, oregano, and cayenne pepper. Cook and stir for 2 minutes. Add 1 can of beans to the pot; mash with a potato masher or fork. Stir in remaining beans, the two cans chiles, and chicken stock. Bring to boiling; reduce heat. Simmer, uncovered, for 5 minutes. Stir in chicken and heat through.

3 Ladle chili into bowls. Top each serving with ¼ cup cheese. If desired, top with sour cream and additional canned chiles.

PER 1 CUP: 471 cal., 16 g total fat (7 g sat. fat, 0 g trans fat), 76 mg chol., 468 mg sodium, 43 g carbo., 9 g fiber, 38 g pro. EXCHANGES: 3 Starch, 4 Lean Meat, ½ Fat

USE UP ALL THE GOOD STUFF

GIVE LEFTOVER FOODS A SECOND WIND BY STIRRING THEM INTO SOUPS.

Soups are infinitely adaptable and can accommodate leftover meats and vegetables you might have on hand. For example, if you have fresh spinach or other sturdy greens in danger of wilting before you can use them, toss them into a soup toward the end of cooking time for added color. Extra cooked chicken or turkey can help turn a side-dish soup into a main dish.

SALMON AND ASPARAGUS CHOWDER

PREP: 20 MINUTES **COOK:** 23 MINUTES
MAKES: 8 MAIN-DISH SERVINGS

- 1 pound fresh skinless salmon fillets or one 15-ounce can salmon, rinsed, drained, flaked, and skin and bones removed
- 2 14-ounce cans vegetable broth or 3½ cups vegetable stock
- 2 cups frozen whole small onions or 1 cup chopped onion (not frozen)
- 2½ cups cubed red-skin potatoes (3 medium)
- 1 tablespoon snipped fresh dill or ½ teaspoon dried dillweed
- 1 teaspoon finely shredded lemon peel
- 2½ cups whole milk, half-and-half, or light cream
- 2 tablespoons cornstarch
- 1 10-ounce package frozen cut asparagus, thawed and well drained, or 2 cups cut-up fresh trimmed asparagus
  Fresh dill sprigs (optional)

1 Rinse fresh salmon; pat dry. To poach fresh salmon, in a large skillet bring 1½ cups water to boiling. Add salmon. Return to boiling; reduce heat. Simmer, covered, for 6 to 8 minutes or until the salmon flakes easily with a fork (see photo 1, below). Remove salmon from skillet, discarding poaching liquid. Flake salmon into ½-inch pieces; set aside.

2 In a large pot combine vegetable broth, onions, potatoes, snipped dill, lemon peel, and ½ teaspoon each *salt* and *black pepper*. Bring to boiling; reduce heat. Simmer, covered, for 15 minutes or until vegetables are tender, stirring occasionally.

3 In a large screw-top jar combine milk and cornstarch. Cover and shake well; stir into soup (see photo 2, below). Stir in asparagus. Cook and stir until slightly thickened and bubbly. Cook and stir for 2 minutes more. Gently stir in poached salmon or canned salmon (see photo 3, below); heat through. If desired, garnish with dill sprigs.

PER 1⅓ CUPS: 235 cal., 10 g total fat (3 g sat. fat, 0 g trans fat), 39 mg chol., 609 mg sodium, 19 g carbo., 2 g fiber, 16 g pro.
EXCHANGES: ½ Vegetable, 1 Starch, 1½ Medium-Fat Meat, ½ Fat

PREPARING SALMON CHOWDER, STEP-BY-STEP

1. Check salmon for doneness at the minimum cooking time. Salmon is done when it separates easily into flakes when prodded with a fork. **2.** Stir the hot mixture continuously while adding the cornstarch mixture so the sauce thickens smoothly. **3.** Gently stir the salmon in at the end of cooking so your chowder retains the nice chunk-size pieces.

QUICK CIOPPINO WITH BASIL GREMOLATA

START TO FINISH: 25 MINUTES
MAKES: 4 MAIN-DISH SERVINGS

- 6 ounces fresh or frozen cod fillets
- 6 ounces fresh or frozen peeled and deveined shrimp
- 1 cup green sweet pepper strips (1 medium)
- 1 cup chopped onion (1 large)
- 2 cloves garlic, minced
- 1 tablespoon olive oil or vegetable oil
- 2 14.5-ounce cans Italian-style stewed tomatoes, undrained and cut up
- ½ cup water
- ¼ teaspoon salt
- ¼ teaspoon black pepper
- 3 tablespoons snipped fresh basil
- 1 tablespoon finely shredded lemon peel
- 2 cloves garlic, minced

1 Thaw cod and shrimp, if frozen. Rinse cod and shrimp; pat dry with paper towels. Cut cod into 1-inch pieces; set aside.

2 In a large pot cook and stir sweet pepper, onion, and 2 cloves minced garlic in hot oil until tender. Stir in undrained tomatoes, water, salt, and black pepper. Bring mixture to boiling.

3 Stir in cod and shrimp. Return to boiling; reduce heat. Simmer, covered, for 2 to 3 minutes or until cod flakes easily when tested with a fork (see photo, page 311) and shrimp turn opaque.

4 For gremolata, in a small bowl combine snipped basil, finely shredded lemon peel, and 2 cloves minced garlic. Ladle cioppino into bowls. Sprinkle each serving with gremolata.

PER 1⅓ CUPS: 188 cal., 5 g total fat (1 g sat. fat, 0 g trans fat), 83 mg chol., 921 mg sodium, 20 g carbo., 5 g fiber, 19 g pro. EXCHANGES: 1½ Vegetable, 1 Starch, 2 Lean Meat, ½ Fat

OTHER FISH IN THE SEA IF NECESSARY, SUBSTITUTE FLOUNDER, HADDOCK, OR POLLACK FOR COD. KEEP THE GREMOLATA TOPPING IN MIND TO ADD FRESHNESS TO OTHER SOUPS AND STEWS.

QUICK CIOPPINO WITH BASIL GREMOLATA

VEGGIE FISH CHOWDER

PREP: 20 MINUTES **COOK:** 10 MINUTES
MAKES: 4 TO 6 MAIN-DISH SERVINGS

- 1 pound cod, salmon or other firm-texture fish steaks or fillets, cut into 4 pieces
- 1 32-ounce package reduced-sodium chicken broth
- 1 cup thinly sliced carrots (2 medium)
- 1 cup sugar snap peas, halved diagonally
- 1 4-ounce package (or half of a 7.2-ounce package) butter-and-herb-flavored instant mashed potatoes
- ¼ cup finely shredded Parmesan cheese

1 Rinse cod; pat dry. Season fish lightly with *black pepper*; set aside. In a large pot bring broth and 1 cup *water* to boiling. Add carrots; cover and cook for 5 minutes. Add fish and peas. Return to boiling; reduce heat. Simmer, covered, about 3 minutes or until fish flakes easily when tested with a fork (see photo, page 311).

2 Stir in mashed potatoes and simmer for 2 minutes. Flake fish into bite-size pieces. Ladle chowder into bowls. Top each serving with Parmesan cheese.

PER 1¾ CUPS: 269 cal., 5 g total fat (2 g sat. fat, 0 g trans fat), 52 mg chol., 1,269 mg sodium, 28 g carbo., 3 g fiber, 28 g pro. EXCHANGES: ½ Vegetable, 1½ Starch, 3 Lean Meat, ½ Fat

HOT-AND-SOUR SOUP WITH SHRIMP

START TO FINISH: 35 MINUTES
MAKES: 4 MAIN-DISH SERVINGS

- 12 ounces fresh or frozen shrimp in shells
- 4 ounces fresh shiitake mushrooms, stems removed and sliced, or button mushrooms, sliced
- 1 tablespoon vegetable oil
- 2 14-ounce cans chicken broth
- ¼ cup rice vinegar or white vinegar
- 2 tablespoons soy sauce
- 1 teaspoon sugar
- 1 teaspoon grated fresh ginger or ¼ teaspoon ground ginger
- 1 tablespoon cornstarch
- 1 tablespoon cold water
- ½ cup frozen peas
- ½ cup shredded carrot (1 medium)
- 2 tablespoons thinly sliced green onion (1)
- 1 egg, lightly beaten

1 Thaw shrimp, if frozen. Peel and devein shrimp. Rinse shrimp and pat dry; set aside. In a large saucepan cook and stir mushrooms in hot oil until tender. Add chicken broth, vinegar, soy sauce, sugar, ginger, and ½ teaspoon *black pepper*. Bring to boiling; reduce heat. Simmer, covered, for 2 minutes. Stir in shrimp. Return to boiling; reduce heat. Simmer, covered, for 1 minute more.

2 Combine cornstarch and cold water; stir into chicken broth mixture (see photo 2, page 579). Cook and stir until slightly thickened and bubbly. Cook and stir 2 minutes more. Stir in peas, carrot, and green onion. Pour egg into soup in a steady stream, stirring a few times to create shreds.

PER 1⅔ CUPS: 212 cal., 7 g total fat (1 g sat. fat, 0 g trans fat), 184 mg chol., 1,430 mg sodium, 13 g carbo., 2 g fiber, 22 g pro. EXCHANGES: ½ Vegetable, ½ Other Carbo., 3 Lean Meat, 1 Fat

OYSTER STEW

START TO FINISH: 25 MINUTES
MAKES: 6 MAIN-DISH SERVINGS

- 1 pint (about 3 dozen) shucked oysters, undrained (about 1 pound)
- 1 cup finely chopped onion (1 large)
- ½ cup finely chopped celery (1 stalk)
- ¼ cup butter or margarine
- 2 tablespoons all-purpose flour
- ⅛ teaspoon cayenne pepper
- 2 cups whole milk
- 2 cups half-and-half or light cream
  Cream sherry (optional)
  Freshly ground nutmeg (optional)
  Snipped fresh Italian parsley (optional)

1 Drain oysters, reserving liquor. Remove any shell pieces. Set oysters and liquor aside.

2 In a large saucepan cook onion, celery, and ½ teaspoon *salt* in hot butter over medium heat for 10 minutes or until tender. Stir in flour, cayenne pepper, and ¼ teaspoon *black pepper*. Cook and stir for 2 minutes more. Slowly whisk in milk and half-and-half. Bring to a simmer.

3 Stir in drained oysters. Cook for 3 to 5 minutes or until oysters curl around the edges. Stir in oyster liquor; heat through. If desired, add a splash of sherry, the ground nutmeg, and/or parsley.

PER 1¾ CUPS: 294 cal., 21 g total fat (13 g sat. fat, 0 g trans fat), 98 mg chol., 481 mg sodium, 15 g carbo., 1 g fiber, 11 g pro. EXCHANGES: 1 Starch, 1 Lean Meat, 4 Fat

MANHATTAN CLAM CHOWDER

PREP: 30 MINUTES **COOK:** 11 MINUTES
MAKES: 4 MAIN-DISH SERVINGS

- 1 pint shucked clams or two 6.5-ounce cans minced clams
- 1 cup chopped celery (2 stalks)
- ⅓ cup chopped onion (1 small)
- ¼ cup chopped carrot (1 small)
- 2 tablespoons olive oil or vegetable oil
- 1 8-ounce bottle clam juice or 1 cup chicken broth
- 2 cups cubed red potatoes (2 medium)
- 1 teaspoon dried thyme, crushed
- ⅛ teaspoon cayenne pepper
- ⅛ teaspoon black pepper
- 1 14.5-ounce can diced tomatoes, undrained
- 2 tablespoons purchased cooked bacon pieces or cooked crumbled bacon*

1 Chop fresh clams (if using), reserving juice; set clams aside. Strain clam juice to remove bits of shell. (Or drain canned clams, reserving the juice.) If necessary, add enough water to the reserved clam juice to equal 1½ cups; set aside.

2 In a large saucepan cook celery, onion, and carrot in hot oil until tender. Stir in the reserved 1½ cups clam liquid and the 8 ounces clam juice. Stir in potatoes, thyme, cayenne pepper, and black pepper. Bring to boiling; reduce heat. Simmer, covered, for 10 minutes. Stir in clams, undrained tomatoes, and bacon pieces. Return to boiling; reduce heat. Cook for 1 to 2 minutes more or until heated through.

*NOTE: If cooking your own bacon, cook 2 slices, reserving 2 tablespoons drippings. Omit oil and cook the celery, onion, and carrot in the reserved bacon drippings.

PER 1½ CUPS: 252 cal., 9 g total fat (1 g sat. fat, 0 g trans fat), 41 mg chol., 503 mg sodium, 24 g carbo., 3 g fiber, 18 g pro. EXCHANGES: 1 Vegetable, 1½ Starch, 1½ Lean Meat, 1 Fat

NEW ENGLAND CLAM CHOWDER

START TO FINISH: 45 MINUTES
MAKES: 4 MAIN-DISH SERVINGS

- 1 pint shucked clams or two 6.5-ounce cans minced clams
- 2 slices bacon, halved
- 2½ cups chopped, peeled potatoes (3 medium)
- 1 cup chopped onion (1 large)

- 1 teaspoon instant chicken bouillon granules
- 1 teaspoon Worcestershire sauce
- ¼ teaspoon dried thyme, crushed
- ⅛ teaspoon black pepper
- 2 cups milk
- 1 cup half-and-half or light cream
- 2 tablespoons all-purpose flour

1 Chop fresh clams (if using), reserving juice; set clams aside. Strain clam juice to remove bits of shell. (Or drain canned clams, reserving the juice.) If necessary, add enough water to the reserved clam juice to equal 1 cup; set aside.

2 In a large saucepan cook bacon until crisp. Remove bacon, reserving 1 tablespoon drippings in pan. Drain bacon on paper towels; crumble bacon and set aside.

3 Stir the reserved 1 cup clam liquid, potatoes, onion, bouillon granules, Worcestershire sauce, thyme, and pepper into saucepan. Bring to boiling; reduce heat. Simmer, covered, about 15 minutes or until potatoes are tender. Using the back of a fork, mash potatoes slightly against the side of the pan.

4 Stir together milk, half-and-half, and flour; add to potato mixture. Cook and stir until slightly thickened and bubbly. Stir in clams. Return to boiling; reduce heat. Cook for 1 to 2 minutes more or until heated through. Ladle chowder into bowls. Sprinkle each serving with crumbled bacon.

PER 1½ CUPS: 378 cal., 15 g total fat (8 g sat. fat, 0 g trans fat), 78 mg chol., 476 mg sodium, 35 g carbo., 2 g fiber, 25 g pro. EXCHANGES: 2 Starch, 2½ Lean Meat, 2 Fat

CRAB AND POBLANO SOUP

START TO FINISH: 30 MINUTES
MAKES: 8 SIDE-DISH SERVINGS

- ¼ cup butter or margarine
- 2 fresh poblano chile peppers, seeded and chopped (see tip, page 24)
- ¾ cup chopped red sweet pepper (1 medium)
- ½ cup chopped onion (1 medium)
- 2 cloves garlic, minced
- ¼ cup all-purpose flour
- ¼ teaspoon salt
- ¼ teaspoon black pepper
- 1 14-ounce can chicken broth
- 2 cups milk

6 ounces asadero cheese or Monterey Jack cheese, shredded (1½ cups)

1 6.5-ounce can lump crabmeat, drained, or 8 ounces fresh lump crabmeat, picked over and cut into bite-size pieces

1 recipe Fresh Tomato Salsa

1 recipe Crisp Tortilla Strips (optional)

1 In a large saucepan melt butter over medium heat. Add chile peppers, sweet pepper, onion, and garlic. Cook until tender, stirring occasionally. Stir in flour, salt, and black pepper. Add broth all at once; stir to combine. Cook and stir until thickened and bubbly. Cook and stir for 1 minute more.

2 Reduce heat to medium-low. Stir in milk and cheese. Cook and stir for 3 to 5 minutes more or until cheese melts. Gently stir in crabmeat and heat through.

3 Ladle soup into bowls. Top each serving with Fresh Tomato Salsa. If desired, serve with Crisp Tortilla Strips.

FRESH TOMATO SALSA: In a small bowl stir together 3 roma tomatoes, seeded and chopped; 1 green onion, thinly sliced; 1 tablespoon snipped fresh cilantro; 2 teaspoons lime juice; and 1 teaspoon finely chopped fresh jalapeño chile pepper (see tip, page 24). Season to taste with salt and black pepper.

PER ¾ CUP SOUP: 203 cal., 12 g total fat (8 g sat. fat, 0 g trans fat), 60 mg chol., 664 mg sodium, 11 g carbo., 1 g fiber, 14 g pro. EXCHANGES: ½ Vegetable, ½ Starch, 1½ Lean Meat, 2 Fat

CRISP TORTILLA STRIPS: Preheat oven to 350°F. Roll up each of 3 flour tortillas. Using a sharp knife, slice tortilla roll crosswise for long thin strips. Lightly coat tortilla strips with nonstick cooking spray. Spread the strips on a baking sheet. Bake about 5 minutes or until golden. Cool on a wire rack.

A MARVELOUS MELTER YOU MIGHT FIND THE ASADERO CHEESE LABELED AS CHIHUAHUA OR OAXACA. BY ANY NAME, IT'S A GREAT MELTING CHEESE IN THIS SOUP AND OTHER RECIPES.

CRAB AND POBLANO SOUP

MINESTRONE (photo, page 565)

START TO FINISH: 25 MINUTES
MAKES: 6 MAIN-DISH SERVINGS

- 2 cloves garlic, minced
- ½ cup chopped onion (1 medium)
- 1 tablespoon olive oil
- 1 cup chopped yellow sweet pepper (1 large)
- 1¼ cups coarsely chopped zucchini (1 medium)
- 2 14-ounce cans beef broth
- 1 15-ounce can cannellini (white kidney) beans, rinsed and drained
- 8 ounces green beans, trimmed and cut into 1½-inch pieces
- 1 cup dried mostaccioli
- ¼ cup coarsely chopped fresh basil or 2 teaspoons dried basil, crushed
- 2 medium tomatoes, coarsely chopped
- 2 cups packaged fresh baby spinach leaves
   Shaved Parmesan cheese (optional)

1 In a large pot cook garlic and onion in hot oil until tender, stirring occasionally. Add sweet pepper, zucchini, beef broth, and 2 cups *water*. Bring to boiling. Add beans, pasta, and dried basil (if using). Return to boiling; reduce heat. Simmer, covered, for 10 to 12 minutes or until pasta is tender, stirring occasionally.

2 Stir in tomatoes, spinach, and fresh basil (if using). Remove from heat. Season to taste with *salt* and *black pepper*. If desired, top with cheese.

PER 1¾ CUPS: 182 cal., 3 g total fat (0 g sat. fat, 0 g trans fat), 0 mg chol., 717 mg sodium, 33 g carbo., 7 g fiber, 10 g pro. EXCHANGES: 1½ Vegetable, 1½ Starch, 1½ Very Lean Meat, ½ Fat

BEAN SOUP WITH HERBED POLENTA DUMPLINGS

PREP: 30 MINUTES   **STAND:** 60 MINUTES
COOK: 2 HOURS + 40 MINUTES
MAKES: 10 MAIN-DISH SERVINGS

- 8 ounces dried cranberry, red, or pinto beans
- 1 bay leaf
- 1 tablespoon olive oil
- 2 fennel bulbs, trimmed, cored, and thinly sliced
- 1 cup chopped onions (2 medium)
- 1 cup chopped carrots (2 medium)
- 1 cup chopped celery (2 stalks)
- 3 cloves garlic, minced
- 6 cups chicken broth or vegetable broth
- 1 14.5-ounce can diced tomatoes, undrained
- 2 cups shredded cabbage
- 1 cup frozen cut green beans
- 2 tablespoons finely shredded fresh basil
- 1 recipe Herbed Polenta Dumplings
   Shredded Parmesan cheese (optional)

1 Rinse beans. In a large pot combine beans and 6 cups water. Bring to boiling; reduce heat. Simmer, uncovered, for 2 minutes. Remove from heat. Cover and let stand for 60 minutes. Drain; rinse beans.

2 Return beans to pot; add 6 cups fresh *water* and bay leaf. Bring to boiling; reduce heat. Simmer, covered, about 90 minutes or until beans are tender. Drain; rinse beans and set aside. Discard bay leaf.

3 In same pot heat oil over medium heat. Add fennel, onions, carrots, celery, and garlic; saute until vegetables are tender, stirring occasionally (see photo 1, page 585). Stir in broth and undrained tomatoes. Bring to boiling; reduce heat. Simmer, covered, for 30 minutes. Stir in cranberry beans, cabbage, and green beans (see photo 2, page 585). Return to boiling; reduce heat. Simmer, covered, for 30 minutes. Stir in basil.

4 Meanwhile prepare Herbed Polenta Dumplings. Drop dough mounds onto hot bubbling soup (see photo 3, page 585). Simmer, covered, for 10 minutes. (Do not lift cover during cooking.) If desired, sprinkle each serving with Parmesan cheese.

HERBED POLENTA DUMPLINGS: In a large saucepan combine 2 cups chicken broth; ½ teaspoon dried Italian seasoning, crushed; and ¼ teaspoon salt. Bring to boiling. In a medium bowl stir together 1 cup quick-cooking polenta mix or cornmeal and 1 cup chicken broth. Gradually add polenta mixture to broth mixture, stirring constantly. Cook and stir until mixture returns to boiling. Reduce heat to low. Cook about 5 minutes or until thick, stirring frequently (mixture might spatter). Remove from heat. Stir in ⅓ cup grated Parmesan cheese and ¼ cup whipping cream. Using two spoons, drop mixture into 25 to 30 mounds onto a greased baking sheet. (If mixture is soft, cool about 15 minutes before forming mounds.) Cover; chill until ready to add to soup.

PER 1½ CUPS: 280 cal., 5 g total fat (2 g sat. fat, 0 g trans fat), 13 mg chol., 1,102 mg sodium, 47 g carbo., 10 g fiber, 11 g pro. EXCHANGES: 1 Vegetable, 3 Starch, ½ Fat

PREPARING BEAN AND DUMPLING SOUP, STEP-BY-STEP

1. Sauteing hearty vegetables before boiling imparts rich, distinctive flavor to soup. **2.** Add ingredients and bring to boiling. Simmer the soup by adjusting the heat down to a gentle boil, which blends flavors and tenderizes the vegetables. **3.** Be sure the soup is bubbling before dropping the dumplings on top so the dumplings don't deflate.

10 TO TRY—POTATO SOUP TOPPERS

Start with Cream of Potato Soup, page 589. Add one of these toppers before serving. **1.** Dairy sour cream and sliced jalapeño chile peppers. **2.** Cheese-flavored popcorn. **3.** Crumbled crisp-cooked bacon and diced tomato. **4.** Toasted pine nuts and crumbled goat cheese. **5.** A drizzle of olive oil and a sprinkle of shredded Parmesan cheese. **6.** Roasted pumpkin seeds. **7.** Plain or cheese-flavored fish crackers. **8.** Crushed corn chips or tortilla chips and a sprinkle of chili powder. **9.** Snipped fresh herbs and crumbled feta cheese. **10.** Shredded cheese and fresh dill.

CORN CHOWDER

PREP: 30 MINUTES **COOK:** 15 MINUTES
MAKES: 6 SIDE-DISH SERVINGS

- 6 ears fresh sweet corn or 3 cups frozen whole kernel corn
- ½ cup chopped onion (1 medium)
- ½ cup chopped green sweet pepper
- 1 tablespoon vegetable oil
- 1 14-ounce can chicken broth
- 1 cup cubed, peeled potato (1 medium)
- 2 tablespoons all-purpose flour
- 1½ cups half-and-half, light cream, or milk
- 4 ounces white cheddar cheese, shredded (1 cup)
- 3 slices bacon, crisp-cooked, drained, and crumbled

1 If using fresh corn, use a sharp knife to cut the kernels off the cobs (you should have about 3 cups corn kernels). Set corn kernels aside.

2 In a large saucepan cook onion and sweet pepper in hot oil until onion is tender. Stir in corn, broth, and potato. Bring to boiling; reduce heat. Simmer, covered, for 10 to 15 minutes or until vegetables are tender, stirring occasionally.

3 In a small bowl combine flour, ½ teaspoon *salt*, and ¼ teaspoon *black pepper*. Stir half-and-half into flour mixture; add to corn mixture in saucepan. Cook and stir until slightly thickened and bubbly. Cook and stir for 1 minute more. Stir in cheese and heat until melted and smooth. Add bacon; heat through.

PER 1 CUP: 314 cal., 18 g total fat (9 g sat. fat, 0 g trans fat), 47 mg chol., 709 mg sodium, 29 g carbo., 3 g fiber, 12 g pro. EXCHANGES: 2 Starch, 1 High-Fat Meat, 1½ Fat

BAKED POTATO SOUP

PREP: 30 MINUTES **BAKE:** 40 MINUTES **OVEN:** 425°F
MAKES: 5 TO 6 SIDE-DISH SERVINGS

- 2 large baking potatoes (8 ounces each)
- 6 tablespoons thinly sliced green onions (3)
- 3 tablespoons butter or margarine
- 3 tablespoons all-purpose flour
- 2 teaspoons snipped fresh dill or chives or ¼ teaspoon dried dillweed
- 4 cups milk
- 1¼ cups shredded American cheese (5 ounces)

- 4 slices bacon, crisp-cooked, drained, and crumbled

1 Preheat oven to 425°F. Scrub potatoes with a vegetable brush; pat dry. Prick potatoes with a fork. Bake for 40 to 60 minutes or until tender; cool. Cut each potato lengthwise. Scoop out white portion of each potato. Break up any large pieces of potato. Discard potato skins.

2 In a large saucepan cook 3 tablespoons of the green onions in butter over medium heat until tender. Stir in flour, dill, and ¼ teaspoon each *salt* and *black pepper*. Add milk all at once. Cook and stir until thickened and bubbly. Add the potato pieces and 1 cup of the cheese; stir until cheese melts.

3 Top each serving with the remaining ¼ cup cheese and 3 tablespoons green onions, and the crumbled bacon.

PER 1 CUP: 372 cal., 22 g total fat (13 g sat. fat, 0 g trans fat), 68 mg chol., 821 mg sodium, 26 g carbo., 1 g fiber, 17 g pro. EXCHANGES: 2 Starch, 1½ High-Fat Meat, 1½ Fat

FRENCH ONION SOUP

START TO FINISH: 30 MINUTES
MAKES: 4 SIDE-DISH SERVINGS

- 2 tablespoons butter or margarine
- 2 cups thinly sliced yellow onions (2 large)
- 4 cups beef broth
- 2 tablespoons dry sherry (optional)
- 1 teaspoon Worcestershire sauce
  Dash black pepper
- 4 slices French bread, toasted
- ¾ cup shredded Swiss, Gruyère, or Jarlsberg cheese (3 ounces)

1 In a large saucepan melt butter; add onions. Cook, covered, over medium-low heat for 8 to 10 minutes or until tender and golden, stirring occasionally. Stir in broth, sherry (if desired), Worcestershire sauce, and pepper. Bring to boiling; reduce heat. Simmer, covered, for 10 minutes.

2 Meanwhile, preheat broiler. Arrange toasted bread slices on a baking sheet; sprinkle with cheese. Broil 3 to 4 inches from the heat about 1 minute or until cheese melts and turns light brown. Ladle soup into bowls and top each serving with a toasted bread slice.

PER 1 CUP: 274 cal., 13 g total fat (7 g sat. fat, 0 g trans fat), 34 mg chol., 1,201 mg sodium, 26 g carbo., 2 g fiber, 13 g pro. EXCHANGES: ½ Vegetable, 1½ Starch, 1 High-Fat Meat, 1 Fat

MUSHROOM-TOMATO BISQUE

PREP: 20 MINUTES **COOK:** 30 MINUTES
MAKES: 4 SIDE-DISH SERVINGS

- 4 ounces fresh shiitake mushrooms or other mushrooms
- ½ cup sliced leeks or chopped onion
- ½ cup sliced celery (1 stalk)
- 2 cloves garlic, minced
- 2 tablespoons butter or margarine
- 1 14.5-ounce can diced tomatoes, undrained
- 1 14-ounce can chicken broth
- ½ cup whipping cream
- ½ teaspoon dried dillweed

1 If using shiitake mushrooms, remove stems from mushrooms (see photo 1, below); slice mushrooms and set aside.

2 In a large saucepan cook leeks, celery, and garlic in hot butter until tender. Add mushrooms; cook and stir for 5 minutes or until mushrooms are tender. Stir in undrained diced tomatoes, broth, whipping cream, dillweed, and ⅛ teaspoon *black pepper*. Bring to boiling; reduce heat. Simmer, covered, for 30 minutes. Cool mixture slightly.

3 Using a handheld immersion blender, blend soup mixture until nearly smooth (see photo 2, below); heat through. (Or let soup cool slightly. Transfer mixture, half at a time, to a blender or food processor. Cover and blend or process until smooth. Return soup to saucepan; heat through.)

PER 1 CUP: 193 cal., 13 g total fat (8 g sat. fat, 0 g trans fat), 47 mg chol., 605 mg sodium, 17 g carbo., 2 g fiber, 3 g pro.
EXCHANGES: 1 Vegetable, 1 Starch, 2½ Fat

ROASTED RED PEPPER SOUP

PREP: 15 MINUTES **COOK:** 15 MINUTES
MAKES: 4 SIDE-DISH SERVINGS

- 1 cup chopped onion (1 large)
- 4 cloves garlic, minced
- 1 tablespoon olive oil
- 3 14-ounce cans vegetable or chicken broth (5¼ cups)
- 1 12-ounce jar roasted red sweet peppers, drained and sliced
- 1 cup peeled, chopped potato (1 medium)
- 1 teaspoon dried oregano, crushed, or 1 tablespoon snipped fresh oregano
- ½ teaspoon dried thyme, crushed
- ¼ cup dairy sour cream
- 1 tablespoon minced fresh chives

1 In a large saucepan cook and stir onion and garlic in hot oil for 3 to 4 minutes or until tender. Stir in broth, red peppers, potato, oregano, and thyme. Bring to boiling; reduce heat. Simmer, covered, for 15 minutes. Cool mixture slightly.

2 Using a handheld immersion blender, blend until almost smooth (see photo 2, below); heat through. (Or let soup cool slightly. Transfer mixture, one-third at a time, to a blender or food processor. Cover and blend or process until smooth. Return soup to saucepan; heat through.)

3 In a small bowl combine sour cream and chives. Ladle soup into bowls. Top each serving with a tablespoon of sour cream mixture.

PER 1½ CUPS: 137 cal., 6 g total fat (2 g sat. fat, 0 g trans fat), 5 mg chol., 1,181 mg sodium, 18 g carbo., 3 g fiber, 2 g pro.
EXCHANGES: ½ Vegetable, 1 Starch, 1 Fat

MUSHROOM-TOMATO BISQUE, STEP-BY-STEP

1. Shiitake mushrooms are a good choice for soups because of their meaty flavor and texture. Remove and discard the tough stems and use only the caps of this variety. **2.** If you have a handheld immersion blender, you can blend the soup right in the saucepan, which makes the task easy, safe, and mess-free. To use a traditional blender, see tips on page 567.

CREAM OF VEGETABLE SOUP

START TO FINISH: 25 MINUTES
MAKES: 4 SIDE-DISH SERVINGS

    Desired vegetables (see variations)
1½ cups chicken broth or vegetable stock
 1 tablespoon butter or margarine
 1 tablespoon all-purpose flour
    Seasoning (see variations)
 1 cup milk, half-and-half, or light cream

1 In a large saucepan cook desired vegetables, covered, in large amount of boiling water as directed. Drain well. Set aside 1 cup cooked vegetables.

2 In a blender or food processor combine the remaining cooked vegetables and ¾ cup of the chicken broth. Cover and blend or process until smooth; set aside.

3 In the same saucepan melt butter. Stir in flour, desired seasoning, ¼ teaspoon *salt*, and dash *black pepper*. Add 1 cup milk all at once. Cook and stir until slightly thickened and bubbly. Cook and stir for 1 minute more.

4 Stir in the reserved cooked vegetables, the blended vegetable mixture, and the remaining ¾ cup broth. Cook and stir until heated through. If necessary, stir in additional milk to reach desired consistency. Season to taste with additional salt and black pepper.

CREAM OF POTATO SOUP: *(photo, page 586)* Cook 5 medium potatoes, peeled and cubed, and ½ cup chopped onion about 15 minutes or until tender. Blend remaining mixture as directed in Step 2, except use all of the broth. For seasoning, use ¼ teaspoon dried dillweed or basil, crushed, in Step 3.

PER 1 CUP: 185 cal., 4 g total fat (3 g sat. fat, 0 g trans fat), 13 mg chol., 560 mg sodium, 31 g carbo., 3 g fiber, 6 g pro. EXCHANGES: 2 Starch, ½ Fat

CREAM OF CAULIFLOWER-CHEESE SOUP:
Cook 4 cups fresh or frozen cauliflower florets for 8 to 10 minutes or until tender (follow package directions if using frozen cauliflower). Blend remaining cauliflower florets as directed in Step 2. For seasoning, use ½ teaspoon toasted and crushed cumin seeds in Step 3. Stir ½ cup shredded American cheese into soup mixture after broth in Step 4. If desired, top with additional shredded American cheese.

PER 1 CUP: 148 cal., 9 g total fat (5 g sat. fat, 0 g trans fat), 27 mg chol., 792 mg sodium, 10 g carbo., 3 g fiber, 8 g pro. EXCHANGES: ½ Starch, 1 Vegetable, ½ High-Fat Meat, 1 Fat

CREAM OF BROCCOLI-CHEESE SOUP: Cook 4 cups fresh or frozen chopped broccoli for 8 to 10 minutes or until tender (follow package directions if using frozen broccoli). Blend remaining broccoli as directed in Step 2. For seasoning, use ½ teaspoon finely shredded lemon peel in Step 3. Stir ½ cup shredded American cheese into soup mixture after broth in Step 4. If desired, top with additional shredded American cheese.

PER 1 CUP: 153 cal., 9 g total fat (5 g sat. fat, 0 g trans fat), 27 mg chol., 792 mg sodium, 11 g carbo., 2 g fiber, 8 g pro. EXCHANGES: ½ Starch, 1 Vegetable, ½ High-Fat Meat, 1 Fat

RED AND GREEN GAZPACHO

PREP: 30 MINUTES **CHILL:** 1 TO 24 HOURS
MAKES: 6 SIDE-DISH SERVINGS

 3 cups chopped tomatoes (3 large)
 2 11.5-ounce cans tomato juice
    (about 3 cups)
 ½ cup chopped tomatillos (2 medium)
    (optional)
 ½ cup chopped cucumber
 1 fresh jalapeño pepper, seeded and finely
    chopped (see tip, page 24)
 ¼ cup finely chopped green onions (2)
 1 clove garlic, minced
 ¼ cup finely snipped fresh cilantro
 1 tablespoon olive oil
 1 tablespoon lime juice
 ¼ teaspoon salt
 ¼ teaspoon bottled hot pepper sauce
 1 avocado, halved, seeded, peeled, and
    chopped (optional)
    Lime wedges

1 In a large bowl combine tomatoes, tomato juice, tomatillos (if desired), cucumber, jalapeño pepper, green onions, garlic, cilantro, oil, lime juice, salt, and hot pepper sauce. Cover and chill at least 1 hour or up to 24 hours.

2 If desired, top each serving with chopped avocado. Serve with lime wedges.

PER 1 CUP: 62 cal., 3 g total fat (0 g sat. fat, 0 g trans fat), 0 mg chol., 398 mg sodium, 10 g carbo., 2 g fiber, 2 g pro. EXCHANGES: 2 Vegetable

STRAWBERRY-MELON SOUP
WITH GINGER MELON BALLS

4 Meanwhile, in a large bowl stir together sour cream and yogurt; set aside. Place strawberries in a blender or food processor. Cover and blend until smooth; add to sour cream mixture. Place remaining 2 cups cantaloupe pieces in same blender or food processor. Cover and blend until smooth. Add pureed melon and milk to strawberry mixture in bowl; stir to combine. Cover and chill overnight.

5 To serve, drain melon balls, reserving syrup. Stir reserved syrup into the chilled soup. Ladle soup into chilled bowls (see tip, below); top with melon balls. If desired, garnish with mint leaves.

PER 1 CUP: 198 cal., 7 g total fat (4 g sat. fat, 0 g trans fat), 21 mg chol., 78 mg sodium, 30 g carbo., 2 g fiber, 5 g pro.
EXCHANGES: ½ Milk, 1 Fruit, ½ Other Carbo., 1½ Fat

FAST ■ LOW FAT ■ HEALTHY

FALL FRUIT SOUP

PREP: 10 MINUTES COOK: 5 MINUTES
MAKES: 6 SIDE-DISH SERVINGS

- 1 cup cranberries (4 ounces)
- 3 plums, halved, pitted, and cut into thin slices
- 1 medium pear, cored and cut into bite-size pieces
- 1 medium cooking apple (such as Rome, Jonathan, or Fuji), cored and cut into bite-size pieces
- 3 cups cranberry-apple juice
- ¼ cup packed brown sugar
- 1 tablespoon lemon juice
- 2 3-inch pieces stick cinnamon

1 In a large saucepan combine cranberries, plums, pear, and apple. Stir in cranberry-apple juice, brown sugar, lemon juice, and cinnamon stick. Bring to boiling; reduce heat. Simmer, covered, for 5 to 6 minutes or until fruit is tender and skins on cranberries pop. Remove cinnamon sticks; discard.

PER 1 CUP: 169 cal., 0 g total fat, 0 mg chol., 13 mg sodium, 45 g carbo., 3 g fiber, 1 g pro.
EXCHANGES: 2 Fruit, 1 Other Carbo.

STRAWBERRY-MELON SOUP WITH GINGER MELON BALLS

PREP: 40 MINUTES COOK: 5 MINUTES
CHILL: OVERNIGHT MAKES: 8 SIDE-DISH SERVINGS

- 1 small cantaloupe melon
- ½ of a small honeydew melon
- ½ cup unsweetened pineapple juice
- ⅓ cup sugar
- 1 tablespoon grated fresh ginger
- 1 8-ounce carton dairy sour cream
- 1 6-ounce carton vanilla yogurt
- 4 cups fresh or frozen unsweetened strawberries
- 2 cups milk
  Mint leaves (optional)

1 Using a small melon baller, scoop the cantaloupe and the honeydew into balls or use a knife to cut melons into cubes. (You should have about 4 cups cantaloupe and 2 cups honeydew pieces.) Set melon pieces aside.

2 In a small saucepan combine pineapple juice, sugar, and ginger. Bring to boiling, stirring until sugar dissolves; reduce heat. Simmer, uncovered, for 5 to 7 minutes or until the mixture is the consistency of a thin syrup. Remove from heat; cool.

3 Transfer syrup to a storage container. Add 2 cups of the cantaloupe pieces and all of the honeydew pieces. Cover and chill overnight.

KEEP YOUR COOL

TO SERVE COLD SOUPS AT THEIR CHILLIEST BEST, PLACE THE SOUP BOWLS IN THE REFRIGERATOR FOR 10 TO 15 MINUTES BEFORE FILLING.

VEGETABLES & FRUITS

RATATOUILLE, PAGE 617

VEGETABLES & FRUITS

COUNT ON VEGETABLES AND FRUITS TO ADD COLOR, SPARKLE, AND OTHER GOOD THINGS (LIKE NUTRIENTS!) TO YOUR COOKING.

VEGGIES ON THE QUICK

These methods are among the quickest ways to get veggies from the fridge to the table.

STIR-FRY: Cut vegetables into bite-size pieces. If you're cooking more than one type of vegetable, cut them into pieces sized so they will cook at about the same rate. Heat oil in a wok or large skillet over medium-high heat. When hot, add the vegetables in small batches and cook, stirring constantly, until they are just crisp-tender. Note that stir-frying too many vegetables at once causes them to steam and become mushy. If necessary, you can return all cooked vegetables to the wok or skillet and cook them just long enough to reheat.

SAUTE: This method is much like stir-frying; the difference is that you generally use lower heat settings than for stir-frying, so you can stir occasionally rather than constantly. This method works especially well for cooking vegetables in butter, which can burn quickly over medium-high heat.

STEAM, BOIL, MICROWAVE: For know-how on these methods, see the charts, pages 624–627.

WORTH THE WAIT

Roasting vegetables in the oven brings out their natural sweetness while giving them irresistible texture—crispy on the outside, tender on the inside. For this cooking technique, the vegetables are generally tossed with oil, seasoned with salt and pepper, and baked in a hot oven in a shallow pan. For a taste of this marvelous method, try the Thyme-Roasted Beets, page 597, and the Lemon-Roasted Cauliflower, page 600. Once you get the hang of roasting, try it for other vegetables. Dense vegetables, such as potatoes, winter squash, and carrots, are particularly good candidates; tender vegetables, such as asparagus and mushrooms, also transform in the heat of the oven.

GETTING THE MOST FROM YOUR VEGGIES

To get the most nutrition from fresh vegetables, cook and enjoy them soon after purchasing. Frozen vegetables are also good sources of nutrition—they're flash-frozen soon after picking, which retains vitamins and minerals at levels equal to or sometimes greater than when fresh. Canned vegetables can be a good choice too; however, to keep sodium levels in check, look for canned products labeled low sodium or no salt added.

RIPENING FRUITS

Some fruits are picked and shipped while still firm and might need additional ripening. To ripen fruit:

■ Place it in a small, clean paper bag. (A plastic bag is not a good choice; it doesn't allow fruit to breathe, and the trapped moisture can cause the fruit to grow mold.)

■ Loosely close the bag and store it at room temperature. To speed up the ripening, place an apple or ripe banana in the bag with the underripe fruit.

■ Check the fruit daily and remove any that yield to gentle pressure. To check the fruit, cradle it in the palm of your hand and gently squeeze rather than prodding the fruit with your thumb or finger, which can bruise it.

■ Enjoy the ripe fruit immediately or refrigerate it for a couple of days. Refrigeration will slow down further ripening.

ARTICHOKES WITH HERB-BUTTER SAUCE

START TO FINISH: 35 MINUTES **MAKES:** 2 SERVINGS

- 2 artichokes (about 10 ounces each)
  Lemon juice
- ¼ cup butter
- 1 tablespoon lemon juice
- 1 teaspoon snipped fresh dill, tarragon, or oregano, or ¼ teaspoon dried dillweed, tarragon, or oregano, crushed

1 Wash artichokes; trim stems and remove loose outer leaves. Cut 1 inch off the top of each artichoke; snip off the sharp leaf tips. Brush the cut edges with a little lemon juice. In a large saucepan or Dutch oven bring a large amount of lightly salted water to boiling; add artichokes. Return to boiling; reduce heat. Simmer, covered, for 20 to 30 minutes or until a leaf pulls out easily. Drain artichokes upside down on paper towels.

2 Meanwhile, for Herb-Butter Sauce, melt butter. Stir in the 1 tablespoon lemon juice and dill. Turn artichokes right side up; serve with butter sauce.*

***NOTE:** To eat an artichoke, pull off a leaf and dip the leaf base into sauce. Draw the leaf base through your teeth, scraping off only tender flesh. Discard remainder of leaf. Continue removing leaves until fuzzy choke appears. Scoop out choke with a grapefruit spoon and discard. Eat the remaining heart with a fork, dipping each piece into sauce.

PER ARTICHOKE WITH 2 TABLESPOONS SAUCE: 268 cal., 23 g total fat (15 g sat. fat, 0 g trans fat), 61 mg chol., 278 mg sodium, 15 g carbo., 7 g fiber, 4 g pro.
EXCHANGES: 2 Vegetable, 5 Fat

ARTICHOKES WITH LEMON-MUSTARD MAYO: Prepare as directed, except chill artichokes after Step 1 and omit sauce. For Lemon-Mustard Mayo, combine ½ cup mayonnaise, ½ teaspoon finely shredded lemon peel, 2 teaspoons fresh lemon juice, and 1 teaspoon Dijon-style mustard. Season with black pepper. Makes 4 appetizer servings.

PER HALF ARTICHOKE WITH 2 TABLESPOONS MAYO: 466 cal., 44 g total fat (8 g sat. fat, 0 g trans fat), 20 mg chol., 613 mg sodium, 15 g carbo., 7 g fiber, 4 g pro.
EXCHANGES: 2 Vegetable, 9 Fat

FAST • LOW FAT

ROASTED ASPARAGUS

PREP: 15 MINUTES **ROAST:** 15 MINUTES
OVEN: 400°F **MAKES:** 6 SERVINGS

- 2 pounds asparagus spears
- 1 tablespoon olive oil
- ⅛ to ¼ teaspoon salt
- ⅛ to ¼ teaspoon black pepper
- ¼ cup shredded Parmesan or Asiago cheese (1 ounce)

1 Preheat oven to 400°F. Snap off and discard woody bases from asparagus. If desired, scrape off scales (see photos 1 and 2, below). Place asparagus in a 15×10×1-inch baking pan. Drizzle with olive oil; toss to coat. Spread in a single layer. Sprinkle with salt and pepper. Roast, uncovered, for 15 to 20 minutes or until asparagus is crisp-tender, turning once. Transfer to a serving platter; sprinkle with cheese.

PER SERVING: 57 cal., 3 g total fat (1 g sat. fat, 0 g trans fat), 2 mg chol., 107 mg sodium, 5 g carbo., 2 g fiber, 4 g pro.
EXCHANGES: 1 Vegetable, ½ Fat

PREPARING ASPARAGUS, STEP-BY-STEP

1. Starting at the base of each asparagus spear and working toward the tip, bend the spear a few times until you find a place where it breaks easily. Snap off the woody base at that point. **2.** If desired, for a smooth, clean look, use a vegetable peeler to scrape off the scales on the spears.

ASPARAGUS-SNAP PEA STIR-FRY

PREP: 20 MINUTES **COOK:** 6 MINUTES
MAKES: 6 SERVINGS

- 1 pound asparagus spears
- 2 cups fresh or frozen sugar snap peas
- 1 tablespoon vegetable oil
- 2 teaspoons grated fresh ginger
- 2 cloves garlic, minced
- 1 medium red onion, cut into thin wedges
- 1 medium red sweet pepper, cut into 1-inch pieces
- 1 tablespoon sesame seeds
- 2 tablespoons soy sauce
- 2 tablespoons rice vinegar
- 1 tablespoon packed brown sugar
- 1 teaspoon toasted sesame oil

1 Snap off and discard woody bases from asparagus. If desired, scrape off scales (see photos 1 and 2, page 594). Bias-slice asparagus into 2-inch pieces (you should have about 3 cups). Remove strings and tips from peas.

2 In a wok or large skillet heat oil over medium-high heat. Add ginger and garlic; cook and stir for 15 seconds. Add asparagus, onion, and sweet pepper; cook and stir for 3 minutes. Add sugar snap peas and sesame seeds; cook and stir for 3 to 4 minutes more or until vegetables are crisp-tender.

3 Add soy sauce, rice vinegar, brown sugar, and sesame oil to vegetable mixture; toss to coat. Serve with a slotted spoon.

PER ⅔ CUP: 86 cal., 4 g total fat (1 g sat. fat, 0 g trans fat), 0 mg chol., 343 mg sodium, 10 g carbo., 3 g fiber, 3 g pro.
EXCHANGES: 1½ Vegetable, 1 Fat

GREEN BEANS WITH HAZELNUTS

PREP: 15 MINUTES **COOK:** 6 MINUTES
MAKES: 8 SERVINGS

- 2 pounds fresh green beans
- ⅓ cup snipped fresh Italian parsley
- 1 tablespoon snipped fresh rosemary
- 2 teaspoons finely shredded lime peel
- 1 tablespoon fresh lime juice
- 1 clove garlic, minced
- 2 tablespoons olive oil
- ⅓ cup hazelnuts, toasted* and chopped
- Lime wedges (optional)

1 Remove ends and strings from beans. Leave whole or cut into 1-inch pieces. Cook beans, covered, in a small amount of boiling salted water for 3 to 4 minutes or until crisp-tender; drain. Immediately plunge beans in ice water; let sit for 3 minutes or until cool. Drain well; set aside.

2 In a small bowl combine parsley, rosemary, lime peel, lime juice, and garlic; set aside.

3 In a large skillet heat olive oil over medium-high heat. Add beans. Cook, stirring occasionally, 3 to 4 minutes or until heated through. If desired, season with *salt* and *black pepper*. Remove from heat. Stir in lime mixture and hazelnuts. If desired, serve with lime wedges.

*NOTE: Spread hazelnuts in a single layer in a shallow baking pan. Bake in a 350°F oven for 5 to 10 minutes or until light golden brown, watching carefully to avoid burning and stirring once or twice. To remove the papery skins from hazelnuts, rub the nuts with a clean dish towel.

PER ¾ CUP: 98 cal., 7 g total fat (1 g sat. fat, 0 g trans fat), 0 mg chol., 7 mg sodium, 9 g carbo., 4 g fiber, 3 g pro.
EXCHANGES: 1½ Vegetable, 1½ Fat

HOME-STYLE GREEN BEAN BAKE

PREP: 15 MINUTES **BAKE:** 45 MINUTES
OVEN: 350°F **MAKES:** 6 SERVINGS

- 1 10.75-ounce can condensed cream of mushroom soup or cream of celery soup
- ½ cup shredded cheddar cheese or American cheese (2 ounces)
- 1 2-ounce jar sliced pimiento, drained (optional)
- 3 14.5-ounce cans French-cut green beans or cut green beans, drained, or 6 cups frozen French-cut green beans or cut green beans, thawed and drained
- 1 2.8-ounce can french-fried onions

1 Preheat oven to 350°F. In a large bowl stir together soup, cheese, and, if desired, pimiento. Stir in green beans. Transfer bean mixture to a 1½-quart casserole.

2 Bake, uncovered, for 40 minutes. Remove from oven and stir; sprinkle with french-fried onions. Bake for 5 minutes more or until heated through.

PER 1 CUP: 194 cal., 12 g total fat (3 g sat. fat, 0 g trans fat), 12 mg chol., 1,180 mg sodium, 16 g carbo., 2 g fiber, 6 g pro.
EXCHANGES: 1½ Vegetable, ½ Starch, 2½ Fat

ROASTING BEETS, STEP-BY-STEP

1. Trim stems from fresh beets with a sharp knife. Use kitchen shears to trim the root ends. **2.** Drizzle olive oil mixture over beets in baking dish; use a rubber scraper to toss beets and coat evenly. **3.** Use a fork or sharp knife to gently pierce the cooked beets to test for doneness. The utensil should slide easily into beets when they are tender.

THYME-ROASTED BEETS

PREP: 20 MINUTES **ROAST:** 40 MINUTES
COOL: 15 MINUTES **OVEN:** 400°F
MAKES: 8 SERVINGS

3½ to 4 pounds baby beets (assorted colors)
    or small beets
6 cloves garlic, peeled
3 sprigs fresh thyme
5 tablespoons olive oil
½ teaspoon kosher salt
¼ teaspoon black pepper
2 tablespoons lemon juice
1 tablespoon snipped fresh thyme
3 ounces goat cheese, crumbled (optional)
    Snipped fresh thyme (optional)

1 Preheat oven to 400°F. Cut tops off beets and trim root ends (see photo 1, page 596). Halve or quarter beets. Place beets in a 3-quart rectangular baking dish. Add garlic and thyme sprigs. In a small bowl combine 3 tablespoons of the olive oil, the salt, and pepper. Drizzle over beets; toss to coat (see photo 2, page 596). Cover dish with foil.

2 Roast for 40 to 45 minutes or until tender (see photo 3, page 596). Uncover; let beets cool for 15 minutes in dish on a wire rack. If using small beets, remove skins by wrapping the beets, one at a time, in a paper towel and gently rubbing the skins off. (Baby beets do not need to be peeled.)

3 Remove garlic from dish and finely chop. Discard thyme sprigs. In a small bowl combine chopped garlic, the remaining 2 tablespoons olive oil, the lemon juice, and the 1 tablespoon snipped thyme. Drizzle over beets; toss gently to coat.

4 If desired, sprinkle beets with crumbled goat cheese and additional snipped thyme. Serve warm or at room temperature.

PER ¾ CUP: 165 cal., 9 g total fat (1 g sat. fat, 0 g trans fat), 0 mg chol., 246 mg sodium, 20 g carbo., 6 g fiber, 3 g pro. EXCHANGES: 3 Vegetable, 2 Fat

FAST

BROCCOLI SAUTE

START TO FINISH: 20 MINUTES **MAKES:** 4 SERVINGS

2 tablespoons olive oil
5 cups broccoli florets
2 cloves garlic, thinly sliced
¼ cup chicken broth
3 tablespoons water
⅛ teaspoon salt
⅛ teaspoon black pepper
2 tablespoons snipped fresh basil or
    Italian parsley

1 In a large skillet heat 1 tablespoon of the oil over medium-high heat. Add broccoli and garlic; cook for 2 minutes, stirring occasionally. Add broth, water, salt, and pepper. Bring to boiling; reduce heat. Cover and cook for 2 minutes. Uncover; cook for 2 minutes more or until broccoli is tender and liquid is almost gone. Add the remaining 1 tablespoon oil and basil; toss to coat.

PER ¾ CUP: 102 cal., 7 g total fat (1 g sat. fat, 0 g trans fat), 0 mg chol., 171 mg sodium, 8 g carbo., 3 g fiber, 3 g pro. EXCHANGES: 1 Vegetable, 1½ Fat

BEST EVER

BROCCOLI-CAULIFLOWER BAKE

PREP: 25 MINUTES **BAKE:** 20 MINUTES
OVEN: 375°F **MAKES:** 8 SERVINGS

4 cups broccoli florets
3 cups cauliflower florets
½ cup chopped onion (1 medium)
1 tablespoon butter
1 10.75-ounce can condensed cream of
    mushroom or cream of chicken soup
3 ounces American cheese, cubed, or
    process Swiss cheese, torn
¼ cup milk
½ teaspoon dried basil or thyme, crushed
¾ cup soft bread crumbs (1 slice bread)
1 tablespoon butter, melted

1 Preheat oven to 375°F. In a large saucepan cook broccoli and cauliflower, covered, in a small amount of boiling lightly salted water for 6 to 8 minutes or until vegetables are crisp-tender. Drain well. Remove broccoli and cauliflower from saucepan; set aside.

2 In the same saucepan cook onion in 1 tablespoon hot butter over medium heat until tender, stirring occasionally. Stir in soup, cheese, milk, and basil. Cook and stir over medium-low heat until cheese melts. Stir in cooked broccoli and cauliflower. Transfer to a 2-quart casserole. Toss together bread crumbs and the 1 tablespoon melted butter; sprinkle over vegetable mixture.

3 Bake, uncovered, about 20 minutes or until heated through.

PER ⅔ CUP: 137 cal., 9 g total fat (5 g sat. fat, 0 g trans fat), 20 mg chol., 497 mg sodium, 11 g carbo., 3 g fiber, 5 g pro. EXCHANGES: 1 Vegetable, ½ Starch, 1½ Fat

FAST

SAUTEED BROCCOLI RABE

START TO FINISH: 20 MINUTES **MAKES:** 6 SERVINGS

> 2 pounds broccoli rabe
> 1 large red sweet pepper, cut into bite-size strips
> 1 teaspoon dried basil, crushed
> ¼ teaspoon salt
> 3 cloves garlic, minced
> 2 tablespoons olive oil
>   Crushed red pepper
>   Lemon wedges

1 Wash broccoli rabe; remove and discard woody stems. Coarsely chop the leafy greens; set aside.

2 In a very large skillet cook and stir sweet pepper, basil, salt, and garlic in hot oil over medium-high heat for 2 minutes. Add broccoli rabe. Using tongs, toss and cook for 4 to 6 minutes or until broccoli rabe is crisp-tender. Transfer to serving dish. Sprinkle with crushed red pepper. Serve with lemon wedges.

PER ½ CUP: 82 cal., 5 g total fat (1 g sat. fat, 0 g trans fat), 0 mg chol., 148 mg sodium, 6 g carbo., 5 g fiber, 5 g pro.
EXCHANGES: 1 Vegetable, 1 Fat

BEST EVER • FAST

PAN-ROASTED BRUSSELS SPROUTS

START TO FINISH: 30 MINUTES **MAKES:** 8 SERVINGS

> 2 pounds Brussels sprouts
> 7 cloves garlic, minced
> 1 tablespoon olive oil
> 3 tablespoons butter
> 12 sprigs fresh thyme
> 1 large sprig fresh rosemary, halved
> 2 teaspoons fennel seeds
> 1¼ teaspoons kosher salt or 1 teaspoon salt
> 1 tablespoon sherry or white wine vinegar

1 Trim stems and remove any wilted outer leaves from Brussels sprouts; wash. Halve any large Brussels sprouts. In a large pot cook Brussels sprouts, uncovered, in a large amount of boiling lightly salted water for 3 minutes; drain well. Pat dry with paper towels.

2 In a very large heavy skillet cook and stir garlic in hot oil over medium heat for 2 minutes. Add half of the butter, thyme, rosemary, fennel seeds, and salt. Increase heat to medium-high; using tongs, carefully arrange half of the Brussels sprouts, cut sides down, in the skillet. Cook, uncovered, for

4 to 6 minutes or until the Brussels sprouts are well browned. Remove sprouts from pan. Repeat with the remaining butter, thyme, rosemary, fennel seeds, salt, and Brussels sprouts. Return all Brussels sprouts to the skillet along with the vinegar; toss to coat.

MAKE-AHEAD DIRECTIONS: Prepare as directed. Cover and chill for up to 1 day.

PER ½ CUP: 108 cal., 6 g total fat (3 g sat. fat, 0 g trans fat), 11 mg chol., 361 mg sodium, 11 g carbo., 5 g fiber, 4 g pro.
EXCHANGES: 1½ Vegetable, 1½ Fat

FAST • LOW FAT

BROWN SUGAR-GLAZED CARROTS

START TO FINISH: 25 MINUTES **MAKES:** 4 SERVINGS

> 1 pound packaged peeled fresh baby carrots or medium carrots, halved lengthwise and cut into 2-inch pieces
> 1 tablespoon butter or margarine
> 1 tablespoon packed brown sugar
>   Dash salt
>   Black pepper

1 In a medium saucepan cook carrots, covered, in a small amount of boiling salted water for 8 to 10 minutes or until crisp-tender. Drain; remove carrots from pan.

2 In the same saucepan combine butter, brown sugar, and salt. Cook and stir over medium heat until smooth. Add carrots. Cook and stir about 2 minutes or until glazed. Season with pepper.

HERBED-GLAZED CARROTS: Prepare as directed, except substitute 1 tablespoon honey for the brown sugar and add 1 tablespoon snipped fresh thyme or ½ teaspoon dried thyme, crushed, to the butter mixture. Sprinkle with snipped fresh Italian parsley before serving.

PER ¾ CUP BROWN SUGAR OR HERB VARIATION: 85 cal., 3 g total fat (2 g sat. fat, 0 g trans fat), 8 mg chol., 135 mg sodium, 14 g carbo., 3 g fiber, 1 g pro.
EXCHANGES: 1½ Vegetable, ½ Other Carbo., ½ Fat

ORZO-BROCCOLI PILAF

PREP: 20 MINUTES **COOK:** 22 MINUTES
STAND: 5 MINUTES **MAKES:** 6 SERVINGS

- 2 teaspoons olive oil
- 1 cup sliced fresh mushrooms
- ½ cup chopped onion (1 medium)
- ⅔ cup dried orzo
- 1 14-ounce can reduced-sodium chicken broth
- 1 teaspoon dried marjoram, crushed
- ⅛ teaspoon black pepper
- 2 cups small broccoli florets
- ½ cup shredded carrot (1 medium)

1 In a large saucepan heat olive oil over medium-high heat. Add mushrooms and onion; cook for 5 to 7 minutes or until onion is tender, stirring occasionally. Stir in orzo. Cook and stir about 2 minutes more or until orzo is light brown.

2 Stir in broth, marjoram, and pepper. Bring to boiling; reduce heat. Cover; simmer 12 minutes. Stir in broccoli and carrot. Cover; return to simmer. Simmer about 3 minutes or until orzo is tender. Remove from heat. Let stand, covered, 5 minutes.

PER ⅔ CUP: 111 cal., 2 g total fat (0 g sat. fat, 0 g trans fat), 0 mg chol., 176 mg sodium, 19 g carbo., 2 g fiber, 5 g pro.
EXCHANGES: ½ Vegetable, 1 Starch

SWEET-AND-SOUR CABBAGE

START TO FINISH: 15 MINUTES **MAKES:** 4 SERVINGS

- 3 tablespoons packed brown sugar
- 3 tablespoons vinegar
- 3 tablespoons water
- 4 teaspoons vegetable oil
- ¼ teaspoon caraway seeds
- ¼ teaspoon salt
  - Dash black pepper
- 3 cups shredded red or green cabbage
- ¾ cup chopped apple

1 In a large skillet combine brown sugar, vinegar, water, oil, caraway seeds, salt, and pepper. Cook for 2 to 3 minutes or until hot and brown sugar is dissolved, stirring occasionally.

2 Stir in the cabbage and apple. Cook, covered, over medium-low heat about 5 minutes or until cabbage is crisp-tender, stirring occasionally. Serve with a slotted spoon.

PER ½ CUP: 109 cal., 5 g total fat (1 g sat. fat, 0 g trans fat), 0 mg chol., 163 mg sodium, 17 g carbo., 2 g fiber, 1 g pro.
EXCHANGES: 1 Vegetable, ½ Other Carbo., 1 Fat

ADMIRABLE COOKING APPLES THE PHOTO ON PAGE 621 SHOWS APPLES THAT WORK WELL FOR COOKING. TRY GRANNY SMITH APPLES TO ADD TANG AND A JOLT OF GREEN COLOR TO SWEET-AND-SOUR CABBAGE.

ORZO-BROCCOLI PILAF

SWEET-AND-SOUR CABBAGE

LEMON-ROASTED CAULIFLOWER

PREP: 15 MINUTES **ROAST:** 30 MINUTES
OVEN: 450°F **MAKES:** 6 TO 8 SERVINGS

- ¼ cup vegetable oil
- 4 teaspoons finely shredded lemon peel
- 2 cloves garlic, minced
- 1 teaspoon kosher salt or ¾ teaspoon salt
- 1 medium head cauliflower (about 2¾ to 3 pounds), cut into chunks
- 3 tomatoes, cored and quartered
- 2 tablespoons lemon juice

1 Preheat oven to 450°F. In a very large bowl combine oil, 3 teaspoons of the lemon peel, the garlic, and salt. Add cauliflower; toss to coat.

2 Place cauliflower in a 15×10×1-inch baking pan. Roast, uncovered, for 20 minutes. Stir in tomatoes. Roast for 10 to 15 minutes more or until cauliflower is tender and edges are brown. Remove from oven. Add lemon juice and remaining 1 teaspoon lemon peel; toss to coat.

PER 1 CUP: 115 cal., 9 g total fat (1 g sat. fat, 0 g trans fat), 0 mg chol., 349 mg sodium, 7 g carbo., 3 g fiber, 2 g pro.
EXCHANGES: 1 Vegetable, 2 Fat

CREAMED CORN CASSEROLE

PREP: 15 MINUTES **BAKE:** 50 MINUTES
OVEN: 375°F **MAKES:** 12 SERVINGS

- Nonstick cooking spray
- 2 16-ounce packages frozen whole kernel corn
- 2 cups chopped red and/or green sweet peppers (2 large)
- 1 cup chopped onion (1 large)
- 1 tablespoon butter or margarine
- ¼ teaspoon black pepper
- 1 10.75-ounce can condensed cream of celery soup
- 1 8-ounce tub cream cheese spread with chive and onion or cream cheese spread with garden vegetables
- ¼ cup milk

1 Preheat oven to 375°F. Lightly coat a 2-quart casserole with cooking spray; set aside. Place corn in a colander. Run it under cool water to thaw; drain. Set aside.

2 In a large saucepan cook sweet peppers and onion in hot butter until tender. Stir in corn and black pepper. In a medium bowl whisk together soup, cream cheese spread, and milk; stir into corn mixture. Transfer to prepared casserole.

3 Bake, covered, for 50 to 55 minutes or until casserole is heated through, stirring once.

SLOW COOKER DIRECTIONS: Prepare as directed, except do not thaw corn and omit butter. In a 3½- or 4-quart slow cooker combine corn, sweet peppers, onion, and black pepper. In a medium bowl whisk together soup, cheese spread, and milk. Pour over corn mixture in cooker. Cover; cook on low-heat setting for 8 to 10 hours or on high-heat setting for 4 to 5 hours. Stir before serving.

PER ½ CUP: 169 cal., 9 g total fat (4 g sat. fat, 0 g trans fat), 26 mg chol., 270 mg sodium, 21 g carbo., 3 g fiber, 5 g pro.
EXCHANGES: 1½ Starch, 1 Fat

FAST

CORN ON THE COB

START TO FINISH: 20 MINUTES
MAKES: 8 SERVINGS

- 8 ears of corn
- Butter, margarine, or 1 recipe Herb Butter, Cajun Butter, or Chipotle-Lime Butter*

1 Remove husks from the ears of corn. Scrub with a stiff brush to remove silks; rinse. Cook, covered, in enough boiling lightly salted water to cover for 5 to 7 minutes or until tender. Serve with butter, *salt*, and *black pepper*.

HERB BUTTER: In a small mixing bowl beat ½ cup softened butter, 2 teaspoons snipped fresh thyme, and 2 teaspoons snipped fresh marjoram or oregano with an electric mixer on low speed until combined. Cover and chill for 1 to 24 hours.

CAJUN BUTTER: In a small mixing bowl beat ½ cup softened butter, 1 teaspoon garlic salt, ¼ teaspoon black pepper, ¼ teaspoon cayenne pepper, ⅛ teaspoon ground ginger, and ⅛ teaspoon ground cloves with an electric mixer on low speed until combined. Cover; chill for 1 to 24 hours.

CHIPOTLE-LIME BUTTER: In a small mixing bowl beat ½ cup softened butter, 1 teaspoon finely shredded lime peel, ½ teaspoon salt, ⅛ to ¼ teaspoon ground chipotle chile pepper, and dash cayenne pepper with electric mixer on low speed until combined. Cover; chill for 1 to 24 hours.

***NOTE:** If desired, try Onion-Parmesan Butter, Blue Cheese Butter, Lemon-Dill Butter, or Chipotle-Cilantro Butter (page 112).

PER EAR WITH 1 TABLESPOON PLAIN OR FLAVORED BUTTER: 179 cal., 13 g total fat (7 g sat. fat, 0 g trans fat), 31 mg chol., 168 mg sodium, 17 g carbo., 2 g fiber, 3 g pro.
EXCHANGES: 1 Starch, 2 Fat

SKILLET SCALLOPED CORN

START TO FINISH: 15 MINUTES **MAKES:** 4 SERVINGS

- 4 teaspoons butter
- ¼ cup crushed rich round, wheat, or rye crackers
- 1 11-ounce can whole kernel corn with sweet peppers, drained
- 1 7- to 8.75-ounce can whole kernel corn with sweet peppers, whole kernel corn, or white (shoepeg) corn, drained
- 2 1-ounce slices process Swiss cheese, torn
- ⅓ cup crushed rich round, wheat, or rye crackers
- ⅓ cup milk
- ⅛ teaspoon onion powder
  Dash black pepper

1 For topping, in a large skillet melt butter over medium heat. Add the ¼ cup crushed crackers to the skillet. Cook and stir until light brown; set aside.

2 In the same skillet combine the corn, cheese, ⅓ cup crushed crackers, the milk, onion powder, and pepper. Cook, stirring frequently, until cheese melts. Transfer to a serving dish; sprinkle with crumb topping.

PER ½ CUP: 220 cal., 12 g total fat (6 g sat. fat, 0 g trans fat), 23 mg chol., 713 mg sodium, 24 g carbo., 2 g fiber, 7 g pro. EXCHANGES: 1½ Starch, ½ Medium-Fat Meat, 1½ Fat

EGGPLANT PARMIGIANA

PREP: 20 MINUTES **COOK:** 9 MINUTES
MAKES: 4 SERVINGS

- 1 small eggplant (12 ounces)
- 1 egg, lightly beaten
- 1 tablespoon water
- ¼ cup all-purpose flour
- 2 tablespoons vegetable oil
- ⅓ cup grated Parmesan cheese
- 1 cup meatless spaghetti sauce
- ¾ cup shredded mozzarella cheese (3 ounces)
  Shredded fresh basil (optional)

1 Wash and peel eggplant; cut crosswise into ½-inch slices. Combine egg and water; dip eggplant slices into egg mixture, then into flour, turning to coat both sides.

SKILLET SCALLOPED CORN

2 In a large skillet cook eggplant, half at a time, in hot oil over medium-high heat for 4 to 6 minutes or until golden, turning once. (If necessary, add additional oil and reduce heat to medium if eggplant browns too quickly.) Drain on paper towels.

3 Wipe the skillet with paper towels. Arrange the cooked eggplant slices in the skillet; sprinkle with the Parmesan cheese. Top with spaghetti sauce and mozzarella cheese. Cook, covered, over medium-low heat for 5 to 7 minutes or until heated through. If desired, top with basil.

BAKED EGGPLANT PARMIGIANA: Preheat oven to 400°F. Prepare as directed, except in Step 2 place the eggplant slices in a single layer in an ungreased 2-quart rectangular baking dish. (If necessary, cut slices to fit.) Sprinkle with Parmesan cheese. Top with spaghetti sauce and mozzarella cheese. Bake, uncovered, for 12 to 15 minutes or until heated through. If desired, top with basil.

PER SERVING: 250 cal., 15 g total fat (5 g sat. fat, 0 g trans fat), 70 mg chol., 563 mg sodium, 20 g carbo., 5 g fiber, 12 g pro. EXCHANGES: 2 Vegetable, ½ Other Carbo., 1 Medium-Fat Meat, 2 Fat

ROASTED FENNEL AND ONIONS

PREP: 15 MINUTES **ROAST:** 35 MINUTES
OVEN: 400°F **MAKES:** 6 SERVINGS

- 2 medium fennel bulbs
- 1 large onion, cut into 1-inch wedges
- 1 tablespoon olive oil
- ½ teaspoon fennel seeds
- ¼ teaspoon salt
- ¼ teaspoon black pepper

1 Preheat oven to 400°F. Cut off and discard fennel stalks (see photo 1, below). Remove any wilted outer layers; cut a thin slice from base of each bulb (see photo 2, below). Cut bulbs in quarters lengthwise (see photo 3, below). Cut core out of each quarter. Cut quarters lengthwise into 1-inch wedges. Place fennel and onion in a shallow roasting pan. Drizzle with olive oil; sprinkle with fennel seeds, salt, and pepper. Stir to coat.

2 Roast, uncovered, for 35 to 40 minutes or until light brown and tender, stirring twice.

PER ½ CUP: 56 cal., 2 g total fat (0 g sat. fat, 0 g trans fat), 0 mg chol., 139 mg sodium, 8 g carbo., 3 g fiber, 1 g pro.
EXCHANGES: 1½ Vegetable, ½ Fat

BRAISED FENNEL WITH DILL

PREP: 10 MINUTES **COOK:** 30 MINUTES
MAKES: 6 SERVINGS

- 3 medium fennel bulbs
- 2 tablespoons butter
- ½ cup chicken broth
- ¼ cup dry white wine
- 3 tablespoons snipped fresh dill

1 Cut off and discard fennel stalks (see photo 1, below). Remove any wilted outer layers; cut a slice from base of each bulb (see photo 2, below). Cut bulbs in quarters lengthwise (see photo 3, below). Cut core out of each quarter. Cut quarters lengthwise into 1-inch wedges.

2 In a large skillet melt butter over medium heat. Add fennel, broth, wine, ¼ teaspoon *salt,* and *black pepper* to taste. Cook, covered, about 20 minutes or just until tender, stirring occasionally. Cook, uncovered, 10 minutes more or until liquid evaporates. Stir in dill.

PER ¾ CUP: 80 cal., 4 g total fat (2 g sat. fat, 0 g trans fat), 10 mg chol., 266 mg sodium, 9 g carbo., 4 g fiber, 2 g pro.
EXCHANGES: 1½ Vegetable, 1 Fat

PREPARING FENNEL BULBS, STEP-BY-STEP

1. Using a sharp knife, carefully cut about 1 inch above fennel bulb to remove stalks. Discard stalks, saving a few wispy fronds for a garnish if desired. **2.** Cut a thin slice off root end of each bulb. **3.** Cut bulbs in half lengthwise from stalk end to root end. Cut halves in half again to make quarters. Cut away and discard tough core portion from each quarter.

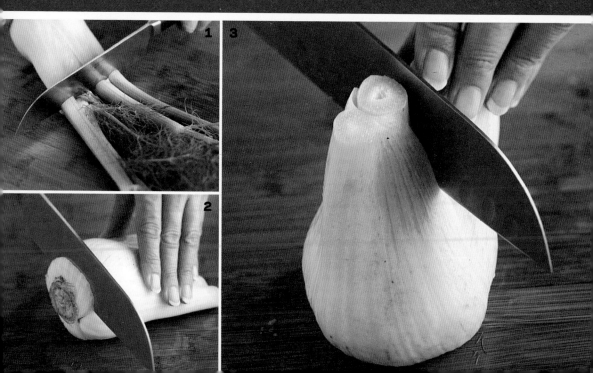

COLLARD GREENS WITH BACON

PREP: 30 MINUTES **COOK:** 60 MINUTES
MAKES: 6 SERVINGS

- 1 pound collard greens
- 3 slices bacon, chopped
- 2 cups water
- 1 8- to 10-ounce smoked pork hock
- ½ cup chopped onion (1 medium)
- ½ cup chopped green sweet pepper (1 small)
- 1 teaspoon sugar
- ¼ teaspoon salt
- ⅛ teaspoon cayenne pepper
- 4 cloves garlic, minced
  Red wine vinegar (optional)

1 Wash collard greens thoroughly in cold water; drain well. Remove and discard stems; trim bruised leaves. Coarsely chop leaves to measure 6 cups, lightly packed; set aside.

2 In a large saucepan cook bacon until crisp. Remove bacon, reserving drippings in saucepan. Drain bacon on paper towels and set aside. Add water, pork hock, onion, sweet pepper, sugar, salt, cayenne pepper, and garlic to saucepan. Bring to boiling; add chopped collard greens. Reduce heat. Simmer, covered, for 60 to 75 minutes or until greens are tender. Remove from heat. Remove pork hock. Cover greens; keep warm.

3 When cool enough to handle, cut meat off pork hock. Chop or shred meat; discard bone and fat. Return meat to greens mixture along with cooked bacon; heat through. Serve with a slotted spoon. If desired, drizzle each serving with a little vinegar.

PER ⅔ CUP: 176 cal., 13 g total fat (4 g sat. fat, 0 g trans fat), 34 mg chol., 312 mg sodium, 6 g carbo., 2 g fiber, 9 g pro. EXCHANGES: 1 Vegetable, 1 High-Fat Meat, 1 Fat

SMOTHERED OKRA

PREP: 20 MINUTES **COOK:** 20 MINUTES
MAKES: 4 SERVINGS

- ½ cup chopped onion (1 medium)
- ½ cup chopped green sweet pepper
- 2 cloves garlic, minced
- 2 tablespoons butter
- 8 ounces whole okra, cut into ½-inch pieces (2 cups), or 2 cups frozen cut okra, thawed
- 2 cups chopped, peeled tomatoes (2 large)
- ½ teaspoon salt
- ⅛ teaspoon black pepper

- ⅛ teaspoon cayenne pepper (optional)
- 2 slices bacon, crisp-cooked, drained, and crumbled (optional)

1 In a large skillet cook and stir onion, sweet pepper, and garlic in hot butter over medium heat about 5 minutes or until tender. Stir in okra, tomatoes, salt, black pepper, and, if desired, cayenne pepper. Bring to boiling; reduce heat. Simmer, covered, about 20 minutes for fresh okra (10 minutes for frozen okra) or until okra is tender. If desired, sprinkle with bacon.

PER ⅔ CUP: 99 cal., 6 g total fat (4 g sat. fat, 0 g trans fat), 15 mg chol., 342 mg sodium, 11 g carbo., 4 g fiber, 2 g pro. EXCHANGES: 1½ Vegetable, 1½ Fat

---

ROASTING GARLIC

HERE'S HOW TO ROAST GARLIC TO BRING OUT ITS SWEETNESS AND CREAMY TEXTURE.

■ Cut off the top ½ inch of a garlic bulb to expose the ends of the individual cloves. Leaving garlic bulb whole, remove any loose, papery outer layers.

■ Place bulb, cut end up, in a muffin cup or custard cup, or on a double thickness of foil. Drizzle bulb with 1 tablespoon olive oil. Sprinkle with salt and black pepper.

■ Cover bulb with foil or bring foil up around bulb and fold edges together to loosely enclose.

■ Roast in a preheated 400°F oven about 25 minutes or until garlic feels soft when squeezed. Cool; squeeze bulb from the bottom of papery husk and cloves will pop out.

■ To serve roasted garlic, simply spread on toasted crusty bread slices or crackers.

■ Roasted garlic can also be used as a recipe ingredient—whisk it into soups and pan sauces. Or combine it with melted butter or olive oil and toss with vegetables, such as asparagus or hot cooked new potatoes.

MUSHROOM MEDLEY AU GRATIN

PREP: 35 MINUTES **BAKE:** 15 MINUTES
OVEN: 350°F **MAKES:** 6 SERVINGS

  2 tablespoons grated Parmesan cheese
  2 tablespoons fine dry bread crumbs
  2 teaspoons butter, melted
  8 ounces fresh shiitake mushrooms
  4 ounces fresh oyster mushrooms
  1 pound fresh button mushrooms, sliced
  1 clove garlic, minced
  2 tablespoons butter
  2 tablespoons all-purpose flour
  2 teaspoons Dijon-style mustard
1½ teaspoons snipped fresh thyme or
       ½ teaspoon dried thyme, crushed
  ¼ teaspoon salt
  ⅔ cup milk

1 Preheat oven to 350°F. In a small bowl stir together Parmesan cheese, bread crumbs, and the 2 teaspoons melted butter; set aside.

2 Separate caps and stems from shiitake and oyster mushrooms. (Reserve stems to use in stocks or discard.) Slice mushroom caps.

3 In a large skillet cook button mushrooms and garlic in the 2 tablespoons butter over medium-high heat about 5 minutes or until tender and most of the liquid evaporates, stirring occasionally. Remove mushrooms from skillet and set aside, reserving drippings in skillet.

4 Add shiitake and oyster mushrooms to the skillet. Cook for 7 to 8 minutes or until tender and most of the liquid has evaporates, stirring occasionally. Stir in the flour, mustard, thyme, and salt. Add milk all at once. Cook and stir until thickened and bubbly. Stir in button mushroom mixture.

5 Transfer mushroom mixture to a 1-quart au gratin dish or 1-quart casserole. Sprinkle with the bread crumb mixture. Bake, uncovered, about 15 minutes or until heated through.

PER ½ CUP: 120 cal., 7 g total fat (4 g sat. fat, 0 g trans fat), 17 mg chol., 237 mg sodium, 10 g carbo., 2 g fiber, 6 g pro.
EXCHANGES: 1½ Vegetable, 1½ Fat

BISTRO MUSHROOMS

START TO FINISH: 20 MINUTES **MAKES:** 4 SERVINGS

  2 tablespoons olive oil, roasted garlic olive oil, or butter
  3 cups sliced cremini, stemmed shiitake, and/or button mushrooms (8 ounces)
  ⅓ cup dry red wine, dry sherry, or beef broth
  1 tablespoon Worcestershire sauce for chicken
  2 teaspoons snipped fresh thyme
       Salt
       Black pepper

1 In a large skillet heat oil over medium-high heat. Add mushrooms; cook and stir for 4 minutes. Stir in wine, Worcestershire sauce, and thyme. Simmer, uncovered, for 3 minutes. Season to taste with salt and pepper. Serve with beef, fish, pork, or poultry.

PER ⅓ CUP: 79 cal., 7 g total fat (1 g sat. fat, 0 g trans fat), 0 mg chol., 210 mg sodium, 3 g carbo., 0 g fiber, 1 g pro.
EXCHANGES: ½ Vegetable, 1½ Fat

GLAZED PARSNIPS AND CARROTS

START TO FINISH: 30 MINUTES **MAKES:** 6 SERVINGS

  8 ounces parsnips, cut into thin strips or sliced (2¼ cups)
  8 ounces carrots, cut into thin strips or sliced (2¼ cups)
  ¾ cup orange juice
  ⅓ cup dried cranberries
  ½ teaspoon ground ginger
  2 firm ripe pears, peeled, if desired, and sliced
  ⅓ cup pecan halves, toasted (see tip, page 20)
  3 tablespoons packed brown sugar
  2 tablespoons butter or margarine

1 In a large nonstick skillet combine parsnips, carrots, orange juice, dried cranberries, and ginger. Bring to boiling; reduce heat to medium. Cook, uncovered, for 7 to 8 minutes or until vegetables are crisp-tender and most of the liquid evaporates, stirring occasionally.

2 Stir pears, pecans, brown sugar, and butter into mixture in skillet. Cook, uncovered, for 2 to 3 minutes more or until vegetables are glazed.

PER ¾ CUP: 213 cal., 9 g total fat (3 g sat. fat, 0 g trans fat), 10 mg chol., 60 mg sodium, 35 g carbo., 6 g fiber, 2 g pro.
EXCHANGES: 1½ Vegetable, 1 Fruit, ½ Other Carbo., 1½ Fat

10 TO TRY— VEGGIE TOPPERS

Top 2 to 3 cups steamed vegetables with ¼ cup of one of the following combinations. **1. ALMOND-CHERRY:** Toasted almonds and dried cherries. **2. GARLIC-PANKO:** Panko bread crumbs toasted in 1 tablespoon olive oil in a skillet with 1 clove garlic, minced. **3. ASIAGO-RAISIN:** Shredded or shaved Asiago cheese and golden raisins. **4. GREEK:** Chopped Kalamata olives and crumbled feta cheese. **5. PEPPER-PEANUT:** Finely chopped red, green, and yellow sweet peppers and chopped honey-roasted peanuts. **6. PINE NUT:** Toasted pine nuts and finely shredded Parmesan cheese. **7. GOUDA-TOMATO:** Shredded smoked Gouda cheese and chopped dried tomatoes (oil pack). **8. BLUE CHEESE-NUT:** Crumbled blue cheese and chopped toasted walnuts. **9. BACON-TOMATO:** Crumbled crisp-cooked bacon and chopped fresh tomato. **10. DILL-POTATO CHIP:** Crushed potato chips and 1 teaspoon snipped fresh dill.

PEAS PARISIENNE

PREP: 20 MINUTES **COOK:** 10 MINUTES
MAKES: 6 SERVINGS

- 1 cup finely chopped onion (1 large)
- 6 cloves garlic, minced
- 2 teaspoons snipped fresh thyme or
  ½ teaspoon dried thyme, crushed
- 2 tablespoons butter
- 1 16-ounce package frozen peas (3¾ cups)
- ½ cup chicken broth
- ¼ teaspoon black pepper
  Pinch ground nutmeg

1 In a large saucepan cook onion, garlic, and thyme in hot butter over medium heat about 5 minutes or until onion is tender and begins to brown, stirring occasionally. Add peas, broth, pepper, and nutmeg. Bring to boiling; reduce heat. Simmer, uncovered, about 5 minutes or until peas are tender and heated through, stirring occasionally.

PER ½ CUP: 108 cal., 4 g total fat (2 g sat. fat, 0 g trans fat), 10 mg chol., 279 mg sodium, 13 g carbo., 4 g fiber, 5 g pro. EXCHANGES: 1 Starch, 1 Fat

PEAS, CARROTS, AND MUSHROOMS

START TO FINISH: 25 MINUTES **MAKES:** 6 SERVINGS

- ½ cup sliced carrot (1 medium)
- 1 10-ounce package frozen peas
- 2 cups sliced fresh mushrooms
- 2 green onions, cut into ½-inch pieces
- 1 tablespoon butter or margarine
- 1 tablespoon snipped fresh basil or
  ½ teaspoon dried basil, crushed
- ¼ teaspoon salt
  Dash black pepper

1 In a medium saucepan cook carrot, covered, in a small amount of boiling salted water for 3 minutes. Add the frozen peas. Return to boiling; reduce heat. Cook about 5 minutes more or until carrot and peas are crisp-tender; drain well. Remove carrot and peas from saucepan; set aside.

2 In the same saucepan cook mushrooms and green onions in hot butter until tender. Stir in basil, salt, and pepper. Return carrot and peas to saucepan; heat through, stirring occasionally.

PER ⅔ CUP: 67 cal., 2 g total fat (1 g sat. fat, 0 g trans fat), 5 mg chol., 226 mg sodium, 9 g carbo., 3 g fiber, 4 g pro. EXCHANGES: ½ Vegetable, ½ Starch, ½ Fat

SUGAR SNAP PEAS WITH ORANGE-GINGER BUTTER

START TO FINISH: 25 MINUTES **MAKES:** 4 SERVINGS

- 3 cups fresh or frozen sugar snap peas
- 1 teaspoon grated fresh ginger
- 1 tablespoon butter or margarine
- 1 tablespoon orange marmalade or peach preserves
- 1 teaspoon cider vinegar
- ⅛ teaspoon black pepper

1 Remove strings and tips from peas. Cook fresh peas, covered, in a small amount of boiling salted water for 3 to 5 minutes or until crisp-tender. (Cook frozen peas according to the package directions.) Drain well.

2 Meanwhile, in a small saucepan cook ginger in hot butter for 1 minute. Stir in marmalade, vinegar, and pepper; cook and stir until marmalade melts. Pour marmalade mixture over hot cooked peas; toss to coat.

PER ⅔ CUP: 58 cal., 3 g total fat (2 g sat. fat, 0 g trans fat), 8 mg chol., 25 mg sodium, 7 g carbo., 1 g fiber, 1 g pro. EXCHANGES: 1½ Vegetable, ½ Fat

MASHING TATERS

USE THE RIGHT UTENSIL TO GET THE DESIRED MASHED-POTATO TEXTURE.

■ For coarser mashed potatoes or when mashing potatoes that still have the skin on, use a potato masher. Push down through the potatoes until potatoes reach desired texture.

■ For very smooth and light mashed potatoes, press peeled cooked potatoes through a ricer. Be gentle when stirring additional ingredients into riced potatoes to maintain their lightness.

MAKE-IT-MINE MASHED POTATOES

CREATIVE BISTRO CHEFS HAVE ELEVATED HUMBLE MASHED POTATOES TO STYLISH, SOUGHT-AFTER SIDES. FOLLOW THEIR LEAD AND COME UP WITH YOUR OWN VERSION OF THIS CLASSIC COMFORT FOOD.

BASIC INGREDIENTS

PREP: 15 MINUTES
COOK: 20 MINUTES
MAKES: 4 SERVINGS

- 1½ pounds (3 large or 4 medium) Potatoes, peeled if desired*
- 2 tablespoons butter or margarine
- ½ teaspoon salt
- ¼ teaspoon black pepper
  Seasoning
  Dairy
- ¼ to ½ cup Stir-In

POTATOES (see tip, right)
(PICK ONE)

Red
Russet
Sweet potato
Yukon gold or other yellow potato

SEASONING (PICK ONE)

- ½ teaspoon ground chipotle chile pepper
- ½ teaspoon chili powder
- ½ teaspoon ground nutmeg
- 1 teaspoon Dijon-style mustard
- 1 teaspoon minced garlic
- 1 teaspoon salt-free seasoning blend
- 1 teaspoon wasabi paste

DAIRY (PICK ONE)

- 3 to 5 tablespoons milk
- 3 to 5 tablespoons half-and-half or light cream
- 3 to 5 tablespoons whipping cream
- 3 to 5 tablespoons buttermilk
- ¼ to ⅓ cup dairy sour cream
- 2 ounces cream cheese plus 3 tablespoons milk

STIR-IN (PICK ONE)

Crumbled crisp-cooked bacon
Shredded cheese, such as cheddar, smoked cheddar, Gouda, blue (crumbled), or Parmesan
Sliced green onions
Chopped caramelized onions
Sauteed leeks or sliced mushrooms
Chopped roasted sweet or hot peppers
Chopped dried tomatoes (oil pack, drained)
2 tablespoons mashed roasted garlic (see tip, page 603)
2 tablespoons snipped fresh chives or parsley
2 tablespoons purchased basil pesto
1 tablespoon snipped fresh rosemary, thyme, or sage

BASIC INSTRUCTIONS

1 In a medium saucepan cook desired Potatoes in lightly salted boiling water, covered, for 20 to 25 minutes or until tender; drain. Mash with a potato masher (see photo 1, page 606), a ricer (see photo 2, page 606), or beat with an electric mixer on low speed. Add butter, salt, pepper, and Seasoning. Gradually beat in Dairy to make mashed potatoes light and fluffy. Add Stir-In.**

*NOTE If you leave the peel on the potato, use a potato masher rather than the ricer or mixer to mash the potatoes.

**NOTE If desired, add more than one Stir-In to mashed potatoes. One tasty combo is crumbled bacon, shredded cheddar cheese, and sliced green onions.

SPUDS FOR MASHING

You can use just about any variety of potatoes for mashed potatoes. With their light, pleasantly mealy texture, russets are classic for mashing. For a creamy texture, choose yellow-flesh or red-skin potatoes. See pages 609 and 623 for more about potatoes.

BAKED POTATOES

PREP: 5 MINUTES **BAKE:** 40 MINUTES
OVEN: 425°F **MAKES:** 4 SERVINGS

4 medium baking potatoes (6 to 8 ounces each)

Shortening, butter, or margarine (optional)

1 Preheat oven to 425°F. Scrub potatoes thoroughly with a brush; pat dry. Prick potatoes with a fork. (If desired, for soft skins, rub potatoes with shortening or wrap each potato in foil.)

2 Bake for 40 to 60 minutes (or in a 350°F oven for 70 to 80 minutes) or until tender. To serve, roll each potato gently under a towel. Using a knife, cut an X in top of each potato. Press in and up on the ends of each potato.

PER POTATO: 131 cal., 0 g total fat, 0 mg chol., 10 mg sodium, 30 g carbo., 4 g fiber, 3 g pro.
EXCHANGES: 2 Starch

BAKED SWEET POTATOES: Prepare as directed, except substitute sweet potatoes or yams for the baking potatoes. If desired, serve sweet potatoes with butter and brown sugar or cinnamon-sugar.

PER SWEET POTATO: 146 cal., 0 g total fat, 0 mg chol., 94 mg sodium, 34 g carbo., 5 g fiber, 3 g pro.
EXCHANGES: 2 Starch

TWICE-BAKED POTATOES

PREP: 20 MINUTES **STAND:** 10 MINUTES
BAKE: 22 MINUTES **OVEN:** 425°F
MAKES: 4 SERVINGS

1 recipe Baked Potatoes (above)
½ cup dairy sour cream or plain yogurt
¼ teaspoon garlic salt
⅛ teaspoon black pepper
Milk (optional)
¾ cup finely shredded cheddar cheese (3 ounces)
1 tablespoon snipped fresh chives (optional)

1 Bake potatoes as directed; let stand about 10 minutes. Cut a lengthwise slice off the top of each baked potato; discard skin from slices and place pulp in a bowl. Scoop out potato pulp (see photo 1, below); add to the bowl.

2 Mash the potato pulp with a potato masher or an electric mixer on low speed. Add sour cream, garlic salt, and pepper; beat until smooth. (If necessary, stir in 1 to 2 tablespoons milk to reach desired consistency.) Season to taste with *salt* and additional black pepper. Stir in ½ cup of the cheddar cheese and, if desired, chives. Spoon the mashed potato mixture into the potato shells (see photo 2, below). Place in a 2-quart baking dish.

3 Bake, uncovered, in the 425°F oven for 20 to 25 minutes or until light brown. Sprinkle with remaining cheese. Bake for 2 to 3 minutes more or until cheese melts.

SOUTHWESTERN TWICE-BAKED POTATOES: Prepare as directed, except in Step 2 substitute Monterey Jack cheese with jalapeños for the cheddar cheese and snipped fresh cilantro for the chives. Serve with purchased salsa.

PER POTATO PLAIN OR SOUTHWESTERN VARIATION: 263 cal., 12 g total fat (7 g sat. fat, 0 g trans fat), 35 mg chol., 221 mg sodium, 31 g carbo., 4 g fiber, 9 g pro.
EXCHANGES: 2 Starch, ½ High-Fat Meat, 1 Fat

TWICE-BAKED POTATOES, STEP-BY-STEP

1. Using a spoon, gently scoop out the cooked potato pulp, leaving ¼-inch shells. You want a shell that's thick enough to stay open by itself.
2. Spoon the mashed potato filling evenly back into the potato shells, mounding the filling slightly above the edges of the potato.

FRENCH FRIES

PREP: 15 MINUTES **COOK:** 5 MINUTES PER BATCH
OVEN: 300°F **MAKES:** 4 TO 6 SERVINGS

  4 medium baking potatoes (1½ pounds)
     Vegetable oil for deep-fat frying
     Salt or seasoned salt (optional)

1 If desired, peel potatoes. To prevent darkening, immerse peeled potatoes in a bowl of ice water until ready to cut. Cut potatoes lengthwise into ⅜-inch-wide strips. Return potatoes to ice water.

2 In a heavy, deep 3-quart saucepan or fryer, heat oil to 365°F. To prevent splattering, pat potatoes dry. Using a spoon, carefully add potatoes, a few at a time, to hot oil. Fry for 5 to 6 minutes or until crisp and golden brown, turning once.

3 Meanwhile, preheat oven to 300°F. Using a slotted spoon, carefully remove fries from hot oil; drain on paper towels. If desired, sprinkle with salt. Keep fries warm in a baking pan in oven while frying remaining potatoes.

PER SERVING: 371 cal., 27 g total fat (3 g sat. fat, 0 g trans fat), 0 mg chol., 10 mg sodium, 30 g carbo., 4 g fiber, 3 g pro. EXCHANGES: 2 Starch, 5 Fat

SWEET POTATO FRIES: Prepare as directed, except use 4 medium sweet potatoes.

PER SERVING: 386 cal., 27 g total fat (3 g sat. fat, 0 g trans fat), 0 mg chol., 94 mg sodium, 34 g carbo., 5 g fiber, 3 g pro. EXCHANGES: 2 Vegetable, 5 Fat

COTTAGE-FRIED POTATOES

PREP: 15 MINUTES **COOK:** 20 MINUTES
MAKES: 4 SERVINGS

  3 tablespoons butter or margarine
  2 cloves garlic, minced
  3 medium potatoes (1 pound), peeled, if
     desired, and thinly sliced
  1 small onion, thinly sliced
  ¼ teaspoon salt
  ⅛ teaspoon black pepper

1 In a large skillet melt butter over medium heat. Add garlic; cook and stir for 15 seconds. Layer sliced potatoes and onion in skillet. Sprinkle with salt and pepper. Cook, covered, for 8 minutes, turning occasionally. Uncover; cook for 12 to 15 minutes more or until potatoes are tender and light brown, turning occasionally. (If necessary, add additional butter during cooking.)

PER ⅔ CUP: 171 cal., 9 g total fat (6 g sat. fat, 0 g trans fat), 23 mg chol., 214 mg sodium, 22 g carbo., 3 g fiber, 3 g pro. EXCHANGES: 1½ Starch, 2 Fat

HASH BROWN POTATOES

PREP: 10 MINUTES **COOK:** 18 MINUTES
MAKES: 4 SERVINGS

  4 medium potatoes (1½ pounds)
  ¼ cup finely chopped onion
  ¼ teaspoon salt
  ⅛ teaspoon black pepper
  3 tablespoons butter or margarine

1 Peel potatoes; coarsely shred to make 4½ cups. Rinse shredded potatoes and pat dry. Combine potatoes, onion, salt, and pepper.

2 In a large skillet melt butter over medium-low heat. Using a pancake turner, pat potato mixture into skillet. Cook about 10 minutes or until bottom of mixture is crisp. With the pancake turner, turn over potato mixture in large sections. Cook for 8 to 10 minutes more or until golden.

PER ¾ CUP: 202 cal., 9 g total fat (6 g sat. fat, 0 g trans fat), 23 mg chol., 214 mg sodium, 30 g carbo., 2 g fiber, 3 g pro. EXCHANGES: 2 Starch, 2 Fat

CHEESE-TOPPED HASH BROWNS: Prepare as directed, except before serving sprinkle with ½ cup finely shredded cheddar cheese (2 ounces). Cover and cook for 1 to 2 minutes more or until cheese melts.

PER ¾ CUP: 260 cal., 13 g total fat (8 g sat. fat, 0 g trans fat), 38 mg chol., 301 mg sodium, 29 g carbo., 2 g fiber, 6 g pro. EXCHANGES: ½ High-Fat Meat, 2 Starch, 2 Fat

PICKING THE RIGHT SPUD

THE BEST POTATO VARIETY FOR ANY GIVEN STYLE OF COOKING DEPENDS ON ITS STARCH CONTENT.

■ High-starch potatoes (russets) have a light, mealy texture. They are best for baked potatoes, french fries, and mashed potatoes.

■ Medium-starch potatoes (Finnish yellow, Yukon gold) are all-purpose potatoes. They contain more moisture than high-starch potatoes, so they don't fall apart as easily. They're a good choice for roasting and scalloped potatoes, and they mash well too.

■ Low-starch potatoes (round red, round white, new potatoes) are often called waxy potatoes. They hold their shape better than other potatoes, making them ideal for salads and roasting.

EASY ROASTED POTATOES

PREP: 10 MINUTES **ROAST:** 25 MINUTES
OVEN: 425°F **MAKES:** 4 SERVINGS

- 3 medium round red or white potatoes (1 pound), cut into eighths, or 10 to 12 tiny new potatoes (1 pound), halved
- 2 tablespoons olive oil
- ½ teaspoon onion powder
- ¼ teaspoon salt
- ¼ teaspoon black pepper
- ⅛ teaspoon paprika
- 1 clove garlic, minced

1 Preheat oven to 425°F. Place potatoes in a 9×9×2-inch baking pan. In a small bowl combine oil, onion powder, salt, pepper, paprika, and garlic. Drizzle oil mixture over potatoes, tossing to coat. Roast, uncovered, for 25 to 30 minutes or until potatoes are tender and brown on the edges, stirring occasionally.

PER ¾ CUP: 150 cal., 7 g total fat (1 g sat. fat, 0 g trans fat), 0 mg chol., 153 mg sodium, 20 g carbo., 3 g fiber, 2 g pro. EXCHANGES: 1 Starch, 1½ Fat

PARMESAN POTATO WEDGES

PREP: 25 MINUTES **BAKE:** 30 MINUTES
OVEN: 425°F **MAKES:** 6 SERVINGS

- 6 medium baking potatoes (about 2 pounds)
- ⅓ cup butter, melted
- ¼ cup grated Parmesan cheese (1 ounce)
- ½ teaspoon Italian seasoning, crushed
- ¼ teaspoon salt
- ⅛ teaspoon black pepper
- 1 clove garlic, minced

1 Preheat oven to 425°F. Line a 15×10×1-inch baking pan with parchment paper or foil; set aside. Cut each potato lengthwise into eight wedges. In a large bowl stir together butter, Parmesan cheese, Italian seasoning, salt, pepper, and garlic. Add potato wedges and stir to coat evenly. Place the wedges on the prepared baking pan. Bake, uncovered, about 30 minutes or until tender.

PER SERVING: 222 cal., 11 g total fat (7 g sat. fat, 0 g trans fat), 30 mg chol., 229 mg sodium, 27 g carbo., 3 g fiber, 4 g pro. EXCHANGES: 1½ Starch, 2 Fat

CREAMY POTLUCK POTATOES

PREP: 10 MINUTES **BAKE:** 75 MINUTES
STAND: 5 MINUTES **OVEN:** 350°F
MAKES: 12 SERVINGS

- 1 32-ounce package frozen diced hash brown potatoes, thawed (7½ cups)
- 1 10.75-ounce can reduced-fat and reduced-sodium condensed cream of chicken soup
- 1 8-ounce carton dairy sour cream
- 2 tablespoons butter or margarine, melted
- 1 cup shredded cheddar cheese (4 ounces)
- ¼ cup sliced green onions (2)
- ¼ cup milk
- ½ teaspoon garlic salt
- ¼ teaspoon black pepper

1 Preheat oven to 350°F. In a large bowl stir together potatoes, soup, sour cream, and butter. Stir in ½ cup shredded cheese, 3 tablespoons green onions, the milk, garlic salt, and pepper. Transfer to a 2-quart rectangular baking dish.

2 Bake, covered, 75 minutes or until potatoes are tender. Sprinkle with remaining cheese. Let stand 5 minutes. Sprinkle with remaining onions.

PER ¾ CUP: 173 cal., 10 g total fat (6 g sat. fat, 0 g trans fat), 26 mg chol., 241 mg sodium, 17 g carbo., 1 g fiber, 5 g pro. EXCHANGES: 1 Starch, 2 Fat

SCALLOPED POTATOES

PREP: 30 MINUTES **BAKE:** 85 MINUTES
STAND: 10 MINUTES **OVEN:** 350°F
MAKES: 10 SERVINGS

- 1 cup chopped onion (1 large)
- 2 cloves garlic, minced
- ¼ cup butter or margarine
- ¼ cup all-purpose flour
- ½ teaspoon salt
- ¼ teaspoon black pepper
- 2½ cups milk
- 8 cups thinly sliced red, white, long white, or yellow potatoes (about 2½ pounds)

1 Preheat oven to 350°F. For sauce, in a medium saucepan cook onion and garlic in hot butter over medium heat until tender. Stir in flour, salt, and pepper. Add milk all at once. Cook and stir until thickened and bubbly. Remove from heat.

2 Place half the potatoes in a greased 3-quart rectangular dish. Top with half the sauce; repeat.

3 Bake, covered, for 45 minutes. Uncover and bake for 40 to 50 minutes more or until potatoes are tender. Let stand, uncovered, for 10 minutes before serving.

PER ABOUT 1 CUP: 182 cal., 6 g total fat (4 g sat. fat, 0 g trans fat), 17 mg chol., 182 mg sodium, 28 g carbo., 3 g fiber, 5 g pro. EXCHANGES: 2 Starch, 1 Fat

BEST EVER

CHEESY GARLIC POTATO GRATIN

PREP: 25 MINUTES **BAKE:** 90 MINUTES
STAND: 10 MINUTES **OVEN:** 350°F
MAKES: 6 SERVINGS

- 4 medium Yukon gold or other yellow-flesh potatoes (1½ pounds), thinly sliced (about 5 cups)
- ⅓ cup sliced green onions (3) or thinly sliced leek
- 4 cloves garlic, minced
- 1 teaspoon salt
- ¼ teaspoon black pepper
- 1½ cups shredded Swiss, Gruyère, provolone, or Jarslberg cheese (6 ounces)
- 1 cup whipping cream

1 Preheat oven to 350°F. Grease a 2-quart baking dish. Layer half of the sliced potatoes and half of the green onions in prepared dish. Sprinkle with half of the garlic, salt, and pepper. Sprinkle with half of the cheese. Repeat layers. Pour whipping cream over top.

2 Bake, covered, for 70 minutes. Uncover; bake for 20 to 30 minutes more or until potatoes are tender when pierced with a fork and top is golden brown. Let stand for 10 minutes before serving.

CHEESY GARLIC SWEET POTATO GRATIN:
Prepare as directed, except substitute sweet potatoes for half of the Yukon gold potatoes.

PER ⅔ CUP PLAIN OR SWEET POTATO VARIATION: 354 cal., 24 g total fat (15 g sat. fat, 0 g trans fat), 85 mg chol., 474 mg sodium, 23 g carbo., 3 g fiber, 12 g pro. EXCHANGES: 1½ Starch, 1 High-Fat Meat, 3 Fat

GO FOR THE GOLD YELLOW-FLESH POTATOES GIVE YOUR POTATO GRATINS WARM AND WINNING COLOR. IF YOU LIKE, SUBSTITUTE HALF THE YUKONS WITH SWEET POTATOES FOR A TWO-TONED TREAT.

CHEESY GARLIC POTATO GRATIN

BAKED SWEET POTATO FRIES

PREP: 15 MINUTES **BAKE:** 25 MINUTES
OVEN: 400°F **MAKES:** 6 SERVINGS

Nonstick cooking spray
4 medium sweet potatoes (about 2 pounds),
  peeled if desired
¼ cup olive oil
1 teaspoon salt
½ teaspoon black pepper
Snipped fresh parsley (optional)
Coarse salt (optional)

1 Preheat oven to 400°F. If desired, line two baking sheets with foil. Lightly coat foil with nonstick spray; set baking sheets aside.

2 Cut sweet potatoes lengthwise into ½-inch-thick strips. Place sweet potatoes in a large bowl. In a small bowl combine oil, salt, and pepper. Drizzle oil mixture over potatoes, tossing to coat. Arrange sweet potatoes in a single layer on prepared baking sheets.

3 Bake for 15 minutes. Turn potatoes over. Bake for 10 to 15 minutes more or until golden brown. If desired, sprinkle with parsley or coarse salt.

BROWN SUGAR-CINNAMON SWEET POTATO FRIES: Prepare as directed, except add 2 tablespoons packed brown sugar and ¼ teaspoon ground cinnamon with the oil.

GARLIC SWEET POTATO FRIES: Prepare as directed, except add 2 cloves garlic, minced, and ¼ teaspoon garlic powder with the oil.

SOUTHWESTERN SWEET POTATO FRIES: Prepare as directed, except before baking sprinkle with a mixture of 1 tablespoon sugar, 1 teaspoon ground cumin, 1 teaspoon chili powder, ¼ teaspoon onion powder, and ⅛ teaspoon cayenne pepper.

PER ⅔ CUP PLAIN, BROWN SUGAR, GARLIC, OR SOUTHWESTERN VARIATIONS: 178 cal., 9 g total fat (1 g sat. fat, 0 g trans fat), 0 mg chol., 450 mg sodium, 23 g carbo., 3 g fiber, 2 g pro. EXCHANGES: 1½ Starch, 2 Fat

SWEET POTATO AND CRANBERRY SAUTE

PREP: 15 MINUTES **COOK:** 19 MINUTES
MAKES: 4 SERVINGS

1¼ cups apple juice or apple cider
1 pound sweet potatoes, peeled and cut
  into ¼-inch slices (about 3 cups)
1 cup coarsely chopped cooking apple
  (1 large)

2 tablespoons dried cranberries
¼ cup maple syrup
¼ teaspoon salt
2 tablespoons chopped hazelnuts (filberts)
  or walnuts, toasted (see tip, page 20)

1 In a large skillet heat apple juice to simmering. Add sweet potatoes, spreading evenly. Cook, covered, over medium-low heat about 12 minutes or until potatoes are nearly tender. Stir in apple, cranberries, maple syrup, and salt. Cook, covered, over low heat for 3 to 4 minutes more or just until apple is tender. Uncover; boil about 4 minutes more or until liquid is syrupy. Sprinkle with nuts.

PER 1 CUP: 238 cal., 3 g total fat (0 g sat. fat, 0 g trans fat), 0 mg chol., 213 mg sodium, 53 g carbo., 5 g fiber, 3 g pro. EXCHANGES: 1 Fruit, 1½ Starch, 1 Other Carbo.

CANDIED SWEET POTATOES

PREP: 30 MINUTES **BAKE:** 30 MINUTES
STAND: 5 MINUTES **OVEN:** 375°F
MAKES: 6 SERVINGS

4 medium sweet potatoes (about 2 pounds)
  or two 18-ounce cans sweet potatoes,
  drained
¼ cup packed brown sugar or pure maple
  syrup
¼ cup butter, melted
¾ cup chopped pecans or walnuts, toasted
  if desired (see tip, page 20), and/or tiny
  marshmallows

1 Preheat oven to 375°F. Peel fresh sweet potatoes; cut into 1½-inch chunks. Cook fresh sweet potatoes, covered, in enough boiling water to cover for 10 to 12 minutes or just until tender; drain. (Cut up canned sweet potatoes.)

2 Transfer potatoes to a 2-quart rectangular baking dish. Add brown sugar and melted butter; stir gently to combine.

3 Bake, uncovered, for 30 to 35 minutes or until potatoes are glazed, stirring gently twice. Sprinkle with nuts and/or marshmallows; let stand for 5 minutes before serving.

MAKE-AHEAD DIRECTIONS: Prepare as directed through Step 2. Cover and chill for up to 24 hours. Bake, uncovered, in a 375°F oven for 35 to 40 minutes or until potatoes are glazed, stirring gently twice. Continue as directed.

PER ¾ CUP: 327 cal., 18 g total fat (6 g sat. fat, 0 g trans fat), 20 mg chol., 140 mg sodium, 41 g carbo., 6 g fiber, 4 g pro. EXCHANGES: 1½ Starch, 1 Other Carbo., 3 Fat

SLIP ME SOME SKIN THERE'S NO NEED TO PEEL SWEET POTATOES IF THEY'RE CUT INTO STRIPS AND ROASTED. THE WELL-SCRUBBED SKIN ADDS FIBER AND GIVES THE FRIES EXTRA CRUNCH.

SWEET POTATO AND
CRANBERRY SAUTE

CREAMY SPINACH

START TO FINISH: 20 MINUTES **MAKES:** 4 SERVINGS

- 2 9-ounce packages prewashed fresh spinach (large stems removed) or two 10-ounce packages frozen chopped spinach, thawed
- ½ cup chopped onion (1 medium)
- 2 to 3 cloves garlic, minced
- 2 tablespoons butter
- 1 cup whipping cream
- ½ teaspoon black pepper
- ¼ teaspoon salt
- ¼ teaspoon ground nutmeg

1 In a large pot cook fresh spinach (if using) in rapidly boiling salted water for 1 minute. Drain well, squeezing out excess liquid. Pat dry with paper towels. Using kitchen shears, coarsely snip spinach; set aside. (If using frozen spinach, drain well after thawing, squeezing out excess liquid.)

2 In a large skillet cook onion and garlic in hot butter about 5 minutes or until onion is tender. Stir in cream, pepper, salt, and nutmeg. Bring to boiling; cook for 3 to 5 minutes or until cream starts to thicken. Add spinach. Simmer until mixture reaches desired consistency, stirring occasionally. Serve immediately.

PER ¾ CUP: 312 cal., 29 g total fat (18 g sat. fat, 0 g trans fat), 97 mg chol., 345 mg sodium, 11 g carbo., 4 g fiber, 7 g pro.
EXCHANGES: 2 Vegetable, 6 Fat

BALSAMIC-GLAZED SQUASH

PREP: 20 MINUTES **ROAST:** 45 MINUTES
OVEN: 425°F **MAKES:** 8 SERVINGS

- 2 tablespoons butter
- 2 medium acorn squash (about 3 pounds)
- 3 tablespoons olive oil
- ½ teaspoon salt
- 1 recipe Balsamic Drizzle

1 Preheat oven to 425°F. Place butter in a 15×10×1-inch baking pan. Heat in the oven for 2 minutes or until butter melts; tilt pan to coat. Set pan aside.

2 Cut squash in half lengthwise;* remove and discard seeds (see photos 1 and 2, below). Cut squash crosswise into 1-inch slices. Place squash in a single layer in prepared pan. Drizzle with olive oil and sprinkle with salt, turning squash to coat.

3 Roast, uncovered, about 45 minutes or until squash is tender, turning squash once or twice. Transfer to a serving platter. Spoon Balsamic Drizzle over squash.

BALSAMIC DRIZZLE: In a saucepan combine 1 cup balsamic vinegar, 2 teaspoons honey, 1 bay leaf, and 1 sprig rosemary. Bring to boiling. Boil gently, uncovered, about 30 minutes or until reduced to ⅓ cup. Remove rosemary and bay leaf.

*NOTE: To make squash easier to cut, microwave whole squash on 50% (medium) power for 5 to 6 minutes., turning once.

PER SERVING: 166 cal., 8 g total fat (3 g sat. fat, 0 g trans fat), 8 mg chol., 176 mg sodium, 22 g carbo., 2 g fiber, 1 g pro.
EXCHANGES: 1½ Starch, 1½ Fat

PREPARING ACORN SQUASH, STEP-BY-STEP

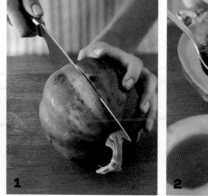

1. Securely hold the acorn squash on the cutting board so it will not roll. Using a large chef's knife, cut squash in half from the stem end to the blossom end. **2.** Using a large spoon, scoop out and discard the seeds and membranes from squash halves.

MAPLE ACORN SQUASH

PREP: 15 MINUTES **BAKE:** 65 MINUTES
OVEN: 350°F **MAKES:** 4 SERVINGS

    1 medium acorn squash (1½ to 2 pounds)

    ¼ cup maple syrup

    2 tablespoons butter or margarine, melted

    ½ teaspoon finely shredded orange peel
       (optional)

    ⅛ teaspoon ground cinnamon or nutmeg

1 Preheat oven to 350°F. Cut squash in half
lengthwise; remove and discard seeds (see photos
1 and 2, page 614). Arrange the squash halves,
cut sides down, in a 2-quart rectangular baking
dish. Bake, uncovered, for 45 minutes. Turn
squash halves cut sides up.

2 Meanwhile, in a small bowl stir together maple
syrup, butter, orange peel (if desired), and cinnamon. Spoon syrup mixture into centers of squash
halves. Bake, uncovered, for 20 to 25 minutes
more or until squash is tender. Cut squash halves
in half and divide pieces among four serving
plates. Spoon syrup mixture over squash pieces.

PER SERVING: 155 cal., 6 g total fat (4 g sat. fat, 0 g trans fat),
15 mg chol., 47 mg sodium, 27 g carbo., 2 g fiber, 1 g pro.
EXCHANGES: 1 Starch, 1 Other Carbo., 1 Fat

FAST

CARAMELIZED ONIONS

START TO FINISH: 21 MINUTES **MAKES:** 1⅓ CUPS

    2 tablespoons butter

    2 large sweet onions (such as Vidalia or
       Walla Walla), halved lengthwise and thinly
       sliced or cut into ¾-inch chunks

1 In a large skillet melt butter over medium-low
heat. Add onions. Cook, covered, for 13 to
15 minutes or until onions are tender, stirring
occasionally. Uncover; cook and stir over medium-
high heat for 3 to 5 minutes or until golden.

PER ⅓ CUP: 104 cal., 6 g total fat (4 g sat. fat, 0 g trans fat),
15 mg chol., 54 mg sodium, 13 g carbo., 1 g fiber, 1 g pro.
EXCHANGES: 1½ Vegetable, 1½ Fat

BUTTERED SPAGHETTI SQUASH

PREP: 20 MINUTES **BAKE:** 30 MINUTES
OVEN: 350°F **MAKES:** 6 SERVINGS

    1 medium spaghetti squash (2½ to
       3 pounds)

    ½ cup finely shredded Parmesan cheese

    3 tablespoons butter or margarine, cut up

    1 tablespoon chopped fresh basil, oregano,
       or parsley

    ¼ teaspoon salt

1 Preheat oven to 350°F. Halve squash lengthwise; remove and discard seeds. Place squash
halves, cut sides down, in a large baking dish.
Using a fork, prick the skin all over. Bake, uncovered, for 30 to 40 minutes or until tender.

2 Using a fork, remove the squash pulp from
shell. Toss squash with ¼ cup of the Parmesan
cheese, the butter, basil, and salt. Sprinkle with
the remaining Parmesan cheese.

PER ¾ CUP: 120 cal., 8 g total fat (5 g sat. fat, 0 g trans fat),
20 mg chol., 274 mg sodium, 10 g carbo., 0 g fiber, 3 g pro.
EXCHANGES: 1½ Vegetable, 1½ Fat

SPAGHETTI SQUASH WITH MARINARA SAUCE:
Bake squash as directed in Step 1. Omit the
Parmesan cheese, butter, basil, and salt. For marinara sauce, in a medium saucepan cook and stir
¼ cup chopped onion and 2 cloves garlic, minced,
in 1 tablespoon olive oil over medium heat until
onion is tender. Stir in one 14.5-ounce can diced
tomatoes, undrained; 1 teaspoon dried Italian
seasoning, crushed; ¼ teaspoon salt; ¼ teaspoon
black pepper; and ⅛ teaspoon fennel seeds,
crushed. Bring to boiling; reduce heat. Simmer,
uncovered, for 10 to 15 minutes or until desired
consistency, stirring often. Remove squash pulp
from shell. Spoon sauce over squash. If desired,
sprinkle with grated Parmesan cheese.

PER ¾ CUP SQUASH WITH ¼ CUP SAUCE: 80 cal., 3 g total
fat (0 g sat. fat, 0 g trans fat), 0 mg chol., 256 mg sodium, 14 g
carbo., 1 g fiber, 2 g pro.
EXCHANGES: 2 Vegetable, ½ Fat

ROASTED SWEET PEPPERS

USE IN SALADS, SOUPS, OR VEGETABLE MEDLEYS AND ON TOP OF PIZZAS.

Preheat oven to 425°F. Cut sweet peppers
in half lengthwise; remove stems, seeds,
and membranes. Place pepper halves, cut
sides down, on a foil-lined baking sheet.
Bake for 20 to 25 minutes or until peppers
are charred and very tender. Bring the foil up
around peppers and fold edges together to
enclose. Let stand about 15 minutes or until
cool enough to handle. Use a sharp knife to
loosen edges of the skins; gently pull off the
skins in strips and discard.

SUMMER SQUASH TOSS

START TO FINISH: 25 MINUTES **MAKES:** 8 SERVINGS

- 1 medium red onion, cut into thin wedges
- 1 tablespoon olive oil or vegetable oil
- 3 medium zucchini and/or yellow summer squash, halved lengthwise and cut into ¼-inch slices (about 5 cups)
- ½ teaspoon salt
- ¼ teaspoon black pepper
- 2 tablespoons snipped fresh basil, thyme, and/or Italian parsley
- 2 ounces goat cheese, crumbled

1 In a very large skillet cook onion in hot oil over medium-high heat for 7 minutes, stirring occasionally. Add zucchini, salt, and pepper to skillet; reduce heat to medium. Cook, uncovered, about 8 minutes or until vegetables are crisp-tender, stirring occasionally. Sprinkle with herb and cheese.

PER ¾ CUP: 52 cal., 3 g total fat (1 g sat. fat, 0 g trans fat), 3 mg chol., 179 mg sodium, 4 g carbo., 1 g fiber, 2 g pro.
EXCHANGES: 1 Vegetable, ½ Fat

GRATIN-STYLE PATTYPAN SQUASH

PREP: 15 MINUTES **COOK:** 6 MINUTES
BROIL: 2 MINUTES **MAKES:** 4 SERVINGS

- 2 tablespoons olive oil
- 1 pound baby pattypan and/or sunburst squash, halved or quartered*
- 2 cloves garlic, minced
- 2 slices bacon, crisp-cooked, drained, and crumbled
- 2 tablespoons grated Parmesan cheese
- 1 tablespoon snipped fresh basil
- ⅛ teaspoon black pepper

1 Preheat broiler. In a large skillet heat 1 tablespoon of the oil over medium heat. Add squash and garlic; cook and stir for 6 to 8 minutes or until tender. Transfer to a 1- to 1½-quart broiler-safe au gratin dish. In a small bowl stir together bacon, Parmesan, basil, and pepper. Sprinkle over squash in dish. Drizzle with remaining 1 tablespoon oil.

2 Broil 3 to 4 inches from the heat for 2 to 3 minutes or until top is golden.

*NOTE: Substitute zucchini or yellow summer squash cut into 1-inch pieces for pattypan squash.

PER ½ CUP: 113 cal., 9 g total fat (2 g sat. fat, 0 g trans fat), 7 mg chol., 133 mg sodium, 5 g carbo., 1 g fiber, 4 g pro.
EXCHANGES: 1 Vegetable, 2 Fat

CRUNCH TIME CRUSHED POTATO CHIPS PROVIDE A CRISP COATING FOR FRIED GREEN TOMATOES. FOR ANOTHER OPTION, TRY CRUSHED CRACKERS OR PANKO—COARSE JAPANESE-STYLE BREAD CRUMBS.

SUMMER SQUASH TOSS

SPICY HERB FRIED GREEN TOMATOES

SPICY HERB FRIED GREEN TOMATOES

PREP: 30 MINUTES **COOK:** 4 MINUTES PER BATCH
MAKES: 6 TO 7 SERVINGS

- 1 8-ounce carton dairy sour cream
- 6 cloves garlic, minced
- 1 tablespoon snipped fresh cilantro
- ⅛ teaspoon salt
- ¼ cup milk
- 2 cups crushed potato chips (about 5 ounces)
- 1 tablespoon snipped fresh thyme
- ½ teaspoon black pepper
- ¼ teaspoon cayenne pepper
- ½ cup all-purpose flour
- 2 large firm green tomatoes (about 1 pound total), sliced ¼ inch thick
- 3 tablespoons butter or margarine
- 3 tablespoons olive oil

1 In a small bowl combine sour cream, garlic, cilantro, and salt. Reserve half of the mixture to serve with fried tomatoes. Place the remaining mixture in a shallow dish and whisk in milk until combined. In another shallow dish combine crushed potato chips, thyme, black pepper, and cayenne pepper. Place flour in a third shallow dish.

2 Dip tomato slices in flour, turning to coat; shake off excess. Dip in milk mixture; dip in potato chip mixture.

3 In a very large skillet heat 2 tablespoons of the butter and 2 tablespoons of the oil over medium heat. Add half of the coated tomato slices; cook about 4 minutes or until crisp and golden, turning once halfway through cooking. Drain on paper towels. Add remaining 1 tablespoon butter and olive oil to skillet. Add remaining tomato slices; cook as directed. Serve with reserved sour cream mixture.

PER 2 SLICES: 376 cal., 29 g total fat (12 g sat. fat, 0 g trans fat), 36 mg chol., 258 mg sodium, 26 g carbo., 2 g fiber, 5 g pro. EXCHANGES: 1 Vegetable, 1½ Starch, 5 Fat

FAST

TOMATO SAUTE

START TO FINISH: 30 MINUTES **MAKES:** 4 SERVINGS

- 2½ cups whole red grape tomatoes, yellow pear tomatoes, cherry tomatoes, and/or small yellow tomatoes
- 1 tablespoon olive oil

- ¼ cup finely chopped onion
- 1 clove garlic, minced
- 1 teaspoon snipped fresh thyme
- ¼ teaspoon salt
- ¼ teaspoon black pepper
- 2 ounces fresh mozzarella cheese, cut into ½-inch cubes

1 Halve the grape, pear, and/or cherry tomatoes or cut small yellow tomatoes into wedges; set aside. In a large skillet heat oil over medium heat. Add onion, garlic, and thyme; cook and stir for 2 to 3 minutes or until onion is tender. Add tomatoes, salt, and pepper. Cook and stir for 1 to 2 minutes or until tomatoes are just warmed. Remove from heat. Stir in mozzarella cheese.

PER ½ CUP: 98 cal., 7 g total fat (2 g sat. fat, 0 g trans fat), 11 mg chol., 241 mg sodium, 6 g carbo., 2 g fiber, 4 g pro. EXCHANGES: 1 Vegetable, ½ Medium-Fat Meat, 1 Fat

RATATOUILLE *(photo, page 591)*

START TO FINISH: 40 MINUTES **MAKES:** 4 SERVINGS

- ½ cup chopped onion (1 medium)
- 1 clove garlic, minced
- 1 tablespoon olive oil or vegetable oil
- 3 cups cubed, peeled eggplant
- 1 medium zucchini or yellow summer squash, halved lengthwise and cut into ¼-inch slices (1½ cups)
- 1 cup chopped, peeled tomatoes (2 medium) or one 14.5-ounce can diced tomatoes, drained
- ¾ cup chopped green sweet pepper (1 medium)
- 3 tablespoons dry white wine, chicken broth, or vegetable broth
- ¼ teaspoon salt
- ⅛ teaspoon black pepper
- 1 tablespoon snipped fresh basil or oregano

1 In a large skillet cook onion and garlic in hot oil over medium heat until onion is tender. Stir in eggplant, zucchini, tomatoes, sweet pepper, wine, salt, and black pepper. Bring to boiling; reduce heat. Simmer, covered, about 10 minutes or until vegetables are tender. Uncover and cook about 5 minutes more or until most of the liquid evaporates, stirring occasionally. Season to taste with additional salt and black pepper. Stir in basil just before serving.

PER ¾ CUP: 85 cal., 4 g total fat (1 g sat. fat, 0 g trans fat), 0 mg chol., 156 mg sodium, 11 g carbo., 4 g fiber, 2 g pro. EXCHANGES: 1½ Vegetable, 1 Fat

MASHED ROOT VEGETABLES

PREP: 25 MINUTES **COOK:** 20 MINUTES
BAKE: 15 MINUTES **OVEN:** 400°F
MAKES: 12 SERVINGS

- 6 pounds assorted root vegetables, such as carrots, parsnips, turnips, rutabagas, and/or red or yellow potatoes
- 6 cloves garlic, peeled
- 1 tablespoon kosher salt
- ½ cup milk, half-and-half, or light cream
- 2 tablespoons olive oil
- 2 tablespoons butter
- ½ to 1 teaspoon black pepper
- ⅓ cup snipped fresh Italian parsley, or 2 tablespoons snipped fresh Italian parsley and 1 tablespoon snipped fresh thyme, basil, oregano, or sage
- 1½ cups shredded Parmesan cheese (6 ounces)

1 Preheat oven to 400°F. Peel root vegetables; cut vegetables into 2- to 3-inch pieces. Place the root vegetables, garlic, and 1½ teaspoons of the salt in a 4- to 6-quart pot and fill with enough cold water to cover. Bring to boiling. Reduce heat and simmer, covered, for 20 minutes or until very tender. Meanwhile, in a small saucepan heat milk, olive oil, and butter until warm and butter melts.

2 Drain vegetables in a colander. Return to pan. Mash vegetables with a potato masher. Stir milk mixture, remaining salt, and the pepper into vegetables. Stir in Italian parsley and half of the cheese. Place mashed vegetable mixture in a 3-quart au gratin dish and spread evenly. Top with remaining cheese.

3 Bake, uncovered, about 15 minutes or until cheese melts and vegetables are heated through. If desired, preheat broiler; place dish 4 to 5 inches from the heat and broil about 2 minutes or until top browns.

PER 1⅓ CUPS: 206 cal., 8 g total fat (3 g sat. fat, 0 g trans fat), 13 mg chol., 727 mg sodium, 29 g carbo., 6 g fiber, 7 g pro. EXCHANGES: 1½ Vegetable, 1½ Starch, ½ Lean Meat, 1 Fat

BEST EVER

OVEN-FRIED VEGGIES

PREP: 25 MINUTES **BAKE:** 20 MINUTES
OVEN: 400°F **MAKES:** 6 SERVINGS

- 1 cup panko (Japanese-style bread crumbs)
- ½ cup grated Parmesan cheese
- 1 teaspoon dried oregano or thyme, crushed
- ½ teaspoon garlic powder
- ½ teaspoon black pepper
- 1 egg, lightly beaten
- 1 tablespoon milk
- 4 cups cauliflower florets, broccoli florets, whole fresh button mushrooms, and/or packaged peeled baby carrots
- ¼ cup butter or margarine, melted
  Easy Aïoli (page 543) or bottled ranch dressing (optional)

1 Preheat oven to 400°F. Lightly grease a 15×10×1-inch baking pan; set aside. In a resealable plastic bag combine panko, Parmesan cheese, oregano, garlic powder, and pepper. In a small bowl combine egg and milk.

2 Toss 1 cup of the vegetables in the egg mixture. Using a slotted spoon, transfer vegetables to the plastic bag. Seal bag; shake to coat with panko mixture. Place coated vegetables on prepared baking pan. Repeat with remaining vegetables, egg mixture, and panko mixture. Drizzle melted butter over vegetables.

3 Bake for 20 to 25 minutes or until golden, stirring twice. If desired, serve with Easy Aïoli.

PER ⅔ CUP: 169 cal., 11 g total fat (6 g sat. fat, 0 g trans fat), 62 mg chol., 222 mg sodium, 12 g carbo., 2 g fiber, 7 g pro. EXCHANGES: 1 Vegetable, ½ Starch, ½ Lean Meat, 2 Fat

FAST ▪ LOW FAT

APPLE-THYME SAUTE

START TO FINISH: 15 MINUTES **MAKES:** 4 SERVINGS

- 1 tablespoon butter
- 2 medium Granny Smith and/or Rome Beauty apples, cored and cut into ½-inch wedges (about 2½ cups)
- ⅓ cup sliced shallots (3)
- 1 tablespoon snipped fresh thyme or 1 teaspoon dried thyme, crushed
- 1 tablespoon lemon juice
- ¼ teaspoon salt
- ⅛ teaspoon black pepper

1 In a large skillet melt butter over medium heat. Add apples, shallots, and thyme. Cook, covered, about 5 minutes or just until apples are tender, stirring occasionally. Stir in lemon juice, salt, and pepper.

PER ¾ CUP: 84 cal., 3 g total fat (2 g sat. fat, 0 g trans fat), 8 mg chol., 168 mg sodium, 15 g carbo., 2 g fiber, 1 g pro. EXCHANGES: 1 Fruit, ½ Fat

AVOCADO WITH RED PEPPER SAUCE

START TO FINISH: 20 MINUTES **MAKES:** 4 SERVINGS

- ½ cup red pepper jelly
- ⅓ cup red wine vinegar
- 2 medium avocados, halved, seeded, peeled, and sliced
- ¼ cup pitted ripe olives, coarsely chopped
- ¼ cup chopped red or green sweet peppers
  Small sage leaves
  Red sweet pepper strips

1 In a small saucepan combine jelly and vinegar. Cook and stir over medium-low heat until jelly melts. Spoon 2 tablespoons of the jelly mixture on each of four salad plates. Arrange a few avocado slices on the jelly mixture on each plate. Top avocado slices with remaining jelly mixture. Sprinkle with chopped olives and sweet peppers. Garnish with sage and pepper strips.

PER SERVING: 320 cal., 16 g total fat (3 g sat. fat, 0 g trans fat), 0 mg chol., 92 mg sodium, 44 g carbo., 10 g fiber, 4 g pro. EXCHANGES: ½ Vegetable, 2½ Other Carbo., 3½ Fat

HONEY-BERRY COMPOTE

PREP: 15 MINUTES **CHILL:** 2 TO 24 HOURS
MAKES: 8 SERVINGS

- 2 teaspoons finely shredded orange peel
- ½ cup orange juice
- ¼ cup honey
- 1 tablespoon snipped fresh mint (optional)
- 2 cups halved green or red seedless grapes
- 2 cups fresh blueberries
- 2 cups halved fresh strawberries
- 2 cups fresh raspberries and/or blackberries

1 For dressing, in a medium bowl whisk together orange peel, orange juice, honey, and, if desired, the mint.

2 In a large serving bowl combine grapes, blueberries, and strawberries. Gently stir in dressing. Cover and chill for 2 to 24 hours. Just before serving stir in raspberries and/or blackberries.

PER 1 CUP: 103 cal., 1 g total fat (0 g sat. fat, 0 g trans fat), 0 mg chol., 2 mg sodium, 26 g carbo., 4 g fiber, 1 g pro. EXCHANGES: 1 Fruit, ½ Other Carbo.

A TANGY TRICK TO KEEP AVOCADOS FROM TURNING BROWN AFTER THEY'RE CUT, RUB A LITTLE LEMON JUICE, LIME JUICE, OR VINEGAR OVER THEM.

AVOCADO WITH RED PEPPER SAUCE

APPLE-GINGER POACHED PEARS

FIG AND WALNUT BAKED APPLES

PREP: 20 MINUTES **BAKE:** 25 MINUTES
COOL: 20 MINUTES **OVEN:** 350°F
MAKES: 6 TO 8 SERVINGS

- 2 pounds cooking apples, such as Rome Beauty, Golden Delicious, McIntosh, or Jonathan
- ½ cup snipped dried figs
- ⅓ cup apple juice
- ¼ cup chopped walnuts
- 2 tablespoons packed brown sugar
- 2 tablespoons butter, melted

1 Preheat oven to 350°F. Using an apple corer or a sharp knife, remove cores from the apples. Cut each apple into eight wedges; set aside.

2 In a large bowl stir together figs, apple juice, walnuts, brown sugar, and melted butter. Add apple wedges; toss to coat. Spoon mixture into a 2-quart square baking dish. Bake, uncovered, for 25 to 30 minutes or until apples are tender, stirring once. Cool slightly and stir before serving.

PER ¾ CUP: 199 cal., 7 g total fat (3 g sat. fat, 0 g trans fat), 10 mg chol., 32 mg sodium, 36 g carbo., 5 g fiber, 2 g pro.
EXCHANGES: 2 Fruit, ½ Other Carbo., 1 Fat

LOW FAT ▪ HEALTHY

APPLE-GINGER POACHED PEARS

PREP: 20 MINUTES **COOK:** 25 MINUTES
CHILL: 2 TO 24 HOURS **MAKES:** 8 SERVINGS

- 8 small to medium red and/or green pears
- 3 cups apple juice
- 2 cups cranberry juice
- 1 cup sugar
- 1 2-inch piece peeled fresh ginger, cut into strips
- 2 3-inch sticks cinnamon, broken

1 Cut thin slices from pear bottoms so pears stand up. Working through bottoms, use a melon baller to remove cores, leaving stems intact.

2 Meanwhile, in a 4-quart pot combine apple juice, cranberry juice, sugar, ginger, and cinnamon. Cook, uncovered, over medium heat until gently boiling, stirring occasionally to dissolve sugar. Add the pears. Return liquid just to boiling. Reduce heat. Simmer, covered, about 15 minutes or until pears are just tender. Remove from heat; cool pears slightly in syrup. Transfer pears and syrup to an extra-large bowl. Cover and chill 2 to 24 hours.

3 Drain pears, reserving 2 cups syrup. Place reserved syrup in a small saucepan. Bring to boiling; reduce heat. Simmer, uncovered, until syrup is reduced to ½ to ¾ cup. Spoon over pears.

PER PEAR: 156 cal., 0 g total fat, 0 mg chol., 6 mg sodium, 41 g carbo., 5 g fiber, 1 g pro.
EXCHANGES: 2½ Fruit

FAST ▪ LOW FAT ▪ HEALTHY

WARM SPICED PEACHES

PREP: 15 MINUTES **BAKE:** 10 MINUTES
OVEN: 350°F **MAKES:** 4 SERVINGS

- 3 cups peeled, pitted, and sliced peaches or pitted and sliced nectarines, plums, and/or apricots
- 2 teaspoons sugar
- ½ teaspoon finely shredded orange peel
- ½ teaspoon vanilla
- ¼ teaspoon ground cinnamon
- ⅛ teaspoon ground nutmeg
- 2 teaspoons snipped fresh basil or 1 teaspoon snipped fresh mint

1 Preheat oven to 350°F. In a medium bowl combine peaches, sugar, orange peel, vanilla, cinnamon, and nutmeg; toss gently to combine. Divide peach mixture among four 5-inch individual quiche dishes or 10-ounce custard cups.

2 Bake, covered, for 10 to 15 minutes or just until warm. Sprinkle with basil.

PER ½ CUP: 56 cal., 0 g total fat, 0 mg chol., 0 mg sodium, 13 g carbo., 2 g fiber, 1 g pro.
EXCHANGES: 1 Fruit

APPLES

Most apples are good for eating out of hand; the ones pictured below are also good for cooking. For sweet apples, choose Gala, Fuji, and Golden Delicious; for sweet-tart apples, try Braeburn, Jonagold, and Jonathan. For a mildly tart choice, go with Rome Beauty, and for tart, reach for Granny Smith.

Braeburn   Fuji   Gala   Golden Delicious

Granny Smith   Jonagold   Jonathan   Rome Beauty

GREENS

These greens are most often cooked before eating—try them in soups, stews, stir-fries, and as a side dish.

Kale

Swiss chard

Bok choy

Collard greens

Beet greens

Mustard greens

Turnip greens

SQUASH

Squash are divided into two categories—summer and winter. Summer squash have thin, edible skins and cook quickly. Winter squash have thick skins, hard seeds, and firm flesh that's usually deep yellow or orange. Because of the firmness of their flesh, winter squash need to cook longer than summer squash.

SUMMER SQUASH

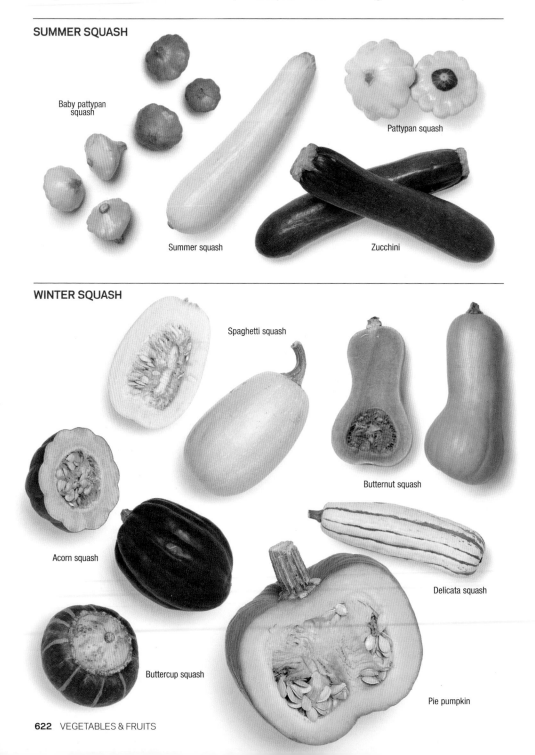

Baby pattypan squash

Pattypan squash

Summer squash

Zucchini

WINTER SQUASH

Spaghetti squash

Butternut squash

Acorn squash

Delicata squash

Buttercup squash

Pie pumpkin

POTATOES

Potatoes vary in texture, shape, and color, which can make some better suited to certain methods of cooking than others. See the tip on page 609 for suggestions on how to best serve some of these varieties.

Sweet potatoes

Long white potato

Russet potatoes

New potatoes

Fingerling potatoes

Yellow-flesh potatoes

Round white potatoes

Round red potatoes

ONIONS

Onions add so much flavor to cooking, it's no wonder many recipes start with chopping one. When a recipe simply calls for an onion, you can use yellow or white; otherwise, use the specific variety called for.

Green onions

Boiling onions

Pearl onions

Shallots

Yellow, white, and red onions

Leek

MUSHROOMS

These varieties add taste and texture to recipes. When a recipe calls for fresh mushrooms, use white button or cremini—choose the latter if you prefer a more earthy flavor.

Oyster

Shiitake

White button

Portobello
(baby)

Cremini

COOKING FRESH VEGETABLES

These charts offer basic cooking directions for fresh vegetables. The amounts given for each vegetable yield enough cooked vegetables for 4 servings, except where noted. To prepare fresh vegetables, wash with cool, clear tap water; scrub firm vegetables with a clean produce brush.

To steam vegetables, place a steamer basket in a saucepan. Add water to just below the bottom of the basket. Bring water to boiling. Add vegetables to steamer basket. Cover and reduce heat. Steam for the time specified in the chart or until vegetables reach desired doneness.

To microwave vegetables, use a microwave-safe baking dish or casserole and follow the directions in the chart, keeping in mind that times might vary depending on the microwave oven. Cover with waxed paper, vented plastic wrap, or the lid of the baking dish or casserole.

Vegetable and Amount	Preparation (Yield)	Conventional Cooking Directions	Microwave Cooking Directions
Artichokes 2 (10 ounces each) (2 servings)	Wash; trim stems. Cut off 1 inch from tops; snip off sharp leaf tips. Brush cut edges with lemon juice.	Cook, covered, in a large amount of boiling salted water for 20 to 30 minutes or until a leaf pulls out easily. (Or steam for 20 to 25 minutes.) Invert artichokes to drain.	Place in a casserole with 2 tablespoons water. Microwave, covered, on 100% power (high) for 7 to 9 minutes or until a leaf pulls out easily, rearranging artichokes once. Invert artichokes to drain.
Asparagus 1 pound (15 to 24 spears)	Wash and break off woody bases where spears snap easily; if desired, scrape off scales (see photos 1 and 2, page 594). Leave spears whole or cut into 1-inch pieces (2 cups pieces).	Cook, covered, in a small amount of boiling salted water for 3 to 5 minutes or until crisp-tender. (Or steam for 3 to 5 minutes.)	Place in a baking dish or casserole with 2 tablespoons water. Microwave, covered, on 100% power (high) for 2 to 4 minutes or until crisp-tender.

COOKING FRESH VEGETABLES *(continued)*

Vegetable and Amount	Preparation (Yield)	Conventional Cooking Directions	Microwave Cooking Directions
Beans: green, Italian green, purple, yellow wax 12 ounces	Wash; remove ends and strings. Leave whole or cut into 1-inch pieces (2½ cups pieces). For French-cut beans, slice lengthwise.	Cook, covered, in a small amount of boiling salted water for 10 to 15 minutes for whole or cut beans (5 to 10 minutes for French-cut beans) or until crisp-tender. (Or steam whole, cut, or French-cut beans for 18 to 22 minutes.)	Place in a casserole with 2 tablespoons water. Microwave, covered, on 100% power (high) for 8 to 12 minutes for whole or cut beans (7 to 10 minutes for French-cut beans) or until crisp-tender, stirring once.
Beets 4 medium (1 pound)	For whole beets, cut off all but 1 inch of stems and roots; wash. Do not peel. Or peel beets; cube or slice (2¾ cups cubes).	Cook, covered, in enough boiling salted water to cover for 35 to 45 minutes for whole beets (about 20 minutes for cubed or sliced beets) or until tender. Slip skins off whole beets.	Place in a casserole with 2 tablespoons water. Microwave cubed or sliced beets, covered, on 100% power (high) for 9 to 12 minutes or until tender, stirring once.
Broccoli 1 pound	Wash; remove outer leaves and tough parts of stalks. Cut lengthwise into spears or cut into 1-inch florets (3½ cups florets).	Cook, covered, in a small amount of boiling salted water for 8 to 10 minutes or until crisp-tender. (Or steam for 8 to 10 minutes.)	Place in a baking dish with 2 tablespoons water. Microwave, covered, on 100% power (high) for 5 to 8 minutes or until crisp-tender, rearranging or stirring once.
Brussels sprouts 12 ounces	Trim stems and remove any wilted outer leaves; wash. Cut large sprouts in half lengthwise (3 cups).	Cook, covered, in enough boiling salted water to cover for 10 to 12 minutes or until crisp-tender. (Or steam for 10 to 15 minutes.)	Place in a casserole with ¼ cup water. Microwave, covered, on 100% power (high) for 5 to 7 minutes or until crisp-tender, stirring once.
Cabbage Half of a 1½-pound head	Remove wilted outer leaves; wash. Cut into 4 wedges or coarsely chop (3 cups coarsely chopped).	Cook, uncovered, in a small amount of boiling water for 2 minutes. Cover; cook for 6 to 8 minutes more for wedges (3 to 5 minutes for pieces) or until crisp-tender. (Or steam wedges for 10 to 12 minutes.)	Place in a baking dish or casserole with 2 tablespoons water. Microwave, covered, on 100% power (high) for 9 to 11 minutes for wedges (4 to 6 minutes for pieces) or until crisp-tender, rearranging or stirring once.
Carrots 1 pound	Wash, trim, and peel or scrub, if necessary. Cut standard-size carrots into ¼-inch slices or into strips (2½ cups slices) or measure 3½ cups packaged peeled baby carrots.	Cook, covered, in a small amount of boiling salted water for 7 to 9 minutes for slices (4 to 6 minutes for strips, 8 to 10 minutes for baby carrots) or until crisp-tender. (Or steam slices or baby carrots for 8 to 10 minutes or strips for 5 to 7 minutes.)	Place in a casserole with 2 tablespoons water. Microwave, covered, on 100% power (high) for 7 to 10 minutes for slices (5 to 7 minutes for strips, 7 to 9 minutes for baby carrots) or until crisp-tender, stirring once.
Cauliflower 12 ounces florets or 1½-pound head	Wash; remove leaves and woody stem. Leave whole or break into florets (3 cups florets).	Cook, covered, in a small amount of boiling salted water for 10 to 15 minutes for head (8 to 10 minutes for florets) or until crisp-tender. (Or steam head or florets for 8 to 12 minutes.)	Place in a casserole with 2 tablespoons water. Microwave, covered, on 100% power (high) for 9 to 11 minutes for head (7 to 10 minutes for florets) or until crisp-tender, turning or stirring once.
Corn 4 ears	Remove husks. Scrub with a stiff brush to remove silks; rinse. Cut kernels from cob (2 cups kernels).	Cook, covered, in a small amount of boiling salted water for 4 minutes. (Or steam for 4 to 5 minutes.)	Place in a casserole with 2 tablespoons water. Microwave, covered, on 100% power (high) for 5 to 6 minutes, stirring once.

COOKING FRESH VEGETABLES (continued)

Vegetable and Amount	Preparation (Yield)	Conventional Cooking Directions	Microwave Cooking Directions
Corn on the cob (1 ear equals 1 serving)	Remove husks from fresh ears of corn. Scrub with a stiff brush to remove silks; rinse.	Cook, covered, in enough boiling lightly salted water to cover for 5 to 7 minutes or until kernels are tender.	Wrap each ear in waxed paper; place on microwave-safe paper towels in the microwave. Microwave on 100% power (high) for 3 to 5 minutes for 1 ear, 5 to 7 minutes for 2 ears, or 9 to 12 minutes for 4 ears, rearranging once.
Greens: beet or chard 12 ounces	Wash thoroughly in cold water; drain well. Remove stems; trim bruised leaves. Tear into pieces (12 cups torn).	Cook, covered, in a small amount of boiling salted water for 8 to 10 minutes or until tender.	Not recommended.
Greens: kale, mustard, or turnip 12 ounces	Wash thoroughly in cold water; drain well. Remove stems; trim bruised leaves. Tear into pieces (12 cups torn).	Cook, covered, in a small amount of boiling salted water for 20 to 25 minutes or until tender.	Not recommended.
Kohlrabi 1 pound	Cut off leaves; wash. Peel; chop or cut into strips (3 cups strips).	Cook, covered, in a small amount of boiling salted water for 4 to 6 minutes or until crisp-tender. (Or steam about 6 minutes.)	Place in a casserole with 2 tablespoons water. Microwave, covered, on 100% power (high) for 5 to 7 minutes or until crisp-tender, stirring once.
Mushrooms 1 pound	Wipe mushrooms with a damp towel or paper towel. Leave whole or slice (6 cups slices).	Cook sliced mushrooms in 2 tablespoons butter or margarine about 5 minutes. (Or steam whole mushrooms for 10 to 12 minutes.)	Place in a casserole with 2 tablespoons butter or margarine. Microwave, covered, on 100% power (high) for 4 to 6 minutes, stirring twice.
Okra 8 ounces	Wash; cut off stems. Cut into ½-inch slices (2 cups slices).	Cook, covered, in a small amount of boiling salted water for 8 to 10 minutes or until tender.	Place in a casserole with 2 tablespoons water. Microwave, covered, on 100% power (high) for 4 to 6 minutes or until tender, stirring once.
Onions: boiling or pearl 8 ounces boiling onions (10 to 12) 8 ounces pearl onions (24 to 30)	Peel boiling onions before cooking; peel pearl onions after cooking (2 cups).	Cook, covered, in a small amount of boiling salted water for 10 to 12 minutes (boiling onions) or 8 to 10 minutes (pearl onions). (Or steam boiling onions for 12 to 15 minutes or pearl onions 10 to 12 minutes.)	Place in a casserole with 2 tablespoons water. Microwave, covered, on 100% power (high) for 3 to 5 minutes.
Parsnips 12 ounces	Wash, trim, and peel or scrub. Cut into ¼-inch slices (2 cups slices).	Cook, covered, in a small amount of boiling salted water for 7 to 9 minutes or until tender. (Or steam for 8 to 10 minutes.)	Place in a casserole with 2 tablespoons water. Microwave, covered, on 100% power (high) for 4 to 6 minutes or until tender, stirring once.
Peas, edible pod: snow peas or sugar snap peas 6 ounces	Remove strings and tips; wash (2 cups).	Cook, covered, in a small amount of boiling salted water for 2 to 4 minutes or until crisp-tender. (Or steam for 2 to 4 minutes.)	Place in a casserole with 2 tablespoons water. Microwave, covered, on 100% power (high) for 2 to 4 minutes or until crisp-tender.

COOKING FRESH VEGETABLES *(continued)*

Vegetable and Amount	Preparation (Yield)	Conventional Cooking Directions	Microwave Cooking Directions
Peas, green 2 pounds	Shell and wash (3 cups shelled).	Cook, covered, in a small amount of boiling salted water for 10 to 12 minutes or until crisp-tender. (Or steam for 12 to 15 minutes.)	Place in a casserole with 2 tablespoons water. Microwave, covered, on 100% power (high) 6 to 8 minutes or until crisp-tender, stirring once.
Potatoes 1 pound	Wash, peel, and remove eyes, sprouts, or green areas. Cut into quarters or cubes (2¾ cups cubes).	Cook, covered, in enough boiling salted water to cover for 20 to 25 minutes for quarters (15 minutes for cubes) or until tender. (Or steam about 20 minutes.)	Place in a casserole with 2 tablespoons water. Microwave, covered, on 100% power (high) for 8 to 10 minutes or until tender, stirring once.
Rutabagas 1 pound	Wash and peel. Cut into ½-inch cubes (3 cups cubes).	Cook, covered, in a small amount of boiling salted water for 18 to 20 minutes or until tender. (Or steam for 18 to 20 minutes.)	Place in a casserole with 2 tablespoons water. Microwave, covered, on 100% power (high) 11 to 13 minutes or until tender, stirring 3 times.
Spinach 1 pound	Wash and drain; remove stems and tear into pieces (12 cups torn).	Cook, covered, in a small amount of boiling salted water for 3 to 5 minutes or until tender; begin timing when steam forms. (Or steam for 3 to 5 minutes.)	Not recommended.
Squash: acorn or delicata One 1¼-pound (2 servings)	Wash, halve, and remove seeds.	Place squash halves, cut sides down, in a baking dish. Bake in a 350°F oven for 45 to 50 minutes or until tender.	Place, cut sides down, in a baking dish with 2 tablespoons water. Microwave, covered, on 100% power (high) for 7 to 10 minutes or until tender, rearranging once. Let stand, covered, for 5 minutes.
Squash: buttercup or butternut One 1½-pound or a 1½-pound piece	Wash, halve lengthwise, and remove seeds.	Place squash halves, cut sides down, in a baking dish. Bake in a 350°F oven for 45 to 50 minutes or until tender.	Place, cut sides down, in a baking dish with 2 tablespoons water. Microwave, covered, on 100% power (high) for 9 to 12 minutes or until tender, rearranging once.
Squash: pattypan, yellow summer, or zucchini 12 ounces	Wash; do not peel. Cut off ends. Cut into ¼-inch slices (3 cups slices) or leave pattypan whole.	Cook, covered, in a small amount of boiling salted water for 3 to 5 minutes or until crisp-tender. (Or steam for 4 to 6 minutes.)	Place in a casserole with 2 tablespoons water. Microwave, covered, on 100% power (high) for 4 to 5 minutes or until crisp-tender, stirring twice.
Squash, spaghetti Half of a 3-pound or a 1½-pound piece	Wash and remove seeds.	Place, cut sides down, in a baking dish. Bake in a 350°F oven for 45 to 50 minutes or until tender.	Place, cut sides down, in a baking dish with ¼ cup water. Microwave, covered, on 100% power (high) for about 15 minutes or until tender.
Sweet potatoes 1 pound	Wash, peel, and cut off woody portions and ends. Cut into quarters for microwave) or into cubes (2¾ cups cubes).	Cook, covered, in enough boiling salted water to cover for 25 to 30 minutes or until tender. (Or steam for 20 to 25 minutes.)	Place in a casserole with ½ cup water. Microwave, covered, on 100% power (high) for 10 to 13 minutes or until tender, stirring once.
Turnips 1 pound	Wash and peel. Cut into ½-inch cubes or strips (2¾ cups cubes).	Cook, covered, in a small amount of boiling salted water for 10 to 12 minutes or until tender. (Or steam for 10 to 15 minutes.)	Place in a casserole with 2 tablespoons water. Microwave, covered, on 100% power (high) 10 to 12 minutes or until tender; stir once.

SELECTING FRESH VEGETABLES

These charts offer specific guidelines for selecting and storing a variety of fresh vegetables. In general, choose vegetables that are plump, crisp, brightly colored, and heavy for their size. Avoid any that are bruised, shriveled, moldy, or blemished. For cooking information, see charts on pages 624–627.

Vegetable	Peak Season	How to Choose	How to Store
Asparagus	Available March through June with peak season in April and May; available year-round in some areas.	Choose crisp, firm, straight stalks with good color and compact, closed tips. If possible, select spears that are the same size for even cooking.	Wrap the bases of fresh asparagus spears in wet paper towels and place in a plastic bag in the refrigerator for up to 3 days.
Beans, green: snap or string	Available April through September; available year-round in some areas.	Select fresh beans that are brightly colored and crisp. Avoid those that are bruised, scarred, or rusty with brown spots or streaks. Bulging, leathery beans are old.	Refrigerate in a covered container for up to 5 days.
Beets	Available year-round with peak season from June through October.	Select small or medium beets; large beets tend to be pithy, tough, and less sweet.	Trim beet greens, leaving 1 to 2 inches of stem. Do not cut the long root. Store unwashed beets in an open container in the refrigerator for up to 1 week.
Bok choy	Available year-round.	Look for firm, white, bulblike bases with deep green leaves. Avoid soft spots on base or wilted, shriveled leaves.	Refrigerate in a plastic bag and use within 3 days.
Broccoli	Available year-round with peak season from October through May.	Look for firm stalks with tightly packed, deep green or purplish green heads. Avoid heads that are light green or yellowing.	Keep unwashed broccoli in a covered container in the refrigerator for up to 4 days.
Brussels sprouts	Available year-round with peak season from August through April.	Pick out the smaller sprouts that are vivid green; they will taste the sweetest. Large ones might be bitter.	Refrigerate in a covered container for up to 2 days.
Cabbage: green, napa, red, or savoy	Available year-round.	The head should feel heavy for its size, and its leaves should be unwithered, brightly colored, and free of brown spots.	Refrigerate in a covered container for up to 5 days.
Carrots	Available year-round.	Select straight, rigid, bright orange carrots without cracks.	Refrigerate in a plastic bag for up to 2 weeks.
Cauliflower	Available year-round.	Look for solid, heavy heads with bright green leaves. Avoid those with brown bruises, yellowed leaves, or speckled appearance.	Refrigerate in a covered container for up to 4 days.
Celery	Available year-round.	Look for crisp ribs that are firm, unwilted, and unblemished.	Refrigerate in a plastic bag or container for up to 2 weeks.
Cucumbers	Available year-round with peak season from late May through early September.	Select firm cucumbers without shriveled or soft spots. Edible wax sometimes is added to prevent moisture loss.	Keep salad cucumbers in refrigerator for up to 10 days. Pickling cucumbers should be picked and used the same day.
Eggplant	Available year-round with peak season from August through September.	Look for plump, glossy eggplants that have fresh-looking, mold-free caps. Skip any that are scarred or bruised.	Refrigerate whole eggplants for up to 2 days.

SELECTING FRESH VEGETABLES *(continued)*

Vegetable	Peak Season	How to Choose	How to Store
Fennel	Available October through April; available year-round in some areas.	Look for crisp, clean bulbs without brown spots or blemishes. Tops should be bright green and fresh looking.	Refrigerate, tightly wrapped, for up to 5 days.
Greens, cooking: beet, chard, collard, kale, mustard, turnip	Most available year-round with peak season in winter months; peak season for chard is during the summer months.	Look for crisp or tender leaves that are brightly or richly colored. Avoid wilted or yellowing leaves.	Cut away center stalk of kale leaves. Refrigerate most greens in plastic bag for up to 3 days; refrigerate mustard greens for up to 1 week.
Leeks	Available year-round.	Look for leeks that have clean white ends and fresh green tops.	Refrigerate, tightly wrapped, for up to 5 days.
Mushrooms (all varieties)	Available year-round; morel mushrooms available April through June.	Mushrooms should be firm, fresh, plump, and bruise-free. Size is a matter of preference. Avoid spotted or slimy mushrooms.	Store unwashed mushrooms in the refrigerator for up to 2 days. A paper bag or, if packaged, the original packaging lets them breathe so they stay firm longer.
Okra	Available year-round with peak season from May through September.	Look for small, crisp, brightly colored pods without brown spots or blemishes. Avoid shriveled pods.	Refrigerate, tightly wrapped, for up to 3 days.
Onions (all varieties)	Variety determines availability. Some varieties, such as white, red, pearl, and boiling onions, are available year-round. Various sweet onion varieties, such as Vidalia and Walla Walla, are available on and off throughout the year.	Select dry bulb onions that are firm, free from blemishes, and not sprouting. They should have papery outer skins and short necks.	Keep in a cool, dry, well-ventilated place for several weeks.
Peas, Pea pods	Peas: Available January through June with peak season from March through May. Pea pods: Available February through August.	Select fresh, crisp, brightly colored peas, snow peas, or sugar snap peas. Avoid shriveled pods or those with brown spots.	Store, tightly wrapped, in the refrigerator for up to 3 days.
Peppers: hot or sweet	Available year-round.	Fresh peppers, whether sweet or hot, should be brightly colored and have a good shape for the variety. Avoid shriveled, bruised, or broken peppers.	Refrigerate in a covered container for up to 5 days.
Potatoes	Available year-round.	Look for clean potatoes that have smooth, unblemished skins. They should be firm and have a shape that is typical for their variety. Avoid those that have green spots or are soft, moldy, or shriveled.	Store for several weeks in a dark, well-ventilated, cool place that is slightly humid but not wet. Do not refrigerate—potatoes tend to get sweet at cold temperatures.
Root vegetables: parsnips, rutabagas, or turnips	Available year-round. Parsnips: Peak season from November through March. Rutabagas: Peak season from September through March. Turnips: Peak season from October through March.	Choose vegetables that are smooth-skinned and heavy for their size. Sometimes parsnips, rutabagas, and turnips are covered with a wax coating to extend storage; cut off this coating before cooking.	Refrigerate for up to 2 weeks.

SELECTING FRESH VEGETABLES *(continued)*

Vegetable	Peak Season	How to Choose	How to Store
Spinach	Available year-round.	Leaves should be crisp and free of moisture. Avoid spinach with broken or bruised leaves.	Rinse leaves in cold water and thoroughly dry. Place the leaves in a storage container with a paper towel and refrigerate for up to 3 days.
Squash, winter	Some varieties available year-round with peak season from September through March.	Choose firm squash that are heavy for their size. Avoid those with soft spots.	Store whole squash in a cool, dry place for up to 2 months. Refrigerate cut squash, wrapped in plastic, for up to 4 days.
Sweet potatoes	Available year-round with peak season from October through January.	Choose small to medium smooth-skinned potatoes that are firm and free of soft spots.	Store in a cool, dry, dark place for up to 1 week.
Tomatoes	Available year-round with peak season from June through early September.	Pick well-shaped, plump, fairly firm tomatoes. Ripe tomatoes yield to slight pressure and smell like a tomato.	Store at room temperature for up to 3 days. Do not store tomatoes in the refrigerator because they lose their flavor.
Zucchini, Summer squash	Some varieties available year-round with peak season from June through September.	It is almost impossible for tender-skinned zucchini to be blemish-free, but look for small ones that are firm and free of cuts and soft spots.	Refrigerate squash, tightly wrapped, for up to 5 days.

SELECTING FRESH FRUITS

These charts offer specific guidelines for selecting and storing a variety of fresh fruits. In general, look for fruits that are plump, tender, and bright in color. Fruits should be heavy for their size and free from mold, mildew, bruises, cuts, or other blemishes. Some fruits are picked and shipped while still firm, so they might need additional ripening (see tip, page, 593).

Fruit	Peak Season	How To Choose	How to Store
Apples	Available year-round with peak season September through November.	Select firm apples, free from bruises or soft spots. Apples are sold ready for eating. Select variety according to intended use.	Refrigerate for up to 6 weeks; store bulk apples in a cool, moist place. Don't store near foods with strong odors that can be absorbed.
Apricots	Available May through July.	Look for plump, fairly firm apricots with deep yellow or yellowish orange skin.	Ripen firm fruit as directed on page 593 until it yields to gentle pressure and is golden in color. Refrigerate ripened fruit for up to 2 days.
Avocados	Available year-round.	Avoid bruised fruit with gouges or broken skin. Soft avocados can be used immediately (and are especially good for guacamole).	Ripen firm fruit as directed on page 593 until it yields to gentle pressure in cradled hands. Store ripened fruit in the refrigerator for up to 3 days.
Bananas	Available year-round.	Choose bananas at any stage of ripeness, from green to yellow.	Ripen at room temperature until they have a bright yellow color. Overripe bananas are brown.

SELECTING FRESH FRUITS *(continued)*

Fruit	Peak Season	How To Choose	How to Store
Berries	Blackberries: Available June through August. Blueberries: Available late May through October. Boysenberries: Available late June through early August. Raspberries: Available year-round with peak season from May through September. Strawberries: Available year-round with peak season from April through June.	If picking your own, select berries that separate easily from their stems.	Refrigerate berries in a single layer, loosely covered, for up to 2 days. Rinse just before using.
Cantaloupe	Available year-round with peak season from June through September.	Select cantaloupe that has a delicate, sweet, aromatic scent; look for cream-color netting over rind that is yellowish green or gray. Melon should feel heavy for its size.	Ripen as directed on page 593. Refrigerate ripened, whole melon up to 4 days. Refrigerate cut fruit in a covered container or tightly wrapped for up to 2 days.
Carambolas (Star fruit)	Available late August through February.	Look for firm, shiny-skinned golden fruit. Some browning on the edge of the fins is natural and does not affect the taste.	Ripen as directed on page 593. Refrigerate ripened fruit in a covered container or tightly wrapped for up to 1 week.
Cherries	Sweet: Available May through August with peak season in June and July. Tart: Available June through August with peak season in June and July.	Select firm, brightly colored fruit.	Refrigerate in a covered container for 2 to 3 days.
Cranberries	Available October through December with peak season in November.	Fruit is ripe when sold. Avoid soft, shriveled, or bruised cranberries.	Refrigerate for up to 4 weeks or freeze for up to 1 year.
Grapefruit	Available year-round.	Choose fully colored grapefruit with a nicely rounded shape. Juicy grapefruit will be heavy for its size.	Refrigerate for up to 2 weeks.
Grapes	Available year-round.	Look for plump grapes without bruises, soft spots, or mold. Bloom (a frosty white cast) is typical and doesn't affect quality.	Refrigerate in a covered container for up to 1 week.
Honeydew melon	Available year-round with peak season from June through September.	Choose one that is firm and a creamy yellow color with a sweet, aromatic scent. Avoid wet, dented, bruised, or cracked fruit.	Ripen as directed on page 593. Refrigerate ripened whole melon up to 4 days. Refrigerate cut fruit in a covered container or tightly wrapped for up to 3 days.
Kiwifruits	Available year-round.	Choose fruit that is free of wrinkles, bruises, and soft spots.	Ripen firm fruit as directed on page 593 until skin yields to gentle pressure; refrigerate for up to 1 week.
Lemons, Limes	Available year-round.	Look for firm, well-shaped fruit with smooth, brightly colored skin. Avoid fruit with shriveled skin.	Refrigerate for up to 2 weeks.
Mangoes	Available April through September with peak season from June through July.	Look for fully colored fruit that smells fruity and feels fairly firm when pressed.	Ripen firm fruit as directed on page 593 and refrigerate for up to 5 days.

SELECTING FRESH FRUITS *(continued)*

Fruit	Peak Season	How to Choose	How to Store
Oranges	Available year-round.	Choose oranges that are firm and heavy for their size. Brown specks or a slight greenish tinge on the surface of an orange will not affect the eating quality.	Refrigerate for up to 2 weeks.
Papayas	Available year-round.	Choose fruit that is at least half yellow and feels somewhat soft when pressed. The skin should be smooth.	Ripen as directed on page 593 until yellow. Refrigerate in a covered container for 1 to 2 days.
Peaches, Nectarines	Peaches: Available May through September. Nectarines: Available May through September with peak season in July and August.	Look for fruit with a golden yellow skin and no tinges of green. Ripe fruit should yield slightly to gentle pressure.	Ripen as directed on page 593. Refrigerate ripened fruit for up to 5 days.
Pears	Available year-round.	Skin color is not always an indicator of ripeness because the color of some varieties does not change much as the pears ripen. Look for pears without bruises or cuts. Choose a variety according to intended use.	Ripen as directed on page 593 until skin yields to gentle pressure at the stem end. Refrigerate ripened fruit for several days.
Pineapple	Available year-round with peak season from March through July.	Look for a plump pineapple with a sweet, aromatic smell. It should be slightly soft to the touch, heavy for its size, and have deep green leaves. Avoid those with soft spots.	Refrigerate for up to 2 days. Cut pineapple lasts a few more days if placed in a tightly covered container and refrigerated.
Plantains	Available year-round.	Choose undamaged plantains. Slight bruises are acceptable because the skin is tough enough to protect the fruit. Choose plantains at any stage of ripeness, from green to dark brown or black, depending on intended use.	Ripen as directed on page 593. Color will change from green to yellow-brown to black. Black plantains are fully ripe. The starchy fruit must be cooked before eating.
Plums	Available May through October with peak season in June and July.	Find firm, plump, well-shaped fresh plums. Each should give slightly when gently pressed. Bloom (light gray cast) on the skin is natural and doesn't affect quality.	Ripen as directed on page 593. Refrigerate ripened fruit for up to 3 days.
Rhubarb	Available February through June with peak season from April through June.	Look for crisp stalks that are firm and tender. Avoid rhubarb that looks wilted or has very thick stalks.	Wrap stalks tightly in plastic wrap and refrigerate for up to 5 days.
Watermelon	Available May through September with peak season from mid-June through late August.	Choose watermelon that has a hard, smooth rind and is heavy for its size. Avoid wet, dented, bruised, or cracked fruit.	Watermelon does not ripen after it is picked. Refrigerate whole melon for up to 4 days. Refrigerate cut fruit in a covered container or tightly wrapped for up to 3 days.

GLOSSARY

AL DENTE: To tell when pasta is done, taste it. It should be tender but slightly firm, a stage Italians call al dente (al-DEN-tay), "to the tooth."

BASTE: To moisten foods during cooking or grilling with fats or seasoned liquids to add flavor and prevent drying. Make sure to clean brushes and basters between useage as they could be sources of bacteria if contaminated with uncooked or undercooked meat and poultry juices, then allowed to sit at room temperature.

BIAS-SLICE: To slice a food at a 45-degree angle.

BLANCH: To partially cook fruits, vegetables, or nuts in boiling water or steam to intensify and set color and flavor. This is an important step in preparing fruits and vegetables for freezing. Blanching also helps loosen skins from tomatoes and peaches.

BLEND: To combine two or more ingredients by hand or with an electric mixer or blender until smooth and uniform in texture, flavor, and color.

BOIL: To cook food in liquid at a temperature that causes bubbles to form in the liquid and rise in a steady pattern, breaking at the surface. A rolling boil occurs when liquid is boiling so vigorously that the bubbles can't be stirred down. Also see Simmer, page 634.

BRAISE: To cook food slowly in a small amount of liquid in a tightly covered pan on the stovetop or in the oven. Braising is recommended for less-tender cuts of meat.

BROWN: To cook food in a skillet, broiler, or oven to add flavor and aroma and develop a rich, desirable color on the outside.

BUTTERFLY: To split food such as shrimp or pork chops through the middle without completely separating the halves. Opened flat, the split halves resemble a butterfly.

CHEESECLOTH: A thin, 100-percent-cotton cloth with a fine or coarse weave. In cooking, cheesecloth is used to bundle herbs, strain liquids, and wrap rolled meats. Look for it in supermarkets and specialty cookware shops.

CHILL: To cool food to below room temperature in the refrigerator or over ice. When recipes in this book call for chilling foods, it should be done in the refrigerator.

COAT (VERB): To evenly cover food with crumbs, flour, or a batter before cooking.

CREAM (VERB): To beat a fat, such as butter or shortening, either alone or with sugar to a light, fluffy consistency. May be done by hand with a wooden spoon or with an electric mixer. This process incorporates air into the fat so baked products have a lighter texture and more volume.

CRIMP: To pinch or press pastry dough together using your fingers, a fork, or another utensil. Usually done for a piecrust edge. Also see Flute.

CRISP-TENDER: The state of vegetables that have been cooked until just tender but still somewhat crunchy. At this stage a fork can be inserted into the vegetables with a little pressure.

CURDLE: To cause semisolid pieces of coagulated protein to develop in a dairy product. This can occur when food such as milk or sour cream is heated to too high a temperature or is combined with an acidic food, such as lemon juice.

DASH: A dash is a small amount between $\frac{1}{16}$ and $\frac{1}{8}$ of a teaspoon.

DOUGH: A mixture of flour and other ingredients that's stiff but pliable enough to work with your hands. Unlike batter, dough is too stiff to pour.

DREDGE: To coat food, either before or after cooking, with a dry ingredient, such as flour, cornmeal, or sugar.

DUST: To sprinkle food with a dry ingredient, such as flour, cornmeal, or powdered sugar, before or after cooking.

FLAKE: To gently break food into small, flat pieces.

FLOUR (VERB): To coat or dust a food or utensil with flour. Food may be floured before cooking to add texture and improve browning. Baking utensils such as pans sometimes are floured to prevent sticking.

FLUTE: See page 446.

FOLD: See page 19.

GARNISH: To add visual appeal to a finished dish.

GIBLETS: The edible internal organs of poultry, including the liver, heart, and gizzard. (The neck is not part of the giblets, though it is sometimes packaged with them.) Giblets sometimes are used to make gravy.

GLAZE: A thin, glossy coating.

GREASE: To coat a utensil, such as a baking pan or skillet, with a thin layer of fat or oil. A pastry brush works well for this. Also refers to fat released from meat and poultry during cooking.

GRIND: To mechanically cut food into smaller pieces, usually with a food grinder or food processor.

ICE (VERB): To drizzle or spread with a thin frosting.

JELLY ROLL: A dessert made by spreading a filling on a sponge cake and rolling it up into a log shape. When other foods are shaped "jelly-roll-style," it refers to rolling them into a log shape with fillings inside.

KNEAD: To work dough with the heels of your hands in a pressing and folding motion until it becomes smooth and elastic. This is an essential step in many yeast breads.

MARBLE: To gently swirl one food into another. Marbling usually is done with light and dark cake or cookie batters.

MARINATE: To soak food in a marinade. When marinating, do not use a metal container that can react with acidic ingredients to give food an off flavor. Always marinate foods in the refrigerator, never on the countertop. To reduce cleanup, contain the food you are marinating in a plastic bag set in a bowl or dish. Discard leftover marinade that has come in contact with raw meat. Or if it's to be used on cooked meat, bring leftover marinade to a rolling boil before using.

MOISTEN: To add enough liquid to a dry ingredient or mixture to make it damp but not runny.

PARBOIL: To boil food, such as a vegetable, only until it is partially cooked.

PARTIALLY SET: A mixture of gelatin and a liquid that has the consistency of unbeaten egg whites.

PINCH: The amount of a dry ingredient you can pinch between your finger and thumb.

PIPE: To force semisoft food, such as frosting or whipped cream, through a pastry bag.

PIT (VERB): To remove the seed from fruit.

PLUMP: To allow dried food, such as raisins, to soak in a liquid, which increases its volume.

POACH: To cook food by partially or completely submerging it in a simmering liquid.

POUND: To strike food with a heavy utensil to crush it or, in the case of meat or poultry, to break up connective tissue to tenderize or flatten it.

PROCESS: To preserve food at home by canning or to prepare food in a food processor.

PROOF: To allow a yeast dough to rise before baking. Proof also indicates the amount of alcohol present in distilled liquor.

PUREE: To process or mash food until it is as smooth as possible. This can be done using a blender, food processor, sieve, or food mill; also refers to the resulting mixture.

RECONSTITUTE: To bring concentrated or condensed food, such as frozen fruit juice, to its original strength by adding water.

REDUCE: To decrease the volume of a liquid by boiling it uncovered to cause evaporation. As moisture evaporates, the liquid thickens and flavor intensifies. The resulting liquid, called a reduction, can be used as a sauce or as the base of a sauce. When reducing liquids, use the pan size specified in the recipe because the surface area of the pan affects how quickly the liquid will evaporate.

RIND: The skin or outer coating—usually rather thick—of food such as melons or citrus fruits.

SCALD: To heat a liquid, often milk, to a temperature just below the boiling point, which is when tiny bubbles just begin to appear around the edge.

SCORE: To cut narrow slits, often in a diamond pattern, through the outer surface of a food to decorate it, tenderize it, help it absorb flavor, or allow fat to drain as it cooks.

SIEVE (VERB): To separate liquids from solids by pressing the mixture through a sieve.

SIFT: To put one or more dry ingredients, especially flour or powdered sugar, through a sifter or sieve to remove lumps.

SIMMER: To cook food in a liquid that is kept just below the boiling point; a liquid is simmering when a few bubbles form slowly and burst just before reaching the surface. See also Boil, page 633.

SKIM: To remove a substance such as fat or foam from the surface of a liquid such as homemade broth or stock. To skim fat from poultry or meat drippings, see page 488. To skim fat from broth, see page 557.

VEGETABLE OIL: An oil made from plant sources, such as vegetables, nuts, or seeds. Common types for general cooking include corn, soybean, canola, sunflower, safflower, peanut, and olive. For baking, oil cannot be used interchangeably with solid fat because oil does not hold air when beaten.

A

Aïoli, Easy, 543
Almonds
Almond Biscotti, 268
Almond Butter Frosting, *179*
Blondies, 275
Cherry-Almond Tart, *460*, 461
Chicken with Almond
Pan Sauce, 479
Cranberry-Almond Cereal Mix, 154
health benefits, 35
Romesco Sauce, *541*
Tilapia with Almond Butter, 318
Angel food cakes
Angel Food Cake, 177
Angel Food Ice Cream Cake, 176
Chocolate Angel Food Cake, 177
Orange Angel Food Sherbet
Cake, 176
Antipasti Platter, 40, *41*
Appetizers and snacks. *See also* Dips
and spreads
Antipasti Platter, 40, *41*
Apricot Sweet-and-Sour
Meatballs, 56
Bacon and Cracked Black Pepper
Biscuits, 128, *129*
Balsamic Shallot and Goat Cheese
Tart, 52, *53*
Brie en Croûte, 49
bruschetta variations, 40, *41*
Buffalo Wings, 56
Cheese and Chile Quesadillas, 54
Chicken Quesadillas, 54
Crab Tartlets, 44
Cranberry-Barbecue Meatballs, 56
Cranberry-Chipotle Meatballs, 56
Deviled Eggs, 43
Deviled Eggs, 10 to Try, *42*
Egg Rolls, 62
Fajita-Style Quesadillas, 54
Flamin' Cajun Riblets, 551
Fried Chicken Tenders, 367
Gingery Apricot-Glazed
Pork Ribs, 55
Lemon-Ginger-Marinated
Shrimp Bowl, 57
Make-It-Mine Party Mix, *61*
Marinated Olives, 40
Mozzarella Cheese Sticks, *366*
nachos variations, 54
Onion Rings, 60
Potato Skins, 58
Praline-Topped Brie, 49
Prosciutto-Wrapped Scallops with
Roasted Red Pepper
Aïoli, 58, *59*
Sausage and Meatball Bites, 553
Savory Nuts, 60
serving amounts, 39
Shrimp Spring Rolls with
Chimichurri Sauce, *37*, 62
Spicy Marinated Shrimp Bowl, 57
Spinach Phyllo Triangles, 52
stuffed mushrooms variations, 69
Sweet-and-Savory
Potato Chips, 366
Vegetarian Spring Rolls, 62
Warm Edamame, 60
Wrap-and-Roll Basil Pinwheels, 43
Zesty Shrimp Cocktail, 56
Apple butter
Apple Butter, *210*
Apple Butter-Glazed Ham, 406
Apple-Pear Butter, 210
Caramel Apple Butter, 210
Apple cider or juice. *See* Cider

Apples
Apple Baked Beans, 73
apple butter variations, *210*
Apple Cake with Buttery Caramel
Sauce, *162*
Apple Chicken Salad, *505*
Apple Crisp, 288
Apple Dumplings, 290
Apple Martinis, *99*
Apple-Pear Praline Pie, *449*
applesauce variations, 208–209
Apple-Thyme Saute, 618
Balsamic-Glazed Flank Steak with
Fall Fruit Salsa, *392*
Beet and Apple Salad, 517
best varieties for cooking, 621
canning, 209
Caramel Apples, 194
Caramel Apples, 10 to Try, *195*
Caramel Apple Tarts, 463
Cranberry Strudel Rolls, 292
Curried Pork and Apple Stew, *576*
Danish Pastry Apple Bars, 282
Fig and Walnut Baked Apples, 620
freezing, 209
Pan-Seared Duck with Apples, 491
preventing discoloration of, 79
selecting, 630
Smoky Apple Mac 'n' Cheese, *237*
Waldorf Salad, 518
Applesauce, 208
Applesauce Bars, 279
Spiced Applesauce, 209
Very Berry Applesauce, 209
Appliances, small, 11
Apricots
Apricot Baked Beans, 73
Apricot Freezer Jam, 215
Apricot-Glazed Holiday Hens, 490
Apricot Meatball Bites, *552*
Apricot-Mustard Meat Loaf, 395
Apricot-Pecan Stuffing, 553
Apricot Sweet-and-Sour
Meatballs, 56
canning and freezing, 209
selecting, 630
Artichokes
Artichoke-Olive Filled French
Omelet, 142, *143*
Artichokes with Herb-Butter
Sauce, 594
Artichokes with Lemon-Mustard
Mayo, 594
Baked Risotto with Sausage and
Artichokes, 226
Cheesy Artichoke and Spinach
Dip, 48
Chicken with Parmesan Rice, 483
cooking methods, 624
Gorgonzola-Sauced Tortellini with
Artichokes, 434
Mediterranean Chicken Salad, *505*
Spinach-Artichoke Dip, 551
Asiago Popovers, 130
Asian Beef Salad, 244
Asian-Style Pork Ribs,
Oven-Roasted, 404
Asparagus
Asparagus Deviled Eggs, *42*
Asparagus-Ham Filled French
Omelet, 142, *143*
Asparagus-Snap Pea Stir-Fry, 595
Chicken and Vegetable
Tetrazzini, 233
cooking methods, 624
freezing, 219
Gingery Vegetable-Tofu
Stir-Fry, 71

Grilled Salmon and Asparagus with
Garden Mayonnaise, *356*, 357
Lemon-Asparagus Risotto, *63*, 77
Potato and Ham Bake, 227
preparing, 594
Roasted Asparagus, 594
Salmon and Asparagus
Chowder, 579
Salmon and Asparagus-Sauced
Pasta, 430
selecting, 628
Avocados
Avocado Butter, 339
Avocado with Red Pepper
Sauce, *619*
California-Style Egg Salad
Sandwiches, 529
Greek Quinoa and Avocados, *81*
guacamole variations, 46
Mexican Deviled Eggs, *42*
Orange-Avocado Salsa, 348
selecting, 630

B

Bacon
Bacon, Spinach, and Tomato Salsa
Wraps, 526
Bacon and Cracked Black Pepper
Biscuits, 128, *129*
Bacon-Cheddar-Stuffed
Mushrooms, 59
Bacon Deviled Eggs, *42*
Bacon-Egg-Tomato Chicken
Salad, *505*
Baked Beans with Bacon, 72
BLT Fish Tacos, *319*
Chicken with Bacon
Pan Sauce, 479
Collard Greens with Bacon, 603
cooking, 133
Eggs Benedict, 135
Fettuccine alla Carbonara, *429*
Meat Lover's Scrambled Eggs, 136
Overnight Breakfast Pie, 139
Potato Skins, 58
Quiche Lorraine, 144
Baked Beans, Classic, 72
Baked Beans, 10 to Try, *73*
Baked Beans with Bacon, 72
Baked Cavatelli, 440
Baked Cheese Grits, 77
Baked Chicken Chile Rellenos, 480
Baked Potatoes, 608
Baked Potato Soup, 587
Baked Sweet Potatoes, 608
Baked Sweet Potato Fries, 612, *613*
Baked Ziti with Three Cheeses, *440*
Bakeware, 14–15
Baking powder, 103
Baking soda, 103
Baklava, 292, *293*
Balsamic BBQ Sauce, 540
Balsamic-Caper Pan Sauce, Chicken
with, 479
Balsamic-Glazed Flank Steak with Fall
Fruit Salsa, *392*
Balsamic-Glazed Squash, 614
Balsamic Shallot and Goat Cheese
Tart, 52, *53*
Balsamic Vinaigrette, 502
Bananas
Banana Bars, 279
Banana-Blueberry Smoothie, *96*
Banana Bread, 124
Banana-Chocolate Smoothie, *96*
Banana Cream Pie, 453
Caramel-Frosted Hummingbird
Cake, 167

Note: Numbers in *italics* indicate photo pages for finished dishes.

INDEX   **635**

Note: Numbers in *italics* indicate photo pages for finished dishes.

INDEX **637**

Note: Numbers in *italics* indicate photo pages for finished dishes.

INDEX **639**

Note: Numbers in *italics* indicate photo pages for finished dishes.

INDEX **643**

Note: Numbers in *italics* indicate photo pages for finished dishes.

INDEX **645**

Note: Numbers in *italics* indicate photo pages for finished dishes.

Note: Numbers in *italics* indicate photo pages for finished dishes.

Note: Numbers in *italics* indicate photo pages for finished dishes.

INDEX **651**

Note: Numbers in *italics* indicate photo pages for finished dishes.

Note: Numbers in *italics* indicate photo pages for finished dishes.

Note: Numbers in *italics* indicate photo pages for finished dishes.

COOKING AT HIGH ALTITUDES

WHEN YOU COOK AT HIGH ALTITUDES, RECIPE ADJUSTMENTS NEED TO BE MADE TO ENSURE THE BEST RESULTS POSSIBLE.

Unfortunately, no simple formula exists for converting all recipes to high altitude recipes. If you live more than 1,000 feet above sea level, it will help you to understand ways in which altitude affects cooking and to become familiar with common cooking adjustments.

GENERAL HIGH-ALTITUDE ISSUES

Higher than 3,000 feet above sea level:

☒ Water boils at lower temperatures, causing moisture to evaporate more quickly. This can cause food to dry out during cooking and baking.

☒ Because of a lower boiling point, foods cooked in steam or boiling liquids take longer to cook.

☒ Lower air pressure may cause baked goods that use yeast, baking powder, baking soda, egg whites, or steam to rise excessively, then fall.

SUGGESTIONS FOR BAKING

☒ For cakes leavened by air, such as angel food, beat the egg whites only to soft peaks; otherwise, the batter may expand too much.

☒ For cakes made with shortening, you may want to decrease the baking powder (start by decreasing it by ⅛ teaspoon per teaspoon called for); decrease the sugar (start by decreasing by about 1 tablespoon for each cup called for); and increase the liquid (start by increasing it 1 to 2 tablespoons for each cup called for). These estimates are based on an altitude of 3,000 feet above sea level—at higher altitudes you may need to alter these measures proportionately. You can also try increasing the baking temperature by 15°F to 25°F to help set the batter.

☒ When making a rich cake, reduce the shortening by 1 to 2 tablespoons per cup and add one egg (for a 2-layer cake) to prevent cake from falling.

☒ Cookies generally yield acceptable results, but if you're not satisfied, try slightly increasing baking temperature; slightly decreasing the baking powder or soda, fat, and/or sugar; and/or slightly increasing the liquid ingredients and flour.

☒ Muffinlike quick breads and biscuits generally need little adjustment, but if you find that these goods develop a bitter or alkaline flavor, decrease the baking soda or powder slightly. Because cake-like quick breads are more delicate, you may need to follow adjustment guidelines for cakes.

☒ Yeast breads will rise more quickly at high altitudes. Allow unshaped dough to rise only until double in size, then punch the dough down. Repeat this rising step once more before shaping dough. Flour tends to be drier at high altitudes and sometimes absorbs more liquid. If your yeast dough seems dry, add more liquid and reduce the amount of flour the next time you make the recipe.

☒ Large cuts of meat may take longer to cook. Be sure to use a meat thermometer to determine proper doneness.

SUGGESTIONS FOR RANGE-TOP COOKING

CANDY-MAKING: Rapid evaporation caused by cooking at high altitudes can cause candies to cook down more quickly. Therefore, decrease the final cooking temperature by the difference in boiling water temperature at your altitude and that of sea level (212°F). This is an approximate decrease of 2°F for every increase of 1,000 feet in elevation above sea level.

CANNING AND FREEZING FOODS: When canning at high altitudes, adjustments in processing time or pressure are needed to guard against contamination; when freezing, an adjustment in the blanching time is needed. See the Canning and Freezing chapter, especially the tip on page 211.

DEEP-FAT FRYING: At high altitudes, deep-fried foods can overbrown on the outside but remain underdone inside. While foods vary, a rough guideline is to lower the temperature of the fat about 3°F for every 1,000 feet in elevation above sea level.

COOKING ABOVE 6,000 FEET

Cooking at altitudes higher than 6,000 feet above sea level poses further challenges because the dry air found at such elevations influences cooking. Call your local United States Department of Agriculture Extension Service Office for advice.

Further Information

For more information on cooking at high altitudes, contact your county extension office or write to Colorado State University, Department of Food Science and Human Nutrition Cooperative Extension, Fort Collins, CO 80523-1571. Please use this contact only for queries regarding high-altitude cooking.

METRIC
INFORMATION

PRODUCT DIFFERENCES

Most of the ingredients called for in the recipes in this book are available in most countries. However, some are known by different names. Here are some common American ingredients and their possible counterparts:

☒ Sugar (white) is granulated, fine granulated, or castor sugar.

☒ Powdered sugar is icing sugar.

☒ All-purpose flour is enriched, bleached or unbleached white household flour. When self-rising flour is used in place of all-purpose flour in a recipe that calls for leavening, omit the leavening agent (baking soda or baking powder) and salt.

☒ Light-color corn syrup is golden syrup.

☒ Cornstarch is cornflour.

☒ Baking soda is bicarbonate of soda.

☒ Vanilla or vanilla extract is vanilla essence.

☒ Green, red, or yellow sweet peppers are capsicums or bell peppers.

☒ Golden raisins are sultanas.

VOLUME AND WEIGHT

The United States traditionally uses cup measures for liquid and solid ingredients. The chart below shows the approximate imperial and metric equivalents. If you are accustomed to weighing solid ingredients, the following approximate equivalents will be helpful.

☒ 1 cup butter, castor sugar, or rice = 8 ounces = ½ pound = 250 grams

☒ 1 cup flour = 4 ounces = ¼ pound = 125 grams

☒ 1 cup icing sugar = 5 ounces = 150 grams

☒ Canadian and U.S. volume for a cup measure is 8 fluid ounces (237 ml), but the standard metric equivalent is 250 ml.

☒ 1 British imperial cup is 10 fluid ounces.

☒ In Australia, 1 tablespoon equals 20 ml, and there are 4 teaspoons in the Australian tablespoon.

☒ Spoon measures are used for smaller amounts of ingredients. Although the size of the tablespoon varies slightly in different countries, for practical purposes and for recipes in this book, a straight substitution is all that's necessary. Measurements made using cups or spoons always should be level unless stated otherwise.

COMMON WEIGHT RANGE REPLACEMENTS

Imperial / U.S.	Metric
½ ounce	15 g
1 ounce	25 g or 30 g
4 ounces (¼ pound)	115 g or 125 g
8 ounces (½ pound)	225 g or 250 g
16 ounces (1 pound)	450 g or 500 g
1¼ pounds	625 g
1½ pounds	750 g
2 pounds or 2¼ pounds	1,000 g or 1 Kg

OVEN TEMPERATURE EQUIVALENTS

Fahrenheit Setting	Celsius Setting	Gas Setting
300°F	150°C	Gas Mark 2 (very low)
325°F	160°C	Gas Mark 3 (low)
350°F	180°C	Gas Mark 4 (moderate)
375°F	190°C	Gas Mark 5 (moderate)
400°F	200°C	Gas Mark 6 (hot)
425°F	220°C	Gas Mark 7 (hot)
450°F	230°C	Gas Mark 8 (very hot)
475°F	240°C	Gas Mark 9 (very hot)
500°F	260°C	Gas Mark 10 (extremely hot)
Broil	Broil	Grill

*Electric and gas ovens may be calibrated using celsius. However, for an electric oven, increase celsius setting 10 to 20 degrees when cooking above 160°C. For convection or forced air ovens (gas or electric), lower the temperature setting 25°F/10°C when cooking at all heat levels.

BAKING PAN SIZES

Imperial / U.S.	Metric
9×1½-inch round cake pan	22- or 23×4-cm (1.5 L)
9×1½-inch pie plate	22- or 23×4-cm (1 L)
8×8×2-inch square cake pan	20×5-cm (2 L)
9×9×2-inch square cake pan	22- or 23×4.5-cm (2.5 L)
11×7×1½-inch baking pan	28×17×4-cm (2 L)
2-quart rectangular baking pan	30×19×4.5-cm (3 L)
13×9×2-inch baking pan	34×22×4.5-cm (3.5 L)
15×10×1-inch jelly roll pan	40×25×2-cm
9×5×3-inch loaf pan	23×13×8-cm (2 L)
2-quart casserole	2 L

U.S. / STANDARD METRIC EQUIVALENTS

⅛ teaspoon = 0.5 ml	
¼ teaspoon = 1 ml	
½ teaspoon = 2 ml	
1 teaspoon = 5 ml	
1 tablespoon = 15 ml	
2 tablespoons = 25 ml	
¼ cup = 2 fluid ounces = 50 ml	
⅓ cup = 3 fluid ounces = 75 ml	
½ cup = 4 fluid ounces = 125 ml	
⅔ cup = 5 fluid ounces = 150 ml	
¾ cup = 6 fluid ounces = 175 ml	
1 cup = 8 fluid ounces = 250 ml	
2 cups = 1 pint = 500 ml	
1 quart = 1 litre	